SIPRI Yearbook 1998
Armaments, Disarmament and International Security

sipri
Stockholm International Peace Research Institute

SIPRI is an independent international institute for research into problems of peace and conflict, especially those of arms control and disarmament. It was established in 1966 to commemorate Sweden's 150 years of unbroken peace.

The Institute is financed mainly by the Swedish Parliament. The staff and the Governing Board are international. The Institute also has an Advisory Committee as an international consultative body.

The Governing Board is not responsible for the views expressed in the publications of the Institute.

Governing Board
Professor Daniel Tarschys, Chairman (Sweden)
Dr Oscar Arias Sánchez (Costa Rica)
Mr Marrack Goulding (United Kingdom)
Dr Ryukichi Imai (Japan)
Dr Catherine Kelleher (United States)
Dr Marjatta Rautio (Finland)
Dr Lothar Rühl (Germany)
Dr Abdullah Toukan (Jordan)
The Director

Director
Dr Adam Daniel Rotfeld (Poland)

Adam Daniel Rotfeld, Director, *Yearbook Editor and Publisher*
Connie Wall, *Managing Editor*
Coordinators
Ian Anthony, Eric Arnett, Peter Jones, Zdzislaw Lachowski
Editors
Billie Bielckus, Jetta Gilligan Borg, Eve Johansson
Editorial Assistant
Rebecka Charan

sipri
Stockholm International Peace Research Institute
Frösunda, S-169 70 Solna, Sweden
Cable: SIPRI
Telephone: 46 8/655 97 00
Telefax: 46 8/655 97 33
E-mail: sipri@sipri.se
Internet URL: http://www.sipri.se

SIPRI Yearbook 1998

Armaments, Disarmament and International Security

Stockholm International Peace Research Institute

OXFORD UNIVERSITY PRESS
1998

Oxford University Press, Great Clarendon Street, Oxford OX2 6DP
Oxford New York
Athens Auckland Bangkok Bagotá Bombay
Buenos Aires Calcutta Cape Town Dar es Salaam
Delhi Florence Hong Kong Istanbul Karachi
Kuala Lumpur Madras Madrid Melbourne
Mexico City Nairobi Paris Singapore
Taipei Tokyo Toronto Warsaw
and associated companies in
Berlin Ibadan

Oxford is a trade mark of Oxford University Press

Published in the United States
by Oxford University Press Inc., New York

© SIPRI 1998

Yearbooks before 1987 published under title
'World Armaments and Disarmament:
SIPRI Yearbook [year of publication]'

All rights reserved. No part of this publication may be reproduced, stored in a retrieval system, or transmitted, in any form or by any means, without the prior permission in writing of Oxford University Press. Within the UK, exceptions are allowed in respect of any fair dealing for the purpose of research or private study, or criticism or review, as permitted under the Copyright, Designs and Patents Act, 1988, or in the case of reprographic reproduction in accordance with the terms of the licences issued by the Copyright Licensing Agency. Enquiries concerning reproduction outside these terms should be sent to the Rights Department, Oxford University Press, at the address above. Enquiries concerning reproduction in other countries should be sent to SIPRI.

British Library Cataloguing in Publication Data

Data available
ISSN 0953–0282
ISBN 0–19–829454–9

Library of Congress Cataloging in Publication Data

Data available
ISSN 0953–0282
ISBN 0–19–829454–9

Typeset and originated by Stockholm International Peace Research Institute
Printed and bound in Great Britain by
Biddles Ltd., Guildford and King's Lynn

Contents

Preface	xiii
Acronyms	xiv
Glossary Ragnhild Ferm and Connie Wall	xviii
Introduction: Transformation of the world security system Adam Daniel Rotfeld	1
I. Achievements and failures	1
II. The driving forces of change	2
III. A trans-governmental order	3
IV. The agenda ahead	5
V. SIPRI findings	8
VI. Conclusions	14

Part I. Security and conflicts, 1997

1. Major armed conflicts — 17
Margareta Sollenberg and Peter Wallensteen

    I. Global patterns of major armed conflicts, 1989–97 — 17
    II. Changes in the table of conflicts — 18
        New conflicts—Conflicts recorded for 1996 that were not recorded for 1997—Conflict activity and peace efforts
    III. Regional patterns of major armed conflicts, 1989–97 — 22
    IV. Conclusions — 23
    Table 1.1. Regional distribution of locations with at least one major armed conflict, 1989–97 — 20
    Table 1.2. Regional distribution, number and types of major armed conflicts, 1989–97 — 20

Appendix 1A. Major armed conflicts, 1997 — 24
Margareta Sollenberg, Ramses Amer, Carl Johan Åsberg, Ann-Sofi Jakobsson and Andrés Jato

    Table 1A. Table of conflict locations with at least one major armed conflict in 1997 — 26

2. Armed conflict prevention, management and resolution — 31
Trevor Findlay

    I. Introduction — 31
    II. The United Nations — 32
        Restructuring and reform—The Secretary-General and the Secretariat—The Security Council and General Assembly—International legal mechanisms
    III. UN peacekeeping operations — 40
        Continuing peacekeeping reforms—Peacekeeping finance—Improvements in UN peacekeeping capability through national and cooperative efforts
    IV. UN peace-enforcement measures — 52
        Sanctions—Military enforcement
    V. Regional and other multilateral organizations — 54
        Europe and the CIS—Africa—Latin America—Asia
    VI. Other players — 65

VII.	Conclusions: conflict prevention, management and resolution in the 1990s Sovereignty challenged—Globalization and regionalization—Conflict prevention—Peacekeeping—Conflict resolution—Peace-building—The fate of the UN—Assessment	69
Table 2.1.	Cases before the International Court of Justice, 1997	39
Figure 2.1.	UN peacekeeping operations in 1988–97: costs, number of operations and number of military and civilian police personnel	42
Figure 2.2.	UN peacekeeping operations in the field, as of 31 December 1997	44
Figure 2.3.	Other multilateral peacekeeping operations in the field, as of 31 December 1997	56

Appendix 2A. Multilateral peace missions, 1997 — 75
Susanna Eckstein

Table 2A.	Multilateral peace missions	76

3. The Middle East peace process — 91
Peter Jones and Gunilla Flodén

I.	Introduction	91
II.	The Israeli–Palestinian track The Hebron Accord—A new Israeli settlement—Renewed terrorism and an Israeli proposal—Internal problems for Netanyahu and Arafat—The USA resumes its role	91
III.	The other tracks of the peace process The Israeli–Syrian track and events in Lebanon—Lebanon—The Israeli–Jordanian talks—The multilateral track	97
IV.	Wider regional events The Iranian election—The Iraqi situation—Other events in the region	102
V.	Conclusions	106

Appendix 3A. Documents on the Middle East peace process — 108

Note for the Record (attached to the Protocol concerning the redeployment in Hebron)—US Secretary of State Warren Christopher, US letter of assurance to Israel

4. Russia: conflicts and peaceful settlement of disputes — 111
Vladimir Baranovsky

I.	Introduction	111
II.	Post-war accommodation in Chechnya Domestic developments—Political aspects of relations—The transit of oil—The regional context	111
III.	Russia's relations with its post-Soviet European neighbours Ukraine—Belarus—The Baltic states—The Trans-Dniester region	118
IV.	Conflicts in the Transcaucasus A volatile geopolitical landscape—Abkhazia—Nagorno-Karabakh	125
V.	Tajikistan	135
VI.	The CIS: a lower profile?	137
VII.	Conclusions	138
Figure 4.1.	Existing and possible future oil routes from Central Asia and the Caucasus	126

5. Europe: the transition to inclusive security — 141
Adam Daniel Rotfeld

I.	Introduction	141
II.	NATO: enlargement and new security arrangements The NATO–Russia Founding Act—The NATO–Ukraine Charter—NATO and the Baltic states—The Euro-Atlantic Partnership Council—	142

	The Madrid Declaration—A new NATO in the new Europe—Costs of NATO enlargement	
III.	The European Union: the security dimension	154
	The EU enlargement process—The EU and NATO—The two enlargement processes: differences and similarities	
IV.	The OSCE: pan-European security cooperation	160
	OSCE activities—A Charter on European Security	
V.	Conclusions	166
Figure 5.1.	The overlapping membership of multilateral Euro-Atlantic security organizations, as of 1 January 1998	142

Appendix 5A. Documents on European security 168

Founding Act on Mutual Relations, Cooperation and Security between the North Atlantic Treaty Organization and the Russian Federation (NATO–Russia Founding Act)—Basic Document of the Euro-Atlantic Partnership Council—Madrid Declaration on Euro-Atlantic Security and Cooperation—Treaty of Amsterdam Amending the Treaty on European Union, the Treaties Establishing the European Communities and Certain Related Acts—Protocol to the North Atlantic Treaty on the Accession of Poland

Part II. Military spending and armaments, 1997

6. Military expenditure and arms production 185
Elisabeth Sköns, Agnès Courades Allebeck, Evamaria Loose-Weintraub and Reinhilde Weidacher

I.	Introduction	185
II.	The military expenditure data	187
	Utility of data—Available data	
III.	Global and regional trends in military expenditure	191
	Asia—Africa	
IV.	Military expenditure by country income group	196
V.	Arms production in OECD and developing countries	198
	The SIPRI top 100—Restructuring of the arms industry in 1996 and 1997	
VI.	The candidates for NATO membership in Central and Eastern Europe	207
	NATO requirements—Military expenditure and procurement in the prospective member states	
Table 6.1.	Regional military expenditure estimates, 1988–97	192
Table 6.2.	Military expenditure estimates for Africa, 1988–97	195
Table 6.3.	Military expenditure estimates by country income group, 1988–97	197
Table 6.4.	Regional/national shares of arms sales for the top 100 arms-producing companies in the OECD and the developing countries, 1996 compared to 1995	200
Table 6.5.	The major companies by military industrial sector, 1996–97	202
Table 6.6.	Procurement and total military expenditure for the Czech Republic, Hungary and Poland, 1993–98	210

Appendix 6A. Tables of military expenditure 214
Elisabeth Sköns, Agnès Courades Allebeck, Evamaria Loose-Weintraub and Petter Stålenheim

Table 6A.1.	Military expenditure by region, in constant US dollars, 1988–97	214
Table 6A.2.	Military expenditure by region and country, in local currency, 1988–97	216
Table 6A.3.	Military expenditure by region and country, in constant US dollars, 1988–97	222

Table 6A.4. Military expenditure by region and country, as percentage of gross domestic product, 1988–96 — 228

Appendix 6B. Tables of NATO military expenditure — 236
Table 6B.1. NATO distribution of military expenditure by category, 1988–97 — 236
Table 6B.2. Military equipment expenditure of France, 1988–97 — 239

Appendix 6C. Sources and methods for military expenditure data — 240
    I. Purpose of the data — 240
   II. Sources — 240
  III. Methods — 241
       Definition of military expenditure—Calculations—Estimates and the use of brackets

Appendix 6D. The military expenditure of the USSR and the Russian Federation, 1987–97 — 243
Julian Cooper

    I. Introduction — 243
   II. Soviet military expenditure, 1987–91 — 244
  III. Military expenditure in the Russian Federation, 1992–97 — 246
       The budgetary process—The budget chapter 'national defence'—Other sources of funding for the military—Actual expenditure—The military burden
  IV. The trend of Soviet and Russian military expenditure in 1995 dollar terms — 257
       Current issues of Russian military expenditure

Table 6D.1. Expenditure of the Ministry of Defence and Ministry of Atomic Energy of the USSR, 1987–90 — 244
Table 6D.2. Estimated total military expenditure of the USSR, 1987–90 — 246
Table 6D.3. The original budget request of the Russian Ministry of Defence and the final budget allocation to national defence, 1992–97 — 247
Table 6D.4. Military expenditure in the Russian federal budget, 1992–97 — 250
Table 6D.5. Actual outlays on Russian national defence and Ministry of Defence, 1992–97 — 252
Table 6D.6. Structure of actual and planned expenditure of the Russian Ministry of Defence, 1992–97 — 254
Table 6D.7. USSR and Russia, expenditure by service, 1990–97 — 255
Table 6D.8. Estimated actual total Russian military-related expenditure, 1992–96 — 256
Table 6D.9. Soviet and Russian military expenditure, 1987–96 — 257
Table 6D.10. Military expenditure in the Russian Federation and the USSR, 1987–97 — 258

Appendix 6E. The 100 largest arms-producing companies, 1996 — 260
Elisabeth Sköns, Reinhilde Weidacher and the SIPRI Arms Industry Network

Table 6E. The 100 largest arms-producing companies in the OECD and developing countries, 1996 — 261

7. Military research and development — 267
Eric Arnett

    I. Introduction — 267
   II. Global trends — 269
       A note on sources of information—New sources of support for the Russian military technology base—Military R&D and national technology bases
  III. The USA — 275
       The Quadrennial Defense Review—Ballistic missile defence—Cruise missile defence—Anti-satellite weapons

	IV.	Conclusions	288
Table 7.1.		Official figures for government military R&D expenditure	268
Table 7.2.		Government expenditure on military R&D in select countries, 1983–96	269
Table 7.3.		Government expenditure on military R&D as a fraction of total government R&D expenditure in select countries, 1983–96	273
Table 7.4.		Government expenditure on military R&D as a fraction of national R&D expenditure in select countries, 1983–96	274
Table 7.5.		Appropriations for major US R&D programmes, 1998	278
Table 7.6.		Ballistic missile programmes in select countries and corresponding tactical ballistic missile defence programmes	280
Table 7.7.		Chinese anti-ship missiles	286

8. Transfers of major conventional weapons 291
Siemon T. Wezeman and Pieter D. Wezeman

	I.	Introduction	291
	II.	Main developments in 1997	292
		The suppliers of major conventional weapons—The recipients of major conventional weapons	
	III.	Arms transfers to Sub-Saharan Africa	302
		Arms transfers to countries in conflict	
	IV.	International embargoes on arms transfers	305
	V.	National and international transparency in transfers of conventional weapons	306
		Official data on arms exports—The UN Register of Conventional Arms	
Table 8.1.		The 30 leading suppliers of major conventional weapons, 1993–97	294
Table 8.2.		The 72 leading recipients of major conventional weapons, 1993–97	300
Table 8.3.		Suppliers of major conventional weapons to Sub-Saharan countries engaged in conflicts, 1993–97	304
Table 8.4.		Arms embargoes by international organizations in effect, 1993–97	306
Table 8.5.		Official data on arms exports, 1992–96	308
Table 8.6.		Government returns to the UN Register for calendar years 1992–96, as of 1 April 1998	312
Figure 8.1.		The trend in transfers of major conventional weapons, 1983–97	292

Appendix 8A. The volume of transfers of major conventional weapons, 1988–97 318
Ian Anthony, Pieter D. Wezeman and Siemon T. Wezeman

Table 8A.1.	Volume of imports of major conventional weapons	318
Table 8A.2.	Volume of exports of major conventional weapons	319

Appendix 8B. Register of the transfers and licensed production of major conventional weapons, 1997 322
Ian Anthony, Pieter D. Wezeman and Siemon T. Wezeman

Appendix 8C. Sources and methods 369

	I.	The SIPRI sources	369
	II.	Selection criteria	369
	III.	The SIPRI trend-indicator value	370

Part III. Non-proliferation, arms control and disarmament, 1997

9. Multilateral security-related export controls 373
Ian Anthony and Jean Pascal Zanders

	I.	Introduction	373
	II.	The Wassenaar Arrangement	375
		Controls on encryption technology	

x SIPRI YEARBOOK 1998

III.	Nuclear export controls	380
	The Zangger Committee—The Nuclear Suppliers Group	
IV.	Export control regimes for chemical and biological weapons and technologies	386
	The Australia Group—The legal status of CBW-related export control mechanisms—The international debate concerning the Australia Group	
V.	The Missile Technology Control Regime	394
VI.	European Union dual-use export controls	399
	Further steps	
Table 9.1.	Membership of multilateral military-related export control regimes, as of 1 January 1998	374

Appendix 9A. Nuclear Suppliers Group consultation and information exchange procedure guidelines — 401

Memorandum of Understanding on Implementation of 'Dual-Use' Guidelines

10. Nuclear arms control — 403
Shannon Kile

I.	Introduction	403
II.	The START treaties	404
	Implementation of the START I Treaty—The START II Treaty—The START reductions and changes in US nuclear doctrine—Reducing alert rates	
III.	The ABM Treaty and ballistic missile defence	419
	The ABM Treaty demarcation agreement	
IV.	Cooperative threat reduction	425
	The Nunn–Lugar programme—The reactor conversion agreement	
V.	Other nuclear non-proliferation and disarmament developments	428
	The Comprehensive Nuclear Test-Ban Treaty—A ban on the production of fissile material for nuclear explosives—The NPT Preparatory Committee	
VI.	Conclusions	432
Table 10.1.	START I limits in 1997, 1999 and 2001	405
Table 10.2.	START I aggregate numbers of strategic nuclear delivery vehicles and accountable warheads, 1 January 1998	406
Figure 10.1.	US and Soviet/Russian strategic nuclear forces: deployed warheads, 1990, 1998 and after implementation of the START II Treaty	412

Appendix 10A. Tables of nuclear forces — 434
Robert S. Norris and William M. Arkin

Table 10A.1. US strategic nuclear forces, January 1998	434
Table 10A.2. Russian strategic nuclear forces, January 1998	437
Table 10A.3. British nuclear forces, January 1998	439
Table 10A.4. French nuclear forces, January 1998	440
Table 10A.5. Chinese nuclear forces, January 1998	442

Appendix 10B. The nuclear weapon-free zones in South-East Asia and Africa — 443
Amitav Acharya and Sola Ogunbanwo

I.	Introduction	443
II.	South-East Asia	443
	Background—The treaty provisions—The attitude of the nuclear weapon states—Prospects—Conclusions	
III.	Africa	450
	Background—The treaty provisions—The attitude of the nuclear weapon states—Conclusions	

11. Chemical and biological weapon developments and arms control 457
Jean Pascal Zanders and John Hart

I.	Introduction	457
II.	Chemical weapon disarmament	457
	The creation of a disarmament regime—Declarations of CW possession and programmes—Destruction of chemical weapons—Old and abandoned chemical weapons—The CWC and the use of riot-control agents in peacekeeping operations	
III.	Biological weapon disarmament	470
IV.	Chemical and biological warfare proliferation concerns	474
	Threat and response—Allegations of CBW programmes—The Cuban allegation of biological warfare—Other events related to CBW proliferation	
V.	UNSCOM developments	481
VI.	The Gulf War illnesses	486
VII.	Conclusions	488
Table 11.1.	UNSCOM inspections, 1997	482

Appendix 11A. Entry into force of the Chemical Weapons Convention 490
Robert J. Mathews

I.	Introduction	490
II.	The First Conference of the States Parties	491
	The Executive Council—Action on PrepCom recommendations—The OPCW programme and budget	
III.	The Second Conference of the States Parties	495
IV.	Future issues and concerns	497
	OPCW analytical database—Schedules of chemicals—Refinement of the inspection procedures—Relative proportion of inspection effort for Article I verification activities—Off-site analysis	
V.	Conclusions	500

12. Conventional arms control 501
Zdzislaw Lachowski

I.	Introduction	501
II.	Conventional arms control in Europe: the CFE Treaty	502
	Compliance issues—Entry into force of the Flank Document—Towards adaptation of the CFE Treaty—The NATO–Russia Founding Act and the 'basic elements' decision—The status of the negotiations	
III.	Regional arms control in Europe	517
	Phase II of the implementation of the Florence Agreement—The Train and Equip Program—Russian arms control and security initiatives in the Baltic Sea region	
IV.	Open Skies	524
V.	Conventional arms control endeavours outside Europe	525
	Russia–China—Asia–Pacific—South Asia	
VI.	Conclusions	530
Table 12.1.	Accommodation of new members' holdings and allocations within NATO TLE headroom	509
Table 12.2.	Current entitlements and adjusted national ceilings proposed by NATO states, July–September 1997	515
Table 12.3.	'Initial illustrative ceilings' proposed by Germany	516
Table 12.4.	Five per cent exemptions under Article III of the Florence Agreement, as agreed on 30 January 1997	518

xii SIPRI YEARBOOK 1998

Table 12.5.	Reductions completed under the Florence Agreement, as of 31 October 1997	520

Appendix 12A. Confidence- and security-building measures in Europe 531
Zdzislaw Lachowski and Patrick Henrichon

I.	Introduction	531
II.	The Annual Implementation Assessment Meeting	531
III.	Improving and reviewing the Vienna Document 1994	532
	Amending the Vienna Document—Towards a new Vienna Document	
IV.	The implementation record for 1997	535
V.	Regional CSBMs	536
	Agreement on CSBMs in Bosnia and Herzegovina—Russia's CSBM initiative in the Baltic Sea region—South-eastern Europe	
VI.	Conclusions	540
Table 12A.	Calendar of planned notifiable military activities in 1998, exchanged by 18 December 1997	534

Appendix 12B. Basic elements for CFE Treaty adaptation 541

Decision of the Joint Consultative Group concerning certain Basic Elements for Treaty Adaptation

13. The ban on anti-personnel mines 545
Zdzislaw Lachowski

I.	Introduction	545
II.	A two-track approach	546
	The Conference on Disarmament—The Ottawa Process	
III.	From Oslo to Ottawa	553
	The Oslo Conference: the US end-game thwarted—The APM Convention—Demining	
IV.	Conclusions	557

Appendix 13A. Documents on the prohibition of anti-personnel mines 559

Protocol on Prohibitions or Restrictions on the Use of Mines, Booby-traps and other Devices as Amended on 3 May 1996 (Protocol II as Amended on 3 May 1996)—Convention on the Prohibition of the Use, Stockpiling, Production and Transfer of Anti-personnel Mines and on their Destruction

Annexes

Annexe A. Arms control and disarmament agreements 577
Ragnhild Ferm

Annexe B. Chronology 1997 599
Ragnhild Ferm

About the contributors	611
Abstracts	616
Errata	621
Index	622

Preface

The Stockholm International Peace Research Institute presents in this volume the 29th edition of the SIPRI Yearbook. In his essay on the first 30 years of SIPRI's activities, Professor Francesco Calogero, Chairman of the Pugwash Council on Science and World Affairs and for many years a member of the SIPRI Governing Board, noted: 'The positive impact of SIPRI has mainly derived from the original policy choice, that made of it an important source of objective and reliable data on armaments and conflicts'. What is needed is 'information on the facts: the hard data; the objective chronicle of events'. It is this philosophy which guides the work of SIPRI that is presented in the Yearbook.

The introductory chapter highlights the factors of global change in the broad political context as well as the new threats to international security and presents the main findings of the Yearbook.

The Yearbook contains analyses and assessments, supported by data and documentation. Part I of this volume deals with security; major armed conflicts; and conflict prevention, management and resolution. It contains chapters on the Middle East peace process; developments in Russia, particularly those concerning the conflicts waged on its periphery; and Europe's progress in moving away from bloc divisions and a balance of forces towards a new security order based on inclusiveness and cooperativeness. Part II presents SIPRI's traditional studies of military expenditure; arms production, including the list of the 100 largest arms-producing companies; military research and development; and transfers of major conventional weapons. Part III deals with multilateral security-related export controls and developments in arms control and disarmament, including weapons of mass destruction—nuclear, biological and chemical—and conventional weapons, the latter covering confidence- and security-building measures and anti-personnel mines. The Yearbook also contains a comprehensive glossary of the terms and security-oriented organizations discussed in the volume. It concludes with annexes on the implementation of arms control and disarmament agreements and a chronology of the important events in 1997 in armaments, disarmament and international security.

Nearly all the chapters reflect the results of research conducted at SIPRI. A number of other experts contributed material. I would like to express our gratitude to Peter Wallensteen and his collaborators for the chapter on major armed conflicts and to Amitav Acharya, William M. Arkin, Julian Cooper, Robert J. Mathews, Robert S. Norris and Sola Ogunbanwo for the appendices they prepared for SIPRI.

The Yearbook editorial team—Billie Bielckus, Jetta Gilligan Borg, Eve Johansson and Rebecka Charan, editorial assistant—led by Connie Wall, are to be thanked for their competence and devotion to the difficult task of editing this comprehensive volume. I would also like to thank the coordinators—Ian Anthony, Eric Arnett, Peter Jones and Zdzislaw Lachowski—for their editorial support in addition to the chapters they contributed to the book. I am grateful to Gerd Hagmeyer-Gaverus, information technology manager; Billie Bielckus, cartographer; Peter Rea, indexer; and all the other members of the SIPRI staff who provided the necessary support for the production of this Yearbook.

Adam Daniel Rotfeld
Director
April 1998

Acronyms

Acronyms for UN observer, peacekeeping and electoral operations and weapon systems are given in appendix 2A and appendix 8B, respectively. Acronyms not defined in this list are defined in the chapters of this volume.

ABACC	Brazilian–Argentine Agency for Accounting and Control of Nuclear Materials	CBW	Chemical and biological weapon/warfare
ABM	Anti-ballistic missile	CCW	Certain Conventional Weapons (Convention)
ACM	Advanced cruise missile	CD	Conference on Disarmament
ACV	Armoured combat vehicle	CEE	Central and Eastern Europe
ADM	Atomic demolition munition	CFE	Conventional Armed Forces in Europe (Treaty)
AG	Australia Group	CFSP	Common Foreign and Security Policy
AIFV	Armoured infantry fighting vehicle	CIO	Chairman-in-Office
ALCM	Air-launched cruise missile	CIS	Commonwealth of Independent States
APC	Armoured personnel carrier		
APEC	Asia–Pacific Economic Co-operation	CivPol	Civilian police
APM	Anti-personnel mine	CJTF	Combined Joint Task Forces
ARF	ASEAN Regional Forum	CPC	Conflict Prevention Centre
ARV	Armoured recovery vehicle	CPI	Consumer price index
ASEAN	Association of South-East Asian Nations	CSBM	Confidence- and security-building measure
ASEAN–PMC	ASEAN Post Ministerial Conference	CSCAP	Council for Security Cooperation in the Asia Pacific
ATBM	Anti-tactical ballistic missile	CSCE	Conference on Security and Co-operation in Europe
ATC	Armoured troop carrier		
ATTU	Atlantic-to-the-Urals (zone)	CTB	Comprehensive test ban
BIC	Bilateral Implementation Commission	CTBT	Comprehensive Nuclear Test-Ban Treaty
BMD	Ballistic missile defence	CTBTO	Comprehensive Nuclear Test-Ban Treaty Organization
BTWC	Biological and Toxin Weapons Convention	CTR	Cooperative Threat Reduction
BW	Biological weapon/warfare	CW	Chemical weapon/warfare
CBM	Confidence-building measure	CWC	Chemical Weapons Convention
CBSS	Council of the Baltic Sea States		

CWPF	Chemical weapons production facility
DOD	Department of Defense
DOE	Department of Energy
DPKO	Department of Peacekeeping Operations
DPSS	Designated permanent storage site
EAEC	European Atomic Energy Community (Euratom)
EAPC	Euro-Atlantic Partnership Council
ECOMOG	ECOWAS Monitoring Group
ECOWAS	Economic Community of West African States
EEZ	Exclusive economic zone
Enmod	Environmental modification
ESDI	European Security and Defence Identity
EU	European Union
Euratom	European Atomic Energy Community (EAEC)
FMCT	Fissile Material Cut-off Treaty
FSC	Forum for Security Co-operation
FY	Fiscal year
G7	Group of Seven
G8	Group of Eight
G-21	Group of 21
GCC	Gulf Co-operation Council
GDP	Gross domestic product
GLCM	Ground-launched cruise missile
GNP	Gross national product
GUAM	Georgia–Ukraine–Azerbaijan–Moldova
HACV	Heavy armoured combat vehicle
HCNM	High Commissioner on National Minorities
HEU	Highly enriched uranium
HLTF	High Level Task Force
IAEA	International Atomic Energy Agency
IBRD	International Bank for Reconstruction and Development
ICBL	International Campaign to Ban Landmines
ICBM	Intercontinental ballistic missile
ICJ	International Court of Justice
ICRC	International Committee of the Red Cross
IFOR	Implementation Force
IFV	Infantry fighting vehicle
IGC	Intergovernmental Conference
IMF	International Monetary Fund
INF	Intermediate-range nuclear forces
IPTF	International Police Task Force
IRA	Irish Republican Army
IRBM	Intermediate-range ballistic missile
JACADS	Johnston Atoll Chemical Agent Disposal Systems
JCC	Joint Consultative Commission
JCG	Joint Consultative Group
JCIC	Joint Compliance and Inspection Commission
LCA	Light Combat Aircraft
LDC	Least developed country
MBT	Main battle tank
MCG	Mediterranean Cooperation Group
MD	Military District
Minatom	Ministry of Atomic Energy

MIRV	Multiple independently targetable re-entry vehicle	ODIHR	Office for Democratic Institutions and Human Rights
MNLH	Maximum National Levels for Holdings	OECD	Organisation for Economic Co-operation and Development
MOD	Ministry of Defence		
MOU	Memorandum of Understanding	OIC	Organization of the Islamic Conference
MTCR	Missile Technology Control Regime	O&M	Operation and maintenance
MTM	Multinational technical means (of verification)	OPANAL	Agency for the Prohibition of Nuclear Weapons in Latin America and the Caribbean
NAC	North Atlantic Council	OPCW	Organisation for the Prohibition of Chemical Weapons
NACC	North Atlantic Cooperation Council		
NAM	Non-Aligned Movement	OPEC	Organisation of Petroleum Exporting Countries
NATO	North Atlantic Treaty Organization	OSCC	Open Skies Consultative Commission
NBC	Nuclear, biological and chemical (weapons)	OSCE	Organization for Security and Co-operation in Europe
NGO	Non-governmental organization	OSI	On-site inspection
NIC	Newly industrialized countries	P5	Permanent Five (members of the UN Security Council)
NNSC	Neutral Nations Supervisory Commission	PA	Palestinian Authority
		PFP	Partnership for Peace
NNWS	Non-nuclear weapon state	PJC	Permanent Joint Council (NATO–Russia)
NPT	Non-Proliferation Treaty		
NSG	Nuclear Suppliers Group	PLO	Palestine Liberation Organization
NSIP	NATO Security Investment Programme	PNC	Palestinian National Council
NTM	National technical means (of verification)	PNE(T)	Peaceful Nuclear Explosions (Treaty)
NWFZ	Nuclear weapon-free zone	PPP	Purchasing power parity
NWS	Nuclear weapon state/states	PrepCom	Preparatory Commission
OAS	Organization of American States	PTB(T)	Partial Test Ban (Treaty)
		QDR	Quadrennial Defense Review
OAU	Organization of African Unity	R&D	Research and development
OCCAR	Organisme Conjoint de Coopération en Matière d'Armement	RDT&E	Research, development, testing and evaluation
		RPV	Remotely piloted vehicle
		RV	Re-entry vehicle

SAM	Surface-to-air missile	UNSCOM	UN Special Commission on Iraq
SBSS	Science Based Stockpile Stewardship (programme)	WEAG	Western European Armaments Group
SCC	Standing Consultative Commission	WEU	Western European Union
SFOR	Stabilization Force	WMD	Weapon of mass destruction
SITC	Standard International Trade Classification	WTO	Warsaw Treaty Organization (Warsaw Pact)
SLBM	Submarine-launched ballistic missile	WTO	World Trade Organization
SLCM	Sea-launched cruise missile	ZOPFAN	Zone of Peace, Freedom and Neutrality
SLV	Space launch vehicle		
SNDV	Strategic nuclear delivery vehicle		
SNF	Short-range nuclear forces		
SRAM	Short-range attack missile		
SRCC	Sub-Regional Consultative Commission		
SRBM	Short-range ballistic missile		
SSBN	Nuclear-powered, ballistic-missile submarine		
SSM	Surface-to-surface missile		
START	Strategic Arms Reduction Talks/Treaty		
THAAD	Theater High-Altitude Area Defense		
TIPH	Temporary International Presence in Hebron		
TLE	Treaty-limited equipment		
TMD	Theatre missile defence		
TNF	Theatre nuclear forces		
TTB(T)	Threshold Test Ban (Treaty)		
UNCLOS	UN Convention on the Law of the Sea		
UNCTAD	UN Conference on Trade and Development		
UNDP	UN Development Programme		
UNHCR	UN High Commissioner for Refugees		
UNROCA	UN Register of Conventional Arms		

Glossary

RAGNHILD FERM and CONNIE WALL

The main terms discussed in this Yearbook are defined in the glossary. For acronyms that appear in the definitions, see page xiv. For the members of global, regional and subregional organizations, see page xxix. For summaries of and parties to the arms control and disarmament agreements mentioned in the glossary, see annexe A.

Agency for the Prohibition of Nuclear Weapons in Latin America and the Caribbean (OPANAL)	Established by the 1967 Treaty of Tlatelolco to resolve, together with the IAEA, questions of compliance with the treaty.
Amsterdam Treaty	The 1997 Treaty of Amsterdam Amending the Treaty on European Union. *See* European Union.
Anti-ballistic missile (ABM) system	*See* Ballistic missile defence.
Anti-personnel mine (APM)	A mine designed to be exploded by the presence, proximity or contact of a person and that will incapacitate, injure or kill one or more persons. The 1997 APM Convention prohibits the use, stockpiling, production and transfer of APMs, and Protocol II (as amended in 1996) of the 1981 Inhumane Weapons Convention prohibits or restricts their use.
Anti-Personnel Mine (APM) Convention	The 1997 Convention on the Prohibition of the Use, Production, Transfer and Stockpiling of Anti-Personnel Landmines and on their Destruction.
Anti-tactical ballistic missile (ATBM) system	*See* Theatre missile defence.
Arab League	The League of Arab States, known as the Arab League and with Permanent Headquarters in Cairo, was established in 1945. Its principal objective is to form closer union among Arab states and foster political and economic cooperation. An agreement for collective defence and economic cooperation among the members was signed in 1950. *See* the list of members.
Asia–Pacific Economic Co-operation (APEC)	Established in 1989 for Asia–Pacific 'participating economies' to promote trade and growth in the region. The Secretariat is in Singapore; it holds annual ministerial meetings. *See* the list of participating economies.
Asia–Pacific region	The Pacific rim states of Asia, North and South America, and Oceania. It is defined differently by the membership of different Asia–Pacific organizations (*see*, e.g., the lists of members of APEC and CSCAP).

GLOSSARY

Association of South-East Asian Nations (ASEAN)	Established in 1967 to promote economic, social and cultural development as well as regional peace and security in South-East Asia. The seat of the Secretariat is in Jakarta. ASEAN proposed and negotiated the South-East Asia nuclear weapon-free zone, embodied in the 1995 Treaty of Bangkok. The ASEAN Regional Forum (ARF) was established in 1993 to address security issues in a multilateral forum, with an official and a non-official programme. The ASEAN Post Ministerial Conference (ASEAN–PMC) was established in 1979 as a forum for discussions of political and security issues with dialogue partners. *See* the lists of the members of ASEAN, ARF and ASEAN–PMC.
Atlantic-to-the-Urals (ATTU) zone	Zone of application of the 1990 CFE Treaty and the 1992 CFE-1A Agreement, stretching from the Atlantic Ocean to the Ural Mountains. It covers the entire land territory of the European NATO states (excluding part of Turkey); the former non-Soviet WTO states; and Armenia, Azerbaijan, Belarus, Georgia, Moldova and Ukraine. It also includes the territory of Russia and Kazakhstan west of the Ural River.
Australia Group	Group of states, formed in 1985, which meets informally each year to monitor the proliferation of chemical and biological products and to discuss chemical and biological weapon-related items which should be subject to national regulatory measures. *See* the list of members.
Balkan states	States in south-eastern Europe bounded by the Adriatic, Aegean and Black seas: Albania, Bosnia and Herzegovina, Bulgaria, Croatia, Greece, Macedonia (Former Yugoslav Republic of), Romania, Slovenia, Turkey and Yugoslavia (Serbia and Montenegro).
Ballistic missile	Missile which follows a ballistic trajectory (part of which may be outside the earth's atmosphere) when thrust is terminated.
Ballistic missile defence (BMD)	Weapon system designed to defend against a ballistic missile attack by intercepting and destroying ballistic missiles or their warheads in flight.
Baltic Council	Established in 1990 for the promotion of democracy and development of cooperation between the three Baltic states, it consists of the Baltic Assembly (established in 1991, for cooperation between the parliaments) and the Baltic Council of Ministers (established in 1994, for cooperation between the governments). The Baltic Council Secretariat is in Riga. *See* list of members.
Bilateral Implementation Commission (BIC)	Established by the 1993 START II Treaty to resolve questions of compliance with the treaty.
Binary chemical weapon	A shell or other device filled with two chemicals of relatively low toxicity which mix and react while the device is being delivered to the target, the reaction product being a super-toxic chemical warfare agent, such as a nerve agent.

Biological weapon (BW)	Weapon containing infectious agents or living organisms, whatever their nature, or infective material derived from them, when used or intended to cause disease or death in humans, animals or plants, as well as their means of delivery.
Central and Eastern Europe (CEE)	Bulgaria, the Czech Republic, Hungary, Poland, Romania and Slovakia. The term is sometimes also taken to include the European former Soviet republics—Armenia, Azerbaijan, Belarus, Georgia, Moldova, the European part of Russia and Ukraine—and sometimes also the Baltic states.
Central Asia	Kazakhstan, Kyrgyzstan, Tajikistan, Turkmenistan and Uzbekistan.
Chemical weapon (CW)	Chemical substances—whether gaseous, liquid or solid—when used or intended for use as weapons because of their direct toxic effects on humans, animals or plants, as well as their means of delivery.
Combined Joint Task Forces (CJTF)	Concept declared at the June 1996 Berlin meeting of NATO foreign ministers to facilitate NATO contingency operations, including the use of 'separable but not separate' military capabilities in operations led by the Western European Union (WEU), with the participation of states outside the NATO Alliance.
Common Foreign and Security Policy (CFSP)	Institutional framework, established by the 1992 Maastricht Treaty, for consultation and development of common positions and joint action on European foreign and security policy. It constitutes the second of the three 'pillars' of the European Union. The CFSP is further elaborated in the 1997 Amsterdam Treaty. *See also* European Union.
Commonwealth of Independent States (CIS)	Established in 1991 as a framework for multilateral cooperation among former Soviet republics. *See* the list of members.
Comprehensive Nuclear Test-Ban Treaty Organization (CTBTO)	Established by the 1996 Comprehensive Nuclear Test-Ban Treaty to resolve questions of compliance with the treaty and as a forum for consultation and cooperation among the states parties.
Conference on Disarmament (CD)	A multilateral arms control negotiating body, based in Geneva, composed of states representing all the regions of the world and including the permanent members of the UN Security Council. The CD reports to the UN General Assembly. *See* the list of members under United Nations.
Conference on Security and Co-operation in Europe (CSCE)	*See* Organization for Security and Co-operation in Europe.
Confidence- and security-building measure (CSBM)	Measure undertaken by states to promote confidence and security through military transparency, openness, constraints and cooperation. CSBMs are militarily significant, politically binding, verifiable and, as a rule, reciprocal.
Confidence-building measure (CBM)	Measure undertaken by states to help reduce the danger of armed conflict and of misunderstanding or miscalculation of military activities.

GLOSSARY xxi

Conventional weapon	Weapon not having mass destruction effects. *See also* Weapon of mass destruction.
Conversion	Term used to describe the shift in resources from military to civilian use. It usually refers to the conversion of industry from military to civilian production.
Cooperative Threat Reduction (CTR) programme	Programme established in 1991 to facilitate bilateral cooperation between the USA and the former Soviet republics with nuclear weapons on their territories (Belarus, Kazakhstan, Russia and Ukraine), primarily for US assistance in the safe and environmentally responsible storage, transportation, dismantlement and destruction of former Soviet nuclear weapons. The programme now also provides assistance to Georgia, Moldova, Turkmenistan and Uzbekistan as well as assistance for the destruction of chemical weapons in Russia.
Council for Security Cooperation in the Asia Pacific (CSCAP)	Established in 1993 as an informal, non-governmental process for regional confidence building and security cooperation through dialogue, consultation and cooperation in Asia–Pacific security matters. *See* the list of members.
Council of Europe	Established in 1949, with its seat in Strasbourg. Its main aims are defined in the 1950 European Convention on Human Rights and the 1953 Convention for the Protection of Human Rights and Fundamental Freedoms. Among its organs is the European Court of Human Rights. The European Council is open to membership of all the European states which accept the principle of the rule of law and guarantee their citizens human rights and fundamental freedoms. *See* the list of members.
Council of the Baltic Sea States (CBSS)	Established in 1992 to promote common strategies for political and economic cooperation and development among the states bordering on the Baltic Sea, Iceland and Norway. *See* the list of members.
Counter-proliferation	Measures or policies to prevent the proliferation or enforce the non-proliferation of weapons of mass destruction.
Cruise missile	Guided weapon-delivery vehicle which sustains flight at subsonic or supersonic speeds through aerodynamic lift, generally flying at very low altitudes to avoid radar detection, sometimes following the contours of the terrain. It can be air-, ground- or sea-launched (ALCM, GLCM and SLCM, respectively) and carry a conventional, nuclear, chemical or biological warhead.
Dayton Agreement	The General Framework Agreement for Peace in Bosnia and Herzegovina was agreed at Dayton, Ohio, and signed in Paris in 1995. As stipulated in the Dayton Agreement, the Agreement on Sub-Regional Arms Control (Florence Agreement) was signed in 1996.
Dual-capable	Term that refers to a weapon system or platform that can carry either conventional or non-conventional explosives.
Dual-use technology	Technology that can be used for both civilian and military applications.

Economic Community of West African States (ECOWAS)	A regional organization established in 1975 with its Executive Secretariat in Lagos, Nigeria, to promote cooperation and development in economic activity, improve relations among its member countries and contribute to development in Africa. In 1981 it adopted the Protocol on Mutual Assistance in Defence Matters. In 1990 the ECOWAS Cease-fire Monitoring Group (ECOMOG) was established to restore the peace process in Liberia. In 1997 the UN Security Council asked ECOWAS to assist in monitoring the sanctions on Sierra Leone. *See* the list of members.
Euro-Atlantic Partnership Council (EAPC)	Established in 1997, the EAPC succeeded the North Atlantic Cooperation Council (NACC). The EAPC provides the overarching framework for practical cooperation between NATO and its PFP partners, with an expanded political dimension. *See* the list of members under North Atlantic Treaty Organization.
European Atomic Energy Community (Euratom or EAEC)	Based on the 1957 Treaty Establishing the European Atomic Energy Community (Euratom Treaty), Euratom was established to promote common efforts between EU member states in the development of nuclear energy for peaceful purposes. Euratom is located in Brussels. It has an agreement with the IAEA for joint application of safeguards in the territories of the members.
European Security and Defence Identity (ESDI)	Concept aimed at strengthening the European pillar of NATO while reinforcing the transatlantic link. Militarily coherent and effective forces, capable of conducting operations under the control of the Western European Union, are to be created.
European Union (EU)	Organization of European states. The 1992 Treaty on European Union (Maastricht Treaty), which created the EU, entered into force in 1993. The 1997 Amsterdam Treaty strengthens the political dimension of the EU and prepares the EU for enlargement. It also confirms that the EU will avail itself of the WEU to elaborate and implement those decisions and actions of the EU which have defence implications, but the operational responsibilities will remain within the WEU. The European Council and the European Commission are in Brussels. The three EU pillars are: cooperation in economic and monetary affairs and Euratom; the common foreign and security policy (CFSP); and cooperation in justice and home affairs. *See* the list of members.
Fissile material	Material composed of atoms which can be split by either fast or slow (thermal) neutrons. Uranium-235 and plutonium-239 are the most common examples of fissile material.
Group of Seven (G7)	Group of leading industrialized nations which have met informally, at the level of heads of state or government, since the 1970s. From 1997 Russia has participated with the G7 in meetings of the G8. *See* the list of members.
Intercontinental ballistic missile (ICBM)	Ground-launched ballistic missile with a range greater than 5500 km.

GLOSSARY xxiii

Intermediate-range nuclear forces (INF)	Theatre nuclear forces with a range of from 1000 km up to and including 5500 km.
International Atomic Energy Agency (IAEA)	An independent, intergovernmental organization within the UN system, with headquarters in Vienna. The IAEA is endowed by its Statute, which entered into force in 1957, to promote the peaceful uses of atomic energy and ensure that nuclear activities are not used to further any military purpose. It has also cooperated with the UN Special Commission on Iraq (UNSCOM) in carrying out the removal of nuclear weapon-usable material from Iraq. Under the NPT and the nuclear weapon-free zone treaties, non-nuclear weapon states must accept IAEA nuclear safeguards to demonstrate the fulfilment of their obligation not to manufacture nuclear weapons. In 1997 the IAEA safeguards were strengthened by the Model Protocol Additional to Safeguards Agreements. *See* the list of members under United Nations.
International Court of Justice (ICJ)	One of the principal organs of the United Nations, set up in 1945 and located in The Hague. Its Statute forms an integral part of the UN Charter.
International Criminal Tribunal for the Former Yugoslavia	The international tribunal tasked with prosecuting those who committed war crimes during the conflict in the former Yugoslavia.
Joint Consultative Group (JCG)	Established by the 1990 CFE Treaty to promote the objectives and implementation of the treaty by reconciling ambiguities of interpretation and implementation.
Joint Compliance and Inspection Commission (JCIC)	Established by the 1991 START I Treaty to resolve questions of compliance, clarify ambiguities and discuss ways to improve implementation of the treaty. It convenes at the request of at least one of the parties.
Kiloton (kt)	Measure of the explosive yield of a nuclear weapon equivalent to 1000 tonnes of trinitrotoluene (TNT) high explosive. The bomb detonated at Hiroshima in World War II had a yield of about 12–15 kilotons.
Landmine	*See* Anti-personnel mine (APM).
London Guidelines for Nuclear Transfers	*See* Nuclear Suppliers Group.
Maastricht Treaty	The 1992 Treaty on European Union. *See* European Union.
Megaton (Mt)	Measure of the explosive yield of a nuclear weapon equivalent to 1 million tonnes of trinitrotoluene (TNT) high explosive.
Minsk Group	Group of states created in 1992 which act together in the OSCE for political settlement of the conflict in the Armenian enclave of Nagorno-Karabakh in Azerbaijan. *See* the list of members under Organization for Security and Co-operation in Europe.

Missile Technology Control Regime (MTCR)	An informal military-related export control regime, established in 1987, which produced the Guidelines for Sensitive Missile-Relevant Transfers. Its goal is to limit the spread of weapons of mass destruction by controlling their delivery systems. *See* the list of members.
Multiple independently targetable re-entry vehicles (MIRVs)	Re-entry vehicles, carried by a single ballistic missile, which can be directed to separate targets along separate trajectories. A missile can carry two or more re-entry vehicles.
National technical means (NTM) of verification	Technical means of intelligence, under the national control of a state, which are used to monitor compliance with an arms control treaty to which the state is a party.
NATO–Russia Permanent Joint Council (PJC)	Established by the 1997 NATO–Russia Founding Act on Mutual Relations, Cooperation and Security for consultation and cooperation between NATO and Russia.
NATO–Ukraine Commission	The NATO North Atlantic Council meets periodically with Ukraine as the NATO–Ukraine Commission, to ensure that NATO and Ukraine are implementing the provisions of the 1997 NATO–Ukraine Charter on a Distinctive Partnership.
Non-Aligned Movement (NAM)	Group established at Belgrade in 1961, sometimes referred to as the Movement of Non-Aligned Countries. NAM is a forum for consultations and coordination of positions on political and economic issues. The Coordinating Bureau of the Non-Aligned Countries (also called the Conference of Non-Aligned Countries) is the forum in which NAM coordinates its actions within the UN. *See* the list of members.
Non-governmental organization (NGO)	A national or international organization of individuals or organizations whose aim is to provide advice and present positions to national and international bodies and to inform the public about specific issues. Some NGOs are accredited by international organizations such as the UN and the OSCE, which seek their advice and assistance.
Non-strategic nuclear forces	*See* Theatre nuclear forces.
Nordic Council	Political advisory organ for cooperation between the parliaments of the Nordic states, founded in 1952 and with its Secretariat in Copenhagen. The Nordic Council of Ministers, established in 1971, is an organ for cooperation between the governments of the Nordic countries and between these governments and the Nordic Council. *See* the list of members.
North Atlantic Cooperation Council (NACC)	*See* Euro-Atlantic Partnership Council.
North Atlantic Treaty Organization (NATO)	Established in 1949 by the North Atlantic Treaty as a political and military defence alliance. NATO has 16 member nations (West European states, the USA and Canada) and its headquarters are in Brussels. In July 1997 the Czech Republic, Hungary and Poland were invited to begin NATO accession negotiations. The three Protocols of Accession were signed in December 1997 and are to be ratified by the parliaments of all NATO states. *See* the list of members.

GLOSSARY

Nuclear Suppliers Group (NSG)	Also known as the London Club, the NSG, established in 1975, coordinates multilateral export controls on nuclear materials. In 1977 it agreed on the Guidelines for Nuclear Transfers (London Guidelines, subsequently revised). The Guidelines contain a 'trigger list' of materials which should trigger IAEA safeguards when exported for peaceful purposes to any non-nuclear weapon state. In 1992 the NSG agreed the Guidelines for Transfers of Nuclear-Related Dual-Use Equipment, Material and Related Technology (Warsaw Guidelines, subsequently revised). *See* the list of members.
Open Skies Consultative Commission (OSCC)	Established by the 1992 Open Skies Treaty to resolve questions of compliance with the treaty.
Organisation for Economic Co-operation and Development (OECD)	Established in 1961 to replace the Organisation for European Economic Co-operation, the OECD's objectives are to promote economic and social welfare by coordinating policies. Its headquarters are in Paris. *See* the list of members.
Organisation for the Prohibition of Chemical Weapons (OPCW)	Established by the 1993 Chemical Weapons Convention to resolve questions of compliance with the convention. Its seat is in The Hague.
Organisme Conjoint de Coopération en Matière d'Armement (OCCAR)	Established in 1996 as a management structure for international cooperative armaments programmes between France, Germany, Italy and the UK. It is also known as the Joint Armaments Cooperation Organization (JACO).
Organization for Security and Co-operation in Europe (OSCE)	Established in 1973 as the Conference on Security and Co-operation in Europe (CSCE), which adopted the Helsinki Final Act in 1975. Since 1995 it transformed into an organization, as a primary instrument for early warning, conflict prevention and crisis management in the OSCE region. The OSCE is concerned with implementation of the principles guiding relations between the member states, human rights, pluralistic democracy (election monitoring), and economic and environmental security. Its Forum for Security Co-operation (FSC) deals with arms control and CSBMs. The OSCE comprises several institutions, all located in Europe. *See* the list of members.
Organization of African Unity (OAU)	Established in 1963 as a union of African states with the objective of promoting cooperation among them. The seat of the Secretary-General is in Addis Ababa. The OAU, in cooperation with the UN, negotiated the Africa nuclear weapon-free zone, embodied in the 1996 Treaty of Pelindaba. *See* the list of members.
Organization of American States (OAS)	Group of states in the Americas which adopted a charter in 1948. The objective of the OAS is to strengthen peace and security in the western hemisphere. The General Secretariat is in Washington, DC. *See* the list of members.
Organization of the Islamic Conference (OIC)	Established in 1971 by Islamic states to promote cooperation among the member states and to support peace, security and the struggle of the people of Palestine and all Muslim people. Its Secretariat is in Jedda, Saudi Arabia. *See* the list of members.

Pact on Stability in Europe	The French proposal presented in 1993 as part of the cooperation in the framework of the EU Common Foreign and Security Policy (CFSP). Its objective is to contribute to stability by preventing tension and potential conflicts connected with border and minorities issues. The Pact was adopted in 1995, and the instruments and procedures were handed over to the OSCE.
Partnership for Peace (PFP)	The NATO programme launched in 1994 for cooperation with NACC and other OSCE states in such areas as military planning, budgeting and training, under the authority of the North Atlantic Council. It provides for cooperation to prepare for and undertake multilateral crisis-management activities such as peacekeeping. The aims of the Enhanced PFP programme, adopted in May 1997, are to strengthen political consultation, develop a more operational role, and provide for greater involvement of partners in PFP decision making and planning. The activities of the PFP and NACC were merged in the EAPC. *See* the list of members under North Atlantic Treaty Organization.
Peaceful nuclear explosion (PNE)	A nuclear explosion for non-military purposes, such as digging canals or harbours or creating underground cavities. The USA terminated its PNE programme in 1973. The USSR conducted its last PNE in 1988.
Petersberg tasks	Tasks emanating from the 1992 meeting of the WEU Council at Petersberg, Germany. Under a UN mandate, WEU members will engage in humanitarian and rescue tasks, peacekeeping operations and tasks of combat forces in crisis management, including peacemaking. NATO will also engage in these tasks. The 1997 Amsterdam Treaty provides the EU with access to an operational capability in the context of the Petersberg tasks.
Re-entry vehicle (RV)	The part of a ballistic missile which carries a nuclear warhead and penetration aids to the target. It re-enters the earth's atmosphere and is destroyed in the final phase of the missile's trajectory. A missile can have one or several RVs and each RV contains a warhead.
Safeguards agreements	*See* International Atomic Energy Agency.
Short-range nuclear forces (SNF)	Nuclear weapons, including artillery, mines, missiles, etc., with ranges of up to 500 km.
South Pacific Forum	Group of South Pacific states created in 1971 which i.a. negotiated the 1985 South Pacific Nuclear Free Zone Treaty (Treaty of Rarotonga). The Secretariat is in Suva, Fiji. *See* the list of members.
Standing Consultative Commission (SCC)	Established by a 1972 US–Soviet Memorandum of Understanding. The USA and Russia refer issues regarding implementation of the 1972 ABM Treaty to the SCC.
Strategic nuclear weapons	ICBMs and SLBMs with a range usually of over 5500 km, as well as bombs and missiles carried on aircraft of intercontinental range.

GLOSSARY

Subcritical experiments	Experiments designed not to reach nuclear criticality, i.e., there is no nuclear explosion and no energy release.
Submarine-launched ballistic missile (SLBM)	A ballistic missile launched from a submarine, usually with a range in excess of 5500 km.
Sub-Regional Consultative Commission (SRCC)	Established by the 1996 Agreement on Sub-Regional Arms Control (Florence Agreement) as a forum for the parties to resolve questions of compliance with the agreement.
Tactical nuclear weapon	A short-range nuclear weapon which is deployed with general-purpose forces along with conventional weapons.
Theatre missile defence (TMD)	Weapon systems designed to defend against non-strategic nuclear missiles by intercepting and destroying them in flight.
Theatre nuclear forces (TNF)	Nuclear weapons with ranges up to and including 5500 km.
Throw-weight	Sum of the weight of a ballistic missile's re-entry vehicle(s), dispensing mechanisms, penetration aids, and targeting and separation devices.
Toxins	Poisonous substances which are products of organisms but are not living or capable of reproducing themselves, as well as chemically created variants of such substances. Some toxins may also be produced synthetically.
Treaty-limited equipment (TLE)	Five categories of equipment on which numerical limits are established by the 1990 CFE Treaty: battle tanks, armoured combat vehicles, artillery, combat aircraft and attack helicopters.
United Nations Register of Conventional Arms (UNROCA)	A voluntary reporting mechanism set up in 1992 for member states of the United Nations to report annually their imports and exports of seven categories of weapons or systems: battle tanks, armoured combat vehicles, large-calibre artillery systems, attack helicopters, combat aircraft, warships, and missiles and missile launchers.
Visegrad Group	Group of states comprising the Czech Republic, Hungary, Poland and Slovakia, formed in 1991 with the aim of intensifying subregional cooperation in political, economic and military areas and coordinating relations with multilateral European institutions.
Warhead	The part of a weapon which contains the explosive or other material intended to inflict damage.
Warsaw Guidelines	*See* Nuclear Suppliers Group.
Warsaw Treaty Organization (WTO)	The WTO, or Warsaw Pact, was established in 1955 by the Treaty of Friendship, Cooperation and Mutual Assistance between eight countries: Albania (withdrew in 1968), Bulgaria, Czechoslovakia, the German Democratic Republic, Hungary, Poland, Romania and the USSR. The WTO was dissolved in 1991.

Wassenaar Arrangement	The Wassenaar Arrangement on Export Controls for Conventional Arms and Dual-Use Goods and Technologies was formally established in 1996. It aims to prevent the acquisition of armaments and sensitive dual-use goods and technologies for military uses by states whose behaviour is cause for concern to the Wassenaar members. *See* the list of members.
Weapon of mass destruction	Nuclear weapon and any other weapon, such as chemical and biological weapons, which may produce comparable effects.
Western European Union (WEU)	Established by the 1954 Protocols to the 1948 Brussels Treaty of Economic, Social and Cultural Collaboration and Collective Self-Defence among Western European States. The seat of the WEU has been in Brussels since 1993. Within the EU Common Foreign and Security Policy (CFSP) and at the request of the EU, the WEU is to elaborate and implement EU decisions and actions which have defence implications. The Western European Armaments Group (WEAG) is the WEU armaments cooperation forum. The Western European Armaments Organization (WEAO) was established in 1997 (as a subsidiary body of the WEU) to provide a legal framework for the cooperative armaments activities of WEAG. Initially, its main task is the management of WEAG military research and technology activities. *See* the list of members.
Yield	Released nuclear explosive energy expressed as the equivalent of the energy produced by a given number of tonnes of trinitrotoluene (TNT) high explosive.
Zangger Committee	Established in 1971, the Nuclear Exporters Committee, called the Zangger Committee after its first chairman, is a group of nuclear supplier countries that meets informally twice a year to coordinate export controls on nuclear materials. *See* the list of members.

Membership of international organizations, as of 1 January 1998

The UN member states and organizations within the UN system are listed first, followed by all other organizations in alphabetical order. Note that not all the members of organizations are UN member states. Where confirmed information on new members became available in early 1998, this is given in notes.

United Nations (UN) and year of membership

Afghanistan, 1946
Albania, 1955
Algeria, 1962
Andorra, 1993
Angola, 1976
Antigua and Barbuda, 1981
Argentina, 1945
Armenia, 1992
Australia, 1945
Austria, 1955
Azerbaijan, 1992
Bahamas, 1973
Bahrain, 1971
Bangladesh, 1974
Barbados, 1966
Belarus, 1945
Belgium, 1945
Belize, 1981
Benin, 1960
Bhutan, 1971
Bolivia, 1945
Bosnia and Herzegovina, 1992
Botswana, 1966
Brazil, 1945
Brunei Darussalam, 1984
Bulgaria, 1955
Burkina Faso, 1960
Burundi, 1962
Cambodia, 1955
Cameroon, 1960
Canada, 1945
Cape Verde, 1975
Central African Republic, 1960
Chad, 1960
Chile, 1945
China, 1945
Colombia, 1945
Comoros, 1975
Congo (Brazzaville), 1960
Congo, Democratic Republic of the, 1960
Costa Rica, 1945
Côte d'Ivoire, 1960
Croatia, 1992
Cuba, 1945
Cyprus, 1960

Czech Republic, 1993
Denmark, 1945
Djibouti, 1977
Dominica, 1978
Dominican Republic, 1945
Ecuador, 1945
Egypt, 1945
El Salvador, 1945
Equatorial Guinea, 1968
Eritrea, 1993
Estonia, 1991
Ethiopia, 1945
Fiji, 1970
Finland, 1955
France, 1945
Gabon, 1960
Gambia, 1965
Georgia, 1992
Germany, 1973
Ghana, 1957
Greece, 1945
Grenada, 1974
Guatemala, 1945
Guinea, 1958
Guinea-Bissau, 1974
Guyana, 1966
Haiti, 1945
Honduras, 1945
Hungary, 1955
Iceland, 1946
India, 1945
Indonesia, 1950
Iran, 1945
Iraq, 1945
Ireland, 1955
Israel, 1949
Italy, 1955
Jamaica, 1962
Japan, 1956
Jordan, 1955
Kazakhstan, 1992
Kenya, 1963
Korea, Democratic People's Republic of (North Korea), 1991

Korea, Republic of (South Korea), 1991
Kuwait, 1963
Kyrgyzstan, 1992
Lao People's Democratic Republic, 1955
Latvia, 1991
Lebanon, 1945
Lesotho, 1966
Liberia, 1945
Libya, 1955
Liechtenstein, 1990
Lithuania, 1991
Luxembourg, 1945
Macedonia, Former Yugoslav Republic of (FYROM), 1993
Madagascar, 1960
Malawi, 1964
Malaysia, 1957
Maldives, 1965
Mali, 1960
Malta, 1964
Marshall Islands, 1991
Mauritania, 1961
Mauritius, 1968
Mexico, 1945
Micronesia, 1991
Moldova, 1992
Monaco, 1993
Mongolia, 1961
Morocco, 1956
Mozambique, 1975
Myanmar (Burma), 1948
Namibia, 1990
Nepal, 1955
Netherlands, 1945
New Zealand, 1945
Nicaragua, 1945
Niger, 1960
Nigeria, 1960
Norway, 1945
Oman, 1971
Pakistan, 1947
Palau, 1994
Panama, 1945
Papua New Guinea, 1975

Paraguay, 1945
Peru, 1945
Philippines, 1945
Poland, 1945
Portugal, 1955
Qatar, 1971
Romania, 1955
Russia, 1945[a]
Rwanda, 1962
Saint Kitts (Christopher) and Nevis, 1983
Saint Lucia, 1979
Saint Vincent and the Grenadines, 1980
Samoa, Western, 1976
San Marino, 1992
Sao Tome and Principe, 1975
Saudi Arabia, 1945
Senegal, 1960
Seychelles, 1976

Sierra Leone, 1961
Singapore, 1965
Slovakia, 1993
Slovenia, 1992
Solomon Islands, 1978
Somalia, 1960
South Africa, 1945
Spain, 1955
Sri Lanka, 1955
Sudan, 1956
Suriname, 1975
Swaziland, 1968
Sweden, 1946
Syria, 1945
Tajikistan, 1992
Tanzania, 1961
Thailand, 1946
Togo, 1960
Trinidad and Tobago, 1962
Tunisia, 1956

Turkey, 1945
Turkmenistan, 1992
Uganda, 1962
UK, 1945
Ukraine, 1945
United Arab Emirates, 1971
Uruguay, 1945
USA, 1945
Uzbekistan, 1992
Vanuatu, 1981
Venezuela, 1945
Viet Nam, 1977
Yemen, 1947
Yugoslavia, 1945[b]
Zaire see Congo, Democratic Republic of the
Zambia, 1964
Zimbabwe, 1980

[a] In Dec. 1991 Russia informed the UN Secretary-General that it was continuing the membership of the USSR in the Security Council and all other UN bodies.

[b] A claim by Yugoslavia (Serbia and Montenegro) in 1992 to continue automatically the membership of the former Yugoslavia was not accepted by the UN General Assembly. It was decided that Yugoslavia should apply for membership, which it had not done by 1 Jan. 1998. It may not participate in the work of the General Assembly, its subsidiary organs or the conferences and meetings it convenes.

UN Security Council

Permanent members (the P5): China, France, Russia, UK, USA

Non-permanent members in 1997 (elected by the UN General Assembly for two-year terms; the year in brackets is the year at the end of which the term expires): Chile (1997), Costa Rica (1998), Egypt (1997), Guinea-Bissau (1997), Japan (1998), Kenya (1998), Korea (South) (1997), Poland (1997), Portugal (1998), Sweden (1998)

Note: Bahrain, Brazil, Gabon, Gambia and Slovenia were elected non-permanent members for 1998–99.

Conference on Disarmament (CD)

Members: Algeria, Argentina, Australia, Austria, Bangladesh, Belarus, Belgium, Brazil, Bulgaria, Cameroon, Canada, Chile, China, Colombia, Cuba, Egypt, Ethiopia, Finland, France, Germany, Hungary, India, Indonesia, Iran, Iraq, Israel, Italy, Japan, Kenya, Korea (North), Korea (South), Mexico, Mongolia, Morocco, Myanmar (Burma), Netherlands, New Zealand, Nigeria, Norway, Pakistan, Peru, Poland, Romania, Russia, Senegal, Slovakia, South Africa, Spain, Sri Lanka, Sweden, Switzerland, Syria, Turkey, UK, Ukraine, USA, Venezuela, Viet Nam, Yugoslavia,* Zaire, Zimbabwe

* Yugoslavia (Serbia and Montenegro) has been suspended since 1992.

International Atomic Energy Agency (IAEA)

Members: Afghanistan, Albania, Algeria, Argentina, Armenia, Australia, Austria, Bangladesh, Belarus, Belgium, Bolivia, Bosnia and Herzegovina, Brazil, Bulgaria, Cambodia, Cameroon, Canada, Chile, China, Colombia, Costa Rica, Côte d'Ivoire, Croatia, Cuba, Cyprus, Czech Republic, Denmark, Dominican Republic, Ecuador, Egypt, El Salvador, Estonia, Ethiopia, Finland, France, Gabon, Georgia, Germany, Ghana, Greece, Guatemala, Haiti, Holy See, Hungary, Iceland, India, Indonesia, Iran, Iraq, Ireland, Israel, Italy, Jamaica, Japan, Jordan, Kazakhstan, Kenya, Korea (South), Kuwait, Latvia, Lebanon, Liberia, Libya, Liechtenstein, Lithuania, Luxembourg, Macedonia (Former Yugoslav Republic of), Madagascar, Malaysia, Mali, Malta, Marshall Islands, Mauritius, Mexico, Moldova, Monaco, Mongolia, Morocco, Myanmar (Burma), Namibia, Netherlands, New Zealand, Nicaragua, Niger, Nigeria, Norway, Pakistan, Panama,

Paraguay, Peru, Philippines, Poland, Portugal, Qatar, Romania, Russia, Saudi Arabia, Senegal, Sierra Leone, Singapore, Slovakia, Slovenia, South Africa, Spain, Sri Lanka, Sudan, Sweden, Switzerland, Syria, Tanzania, Thailand, Tunisia, Turkey, Uganda, UK, Ukraine, United Arab Emirates, Uruguay, USA, Uzbekistan, Venezuela, Viet Nam, Yemen, Yugoslavia,* Zaire, Zambia, Zimbabwe

* Yugoslavia (Serbia and Montenegro) has been suspended since 1992. It is deprived of the right to participate in the IAEA General Conference and the Board of Governors' meetings but is assessed for its contribution to the budget of the IAEA.

Note: North Korea was a member of the IAEA until Sep. 1994.

Arab League

Members: Algeria, Bahrain, Comoros, Djibouti, Egypt, Iraq, Jordan, Kuwait, Lebanon, Libya, Mauritania, Morocco, Oman, Palestine, Qatar, Saudi Arabia, Somalia, Sudan, Syria, Tunisia, United Arab Emirates, Yemen

Asia–Pacific Economic Co-operation (APEC)

Participating economies: Australia, Brunei, Canada, Chile, China, Hong Kong (China), Indonesia, Japan, Korea (South), Malaysia, Mexico, New Zealand, Papua New Guinea, the Philippines, Singapore, 'Chinese Taipei' (Taiwan), Thailand, USA

Association of South-East Asian Nations (ASEAN)

Members: Brunei, Indonesia, Laos, Malaysia, Myanmar (Burma), Philippines, Singapore, Thailand, Viet Nam

ASEAN Regional Forum (ARF)

Members: The ASEAN states plus Australia, Cambodia, Canada, China, European Union (EU), India, Japan, Korea (South), New Zealand, Papua New Guinea, Russia, USA

ASEAN Post Ministerial Conference (ASEAN–PMC)

Members: The ASEAN states plus Australia, Canada, European Union (EU), Japan, Korea (South), New Zealand, USA

Australia Group

Members: Argentina, Australia, Austria, Belgium, Canada, Czech Republic, Denmark, Finland, France, Germany, Greece, Hungary, Iceland, Ireland, Italy, Japan, Korea (South), Luxembourg, Netherlands, New Zealand, Norway, Poland, Portugal, Romania, Slovakia, Spain, Sweden, Switzerland, UK, USA

Observer: European Commission

Baltic Council

Members: Estonia, Latvia, Lithuania

Commonwealth of Independent States (CIS)

Members: Armenia, Azerbaijan, Belarus, Georgia, Kazakhstan, Kyrgyzstan, Moldova, Russia, Tajikistan, Turkmenistan, Ukraine, Uzbekistan

Council for Security Cooperation in the Asia Pacific (CSCAP)

Members: Australia, Canada, China, Indonesia, Japan, Korea (North), Korea (South), Malaysia, Mongolia, New Zealand, Philippines, Russia, Singapore, Thailand, USA, Viet Nam

Council of Europe

Members: Albania, Andorra, Austria, Belgium, Bulgaria, Croatia, Cyprus, Czech Republic, Denmark, Estonia, Finland, France, Germany, Greece, Hungary, Iceland, Ireland, Italy, Latvia, Liechtenstein, Lithuania, Luxembourg, Macedonia (Former Yugoslav Republic of), Malta, Moldova, Netherlands, Norway, Poland, Portugal, Romania, Russia, San Marino, Slovakia, Slovenia, Spain, Sweden, Switzerland, Turkey, UK, Ukraine

Observers: Canada, Holy See, Japan, USA

Council of the Baltic Sea States (CBSS)

Members: Denmark, Estonia, European Commission, Finland, Germany, Iceland, Latvia, Lithuania, Norway, Poland, Russia, Sweden

Economic Community of West African States (ECOWAS)

Members: Benin, Burkina Faso, Cape Verde, Côte d'Ivoire, Gambia, Ghana, Guinea, Guinea-Bissau, Liberia, Mali, Mauritania, Niger, Nigeria, Senegal, Sierra Leone, Togo

European Union (EU)

Members: Austria, Belgium, Denmark, Finland, France, Germany, Greece, Ireland, Italy, Luxembourg, Netherlands, Portugal, Spain, Sweden, UK

Group of Seven (G7)

Members: Canada, France, Germany, Italy, Japan, UK, USA

Missile Technology Control Regime (MTCR)

MTCR partners: Argentina, Australia, Austria, Belgium, Brazil, Canada, Denmark, Finland, France, Germany, Greece, Hungary, Iceland, Ireland, Italy, Japan, Luxembourg, Netherlands, New Zealand, Norway, Portugal, Russia, South Africa, Spain, Sweden, Switzerland, Turkey, UK, USA

Non-Aligned Movement (NAM)

Members: Afghanistan, Algeria, Angola, Bahamas, Bahrain, Bangladesh, Barbados, Belize, Benin, Bhutan, Bolivia, Botswana, Brunei, Burkina Faso, Burundi, Cambodia, Cameroon, Cape Verde, Central African Republic, Chad, Chile, Colombia, Comoros, Congo (Brazzaville), Congo, Democratic Republic of (formerly Zaire), Côte d'Ivoire, Cuba, Cyprus, Djibouti, Ecuador, Egypt, Equatorial Guinea, Eritrea, Ethiopia, Gabon, Gambia, Ghana, Grenada, Guatemala, Guinea, Guinea-Bissau, Guyana, Honduras, India, Indonesia, Iran, Iraq, Jamaica, Jordan, Kenya, Korea (North), Kuwait, Laos, Lebanon, Lesotho, Liberia, Libya, Madagascar, Malawi, Malaysia, Maldives, Mali, Malta, Mauritania, Mauritius, Mongolia, Morocco, Mozambique, Myanmar (Burma), Namibia, Nepal, Nicaragua, Niger, Nigeria, Oman, Pakistan, Palestine, Panama, Papua New Guinea, Peru, Philippines, Qatar, Rwanda, Saint Lucia, Sao Tome and Principe, Saudi Arabia, Senegal, Seychelles, Sierra Leone, Singapore, Somalia, South Africa, Sri Lanka, Sudan, Suriname, Swaziland, Syria, Tanzania, Thailand, Togo, Trinidad and Tobago, Tunisia, Turkmenistan, Uganda, United Arab Emirates, Uzbekistan, Vanuatu, Venezuela, Viet Nam, Yemen, Yugoslavia,* Zambia, Zimbabwe

* Yugoslavia (Serbia and Montenegro) has not been permitted to participate in NAM activities since 1992.

Nordic Council

Members: Denmark (including the Faroe Islands and Greenland), Finland (including Åland), Iceland, Norway, Sweden

North Atlantic Treaty Organization (NATO)

Members: Belgium, Canada, Denmark, France,* Germany, Greece, Iceland, Italy, Luxembourg, Netherlands, Norway, Portugal, Spain,* Turkey, UK, USA

* France and Spain are not in the integrated military structures of NATO, but in December 1997 the Government of Spain approved Spain's full participation.

Note: In December 1997, Protocols of Accession to NATO for the Czech Republic, Hungary and Poland were signed by all the NATO member states.

Euro-Atlantic Partnership Council (EAPC)

Members: Albania, Armenia, Austria, Azerbaijan, Belarus, Bulgaria, Czech Republic, Estonia, Finland, Georgia, Hungary, Kazakhstan, Kyrgyzstan, Latvia, Lithuania, Macedonia (Former Yugoslav Republic of), Moldova, Poland, Romania, Russia, Slovakia, Slovenia, Sweden, Switzerland, Tajikistan, Turkmenistan, Ukraine, Uzbekistan

Partnership for Peace (PFP)

Partner states: Albania, Armenia, Austria, Azerbaijan, Belarus, Bulgaria, Czech Republic, Estonia, Finland, Georgia, Hungary, Kazakhstan, Kyrgyzstan, Latvia, Lithuania, Macedonia (Former Yugoslav Republic of), Moldova, Poland, Romania, Russia, Slovakia, Slovenia, Sweden, Switzerland, Turkmenistan, Ukraine, Uzbekistan

Nuclear Suppliers Group (NSG)

Members: Argentina, Australia, Austria, Belgium, Brazil, Bulgaria, Canada, Czech Republic, Denmark, Finland, France, Germany, Greece, Hungary, Ireland, Italy, Japan, Korea (South), Luxembourg, Netherlands, New Zealand, Norway, Poland, Portugal, Romania, Russia, Slovakia, South Africa, Spain, Sweden, Switzerland, UK, Ukraine, USA

Organisation for Economic Co-operation and Development (OECD)

Members: Australia, Austria, Belgium, Canada, Czech Republic, Denmark, Finland, France, Germany, Greece, Hungary, Iceland, Ireland, Italy, Japan, Korea (South), Luxembourg, Mexico, Netherlands, New Zealand, Norway, Poland, Portugal, Spain, Sweden, Switzerland, Turkey, UK, USA

The European Commission participates in the work of the OECD.

Organization for Security and Co-operation in Europe (OSCE)

Members: Albania, Andorra, Armenia, Austria, Azerbaijan, Belarus, Belgium, Bosnia and Herzegovina, Bulgaria, Canada, Croatia, Cyprus, Czech Republic, Denmark, Estonia, Finland, France, Georgia, Germany, Greece, Holy See, Hungary, Iceland, Ireland, Italy, Kazakhstan, Kyrgyzstan, Latvia, Liechtenstein, Lithuania, Luxembourg, Macedonia (Former Yugoslav Republic of), Malta, Moldova, Monaco, Netherlands, Norway, Poland, Portugal, Romania, Russia, San Marino, Slovakia, Slovenia, Spain, Sweden, Switzerland, Tajikistan, Turkey, Turkmenistan, UK, Ukraine, USA, Uzbekistan, Yugoslavia*

* Yugoslavia (Serbia and Montenegro) has been suspended since 1992.

Members of the Minsk Group: Armenia, Azerbaijan, Belarus, Denmark, Finland, France, Germany, Italy, Norway, Poland, Russia, Sweden, Turkey, USA

Partners for Co-operation: Algeria, Egypt, Israel, Japan, Korea (South), Morocco, Tunisia

Organization of African Unity (OAU)

Members: Algeria, Angola, Benin, Botswana, Burkina Faso, Burundi, Cameroon, Cape Verde, Central African Republic, Chad, Comoros, Congo (Brazzaville), Congo, Democratic Republic of (formerly Zaire), Côte d'Ivoire, Djibouti, Egypt, Equatorial Guinea, Eritrea, Ethiopia, Gabon, Gambia, Ghana, Guinea, Guinea-Bissau, Kenya, Lesotho, Liberia, Libya, Madagascar, Malawi, Mali, Mauritania, Mauritius, Mozambique, Namibia, Niger, Nigeria, Rwanda, Western Sahara (Saharawi Arab Democratic Republic, SADR*), Sao Tome and Principe, Senegal, Seychelles, Sierra Leone, Somalia, South Africa, Sudan, Swaziland, Tanzania, Togo, Tunisia, Uganda, Zambia, Zimbabwe

* The Western Sahara was admitted in 1982. Its membership was disputed by Morocco and other states. Morocco withdrew from the OAU in 1985.

Organization of American States (OAS)

Members: Antigua and Barbuda, Argentina, Bahamas, Barbados, Belize, Bolivia, Brazil, Canada, Chile, Colombia, Costa Rica, Cuba,* Dominica, Dominican Republic, Ecuador, El Salvador, Grenada, Guatemala, Guyana, Haiti, Honduras, Jamaica, Mexico, Nicaragua, Panama, Paraguay, Peru, Saint Kitts (Christopher) and Nevis, Saint Lucia, Saint Vincent and the Grenadines, Suriname, Trinidad and Tobago, Uruguay, USA, Venezuela

* Cuba has been excluded from participation since 1962.

Permanent observers: Algeria, Angola, Austria, Belgium, Bosnia and Herzegovina, Bulgaria, Croatia, Cyprus, Czech Republic, Egypt, Equatorial Guinea, EU, Finland, France, Germany, Ghana, Greece, Holy See, Hungary, India, Israel, Italy, Japan, Kazakhstan, Korea (South), Latvia, Lebanon, Morocco, Netherlands, Pakistan, Poland, Portugal, Romania, Russia, Saudi Arabia, Spain, Sri Lanka, Sweden, Switzerland, Tunisia, UK, Ukraine, Yemen

Organization of the Islamic Conference (OIC)

Members: Afghanistan, Albania, Algeria, Azerbaijan, Bahrain, Bangladesh, Benin, Bosnia and Herzegovina, Brunei, Burkina Faso, Cameroon, Chad, Comoros, Djibouti, Egypt, Gabon, Gambia, Guinea, Guinea-Bissau, Indonesia, Iran, Iraq, Jordan, Kazakhstan, Kuwait, Kyrgyzstan, Lebanon, Libya, Malaysia, Maldives, Mali, Mauritania, Morocco, Mozambique, Niger, Nigeria, Oman, Pakistan, Palestine, Qatar, Saudi Arabia, Senegal, Sierra Leone, Somalia, Sudan, Suriname, Syria, Tajikistan, Tunisia, Turkey, Turkmenistan, Uganda, United Arab Emirates, Uzbekistan, Yemen

South Pacific Forum

Members: Australia, Cook Islands, Fiji, Kiribati, Marshall Islands, Micronesia, Nauru, New Zealand, Niue, Palau, Papua New Guinea, Samoa (Western), Solomon Islands, Tonga, Tuvalu, Vanuatu

Wassenaar Arrangement

Members: Argentina, Australia, Austria, Belgium, Bulgaria, Canada, Czech Republic, Denmark, Finland, France, Germany, Greece, Hungary, Ireland, Italy, Japan, Korea (South), Luxembourg, Netherlands, New Zealand, Norway, Poland, Portugal, Romania, Russia, Slovakia, Spain, Sweden, Switzerland, Turkey, UK, Ukraine, USA

Western European Union (WEU)

Members: Belgium, France, Germany, Greece, Italy, Luxembourg, Netherlands, Portugal, Spain, UK

Associate Members: Iceland, Norway, Turkey

Observers: Austria, Denmark, Finland, Ireland, Sweden

Associate Partners: Bulgaria, Czech Republic, Estonia, Hungary, Latvia, Lithuania, Poland, Romania, Slovakia, Slovenia

Members of WEAG and WEAO: Belgium, Denmark, France, Germany, Greece, Italy, Luxembourg, Netherlands, Norway, Portugal, Spain, Turkey, UK

Zangger Committee

Members: Argentina, Australia, Austria, Belgium, Bulgaria, Canada, China, Czech Republic, Denmark, Finland, France, Germany, Greece, Hungary, Ireland, Italy, Japan, Luxembourg, Netherlands, Norway, Poland, Portugal, Romania, Russia, Slovakia, South Africa, Spain, Sweden, Switzerland, UK, USA

Conventions in tables

. .	Data not available or not applicable
–	Nil or a negligible figure
( )	Uncertain data
b.	Billion (thousand million)
m.	Million
th.	Thousand
tr.	Trillion (million million)
$	US dollars, unless otherwise indicated

Introduction
Transformation of the world security system

ADAM DANIEL ROTFELD

Today the international security environment is far more complex than it was in the cold war era of bipolarity. This is confirmed by the developments of 1997 which are presented and analysed in this Yearbook. The data and facts on armaments, arms control, international security and major armed conflicts in this volume reveal the basic, often contradictory elements of the emerging international security regime: it is characterized by both globalization and fragmentation. The radically diminished threat of a world war has been replaced by the reality of intra-state conflicts which undermine stability and security at the domestic and regional levels. A serious challenge for the international system is the increasing number of weak or even failed states and their inability to control developments on their own territory. The positive forces behind these negative developments are the trend towards democratization, civil society and respect for human rights and the increasing role of multilateral security institutions and their concerted efforts to achieve benefits for the international community of nations.[1]

I. Achievements and failures

Events in 1997 did not support the conventional wisdom that multilateral organizations are ineffective, if not helpless, in dealing with domestic armed conflicts. Indeed, the progress made in conflict management and settlement was possible largely because of the commitment of the United Nations and regional organizations. In other efforts, contacts were established or negotiations launched which opened prospects for settling conflicts that were previously considered insoluble. Peace or cease-fire agreements were reached in a number of cases.[2]

The year also witnessed the outbreak of new disputes and major armed conflicts and the continuation of others, several of which were characterized by large-scale massacres and other atrocities. The situation in the Kosovo province of Yugoslavia (Serbia and Montenegro) became aggravated, the peace process between Israel and the Palestinians came to a halt, and Saddam Hussein's policy towards the United Nations Special Commission on Iraq (UNSCOM) led Iraq to the brink of war in 1997.

---

[1] United Nations, Report of the Secretary-General on the Work of the Organization, UN document A/52/1, 1997, pp. 1–4.
[2] See chapters 1 and 2 in this volume.

SIPRI Yearbook 1998: Armaments, Disarmament and International Security

Alongside these developments in regions of conflict, significant progress was achieved in arms control and disarmament during the year. The 1993 Chemical Weapons Convention (CWC) entered into force, and agreement was reached by the parties to the 1972 Biological and Toxin Weapons Convention (BTWC) to intensify their efforts to negotiate verification procedures.[3] The 1995 Treaty of Bangkok, establishing a nuclear weapon-free zone in South-East Asia, entered into force during the year. As the result of a global campaign, the 1997 Convention on the Prohibition of the Use, Stockpiling, Production and Transfer of Anti-Personnel Mines and their Destruction (APM Convention) was opened for signature,[4] and the basic elements for adaptation of the 1990 Treaty on Conventional Armed Forces in Europe (CFE Treaty) were agreed by the parties. Among the achievements in early 1998, the Protocol on Environmental Protection to the Antarctic Treaty (Madrid Protocol) entered into force. With the required 20 ratifications attained, Protocol IV of the 1981 Convention on Prohibitions or Restrictions on the Use of Certain Conventional Weapons which may be Deemed to be Excessively Injurious or to have Indiscriminate Effects, prohibiting the employment of laser weapons designed to cause permanent blindness, will enter into force on 30 July 1998.[5]

II. The driving forces of change

In his first report on the work of the United Nations, in 1997 Secretary-General Kofi Annan defined some of the key forces that are transforming the world and thus the UN agenda. One of the fundamental factors which he listed is the inter-ethnic conflicts that erupted after the break-up of several multi-ethnic states and the collapse of bipolarity. Another is globalization, the most profound source of international transformation since the industrial revolution. Other shifts in the world today include the revolution in information technology and the intensification of global environmental interdependence. The transnational expansion of civil society and the closely related trend towards democratization and respect for human rights are evidenced by the fact that some 120 countries now hold free and fair elections, the highest number in history. The final factor listed in the Secretary-General's report is the expanding global networks of 'uncivil society'—organized crime, drug traffic, money laundering and internationally organized terrorism.

Paradoxically, the integrative trends are accompanied by fragmentation. However, as the Secretary-General rightly noted, '[i]n some instances, what appears to be fragmentation is in fact a move towards decentralization in policy-making and administration due to the desire for greater efficiency, effectiveness and accountability, thus posing no grounds for concern'.[6] In some parts of the world fragmentation is a by-product of the collapse of

---

[3] See chapter 11 in this volume.
[4] See chapter 13 in this volume.
[5] For the parties to the arms control and disarmament agreements, see annexe A in this volume.
[6] United Nations (note 1), p. 3.

bipolarity and the erosion of state power. The latter—alongside the lack of deep-rooted democratic institutions and abuses of human rights, civil freedoms and the rights of minorities in particular—contributes to the aggravation of domestic conflicts of an ethnic, national or religious nature. In extreme situations, as in Albania, Bosnia and Herzegovina, Cambodia and Rwanda, the conflicts have led to general chaos and the breakdown of the state, rendering it unable, without external intervention, to restore order based on respect for democratic norms and principles and for the rights of individuals and minority groups. In summary, the new world security environment has generated internal destabilization in some states, with uncertainties and insecurities that affect not only states but also regions and even the entire international community, as in the case of dictatorial regimes such as that of Iraq.

It is increasingly recognized that good governance, human rights and democratization are essential building blocks for the attainment of international peace and security. Good governance comprises the rule of law, effective state institutions, transparency and accountability in the management of public affairs, respect for human rights and meaningful participation by all citizens in national political processes.[7] The obligations of states in this regard are regulated by both national legal instruments and treaties under international law. Thus, the principles of sovereignty and non-intervention in internal affairs cannot prevent multilateral organizations and states from showing interest or becoming involved in the affairs of other states.[8]

In an analysis of the intra-state conflicts that have flared up since the cold war, two often underestimated aspects deserve attention. First, whatever the banner under which they are waged—ethnic, national, religious or any other—civil wars today occur chiefly in failed states. This is especially true when the state's economy and the institutions guarding law and order and respect for civil rights and freedoms have broken down. Second, unlike 'classic wars', in the post-cold war conflicts the combating parties do not abide by legal principles or norms or the humanitarian laws which determine the code of conduct in wartime. The barbaric practices of parties to a conflict, accompanied by the spread of organized crime and disregard for the law, make it extremely difficult for international institutions to intervene effectively to achieve peaceful settlement of disputes.

III. A trans-governmental order

It would be naïve to believe that the response to the new security challenges should be the creation of a hierarchical supra-state structure, a *sui generis* world government. While the international system is jeopardized by the exis-

---

[7] United Nations (note 1), p. 5.
[8] According to the UN Charter (Article 2, para. 7), 'Nothing contained in the present Charter shall authorize the United Nations to intervene in matters which are essentially within the domestic jurisdiction of any state'. Similar provisions are reflected in the Declaration on Principles Guiding Relations between Participating States (Principle VI on non-intervention in internal affairs) of the Helsinki Final Act of the Conference on Security and Co-operation in Europe, Helsinki, 1 Aug. 1975.

tence of weak states, particularly those which have recently gained independence, the number of sovereign states is not decreasing but growing. In 1945 the UN Charter was signed and adopted by 53 nations; today there are 185 UN member states.

In the search for solutions to global trans-border problems such as organized crime, international terrorism, endangered natural environments, and so on, states have developed cooperation between their police, judicial, ministerial and parliamentary agencies. As one author noted, '[t]he result is not world government, but global governance . . . The state is not disappearing, it is disaggregating into its separate, functionally distinct parts'.[9]

In his work on the clash of civilizations, Samuel Huntington recommended adherence to an 'abstention rule' by which the USA and other Western powers, in order to avoid a major inter-civilizational war, should 'refrain from intervening in conflicts in other civilizations'.[10] His second recommendation is a 'joint mediation rule', by which the 'core' states would negotiate with each other to contain or to stop 'fault-line' wars from breaking out between states or groups of states in their respective civilizations. This may be seen as a new version of the United States's Monroe Doctrine, expanded in our times to cover Western civilization, that is, mainly the states of Europe and North America. However, while it is true that regional, national or local action is needed to solve most security problems, including those of global relevance, the global interdependence and integration of states are growing at different levels. The rich developed nations cannot isolate themselves from the problems of the poor developing world—of the African, Asian and Latin American states. In this regard, the proposition of openness and partnership between the nations of the poor South and the wealthy North is much more promising.

Swedish Under-Secretary of State Mats Karlsson listed five qualitative elements required for a genuine North–South partnership. He claimed that there is a need (*a*) for a real change of attitude—a 'subject-to-subject attitude'; (*b*) to be explicit about shared values; (*c*) for transparency in interests, which requires openness; (*d*) for clear contractual standards, in order to avoid the host of conditionalities that now hamstring the politics of cooperation, and for these standards to be upheld jointly by all parties; and (*e*) equality of the capacity to analyse and judge the terms of a contract. In other words, a code of conduct should be developed to make the partnership more explicit and concrete.[11] The essence of such a partnership is mutual respect and equality. In place of relationships focused on aid, there is a need to develop a more comprehensive approach in which African, Asian and Latin American partners are treated as the subjects rather than the objects of development. The relationship should be based on trade, investments and closer links to the global economy.

---

[9] Slaughter, A.-M., 'The real new world order', *Foreign Affairs*, vol. 76, no. 5 (Sep./Oct. 1997), p. 184.

[10] Huntington, S., *The Clash of Civilizations and the Remaking of World Order* (Simon and Schuster: New York, 1996), p. 316.

[11] Karlsson, M., 'Foreword', eds H. Kifle, A. O. Olukoshi and L. Wohlgemuth, *A New Partnership for African Development: Issues and Parameters* (Nordic Africa Institute: Uppsala, 1997), pp. 6–8.

As regards Euro-Asian relations, the heads of state and government of 10 Asian and 15 European nations and the President of the European Commission, meeting at the Second Asia–Europe Meeting in London on 3–4 April 1998,[12] recognized the growing interdependence of the economies and economic policies of their countries. They agreed on a collective effort to enhance understanding of the consequences of the present economic conditions in Asia.[13] Under the philosophy of inclusiveness, they agreed a number of joint principles, directions and action programmes.

IV. The agenda ahead

Crises, risks and challenges—rather than abstract constructs and proposals—determine the priorities in the field of security, arms control and disarmament. The main challenge to world security at the turn of the century will be posed not so much by rivalries between the great powers or the accelerated revolution in military technology as by human poverty. More than one-quarter of the developing world's population still lives in poverty. About 1.3 billion people—one-third of the global population—subsist on incomes of less than $1 a day,[14] and global pressures are creating or threatening further increases in poverty. There is a clear relationship between domestic and regional conflicts and the spread of poverty and stagnation or decline in some 100 developing countries. Eradicating human poverty worldwide should therefore be seen not only as a moral imperative and a commitment to human solidarity but also as a practical political strategy. Such a strategy was adopted in the programme of the 1995 Copenhagen World Summit for Social Development. Implementing this programme will not be an easy task.[15]

The adoption by the UN General Assembly of its Agenda for Development and the 19th General Assembly special session to review the implementation of agreements reached at the 1992 Rio Conference on Environment and Development may be seen as two major events of 1997 aimed at international economic cooperation and sustainable development. A self-sustaining 'pro-poor' growth strategy should be implemented with strong external support.[16] An increase in public spending on human development and a decrease in military expenditures should be seen as an integral part of this strategy. However, although the decline in world military spending over the period 1988–97 by more than one-third in real terms did bring real economic advantages for many

---

[12] The first summit meeting was held in Bangkok on 1–2 Mar. 1996.

[13] Chairman's Statement, London, 4 April 1998. URL <http://asem2.fco.gov.uk/asem2/texts/closing/chairmans.statement.shtml>, version current on 7 Apr. 1998.

[14] The worst situation prevails in South-East Asia and Sub-Saharan Africa (it is estimated that by 2000 half the population of Sub-Saharan Africa will be living below the poverty level). United Nations Development Programme (UNDP), *Human Development Report 1997* (Oxford University Press: Oxford and New York, 1997), p. 3.

[15] However, the cost of eliminating poverty is estimated at only about 1 per cent of the global income, or no more than 2–3 per cent of the national income of all but the poorest countries. United Nations Development Programme (note 14), p. 116.

[16] United Nations Development Programme (note 14), pp. 7, 110.

states, not all the hoped-for immediate benefits or utopian visions of a peace dividend were realized.

According to the findings presented in this volume, Russia's military spending in 1997 was less than one-tenth of that of the USSR in 1988.[17] However, this radical reduction did not result from a programme of conversion to civilian production but from Russia's economic collapse. As a consequence, poverty has spread from a small part of the population of the former USSR and some countries of Central and Eastern Europe to about one-third of this combined area—120 million people of the region have incomes of no more than $4 a day.[18] The cost of moving from a totalitarian state to a democratic state or from a centrally steered economy to a market economy has been much higher than expected.

Other major challenges which affect the security agenda are related to domestic transformations, or shaping the rule of law and consolidating democracy. The challenges cannot be met by merely rewriting constitutions and laws or implementing institutional reform, although both are necessary. If significant change could be brought about by such measures alone, this would mean that implementing democracy and the rule of law were merely technical and financial problems. The experience of recent years shows that the greatest obstacle to overcome in the process of transformation is people—their mentality and ways of carrying out policy.

Rule-of-law reform will succeed only if it gets at the fundamental problem of leaders who refused to be ruled by the law. Respect for the law will not easily take root in systems rife with corruption and cynicism, since entrenched elites cede their traditional impunity and vested interests only under great pressure. Even the new generation of politicians arising out of the political transitions of recent years are reluctant to support reforms that create competing centers of authority beyond their control.[19]

In other words, the rule of law—defined as a system in which 'the laws are public knowledge, are clear in meaning and apply equally to everyone'[20]—should be based on public control, transparency and accountability of governments. This applies particularly to the military. Democracy cannot be consolidated until the military becomes firmly subordinated to civilian control and committed to democratic constitutional order.[21] The rule of law and democracy cannot be reduced to or identified solely with free elections.

Security analysts consider the geo-strategic revolution as one of the most serious challenges to the emerging world system. The superpower confrontation of the cold war era is being replaced by a world of asymmetrical multipolarity in which the United States is the strongest power. As a result of its

---

[17] See chapter 6 in this volume.
[18] United Nations Development Programme (note 14), p. 3.
[19] Carothers, T., 'The rule of law revival', *Foreign Affairs*, vol. 77, no. 2 (Mar./Apr. 1998), p. 96. See also Eatwell, J. et al., *Transformation and Integration: Shaping the Future of Central and Eastern Europe* (Institute for Public Policy Research: London, 1996).
[20] Carothers (note 18), p. 96.
[21] Diamond, L. et al. (eds), *Consolidating the Third Wave Democracies: Themes and Perspectives* (Johns Hopkins University Press: Baltimore, Md., and London, 1997), p. xxviii.

internal developments, Russia has lost its position as a superpower and perceives that other global actors are taking advantage of its difficulties.[22] In this context, a Euro-Asian strategy is gaining in popularity as a basis for Russian domestic and foreign policy.[23]

The spectacular political development and economic growth of China are raising the question of how to ensure its peaceful integration into the international system. In the US assessment, during the next decade China and Russia are more likely to mount 'a low-intensity strategic competition with the United States designed to reduce or offset US influence in the regions they regard as their special spheres of influence'.[24] According to prominent Russian security analysts, a breakthrough was achieved in 1997 in determining the new priorities of Russian political strategy. The main assumption upon which this strategy is based was described as a multipolar world regulated by global and regional multilateral security systems, peace-shaping and disarmament. In effect, Russia is compensating for its excessively close and unbalanced relations with the USA immediately after the end of the cold war (although cooperation with the USA remains a priority of Russian foreign policy). It has also elevated its relations with China to a 'strategic partnership'; has a *rapprochement* with France, the UK, and other medium-sized and small nations of Europe; has accelerated its dialogue with Japan; has restored its traditional links with India and Arab states; and is developing its cooperation with Iran.[25] Russia's privileged partner in Europe, Germany, should be added to this list.

Another serious challenge to global security is the attempts to undermine UN Security Council decisions. The experience of UNSCOM and the agreement achieved by Secretary-General Annan between the UN and Iraq on complete access to the sites in Iraq suspected of storing weapons of mass destruction are a starting-point that may be useful in the effort to strengthen the global non-proliferation regime and as a step towards their elimination.

A matter of serious concern to the international community is the unresolved question of how to curb the rapidly escalating proliferation of small arms.[26] This question is all the more acute since they are the primary or sole tools of violence used in most armed conflicts. At the other extreme, the long-standing objective of eliminating nuclear weapons remains on the arms control and disarmament agenda.[27] However, it is not likely to be achieved in the immediate future.

---

[22] Binnendijk, H. (ed.), *Strategic Assessment 1997: Flashpoints and Force Structure* (National Defence University: Washington, DC, 1997), p. 1.
[23] Rogov, S. M., *Yevraziyskaya strategiya dlya Rossii* [A Euro-Asian strategy for Russia] (Institute of the USA and Canada, Russian Academy of Sciences: Moscow, 1998), p. 55.
[24] Binnendijk (note 21), p. xii.
[25] Martynov, V., Arbatov, A. and Pikayev, A., 'Rossiya v sisteme mezhdunarodnoy bezopasnosti i razoruzheniya' [Russia in the system of international security and disarmament], *Yezhegodnik SIPRI 1997: Vooruzheniya, Razoruzheniye y Mezhdunarodnaya Bezopasnost* [Russian edition of the *SIPRI Yearbook 1997*] (IMEMO: Moscow, 1997), p. 17.
[26] United Nations, Report of the Panel of Governmental Experts on Small Arms, UN document A/52/298, 28 Aug. 1997; and Regehr, E., 'Militarizing despair: the politics of small arms', *Ploughshares Monitor*, Dec. 1997, pp. 13–16.
[27] 'The opportunity now exists, perhaps without precedent or recurrence, to make a new and clear choice to enable the world to conduct its affairs without nuclear weapons.' Statement of the Canberra

At their March 1997 summit meeting, the US and Russian presidents agreed to synchronize the START II and III nuclear disarmament processes.[28] In addition, the possibility of using reciprocal unilateral measures such as taking nuclear weapons off alert status rather than treaties to achieve arms control is now under examination.[29] Although the cold war ended nearly 10 years ago, the philosophy and basic structure of the plans developed during that period for the use of nuclear weapons remain unchanged. If the promises and commitments of the nuclear weapon states to pursue the elimination of nuclear weapons are to be credible, they call for not only a serious debate but also a new arms control agenda.

In summary, the agenda ahead must include serious consideration of at least four major security issues: the abolition of nuclear weapons, unilateral nuclear arms control initiatives, prevention of armed conflicts and control of the trade in small arms.

V. SIPRI findings

The authors of this Yearbook present original data, facts and analyses of developments in 1997 in security and conflicts; military spending and armaments; and non-proliferation, arms control and disarmament.

Conflicts.[30] In 1997 there were 25 major armed conflicts worldwide; in 1996 there were 27 conflicts, while 36 conflicts were registered for 1989, the first year of the conflict data series. As in 1996, all but one of the conflicts of 1997 were intra-state in nature.

Conflict prevention, management and resolution.[31] Important successes during 1997 were balanced by less welcome developments in which peace processes ran into difficulties, peace settlements unravelled, fighting continued in a number of countries and new intra-state conflicts erupted. Notable achievements were the reinstatement of a cease-fire and the commencement of the first negotiations in decades between the parties to the Northern Ireland conflict; the agreement by North Korea to enter negotiations on a Korean peace treaty; agreement by Russia and Japan to seek a peace settlement; and the achievement of peace accords in Bangladesh, Liberia, Nicaragua and Tajikistan.

In contrast, military coups unravelled the peace settlements in Cambodia and Sierra Leone; the peace processes in Angola, Bosnia and Herzegovina, Chechnya and the Middle East remained deeply troubled; and diplomatic efforts failed to prevent or halt civil wars in Central Africa. Fighting erupted in

---

Commission on the Elimination of Nuclear Weapons, Canberra, Aug. 1996. See also chapter 10 in this volume.

[28] See chapter 10 in this volume.

[29] Bunn, G. and Holloway, D., *Arms Control without Treaties? Rethinking US–Russian Strategic Negotiations in light of the Duma–Senate Showdown in Treaty Appoval*, CISAC Working Paper (Center for International Security and Arms Control (CISAC), Stanford University: Stanford, Calif., Feb. 1998).

[30] A 'major armed conflict' is defined as one which has incurred the battle-related deaths of at least 1000 people; see chapter 1 in this volume.

[31] See chapter 2 in this volume.

the Central African Republic, western China and Comoros; the beginnings of armed resistance appeared in Kosovo; and fighting continued or was resumed in a number of other countries. The largest peace enforcement/peacekeeping mission, involving 31 000–36 000 troops, was the NATO-led Stabilization Force in Bosnia and Herzegovina. While most of the regional initiatives continued to stem from Europe and the Commonwealth of Independent States (CIS), there were a number from African, Latin American and Asian organizations.

UN Secretary-General Annan presented the most sweeping reform package in UN history, the Secretariat continued its involvement in electoral assistance and observation, and human rights field operations were deployed in a dozen or so countries. The post-cold war boom in UN peacekeeping ended in 1997, however, with the Security Council unprepared to maintain the required level of funding. At the end of the year 15 peacekeeping operations were running, with overall personnel numbers reduced to 1989 levels. The UN financial crisis was thus somewhat eased.

The Middle East.[32] Despite a promising start to the year with the successful Israeli redeployment in Hebron, the Middle East peace process suffered from the considerable violence in the region in 1997. Israel's decision to begin building a new Jewish settlement in an Arab sector of east Jerusalem caused the Palestinians to suspend the peace talks. Israel blamed the Palestinian Authority for not doing enough to fight terrorism. The Israeli–Syrian talks were similarly suspended after the Netanyahu Government indicated that it wished to revise the commitments made by its predecessor. The multilateral talks were essentially dormant in 1997.

A number of events in the region made headlines in 1997: Iran's election ushered in a more moderate president, although ultimate power in that country still resides with the conservative clergy; fighting intensified in Algeria, with tragic consequences for thousands of people; and Iraq's stand-off with the international community reached a crisis point. All these trends continued in early 1998, and there is little reason for optimism unless significant changes take place at the political level throughout the region.

Russia.[33] Russia was active in 1997 in addressing the conflicts in the post-Soviet states. It played a prominent role in promoting political reconciliation in Tajikistan, although the result achieved is fragile, and it increased its efforts to bring the parties to negotiate in Abkhazia, Nagorno-Karabakh and Trans-Dniester, although these conflicts have not been resolved. The settlement of the dispute over the Black Sea Fleet opened the way for the signing of a basic treaty with Ukraine, while the 1997 Charter of Union with Belarus is already a dead letter. The general issue of the enlargement of NATO onto the territory of the former USSR still has explosive potential. Russia's relationship with the Baltic countries became more constructive and pragmatic but was dominated by Russia's fear of their eventual membership in NATO.

[32] See chapter 3 in this volume.
[33] See chapter 4 in this volume.

The CIS continued to be a weak organization. There were signs that Ukraine seeks to build a counterbalance to it within the post-Soviet space and of the emergence of an alternative grouping of Georgia, Ukraine, Azerbaijan and Moldova (GUAM) which could change the political balance and move its centre of gravity away from Russia. The question of the ownership, exploitation and transport of the oil reserves of the Transcaucasus and Central Asia began to emerge as a major factor in relations between the post-Soviet states. Russia in particular began to fear the consequent interest of the USA in the region.

Europe.[34] Enlargement of the membership of NATO and the European Union (EU) dominated the European security agenda in 1997. Protocols of accession to NATO were signed with the Czech Republic, Hungary and Poland, to be submitted to the parliaments of the NATO members for ratification in 1998. The Euro-Atlantic Partnership Council was established to replace the North Atlantic Co-operation Council and provide the framework for enhanced cooperation between NATO and its Partnership for Peace partners. With the non-military elements of stability gaining in importance, NATO is embarking on a change 'from defence of member territory to defence of common interests'. The EU decided to open accession talks in the spring of 1998. Thus, although final decisions were not made in 1997, the directions of NATO and EU evolution were mapped out. With the absence of an external threat and the codification of relationships within NATO and between the alliance and several former Soviet republics in documents signed in 1997, the divide between the states belonging to NATO and those remaining outside it is becoming less distinct. The difference between EU member and non-member states is still distinct, however. This enlargement process is more complex since both current and new members must undergo significant adjustments to accommodate an expanded organization.

The Organization for Security and Co-operation in Europe (OSCE) decided to contribute to a strengthening of the relationship between all the European security-related organizations and continued its negotiations on a Charter on European Security.

Military expenditure and arms production.[35] World military expenditure continued to decline in 1997 but the rate of decline decelerated to less than 1 per cent in real terms. The total amount of money devoted to military activities in 1997 is estimated to be around $740 billion, corresponding on average to 2.6 per cent of global gross national product. The decline began in 1988 after a long period of rapid growth. The sharpest decline took place in 1992, when Russia cut its arms procurement expenditure by two-thirds as part of a budget reduction strategy. Its actual military expenditure in 1997 was less than one-tenth of that of the USSR in 1988. US military expenditure also shows a considerable decline, by 31 per cent over the period, but is still at about the same level as in 1980. Total military expenditure in Europe, apart from Russia

[34] See chapter 5 in this volume.
[35] See chapter 6 in this volume.

and other former Soviet states, declined by only 14 per cent in real terms during 1988–97.

Arms production is characterized by continued structural changes in most parts of the world. With the global demand for weapons having been reduced by roughly one-quarter since 1990 and competition increasingly intense, the company strategies are becoming more aggressive. The combined arms sales of the 'top 100' arms-producing companies in the Organisation for Economic Co-operation and Development (OECD) countries and the developing countries amounted to $156 current billion in 1996, a slight fall in real terms compared with 1995. The arms sales of the 'top 100' have been on a declining trend since at least 1989 but appear to be bottoming out.

Military research and development.[36] Global spending on military research and development (R&D) continued to decline in 1997, mainly because of reductions in the US budget. The 1997 US Quadrennial Defense Review emphasized continuity in R&D programmes at the expense of technologies often grouped under the rubric of the Revolution in Military Affairs. Critics claimed that the review and related policies of the Clinton Administration would leave US forces vulnerable to new threats, in particular from ballistic and cruise missiles, but these fears are exaggerated.

Most members of the OECD have returned to spending less than 110 per cent of their 1983 funding levels. The fear commonly expressed that science would be irreversibly militarized by the build-up of the 1980s has not been borne out, the military share of government and national R&D having returned to its previous level or lower in most cases. Contrary to expectations, the 1991 Persian Gulf War did not lead second-tier arms producers to increase their R&D budgets in the hope of developing or countering technologies demonstrated by the USA, which itself cancelled several programmes at that time. While Russia's new willingness to allow its design bureaux to sell their expertise on the international market was a notable development of 1997, the more important trends are towards tighter technology controls, even as the Russian technology base quickly falls further behind the state of the art.

Arms transfers.[37] The SIPRI global trend-indicator value of the international transfers of major conventional weapons in 1997 was $25 156 million. This figure is 24 per cent higher than the value for 1994, which was the lowest since 1970. However, the figure for 1997 is still only 62 per cent of the value for 1987, when arms transfers reached their highest level since 1950. There were no major changes in the ranked list of arms exporters in 1997. Nearly all transfers originate from a small number of supplier countries, mainly the USA, Russia, the UK, France, China and Germany. Among the arms recipients, countries in North-East Asia and the Middle East are the leading importers.

While plagued by many serious armed conflicts, the countries in Sub-Saharan Africa are not major recipients of major conventional weapons and

---

[36] See chapter 7 in this volume.
[37] See chapter 8 in this volume.

there seems to be no indication that these weapons have played an important role in the outbreak or outcome of these conflicts.

In 1997 there was an improvement in the transparency of arms exports. Several arms-exporting countries in Europe and North America published or promised to publish new and better data on arms transfers. On the other hand, a review of the UN Register of Conventional Arms did not achieve the hoped-for and much needed improvements or expansion of its coverage. After a promising start, the future of the UN Register is now uncertain; its intended role of preventing conflicts through exposing possibly destabilizing accumulations of certain major conventional weapons has not been fulfilled.

Multilateral security-related export controls.[38] The Australia Group, the Missile Technology Control Regime (MTCR), the Nuclear Suppliers Group (NSG), the Zangger Committee and the Wassenaar Arrangement on Export Controls have all played an important part in creating conditions for more effective supply-side approaches to non-proliferation. Exchanges of information and experience and the joint development of common control lists in the framework of these regimes have allowed countries to improve their national export control systems. The European Union export control system for dual-use items also helps EU member states to meet their non-proliferation commitments without undermining their single market.

The membership of the regimes continued to expand in 1997. Two countries which had not previously participated in any of the regimes—China and Latvia—joined or were approved for entry into two regimes: China joined the Zangger Committee and Latvia was accepted for membership of the NSG. In addition, South Korea and Ukraine became members of the Zangger Committee while Turkey became a member of the MTCR. The decision of China to participate in a multilateral regime is a particularly important development given its role as a supplier of nuclear technologies. China is also an important supplier of missile delivery systems and conventional arms, and it is possible that in time the experience gained from the Zangger Committee will lead China to participate in other multilateral regimes.

Nuclear arms control.[39] The year ended with key pieces of 'unfinished business' still unfinished. In 1997 efforts to advance the nuclear arms control and non-proliferation agenda yielded mixed results. Implementation of the 1991 Treaty on the Reduction and Limitation of Strategic Offensive Arms (START I Treaty) continued to proceed, with the USA and the former Soviet parties to the treaty completing the Phase I reductions in their strategic nuclear forces ahead of the deadline. At the Helsinki summit meeting, the US and Russian presidents agreed on measures to boost the 1993 START II Treaty's ratification prospects in the Russian Parliament, in particular by extending the deadline for implementing the reductions. They also agreed on the outline of a START III accord that could bring about deep reductions in the US and Russian nuclear arsenals. The impasse in the negotiations between Russia and

---

[38] See chapter 9 in this volume.
[39] See chapter 10 in this volume.

the USA over a US proposal to clarify the scope of the 1972 Anti-Ballistic Missile Treaty (ABM Treaty) was formally resolved when they reached agreement on the demarcation between strategic and theatre (non-strategic) missile defence systems. A potential breakthrough was the agreement in principle to establish a warhead dismantlement regime within the START III framework.

The 1996 Comprehensive Nuclear Test-Ban Treaty (CTBT) had not entered into force, and the Conference on Disarmament (CD) had still not formed a committee to negotiate a global convention banning the production of fissile material for nuclear explosives.

Chemical and biological arms control.[40] The most notable achievement of the year was the entry into force of the CWC. By the end of the year all five permanent members of the UN Security Council as well as many other key countries in regions of conflict had become parties to the convention. The CWC states parties met in two conferences in 1997 to establish the new disarmament regime.

More information about old and abandoned chemical weapons became public in 1997. There were reports of past use of chemical weapons in Africa and the former Yugoslavia, and claims were made that Russia continues to conduct a CBW programme. In the USA, CW destruction continued in 1997, but total destruction of the US CW stockpile by 2007, the CWC deadline, appears difficult to achieve. Russia enacted legislation on CW destruction in 1997, and Finland, Germany, the Netherlands, Sweden and the USA continued to provide CW destruction assistance to Russia.

Throughout 1997 officials in Iraq continued to obstruct inspections by the UNSCOM teams. At the end of the year, as inspectors were apparently closing in on new elements of Iraq's still hidden chemical and biological weapon (CBW) programmes, Iraq refused access to several sites, and the crisis with the UN escalated to the point where a military intervention became a serious possibility. Despite efforts to establish or strengthen CBW disarmament regimes, concern about their proliferation or use increased in 1997.

Progress in the negotiations on a legally binding verification protocol to the BTWC was modest, although the introduction of a 'rolling text' allows for a more structured approach. The treaty regime was tested for the first time when Cuba formally accused the United States of waging biological warfare and initiated the procedure to investigate the allegations.

Conventional arms control.[41] Despite fears that Russia's opposition to NATO enlargement would adversely affect the negotiations on adaptation of the CFE Treaty, developments in 1997 were characterized by *rapprochement* between NATO and Russia. In July agreement was reached on the Decision of the Joint Consultative Group concerning Certain Basic Elements for Treaty Adaptation, mapping out the course of future talks. Implementation of the 1996 Agreement on Sub-Regional Arms Control established a balance of

---

[40] See chapter 11 in this volume.
[41] See chapters 12 and 13 in this volume.

armed forces and increased transparency and predictability in the former Yugoslavia and will hopefully facilitate further steps towards a stable military balance in South-Eastern Europe.

The Baltic Sea region offers prospects for a genuine dialogue, especially in the wake of the substantial cuts that Russia has promised to make in its land and naval forces deployed in the north-west. Outside Europe, only the Asia–Pacific region witnessed a promising dialogue on conventional arms control. Other parts of the world are either bogged down in political and security crises or facing the risk of rearmament, as in Latin America.

The 1997 APM Convention emphasizes the humanitarian benefits of the ban on anti-personnel landmines and thus differs from traditional arms control agreements which sought to reduce unnecessary suffering on the battlefield. For the first time, a grassroots campaign cum interstate negotiation led to a disarmament agreement outside the UN framework and without the decisive involvement of the major powers.

VI. Conclusions

The post-cold war transnational threats and challenges call urgently for a redefinition of the traditional concept of international security. The security agenda ahead must be founded on a new political philosophy, encompassing a common, institutionalized system of standards and shared values rather than concepts based on the balance of power.

In the cold war period, international security was seen by states exclusively from the national perspective and nearly exclusively in its military dimension. Today, with global interdependence and risks, this approach is no longer adequate. It is now commonly understood that security comprises much more than military security, although the military dimension—particularly the need to strengthen the non-proliferation regime for weapons of mass destruction—is still relevant. Consequently, a new arms control agenda must be set for the 21st century; one of the top priorities must be the complete elimination of nuclear weapons, now that the production, possession and use of chemical and biological weapons have been prohibited in international agreements. Only in this way can the intentional and accidental use of weapons of mass destruction be prevented. The success of the new security agenda will require the cooperation of all states and substantive coordination of the work of global and regional security organizations.

Part I. Security and conflicts, 1997

Chapter 1. Major armed conflicts

Chapter 2. Armed conflict prevention, management and resolution

Chapter 3. The Middle East peace process

Chapter 4. Russia: conflicts and peaceful settlement of disputes

Chapter 5. Europe: the transition to inclusive security

1. Major armed conflicts

MARGARETA SOLLENBERG and PETER WALLENSTEEN

I. Global patterns of major armed conflicts, 1989–97

In 1997 there were 25 major armed conflicts in 24 locations throughout the world. The number of major armed conflicts was lower than for the previous year, but the number of conflict locations remained the same (in 1996 there were 27 major armed conflicts in 24 locations).[1] Both figures for 1997 are also significantly lower than those for 1989, the first year of the period covered in the conflict statistics. The conflicts and locations for 1997 are presented in table 1A, appendix 1A.

A 'major armed conflict' is defined as prolonged combat between the military forces of two or more governments, or of one government and at least one organized armed group, incurring the battle-related deaths of at least 1000 people during the entire conflict and in which the incompatibility concerns government and/or territory.[2] A conflict 'location' is the territory of at least one state. Since certain states are the location of more than one conflict, the number of conflicts reported is greater than the number of locations.[3] A major armed conflict is removed from the table when the contested incompatibility has been resolved and/or when there is no recorded use of force related to the incompatibility between the parties during the year. The same conflict may reappear in the table for subsequent years if there is any renewed use of armed force.

All but one of the conflicts in 1997 were internal, that is, the issue concerned control over the government or territory of one state.[4] The sole interstate conflict in 1997, that between India and Pakistan, was also recorded for 1996. This conflict focused on the Kashmir issue, which generated tension both internally in both countries and between the two states. Most of the fighting at the interstate level involved artillery exchanges. There was foreign intervention in two conflicts: Congo (Brazzaville)—troops from Angola—and Zaire—troops from Rwanda. In 1997 there were more conflicts over incompatibilities

---

[1] It should be noted that they were not the same 24 locations in both years; see table 1.1.

[2] See appendix 1A in this volume for definitions of the criteria. See also Heldt, B. (ed.), *States in Armed Conflict 1990–91* (Department of Peace and Conflict Research, Uppsala University: Uppsala, 1992), chapter 3, for the full definitions.

[3] Some countries may also be the location of minor armed conflicts. The table in appendix 1A presents only the major armed conflicts in the countries listed.

[4] A distinction is made between 'internal conflicts' and 'internal conflicts with foreign intervention'. Internal conflicts are determined by the incompatibility and whether it is internally defined, i.e., if there are incompatible positions stated by parties within a state and regarding a governmental or territorial issue within that state. When an internal conflict involves forces from other states on the side of either of the internal parties, it is treated in this chapter as an internal conflict with foreign intervention.

SIPRI Yearbook 1998: Armaments, Disarmament and International Security

concerning government than territory for the first time since 1990 (see table 1.2).

II. Changes in the table of conflicts

New conflicts

All the new conflicts in 1997 were located on the African continent. Four major armed conflicts were recorded for 1997 that were not listed for 1996.[5] In Burundi, the government of Tutsi leader Pierre Buyoya became involved in heightened armed conflict with the National Council for the Defence of Democracy (CNDD), the Hutu-based opposition formed in 1994 and led by Leonard Nyangoma. In Congo (Brazzaville), a short but severe civil war erupted in 1997, resulting in the victory of the Angola-supported opposition led by Denis Sassou-Nguesso. This conflict had been successfully contained by international mediation since 1993. The conflict in Zaire, which began in late 1996, ended on 16 May 1997 with the victory of the forces of the Alliance of Democratic Forces for the Liberation of Congo-Kinshasa (ADFL), led by Laurent Kabila. The ADFL received support from Rwanda and indirect support from Angola, Burundi and Uganda. On 17 May Kabila changed the name of the country, announcing the establishment of the Democratic Republic of the Congo. The protracted conflict in Senegal over the territory of Casamance, which began in 1982, reached the threshold of 1000 deaths in 1997 and there were no signs of an early end to this conflict.

Conflicts recorded for 1996 that were not recorded for 1997

Six conflicts recorded for 1996 do not appear in the data for 1997. In four of these conflicts—Guatemala, Russia (Chechnya) and Tajikistan—this was because of peace agreements concluded in late 1996.[6] The two remaining conflicts involved the Kurds in Iran and Iraq. In the Iranian case, the Kurdish Democratic Party of Iran (KDPI) has been largely suppressed but bases remain in Iraqi Kurdistan.[7] In Iraqi Kurdistan, there was no fighting between the Iraqi Government and Kurdish groups. The USA had responded militarily to the Iraqi invasion of Iraqi Kurdistan in 1996, when Iraq had supported one group against the other. Following this, the government was forced to leave rival Kurdish groups to fight among themselves. In Somalia, there was no fighting between the previously recorded parties but small-scale fighting continued between some of the warlords, mainly concerning private gains rather than governmental power. The Ethiopian-backed Sodere Declarations of January 1997, uniting 26 Somali factions in the National Salvation Council, changed

---

[5] As noted below, some of these conflicts began before 1997 but did not reach the threshold of 1000 battle-related deaths until 1997.

[6] See also chapters 2 and 4 in this volume.

[7] There are indications of possible activity in the Kurdish–Iranian conflict. However, since none of the reports can be verified, the conflict is not included in the table.

the political situation towards a climate of negotiation. The Hussein Aideed faction, one of the two major factions which did not join the Council, became involved in subsequent negotiations in Cairo in November. The only major faction rejecting all the negotiations was the Somali National Movement of Somaliland, because it considers Somaliland to be independent and no longer part of Somalia.

Conflict activity and peace efforts

In some of the conflicts the intensity of the fighting in 1997 increased to higher levels than in previous years. Seven of the major armed conflicts incurred at least 1000 battle-related deaths in 1997 alone:[8] Afghanistan, Algeria, Congo (Brazzaville), Sri Lanka, Sudan, Turkey and Zaire. Five of these conflicts were among the six wars reported for 1996: Afghanistan, Algeria, Sri Lanka, Sudan, Turkey and the Russian conflict over Chechnya which was ended in 1997.

In some conflicts there was also a change in the constellations of warring parties. This was true for Afghanistan (where events turned in late 1996 when the Taleban took control of large parts of Afghanistan, including the capital, and other groups united against them).[9] In Sudan, the Sudanese People's Liberation Movement (SPLM), which had been fighting for secession of the south, had in 1996 entered into an alliance with leaders from the north in the hope of overthrowing the National Islamic Front Government in Khartoum.[10] By the end of 1997 the military situation on the ground had not changed significantly. In the case of Sierra Leone, a complicated chain of events resulted in a reduction of the fighting between the previous parties after the peace agreement of 1996 but also led to the formation of a new alliance after the May 1997 military coup when the former opposition organization, the Revolutionary United Front (RUF), and the army joined together in the new government. The conflict also became further complicated as Nigerian forces, under the umbrella of ECOMOG,[11] confronted the government on the side of the overthrown civilian government.[12] In Guinea, an agreement was concluded by the warring parties in October 1997 to reinstate the overthrown civilian government, but implementation of this agreement seemed to be stalled by the end of the year.

---

[8] These conflicts are classified as 'wars'. This term is also used by other conflict researchers, e.g., the Correlates of War Project, University of Michigan.

[9] The government of a state is that party which is generally regarded as being in central control even by those organizations seeking to assume power. If this criterion is not applicable, the government is that party controlling the capital. In most cases the two criteria coincide.

[10] In previous SIPRI Yearbooks, the SPLM was listed as the SPLA (Sudanese People's Liberation Army, the military wing of the SPLM). As political rather than military organizations are listed as parties to conflicts, the correct name of this party in the Sudan conflict is the SPLM.

[11] ECOMOG is the Economic Community of West African States (ECOWAS) Monitoring Group, established in 1990. For the members of ECOWAS, see the glossary in this volume; see also chapter 2.

[12] Conflict developments in Sierra Leone after the May 1997 coup are not included in the data presented in the table in appendix 1A since they constitute a new armed conflict. The new conflict did not incur 1000 deaths in 1997.

Table 1.1. Regional distribution of locations with at least one major armed conflict, 1989–97

Region[a]	1989	1990	1991	1992	1993	1994	1995	1996	1997
Africa	9	10	10	7	7	6	6	5	8
Asia	11	10	8	11	9	9	9	10	9
Central and South America	5	5	4	3	3	3	3	3	2
Europe	2	1	2	4	5	4	3	2	1
Middle East	5	5	5	4	4	5	4	4	4
Total	**32**	**31**	**29**	**29**	**28**	**27**	**25**	**24**	**24**

Table 1.2. Regional distribution, number and types of major armed conflicts, 1989–97[b]

Region[a]	1989		1990		1991		1992		1993		1994		1995		1996		1997	
	G	T	G	T	G	T	G	T	G	T	G	T	G	T	G	T	G	T
Africa	7	3	8	3	8	3	6	1	6	1	5	1	5	1	4	1	7	1
Asia	6	8	5	10	3	8	5	9	4	7	4	7	4	8	4	7	3	7
Central and South America	5	–	5	–	4	–	3	–	3	–	3	–	3	–	3	–	2	–
Europe	1	1	–	1	–	2	–	4	–	6	–	5	–	3	–	2	–	1
Middle East	1	4	1	4	2	5	2	3	2	4	2	4	2	4	2	4	2	2
Total	**20**	**16**	**19**	**18**	**17**	**18**	**16**	**17**	**15**	**18**	**14**	**17**	**14**	**16**	**13**	**14**	**14**	**11**
Total	**36**		**37**		**35**		**33**		**33**		**31**		**30**		**27**		**25**	

G = Government and T = Territory, the two types of incompatibility.

[a] Only those regions of the world in which a conflict was recorded for the period 1989–97 are included in the tables.
[b] The total annual number of conflicts does not necessarily correspond to the number of conflict locations in table 1.1 or table 1A, appendix 1A, since there may be more than 1 major armed conflict in each location.

Source: Uppsala Conflict Data Project.

Two conflicts ended in 1997 through comprehensive peace agreements which included provisions on military settlements and the incompatibility: the Chittagong Hill Tracts dispute in Bangladesh and the conflict over government in Tajikistan.[13] However, because a few instances of fighting occurred in Bangladesh, this conflict still appears in the table. In Tajikistan no fighting between the parties was recorded, although it appeared that the parties to the agreement, the Government of Tajikistan and the United Tajik Opposition, no longer controlled all their respective armed supporters. Some factions led by warlords were involved in sporadic violence when guarding positions gained during the conflict.

Several of the peace agreements concluded in previous years were in the process of implementation in 1997. In the Israel–Palestine conflict, suicide bombings and the continued construction of new Israeli settlements on the West Bank and in the Jerusalem area seriously damaged the peace process.[14] In Angola, the peace process ran into renewed troubles. The government's involvement in the war in Congo (Brazzaville) and its support for the ADFL in Zaire were related to the conflict with its Angolan opponent, the National Union for the Total Independence of Angola (União Nacional para a Independência Total de Angola, UNITA), which in turn was associated with the Mobutu regime in Zaire. In other cases, negotiations continued without immediate success. In Northern Ireland, a new cease-fire by the Provisional Irish Republican Army (Provisional IRA) was proclaimed on 19 July 1997. The new British Government, under Prime Minister Tony Blair, initiated multi-party round-table discussions involving among others Sinn Féin and Unionist political parties. In the Philippines, talks with the Communist National Democratic Front continued but resulted in only periodic cease-fires.

Other conflicts seemed to be on the verge of resolution after having been stalemated for years. In Western Sahara, a conflict last recorded for 1991, the referendum originally scheduled for early 1992 and postponed since then was finally scheduled for late 1998 after an agreement was brokered by UN Special Envoy James Baker.

One of the few cases of direct international involvement in a conflict in 1997 was Tajikistan, where Iran, Russia and the UN mediated an agreement. Otherwise, the trend was towards agreements concluded by the parties directly and without outside assistance, as for example in the case of Bangladesh. This trend towards self-reliance in dispute settlement is in contrast to events at the beginning of the decade, when outside mediation was the norm. Attempts at other types of international involvement, such as humanitarian interventions in Congo (Brazzaville) and Zaire, were also unsuccessful in 1997.

[13] See also chapter 4, section V, in this volume.
[14] See also chapter 3 in this volume.

III. Regional patterns of major armed conflicts, 1989–97

The regional distribution of locations and major armed conflicts in the period 1989–97 is shown in tables 1.1 and 1.2, respectively. The global trend is that of a decline in the total number of conflicts since 1990. In 1997 none of the regions was entirely spared armed conflict.

As can be seen from table 1.2, the number of major armed conflicts in Europe has fallen since the peak year 1993. After the re-establishment of the cease-fire in July by the Provisional IRA and paramilitary groups associated with the Ulster Unionist Party in Northern Ireland, Europe had by the end of 1997 no active major armed conflict. Also, with the resolution of the conflict in Tajikistan, there are no active major armed conflicts stemming from the breakup of the Soviet Union or Yugoslavia. However, the underlying political disputes behind several of these conflicts remain to be resolved.

The trend of declining numbers of conflicts in Africa was ended during the year. All the new conflicts in 1997 were located on the African continent. There were spillover effects as in previous years, but there was also a change in the conflict patterns in which states increasingly became involved in disputes in neighbouring countries. Such involvement often included economic or political support for either of the warring parties. This was particularly obvious in the region stretching from Angola and Congo (Brazzaville) in the west to Kenya, Sudan and Tanzania in the east, where complex links emerged which had an effect on the development of three of the new conflicts, that is, Burundi, Congo (Brazzaville) and Zaire. Direct foreign intervention by regular troops was recorded only for Congo (Brazzaville) and Zaire. In Algeria, the conflict had involved massacres in previous years, but in 1997 there was a dramatic increase in the number and scale of the massacres, which claimed thousands of lives. Most of the massacres were blamed on the Armed Islamic Group (GIA), but the identity of the perpetrators is not known. Although one conflict in Africa was removed from the list in 1997 (Somalia), the number of conflicts in Africa sharply increased.

The Middle East region shows little variation in the number of major armed conflicts during this period. All the conflicts active in 1997 had been active for the majority of the years covered. Although there was no involvement in Iraqi Kurdistan by the Iraqi Government, the territory continued to be the battleground for intra-Kurdish fighting involving both major Iraqi Kurdish groups and the Kurdish Worker's Party (PKK), which seeks independence for the Kurdish region of Turkey. The Turkish Army continued making large-scale offensives into Iraqi Kurdistan which were strongly condemned by the Iraqi Government as well as by Iran and Syria. Conflict with the Israeli Government continued both within Israel and in southern Lebanon.

Asia is the region that has had the highest number of major armed conflicts every year in the period 1989–97 except for 1991, when Africa had as many. In addition to the protracted conflicts over Afghanistan and Kashmir, 1997 saw the return of major fighting in Cambodia, in spite of previous United

Nations efforts to forge a democratic and legitimate government.[15] Although some conflicts increased slightly in intensity compared to 1996, several continued on a comparatively low level of intensity, partly because they were contained by a strong state military presence (India, Indonesia[16] and Myanmar) and partly because of ongoing negotiations (the Philippines).

In Central and South America the pattern was of an overall decline in the number of major armed conflicts from 1989 to 1997, with a stable number in the period 1992–96 and a decline of one in 1997. Negotiations on a comprehensive peace accord were successfully concluded in Guatemala in 1996. In Peru, the occupation of the Japanese Embassy in Lima by the Tupac Amaru Revolutionary Movement (MRTA) in late 1996 was followed in April 1997 by an attack by government forces on the embassy in which all the guerrillas were killed. The rival Sendero Luminoso group later resurfaced after a period of inactivity. In Colombia, guerrilla forces had become stronger and were able to attack all parts of the country. Affected by the activity of both left-and right-wing paramilitary groups and groups involved in the drug trade, the internal security situation in Colombia in 1997 was worse than it had been for many years.

IV. Conclusions

The promising trend of a global decline in the number of conflicts continued in 1997. However, there were more conflicts in Africa in 1997 than in any year since 1991.

A striking feature of the conflicts in Africa, and to some extent in Asia and South America, is the link between armed conflict and a weak state. All the new conflicts in Africa, for example, took place in severely weakened states. While the existence of a weakened state is not a guarantee that conflict will occur, just as strong states also experience conflict, the correlation is noticeable and raises difficult issues for the international community. In an immediate sense, the most crucial of these is whether that community is prepared to make the necessary commitment of resources to disarm the warlords and criminal elements which arise to fill the power vacuum left behind by collapsing states before any effective rebuilding can occur.

---

[15] The fighting between the government and the Funcinpec faction of First Prime Minister Norodom Ranariddh, after Ranariddh was ousted from the government in July, is not included in the table since it constitutes a new armed conflict.

[16] As a part of the dissolution of the Portuguese colonial empire in 1975, East Timor was to be granted independence. An independent state was declared in Nov. 1975. Indonesia invaded the territory in Dec. 1975, annexed it and declared East Timor an Indonesian province in 1977. Since the invasion, Indonesian rule over East Timor has been disputed by the United Nations.

Appendix 1A. Major armed conflicts, 1997

MARGARETA SOLLENBERG, RAMSES AMER, CARL JOHAN
ÅSBERG, ANN-SOFI JAKOBSSON and ANDRÉS JATO*

The following notes and sources apply to table 1A. Note that, although some countries are also the location of minor armed conflicts, the table lists only the major armed conflicts in those countries. Reference to the tables of major armed conflicts in previous SIPRI Yearbooks is given in the list of sources.

[a] The stated general incompatible positions. 'Govt' and 'Territory' refer to contested incompatibilities concerning government (type of political system, a change of central government or in its composition) and territory (control of territory [interstate conflict], secession or autonomy), respectively.

[b] 'Year formed' is the year in which the incompatibility was stated. 'Year joined' is the year in which use of armed force began or recommenced.

[c] The non-governmental warring parties are listed by the name of the parties using armed force. Only those parties which were active during 1997 are listed in this column.

[d] The figure for 'No. of troops in 1997' is for total armed forces (rather than for army forces, as in the *SIPRI Yearbooks 1988–1990*) of the government warring party (i.e., the government of the conflict location), and for non-government parties from the conflict location. For government and non-government parties from outside the location, the figure in this column is for total armed forces within the country that is the location of the armed conflict. Deviations from this method are indicated by a note (*) and explained.

[e] The figures for deaths refer to total battle-related deaths during the conflict. 'Mil.' and 'civ.' refer, where figures are available, to *military* and *civilian* deaths, respectively; where there is no such indication, the figure refers to total military and civilian battle-related deaths in the period or year given. Information which covers a calendar year is necessarily more tentative for the last months of the year. Experience has also shown that the reliability of figures improves over time; they are therefore revised each year.

[f] The 'change from 1996' is measured as the increase or decrease in the number of battle-related deaths in 1997 compared with the number of battle-related deaths in 1996. Although based on data that cannot be considered totally reliable, the symbols represent the following changes:

+ +   increase in battle deaths of > 50%
+   increase in battle deaths of > 10 to 50%
0   stable rate of battle deaths ($\pm$ 10%)
–   decrease in battle deaths of > 10 to 50%
– –   decrease in battle deaths of > 50%
n.a.   not applicable, since the major armed conflict was not recorded for 1996.

Note: In the last three columns ('Total deaths', 'Deaths in 1997' and 'Change from 1996'), '. .' indicates that no reliable figures, or no reliable disaggregated figures, were given in the sources consulted.

* R. Amer was responsible for the data for the conflict location of Cambodia; C. J. Åsberg for India and India–Pakistan; A.-S. Jakobsson for the United Kingdom and Israel; and Andrés Jato for Angola, Burundi, Congo (Brazzaville), Rwanda, Sierra Leone, Somalia, Sudan, Uganda and Zaire. M. Sollenberg was responsible for the remaining conflict locations. Ylva Nordlander, Ulrika Gustin and Johanna Wallin provided assistance in the data collection.

Sources: For additional information on these conflicts, see chapters in previous editions of the *SIPRI Yearbook:* Sollenberg, M. and Wallensteen, P., 'Major armed conflicts', *SIPRI Yearbook 1997: Armaments, Disarmament and International Security* (Oxford University Press: Oxford, 1997), chapter 1; Sollenberg, M. and Wallensteen, P., 'Major armed conflicts', *SIPRI Yearbook 1996* (Oxford University Press: Oxford, 1996), chapter 1; Sollenberg, M. and Wallensteen, P., 'Major armed conflicts', *SIPRI Yearbook 1995* (Oxford University Press: Oxford, 1995), chapter 1; Wallensteen, P. and Axell, K., 'Major armed conflicts', *SIPRI Yearbook 1994* (Oxford University Press: Oxford, 1994), chapter 2; Amer, R., Heldt, B., Landgren, S., Magnusson, K., Melander, E., Nordquist, K.-Å., Ohlson, T. and Wallensteen, P., 'Major armed conflicts', *SIPRI Yearbook 1993: World Armaments and Disarmament* (Oxford University Press: Oxford, 1993), chapter 3; Heldt, B., Wallensteen, P. and Nordquist, K.-Å., 'Major armed conflicts in 1991', *SIPRI Yearbook 1992* (Oxford University Press: Oxford, 1992), chapter 11; Lindgren, K., Heldt, B., Nordquist, K.-Å. and Wallensteen, P., 'Major armed conflicts in 1990', *SIPRI Yearbook 1991* (Oxford University Press: Oxford, 1991), chapter 10; Lindgren, K., Wilson, G. K., Wallensteen, P. and Nordquist, K.-Å., 'Major armed conflicts in 1989', *SIPRI Yearbook 1990* (Oxford University Press: Oxford, 1990), chapter 10; Lindgren, K., Wilson, G. K. and Wallensteen, P., 'Major armed conflicts in 1988', *SIPRI Yearbook 1989* (Oxford University Press: Oxford, 1989), chapter 9; Wilson, G. K. and Wallensteen, P., 'Major armed conflicts in 1987', *SIPRI Yearbook 1988* (Oxford University Press: Oxford, 1988), chapter 9; and Goose, S., 'Armed conflicts in 1986, and the Iraq–Iran War', *SIPRI Yearbook 1987* (Oxford University Press: Oxford, 1987), chapter 8.

The following journals, newspapers and news agencies were consulted: *Africa Confidential* (London); *Africa Events* (London); *Africa Reporter* (New York); *Africa Research Bulletin* (Oxford); *AIM Newsletter* (London); *Asian Defence Journal* (Kuala Lumpur); *Asian Recorder* (New Delhi); *Balkan War Report* (London); *Burma Focus* (Oslo); *Burma Issues* (Bangkok); *Conflict International* (Edgware); *Dagens Nyheter* (Stockholm); Dialog Information Services Inc. (Palo Alto); *The Economist* (London); *Facts and Reports* (Amsterdam); *Far Eastern Economic Review* (Hong Kong); *Financial Times* (Frankfurt); *Fortnight Magazine* (Belfast); *The Guardian* (London); *Horn of Africa Bulletin* (Uppsala); *Jane's Defence Weekly* (Coulsdon, Surrey); *Jane's Intelligence Review* (Coulsdon, Surrey); *The Independent* (London); *International Herald Tribune* (Paris); *Kayhan International* (Teheran); *Keesing's Contemporary Archives* (Harlow, Essex); *Latin America Weekly Report* (London); *Le Monde Diplomatique* (Paris); *Mexico and Central America Report* (London); *Middle East International* (London); *Monitor* (Washington, DC); *Moscow News* (Moscow); *Newsweek* (New York); *New Times* (Moscow); *New York Times* (New York); *OMRI (Open Media Research Institute) Daily Digest* (Prague); *Pacific Report* (Canberra); *Pacific Research* (Canberra); *Reuter Business Briefing* (London); *Prism* (Washington, DC); *RFE/RL (Radio Free Europe/Radio Liberty) Research Report* (Munich); *S.A. Barometer* (Johannesburg); *Selections from Regional Press* (Institute of Regional Studies: Islamabad); *Southern African Economist* (Harare); *Southern Africa Political & Economic Monthly* (Harare); *SouthScan* (London); *Sri Lanka Monitor* (London); *The Statesman* (Calcutta); *Sudan Update* (London); *Svenska Dagbladet* (Stockholm); *Tehran Times* (Teheran); *The Times* (London); *Transition* (Prague); *World Aerospace & Defense Intelligence* (Newtown, Conn.).

Table 1A. Table of conflict locations with at least one major armed conflict in 1997

Location	Incompat-ibility[a]	Year formed/ year joined[b]	Warring parties[c]	No. of troops in 1997[d]	Total deaths[e] (incl. 1997)	Deaths in 1997	Change from 1996[f]
Europe							
United Kingdom	Territory	1969/1969	Govt of UK vs. Provisional IRA	214 000 ..	1 500*	3	– –

Provisional IRA: Provisional Irish Republican Army
* The total number of deaths in political violence in Northern Ireland is approximately 3200. The figure given here is an estimate of the deaths incurred between the Government of the UK and the Provisional IRA; the remaining deaths were mainly caused by other paramilitary organizations such as the Ulster Volunteer Force (UVF) and the Ulster Freedom Fighters (UFF).

Location	Incompat-ibility	Year formed/ year joined	Warring parties	No. of troops in 1997	Total deaths (incl. 1997)	Deaths in 1997	Change from 1996
Middle East							
Iran	Govt	1970/1991	Govt of Iran vs. Mujahideen e-Khalq	500 000* ..	..	..	..

* Including the Revolutionary Guard.

| Iraq | Govt | 1980/1991 | Govt of Iraq vs. SAIRI | 350 000–400 000 .. | .. | .. | .. |

SAIRI: Supreme Assembly for the Islamic Revolution in Iraq

| Israel | Territory | 1964/1964 | Govt of Israel vs. Non-PLO groups* | 170 000–180 000 .. | 1948–: > 13 000 | 100–150 (mil.) 75–100 (civ.) | – |

PLO: Palestine Liberation Organization
* Examples of these groups are Hamas, PFLP-GC (Popular Front for the Liberation of Palestine–General Command), Islamic Jihad, Hizbollah and Amal.

| Turkey | Territory | 1974/1984 | Govt of Turkey vs. PKK | 800 000* 6 000–10 000 | > 30 000 | > 1 000 | – |

PKK: Partiya Karkeren Kurdistan, Kurdish Worker's Party, or Apocus
* Including the Gendarmerie/National Guard.

MAJOR ARMED CONFLICTS 27

Asia

Location		Year formed/Year joined	Warring parties	Troops 1996	Deaths 1996
Afghanistan	Govt	1992/1992	Govt of Afghanistan	20 000	>20 000*
		1978/1978	vs. Jumbish-i Milli-ye Islami, Jamiat-i-Islami,		>2 000
		1990/1990	Hezb-i-Wahdat		+

* Note that this figure includes deaths in the fighting since 1992 in which other parties than those listed above also participated.

| Bangladesh | Territory | 1971/1982 | Govt of Bangladesh vs. JSS/SB | 120 000 2 000–5 000 | 1975–: 3 000–3 500 | <25 0 |

JSS/SB: Parbatya Chattagram Jana Sanghati Samiti (Chittagong Hill Tracts People's Co-ordination Association/Shanti Bahini [Peace Force])

| Cambodia | Govt | 1979/1979 | Govt of Cambodia vs. PDK | 140 000* 1 000–4 000 | >25 500** | .. |

PDK: Party of Democratic Kampuchea (Khmer Rouge)
* Including all militias.
** For figures for battle-related deaths in this conflict prior to 1979, see *SIPRI Yearbook 1990*, p. 405, and note *p*, p. 418. Regarding battle-related deaths in 1979–89, i.e., not only involving the Govt and PDK, the only figure available is from official Vietnamese sources, indicating that 25 300 Vietnamese soldiers died in Cambodia. An estimated figure for the period 1979–89, based on various sources, is > 50 000, and for 1989 >1000. The figures for 1990, 1991 and 1992 were lower.

India	Territory	../1989	Govt of India vs. Kashmir insurgents**	1 145 000 ..	>20 000*	0
	Territory	../1992	vs. BdSF	..		
	Territory	1982/1988	vs. ULFA	..		>500

BdSF: Bodo Security Force
ULFA: United Liberation Front of Assam
* Only the Kashmir conflict.
** Several groups are active, some of the most important being the Jammu and Kashmir Liberation Front (JKLF), the Hizb-e-Mujahideen and the Harkat-ul-Ansar.

| India–Pakistan | Territory | 1947/1996 | Govt of India vs. Govt of Pakistan | 1 145 000 587 000 | .. | .. |

Location	Incompat-ibility[a]	Year formed/ year joined[b]	Warring parties[c]	No. of troops in 1997[d]	Total deaths[e] (incl. 1997)	Deaths in 1997	Change from 1996[f]
Indonesia	Territory	1975/1975	Govt of Indonesia vs. Fretilin	310 000 100–200	15 000–16 000 (mil.)	50–100	+
Myanmar	Territory	1948/1948	Govt of Myanmar vs. KNU	300 000–400 000 2 000–4 000	1948–50: 8 000 1981–88: 5 000–8 000	50–200	+
Philippines	Govt	1968/1968	Govt of the Philippines vs. NPA	110 000 ..	21 000–25 000	< 100	+
Sri Lanka	Territory	1976/1983	Govt of Sri Lanka vs. LTTE	110 000 5 000–8 000	> 40 000	> 4 000	+
Africa							
Algeria	Govt	1992/1992 1993/1993	Govt of Algeria vs. FIS* vs. GIA	170 000**	40 000–80 000	> 3 000	..***

Fretilin: Frente Revolucionária Timorense de Libertação e Independência (Revolutionary Front for an Independent East Timor)
KNU: Karen National Union
NPA: New People's Army
LTTE: Liberation Tigers of Tamil Eelam
FIS: Front Islamique du Salut, Jibhat al-Inqath (Islamic Salvation Front)
GIA: Groupe Islamique Armé (Armed Islamic Group)

* The Islamic Salvation Army (Armée Islamique du Salut, AIS) is considered to be the armed wing of the FIS. There are also several other armed Islamic groups under the FIS military command.
** Including the Gendarmerie and the National Security Forces.
*** The minimum number of deaths in 1997 is 3000, but it has not been possible to determine the change from 1996.

MAJOR ARMED CONFLICTS   29

Location	Govt/ Territory	Year formed/ Year joined	Warring parties	No. of troops in 1997	Total deaths	Deaths in 1997	Change from 1996
Burundi	Govt	1994/1994	Govt of Burundi vs. CNDD	40 000 / ..	>1 000*	800	n.a.

CNDD: Conseil national pour la défense de la démocratie (National Council for the Defence of Democracy)
* Political violence in Burundi since 1993, involving other groups than the CNDD, has claimed a total of at least 100 000 lives.

| Congo (Brazzaville) | Govt | ../1997 | Govt of Congo vs. FDU,* Angola | 10 000 / 1 500–3 000, 3 500 | 4 000–7 000 | 4 000–7 000 | n.a. |

FDU: Forces démocratiques unies (United Democratic Forces)
* Armed action was primarily carried out by the Cobras, the private militia of FDU leader Sassou-Nguesso.

| Senegal | Territory | 1982/1982 | Govt of Senegal vs. MFDC | 13 000 / 500–1 000 | >1 000 | 200–500 | n.a. |

MFDC: Mouvement des forces démocratiques de la Casamance (Casamance Movement of Democratic Forces)

| Sierra Leone | Govt | 1991/1991 | Govt of Sierra Leone vs. RUF | 14 000 / 3 000–5 000 | >3 000 | <100 | – – |

RUF: Revolutionary United Front

| Sudan | Govt | 1980/1983 | Govt of Sudan vs. NDA* | 80 000–100 000 / .. | 37 000– 40 000 (mil.)** | >5 000 | ++ |

NDA: National Democratic Alliance
* The June 1995 Asmara Declaration forms the basis for the political and military activities of the NDA. The NDA is an alliance of several southern and northern opposition organizations, of which the SPLM (Sudan People's Liberation Movement) is the largest, with 30 000–50 000 troops. SPLM leader John Garang is also the leader of the NDA.
** Figure for up to 1991.

| Uganda | Govt | 1993/1994 | Govt of Uganda vs. LRA | 40 000–50 000 / 1 000–4 000 | >1 000 | 250 | 0 |

LRA: Lord's Resistance Army

Location	Incompat-ibility[a]	Year formed/ year joined[b]	Warring parties[c]	No. of troops in 1997[d]	Total deaths[e] (incl. 1997)	Deaths in 1997	Change from 1996[f]
Zaire*	Govt	1996/1996	Govt of Zaire vs. ADFL, Rwanda	28 000 20 000–40 000 ..	4 000–9 000	>2 000	n.a.

ADFL: Alliance des forces démocratiques pour la libération du Congo-Kinshasa (Alliance of Democratic Forces for the Liberation of Congo-Kinshasa)
* After the ADFL victory of May 1997, the name of the country was changed to the Democratic Republic of the Congo.

Central and South America

Location	Incompat-ibility[a]	Year formed/ year joined[b]	Warring parties[c]	No. of troops in 1997[d]	Total deaths[e] (incl. 1997)	Deaths in 1997	Change from 1996[f]
Colombia	Govt	1949/1978 1965/1978	Govt of Colombia vs. FARC vs. ELN	140 000 7 000 3 000	..*	500–1 000	0

FARC: Fuerzas Armadas Revolucionarias Colombianas (Revolutionary Armed Forces of Colombia)
ELN: Ejército de Liberación Nacional (National Liberation Army)
* In the past 3 decades the civil wars of Colombia have claimed a total of some 30 000 lives.

| Peru | Govt | 1980/1981 1984/1986 | Govt of Peru vs. Sendero Luminoso vs. MRTA | 125 000 500–1 500 200 | >28 000 | 50–200 | 0 |

Sendero Luminoso: Shining Path
MRTA: Movimiento Revolucionario Tupac Amaru (Tupac Amaru Revolutionary Movement)

2. Armed conflict prevention, management and resolution

TREVOR FINDLAY*

I. Introduction

Efforts at conflict prevention, management and resolution in 1997 were crowned by the reinstatement of a cease-fire and commencement of the first negotiations in decades between the parties to the conflict in Northern Ireland. Also historic were the agreement by North Korea to begin negotiations on a Korean peace treaty and that by Russia and Japan to aim for a peace agreement by 2000. Actual peace accords were achieved in Bangladesh, Liberia, Nicaragua and Tajikistan and a cease-fire agreement was signed for the island of Bougainville, Papua New Guinea. Talks were resumed to settle the long-running Western Sahara, Cyprus and Kashmir disputes, in the latter two cases to little avail. The implementation of recently achieved peace agreements proceeded well in Guatemala, Eastern Slavonia and the Philippines, and the peace process was revived in Niger. Peace accords involving some of the parties in conflict were achieved in Somalia and Sudan, even while armed conflict continued among others. Cease-fires largely held in Azerbaijan, Georgia and Moldova, and some progress towards peace settlements was registered.

As usual such promising developments were balanced by others less welcome. What had been counted as peace settlements in Cambodia and Sierra Leone unravelled as coups took place. Peace processes continued to be deeply troubled in Angola, Bosnia and Herzegovina, Chechnya and the Middle East.[1] Civil wars in Zaire (renamed the Democratic Republic of the Congo in May 1997) and in its smaller neighbour, Congo (Brazzaville), were both ended, not as a result of the numerous international attempts at conflict resolution, but through military victory by one side.

In 1997 new intra-state armed conflicts broke out in the Central African Republic, western China and Comoros.[2] The beginnings of armed resistance were apparent in the largely Albanian Kosovo province of Serbia in Yugoslavia (Serbia and Montenegro).[3] Fighting continued or was renewed in Afghanistan, Algeria, Burundi, Chad, Colombia, India, Myanmar, Peru,

[1] For a full account of developments in the Middle East peace process, see chapter 3 in this volume.
[2] For developments in major armed conflicts which had led to 1000 or more deaths by the end of 1997, see chapter 1 in this volume.
[3] There were guerrilla operations by the ethnic Albanian Kosovo Liberation Army. Hedges, C., 'In Kosovo, war by night', *International Herald Tribune*, 20 Oct. 1997, p. 5.

* Susanna Eckstein of the SIPRI Project on Peacekeeping and Regional Security assisted in researching this chapter.

SIPRI Yearbook 1998: Armaments, Disarmament and International Security

Rwanda and Senegal. Fighting among the Kurds in Iraq resumed. In the Great Lakes Region of Africa there were many new and continuing small-scale armed uprisings, some of them with seemingly unfathomable aims, such as the Lord's Resistance Army in Uganda. In Spain the Basque separatist movement (Euzkadi ta Azkatasuna, ETA) continued its terrorist campaign for independence. Ethnic violence also erupted in the northern Indian state of Bihar and on the Indonesian island of Kalimantan.[4]

Although there were again no major interstate military engagements in 1997, several minor interstate or cross-border military engagements occurred, including the perennial shelling of each other's border positions by India and Pakistan; clashes between Israel and Hezbollah in Lebanon; infiltration by North Korea into South Korea and artillery exchanges between them; clashes on the Thai–Cambodian border; a brief naval skirmish between Honduras and Nicaragua; naval and air incidents between Greece and Turkey; and incidents between the Philippine Navy and Chinese fishing boats around the Spratly Islands. Border incursions were conducted by both Turkey and Iran into Iraq in pursuit of Kurdish rebels.

This chapter surveys efforts undertaken in 1997 to prevent, manage or resolve armed conflict.[5] Section II focuses on the United Nations, the key multilateral actor, while section III deals separately with peacekeeping. Section IV surveys the UN role in peace enforcement, while section V analyses the role of regional and other multilateral organizations. Section VI provides an overview of the role of other actors, comprising individual states, ad hoc groupings of states, non-governmental organizations (NGOs) and prominent individuals. The conclusion proffers some thoughts on conflict prevention, management and resolution so far in the 1990s.

II. The United Nations

Under a new Secretary-General, Kofi Annan of Ghana, and relieved of direct responsibility for some of the most difficult peace operations (in Albania, Bosnia and Herzegovina and most African conflicts), the UN was able to turn its attention to restructuring and reform. The Secretary-General began implementing some reforms immediately and presented a further comprehensive reform package in mid-year. The UN remained, of course, involved in a wide range and number of conflict prevention, management and resolution efforts, either alone or in cooperation with regional or other organizations.

Restructuring and reform

On 16 July 1997 Annan presented to the General Assembly a comprehensive reform package, the most sweeping in UN history. It comprised reforms which

[4] *Far Eastern Economic Review*, 20 Feb. 1997, pp. 26–27; and *The Economist*, 15 Feb. 1997, p. 57.
[5] Institutionalized disarmament and arms control measures, including confidence- and security-building measures, while clearly a form of conflict prevention, are considered in chapter 12 and appendix 12A in this volume.

he himself could initiate, those which required the approval of the UN General Assembly and/or Security Council and those which required agreement from various other parts of the UN system.[6] While the implementation of all the proposals would make the UN as a whole more effective and efficient and thereby contribute to its efforts to prevent, manage and resolve conflict, there were particular proposals which would have a direct effect on such efforts:

1. A new leadership and management structure was proposed, including the position of Deputy Secretary-General to relieve the Secretary-General of administrative burden; establishment of a Senior Management Group (a type of cabinet); decentralization of decision making for UN missions in the field; and consolidation of the UN presence in each country under 'one flag' (usually that of the representative of the UN Development Programme).

2. A new management culture was to be accompanied by management and efficiency measures which would eliminate at least 1000 staff posts, reduce administrative costs by one-third, improve performance and effect additional savings in personnel and costs.

3. Human resources policies and practices were to be thoroughly overhauled to ensure that UN staff had the necessary skills and enjoyed the requisite conditions for effective service.

4. UN funds and programmes with development responsibilities were to be organized into a UN Development Group to facilitate cooperation, including that for peace-building activity undertaken during UN peace operations.

5. The organization's ability to deploy peacekeeping and other field operations rapidly, including its rapid-reaction capability, was to be improved.

6. Capacity for post-conflict peace-building was to be strengthened by designating the Department of Political Affairs as a focal point; an Executive Committee for Peace and Security was to be convened to ensure a unified effort across the entire UN system in all peacekeeping and peace-building, both in the field and at headquarters; and steps were to be taken to improve the UN's 'global watch' to detect threats to peace and security.

7. The UN's response to humanitarian needs, including its response during UN peace operations, was to be enhanced through the establishment of a new Emergency Relief Coordination Office to replace the Department of Humanitarian Affairs (DHA).

8. The Office of the High Commissioner for Human Rights and the Centre for Human Rights were to be consolidated into a single Office of the High Commissioner, to be located in Geneva.

The plan was welcomed by the United States Administration, which had pressed the UN for radical reform both for its own sake and to induce the US Congress to approve payment of US arrears to the UN.[7] Congress remained

---

[6] United Nations, Report of the Secretary-General, Renewing the United Nations: a programme for reform, UN document A/51/950, 16 July 1997.
[7] US Secretary of State Madeleine Albright, 'US policy and reform agenda on the United Nations', remarks to the press, Washington, DC, 19 Sep. 1997, *US Department of State Dispatch*, no. 42 (Aug./Sep. 1997), pp. 1–2.

unmoved, however, still refusing by the end of 1997 to authorize such payments. While most other developed countries supported Annan's package, some developing countries expressed concern that cuts would be at the expense of development activities, despite the Secretary-General's explicit pledge that savings on administrative expenses would become a 'development dividend'. Privately, developing states were also concerned that their nationals would lose key appointments in the UN bureaucracy as a result of staff cuts. At the General Assembly session which began in September the Secretary-General's plan was dissected minutely by the 185 UN member states to the point that agreement on those reform measures requiring the Assembly's approval seemed depressingly unlikely.

The Secretary-General and the Secretariat

The new Secretary-General continued, like his predecessor, to devote considerable attention to peace and security issues, in some cases intervening personally with good offices and mediation. During 1997 the Secretary-General and/or his representatives continued their efforts to settle the conflicts in Afghanistan, Burundi, Cyprus, East Timor, Iraq, Rwanda, Sierra Leone, Tajikistan, Western Sahara and Zaire. The principal new UN mediatory effort was in Congo (Brazzaville). In three cases—Cyprus, Western Sahara and East Timor—the Secretary-General attempted to revitalize flagging peace processes by the appointment of new high-level emissaries. In November the UN was itself forced to rely on the good offices of representatives of Algeria, Argentina, Russia and Sweden to help it negotiate with Iraq over its refusal to permit US inspectors to be part of the monitoring of Iraq's weapons of mass destruction potential by the UN Special Commission on Iraq (UNSCOM).[8]

Jamsheed Marker of Pakistan, the Secretary-General's new personal representative, embarked on an intensive series of consultations with Indonesia and Portugal to reinvigorate the tripartite talks on East Timor held under UN auspices since 1983. At the ninth annual round of talks in June it was agreed that such biannual diplomatic summit meetings should be replaced by technical expert meetings.[9] On 20–23 October the third meeting of the All-Inclusive Intra-East Timorese Dialogue (AIETD) was held in Krumbach, Austria.[10] As in the earlier AIETD meetings there was agreement on a number of social, cultural and human rights issues but not on a joint East Timorese position on political issues, which was their original goal.[11] The prospects of a settlement appeared to improve, however, when leader of the Revolutionary Front for an

[8] For details of UNSCOM's activities see chapter 11 in this volume.

[9] 'Indonesia: Timorese resistance official pleased with outcome of talks', RDP Antena 1 Radio Network (Lisbon), 20 June 1997, in Foreign Broadcast Information Service, *Daily Report–East Asia (FBIS-EAS)*, FBIS-EAS-97-120, 8 July 1997.

[10] An offer by South Africa to host future talks was rejected.

[11] On the AIETD meetings in 1995 and 1996 in Burg Schlaining, see Salla, M. E., 'Creating the "ripe moment" in the East Timor conflict', *Journal of Peace Research*, vol. 34, no. 4 (1997), p. 457. 'AIETD ends agreeing to seven-point Krumbach Declaration', Embassy of the Republic of Indonesia, Washington, DC, 24 Oct. 1997, URL <http://www.kbri.org/releases/others/timor110497.html>, version current on 3 Mar. 1997.

Independent East Timor (Frente Revolucionára Timorense de Libertação e Independência, Fretilin) and Nobel Peace Prize laureate José Ramos Horta offered a cease-fire and another spokesperson indicated that instead of independence the guerrilla group might be satisfied with autonomy along the lines of Puerto Rico's links with the USA.[12] However, the Timorese remained as divided as ever over such concessions.

In January the Secretary-General announced the appointment of a joint UN/Organization of African Unity (OAU) Special Representative for the Great Lakes Region of Africa, Mohammed Sahnoun of Algeria.[13] Such an appointment represented a new development in cooperation between the UN and a regional organization. However, neither Sahnoun nor his collaborators were able to negotiate an end to the civil wars in Congo (Brazzaville) and Zaire.

The Secretary-General's UN Special Mission to Afghanistan (UNSMA), headed by Norbert Holl, also struggled unsuccessfully to nourish moves towards a cease-fire and settlement, succeeding only in negotiating exchanges of prisoners of war. In April the Secretary-General convened a meeting in New York of member states with influence in Afghanistan, using the same formula as for a previous meeting in 1996.[14] The waxing and waning of the battlefield fortunes of the parties in Afghanistan prevented any significant progress being made. Holl declared in October that there was a 'standstill' in the negotiation process because the parties were being egged on by neighbouring Pakistan and Iran.[15]

The Secretariat continued its involvement in electoral assistance and observation. The recent global trend towards democratization was illustrated by the UN's report that it had received at least 80 requests for electoral assistance in the past five years.[16] The Secretary-General also reported that some 120 countries now hold generally free and fair elections, the highest number in history.[17] International observation of elections occurred during 1996–97 in Algeria, Ghana, Madagascar, Mali and Yemen, while electoral assistance was provided to Bangladesh, Comoros, Gambia, Guyana, Haiti, Liberia, Mali and Mexico.

In the field of human rights promotion and protection, the UN deployed human rights field operations in Abkhazia (Georgia), Burundi, Cambodia, Colombia, the Democratic Republic of the Congo, Gaza, Guatemala, Haiti, Malawi, Mongolia, Rwanda and the former Yugoslavia.[18] This represented a quantum leap in UN human rights activities in just a few years.

[12] 'Portugal: Timor: UDT opposes cease-fire before Indonesian withdrawal', RDP Antena 1 Radio Network (Lisbon), 3 Oct. 1997, in Foreign Broadcast Information Service, *Daily Report–West Europe (FBIS-WEU)*, FBIS-WEU-97-276, 6 Oct. 1997.
[13] United Nations, Letter dated 22 January 1997 from the Secretary-General addressed to the President of the Security Council, UN document S/1997/73, 24 Jan. 1997.
[14] United Nations, Report of the Secretary-General: The situation in Afghanistan and its implications for international peace and security, UN document A/51/929, 16 June 1997.
[15] Rashid, A., 'Agonizing aftermath', *The Economist*, 30 Oct. 1997, p. 31.
[16] United Nations, Report of the Secretary-General on the work of the organization, UN document A/52/1, 3 Sep. 1997, para. 38.
[17] United Nations (note 16), para. 15.
[18] United Nations (note 16), para. 31.

Despite the ubiquitous rhetoric about the need for improving the UN's capacity for 'preventive action', there was very little advance in 1997. The UN Trust Fund for Preventive Action Against Conflicts, established in 1996, had received contributions only from the Netherlands and Norway, amounting to just $4.5 million.[19] The funds were to be used by the Secretary-General for urgent conflict prevention efforts such as the dispatch of mediators.

The Security Council and General Assembly

The Security Council, while continuing to remain seized of a vast range of peace and security issues, again adopted a conservative stance towards intervention in internal conflicts. It again focused much attention on Africa, holding a ministerial meeting in September, only the third in its history, on the situation in that continent.[20] The Council continued to act conservatively towards new peacekeeping proposals. In the cases of Albania and the Central African Republic (CAR) it opted for 'contracting out' peacekeeping to coalitions of the willing and able. It also declined to support the Secretary-General's proposals for deployment of UN peacekeepers to Sierra Leone (giving a de facto mandate to a subregional organization instead) and Congo (Brazzaville). Senegal's offer to lead an operation in Congo (Brazzaville), the first ever by a developing country, was unceremoniously turned down because of its perceived inability to fulfil such a role. Annan also advocated resurrecting plans made in 1996 for deploying a Canadian-led multinational force to eastern Zaire, because of the serious humanitarian situation there following the outbreak of civil war. This was also rejected by the Council. This aversion to the deployment of new peace operations was attributable to the earlier Council experience with Bosnia and Herzegovina, Rwanda and Somalia, as well as the US reluctance to provide the bulk of the funding and become involved on the ground for fear of casualties. China continued to oppose any peace operation it regarded as involving interference in the internal affairs of a sovereign UN member state but, as in the past, abstained rather than vetoing them.

The 'contracting out' alternative increasingly favoured by the Council continued to attract criticism on the grounds that such operations ran the risk of being subverted by national priorities, that the Council and Secretariat were unable to exert the same control over them as over UN operations, and that they were invariably commanded and dominated by Western states, with developing states providing the peacekeeping equivalent of 'cannon fodder'.

The Council also devoted considerable time to discussing the situation in Iraq, particularly with regard to Iraq's continued failure to permit the UN Special Commission to carry out its verification and monitoring efforts to determine that Iraq had destroyed its weapons of mass destruction and long-range missile programmes. One crisis in relations with Iraq having been

[19] *Jane's Defence Weekly*, 11 June 1997, p. 5.
[20] United Nations, *Security Council 1997 Round-up* (United Nations Information Centre for the Nordic Countries: Copenhagen, 9 Jan. 1998), p. 1.

averted during 1997, as the year closed another was on the horizon as Iraq refused inspectors access to presidential sites in the country and attempted to bar US inspectors from UNSCOM teams.

The Council witnessed three vetoes during the year, the highest number since 1989.[21] Two were by the USA on the same issue, the refusal of Israel to halt the building of new settlements in east Jerusalem or extension of existing ones on the West Bank, while one was China's temporary veto of a new peacekeeping mission in Guatemala.[22] Showing new openness, the Council took the unprecedented step in February of allowing itself to be briefed by NGOs—including CARE International, Oxfam and Médecins sans Frontières (MSF, Doctors without Borders)—about their efforts in the Great Lakes Region of Africa.[23]

Reform of the Security Council still eluded the UN membership. Opinion seemed more divided than ever. Italy, seeking a seat of its own, attempted to postpone a decision purportedly on the grounds that agreement was nowhere in sight. The USA on the other hand, in finally announcing its own position on enlarging Council membership, attempted to bring the process to a close. It favoured adding five new permanent seats to the 15-member Council, one each for Japan and Germany and the remaining three for representatives of Africa, Asia and Latin America.[24] The USA was reportedly flexible on whether all the new permanent members would acquire the right of veto currently held by the Permanent Five (China, France, Russia, the UK and the USA). The President of the General Assembly for 1997, Malaysian Ambassador Razali Ismail, also sought a quick decision on Council membership but favoured increasing it to 24 by adding five permanent and four non-permanent members.

The General Assembly's most significant act during 1997 in considering conflict situations occurred when, following the US veto of draft Security Council resolutions on east Jerusalem, the Assembly convened its 10th emergency session.[25] It met three times during the year but failed to contribute a solution to the problem.

International legal mechanisms

The International Court of Justice (ICJ) had fewer cases before it in 1997 since several were removed from its docket in 1996 and no new ones were added. Public hearings were concluded on the Lockerbie cases between Libya and the UK and the USA, enabling the judges to begin deliberations on whether the ICJ had jurisdiction to deal with the merits of the cases and

---

[21] *UN Chronicle*, no. 1 (1997), p. 20. For details of pre-1991 vetoes, see Evans, G., *Cooperating for Peace: The Global Agenda for the 1990s and Beyond* (Allen & Unwin: Sydney, 1993), p. 21.

[22] United Nations, Dag Hammarskjöld Library Research Guide: List of matters considered/action taken by the Security Council in 1997, 7 Nov. 1997, URL <http://www.un.org/Depts/dhl/resguide/sact.htm>, version current on 7 Nov. 1997.

[23] *UN Chronicle* (note 21), p. 7.

[24] Crosette, B., 'US to seek 3 seats for poor nations on UN Council', *International Herald Tribune*, 18 July 1997, p. 1.

[25] United Nations (note 20), p. 2.

whether the Libyan complaints against the other two parties were admissible.[26] A decision was expected in early 1998. In September a judgement was delivered, 14 votes to 1, on the dispute between Hungary and Slovakia over the Gabcíkovo–Ngymaros dam project on the Danube River.[27] The ICJ ruled against Hungary, finding that it was not entitled to suspend work on the project, since it was obliged by treaty to continue regardless of changed circumstances.

Two international tribunals were involved not in resolving international conflicts but in putting on trial individuals suspected of war crimes and gross violations of human rights. The aim was not only to seek justice but also to deter such acts in future. The International Criminal Tribunal for the Former Yugoslavia marked a major milestone by delivering in May the first determination by an international tribunal of individual guilt or innocence in connection with serious violations of international humanitarian law.[28] It was also the first judgement and sentencing in a case of 'ethnic cleansing'. Another sentence for ethnic cleansing was handed down in July.[29] The tribunal's relationship with Croatia improved after Croatia handed over several indicted persons. The Bosnian Serb entity of Bosnia and Herzegovina, the Republika Srpska, continued to refuse to cooperate with the tribunal. NATO-led Stabilization Force (SFOR) troops, however, began arresting war crimes suspects for the first time.[30] In July British troops arrested one indictee and killed another who resisted arrest, while in December SFOR arrested two Croats in Vitez, one after a struggle. Ten Croat indictees were later arrested and detained for trial.[31] Three Bosnian Croat suspects were released owing to lack of evidence.

The International Criminal Tribunal for Rwanda, based in Arusha, Tanzania, resumed its work in better shape after the unprecedented sacking by Annan of two tribunal officials—deputy prosecutor Honore Rakotomanana of Madagascar and registrar Andronico Adede of Kenya—for serious mismanagement.[32] Although the investigation by Under-Secretary-General Karl Paschke found no evidence of corruption or misuse of funds, he reported 'mismanagement in almost all areas of the tribunal and frequent violations of UN rules and regulations'.[33] Bernard Muna of Cameroon took over as deputy prosecutor and immediately reinvigorated proceedings by proposing group trials, on the basis that the Rwandan massacres had been the result of a conspiracy.[34] Overturning its previous non-cooperation with the tribunal, Kenya in July arrested several former Rwandan officials on genocide charges and turned

---

[26] International Court of Justice, Communiqué no. 97/13, The Hague, 22 Oct. 1997.
[27] International Court of Justice, Communiqué no. 97/10 bis, The Hague, 25 Sep. 1997.
[28] *Daily Highlights* (UN Department of Public Information), 7 May 1997. Last year the ICJ handed down its first sentence for a crime against humanity since the Nuremberg and Tokyo trials after World War II.
[29] *Daily Highlights* (UN Department of Public Information), 14 July 1997.
[30] See section V in this chapter.
[31] United Nations, Report of the Secretary-General on the United Nations Mission in Bosnia and Herzegovina, UN document S/1997/966, 10 Dec. 1997, p. 6.
[32] *Jane's Defence Weekly*, 5 Mar. 1997, p. 6.
[33] Note 32.
[34] Cruvellier, T., 'Muna goes for mega-trials', *Tribunal*, no. 10 (Aug./Sep. 1997), pp. 6–7.

Table 2.1. Cases before the International Court of Justice, 1997

- Application of the Convention on the Prevention and Punishment of the Crime of Genocide (Bosnia and Herzegovina v. Yugoslavia)
- Maritime Delimitation and Territorial Questions between Qatar and Bahrain (Qatar v. Bahrain)
- Questions of Interpretation and Application of the 1971 Montreal Convention arising from the Aerial Incident at Lockerbie (Libya v. United Kingdom)
- Questions of Interpretation and Application of the 1971 Montreal Convention arising from the Aerial Incident at Lockerbie (Libya v. USA)
- Oil Platforms (Iran v. USA)
- Land and Maritime Boundary between Cameroon and Nigeria (Cameroon v. Nigeria)
- Fishing Jurisdiction (Spain v. Canada)
- Kasikili/Sedudu Island (Botswana/Namibia)

Note: Cases listed as one party versus another are those in which one party (the first mentioned) brought to the ICJ a case against another party; in the other case both parties jointly sought a Court ruling.

them over to UN investigators, as did Cameroon, Namibia and the USA.[35] Kenya also arrested a Belgian citizen, Georges Ruggiu, formerly a reporter at the Rwandan Government radio station, Radio Milles Collines, which had broadcast incitement to violence and racial hatred against Tutsis, moderate Hutus and Belgians.[36] As of September the tribunal had three trials under way and 21 accused persons awaiting trial.[37]

Meanwhile, negotiations between more than 100 countries began in New York in December on the statute for a permanent International Criminal Court.[38] Such a court would obviate the need for the establishment of special tribunals and constitute a standing deterrent to the commission of war crimes. Debate continued over whether states would be able to lodge complaints against individuals with the court (as provided for in the current draft statute) or whether the court would independently investigate individuals once a 'situation', such as genocide in a particular location, had been referred to it by the Security Council. The negotiations are to resume in Rome in mid-1998.

Following a trend in attempts to resolve maritime disputes arising from the 1982 UN Law of the Sea Convention, Eritrea and Yemen established an ad hoc arbitration panel in London, comprising an Egyptian, two Americans and a Briton, with British judge Sir Robert Jennings presiding, to arbitrate their dispute over the Hanish islands in the Red Sea.[39] A special Arbitral Tribunal established by the 1995 General Framework Agreement for Peace in Bosnia and Herzegovina (the Dayton Agreement) also ruled on the situation of Brcko in Bosnia and Herzegovina, deciding to keep it under temporary international

---

[35] *International Herald Tribune*, 19–20 July 1997, p. 1.
[36] *The Guardian*, 24 July 1997, p. 7.
[37] United Nations (note 16), para. 128.
[38] *The Economist*, 6 Dec. 1997, pp. 16 and 45. For background, see Findlay, T., 'Conflict prevention, management and resolution', *SIPRI Yearbook 1997*: *Armaments, Disarmament and International Security* (Oxford University Press: Oxford, 1997), p. 39.
[39] *Horn of Africa Bulletin*, vol. 9, no. 1 (Jan./Feb. 1997), p. 5.

supervision until March 1998, rather than handing it to the Bosnian Serbs or the Government of Bosnia and Herzegovina.[40]

III. UN peacekeeping operations

The great post-cold war boom in UN peacekeeping, in which large, multi-component missions were dispatched to deal with complex civil wars by engaging in peace-building and peacekeeping, ended in 1997 with the scaling down of the last such missions in Angola, Haiti and Eastern Slavonia. These were drawn down not because they had achieved complete success, but because the Security Council was unprepared to fund them at the same level indefinitely. The 15 extant operations in the field as 1997 ended comprised: small observer missions characteristic of the cold war era, many of them established decades ago; remnants of previously large-scale missions; two entirely civilian police (CivPol) missions, in Bosnia and Herzegovina and Haiti; and two missions, in Georgia and Tajikistan, mostly engaged in observing peacekeeping efforts conducted by a regional organization. The largest peace operation in existence at the end of 1997, but one commonly judged to be a mixture of peacekeeping and peace enforcement, was SFOR and its accompanying civilian components in Bosnia and Herzegovina, but this was a non-UN operation led by NATO.

The number of troops involved in UN peacekeeping continued to drop, as did the costs (see figure 2.1). As of 31 December 1997 there were fewer than 15 000 military and civilian police personnel in the field, compared with 25 000 troops at the end of 1996.[41] The estimated cost of peacekeeping was $1.3 billion in 1997, the first time in many years that it had fallen below the annual UN regular budget.[42]

In the roughly 10 years since the end of the cold war, peacekeeping has experienced an unprecedented boom, followed by a contraction to its previous levels. The number of operations peaked in 1995. Although the numbers have not fallen dramatically since then, they mask a shrinkage in the size, complexity and cost of missions. The number of troops, military observers and civilian police has plunged dramatically, nearly to the level of 1989, while costs have plummeted accordingly.

The continued contraction in UN peacekeeping has been compounded by the Security Council's continuing reluctance to authorize major new UN operations. Although the UN Secretariat in 1997 carried out planning and preparations for a mission in Sierra Leone and contingency planning for missions in Burundi and Zaire, none of these came about.[43] The Council authorized only one new UN mission in 1997, a small one in Guatemala.

[40] United Nations, Cooperation between the United Nations and the Organization for Security and Co-operation in Europe, Report of the Secretary-General, UN document A/52/450, 10 Oct. 1997, p. 3.
[41] United Nations, Monthly summary of troop contributions to peacekeeping operations as of 31 December 1997 (UN: New York, 31 Dec. 1997).
[42] United Nations, *1997 Year in Review: United Nations Peace Missions* (United Nations Information Centre for the Nordic Countries: Copenhagen, Dec. 1997), p. 2.
[43] United Nations (note 16), para. 116.

The Guatemala operation, the United Nations Verification Mission in Guatemala (MINUGUA), was unique in the history of peacekeeping in evolving from a solely human rights mission, also called MINUGUA, through the addition of 155 military observers.[44] China originally vetoed its establishment because of Guatemala's pro-Taiwan activities but later concurred when Guatemala agreed not to co-sponsor the annual General Assembly resolution calling for Taiwan's re-admission to the UN. The new mission was deployed for only three months from March 1997 for the purpose of verifying compliance with the Agreement on the Definitive Ceasefire, sign ed at Oslo, Norway, on 4 December 1996, by the Guatemalan Government and its rebel opposition, the Guatemalan National Revolutionary Unity (Unidad Revolucionaria Nacional Guatemalteca, URNG).[45] Its main task was to collect weapons from the URNG as it disarmed and demobilized and to transfer them to the Guatemalan Government. When the military observers withdrew at the end of May MINUGUA resumed its previous human rights role. There were unconfirmed reports in August of two new guerrilla groups resuming the armed struggle, which had lasted 36 years until the 1996 peace agreement.[46]

With regard to Angola, the Security Council was finally sufficiently convinced of the sturdiness of the peace process, after so many years of false hopes, to downgrade the third peacekeeping operation stationed there, the UN Angola Verification Mission (UNAVEM III), into the small UN Observer Mission in Angola (Missao de Observação das Nações Unidas em Angola, MONUA). Its authorized strength would be just 86 military observers (down from UNAVEM's 350) and 345 CivPols (up from 260).[47] Having devoted substantial resources and four peacekeeping missions to Angola, the international community could have expected peace to ensue. Under the terms of the 1994 Lusaka Protocol a Government of Unity and National Reconciliation (GURN) had been established by the two opposing forces, the Angolan Government and the National Union for the Total Independence of Angola (União Nacional para a Independência Total de Angola, UNITA), and the latter's forces had reportedly been largely demobilized under UN supervision. However, no sooner had MONUA been established than fighting resumed after UNITA refused the government access to its economic, military and political redoubt in the diamond-rich north-east and began backtracking on other aspects of the peace process. UNITA troops also attacked and harassed MONUA personnel. The Secretary-General described these developments as 'some of the most serious difficulties' since the signing of the Lusaka

---

[44] United Nations, Report of the Secretary-General on the Group of Military Observers attached to MINUGUA, UN document S/1997/432, 4 June 1997.
[45] For details see Findlay (note 38), pp. 64–65.
[46] 'Guatemala: new guerrilla groups cause army to reopen some garrisons', Prensa Libre (Guatemala City), 2 Aug. 1997, in Foreign Broadcast Information Service, *Daily Report–Latin America (FBIS-LAT)*, FBIS-LAT-97-214, 19 Aug. 1997.
[47] United Nations, Progress Report of the Secretary-General on the United Nations Angola Verification Mission (UNAVEM III), UN document S/1997/438/Add. 1, 5 June 1997, para. 45.

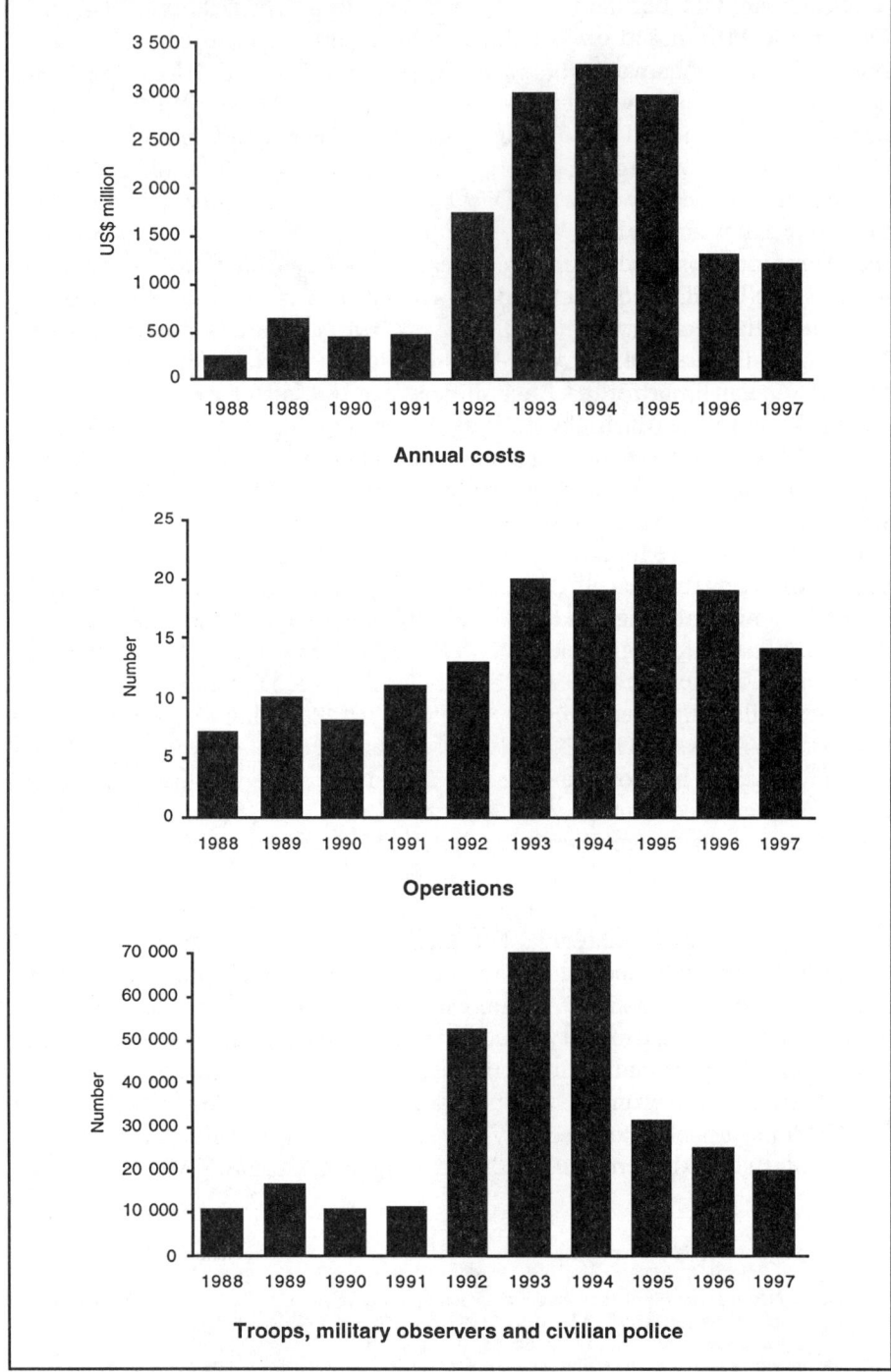

Figure 2.1. UN peacekeeping operations in 1988–97: costs, number of operations and number of military and civilian police personnel

Protocol.⁴⁸ By October the Council's patience finally ran out and additional sanctions were imposed on UNITA (the arms embargo remained in force). UNITA's leadership was subject to international travel restrictions and its offices outside Angola were to be closed. Foreign air traffic into UNITA-held territory was prohibited to prevent food, supplies and arms being delivered. UNITA's cooperation in the peace process remained frustratingly patchy as the year ended. The downsizing of MONUA's military component began in December and was expected to be completed by February 1998.

The previously scaled-back UN Mission for the Referendum in Western Sahara (MINURSO) received a new lease of life as the new Special Representative of the Secretary-General for Western Sahara, former US Secretary of State James Baker, brokered an accord between the Moroccan Government and the Popular Front for the Liberation of Saguía el-Hamra and Rio de Oro (Frente Popular para la Liberación de Saguía el-Hamra y del Rio de Oro, Frente Polisario) that would permit the long-delayed referendum on Western Saharan independence to be held in 1998.⁴⁹ The process was engendered by 'proximity talks' held in Lisbon in June involving the foreign ministers of Algeria, Mauritania, Morocco and the Polisario and followed indications from the Security Council that its patience and willingness to deploy MINURSO indefinitely were running out.⁵⁰

The UN Peacekeeping Force in Cyprus (UNFICYP) also remained hostage to political fortune as the Greek Cypriots and Turkey undertook mutually unsettling military preparations to preserve their positions on the island. As a result of the August 1996 riots and the subsequent prolonged state of alert, UNFICYP was to be returned to its authorized strength of 1236 military personnel (in addition to its 35 Australian and Irish CivPols).⁵¹ Fortunately, in 1997 there was also more diplomatic activity aimed at settling the Cyprus dispute than had been seen for many years. Annan invited the leaders of the two communities, Turkish Cypriot Rauf Denktash and Greek Cypriot Glafkos Clerides, to a series of talks in Switzerland and the USA, their first in three years, under the chairmanship of UN Special Advisor on Cyprus, Diego Cordovez.⁵² The US Presidential Envoy on Cyprus, Richard Holbrooke, made his first visit to the island in November, also in an attempt to stimulate negotiations.⁵³ At the end of the year it was reported that Holbrooke, Britain's special representative on the Cyprus issue, Sir David Hannay, and the UN were working on a draft constitution for Cyprus which would form part of a comprehensive settlement package for negotiation in 1998.⁵⁴ Meanwhile the

---

⁴⁸ United Nations, Progress report of the Secretary-General on the United Nations Observation Mission in Angola (MONUA), UN document S/1997/640, 13 Aug. 1997, para. 38.

⁴⁹ United Nations (note 20), p. 9.

⁵⁰ *UN Chronicle*, vol. 34, no. 1 (1997), p. 19; and *The Guardian*, 11 June 1997, p. 7.

⁵¹ United Nations, Report of the Secretary-General on the United Nations Operation in Cyprus, UN document S/1997/437, 5 June 1997, p. 6.

⁵² United Nations (note 16), para. 88.

⁵³ *International Herald Tribune*, 10 Nov. 1997, p. 5.

⁵⁴ 'Cyprus: Britain, UN prepare joint plan for Cyprus solution', *O Filelevtheros* (Nicosia), 23 June 1997, in FBIS-WEU-97-174, 24 June 1997.

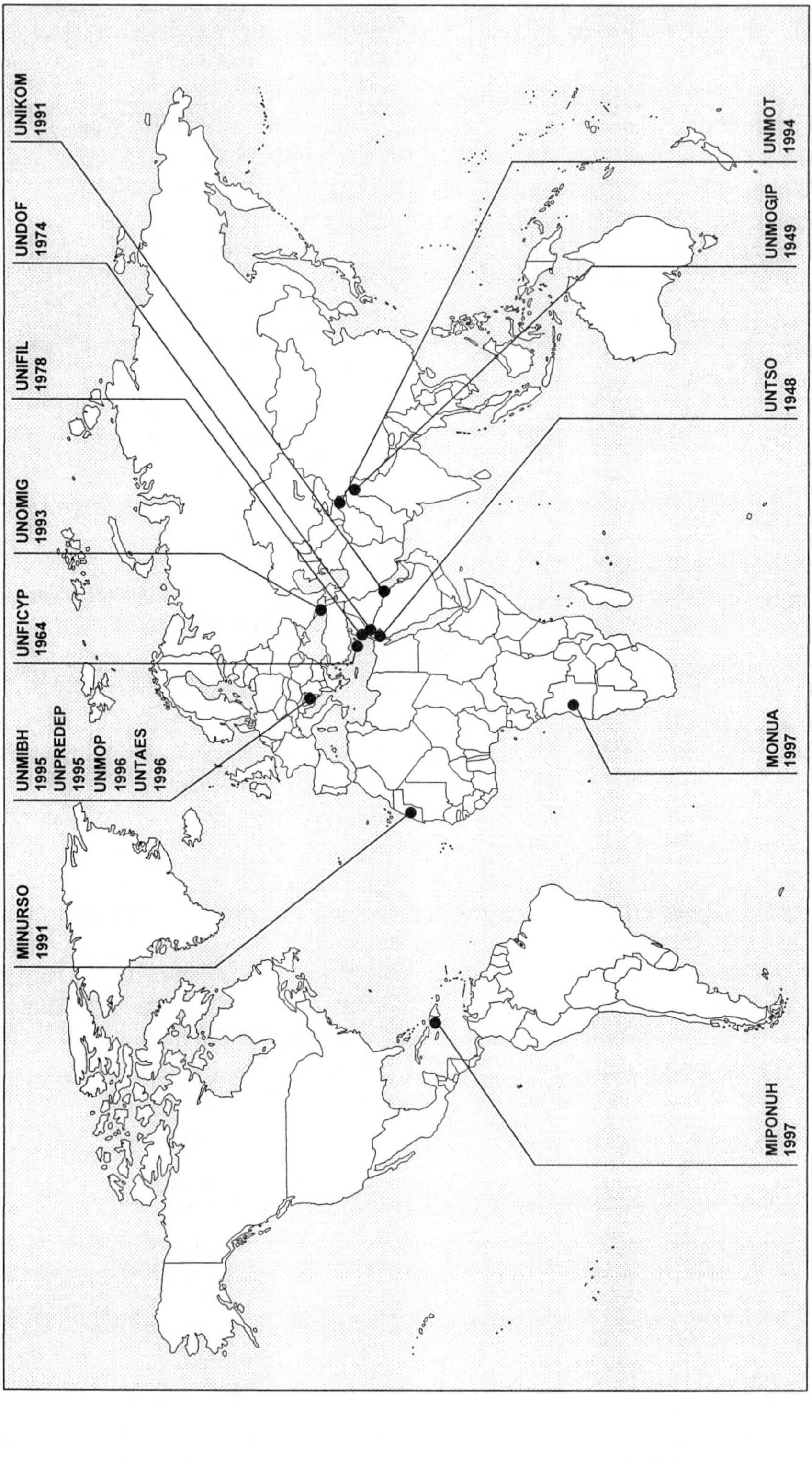

44 SECURITY AND CONFLICTS, 1997

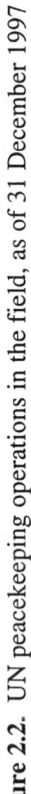

Figure 2.2. UN peacekeeping operations in the field, as of 31 December 1997

UN attempted to obtain agreement between the military establishments of the two sides on military confidence-building measures.[55]

One mission area in which there was a peace settlement, albeit a shaky one, was Tajikistan, where the UN Military Observers in Tajikistan (UNMOT) had been monitoring both the situation and the activities of a Russian-led Commonwealth of Independent States (CIS) peacekeeping force since 1994.[56] On 28 May, largely as a result of a mix of mediation and pressure by Iran and Russia, an agreement paving the way to a final peace agreement was signed in the presence of a UN representative by the Tajik Government and the Union of Tajik Opposition in Tehran.[57] Afghanistan, Iran, Kazakhstan, Kyrgyzstan, Russia, Turkmenistan and Uzbekistan, as well as the Organization for Security and Cooperation in Europe (OSCE) and the Organization of the Islamic Conference (OIC), signed the document as guarantors and formed a Contact Group to keep the peace process on track.[58] The final General Agreement on Peace Settlement and National Accord in Tajikistan was signed in Moscow by the two sides on 27 June. A National Reconciliation Commission was to be charged with preparing for a constitutional referendum and parliamentary elections. UNMOT military observers, who were withdrawn temporarily to Tashkent in February when UN employees were taken hostage, were redeployed throughout Tajikistan after the agreement was signed, their mandate enlarged to permit them to investigate cease-fire violations and their numbers expanded from 45 to 120.[59]

Of the four UN missions deployed in the republics of the former Yugoslavia, only the UN Mission in Bosnia and Herzegovina (UNMBIH), which comprised civilians and the International Police Task Force (IPTF), increased in size in 1997. It was given 186 additional CivPols and 11 civilians to help it better monitor, restructure and retrain police in the disputed Brcko area and carry out its continuing mandate under the Dayton Agreement. The IPTF had already successfully assisted in down-sizing from 23 000 to 11 500 the police force of the Federation of Bosnia and Herzegovina, the new force being subject to a 'substantial' vetting process involving psychological tests and examinations in the principles of democratic policing and human rights.[60] In Macedonia, the UN's only explicitly styled conflict prevention force, the UN Preventive Deployment Force (UNPREDEP), continued to act as an element of stability in a delicate internal and external environment. In view of the situation in neighbouring Albania, in April the Security Council decided to

---

[55] 'Cyprus: UN urges military dialogue progress before Cyprus talks', *Cyprus Mail* (Nicosia), 22 June 1997, in FBIS-WEU-97-173, 24 June 1997.

[56] For details of conflicts in the former Soviet republics see chapter 4 in this volume.

[57] Abdullaev, R. and Babakhanov, U., 'Thank the Taliban for the Tajik peace agreement', *Transitions*, Oct. 1997, pp. 46–51.

[58] 'Iran: Velayati tells UN's Annan of progress in Tajik peace talks', IRNA (Tehran), 31 May 1997, in Foreign Broadcast Information Service, *Daily Report–Near East and South Asia (FBIS-NES)*, FBIS-NES-97-151, 3 June 1997. For the members of the OSCE and the OIC see the glossary in this volume.

[59] 'Tajikistan: UN envoy discusses increase in Tajikistan presence', Interfax (Moscow), 1 July 1997, in Foreign Broadcast Information Service, *Daily Report–Central Eurasia (FBIS-SOV)*, FBIS-SOV-97-182, 2 July 1997; and United Nations (note 42), p. 23.

[60] *UN Chronicle*, vol. 34, no. 1 (1997), p. 22.

suspend the planned reduction in UNPREDEP's strength.[61] However, by the end of the year the situation had stabilized sufficiently for the Council to authorize the reduction to proceed and to accord the mission one last mandate, to 31 August 1998, after which the military component would be withdrawn and the nature of the mission reconsidered. The UN Transitional Administration for Eastern Slavonia, Baranja and Western Sirmium (UNTAES) was scheduled to end on 15 January 1998 after a surprisingly successful mission involving the facilitation of elections in April and preparations for the handover of the Croatian Serb-occupied area to Croatian Government control. The UNTAES military mission ended in October, when the bulk of its military component was withdrawn. However, there remained grave fears for the future of the Serb community under Croatian rule. Hence the Security Council decided to maintain a support group of 180 CivPols in the area after the withdrawal of UNTAES.[62] The mandate of the UN Mission of Observers in Prevlaka (UNMOP) on the Prevlaka peninsula was again extended by the Security Council because of continuing violations of the demilitarized zone by both Croatia and Yugoslavia (Serbia and Montenegro) and the lack of progress in settling the dispute over ownership of the territory.[63]

The UN Support Mission in Haiti (UNSMIH) was transformed twice during the year. In July the Security Council responded favourably to the request of Haitian President René Préval for the UN mission to remain to continue training the Haitian National Police but reduced its strength to just 250 CivPols and 50 military personnel, renamed it the UN Transitional Mission in Haiti (UNTMIH) and gave it a four-month non-renewable mandate.[64] In November the mission became an entirely CivPol operation, was renamed the UN Civilian Police Mission in Haiti (to be known by its French acronym MIPONUH, Mission de police civile des Nations Unies en Haïti) and was given a six-month extendable mandate. The Council was forced to take such a step because peace-building and peacemaking remained far from concluded in Haiti, with crime on the rise and political paralysis hindering economic recovery.[65] Five hundred US troops remained in the country under bilateral arrangements to assist in rehabilitation, as did UN agencies.

Continuing peacekeeping reforms

The UN Secretariat, now guided by a Secretary-General with long experience of peacekeeping operations, continued to pursue more efficient and effective peacekeeping. The Department of Peacekeeping Operations (DPKO) acquired a new Under-Secretary-General in February, Frenchman Bernard Miyet, after Annan was appointed Secretary-General. The DPKO continued to review

---

[61] *UN Chronicle*, vol. 34, no. 2 (1997), p. 73.

[62] United Nations, Report of the Secretary-General on the United Nations Transitional Administration for Eastern Slavonia, Baranja and Western Sirmium, UN document S/1997/953, 4 Dec. 1997.

[63] United Nations, Report of the Secretary-General on the United Nations Mission in Prevlaka, UN document S/1997/311, 14 Apr. 1997.

[64] UN Security Council Resolution 1123, UN document S/RES/1123, 30 July 1997.

[65] *The Economist*, 1 Nov. 1997, pp. 62–63.

cumbersome or inappropriate rules and procedures governing support for field operations, such as recruitment of personnel, procurement of supplies and settlement of third-party liability claims.[66]

Concerns among the developing countries about what they perceived to be differential treatment of their peacekeepers compared with those from developed countries persisted. An example was the compensation the UN pays for death or injury of peacekeepers.[67] Since the UN's death and disability awards are based on the national legislation of the contributing state, payments to troops from developed states have been 50 to 60 times higher than payments to developing states. Ambassador Anwarul Karim Chowdhury of Bangladesh, which has provided the second largest number of UN peacekeepers in recent years (after Pakistan), argued that 'This is serious discrimination. A life lost is a life lost'.[68] While the Group of 77 developing states[69] demanded that the present system be replaced with a standardized rate for all countries, and the Secretariat proposed a figure of $50 000, some industrialized states continued to argue that since living standards differed across countries differential rates should continue to apply. Developing countries also expressed concern about the significant number of military personnel from developed countries seconded to the DPKO.

In a move given greater urgency by new allegations of misconduct by Belgian and Italian peacekeepers in Somalia, a code of conduct for peacekeepers was under preparation by the DPKO to ensure compliance with human rights norms and encourage sensitivity towards the moral and cultural norms of host countries.[70] Another Secretariat initiative was the development of doctrine and guidelines for future UN peacekeeping operations deployed in conjunction with regional organizations, such as those in Georgia, Liberia and Tajikistan.[71] Standard guidelines and a manual for public information components in the field were being finalized to meet a long-standing criticism that the UN has usually handled public information in the field poorly.[72]

Meanwhile the UN Stand-by Arrangements System (UNSAS), which permits states to make non-binding pledges of contributions to future peacekeeping missions, continued to slowly attract additional pledges. As of 3 December 1997, 67 countries had officially expressed their willingness to participate, compared with 62 in November 1996. Twelve countries—Argentina, Austria, Bolivia, Denmark, Ghana, Italy, Jordan, Malaysia, Nepal, Singapore, Ukraine and Uruguay—had signed a Memorandum of Understanding with the UN confirming participation in the system, compared with just five in 1996.[73]

---

[66] United Nations (note 16), para. 117.
[67] Deen, T., 'UN discriminates on race in cost of dying for peace', *Jane's Defence Weekly*, 21 May 1997, p. 5.
[68] *Jane's Defence Weekly*, 21 May 1997, p. 5.
[69] Established in 1964, the Group of 77 promotes the economic interests of the developing world within the UN system. Its membership has increased to 132 countries.
[70] *Jane's Defence Weekly*, 19 Feb. 1997, p. 5.
[71] United Nations (note 16), para. 120.
[72] United Nations (note 16), para. 164.
[73] United Nations, Monthly Status Report, UN Standby Arrangements, 3 Dec. 1997.

China announced in May that it would 'in principle' participate.[74] The Secretariat continued to report that some support functions were still not pledged in sufficient numbers to allow for 'optimum system efficiency', including headquarters support, communications, engineering, air services, CivPols and logistics. Moreover, only 40 per cent of the pledged resources could be ready for use in the mission area within 30 days or less.[75] However, the Military Advisor to the Secretary-General, Major-General Franklin van Kappen of the Netherlands, reported that UNSAS had already proved 'most helpful' in planning for and subsequent deployment of peacekeepers to Angola, Haiti and the former Yugoslavia.

Planning for the establishment of a Rapidly Deployable Mission Headquarters (RDMHQ) to accelerate deployment of future peace operations was, according to van Kappen, 'pretty far advanced', with screening of candidates for the headquarters posts well under way.[76] By the end of 1997 the UN reported that the system was ready for implementation when funding became available.[77]

A report by the UN Office of Internal Oversight Services was critical of the operation of the UN Logistics Base at Brindisi, Italy,[78] largely the result of financial and staff shortages, stating that much of the equipment from defunct peacekeeping missions was in poor condition and would have to be written off. Moreover, the mission-ready start-up kits supposed to have been prepared for future missions remained incomplete because of the lack of reserve equipment and funds. The report recommended improved procedures and funding, renewed efforts to complete the start-up kits and the sending only of reusable equipment to the base in future.

Peacekeeping finance

As the costs of peacekeeping continued to fall, the financial crisis of the UN continued to ease. The USA remained the largest peacekeeping debtor, owing $1.3 billion by the end of 1997.[79] The next largest were Japan, Russia and Ukraine. In the USA, while influential voices continued to be raised in support of the UN and the payment of the outstanding US debt, the Congress voted in November not to repay it.[80] Ted Turner, founder of Cable News Network

---

[74] 'China: PRC to participate in UN peacekeeping operations', Xinhua (Beijing), 29 May 1997, in Foreign Broadcast Information Service, *Daily Report–China (FBIS-CHI)*, FBIS-CHI-97-149, 2 June 1997.

[75] 'Standby arrangement system: enhancing deployment capacity', *UN Chronicle*, vol. 34, no. 1 (1997), pp. 13–14.

[76] *1996 Annual Report to Congress on Peacekeeping*, Washington DC, 1996, p. 10.

[77] United Nations (note 42), p. 4. For background to the RDMHQ see Findlay (note 38), pp. 45–46.

[78] United Nations, Administrative and budgetary aspects of the financing of the United Nations peacekeeping operations: Report of the Secretary-General on the activities of the Office of Internal Oversight Services, UN document A/51/803, 20 Feb. 1997.

[79] United Nations, Outstanding contributions to the regular budget, international tribunals and peacekeeping operations as of 31 October 1997 (United Nations Information Centre for the Nordic Countries: Copenhagen, Jan. 1998), p. 24.

[80] See, e.g., *American National Interest and the United Nations*, Statement and report of an Independent Task Force (Council on Foreign Relations: New York, 1996).

(CNN), stunned the Secretary-General in September by pledging a donation of $1 billion to the UN, spread over 10 years.[81] However, since it would go towards children, refugee and landmine programmes funded by voluntary contributions rather than to the UN regular budget, it would not directly affect the overall UN financial situation or that of peacekeeping.

Earlier, a report by the Management Reform Group of the Department of Administration and Management (renamed the Department of Management in Annan's reform package) had announced in April that managerial reform at UN Headquarters would save $100 million in 1997.[82] A $1.7 million saving by the DPKO alone was achieved through improved selection and training of CivPols. The UN's powerful Advisory Committee on Administrative and Budgetary Questions reported that essential improvements were still needed in administrative and management techniques for UN peacekeeping.[83] It called for more involvement of field missions in preparation of cost estimates and budget performance reports, compilation of a roster of qualified administrators to be assigned to missions, and improved cooperation between UN administration in the field and the military, especially on matters with financial and/or legal implications. It also suggested that the UN become tougher with the host governments of peacekeeping operations in ensuring that they meet their obligations under Status of Forces Agreements signed with the UN.

Improvements in UN peacekeeping capability through national and cooperative efforts

National and cooperative efforts outside the UN framework also continued to promise a rise in the effectiveness of UN peacekeepers and associated mission personnel. The Council of Defence Ministers of the CIS, for instance, agreed to establish four peacekeeping training centres, two in Russia and one each in the Caucasus and Central Asia.[84]

Establishment of joint peacekeeping units became more popular. The NATO–Russia Permanent Joint Council (PJC) decided in September in New York to create a peacekeeping task force, as well as to discuss future possibilities such as joint exercises, training and even combined units.[85] The Baltic states, Estonia, Latvia and Lithuania, signed further agreements relating to the establishment of their joint peacekeeping battalion in 1998.[86] The Czech Republic and Poland agreed to form a joint peacekeeping unit, while Hungary

---

[81] *The Economist*, 27 Sep. 1997, p. 53.

[82] *UN Chronicle*, no. 1 (1997), p. 35.

[83] United Nations, Administrative and budgetary aspects of the financing of the UN peacekeeping operations: Report of the Advisory Committee on Administrative and Budgetary Questions, UN document A/51/892, 8 May 1997, pp. 3–4.

[84] Remarks of Maj.-Gen. Andrei Marshankin, Chief for Coordination of Military Cooperation of the CIS Member States, Moscow, at the Workshop on Challenges of Peace Support Operations into the 21st Century, National Defence College, Stockholm, 26–27 Sep. 1997.

[85] 'Russia: Russia, NATO Council support creating peacekeeping force', Interfax (Moscow), 29 Sep. 1997, in FBIS-SOV-97-272, 1 Oct. 1997. On the PJC see also chapter 5 in this volume.

[86] 'Lithuania: Baltic states reach accord on joint peacekeeping battalion', Radio Riga Network (Riga), 16 Oct. 1997, in FBIS-SOV-97-289, 20 Oct. 1997.

and Romania discussed a similar venture, as did Hungary, Italy and Slovenia.[87] The states involved in the Multinational United Nations Stand-by Forces High Readiness Brigade (SHIRBRIG), which will be available to the UN for six-month peacekeeping deployments pending the arrival of regular peacekeeping forces, took more steps during the year towards operability.[88] The headquarters in Denmark began to function and several participating states signed various implementation agreements.

Japan and the USA agreed to cooperate more closely in peacekeeping under the 1997 revised Guidelines for US–Japan Defense Cooperation.[89] As a result, the Japanese Government decided to formulate new regulations concerning the use of force by Japanese troops in peacekeeping operations, to accommodate the constitutional ban on the use of force except in self-defence.[90] To date, Japanese troops have been strictly prohibited from using force except in cases of personal self-defence or defence of other Japanese military personnel. Japan also sent troops for additional training to the Malaysian Peacekeeping Training Centre.[91]

Canada continued efforts to repair the damage done to its proud and long-standing peacekeeping reputation when Canadian troops tortured to death a Somali civilian and killed another in 1992. A Commission of Enquiry not only criticized the conduct of Canadian peacekeepers in Somalia but accused the armed forces of flagrantly covering up their misdeeds.[92] Training and selection procedures are being changed to prevent a repetition of the incidents. A Belgian enquiry into the behaviour of its troops in Somalia led to the charging but subsequent acquittal of several soldiers.

New peacekeepers and new peacekeeping partners continued to appear. The Government of Mozambique presented a bill to parliament that would permit Mozambican troops to participate in peacekeeping operations.[93] This was yet another case, like that of Namibia, of a former beneficiary of peacekeeping contributing to peacekeeping operations elsewhere. New peacekeeper South Africa completed training of two battalions for peacekeeping.[94]

The pace of peacekeeping exercises accelerated during the year. As part of NATO's Partnership for Peace (PFP), several exercises were conducted, including two by a group of Central Asian states, exercising together as the

---

[87] 'Poland: ministers agree to form joint peacekeeping force', PAP (Warsaw), 30 May 1997, in Foreign Broadcast Information Service, *Daily Report–East Europe (FBIS-EEU)*, FBIS-EEU-97-150, 2 June 1997; 'Hungary: Vegh, Romanian general confer on joint peacekeeping unit', Rompres (Bucharest), 25 June 1997, in FBIS-EEU-97-176, 26 June 1997; and Radio Free Europe/Radio Liberty, *RFE/RL Newsline*, vol. 1, no. 160, part II (14 Nov. 1997).

[88] Its members are Austria, Canada, Denmark, the Netherlands, Norway, Poland and Sweden.

[89] *Jane's Defence Weekly*, 18 June 1997, p. 14; and 'Completion of the review of the Guidelines for US–Japan Defense Cooperation', *News Release* (US Department of Defense), no. 507–97 (23 Sep. 1997), URL <http://www.defenselink.mil/news/Sep1997/b09231997_bt50797b.html>, version current on 4 Mar. 1998.

[90] 'Japan: Tokyo to draw up rules on SDF weapon use', *Mainichi Shimbun* (Tokyo), 28 July 1997, in FBIS-EAS-97-209, 29 July 1997.

[91] *International Peacekeeping News*, vol. 2, no. 6 (Jan./Feb. 1997), p. 13.

[92] *Financial Times*, 4 July 1997, p. 5.

[93] *International Security Digest*, vol. 4, no. 6 (Aug. 1997), p. 1.

[94] *International Security Digest*, vol. 4, no. 2 (Apr. 1997), p. 1.

CONFLICT PREVENTION, MANAGEMENT AND RESOLUTION 51

Central Asian Battalion (Centrasbat), in Kazakhstan and Uzbekistan in September.[95] They were joined by troops from the Baltic states, Georgia, Germany, Russia, Turkey and the USA. Centrasbat was formed in 1996 by Kazakhstan, Kyrgyzstan and Uzbekistan. Another PFP exercise was 'Baltic Challenge' in Estonia in July, involving the Baltic and Nordic states, Ukraine and the USA.[96] In October military units from Argentina, Brazil and Uruguay exercised together in 'Operation Southern Cross 97' in Rio Grande do Sul state, with Bolivia and Paraguay observing.[97] In May the Brazilian Navy joined 13 NATO countries in 'Exercise Linked Seas' in the sea and coastal waters of the Iberian peninsula to practice joint peace support operations.[98]

The USA continued to promote its idea of an African peacekeeping force, although its earlier African Crisis Response Force proposal was renamed the African Crisis Response Initiative (ACRI) after criticism from African states sensitive to external meddling. ACRI is designed to train and equip African peacekeepers, stationed but ready in their nation of origin, for rapid deployment to areas of crisis in Africa. The components of the programme, estimated to cost $25–40 million, include: (a) a force of 5000–10 000 (c. 8–10 battalions); (b) training to be conducted by US Special Forces in joint exercises on a 60-day training cycle; and (c) compatible communications and training equipment (such as mine-detection equipment, night-vision goggles, uniforms, computers and language training).[99] Ethiopia, Malawi, Mali, Senegal, Tunisia and Uganda began receiving training in 1997, while Ghana was scheduled for 1998. African critics of the programme feared that it was simply designed to avoid Western involvement in future African crises.

France conducted 'Operation Nangbeto', its first large humanitarian training exercise with its former colonies in West Africa, from 19 to 21 March.[100] Nearly 4500 troops from Benin, Burkina Faso, France and Togo rehearsed the establishment of a security zone and provision of humanitarian aid in a country torn by internal strife. France also organized a seminar in Dakar, Senegal, in October to 'reinforce' African peacekeeping capabilities.[101] The UN was similarly involved in attempting to improve African capabilities, holding a seminar in Egypt on peacekeeping training and establishing training teams.[102] The Secretary-General also established a voluntary fund for enhancing African peacekeeping preparedness, to be used to strengthen institutional collaboration through staff exchanges and enhanced liaison arrangements between the UN and the OAU. Under British sponsorship, a joint peacekeep-

[95] 'Kyrgyzstan: NATO commander views Central Asian peacekeeping exercise', Interfax (Moscow), 16 Feb. 1996, in FBIS-SOV-97-033, 16 Feb. 1997; and Smith, J. R., 'Central Asian war game tests Pentagon's reach', *International Herald Tribune*, 16 Sep. 1997, p. 2.
[96] 'Estonia: international military peacekeeping exercises to be staged', Interfax (Moscow), 3 July 1997, in FBIS-SOV-97-184, 7 July 1997.
[97] 'Argentina: Mercosur member countries starting military exercise', TELAM (Buenos Aires), 7 Oct. 1997, in FBIS-LAT-97-280, 9 Oct. 1997.
[98] *Jane's Defence Weekly*, 6 Aug. 1997, p. 27.
[99] Information from Project on Peacekeeping and the United Nations, Council for a Livable World Education Fund, Washington, DC, July 1997.
[100] *Jane's Military Exercise & Training Monitor*, Jan.–Mar. 1997, p. 1.
[101] *Defense News*, vol. 12, no. 42 (1997), p. 2.
[102] *Track Two*, Apr. 1997, p.2.

ing exercise, 'Blue Hungwe', was held in Zimbabwe in April by troops and observers from Angola, Botswana, Lesotho, Malawi, Mozambique, Namibia, South Africa, Swaziland, Tanzania, the UK and Zimbabwe.[103] The aim was to develop operational, logistics and communications doctrines for joint operations. The UK also agreed to train two battalions in Sierra Leone but the coup there ended such plans for the moment.

With France, the UK, the USA and the UN all involved in preparing Africans for peacekeeping, there was a clear need for coordination. The Group of Seven (G7) industrialized countries, plus Russia, at the summit meeting in Denver, Colorado in June, agreed to support ACRI.[104] France organized a coordination meeting in November in New York, although it stressed that it was not proposing the establishment of an African force but rather a 'framework' for future African peacekeeping efforts.[105]

IV. UN peace-enforcement measures

The two principle means which the UN Charter envisages for 'enforcing' peace are sanctions and the threat or use of military force.[106]

Sanctions

Sanctions regimes of various sorts remained in place in 1997 against Iraq, Libya, Liberia, Somalia, Sudan and non-governmental forces in Rwanda. The existing arms embargo on UNITA in Angola was supplemented with additional sanctions. Sanctions were imposed on Sierra Leone after the military coup there in May, prohibiting the import of petroleum products, arms and all other military equipment and strictly limiting the international travel of members of the military regime.[107] The Economic Community of West African States (ECOWAS) was asked by the Security Council to assist in monitoring them.[108] While the Council failed to agree to tighten sanctions on Sudan because of its alleged continuing support for terrorism, and did not implement the air embargo it had threatened to impose in August 1996, the USA imposed its own sanctions unilaterally. The USA and the UK strongly resisted pressure from African and Asian states to compromise with Libya over its refusal to extradite suspects in the Lockerbie bombing to Scotland, thereby permitting sanctions to be lifted.

---

[103] *Jane's Intelligence Review and Jane's Sentinel Pointer*, June 1997, p. 11.
[104] *Jane's Defence Weekly*, 13 Aug. 1997, p. 17. For list of members of the G7 see the glossary in this volume.
[105] 'South Africa: permanent African intervention force said not planned', South African Press Agency (Johannesburg), 5 Nov. 1997, in Foreign Broadcast Information Service, *Daily Report–Africa (FBIS-AFR)*, FBIS-AFR-97-309, 6 Nov. 1997.
[106] 'Enforce' is used here in the sense of coercing a party to do something it would otherwise not wish to do or to refrain from doing something it does wish to do. The difference between an enforcement activity and a non-enforcement activity turns on the question of consent. If the consent of the party is not forthcoming then the action taken is necessarily an enforcement activity.
[107] *International Herald Tribune*, 9 Oct. 1997, p. 7.
[108] UN Security Council Resolution 1132, UN document S/RES/1132, 8 Oct. 1997.

Although sanctions against Iraq resulting from the 1991 Persian Gulf War were retained, the oil-for-food programme begun in December 1996, which allowed Iraq to sell oil under UN supervision to buy essential commodities for its population, was extended in June. According to Annan it was the 'first systematic attempt by the Council to address the humanitarian needs of a civilian population in a country remaining subject to sanctions' and thus represented overdue implementation of Article 50 of the UN Charter.[109] In November the Security Council tightened sanctions on Iraq after it attempted to ban US personnel from UNSCOM verification activities, by imposing travel restrictions on the Iraqi officials involved.

Military enforcement

In 1997 five UN or UN-authorized missions—the Iraq–Kuwait Observation Mission (UNIKOM) on the Iraq–Kuwait border, SFOR in Bosnia and Herzegovina, UNTAES in Eastern Slavonia, the Inter-African Mission to Monitor the Implementation of the Bangui Agreements (Mission interafricaine de surveillance des accords de Bangui, MISAB) in the Central African Republic and the Multinational Protection Force (MPF) for Albania—were mandated to use force under Chapter VII, the enforcement chapter of the UN Charter. While the threat of force was implicit in many of the actions undertaken by such missions, such as the arrest of war criminals and seizure of weapons by SFOR, there was no use of force other than in self-defence.[110]

MISAB and the MPF were in fact only authorized to use force in self-defence—to ensure the security and freedom of movement of their own personnel.[111] As in the cases of Bosnia and Herzegovina and Somalia in previous years, this was arguably a misuse of Chapter VII, since normal peacekeeping operations authorized under Chapter VI already have the right to use force in self-defence.

The Multinational Interception Force (MIF), one of the largest maritime sanctions monitoring and verification efforts in history, established to prevent Iraq from flouting the sanctions regime, continued its operations in the Persian Gulf, little noticed outside the region. Mandated by the Security Council in 1990 and under US command, it had by 1997 involved 15 countries on a rotational basis.[112] In a purely quadripartite arrangement, British and French naval forces patrolled the Hanish islands area of the Red Sea to enforce the peace agreement between Yemen and Eritrea over sovereignty over the island, but no force was used in doing so.[113]

---

[109] United Nations (note 16), para. 89.
[110] On the use of riot-control agents in peacekeeping operations see chapter 11 in this volume.
[111] UN Security Council Resolution 1101, UN document S/RES/1101, 28 Mar. 1997, para. 2; and UN Security Council Resolution 1125, UN document S/RES/1125, 6 Aug. 1997.
[112] *UN Chronicle*, no. 1 (1997), p. 28. Authorized by UN Security Council Resolution 665, UN document S/RES/665, 25 Aug. 1990.
[113] *Horn of Africa Bulletin*, vol. 8, no. 6 (Nov./Dec. 1996), p. 5.

V. Regional and other multilateral organizations

Regional organizations played a noticeably increased role in conflict prevention, management and resolution efforts in 1997. As in previous years most of the regional initiatives stemmed from Europe and the CIS, but there were also a number of missions from African, Latin American and Asian organizations.

Europe and the CIS

The largest peace operation during the year, whose strength—between 31 000 and 36 000 troops—eclipsed by a long way any UN mission, was the NATO-led SFOR in Bosnia and Herzegovina. It was a hybrid peace enforcement/ peacekeeping mission, with the power to enforce its will on the parties but with many traditional peacekeeping tasks as well. SFOR had taken over from the larger but similarly constituted Implementation Force (IFOR) in December 1996 to continue implementation of the Dayton Agreement. SFOR faced a number of challenges during the year which engendered increasing Bosnian Serb opposition. SFOR troops were taunted and attacked by hostile Serb crowds and several other incidents of harassment of international personnel occurred. There were several causes. First, British troops killed a suspected Bosnian Serb war criminal who resisted arrest and arrested another. Second, in response to the attempt by former Bosnian Serb President Radovan Karadzic (still in effective control of many of the levers of power in the Republika Srpska) to oust his elected successor, Biljana Plavsic, SFOR seized control of television transmitters broadcasting anti-SFOR and anti-Plavsic propaganda. It intervened to prevent Karadzic forces from kidnapping Plavsic in Banja Luka in an attempted coup in September.[114] SFOR also seized police stations under Karadzic's control and handed them to police under Plavsic's authority and moved to place under international control the Bosnian Serb 'special police', some of whom guard Karadzic.[115] At other times, acting inconsistently and worryingly like its predecessor, the UN Protection Force (UNPROFOR), SFOR shrank from forceful action when confronted by Serb resistance. While there was criticism that SFOR seemed to be siding with one party in an internal dispute, SFOR argued that it was its duty to uphold the legitimate authorities in all of Bosnia and Herzegovina. SFOR's enforcement mandate and overwhelming military strength allowed it to do so. Its actions were, however, impossible to disentangle from the USA's political support for Plavsic who, despite her past record of inciting ethnic cleansing, was apparently willing to tolerate implementation of the Dayton Agreement.

SFOR also helped provide security for the first municipal elections held in Bosnia and Herzegovina since the war, as well as parliamentary elections in the Republika Srpska. The elections themselves went smoothly, although in the municipal elections the right of voters to cast their ballots in their former

---

[114] Steele, J., 'How S-For foiled coup by Karadzic', *The Guardian*, 15 Sep. 1997, p. 6.
[115] Cody, E., 'Allies tighten squeeze on Karadzic', *International Herald Tribune*, 14 Aug. 1997, p. 1.

places of residence—before ethnic cleansing and fighting forced them to move—produced election results which were unlikely ever to be implemented. For example, Muslim councillors were elected in the former UN Safe Area of Srebrenica, now totally devoid of Muslims. SFOR was unlikely to be able to enforce such results on an unwilling local populace.

Both the UN's IPTF and SFOR continued to attempt to provide security for those wishing to return to live in their former homes across the ethnic divide. Around the disputed city of Brcko, arguably exceeding their mandate, US troops quietly expanded their activities to furnish almost constant protection for returning refugees.[116] SFOR also provided particularly heavy security in the divided city of Mostar. A new initiative was begun in March to offer aid to municipalities which declared themselves 'open cities' willing to take back and embrace minorities. Several did so and dozens were seeking such status by the end of 1997.[117] However, SFOR clearly could not provide complete protection to all returnees and in any event will not be deployed permanently in the country.

While there were only relatively minor violations of the military aspects of the Dayton Agreement in 1997 and the various levels of government specified in the accord were now in place, a major strategic goal, the integration of the Federation of Bosnia and Herzegovina and the Republika Srpska into a functioning state of Bosnia and Herzegovina, remained as distant as ever. Even the federation remained more apparent than real. Dayton Agreement negotiator Richard Holbrooke was re-enlisted to persuade the parties to fulfil their commitments, but even he had limited success. While there were some calls for the agreement to be abandoned and negotiations held to institutionalize the de facto division of the country into three independent 'statelets'[118]—Croat, Muslim and Serb—NATO remained firm that the agreement would be proceeded with. This raised the question of how long SFOR would need to be stationed in the country beyond its June 1998 deadline to prevent a reversion to war. Such concerns were heightened by the US Train and Equip Program for the forces of the Federation of Bosnia and Herzegovina which, while designed to balance their forces with those of the Bosnian Serbs, provided new equipment and advanced training which may tip the military balance and provide incentives for an attempt to seize Bosnian Serb territory. A decision on an extension of SFOR's mandate depended on the US Administration, since its NATO partners continued to indicate that they would not stay in Bosnia if US troops were withdrawn. In December President Clinton conceded that some form of international force, including US troops, would have to remain in Bosnia for the foreseeable future. At the weekly meeting of NATO's Permanent Council on 10 December the USA presented four options for a follow-on force; the zero option seemed the least likely to be adopted.[119]

---

[116] O'Connor, M., 'Quiet protection in Brcko', *International Herald Tribune*, 30 July 1997, p. 2.
[117] *The Economist*, 9 Aug. 1997, pp. 23–24.
[118] Mearsheimer, J. J., 'Since Dayton is doomed, get on with the partition of Bosnia', *International Herald Tribune*, 8 Oct. 1997, p. 10.
[119] *Atlantic News*, no. 2973 (12 Dec. 1997), p. 1.

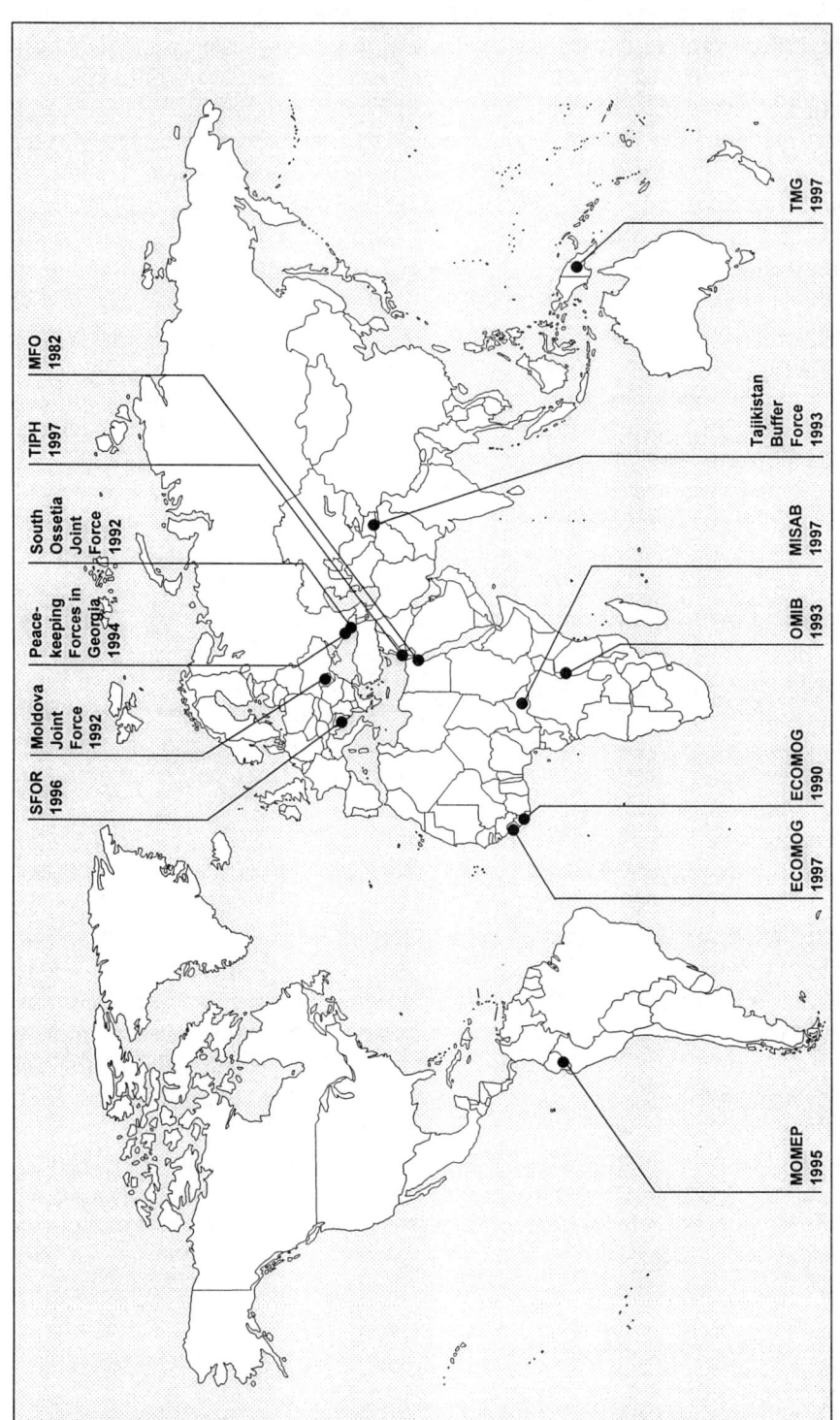

Figure 2.3. Other multilateral peacekeeping operations in the field, as of 31 December 1997

Europe acquired its second peacekeeping mission 'contracted out' to a group of interested states when the Security Council in March authorized Italy to lead a 7000-strong MPF in Albania. For weeks the country had been wracked by dissolution and anarchy, triggered by the collapse of pyramid investment schemes—a prime example of the diversity of early-warning indicators of crises. The Security Council mandated the MPF, in a 'temporary and limited operation', to 'facilitate the safe and prompt delivery of humanitarian assistance, and to help create a secure environment for the missions of international organizations'.[120] Italy provided the bulk of the forces and logistical support. An unusual feature was the participation of troops from Greece and Turkey, which are at loggerheads in their bilateral relations. The operation was guided by a Steering Committee consisting of representatives of the troop-contributing countries and the Italian Force Commander, with observers from the UN, the OSCE, the Western European Union (WEU), the European Union (EU) and the International Committee of the Red Cross (ICRC). Although such a committee was not unprecedented—the UN had such committees for its early operations in the Sinai and in the former Belgian Congo—it was a relatively rare attempt to give troop-contributing countries a say in the strategic management of a peace operation.

The MPF's mode of operation was to secure control of main roads and other avenues of communication and provide a 'security framework' to civil and humanitarian convoys, UN agencies and NGOs. The MPF also protected and assisted with the national elections held in July which led to a peaceful transfer of power. The force was on occasions fired on and used lethal force but sustained no fatalities itself. While it had its mandate extended once by the Security Council, it ultimately staged a successful withdrawal. The OSCE also fielded a 'Presence in Albania' which assisted the Albanian authorities, including in organizing the elections.[121] The WEU provided a Multinational Advising Police Element (MAPE).[122]

The proposal to deploy the MPF was criticized on the grounds that there was no need for such a force, since mass starvation was not imminent, and that its limited mandate and rules of engagement prevented it from dealing directly with those responsible for the anarchic situation. The force was not permitted to engage in peace enforcement and was therefore, apart from its protective functions, mostly a symbol of international, especially European, concern. The role of Italy was also criticized on the grounds that it had direct national interests at stake which would not always coincide with those of the UN, such as preventing waves of refugees reaching the Italian coast, and that as a former colonial power it would not be suitably impartial. Despite these concerns the mission was generally judged successful within the constraints of its mandate. As a precedent for future operations, however, it left much to be

---

[120] UN Security Council Resolution 1101, UN document S/RES/1101, 28 Mar. 1997, para. 2.

[121] Bloed, A., 'OSCE presence in Albania successful', *Helsinki Monitor*, vol. 8, no. 3 (1997), pp. 82–86. See also chapter 5 in this volume.

[122] 'Albania: Albania, WEU sign accord on multinational police status', ATA (Tirana), 25 June 1997, in FBIS-WEU-97-176, 26 June 1997.

desired, especially since disarmament was never achieved and once the force withdrew anarchic conditions began to return, especially in the south. This forced Italy to provide 600 troops bilaterally to help with security.[123]

As for other regional organizations in Western Europe, the *European Union*, in its Treaty of Amsterdam of 22 July, included for the first time, as part of its quest for a common foreign and security policy, a reference to 'peacekeeping tasks and tasks of combat forces in crisis management, including peacemaking'.[124] This was made possible by a policy change by the new British Labour Government.

The Organization for Security and Co-operation in Europe maintained its various missions designed to prevent, manage or resolve conflict, adding a new one in Albania and an OSCE centre in the disputed area of Brcko in Bosnia and Herzegovina.[125] The OSCE continued its division of labour with the UN, with the UN taking the lead in Abkhazia, Macedonia and Tajikistan and the OSCE in Moldova, Nagorno-Karabakh and South Ossetia. However, the OSCE was still unable to deploy its first peacekeeping mission, to Nagorno-Karabakh, because of continuing disagreement between the warring parties,[126] even though the May 1994 cease-fire continued to hold. Its greatest challenge during the year was to oversee the holding of municipal elections in Bosnia and Herzegovina. These had been postponed from 1996 when it was apparent that the OSCE was having enough difficulty organizing national elections without the extra burden of municipal ones.

The Commonwealth of Independent States continued to maintain two peace operations, in Abkhazia (Georgia) and in Tajikistan, both monitored and assisted by accompanying UN missions, the UN Observer Mission in Georgia (UNOMIG) and UNMOT, respectively.[127] Both remained controversial. The mission in Georgia, the Collective Peacekeeping Forces, faced a crisis as a result of increasing pressure from the Georgian Parliament and public opinion to withdraw. Being deployed along the border between the breakaway region of Abkhazia and Georgia proper, it was perceived as contributing to the partition of the country and failing to facilitate the return of Georgian refugees to their homes in Abkhazia. In last-minute UN-sponsored talks in Geneva, representatives of Georgia, Abkhazia, the OSCE and Friends of Georgia (the USA, UK, France, Germany and Russia) helped defuse tension.[128] Trilateral talks were also held in Moscow between Russia, Georgia and Abkhazia.[129] In the event the expiry of the force's mandate on 31 July passed without incident and the force remained deployed, its mandate extended to 31 December by the

---

[123] *The Economist*, 9 Aug. 1997, p. 24.

[124] European Union, Treaty of Amsterdam amending the Treaty on European Union, the Treaties Establishing the European Communities and certain related Acts, Amsterdam, 2 Oct. 1997, Title V, Article J.7 (2). Extracts from the Amsterdam Treaty are reproduced in appendix 5A in this volume.

[125] For details of OSCE activities see chapter 5 in this volume.

[126] For background see Nowak, J. M., 'The Organization for Security and Co-operation in Europe', ed. T. Findlay, *Challenges for the New Peacekeepers*, SIPRI Research Report no. 12 (Oxford University Press: Oxford, 1995).

[127] For further details of conflicts in the former Soviet republics, see chapter 4 in this volume.

[128] Dale, C., 'Abkhazia: the war that wasn't', *War Report*, no. 54 (Sep. 1997), p. 11.

[129] *Financial Times*, 3 Aug. 1997, p. 2.

CIS summit meeting in Kishinev.[130] The OSCE's Minsk Group continued unsuccessfully its attempts to negotiate a settlement.

Africa

The principal regional organization in Africa, the *Organization of African Unity*, continued to struggle to revamp and revitalize itself in order to meet the grave challenges facing African peace and security. The 33rd OAU summit meeting, held in Harare, Zimbabwe in June, was exceptional. For the first time in its history, it mandated a regional African force to undertake peace enforcement. In response to the military coup in Sierra Leone in late May which overturned a recently elected government, the OAU authorized the ECOWAS Monitoring Group (ECOMOG) peacekeeping force based in Liberia to remove the illegal government of Major Johnny Koroma by force. As demonstrated by its action over Sierra Leone, the OAU appeared to be overturning its traditional reluctance to countenance intervention in the internal affairs of its member states, at least in the case of military coups. Zimbabwean Prime Minister Robert Mugabe declared in closing the summit meeting that future coups in Africa would be handled in a 'hard way'.[131]

Further progress was made in plans to fully develop and institutionalize the OAU's Mechanism on Conflict Prevention, Management and Resolution, established in 1993. The New York-based International Peace Academy (IPA) assisted in this process. A fourth meeting, in New York, of the OAU/IPA Joint Task Force on Peacemaking and Peacekeeping in Africa finalized a report on measures to improve the mechanism and agreed a plan to publicize these among African governments and external supporters.[132] The mechanism remained desperately short of experienced personnel, equipment and funding. One initiative being developed was the establishment of logistical stores in Addis Ababa for the deployment of a 100-person OAU military observer force at short notice.[133] The observers themselves would be identified and placed on standby in their respective countries.

In addition to these efforts the OAU was also stretched coping with new and ongoing African crises. In September it attempted to mediate between the Government of Comoros and rebels on the breakaway island of Anjouan, but was thwarted by the government attempt to use force to end the two-month secession.[134] The rebels were not seeking independence but rather to re-enter a union with France, an idea France rejected. OAU envoy Pierre Yere had arranged a mediation conference in Addis Ababa and had warned on the eve of the attack that an invasion would be a disaster for the tiny Indian Ocean

---

[130] 'Moldova: CIS summit extends Abkhazia mandate of Russian peacekeepers', ITAR-TASS (Moscow), 23 Oct. 1997, in FBIS-SOV-97-296, 27 Oct. 1997.
[131] 'Zimbabwe: OAU summit ends with promise to get 'tougher' on coups', South African Press Agency (Johannesburg), 4 June 1997, in FBIS-AFR-97-155, 4 June 1997.
[132] *Newsletter of the International Peace Academy*, summer 1997, p. 3.
[133] International Peace Academy, IPA Seminar on Peacemaking and Peacekeeping Addis Ababa, UN Conference Center, Addis Ababa, 13–21 Dec. 1996, IPA Training Seminar Report, New York, Dec. 1996, p. 10.
[134] *International Herald Tribune*, 3 Sep. 1997, p. 2.

state.[135] Comoran troops withdrew from the island after an embarrassingly incompetent raid in which, according to the Comoran Red Crescent, at least 56 people were killed.[136] In November the rebels first rejected an OAU proposal to deploy 25 military observers to Anjouan but in December joined reconciliation talks with the government in Addis Ababa.[137]

In a joint effort with the UN and South African Deputy Foreign Minister Aziz Pahad, the OAU also attempted to negotiate a settlement of the civil war which wracked Zaire in the first half of 1997. Talks were held by the UN/OAU Special Representative Mohammed Sahnoun with the Zairean Government of President Mobutu Sese Seko and the rebel Alliance of Democratic Forces for the Liberation of Congo-Kinshasa (ADFL), led by Laurent Kabila. This included a one-day summit meeting of the Central Organ of the OAU Mechanism for Conflict Prevention, Management and Resolution in Lomé, Togo, attended by the UN Secretary-General, and talks in South Africa hosted by Deputy President Thabo Mbeki.[138] Initially both sides accepted a cease-fire and a UN/OAU five-point peace plan endorsed by the Security Council. However, Kabila's military gains were so swift and seemingly inevitable that there was no incentive for his side to negotiate in earnest. Mobutu, for his part, clung desperately to power until fleeing in May. Annan had attempted to negotiate a 'soft landing' to the fall of the capital, Kinshasa, but in the event this proved both impossible and unnecessary. With the departure of Mobutu the UN immediately came into dispute with the new Kabila Government in attempting to send a UN team to investigate massacres of Hutu and other refugees in eastern Zaire, suspected to be the work of the Kabila forces. After weeks of negotiations and two failed attempts by teams to enter the country Kabila gave in to US diplomatic pressure in late October. The Secretary-General's Investigative Team did not deploy until December.[139] There were fears that by this stage key evidence had disappeared or been tampered with.

In neighbouring Congo (Brazzaville), when conflict between former President Denis Sassou-Nguesso and his successor President Pascal Lissouba erupted in June, an International Mediation Committee (IMC) was established, led by President Omar Bongo of Gabon. Mediation was also attempted by French President Jacques Chirac, Sahnoun and Brazzaville mayor Bernard Kolelas.[140] Several cease-fires were agreed to and broken. The IMC asked the Security Council to authorize the rapid deployment to Brazzaville of an inter-African force (under either UN or national command) to at least secure the international airport.[141] Senegal offered to lead and contribute to the force, while Mali offered to provide troops and Algeria and France logistical sup-

---

[135] *Financial Times*, 4 Sep. 1997, p. 5.
[136] Daley, S., 'Comoran throwback to colonialism', *International Herald Tribune*, 30 Sep. 1992, p. 9.
[137] *International Herald Tribune*, 11 Nov. 1997, p. 6; and 9 Dec. 1997, p. 10.
[138] *UN Chronicle*, no. 1 (1997), p. 6.
[139] United Nations (note 20), p. 4.
[140] Pitman, J., 'UN peacekeepers', Voice of America correspondent report (Kinshasa), 23 June 1997.
[141] United Nations, Letter dated 20 June 1997 from the Secretary-General to the President of the Security Council, UN document S/1997/484, 20 June 1997.

port.[142] The Council declined the request—the UK and the USA were opposed. The issue was decided on the battlefield in October when the forces of Sassou-Nguesso seized Brazzaville and, with Angolan assistance, the country's only port, Pointe-Noire, thereby ending the conflict.

Ethiopia, mandated by the OAU and the subregional Intergovernmental Authority for Development (IGAD)[143] to mediate between Somalia's still warring factions, helped produce the Sodere declarations in early January establishing a National Salvation Council—but without two of the main factions, those led by Hussein Aideed and Mohamed Ibrahim Egal.[144] Italian mediation in January produced a temporary new cease-fire between the Aideed faction and that of Ali Mahdi Mohamed.[145] On 22 December, after several weeks of talks mediated by Egypt, all the Somalian factions signed the Cairo Declaration on Somalia committing them to power-sharing, the establishment of a federal system and the formation of a transitional government pending democratic elections.[146]

IGAD was also involved in negotiations between the Sudanese Government and the Sudan People's Liberation Movement (SPLM) aimed at ending the 14-year conflict. Former US President Jimmy Carter visited Sudan during the year to promote the IGAD process.[147] In April the Sudanese Government and five rebel factions signed a peace accord but it excluded the SPLM, the largest faction, based in southern Sudan.[148] In July the government accepted a Declaration of Principles on Peace drafted by the IGAD summit meeting (involving Djibouti, Eritrea, Ethiopia, Kenya, Sudan and Uganda) in Nairobi, as the basis for negotiations with the SPLM. These provided for a secular state and the right of the people in the south to vote on whether to remain part of that state. While President Lieutenant-General Omar Hassan al-Bashir of Sudan said that the principles were not binding, the SPLM said that it could not negotiate unless they were.[149] The IGAD chairman, Kenyan President Daniel Arap Moi, was mandated to pursue such negotiations in October in Nairobi. These resulted only in a commitment to restart negotiations in April 1998, with shuttle diplomacy taking place in the meantime.[150] Eritrea, Saudi Arabia and the United Arab Emirates also attempted to encourage the peace process in their own ways.[151] The willingness of the government to negotiate was undoubtedly inspired by the SPLM's impressive military gains during the year: 'the war is over', boasted rebel leader Colonel John Garang.[152]

[142] 'Senegal: Senegal agrees to head Congo intervention force', Agence France-Presse (Paris), 8 July 1997, in FBIS-AFR-97-189, 10 July 1997.
[143] Formerly the Intergovernmental Authority on Drought and Development (IGADD).
[144] *UN Chronicle*, no. 1 (1997), pp. 18–19; and *Horn of Africa Bulletin* (note 39), pp. 18–19.
[145] *International Peacekeeping News*, vol. 2, no. 6 (Jan./Feb. 1997), p. 11.
[146] UN Security Council, 'Security Council welcomes results of Somali leaders' meetings in Cairo', Press Release SC/6459, 23 Dec. 1997.
[147] *Horn of Africa Bulletin*, vol. 9, no. 2 (Mar./Apr. 1997), p. 30.
[148] *Horn of Africa Bulletin* (note 147), p. 29.
[149] *Financial Times*, 10 July 1997, p. 4.
[150] 'Kenya: Sudanese peace talks to reconvene in '98; communiqué issued', Kenya Broadcasting Corporation Network (Nairobi), 11 Nov. 1997, in FBIS-AFR-97-315, 12 Nov. 1997.
[151] *Horn of Africa Bulletin* (note 147), p. 26.
[152] Daniszewski, J., 'High hopes in south Sudan', *International Herald Tribune*, 31 Oct. 1996, p. 6.

In the Central African Republic a new regional African peacekeeping operation, MISAB, was set up in February as a result of France's decision to withdraw its own forces from the country as part of its general military drawdown in its former African colonies. The 800-strong force, comprising contingents from six neighbouring states, was commanded by a Malian but assisted by French advisers and paid for by France.[153] Its mandate was to help implement the Bangui Agreements between the CAR Government and mutinous troops from a southern tribe, negotiated with French encouragement by Burkina Faso, Chad, Gabon and Mali in January.[154] Those states, plus Senegal and Togo, provided the peacekeeping force. The UN Security Council welcomed the establishment of MISAB, approved its conduct as a neutral and impartial implementation force, and acting under Chapter VII of the Charter authorized participating states to ensure the security and freedom of movement of their personnel.[155] This was an authorization to use force only in self-defence, not for enforcement. MISAB became involved in fierce battles with army mutineers in June, reportedly after coming under attack.[156]

West Africa's regional peacekeeping force, ECOMOG, finally met with success in Liberia. Remarkably, the peace process, which had been patched up again in 1996, was sustained in 1997, producing disarmament of the factions, orderly and apparently free and fair (albeit rescheduled) elections, and a peaceful assumption of power by a democratically elected government. The elections were monitored by the OAU and other international observers. Disappointingly, the overwhelming winner of the July presidential elections was Charles Taylor, the warlord who had begun the brutal seven-year civil war. This boded ill for the future of Liberian democracy. ECOMOG had been reinforced for the election period by troops from Benin, Burkina Faso, Ghana, Mali, Niger and a medical unit from Côte d'Ivoire.[157] It was due to remain in Liberia for a further six months to organize and train a new Liberian army and police force.[158] The UN Observer Mission in Liberia (UNOMIL), the mission which had been observing ECOMOG's activities and assisting the peace process (in much more significant ways than originally envisaged), was withdrawn by 30 September. A small UN mission was to replace it to assist in post-conflict peace-building.[159]

Following the military coup in Sierra Leone on 25 May, the peace process, which had begun with the signing of the Abidjan Agreement in November 1996 and had led to elections and an apparently peaceful transfer of power, was abruptly reversed. Once Annan's proposal for a UN peacekeeping opera-

[153] *The Economist*, 18 Oct. 1997, p. 55.
[154] Rupert, J., 'Africans taking over peacekeeping role on their continent', *Washington Post*, Foreign Service, 6 Oct. 1997, page A15; and Lewis, J. A. C., 'France keeps to pull-out plan amid CAR demands', *Jane's Defence Weekly*, 15 Oct. 1997, p. 16.
[155] UN Security Council Resolution 1125, UN document S/RES/1125, 6 Aug. 1997.
[156] *International Herald Tribune*, 25 June 1997, p. 6.
[157] *Jane's Defence Weekly*, 5 Mar. 1997, p. 15.
[158] Rupert, J., 'Liberia, calmed by elections, steps back from the brink of catastrophe', *International Herald Tribune*, 29 July 1997, p. 7.
[159] United Nations, Final Report of the Secretary-General on the United Nations Observer Mission in Liberia, UN document S/1997/712, 12 Sep. 1997.

tion to oversee the peace process was rejected by the Security Council (although supported by the UK), ECOMOG was the only viable alternative. Nigerian troops already in the country (Sierra Leone being the transit point for ECOMOG deployments to Liberia) and additional Ghanaian and Nigerian troops hurriedly deployed from Liberia began to assume a peacekeeping role. In June the OAU summit meeting in Harare authorized ECOMOG to restore 'legality and constitutionality' to the country.[160] The Security Council, while expressing 'full support' for the attempts by ECOWAS to mediate, declined to authorize ECOMOG activities.[161] After military clashes between ECOMOG troops and the rebels and the shelling and bombing of the capital Freetown by the Nigerian Navy and Air Force, several cease-fires were negotiated by ECOWAS in July. Talks in Conakry, Guinea, conducted by the foreign ministers of the ECOWAS Committee of Five (Côte d'Ivoire, Ghana, Guinea, Liberia and Nigeria) eventually negotiated the reinstatement of ousted Sierra Leonian President Ahmed Tejan Kabbah, along with an amnesty for the rebels. The UN's role was limited to the establishment of a small liaison office and dispatch of a fact-finding mission to report on possible UN assistance in implementing the Conakry Agreement.

The use of ECOMOG in Sierra Leone, while in this case felicitous, portended the possible emergence of a permanent West African peacekeeping force, dominated by regional heavyweight Nigeria and available for both meritorious and potentially mischievous purposes. The Nigerian Government's enthusiasm for ending the military take-over in Sierra Leone and its persistence in bringing peace to Liberia were starkly at odds with its failure to reinstate democracy within Nigeria. Nigerian leader General Sani Abacha had himself come to power in a coup and had executed human rights activists in defiance of international opinion. Nigeria remained under EU, US and Commonwealth sanctions, including visa restrictions and an arms embargo, during the year. It was threatened with further sanctions, including possible expulsion, at the Commonwealth's Edinburgh summit meeting in October 1997, if its human rights record did not improve and its halting moves towards democratization did not accelerate.

Meanwhile, the UN Consultative Committee on Security in Central Africa appeared to spring to life during its annual meeting in Libreville, Gabon. It drew up peace plans for a conference in Equatorial Guinea on the establishment of democratic institutions and peace in Central Africa.[162]

Latin America

The Military Observer Mission Ecuador/Peru (MOMEP), comprising observers from the four guarantor parties to the 1942 Rio Protocol—Argentina,

---

[160] 'Zimbabwe: OAU gives "green light" to use force in Sierra Leone', South African Press Agency (Johannesburg), 4 June 1997, in FBIS-AFR-97-155, 4 June 1997.

[161] UN Security Council Resolution 1132, UN document S/RES/1132, 8 Oct. 1997.

[162] 'Gabon: Gabon—Central African security ministers end meeting', Africa No. 1 (Libreville), 11 July 1997, in FBIS-AFR-97-192, 14 July 1997.

Brazil, Chile and the USA—and from the two parties in conflict, continued to monitor the cease-fire, withdrawal and demilitarization agreement reached between Ecuador and Peru in February 1995 after their brief military clash earlier that year. Negotiations on a settlement, postponed because of domestic difficulties in both countries, finally began in Brasilia but progress was slow and complicated by border incidents and military manoeuvres.[163]

Elsewhere in the continent several initiatives were taken to prevent or resolve armed conflicts. After fruitless attempts by Bolivia and Chile bilaterally to negotiate a settlement of their 100-year old territorial dispute, Bolivia, which has for decades sought an outlet to the sea, asked Peru and the Organization of American States (OAS) to become involved.[164] Nicaragua negotiated a peace agreement with the 3-80 Northern Front with the assistance of the joint UN–OAS International Verification and Support Commission (Comisión Internacional de Apoyo y Verificación, CIAV), which since May 1990 had helped implement the Esquipulas and Tela agreements.[165] The Managua Agreement was signed on 30 May in Nicaragua's capital and represented a further important step in normalizing the situation there after decades of civil strife.

Asia

Asia's principal regional organization, the Association of South-East Asian Nations (ASEAN), responded helplessly to events in Cambodia. An internal state coup was staged in Phnom Penh on 5 July against First Prime Minister Prince Norodom Ranariddh, winner of the UN-supervised elections in 1994, by his power-sharing Second Prime Minister, Hun Sen. Scores of Ranariddh's supporters were killed and looting broke out in the capital, Phnom Penh. Clashes erupted between troops loyal to each side, again splitting the purportedly integrated Royal Cambodian Armed Forces. The coup was apparently intended to head off a peace agreement between the Cambodian Government and the last hold-outs of the notorious Khmer Rouge, a development which Hun Sen feared would weaken him politically and militarily. A split in the Khmer Rouge earlier in the year had led to the arrest of former leader Pol Pot and to a formal request to the UN by both Cambodian prime ministers for him to be tried by an international tribunal. It had also facilitated peace talks with Prince Ranariddh on an end to the conflict. Just before the coup the Khmer Rouge had reportedly agreed to integrate its remaining forces into the Cambodian Army and to recognize the government.[166]

---

[163] 'Ecuador: Ecuador's Ayala Lasso views prospects for peace with Peru', *Voz de los Andes* (Quito), 2 Aug. 1997, in FBIS-LAT-97-214, 5 Aug. 1997.
[164] 'Bolivia: Bolivia asks Peru, OAS for help to solve dispute with Chile', Radio Cadena Nacional Network (La Paz), 4 June 1997, in FBIS-LAT-97-155, 6 June 1997.
[165] 'Nicaragua: Aleman signs peace agreement with 3-80 Northern Front', Radio Nicaragua Network (Managua), 2 June 1997, in FBIS-LAT-97-153, 19 June 1997.
[166] Thayer, N., 'Cambodian coup upset ending of the civil war', *International Herald Tribune*, 18 Aug. 1997, p. 4.

Following the coup, ASEAN and Japan sent delegations to Phnom Penh to mediate, but Hun Sen refused to budge from his position that this was an internal matter.[167] Australia and the USA halted military assistance. The USA tried to rally a 'Friends of Cambodia' group for a joint approach but was stymied by potential members' fears of upsetting ASEAN's initiative. ASEAN postponed admitting Cambodia to membership because of the coup (although it did admit equally troubled Myanmar). As the year ended it looked increasingly unlikely that Ranariddh would ever be reinstated. International opinion remained divided on whether the Hun Sen Government should be assisted in running scheduled elections in 1998 or whether, since their outcome was likely to be a foregone conclusion, they should be boycotted.[168]

VI. Other players

As usual a multitude of other players besides regional organizations were active in 1997 in conflict prevention, management and resolution.

Individual states were most active. South Africa appeared to be emerging as a ubiquitous peacemaker, with attempts to mediate in the Zaire and East Timor conflicts, and reportedly (although this was denied) in the dispute between Libya and the UN over the trial of suspects in the Lockerbie aircraft bombing in December 1988. One of the more unusual unilateral attempts of the year at peacemaking was its hosting in June of a four-day workshop in Cape Town of political leaders from Northern Ireland.[169] The new British Labour Government's Foreign Secretary, Robin Cook, was also active as a potential conflict resolver. However, he ruffled Indian sensibilities by appearing to offer British mediation in the Kashmir dispute. The British Conservative Government had offered earlier in the year to mediate in the Sri Lankan civil war, which continued unabated during 1997.[170] Iran meanwhile mediated in the conflict between Sudan and Uganda at talks in north-western Uganda.[171] Pakistan launched an initiative in July to promote new intra-Afghan talks.[172] Tanzania, in cooperation with the OAU, continued its efforts to encourage the peace process in Burundi.[173]

Algeria firmly rejected offers by France, Italy and the UN to help mediate an end to the country's brutal civil war, characterized by mass killings of civilians by often unidentified groups. These atrocities escalated in number, frequency and perversity in 1997 as the international community watched, apparently helplessly, despite calls for international action by the new UN

[167] Richardson, M., 'ASEAN opts for continued mediation in Cambodia', *International Herald Tribune*, 12 Aug. 1997, p. 6.
[168] In early 1998 the EU did agree to provide substantial funding for the elections.
[169] 'South Africa: N. Ireland conference an "overwhelming success"', South African Press Agency (Johannesburg), 2 June 1997, in FBIS-AFR-97-108, 20 June 1997.
[170] Jayasinghe, A., 'Britain sets up deal to end Tamil conflict', *Financial Times*, 4 Apr. 1997, p. 4.
[171] *Horn of Africa Bulletin* (note 147), p. 26.
[172] 'Afghanistan: Fresh initiative launched to promote intra-Afghan talks', Radio Pakistan Network (Islamabad), 1 July 1997, in FBIS-NES-97-182, 2 July 1997.
[173] 'Burundi: Burundi—Tanzanian team arrives for talks on peace process', Radio-Télévision Nationale du Burundi (Bujumbura), 6 July 1997, in FBIS-AFR-97-187, 8 July 1997.

Human Rights Commissioner, former Irish President Mary Robinson, Amnesty International and other human rights groups.[174]

As usual the USA was seemingly omnipresent in important peacemaking efforts. While failing dismally in the Middle East, its perseverance paid off in regard to Korea. Under US leadership and with Chinese assistance, unprecedented talks were held in New York in August and September between North and South Korea, China and the USA. Although reeling under famine and catastrophic economic decline, North Korea proved to be a stubborn negotiator. Agreement was eventually reached that full-fledged quadripartite talks would begin in Geneva in December on a Korean peace agreement.[175] Agreement was not reached on an agenda, since the North demanded that the deployment of US troops in the South be discussed and that a separate North Korea–US peace treaty be negotiated. Key developments in producing the agreement were: North Korea's dropping of its long-standing position that South Korea should not be involved in any Korean peace treaty; its agreement to abide by the 1953 Armistice Agreement until a replacement could be negotiated; and its apology for a submarine incursion into South Korean waters in 1996. The Neutral Nations Supervisory Commission (NNSC) for Korea continued its thankless task of attempting to monitor the so-called truce between the two Koreas.

Former US Senator George Mitchell chaired the historic Northern Ireland peace talks which began in Belfast in September. This was the first time in decades that all the parties to the Northern Ireland conflict had convened for talks. The breakthrough came after the Irish Republican Army (IRA) agreed to renew its cease-fire and Sinn Fein, its political wing, signed the Mitchell Principles, among which was the renunciation of violence.[176] Although initially boycotted by some of the unionist parties, all the significant ones were eventually involved in the talks. By the end of the year there were few signs of any imminent agreement, although British Prime Minister Tony Blair did meet with all the parties, including Sinn Fein, bilaterally and Northern Ireland Affairs Minister Mo Mowlam was also active in seeking to keep the momentum of peace going. The Independent International Commission on Decommissioning was established in the meantime, with representatives of Canada, Finland and the USA, to prepare for verifying the decommissioning of paramilitary weaponry in the province and in the Republic of Ireland.

Surprisingly, a number of new players attempted to become involved in the East Timor issue.[177] South African President Nelson Mandela offered to mediate directly between Indonesia, Portugal and East Timorese factions and during a visit to Jakarta convinced President Suharto to let him meet jailed

---

[174] Khalaf, R., 'Panic and confusion over Algiers killings', 24 Sep. 1997, p. 8; and *The Economist*, 11 Oct. 1997, pp. 52–53.

[175] *Newsreview*, vol. 26, no. 32 (9 Aug. 1997), pp. 6–7.

[176] Balz, D., 'Sinn Fein vows to end violence for Ulster aims', *International Herald Tribune*, 10 Sep. 1997, p. 1.

[177] For background, see Salla, M. E., 'Creating the "ripe moment" in the East Timor conflict', *Journal of Peace Research*, vol. 34, no. 4 (1997), pp. 44–66.

CONFLICT PREVENTION, MANAGEMENT AND RESOLUTION 67

Fretilin leader Xanana Gusmao.[178] British Foreign Secretary Robin Cook proposed an EU fact-finding mission to East Timor, a suggestion supported by Indonesia.[179] A group of prominent figures, including the former presidents of Chile, Costa Rica, Germany and South Africa and former Australian Foreign Minister Gareth Evans, wrote to President Suharto suggesting that East Timor be given special autonomous status.[180] Indonesian Foreign Minister Ali Alatas appeared not to rule out such an idea as long as it formed part of an overall settlement and the status of East Timor did not differ from that proposed for Aceh and Jogjakarta, two other areas which have resisted rule from Jakarta.

New Zealand managed to succeed where it had previously failed in helping mediate a cease-fire for Bougainville, the secessionist island of Papua New Guinea.[181] The Burnham Declaration, negotiated at a New Zealand army base, Burnham Camp, south of Christchurch, called for a cease-fire, demilitarization of the island, an end to the military blockade by Papua New Guinea and the deployment of a UN peacekeeping force. In late November an unarmed regional peacekeeping force, comprising 230 troops and civilians from Australia, Fiji, New Zealand, Tonga and Vanuatu, was deployed to Bougainville.[182] A meeting was held in Cairns, Australia, to plan negotiations on a permanent settlement to be held in January 1998.

In addition to its predominance in CIS missions, Russia continued its peacekeeping/peacemaking efforts in two former Soviet republics: concerning Georgia's South Ossetia region and the Trans-Dniester region of eastern Moldova.[183] Russia maintained approximately 11 000 troops deployed in peacekeeping operations in the former Soviet republics at a cost in 1996 of 600 billion roubles.[184] Russia also continued to attempt to broker settlements in armed conflicts around the its periphery, finally succeeding in Tajikistan but facing continuing difficulties in relation to Abkhazia, Moldova, Nagorno-Karabakh and South Ossetia. France, Russia and the USA attempted to resolve the impasse in talks over the Nagorno-Karabakh conflict by proposing that Armenia recognize the territorial integrity of Azerbaijan, while the latter should grant Nagorno-Karabakh an exceptionally high degree of autonomy.[185]

The Temporary International Presence in Hebron (TIPH), first deployed in 1994, was expanded beyond its existing Norwegian contingent to include participation from Denmark, Italy, Sweden, Switzerland and Turkey, after Israel

[178] Richardson, M., 'Notables seek solution to East Timor rebellion', *International Herald Tribune*, 11 Sep. 1997, p. 1; and McBeth, J., 'Good offices', *Far Eastern Economic Review*, 14 Aug. 1997, p. 21.
[179] Cummings-Bruce, N., 'Jakarta supports Cook's Timor plan', *The Guardian*, 30 Aug. 1997, p. 6.
[180] Richardson (note 178), p. 1.
[181] Field, M., 'Peace—a real prospect at last', *Pacific Islands Monthly*, Sep. 1997, pp. 26–28; and Oct. 1997, pp. 31–32.
[182] *South China Morning Post*, 18 Nov. 1997.
[183] Russian political parlance does not differentiate between peacekeeping, peace making and peace enforcement. The term used in Russia—*mirotvorchestvo*—means, if directly translated, 'peace creation'; this could cover a very broad range of activities, from political mediation to combat operations aimed at 'imposing peace'.
[184] Korestsky, A. and Vignansky, M., 'Russian peace-keeping operations are expensive', *Daily Review*, 7 Apr. 1997, URL <http://www.ria-novosti.com/dr/dg07043.htm>, version current on 10 Apr. 1997.
[185] *International Herald Tribune*, 25–26 Oct. 1997, p. 2. See also chapter 4 in this volume.

and the Palestinian Authority signed an agreement allowing for 180 observers to patrol the West Bank town of Hebron after Israel's withdrawal.[186] In the Balkans an unprecedented two-day summit meeting was held on Crete, involving Albania, Bosnia and Herzegovina, Bulgaria, Greece, Macedonia, Romania, Turkey and Yugoslavia (Serbia and Montenegro), which agreed to create a framework for economic growth and political cooperation. Notably absent were Croatia and Slovenia, two former Yugoslav republics. A bilateral meeting between the Greek and Turkish prime ministers held in conjunction with the summit meeting reportedly made 'scant progress' but they did agree to pursue confidence-building measures.[187]

Some states simply conducted their own peacemaking, in regard to both interstate and intra-state conflicts. After seven years of bilateral negotiations, in November China and Russia signed a landmark agreement ending a decades-old border dispute. The treaty established an agreed 4000-km eastern border from Mongolia to where the Tumen River meets the Sea of Japan and included territory fought over as recently as 1969.[188] The western border question remained to be resolved. The 10th round of the Sino-Indian Joint Working Group talks on the unresolved border dispute between China and India opened in New Delhi in August.[189] During the year China and Viet Nam also began talks on their border and maritime disputes.[190] India and Pakistan initiated a new attempt at resolving the Kashmir issue, despite continuing border clashes, meeting three times during the year at foreign secretary level.[191] India and Bangladesh negotiated an agreement to end their dispute over sharing of the Teesta River waters.[192] In November Japan and Russia agreed to work towards concluding a peace treaty formally ending their World War II belligerency by 2000.[193]

Mali, Mauritania and Senegal held a trilateral meeting of military chiefs regarding security problems in their border area along the Senegal River and contemplated integrating their armed forces.[194] Kenya and Uganda agreed to establish a Peace Monitoring Committee to meet four times a year to maintain peace on their common border, while Kenya also held talks with Ethiopia on how to avoid border incidents like the one that resulted in the deaths of Kenyan soldiers earlier in the year.[195] Meanwhile, Honduras and Nicaragua appeared ready to resume negotiations in their bilateral technical commission

---

[186] *International Peacekeeping News*, vol. 2, no. 6 (Jan./Feb. 1997), p. 21.
[187] *International Herald Tribune*, 5 Oct. 1997, p. 6; and *Jane's Defence Weekly*, 12 Nov. 1997, p. 5.
[188] *International Herald Tribune*, 11 Nov. 1997, p. 4.
[189] *International Security Digest*, vol. 4, no. 7 (Sep. 1997), p. 3.
[190] *International Security Digest* (note 189), p. 2.
[191] *Jane's Defence Weekly*, 9 Oct. 1997, p. 8; and *International Herald Tribune*, 23 June 1997, p. 5.
[192] *International Herald Tribune*, 21 July 1997, p. 4.
[193] *Jane's Defence Weekly*, 4 Feb. 1998, p. 16.
[194] 'Mali: Malian, Senegalese, Mauritanian army heads discuss security', Radiodiffusion-Télévision du Mali Radio (Bamako), 15 July 1997, in FBIS-AFR-97-196, 15 July 1997.
[195] 'Uganda: Uganda, Kenya agree to set up peace monitoring committee', Radio Uganda Network (Kampala), 5 Oct. 1997, in FBIS-AFR-97-278, 7 Oct. 1997; and 'Ethiopia: Ethiopian, Kenyan officials discuss conflict resolution', Radio Ethiopia Network (Addis Ababa), 4 July 1997, in FBIS-AFR-97-185, 8 July 1997.

to demarcate their maritime boundary after naval clashes in May.[196] Japan was to fund the demarcation exercise.

The Philippine Government in July signed a cease-fire agreement with the Moro Islamic Liberation Front, one of the groups that had not joined the peace agreement signed with other Moro rebels in 1996.[197] It continued to negotiate episodically and in vain with the Communist Party of the Philippines–National Democratic Front–New People's Army to end the ageing communist insurgency in Luzon.[198] The Sri Lankan Government pressed ahead with a power-sharing 'peace package' to end the island's 14-year war, despite a devastating bombing in the capital, Colombo, believed to be the work of the Tamil Tigers.[199] The plan would give autonomy to the Tamil and Muslim minorities. The Government of Bangladesh in December signed a historic agreement with the Shanti Bahini rebels, ending a 22-year separatist war.[200] The Ethiopian Government negotiated in January with the Afar Revolutionary Democratic Unity Front.[201] In Cambodia talks took place between the Khmer Rouge and the government after the latter had purged Prince Ranariddh and his close supporters from its ranks.

VII. Conclusions: conflict prevention, management and resolution in the 1990s

Several clear trends have emerged so far in the 1990s in conflict prevention, management and resolution as the international community has attempted to come to grips with the post-cold war era. Far from heralding the end of history or a new world order, the 1990s have witnessed a series of vicious internal armed conflicts, gross violations of human rights such as have not been seen since World War II, complex humanitarian emergencies and instances of collapsing states. Sometimes these have occurred simultaneously, as in the case of the former Yugoslavia and the Great Lakes Region of Africa. No international institutions were well prepared. All were reluctant to intervene openly in the internal affairs of sovereign states unless asked to do so. The United Nations, traditionally oriented towards interstate conflict, still ran peacekeeping, its truly unique contribution to conflict prevention, management and resolution, amateurishly and on a shoestring. In Europe the OSCE had barely established its Conflict Prevention Centre when war erupted in Bosnia and Herzegovina and Croatia. Other regions, such as Africa, possessed practically no mechanisms at all. By the end of 1997, the picture, while hardly revolutionized, was encouragingly different.

---

[196] 'Honduras: Honduras complains to Nicaragua for attacks to navy', *La Tribuna* (Tegucigalpa), 3 June 1997, in FBIS-LAT-97-154, 19 June 1997.
[197] *International Herald Tribune*, 19–20 July 1997, p. 6. For details of the 1996 agreement see Findlay (note 38), p. 64.
[198] 'Philippines: Communist negotiator: peace accord prospects "very bleak"', *Business News* (Manila), 1 Sep. 1997, in FBIS-EAS-97-244, 17 Sep. 1997.
[199] *International Herald Tribune*, 3 Oct. 1997, p. 4.
[200] *International Herald Tribune*, 3 Dec. 1997, p. 6; and *Jane's Defence Weekly*, 28 May 1997, p. 15.
[201] *Horn of Africa Bulletin* (note 39), pp. 11–12.

Sovereignty challenged

An enormously significant development has been the increased willingness of the United Nations and regional organizations, in preventing, managing or ending conflict, to challenge the claim by states that they are immune from interference in their internal affairs. The Security Council has demonstrated its preparedness to use the enforcement provisions of Chapter VII of the UN Charter to forcibly provide humanitarian assistance, attempt to guard populations at risk in civil wars, protect peacekeepers and capture renegade factional leaders. It has deployed peace operations without obtaining consent from the country or parties concerned and authorized member states to use force to punish a recalcitrant party in an internal conflict. It has authorized a group of states to roll back an invasion and then imposed the most intrusive verification regime in history on the defeated state to prevent the threat of weapons of mass destruction from that quarter.

Less visible, but with similar implications for state sovereignty, has been the UN's willingness to investigate human rights violations and deploy human rights missions in the field. Naturally, given the disparities of power in the international system, these initiatives have not affected all states evenly. Nonetheless even great powers like China have felt pressure to improve their human rights record and to support intrusive peace operations such as that in Cambodia even while protesting the sanctity of state sovereignty. Regional organizations such as the OAU and the OAS, long committed to protecting their members' sovereignty to the point of totally ignoring internal developments, have also embarked on increasingly intrusive measures to promote democratization, good governance and human rights.

It remains the case that, as long as international society comprises sovereign states which guard their independence and decline to recognize supranational authority, international institutions will perforce rely on voluntarism, compliance with norms and laws will be patchy, and sanctions will necessarily be episodic and inconsistently applied.

Globalization and regionalization

Another astounding development is the extraordinary range and reach of the players which now engage in conflict prevention, management and resolution efforts. Almost all nations of any prominence seem to be involved, even if they themselves have unresolved internal armed conflicts or conflicts with their neighbours which require the mediatory efforts of others. Non-governmental organizations, regional organizations and individuals are increasingly participating. Location seems not to matter, with actors reaching around the globe to become involved. This globalization mirrors and benefits from other globalizing trends, such as those in telecommunications and finance. NGOs in the field now communicate with their headquarters by portable satellite dish, the Internet enables information on conflicts to be disseminated in an instant and air travel enables international negotiations to be conducted almost anywhere on the planet. While there are risks that too many players might spoil the chances of successful conflict resolution, there are also synergies to be harvested, such as the growing cooperation between the United Nations, NGOs and regional organizations in Africa.

Regionalization is itself a new trend in conflict prevention, management and resolution. With the realization that the UN is unable to intervene in every conflict, regional organizations have been slowly but surely improving their own capabilities, focusing on their areas of greatest perceived need. Europe now has the entire range of conflict prevention, management and resolution capacities built into its multiple institutions, including the OSCE, the EU, NATO and the CIS. Africa has concentrated on establishing a conflict prevention capacity within the OAU and lately on improving African peacekeeping capabilities. More generally its focus has been on the growth of civil society, democratization and general nation-building and development. African sub-regional bodies are showing considerable inventiveness and agility in these areas. Latin America has devoted most of its energy to democratization, given its past difficulties in maintaining civilian governments. Asia now has ASEAN and the ASEAN Regional Forum (ARF), both of which are moving slowly to tackle more difficult conflict issues.[202]

Conflict prevention

If there is one lesson that has been thoroughly absorbed by the international community during the 1990s, it is that an ounce of prevention is worth a pound of cure. Driven home by the enormous cost of peacekeeping and peace-building efforts, the conclusion has been reached that early conflict prevention can save lives and resources out of all proportion to its cost. Yet, despite the rhetoric devoted to it, neither the UN nor regional organizations have developed the means for effective conflict prevention. The UN still lacks a capable early-warning mechanism, a conflict prevention centre or conflict prevention units in regions at risk. One encouraging development, however, has been the establishment of international tribunals to try individuals suspected of war crimes, crimes against humanity or other gross violations of human rights. Such bodies not only help to achieve justice; they also serve as a warning to future would-be violators of international law. The establishment of a permanent International Criminal Court would make the link between justice and deterrence even stronger.

Peacekeeping

Peacekeeping since the end of the cold war has been on a roller-coaster ride of increased fame and fortune, followed by disaster, retreat, lowered expectations and cynicism. The explosion in the number, size and complexity of UN peacekeeping operations coincided with their deployment in situations which would

---

[202] For lists of the members of ASEAN and ARF see the glossary in this volume.

not previously have been considered appropriate. Thrust into humanitarian disasters and political anarchy (Somalia), vicious ongoing ethnic warfare (the former Yugoslavia) and genocide (Rwanda), UN peacekeepers were given responsibilities well beyond their capabilities and resources. They were authorized to use force in ways which impaired their ability to be impartial, and asked to perform peacekeeping and peace enforcement at the same time, or to work closely with national military commands or military alliances with their own agendas to pursue. The considerable successes of UN peacekeeping, including operations in Cambodia, El Salvador and Mozambique, were overshadowed by the disasters.

Then, as is often the case in human affairs, the pendulum swung too far the other way. Peacekeeping was seen by the UN and its critics alike as suitable only for situations in which consensus was absolutely guaranteed, peacekeepers would be in no danger whatsoever and missions would be short and cheap. Any mission that failed to meet these criteria would be 'contracted out' to a coalition of the willing and able, authorized by the Security Council but led by a member state and subject to the whims of national policy. Traditional peacekeeping was seen to be UN business and enhanced peacekeeping or peace enforcement the business of others. Hence the Security Council has lately rejected all proposals for UN peace operations in African conflicts and severely constrained some of those already operating there.

Meanwhile the UN, individual states and regional organizations have been quietly building their capacities for peacekeeping, establishing doctrine, training troops, purchasing peacekeeping equipment, conducting joint exercises and establishing peacekeeping schools. The concept of 'peace operations', including peacekeeping, humanitarian missions and peace enforcement, has been absorbed into Western military doctrine (although it has yet to spread beyond). To the extent that they are among the clearest roles required of the military in the present era of down-sizing and budget cuts, peace operations are taken increasingly seriously. The UN itself has reformed its peacekeeping department and gained a situation room, standby arrangements and soon a rapidly deployable headquarters. Its procedures are better, its concepts of operations clearer and its personnel more capable and alert to the pitfalls than ever before. Ironically, all of this has occurred as the great wave of post-cold war UN peacekeeping has ended in contraction and apparently endemic timidity.

One encouraging development is the growth in regional peacekeeping initiatives. While these rarely match the size and complexity of UN second-generation operations (IFOR and SFOR in Bosnia and Herzegovina being the main exceptions), there are more such operations, located in more regions, than ever before. This has to some extent made up for the decline in UN peacekeeping activity.

In principle, however, there is no reason why the United Nations should not be entrusted with the harder tasks of peacekeeping or even peace enforcement in the right circumstances (although not enforcement operations like that against Iraq in the 1991 Persian Gulf War). Given the proper mandate and rules of engagement and the personnel and resources to match, especially proper command and control, there would seem to be no practical impediments either. The UN could as readily have handled the recent missions in Albania, Sierra Leone and the Central African Republic as it has the equally challenging missions in Eastern Slavonia and Haiti. It urgently needs a difficult new mission to prove itself and help swing the pendulum back.

Conflict resolution

Despite the growth in activity in conflict resolution, much of it remains surprisingly amateurish. The vast majority of those involved are untrained as negotiators or conflict resolvers. Instead they are diplomats used to representing their own countries, international civil servants experienced in running bureaucracies or, increasingly, self-appointed employees of NGOs. Despite the wealth of theory, knowledge and experience among conflict-resolution professionals at the local and national levels, this is rarely used in international negotiations. The UN itself does not have a dedicated corps of trained conflict-resolution specialists at headquarters, much less in the field where they would be of most use. Such amateurism must be addressed and increased resources devoted to ending this lacuna in UN capabilities.

Peace-building

Peace-building has come increasingly into vogue as a means of preventing recidivism in conflict-torn countries which have achieved a peace settlement. This involves the restoration and maintenance of civil society, law and order, human rights promotion and protection, arrangements for refugees and displaced persons, the holding of elections, re-establishment of local administration and government utilities, de-mining, and reconstruction and development. Some of these peace-building activities are also useful in preventing conflict from occurring in the first place. One particularly notable peace-building trend is democratization. Even the UN is active in promoting and assisting in the establishment of democratic electoral processes, something that would have been unthinkable during the ideological stand-off of the cold war. It is also a welcome development that the World Bank, the International Monetary Fund and the Organisation for Economic Co-operation and Development have recognized that their decisions can have a significant impact on conflict prevention and peace-building. Seen in this context peace-building is a never-ending project but one which ultimately saves lives and resources.

The fate of the UN

The future of the United Nations is critical to global conflict prevention, management and resolution efforts. While the institution itself is under new stewardship and seized of the need for change, the prospects for meaningful reform still remain clouded by the persistence of national interests: from the

USA's enthusiasm for reform but unwillingness to pay, through some key developing states' unavailing suspicion of all reform proposals, to the indifference of the vast majority of member states. Reform and expansion of the increasingly vital Security Council would be encouraging but insufficient. Without meaningful, wholesale reform of its entire system the United Nations will continue to suffer a loss of moral stature and capability which will not augur well for peace and security in the 21st century.

Assessment

Conflict prevention, management and resolution have advanced considerably in the 1990s. There is heightened awareness of at least the need for early conflict prevention. This has been accompanied by a new appreciation of the value of a holistic and integrated approach to prevention, management and resolution through the life-cycle of a conflict, to ensure that enduring solutions are found and maintained. There is a new-found realization that peace-building can be effective before, during and after armed conflicts. Peacekeeping, after much trial and error, has become more capable and efficient, regional organizations have become at least more aware of their own responsibilities and needs, and the UN has embarked on reform with a conviction that has been absent previously. While the age-old scourge of armed conflict is not likely to be removed any time soon, the international tools for preventing, managing and resolving it are better than they have ever been and are evolving in the right direction.

Appendix 2A. Multilateral peace missions, 1997

SUSANNA ECKSTEIN

Table 2A lists multilateral observer, peacekeeping, peacebuilding and combined peacekeeping and peace-enforcement missions initiated, continuing or terminated in 1997, by international organization and by starting date. Five groups of mission are presented. The 25 run by the United Nations are divided into two sections: UN peacekeeping operations (20) are those so designated by the UN itself (see figure 2.2 in chapter 2), although they may include some missions more properly described as observer missions; the other 5 UN operations comprise missions not officially described by the UN as peacekeeping operations (2 of these are operated in cooperation with the Organization of American States, OAS). Of the remaining missions, 12 are run by the Organization for Security and Co-operation in Europe (OSCE), 4 by the Commonwealth of Independent States (CIS)/Russia and 13 by other organizations or ad hoc groups of states. Peace missions comprising individual negotiators or teams of negotiators not resident in the mission area are not included.

Legal instruments underlying the establishment of an operation, such as relevant resolutions of the UN Security Council, are cited in the first column.

The names of missions that ended in 1997 and of individual countries that ended their participation in 1997 are italicized, while new missions and individual countries participating for the first time in 1997 are listed in bold text. Numbers of civilian observers and international and local civilian staff are not included.

Mission fatalities are recorded from the beginning of the conflict until the last reported date for 1997 ('to date'), and as a total for the year ('in 1997'). Information on the approximate or estimated annual cost of the missions ('yearly') and the approximate outstanding contributions ('unpaid') to the operation fund at the close of the 1997 budget period (the date of which varies from operation to operation) is given in millions of current dollars. In the case of UN missions, unless otherwise noted, UN data on contributing countries and on numbers of troops, military observers and civilian police as well as on fatalities and costs are as of 31 December 1997. UN data on total mission fatalities ('to date') are for all UN missions since 1948.

Figures on the number of personnel in/for OSCE missions are totals for each mission, and include both military and civilian staff in 1997.

Table 2A. Multilateral peace missions

Acronym/ (Legal instrument[a])	Name/type of mission (O: observer) (PK: peacekeeping)	Location	Start date	Countries contributing troops, military observers (mil. obs) and/or civilian police (CivPol) in 1997	Troops/ Mil. obs/ CivPol	Deaths: To date In 1997	Cost: Yearly Unpaid
United Nations (UN) peacekeeping operations[1] (20 operations) (UN Charter, Chapters VI and VII)					10 672[2] 1 075 3 132	1 546[3] 37	1 200[4] 1 574[5]
UNTSO (SCR 50)	UN Truce Supervision Organization (O)	Egypt/Israel/ Lebanon/Syria	June 1948	Argentina, Australia, Austria, Belgium, Canada, Chile, China, Denmark, **Estonia**, Finland, France, Ireland, Italy, Netherlands, New Zealand, Norway, Russia, Sweden, Switzerland, USA	– 153 –	38 –	24 –
UNMOGIP (SCR 91)	UN Military Observer Group in India and Pakistan (O)	India/Pakistan (Kashmir)	Jan. 1949	Belgium, Chile, Denmark, Finland, Italy, South Korea, Sweden, Uruguay	– 44 –	9 –	6 –
UNFICYP (SCR 186)	UN Peacekeeping Force in Cyprus (PK)	Cyprus	Mar. 1964	Argentina, Australia, Austria, Canada, Finland, Hungary, Ireland, **Slovakia, Slovenia**, UK	1 217 – 35	168 –	48[6] 15
UNDOF (SCR 350)	UN Disengagement Observer Force (O)	Syria (Golan Heights)	June 1974	Austria, Canada, Japan, Poland	1 049 –[7] –	39 3	34[8] 13[9]
UNIFIL (SCR 425, 426)	UN Interim Force in Lebanon (PK)	Lebanon (Southern)	Mar. 1978	**Estonia**, Fiji, Finland, France, Ghana, Ireland, Italy, Nepal, Norway, Poland	4 468 –[10] –	223 10	125 111
UNIKOM (SCR 689)	UN Iraq–Kuwait Observation Mission (O)	Iraq/Kuwait (Khawr 'Abd Allah waterway and UN DMZ)[11]	Apr. 1991	Argentina, Austria, Bangladesh, Canada, China, Denmark, Fiji, Finland, France, Germany, Ghana, Greece, Hungary, India, Indonesia, Ireland, Italy, Kenya, Malaysia, Nigeria, Pakistan, Poland, Romania, Russia, Senegal, Singapore, Sweden, Thailand, Turkey, UK, USA, Uruguay, Venezuela	890[12] 192 –	10 2	52[13] 11
MINURSO (SCR 690)	UN Mission for the Referendum in Western Sahara (O)	Western Sahara	Sep. 1991	Argentina, Austria, Bangladesh, Canada, China, Egypt, El Salvador, France, Ghana, Greece, Guinea, Honduras, *Hungary*, **India**, Ireland, Italy, Kenya, South Korea, Malaysia, Nigeria, *Norway*, Pakistan, Poland, Portugal, Russia, **Sweden**, *Togo, Tunisia*, USA, Uruguay, ***Venezuela***	21[14] 200 78	7 –	30[15] 49

CONFLICT PREVENTION, MANAGEMENT AND RESOLUTION

Acronym (SCR)	Name	Location	Start	Countries contributing						
UNOMIG (SCR 849, 858)	UN Observer Mission in Georgia (O)	Georgia (Abkhazia)	Aug. 1993	Albania, Austria, Bangladesh, *Cuba*, Czech Rep., Denmark, Egypt, France, Germany, Greece, Hungary, Indonesia, Jordan, South Korea, Pakistan, Poland, Russia, Sweden, Switzerland, Turkey, UK, USA, Uruguay	–	106[16]	–	3	–	19[17]	6
UNOMIL (SCR 866)[18]	UN Observer Mission in Liberia (O)	Liberia	Sep. 1993	Bangladesh, China, Czech Rep., Egypt, India, Kenya, Malaysia, Nepal, Pakistan, Uruguay	–	9	–	–	–	20[19]	8
UNMOT (SCR 968)[20]	UN Mission of Observers in Tajikistan (O)	Tajikistan	Dec. 1994	Austria, Bangladesh, Bulgaria, Denmark, **Ghana**, **Indonesia**, Jordan, **Nigeria**, Poland, Switzerland, Ukraine, Uruguay	–	57[21]	–	1	–	8[22]	3
UNAVEM III (SCR 976)	UN Angola Verification Mission III (O)	Angola	Feb. 1995[23]	Algeria, Bangladesh, Brazil, Bulgaria, Congo, Egypt, France, Guinea-Bissau, Hungary, India, Jordan, Kenya, South Korea, Malaysia, Mali, Namibia, Netherlands, New Zealand, Nigeria, Norway, Pakistan, Poland, Portugal, Romania, Russia, Senegal, Slovakia, Sweden, Tanzania, Ukraine, Uruguay, Zambia, Zimbabwe	3 649[24]	283	288	33	6	–[25]	59
UNPREDEP (SCR 983)	UN Preventive Deployment Force[26] (PK)	Macedonia	Mar. 1995	Argentina, Bangladesh, Belgium, Brazil, Canada, Czech Rep., Denmark, Egypt, Finland, Ghana, Indonesia, Ireland, Jordan, Kenya, Nepal, New Zealand, Nigeria, Norway, Pakistan, Poland, Portugal, Russia, Sweden, Switzerland, Turkey, Ukraine, USA	748[27]	34	25	4	4	46[28]	7
UNMIBH (SCR 1035)[29]	UN Mission in Bosnia and Herzegovina (O)	Bosnia and Herzegovina	Dec. 1995	Argentina, Austria, Bangladesh, Bulgaria, Canada, **Chile**, Denmark, Egypt, Estonia, Finland, France, Germany, Ghana, Greece, Hungary, **Iceland**, India, Indonesia, Ireland, **Italy**, Jordan, Malaysia, Nepal, Netherlands, Nigeria, Norway, Pakistan, Poland, Portugal, Russia, Senegal, Spain, Sweden, Switzerland, **Thailand**, Tunisia, Turkey, **UK**, Ukraine, USA	3	–	1 976[30]	4	1	190	34
UNTAES (SCR 1037)[31]	UN Transitional Administration for Eastern Slavonia, Baranja and Western Sirmium (PK)	Croatia	Jan. 1996	Argentina, Austria, Bangladesh, Belgium, Brazil, Czech Rep., Denmark, Egypt, Fiji, Finland, Ghana, *Greece*, Indonesia, Ireland, Jordan, Kenya, Lithuania, Nepal, *Netherlands*, New Zealand, Nigeria, Norway, Pakistan, Poland, *Portugal*, Russia, Slovakia, Sweden, Switzerland, Tunisia, *UK*, Ukraine, USA	716[32]	97	378[33]	10	6	275	57

78 SECURITY AND CONFLICTS, 1997

Acronym/ (Legal instrument[a])	Name/type of mission (O: observer) (PK: peacekeeping)	Location	Start date	Countries contributing troops, military observers (mil. obs) and/or civilian police (CivPol) in 1997	Troops/ Mil. obs/ CivPol	Deaths: To date In 1997	Cost: Yearly Unpaid
UNMOP (SCR 1038)	UN Mission of Observers in Prevlaka (O)	Croatia	Jan. 1996	Argentina, Bangladesh, Belgium, Brazil, Canada, Czech Rep., Denmark, Egypt, Finland, Ghana, Indonesia, Ireland, Jordan, Kenya, Nepal, New Zealand, Nigeria, Norway, Pakistan, Poland, Portugal, Russia, Sweden, Switzerland, Ukraine	– 28 –	– –	–[34] –
UNSMIH (SCR 1063)[35]	UN Support Mission in Haiti (PK)	Haiti	July 1996	Algeria, Bangladesh, *Benin*, Canada, France, India, Mali, Pakistan, Togo, USA	1 287[36] – 222	– –	14[37] 10
MINUGUA (SCR 1094)[38]	UN Verification Mission in Guatemala (PK)	Guatemala	Mar. 1997	*Argentina, Australia, Brazil, Canada, Ecuador, Norway, Russia, Spain, Sweden, Ukraine, Uruguay, USA, Venezuela*	– 132[39] –	– –	5[40] 0.3
MONUA (SCR 1118)[41]	UN Observer Mission in Angola[42] (O)	Angola	July 1997	Bangladesh, Brazil, Bulgaria, Congo, Egypt, France, Guinea-Bissau, Hungary, India, Jordan, Kenya, Malaysia, Mali, Namibia, *Netherlands*, New Zealand, Nigeria, Norway, Pakistan, Poland, Portugal, Romania, Russia, Senegal, Slovakia, Sweden, Tanzania, Ukraine, Uruguay, Zambia, Zimbabwe	1 558[43] 164 361	5 5	155[44] 68[45]
UNTMIH (SCR 1123)[46]	UN Transition Mission in Haiti (PK)	Haiti	Aug. 1997	*Argentina, Benin, Canada, France, India, Mali, Nigeria, Niger, Pakistan, Senegal, Togo, Tunisia, Uruguay*	1 193[47] – 156	– –	10 –[48]
MIPONUH (SCR 1141)[49]	UN Civilian Police Mission in Haiti[50]	Haiti	Nov. 1997	Argentina, Benin, Canada, France, India, Mali, Niger, Senegal, Togo, Tunisia, USA	– – 279[51]	– –	14[52] –[53]

Other United Nations (UN) operations (5 operations)[54]

CIAV/OAS[55]	*International Commission for Support and Verification*	Nicaragua	May 1990	–[56]	– – –	2 –	1.4[57] ..
MICIVIH (GAR 47/20B)[58]	*International Civilian Mission to Haiti* (O)	Haiti	Feb. 1993	–[59]	– 60 –	– –	8.6[61] ..

Acronym/Resolution	Mission	Location	Start	Contributors				
UNSMA (GAR 48/208)	UN Special Mission to Afghanistan	Afghanistan/ Pakistan[62]	Mar. 1994	Bangladesh, Ghana, Ireland, Singapore[63]	..	–	..	–
					–	5[64]	–	
MINUGUA (GAR 48/267)[65]	UN Verification Mission in Guatemala	Guatemala	Oct. 1994	Argentina, Brazil, Canada, Colombia, Italy, Spain, Sweden, Uruguay, Venezuela[66]	28	–	..	–
					–	17		
					–	38		
(GAR 51/199)[67]	UN Support Unit in El Salvador	El Salvador	Jan. 1997[68]	[69]	0.4	–	..	–
					–	–		
					–	–		

Organization for Security and Co-operation in Europe (OSCE) (12 operations)[70]

Acronym	Mission	Location	Start	Contributors				
– (CSO 18 Sep. 1992)[71]	OSCE Spillover Mission to Skopje (O)	Former Yugoslav Rep. of Macedonia	Sep. 1992	..	0.4[73]	–	..	–
					–	4[72]		
					–	–		
– (CSO 6 Nov. 1992)[74]	OSCE Mission to Georgia (O)	Georgia (S. Ossetia; Abkhazia)[75]	Dec. 1992	..	1.5[77]	1	..	–
					–	19[76]		
					–	–		
– (CSO 13 Dec. 1992)[78]	OSCE Mission to Estonia (O)	Estonia	Feb. 1993	..	0.5[79]	–	..	–
					–	6		
					–	–		
– (CSO 4 Feb. 1993)[80]	OSCE Mission to Moldova (O)	Moldova	Apr. 1993	..	0.5[81]	–	..	–
					–	8		
					–	–		
– (CSO 23 Sep. 1993)[82]	OSCE Mission to Latvia (O)	Latvia	Nov. 1993	..	0.5[83]	–	..	–
					–	7		
					–	–		
– (1 Dec. 1993)[84]	OSCE Mission to Tajikistan (O)	Tajikistan	Feb. 1994	..	0.9[86]	–	..	–
					–	8[85]		
					–	–		
– (2 June 1994)[87]	OSCE Mission in Sarajevo (O)	Bosnia and Herzegovina	Oct. 1994	..	0.8[88]	–	..	–
					–	6		
					–	–		

80 SECURITY AND CONFLICTS, 1997

Acronym/ (Legal instrument*)	Name/type of mission (O: observer) (PK: peacekeeping)	Location	Start date	Countries contributing troops, military observers (mil. obs) and/or civilian police (CivPol) in 1997	Troops/ Mil. obs/ CivPol	Deaths: To date In 1997	Cost: Yearly Unpaid
— (CSO 15 June 1994)[89]	OSCE Mission to Ukraine (O)	Ukraine	Nov. 1994	..	— 4 —	— —	0.5[90] ..
— (11 Apr. 1995)[91]	OSCE Assistance Group to Chechnya (O)	Chechnya	Apr. 1995	..	— 8[92] —	— —	1.5[93] ..
— (8 Dec. 1995)[94]	OSCE Mission to Bosnia and Herzegovina (O)	Bosnia and Herzegovina[95]	Dec. 1995	..	— _[96] —	— —	20[97] ..
— (18 Apr. 1996)[98]	OSCE Mission to Croatia (O)	Croatia	July 1996	..	— _[99] —	— —	1[100] ..
— **(27 Mar. 1997)[101]**	**OSCE Presence in Albania** (O)	**Albania**	**Apr. 1997**	..	— 8 —	— —	1.9[102] ..
CIS/Russia (4 operations)[103]							
— (Bilateral agreement)[104]	'South Ossetia Joint Force' (PK)	Georgia (S. Ossetia)	July 1992	Georgia, Russia, North and South Ossetia	..[105] .. —	.. ..	.. ..
— (Bilateral agreement)[106]	'Moldova Joint Force' (PK)	Moldova (Trans-Dniester)	July 1992	Moldova, Russia, 'Trans-Dniester Republic'	..[107] .. —	.. ..	.. ..
— (CIS 24 Sep. 1993)[108]	CIS 'Tajikistan Buffer Force' (PK)	Tajikistan (Afghan border[109])	Aug. 1993	Kazakhstan, Kyrgyzstan, Russia, Uzbekistan	..[110] .. —	..[111] ..	1[112] ..
— (CIS 15 Apr. 1994)[113]	CIS 'Peacekeeping Forces in Georgia' (PK)	Georgian–Abkhazian border	June 1994	Russia	..[114] .. —	.. ..	.. ..

Other (13 operations)

Acronym (Legal basis)	Location	Start date	Countries contributing	Troops	Mil. Obs.	Civ. Pol.	Col 1	Col 2
NNSC Neutral Nations Supervisory Commission[115] (Armistice Agreement) (O)	North Korea/ South Korea	July 1953	Sweden, Switzerland[116]	—	10	—	1.5[117]	..
MFO Multinational Force and Observers in the Sinai[118] (Protocol to treaty) (O)	Egypt (Sinai)	Apr. 1982	Australia, Canada, Colombia, Fiji, France, Hungary, Italy, New Zealand, Norway, Uruguay, USA	1 896[119]	—	—	51[120]	—
ECOMOG ECOWAS[122] Monitoring Group[121] (ESMC 7 Aug. 1990) (PK)	Liberia	Aug. 1990	**Benin**, **Burkina Faso**, Gambia, Ghana, Guinea, Mali, Niger, Nigeria, Sierra Leone[123]	11 000[124]	—	—	..[125]	..[126]
ECMM European Community Monitoring Mission[127] (Brioni Agreement) (O)	Former Yugoslavia	July 1991	Austria, Belgium, Denmark, Finland, France, Germany, Greece, Ireland, Italy, **Luxembourg**, Netherlands, Norway, Portugal, Slovakia, Spain, Sweden, UK	241[128]	—	6	—	17
OMIB[129] OAU Mission in Burundi (OAU 1993) (O)	Burundi	Dec. 1993	..	—[130]	—	1	..	..[131]
MOMEP Mission of Military Observers Ecuador/ Peru[132] (Decl. of Itamaraty) (O)	Ecuador/Peru	Mar. 1995	Argentina, Brazil, Chile, Ecuador, Peru, USA	34[133]	—	—	—	5.4[134]
SFOR Stabilization Force (SCR 1088) (PK)	Bosnia and Herzegovina	Dec. 1996	Albania, Austria, Belgium, Bulgaria, Canada, Czech Rep., Denmark, Egypt, Estonia, Finland, France, Germany, Greece, Hungary, **Ireland**, Italy, Jordan, Latvia, Lithuania, Luxembourg, Malaysia, Morocco, Netherlands, Norway, Poland, Portugal, Romania, Russia, **Slovenia**, Spain, Sweden, Turkey, UK, Ukraine, USA[135]	36 300[136]	—	—	78[137]	..
TIPH 2 Temporary International Presence in Hebron[138] (O)	Hebron	Jan. 1997[139]	Denmark, Italy, Norway, Sweden, Switzerland, Turkey	—	132	—	..	..
MISAB Inter-African Mission to Monitor the Implementation of the Bangui Agreements[141] (S/1997/561, SCR1125)[140] (PK)	Central African Republic	Feb. 1997	Burkina Faso, Chad, Gabon, Mali, Senegal, Togo	800[142]	—	—	..[143]	..[144]

Acronym/ (Legal instrument[a])	Name/type of mission (O: observer) (PK: peacekeeping)	Location	Start date	Countries contributing troops, military observers (mil. obs) and/or civilian police (CivPol) in 1997	Troops/ Mil. obs/ CivPol	Deaths: To date In 1997	Cost: Yearly Unpaid
MPF (SCR 1101)[145]	Multinational Protection Force (PK)	Albania	Apr. 1997[146]	Austria, Denmark, France, Greece, Italy, Portugal, Romania, Spain, Turkey[147]	_[148] – –	.. ..	.149 .. ..
ECOMOG (OAU mandate)[150]	ECOWAS Monitoring Group (PK)	Sierra Leone	May 1997	Ghana, Guinea, Nigeria[151]	_[152] – –	.. ..	.. .. ..
TMG (Burnham Declaration)[153]	Bougainville Truce Monitoring Group (PK)	Papua New Guinea	Nov. 1997	Australia, Fiji, New Zealand, Vanuatu[154]	328 – –	– –	4 .. ..
OMIC (OAU 1997)[155]	OAU Observer Mission in the Comoros (O)	Comoros	Nov. 1997	Egypt, Nigeria, Senegal, Tunisia	– 20 –	– –	.156 .. ..

Notes for table 2A

[a] GAR = General Assembly Resolution; SCR = Security Council Resolution; SG = Secretary-General

[1] Sources for this section, unless otherwise noted: United Nations, Department of Peacekeeping Operations, Monthly summary of troop contributions to peace-keeping operations; United Nations, United Nations Peace-keeping Operations, Background Note, DPI/1634/Rev. 5, Dec. 1997; United Nations, Status of contributions as at 31 December 1997, UN document ST/ADM/SER.B/521, 8 Jan. 1998; and information from UN Department of Public Information, Peace and Security Section, New York and UN Information Centre for the Nordic Countries, Copenhagen.

[2] As of 31 Dec. 1997. Operational strength varies from month to month because of rotation.

[3] Casualty figures are valid 31 Dec. 1997 and include military, civilian police and civilian international and local staff. The figures, from the UN Situation Centre, are based on information from the Peace-Keeping Data-Base covering the period 1948–97. This database is still under review and there may be some errors or omissions.

[4] 18 of the 20 UN peacekeeping operations conducted or ongoing in 1997 are financed from their own separate accounts on the basis of legally binding assessments on all member states in accordance with Article 17 of the UN Charter. UNTSO and UNMOGIP are funded from the UN regular budget. Some missions, as noted in the relevant footnote, are partly funded by voluntary contributions. Figures are annualized budget estimates.

[5] Outstanding contributions to UN peacekeeping operations as of 31 Dec. 1997.

[6] This amount includes the voluntary contribution from the Government of Cyprus of one-third of the cost of the force, and the annual amount of $6.5 m. contributed by the Government of Greece. United Nations, Report of the Secretary-General on the United Nations Operation in Cyprus, UN document S/1997/962, 8 Dec. 1997, p. 6.

[7] UNDOF was assisted by 78 military observers detailed from UNTSO. United Nations, Report of the Secretary-General on the United Nations Disengagement Observer Force, UN document S/1997/884, 14 Nov. 1997.

[8] Initially financed from a special account established for UNEF II (Second UN Emergency Force, Oct. 1973–July 1979), which remained open for UNDOF.

[9] Total approximate value of outstanding contributions to UNEF II and UNDOF.

10 UNIFIL was assisted by 55 military observers of the Observer Group Lebanon of UNTSO. In addition, UNIFIL employed 455 civilian staff. United Nations, Report of the Secretary-General on the United Nations Interim Force in Lebanon, UN document S/1998/53, 20 Jan. 1998.

11 Demilitarized zone (DMZ).

12 Authorized strength: 910 troops and 300 military observers. Financing of the activities arising from SCR 687 (1991): United Nations Iraq–Kuwait Observation Mission, Report of the Secretary-General, UN document A/49/863, 20 Mar. 1995, p. 5.

13 Two-thirds of the cost of the mission, equivalent to some $33 m., is funded through voluntary contributions from the Government of Kuwait. United Nations, Report of the Secretary-General on the United Nations Iraq–Kuwait Observation Mission, UN document S/1997/740, 24 Sep. 1997.

14 SCR 1133 (20 Oct. 1997) extended the mandate of MINURSO until 20 Apr. 1998, enabling the mission to resume its task of identifying prospective voters and authorizing the increase of its size. The identification process, which was suspended in May 1996, was resumed on 3 Dec. 1997 and is to be completed by 31 May 1998.

15 The cost of the expansion of MINURSO for the full implementation of the settlement plan is estimated at $129 m. The estimate provides for the emplacement of 347 military observers, 1273 military contingent personnel, 319 civilian police observers and 960 support staff. United Nations, Report of the Secretary-General on the situation concerning Western Sahara, Addendum, S/1997/882/Add.1, 19 Nov. 1997. Proposed additional requirements requested due to resumption of identification process: $17.9 m.

16 It was decided to bring the number of observers back to 136, as authorized by SCR 937 (21 July 1994). United Nations, Report of the Secretary-General concerning the situation in Abkhazia, Georgia, UN document S/1998/51, 19 Jan. 1998.

17 The financial implications of to the planned expansion of UNOMIG are indicated to be c. $1.7 m.

18 SCR 1116 (27 June 1997) extended the mandate of UNOMIL for a final period to 30 Sep. 1997, by which time withdrawal was substantially completed. A continued UN presence was agreed by the Secretary-General and the Government of Liberia. A UN Peace-Building Support Office will be the focal point for the UN's post-conflict peace-building activities and will coordinate UN activities in Liberia. United Nations, Final Report of the Secretary-General on the United Nations Observer Mission in Liberia, UN document S/1997/712, 12 Sep. 1997.

19 By 31 Aug. 1997, $115 m. had been assessed on member states for the operation of UNOMIL from inception to 30 Sep. 1997, of which $97 m. has been received. United Nations, Final Report of the Secretary-General on the United Nations Observer Mission in Liberia, UN document S/1997/712, 12 Sep. 1997. In Oct. the General Assembly's Fifth Committee (Administrative and Budgetary) recommended a reduction to $9 m. for the period 1 July 1997–30 June 1998. Press Release GA/AB/3180, 30 Oct. 1997.

20 SCR 1138 (14 Nov. 1997) expanded the size and the mandate of UNMOT to enhance the mission's ability to assist in the implementation of the General Agreement on the Establishment of Peace and National Accord in Tajikistan, signed on 27 June 1997 (A/52/219–S/1997/510, annex I).

21 The increase in personnel authorized by SCR 1138 comprises 75 military observers, 2 civilian police and 146 international and locally recruited staff. Support to the Joint Security Unit, established by the parties to the peace agreement in order to provide security to UNMOT personnel, is also included. It includes the assignment of UNMOT military observers to the unit on a permanent basis. United Nations, Report of the Secretary-General on the situation in Tajikistan, UN document S/1997/859, 5 Nov. 1997.

22 The cost of expanding the size and mandate of UNMOT is estimated at $13.7 m. United Nations, Report of the Secretary-General on the situation in Tajikistan, UN document S/1997/859, 5 Nov. 1997.

23 Pursuant to SCR 1106 (16 Apr. 1997) the mandate of UNAVEM III ended on 30 June 1997 with the understanding that the mission would become an observer mission (see MONUA).

24 The scheduled withdrawal of the UNAVEM III military units by Aug.–Sep. 1997 was postponed because of the deteriorating military situation. Plans for the down-sizing provided for the repatriation of a number of military personnel by the end of Nov. 1997, with a gradual draw-down of the troops between Dec. 1997 and the first week of Feb. 1998, when the strength of the military component of the mission would have been reduced to the level initially envisaged for its successor MONUA. United Nations, Report of the Secretary-General on the United Nations Observer Mission in Angola, UN document S/1997/807, 17 Oct. 1997.

25 No cost estimate was prepared as it was expected that the Security Council would authorize a follow-on mission.

26 SCR 1142 (4 Dec. 1997) extended the mandate of UNPREDEP for a final period until 31 Aug. 1998. The Secretary-General was requested to report to the Security

Council no later than 1 June 1998 on the modalities of the termination of UNPREDEP and to submit recommendations on the type of international presence most appropriate for the Former Yugoslav Republic of Macedonia after 31 Aug. 1998.

[27] In accordance with the provisions of SCR 1110 (28 May 1997) a 2-month phased reduction of the UNPREDEP military component by 300 took place between 1 Oct. and 30 Nov. 1997. United Nations, Report of the Secretary-General on the United Nations Preventive Deployment Force pursuant to Security Council Resolution 1110 (1997), UN document S/1997/911, 20 Nov. 1997. The military component will remain at 750 troops until the mission's mandate expires on 31 Aug. 1998. SCR 1142 (4 Dec. 1997).

[28] The cost of maintaining the UNPREDEP force at its reduced strength until 31 May 1998 is within the original appropriation made by the General Assembly of $46.5 m. for the period 1 July 1997–30 June 1998. United Nations, Report of the Secretary-General on the United Nations Preventive Deployment Force pursuant to Security Council Resolution 1110 (1997), UN document S/1997/911/Add. 1, 25 Nov. 1997.

[29] SCR 1035 (21 Dec. 1995) authorized establishment of the International Police Task Force (IPTF), in accordance with Annex 11 of the General Framework Agreement for Peace in Bosnia and Herzegovina (the Dayton Agreement), plus a civilian mission as proposed in the Secretary-General's report of 13 Dec. 1995, S/1995/1031. The mission was later given the name UNMIBH. UN document S/1996/83, p. 5.

[30] Pursuant to SCR 1103 (31 Mar. 1997) and SCR 1107 (16 May 1997) the authorized strength of IPTF (main component of UNMIBH) increased to 2027 police monitors.

[31] SCR 1120 (14 Jul. 1997) extended the mandate of UNTAES for a final period ending 15 Jan. 1998. SCR 1145 (19 Dec. 1997) authorized the establishment of a support group of 180 civilian police monitors (UN Civilian Police Support Group) for a single period of up to 9 months with effect from 16 Jan. 1998.

[32] A 2-phase exit strategy allowed the progressive reduction of UNTAES personnel and resources. By mid-Oct. the number of military units was reduced to 720 while the number of military observers and civilian police remained unchanged until the mandate expired. United Nations, Report of the Secretary-General on the United Nations Transitional Administration for Eastern Slavonia, Baranja and Western Sirmium, UN document S/1997/953, 4 Dec. 1997. By mid-Jan. the military liquidation force operational since 15 Oct. 1997 was being progressively phased out and complete withdrawal was expected not later than 31 May 1998. United Nations, Report of the Secretary-General on the United Nations Transitional Administration for Eastern Slavonia, Baranja and Western Sirmium, UN document S/1998/59, 22 Jan. 1998.

[33] The reduction of the civilian police component began on 16 Jan. 1998 and was within its authorized strength of 180 by 31 Jan. 1998. United Nations, Report of the Secretary-General on the United Nations Transitional Administration for Eastern Slavonia, Baranja and Western Sirmium, UN document S/1998/59, 22 Jan. 1998.

[34] Cost included in UNMIBH.

[35] Pursuant to SCR 1086 (5 Dec. 1996) the final mandate of UNSMIH expired on 31 July 1997. UNSMIH was succeeded by UNTMIH, a transition mission with an almost identical mandate.

[36] Authorized strength of UNSMIH: 300 civilian police and 500 troops. An additional 800 military personnel were funded voluntarily by Canada and the USA. United Nations, Report of the Secretary-General on the United Nations Support Mission in Haiti, UN document S/1997/564, 19 July 1997.

[37] The 3 missions in Haiti in 1997—UNSMIH, UNTMIH and MIPONUH—were all financed under the same special account.

[38] SCR 1064 (20 Jan. 1997) authorized the attachment for a 3-month period of 155 military observers and requisite medical personnel to the human rights mission MINUGUA, thereby temporarily transforming it into a peacekeeping mission. After successfully completing its mission of verifying the Agreement of the Definitive Ceasefire between the Government of Guatemala and the Unidad Revolucionaria Nacional Guatemalteca (URNG), signed at Oslo, 4 Dec. 1996 (S/1996/1045, annex), the military observers withdrew (on 27 May) and MINUGUA resumed its previous human rights role under its new name. United Nations, Report of the Secretary-General on the Group of Military Observers Attached to MINUGUA, UN document S/1997/432, 4 June 1997.

[39] In addition there were 13 medical personnel from Austria, Germany and Singapore. United Nations, Report of the Secretary-General on the Group of Military Observers attached to MINUGUA, UN document S/1997/432, 4 June 1997.

[40] Military observer component only.

[41] SCR 1118 (30 June 1997) authorized the establishment of MONUA as a follow-on mission to UNAVEM III, for an initial 4-month period which was later extended by SCR 1135 (29 Oct. 1997) until 30 Jan. 1998. It was originally expected that the mission would be completed by 1 Feb. 1998. However, in Jan. 1998 the Secretary-General

recommended an extension of the mandate for an additional 3 months at a reduced level. United Nations, Report of the Secretary-General on the United Nations Observer Mission in Angola, UN document S/1998/17, 12 Jan. 1998.

42 MONUA (Missao de Observacao das Nacoes Unidas em Angola, in Portuguese).

43 Authorized strength of MONUA: 193 troops, 86 military observers and 345 civilian police supported by a civilian establishment of some 310 international civilian staff. United Nations, Progress Report of the Secretary-General on the United Nations Angola Verification Mission (UNAVEM III), UN document S/1997/438/Add.1, 6 June 1997.

44 The estimated cost from 1 July 1997 to 30 June 1998 amounts to $162 m. United Nations, Report of the Secretary-General on the United Nations Observer Mission in Angola, UN document S/1997/807, 17 Oct. 1997. In Oct. the General Assembly's Fifth Committee (Administrative and Budgetary) recommended the appropriation of $155 m. for the period 1 July 1997–30 June 1998. Press Release GA/AB/3180, 30 Oct. 1997.

45 As of 30 Sep. 1997, unpaid assessed contributions to the UNAVEM/MONUA special account for the period since the inception of the mission to 30 June 1997 amounted to $89 m. United Nations, Report of the Secretary-General on the United Nations Observer Mission in Angola, UN document S/1997/807, 17 Oct. 1997.

46 SCR 1123 (30 July 1997) authorized the establishment of UNTMIH as a successor operation to UNSMIH, for a single 4-month period ending 30 Nov. 1997.

47 Authorized strength of UNTMIH: 50 troops and 250 civilian police. An additional 1125 military personnel were funded voluntarily by Canada and the USA. United Nations, Report of the Secretary-General on the United Nations Transition Mission in Haiti, UN document S/1997/832, 31 Oct. 1997.

48 Included in UNSMIH.

49 SCR 1141 (28 Nov. 1997) authorized the establishment of MIPONUH as a follow-on mission to UNTMIH, for a single 12-month period ending 30 Nov. 1998.

50 MIPONUH (Mission de police civile des Nations Unies en Haiti, in French).

51 Authorized strength of MIPONUH: up to 300 civilian police including a 90-strong special police unit. United Nations, Report of the Secretary-General on the United Nations Transition Mission in Haiti, UN document S/1997/832/Add. 1, 20 Nov. 1997.

52 The estimated cost for a 6-month period includes support by some 222 civilian international and local staff. United Nations, Report of the Secretary-General on the United Nations Transition Mission in Haiti, UN document S/1997/832/Add. 1, 20 Nov. 1997.

53 Included in UNSMIH.

54 Comprises substantial UN peace missions (2 in cooperation with the Organization of American States, OAS) not officially described by the UN as peacekeeping. All information on CIAV/OAS and MICIVIH from the Organization of American States, Information and Dialogue Unit for the Promotion of Democracy, Washington, DC.

55 Established jointly by the UN and the OAS to verify compliance with the Tela Agreement signed in Honduras, 7 Aug. 1989. Conclusion of the mandate 30 June 1997 following the Managua Agreement signed by the Government of Nicaragua and the 3-80 Northern Front, 30 May 1997. Resolution adopted at the sixth plenary session of the General Assembly of the Organization of American States (OAS), held on 4 June 1997, AG/RES. 1467 (XXVII-O/97).

56 As of 30 June 1997 staff members (including head of mission) were from: Argentina 3, Colombia 1, Nicaragua 14, Uruguay 1, USA 1.

57 Cost of mission 1 Jan.–30 June 1997, not including final closing costs.

58 Joint UN participation with OAS was authorized by the resolution.

59 At the end of 1997 staff members were from: Argentina, Barbados, Canada, Chile, El Salvador, Grenada, Mexico, St. Lucia, St. Vincent, Trinidad and Tobago, USA.

60 The mission consists of 64 civilian observers, 32 from the UN and 32 from the OAS. As of 31 Dec. 1997 the OAS had 27 international civilian observers.

61 Cost to the UN: $4.4 m. Cost to the OAS: c. $4.2 m. Since 1991, 14 countries have contributed to the financing : (in US$) Bolivia 5000, Brazil 50 000, Canada 1.1 m., Chile 20 000, Colombia 25 000, Dominica 1000, France 350 000, Germany 130 000, Italy 92 000, Netherlands 106 000, Panama 45 000, St. Kitts and Nevis 3000, USA 29 m.).

62 UNSMA maintains a temporary headquarters in Islamabad, Pakistan. The Secretary-General has suggested the opening of an office in Turkmenistan. United Nations, Report of the Secretary-General on the Situation in Afghanistan and its Implications for International Peace and Stability, UN document S/1997/894, 14 Nov. 1997.

63 Information from UN Department of Political Affairs, New York.

64 Information from UN Department of Political Affairs, New York.

65 The mandate of MINUGUA was renewed with expanded responsibilities, enabling the mission to carry out broader verification tasks, for a further period of 1 year ending 31 Mar. 1998. In order to reflect its new mandate, its name was changed to United Nations Verification Mission in Guatemala as from 1 Apr. In late Oct., the Secretary-General recommended that the General Assembly authorize the renewal of the mandate beyond 31 Mar. 1998 until 31 Dec. 1999. This would enable MINUGUA to carry out verification of the peace agreements between the Government of Guatemala and the URNG, signed in Guatemala City, 29 Dec. 1996, while conforming to the timetable for their implementation. United Nations, Report of the Secretary-General, United Nations Verification Mission in Guatemala, UN document A/52/554, 31 Oct. 1997.
66 Countries providing military observers and civilian police. In addition 27 countries contributed civilian personnel. UN Department of Political Affairs, New York.
67 GAR 51/199 (17 Dec. 1996) authorized the establishment of a small support unit to assist the UN Special Envoy for a period of 6 months. The tasks of the Special Envoy were previously carried out by the United Nations Office of Verification in El Salvador (ONUV), 1 May–31 Dec. 1996.
68 Established 1 Jan. 1997. Mandate expired 30 June 1997.
69 Staff consisted of 3 international officials from Brazil, Switzerland and Uruguay, 1 civilian police consultant from Chile, 2 local consultants and a small number of administrative staff. United Nations, Report of the General-Secretary, Assessment of the peace process in El Salvador, UN document A/51/917, 1 July 1997 and information from UN Department of Political Affairs, New York.
70 32 countries contributed personnel to OSCE long-term missions in 1997: Armenia, Austria, Azerbaijan, Belgium, Bulgaria, Canada, Czech Rep., Finland, France, Georgia, Germany, Greece, Hungary, Ireland, Italy, Latvia, Lithuania, Macedonia, Moldova, Netherlands, Norway, Poland, Romania, Russia, Slovakia, Spain, Sweden, Switzerland, Turkey, Ukraine, UK, USA. As country representation is constantly changing there is no OSCE information on current mission composition. The mission to Kosovo, Sandjak and Vojvodina, expelled on 28 June 1993, could not be redeployed because of a lack of agreement on its extension. *Sources*: OSCE, Survey of OSCE Long-Term Missions and other OSCE Field Activities (Conflict Prevention Centre, CPC: Vienna, 7 Oct. 1997 and 5 Mar. 1998); and specific information from the CPC. Note: Information on fatalities in OSCE missions to 31 Dec. 1997 was available only for Albania; for other missions the data here are valid as from spring 1997.
71 Decision to establish the mission taken at 16th CSO meeting, 18 Sep. 1992, Journal no. 3, Annex 1. Authorized by the Government of the Former Yugoslav Republic of Macedonia (FYROM) through Articles of Understanding (corresponding to an MOU) agreed by exchange of letters, 7 Nov. 1992.
72 Authorized strength: 8 members. Supplemented by 2 monitors from the European Community Monitoring Mission (ECMM) under operational command of OSCE Head of Mission.
73 Budget adopted for 1997.
74 Decision to establish the mission taken at 17th CSO meeting, 6 Nov. 1992, Journal no. 2, Annex 2. Authorized by Government of Georgia through MOU, 23 Jan. 1993 and by 'Leadership of the Republic of South Ossetia' by exchange of letters on 1 Mar. 1993. Mandate expanded on 29 Mar. 1994 to include *inter alia* monitoring of Joint Peacekeeping Forces in South Ossetia.
75 The mission is based in Tbilisi. In Apr. 1997, a branch office in Tskhinvali became operational.
76 The authorized strength increased by 2 officers when the branch office in Tskhinvali became operational.
77 Budget adopted for 1997. In addition the Permanent Council decided to release the $0.2 m. reserved in the 1997 budget for the opening of the branch office in Tskhinvali.
78 Decision to establish the mission taken at 18th CSO meeting, 13 Dec. 1992, Journal no. 3, Annex 2. Authorized by Estonian Government through MOU, 15 Feb. 1993.
79 Budget adopted for 1997.
80 Decision to establish the mission taken at 19th CSO meeting, 4 Feb. 1993, Journal no. 3, Annex 3. Authorized by Government of Moldova through MOU, 7 May 1993. An 'Understanding of the Activity of the CSCE Mission in the Pridnestrovian [Trans-Dniester] Region of the Republic of Moldova' came into force on 25 Aug. 1993 through an exchange of letters between the Head of Mission and the 'President of the Pridnestrovian Moldovan Republic'.
81 Budget adopted for 1997.
82 Decision to establish the mission taken at 23rd CSO meeting, 23 Sep. 1993, Journal no. 3, Annex 3. Authorized by Government of Latvia through MOU, 13 Dec. 1993.
83 Budget adopted for 1997.

84 Decision to establish the mission taken at 4th meeting of the Council, Rome (CSCE/4-C/Dec. 1), Decision I.4, 1 Dec. 1993. No MOU signed.
85 At its 118th Plenary Meeting on 5 June 1997 the OSCE Permanent Council approved the augmentation of the mission by 3 international staff members.
86 Budget adopted for 1997. In addition the Permanent Council decided to release $0.2 m. for the increase in staff.
87 Decision to establish the mission taken by the Permanent Council (formerly Permanent Committee), 2 June 1994, Journal No. 23, Annex. According to Article 18 of 'Decision on OSCE Action for Peace, Democracy and Stability in Bosnia and Herzegovina' (MC(5).DEC/1) by the Budapest Ministerial Council on 8 Dec. 1995, the present OSCE Mission in Sarajevo is now a distinct section of the Mission to Bosnia and Herzegovina.
88 Budget adopted for 1996.
89 Decision to establish the mission taken at 27th CSO meeting, 15 June 1994, Journal no. 3, Decision (c). Authorized by Government of Ukraine through MOU, 24 Jan. 1995.
90 Budget adopted for 1997.
91 Decision to establish the mission taken at 16th meeting of the Permanent Council, 11 Apr. 1995, Decision (a). No MOU signed.
92 72 observers were sent to monitor the elections held on 27 Jan. 1997. *Keesing's Record of World Events*, vol. 43, no. 1 (Jan. 1997).
93 Budget adopted for 1997.
94 Decision to establish the mission taken at 5th meeting, Ministerial Council, Budapest, 8 Dec. 1995 (MC(5).DEC/1) in accordance with Annex 6 of the Dayton Agreement.
95 The mission is based in Sarajevo. In June 1997, an additional centre opened in Brcko.
96 The composition of the mission during the municipal elections was 246 internationally seconded members. For the rest of the year the mission was reduced to 194.
97 Budget adopted for 1997.
98 Decision to establish the mission taken by Permanent Council, 18 Apr. 1996, Journal no. 65 (PC.DEC/112). Adjustment of the mandate by the Permanent Council, 26 June 1997, Journal no. 121 (PC.DEC/176).
99 The mission was authorized to increase its personnel, starting July 1997, to a ceiling of 250 expatriates with a view to full deployment by 15 Jan. 1998. PC.DEC/176, 26 June 1997. According to PC.DEC/181, 17 July 1997, the Secretariat may recruit a maximum of 4 key administrative and support staff at the mission headquarters.
100 Budget adopted for 1997. In addition PC.DEC/181, 17 July 1997, authorized the Secretary-General to incur commitments and make expenditures up to the level of $3.6 m. pending the approval of a revised budget line for the mission for the remaining part of the financial year 1997.
101 Decision to establish the mission taken at 108th meeting of the Permanent Council, 27 Mar. 1997 (PC.DEC/160).
102 Budget valid 22 Apr.–31 Dec. 1997.
103 Figures used in this section could not be verified by official sources. Russian-dominated peacekeeping efforts in South Ossetia and Moldova cannot be described as CIS peacekeeping operations as the agreements establishing them were bilateral, they are being undertaken by a mixture of CIS and non-CIS forces, or they came into being before general CIS peacekeeping agreements were implemented. Crow, S., 'Russia promotes CIS as an international organization', *RFE/RL Research Report*, vol. 3, no. 11 (18 Mar. 1994), p. 35, note 10.
104 Agreement on the Principles Governing the Peaceful Settlement of the Conflict in South Ossetia, signed in Dagomys, 24 June 1992, by Georgia and Russia. A Joint Monitoring Commission with representatives of Russia, Georgia and North and South Ossetia was established to oversee the implementation of the Agreement.
105 700 Russian troops and 700 Georgian and joint N/S Ossetian units in 1995. O'Prey, K., *Keeping the Peace in the Borderlands of Russia*, Occasional paper no. 23 (Henry L. Stimson Center: Washington, DC, July 1995), p. 16.
106 Agreement on the Principles Governing the Peaceful Settlement of the Armed Conflict in the Trans-Dniester Region, signed in Moscow, 21 July 1992 by the presidents of Moldova and Russia. A Joint Control Commission with representatives of Russia, Moldova and Trans-Dniester was established to coordinate the activities of the joint peacekeeping contingent.
107 Originally comprised 6 Russian battalions (2400 troops), reportedly reduced to 630 troops in 1993–94; 3 Moldovan battalions (1200 troops); 3 Trans-Dniester battalions

(1200 troops); and 10 military observers from each of the parties involved in the conflict. Gribincea, M., 'Rejecting a new role for the former 14th Russian Army', *Transition*, vol. 2, no. 6 (22 Mar. 1996), pp. 38–39. The Russian contingent has gradually shrunk to 2 battalions because of financial constraints. At the end of Nov., Ukrainian President Kuchma announced the intention to send a peacekeeping unit to add to but not replace the existing Russian contingent. 'Ukraine ready to send peacekeepers to Moldova', Norwegian Institute of International Affairs (NUPI) Centre for Russian Studies Database, URL: <http://www.nupi.no/cgi-win/Russland/krono.exe/1426>, version current on 25 Nov. 1997.

[108] CIS Agreement on the Collective Peace-keeping Forces and Joint Measures on their Logistical and Technical Maintenance, signed in Moscow, 24 Sep. 1993. The operation is the first application of the Agreement on Groups of Military Observers and Collective Peacekeeping Forces in the CIS, signed in Kiev, 20 Mar. 1992.

[109] The Russian Border Troops and other CIS forces stationed or operating elsewhere in Tajikistan are not part of this operation.

[110] The Russian 201st Motorized Rifle Division (MRD) constitutes the core of the CIS Collective Peacekeeping Forces (CPF). Reportedly the CPF consists of 5500 men of the MRD plus 500 men in a Kazakh and a Kyrgyz battalion respectively, and an Uzbek unit of 300 men. Jonson, L., 'Peace support flexibility—different military traditions and operational landscapes: the case of Russia in Tajikistan', paper presented at the Workshop on Challenges of Peace Support Operations into the 21st Century, National Defence College, Stockholm, 26–27 Sep. 1997.

[111] 75 peacekeepers were killed between the beginning of the operation and the end of Sep. 1995. Masyuk, Y., video report, NTV (Moscow), 23 Oct. 1995, Foreign Broadcast Information Service, *Daily Report–Central Eurasia* (*FBIS-SOV*), FBIS-SOV-95-207, 26 Oct. 1995, p. 14. As of the end of Nov., more than 30 soldiers and officers had been killed in 1995. Gridneva, G., ITAR-TASS (Moscow) 30 Nov. 1995, FBIS-SOV-95-231, 1 Dec. 1995, p. 55. Fatal casualties in the 201st MRD reportedly numbered 39 in 1993, 35 in 1994 and 23 in 1995. *Krasnaya Zvezda*, 19 Jan. 1996, p. 2. More than 60 Russians were killed during 1995–96. 'Suspect sentenced to death for killing Russian soldiers', *OMRI Daily Digest*, no. 24, part I (4 Feb. 1997).

[112] National contingents are fully financed by the state sending them. Only the command of the collective force and combat support units are financed from a joint budget, shared as follows: Kyrgyzstan 10%; Tajikistan 10%; Kazakhstan 15%; Uzbekistan 15%; and Russia 50%. O'Prey (note 105), p. 38.

[113] Georgian–Abkhazian Agreement on a Cease-fire and Separation of Forces, signed in Moscow, 14 May 1994. Mandate approved by Heads of States members of the CIS Council of Collective Security, 21 Oct. 1994. Endorsement by the UN Security Council through SCR 937 (21 July 1994).

[114] Estimated number of troops in 1997: 1600. Yurkin, A., 'Russia: Rotation of Russian peacekeepers begins in Abkhazia', ITAR-TASS (Moscow), 15 Apr. 1997, FBIS-SOV-97-105, 15 Apr. 1997.

[115] Agreement concerning a military armistice in Korea, signed at Panmunjom on 27 July 1953 by the Commander-in-Chief, UN Command; the Supreme Commander of the Korean People's Army; and the Commander of the Chinese People's Volunteers. Entered into force on 27 July 1953.

[116] The Neutral Nations Supervisory Commission entrusted to oversee the armistice agreement originally consisted of representatives from 4 countries: Czechoslovakia, Poland, Sweden and Switzerland. The Czechoslovak delegation was forced to leave in Apr. 1993 and by the end of 1997 the Korean People's Army/Chinese People's Volunteers had not yet nominated a replacement. The Polish delegation was forced to leave in Feb. 1995. Poland, however, remains a Commission member, maintaining an office in Warsaw and participating in the work of the Commission in Panmunjom. Information from Swedish Delegation to the NNSC, Panmunjom, South Korea.

[117] Approximate cost of Swedish and Swiss delegations. Information from Swedish delegation to the NNSC, Panmunjom, South Korea.

[118] 1981 Protocol to the Treaty of Peace between Egypt and Israel, signed 26 Mar. 1979. Established following withdrawal of Israeli forces from Sinai. Deployment began 20 Mar. and mission commenced on 25 Apr. 1982. 'The Multinational Force and Observers', Report from the Office of Personnel and Publications, MFO, Rome, June 1993.

[119] Strength as of Nov. 1997.

[120] Operating budget for FY 1997. Force funded by Egypt, Israel and the USA (31% each). Voluntary contributions from Germany (since 1992), Japan (since 1989) and Switzerland (since 1994) amounted to $2 m. in 1997. Annual Report of the Director General, MFO, Rome, Jan. 1998.

[121] Decision A/DEC.1/8/90 on the cease-fire and establishment of an ECOWAS Monitoring Group (ECOMOG) for Liberia. Economic Community of West African States. First Session of the Community Standing Mediation Committee, Banjul, 6–7 Aug. 1990. The ECOWAS Standing Mediation Committee (ESMC) is composed of Gambia,

Ghana, Guinea, Mali, Nigeria, Sierra Leone and Togo.

122 ECOWAS membership: Benin, Burkina Faso, Cape Verde, Côte d'Ivoire, Gambia, Ghana, Guinea, Guinea-Bissau, Liberia, Mali, Mauritania, Niger, Nigeria, Senegal, Sierra Leone and Togo.

123 A 35-man medical unit from Côte d'Ivoire joined in Apr. 1997. United Nations, Twenty-third progress report of the Secretary-General on the United Nations Observer Mission in Liberia, UN document S/1997/478, 19 June 1997.

124 As of June 1997. United Nations (note 123), 19 June 1997.

125 ECOMOG has lost about 700 men in combat while trying to establish a cease-fire. Howe, H., 'Lessons of Liberia–ECOMOG and regional peacekeeping', *International Security*, vol. 21, no. 3 (winter 1996/97), pp. 145–76.

126 Originally financed by ECOWAS countries with additional voluntary contributions from UN member states through the Trust Fund for the Implementation of the Cotonou Agreement. At the summit meeting of the Heads of State and Government of ECOWAS, held in Abuja 28–29 Aug. 1997, the ECOWAS leaders decided that the costs of the continued ECOMOG presence in Liberia will be financed mainly by the Government of Liberia. United Nations, Final report of the Secretary-General on the United Nations Observer Mission in Liberia, UN document S/1997/712, 12 Sep. 1997.

127 Mission established by the Brioni Agreement, signed at Brioni (Croatia), 7 July 1991 by representatives of the European Community (EC) and the governments of Croatia, Slovenia and federal Yugoslavia. Mandate confirmed by the EC meeting of foreign ministers, The Hague, 10 July 1991. Mission authorized by governments of Croatia, Slovenia and Yugoslavia through MOU, 13 July 1991. Information from Swedish delegation to the ECMM, Sarajevo.

128 Total number of personnel: 341 of whom 241 are observers. Information from Swedish delegation to the ECMM, Sarajevo.

129 MIOB (Mission de l'OUA au Burundi, in French). Both names are official.

130 Following the 1996 coup in Burundi, the Organization of African Unity (OAU) decided to withdraw the military component of OMIB and to reinforce the civilian component. This latter decision had not been implemented by Jan. 1997 when the number of civilian observers was 5.

131 Funded by the regular budget of the OAU and voluntary contributions.

132 The first article of the Declaration, dated 17 Feb. 1995, states the willingness of the guarantor countries of the 1942 Protocol of Rio de Janeiro—Argentina, Brazil, Chile and USA—to send an observer mission to the region in conflict, as well as the acceptance of this offer by the conflicting parties. Information from Brazilian Embassy in Stockholm.

133 In addition c. 110 personnel from Argentina, Brazil, Chile and the USA provide logistical and communications support. Brazil acts as overall coordinator for MOMEP.

134 The cost was divided between the governments of Ecuador and Peru. Brazil and the USA provided helicopter support.

135 Iceland provided medical support.

136 Troops were temporarily reinforced during the elections held in Bosnia (13–14 Sep.) and the Republika Srpska (22–23 Nov.). United Nations, Letter dated 14 Oct. 1997 from the Secretary-General addressed to the President of the Security Council, UN document S/1997/794, 14 Oct. 1997; and United Nations, Letter dated 12 Dec. 1997 from the Secretary-General addressed to the President of the Security Council, UN document S/1997/975, 13 Dec. 1997.

137 Information from North Atlantic Treaty Organization (NATO) Press Office, Brussels.

138 Protocol Concerning the Redeployment in Hebron, signed 15 Jan. 1997.

139 In May 1996, a group of Norwegian observers were sent to Hebron. After Israel and the Palestinian Authority signed and implemented the Hebron Protocol in Jan. 1997, the mission was expanded to include observers from 5 additional countries. The current mandate expires at the end of Jan. 1998 and may be extended for an additional 6-month period. Information from Ambassador Mona Juul, Middle East Coordinator, Royal Ministry of Foreign Affairs, Oslo.

140 MISAB was originally set up by the Presidents of Burkina Faso, Chad, Gabon and Mali (original mandate S/1997/561, Appendix I), to monitor the implementation of the Bangui Agreements signed on 25 Jan. 1997 (S/1997/561, Appendixes III–VI). Upon request (S/1997/543), the Security Council authorized MISAB (SCR 1125) on 6 Aug. 1997. The mandate was later extended for a further period of 3 months, to 6 Feb. 1998. SCR 1136 (6 Nov. 1997).

141 MISAB (Mission Interafricaine de Surveillance des Accords de Bangui, in French).
142 On 8 Feb. 1997, MISAB was deployed in Bangui, comprising a total of some 800 troops under the military command of Gabon and with logistical and financial support provided by France. United Nations, Report of the Secretary-General pursuant to SCR 1136 (6 Nov. 1997) concerning the situation in the Central African Republic, UN document S/1998/61, 23 Jan. 1998.
143 MISAB suffered some casualties in particular during confrontations in Bangui in Mar. and June 1997. United Nations, Report of the Secretary-General pursuant to SCR 1136 (6 Nov. 1997) concerning the situation in the Central African Republic, UN document S/1136 (6 Nov. 1997). In addition, a Trust Fund for the Central African Republic was established by the UN Secretary-General. The Organization of African Unity supported MISAB with special grants. United Nations, Report of the Secretary-General pursuant to SCR 1136 (6 Nov. 1997) concerning the situation in the Central African Republic, UN document S/1998/61, 23 Jan. 1998.
145 The Permanent Council of the OSCE decided to establish the conditions for launching an assistance effort to Albania at its 108th meeting, 27 Mar. 1997 (PC.DEC/160). SCR 1101 (28 Mar. 1997) authorized the establishment of the MPF for a period of 3 months. SCR 1114 (19 June 1997) extended the mandate by 45 days ending on 12 Aug. 1997.
146 Complete withdrawal was achieved on 11 Aug. 1997. United Nations, Eleventh and final report to the Security Council on the operation of the multinational protection force in Albania, UN document S/1997/632, 12 Aug. 1997, appendix.
147 The mission was under the command of Italy. Belgium and Slovenia contributed with medical units. United Nations (note 146), appendix.
148 Authorized strength of MPF: 6000. Letter dated 9 Apr. 1997 from the Chargé d'Affaires A.I. of the permanent mission of Italy to the United Nations addressed to the Secretary-General, UN document S/1997/296, 10 Apr. 1997. During the elections in June–July the force reached its maximum strength of 7215. United Nations, Eighth report to the Security Council on the operation of the multinational protection force in Albania, UN document S/1997/513, 3 July 1997, appendix.
149 The cost of the mission will be borne by the participating member states. SCR 1101 (28 Mar. 1997).
150 Following a military coup on 25 May 1997 ECOMOG peacekeeping forces intervened in Sierra Leone on 2 June 1997. Authorization was given by the OAU at the 33rd annual summit in Harare, 2–4 June 1997. 'Zimbabwe: OAU gives "green light" to use force in Sierra Leone', SAPA (Johannesburg), 3 June 1997, in Foreign Broadcast Information Service, *Daily Report–Africa (FBIS-AFR)*, FBIS-AFR-97-155, 4 June 1997. The decision of the OAU was supported by the UN Security Council. S/PRST/1997/36 (11 July 1997). The Conakry Agreement signed in Guinea, 23 Oct. 1997, by the ECOWAS Committee of Five on Sierra Leone and a delegation representing Major Johnny Koroma, Chairman of the Armed Forces Revolutionary Council (AFRC) regime in Sierra Leone, called for a cease-fire to be monitored by ECOMOG forces. United Nations, Second Report of the Secretary-General on the situation in Sierra Leone, UN document S/1997/958, 5 Dec. 1997.
151 The mission is headed by Nigeria. Interview with Malian President Alpha Oumar Konare by RFI correspondent Farida Ayari in Harare, Radio France Internationale (Paris), 3 June 1997, in 'Mali: Mali's Konare on Sierra Leone, OAU responsibility', FBIS-AFR-97-155, 4 June 1997.
152 A total of 700 Nigerian troops arrived in Freetown on 26 May 1997, bringing the total strength to 1600 men. Guinea was reported on 31 May 1997 to have dispatched 1500 troops to support the Nigerian force. *Keesing's Record of World Events*, vol. 43, no. 5 (May 1997), pp. 41625–26. A further reinforcement of 3000 Nigerian and other ECOMOG troops, bringing their number to more than 4600, was reported on 4 June 1997. *Keesing's Record of World Events*, vol. 43, no. 6 (June 1997), p. 41672.
153 TMG was established in order to monitor the implementation of the Burnham Truce signed by the Government of Papua New Guinea and the Bougainville parties (the Bougainville Transitional Government, the Bougainville Interim Government and the Bougainville Revolutionary Army) at Burnham, New Zealand, 1–10 Oct. 1997.
154 The mission is headed by New Zealand.
155 Mission established by decision of the OAU at its 36th Ordinary Session at Ambassadorial Level in Addis Ababa, Ethiopia, 22 Aug. 1997. Information from OAU Political Department, Addis Ababa, Ethiopia.
156 Monthly operational cost estimates at $160 000.

3. The Middle East peace process

PETER JONES and GUNILLA FLODÉN

I. Introduction

The overall assessment of the Middle East peace process in 1997 is negative, especially as regards the Israeli–Palestinian talks. Despite the signing of the long delayed Protocol Concerning the Redeployment in Hebron (known as the Hebron Accord), renewed Israeli settlement activity brought the peace process to a halt. Israel's interpretation of commitments to make further troop redeployments on the West Bank was a source of tension. Israel charged that the Palestinian Authority (PA) had not changed the sections of the Palestine Liberation Organization (PLO) Charter calling for the destruction of Israel and was not doing enough to fight terrorism. Importantly, the credibility of the United States as an arbiter of the process descended to new low levels in 1997, and there were signs at the end of the year that the Clinton Administration was increasingly frustrated with Prime Minister Benjamin Netanyahu.

Progress on the other tracks of the peace process was limited. Despite hope of a resumption of the Israeli–Syrian talks, this did not occur. Violence continued in southern Lebanon. The Israeli–Jordanian peace process also slowed, with King Hussein publicly expressing frustration with Netanyahu. No progress was made in the multilateral talks.

The wider regional events were also troubling. Tension rose in the Persian Gulf region, and internal fighting in Algeria, Egypt and the Kurdish regions of Iraq and Turkey persisted. Iraq continued to evade commitments to reveal the full nature of its weapons of mass destruction programmes. One hopeful note was sounded in Iran where the moderate Mohammed Khatami was elected president by an overwhelming majority. Time will tell whether he is able to enact reform or whether less moderate elements will force him to retreat.

This chapter reviews and analyses events in the region in 1997, with primary emphasis on the peace process. Section II concerns events in the Israeli–Palestinian talks. Section III reviews the other tracks of the peace process. Section IV reviews wider regional events. Section V offers some conclusions and points to areas of future concern.

II. The Israeli–Palestinian track

The Hebron Accord

As 1997 began it seemed possible that a new spirit would energize the peace process. Most importantly, agreement was reached on 15 January 1997 on the

SIPRI Yearbook 1998: Armaments, Disarmament and International Security

long-disputed Israeli troop redeployment from the West Bank city of Hebron.[1] The Hebron Accord specified that Israel would withdraw from most of Hebron within 10 days.[2] Furthermore, a Note for the Record,[3] prepared by the US Special Middle East Coordinator Dennis Ross, guaranteed continuing Israeli troop withdrawal from the West Bank. Israel agreed to carry out three stages of additional troop redeployments. The initial stage was set for the first week of March 1997, and the other two stages were to be completed not later than mid-1998.[4] However, the size of these troop redeployments was not specified, and neither party seemed satisfied with the Accord.[5]

Many Arab countries were ambivalent about the Hebron Accord. The credibility and the seriousness of US guarantees that the Accord would be implemented were questioned, and fears existed that it would not be honoured. On the positive side, there were hopes of a change in Netanyahu's hard-line policy towards the peace process. The Israeli agreement to withdraw from most of Hebron and Israel's commitment to further West Bank pull-outs appeared to mark a shift in Netanyahu's approach to the peace process. Hopes rose that further redeployment would occur and that ongoing negotiations to create air- and seaports in Gaza and a safe corridor for Palestinian transit between Gaza and the West Bank would bear fruit in 1997.

A new Israeli settlement

The renewed momentum of the peace process was shattered on 26 February 1997 when Netanyahu announced a decision to build 6500 Jewish housing units in an Arab sector of east Jerusalem at a site Israel called Har Homa—known as Jabal Abu Ghneim to the Palestinians.[6] The settlement plan cut off much of east Jerusalem and its Palestinian residents from the rest of the West Bank. The Palestinians warned of renewed violence, claiming that the Har Homa settlement was designed to pre-empt determination of the final borders

---

[1] For further information, see Jones, P., 'The Middle East peace process', *SIPRI Yearbook 1997: Armaments, Disarmament and International Security* (Oxford University Press: Oxford, 1997), pp. 92, 95–96.

[2] The Accord was prepared primarily in accordance with Article VII, Annex I of the 1995 Israeli–Palestinian Interim Agreement on the West Bank and the Gaza Strip (known as the Interim Agreement or Oslo II Agreement). The 400-page Interim Agreement was signed in Washington, DC, on 28 Sep. 1995. Excerpts from it are reproduced in Jones, P., 'The Middle East peace process', *SIPRI Yearbook 1996: Armaments, Disarmament and International Security* (Oxford University Press: Oxford, 1996), pp. 191–202. The text of Article VII, Annex I is available at Israel Ministry of Foreign Affairs, 'The Israeli–Palestinian Interim Agreement on the West Bank and the Gaza Strip', URL <http://www.israel-mfa.gov.il/peace/iaannex1.html#article7>, version current on 24 Feb. 1998.

[3] For the text of the Note for the Record see appendix 3A in this volume.

[4] The timetable was a compromise agreed by Arafat and Netanyahu. The PA's initial demand was for the withdrawal to be completed by Sep. 1997 as stipulated in the Interim Agreement, while Israel proposed that it be delayed until May 1999.

[5] The most important achievement on the part of Israel was a letter from then US Secretary of State Warren Christopher which recognized Israel's right to decide the area and size of the next 3 agreed phases of redeployment. See appendix 3A in this volume. See also 'New Hebron deal leaves Arafat with less West Bank land than he bargained for', *Mideast Mirror*, 15 Jan. 1997, pp. 2–3.

[6] For the official announcement see 'Ministerial Committee on Jerusalem Affairs Communiqué' (communicated by the Cabinet Secretariat), 26 Feb. 1997, URL <http://www.israel-mfa.gov.il/news/hhoma.html>, version current on 23 Jan. 1998.

of Jerusalem and would therefore violate the Oslo agreements.[7] Netanyahu approved the construction to shore up his coalition and to show that he was able to impose his strategy on Jerusalem. Various Arab countries accused Netanyahu of deliberately trying to stop the peace process.[8] US President Bill Clinton was also critical. The USA, however, used its veto against a draft United Nations Security Council resolution which criticized Har Homa, the first veto of two it would exercise in the Security Council on this issue in 1997.[9]

Renewed terrorism and an Israeli proposal

Compounding the Har Homa decision, Netanyahu announced in early March 1997 that Israel would withdraw from a further 9 per cent of the West Bank, but that only a small portion of the 9 per cent would be from areas exclusively controlled by Israel.[10] The Palestinians regarded the proposal as insufficient as they had expected a troop withdrawal from approximately one-third of the territory in question. These events sparked a new crisis and stirred frustration and despair in the Palestinian camp. When the negotiations stalled President Yasser Arafat suspended both security and intelligence cooperation with Israel.[11] Many Palestinians were convinced that Israel's Likud Government would never offer them anything that matched even their lowest aspirations.

In mid-March a new round of terrorism was launched against Israel.[12] Netanyahu argued that Arafat had indirectly given the 'green light' to terrorist groups. This accusation appeared to be corroborated later in 1997 when Arafat publicly embraced Abdel-Aziz Rantisi, founder of Hamas and leader of its political wing, the Islamic Resistance Movement.[13] The fear of new terrorist

[7] The text of the 13 Sep. 1993 Declaration of Principles on Interim Self-Government Arrangements (known as the DOP or Oslo Agreement) and the Interim Agreement (note 2) are together known as the Oslo agreements. The DOP is reproduced in *SIPRI Yearbook 1994* (Oxford University Press: Oxford, 1994), pp. 117–22.
[8] 'Time for the Arabs to respond to Netanyahu with actions rather than words—but how?', *Mideast Mirror*, 21 Mar. 1997, pp. 7–12; and Muncif al-Sulaymi, M., 'Interview with Usamah al-Baz, head of the Egyptian President's Office for Political Affairs', *al-Sharq* (London), 18 Mar. 1997, p. 6, in 'Egypt: Mubarak aide on peace process, Arab issues', Foreign Broadcast Information Service, *Daily Report– Near East and South Asia (FBIS-NES)*, FBIS-NES-97-054, 21 Mar. 1997.
[9] United Nations Security Council, 'Security Council fails to adopt resolution calling on Israel to refrain from East Jerusalem settlement activity', Press Release no. SC/6335 (7 Mar. 1997); and United Nations Security Council, 'Security Council again fails to adopt resolution on Israeli settlement', Press Release no. SC/6345 (21 Mar. 1997).
[10] Israel stated that it would withdraw from 9% of the West Bank, but 7% of the land came from Area B (territories under shared Israeli–Palestinian control) and only 2% from Area C (land controlled exclusively by Israel). For an explanation of the different areas see Jones (note 2), pp. 169–71.
[11] 'Palestinian crackdown on militants is refused', *International Herald Tribune*, 25 Mar. 1997, p. 8.
[12] On 21 Mar. a suicide bomber killed 3 people and injured 48 in a Tel Aviv café. On 30 July a bomb detonated leaving 13 dead and 168 wounded. In a 4 Sep. bombing 7 people died and 192 were injured. Marcus, R. and Yudelman, M., 'Bomb kills 3 in TA cafe', *Jerusalem Post* (international edn), 29 Mar. 1997, pp. 1–2; '"Walking bombs", live bullets, stones and barbs muddy the peacemaking', *Mideast Mirror*, 1 Apr. 1997, pp. 2–5; Borger, J., 'Israel caught in a cycle of barbarism', *The Guardian*, 31 July 1997, p. 6; and 'Netanyahu: we can't continue this way', *Jerusalem Post* (international edn), 13 Sep. 1997, pp. 1–2.
[13] Rodan, S. and Najib, M., 'Deal with the devil', *Jerusalem Post* (international edn), Aug. 1997, p. 7; and Dempsey, J., 'The fraternal thorn in Arafat's side', *Financial Times*, 29 Aug. 1997, p. 4.

attacks permeated 1997 and reduced confidence between Arafat and Netanyahu to the lowest level yet. In response to the attacks Israel sealed off the West Bank and Gaza Strip and withheld tax revenues from the PA, in contravention of the Oslo agreements.[14] Netanyahu also raised anew his claim that the PA had not unequivocally renounced the sections of the PLO Charter calling for the destruction of Israel. Arafat denied this and pointed to the vote which had been taken by an extraordinary meeting of the Palestinian National Council (PNC) on 24 April 1996, declaring the offending sections of the Charter null and void.[15] The Israeli Government responded that the PNC vote only expressed willingness to alter the Charter but had not amended it, a process which Israel believes will require the establishment of a legal committee to redraft the Charter and ratification of the new document by the PNC.[16]

During this period Netanyahu expressed the opinion that the 'Oslo formula' was not working and proposed that it should be abandoned in favour of a 'fast track' to the so-called Final Status issues.[17] He argued that the strategy of incremental concessions by each side, which was intended to build confidence, was not working and that each increment had become a source of tension and disagreement. The PA was deeply suspicious that the idea was a way for Israel to move to discussion of the Final Status issues without handing over the territory it had agreed to cede to the Palestinians under the Interim Agreement, and the USA tended to agree with this assessment.[18] The stage was thus set for a summer of deadlock in the peace process.

Internal problems for Netanyahu and Arafat

Netanyahu's decision to build Jewish settlements at Har Homa, coming so soon after the signing of the Hebron Accord, demonstrated his need to satisfy different constituencies within his coalition. His difficulties intensified after the appointment of Roni Bar-On as attorney-general in January 1997. Bar-On resigned immediately following the public outcry over his lack of qualifications for the post. The opposition claimed it was a politically motivated

---

[14] It is difficult to assess the economic effect of these actions, but the UN estimates that during the 38.5 effective closure days between 31 July and 17 Sep. the direct loss to West Bank and Gaza workers and businesses was $102 million ($2.65 million per day). For further information, see 'Closure on the West Bank and Gaza, August–September 1997', United Nations Office of the Special Coordinator in the Occupied Territories, the World Bank, URL <http://www.arts.mcgill.ca/MEPP/unsco/closure001097.html>, version current on 8 Jan. 1998.

[15] Jones (note 1), pp. 89–90.

[16] For further information, see Embassy of Israel, Stockholm, 'Arafat's letters to Clinton and Blair fail to amend the PLO Covenant', *PMR* [Prime Minister's Report], vol. 2, no. 3 (29 Jan. 1998). For opposition to Netanyahu's policy on this issue, see Commentary by Hemi Shalev, 'The propaganda has become policy', *Ma'ariv*, Hayom supplement (Tel Aviv), 4 Feb. 1998, p. 6, in 'Israel: Government's "propaganda" on peace process criticized', FBIS-NES-98-036, 6 Feb. 1998.

[17] Dowek, N., *Yedi'ot Aharonot*, Leshabat supplement (Tel Aviv), 21 Mar. 1997, p. 2, in 'Israel: full text of PM letter on Har Homa, Final Status', FBIS-NES-97-080, 24 Mar. 1997. These issues include: the status of the Palestinian Government, Jerusalem, Israeli settlements, borders, water, security arrangements and the rights of return of Palestinian refugees. Jones (note 2), pp. 162.

[18] Agence France Presse (Paris), 1403 GMT, 9 Apr. 1997, in 'West Bank: Arafat envoys take hard line ahead of crisis talks', FBIS-NES-97-099, 10 Apr. 1997; and Knowlton, B., 'Clinton sees Netanyahu, calling talks very specific', *International Herald Tribune*, 8 Apr. 1997, p. 1.

appointment in that Shas, the largest orthodox party in Netanyahu's coalition, had threatened to withdraw support for Israeli troop redeployment from Hebron if Bar-on were not appointed.[19] In April a police investigation was launched and recommended that Netanyahu be charged with breach of public trust. Prosecutors decided not to press charges against Netanyahu because of insufficient evidence, but he faced vigorous calls for his resignation.[20] The affair, known as 'Bar-On for Hebron', weakened Netanyahu and made him more dependent on support from the minority, nationalist and religious parties. Perhaps most importantly for the peace process, the hope of a joint Likud–Labour government was dashed. By November the Israeli–US relationship had deteriorated so far that Clinton refused to meet Netanyahu when he travelled to the USA. Subsequently, it deteriorated further when Netanyahu announced additional settlements on occupied land.[21]

The PA seemed to be waiting to find out whether there would be any substantial changes in the government as a result of the Bar-On affair. By the end of July, however, it was Arafat's turn to face a crisis when it was estimated in a report by a Palestinian commission of inquiry that up to one-half of the PA's budget had been misspent by corrupt members of the cabinet. The commission urged Arafat to dissolve the cabinet and put some of its ministers on trial for alleged wrongdoing.[22] Shortly thereafter, speculation arose about Arafat's health. The reports were denied by Palestinian officials who also dismissed rumours that a search for Arafat's successor had begun.[23]

The USA resumes its role

The United States played a limited public role during the summer stalemate, having decided to assume a behind-the-scenes role in the negotiations. By August, however, the USA had become more publicly active.[24] This was possibly because of the fear that the US status in the Arab countries was deteriorating along with the peace process, thus posing a growing danger to broader US strategic interests in the region. At the same time, the European Union (EU) was making efforts to assume a greater role as an arbiter in the peace process, a move welcomed by the Arab governments. The EU is seen as a possible counterpart to what the Arab countries regard as the USA's blatantly

---

[19] It was further rumoured that Bar-On had promised Aryeh Deri, founder and leader of Shas and on trial for corruption since 1993, a plea bargain if Deri were made attorney-general. See report by A. Hasson of Israeli Channel 1 television, cited in 'Elyakim Rubinstein named attorney-general as police investigate "Bar-On for Hebron" affair', *Mideast Mirror*, 27 Jan. 1997, pp. 5–6.

[20] Dempsey, J. and Machlis, A., 'No charges for Netanyahu', *Financial Times*, 21 Apr. 1997, p. 1.

[21] Sharrock, D., 'Netanyahu defies US in pledge on settlements', *The Guardian*, 24 Nov. 1997, p. 7.

[22] Borger, J., 'Arafat told to sack his cabinet', *The Guardian*, 30 July 1997, p. 7; and Khalifah, I., *al-Hadath* (Amman), 28 July 1997, p. 10, in 'West Bank: report "uncovered" "corruption" cases in PA', FBIS-NES-97-211, 31 July 1997.

[23] Zananiri, E. M., 'Power struggle within the PLO', *Jerusalem Times* (Jerusalem), 21 Nov. 1997, p. 3, in 'West Bank: article views reports of PLO "power struggle"', FBIS-NES-97-328, 26 Nov. 1997; and *al-Hayat*, cited in 'Security chiefs are reported maneuvering to succeed Arafat', *International Herald Tribune*, 12 Nov. 1997, p. 1.

[24] Erlanger, S. and Mitchell, A., 'U.S. decided to spur Mideast talks', *International Herald Tribune*, 11 Aug. 1997, p. 9.

pro-Israel stance. However, Arab governments are aware that the EU does not have the same ability to decisively influence the region's security as does the USA. The major role that the EU plays in the peace process is on the economic level, while simultaneously maintaining a supportive and complementary political role.[25] With the assistance of the EU Middle East envoy, Miguel Moratinos, Israeli Foreign Minister David Levy and Arafat agreed to meet in late July in Brussels and resume high-level negotiations.[26]

The first public sign of US activity came in early August when US Secretary of State Madeleine Albright gave her first major speech on the peace process.[27] She rejected Netanyahu's proposal to expedite the talks, outlining instead a blueprint which featured a two-track approach: accelerating negotiations on a permanent settlement while simultaneously carrying through the commitments of the Interim Agreement. Albright made it clear that it was essential for both parties to honour their commitments. For the Palestinians, this involved a total effort to combat terrorist infrastructure. For Israel, a thinly veiled reference was made to the need to halt settlement activity.[28] Albright promised to go to the region if there was hope of progress, and it was rumoured that a compromise formula to restart the talks was being developed.

By the time Albright went to the Middle East, however, renewed terrorism had caused tension to mount.[29] Albright visited several regional capitals and was commended by many observers for her even-handed approach to the issues. Her only achievement, however, was in laying the foundation for Levy and Palestinian senior official Mahmoud Abbas (known as Abu Mazen) to meet in New York shortly thereafter.[30]

A round of meetings was launched which did not make significant progress. As the November Middle East/North Africa Economic Conference in Doha, Qatar,[31] approached, the USA appeared to accept some Israeli ideas regarding the need to break down the issues into more manageable topics. Palestinians charged that this was giving in to Israel's desire to separate the day-to-day process from the main issues of Israeli settlements and redeployment. Arab states saw the new approach as an effort by the USA to save the economic

---

[25] For more detailed information, see 'The role of the European Union in the Middle East peace process and its future assistance', 16 Jan. 1998, URL <http://europa.eu.int/rapid/start/cgi/guesten.ksh?p-action.gettxt=g&doc=IP/98/37>, version current on 26 Jan. 1998.

[26] Radio Monte Carlo (Paris), 1530 GMT, 25 July 1997, in 'West Bank: Moratinos on 'Arafat–Levi meeting, coordination with US', FBIS-NES-97-206, 29 July 1997.

[27] The 6 Aug. 1997 speech was delivered at the National Press Club in Washington, DC. US Department of State, 'The Israeli–Palestinian peace process', URL <http://secretary.state.gov/www/statements/970806.html>, version current on 24 Feb. 1998.

[28] This was expressed by Albright in her speech as a need for Israel to halt 'unhelpful unilateral acts [which] is central to maintaining mutual confidence'. However, during her visit to the region Albright publicly demanded that Israel refrain from expanding or building new Jewish settlements on disputed land to create a suitable climate for talks.

[29] Borger, J., 'Seven dead, 192 hurt in triple suicide bombing in Jerusalem', *The Guardian*, 5 Sep. 1997.

[30] US Department of State, 'Secretary of State Madeleine K. Albright: Statement and Press Conference following meeting with Israeli Foreign Minister Levy and PLO Secretary General Abu Mazen', 29 Sep. 1997, URL <http://secretary.state.gov/www/statements/970929.html>, version current on 24 Feb. 1998.

[31] The conference is discussed further in the subsection 'The multilateral track' in this chapter.

conference by giving an illusion of progress. There were also rumours that the USA was eager to show an accomplishment in the Israeli–Palestinian negotiations because of the worsening confrontation between it and Iraq.[32]

In late November the Israeli Cabinet gave conditional approval to a long-delayed second redeployment without setting a timetable or specifying its scope. The process was prolonged by continuing disagreement within the government over the principles of a final settlement, which in turn would be the basis for a specific decision on troop withdrawal.[33] The approval was also coupled with tough demands on the Palestinians to fight terrorism. It was rumoured that Netanyahu was considering a withdrawal from an additional 6–8 per cent of the West Bank, despite the fact that the USA suggested withdrawal from at least 12 per cent of the area.[34] The Palestinian negotiators accused Netanyahu of insincerity in using the proposal to try to divert attention from his internal political troubles (which included a nationwide strike and the threatened resignation of his foreign minister and, subsequently, his defence minister[35]) and to rebuild his deteriorating relationship with the USA.

Several meetings between Albright and Arafat and Albright and Netanyahu were held near the end of 1997. Only slight progress was made, however, and it was decided that Clinton would meet Arafat and Netanyahu separately in Washington in mid-January 1998.[36] At the end of the year the hope of progress on a safe corridor between Gaza and the West Bank and the opening of air- and seaports in Gaza were still unrealized. Efforts to secure a timetable for Israeli redeployment and to reach an agreement on how much land would be handed over to the Palestinians had also failed.

III. The other tracks of the peace process

The Israeli–Syrian track and events in Lebanon

The overall tone of 1997 on this track ranged from tentative hints of a possible renewal of talks to warnings that armed conflict was a distinct possibility in the foreseeable future. However, no official talks were held between Israel and Syria in 1997, and the level of violence in Lebanon remained high.

On the hopeful side, rumours emerged in January of a possible resumption of talks. By February, reportedly under pressure from the USA, Netanyahu

---

[32] 'Sudden and suspicious US pampering of Palestinians', *al-Quds al-Arabi*, (London), 5 Nov. 1997, in 'West Bank: US seen "pampering" Palestinian delegation to talks', FBIS-NES-97-310, 6 Nov. 1997; and Erlanger, S., 'US feels the pressure to break deadlock in Mideast peace talks', *International Herald Tribune*, 8–9 Nov. 1997, p. 6. See also the subsection 'The Iraqi situation' in this chapter.

[33] Bushinsky, J. et al., 'Cabinet expected to okay redeployment package', *Jerusalem Post* (international edn), 6 Dec. 1997, pp. 1–2; and Schmemann, S., 'Israeli cabinet supports conditional withdrawal', *International Herald Tribune*, 1 Dec. 1997, pp 1, 4.

[34] Schmemann, S., 'Netanyahu is threatened on new front', *International Herald Tribune*, 26 Nov. 1997, pp. 1, 6.

[35] Levy resigned on 4 Jan. 1998, and shortly thereafter Defence Minister Yitzhak Mordechai also threatened to resign unless progress was made in the peace process. Sharrock, D., 'Israeli coalition crumbles', *The Guardian*, 5 Jan. 1997, p. 3.

[36] Erlanger, S., 'Clinton to see Netanyahu and Arafat separately', *International Herald Tribune*, 19 Dec. 1997, p. 6.

hinted that renewed talks might be possible and that Israel was prepared to accept UN Security Council Resolution 242 as the basis for discussions.[37] Resolution 242 mandates the return of all territory seized in conflict in exchange for peace and is seen by many as one of the fundamental bases of the peace process. Hope that a breakthrough had been achieved was dashed when it became clear that Netanyahu had his own interpretation of the resolution: that it meant giving back some territory but not necessarily all of it.[38]

This stand ended the possibility of a resumption of the talks. Syria stated that it would not return to the talks unless they resumed on the basis of the progress made before the Israeli elections, which Syria claimed included a commitment by then Prime Minister Shimon Peres to withdraw from the Golan Heights to the 4 June 1967 border in return for full peace. Senior Syrian officials were critical of Netanyahu for trying to avoid this 'basic' commitment and of the USA for not putting pressure on him.[39] The Syrian Government began circulating accounts of these talks.[40] If Syria hoped to bring Netanyahu back to the table with these detailed leaks, the tactic was a failure. There was no more talk of possible compromise in 1997.

Meanwhile, there was considerable talk, most of it from Israel, of a renewed threat of conflict.[41] Israel also pointed to intensive efforts in Syria's chemical weapon and missile programmes and to Syria's renewed ties to its traditional supplier of arms, Russia, to bolster claims that Syria was preparing an attack to force a breakthrough in the talks.[42] Israeli officials pointed out that there was no hope of Syria defeating Israel but expressed fear that Syria was calculating that it could impose a heavy price on Israel's intransigence in the negotiations, thereby forcing a more moderate approach. Nothing seems to have come of these claims. It was later revealed that at least one source of fear regarding Syrian intentions was suspect. An Israeli agent was arrested for having passed false intelligence which wrongly claimed that Syria was not serious about the peace process and was still reserving the military option.[43] In 1997 Syria made use of a little-known and rarely invoked provision of the 1974 Separation of Forces Agreement between Israel and Syria when it requested

[37] Makovsky, D., Kuttler, H. and David, D., 'Netanyahu optimistic for restart of Syrian track', *Jerusalem Post* (international edn), 8 Feb. 1997, p. 1; Waldmeir, P., 'Netanyahu hints at softer line on Golan', *Financial Times*, 16 Feb. 1997, p. 3; and UN Security Council Resolution 242, UN document S/RES/242, 22 Nov. 1967.

[38] Makovsky, D., 'Netanyahu "accepts" that 242 applies to Golan Heights', *Jerusalem Post* (international edn), 8 Mar. 1997.

[39] See the remarks of Syrian Vice-President Abdelhalim Khaddam in a 7 Feb. interview. MBC Television (London), 1800 GMT, 7 Feb. 1997, in 'Syria, Israel: Khaddam says no signs yet of change in U.S. stand', FBIS-NES-97-027, 11 Feb. 1997.

[40] Lippman, T., 'Syrian says Peres agreed to Golan deal', *International Herald Tribune*, 30 Jan. 1997, p. 2.

[41] Rodan, S., '"It is not a game anymore": the Israeli Army is preparing for war with Syria this year', *Jerusalem Post* (international edn), 11 Jan. 1997; and Collins, L., 'Shahak: Syria is preparing for war', *Jerusalem Post* (international edn), 9 Aug. 1997. Lt.-Gen. Amnon Shahak is Israel's Chief of Staff.

[42] Comments of Israeli Defence Minister Yitzhak Mordechai in 'Israel claims that Syria is making VX nerve gas', *Jane's Defence Weekly*, 7 May 1997, p. 6; and Finnegan, P. and Rodan, S., 'Syria, Russia SA-12 missile talks worry Israel', *Defense News*, 30 June–6 July 1997, p. 4. See also chapter 11 in this volume.

[43] Schiff, Z., 'False information influenced Israel's moves with Syria', *Haaretz* (English edn), 3 Dec. 1997.

the UN Disengagement Observer Force to conduct a short-notice inspection of Israeli positions on the Golan.[44]

Rumours surfaced of crack-downs on opposition figures and corrupt officials in the Syrian capital, which may have signalled that President Hafez-al Assad was either preparing the ground for his succession or seeking to prevent it.[45] Such reports must be read with scepticism. The idea that the Syrian regime may be unstable after Assad leaves office has been raised by Israel before as a way of saying that it cannot make security concessions which could be taken advantage of by a successor who does not regard himself as committed to peace.

Whatever the truth of such claims, 1997 ended as it began on the Israeli–Syrian track: with no apparent progress or prospect of the talks resuming, despite rumours of infrequent 'secret' meetings between Israeli and Syrian emissaries.

Lebanon

Meanwhile, the stalemate in Lebanon dragged on. Israel continued to say that it would withdraw unilaterally from its self-proclaimed security zone in the south of the country, provided adequate security guarantees could be obtained from the guerrilla groups operating there and from the Lebanese and Syrian governments. Each of these parties refused, the Lebanese Government probably at the insistence of Syria, which views Israel's presence in southern Lebanon as a way of embroiling the Israeli Army in an unpopular and costly occupation.[46]

The sporadic violence was punctuated by deadly incidents. In February two Israeli military helicopters ferrying troops to southern Lebanon collided, killing over 70 people. Although these deaths were not the result of enemy action, they shocked the nation and gave rise to another round of questioning over the seemingly endless operation.[47] As casualties mounted, Israelis routinely began to refer to Lebanon as Israel's 'Viet Nam', a place where they could not win but from which they could not withdraw.[48]

---

[44] Blanche, E., 'Syrian fears checked by inspection of the Golan', *Jane's Defence Weekly*, 24 Sep. 1997, p. 14. The inspection reportedly took place over 2 days approximately 6 months before it became public knowledge. A senior Israeli officer said that it helped to 'calm the security situation'. For background, see Israel Ministry of Foreign Affairs, 'Separation of Forces Agreement between Israel and Syria', 31 May 1974, URL <http://www.israel-mfa.gov.il/prace/syr1974.html>, version current on 2 Feb. 1998; and United Nations Peacekeeping Operations, 'United Nations Disengagement Observer Force', URL <http://www.un.org/Depts/DPKO/Missions/undof.htm>, version current on 10 Feb. 1998.

[45] Jehl, D., 'New riddles in Assad's Damascus', *International Herald Tribune*, 29 Jan. 1997, p. 1.

[46] For more background on the Lebanese situation, see Jones (note 1), pp. 87–89.

[47] Collins, L., O'Sullivan, A. and Keinon, H., 'Nation unites in mourning', *Jerusalem Post* (international edn), 15 Feb. 1997, pp. 1–2; and Dempsey, J., 'Israel agonises over presence in south Lebanon', *Financial Times*, 11 Feb. 1997, p. 4.

[48] Hirst, D., 'War wins in "Valley of Death"', *The Guardian*, 4 Mar. 1997. Against these developments, some Israeli officers did comment that the monitoring committee established after Israel's invasion of Lebanon in 1996 was doing a creditable job in at least holding down the number of civilian casualties in the area. O'Sullivan, A., 'Against all odds', *Jerusalem Post* (international edn), 26 Apr. 1997.

In August, after a particularly heavy round of fighting between Israeli forces and guerrilla groups in southern Lebanon, Katyusha rockets were launched against a town in the upper Galilee area.[49] This attack was followed on 19 August 1997 by a barrage of over 80 missiles, prompting Netanyahu to vow revenge.[50] Most observers thought this would take the, by now, standard form of aerial bombardment of suspected Hezbollah sites and surrounding villages by the Israeli Air Force. Although such strikes were launched as a matter of course, it soon became clear that Netanyahu had something else in mind. Unfortunately, the commando raid Netanyahu ordered to carry out his threat went terribly wrong. The seaborne Israeli force encountered a group of Lebanese Army soldiers and Hezbollah fighters. Israel was forced to withdraw ignominiously after suffering 11 deaths in a fierce fire-fight.[51] Coming on the heels of another terrorist attack in Israel, the news from Lebanon contributed to Netanyahu's decision to halt moves to restart the Palestinian track of the peace process.[52]

The Israeli–Jordanian talks

Despite the willingness of Jordan's King Hussein to develop closer relations with Israel than any other Arab state has done, 1997 was a difficult year for the Israeli–Jordanian relationship. Efforts to develop the relationship centred on the various working groups established by their peace treaty.[53] While much of this work was successful, it went on behind closed doors. The publicly known events of the year were discouraging.

On 13 March a Jordanian soldier, who was later found to be mentally disturbed, opened fire on a group of Israeli schoolgirls touring Jordan, killing seven of them. King Hussein was deeply shocked by the incident, and his decision to visit Israel and personally apologize to the families for the outrage did much to preserve his image as a leader committed to peace.[54] The king was, however, criticized by some in Jordan for going to Israel.

The pressures to which King Hussein was subject grew dramatically in late September when Israel attempted to assassinate the political leader of Hamas in Amman. Two Israeli agents, who had used faked Canadian passports to enter Jordan, approached Khaled Meshal on the street and injected him with a poison. The agents were caught, and their identities soon became apparent. This resulted in reportedly furious calls from King Hussein to Netanyahu and a visit to Israel by the Crown Prince of Jordan to demand that Israel supply an

---

[49] Jehl, D., 'Rockets from Lebanon hit Israel', *International Herald Tribune*, 9–10 Aug. 1997, p. 2.

[50] Borger, J., 'Israel "will strike back" at Hizbullah', *The Guardian*, 20 Aug. 1997, p. 7.

[51] 'Eleven Israeli commandos die in south Lebanon ambush', *Jane's Defence Weekly*, 10 Sep. 1997, p. 3.

[52] Borger, J., 'Killings wreck Israel peace', *The Guardian*, 6 Sep. 1997, p. 1.

[53] The text of the Treaty of Peace Between the State of Israel and the Hashemite Kingdom of Jordan, 26 Oct. 1994, is reproduced in *SIPRI Yearbook 1995: Armaments, Disarmament and International Security* (Oxford University Press: Oxford, 1995), pp. 197–203.

[54] 'Seven schoolgirls shot dead on Jordanian border', *Mideast Mirror*, 13 Mar. 1997, pp. 1–4.

antidote to the poison, threatening to cut diplomatic ties with Israel if it were not forthcoming.[55]

Over the next week it became clear that a larger deal was being worked out as Israel released Sheikh Ahmad Yassin, the spiritual leader of Hamas, who had been languishing in poor health in an Israeli prison for eight years. He was serving a life sentence for ordering suicide bombings. Yassin was flown to Amman, where he was greeted by King Hussein and Arafat.[56] He then returned to Gaza. Compounding the fiasco, from Israel's point of view, Netanyahu released over 50 more Palestinian prisoners as part of an apparent exchange. The undoubted 'winner' in the incident was King Hussein, who managed to secure the freedom of Yassin after many years of ineffectual attempts by Arafat. For Netanyahu, the affair was a disaster.[57]

Perhaps the greatest long-term consequence of the affair was that it appears to have been the 'final straw' for King Hussein. In an extraordinary interview with a Western journalist some weeks later he bluntly said that he was fed up with Netanyahu and no longer felt he could trust the Israeli Prime Minister as a partner in negotiations, although he did make the point that there was no going back in the peace process and that he still believed that the Israeli people wanted peace even if Netanyahu did not.[58] If these remarks truly reflect the king's thinking, they signal that Israel's sole real friend in the Arab world is no longer willing to give the Israeli Government the benefit of the doubt, at least as long as the present government is in office.

The multilateral track

The multilateral track of the peace process has suffered greatly as a result of the slow-down in the bilateral talks. Originally intended to serve as a mechanism for involving a greater number of states in the peace process and allowing certain issues to be tackled on a wider regional basis, the multilateral talks are dependent on progress in the bilateral talks for their political sanction.[59]

Composed of five working groups and a steering committee, the multilateral groups met rarely in 1997 and accomplished little of substance.[60] The Refugee Working Group did hold two meetings in 1997, both at the working level. The

[55] LaGuardia, A., 'Sick Hamas chief flown to Jordanian "peace deal"', *Electronic Telegraph*, issue 861 (2 Oct. 1997), URL <http://www.telegraph.co.uk>, version current on 2 Oct. 1997; and Schmemann, S., 'Netanyahu faces crisis over failed Hamas hit', *International Herald Tribune*, 6 Oct. 1997, p. 1. The incident also caused a minor flap in Israel's normally good relations with Canada, which recalled its ambassador for a period of 'consultations'.

[56] Dempsey, J., 'Ailing Hamas leader freed "in shady deal"', *Financial Times*, 2 Oct. 1997, p. 6.

[57] Ayub, T., *Jordan Times* (Amman), Internet version, 5 Oct. 1997, in 'Jordan: Jordanian minister: Israel to release Palestinian prisoners', FBIS-NES-97-278, 7 Oct. 1997.

[58] Lancaster, J., 'Hussein accuses Netanyahu of betraying him', *International Herald Tribune*, 1–2 Nov. 1997, pp. 1, 4.

[59] Jones (note 2), pp. 181–88; Jones (note 1) pp. 97–100; and Peters, J., *Pathways to Peace: The Multilateral Arab–Israeli Peace Talks* (Royal Institute of International Affairs: London, 1996).

[60] The working groups are the Arms Control and Regional Security Working Group (ACRS), the Environment Working Group, the Refugee Working Group, the Regional Economic Development Working Group (REDWG) and the Working Group on Water Resources. They are discussed in Jones (note 1), pp. 97–100.

first meeting was held in Paris in May and the second in Aqaba in December. Neither meeting produced any results of note. None of the other multilateral groups met in 1997, the first year this had happened since the peace process began.

An offshoot of the multilateral talks are the annual regional economic meetings sponsored by the Geneva-based World Economic Forum. The first two summit meetings (held in Casablanca in 1994, and in Amman in 1995) had been successful in bringing together regional businesses to explore the new opportunities provided by the peace process. The third meeting, held in Cairo in 1996, was less successful, as the difficulties of the process had already begun to be felt. The 1997 conference was held in Doha, Qatar, and was not well attended. Many Arab states, including key powers such as Egypt and Saudi Arabia, refused to participate. Ministerial participation was weak, with Israel's Foreign Minister Levy staying away and US Secretary of State Albright only making a perfunctory appearance. Although business deals were entered into, the wider political objectives of the peace process were not met. The conference issued a final communiqué in which, for the first time, the host of the next meeting was not named, thereby causing speculation as to whether or not a fourth meeting would take place.[61]

A final set of multilateral discussions involving some regional states also moved slowly in 1997. The European Union's Euro-Mediterranean Partnership (also known as the Barcelona Initiative) continued to search for ways to promote dialogue and development between Europe and the southern side of the Mediterranean.[62] Although a number of academic workshops were held, official discussions were slow for two reasons. First, the slow-down of the peace process also affected the Euro-Mediterranean Partnership talks. Second, many regional states continued to protest at Europe's unwillingness to allow them to export agricultural goods to Europe without tariffs, while insisting that regional tariffs on European finished goods should be lowered.

IV. Wider regional events

The peace process did not exist in a vacuum. Other events took place and affected the process, as they, in turn, were affected by it. Critical events of note were: the Iranian presidential election, the ongoing dispute between the international community and Iraq, the emerging relationship between Israel and Turkey, and continuing violence in several countries.

---

[61] Doha Declaration, MENA Economic Summit, 16–18 Nov. 1997, URL <http://www.usis.usemb.se/regional/nea/econmena/dohadecl.htm>, version current on 10 Feb. 1998.

[62] On 28 Nov. 1995, in Barcelona, the EU and 12 Mediterranean participants (Algeria, Cyprus, Egypt, Israel, Jordan, Lebanon, Malta, Morocco, the Palestinian Authority, Syria, Tunisia and Turkey) signed a declaration concerning the new Euro-Mediterranean Partnership which creates a framework for political, economic, cultural and social ties between the partners. European Union, 'Euro-Mediterranean Partnership: implementation of the multilateral aspects of the Barcelona Declaration', 10 Feb. 1997, URL <http://europa.eu.int/rapid/start/cgi/guesten.ksh?p_action.gettxt=gt&doc=MEMO/97/15|0|AGED&lg=EN>, version current on 26 Jan. 1998; and Jones (note 2), p. 100.

The Iranian election

The election of Mohammed Khatami as President of Iran was a hopeful sign for Iranian moderates. Khatami won the post on 23 May 1997, soundly and unexpectedly defeating the candidate of the more hard-line faction, Parliamentary Speaker Akbar Nateq Nouri. Khatami polled 70 per cent of the vote, all the more impressive as it included an overwhelming majority of the young and women, who comprise the two largest and fastest-growing groups of voters. Even those who opposed Khatami were forced to concede that his victory constituted a clear signal that the people of Iran want change.[63] It also seems to indicate widespread revulsion with the high levels of corruption and favouritism of the religious élite and their allies.

However, Khatami's election victory does not guarantee that reforms will succeed. Conservative forces and the clerical establishment still hold most of the power in Tehran. When Khatami named his new cabinet in August 1997 conservative opponents criticized it for 'ideological weakness' and called for its more liberal members to be ousted.[64] Although the cabinet survived, the beginnings of a conservative backlash were apparent. Perhaps the greatest problem which Khatami faces is that Iran's supreme leader, Ayatollah Khamenei, opposes the economic and social reforms for which the new president stands. Khatami will need all his skills and allies to translate his election victory into far-reaching reforms.

Other news involving Iran in 1997 was mixed. A German court ruled in April 1997 that Iran had sponsored the 1992 assassination of political opponents who had taken refuge in Germany. The ruling sparked a crisis in Iran–EU relations, as members of the EU withdrew their ambassadors.[65] Iran accused the court of issuing a false verdict under political pressure. The dispute was not resolved until the end of 1997, when EU ambassadors returned to Iran with neither side accepting that it had acted wrongly.

Meanwhile, the USA and Israel continued to accuse Iran of trying to acquire weapons of mass destruction and missiles and of supporting terrorists opposed to the peace process, both of which accusations Iran denies.[66] At the same time, many commentators in the USA called upon the Clinton Administration to review its Iran policy, criticizing it as ineffective and detrimental to long-

---

[63] *Tehran Times*, 14 May 1997, p. 4, in 'Iran: women's society backs Khatami for president', FBIS-NES-97-139, 22 May 1997; *Asharq al-Awsat* and *al-Hayat* cited in 'Iran: a scent of freedom in the air', *Mideast Mirror*, 22 Aug. 1997, p. 14; and IRNA (Tehran), 26 May 1997, in 'Iran: congratulatory messages "pour in" for Khatami', FBIS-NES-97-146, 28 May 1997.

[64] Hirst, D., 'Khatami's new cabinet will test the power of ayatollahs in Iran', *The Guardian*, 19 Aug. 1997, p. 7; and 'Editorial: "nightmare awaits those who misinterpret Khatami's victory"', *Iran News* (Tehran), 23 Aug. 1997, pp. 2, 13, in 'Iran: article warns West not to overestimate Khatami's victory', FBIS-NES-97-240, 29 Aug. 1997.

[65] Norton-Taylor, R. and Staunton, D., 'Iranian terror sparks crisis', *The Guardian*, 11 Apr. 1997, p. 1. The USA quickly praised the EU for this action, claiming vindication of its policies towards Iran. Clark, B., 'US applauds European stand on Iran', *Financial Times*, 12–13 Apr. 1997, p. 3. Greece was the only EU state not to withdraw its ambassador.

[66] Rodan, S. and Yudin, P., 'Lawmakers, Israel lambaste slow U.S. action on Russia–Iran trade', *Defense News*, 29 Sep.–5 Oct. 1997.

term US interests.⁶⁷ Although the administration maintained its hard line on Iran, there were also signs that the USA was prepared to explore ways of coexisting with Tehran. In April, for example, the US Government officially placed the Mujahideen-e Khalq on its list of terrorist organizations.⁶⁸ Based largely in Iraq, the Mujahideen-e Khalq has been one of the Iranian Government's most vicious opponents and has been responsible for numerous terrorist attacks against Iranian leaders and targets. The US Government's decision to place it on a list of terrorist organizations which it is illegal for US citizens to be involved with or support may have been a signal to Iran regarding the USA's desire to explore the possibility of coexistence.

For its part, Iran maintained its criticism of the USA, Israel and the peace process and moved to develop closer ties with its Persian Gulf neighbours. This last policy was motivated by a desire to persuade the other states of the region that US forces should leave the area. Interestingly, however, President Khatami did indicate in December 1997 that he would welcome the idea of a 'dialogue' between individual citizens of Iran and the USA on 'civilizational issues'.⁶⁹

The Iraqi situation

Iraqi President Saddam Hussein continued to play 'cat and mouse' with the international community in 1997. In particular, he spent much of the year trying to get the United Nations Special Commission on Iraq (UNSCOM) out of the country, despite the fact that the UN believes that he has not revealed the true extent of his weapons of mass destruction programmes.⁷⁰ Appealing to the undoubted suffering which ordinary Iraqis have suffered during the sanctions (although neglecting to mention that his own policies are responsible for intensifying and prolonging that suffering), President Hussein complained that they appeared to be without end. He said that his regime required a cut-off date by which it could expect sanctions to be lifted and increasingly urged that future cooperation would be based on the provision of such a date. Although the UK and the USA remained firm, other countries such as France and Russia appeared willing to concede that Hussein's arguments were valid. France and Russia were doubtless influenced by their economic interest in rehabilitating Iraq to allow it to pay off the debts it owes them and become once again a customer for their goods and services. Many Arab commentators also decried the hardships being suffered by the Iraqi people and pointed to US support of Israel and a desire to 'crush' Iraq as evidence of an anti-Arab bias.⁷¹

⁶⁷ See, e.g., Brzezinski, Z., Scowcroft, B. and Murphy, R., 'Differentiated containment', *Foreign Affairs*, vol. 76, no. 3 (May/June 1997).
⁶⁸ US Department of State, Office of the Coordinator for Counterterrorism, 'Patterns of global terrorism 1996', release date Apr. 1997, URL <http://www.usis.usemb.se/terror/rpt1996/appb.html>, version current on 15 Jan. 1998.
⁶⁹ While noting that it would prefer an official dialogue, the USA did 'welcome' Khatami's remarks. Jehl, D., 'Iran leader extends hand to Americans', *International Herald Tribune*, 5 Dec. 1997.
⁷⁰ See also chapter 11 in this volume.
⁷¹ 'Editorial: "collective Arab responsibility"', *Jordan Times* (Amman), Internet version, 13 Oct. 1997, in 'Jordan: *Jordan Times* urges Arabs to intervene with UN to save Iraq', FBIS-NES-97-286,

By 29 October the tension had reached a head. Hussein ordered the US members of UNSCOM to leave Iraq, a clear violation of his authority under the terms of UNSCOM's establishment.[72] Rather than accept Iraqi ultimatums as to how he should conduct operations the head of UNSCOM withdrew the entire operation and referred the matter to the Security Council.[73] Tension increased when the UK and the USA augmented their forces in the region in anticipation of violence. Hussein appeared to back down on 17 November and went on to accept a compromise brokered by Russia by which UNSCOM would resume its operations while Russia would work to have the sanctions eased.[74] By early 1998, however, it was becoming clear that this was a temporary respite and that the crisis was moving towards a confrontation between Iraq and the USA.

Whether this brinkmanship is actually winning anything for Hussein is not clear. He is certainly putting the issue back on the international agenda and exposing weaknesses in the Security Council position against him. However, the sanctions are in place as firmly as ever, and US determination to see them through has not abated. Hussein is also gaining periods of reduced monitoring by UNSCOM during which he is probably re-hiding materials in danger of being discovered, particularly with respect to his biological weapon programme. Indeed, there is some suspicion that Hussein's objections to the activities of the UNSCOM inspectors and to the composition of the UNSCOM inspection teams coincide with impending discoveries of new aspects of his weapon programmes by UNSCOM inspectors.

Other events in the region

The growing defence ties between Israel and Turkey were further strengthened in 1997 and constitute an important long-term trend in regional affairs. The moderate Islamist Turkish Government of Prime Minister Necmettin Erbakan, although clearly uncomfortable with these ties, could do little to stop its generals from pursuing them. Indeed, by 18 June 1997 Erbakan had been forced to resign by those same generals, concerned that his party represents a possible abandonment of the strict policy of secularism which is one of the foundations of the modern Turkish state.[75] Seeing in its ties with Israel and the USA a bulwark against Islamic movements in the region, and a useful counter to other regional states with whom Turkey has disputes (such as Syria), Turkey placed large orders with Israeli defence industries in 1997 and announced that a maritime search-and-rescue exercise with Israel and the USA would take

---

15 Oct. 1997; and Barakat, H., 18 July, in *al-Hayat* cited in 'Arab leaders urged to work for end of Iraq sanctions', *Mideast Mirror*, 25 July 1997, pp. 15–17.

[72] United Nations Security Council Resolution 687, UN document S/RES/687, 3 Apr. 1991; and United Nations Security Council Resolution 1137, UN document S/RES/1137, 12 Nov. 1997.

[73] United Nations Security Council, 'Security Council condemns Iraq's expulsion of Special Commission members', Press Release no. SC/6442 (13 Nov. 1997); and Silber, L., Littlejohns, M. and Clark, B., 'Iraq expels US inspectors', *Financial Times*, 14 Nov. 1997.

[74] Fitchett, J., 'Iraq hints at a compromise', *International Herald Tribune*, 17 Nov. 1997; and Silber, L. and Gardner, D., 'Russia acts to defuse Iraq conflict', *Financial Times*, 18 Nov. 1997.

[75] 'Outlook for Turkey: more of the same', *Mideast Mirror*, 24 June 1997, pp. 13–18.

place in early 1998. This latter event was greeted with particular suspicion by many Arab states, seeing in it the beginnings of a military pact between the three states, despite vigorous denials.[76]

Algeria's bloody civil war continued in 1997, despite elections which seemed to hold the promise of political normalization. As the year ended, the levels of violence reached new and appalling heights, prompting the international community to take renewed interest. The Algerian Government maintained that the terrorism was the work of Islamic extremists, but suspicions were raised that the government was using the problem to justify a continuing suspension of democratic reforms. The year ended with growing calls for an international presence or fact-finding mission, which the Algerian Government rejects.[77] In Egypt, Islamic terrorists struck in Cairo and in Luxor, despite the government's recent record of success in crushing their movement. The second of these two attacks was particularly vicious and may have serious consequences for the important tourist industry. In both cases, the continuing violence was partly blamed on outside support, but these claims do not completely answer the question as to how such movements could be spawned in these countries. Finally, fighting in the Kurdish regions of Iraq and Turkey continued, sometimes quite fiercely.

V. Conclusions

It is now six years since the Middle East peace process began. That period has witnessed compelling breakthroughs on a series of disputes which were once thought to be intractable. However, a sense of foreboding has again descended on the region. Although there does not seem to be any prospect of 'going back' to the way things were before the 1991 Madrid conference, which launched the Middle East peace talks, and the 1993 and 1995 Oslo agreements, this does not mean that progress towards a peaceful resolution of the Arab–Israeli conflict is inevitable. The experience of 1997 shows that the failure of the peace process can mutate into a new basis for confrontation and violence which is made more destructive by the new situation in which Israelis and Palestinians find themselves and the crushed hopes of a destroyed peace process.

Although there is ample blame for all the parties involved, the conclusion cannot be escaped that Netanyahu's commitment to the peace process has never been more than equivocal. This and his determination to cling to power

---

[76] 'Turkey, Israel and US seen joining forces to target Syria and Iran', *Mideast Mirror*, 8 May 1997, pp. 6–10; 'Turkey's alliance with Israel alarms Egypt too', *Mideast Mirror*, 13 May 1997, pp. 12–13; 'Joint naval exercise by the US, Israel and Turkey angers Syria', *Financial Times*, 3 Sep. 1997, p. 6; and 'Political analysis: "weird contradictions"', *Tishrin* (Damascus), 4 Dec. 1997, pp. 1, 11, in 'Syria: article assails Turkish–Israeli military "alliance"', FBIS-NES-97-341, 9 Dec. 1997.

[77] Harris, P., 'Algerian election pits democracy against terrorism', *Jane's Intelligence Review*, vol. 9, no. 9 (Sep. 1997), pp. 422–25; Boukrine, D., 'Algeria–EU, the misunderstandings have been eliminated', *Le Matin* (Algiers), 7 Dec. 1997, p. 4, in 'Algeria: daily notes talks with EU on terrorism, human rights', FBIS-NES-97-354, 23 Dec. 1997; and La Une Radio Network (Brussels), 27 Nov. 1997, in 'Algeria: Algeria's Attaf on "complicity" with terrorists', FBIS-NES-97-334, 7 Dec. 1997.

at the head of an unwieldy coalition, rather than exploring the options which Israel's electoral laws give him for compromise with more moderate parties, have been major factors in the deterioration of the peace process.

Looking to the wider issues which may affect the Middle East in 1998, the prospect of opening a dialogue between Iran and the United States is significant. On the other hand, the chance of a confrontation between Iraq and the United Nations, or some of its members, seems high. Internal fighting is likely to continue in Algeria.

More generally, and over a longer time-frame, the Middle East faces a variety of social, economic, demographic, environmental and other challenges as the next millennium approaches. The resolution of these wider problems will not be easy even under the best of circumstances. Indeed, it will probably prove impossible to tackle these broader challenges unless the more immediate political differences which trouble the region move towards a just resolution through the peace process. Unfortunately, 1997 was largely squandered; it was not a year in which any real progress was made. There may not be many more years left for the peace process unless leaders from throughout the region rededicate themselves to it.

Appendix 3A. Documents on the Middle East peace process

NOTE FOR THE RECORD (ATTACHED TO THE PROTOCOL CONCERNING THE REDEPLOYMENT IN HEBRON)

15 January 1997

The two leaders met on January 15, 1997, in the presence of the US Special Middle East Coordinator. They requested him to prepare this Note for the Record to summarize what they agreed upon at their meeting.

Mutual Undertakings

The two leaders agreed that the Oslo peace process must move forward to succeed. Both parties to the Interim Agreement have concerns and obligations. Accordingly, the two leaders reaffirmed their commitment to implement the Interim Agreement on the basis of reciprocity and, in this context, conveyed the following undertakings to each other:

Israeli Responsibilities

The Israeli side reaffirms its commitments to the following measures and principles in accordance with the Interim Agreement:

Issues for Implementation

1. Further Redeployment Phases
   The first phase of further redeployments will be carried out during the first week of March.
2. Prisoner Release Issues
   Prisoner release issues will be dealt with in accordance with the Interim Agreement's provisions and procedures, including Annex VII.

Issues for Negotiation

3. Outstanding Interim Agreement Issues
   Negotiations on the following outstanding issues from the Interim Agreement will be immediately resumed. Negotiations on these issues will be conducted in parallel:
   a. Safe Passage
   b. Gaza Airport
   c. Gaza port
   d. Passages
   e. Economic, financial, civilian and security issues
   f. People-to-people

4. Permanent Status Negotiations
   Permanent status negotiations will be resumed within two months after implementation of the Hebron Protocol.

Palestinian Responsibilities

The Palestinian side reaffirms its commitments to the following measures and principles in accordance with the Interim Agreement:

1. Complete the process of revising the Palestinian National Charter
2. Fighting terror and preventing violence
   a. Strengthening security cooperation
   b. Preventing incitement and hostile propaganda, as specified in Article XXII of the Interim Agreement
   c. Combat systematically and effectively terrorist organizations and infrastructure
   d. Apprehension, prosecution and punishment of terrorists
   e. Requests for transfer of suspects and defendants will be acted upon in accordance with Article II(7)(f) of Annex IV to the Interim Agreement
   f. Confiscation of illegal firearms
3. Size of Palestinian Police will be pursuant to the Interim Agreement.
4. Exercise of Palestinian governmental activity, and location of Palestinian governmental offices, will be as specified in the Interim Agreement.

The aforementioned commitments will be dealt with immediately and in parallel.

Other Issues

Either party is free to raise other issues not specified above related to implementation of the Interim Agreement and obligations of both sides arising from the Interim Agreement.

Prepared by Ambassador Dennis Ross at the request of Prime Minister Benjamin Netanyahu and Ra'ees Yasser Arafat.

Source: United States Information Service, United States Embassy, Stockholm, 'Note for the Record', URL <http://www.usis.usemb.se/regional/nea/peace/hebprot.htm#document3>, version current on 8 Apr. 1998.

US SECRETARY OF STATE WARREN CHRISTOPHER, US LETTER OF ASSURANCE TO ISRAEL

Washington, 15 January 1997

(Letter to be provided by US Secretary of State [Warren] Christopher to Benjamin Netanyahu at the time of signing of the Hebron Protocol)

Dear Mr Prime Minister,

I wanted personally to congratulate you on the successful conclusion of the 'Protocol Concerning the Redeployment in Hebron'. It represents an important step forward in the Oslo peace process and reaffirms my conviction that a just and lasting peace will be established between Israelis and Palestinians in the very near future.

In this connection, I can assure you that it remains the policy of the United States to support and promote full implementation of the Interim Agreement in all of its parts. We intend to continue our efforts to help ensure that all outstanding commitments are carried out by both parties in a cooperative spirit and on the basis of reciprocity.

As part of this process, I have impressed upon Chairman Arafat the imperative need for the Palestinian Authority to make every effort to ensure public order and internal security within the West Bank and Gaza Strip. I have stressed to him that effectively carrying out this major responsibility will be a critical foundation for completing implementation of the Interim Agreement, as well as the peace process as a whole.

I wanted you to know that, in this context, I have advised Chairman Arafat of US views on Israel's process of redeploying its forces, designating specified military locations and transferring additional powers and responsibilities to the Palestinian Authority. In this regard, I have conveyed our belief, that the first phase of further redeployments should take place as soon as possible, and that all three phases of the further redeployments should be completed within twelve months from the implementation of the first phase of the further redeployments but not later than mid-1998.

Mr Prime Minister, you can be assured that the United States' commitment to Israel's security is ironclad and constitutes the fundamental cornerstone of our special relationship. The key element in our approach to peace, including the negotiation and implementation of agreements between Israel and its Arab partners, has always been a recognition of Israel's security requirements. Moreover, a hallmark of US policy remains our commitment to work cooperatively to seek to meet the security needs that Israel identifies. Finally, I would like to reiterate our position that Israel is entitled to secure and defensible borders, which should be directly negotiated and agreed with its neighbors.

Source: United States Information Service, United States Embassy, Stockholm, 'Secretary of State Christopher's Letter of Congratulations to Benjamin Netanyahu', URL <http://www.usis.usemb.se/regional/nea/peace/hebprot.htm#document3>, version current on 8 Apr. 1998.

4. Russia: conflicts and peaceful settlement of disputes

VLADIMIR BARANOVSKY

I. Introduction

Maintaining and consolidating stability on the territory of the former USSR remain formidable tasks, involving both domestic developments in the new states and their external interactions. Russia plays the central role in this part of the world. Its aim of creating a secure immediate environment for itself and establishing itself as an influential international actor requires significant efforts at conflict management both inside the country and on its periphery. Russia's policy had considerable impact on developments within the post-Soviet geopolitical space in 1997.

Section II of this chapter analyses the new situation in and around Chechnya after the end of hostilities. Section III addresses Russia's relations with its European post-Soviet neighbours—Ukraine, Belarus, Moldova (with a focus on the Trans-Dniester region) and the Baltic states. Section IV deals with the Transcaucasus—both in terms of Russia's strategic interests and with respect to conflict management in Abkhazia and Nagorno-Karabakh. Section V concentrates on the ongoing peace settlement in Tajikistan, and section VI presents an assessment of Russia's position on the Commonwealth of Independent States (CIS). Conclusions are presented in section VII.

II. Post-war accommodation in Chechnya

The end of the two-and-a-half-year war in Chechnya left unsettled the basic problem at the source of the conflict—that of Chechnya's status.[1] Consequently, although hostilities had stopped, the situation remained politically fragile throughout 1997. The two sides had been proceeding from incompatible starting-points, Chechnya asserting its independence and Russia proclaiming its territorial integrity, but seemed now to be forging a certain *modus vivendi* in their practical relationship.

Domestic developments

The presidential election in Chechnya on 27 January 1997 played a crucial role in legitimizing the political power of the separatist leadership. Indeed, the election was held after the withdrawal of all Russian troops. It received politi-

---

[1] Baranovsky, V., 'Russia: conflicts and its security environment', *SIPRI Yearbook 1997: Armaments, Disarmament and International Security* (Oxford University Press: Oxford, 1997), pp. 105–12.

cal support from Moscow, which was in need of viable and responsible partners with whom to conduct a dialogue. Although the period of preparation for the election was too short, 16 candidates stood for the presidency; 72 observers from the Organization for Security and Co-operation in Europe (OSCE) monitored the vote and did not report significant infringements of procedures. The officially announced turnout was 79.4 per cent of registered voters; however, polling stations for refugees from Chechnya were established only in neighbouring Ingushetia, whereas significant numbers of them are settled further away in Russia and were thus unable to vote.[2]

Aslan Maskhadov, Chechnya's military leader and chief negotiator with Moscow, won the election with an impressive 59.3 per cent of the vote. Nevertheless, the ability of his government to control the situation in the republic remains questionable. There have been numerous indications that political developments in Chechnya are determined more by the interaction of traditional clans than by state structures. Indeed, a number of President Maskhadov's political rivals have distanced themselves from the new leadership,[3] influential field commanders have proved reluctant to accept the authority of the 'centre',[4] and divisions between the newly emerged authorities have more than once rendered them unable to carry out a coherent policy. Furthermore, criminal groups continue to operate all over Chechnya—a situation which is only aggravated by the considerable amounts of weapons still in private hands. Another manifestation of the weakness of the political regime has been its inability to prevent or deal with numerous hostage-takings, especially of Russian television journalists, most probably undertaken for large sums in ransom.[5]

Although fighting criminal activity and civil disorder has, rightly, become one of the top domestic priorities of the Chechnyan leadership, the forcible introduction and implementation of the rigid Islamic norms and laws (shariah) risk doing grave damage to Chechnya's international image insofar as they are associated with Islamic militancy. Widespread condemnation followed the public execution of common criminals in Grozny in September. Meanwhile,

[2] In all, 513 585 voters were registered for the election. The pre-war population of Chechnya was over 1 million. Curran, D., Hill, F. and Kostritsyna, E., *The Search for Peace in Chechnya: A Sourcebook 1994–1996* (Harvard University, John F. Kennedy School of Government: Cambridge, Mass., Mar. 1997), p. 61.

[3] In particular, this was true of Shamil Basayev, one of the most popular Chechen leaders, and former President Zelimkhan Yandarbiyev. Basayev's later involvement in the leadership in the capacity of de facto head of government was interpreted as an indication of this ability seriously to challenge Maskhadov's power.

[4] Maskhadov was reported to have secured the support of all Chechen field commanders and their commitment to the creation of a 2000-strong national army and the disbanding of all local armed formations. To what extent these decisions have been implemented is unclear.

[5] Between Jan. and Nov. 1997, more than 170 people were kidnapped in Chechnya. In some cases the ransom required (and apparently paid) amounted to millions of dollars. A decision by the Chechnyan Government to make kidnapping punishable by death did not seem to discourage this profitable 'business'. Russian officials accused top Chechnyan leaders, including Vice-President Vakha Arsanov, of direct involvement in hostage-takings. 'Yeltsin aide implicates Chechen leaders in hostage-taking', Radio Free Europe/Radio Liberty, *RFE/RL Newsline*, vol. 1, no. 154, part I (6 Nov. 1997), URL <http.//www.rferl.org/newsline> (hereafter, references to *RFE/RL Newsline* refer to the Internet edition at this address).

Maskhadov proclaimed Chechnya an Islamic republic and the parliament was reported to be drafting constitutional amendments intended to eliminate contradictions between some of the articles of the basic law and the Koran.

The 'information war' was undoubtedly won by the separatists during the period of hostilities, but by the end of 1997 comments in the Russian media had changed radically and were portraying Chechnya as an area of chaos, anarchy, officially sponsored terrorism and banditry.

Political aspects of relations

In contrast to previous years, in 1997 Russia proceeded from an acknowledgement of the real situation in Chechnya and an effort to make the Chechnyan leadership dependent on practical working relations with Moscow. It was also interested in consolidating Maskhadov's government in order to marginalize extremist factions and leaders in Chechnya.[6]

On 12 May 1997 in Moscow, Russian President Boris Yeltsin and Maskhadov signed a treaty on peace and the principles of Russian–Chechnyan relations.[7] Both sides stated their aim of 'firm and equal relations' based on the principles of international law and stressed their rejection of the use of force. Advertised as a 'historic step' putting an end to the state of war, this accord contained no mention of Chechnya's status.

Meanwhile, the Chechnyan leadership was trying to exploit Moscow's interest in building workable relations by intensifying its claims for independence. Russia considered the Khasaviurt agreement, signed in August 1996, effectively terminating the war,[8] as postponing the definition of Chechnya's status until 31 December 2001; the Chechnyan side interpreted it as only setting the final date by which the issue must be settled and not precluding an earlier settlement. Moreover, the Khasaviurt agreement was announced by the Chechnyan side to be no longer valid and superseded by the new treaty. The reference in the treaty to the principles of international law as the basis for mutual relations was presented as a clear indication that Chechnya should no longer be considered a subject (constituent part) of the Russian Federation.[9]

In August 1997, in Moscow, Maskhadov handed Yeltsin a draft treaty on the establishment of interstate relations between Russia and Chechnya, envisaging, *inter alia*, recognition of Chechnya's independence and the exchange

---

[6] Popular field commander Salman Raduyev was reported to be threatening Russia with further terrorist attacks and continuing the fight until full political independence for Chechnya was achieved.

[7] Treaty on Peace and Principles of Mutual Relations between the Russian Federation and the Chechen Republic Ichkeria. The text was published in *Izvestiya*, 14 May 1997, p. 1.

[8] Baranovsky (note 1), pp. 108–10.

[9] 'Russia: Chechen leader stresses treaty with Russia', Radiostantsiya Ekho Moskvy, GMT 12.18, 17 Aug. 1997, in Foreign Broadcast Information Service, *Daily Report–Central Eurasia (FBIS-SOV)*, FBIS-SOV-97-229, 17 Aug. 1997. Chechnya used the term 'reparations', which implies a transaction between 2 sovereign states, in a request for $260 billion for war-related damages as another means of pressurizing Russia on the issue of independence. FBIS-SOV-97-218, 6 Aug. 1997. Russia is not refusing to participate in post-war reconstruction, but is prepared to do so only on a more modest scale. According to Ivan Rybkin, then Secretary of the Russian Security Council, the Russian Government allocated 847 billion roubles ($148 million) to this goal in the period Jan.–Aug. 1997. 'Russian, Chechen presidents meet', *RFE/RL Newsline*, vol. 1, no. 97, part I (18 Aug. 1997).

of diplomatic representatives.[10] Yeltsin rejected this but agreed that a new bilateral treaty should be concluded to define relations between Russia and Chechnya and to give broad autonomy to the latter and that a joint committee should be set up to draft the treaty. It was significant that the two presidents, according to Maskhadov, agreed on the need for defence cooperation on the ground that 'our strategic interests coincide'.[11] Negotiations, predictably, revealed basic incompatibilities. While Chechnya insisted on a formal document with both sides treating each other as independent sovereign states, Russia wanted a treaty on a division of powers between the federal and republican authorities similar to the treaties signed by Moscow with Tatarstan, the Bashkir Republic and other subjects of the Russian Federation. Moscow took the firm position that 'the Chechen Republic will be gaining its sovereignty as part of the Russian Federation'. It was, however, ready to provide Chechnya with special status much higher than that enjoyed by any other subject of the Federation and seemed to be open to negotiating any political formula short of formal independence.[12]

In Russia numerous critics of government policy continued to present the negotiations with Chechnya as threatening the integrity and the very future of the country but were unable to suggest any realistic alternative to political accommodation with the separatist regime. Accommodation, however, would contradict the provisions of the Russian Constitution. Moscow faces a difficult choice between two options (excluding that of recognizing Chechnya's independence): building a political settlement on an ad hoc basis or changing the constitution in order to adapt it to the new reality. In any case, the need for a status for Chechnya that is very different from the one outlined in the present constitution must be the starting-point. This is recognized by at least part of the political establishment in Moscow.[13]

In contrast to the war period, Russian public opinion and political quarters seemed to be feeling growing irritation at Chechnya's lack of cooperativeness. Furthermore, as instability in the rebellious republic persisted, so did its spillover onto neighbouring territories of the Russian Federation, prompting them to organize self-defence at the local level, independently of Moscow and

---

[10] 'Russia: Maskhadov asks Yeltsin for Russia–Chechnya treaty', FBIS-SOV-97-230, 18 Aug. 1997.

[11] 'Yeltsin, Maskhadov agree on economic, defense cooperation', *RFE/RL Newsline*, vol. 1, no. 98, part I (19 Aug. 1997). Later, the Chechnyan side was reported to be drafting a protocol on a joint defence space (alongside an interstate treaty and protocol on a joint economic space). 'Chechen President orders "interstate treaty" with Moscow', FBIS-SOV-97-272, 29 Sep. 1997.

[12] In particular, Chechnya was offered the status of 'self-ruling republic' within the Russian Federation. 'Yeltsin to visit Chechnya', *RFE/RL Newsline*, vol. 1, no. 168, part I (26 Nov. 1997). According to Rybkin, Chechnya 'can obtain maximum independence and powers within the confines of Russian territory'. FBIS-SOV-97-268, 25 Sep. 1997.

[13] Marat Baglay, the newly elected Chairman of the Constitutional Court, has virtually admitted that Chechnya can no longer be called a subject of the Federation as it is in the present constitution and argued for the definition of some intermediate option between the status of a component part of the Federation and that of an independent state. FBIS-SOV-97-062, 3 Mar. 1997. Russian Deputy Prime Minister Ramazan Abdulatipov stated that 'it is utopian to regard Chechnya as a member of the federation now'. 'Abdulatipov says "utopian" to view Chechnya as part of Russia', *RFE/RL Newsline*, vol. 1, no. 106, part I (29 Aug. 1997).

apparently in violation of the constitution.[14] The arguments in favour of 'isolating' the trouble-making area and 'sealing' its border, not spending resources on its reconstruction and, eventually, even 'letting it go'[15] were heard increasingly, undermining the longer-term strategy of 'taming' or domesticating Chechnya and promoting its interdependence with Russia.

The transit of oil

While negotiations on political issues could not solve the most controversial problems, economic cooperation had more chance of success. Both sides agreed on coordination between Russian and Chechnyan ministries with respect to post-war reconstruction, pensions, compensation to those who had suffered during the fighting, and banking.

One of the central issues in the negotiations was the transit of oil via the territory of Chechnya. This problem touches upon the considerable long-term strategic and financial interests associated with the delivery to the West of the presumed huge oil resources under the Caspian Sea shelf.[16] The most rational route via Russia passes through Chechnya and requires the restoration of a 147-km pipeline destroyed during the war.

Uncertainty about the status of Chechnya complicated negotiations. The Chechnyan leadership attempted to link the practical problems with symbolic gestures intended to consolidate the de facto political independence of the republic. It insisted that the agreement on oil transit should have the character of an interstate treaty; that Russia should pay for transit on the basis of international tariffs rather than domestic ones; and that the forms of financial transfers for the restoration of the pipeline should be different from those normally used by Moscow in transactions with the constituent parts of the Russian Federation. Since Russia was interested in consolidating its participation in the Caspian oil project and to have the routes ready for the beginning of 'early oil' deliveries expected in late 1997,[17] the Chechnyan negotiators apparently counted on pressure of time making Moscow more compliant. Moscow, in response, used the argument that it could choose to invest in the construction of an alternative pipeline bypassing Chechnya, thus keeping open the option of cutting the separatists off from the oil project. Finally, all Grozny's political rhetoric notwithstanding, it had to accept Moscow's basic conditions. Agree-

[14] In response to murders, terrorist acts and acts of banditry attributed to Chechens, the Dagestan Government banned all motor traffic to and from Chechnya and decided to create a 5000-strong volunteer militia to patrol the border area; the authorities of Stavropol *krai* (territory) ordered the digging of a ditch along the whole administrative line separating it from Chechnya. 'Chechnya-Dagestan border closed to motor traffic', *RFE/RL Newsline*, vol. 1, no. 147, part I (27 Oct. 1997); Maksakov, I., 'Chechenskiy krizis vyshel za predely Ichkerii' [The Chechnyan crisis has gone beyond Ichkeria's borders], *Nezavisimaya Gazeta*, 10 Nov. 1997, pp. 1, 3; and 'Dagestan encounters problems in creating self-defense forces', *RFE/RL Newsline*, vol. 1, no. 158, part I (12 Nov. 1997).

[15] High-ranking Russian officials and politicians, including Ivan Rybkin, were reported as proposing a referendum on whether Chechnya should be independent. Paradoxically, this was rejected bluntly by the Chechnyan side. Rogozin, D., 'Komu vygoden referendum o nezavisimosti Chechni?' [Who will profit from a referendum on Chechnya's independence?], *Nezavisimaya Gazeta*, 10 Nov. 1997, p. 2.

[16] See also section IV in this chapter.

[17] Deliveries began in Oct. 1997.

ment was reached on 9 September 1997. In particular, both sides will use Russian domestic tariffs and not international ones.[18] It was also reported that the safety of the pipeline against possible terrorist attacks will be ensured by Russian military personnel (440 servicemen plus the necessary armaments and combat equipment).[19]

Nevertheless, the question of the transit of oil remains hostage to the broader political relationship between Russia and Chechnya,[20] especially in the light of further complications which emerged at the end of the year. On the one hand, Moscow has reasons to consider the issue as giving it important political leverage over Chechnya; on the other hand, Russia (as well as Azerbaijan and the recipients of the oil) could at any moment face a political ultimatum from Grozny, which effectively controls the pipeline. However, Chechnya's economic interest in the normal functioning of the pipeline is considerably greater than that of Russia and there are limits to the extent to which Chechnya can blackmail Moscow without damaging its own economy. On the positive side, a common interest in the oil pipeline could change their alienation from each other and promote the logic of economic pragmatism in place of the painful political and psychological heritage of the war.

The regional context

For Moscow, one of the strongest incentives to seek a peaceful settlement in and with Chechnya is to prevent or minimize destabilizing developments in adjacent areas of the North Caucasus. The termination of hostilities undoubtedly had a positive effect for the whole region. However, some worrying developments continued, especially in Dagestan, which borders on Chechnya and risks becoming a new 'hot spot' in the North Caucasus.[21]

New tensions were registered in the area disputed between Ingushetia and North Ossetia, where the consequences of the violent clashes in October–November 1992 endure. Thirty thousand Ingushi refugees have been prevented from returning to their homes in the Prigorodny district of North Ossetia,[22] while over 100 decisions and resolutions of the central government

---

[18] Moscow was ready to pay $0.43 per tonne for oil pumped through the Chechnyan section of the oil pipelene, whereas Chechnya proposed a tariff of $4.27 per tonne. 'Russian–Chechen commission to continue work on oil treaty', FBIS-SOV-97-245, 2 Sep. 1997.

[19] Becker, A., 'Neft poidet v obkhod Chechni' ['The oil will go round Chechnya'], *Segodnya*, 1 Sep. 1997, p. 1. Whether Russian military personnel will actually be allowed into Chechnya is not, however, clear; for instance, the Russian workmen carrying out repairs on the pipeline in the autumn of 1997 were protected by 400 members of the Chechnyan national guard. *Inside (and Beyond) Russia and FSU*, vol. 5, no. 10 (Oct. 1997), p. 14.

[20] While professing at the time of signing to be satisfied with the 9 Sep. accord, both sides began to insist on additional conditions and to threaten to abrogate the agreement if they were not met. Fuller, E., 'The great poker game', *RFE/RL Newsline*, vol. 1, no. 120, part I (18 Sep. 1997).

[21] Rotar, I., 'Voyna na territorii Dagestana fakticheski neizbezhna' [War on Dagestan's territory is actually inevitable], *Nezavisimaya Gazeta*, 11 Sep. 1997, p. 1; and Ilyin, V., 'Na yuge Dagestana gotovyatsa provokatsii' [Provocation being prepared in southern Dagestan], *Nezavisimaya Gazeta*, 4 Oct. 1997, p. 3.

[22] Gadaborshev, A., 'Glavnye problemy—bezhentsy i prestupnost' [The main problems are refugees and criminality], *Nezavisimaya Gazeta*, 25 Sep. 1997, p. 3. The number of returned refugees is estimated at 13 000. '"Positive changes" in Ossetian–Ingush conflict area', FBIS-SOV-97-306, 2 Nov. 1997.

remain unimplemented.²³ Nevertheless, the suggestion of introducing presidential rule in the contested district was rejected as being likely to mean the use of force; instead, on 4 September 1997 the presidents of Ingushetia and North Ossetia, under strong pressure from Moscow, signed an agreement aimed at overcoming tensions between them.²⁴

Russia has succeeded in preventing international recognition of Chechnya, despite the efforts of the separatist leaders, and has here achieved an important goal. Nevertheless, the international dimension of the conflict with Chechnya is still very real. In particular, Chechnya has made advances to Azerbaijan and Georgia, apparently aiming both to challenge Moscow further and to promote its own involvement, as an independent actor, in two issues which are of special relevance for them—a settlement in Abkhazia and the Caspian oil pipeline deals.²⁵ Another example of its international activism is the idea, launched by Maskhadov, of a pan-Caucasus organization resembling the OSCE.²⁶ Interestingly, the separatist leadership has tried to convince Moscow that Chechnya, if able to operate independently, would contribute to stability in the Caucasus area generally and could become a valuable asset for promoting Russia's interests in the region.²⁷ Russia, however, may have serious reasons to believe that this proposal is intended to neutralize the Caucasus 'quadrilateral' (Armenia, Azerbaijan, Georgia and Russia) security pattern within which it has an assured and prominent place.²⁸

Throughout 1997 Russia has faced the extremely challenging task of adjusting to a new situation after its spectacular military and political defeat in Chechnya. Its active efforts to promote stability in the North Caucasus achieved certain results; at the same time, they clearly reflect its concern about the implications of the situation in Chechnya for its prospects in the Transcaucasus and in the broader international context.²⁹

---

²³ 'Russia: Mityukov on Ingush–Ossetian conflict', FBIS-SOV-97-217, 5 Aug. 1997.

²⁴ This document, full of general declarations of goodwill and committing the participants to fulfil the decisions already taken, fails to address the most sensitive issues—the territorial claims, the status of borders and the repatriation of the refugees. The allocation of funds (200 billion roubles) to restore the destroyed houses of Ingush in North Ossetia and a decision on joint patrols and police offices to protect the resettlement of refugees should prove to be of more practical use. Gorodetskaya, N., 'Nazran i Valdikavkaz poobeschayut liubit drug druga' [Nazran and Vladikavkaz promise to love each other], *Segodnya*, 29 Aug. 1997, pp. 1, 4.

²⁵ Kharket, Ye., 'Chechnya pretenduyet na rol posrednika' [Chechnya aspires to play a role as mediator], *Nezavisimaya Gazeta*, 3 Oct. 1997, p. 3.

²⁶ Viganskiy, M., 'Aslan Maskhadov khochet sozdat kavkazskuyu OBSE' [Aslan Maskhadov wants to create a Caucasian OSCE], *Segodnya*, 1 Sep. 1997, p. 1.

²⁷ According to First Deputy Prime Minister of Chechnya Movladi Udugov, 'the Chechens could play the role of a reliable partner [of Russia]. And if Russia has a real, strong partner in the Caucasus, who knows what he wants and knows what he plans today and will have honest and equal relations with Russia, then I think Russia's military, economic and political interests in the Caucasus will be assured'. 'Russia: Chechen leader stresses treaty with Russia' (note 9).

²⁸ The first meeting of the presidents of Armenia, Azerbaijan, Georgia and Russia was held in Kislovodsk in 1996. 'Armenia: Ter-Petrosyan opposes Chechen Caucasus OSCE proposal', FBIS-SOV-97-270, 27 Sep. 1997.

²⁹ Yeltsin was reported to have said at a meeting of the Russian Security Council on 20 Aug.: 'The interests not only of our Commonwealth [the CIS] but of the "far abroad" are also concentrated in the North Caucasus . . . The United States is already stating that this is a zone of its interests . . . the Americans . . . are beginning to penetrate this zone and are unabashedly declaring this'. Yunanov, B., 'Clinton's crossing of the Caucasus Range', *Literaturnaya Gazeta*, 27 Aug. 1997, p. 9, in FBIS-SOV-

III. Russia's relations with its post-Soviet European neighbours

Developments in Russia's relations with its post-Soviet European vicinity in 1997 followed various patterns. The overall normalization of relations with Ukraine can be considered a significant achievement, although it did not eliminate persisting long-term uncertainties. Belarus, behind a widely advertised alliance-type rapprochement, has turned out to be a difficult partner. The questions at issue in relations with the three Baltic states seemed to take on a lower profile, without being removed from the political agenda. Russia's routine involvement in efforts to promote conflict settlement with respect to the Trans-Dniester region of Moldova seem to have contributed to the negotiations, although that process is slow and the outcome still uncertain.

Ukraine

The year 1997 saw the resolution of the Black Sea Fleet issue, one of the most controversial problems in Russian–Ukrainian relations since the demise of the Soviet Union. On 28 May 1997, the prime ministers of the two countries signed three agreements: on the division of the fleet, on the status of the Russian Black Sea Fleet on the territory of Ukraine, and on related settlement of debts.[30] These agreements settled the matters in serious dispute.[31]

In particular, it was agreed that Sevastopol will be the main basing point for the Russian Black Sea Fleet and will be leased to Russia by Ukraine for 20 years with a possibility of automatic extension. The Russian Black Sea Fleet will also be allowed to use six other facilities on Ukrainian territory.[32] The total number of weapons and military equipment of the Russian Black Sea Fleet deployed on the territory of Ukraine will not exceed the levels set by the 1990 Treaty on Conventional Armed Forces in Europe (CFE Treaty). Russia pledges not to deploy nuclear weapons on its Black Sea Fleet. Military exercises and passage through the territorial waters of Ukraine will be carried out in coordination with the authorities of the latter. Financial accounts are to be settled by reducing Ukraine's indebtedness to Russia[33]—by $526.5 million in 1998 as compensation for the ships transferred to Russia (approximately

---

97-252, 9 Sep. 1997. (Yeltsin made a slip in speaking and was referring to US activism in the Caucasian–Caspian area as a whole, not only Russia's North Caucasus.)

[30] For the texts of the agreements, see *Diplomaticheskiy Vestnik*, no. 8 (Aug. 1997), pp. 29–40.

[31] Baranovsky, V., 'Conflict developments on the territory of the former Soviet Union', *SIPRI Yearbook 1994* (Oxford University Press: Oxford, 1994), pp. 183–85; Baranovsky, V., 'Russia and its neighbourhood: conflict developments and settlement efforts', *SIPRI Yearbook 1995: Armaments, Disarmament and International Security* (Oxford University Press: Oxford, 1995), pp. 250–51; Baranovsky, V., 'Conflicts in and around Russia', *SIPRI Yearbook 1996: Armaments, Disarmament and International Security* (Oxford University Press: Oxford, 1996), p. 274; and Baranovsky (note 1), p. 121.

[32] Altogether, the facilities leased to Russia cover 185 km². Russia will have exclusive basing rights in 3 bays of Sevastopol and will share the 4th bay with the Ukrainian Navy.

[33] Ukraine's recognized state indebtness to Russia, at the time the agreements on the Black Sea Fleet were signed, amounted to $3074 million and was to be settled by the end of the year 2007.

one-third of Ukraine's half-share of the Black Sea Fleet) and by $97.75 million annually as rent payments.

Resolution of the Black Sea Fleet issue was a precondition for the conclusion of the Treaty on Friendship, Cooperation and Partnership between the two countries that had waited for signature for three years. Signed by presidents Boris Yeltsin of Russia and Leonid Kuchma of Ukraine on 31 May 1997, the treaty stipulated, *inter alia*, respect for each other's territorial integrity and the inviolability of frontiers (Article 2). Both sides pledged to refrain from supporting or participating in any actions against each other, not to allow their territory to be used to the detriment of each other's security nor to conclude treaties with third countries against each other (Article 6). Both proclaimed their intention to develop military and military–technical cooperation and cooperation on state security and border control issues (Article 8).[34]

The treaty creates a general framework for an intensive and constructive relationship between the two major post-Soviet states, although it does not preclude disputes and conflicts. While Ukraine recognizes that 'Russia is unquestionably Ukraine's strategic partner',[35] concerns seem to persist over Russia's ability to use economic leverage over it.[36] Uncertainty also persists as to Russia's readiness to adjust finally to the fact of Ukraine's independence and overcome its residual superiority complex. Russia's apprehension at Ukraine's possibly getting a 'free ride' in the international arena has apparently been only partially eased by the treaty.

Ironically, by signing the Founding Act with NATO, Russia deprived itself of coherent arguments against Ukraine's drift westwards, in particular regarding its relations with NATO.[37] However, Ukraine's rapprochement with NATO apparently continues to be one of Russia's most serious concerns, especially in its military and security aspects. Thus, Russia declined an invitation to take part in the NATO-led 'Sea Breeze' naval exercises scheduled for August 1997 off the Crimean coast and condemned by some Russian official commentators as anti-Russian and provocative. It is true that joint Russian–Ukrainian naval manoeuvres (the first in post-Soviet history) followed in October, reflecting the common security interests of the two countries in the Black Sea area,[38] but at the same time Ukrainian officials stress that 'the country has no right to stay aloof from NATO, which is the core of the emerging European security system of the 21st century'.[39] Furthermore, some high-

---

[34] For the text of the treaty, see *Diplomaticheskiy Vestnik*, no. 7 (July 1997), pp. 35–41.

[35] Statement of the Ukrainian Prime Minister, Valeriy Pustovoitenko, 'Ukrainian Prime Minister in Moscow', *RFE/RL Newsline*, vol. 1, no. 119, part I (17 Sep. 1997).

[36] The issue of Ukraine's debt to Russia for gas supplies remains unsettled. Uncoordinated taxes are seriously slowing down Russian–Ukrainian economic cooperation; the volume of trade between the 2 countries in the first half of 1997 was down 22% on the same period of 1996. 'Makes sugar a priority issue', *RFE/RL Newsline*, vol. 1, no. 119, part I (17 Sep. 1997).

[37] The NATO–Russia Founding Act, 27 May 1997, is reproduced in appendix 5A of this volume. On 9 July 1997 Ukraine and NATO signed a Charter on a Distinctive Partnership 'modelled' on the agreement with Russia. *NATO Review*, July–Aug. 1997, Documentation, pp. 5–6.

[38] Georgiev, V., 'Ucheniya v interesakh dvukh stran' [Exercises in the interest of two countries], *Nezavisimaya Gazeta*, 22 Oct. 1997, p. 3.

[39] Statement of Vladimir Gorbulin, Secretary of the National Security and Defence Council of Ukraine, *Nezavisimaya Gazeta*, 7 Oct. 1997, p. 3.

ranking Ukrainian military argue in favour of improving the compatibility of their military structures with those of NATO member states and standardizing armaments and military equipment.[40]

President Kuchma, while assessing the development of Russian–Ukrainian relations as highly positive during 1997, continued to express serious reservations and scepticism with respect to the CIS. Ukraine is clearly reluctant to associate itself too closely with the CIS, which (*a*) is at present remarkably ineffective, and (*b*) has the potential to turn into a Russian-dominated alliance. Russia may have serious reasons to believe that Ukraine is trying to build a certain counterbalance to the CIS within the post-Soviet geopolitical space. One example is the idea of Baltic–Black Sea cooperation, met without any enthusiasm in Russia but strongly advocated by Ukraine.[41]

Belarus

Throughout 1997 Russia experienced considerable problems in dealing with the regime of President Alexander Lukashenko in Belarus.

On the one hand, the theme of consolidating the historical ties between the peoples of Belarus and Russia, articulated by Lukashenko in order to trump his domestic opponents, is undoubtedly popular with Russian public opinion. A general rapprochement with Belarus may also be attractive to Russia for a number of reasons. On the western edge of Russia, playing a vital role in many respects—communications to and from Europe, transit links with the Kaliningrad exclave, border control, air defence[42] and so on—it can be regarded as strategically important. It is the only state openly supportive of the Russian campaign against the enlargement of NATO. Furthermore, relations with Belarus can be seen as critical in the light of persisting uncertainties in relations with Ukraine.

On the other hand, Lukashenko has turned out to be an extremely inconvenient ally. Russia could be discredited by his scandalous record on democracy and human rights, which has been broadly condemned by the international community.[43] The Yeltsin Administration has had to take into account the very critical assessment of Lukashenko's regime by the Russian media, as well as the clear (and apparently reciprocal) sympathy of the communist opposition towards it. The financial costs of integration are also a concern: Lukashenko is

---

[40] Statement of the Chairman of the General Staff of Ukraine's Armed Forces Alexander Zatynaiko. Timoshenko, V., 'Vlasti nedovolny silovymi strukturami' [Authorities dissatisfied with force structures], *Nezavisimaya Gazeta*, 7 Oct. 1997, p. 3.

[41] The proposal of President Kuchma to convene a summit meeting of 11 Baltic and Black Sea countries in Crimea in 1999 was actively backed by Azerbaijan, Georgia and Moldova. See section VI in this chapter.

[42] The Minister of Defence of Belarus stated that Russian air defence forces, especially units involved in reconnaissance, may be stationed on the territory of the country. 'Russian air defense units may be stationed in Belarus', FBIS-SOV-97-034, 19 Feb. 1997. Joint air defence exercises were held in Aug. 1997.

[43] 'Belarus is moving towards a dictatorship. Any organization, movement or individual that appears even mildly critical of the administration is being targeted.' Marples, D. R., 'Belarus: an analysis of the Lukashenka regime', *Harriman Review*, vol. 10, no. 1 (spring 1997), p. 28.

generally suspected of aiming to get access to Russia's economic potential and natural resources in order to maintain Belarus' outdated, unreformed and highly inefficient economic system.

Lukashenko initiated a widely advertised campaign to establish a 'Union of Russia and Belarus' as a step further after their 'commonwealth' was officially created in April 1996.[44] Russia responded with confusion and ambivalence. An ambitious 18-page draft treaty reportedly submitted to Yeltsin by Lukashenko was reduced to a noncommittal, three-page 'charter' initialled by Yeltsin and Lukashenko on 2 April 1997.[45] To make up for this rebuff to the ambitious Lukashenko and to the Russian proponents of 'unification', a more detailed Charter of the Union was signed on 23 May 1997. It enumerated the aims of the union in the political, economic, social, legal and security fields, defined the competences delegated to it by the participating states, established a 'union citizenship', and set out the joint bodies to be created in the union (a supreme council, a parliamentary assembly and an executive committee).[46] However, the union remains ephemeral, and the practical implications are assessed by most commentators and analysts with the profoundest scepticism.

The union proved to be a dead letter in the autumn of 1997, when crisis erupted over Lukashenko's provocative suppression of journalists' rights in Belarus. The arrest and detention for more than two months of Pavel Sheremet, correspondent of the Russian ORT television channel, by the Belarussian authorities, on far-fetched charges—in fact because of highly critical coverage of the political regime in Belarus by the Russian media—forced Russia to question the validity of the union, since the principles of democracy and respect for human and civil rights stipulated in the charter were being flagrantly violated. The episode showed clearly that Russia might face serious challenges in dealing with a Belarussian president who is authoritarian, lacking in restraint and inclined to primitive populism—all the possible advantages of an alliance relationship notwithstanding.

The Baltic states

Russia's relations with the three Baltic states were characterized by gradual progress in overcoming continuing problems and the adoption of a more working-style type of interaction. Officials of the Baltic states pointed to a certain normalization of their relations with Russia, and Russia moderated its

---

[44] Baranovsky (note 1), pp. 122–23.

[45] For the text of the Treaty on the Union of Belarus and Russia, see *Diplomaticheskiy Vestnik*, no. 4 (Apr. 1997), pp. 41–43. It did not mention the possibility of a merger of the 2 states even in the most general way: Lukashenko was apparently disturbed by proposals that the Belarussian authorities would be dismissed and the 6 Belarussian regions subordinated directly to Moscow, while he himself would become Russian Vice-President. 'Belarus: spokesman reports proposal for unification with Russia', FBIS-SOV-97-039, 21 Feb. 1997. Meanwhile on 4 Apr. the Russian Duma (the lower house of the Russian Parliament) adopted a statement appealing for 'step-by-step reunification'. For the text of the Duma's statement, see *Diplomaticheskiy Vestnik*, no. 4 (Apr. 1997), pp. 32–33.

[46] For the text, see *Diplomaticheskiy Vestnik*, no. 6 (June 1997), pp. 30–39. For the draft initialled by the two presidents on 2 Apr. 1997, see *International Observer*, vol. 16, no. 325 (Sep. 1997), pp. 788–94 (in English).

tough rhetoric and hard-line policy.[47] In Russia, arguments in favour of developing a more constructive relationship with them became more salient.[48]

At the same time, the issue of their possibly joining NATO continued to be a disturbing factor. The NATO Madrid summit meeting of 8–9 July 1997 refrained from including the Baltic states in the first round of enlargement, so that Russia's concerns became less vociferous, although they were not driven away. Russian officials continued to warn that if NATO enlargement included the Baltic states Russia would have to revise its relations both with NATO member states and with the states that aspire to become members.[49]

Warnings, however, went in parallel with attempts to design positive alternatives. At a summit meeting of 12 Baltic and Black Sea countries in Vilnius in September 1997, then Russian Prime Minister Viktor Chernomyrdin offered 'any kind of security guarantees' and a set of confidence- and security-building measures (CSBMs) for the region to the Baltic states—provided they would maintain their non-bloc status.[50] Significantly, this linkage was apparently removed later. On 3 December 1997 President Yeltsin also proposed arms reductions in the Baltic Sea region. The initiative met with a cold reaction; it was considered as undermining the Baltic states' prospect of getting 'real' security guarantees by 'joining Europe'[51] and imposing on them unwanted protection from Russia, and was finally rejected.[52]

Although basically latent for the time being, the problem has explosive potential unless there are radical changes in relations between NATO and Russia. Russia's instinct for a predominant role in the post-Soviet geopolitical space, coupled with the Baltic states' desire to distance themselves from Russia, makes a troublesome background for their relations.

Against the background of the possible enlargement of NATO onto the territory of the former USSR, Russia's persisting concerns about the rights of the Russian-speaking population have often been interpreted as a deliberate attempt to maintain a certain leverage over the Baltic states. However, the

---

[47] 'Estonia: Foreign Minister on relations with Russia', in *Foreign Broadcast Information Service, Daily Report–Western Europe (FBIS-WEU)*, FBIS-WEU-97-190, 27 Aug. 1997.

[48] Russian Council on Foreign and Defense Policy, 'Rossiya i Pribaltika' [Russia and the Baltic states], Moscow, Oct. 1997. The report was also published in *Nezavisimaya Gazeta*, 28 Oct. 1997, pp. 4–5. See also *Russia and the Baltic States*, Executive Summary of the Report by the Council on Foreign and Defence Policy of Russia (Council on Foreign and Defence Policy of Russia: Moscow, 1997, in English). The Executive Summary was also reproduced in *Second Annual Conference on Baltic Sea Security and Co-operation* (Embassy of the USA in Stockholm, SIPRI and Swedish Institute of International Affairs: Stockholm, 1998), pp. 139–53, appendix E.

[49] Statement of Russian Deputy Foreign Minister Alexander Avdeyev at the Nordic Council Security Conference in Helsinki on 26 Aug. 'Russian official warns against Baltics' joining NATO', *RFE/RL Newsline*, vol. 1, no. 104, part II (27 Aug. 1997).

[50] See also chapter 5, section II and chapter 12, section IV in this volume.

[51] Presentations of the foreign ministers of the 3 Baltic states in *Second Annual Conference on Baltic Sea Security and Co-operation* (note 48), pp. 27–31, 53–62, 79–81.

[52] The presidents of the 3 Baltic States formally rejected Russia's offer of security guarantees in a statement at their semi-annual summit meeting in the Lithuanian resort of Palanga on 10 Nov. Vinogradov, B., 'Baltii ne nuzhen rossiyskiy "zontik"' [The Baltics do not need a Russian 'umbrella'], *Izvestiya*, 11 Nov. 1997, p. 3.

continuing discriminatory legal provisions and practical policies of the authorities do provide ground for criticism and complaint.[53]

Another contentious issue, the border/territorial one, was by and large more successfully addressed in 1997—although in Russia routine appeals continued for pressure to be put on the Baltic states on territorial matters. However, following bilateral meetings with Chernomyrdin at the Vilnius summit meeting in September 1997, each of the three Baltic presidents announced the forthcoming signing of a border agreement with the Russian Federation. The first, between Lithuania and Russia, was signed on 24 October 1997 during an official visit of President Algirdas Brazauskas of Lithuania to Moscow.[54] With Estonia and Latvia, as in previous years, Russia insisted that documents ratifying the border agreement or other related documents would not mention the 1920 Tartu Peace Treaty (considered by Russia to have been invalid since 1940).[55] The delay in finalizing the border issues with Estonia and Latvia may reflect a rationale on Russia's part of treating the three Baltic states in different ways, rewarding Lithuania, which has been the most cooperative, while putting pressure on the other two.[56]

The Trans-Dniester region

During 1997 Russia made considerable efforts to push through a settlement for the Trans-Dniester region of Moldova. On 8 May 1997 in Moscow Moldovan President Petru Lucinschi and Igor Smirnov, the leader of the breakaway region, signed a memorandum on the basis for normalization of relations between the two entities.[57]

---

[53] In Latvia, 700 000 non-citizens out of the total 2.6 million population are subjects of discriminatory treatment in about 80 areas (for instance, pensions, the right to practise some professions, to participate in elections or start private businesses, and so on). In Oct., the OSCE mission in Latvia pointed to the slow rate of naturalization in the country. *Inside (and Beyond) Russia and FSU*, vol. 5, no. 10 (Oct. 1997), p. 9. The OSCE High Commissioner on National Minorities, Max van der Stoel, urged Latvia to amend its controversial draft language law which is in 'contradiction of international conventions Latvia has signed'. 'OSCE criticizes Latvian language bill', *RFE/RL Newsline*, vol. 1, no. 150, part II (31 Oct. 1997). In Estonia, long-resident Russians who claim citizenship continue to be treated as aliens; the citizenship examination in Estonian language and history is often considered too difficult and therefore discriminatory against the Russian-speaking minorities. Estonian citizenship is denied the children of persons resident in Estonia who have Russian citizenship. 'Estonia: Foreign Minister on relations with Russia' (note 47).

[54] 'Lithuania: Brazauskas hopes Russia will ratify border treaty', FBIS-SOV-97-270, 27 Sep. 1997; and Brazauskas, A., 'Mezhdu Rossiyey i Litvoy uzhe net territorialnykh sporov' [No more territorial disputes between Russia and Lithuania], *Izvestiya*, 21 Oct. 1997, pp. 1, 3.

[55] Sergounin, A., 'In search of a new strategy in the Baltic/Nordic area', ed. V. Baranovsky, SIPRI, *Russia and Europe: The Emerging Security Agenda* (Oxford University Press: Oxford, 1997), pp. 346–47.

[56] This 'differentiated policy' was highlighted in a document of the Ministry for Foreign Affairs, 'Russia's long-term line with respect to the Baltic states', adopted in Feb. 1997. See also Russian Council on Foreign and Defence Policy (note 48); and Goble, P., 'Drawing borders geographic and political', *RFE/RL Newsline*, vol. 1, no. 145, part II (23 Oct. 1997). The Latvian–Russian border treaty was reported to have been fully coordinated by the end of Oct. 'Latvian, Russian delegations agree draft border treaty', FBIS-SOV-97-302, 29 Oct. 1997.

[57] President Yeltsin, President Kuchma and Niels Helveg Petersen, the acting chief of the OSCE mission to Moldova, also signed the memorandum as guarantors.

However, the two sides differed considerably in their interpretations of the memorandum.[58] Another round of mediation efforts by Russia, combined with strong pressure on the separatist leaders, took place in September, when Russian Deputy Prime Minister Valeriy Serov, on a visit to Chisinau, was reported to have persuaded both sides to agree on negotiations to begin in Moscow on competence-sharing between the 'centre' and Trans-Dniester. It was also decided to establish a mechanism for regular consultations, with monthly meetings between the presidents, prime ministers and parliamentary leaders of both sides. A Trilateral Joint Control Commission was to be set up to analyse the implementation of the principles of a peace settlement and provisions for reducing military confrontation.[59]

The negotiations in Moscow on 5–9 October produced confusing results.[60] On the positive side, however, the Moldovan Defence Minister and his Trans-Dniestrian counterpart were reported to have agreed on a number of confidence-building measures, including a reduction in the size of the security zone set up in 1992 separating the two sides' troops, exchange visits to military units in the security zone and military manoeuvres. On 10 November Prime Minister Ion Ciubuc of Moldova and Smirnov signed an agreement 'on the organizational principles of social and economic cooperation'.[61]

The issue of the Russian troops, arms and military equipment deployed in Trans-Dniester since Soviet times persists.[62] The agreement of 21 October 1994 on the withdrawal of Russian forces remains unratified; practical aspects of the transfer of weapons and equipment to Moldova and/or their withdrawal have not been settled and are being obstructed by the Trans-Dniester side, which claims them as its property.[63] In September 1997, however, Moldova and Russia were reported to have reached agreement on which military equipment will be destroyed or withdrawn to Russia or sold to third parties (to

---

[58] According to Moldova, the document committed both sides to developing 'relations within the framework of a single state', while the separatist leaders assessed it as a recognition of the existence of 2 independent states which had to establish relations 'within a single entity' as equal partners. In particular, Trans-Dniester insisted on having its own constitution, state symbols, armed forces and currency and the right to maintain external relations separately in the economic, scientific, cultural, technological and other fields. A document providing for special status for the Trans-Dniester region had still to be negotiated. 'Moldova: deadlock in Dniester conflict settlement viewed', FBIS-SOV-97-253, 10 Sep. 1997.

[59] Kuzmichev, V., 'Soglashenie Kishineva i Tiraspolya' [Agreement between Chisinau and Tiraspol], *Nezavisimaya Gazeta*, 26 Sep. 1997, p. 1.

[60] Experts on both sides were reported to be drafting a power-sharing agreement, the text of which, however, was not revealed. The separatist authorities rejected it some days later, and the meeting of Lucinschi and Smirnov scheduled for 16 Oct. to endorse the agreed document did not take place.

[61] 'Chisinau, Tiraspol sign cooperation agreement', *RFE/RL Newsline*, vol. 1, no. 157, part II (11 Nov. 1997).

[62] Baranovsky (1994, note 31), pp. 189–90; Baranovsky (1995, note 31), p. 249; Baranovsky (1996, note 31), p. 261; and Baranovsky (note 1), p. 118.

[63] The withdrawal of all military equipment (which includes 119 tanks, 155 armoured combat vehicles, 33 anti-tank rocket systems, 14 Grad multiple rocket-launched systems, 83 howitzers, 35 000 trucks and millions of other items) will require 2500 heavy railway wagons. Its continuing deployment on Trans-Dniestrian soil risks becoming a serious problem because of insecure storage conditions. Vinogradov, B., 'Komu dostanutsa tanki i sapogi 14-y armii?' [Who will get the tanks and boots of the 14th Army?], *Izvestiya*, 24 Sep. 1997, p. 3.

avoid its being appropriated by the conflicting parties in Trans-Dniester).[64] At the CIS summit meeting at Chisinau in October 1997, Yeltsin reiterated Russia's readiness to withdraw the troops either 'immediately' or within two to three months if Moldova was ready to wait until the situation stabilized.[65]

While it is putting pressure on the separatists, Russia is clearly backing the Moldovan leadership.[66] The latter, however, has to face considerable domestic opposition. It is criticized both for seeking compromise with Trans-Dniester, which, allegedly, would mean the federalization of Moldova, and for bringing about the incorporation of Moldova into a Russian-dominated economic, political and military sphere. To neutralize such criticism the government stresses its readiness to involve other actors (such as Ukraine) and international organizations (such as the Council of Europe) in the settlement process. Moldova's Foreign Minister, Nicolae Tabacaru, speaking at the 52nd session of the UN General Assembly, attacked Russia's 'illegal military presence on Moldovan territory' and accused it of 'reluctance to withdraw its troops and armaments'.[67]

IV. Conflicts in the Transcaucasus

Russia's policy in the Transcaucasus in 1997 was greatly affected by growing concern over the competing influences in the area. Russia seemed to be paying closer attention to: (*a*) apprehended or actual shifts in the foreign policy orientation of the newly independent states; (*b*) efforts to promote a role for Russia in the settlement of the ongoing territorial/status conflicts; and (*c*) ways in which to consolidate its stakes in the dispute over the demarcation of maritime boundaries in the Caspian Sea and ownership of oil resources.

A volatile geopolitical landscape

In the initial post-Soviet period Russia seemed to assume that its dominant position in the Transcaucasus could not be seriously challenged, however troublesome the developments in the region. However, in 1997 it seems to have renounced any complacency in that regard and became extremely sensitive to what is perceived as the growing involvement of out-of-area actors in the region.

---

[64] Kuzmichev (note 59). In Oct., Smirnov was reported to have agreed that the Russian military equipment must be evacuated from the region.
[65] 'Yeltsin on troop withdrawal from Trans-Dniester', *RFE/RL Newsline*, vol. 1, no. 146, part II (24 Oct. 1997).
[66] At the CIS summit meeting in Chisinau in Oct. 1997, Yeltsin declared that 'the policy of Russia is clearly defined: a united and indivisible Moldova' and stressed that all the problems in the region were to be settled via Chisinau. Vinogradov, B., 'Na sammite SNG Rossiya okazalas edinstvennym mirotvortsom' [Russia seen to be the only peacekeeper at the CIS summit], *Izvestiya*, 24 Oct. 1997, p. 3. Not surprisingly, the Trans-Dniestrian application to join the CIS was rejected. Earlier, on 28 July, a Russian–Moldovan bilateral agreement on military cooperation was signed envisaging joint peacekeeping exercises, information exchange, the training of Moldovan personnel in Russian institutions of higher military education and advanced training for officers. *Nezavisimoye Voyennoye Obozreniye*, no. 32 (29 Aug.–4 Sep. 1997), p. 1.
[67] 'Tabacaru accuses Russia of "illegal military presence"', FBIS-SOV-97-274, 1 Oct. 1997.

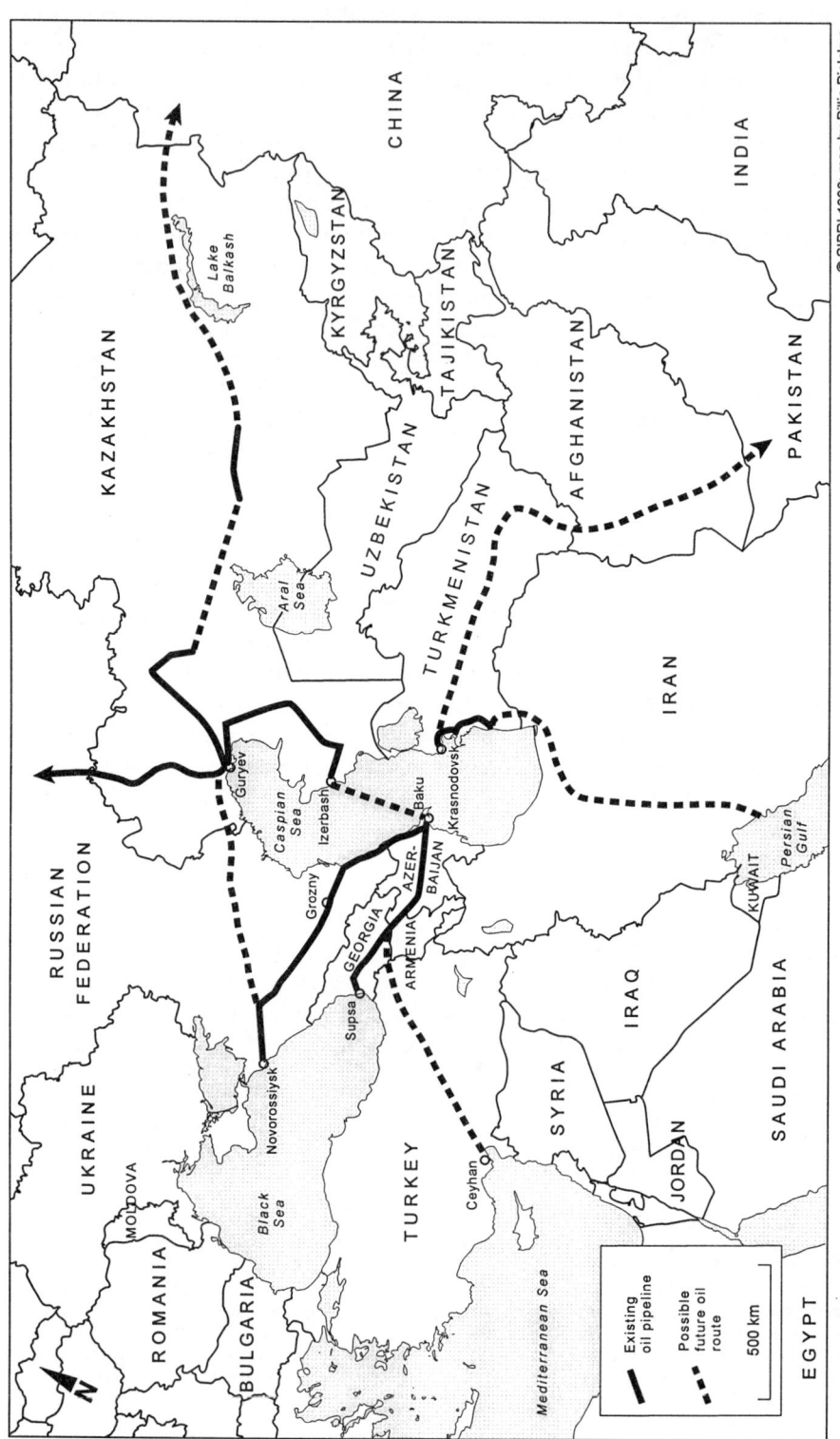

Figure 4.1. Existing and possible future oil routes from Central Asia and the Caucasus

US activism in the region is of special concern. Russia is clearly irritated by the fact that the Transcaucasus is increasingly regarded by the USA in terms of its vital interests. Rapidly developing US investments there are viewed as proof of this trend, indicating that the United States is obtaining powerful levers of influence over the strategically important region and allowing Russia to be squeezed out of the Transcaucasus. The spectacular visit of Azerbaijani President Heidar Aliev to the USA in July–August 1997 was seen in Moscow as clearly signalling forthcoming shifts in the region.[68]

A dramatic reading of this phenomenon, increasingly common in Moscow, suggests that the Transcaucasus is on the brink of fundamental changes tending towards an irrevocable reduction of Russia's position. There is a widespread and growing understanding in political quarters in Moscow that the next twist of the spiral of Russian–US rivalry for spheres of influence on the post-Soviet territory will be in the Transcaucasus. The volatile situation in the region, uncertainties about domestic developments in all three Transcaucasian states, the existence of unsettled conflicts and, last but not least, the prospects of extracting energy resources from the Caspian oilfields—all these factors could turn the Transcaucasus into the stage of intense geopolitical rivalry and require the urgent development of a more activist policy on Russia's part.[69]

There are reasons to believe that 1997 was a year of serious (although often hidden) disputes in political quarters in Moscow over strategy with respect to the Transcaucasus, the arguments being strongly influenced both by differing geopolitical considerations and by the pragmatic interests of the competing economic clans.[70]

A policy of pushing Georgia towards an alliance-type relationship might be rationalized by, and based on, Russia's ability to influence the development of two separatist conflicts there, in Abkhazia and in South Ossetia. However, even if the strategy of pressuring Georgia to look to Russia for its security was successful in 1993–94, when Georgia was in a desperate situation and its President, Eduard Shevardnadze, was virtually forced to agree to a Russian military presence, in 1997 it led to the alienation and reorientation of Georgia. In this respect Georgia's involvement in the development of alternative oil transit routes from the Caspian Sea, bypassing Russia, may be indicative

---

[68] 'US should move to "strategic partnership" with Azerbaijan', FBIS-SOV-97-224, 12 Aug. 1997; Ismailzade, E., ['Has the United States taken Russia's place?'], *Moskovskaya Pravda*, 4 Sep. 1997, p. 6; and 'Azerbaijan: growing US role in Transcaucasus examined', FBIS-SOV-97-266, 23 Sep. 1997.

[69] Yunanov, B., 'Clinton's crossing of the Caucasus Range', *Literaturnaya Gazeta*, 27 Aug. 1997, p. 9, in FBIS-SOV-97-252, 9 Sep. 1997; and 'Azerbaijan: commentary on US, Russian Caucasus plans', FBIS-SOV-97-252, 9 Sep. 1997. On Russia's oil stakes in the region, see Holoboff, E. M., URL <http://www.agora.stm.it/limes/holobof.htm>, 11 Mar. 1997.

[70] The oil and gas lobby has played a dominant role in shaping Russia's policy towards the near abroad, its powerful financial groups trying to gain control over natural resources and exert pressure on the government. Indeed, both Gazprom and the Lukoil seem to be increasingly engaged in pursuing a foreign policy of their own. Conflicts between competing financial groups may become a serious factor of Russia's policy with respect to post-Soviet conflicts and disputes, in the Transcaucasus and elsewhere. See, e.g., Narzikulov, R., 'Neft, gaz i vneshnyaya politika Rossii' [Oil, gas and Russia's foreign policy], *Nezavisimaya Gazeta*, 29 Oct. 1997, p. 5.

indeed. Another worrying trend, as seen from Moscow, is Georgia's increasing links with Azerbaijan and Ukraine.[71]

The choice between Armenia and Azerbaijan, two sworn enemies, is another, more acute problem for Russia. On the one hand, the 'oil factor'[72] and Muslim connections are the strongest arguments for considering Azerbaijan as the most important would-be strategic ally in the region; on the other hand, Armenia's geopolitical isolation and its desperate need for an outsider's protection can be viewed (or presented) as guarantees of a pro-Russian orientation in future, creating a solid basis for a counterbalance to Turkey.

Against this background, Russia seemed to be aiming to keep a certain balance in the region, both politically and militarily. This policy line, however, because it was subject to different and conflicting pressures, often appeared erratic and was much criticized by domestic opponents of the government and by the governments of the Transcaucasus, all of them criticizing Russia for partiality, inconsistency and lack of vision.[73]

On 29 August 1997, the Armenian and Russian presidents signed the Treaty of Friendship, Cooperation and Mutual Assistance and a joint declaration.[74] Azerbaijan stated that it regards the treaty (alongside 14 other Armenian–Russian documents boosting military cooperation) as aiming at the formation of a hostile military alliance.[75] Indeed, Armenia's and Russia's undertaking to assist each other in the event of armed aggression by a third state is certainly more weighty than the ritual provision for 'urgent consultations' in the Russian–Azerbaijani Treaty on Friendship, Cooperation and Mutual Security of 3 July 1997,[76] especially since confrontation between Armenia and Azerbaijan continues. Other disturbing factors for Azerbaijan included the disclosure in April 1997 of large-scale deliveries of Russian weapons to Armenia[77] and the decision of Yeltsin to annul an agreement on Russia's involvement in

---

[71] Korbut, A., 'Shevardnadze i Kuchma nedovolny Kremlem' [Shevardnadze and Kuchma dissatisfied with the Kremlin], *Nezavisimaya Gazeta*, 30 Oct. 1997, p. 3.

[72] In addition to production from Azerbaijan's offshore fields, significant revenues could accrue from the transit of Central Asian oil and gas through its territory. Some experts, however, ascribe the widespread excitement about the 'brilliant prospects' of the Caspian oil reserves to an adroit propaganda campaign initiated by Azerbaijan.

[73] Vinogradov, B., 'Trudny razgovor v Baku o svyazyakh Moskvy s Yerevanom' [Difficult discussion in Baku on the links between Moscow and Yerevan], *Izvestiya*, 9 Oct. 1997, p. 3.

[74] For the texts, see *Rossiyskaya Gazeta*, 13 Sep. 1997; and *Diplomaticheskiy Vestnik*, no. 9 (Sep. 1997), pp. 31–38. The treaty states that each party will immediately contact the other in the event of a threat of military invasion. If either country is attacked by a third party, the other will make available its military facilities and equipment for joint use. The treaty also states that military–technical policy will be coordinated, defence industries developed in tandem, military hardware standardized, and military projects jointly financed. Another important provision of the treaty covers cooperation in foreign policy.

[75] 'Azeris view Russo-Armenia pact as military alliance', FBIS-SOV-97-275, 2 Oct. 1997.

[76] For the text, see *Diplomaticheskiy Vestnik*, no. 8 (Aug. 1997), pp. 40–45.

[77] According to Lev Rokhlin, Chairman of the Duma Defence Committee, between 1993 and 1996 Russia supplied Armenia with weaponry from the Group of Russian Forces in the Caucasus. Anthony, I., 'Introduction', ed. I. Anthony, SIPRI, *Russia and the Arms Trade* (Oxford University Press: Oxford, 1998), p. 13; and Anthony, I., 'Illicit arms transfers', ed. Anthony, pp. 224–25. Azerbaijani Foreign Minister Hasan Hasanov claimed in Sep. that Russia had supplied Armenia with medium-range missiles capable of carrying nuclear warheads—an allegation which was absolutely rejected by Russia. 'Russia denies supplying Armenia with medium-range nukes', *RFE/RL Newsline*, vol. 1, no. 131, part I (3 Oct. 1997). See also chapter 12, section II in this volume.

one important Caspian oil contract.[78] Russia attempted to neutralize the increasing alienation of Azerbaijan by expressing readiness to conclude a treaty similar to the one signed with Armenia.[79] The arms deliveries to Armenia were condemned as illegal, and a joint trilateral commission was set up to investigate the case.[80] Whether these steps can help to prevent Azerbaijan from drifting further away remains highly questionable.

Another remarkable manifestation of Russia's attempts to broaden its room for manoeuvre in the Transcaucasus was its growing interaction with Iran— with respect to demarcation of the Caspian Sea shelf, cooperation on the construction of nuclear facilities in Iran and investment in Iran.[81] Apart from immediate economic gains, this policy line may be explained by the desire to establish a counterbalance to what is perceived as threatening Turkish and/or Western influence to the south of Russia.

Abkhazia

Political developments in the conflict in Abkhazia[82] were characterized by intensive negotiations pushed forward by Russia. The Russian Ministry of Foreign Affairs drafted a protocol that was intended to pave the way for a solution to the conflict, and after June 1997 it promoted regular discussions between Abkhazian and Georgian diplomats in Moscow.[83] Some of the seemingly irreconcilable differences between the two sides were reported to have been overcome at these talks.

The culmination of this development was positive and dramatic: the Abkhaz leader, Vladislav Ardzinba, met Shevardnadze in Tbilisi on 14 August, the fifth anniversary of the Georgian attack on Sukhumi.[84] Arranged and mediated by Russian Foreign Minister Yevgeniy Primakov, the meeting resulted in a declaration by the two sides abjuring the use or threat of force against each other. Government-level meetings followed aimed at restoring economic ties,

[78] During the visit of Heidar Aliev to Moscow in early July 1997 the Azerbaijani State Oil Company SOCAR signed contracts with Russia's Rosneft and Lukoil companies on joint exploitation of the Kyapaz deposit in the Caspian Sea. Because the question of the ownership of the Caspian Sea bed is not settled, and in response to protests from Turkmenistan (which claims the oil deposit), the Russian side was instructed to pull out of the contract on 1 Aug. 'Azeris, Turkmens to reach accord on disputed oil deposit', FBIS-SOV-97-270, 27 Sep. 1997.

[79] Azerbaijan was reported to have reacted without enthusiasm, pointing to the fact that it does not offer its territory for Russian military bases (in contrast to Armenia).

[80] The Russian authorities dismissed an unspecified number of military officials responsible for the clandestine transfer to Armenia.

[81] Russia denies allegations that its nuclear technology supplies to Iran might be used for military purposes. Statement of the Russian Ministry for Foreign Affairs, 9 July 1997, *Yadernoye Nerasprostraneniye* (Carnegie Moscow Center), no. 18 (July 1997), pp. 33–34. Yeltsin denounced US criticism of the $2 billion gas deal concluded at the end of Sep. by Gazprom, France's Total, Malaysia's Petronas and the National Iranian Oil Company.

[82] Amer, R. et al., 'Major armed conflicts', *SIPRI Yearbook 1993: World Armaments and Disarmament* (Oxford University Press: Oxford, 1993), pp. 99–100; Baranovsky (1994, note 31), pp. 193–95; Baranovsky (1995, note 31), pp. 251–53; Baranovsky (1996, note 31), pp. 261–65; and Baranovsky (note 1), pp. 115–17.

[83] 'Abkhazia ... what now?', *Georgia Profile*, vol. 2, no. 4 (Aug. 1997), pp. 21–25.

[84] 'The third coming', *Georgia Profile*, vol. 2, no. 5 (Sep. 1997), pp. 7–9. See also Amer (note 82), pp. 99–100.

transport links and communications between the central government in Tbilisi and the breakaway province. The Abkhaz leadership also agreed that Sukhumi and Tbilisi should have common defence and foreign policies. The Abkhaz and Georgian representatives pledged themselves to coordinate efforts to prevent terrorist activities by guerrilla formations in the border region.[85]

Nevertheless, the long-awaited political settlement did not occur in 1997. The conflicting sides continued to disagree over the key issue, the status of Abkhazia and the character of its relations with Georgia. Abkhazia reasserted that it would never accept 'even the broadest autonomous status' within Georgia: the only acceptable status for it is that of equal partner with Georgia within a confederation, which would imply common foreign and defence policies and policy on minority rights, foreign trade, border control, customs and environmental issues. Georgia interprets the 'common state' as a federation with Abkhazia as a constituent part, even if it has considerable autonomy.

The search for a solution was hampered by militant rhetoric from hard-line elements, increasing the pressure on the leaders of both sides and reducing their ability and willingness to make further concessions. The hard-liners rejected the Moscow-drafted protocol as the basis for a compromise. The talks were further complicated by the declared intention of the Abkhaz leadership to demand from Georgia $60 billion in compensation for war damage or to hold a referendum to ask whether Abkhazia should be part of Georgia, part of Russia or an independent state; by a large-scale military exercise, the first since independence, conducted by the Georgian Army in early October on territory bordering Abkhazia;[86] and by regularly repeated speculation in Tbilisi about a possible armed attack against Abkhazia.[87]

Georgia refused to lift economic sanctions on Abkhazia until an estimated 200 000 ethnic Georgian displaced persons were allowed to return to the homes they were forced to flee during the 1992–93 war. The Abkhaz side insisted on their return being delayed until sanctions had been lifted and blamed Georgian guerrilla formations for explosions and other subversive activities in the Gali district in the south of Abkhazia. In November, Russia's decision to buy Abkhaz agricultural produce without Georgia's prior permission provoked an outraged response from Georgia.[88] Meanwhile Georgia was trying to broaden international involvement in efforts at conflict settle-

[85] Fuller, E., 'Walking the Abkhaz tightrope', *RFE/RL Newsline*, vol. 1, no. 133, part I (7 Oct. 1997).

[86] Georgia, in the course of the exercise involving *c*. 12 000 troops, moved heavy weapons into the limited armaments zone, thereby violating the Agreement on a Cease-fire and Separation of Forces of 14 May 1994 and provoking protests by the commander of the Russian (CIS) peacekeeping force and the UN military observers. 'Russian gen. protests against Georgian military exercises', FBIS-SOV-97-280, 7 Oct. 1997; and Denisov, V., 'V Gruzii zavershilis voyennye ucheniya' [Military exercises in Georgia over], *Krasnaya Zvezda*, 15 Oct. 1997, p. 1.

[87] Georgian Defence Minister Vardiko Nadibaidze said his army is ready to 'resolve the Abkhaz problem by force'. Georgia's military doctrine approved in early Oct. 1997 envisages the use of the armed forces for the 'restoration of the territorial integrity' of the republic. 'Georgia: Parliament approves country's military doctrine', FBIS-SOV-97-275, 2 Oct. 1997.

[88] Georgia accused Russia of violating the decision of the CIS summit meeting of 19 Jan. 1996 stipulating that any interaction with Abkhazia, including trade, was only allowed by permission of the Government of Georgia. Sokolov, V. and Broladze, N., 'Obrazovan koordinatsionny sovet' [Coordination council established], *Nezavisimaya Gazeta*, 21 Nov. 1997, p. 3.

ment, supposedly both to encourage a less ambivalent and more supportive policy line on Russia's part and to challenge, even if indirectly, its exclusive role in the area. These efforts included: (*a*) appeals to the UN to take a more active part in the settlement process; (*b*) the emergence of the Friends of the Secretary-General on Georgia group, including France, Germany, Russia, the UK and the USA;[89] and (*c*) confirmation by Ukraine of its readiness to participate in peacekeeping operations in Abkhazia provided a corresponding decision was made by the UN.[90]

The role of peacekeeping in the area of the conflict continued to be a matter of dispute. The Russian peacekeeping contingent with a CIS mandate had been deployed in Abkhazia in June 1994 at the request of both sides in the conflict, but they differ as to its functions and area of operation.[91] In March 1997 the area of operation was extended by the CIS, in response to persistent demands from Georgia, to cover the whole of the Gali district, to which Georgian refugees are supposed to return *en masse* with peacekeepers entitled to promote and protect their return.[92] This was in practice not fulfilled: the Abkhaz authorities argued that the peacekeepers' mandate could not be amended without Abkhaz consent and this prompted the Georgian side to threaten to demand their withdrawal. The mandate of the peacekeeping forces was extended to the end of the year at the CIS summit meeting on 23 October 1997,[93] but Georgia is expected to bring pressure to bear to provide them either with a more intrusive competence or with a 'truly CIS-wide character'.[94]

The situation in another conflict area in Georgia, in South Ossetia,[95] has been mostly quiet and has allowed for further, if slow, progress towards a political settlement. The first round of negotiations between Georgia and South Ossetia began in March 1997 in Moscow. In November 1997 Presidents Shevardnadze of Georgia and Ludwig Chibirov of South Ossetia held a summit meeting. It was decided to promote the return of refugees and to accelerate the search for consensus as to South Ossetia's status within Georgia.[96]

Nagorno-Karabakh

The situation in this Armenian-populated enclave, which seeks separation from Azerbaijan, has been at a standstill since the cease-fire agreement of

---

[89] Established in 1994 to assist negotiations.
[90] 'Georgia welcomes UN efforts to settle Abkhazian conflict', FBIS-SOV-97-274, 1 Oct. 1997. At the end of Oct., Georgia and Ukraine were reported to have agreed to create a joint peacekeeping battalion with the primary task of safeguarding transport routes through Abkhazia.
[91] Baranovsky (note 1), p. 116.
[92] Tesemnikova, Ye., 'Tbilisi ne zhdyot kardinalnykh reshenii' [Tbilisi does not expect radical decisions], *Nezavisimaya Gazeta*, 18 Oct. 1997, p. 3.
[93] 'Departure of Russian peacekeepers from Abkhazia mooted', FBIS-SOV-97-301, 28 Oct. 1997.
[94] Korbut (note 71).
[95] Baranovsky (1995, note 31), p. 253; Baranovsky (1996, note 31), p. 265; and Baranovsky (note 1), p. 117.
[96] Broladze, N. and Kasayev, A., 'Esche odin shag k miru' [One more step towards peace], *Nezavisimaya Gazeta*, 18 Nov. 1997, p. 3.

16 May 1994.⁹⁷ The Karabakh forces achieved a victory over Azerbaijan and control several districts outside the enclave; their withdrawal is contingent on a satisfactory political settlement of the conflict. The political issues prominent during 1997 are described in the following sections.

Russia's 'settlement enforcement'

Seeking to promote its own leadership in the CIS and to consolidate its position in the Transcaucasus, Russia was diplomatically active on the issue of Nagorno-Karabakh throughout 1997 at different levels—from putting pressure on the presidents of Armenia and Azerbaijan to a kind of shuttle diplomacy of the part of Foreign Minister Primakov.⁹⁸ In October, Yeltsin won French President Jacques Chirac's endorsement of the idea of inviting the presidents of Armenia and Azerbaijan to Moscow for quadrilateral talks on the Karabakh conflict, with the possible involvement of the USA as well.

Having officially taken a firm stand against separatism, not least in the light of its own experience in Chechnya, Russia appeared to consider settlement contingent upon a compromise to be reached by Armenia and Azerbaijan and not to regard Nagorno-Karabakh as a full-fledged negotiating partner (which, in fact, is also Azerbaijan's approach).⁹⁹ The proposal for a high-level conference on Nagorno-Karabakh did not, therefore, envisage the participation of the Karabakh leadership.¹⁰⁰ Not surprisingly, newly elected President Arkadiy Ghukasian of the unrecognized Nagorno-Karabakh Republic complained that the Russian Ministry of Foreign Affairs had 'a monopoly' on mediating a solution to the conflict.¹⁰¹

A phased approach

The OSCE Minsk Group was set up in Mar. 1992 to monitor the situation in Nagorno-Karabakh.¹⁰² The initial logic of its mediation work was that a 'package deal' would address all the major aspects of the settlement—the political status of Karabakh, troop withdrawals from occupied territories, the return of refugees and security guarantees against the resumption of hostilities. In June 1997 the co-chairmen of the OSCE Minsk Conference on Nagorno-Karabakh (France, Russia and the USA) presented the conflicting parties with

---

⁹⁷ Baranovsky (1995, note 31), pp. 254–55; Baranovsky (1996, note 31), pp. 265–67; and Baranovsky (note 1), pp. 113–15.

⁹⁸ 'Aliyev, Yeltsin agree on Russia's shuttle diplomacy', FBIS-SOV-97-281, 8 Oct. 1997.

⁹⁹ As President Ter-Petrosian of Armenia pointed out, Russia cannot be expected to recognize Karabakh's independence when it has 20 Karabakhs of its own. 'Voyna ili mir?' [War or peace?], *Nezavisimaya Gazeta*, 5 Nov. 1997, p. 5.

¹⁰⁰ Armenia agreed to attend the Moscow summit meeting on Karabakh only if representatives from Nagorno-Karabakh are also invited.

¹⁰¹ Ghukasian wanted the OSCE Minsk Group to be promoted as the best forum for mediation, although it had proved to be sympathetic to Azerbaijan's position. In another official statement by Karabakh, Iran was proposed as a possible co-guarantor of a settlement.

¹⁰² For the membership of the Minsk Group in 1997, see the glossary.

new proposals based on a phased approach.[103] It was proposed to proceed with the settlement on a step-by-step basis, starting by withdrawing the troops of Nagorno-Karabakh from six Azerbaijani districts which do not belong to Nagorno-Karabakh proper and by allowing the return of all refugees, Azeris as well as Armenians. Military forces would be withdrawn later from the areas of Lachin, which links the enclave of Nagorno-Karabakh with Armenia, and Shusha, which allows for strategic control over the contested region, in parallel with negotiations on Nagorno-Karabakh's status. International peacekeepers would be deployed in those districts, while Karabakh's armed forces would be maintained until an agreement on status was reached, to be reduced to a military police force afterwards.

Azerbaijan agreed to a phased approach, although initially it had demanded unconditional troop withdrawal from all non-Karabakh territories.[104] Armenia expressed serious reservations and only reluctantly supported the plan later.[105] The most intransigent position was taken by Nagorno-Karabakh, which argued that all aspects of the conflict must be resolved simultaneously—or, alternatively, the issue of status should be decided first and withdrawal of Armenian forces from occupied Azerbaijani territory only envisaged for the third phase.[106]

Control over occupied territories is the main bargaining chip for Nagorno-Karabakh, which will not be keen to deprive itself of the principal leverage it has to trade against satisfactory political status. Furthermore, given the dynamics of its military buildup, its oil wealth and its prospect of regaining lost territories, which would allow for strategic dominance over Nagorno-Karabakh, Azerbaijan may be tempted to resolve the dispute by force after the first stage of the peace process. Finally, Nagorno-Karabakh considered that a phased approach could result in a division, analogous to that of Cyprus, into Armenian and Azerbaijani sectors.

The status of Nagorno-Karabakh

Nagorno-Karabakh has maintained de facto independence for five years and is by no means enthusiastic about the 'broadest possible autonomy' formula suggested by Azerbaijan. Its Armenian population may have good reason to fear ethnically based discrimination if Nagorno-Karabakh is re-established as part of Azerbaijan.[107] Azerbaijan, however, has been successful in promoting the principle of the territorial integrity of states and getting the support of the

---

[103] The exact terms of the new proposal were not made public officially, but became the subject of numerous comments and interpretations. The idea of a phased approach was reiterated later, in the Minsk Group co-chairmen's proposal of 21 Sep.

[104] Gadzhizade, A., 'Visit Minskoy gruppy v Baku' [Minsk Group's visit to Baku], *Nezavisimaya Gazeta*, 25 Sep. 1997, p. 3.

[105] 'Armenian deputy minister criticises OSCE Karabakh decision', FBIS-SOV-97-277, 4 Oct. 1997; and 'Armenia accepts OSCE initiative on Nagorno-Karabakh', FBIS-SOV-97-305, 1 Nov. 1997.

[106] 'Azerbaijan: Karabakh President rejects OSCE mediators' proposals', FBIS-SOV-97-281, 8 Oct. 1997.

[107] The Karabakh authorities blame Azerbaijan for a deliberate 'policy of creating anti-Armenian stereotypes and sowing chauvinistic feelings'. 'Armenia: NKR mission claims Azerbaijan prepares war', FBIS-SOV-97-281, 8 Oct. 1997.

international community on that account. Especially significant was the endorsement of this principle, with respect to the issue of Nagorno-Karabakh, by the OSCE Lisbon summit meeting in December 1996. Significantly, Russia's official stand is that it 'does not doubt the need to ensure Azerbaijan's territorial integrity'.[108] Armenia is also aware that supporting either the independence of Nagorno-Karabakh or its incorporation into Armenia would inevitably be followed by sanctions.[109]

Against this background, an important new theme was developed by Karabakh officials. In September Ghukasian suggested possible alternatives to the extremes of *de jure* independence for Nagorno-Karabakh or its subordination again to Azerbaijan, advocating 'limited sovereignty' in a quasi-federal state with a single parliament. The central government would be responsible for certain policy areas, including the environment, energy, communications and possibly even the economy. Furthermore, in October 1997 Ghukasian was reported to have declared for the first time that full statehood for Nagorno-Karabakh was 'inconceivable' and that some kind of status within Azerbaijan must be considered. Azerbaijan, however, may see this new approach as leading to a 'confederation option', similar to those discussed for Abkhazia and the Trans-Dniester region, that will not be acceptable.

Domestic constraints

Attempts to reach a compromise are complicated by the intransigent demands of all the parties involved. The radical faction of the leadership of Nagorno-Karabakh seems to be against any attempts to lower the stakes on the issue of status; it is indicative that the statement of Ghukasian mentioned above was followed by an official denial that Nagorno-Karabakh was 'ready to submit to Azerbaijan's authority'. Similarly, in Azerbaijan, the Round Table opposition coalition called for the OSCE peace plan to be rejected; Aliev's potential rival, former President Ebulfez Elcibey, called it unacceptable because it would undermine Azerbaijan's territorial integrity and advocated military action to resolve the conflict if it proved impossible to do so by peaceful means.

The most serious domestic protests against compromise over Nagorno-Karabakh were levelled at President Levon Ter-Petrosian of Armenia. He was accused of capitulating to Azerbaijan and urged to reject the OSCE peace proposal; the opposition parties organized massive demonstrations and rallies, called him a traitor to the national interest and demanded his resignation. A further obstacle to the peace process was diverging views within the Armenian leadership: some of its influential members, including the prime minister and the ministers of the interior and national security, were prominent wartime leaders in Nagorno-Karabakh, and others (such as the defence minister) urged the Armenian people 'to fight our last war to the finish'. As a result, on

---

[108] Statement of Russian Foreign Minister Primakov. 'Baku urges Russia to step up arms to Armenia investigation', FBIS-SOV-97-280, 7 Oct. 1997.
[109] Matevosian, G., 'Utrom—dogovor, vecherom—soyuz' [A treaty in the morning, a union in the evening], *Segodnya*, 30 Sep. 1997, p. 3.

4 February 1998 Ter-Petrosian was forced to resign. None of the candidates in the presidential elections on 16 March endorsed the Minsk Group's plan for Nagorno-Karabakh.

V. Tajikistan

The process of political settlement in Tajikistan in 1997 basically followed the lines established by the breakthrough agreement between the government in Dushanbe and the United Tajik Opposition, reached in Moscow in December 1996.[110] The Statute of the National Reconciliation Commission was adopted on 21 February 1997. At the Inter-Tajik negotiations, held in Moscow on 26 February–8 March 1997 under the auspices of the UN, the parties signed a protocol on military problems envisaging the integration of the opposition and government armed units by 1 July 1998.[111] At the next round of negotiations, in Bishkek, on 16–18 May 1997 the parties adopted a protocol on political issues which included an amnesty for political opponents of the government, the establishment of a central electoral commission, the inclusion of representatives of the opposition in the government, freedom of operation for the opposition parties and movements, and access to the media. It was also agreed to deploy opposition armed units (with 460 personnel) in Dushanbe.[112] Finally, a general agreement on establishing peace and national reconciliation in Tajikistan was signed at a ceremony in Moscow on 27 June 1997.[113]

Both parties seemed determined to proceed with implementation of the political decisions. The leader of United Tajik Opposition, Said Abdullo Nuri, returned to Dushanbe in September to head the National Reconciliation Commission, composed of representatives of the government and the opposition. The commission formed four subcommittees to deal with legal, military, political and refugee issues; on 9 October it started to discuss, together with OSCE and UN representatives, the constitutional arrangements for Tajikistan, including the problems of creating a parliament.[114] Starting in October, the government began to release jailed opposition supporters on the basis of an amnesty for participants in the 1992–93 fighting. By the end of the year the parties were discussing the possibility of reserving 30 per cent of government posts for the opposition.[115]

The parties also cooperated in promoting the return of Tajik refugees from Afghanistan, which began on 17 July. By mid-November, nearly 10 000 had been repatriated.

The difficult matter of organizing interaction between and eventual merger of government and opposition forces, fierce enemies until recently, will be one of the key tests for the settlement process. It was confirmed that the military

---

[110] Baranovsky (note 1), pp. 119–20.
[111] For the text, see *Diplomaticheskiy Vestnik*, no. 4 (Apr. 1997), pp. 45–46.
[112] *Diplomaticheskiy Vestnik*, no. 6 (June 1997), pp. 39–40.
[113] For the text, see *Diplomaticheskiy Vestnik*, no. 7 (July 1997), pp. 45–46.
[114] Kharvet, Ye., 'Zalozhnikov pytayutsa osvobodit'' [Attempts to liberate the hostages], *Nezavisimaya Gazeta*, 10 Oct. 1997, p. 3.
[115] 'Tajik President Rakhmanov says peace process "irreversible"', FBIS-SOV-97-308, 4 Nov. 1997.

units of the opposition were gradually to become part of the government force structures.[116] Armed groups were asked to declare their loyalties to either the government or the United Tajik Opposition by 16 November 1997; groups not responding would be disarmed by force. President Imomali Rakhmonov of Tajikistan and Said Abdullo Nuri were reported to be discussing how to repatriate opposition fighters still in Afghanistan and where they should be stationed once back in Tajikistan.

While the principal rivals seemed to be engaged in overcoming confrontation and searching for accommodation, numerous reports pointed to the reluctance of independent field commanders on both sides to follow the logic of reconciliation. Armed clashes, terrorist actions, hostage-takings, pillaging and explosions continued and intensified in different areas of the country, prompting the government and the opposition to develop joint operations to restore order and fight crime.[117] The weakness of the 'official' political regime became only more obvious in the light of the continuing struggle between rival clans attempting to shore up President Rakhmonov's hold on power. Local commanders and political bosses frequently challenged the authority of Dushanbe, even using force to keep control of their respective territories or eventually to overthrow the government.[118] On the opposition side, a major split was caused by the absence of charismatic leader Hoji Akbar Turajonzoda from power sharing.[119] There were also reports accusing the government of maintaining strict control over the media and not allowing adequate information on the reconciliation process.[120]

Russia has played a significant role in promoting the settlement process in all its elements, from actively mediating in the negotiations (indeed, pushing the government to adopt a more conciliatory approach) to assisting in the transfer of opposition combatants to Dushanbe.[121] The mandate of the CIS Collective Peacekeeping Forces in Tajikistan, whose composition and financing are predominantly Russian, includes the promotion of dialogue between the conflicting parties, humanitarian supply and assistance to the return of refugees.[122] While proceeding in its policy from broader geopolitical rationales, such as preventing the destabilization of the whole of Central Asia and maintaining Russia's future role in the area,[123] Russia has apparently not

[116] Vinogradov, B., 'Nochnoy boy v Dushanbe' [Fighting at night in Dushanbe], *Izvestiya*, 17 Oct. 1997, p. 3.
[117] Vinogradov (note 116).
[118] Grankina, V., 'Borba za vliyanie prodolzhayetsa' [The struggle for influence continues], *Nezavisimaya Gazeta*, 2 Oct. 1997, p. 3; and Zadonov, A., 'V Tadzhikistane po-prezhnemu delyat vlast' [Power-sharing continues in Tajikistan], *Nezavisimaya Gazeta*, 4 Nov. 1997, p. 3.
[119] In Mar. 1998, Turajonzoda returned to Dushanbe and was appointed to the government.
[120] Grankina, V., 'Mezhdunarodnye organizatsii bespokoyatsa' [International organizations worry], *Nezavisimaya Gazeta*, 21 Nov. 1997, p. 3.
[121] Tesemnikova, Ye., 'Razgromlena antipravitelstvennaya gruppirovka' [An anti-government group is defeated], *Nezavisimaya Gazeta*, 31 Oct. 1997, p. 3.
[122] The total number of peacekeepers is *c*. 8000. Zavarin, V., 'Mirotvorcheskiye sily v Tadzhikistane' [Peacekeeping forces in Tajikistan], *Nezavisimoye Voyennoye Obozreniye*, no. 41 (31 Oct.–13 Nov. 1997), p. 2. See also Baranovsky (1996, note 31), p. 268.
[123] In particular, the Russian peacekeeping forces currently deployed along the Tajik–Afghan frontier are viewed as an important source of leverage for Russia; it is popularly believed among Moscow's politicians that their withdrawal would mean that 'we lose Central Asia for good'.

felt seriously challenged by the modest intermediary efforts of other international actors (in particular the UN and the OSCE).[124] In any case, it can be given credit for its contribution to the prospects of re-establishing Tajikistan from the ruins of its devastating civil war.

Stability in the country, however, is still to be consolidated; failure to do this could have negative international implications. Significantly, Tajik officials claimed in October that Uzbekistan was aiding and abetting anti-government forces in Tajikistan. This allegation was widely commented on by the Russian media as a worrying external involvement; the Russian Ministry of Foreign Affairs expressed concern about reported clashes on the Tajik–Uzbek frontier. Uzbekistan denied all accusations on that account and the most notorious of the Tajik anti-government rebels stated that 'the current regime is interested in giving the conflict an inter-ethnic dimension and presenting the situation as if Tajiks were fighting with Uzbeks'.[125] One interpretation of these developments is that Uzbekistan may be interested in undermining the peace process in Tajikistan because the forthcoming legalization of the Islamic Resurrection Party there and its possible inclusion in the government could lead to the appearance of extremist Islamic forces in the underground in Uzbekistan.[126]

VI. The CIS: a lower profile?

Russia's official position of giving priority to the CIS in its foreign policy is unchanged. In terms of practical policy, however, Russia seems to be facing increasing problems in relations with its post-Soviet neighbours rather than considering the 'near abroad' as a reliable power pole.

Economic interdependence is without doubt a major factor in the development of the CIS. Some of Russia's partners, however, are increasingly determined to use their resources to achieve a more independent position, even if officially their attitude towards Russia is loyal. Azerbaijan's policy of using the 'big oil' argument in order to distance itself from Russia is a case in point. Russia, meanwhile, is not in a position to play the role of economic sponsor with its less developed CIS partners. Indeed, a considerable section of the pragmatically oriented Russian élites seems to be less enthusiastic about the prospects of 'integration' than it was two years ago: other CIS states, with few exceptions, are regarded as a burden rather than an asset. The CIS summit meeting in Chisinau in October 1997 saw Russia's CIS partners for the first time in the history of the organization presenting a united front against Russia and accusing it in harsh terms of lack of determination in its CIS policy.

Neither is 'variable geometry' conducive to the further consolidation of the CIS. The 'union of two' (Belarus and Russia) and a 'union of four' (Belarus,

---

[124] On the UN Mission of Observers in Tajikistan (UNMOT), see appendix 2A in this volume. UN Security Council Resolution no. 1138 of 14 Nov. 1997 authorized an increase in the number of UN military observers by 75 to 132.
[125] Interview with Col Khudoyberdiyev, commander of the brigade revolting against the Tajik Government, in *Nezavisimaya Gazeta*, 31 Oct, 1997, p. 3.
[126] Zadonov (note 118).

Kazakhstan, Kyrgyzstan and Russia)[127] are both of doubtful vitality and exist on paper rather than in reality. Nor will they contribute to forging a sustainable cooperation pattern on the level of the whole CIS. In practical policy, both Russia and other CIS member states clearly prefer bilateral links to troublesome and ineffective multilateralism.

Russia's role in the ongoing conflicts on the territory of the CIS is recognized as essential, in terms both of peacekeeping and of efforts for political settlement.[128] However, its support for the principle of territorial integrity is not always decisive in undermining separatist claims in the post-Soviet states. In some cases Russia is criticized for ambivalence in implementing this policy line; attempts to work out political compromises and reluctance to give peacekeepers enforcement missions are interpreted as freezing the status quo and perpetuating conflicts.

Russia seems to be seriously concerned about those developments within the CIS that are neither initiated nor guided by itself. An informal alignment of Azerbaijan, Georgia and Ukraine is reported to have existed since late 1996, with Moldova apparently moving closer to it. An unofficial 'group of four' (GUAM—Georgia, Ukraine, Azerbaijan and Moldova) emerged on 15 May 1997 in the course of discussions on the CFE Treaty flank limits; since then the participants have shown a clear interest in developing broader regional cooperation in order to build a 'stable and secure Europe'.[129] This is apparently seen in Moscow as an anti-Russian axis and in the capitals of the countries involved as a means of pressurizing Russia.[130] Whether it will change the political balance within the CIS and move its centre of gravity away from Russia, as is feared in Moscow,[131] is an open question. The prospects of this post-Soviet quasi-alliance, whose members were 'dispersing to different corners',[132] looked by no means brilliant at the end of 1997.

VII. Conclusions

Throughout 1997, Russia showed spectacular activity in addressing the past, ongoing and potential conflicts in the post-Soviet territories. It played a

[127] Baranovsky (note 1), p. 120.

[128] Jonson, L. and Archer, C. (eds), *Peacekeeping and the Role of Russia in Eurasia* (Westview Press: Boulder, Colo., 1996).

[129] Akhundova, E., 'Kiev i Kishinev ischut svoy put v obkhod Rossii' [Kiev and Chisinau are looking for ways to bypass Russia], *Izvestiya*, 15 Oct. 1997, p. 3; 'Azerbaijan, Georgia, Moldova favor Black Sea summit', FBIS-SOV-97-287, 14 Oct. 1997; and Gadzhizade, A., 'Aktiviziruyutsa kontakty Armenii i Azerbaijana' [More active contacts between Armenia and Azerbaijan], *Nezavisimaya Gazeta*, 16 Oct. 1997, p. 3. On the CFE Treaty flank limits, see also chapter 12 in this volume.

[130] Ivzhenko, T., 'SNG dlya Ukrainy—regionalnaya struktura' [The CIS is only a regional structure for Ukraine], *Nezavisimaya Gazeta*, 23 Oct. 1997, p. 3. According to a Ukrainian commentator, the political goals of participants to the GUAM informal association are obvious: 'it is easier for them to jointly support their interests in the region where Moscow's influence is quite considerable'. Ukraine's support is regarded by the 3 other countries 'as a weighty anti-Russian argument in negotiations with Moscow'. 'Ukraine: daily describes agreement with Georgia, Azerbaijan, Moldova', FBIS-SOV-97-314, 10 Nov. 1997.

[131] Korbut (note 71).

[132] This was the assessment of then Prime Minister Chernomyrdin. 'Stroev, Chernomyrdin on GUAM', *RFE/RL Newsline*, vol. 1, no. 174, part I (8 Dec. 1997).

prominent role in launching and promoting a political reconciliation process in Tajikistan; it increased efforts to bring the conflicting parties to negotiate in the Trans-Dniester region, Abkhazia and Nagorno-Karabakh; and a painful accommodation to the new situation in breakaway Chechnya is under way. Successful resolution of the dispute over the Black Sea Fleet opened the way for the signing of a basic treaty with Ukraine. The tone of its interaction with the Baltic states is becoming more constructive and pragmatic.

The 1997 record, however, includes some unfulfilled expectations and persistent worrying problems. In some conflict areas the process of political settlement is very fragile and the possibility of a resumption of hostilities persists; the prospects of defining an acceptable status for breakaway regions are uncertain and Russia's ability to put pressure on separatists has turned out to be rather limited. Chechnya's status remains a big question mark, as do instabilities in the whole North Caucasus area of Russia. Although the CIS was proclaimed Russia's highest foreign policy priority, it does not appear to be a reliable means of forging a Russia-centred power pole. Other member states are looking for alternative options. In Russia's southern vicinity, its sensitivity is focused on the Caspian oil reserves. In Europe, the prospect of NATO enlargement to include the Baltic states, even if not on the immediate political agenda, still has explosive potential—unless considerable progress takes place in involving Russia in a pan-European security architecture.

Russia's policy is apparently following two lines of thinking: putting the developments along its periphery into a broader geopolitical context, on the one hand, and looking for immediate economic gains, on the other hand. On both tracks, Russia seems to be operating more consistently, but also to be experiencing growing concern about competing influences practically everywhere—in the Transcaucasus, Central Asia and the European part of the former Soviet Union.

5. Europe: the transition to inclusive security

ADAM DANIEL ROTFELD

I. Introduction

Enlargement of the membership of the North Atlantic Treaty Organization (NATO) and the European Union (EU) dominated the European security agenda in 1997. The two processes are independent, although they were started almost in parallel. The critical element which they have in common is that they are institutional expressions of integration in the sphere of international security, not only in economic, social or legal affairs. In the long term, these processes—as understood by the politicians who set them in motion—are intended to contribute to overcoming the divisions of the cold war era.[1] They are the most profound and complex elements of the remodelling of European security institutions since the collapse of the Berlin Wall and the dissolution of the Soviet Union at the turn of the decade.[2]

Three protocols of accession to NATO were signed in 1997 and will be submitted to the parliaments of the NATO members in 1998 for ratification. In the EU, a decision was taken to open accession talks with applicant countries in the spring of 1998. Thus, although final decisions about the enlargement of the two organizations were not made in 1997, the directions of their further political evolution were mapped out.

With the absence of an external threat and the codification of relationships within NATO and between the alliance and several former Soviet republics in documents signed in 1997, the divide between the states belonging to NATO and those outside it is becoming less distinct. In the case of the EU, however, the difference between member and non-member states is still quite distinct. The EU process is more complex since both current and new members must undergo significant adjustments to accommodate an expanded organization.

The Euro-Atlantic security organization with the most inclusive membership is the Organization for Security and Co-operation in Europe (OSCE). In 1997 the OSCE Ministerial Council decided that the OSCE would strengthen the non-hierarchical and mutually reinforcing nature of the relationship between all the security-related organizations and continued its negotiations on a Charter on European Security.

---

[1] In a statement before the Senate Armed Services Committee on 23 Apr. 1997, US Secretary of State Madeleine Albright explained why, in the US view, NATO should be enlarged: 'The people of central Europe have a chance to see the erasure of a Cold War dividing line that has cut them off from the European mainstream. The people of Russia have a chance to achieve the deepest and most genuine integration with the West that their nation has ever enjoyed'. Office of the Spokesman, US Department of State, Washington, DC, 23 Apr. 1997.

[2] Eyal, J., 'NATO's enlargement: anatomy of a decision', *International Affairs*, vol. 73, no. 4 (1997), pp. 645–719.

SIPRI Yearbook 1998: Armaments, Disarmament and International Security

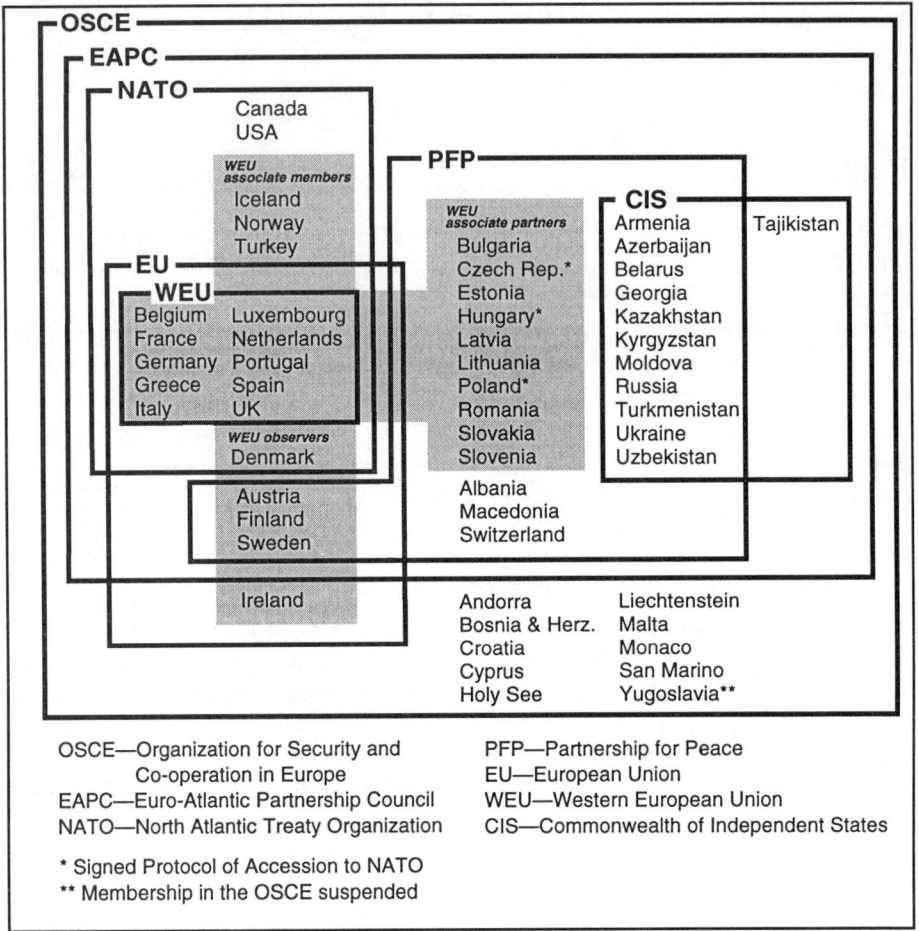

Figure 5.1. The overlapping membership of multilateral Euro-Atlantic security organizations, as of 1 January 1998

Sections II and III of this chapter discuss the enlargement processes of NATO and the EU, respectively. Section IV describes and analyses the activities of the OSCE and section V presents the conclusions. Figure 5.1 shows the current membership of seven Euro-Atlantic organizations.

II. NATO: enlargement and new security arrangements

After the dissolution of the Warsaw Treaty Organization (WTO) and the breakup of the Soviet Union in 1991, the issue of the mandate of the Atlantic Alliance came to the fore. Since the external threat to NATO had disappeared, NATO's main future tasks were reoriented from deterrence or the defence of Western nations against aggression from the east to stability in Europe and cooperation between the United States and European states in wider security matters. The new challenge for NATO is cooperation among its member states and with those states which wish to join it as well as between the alliance and those states which wish or will have to remain outside it.

A central issue of 1997 in this regard was that of the forms and scope of cooperation between NATO and Russia. The general directions of NATO–Russia collaboration were discussed by Russian President Boris Yeltsin and US President Bill Clinton at the summit meeting in Helsinki on 20–21 March 1997.[3] The outcome was that: (*a*) NATO enlargement will go forward; (*b*) no European nation will be excluded from consideration; (*c*) there will be no 'second-class' membership—NATO's new members will enjoy the same benefits and obligations as its current members; (*d*) a new forum will be established for consultation and cooperation between and, where possible, joint action by Russia and NATO;[4] and (*e*) NATO will continue to evolve but its core function of collective defence will be maintained and enhanced.

Russia also wanted the USA and other NATO members to undertake, without reservations, commitments regarding the non-deployment of nuclear and conventional forces on the territories of new NATO member states. NATO offered instead to confirm the 1996 statement of the North Atlantic Council (NAC) that currently and in the foreseeable future there is 'no intention, no plan, and no reason' to station nuclear weapons in the new member states.[5] NATO also declared that it did not contemplate a 'permanent stationing of substantial combat forces' on the territories of new member states.[6] The binding limits on conventional armed forces in Europe were to be agreed under the adapted Treaty on Conventional Armed Forces in Europe (the 1990 CFE Treaty).[7] After the Helsinki summit meeting it became clear that the USA was interested in engaging Russia in an active, constructive and cooperative relationship, with the understanding that the new NATO–Russia security arrangement would offer Russia neither a veto right nor a *droit de regard* over NATO enlargement.

The NATO–Russia Founding Act

Following several rounds of negotiations initiated in January 1997 between NATO Secretary General Javier Solana and Russian Foreign Minister Yevgeniy Primakov, the text of the NATO–Russia Founding Act on Mutual Relations, Cooperation and Security was completed in Moscow on 14 May and

---

[3] At the Helsinki summit meeting the Russian and US presidents issued a joint statement which contained the following information: '[w]hile they continue to disagree on the issue of NATO enlargement, in order to minimize the consequence of this disagreement, they agreed to work, together with others, on a document to establish a cooperative relationship between NATO and Russia as an important part of a new European security system'. Joint Statement on European Security released at the US–Russian summit meeting in Helsinki, 21 Mar. 1997, in *Arms Control Today*, vol. 27, no. 1 (1997), pp. 20–21. For the discussions of nuclear arms control at the Helsinki summit meeting, see chapter 10 in this volume.

[4] Such a forum will not have the power 'to dilute, delay or block NATO decisions', nor will it supplant NATO's North Atlantic Council. Albright, in Office of the Spokesman (note 1).

[5] NATO Press Communiqué M-NAC-2(96)165, 10 Dec. 1996.

[6] NATO Press Release 97(27), 14 Mar. 1997.

[7] See also chapter 12 in this volume.

signed in Paris on 27 May 1997.[8] The document established a permanent institutional framework for a security partnership between NATO and Russia.

The aim of the Founding Act is to 'build together a lasting and inclusive peace in the Euro-Atlantic area on the principles of democracy and cooperative security' (Preamble). NATO and Russia agreed to develop their relations around a shared commitment to seven principles defined in the Founding Act and based on an allegiance to shared values, commitments and norms of behaviour.

The main operational instrument for consultation and cooperation is the NATO–Russia Permanent Joint Council (PJC), established in Section II of the Founding Act. The signatories agreed that their consultations will not extend to the internal affairs of NATO, its member states or Russia. The key provision is that neither NATO nor Russia has 'a right of veto over the actions of the other'. None of the provisions can be used 'as a means to disadvantage the interests of other states'. In the Founding Act the two parties are committed to identify and pursue as many opportunities for joint action as possible. They will inform each other of the security-related challenges they face and the measures that each intends to take to address them. The PJC is to meet twice annually at the level of foreign ministers and defence ministers and monthly at the level of ambassadors/permanent representatives to the NAC.

In order to implement these decisions, a working programme was agreed by the parties.[9] Headed by Ambassador Vitaliy Churkin, the Russian mission to NATO included a senior military representative and staff for military cooperation. Russia has also established working contacts and consultations with NATO. Nonetheless, its view of NATO enlargement to the east is still negative. Russia is also critical of NATO's internal transformation because, in its view, NATO should become a political rather than a military organization.[10]

Nineteen areas for consultation and cooperation at PJC meetings were defined in Section III of the Founding Act. In political–military matters, NATO and Russia committed themselves to 'work together in Vienna with the other States Parties to adapt the CFE Treaty to enhance its viability and effectiveness, taking into account Europe's changing security environment and the legitimate security interests of all OSCE participating States' (Section IV).[11]

[8] The text of the NATO–Russia Founding Act is reproduced in appendix 5A in this volume.

[9] NATO Secretary General Javier Solana informed the Conference on European Security with an Enlarged NATO, held in Rome on 3 Oct. 1997, that 'A very ambitious and detailed work programme has already been agreed between the two parties until the end of the year, covering issues for NATO–Russia consultations, issues for practical cooperation between NATO and Russia and the implementation of the structures mentioned in the Founding Act. . . . All in all, six months since the signing of the Founding Act, the PJC will have met three times at ministerial level and five times at ambassadorial level'. Text of the keynote speech delivered by the NATO Secretary General to the Conference on European Security with an Enlarged NATO, Rome, 3 Oct. 1997. After the second NATO–Russia PJC meeting at the level of foreign ministers, held in Brussels on 17 Dec. 1997, the ministers noted 'the positive development of NATO–Russia relations and the substantial increase of consultation and cooperation achieved over the last few months, at the level of Foreign Ministers, Defense Ministers, Chiefs of General Staff, and Ambassadors'. NATO Press Summary, 17 Dec. 1997, URL <http://www.nato.int/docu/pr/pr97e.htm>, version current on 3 Apr. 1998.

[10] Sergeyev, I., 'We are not adversaries, we are partners', *NATO Review*, no. 1 (spring 1998), p. 17.

[11] In this context Russia and NATO stated that they share the objective of concluding an adaptation agreement 'as expeditiously as possible and, as a first step in this process, they will, together with other

The Founding Act encouraged other parties to the CFE Treaty to lower their levels of armaments and armed forces in the area of application of the treaty. NATO and Russia committed themselves to exercise restraint in relation to their current postures and capabilities during the period of negotiations.[12]

The Founding Act also contains other recommendations for giving the concept of inclusiveness a more concrete operational meaning and removing Russia's resistance and fears regarding NATO enlargement. Whether the accord will meet the expectations of both sides will be determined by how it is implemented. Although there were indications that they had different interpretations of some issues even before the Founding Act was signed—primarily regarding whether the NATO enlargement process is open-ended—there are many indications that Russia has reconciled itself to the fact that some or all of the former non-Soviet WTO countries may join NATO.

The NATO–Ukraine Charter

On 9 July 1997, soon after the signing of the NATO–Russia Founding Act, the Charter on a Distinctive Partnership between NATO and Ukraine was signed in Madrid.[13] However, the institutionalization of relations between NATO and Ukraine is different from that of relations between NATO and Russia. While the NATO–Russia document is considered by Russia as a kind of 'containment' of the alliance, the NATO–Ukraine Charter is oriented towards 'convergence' of Ukraine in a closer relationship to the alliance.[14] One of the indirect effects of the charter is that Ukraine has become more self-confident in pursuing a constructive partnership with Russia.

As stipulated in Article IV of the charter, consultations and cooperation will be implemented through meetings between NATO and Ukraine at different levels: with the North Atlantic Council and with appropriate NATO committees at intervals to be mutually agreed; in exchanges of military liaison missions in Brussels and Kiev; in reciprocal high-level visits, and so on. The NAC will meet periodically with Ukrainian representatives in the NATO–Ukraine Commission, as a rule at least twice a year, to assess the development

---

States Parties to the CFE Treaty, seek to conclude as soon as possible a framework agreement setting forth the basic elements of an adapted CFE treaty, consistent with the objectives and principles of the Document on Scope and Parameters agreed at Lisbon in December 1996'. NATO–Russia Founding Act, Section IV. See also chapter 12 in this volume.

[12] This commitment was earlier expressed in the 1996 OSCE Lisbon Summit Declaration. Document adopted by the States Parties to the Treaty on Conventional Armed Forces in Europe on the Scope and Parameters of the Process Commissioned in Paragraph 19 of the Final Document of the first CFE Treaty Review Conference, of the 1996 Lisbon Summit Declaration, reproduced in *SIPRI Yearbook 1997: Armaments, Disarmament and International Security* (Oxford University Press: Oxford, 1997), pp. 157–59.

[13] For the text of the NATO–Ukraine Charter, see *NATO Review*, July/Aug. 1997, Documentation, pp. 5–6. The idea that the Western countries, in their dialogue on security, treat Russia, Ukraine and the Baltic states equally was reflected in the conclusions of *A Future Security Agenda for Europe: Report of the Independent Working Group established by the Stockholm International Peace Research Institute* (SIPRI: Stockholm, Oct. 1996), p. 11.

[14] Alexandrova, O., 'The NATO–Ukraine Charter: Kiev's Europe–Atlantic integration', *Aussenpolitik*, no. 4, vol. 48 (4th quarter 1997), pp. 325–34.

of NATO–Ukraine relations and the implementation of the charter and to survey planning for the future.

NATO and the Baltic states

For NATO, enlargement to the east—particularly the prospect of admitting Estonia, Latvia and Lithuania—was much more controversial than establishing relations with Ukraine. This was mainly because of the reaction of Russia.[15] On the other hand, from NATO's overall perspective, admission of the Baltic states would be less controversial if the Nordic non-aligned countries (Finland and Sweden) were to join.

Before the NATO–Russia Founding Act was signed, Russian Foreign Minister Primakov warned that if NATO were to consider admitting any of the former Soviet republics (in fact referring to the Baltic states) Russia would reconsider its entire relationship with NATO.[16] In 1997, however, Russia's position *vis-à-vis* the Baltic states underwent an important evolution. In response to the reorientation of the Baltic states' policies towards closer integration with the West, Russia resorted to political, diplomatic and economic pressure and aggressive rhetoric, taking advantage of the fact that NATO will not admit countries with outstanding national minorities problems or those without definitively demarcated borders. Both these issues, alongside economic issues, became Russia's main leverage against the Baltic states and at the multilateral level—in the Council of Europe and the OSCE as well as in the security dialogue between Russia and other countries in the Baltic Sea region.[17]

In 1997 Russia undertook a series of initiatives to obstruct the diplomatic efforts of the Baltic states to be included among the candidates for NATO membership. The most important of these were the proposals presented by Prime Minister Viktor Chernomyrdin in early September and a set of proposals presented by Russia to Lithuanian President Algirdas Brazauskas during his visit to Moscow on 23–24 October. President Yeltsin offered unilateral Russian security guarantees to the Baltic states[18] which would be strengthened under international law.[19] As a rule, guarantees are offered to states threatened by third countries, but in this case Russia proposed guarantees aimed at deterring threats which the Baltic states perceive to emanate from Russia itself. Moreover, Russia expressed its willingness to include France, Germany, the USA and other Western states in the regime of security guarantees. Finally, it contemplated the idea of establishing a Baltic regional stability and security

---

[15] See also chapter 4 in this volume.

[16] *Nezavisimaya Gazeta*, 25 May 1997.

[17] *Russia and the Baltic States*, Executive Summary of the Report by the Council on Foreign and Defence Policy of Russia (Council on Foreign and Defence Policy of Russia: Moscow, 1997), pp. 6–15.

[18] For the text of Yeltsin's offer see 'Yeltsin offers unwanted security to the Baltics', *Baltic Times*, vol. 2 (30 Oct.–5 Nov. 1997), p. 8.

[19] Shustov, V., 'The Russian attitude towards the security problem—measures to strengthen confidence and stability in the Baltic region', eds J. P. Kruzich and A. Fahraeus, *2nd Annual Stockholm Conference on Baltic Sea Security and Cooperation: Towards an Inclusive Security Structure in the Baltic Sea Region* (US Embassy in Sweden, Swedish Institute of International Affairs and SIPRI: Stockholm, 1997), p. 19.

space which would include the Nordic states. Russia proposed nearly 30 specific regional measures in the security, economic, humanitarian and ecological spheres, all intended to constitute a kind of future regional stability and security pact.[20] As a manifestation of Russia's good intentions, during Brazauskas' visit to Moscow Lithuania and Russia signed a treaty confirming the demarcation of the border between the two states and the delimitation of the exclusive economic zone and continental shelf in the Baltic Sea.[21] These Russian initiatives were not well received in the three Baltic capitals; they were seen as an attempt to 'single out' the Baltic states and impose on them uni- or multilateral guarantees which would make it impossible for them to be integrated in the Western security structures even in the long term.[22]

In his diplomatic offensive to the North European states, during a visit to Sweden on 3–4 December 1997 President Yeltsin outlined a number of proposals for cooperation and made a unilateral declaration regarding a 40 per cent reduction of land and naval forces in north-western Russia, to be completed within a year. This declaration should be seen, however, in the light of the reductions in armed forces already envisaged in both the NATO–Russia Founding Act and the framework agreement outlining the basic elements for adaptation of the CFE Treaty[23] as well as the reform of the Russian Army and reduction of manpower and armaments.[24] At the same time Russia linked the improvement of its relations with Estonia and Latvia—including the conclusion of border treaties and the development of economic cooperation—to acceptance of its demands concerning the status of the Russian-language population in these countries. Such a linkage has been rejected by the states directly concerned and by those with which it is engaged in a dialogue on security in the Baltic Sea region.

In the view of the Nordic states, while constructive Russian involvement in the Baltic region is a positive development, there is no room or need for separate regional security pacts in the new Europe nor any reason to treat Baltic security in isolation from that of the rest of Europe.[25]

[20] *Baltic Times* (note 18); and Shustov (note 19).

[21] The border agreement between Lithuania and Russia was signed by the 2 presidents in Moscow on 24 Oct. 1997; it determines the south-western border of Lithuania with the Russian Kaliningrad *oblast*. 'Is Russia's Baltic policy changing?', *Baltic Review*, vol. 13 (1997), p. 6. Russia did not sign a border agreement with the other 2 Baltic states.

[22] In the highly critical rhetoric on the guarantees proposed by Russia, the experience of the Molotov–Ribbentrop Pact of 1939 was recalled; the 'security guarantees' given at that time eventually led to the incorporation of these states into the Soviet Union in 1940.

[23] See chapter 12 in this volume. The framework agreement, as laid down in the 1997 Decision of the Joint Consultative Group Concerning Certain Basic Elements for Treaty Adaptation, is reproduced in appendix 12A in this volume.

[24] See also *Kontseptsiya Voyennoy Reformy Rossiyskoy Federatsii* [The concept of military reform of the Russian Federation], elaborated by the Institute of World Economy and International Relations (IMEMO) of the Russian Academy of Sciences (IMEMO: Moscow, 1997) and published as an annex in *Yezhegodnik SIPRI 1997: Vooruzheniya, Razoruzheniye y Mezhdunarodnaya Bezopasnost* [Russian edition of the *SIPRI Yearbook 1997*] (IMEMO: Moscow, 1997), pp. 445–76.

[25] See, e.g., 'Finland: Nordic ministers on Russian Baltic security initiative', 13 Nov. 1997, in Foreign Broadcast Information Service, *Daily Report–West Europe (FBIS-WEU)*, FBIS-WEU-97-317, 13 Nov. 1997, for statements by the Swedish, Finnish and Danish foreign ministers. For the Swedish position, see also Presentation by Swedish Minister for Foreign Affairs Lena Hjelm-Wallén at the Central Defence and Society Federation National Conference, Sälen, Sweden, 19 Jan. 1998; and Utrikesdeklarationen

The US–Baltic Charter of Partnership

A new element of Russia's position on the Baltic states was its willingness to enter into talks with NATO and the USA on Baltic security. In turn, the Baltic states, wishing to be admitted to the Western security structures, have begun an intensive dialogue with the United States. This dialogue resulted in the signing by the US and three Baltic presidents of a Charter of Partnership on 16 January 1998.[26] The credibility of the US position on the Baltic states stems from the fact that the USA never recognized the forcible incorporation of the three republics into the Soviet Union and 'regards their statehood as uninterrupted since the establishment of their independence' (Preamble). The aim of the Baltic states in signing the charter was to obtain a formal commitment by the USA that an invitation to join NATO would eventually be extended to them, but it contains a general statement of the principle that security institutions 'should be open to all European democracies' (Article III). For its part, the USA reiterated, in carefully worded phrases, its view that 'NATO's partners can become members as each aspirant proves itself able and willing to assume the responsibilities and obligations of membership, and as NATO determines that the inclusion of these nations would serve European stability and the strategic interests of the Alliance' (Article III). The US–Baltic Charter of Partnership thus confirmed the 'open door policy' of NATO but did not offer any binding commitments from the USA regarding admission of the Baltic states to the Atlantic Alliance.

In this context, the USA and the Baltic states underscored their interest in Russia's democratic and stable development and stated their support for a strengthened NATO–Russia relationship 'as a core element of their shared vision of a new and peaceful Europe' (Article III). The USA left its Baltic partners with no doubts that, in the US perspective, Russia occupies a critical place in Europe. In 1997 it was demonstrated that both the USA and NATO consider relations with Russia to be of key importance and that the security of Russia's neighbours on its western frontier is treated in large measure as dependent on NATO–Russian relations.

The Euro-Atlantic Partnership Council

NATO took additional steps during the year to include the countries of the former eastern bloc in an enhanced security partnership. In order to unite the positive experience of the North Atlantic Cooperation Council (NACC) and the Partnership for Peace (PFP), the ministerial meeting of the North Atlantic Council—held in Sintra, Portugal, on 29 May 1997—proposed that the NACC and PFP partners launch the Euro-Atlantic Partnership Council (EAPC) at

---

1998 [Swedish foreign policy statement 1998], 11 Feb. 1998, URL <http://www.ud.se/utrpolit/utrdekla/utrdek98.htm>, version current on 27 Mar. 1998.

[26] A Charter of Partnership Among the United States of America and the Republic of Estonia, Republic of Latvia, and Republic of Lithuania was signed in Washington, DC, on 16 Jan. 1998. For the text of the charter see *Washington File*, 16 Jan. 1998, URL <http://www.usia.gov/regional/eur/baltics/tables/gendocs/charter.htm>, version current on 10 Feb. 1998.

their meeting the next day. The EAPC is meant to provide 'the overarching framework for political and security-related consultations and for enhanced cooperation under PFP, whose basic elements will remain valid'. The Basic Document of the Euro-Atlantic Partnership Council was agreed on 30 May 1997[27] and the inaugural meeting of the EAPC was held the same day. As a result of this decision, NACC ceased to exist and the EAPC took over its mandate. The basic principles of NACC and the PFP will be applicable to the EAPC: *inclusiveness*, with an understanding that opportunities for political consultations and political cooperation will be open to all NATO Allies and partners equally; and *self-differentiation*, in the sense that partners will be able to decide for themselves the level and areas of their cooperation with NATO.

The Madrid Declaration

The Madrid Declaration on Euro-Atlantic Security and Cooperation was approved at the NATO summit meeting held on 8–9 July 1997.[28] It contains two major decisions. First, the NATO heads of state and government invited the Czech Republic, Hungary and Poland to start accession talks with the aim of joining the Atlantic Alliance in 1999 (paragraph 6); NATO also agreed to review the process of enlargement at its next summit meeting, to be held in 1999, and in this context Romania and Slovenia were mentioned as possible new candidates for membership (paragraph 8).[29] Second, the essence and scope of the partnership with non-NATO countries in Europe were expanded, in particular the PFP.

A new NATO in the new Europe

NATO's inclusion of three Central and East European (CEE) states, its new relationships with Russia and Ukraine, its cooperation and partnership with the states in the north and south that remain outside the alliance, and its dialogue with its Mediterranean partners will all be determinants of the future role of NATO in Europe. At the same time, a process of internal adaptation is underway, with its own political and military dimensions.

Twelve European countries have so far submitted requests to join NATO.[30] In other states—mainly the traditionally neutral and non-aligned states—public debates are under way about whether to apply for NATO membership.[31] At

---

[27] The text of the Basic Document of the Euro-Atlantic Partnership Council is reproduced in appendix 5A in this volume.

[28] Excerpts from the Madrid Declaration on Euro-Atlantic Security and Cooperation are reproduced in appendix 5A in this volume.

[29] This was a compromise formula to address the French endeavours to get Romania included in the first round of new NATO members and the proposal to invite Slovenia to ensure territorial continuity between Hungary and the other NATO Allies.

[30] These 12 countries are: the 3 invited candidates (the Czech Republic, Hungary and Poland), Slovakia, the 3 Baltic states (Estonia, Latvia and Lithuania) and 5 Balkan states (Albania, Bulgaria, Croatia, Romania and Slovenia).

[31] Although the Minister of Foreign Affairs of Sweden stated on 19 Jan. 1998 that the official Swedish position remains unaltered ('Sweden's policy of non-participation in military alliances remains

the Brussels NAC ministerial meeting, identical protocols of accession were signed with the Czech Republic, Hungary and Poland on 16 December 1997.[32] At the Madrid meeting it was decided that, pending accession, the applicant countries will become involved in NATO activities 'to ensure that they are best prepared to undertake the responsibilities and obligations of membership in an enlarged Alliance'.[33] The participants also gave assurances that the process of enlargement will be continued.[34] The open character of NATO was confirmed in the statement that no European democratic country whose admission would fulfil the objectives of the 1949 North Atlantic Treaty will be excluded from consideration.

The Madrid Declaration indicates that the main candidates for the second phase of NATO enlargement are Romania, Slovenia and other south-east European countries.[35] In this context, the dialogue between NATO and six states in the Mediterranean region is noteworthy. Initiated in 1995, it aims at dispelling misconceptions about NATO.[36] As proposed at the Sintra NAC ministerial meeting, the Mediterranean Cooperation Group (MCG) was established in Madrid. This initiative should be seen as complementary to the efforts undertaken by the EU, the Western European Union (WEU) and the OSCE. The purpose of the MCG is to take overall responsibility for the dialogue as well as for holding political discussions with individual partners in a '16+1' format.[37] Following the Sintra decision, certain military activities will added to the content of the dialogue.[38]

NATO's involvement in overcoming the crisis in the former Yugoslavia is crucial for the success of its enlargement and reform. The Yugoslav crisis has required the adaptation of political and military mechanisms to the measures called for in UN Security Council resolutions and a selective and restrained

unchanged'; see note 25), a different position is taken by the leader of the Conservative Party (Moderates), Carl Bildt. *Dagens Nyheter* (Stockholm), 28 Jan. 1998. Accession to NATO is also the subject of an open debate in Austria and, to a lesser degree, in Finland. In all these countries the restraint with regard to joining NATO, manifested chiefly by the Social Democrats, stems more from psychological and historical motives than from an assessment of the new situation in Europe.

[32] The 3 protocols will enter into force 'when each of the Parties to the North Atlantic Treaty has notified the Government of the United States of America of its acceptance thereof'. For the text of Poland's accession protocol, see appendix 5A in this volume.

[33] Madrid Declaration on Euro-Atlantic Security and Cooperation, para. 6.

[34] Madrid Declaration on Euro-Atlantic Security and Cooperation, para. 8. The understanding that the current round of accessions is only the beginning of the process was confirmed by the NATO foreign ministers at the NAC meeting in Brussels on 16 Dec. 1997. Excerpts from the text of the final communiqué of the NAC meeting of foreign ministers are reproduced in appendix 5A in this volume.

[35] With regard to aspiring members, the Madrid summit meeting recognized 'with great interest' and took account of positive developments 'in a number of southeastern European countries, especially Romania and Slovenia'. It is symptomatic that the formula regarding the Baltic states is different: 'we recognise the progress achieved towards greater stability and cooperation by the states in the Baltic region which are also aspiring members'. Madrid Declaration on Euro-Atlantic Security and Cooperation, para. 8.

[36] On 8 Feb. 1995 the North Atlantic Council in Permanent Session invited Egypt, Israel, Mauritania, Morocco and Tunisia to the initial round of the Mediterranean dialogue. In Nov. 1995 Jordan was also invited to join the dialogue. Nordam, J., 'The Mediterranean dialogue: dispelling misconceptions and building confidence', *NATO Review*, vol. 45, no. 4 (July/Aug. 1997), p. 26.

[37] See also de Santis, N., 'The future of NATO's Mediterranean initiative', *NATO Review*, no. 1 (spring 1998), p. 32.

[38] Nordam (note 36), p. 29. Egypt, Jordan and Morocco already cooperate with NATO through their participation in SFOR.

use of force in order to achieve two goals—to protect UN safe areas and to bring warring parties to the negotiating table. Moreover, NATO's military involvement was based on the assumptions that mechanisms for cooperation with the EU in enforcing UN sanctions would be set up; the framework for cooperation between the 16 NATO members and 17 other countries in the Implementation Force/Stabilization Force (IFOR/SFOR) would be determined; and implementation and enforcement of the military aspects of the 1995 Dayton Peace Agreement would be monitored and supervised in cooperation with the High Representative, UN agencies and the OSCE. The situation requires a mix of ad hoc decisions, new structures, and the coordination and, where necessary, adjustment of existing organizations.

A new military posture for Europe

The Madrid summit meeting provided the catalyst for reshaping NATO's military posture towards smaller but more flexible and mobile forces and adapting its multinational command structure accordingly. Development of the European Security and Defence Identity (ESDI) within NATO is one of the three fundamental objectives of the alliance adaptation process, as identified by the NATO ministers in Berlin on 3 June 1996.[39]

In a broader context, the Madrid summit meeting called for a more prominent role for the European members of NATO and greater inclusion of the non-NATO WEU states in military and operational activities. The NATO leaders endorsed the concept of the Combined Joint Task Forces (CJTF), which will act under the operational command of the WEU,[40] with the objective of adapting NATO's structures to new missions, improving cooperation with the WEU and reflecting the emerging ESDI.[41] The CJTF concept is intended to enhance NATO's ability to command and control multinational and multi-service forces and to deploy them at short notice for a wide range of military operations. There are also two political aspects: (*a*) it will facilitate the possible participation of non-NATO nations in operations; and (*b*) it will promote the development of the ESDI within NATO.[42] In this regard, the Madrid decisions mark a significant step forward, further blurring the distinction between the members and non-members of the alliance.

At the Madrid meeting, Spain expressed its readiness to participate fully in NATO's new military and command structures. This was viewed as helpful for the development of the ESDI within NATO and for strengthening the transatlantic link.

---

[39] The adaptation process is described in Rotfeld, A. D., 'Europe: in search of cooperative security', *SIPRI Yearbook 1997* (note 12), p. 131. See also Cragg, A., 'Internal adaptation: reshaping NATO for the challenges of tomorrow', *NATO Review*, July/Aug. 1997, p. 30.
[40] *WEU Today,* Mar. 1998, p. 31.
[41] Rotfeld (note 39), pp. 131–32.
[42] For further information on the ESDI see a set of articles in 'Focus—European Security and Defence Identity', *RUSI Journal,* Apr. 1997, pp. 45–56; and Foster, E., 'In search of Europe's security and defence identity', *The New International Security Review 1998* (Royal United Services Institute for Defence Studies (RUSI): London, 1997), pp. 150–68.

The Madrid meeting also decided to direct the NATO Council in Permanent Session to examine the 1991 Alliance Strategic Concept.[43] The work on a new strategic concept will be carried out in 1998 with the aim of presenting it to the next NATO summit meeting, to be held in April 1999.

The December 1997 Brussels NAC ministerial meeting received a comprehensive report describing the progress made since the Madrid summit meeting in three main areas: (*a*) development of the future command structure; (*b*) implementation of the CJTF concept; and (*c*) building the ESDI within NATO. Some progress in all these fields was achieved in close cooperation with the WEU.[44]

Costs of NATO enlargement

The costs that NATO enlargement will incur were presented in 1997 as one of the main obstacles to the process of ratification of the three accession protocols. The cost issue was intensively debated by experts and politicians.[45] Opponents of NATO enlargement raised various arguments, such as why the cost should have to be paid if there is no threat, whether the cost is affordable or excessive, whether published estimates are accurate or will escalate with inflation, whether such estimates are politically motivated or reliable in economic terms, and whether enlargement will require larger defence budgets.[46] Attention was also drawn to the fact that the countries aspiring to join NATO are in a difficult stage of transformation. It was claimed that the costs of adjusting their armies to NATO requirements, especially modernization of weapon systems and infrastructure, are bound to be an excessive burden for their economies. It was also argued that the United States should not 'carry an unfair share of the burden'.[47]

---

[43] The Alliance's Strategic Concept, agreed by the heads of state and government participating in the meeting of the NAC in Rome, 7–8 Nov. 1991, is reproduced in *The Transformation of an Alliance: The Decisions of NATO's Heads of State and Government* ([NATO Secretariat]: Rome, 1991), pp. 29–54.

[44] This cooperation is being developed under the auspices of the NATO–WEU Joint Council. The Final Communiqué of the Dec. 1997 NAC ministerial meeting states: 'We will continue to develop the arrangements and procedures necessary for the planning, preparation, conduct and exercise of WEU-led operation using NATO assets and capabilities' (para. 14). Final Communiqué of the Ministerial Meeting of the North Atlantic Council, Brussels, 16 Dec. 1997, *NATO Review,* Documentation Special Supplement, no. 1 (1998), p. D.4.

[45] See also chapter 6, section VI, in this volume.

[46] The answers to some of these questions are contained in: Kugler, R. L., 'Costs of NATO enlargement: moderate and affordable', *Strategic Forum*, no. 128 (Oct. 1997); and Gompert, D. C., 'NATO enlargement: putting the costs in perspective', *Strategic Forum* (National University, Institute for National Strategic Studies), no. 129 (Oct. 1997). See also 'Statement of Secretary of Defense William S. Cohen before the Senate Committee on Appropriations on the topic of NATO Enlargement, 21 October 1997', News Release, Office of Assistant Secretary of Defense, No. 570-97, 23 Oct. 1997, URL <http://www.defenselink.mil/news/Oct1997/b10231997_btnato.html>, version current on 3 Apr. 1998; 'NATO—the price of expansion', *The Economist*, vol. 342 (15 Nov. 1997), p. 29; and British American Security Information Council (BASIC), *NATO U-Turn on Cost Study,* BASIC Reports (BASIC: London, 15 Dec. 1997). Some of the estimates were based on the cold war era assumptions about the roles and missions of armed forces of the new members. In fact, they were irrelevant in the face of the virtual disappearance of a military threat to the alliance.

[47] Kugler (note 46).

The participants at Madrid were confident that, in line with the new European security environment, 'Alliance costs associated with the integration of new members will be manageable and the resources necessary to meet these costs will be provided'.[48] In the view of the NATO Secretary General, while the additional costs have to be seriously considered, some of the figures that have been quoted by private think-tanks 'are grossly exaggerated, and are based somewhat on mistaken assumptions'.[49] In February 1997 the US President sent to the Senate a report on NATO enlargement containing the Department of Defense estimates of $27–35 billion for the period 1997–2009. Accordingly, the average annual cost envisaged for NATO as a whole was given as $2.1–2.7 billion. The lion's share of the total amount would be paid by the new members—$13–17.5 billion by the year 2009; the non-US NATO members would pay $12.5–15.5 billion; and the United States would cover the remainder of the cost.[50]

The assessment in a report by the NATO Secretary General presented to the Brussels NAC ministerial meeting on the resource implications of the accession of the three invited states is quite different. According to this report, the total cost to be borne by all NATO members is equivalent to about $1.5 billion over a period of 10 years, of which $1.3 billion would be for the NATO Security Investment Programme. The ministers came to the conclusion that 'Alliance costs associated with the accession of the three invitees will be manageable, and . . . the resources necessary to meet these costs will be provided'.[51] These estimates were a final response to the reports and studies debated in 1996 and 1996 which envisaged much greater expenditure.[52]

The cost issue tended to be perceived both by opponents of NATO enlargement before ratification of the accession protocols and by adherents not so much in economic as in political terms.[53]

The key question for those in favour of enlarging NATO was to prevent the debate about the costs from causing the US Senate and the parliaments of other NATO states to reject ratification.[54] A belief prevailed among the NATO members and invited candidates that, although the costs of admission could be considerable, the political and military cost of a failure to enlarge the alliance would be much higher.[55]

---

[48] Madrid Declaration on Euro-Atlantic Security and Cooperation, para. 7.
[49] Text of the keynote speech . . . (note 9).
[50] 'NATO enlargement's military implications and financial costs' (United States Information Service: Stockholm, Sweden), URL <http://www.usis.usemb.se/nato/finance.htm>, version current on 24 Feb. 1997.
[51] Final Communiqué (para. 5) (note 44).
[52] See also Rotfeld (note 39).
[53] Paraphrasing the famous French saying about war and the military, the NATO Secretary General stated at the Conference on European Security with an Enlarged NATO on 3 Oct. 1997: 'Enlargement is too important a subject to leave to bookkeepers'. Text of the keynote speech . . . (note 9).
[54] This is the explanation for the NATO decision not to make public the report on the costs prepared for the Dec. 1997 NAC ministerial meeting. *NATO U-Turn on Cost Study* (note 46).
[55] Albright, M., 'Enlarging NATO: why bigger is better', *The Economist*, 15 Feb. 1997, p. 20; and 'Statement of Secretary of Defense William S. Cohen . . .' (note 46).

III. The European Union: the security dimension

The negotiations of the EU Intergovernmental Conference (IGC), established in 1996 to review the 1992 Treaty on European Union (Maastricht Treaty), were concluded at the European Council meeting in Amsterdam, held on 16–17 June 1997. The Amsterdam Treaty was signed on 2 October 1997 by all the EU member states.[56]

The Maastricht Treaty states the objective of the EU in foreign and security policy: 'to assert its identity on the international scene, in particular through the implementation of a common foreign and security policy [CFSP] including the eventual framing of a common defence policy, which might in time lead to a common defence' (Title I, Article B).[57] The future-oriented CFSP concept has two dimensions: a political and diplomatic dimension based on the earlier system of European Political Cooperation, and a new security and defence dimension which would in large part be implemented by the WEU and partly by development of the ESDI.[58] The Amsterdam Treaty reflects a more pragmatic approach to implementation of the CFSP 'with fairly limited functional improvements to external policy mechanisms and a strengthening of the Presidency in its external role'.[59] However, the CFSP concept has retained its mainly declarative character.

The EU enlargement process

Enlargement has been on the agenda of the EU since the decision of the European Council summit meeting in Copenhagen in June 1993. This meeting decided that the states with which the EU has bilateral Europe Agreements or Association Agreements were eligible for full EU membership.[60]

In July 1997, following the conclusion of the IGC, the European Commission presented its comprehensive *Agenda 2000*. The European Commission had been invited to prepare such a document by the time of the Madrid European Council meeting (16–17 December 1995). The aim of Part Two of

---

[56] The full name of the treaty is the Treaty of Amsterdam Amending the Treaty on European Union, the Treaties Establishing the European Communities and Certain Related Acts. Excerpts are reproduced in appendix 5A in this volume. See also Rotfeld (note 39), pp. 140–42.

[57] The relevant excerpts from the Maastricht Treaty are reproduced in *SIPRI Yearbook 1994* (Oxford University Press: Oxford, 1994), pp. 251–54.

[58] See also Dodd, T., Ware, R. and Weston, A., 'The European Communities (Amendment) Bill: Implementing the Amsterdam Treaty', House of Commons Library, Research Paper no. 97/112, London, 5 Nov. 1997, pp. 24–34.

[59] Comments to Title V, Article J of the Amsterdam Treaty in Dodd *et al.* (note 58), p. 24. A different view is presented in Herolf, G. (ed.), *The Security and Defence Policy of the EU—The Intergovernmental Conference and Beyond*, Conference Papers 21 (Swedish Institute of International Affairs: Stockholm, 1997), pp. 60–62.

[60] German Chancellor Helmut Kohl and French President Jacques Chirac defined the target date for Poland's EU membership as the year 2000. EU Commissioner Hans van der Broek spoke of the period 2002–2003 for the first group of applicants, dismissed by many as unrealistic. Serfaty, S., 'The logic of dual enlargement', Paper presented at the Conference in Rome on the Fifth Castelgandolfo Colloquium on Transatlantic Affairs, 3–4 Oct. 1997.

Agenda 2000, 'Challenge of Enlargement', was to explain the way in which the Commission had examined the different applications for accession, the main questions they raised and the timetable for opening negotiations which appeared most realistic. Among the criteria for EU membership defined in 1993 at the Copenhagen European Council summit meeting, the candidate must have 'achieved stability of institutions guaranteeing democracy, the rule of law, human rights, and respect for and protection of minorities'.[61] The Commission evaluated the progress made under the bilateral agreements. Since the previous enlargement (in 1995, when Austria, Finland and Sweden joined the EU) the *acquis communautaire* has expanded considerably. It now includes the CFSP, justice and home affairs, and the progressive realization of a political, economic and monetary union. The Amsterdam Treaty enshrined in Article F a constitutional principle that 'the Union is founded on the principles of liberty, democracy, respect for human rights and fundamental freedoms and the rule of law'.[62] In other words, the political conditions defined at the Copenhagen meeting are necessary but not sufficient for opening accession negotiations.

In the Final Recommendations of *Agenda 2000* the European Commission concluded that the Czech Republic, Estonia, Hungary, Poland and Slovenia could be in a position 'to satisfy all the conditions of membership in the medium term if they maintain and strongly sustain their efforts of preparation'. It also confirmed the decision of the European Council to open accession negotiations with Cyprus six months after the closing of the 1996/97 IGC, that is, by March 1998.[63]

Agenda 2000 has been dealt with in detail by the European Council and the Committee of Permanent Representatives. The EU foreign ministers held an in-depth debate at their informal meeting at Mondorf in October 1997, and the heads of state and government discussed it informally at the European Council meeting on employment on 20 November. A week later, Denmark and Sweden presented their joint position on the model for launching the enlargement negotiations, which should meet the following criteria:

1. *Inclusiveness*. The enlargement process must include all candidate countries, irrespective of their present stage of preparations.
2. *Non-discrimination*. All candidate states must be measured by the same yardsticks and treated on an equal basis.

---

[61] European Commission, *Agenda 2000*, Communication of the Commission, DOC 97/6, Strasbourg, 15 July 1997, Part Two: The Challenge of Enlargement, Section VII. URL <http://europa.eu.int/comm/dg1a/agenda2000/en/strong/2.htm>, version current on 1 Apr. 1998.

[62] *Agenda 2000* (note 61), Part Two, Section I.

[63] *Agenda 2000* concludes that 'if current efforts are reinforced' the Czech Republic, Hungary and Poland should be able in the medium term to take on the major part of the *acquis* and to establish the administrative structure to apply, while Estonia, Latvia, Lithuania, Slovakia and Slovenia would be able to do so 'only if there is a considerable and sustained increase in their efforts'. *Agenda 2000*, Part Two, Section I (Conclusion), (note 61).

3. *Credibility*. The model must make it clear to all candidate states—and to their populations—that they are part of the enlargement process and will become members of the EU once they fulfil the criteria for membership.[64]

The European Commission considered that none of the applicants fully satisfied the criteria, but the decision to launch the enlargement process was taken by the European Council at its meeting in Luxembourg on 12–13 December 1997. It was decided to initiate an accession process comprising the 10 CEE applicant states and Cyprus.[65] The European Council pointed out that 'all these States are destined to join the European Union on the basis of the same criteria' and that they will participate in the accession process on 'an equal footing'. The process will be 'evolutive and inclusive'.[66] It was formally opened on 30 March 1998 at a meeting of the ministers of foreign affairs of the 15 EU members, the 10 CEE applicants and Cyprus. However, only six applicants (the Czech Republic, Cyprus, Estonia, Hungary, Poland and Slovenia) started full negotiations in March 1998.

The Luxembourg European Council meeting also decided to establish the European Conference as a multilateral forum for political consultations to address questions of general concern; its first meeting was held in London in March 1998.[67] The members of the conference must share 'a common commitment to peace, security and good-neighbourliness, respect for other countries' sovereignty, the principles upon which the European Union is founded, the integrity and inviolability of external borders and the principles of international law and a commitment to the settlement of territorial disputes by peaceful means, in particular through the jurisdiction of the International Court of Justice in the Hague'.[68] Cyprus, Turkey and the 10 CEE candidates were invited to participate in the first meeting. The concept of the European Conference meets the criteria of inclusiveness, non-discrimination and credibility. However, it was conceived mainly as a gesture to Turkey. Turkey's request to begin EU accession negotiations was turned down in December 1997. Turkey objected to this decision and did not attend the 1998 meeting of the European Conference.

In spite of these declarations of principles, the fact is that the European states applying for EU membership are at different stages in adjusting their economies and legislation to the criteria laid down at the Luxembourg European Council meeting. The negotiations are to begin at different times and the

[64] 'Draft on The Launching of the Enlargement Process presented by Denmark and Sweden as a non-paper before the Luxembourg European Council', 27 Nov. 1997. Denmark and Sweden consistently argued that the best way to meet these criteria would be to start negotiations with all the applicant countries simultaneously.

[65] The 10 CEE applicant states are: the Czech Republic, Estonia, Hungary, Poland and Slovenia (the first group) and Bulgaria, Latvia, Lithuania, Romania and Slovakia (the second group). Presidency Conclusions of the Luxembourg European Council, 12–13 Dec. 1997, URL <http://www.uepres.etat.lu/uepres/textes/frame.htm>, version current on 9 Apr. 1998.

[66] Presidency Conclusions (note 65).

[67] The specific mandate of the European Conference is 'to broaden and deepen [the participants'] cooperation on foreign and security policy, justice and home affairs and other areas of common concern, particularly economic matters and regional cooperation'. Presidency Conclusions (note 65).

[68] Presidency Conclusions (note 65), para. 4.

dates of conclusion of the negotiations will vary even more widely. An additional problem is the position of Turkey, which has for a long time signalled its interest in membership of the EU, while at the same time being opposed to the admission of Cyprus.[69] The establishment of the European Conference was intended to facilitate the process of enlargement because it provides for identical treatment for all the applicants and removes from the agenda all the problems stemming from the fact that the negotiations with the candidates will not start simultaneously in the '15+11' format proposed by Denmark and Sweden.

The EU and NATO

The relationship between the EU and NATO is determined not so much by their different mandates as by the substantially different perceptions of the role of NATO and the USA by the proponents of the 'Atlantic option' (led by the UK) and the 'European option' (favoured by France). The test of the practical capabilities of the two organizations was the crisis in Bosnia and Herzegovina. While the enforcement of peace was possible because of NATO's presence there, peace reconstruction, rehabilitation and the shaping of democratic institutions would be impossible without the European Union.

Meanwhile, the functions and structures of both organizations are undergoing an essential transformation: in NATO activities, political security aspects are gaining in significance; and in EU efforts, since the 1992 Petersberg decisions,[70] crisis management and humanitarian intervention have come to the fore. Against this background, two concepts of security policy have emerged: (*a*) that of a European Common Defence Policy, and (*b*) that of conducting joint WEU–NATO military operations under the auspices of the CJTF. In the debate on the roles of and relationships between the EU, the WEU and NATO in the sphere of security, the central issue in 1997 was that of a diminishing role for the USA and concomitant 'Europeanization' of NATO, that is, enhancement of the role of Western Europe in the command structures.[71] Although the NATO documents adopted at the 1997 Madrid summit meeting and Brussels NAC ministerial meeting underline the importance of the decisions agreed at the 1996 Berlin NAC ministerial meeting, in

[69] In both cases, the Luxembourg European Council meeting decided as follows: 'Turkey will be judged on the basis of the same criteria as other applicant States. While the political and economic conditions allowing accession negotiations to be envisaged are not satisfied, the European Council considers that it is nevertheless important for a strategy to be drawn up to prepare Turkey for accession by bringing it closer to the European Union in every field'. Presidency Conclusions (note 65). In turn, Cyprus was advised to include representatives of the Turkish Cypriot community in its accession negotiating delegation.

[70] The Petersberg tasks emanate from the meeting of the WEU Council held at Petersberg, Germany, in June 1992. The WEU members stated their determination to engage in humanitarian and rescue tasks, peacekeeping operations, and tasks of combat forces in crisis management, including peacemaking. Shortly after the Petersberg meeting NATO also declared its intention to perform such operations. At the 1997 European Council meeting in Amsterdam, the decision was made to include these tasks in the Amsterdam Treaty as EU membership tasks.

[71] Foster, E. and Wilson, G., *CJTF—A Lifeline for a European Defence Policy?*, RUSI Whitehall Paper Series (Royal United Services Institute for Defence Studies (RUSI): London, 1997); and Volbracht, B., *Die Reform der WEU: Papiertiger oder Konkurent der NATO?* [Reform of the WEU: a paper tiger or competitor to NATO?] (LIT Verlag: Münster, 1997).

practice there was a lack of concrete new arrangements in this regard. The circumstances under which the CJTF operational activities, under WEU command and in cooperation with NATO, may be set in motion are unclear. Many factors are involved, not the least of which is the outcome of the reform of the Integrated Military Structure within NATO. The reintegration of France into the military structures of NATO—previously announced and expected to materialize in 1997—has effectively been frozen.[72] In practice, the military dependence of the NATO European members on the USA has not decreased but is on the increase.

The agendas of the two summit meetings of 1997—the Amsterdam EU meeting and the Madrid NATO meeting—were dominated by the prospect of enlargement to the east and the need to reform the two organizations. In fact, however, defence spending and demonstrated capabilities—which will dictate whether the ESDI takes shape and is taken seriously—are much more critical factors than procedural decisions, resolutions or political declarations.[73] In all the EU countries, serious reforms have been announced or initiated. They are intended to result in reductions in armed forces, increased professionalization and political readiness to contribute to cooperative military interventions under the auspices of such multilateral organizations as the UN, NATO, the PFP, the WEU and the OSCE. However, the European defence identity has not yet become a political reality and will be postponed by the enlargement of the EU and NATO to an undetermined future time.

The role of the WEU and its relationship with the EU, as well as the links between the WEU, the EU and NATO, have been developed.[74] In short, the arrangements for a coordinated approach to foreign and defence policies will be strengthened. The WEU may serve in the future as a bridge between the EU and NATO.[75] It may ensure the political control and strategic direction of the crisis-management military operations that European states decide to undertake collectively and in which the North American states will not wish to participate directly.[76]

The two enlargement processes: differences and similarities

The nature and aims of EU and NATO enlargement are quite different. However, in the post-cold war period, as a result of their internal transformations and expansion of participation, the two organizations have each acquired a new function in the shaping of European security. NATO—along with the PFP, the EAPC and its bilateral security arrangements with Russia, Ukraine

[72] On 17 Feb. 1997 President Jacques Chirac informed US Secretary of State Albright that, in the absence of agreement concerning the command of the Allied Forces Southern Europe (AFSOUTH) by Apr. or May 1997, France's reintegration would be frozen 'without hard feelings' in the hope that renewed efforts in 2 or 3 years' time would be more fruitful. Foster (note 42), p. 152.

[73] Foster (note 42), p. 155.

[74] Protocol 1 to Article 17(J.7) of the Amsterdam Treaty.

[75] Dodd *et al.* (note 58), p. 74.

[76] Cutileiro, J., 'WEU: a success story', *NATO's Sixteen Nations,* Special Supplement: 50 Years of European Security, 1998, p. 8.

and the Baltic states—has become more than just a defence alliance: it is now the centre of gravity in the search for a new security order in Europe. The EU is facing the challenge of creating new capabilities within the framework of the CFSP and, in close cooperation with the WEU, moving beyond rhetoric and declaratory policies to give a genuine meaning to the vision of a European Security and Defence Identity.

With the Amsterdam Treaty, the implications of EU enlargement will be visible mainly in the political, economic and legal spheres. The process will be determined to a great extent by the Common Agricultural Policy, the European Monetary Union (EMU) and common policies on structural subsidies.[77] In the case of NATO, the decision about the accession of new members, motivated by the new security environment, is 'more demanding in some ways and less complex in others'.[78] Although the decision-making process of both organizations is based on consensus, NATO is much more dependent on the decisions of the big powers in the alliance.

The NATO enlargement decisions are expressions of arbitrary political will, while the EU requires its new members to undergo much more complex adjustment processes. In NATO, the external and internal adaptations of the alliance's structure are seen as complementary, mutually reinforcing processes, but in the EU tension and contradictions continue to permeate the 'widening *versus* deepening' dilemma.

Enlargement of NATO, by its very nature, affects the security interests of both members and applicants as well as the interests of countries remaining outside the alliance. This was the rationale behind the documents that define the new relations and cooperation between NATO and Russia, Ukraine and the Baltic states. The implications of EU enlargement are of a different nature and call for different solutions. In the historical perspective, both processes will overcome the divisions in Europe and enhance stability throughout the continent.[79] It may also be noted, for example, that Russia, which sees new threats in NATO's eastward enlargement, has not voiced fears concerning EU enlargement and has officially declared its interest in promoting it.

Three aspects of institutional cooperation were highlighted in the 1997 NATO Madrid Declaration: close cooperation with the WEU, integrated within the EU; the building of a European Security and Defence Identity within NATO; and the strengthening of the OSCE as a regional organization and as 'a primary instrument for preventing conflict, enhancing cooperative security and advancing democracy and human rights'.[80] The role and place of the OSCE have undergone a necessary evolution in recent years. It is worth

---

[77] Simon Serfaty rightly concluded that 'it is the specific interests of each member state, and the perceptions of these interests by all its partners, that will condition and ultimately produce the compromises and trade-offs over the terms, conditions and timing of enlargement'. Serfaty (note 60).

[78] Serfaty (note 60).

[79] The Swedish Minister for Foreign Affairs has stressed the significance of EU membership 'as part of a deliberate endeavour to make warfare between European countries inconceivable throughout our continent'. Presentation by Swedish Minister for Foreign Affairs Lena Hjelm-Wallén (note 25).

[80] Madrid Declaration on Euro-Atlantic Security and Cooperation, para. 21.

considering the function this organization plays today and should play in the context of NATO and EU enlargement.

IV. The OSCE: pan-European security cooperation

In 1997 the trend observed in recent years continued: the role and significance of the OSCE were underscored by the documents it adopted and its activities. In practice, however, European security was sought through NATO and EU enlargement. Nonetheless, both NATO and the EU have described the OSCE as 'the most inclusive European-wide security organization'[81] and have ascribed it an essential role in securing peace, stability and security in Europe. They have acknowledged that OSCE principles and commitments provide a foundation for the development of a comprehensive and cooperative European security architecture.

At the same time, however, the OSCE is seen by many—decision makers and experts alike—as a fair-weather, loosely organized body. They have noted various weaknesses of the organization: its lack of strong instruments similar to those provided by Chapter VII of the UN Charter; its consensus-based decision-making process; its lack of authority (it has no organ comparable to the UN Security Council); and the gap between many accomplishments in conflict prevention, crisis management and post-conflict rehabilitation, on the one hand, and their coverage in the media and information provided to the broader public about the organization, on the other hand. It is also the 'youngest' European security institution, undertakes activities mainly on an ad hoc basis and lacks a firm bureaucratic structure.

The OSCE is associated mainly with the human dimension of security (human rights and 'Basket 3' issues—contacts among people, information, culture and education), which attracted much public and media attention during the last stages of the cold war. The public is less apprised of the OSCE's role in the achievement of accords on confidence- and security-building measures—the Vienna Documents 1990, 1992 and 1994—and on conventional armaments in Europe—the 1990 CFE Treaty—or in monitoring their implementation. The public is even less aware of OSCE activities under its new mandate as 'a primary instrument for early warning, conflict prevention and crisis management'.[82]

---

[81] E.g., on the part of NATO, see the Madrid Declaration on Euro-Atlantic Security and Cooperation, para. 21.

[82] Budapest Document 1994, Budapest Summit Declaration: Towards a Genuine Partnership in a New Era, para. 8, reproduced in *SIPRI Yearbook 1995: Armaments, Disarmament and International Security* (Oxford University Press: Oxford, 1995), pp. 309–13; and Rotfeld, A. D., 'Europe: the multilateral process', *SIPRI Yearbook 1995,* pp. 265–301. See also Rotfeld, A. D., 'Europe: towards new security arrangements', *SIPRI Yearbook 1996: Armaments, Disarmament and International Security* (Oxford University Press: Oxford, 1996), pp. 279–324; and Document adopted by the States Parties to the Treaty on Conventional Armed Forces in Europe on the Scope and Parameters of the Process Commissioned in Paragraph 19 of the Final Document of the first CFE Treaty Review Conference, of the 1996 Lisbon Summit Declaration, *SIPRI Yearbook 1997* (note 12). A systematic review and assessment of OSCE activities are presented in 2 regular publications: Bloed, A. (ed.), Netherlands Helsinki Committee and International Helsinki Federation for Human Rights, *Helsinki Monitor: Quarterly on Security and Cooperation in Europe* (Helsinki Monitor: Utrecht); and Lutz, D. S. and Tudyka, K. (eds), Institute for

OSCE activities

In 1997 the activities of the OSCE were oriented towards early warning, conflict prevention, crisis management and post-conflict rehabilitation.[83] During the year, the number of its field operations increased through the establishment of the OSCE Presence in Albania, created in response to the serious political crisis that erupted in February 1997,[84] and the Advisory and Monitoring Group in Belarus. The OSCE monitored elections in Bosnia and Herzegovina, Yugoslavia (Serbia and Montenegro) and Chechnya (Russia). The establishment of the Mission to Croatia in 1996 becomes more important in view of the expiry of the mandate of the United Nations Transitional Administration for Eastern Slavonia, Baranja and Western Sirmium (UNTAES) on 15 January 1998.[85]

The effectiveness of the OSCE missions results from the working cooperation between the organization and the UN and the Council of Europe. In the OSCE Secretary General's assessment, the reinforcement of cooperation with intergovernmental bodies was remarkable in 1997.[86]

OSCE missions

In 1997 the OSCE operated long-duration missions in Skopje (the Spillover Monitor Mission), Bosnia and Herzegovina (including a separate mission to Sarajevo), Croatia, Estonia, Georgia, Latvia, Moldova, Tajikistan and Ukraine. The other OSCE field activities were the OSCE Assistance Group to Chechnya, activities of the Personal Representative of the OSCE Chairman-in-Office (CIO) on the Nagorno-Karabakh conflict, dealt with by the Minsk Group,[87] and the newly established operations in Albania and Belarus.

One of the OSCE's achievements in 1997 was a peace plan for solution of the dispute over Nagorno-Karabakh between Armenia and Azerbaijan, prepared by the Minsk Group with the strong support of France, Russia and the USA. However, the plan generated a serious political crisis in Armenia and was not implemented. As a result, the President of Armenia was dismissed in

Peace Research and Security Policy, University of Hamburg (IFHS), *OSCE Yearbook* (published since 1995, in German, English and Russian) (Nomos Verlagsgesellschaft: Baden-Baden).

[83] See also chapters 2 and 4 in this volume.

[84] The chaos and crisis in Albania broke out in Jan. 1997 in the wake of mass protests of people who had lost their lifetime savings as a result of fraudulent pyramid investment schemes and the complete loss of control over the developments by the government. In effect the state collapsed as an institution. The greatest exodus of Albanians to Italy since the end of World War II forced international security institutions to undertake actions in accordance with Chapter VII of the UN Charter. In its Resolution 1101, the UN Security Council voted in favour of the OSCE proposal for a 3-month deployment of a Multinational Protection Force to create a secure environment for the work of EU and OSCE assistance missions and UN and NGO humanitarian activities in Albania. Forces from France, Greece, Romania, Spain and Turkey participated in the military operation, under Italian leadership. See also Foster, E., 'Intervention in Albania', *The New International Security Review 1998* (note 42), pp. 208–16.

[85] According to the OSCE Secretary General, UNTAES has been, along with the Albanian mission, the biggest and the most efficient mission ever to have operated under OSCE auspices. OSCE, *The Secretary General Annual Report 1997 on OSCE Activities (1 Nov. 1996–30 Nov. 1997)*, (OSCE: Vienna, 1997), p. 2. It should be noted that the UN decided to establish a support group of 180 civilian police monitors for a single period of up to 9 months, with effect from 16 Jan. 1998, to monitor the performance of the Croatian police in the Danube region. UN Security Council Resolution 1145, 19 Dec. 1997.

[86] *The Secretary General Annual Report 1997* (note 85), pp. 37–39.

[87] For the members of the Minsk Group in 1997, see the glossary in this volume.

early February 1998. The plan offered broad autonomy to the Armenian population of Nagorno-Karabakh (including an independent military police formation) with the understanding that this territory is under the sovereignty of Azerbaijan.[88]

OSCE Presence in Albania

On 4 March 1997 the OSCE Chairman-in-Office, Danish Foreign Minister Niels Helveg Petersen, responding to the crisis in Albania, appointed former Austrian Chancellor Franz Vranitzky as his Personal Representative. On 27 March the Permanent Council, the central OSCE decision-making body, established the OSCE Presence in Albania to provide Albania with advice and assistance in democratization, establishment of independent media, protection of human rights, and preparation and monitoring of elections. The OSCE also functioned as the coordinating framework for the work of other international organizations regarding Albania. The offices of the OSCE Presence in Albania worked in close coordination with such intergovernmental institutions as the Council of Europe, the WEU (its Multinational Advisory Policy Element) and the EU (its Customs Advisory Mission and the European Community Monitoring Mission, ECMM).

The activity in Albania was effective for several reasons: primarily because of the heavy political, military and financial involvement of Italy and four other European states (France, Greece, Romania and Spain) but also because three international organizations (the OSCE, the Council of Europe and the European Parliament) were represented by prominent persons with authority.[89] In addition to the main office of the OSCE Presence in Tirana, two field offices were opened in October 1997. They work in the areas of human rights and the rule of law, democratization and civil rights, electoral assistance, media monitoring and institution building. The Administrative Centre for the Coordination of Assistance and Public Participation, sponsored by the OSCE, coordinates foreign and domestic assistance and public participation in the constitutional drafting process.

Mission to Croatia

The mandate of the Mission to Croatia was to monitor the return of refugees and displaced persons on a case-by-case basis by studying the existing property law.[90] In cooperation with the OSCE Office for Democratic Institutions and Human Rights (ODIHR), the mission participated in monitoring the April

---

[88] *Izvestiya*, 6 Feb. 1998.

[89] In addition to the key role played by Vranitzky, the group of international observers to the elections in Albania was led by Catherine Lalumière, former Secretary General of the Council of Europe and member of the European Parliament, as the OSCE Special Coordinator. Lord Russell-Johnston, Head of the Council of Europe Parliamentary Assembly, and Javier Ruperez, President of the OSCE Parliamentary Assembly, also participated. See also 'Vranitzky bids farewell to Albania', *OSCE Newsletter*, vol. 4, no. 10 (Oct. 1997).

[90] The activity resulted in a detailed background report on 'The protection of property rights in the Republic of Croatia'. *The Secretary General Annual Report 1997* (note 85), p. 13.

1997 elections to the Croatian House of Counties and the June 1997 presidential election. The Special Coordinator for the OSCE Observer Mission, US Senator Paul Simon, declared the elections to have been 'free, but not fair'— with candidates being able to speak freely but with the process leading up to the elections being fundamentally flawed.[91] In view of the imminent termination of UNTAES, the Permanent Council authorized the OSCE mission to gradually increase its personnel up to a 250-member international staff.[92] The mission was also tasked in 1997 with assisting in the drafting of Croatian legislation and monitoring implementation of agreements on the two-way return of all refugees and displaced persons and the protection of persons belonging to national minorities. In its activities, the mission cooperated with the ECMM and many other governmental and non-governmental organizations.

Mission to Belgrade

As a result of the protests and tensions generated by the decision of the Yugoslav authorities to annul the results of the November 1996 municipal elections, the OSCE was committed to obtaining the facts. On 17 December 1996 the Chairman-in-Office appointed former Spanish Prime Minister Felipe González as his Personal Representative, with the mandate to investigate the situation and present conclusions to both Yugoslavia (Serbia and Montenegro) and the OSCE. After extensive talks with government officials, opposition leaders and media representatives, González reported his findings. In his view, the elections reflected the will of the majority of citizens and the authorities should accept and respect their outcome; on 4 February 1997 the Yugoslav authorities agreed to acknowledge the results. The CIO Personal Representative also concluded that the current electoral system should be improved as soon as possible and steps should be taken towards democratic reform.[93]

Other OSCE activities

In 1997 OSCE activities also involved assistance in the implementation of Russian–Estonian and Russian–Latvian agreements on retired military personnel and in promoting democratic institutions in Belarus. On 18 September 1997 the Permanent Council decided to establish an OSCE Advisory and Monitoring Group in Minsk.

As in previous years, activities developed by the OSCE High Commissioner on National Minorities (HCNM) in Croatia, Estonia, Georgia, Greece, Hungary, Kazakhstan, Kyrgyzstan, Latvia, Macedonia, Romania, Slovakia and Ukraine were praised by the OSCE participating states.[94] The CIO Personal Representative for Kosovo (Federal Republic of Yugoslavia), former Dutch

---

[91] *The Secretary General Annual Report 1997* (note 85), p. 13.
[92] OSCE document PC Decision no. 176, 26 June 1997. The Zagreb headquarters is supported by coordination centres in Vukovar, Knin, Sisak and Daruvar and by field offices in 16 other locations.
[93] *The Secretary General Annual Report 1997* (note 85), p. 17.
[94] See also *The Secretary General Annual Report 1997* (note 85), pp. 19–24; and Report of Max van der Stoel, OSCE High Commissioner on National Minorities, OSCE Implementation Meeting on Human Dimension Issues, Warsaw, 12–28 Nov. 1997.

Foreign Minister Max van der Stoel, was authorized to explore possibilities for reducing tensions in Kosovo; the Yugoslav Government continued to link the renewal of the activities of the missions to Kosovo, Sandjak and Vojvodina with Yugoslavia's participation in the OSCE.[95] It is noteworthy that the Kosovo case calls into question the conventional wisdom that early warning is of key importance in preventing conflicts. It is a necessary—but not sufficient—condition for actions aimed at preventing conflicts. However, the international community does not possess adequate instruments to prevent tensions from escalating to a conflict.

In 1997 the OSCE was engaged in significant activities in Central Asia. Most importantly, it was a signatory to the General Agreement on the Establishment of Peace and National Accord in Tajikistan on 27 June 1997.[96] The ODIHR increased its involvement in the promotion of democratic institutions and human rights in Central Asia. Although the ODIHR was active mainly in the field,[97] some activities were oriented towards integration of the new OSCE participating states.

Cooperation between the OSCE, the UN and the Council of Europe improved qualitatively during the year.[98] The annual High-Level Tripartite Meeting in Geneva, in 1997 held on 24 January, was attended by the representatives of the International Organization of Migration and the International Committee of the Red Cross. Cooperation in the field between the UN and the OSCE was developed in Georgia, Moldova and Tajikistan.[99] The working meetings of the chairmen and secretaries general of the OSCE and the Council of Europe in Oslo on 4 February 1997 and of experts in Strasbourg on 10 March paved the road to the close collaboration of these organizations in Albania, Belarus, Bosnia and Herzegovina, Croatia and the Caucasus.

A Charter on European Security

The 1994 OSCE Budapest summit meeting took decisions on a Common and Comprehensive Security Model for Europe for the 21st Century which in 1997 led to the adoption of the OSCE Guidelines on a Charter on European Security, adopted on 19 December at the Copenhagen OSCE Ministerial Council

---

[95] Yugoslavia (Serbia and Montenegro) has been suspended from participation in the OSCE since 1992.

[96] The OSCE Mission to Tajikistan was also a signatory to the Protocol on the Guarantees of Implementation of the General Agreement, signed in Tehran in May 1997. In addition, the mission provided assistance to the Commission for National Reconciliation, established in Sep. 1997.

[97] *The Secretary General Annual Report 1997* (note 85), pp. 25–29. In 1997 election processes were monitored in Croatia (13 Apr.), Bulgaria (19 Apr.), Croatia (15 June), Albania (29 June–6 July), Bosnia and Herzegovina (13–14 Sep.), Serbia (21 Sep.–5 Oct.), Montenegro (5–19 Oct.), the Republika Srpska (22–23 Nov.) and Serbia (7 Dec.).

[98] For a detailed review of all such forms of cooperation see 'The OSCE in the web of interlocking institutions', OSCE document PC/SM/7/97, Vienna, 19 Sep. 1997; and 'Reports from the OSCE Seminar on Co-operation among International Organizations and Institutions: Experience in Bosnia and Herzegovina, Portoroz, Slovenia, 29–30 Sep. 1997', *Consolidated Summary* (OSCE Secretariat: Vienna, 1997).

[99] The 52nd session of the UN General Assembly adopted Resolution A/RES/52/22 on cooperation between the United Nations and the OSCE, New York, 16 Jan. 1998.

meeting.[100] The Ministerial Council referred to two documents: the 1992 Helsinki Summit Declaration (paragraph 22),[101] according to which 'the OSCE is a forum . . . providing direction and giving impulse to the shaping of the new Europe'; and the 1994 Budapest Summit Declaration (paragraph 8), which states that primary new task of the OSCE is early warning, conflict prevention and crisis management.[102] In addition, the 1996 Lisbon Declaration on a Security Model[103] pledged a central role for the OSCE in ensuring security and stability.

Reaffirming the significance of the basic documents of the process initiated in Helsinki (the 1975 Final Act and the 1990 Charter of Paris), the ministers decided to develop a Charter on European Security as 'a comprehensive and substantive' new OSCE document. The charter is to 'be politically binding and take a further step with regard to standards and practices of OSCE participating States'.[104] By addressing the risks and challenges to European security in the next century, it is intended to contribute to 'a common security space within the OSCE area'. The OSCE should be able to achieve this aim through a strengthened organization, undertaking mutually supportive cooperation with other competent organizations on an equal basis. This should complement the processes of integration across the OSCE area and promote adherence to common values and implementation of commitments. The Charter on European Security should continue to uphold consensus as the basis for OSCE decision making. Flexibility and the ability to respond quickly to a changing political environment are seen as the main quality and advantage of the OSCE in comparison to other European security institutions.

The Ministerial Council presented a catalogue of 10 measures to turn this vision into reality. Unfortunately, like many previous OSCE documents, it contained a menu of wishful thinking rather than operational means to make the OSCE an effective European security organization. The paradox is that the element which determines the authority of the OSCE is at the same time its weakness—its decisions by consensus. While consensus decision making is rooted in the democratic principles of respect for the equality of states, it fails or becomes hamstrung in crisis situations. The comprehensive nature of the organization, embracing nearly all aspects of interstate security—political, economic, legal, military, civilizational and human—provides an opportunity to seek comprehensive solutions. This is important for conflict prevention, crisis management and post-conflict rehabilitation activities, but it is not helpful for concentrating limited resources on systematic activities in innovative approaches to problems. Ad hoc measures often facilitate flexibility, improvi-

---

[100] OSCE, Guidelines on an OSCE Document–Charter on European Security, OSCE document MC(6).DEC/5, *Journal No. 2*, 19 Dec. 1997.
[101] The Helsinki Summit Declaration is reproduced in *SIPRI Yearbook 1993: World Armaments and Disarmament* (Oxford University Press: Oxford, 1993), pp. 190–94.
[102] Budapest Summit Declaration (note 82), p. 310.
[103] The Lisbon Declaration on a Common and Comprehensive Security Model for Europe for the 21st Century is reproduced in *SIPRI Yearbook 1997* (note 12), pp. 153–55.
[104] Guidelines on an OSCE Document–Charter on European Security (note 100), paras 3 and 4.

sation and novel solutions, but they also expose the organizational weaknesses of structures and the lack of resources.

In 1997 the OSCE demonstrated new approaches to fulfilling its tasks by: close interaction with other European security structures, including efforts towards institutionalized cooperation;[105] more efficient early-warning systems and conflict-prevention activities (involving all the OSCE bodies, e.g., the Conflict Prevention Centre, the HCNM and the ODIHR); periodical evaluation and assessment of the implementation of decisions of the Permanent Council; and the direct involvement of high-ranking persons in operational activities in the field.[106]

V. Conclusions

Developments in 1997 in the parallel processes of EU and NATO enlargement brought Europe a step closer to establishing a system of inclusive security. While there was no real breakthrough in the shaping of such a security system, the potential for enhanced Europe-wide cooperation was advanced by the establishment of the EAPC. In addition, the 1997 NATO–Russia Founding Act offers a basis for 'a lasting and inclusive peace' and opens prospects for a greater sharing of values and commitments in the Euro-Atlantic area.

At the same time, the EU Intergovernmental Conference did not result in implementation of the CFSP, which remained largely declaratory. While the tasks defined for the OSCE during the cold war period were largely fulfilled or had outlived their relevance, it conducted significant activities in conflict prevention, crisis management and resolution of disputes, and its work on a Charter on European Security seek to identify new tasks for the organization. All the European security organizations are actively involved in an effort to strengthen security and cooperation in adjacent areas such as the Mediterranean region.

A new phenomenon in the search for regional security is the disappearance of an external threat to Europe. The main challenges and risks are now of a domestic nature, stemming from economic and social problems. For this reason, the non-military elements of stability are gaining in importance, in particular the attempts to institutionalize the changes taking place in NATO 'from defence of member territory to defence of common interests'.[107] Indeed, NATO has outgrown its mission as a defence alliance; it will have to combine treaty-based territorial defence with new tasks. NATO is currently both the centre of gravity and the centrepiece of a qualitatively new European security

---

[105] In this context, instead of separate summit meetings for each organization, bi-annual joint summits of the OSCE and the Council of Europe might be considered, as this could inject more coordination and economy into their decision making.

[106] See also the address by the new OSCE Chairman-in-Office, Bronislaw Geremek, Minister for Foreign Affairs of Poland to the Permanent Council, Vienna, 15 Jan. 1998, OSCE document CIO.Gal/98.

[107] 'NATO after Madrid: looking to the future', Report based on a conference organized by the Stanford–Harvard Preventive Diplomacy Project, Stanford University, Stanford, Calif., 19–20 Sep. 1997, p. 3.

order which is developing an unprecedented degree of mutual confidence and transparency.

In 1997 inclusive security was oriented mainly towards solutions of a procedural and institutional nature. However, a redefinition of the real new threats and adaptation of the ways and means with which to meet them together are decisive for the future. An inclusive and cooperative security order in Europe requires the promotion of a community of shared values and management of national political and economic interests. A system must be sought in which the equality of states and democratic principles are reconciled with acknowledged leadership and efficient decision making.

Appendix 5A. Documents on European security

FOUNDING ACT ON MUTUAL RELATIONS, COOPERATION AND SECURITY BETWEEN THE NORTH ATLANTIC TREATY ORGANIZATION AND THE RUSSIAN FEDERATION (NATO–RUSSIA FOUNDING ACT)

Paris, 27 May 1997

The North Atlantic Treaty Organization and its member States, on the one hand, and the Russian Federation, on the other hand, hereinafter referred to as NATO and Russia, based on an enduring political commitment undertaken at the highest political level, will build together a lasting and inclusive peace in the Euro-Atlantic area on the principles of democracy and cooperative security.

NATO and Russia do not consider each other as adversaries. They share the goal of overcoming the vestiges of earlier confrontation and competition and of strengthening mutual trust and cooperation. The present Act reaffirms the determination of NATO and Russia to give concrete substance to their shared commitment to build a stable, peaceful and undivided Europe, whole and free, to the benefit of all its peoples. Making this commitment at the highest political level marks the beginning of a fundamentally new relationship between NATO and Russia. They intend to develop, on the basis of common interest, reciprocity and transparency a strong, stable and enduring partnership.

This Act defines the goals and mechanism of consultation, cooperation, joint decision-making and joint action that will constitute the core of the mutual relations between NATO and Russia.

NATO has undertaken a historic transformation—a process that will continue. In 1991 the Alliance revised its strategic doctrine to take account of the new security environment in Europe. Accordingly, NATO has radically reduced and continues the adaptation of its conventional and nuclear forces. While preserving the capability to meet the commitments undertaken in the Washington Treaty, NATO has expanded and will continue to expand its political functions, and taken on new missions of peacekeeping and crisis management in support of the United Nations (UN) and the Organisation for Security and Cooperation in Europe (OSCE), such as in Bosnia and Herzegovina, to address new security challenges in close association with other countries and international organisations. NATO is in the process of developing the European Security and Defence Identity (ESDI) within the Alliance. It will continue to develop a broad and dynamic pattern of cooperation with OSCE participating States in particular through the Partnership for Peace and is working with Partner countries on the initiative to establish a Euro-Atlantic Partnership Council. NATO member States have decided to examine NATO's Strategic Concept to ensure that it is fully consistent with Europe's new security situation and challenges.

Russia is continuing the building of a democratic society and the realisation of its political and economic transformation. It is developing the concept of its national security and revising its military doctrine to ensure that they are fully consistent with new security realities. Russia has carried out deep reductions in its armed forces, has withdrawn its forces on an unprecedented scale from the countries of Central and Eastern Europe and the Baltic countries and withdrawn all its nuclear weapons back to its own national territory. Russia is committed to further reducing its conventional and nuclear forces. It is actively participating in peacekeeping operations in support of the UN and the OSCE, as well as in crisis management in different areas of the world. Russia is contributing to the multinational forces in Bosnia and Herzegovina.

I. Principles

Proceeding from the principle that the security of all states in the Euro-Atlantic community is indivisible, NATO and Russia will work together to contribute to the establishment in Europe of common and comprehensive security based on the allegiance to shared values, commitments and norms of behaviour in the interests of all states.

NATO and Russia will help to strengthen the Organisation for Security and Cooperation in Europe, including developing further its role as a primary instrument in preventive diplomacy, conflict prevention, crisis management, post-conflict rehabilitation and regional security cooperation, as well as in enhancing its operational capabilities to carry out these tasks. The OSCE, as the only pan-European security organisation, has a key role in European peace and stability. In strengthening the OSCE, NATO and Russia will cooperate to prevent any possibility of returning to a Europe of division and confrontation, or the isolation of any state.

Consistent with the OSCE's work on a Common and Comprehensive Security Model for Europe for the Twenty-First Century, and taking into account the decisions of the Lisbon Summit concerning a Charter on European Security, NATO and Russia will seek the widest possible cooperation among participating States of the OSCE with the aim of creating in Europe a common space of security and stability, without dividing lines or spheres of influence limiting the sovereignty of any state.

NATO and Russia start from the premise that the shared objective of strengthening security and stability in the Euro-Atlantic area for the benefit of all countries requires a response to new risks and challenges, such as aggressive nationalism, proliferation of nuclear, biological and chemical weapons, terrorism, persistent abuse of human rights and of the rights of persons belonging to national minorities and unresolved territorial disputes, which pose a threat to common peace, prosperity and stability.

This Act does not affect, and cannot be regarded as affecting, the primary responsibility of the UN Security Council for maintaining international peace and security, or the role of the OSCE as the inclusive and comprehensive organisation for consultation, decision-making and cooperation in its area and as a regional arrangement under Chapter VIII of the United Nations Charter.

In implementing the provisions in this Act, NATO and Russia will observe in good faith their obligations under international law and international instruments, including the obligations of the United Nations Charter and the provisions of the Universal Declaration on Human Rights as well as their commitments under the Helsinki Final Act and subsequent OSCE documents, including the Charter of Paris and the documents adopted at the Lisbon OSCE Summit.

To achieve the aims of this Act, NATO and Russia will base their relations on a shared commitment to the following principles:

– development, on the basis of transparency, of a strong, stable, enduring and equal partnership and of cooperation to strengthen security and stability in the Euro-Atlantic area;

– acknowledgement of the vital role that democracy, political pluralism, the rule of law, and respect for human rights and civil liberties and the development of free market economies play in the development of common prosperity and comprehensive security;

– refraining from the threat or use of force against each other as well as against any other state, its sovereignty, territorial integrity or political independence in any manner inconsistent with the United Nations Charter and with the Declaration of Principles Guiding Relations Between Participating States contained in the Helsinki Final Act;

– respect for sovereignty, independence and territorial integrity of all states and their inherent right to choose the means to ensure their own security, the inviolability of borders and peoples' right of self-determination as enshrined in the Helsinki Final Act and other OSCE documents;

– mutual transparency in creating and implementing defence policy and military doctrines;

– prevention of conflicts and settlement of disputes by peaceful means in accordance with UN and OSCE principles;

– support, on a case-by-case basis, of peacekeeping operations carried out under the authority of the UN Security Council or the responsibility of the OSCE.

II. Mechanism for Consultation and Cooperation, the NATO–Russia Permanent Joint Council

To carry out the activities and aims provided for by this Act and to develop common approaches to European security and to political problems, NATO and Russia will create the NATO–Russia Permanent Joint Council. The central objective of this Permanent Joint Council will be to build increasing levels of trust, unity of purpose and habits of consultation and cooperation between NATO and Russia, in order to enhance each other's security and that of all nations in the Euro-Atlantic area and diminish the security of none. If disagreements arise, NATO and Russia will endeavour to settle them on the basis of goodwill and mutual respect within the framework of political consultations.

The Permanent Joint Council will provide a mechanism for consultations, coordination and, to the maximum extent possible, where appropriate, for joint decisions and joint action with respect to security issues of common concern. The consultations will not extend to internal matters of either NATO, NATO member States or Russia.

The shared objective of NATO and Russia is to identify and pursue as many opportunities for joint action as possible. As the relationship develops, they expect that additional opportunities for joint action will emerge.

The Permanent Joint Council will be the principal venue of consultation between NATO and Russia in times of crisis or for any other situation affecting peace and stability. Extraordinary meetings of the Council will take place in addition to its regular meetings to allow for prompt consultations in case of emergencies. In this context, NATO and Russia will promptly consult within the Permanent Joint Council in case one of the Council members perceives a threat to its territorial integrity, political independence or security.

The activities of the Permanent Joint Council will be built upon the principles of reciprocity and transparency. In the course of their consultations and cooperation, NATO and Russia will inform each other regarding the respective security-related challenges they face and the measures that each intends to take to address them.

Provisions of this Act do not provide NATO or Russia, in any way, with a right of veto over the actions of the other nor do they infringe upon or restrict the rights of NATO or Russia to independent decision-making and action. They cannot be used as a means to disadvantage the interests of other states.

The Permanent Joint Council will meet at various levels and in different forms, according to the subject matter and the wishes of NATO and Russia. The Permanent Joint Council will meet at the level of Foreign Ministers and at the level of Defence Ministers twice annually, and also monthly at the level of ambassadors/permanent representatives to the North Atlantic Council.

The Permanent Joint Council may also meet, as appropriate, at the level of Heads of State and Government.

The Permanent Joint Council may establish committees or working groups for individual subjects or areas of cooperation on an ad hoc or permanent basis, as appropriate.

Under the auspices of the Permanent Joint Council, military representatives and Chiefs of Staff will also meet; meetings of Chiefs of Staff will take place no less than twice a year, and also monthly at military representatives level. Meetings of military experts may be convened, as appropriate.

The Permanent Joint Council will be chaired jointly by the Secretary General of NATO, a representative of one of the NATO member States on a rotation basis, and a representative of Russia.

To support the work of the Permanent Joint Council, NATO and Russia will establish the necessary administrative structures.

Russia will establish a Mission to NATO headed by a representative at the rank of Ambassador. A senior military representative and his staff will be part of this Mission for the purposes of the military cooperation. NATO retains the possibility of establishing an appropriate presence in Moscow, the modalities of which remain to be determined.

The agenda for regular sessions will be established jointly. Organisational arrangements and rules of procedure for the Permanent Joint Council will be worked out. These arrangements will be in place for the inaugural meeting of the Permanent Joint Council which will be held no later than four months after the signature of this Act.

The Permanent Joint Council will engage in three distinct activities:

– consulting on the topics in Section III of this Act and on any other political or security issue determined by mutual consent;

– on the basis of these consultations, developing joint initiatives on which NATO and Russia would agree to speak or act in parallel;

– once consensus has been reached in the course of consultation, making joint decisions and taking joint action on a case-by-case basis, including participation, on an equitable basis, in the planning and preparation of joint operations, including peacekeeping operations under the authority of the UN Security Council or the responsibility of the OSCE.

Any actions undertaken by NATO or Russia, together or separately, must be consistent with the United Nations Charter and the OSCE's governing principles.

Recognizing the importance of deepening contacts between the legislative bodies of the participating States to this Act, NATO and Russia will also encourage expanded dialogue and cooperation between the North Atlantic Assembly and the Federal Assembly of the Russian Federation.

III. Areas for Consultation and Cooperation

In building their relationship, NATO and Russia will focus on specific areas of mutual interest. They will consult and strive to cooperate to the broadest possible degree in the following areas:

– issues of common interest related to security and stability in the Euro-Atlantic area or to concrete crises, including the contribution of NATO and Russia to security and stability in this area;

– conflict prevention, including preventive diplomacy, crisis management and conflict resolution taking into account the role and responsibility of the UN and the OSCE and the work of these organisations in these fields;

– joint operations, including peacekeeping operations, on a case-by-case basis, under the authority of the UN Security Council or the responsibility of the OSCE, and if Combined Joint Task Forces (CJTF) are used in such cases, participation in them at an early stage;

– participation of Russia in the Euro-Atlantic Partnership Council and the Partnership for Peace;

– exchange of information and consultation on strategy, defence policy, the military doctrines of NATO and Russia, and budgets and infrastructure development programmes;

– arms control issues;

– nuclear safety issues, across their full spectrum;

– preventing the proliferation of nuclear, biological and chemical weapons, and their delivery means, combatting nuclear trafficking and strengthening cooperation in specific arms control areas, including political and defence aspects of proliferation;

– possible cooperation in Theatre Missile Defence;

– enhanced regional air traffic safety, increased air traffic capacity and reciprocal exchanges, as appropriate, to promote confidence through increased measures of transparency and exchanges of information in relation to air defence and related aspects of airspace management/control. This will include exploring possible cooperation on appropriate air defence related matters;

– increasing transparency, predictability and mutual confidence regarding the size and roles of the conventional forces of member States of NATO and Russia;

– reciprocal exchanges, as appropriate, on nuclear weapons issues, including doctrines and strategy of NATO and Russia;

– coordinating a programme of expanded cooperation between respective military establishments, as further detailed below;

– pursuing possible armaments-related cooperation through association of Russia with NATO's Conference of National Armaments Directors;

– conversion of defence industries;

– developing mutually agreed cooperative projects in defence-related economic, environmental and scientific fields;

– conducting joint initiatives and exercises in civil emergency preparedness and disaster relief;

– combatting terrorism and drug trafficking;

– improving public understanding of evolving relations between NATO and Russia, including the establishment of a NATO documentation centre or information office in Moscow.

Other areas can be added by mutual agreement.

IV. Political–Military Matters

NATO and Russia affirm their shared desire to achieve greater stability and security in the Euro-Atlantic area.

The member States of NATO reiterate that they have no intention, no plan and no reason to deploy nuclear weapons on the territory of new members, nor any need to change any aspect of NATO's nuclear posture or nuclear policy—and do not foresee any future need to do so. This subsumes the fact that NATO has decided that it has no intention, no plan, and no reason to establish nuclear weapon storage sites on the territory of those members, whether through the construction of new nuclear storage facilities or the adaptation of old nuclear storage facilities. Nuclear storage sites are understood to be facilities specifically designed for the stationing of nuclear weapons, and include all types of hardened above or below ground facilities (storage bunkers or vaults) designed for storing nuclear weapons.

Recognising the importance of the adaptation of the Treaty on Conventional Armed Forces in Europe (CFE) for the broader context of security in the OSCE area and the work on a Common and Comprehensive Security Model for Europe for the Twenty-First Century, the member States of NATO and Russia will work together in Vienna with the other States Parties to adapt the CFE Treaty to enhance its viability and effectiveness, taking into account Europe's changing security environment and the legitimate security interests of all OSCE participating States. They share the objective of concluding an adaptation agreement as expeditiously as possible and, as a first step in this process, they will, together with other States Parties to the CFE Treaty, seek to conclude as soon as possible a framework agreement setting forth the basic elements of an adapted CFE Treaty, consistent with the objectives and principles of the Document on Scope and Parameters agreed at Lisbon in December 1996.

NATO and Russia believe that an important goal of CFE Treaty adaptation should be a significant lowering in the total amount of Treaty-Limited Equipment permitted in the Treaty's area of application compatible with the legitimate defence requirements of each State Party. NATO and Russia encourage all States Parties to the CFE Treaty to consider reductions in their CFE equipment entitlements, as part of an overall effort to achieve lower equipment levels that are consistent with the transformation of Europe's security environment.

The member States of NATO and Russia commit themselves to exercise restraint during the period of negotiations, as foreseen in the Document on Scope and Parameters, in relation to the current postures and capabilities of their conventional armed forces—in particular with respect to their levels of forces and deployments—in the Treaty's area of application, in order to avoid developments in the security situation in Europe diminishing the security of any State Party. This commitment is without prejudice to possible voluntary decisions by the individual States Parties to reduce their force levels or deployments, or to their legitimate security interests.

The member States of NATO and Russia proceed on the basis that adaptation of the CFE Treaty should help to ensure equal security for all States Parties irrespective of their membership of a politico-military alliance, both to preserve and strengthen stability and continue to prevent any destabilizing increase of forces in various regions of Europe and in Europe as a whole. An adapted CFE Treaty should also further enhance military transparency by extended information exchange and verification, and permit the possible accession by new States Parties.

The member States of NATO and Russia propose to other CFE States Parties to carry out such adaptation of the CFE Treaty so as to enable States Parties to reach, through a transparent and cooperative process, conclusions regarding reductions they might be prepared to take and resulting national Treaty-Limited Equipment ceilings. These will then be codified as binding limits in the adapted Treaty to be agreed by consensus of all States Parties, and reviewed in 2001 and at five-year intervals thereafter. In doing so, the States Parties will take into account all the levels of Treaty-Limited Equipment established for the Atlantic-to-the-Urals area by the original CFE Treaty, the substantial reductions that have been carried out since then, the changes to the situation in Europe and the need to ensure that the security of no state is diminished.

The member States of NATO and Russia reaffirm that States Parties to the CFE Treaty should maintain only such military capabilities, individually or in conjunction with others, as are commensurate with individual or collective legitimate security needs, taking into account their international obligations, including the CFE Treaty.

Each State Party will base its agreement to the provisions of the adapted Treaty on all national ceilings of the States Parties, on its projections of the current and future security situation in Europe.

In addition, in the negotiations on the adaptation of the CFE Treaty, the member States of NATO and Russia will, together with other States Parties, seek to strengthen stability by further developing measures to prevent any potentially threatening build-up of conventional forces in agreed regions of Europe, to include Central and Eastern Europe.

NATO and Russia have clarified their intentions with regard to their conventional force postures in Europe's new security environment and are prepared to consult on the evolution of these postures in the framework of the Permanent Joint Council.

NATO reiterates that in the current and foreseeable security environment, the Alliance will carry out its collective defence and other missions by ensuring the necessary interoperability, integration, and capability for reinforcement rather than by additional permanent stationing of substantial combat forces. Accordingly, it will have to rely on adequate infrastructure commensurate with the above tasks. In this context, reinforcement may take place, when necessary, in the event of defence against a threat of aggression and missions in support of peace consistent with the United Nations Charter and the OSCE governing principles, as well as for exercises consistent with the adapted CFE Treaty, the provisions of the Vienna Document 1994 and mutually agreed transparency measures. Russia will exercise similar restraint in its conventional force deployments in Europe.

The member States of NATO and Russia

will strive for greater transparency, predictability and mutual confidence with regard to their armed forces. They will comply fully with their obligations under the Vienna Document 1994 and develop cooperation with the other OSCE participating States, including negotiations in the appropriate format, inter alia within the OSCE to promote confidence and security.

The member States of NATO and Russia will use and improve existing arms control regimes and confidence-building measures to create security relations based on peaceful cooperation.

NATO and Russia, in order to develop cooperation between their military establishments, will expand political–military consultations and cooperation through the Permanent Joint Council with an enhanced dialogue between the senior military authorities of NATO and its member States and of Russia. They will implement a programme of significantly expanded military activities and practical cooperation between NATO and Russia at all levels. Consistent with the tenets of the Permanent Joint Council, this enhanced military-to-military dialogue will be built upon the principle that neither party views the other as a threat nor seeks to disadvantage the other's security. This enhanced military-to-military dialogue will include regularly-scheduled reciprocal briefings on NATO and Russian military doctrine, strategy and resultant force posture and will include the broad possibilities for joint exercises and training.

To support this enhanced dialogue and the military components of the Permanent Joint Council, NATO and Russia will establish military liaison missions at various levels on the basis of reciprocity and further mutual arrangements.

To enhance their partnership and ensure this partnership is grounded to the greatest extent possible in practical activities and direct cooperation, NATO's and Russia's respective military authorities will explore the further development of a concept for joint NATO–Russia peacekeeping operations. This initiative should build upon the positive experience of working together in Bosnia and Herzegovina, and the lessons learned there will be used in the establishment of Combined Joint Task Forces.

The present Act takes effect upon the date of its signature.

NATO and Russia will take the proper steps to ensure its implementation in accordance with their procedures.

The present Act is established in two originals in the French, English and Russian language.

The Secretary General of NATO and the Government of the Russian Federation will provide the Secretary General of the United Nations and the Secretary General of the OSCE with the text of this Act with the request to circulate it to all members of their Organisations.

Source: United Nations General Assembly document A/52/161, 30 May 1997.

BASIC DOCUMENT OF THE EURO-ATLANTIC PARTNERSHIP COUNCIL

Sintra, Portugal, 30 May 1997

1. The member countries of the North Atlantic Cooperation Council and participating countries of the Partnership for Peace, determined to raise to a qualitatively new level their political and military cooperation, building upon the success of NACC and PfP, have decided to establish a Euro-Atlantic Partnership Council. In doing so, they reaffirm their joint commitment to strengthen and extend peace and stability in the Euro-Atlantic area, on the basis of the shared values and principles which underlie their cooperation, notably those set out in the Framework Document of the Partnership for Peace.

2. The Euro-Atlantic Partnership Council will be a new cooperative mechanism which will form a framework for enhanced efforts in both an expanded political dimension of partnership and practical cooperation under PfP. It will take full account of and complement the respective activities of the OSCE and other relevant institutions such as the European Union, the Western European Union and the Council of Europe.

3. The Euro-Atlantic Partnership Council, as the successor to NACC, will provide the overarching framework for consultations among its members on a broad range of political and security-related issues, as part of a process that will develop through practice. PfP in its enhanced form will be a clearly identifiable element within this flexible framework. Its basic elements will remain valid. The Euro-Atlantic Partnership Council will build upon the existing framework of NATO's outreach activities preserving their advantages to promote cooperation in a transparent way. The expanded political dimension

of consultation and cooperation which the Council will offer will allow Partners, if they wish, to develop a direct political relationship individually or in smaller groups with the Alliance. In addition, the Council will provide the framework to afford Partner countries, to the maximum extent possible, increased decision-making opportunities relating to activities in which they participate.

4. The Euro-Atlantic Partnership Council will retain two important principles which have underpinned the success of cooperation between Allies and Partners so far. It will be inclusive, in that opportunities for political consultation and practical cooperation will be open to all Allies and Partners equally. It will also maintain self-differentiation, in that Partners will be able to decide for themselves the level and areas of cooperation with NATO. Arrangements under the Council will not affect commitments already undertaken bilaterally between Partners and NATO, or commitments in the PfP Framework Document including the consultation provisions of its article 8.

5. The Euro-Atlantic Partnership Council will meet, as required, in different formats:

– In plenary session to address political and security-related issues of common concern and to provide information as appropriate on activities with limited participation.

– In a limited format between the Alliance and open-ended groups of Partners to focus on functional matters or, on an ad hoc basis, on appropriate regional matters. In such cases, the other EAPC members will be kept informed about the results.

– In a limited format between the Alliance and groups of Partners who participate with NATO in a peace support operation or in the Planning and Review Process, or in other cases for which this format has been agreed. The other members of the EAPC will be informed as appropriate.

– In an individual format between the Alliance and one Partner.

Structure

6. The Euro-Atlantic Partnership Council will meet, as a general rule, at Ambassadorial level in Brussels and on a monthly basis.

7. The Council will meet twice a year at both Foreign Ministers and Defence Ministers level; additional meetings can be envisaged as required. It may also meet at the level of Heads of State or Government, when appropriate.

8. The Council will be chaired by the Secretary General of the North Atlantic Alliance or his Deputy. The representative of a member country will be named President d'Honneur for six months according to modalities to be determined.

9. The work of the Euro-Atlantic Partnership Council will be supported regularly by the Political–Military Steering Committee (PMSC) and the Political Committee (PC) in their configurations at Alliance with all Partners. On an ad hoc basis an EAPC Senior Political Committee would address issues referred to it, as required. The EAPC will consider, based on evolving practical experience, whether this support could be improved by an EAPC Steering Committee (EAPC–SC) which would integrate the functions of the former enlarged Political Committee and the PMSC in NACC/PfP format.

The PMSC will meet, as appropriate, in an Alliance with individual Partners or Alliance with groups of Partners (e.g. PARP [Planning and Review Process]) configuration. The PMSC and PC with Partners will meet at least once a month, or more frequently if required. Other NATO Committees will expand opportunities for work with Partners on cooperation issues and will inform the EAPC on their work in this regard. Their activities will become part of the Euro-Atlantic Partnership Council framework. An important part of this framework will be new opportunities for Partner consultations with the Military Committee. The Military Committee will also play a major role in the expanded range of opportunities for consultation and cooperation provided by the future support structure for the EAPC.

Substance

10. The Euro-Atlantic Partnership Council will adopt at the time of its establishment the NACC Work Plan for Dialogue, Partnership and Cooperation and will replace it with an EAPC Work Plan as part of its future work. The activities included in the Partnership Work Programme (PWP) will also come under the general purview of the EAPC.

11. Specific subject areas on which Allies and Partners would consult, in the framework of the EAPC, might include but not be limited to: political and security related matters; crisis management; regional matters; arms control issues; nuclear, biological and chemical (NBC) proliferation and defence issues; international terrorism; defence planning and budgets and defence policy and strategy; security impacts of economic developments. There

will also be scope for consultations and cooperation on issues such as: civil emergency and disaster preparedness; armaments cooperation under the aegis of the Conference of National Armaments Directors (CNAD); nuclear safety; defence related environmental issues; civil–military coordination of air traffic management and control; scientific cooperation; and issues related to peace support operations.

Eligibility

12. Present NACC members and PfP participating countries automatically become members of the Euro-Atlantic Partnership Council if they so desire. The Euro-Atlantic Partnership Council is open to the accession of other OSCE participating states able and willing to accept its basic principles and to contribute to its goals. New members may join the EAPC by joining the Partnership for Peace through signing the PfP Framework Document and by stating their acceptance of the concept of the EAPC as laid out in this document. The EAPC would be invited to endorse the accession of its new members.

Source: NATO Press and Media Service, Press Communiqué M-NACC-EAPC-1(97)66, 30 May 1997.

MADRID DECLARATION ON EURO-ATLANTIC SECURITY AND COOPERATION

Madrid, 8 July 1997

Excerpts

1. We, the Heads of State and Government of the member countries of the North Atlantic Alliance, have come together in Madrid to give shape to the new NATO as we move towards the 21st century. Substantial progress has been achieved in the internal adaptation of the Alliance. As a significant step in the evolutionary process of opening the Alliance, we have invited three countries to begin accession talks. We have substantially strengthened our relationship with Partners through the new Euro-Atlantic Partnership Council and enhancement of the Partnership for Peace. The signature on 27th May of the NATO–Russia Founding Act and the Charter we will sign tomorrow with Ukraine bear witness to our commitment to an undivided Europe. We are also enhancing our Mediterranean dialogue. Our aim is to reinforce peace and stability in the Euro-Atlantic area.

A new Europe is emerging, a Europe of greater integration and cooperation. An inclusive European security architecture is evolving to which we are contributing, along with other European organisations. Our Alliance will continue to be a driving force in this process.

2. We are moving towards the realisation of our vision of a just and lasting order of peace for Europe as a whole, based on human rights, freedom and democracy. In looking forward to the 50th anniversary of the North Atlantic Treaty, we reaffirm our commitment to a strong, dynamic partnership between the European and North American Allies, which has been, and will continue to be, the bedrock of the Alliance and of a free and prosperous Europe. The vitality of the transatlantic link will benefit from the development of a true, balanced partnership in which Europe is taking on greater responsibility. In this spirit, we are building a European Security and Defence Identity within NATO. The Alliance and the European Union share common strategic interests. We welcome the agreements reached at the European Council in Amsterdam. NATO will remain the essential forum for consultation among its members and the venue for agreement on policies bearing on the security and defence commitments of Allies under the Washington Treaty.

3. While maintaining our core function of collective defence, we have adapted our political and military structures to improve our ability to meet the new challenges of regional crisis and conflict management. NATO's continued contribution to peace in Bosnia and Herzegovina, and the unprecedented scale of cooperation with other countries and international organisations there, reflect the cooperative approach which is key to building our common security. A new NATO is developing: a new NATO for a new and undivided Europe.

4. The security of NATO's members is inseparably linked to that of the whole of Europe. Improving the security and stability environment for nations in the Euro-Atlantic area where peace is fragile and instability currently prevails remains a major Alliance interest. The consolidation of democratic and free societies on the entire continent, in accordance with OSCE principles, is therefore of direct and material concern to the Alliance. NATO's policy is to build effective cooperation through its outreach activities, including the Euro-Atlantic Partnership Council, with

free nations which share the values of the Alliance, including members of the European Union as well as candidates for EU membership.

5. At our last meeting in Brussels, we said that we would expect and would welcome the accession of new members, as part of an evolutionary process, taking into account political and security developments in the whole of Europe. Twelve European countries have so far requested to join the Alliance. We welcome the aspirations and efforts of these nations. The time has come to start a new phase of this process. The Study on NATO Enlargement—which stated, inter alia, that NATO's military effectiveness should be sustained as the Alliance enlarges—the results of the intensified dialogue with interested Partners, and the analyses of relevant factors associated with the admission of new members have provided a basis on which to assess the current state of preparations of the twelve countries aspiring to Alliance membership.

6. Today, we invite the Czech Republic, Hungary and Poland to begin accession talks with NATO. Our goal is to sign the Protocol of Accession at the time of the Ministerial meetings in December 1997 and to see the ratification process completed in time for membership to become effective by the 50th anniversary of the Washington Treaty in April 1999. During the period leading to accession, the Alliance will involve invited countries, to the greatest extent possible and where appropriate, in Alliance activities, to ensure that they are best prepared to undertake the responsibilities and obligations of membership in an enlarged Alliance. We direct the Council in Permanent Session to develop appropriate arrangements for this purpose.

7. Admitting new members will entail resource implications for the Alliance. It will involve the Alliance providing the resources which enlargement will necessarily require. We direct the Council in Permanent Session to bring to an early conclusion the concrete analysis of the resource implications of the forthcoming enlargement, drawing on the continuing work on military implications. We are confident that, in line with the security environment of the Europe of today, Alliance costs associated with the integration of new members will be manageable and that the resources necessary to meet those costs will be provided.

8. We reaffirm that NATO remains open to new members under Article 10 of the North Atlantic Treaty. The Alliance will continue to welcome new members in a position to further the principles of the Treaty and contribute to security in the Euro-Atlantic area. The Alliance expects to extend further invitations in coming years to nations willing and able to assume the responsibilities and obligations of membership, and as NATO determines that the inclusion of these nations would serve the overall political and strategic interests of the Alliance and that the inclusion would enhance overall European security and stability. To give substance to this commitment, NATO will maintain an active relationship with those nations that have expressed an interest in NATO membership as well as those who may wish to seek membership in the future. Those nations that have previously expressed an interest in becoming NATO members but that were not invited to begin accession talks today will remain under consideration for future membership. The considerations set forth in our 1995 Study on NATO Enlargement will continue to apply with regard to future aspirants, regardless of their geographic location. No European democratic country whose admission would fulfil the objectives of the Treaty will be excluded from consideration. Furthermore, in order to enhance overall security and stability in Europe, further steps in the ongoing enlargement process of the Alliance should balance the security concerns of all Allies.

To support this process, we strongly encourage the active participation by aspiring members in the Euro-Atlantic Partnership Council and the Partnership for Peace, which will further deepen their political and military involvement in the work of the Alliance. We also intend to continue the Alliance's intensified dialogues with those nations that aspire to NATO membership or that otherwise wish to pursue a dialogue with NATO on membership questions. To this end, these intensified dialogues will cover the full range of political, military, financial and security issues relating to possible NATO membership, without prejudice to any eventual Alliance decision. They will include meeting within the EAPC as well as periodic meetings with the North Atlantic Council in Permanent Session and the NATO International Staff and with other NATO bodies as appropriate. In keeping with our pledge to maintain an open door to the admission of additional Alliance members in the future, we also direct that NATO Foreign Ministers keep that process under continual review and report to us.

We will review the process at our next meeting in 1999. With regard to the aspiring members, we recognise with great interest and take account of the positive developments towards democracy and the rule of law in a number of southeastern European countries, especially Romania and Slovenia.

The Alliance recognises the need to build greater stability, security and regional cooperation in the countries of southeast Europe, and in promoting their increasing integration into the Euro-Atlantic community. At the same time, we recognise the progress achieved towards greater stability and cooperation by the states in the Baltic region which are also aspiring members. As we look to the future of the Alliance, progress towards these objectives will be important for our overall goal of a free, prosperous and undivided Europe at peace.

(...)

23. We continue to attach greatest importance to further the means of non-proliferation, arms control and disarmament.

We welcome the progress made since the Brussels Summit, as an integral part of NATO's adaptation, to intensify and expand Alliance political and defence efforts aimed at preventing proliferation and safeguarding NATO's strategic unity and freedom of action despite the risks posed by nuclear, biological and chemical (NBC) weapons and their means of delivery. We attach the utmost importance to these efforts, welcome the Alliance's substantial achievements, and direct that work continue.

We call on all states which have not yet done so to sign and ratify the Chemical Weapons Convention. Recognising that enhancing confidence in compliance would reinforce the Biological and Toxin Weapons Convention, we reaffirm our determination to complete as soon as possible through negotiation a legally binding and effective verification mechanism. We urge the Russian Federation to ratify the START II Treaty without delay so that negotiation of START III may begin.

(...)

Source: NATO, Press Release M-1 (97)81, Meeting of the North Atlantic Council, Madrid, 8 July 1997, URL <http://www.nato.int/docu/pr/1997/p97-081e.htm>, version current on 3 Apr. 1998.

TREATY OF AMSTERDAM AMENDING THE TREATY ON EUROPEAN UNION, THE TREATIES ESTABLISHING THE EUROPEAN COMMUNITIES AND CERTAIN RELATED ACTS

Amsterdam, 2 October 1997

Excerpts

10) Title V shall be replaced by the following:

"**Title V**

PROVISIONS ON A COMMON FOREIGN AND SECURITY POLICY

Article J.1

1. The Union shall define and implement a common foreign and security policy covering all areas of foreign and security policy, the objectives of which shall be:
– to safeguard the common values, fundamental interests, independence and integrity of the Union in conformity with the principles of the United Nations Charter;
– to strengthen the security of the Union in all ways;
– to preserve peace and strengthen international security, in accordance with the principles of the United Nations Charter, as well as the principles of the Helsinki Final Act and the objectives of the Paris Charter, including those on external borders;
– to promote international cooperation;
– to develop and consolidate democracy and the rule of law, and respect for human rights and fundamental freedoms.

2. The Member States shall support the Union's external and security policy actively and unreservedly in a spirit of loyalty and mutual solidarity.

The Member States shall work together to enhance and develop their mutual political solidarity. They shall refrain from any action which is contrary to the interests of the Union or likely to impair its effectiveness as a cohesive force in international relations.

The Council shall ensure that these principles are complied with.

Article J.2

The Union shall pursue the objectives set out in Article J.1 by:
– defining the principles of and general

guidelines for the common foreign and security policy;
– deciding on common strategies;
– adopting joint actions;
– adopting common positions;
– strengthening systematic cooperation between Member States in the conduct of policy.

Article J.3

1. The European Council shall define the principles of and general guidelines for the common foreign and security policy, including for matters with defence implications.

2. The European Council shall decide on common strategies to be implemented by the Union in areas where the Member States have important interests in common.

Common strategies shall set out their objectives, duration and the means to be made available by the Union and the Member States.

3. The Council shall take the decisions necessary for defining and implementing the common foreign and security policy on the basis of the general guidelines defined by the European Council.

The Council shall recommend common strategies to the European Council and shall implement them, in particular by adopting joint actions and common positions.

The Council shall ensure the unity, consistency and effectiveness of action by the Union.

Article J.4

1. The Council shall adopt joint actions. Joint actions shall address specific situations where operational action by the Union is deemed to be required. They shall lay down their objectives, scope, the means to be made available to the Union, if necessary their duration, and the conditions for their implementation.

2. If there is a change in circumstances having a substantial effect on a question subject to joint action, the Council shall review the principles and objectives of that action and take the necessary decisions. As long as the Council has not acted, the joint action shall stand.

3. Joint actions shall commit the Member States in the positions they adopt and in the conduct of their activity.

4. The Council may request the Commission to submit to it any appropriate proposals relating to the common foreign and security policy to ensure the implementation of a joint action.

5. Whenever there is any plan to adopt a national position or take national action pursuant to a joint action, information shall be provided in time to allow, if necessary, for prior consultations within the Council. The obligation to provide prior information shall not apply to measures which are merely a national transposition of Council decisions.

6. In cases of imperative need arising from changes in the situation and failing a Council decision, Member States may take the necessary measures as a matter of urgency having regard to the general objectives of the joint action. The Member State concerned shall inform the Council immediately of any such measures.

7. Should there be any major difficulties in implementing a joint action, a Member State shall refer them to the Council which shall discuss them and seek appropriate solutions. Such solutions shall not run counter to the objectives of the joint action or impair its effectiveness.

Article J.5

The Council shall adopt common positions. Common positions shall define the approach of the Union to a particular matter of a geographical or thematic nature. Member States shall ensure that their national policies conform to the common positions.

Article J.6

Member States shall inform and consult one another within the Council on any matter of foreign and security policy of general interest in order to ensure that the Union's influence is exerted as effectively as possible by means of concerted and convergent action.

Article J.7

1. The common foreign and security policy shall include all questions relating to the security of the Union, including the progressive framing of a common defence policy, in accordance with the second subparagraph, which might lead to a common defence, should the European Council so decide. It shall in that case recommend to the Member States the adoption of such a decision in accordance with their respective constitutional requirements.

The Western European Union (WEU) is an integral part of the development of the Union providing the Union with access to an operational capability notably in the context of paragraph 2. It supports the Union in framing the defence aspects of the common foreign and security policy as set out in this Article. The Union shall accordingly foster closer institutional relations with the WEU with a view to the possibility of the integration of the WEU into the Union, should the European Council so decide. It shall in that case recommend to the Member States the adoption of such a decision in accordance with their respective constitutional requirements.

The policy of the Union in accordance with this Article shall not prejudice the specific character of the security and defence policy of certain Member States and shall respect the obligations of certain Member States, which see their common defence realised in the North Atlantic Treaty Organisation (NATO), under the North Atlantic Treaty and be compatible with the common security and defence policy established within that framework.

The progressive framing of a common defence policy will be supported, as Member States consider appropriate, by cooperation between them in the field of armaments.

2. Questions referred to in this Article shall include humanitarian and rescue tasks, peacekeeping tasks and tasks of combat forces in crisis management, including peacemaking.

3. The Union will avail itself of the WEU to elaborate and implement decisions and actions of the Union which have defence implications.

The competence of the European Council to establish guidelines in accordance with Article J.3 shall also obtain in respect of the WEU for those matters for which the Union avails itself of the WEU.

When the Union avails itself of the WEU to elaborate and implement decisions of the Union on the tasks referred to in paragraph 2 all Member States of the Union shall be entitled to participate fully in the tasks in question. The Council, in agreement with the institutions of the WEU, shall adopt the necessary practical arrangements to allow all Member States contributing to the tasks in question to participate fully and on an equal footing in planning and decision-taking in the WEU.

Decisions having defence implications dealt with under this paragraph shall be taken without prejudice to the policies and obligations referred to in paragraph 1, third subparagraph.

4. The provisions of this Article shall not prevent the development of closer cooperation between two or more Member States on a bilateral level, in the framework of the WEU and the Atlantic Alliance, provided such cooperation does not run counter to or impede that provided for in this Title.

5. With a view to furthering the objectives of this Article, the provisions of this Article will be reviewed in accordance with Article N.

Article J.8

1. The Presidency shall represent the Union in matters coming within the common foreign and security policy.

2. The Presidency shall be responsible for the implementation of decisions taken under this Title; in that capacity it shall in principle express the position of the Union in international organisations and international conferences.

3. The Presidency shall be assisted by the Secretary-General of the Council who shall exercise the function of High Representative for the common foreign and security policy.

4. The Commission shall be fully associated in the tasks referred to in paragraphs 1 and 2. The Presidency shall be assisted in those tasks if need be by the next Member State to hold the Presidency.

5. The Council may, whenever it deems it necessary, appoint a special representative with a mandate in relation to particular policy issues.

Article J.9

1. Member States shall coordinate their action in international organisations and at international conferences. They shall uphold the common positions in such fora.

In international organisations and at international conferences where not all the Member States participate, those which do take part shall uphold the common positions.

2. Without prejudice to paragraph 1 and Article J.4(3), Member States represented in international organisations or international conferences where not all the Member States participate shall keep the latter informed of any matter of common interest.

Member States which are also members of the United Nations Security Council will concert and keep the other Member States fully informed. Member States which are permanent members of the Security Council will, in the execution of their functions, ensure the defence of the positions and the interests of the Union, without prejudice to their responsibilities under the provisions of the United Nations Charter.

Article J.10

The diplomatic and consular missions of the Member States and the Commission Delegations in third countries and international conferences, and their representations to international organisations, shall cooperate in ensuring that the common positions and joint actions adopted by the Council are complied with and implemented.

They shall step up cooperation by exchanging information, carrying out joint assessments and contributing to the implementation of the provisions referred to in Article 8c of the Treaty establishing the European Community.

Article J.11

The Presidency shall consult the European Parliament on the main aspects and the basic choices of the common foreign and security policy and shall ensure that the views of the European Parliament are duly taken into consideration. The European Parliament shall be kept regularly informed by the Presidency and the Commission of the development of the Union's foreign and security policy.

The European Parliament may ask questions of the Council or make recommendations to it. It shall hold an annual debate on progress in implementing the common foreign and security policy.

Article J.12

1. Any Member State or the Commission may refer to the Council any question relating to the common foreign and security policy and may submit proposals to the Council.

2. In cases requiring a rapid decision, the Presidency, of its own motion, or at the request of the Commission or a Member State, shall convene an extraordinary Council meeting within forty-eight hours or, in an emergency, within a shorter period.

Article J.13

1. Decisions under this Title shall be taken by the Council acting unanimously. Abstentions by members present in person or represented shall not prevent the adoption of such decisions.

When abstaining in a vote, any member of the Council may qualify its abstention by making a formal declaration under the present subparagraph. In that case, it shall not be obliged to apply the decision, but shall accept that the decision commits the Union. In a spirit of mutual solidarity, the Member State concerned shall refrain from any action likely to conflict with or impede Union action based on that decision and the other Member States shall respect its position. If the members of the Council qualifying their abstention in this way represent more than one third of the votes weighted in accordance with Article 148(2) of the Treaty establishing the European Community, the decision shall not be adopted.

2. By derogation from the provisions of paragraph 1, the Council shall act by qualified majority:
– when adopting joint actions, common positions or taking any other decision on the basis of a common strategy;
– when adopting any decision implementing a joint action or a common position.

If a member of the Council declares that, for important and stated reasons of national policy, it intends to oppose the adoption of a decision to be taken by qualified majority, a vote shall not be taken. The Council may, acting by a qualified majority, request that the matter be referred to the European Council for decision by unanimity.

The votes of the members of the Council shall be weighted in accordance with Article 148(2) of the Treaty establishing the European Community. For their adoption, decisions shall require at least 62 votes in favour, cast by at least 10 members.

This paragraph shall not apply to decisions having military or defence implications.

3. For procedural questions, the Council shall act by a majority of its members.

Article J.14

When it is necessary to conclude an agreement with one or more States or international organisations in implementation of this Title, the Council, acting unanimously, may authorise the Presidency, assisted by the Commission as appropriate, to open negotiations to that effect. Such agreements shall be concluded by the Council acting unanimously on a recommendation from the Presidency. No agreement shall be binding on a Member State whose representative in the Council states that it has to comply with the requirements of its own constitutional procedure; the other members of the Council may agree that the agreement shall apply provisionally to them.

The provisions of this Article shall also apply to matters falling under Title VI.

Article J.15

Without prejudice to Article 151 of the Treaty establishing the European Community, a Political Committee shall monitor the international situation in the areas covered by the common foreign and security policy and contribute to the definition of policies by delivering opinions to the Council at the request of the Council or on its own initiative. It shall also monitor the implementation of agreed policies, without prejudice to the responsibility of the Presidency and the Commission.

Article J.16

The Secretary-General of the Council, High Representative for the common foreign and security policy, shall assist the Council in matters coming within the scope of the common foreign and security policy, in particular through contributing to the formulation, preparation and implementation of policy decisions, and, when appropriate and acting on behalf of the Council at the request of the Presidency, through conducting political dialogue with third parties.

Article J.17

The Commission shall be fully associated with the work carried out in the common foreign and security policy field.

Article J.18

1. Articles 137, 138, 139 to 142, 146, 147, 150 to 153, 157 to 163, 191a and 217 of the Treaty establishing the European Community shall apply to the provisions relating to the areas referred to in this Title.

2. Administrative expenditure which the provisions relating to the areas referred to in this Title entail for the institutions shall be charged to the budget of the European Communities.

3. Operational expenditure to which the implementation of those provisions gives rise shall also be charged to the budget of the European Communities, except for such expenditure arising from operations having military or defence implications and cases where the Council acting unanimously decides otherwise.

In cases where expenditure is not charged to the budget of the European Communities it shall be charged to the Member States in accordance with the gross national product scale, unless the Council acting unanimously decides otherwise. As for expenditure arising from operations having military or defence implications, Member States whose representatives in the Council have made a formal declaration under Article J.13(1), second subparagraph, shall not be obliged to contribute to the financing thereof.

4. The budgetary procedure laid down in the Treaty establishing the European Community shall apply to the expenditure charged to the budget of the European Communities."

(. . .)

A. Protocol annexed to the Treaty on European Union

PROTOCOL ON ARTICLE J.7 OF THE TREATY ON EUROPEAN UNION

THE HIGH CONTRACTING PARTIES,

BEARING IN MIND the need to implement fully the provisions of Article J.7(1), second subparagraph, and (3) of the Treaty on European Union,

BEARING IN MIND that the policy of the Union in accordance with Article J.7 shall not prejudice the specific character of the security and defence policy of certain Member States and shall respect the obligations of certain Member States, which see their common defence realised in NATO, under the North Atlantic Treaty and be compatible with the common security and defence policy established within that framework,

HAVE AGREED UPON the following provision, which is annexed to the Treaty on European Union,

The European Union shall draw up, together with the Western European Union, arrangements for enhanced cooperation between them, within a year from the entry into force of the Treaty of Amsterdam.

Source: European Union, Treaty of Amsterdam (Office for Official Publications of the European Communities: Luxembourg, 1997).

PROTOCOL TO THE NORTH ATLANTIC TREATY ON THE ACCESSION OF POLAND

Identical Protocols of Accession were signed for the Czech Republic, Hungary and Poland

Brussels, 16 December 1997

The Parties to the North Atlantic Treaty, signed at Washington on April 4, 1949,

Being satisfied that the security of the North Atlantic area will be enhanced by the accession of the Republic of Poland to that Treaty,

Agree as follows:

Article I

Upon the entry into force of this Protocol, the Secretary General of the North Atlantic Treaty Organization shall, on behalf of all the Parties, communicate to the Government of the Republic of Poland an invitation to accede to the North Atlantic Treaty. In accordance with article 10 of the Treaty, the Republic of Poland shall become a Party on the date when it deposits its instrument of accession with the Government of the United States of America.

Article II

The present Protocol shall enter into force when each of the Parties to the North Atlantic Treaty has notified the Government of the United States of America of its acceptance thereof. The Government of the United States of America shall inform all the Parties to the North Atlantic Treaty of the date of receipt of each such notification and of the date of the entry into force of the present Protocol.

Article III

The present Protocol, of which the English and French texts are equally authentic, shall be deposited in the Archives of the Government of the United States of America. Duly certified copies thereof shall be transmitted by that Government to the Governments of all the Parties to the North Atlantic Treaty.

In witness whereof, the undersigned plenipotentiaries have signed the present Protocol.

Signed at Brussels on the 16th day of December 1997.

Source: NATO, Protocol to the North Atlantic Treaty on the Accession of the Republic of Poland, Brussels, 16 Dec. 1997, URL <http://www.nato.int/docu/basictxt/b971216c.htm>, version current on 3 Apr. 1998.

Part II. Military spending and armaments, 1997

Chapter 6. Military expenditure and arms production

Chapter 7. Military research and development

Chapter 8. Transfers of major conventional weapons

6. Military expenditure and arms production

ELISABETH SKÖNS, AGNÈS COURADES ALLEBECK,
EVAMARIA LOOSE-WEINTRAUB and REINHILDE
WEIDACHER*

I. Introduction

World military expenditure is still declining but the rate of decline is slowing down. Estimates of world totals indicate that the rate of decline was less than 1 per cent in real terms in 1997, compared to an average annual reduction of 2.5 per cent during the five-year period 1993–97. The best estimates currently available suggest that the total amount of money devoted to military activities amounted to around $740 billion in 1997.[1] This corresponds on average to 2.6 per cent of global gross national product (GNP) and $125 per capita.

The decline in world military spending began in 1988 after a long period of rapid growth. The SIPRI estimate for the 10-year period 1988–97 shows a decline of slightly more than one-third in real terms, corresponding to an average annual decrease of 4.5 per cent per year over the period. The sharpest cut in global military expenditure took place in 1992 when Russia cut its arms procurement expenditure by two-thirds as part of a budget reduction strategy. Its actual military expenditure in 1997 was less than one-tenth of that of the Soviet Union in 1988. US military expenditure also shows a considerable decline, by 31 per cent over the same period, but is still at about the same level as in 1980. Total military expenditure in Europe apart from Russia and other former Soviet states has declined by only 14 per cent in real terms over the 10 years.

The 10-year series of world and regional military expenditure presented in this Yearbook is the result of a major overhaul of the SIPRI military expenditure database, which includes revision of data to improve consistency over time and the calculation of aggregate totals for geographical regions, international organizations and economic groupings.

An essential element in calculating world and regional totals is the estimation of the military expenditure of the Russian Federation. The system of public finance which it inherited from the USSR after its disintegration in 1991 has made it difficult to establish the size of total Russian military expenditure. Above all, it is difficult to trace actual as distinct from budgeted expenditure, since the fiscal problems in Russia have resulted in much lower actual expenditure than provided for in the defence budget as adopted by the Russian Par-

---

[1] This estimate in current dollars is derived from the figure of $704 billion at constant (1995) prices (table 6.1 and appendix 6A) by applying the US inflation between 1995 and 1997 (5.4% over 2 years).

* Section V was written by R. Weidacher and section VI by E. Loose-Weintraub.

SIPRI Yearbook 1998: Armaments, Disarmament and International Security

liament. A special study was therefore commissioned by SIPRI in order to provide the best available estimates of the military expenditure of the Russian Federation and of its predecessor, the USSR, for the period 1987–97. This study makes up appendix 6D to this chapter. The estimates presented there are those used as the new SIPRI series of military expenditure for the USSR and Russia. They show that Russia's total actual military expenditure amounted to 101.5 trillion roubles in 1997, which corresponded to 3.8 per cent of gross domestic product (GDP) and $24.1 billion in constant 1995 dollars.

The data on military expenditure for China also constitute a problem. China does provide a figure for its total defence budget. It is known to be an underestimate, but there is disagreement as to the size of the discrepancy and in particular on the contribution to military revenue made by the commercial activities of the armed forces (the People's Liberation Army) and the extent to which these revenues are used for military activities. Thus, estimates of real Chinese military expenditure range from 50 per cent to 350 per cent higher than the official budget. The SIPRI series is the official Chinese defence budget in yuan converted to US dollars at the official exchange rate.

Arms production is characterized by continued structural changes in most parts of the world. With the global demand for weapons having been reduced by roughly one-quarter since 1990 and competition increasingly intense, the marketing and sales strategies of arms-producing companies are becoming increasingly offensive. The pressure to export is strong and increasing and the terms of export contracts therefore generous. While aggregate data on total national arms production are not readily available, SIPRI collects data and analyses trends among the major arms-producing companies in the Organisation for Economic Co-operation and Development (OECD) countries and in the developing countries (except China). The combined arms sales of the 'top 100' arms-producing companies in these countries amounted to $156 billion in current dollars in 1996, virtually unchanged from 1995. The arms sales of the 'top 100' have been on a declining trend since at least 1989, which is the first year for which SIPRI has data, but appear to be bottoming out, as indicated by the stagnation in 1996, preceded by a slight increase in 1995.

In 1997 the process of restructuring and concentration continued at a rapid pace in the US arms industry; in Europe there was a continued trend of cross-border combinations through joint ventures and armaments cooperation, while smaller producer countries devised strategies to save as much as possible of their military production capability.

Developments in 1997 were in many ways illustrative of the mutual interaction of economic factors and military activities. The fact that the East Asia region had the most rapid growth in military expenditure during the past decade was to a great extent the result of its rapid economic growth. The financial crisis in 1997 forced several countries in the region to cut their military expenditure and cancel or postpone major weapon contracts. This in turn may have an impact on several of the supplier companies in the world. In many of the poor countries in Africa and South Asia the military sector constitutes a substantial economic burden and its consumption of scarce resources is a severe constraint on economic development. In arms-producing countries the cuts in military expenditures have caused a major reorganization of military production with both a national and an international dimension and with an impact also on the commercial parts of the same industries.

This chapter begins with a discussion in section II of the utility and availability of military expenditure data. Section III provides an overview of global and regional trends in military expenditures during the past 10 years and section IV an analysis of countries' military expenditure by income group. Section V presents data and trends among the top 100 companies. Section VI summarizes developments during 1997 in the three countries in Central and Eastern Europe which have been invited to become members of NATO: the Czech Republic, Hungary and Poland. There are five appendices, four of which contain the SIPRI data on which the chapter is based: on world military expenditure by region and by country (appendix 6A); the NATO statistics on expenditure on military personnel and equipment (appendix 6B); the sources and methods for SIPRI military expenditure data (appendix 6C); and financial and employment data for the top 100 companies (appendix 6E). Appendix 6D examines the military expenditure of the USSR and Russia.

II. The military expenditure data

The use of military expenditure data for a wide range of purposes, in research and for policy making, means that the background to the data is vitally important. Two of the more relevant issues are the conceptual issue of the nature of military expenditure data and the empirical issue of their availability. These are treated in this section, which comes to two basic conclusions: (*a*) that there are serious limitations to the usefulness of military expenditure data for many of the purposes for which they are currently being used; and (*b*) that there is a dearth of information about public expenditure for military purposes. Although this is probably primarily due to governments' wish to withhold information from internal public debate, it is also partly due to the failure of researchers in the West to identify relevant national statistical sources, especially for developing countries.

Utility of data

Military expenditure data are often used uncritically, as if they were entirely reliable and appropriate indicators of a multitude of phenomena in the real world. They are neither. Used properly, they can serve as measures or rough indicators of real-world developments, but this requires knowledge of their limitations and therefore in many cases access to additional information and analysis.

Military expenditure data are used both as a dependent and as an independent variable—in the former case as an indicator of other phenomena, such as military strength, militarization, security, conflict potential, governance and government priorities; in the latter case as a determinant of such disparate consequences as arms races, armed conflict and different types of economic performance. Some of these uses involve serious problems of interpretation.

Military expenditure data are an input measure. This fact is crucial to assessments of their utility. They measure resources used for military purposes and are therefore most appropriately used as an indicator of the economic burden imposed by military activities. There is no strong relation between the input of resources into the military establishment and the output in terms of the military strength or military capability or, even less, military security bought by these resources. Military strength depends not only on the input of resources but also on cost-effectiveness. Cost-effectiveness depends in turn on a large number of factors, such as: (*a*) differences in the composition of the defence budget, for instance, in the functional categories personnel, arms procurement, military research and development (R&D), and operations and maintenance (O&M); (*b*) the system of recruitment (professional or conscript armed forces); (*c*) the technological level and performance of weapon systems; and (*d*) the method of arms procurement (imports or domestic production). The link between military expenditure and concepts such as military security or militarization is even more problematic.

Neither is there necessarily any correlation between the occurrence of conflict and military expenditure.[2] A high level of military expenditure, a rising trend or a high 'military burden' can be a sign of emerging conflict but not necessarily so. They may be warning signs that something is likely to happen, but more than statistics is needed for correct judgement to be possible. Thus, the idea that military expenditure statistics can be used as one indicator of early warning of conflict has potential, but they must be used with caution.

The construction of indexes in which military expenditure is one of several components is no solution to the problems described above: it can in fact rather serve to conceal the weaknesses of the indicators included. Military expenditure data yield more focused results, both as an indicator and as a determinant, if disaggregated into spending for domestic arms production, arms imports, military R&D, O&M, the costs of military personnel or conscripts, pensions, administration and so on. However, the lack of uniform definitions of disaggregated items may cause distortions, especially in cross-country comparisons.

As an independent variable, the most appropriate use of military expenditure data is in studies of the economic impact of military expenditure, but then other types of problem are involved, such as reliability and validity of data. Econometric analysis requires familiarity with the data used in order to make proper adjustments to methods and ensure correct interpretation of results.[3]

---

[2] Sköns, E. and Vinai Ström, G., 'Weapon supplies to trouble spots', Background paper prepared for the United Nations Development Programme *Human Development Report 1994*. Unpublished.

[3] A comprehensive account of problems of reliability, validity and comparability is provided in Brzoska, M., 'World military expenditures', eds K. Hartley and T. Sandler, *Handbook of Defense Economics*, vol. 1 (Elsevier: Amsterdam, 1995). The problems involved for econometric analysis are described in Smith, R., 'The demand for military expenditure' in the same volume.

Available data

In spite of the progress made since SIPRI first published its statistics in 1969 in making reliable, consistent and comparable data on military expenditure available from open sources, the situation is still far from satisfactory.

There is a lack of standardized data on a worldwide basis and of data broken down into functional categories or by service. In order to improve information on military expenditure, two major efforts at the intergovernmental level have been launched—by the United Nations and the Organization for Security and Co-operation in Europe (OSCE)—by which member countries are asked to provide such information. Both of these make use of a standardized reporting instrument which was developed by the UN in the late 1970s.

The United Nations: military expenditures in standardized form

All member states of the UN are requested to report to the Secretary-General, by 30 April each year, their military expenditure for the latest fiscal year for which data are available, using the instrument for standardized international reporting of military expenditures adopted by the UN General Assembly on 12 December 1980.[4] The replies are reproduced in annual reports to the UN General Assembly and in subsequent addenda to these reports.[5]

The response rate to the UN reporting instrument has been low. Of the current 185 UN member states, an average of approximately 32 submitted replies during the four years 1994–97 (37, 35, 28 and 27, respectively). This is not much more than during its first three years of existence, 1981–83, when the number of replies ranged from 16 to 24. In 1996 member states were therefore asked by the UN to 'make recommendations on necessary changes to the content and structure' of the UN reporting system 'in order to strengthen and broaden participation' and to report to its 52nd session.[6] In particular, it was believed that the system must be adjusted to take into account different national reporting practices. The only response to this request by the end of 1997 was from the Netherlands on behalf of the European Union (EU) and the associated Central and East European countries, basically agreeing with the analysis of the UN.[7]

OSCE information exchange on military budgets

Information exchange on military expenditure within the OSCE started in 1991 and is part of the broader system of OSCE confidence- and security-

[4] UN General Assembly Resolution 35/142, 12 Dec. 1980. The current request is based on General Assembly Resolution 40/91 B, 12 Dec. 1985, to which the reporting instrument is included as an annex. It is then pursued each year in a *note verbale* by the Secretary-General to all member states.

[5] For the most recent report, see United Nations, Reduction of military budgets: military expenditures in standardized form reported by states. Report by the Secretary-General, UN document A/52/310, 25 Aug. 1997. These reports are also available at the UN Centre for Disarmament Affairs.

[6] This request was made on the basis of General Assembly Resolution 51/38 of 10 Dec. 1996, 'Objective information on military matters, including transparency of military expenditures'.

[7] United Nations, Reduction of military budgets: objective information on military matters, including transparency of military expenditures, UN document A/52/302, 27 Aug. 1997.

building measures (CSBMs). The current obligation to report military expenditure is based on the Vienna Document 1994.[8] The Conflict Prevention Centre in Vienna is the depository for the reports. Their circulation is restricted and they can be released only with the permission of the originating government.

Each member state is obliged to provide every other member government with reports on: (*a*) its military expenditure for the most recent fiscal year on the basis of the categories of the UN reporting instrument (para. 15.3); (*b*) actual expenditure for earlier years when these differ from previously reported budgets; and (*c*) where available and at various levels of detail, data on future budgets (para. 15.4). The implementation of the OSCE exchange of information is reviewed in annual implementation assessment meetings and surveys are prepared of which states have reported for which years.

Information exchange on military expenditure within the OSCE shows a better response rate than reporting to the UN. This is probably explained by two factors: that it is a binding commitment within a regional CSBM system; and that access to information submitted is restricted to the states involved. Even so, only 39 out of the 50 OSCE participating states which had military forces during the three years 1994–96 had provided information on their military expenditure in any of those years by the end of 1996, and only 32 had provided information on military budgets adopted or budget plans (under para. 15.4).[9] In particular, response rates among the countries of Central Asia are low. In addition to a possible unwillingness to provide data, this may have to do with practical difficulties in filling in the reporting instrument. For this reason, various forms of technical assistance have been proposed and carried out to help these countries provide the requested information.

National statistics

Most, although not all, governments in industrialized countries provide aggregate data on their military expenditures. For other countries it can be more difficult to find such data. A few regard military expenditure as confidential and refuse to provide any information. It is often difficult to identify the official sources and get access to them, even with the assistance of the relevant authorities; in the case of some countries the language of publication may be a difficulty. However, surprising amounts of official data are also available for developing countries. This was shown in a data project in the early 1980s, which had two primary purposes: (*a*) to see how far it was possible to produce comparable military expenditure figures for developing countries using their budgets or final expenditure accounts; and (*b*) to provide security expenditure

---

[8] Conference on Security and Co-operation in Europe, Vienna Document 1994 of the Negotiations on Confidence- and Security-Building Measures, CSCE document 1113/94, 28 Nov. 1994, reproduced in *SIPRI Yearbook 1995: Armaments, Disarmament and International Security* (Oxford University Press: Oxford, 1995), pp. 799–820. Para. 15 of the document includes the rules for reporting of military expenditures.

[9] Survey of CSBM information exchanged in preparation for the Annual Implementation Assessment Meeting, 27 Feb. 1997.

data disaggregated by service branch and resource costs.[10] For this purpose a search was made for the relevant national public sources of around 100 developing countries of similar size over the period 1950–80 and estimates were made according to the structure of the UN reporting instrument. The result showed that many developing countries do publish information on military and other security expenditure: data were obtained for 48 countries, covered most of the period and could in several cases be disaggregated.

SIPRI sends out its own questionnaire to most countries, mainly through their diplomatic representation in Stockholm, but also directly to relevant ministries, central banks and national statistical offices. In 1997 the result was 43 replies of substance, of which 21 were from developing countries, 13 from countries in transition and 9 from industrialized countries. The SIPRI questionnaire is much less detailed than the UN reporting instrument, and countries do not always reply by completing the form: some send a copy of their submission to the UN or the OSCE or copies of the relevant official publication instead.

Of the 158 countries included in the SIPRI military expenditure tables, primary sources are available for most industrialized countries and for about half of the developing countries. Standardized data as reported by the International Monetary Fund (IMF) are available for 110 countries, although it is not clear how well the IMF definition is applied.[11] Still, only about one-fifth of these countries provide data tailored to the UN reporting instrument. It is therefore likely that the low response rates to questionnaires may be a question less of confidentiality than of competence, resources and incentives to reply.

III. Global and regional trends in military expenditure

World military expenditure has fallen by about one-third in real terms over the 10-year period 1988–97 to roughly $704 billion in 1997 at constant 1995 prices and exchange rates (see table 6.1), corresponding to $740 billion in current prices. During recent years there has been a deceleration in the rate of decline. According to the best estimates available at the end of 1997, the fall was 1.1 per cent in 1996 and 0.6 per cent in 1997.

The fall has been most dramatic in Russia, where military expenditure has fallen to less than 10 per cent of the 1988 level in the Soviet Union (see appendix 6D). The fall in the aggregate military expenditure of the member states of the Commonwealth of Independent States (CIS) is similar, the military expenditure of the CIS countries other than Russia being small in comparison to Russia's.

Other countries and regions which have contributed significantly to the drop in world military expenditure include Africa, Central America and the USA,

---

[10] Ball, N., *Third World Security Expenditure: A Statistical Compendium*, FOA Report C 10250-M5 (Swedish National Defence Research Establishment: Stockholm, May 1984), p. 34.

[11] Brzoska (note 3), p. 60.

Table 6.1. Regional military expenditure estimates, 1988–97

Figures are in US $b. in constant 1995 prices and exchange rates. Figures in italics are percentages. Figures do not always add up to totals because of the conventions of rounding.

Region[a]	1988	1989	1990	1991	1992	1993	1994	1995	1996	1997	% change 1988–97
Africa	12.6	13.3	12.3	11.2	10.6	10.7	9.7	9.2	9.4	[8.8]	–30
North	2.2	2.8	2.4	2.5	2.7	3.0	3.3	3.0	3.2	3.2	45
Sub-Saharan	10.4	10.4	9.9	8.7	7.9	7.7	6.4	6.1	6.2	[5.6]	–46
Americas	410	405	386	338	358	342	325	309	295	[290]	–29
North	390	385	369	325	342	325	307	289	273	268	–31
Central	0.8	0.8	0.9	0.6	0.6	0.6	0.6	0.6	0.5	0.5	–39
South	19.2	18.9	16.0	12.1	15.3	16.5	16.6	[19.6]	[21.2]	[21.9]	*14*
Asia	95.0	99.5	102	105	108	110	112	115	119	120	*26*
Central	..	..	..	..	..	..	..	..	..	..	..
East	83.8	88.3	90.6	93.4	96.6	98.1	99.7	102	106	106	*27*
South	11.2	11.2	11.4	11.2	11.2	12.2	12.1	12.6	13.0	13.6	*22*
Europe	500	483	447	..	279	265	259	235	235	[234]	–53
Middle East	39.6	36.9	[47.0]	[64.2]	[45.0]	42.1	41.2	38.5	42.1	43.3	*9*
Oceania	8.9	8.8	8.8	8.8	9.1	8.9	9.2	8.9	8.7	8.8	*1*
World total	**1 066**	**1 047**	**1 003**	..	**810**	**779**	**756**	**716**	**708**	**[704]**	**–34**
Change per year (%)	..	–1.8	–4.2	..	..	–3.8	–3.0	–5.2	–1.1	–0.6	–4.5

[a] The countries included in the geographical regions are listed in appendix 8A in this volume. Africa excludes Libya, Asia excludes Central Asia, Afghanistan, Cambodia and Laos, and the Middle East excludes Iraq because of lack of data; and Europe excludes Yugoslavia because of the lack of consistent data over the entire period. World totals exclude all of these.

Source: Appendix 6A, table 6.A1.

with cuts of around one-third in real terms, while there have been smaller reductions in Europe outside the CIS (by 14 per cent). Behind the declining trend in aggregate African military expenditure are several very different developments, including the process of demilitarization in Southern and other parts of Africa and the violent civil wars in Central Africa, where scarcity of resources is combined with extreme poverty among the vast majority of the population. South American military expenditures fell until the early 1990s but have since been rising on aggregate, although the trend continues downwards in several countries.

The exceptions to the downward trend were North Africa, the Middle East, and South and East Asia. These regions have experienced a long-term increase in military expenditure. The increase of 45 per cent in North Africa is due almost entirely to the rise in Algeria. Military expenditure in the Middle East has fluctuated considerably, with a peak in 1991 as a result of the Persian Gulf War, within the limits of a total increase of 9 per cent over the 10 years 1988–97. In Asia the aggregate increase over the same period was more than one-quarter, with both South and East Asia on roughly the same trend. However, in several East Asian countries the military budgets adopted for 1997 were being cut during the second half of the year as a result of the financial crisis in the region and expenditure plans are being revised downwards.

Asia

The financial crisis which ravaged several countries in East Asia during the second half of 1997 will have an impact on the military sectors there because of its effect on their military budgets. It is also likely to have an impact on the arms industries in the countries which supply their weapons, because East Asia constitutes a major share of the world arms import market,[12] has been the region with the most rapid growth of arms imports, and was predicted to remain so in the foreseeable future.

The countries most seriously affected by the financial crisis were Indonesia, South Korea, Malaysia, Thailand and to some extent the Philippines, and there may be side-effects in neighbouring countries, in particular Japan, Singapore and Taiwan. Several of these countries constitute the core of the Association of South-East Asian Nations (ASEAN), the regional organization for economic and political cooperation.

Military expenditure in the ASEAN countries increased by an aggregate of 52 per cent in real terms over the nine-year period 1988–96.[13] The growth in South Korean military expenditure has been roughly the same, while Taiwan's went up by 32 per cent over the six-year period 1988–93 and has declined since. The growth in military expenditures in this region has been absorbed by rapid economic growth. Except in Malaysia, it has been slower than the growth of the national economies, as is illustrated by the declining share of military expenditure in their GDPs (see appendix 6A, table 6A.4).

Assuming a 20–30 per cent procurement share in the total military budgets of these countries, the size of the combined arms markets of the ASEAN countries, South Korea and Taiwan can be estimated at $6–9 billion in 1996. Extending the calculation to all of East Asia, the estimate rises to $21–32 billion, but this would include China and Japan, which meet a significant part of their weapon requirements from domestic production. In spite of its ambitions to build up a domestic arms industry, the region is dependent on arms imports, especially of high-technology weapons. East Asia has therefore been an attractive market for sellers of advanced and expensive weapon systems. Contributing to its attractiveness has been not only its size but also the perceived political and economic stability of this market. The financial crisis, starting in the early summer of 1997, altered this perception.

The economic aid offered by the IMF was associated with its standard conditions: improvements in government budget balances (by reducing expenditure or increasing taxes) and in the balance of payments. Military expenditures in the region were thus affected in two ways: (*a*) by depreciation of the

---

[12] See appendix 8A, table 8A.1 in this volume.
[13] This trend is calculated for the countries which were ASEAN members during the entire period 1988–96, i.e., Brunei, Indonesia, Malaysia, the Philippines, Singapore and Thailand. On the current membership of ASEAN see the glossary in this volume.

currencies, which made arms imports roughly twice as expensive as before; and (*b*) by reductions in central government expenditure. At the same time the burden on the population of these countries increased, both because of the rising cost of living and because of cuts in government social expenditures.

Malaysia, which was the worst affected country but did not call in the IMF during 1997, announced a severe austerity plan in December 1997 including a 5 per cent cut in military expenditure.[14] Thailand, the first country to apply for IMF economic aid, had already cut its defence budget for fiscal year (FY) 1997/98 twice before the IMF agreement. A third cut brought the total reduction to 30 per cent of the original budget.[15] In early 1998 the new government in South Korea presented a revised budget for 1998 in which military expenditure was cut by 4.1 per cent from the original budget. Even so it remained 1.5 per cent higher than the 1997 defence budget and was much less reduced than social expenditures, which were cut by 13 per cent compared to the original budget.[16] Because of the fall in the purchasing power in dollars of the defence budget—by an estimated 15 per cent—almost all new arms procurement projects have been postponed. Arms imports reportedly account for 80 per cent of government foreign currency expenditure and have thus contributed significantly to the outflow of foreign currency and therefore to the financial crisis itself.[17]

Arms import plans altered significantly during 1997 and are likely to be further changed during 1998.[18] In January 1998, US Secretary of State for Defense William Cohen made a tour in the region during which he promised the US Government's support for the renegotiation of weapon contracts with US companies.[19]

Africa

Since the economic upturn in 1994–95, the national economies of Africa have performed better than they have for two decades, and the number of countries of the region which have experienced a 3 per cent growth rate has increased from 17 in 1992 to a forecast 35 in 1997.[20] Nevertheless, the vast majority of the African population, especially in Sub-Saharan Africa, still suffers severe deprivation in terms of income, nutrition, health and education. It is clear that African economies are very vulnerable to any reversal in economic growth and other external factors, such as development aid and debt policy,[21] and are

[14] 'Thailand, Malaysia impose defence purchase freeze', *Defense News*, 27 Oct.–2 Nov. 1997, p. 6.
[15] Interview with the Thai Navy Commander-in-Chief, *Defense News*, 12–18 Jan. 1998, p. 30.
[16] 'South Korea: the government announces supplementary budget bill', *Korea Times* (Internet version), 6 Feb. 1998, in Foreign Broadcast Information Service, *Daily Report–East Asia (FBIS-EAS)*, FBIS-EAS-98-037, 9 Feb. 1998.
[17] 'The national defense budget is not insufficient', *Hangyore*, 3 Feb. 1998, p. 3, in FBIS-EAS-98-034, 4 Feb. 1998.
[18] Changes in import orders of military equipment are listed in chapter 8 in this volume.
[19] Richter, P., 'Crisis thwarts Pentagon efforts to beef up Asia military', *Los Angeles Times*, 15 Jan. 1998.
[20] International Monetary Fund, *World Economic Outlook* (IMF: Washington, DC, May, Oct. 1997).
[21] Hawkins, T., 'Can African economies sustain their recovery?', *Financial Times*, 14 May 1997, p. 6.

Table 6.2. Military expenditure estimates for Africa, 1988–97

Figures are in US $b. in constant 1995 prices and exchange rates. Figures in italics are percentages.

	1988	1989	1990	1991	1992	1993	1994	1995	1996	1997	% change 1988–97
Africa[a]	12.6	13.3	12.3	11.2	10.6	10.7	9.7	9.2	9.4	[8.8]	*– 30*
North[b]	2.2	2.8	2.4	2.5	2.7	3.0	3.3	3.0	3.2	3.2	*45*
Sub-Saharan	10.4	10.4	9.9	8.7	7.9	7.7	6.4	6.1	6.2	[5.6]	*– 46*
SADC[c]	6.9	6.9	6.5	5.5	5.0	4.7	4.4	4.1	4.0	3.5	*– 49*

[a] Excludes Libya because of lack of data. Egypt is included in the Middle East region.

[b] Includes Algeria, Morocco and Tunisia. Excludes Libya because of lack of data.

[c] The members of the Southern African Development Community are Angola, Botswana, Lesotho, Malawi, Mauritius, Mozambique, Namibia, South Africa, Swaziland, Tanzania, Zambia and Zimbabwe.

Source: Appendix 6A, table 6A.3.

increasingly aid-dependent (aid in 1996 accounted for 11 per cent of their GDP).[22] They carry an external debt burden of 63 per cent of GDP and a 22 per cent ratio of debt-service payments to export incomes.[23]

Civil war and political turmoil, as in 1997 in the Democratic Republic of Congo (formerly Zaire) and Congo (Brazzaville), are not always reflected in military expenditure data. This is partly because most civil wars and mutinies are not fought with major conventional weapons but with small arms, which are not always significant in terms of money. Furthermore, during civil wars budgets and economic data generally become highly unreliable (if they are available at all). Even in peacetime, access to figures on the actual military outlays of most African countries is difficult. Many countries have a poor record of public accounting; others, such as Libya, do not disclose their defence budgets at all. When budgetary data on military expenditure are available they are often only preliminary figures. Figures on actual expenditure are seldom published. By definition, budget figures do not include extra-budgetary accounts, and in some cases expenditure would be much higher if those were transparent as well. This is, for example, the case with Nigeria, where allegedly the military are diverting oil revenues into special off-budget accounts.[24]

Overall military expenditure by African countries, excluding Egypt and Libya, fell by 30 per cent in real terms between 1988 and 1997 (see table 6.2). North Africa deviated from that pattern with an increase of 45 per cent over the period. This rise was mostly attributable to Algeria, which tripled its military spending and increased the share of military expenditure in GDP from 1.9 to 3.4 per cent over the 10-year period. The military share in government

---

[22] Compared to 0.7% for Asia and 0.4% for Latin America. Mbaye, S., 'Fausse embellie économique en Afrique subsaharienne', *Le Monde Diplomatique*, June 1997, p. 4.

[23] *World Economic Outlook*, Oct. 1997 (note 20), pp. 207, 212.

[24] 'Nigeria debt arrears up $10 bn over past 3 years', *Financial Times*, 19 June 1997, p. 12.

expenditure increased from 9 to 15 per cent over the period 1991–97.[25] Although the military formally withdrew from politics in 1989, the growing violence in the internal conflict with the Front Islamique du Salut (FIS) has gradually expanded the influence of the military in Algeria.

South Africa remains by far the largest spender in Africa. In 1997 it accounted for 28 per cent of total African military spending and 43 per cent of that of the Sub-Saharan region. Since it embarked on disarmament in 1989 its military expenditure has declined by 53 per cent in real terms. Reallocation of government expenditure has meant a reduction in military expenditure from 4.3 to 2.1 per cent of GDP between 1988 and 1996. Major cuts have been made in the number of civilian and military personnel by the ending of conscription and the closure of military bases and in procurement plans.[26] In January 1998 a restructuring plan was approved, which included further cuts in defence spending and a cut of civilian and military personnel from 95 000 to around 70 000.[27]

Several African countries have followed the trend of demilitarization, although to a lesser extent, especially most of South Africa's neighbours and partners in the Southern African Development Community (SADC).[28] Botswana, Malawi, Mozambique, Namibia, Zambia and Zimbabwe have all experienced a decline in their military spending since the beginning of the 1990s, both in real terms and as a share of their GDP. In Angola, military expenditure continues to place a major burden on the economy. In 1997, 11 per cent of total government expenditure was allocated to the military, less than 4 per cent to education and 2 per cent to health.[29] Until demobilization under the terms of the 1994 Lusaka peace accord is complete the defence spending of Angola is not likely to diminish.

Future levels of military expenditure in the African francophone countries may be influenced by France's reconsideration in 1997 of its engagement in Africa. As a result of its efforts to reduce its defence budget and to reform its armed forces, and reinforced by its policy failure in Central Africa, France decided to reduce significantly its military presence in the region. Implementation began in 1997 of a plan to reduce its current presence of 8000 soldiers in Cameroon, the Central African Republic, Chad, Côte d'Ivoire, Djibouti, Gabon and Senegal to 2000 permanently stationed professional forces.

IV. Military expenditure by country income group

Trends in military expenditure vary considerably with countries' level of income as measured by GNP per capita. The groupings by income level used here are very broad and encompass countries of very different types as regards

[25] Economist Intelligence Unit, *Country Profile 1990–91 Algeria*, p. 34; and 'Budget général de l'État pour 1997', *Journal Officiel de la République Algérienne*, no. 85 (31 Dec. 1996), p. 56.
[26] Batchelor, P. and Willett, S., SIPRI, *Disarmament and Defence Industrial Adjustment in South Africa* (Oxford University Press: Oxford, 1998).
[27] 'South Africa approves restructure blueprint', *Jane's Defence Weekly*, 28 Jan. 1998, p. 14.
[28] For the membership of the SADC, see note (c) to table 6.2.
[29] Economist Intelligence Unit, *Country Profile Angola*, 3rd quarter 1997, p. 16.

Table 6.3. Military expenditure estimates by country income group, 1988–97

Figures are in US $b. in constant 1995 prices and exchange rates. Figures in italics are percentages. Figures do not always add up to totals because of the conventions of rounding.

Income group	1988	1989	1990	1991	1992	1993	1994	1995	1996	1997	% change 1988–97
Low	26	26	29	28	29	30	29	29	30	31	*19*
Middle	292	272	237	..	85	79	81	64	64	[64]	*– 78*
(excl. USSR/CIS)	34	33	34	35	36	36	38	37	38	38	*12*
Upper middle	57	58	55	64	54	57	56	57	62	[62]	*9*
High	691	690	682	639	642	613	591	566	553	548	*– 21*
World total	**1 066**	**1 047**	**1 003**	..	**810**	**779**	**756**	**716**	**708**	**[704]**	***– 34***

a Low-income economies are defined as those with a GNP per capita in 1995 ≤ $765; middle-income: $766–$3035; upper-middle-income: $3036–$9385; and high-income ≥ $9386, as defined in *World Development Report 1997* (World Bank and Oxford University Press: Washington, DC and New York, June 1997).

Source: Appendix 6A, table 6.A1.

political system, regional security context and to some extent economic system. The only characteristic they share is the interval of GNP per capita into which they fit. Nevertheless, there is some interest in analysing countries by income group.

The low-income countries increased their military expenditures over the period 1988–97 (table 6.3). This group is dominated by the 30 poorest countries in Africa and the five countries of South Asia. It also includes China and Mongolia in North-East Asia, Viet Nam in South-East Asia, and Honduras and Nicaragua in Central America. The rise in the military expenditure of this group is due to increases in South Asia, China and some African countries, while other countries in the group, including Mongolia, Viet Nam and the two Central American countries, have made cuts.

The middle-income group of countries had the sharpest reductions in military expenditure. However, this is due only to the reduction in Russian military expenditure compared with that of the Soviet Union. If the USSR/Russia and the other CIS countries in this group are excluded, the group shows a combined increase of 12 per cent over the period. Several of the middle-income countries with major increases in military expenditure are in the Mediterranean region—Algeria, Lebanon, Syria and Turkey. Others which contribute to the increasing military expenditure of middle-income economies are Indonesia and Thailand.

The upper-middle income group consists of 17 countries, those with the highest military expenditure being Argentina, Brazil, Chile, Croatia, the Czech Republic, Greece, Hungary, Malaysia, Mexico, Oman, Saudi Arabia, Slovenia, South Africa and Taiwan. As a group they maintained a low growth rate in their military expenditures over the period 1988–97. However, this conceals wide country variations. The countries with significant military expenditure increases include Brazil, Malaysia, Saudi Arabia, Taiwan and to some extent Greece. Except for Brazil and Saudi Arabia they expanded their military budgets at about the same rate as their economic growth, thus maintaining a fairly constant share of military expenditure in GDP. Other countries in this group have cut their military spending considerably since 1988, in particular Argentina, Hungary and South Africa. A few have kept their defence budgets constant, such as Mexico, Oman and Uruguay.

The 28 high-income countries reduced their military expenditure as a group but include several whose spending has increased. The reduction is accounted for mainly by the USA. Except for Portugal, NATO member countries in this group also reduced their military expenditures. Of non-NATO countries in this group, only three reduced their military budgets between 1988 and 1997—New Zealand, Switzerland and the United Arab Emirates. These cuts outweighed the increases during the period made by several high-income countries in Europe—Austria, Finland, Ireland and Sweden—and in other regions—Australia, Israel, Japan, South Korea, Kuwait and Singapore.

V. Arms production in OECD and developing countries

The dramatic changes in the conditions for arms production beginning in the late 1980s continued to have a strong impact on arms production and the arms industry during 1997. However, the rapidly declining trend in the demand for military equipment, which is the most important factor, appears to be slowing down, and in several major arms-producing countries decline has turned into growth.[30] Even so, the level of demand today is significantly lower than it was in 1987, the peak year of military expenditures. A rough estimate based on trends in the main centres of demand suggests that global demand for weapons dropped by between one-third and one-half between 1987 and 1997.[31] The process of adjusting production to a situation which is fundamentally different from that of the late 1980s is likely to continue for several more years until the industry has moulded itself into a more stable structure.

In the industrialized market economies, the adjustment process is now moving from the early stages of rapid down-sizing, rationalization and concentration into a stage in which those individual companies which have maintained a strong defence orientation are positioning themselves in the smaller market in order to survive as producers of military equipment. This stage is marked by more vigorous pursuit of two types of company strategy: concentration and exports.

---

[30] The return to growth is seen in the equipment expenditures of European members of NATO (appendix 6B) and in SIPRI data on international arms transfers (appendix 8A). Preliminary estimates of Russia's military expenditure also show a return to growth in 1997 (appendix 6D).

[31] NATO expenditures on military equipment fell by one-third and Russia's arms procurement budget has been reduced by more than two-thirds over the period 1988–97 (see appendices 6B and 6D in this volume); and arms imports by developing countries fell by 33% between 1987 and 1997 (SIPRI arms transfers database). These 3 sources account for at least two-thirds of the global demand for military equipment.

While there was room for further national concentration in the United States in 1997, West European companies continued to be confined to the creation of international joint ventures and other forms of armaments cooperation and continued to press for further Europe-wide military industrial integration. There are also indications that there will be a growing number of important exceptions to the trend towards increased diversification into civilian production, and thus reduced dependence on military sales, previously identified for the period 1990–95.[32]

The pressure for increased military exports and for government assistance in the competition for increased shares of the global arms market continued during 1997. The financial crisis in East Asia is likely to have an impact on the arms industries in supplier countries, since the region holds a major share of world arms imports. In several countries, contracts negotiated in East Asia have been an important source of revenue in a period of declining domestic arms procurement.

The SIPRI top 100

Since no worldwide data on national arms production are available, SIPRI collects information on the major arms-producing companies. A list is compiled of the top 100 companies in the countries in the OECD and the developing world except China with the purpose of providing an indication of worldwide trends in the arms industry. This is presented in appendix 6E.

The total volume of arms sales of the top 100 companies were virtually unchanged in 1996, at around $156 current billion,[33] after a slight increase in 1995.[34] Continued rapid concentration in the US arms industry contributed to an increase in the arms sales of the largest companies through mergers and acquisitions while the overall decline in the defence market resulted in reduced arms sales among the smaller companies.

The decline in the share of combined arms sales of the US companies among the top 100 slowed down in 1996: their share was about the same as in 1995 (table 6.4). The number of US companies in the list remained stable but is likely to fall in 1997 as a result of the completion of a large number of major mergers and acquisitions initiated during 1996 and 1997 which have not yet had their full impact. The share of the West European companies in the top 100's combined sales showed a slight increase because of significant growth in the sales of the British companies and a return to growth in the aggregate sales of the German companies, but the French and Swiss companies' shares in sales fell.

---

[32] Sköns, E. and Cooper, J., 'Arms production', *SIPRI Yearbook 1997: Armaments, Disarmament and International Security* (Oxford University Press: Oxford, 1997), pp. 247–49.

[33] The value of total arms sales for this group of companies was $154.3 billion in 1995 at current prices and exchange rates. The 1996 figures thus show a marginal reduction in constant terms.

[34] In 1995 the nominal increase in the arms sales of the top 100 was 5%, which represented a slight increase in real terms. Sköns and Cooper (note 32), p. 240.

Table 6.4. Regional/national shares of arms sales[a] for the top 100 arms-producing companies in the OECD and the developing countries, 1996 compared to 1995[b]

Figures may not add up to totals because of the conventions of rounding.

Number of companies, 1996	Region/ country	Percentage of total arms sales 1995	Percentage of total arms sales 1996	Arms sales 1996 (US current $b.)
38	USA	55.4	55.2	86.3
40	West European OECD	35.0	35.5	55.6
11	France	13.3	12.7	19.9
12	UK	11.7	12.6	19.7
9	Germany	5.2	5.4	8.4
2	Italy	2.4	2.4	3.7
2	Sweden	1.1	1.1	1.8
2	Switzerland	0.9	0.7	1.1
2	Spain	0.4	0.6	1.0
14	Other OECD	6.9	6.7	10.5
7	Japan[c]	4.8	4.6	7.2
3	South Korea[d]	1.3	1.3	2.0
2	Australia	0.4	0.4	0.6
1	Turkey	0.2	0.2	0.4
1	Canada	0.2	0.2	0.3
8	Non-OECD countries	2.8	2.5	4.0
5	Israel	1.7	1.6	2.5
2	India	0.7	0.6	1.0
1	South Africa	0.4	0.3	0.5
100		*100.0*	*100.0*	156.4

[a] Arms sales include both sales for domestic procurement and exports.
[b] China is not included because of the lack of data.
[c] For Japanese companies data in the arms sales column represent new military contracts rather than arms sales.
[d] Data for South Korea are for 1995 in all columns.

Source: Appendix 6E.

Among other OECD countries, the main change is the fall in the share of Japanese companies in sales, as measured in US dollars, but this is mainly an effect of the deterioration in the value of the yen against the dollar. For the same reason the number of Japanese companies among the top 100 fell from nine in 1995 to seven in 1996. The three South Korean and two Australian arms-producing companies which appear in the SIPRI list this year for the first time are not true new entrants, but were excluded in previous years only because of non-availability of data. The share of the three developing countries in the top 100 companies' arms sales fell to 2.5 per cent in 1996.

Restructuring of the arms industry in 1996 and 1997

Among the industrialized market economies, down-sizing and consolidation have been most pronounced in the United States, where this process has led to the formation of a few large conglomerates. Consolidation in Western Europe, although uneven, has been slower. There is therefore a widening size difference between leading US and West European firms. In Western Europe this has led to increased pressure for cross-border consolidation since the imbalances in size are perceived as a major problem by both industry and government. Further consolidation is seen as necessary to strengthen the position of European companies, either in future cooperation schemes with large US companies or as their competitors or both.[35]

It is the balance between cooperation and competition which will determine the future structure of the global arms industry, and in particular the transatlantic balance.[36] First, while there have been and continue to be several transatlantic cooperative armament programmes within the framework of NATO, these have often fallen short of the common goals of NATO states. Second, the principal traditional motivation for these programmes has been the standardization and harmonization of military equipment, not industrial rationalization. Third, although they may have served to reduce duplication in military R&D and involved some technology transfer, most of these programmes have not led to rationalization of production to any significant extent. The failure of governments to promote this rationalization, in combination with the economic pressures on the industry, is leading to more industry-led initiatives, not only in external restructuring (mergers and acquisitions), which until now has been the main trend, but also in transatlantic armaments cooperation.[37]

In Japan, unlike most other arms-producing countries, there has been little pressure for restructuring and consolidation in spite of declining domestic arms procurement and the absence of export opportunities to compensate for this.[38] The lack of pressure for restructuring is mainly the result of two factors: (a) a low degree of dependence on military sales among defence contractors; and (b) the supportive arms procurement regime of the Japan Defense Agency, including payment on a cost-plus-fee basis. The adoption in December 1997 of a series of procurement reform measures may lead to some pressure on

---

[35] There are many examples of this perception. Richard Evans, Chief Executive Officer of British Aerospace (BAe), argues: 'We need to create European entities with the critical mass that in due course will be capable of creating strategic alliances with US companies'. *Defense News*, 2–8 Sep. 1996, p. 62. François Heisbourg, Senior Vice-President for Strategic Development at Matra Défense, argues: 'In financial, industrial and commercial terms only broad-based ventures with ready access to a wide range of defence markets can compete with the new American behemoths.' *Interavia*, July/Aug. 1997, pp. 14–15. German Defence Minister Volker Rühe has said that Europe must tackle the question of 'how to leap over principles of the market economy—aimed at competition within Europe—in favour of achieving competitiveness versus the USA'. *Interavia*, Apr. 1997, p. 3.

[36] Referring, as is common practice, to the US–West European nexus, and thus excluding Canada.

[37] A significant illustration of this new trend in the transatlantic context is a speech by Vance D. Coffman, Chief Executive Officer of Lockheed Martin, the world's largest arms-producing company, in which he argued in favour of transatlantic industry partnerships, primarily in the form of equity investments and joint ventures, and with the cooperation and support of governments in shaping harmonized requirements and eliminating legal and political barriers to such partnerships. 'The future of transatlantic industrial partnerships', Remarks by Vance D. Coffman before the 1998 Wehrkunde Conference, Munich, 7 Feb. 1998.

[38] Japanese expenditure on arms procurement declined by 15% in nominal terms between FY 1992/93 (953 billion yen) and FY 1996/97 (806 billion yen), corresponding to a volume reduction of 17%. 'Japanese defense firms make civil shift', *Defense News*, 31 Mar.–6 Apr. 1997, p. 4.

Table 6.5. The major companies by military industrial sector,[a] 1996–97

Company name[b]	Arms sales (US $m.) 1996	After acq.[c]	Restructuring in 1996–97
Aerospace			
Lockheed Martin, USA	18 010	(28 000)	Acquired military units of Loral in 1996; pending merger with Northrop Grumman
Boeing, USA	4 000	20 000	Acquired military units of Rockwell in 1996; merged with McDonnell Douglas in Aug. 1997
British Aerospace (BAe) UK	8 340	10 500	Joint venture (Matra BAe Dynamics) with Matra HT in 1996; acquired 49% stake in STN Atlas and part of Siemens' military electronics in 1997
DASA (Daimler Benz), Germany	3 330	–	Acquired part of Siemens' military electronics in 1997
Aérospatiale, France	2 310	(3 500)	Merger plans with Dassault Aviation delayed by the French Government's opposition to privatization
Matra BAe Dynamics, France/UK	1 950	2 350	Acquired 30% of DASA's LFK
Dassault Aviation, France	1 230	–	
Alcatel Satellites, France	800	1 200	Joint venture to be formed with Thomson-CSF, Dassault Electronique and Aérospatiale
Electronics			
Raytheon, USA	4 030	14 500	Acquired military units of Texas Instruments and Hughes
Thomson-CSF, France	4 540	6 000	Acquired 33% of Elettronica, Italy; restructuring in 1997/98
GEC, UK	4 460	–	Joint venture (Thomson Marconi Sonar) with Thomson-CSF in 1996; increased its share in Marconi Alenia Communications to 95%; acquired Hazeltine in 1996 and 60% of Italtel's military units in 1997
TRW, USA	3 360	4 000	Acquired BDM International in 1997
Litton, USA	1 920	2 620	Acquired Teldix, Sperry Marine and Systems Business unit of Hughes in 1996, and Racal Marine in 1997
Allied Signal, USA	1 260	–	Sold Ocean Systems to L-3 Communications
Engines			
Pratt & Whitney, USA	1 857	–	Subsidiary of United Technology
General Electric, USA	1 800	–	
Rolls Royce AC, UK	976	–	Acquired Allison, USA, in 1995
SNECMA Groupe, France	914	–	Will acquire 50% in joint venture Messier Dowty from TI Group
Shipbuilding			
DCN, France	3 470	–	French state-owned company
General Dynamics, USA	2 332	–	Owns Bath Iron Works and Electric Boat

Company name[b]	Arms sales (US $m.) 1996	After acq.[c]	Restructuring in 1996–97
Newport News, USA	1 730	–	Spun-off from Tenneco in 1996; acquired Continental Maritime Ind. of San Diego in 1997
Ingalls Shipbuilding, USA	1 296	–	Subsidiary of Litton
Thyssen, Germany	910	(1 600)	Merged shipbuilding activities of Blohm&Voss and Thyssen Nordseewerke; merger plans with HDW
HDW (Preussag), Germany	650	–	Plans to merge with Thyssen Werften
Military vehicles, artillery, ordnance & ammunition			
General Dynamics, USA	1 026	2 000	Acq. units of Teledyne Vehicle Systems in 1996; LM Armaments, Adv. Tech. Systems unit of Lucent Tech. and Ceridian Computer Devices in 1997
Rheinmetall, Germany	542	1 630	Acquired part of STN Atlas (26%, with Badenwerke 25% and BAe 49%)
GKN, UK	1 500	–	Plans to merge military vehicle units with Vickers
GIAT Industries, France	1 340	–	Sold Herstal in 1997; plans to merge Giat Munition with TDA (Thomson/DASA)
Alliant Tech Systems, USA	1 048	–	Sold Marine Systems to Hughes in 1997
United Defense, USA	1 020	–	Acquired by Carlyle Group from FMC in Oct. 1997
Wegmann, Germany	332	(685)	Plans to merge with Krauss-Maffei
Vickers, UK	539	(2 000)	Plans to merge with GKN military vehicle units

[a] The large number of vertical mergers integrating complementary capacities makes it increasingly difficult to distinguish between different military industrial sectors. The classification of this table thus provides only an indication of companies' core business areas.

[b] Japanese arms-producing companies, except for Mitsubishi Electric, are not included in this table because their product ranges are so diversified that they cannot be categorized.

[c] Estimates are for combined sales after the implementation of mergers and acquisitions. Estimates in brackets are for planned mergers.

Source: SIPRI arms production files.

companies to cut costs and to consolidate, especially at the subcontractor level where companies are smaller.[39]

The issues of size and competitiveness are also on the agenda in a number of third-tier arms-producing countries.[40] Consolidation accompanied by priva-

---

[39] Nakamoto, M., 'Cold wind of change sweeps in', *Financial Times*, 16 Dec. 1997, p. V; and Usui, N., 'Japan adopts acquisition reform to cut costs', *Defense News*, 15–21 Dec. 1997, pp. 3, 19.

[40] A rough classification of arms-producing countries into 4 layers, or 'tiers', is provided in Anthony, I., 'The "third tier" countries: production of major weapons', ed. H. Wulf, SIPRI, *Arms Industry Limited* (Oxford University Press: Oxford, 1993), pp. 362–63. According to this scheme, third-tier countries are those which which cannot produce the full spectrum of military technology but nevertheless have significant arms industries (a group of around 20 countries, including Australia, India, Israel, South Korea, South Africa, Spain and Turkey, which appear in the SIPRI 'top 100' list).

tization of large state-owned military industrial assets is being discussed or is under way in Australia, Greece, Israel and Spain.

The government restructuring programme for the Australian defence industry is approaching its final stage in 1998 with the privatization of the state-owned Australian Defence Industries and its partly-owned subsidiary Australian Submarine Corporation, after which a series of restructuring measures is expected.[41] The Greek Government is planning to merge the state-owned arms-producing companies.[42] In Israel there are plans to merge the loss-making state-owned enterprises Israel Aircraft Industries (IAI), Israel Military Industries and Rafael with the profitable private arms-producing companies Tadiran and Elbit Systems.[43] The Spanish Government introduced a Programme for Modernizing State-owned Enterprises in June 1996. According to this programme, profitable arms-producing companies are to be privatized by FY 1998/99 and loss-making companies to be restructured and down-sized.[44]

The arms industries in these countries are to be privatized in the course of consolidation. Finland has moved in the reverse direction, combining the major domestic arms industrial assets in a newly established state-owned holding company.[45]

The USA

The concentration process in the US arms industry has gone on at a rapid pace during the 1990s, probably culminating in 1997 with the announcement of a number of huge take-overs and mergers among the top arms-producing companies. The share of the top five prime contractors in the total volume of US Department of Defense (DOD) prime contract awards to the top 100 companies increased from 33 to 44 per cent between FYs 1990 and 1996.[46] This share will increase significantly in the aftermath of the completion of the takeovers of McDonnell Douglas by Boeing, of the military business of Hughes by Raytheon, and, if it is approved, of Northrop Grumman by Lockheed Martin.[47] These three takeovers will lead to the formation of three giant industrial conglomerates—Lockheed Martin in aerospace and military

[41] Grazebrook, A. W., 'Australian defence industry: major decisions ahead', *Asia–Pacific Defence Reporter,* vol. 24, no. 1 (1998), annual reference edition, pp. 31–33.

[42] Denny, S. and Finnegan, P., 'Greece eyes privatization plan for defense companies', *Defense News,* 24–30 Nov. 1997, p. 26.

[43] Friedlin, J., 'Laying down the sword', *Jerusalem Post,* international edn, 5 July 1997, p. 20; and Rodan, S., 'Biting the bullet', *Jerusalem Post,* international edn, 14 June 1997, p. 20.

[44] The loss-making divisions of Santa Barbara are to be closed down, starting in 1998, while Bazán may initiate diversification into civilian production. Letter from Centre d'Estudis par la Pau i el Desarmamento, 4 Dec. 1997. The state holding company SEPI, which since Sep. 1997 has controlled all 4 leading Spanish defence companies, provides information about the modernization programme on its Internet website at URL <http://www.sepi.se/frames/frame1.htm>.

[45] Patria Industries, created in Oct. 1996 as Suomen Puolustusväline, controls about two-thirds of the Finnish arms industry. Information folder on the reorganization, Patria Industries, 7 May 1997.

[46] US Department of Defense, Directorate for Information Operations and Reports, *100 Companies Receiving the Largest Dollar Volume of Prime Contract Awards* (US Government Printing Office, annual), URL <http://web1.whs.osd.mil/peidhome/procstat/top100/top100.htm>.

[47] The merged Lockheed Martin/Northrop Grumman and Boeing/McDonnell Douglas would account for at least 60% of the top 100 Department of Defense prime contracts, according to reports in 'Mega-mergers: then there were three . . .', *Jane's Defence Weekly,* 22 Oct. 1997, p. 22.

electronics, Boeing in aerospace, and Raytheon in military electronics and missiles (table 6.5).

In 1997 there was an important case of horizontal integration in the US arms industry being limited as a result of anti-trust concerns. General Dynamics, the only US producer of main battle tanks, having acquired the land systems units from Lockheed Martin, lost the bidding for United Defense, the other leading producer of military vehicles, because of the seller's fear of time-consuming anti-trust investigations which might go against it.[48]

With these deals the US concentration process has probably reached its limits, at least in the aerospace and military vehicle sectors. What may follow is a series of divestitures of both civil and military production units from the merged conglomerates in order to fulfil company strategies of 'core defence'—concentration on defence products in which a company has a market lead. In other sectors there may still be some room for further concentration, albeit limited. In the field of military electronics and information technology Northrop Grumman and Raytheon acquired large assets in 1996 and 1997. Raytheon thereby increased its military dependency from 33 to 65 per cent. A large number of minor military electronic units were also purchased by Litton, ITT Industries and TRW. However, at the sub-system supplier level, the rate of consolidation is likely to continue at a high rate.

The evaluation of the restructuring process in the US arms industry has only begun, and a final picture is only gradually emerging of the new structure of the US defence industrial base and the implications for procurement costs, industrial development, and civil and military innovation. As regards the general structure of the industry, concern was expressed in a Defense Science Board report of May 1997 about the impact of vertical integration (acquisition of subcontractors) on competition at the sub-system level.[49] A survey of the mergers and acquisitions in the US arms industry during the period 1989–95 shows that at the prime contractor level many of these have not involved the combining of production lines (horizontal mergers) for specific weapon systems to achieve economies of scale but rather the acquisition of larger positions in a greater number of weapon programmes (market extension-type mergers).[50] No clear efficiency gains have been demonstrated for these mergers, and it is being argued that they could rather lead to higher prices, poorer quality and a diminution in innovation of military technology.[51]

---

[48] A take-over would have turned General Dynamics into the USA's sole producer of tracked military vehicles. 'Unique situation allows Carlyle to purchase United Defense LP', *Defense News*, 1–7 Sep. 1997, p. 21.

[49] The Defense Science Board is a senior advisory panel to the Secretary of Defense. For a summary, see 'US policies, consolidation may pinch subcontractors', *Defense News*, 15–18 May 1997, p. 1, 42.

[50] Oden, M., 'Cashing-in, cashing-out and converting: restructuring of the defense industrial base in the 1990s', Study presented to the Council on Foreign Relations, New York, 9 Feb. 1996 and forthcoming in Markusen, A. and Costigan, S. (eds.), *Arming the Future: A Defense Industry for the 21st Century* (Council on Foreign Relations: New York, 1998).

[51] Markusen, A., 'The post-cold war persistence of defense specialized firms', Paper presented at the Klein Symposium, Penn State University, Dec. 1997, and forthcoming in Susman, G., *Defense Diversification* (Elsevier: Oxford, 1998); and Markusen, A., *The Economics of Defense Industry Mergers and Divestitures*, Working Paper no. 128 (Center for Urban Policy Research, Rutgers State University of New Jersey: New Brunswick, N.J., 1997), also published in *Economic Affairs*, vol. 17, no. 4, pp. 28–32.

Western Europe

Cross-border defence industrial consolidation is still at an early stage in Western Europe and is most advanced in the aerospace and electronics sectors, while consolidation in the production of land systems is occurring mainly at the national level. International joint ventures and consortia, rather than European industrial integration, constitute so far the major form of West European restructuring.

The delay in Europe-wide consolidation has been imputed to the reluctance of the French Government to impose restructuring on its state-owned arms industry, according to a plan launched in February 1996 by the previous government.[52] However, in October 1997 the government finally initiated the consolidation of the domestic aerospace and military electronics industry, announcing the partial privatization of Thomson-CSF and its combination with Dassault Electronique and major segments of the space and military activities of Aérospatiale and Alcatel Alsthom.[53]

Another decisive step was an agreement of December 1997 between the governments of France, Germany and the UK to ask their defence and aerospace industries to prepare a clear plan and timetable for their restructuring by the end of March 1998. The plan should include the expansion of Airbus Industrie activities to the production of helicopters, missiles and fighter aircraft in addition to its current civilian production.[54] In several announcements during 1997 the partner companies of Airbus—Aérospatiale, British Aerospace (BAe), CASA and DASA—showed their determination to transform Airbus from a risk-sharing consortium into a single corporate entity by 1 January 1999.[55] The reorganization is, however, dependent on the French Government's willingness to privatize Aérospatiale, of which there were no clear indications by the end of 1997.[56]

A large number of cross-border partnerships were established in 1996 and 1997 between the leading British companies BAe and GEC, the French Lagardère group, and several German and Italian companies. In the aerospace sector consolidation advanced with the inclusion of the German DASA Dornier in the Franco-British Matra Marconi joint venture and in the missile sector with the formation of Matra BAe Dynamics. In late 1997 the govern-

---

See also Gholz, E., 'National interest should guide defense industry mergers', *Defense News*, 17–23 Feb. 1997, p. 29.

[52] The consolidation plan announced in Feb. 1996 included: (*a*) the privatization of Thomson; and (*b*) the merger of Dassault Aviation and Aérospatiale. 'France sets agenda for industrial consolidation', *Jane's Defence Weekly*, 28 Feb. 1996, p. 25.

[53] Although exact ownership shares were not finalized at the time of the announcement (13 Oct. 1997), the plan was to reduce the government share of 58% in Thomson-CSF to around 30% in the new Thomson (increasing to 40% if the 10% share of state-owned Aérospatiale is counted), while Dassault Industries and Alcatel Alsthom would receive a joint 25% share, and 35% would be sold to private investors. 'France to form world-class defense/space group', *Aviation Week & Space Technology*, 20 Oct. 1997.

[54] 'Euro defence groups ordered to rationalise', *Jane's Defence Weekly*, 17 Dec. 1997, p. 17.

[55] 'Airbus: the next steps', *Interavia*, Nov. 1997, p. 25; and 'Merger wave in Europe steams ahead', *Defense News*, 8–14 Dec. 1997, pp. 8, 13.

[56] 'BAe says consolidation far from certain', *Interavia Air Letter*, 24 Feb. 1998, p. 5; and 'Aérospatiale shake-up is prelude to link-ups', *Jane's Defence Weekly*, 17 Dec. 1997, p. 17.

ments of Germany, Italy, Spain and the UK signed an agreement to start the production investment phase of the Eurofighter 2000 programme.[57] In the field of military electronics, a number of West European industrial alliances were formed in 1996 and 1997, a process which is likely to accelerate after the establishment of a new Thomson-CSF and the sale of Siemens' military branch to BAe and DASA. Consolidation in the field of land systems is still taking place at the national rather than international level in the main West European arms-producing countries. Cross-border consolidation is advancing, however, in the ordnance sector around the Franco-German Thomson DASA Armements (TDA) joint venture established in 1994.

In November 1997 the European Commission made an input in the process by publishing a communication on restructuring of defence-related industry in the EU member states.[58] Acknowledging that essential responsibility for restructuring lies with the member states, but seeking to help them cooperate to this end, it proposed an approach to the implementation of an 'integrated European market for defence products'. It included a common position on drawing up a European armaments policy, covering intra-EU transfers, public procurement and common customs arrangements, and an action plan for industry, which identified the areas in which immediate EU action was seen to be necessary.

VI. The candidates for NATO membership in Central and Eastern Europe

On 16 December 1997 the foreign ministers of the NATO member countries signed the accession protocols for the Czech Republic, Hungary and Poland. The plan is that, following ratification by the present member countries, they will join the alliance in the spring of 1999.[59] These plans have given rise to a debate about the cost of enlarging the membership of NATO for both present and future member countries. Cost estimates have varied widely depending on underlying assumptions. The choice of assumptions, in turn, has a political element. Many of the factors which will determine the ultimate cost of NATO enlargement have yet to be decided and an assessment of future costs can at present be no more than a qualified guess.

This section examines some of the factors which will have an impact on the future military expenditures of the three candidate countries.

NATO requirements

The costs of NATO membership are of two basic types: (*a*) the financial contributions by each member country to the NATO common budgets; and (*b*) the

[57] The production phase began in Dec. 1997 after the German Bundestag's approval of funding for production.
[58] European Commission, Implementing European Union strategy on defence-related industries, COM (97) 583 final, Brussels, 12 Nov. 1997.
[59] See also chapter 5, section II, in this volume.

additional national defence requirements associated with NATO membership, which are financed via national defence budgets. It is possible to specify the former but not the latter. In addition, the size and type of the latter contributions are to some extent subject to negotiation.

The three common budgets are: (*a*) the military budget, which funds primarily O&M for the NATO international military headquarters and programmes; (*b*) the NATO Security Investment Programme (NSIP), which funds infrastructure investments; and (*c*) the civil budget, which pays for civilian personnel and facilities. The common budgets are small compared to the member countries' own defence budgets: the combined 1997 defence budgets of member countries amounted to $466 billion;[60] NATO's common budget for 1998 amounts to around $1.6 billion.[61]

The NATO estimates of the costs of enlargement in the final communiqué from the accession meeting were significantly lower than previous estimates, which ranged from $27 billion to $125 billion over a period of 15 years.[62] They covered only the direct enlargement costs which would be eligible for common funding. NATO estimated about $1.5 billion over a period of 10 years, of which $1.3 billion would be for the NSIP, to be shared by the 19 members.[63] The estimates for NSIP costs were for extending the NATO communication and anti-air defence network, the minimum requirement for the integration of the new members, and were for $266 million, $315 million and $700 million to the Czech Republic, Hungary and Poland, respectively.[64]

NATO did not and will not make any estimates of the cost of the nationally funded military commitments for existing or prospective members.[65] Estimates made by the US DOD included $18–23 billion for nationally funded military modernization out of $27–35 billion estimated total costs of enlargement.[66]

National contributions to common NATO budgets are made according to an agreed formula. The US share, for example, is around 25 per cent. Thus the increase in the US contribution to the common budgets resulting from NATO

---

[60] 'NATO financial and economic data relating to NATO defence, 1975–1997', *Atlantic News*, vol. 31, no. 2973 (12 Dec. 1997). These estimates are calculated at current prices and exchange rates and therefore differ from those in appendix 6A in this volume which are calculated at 1995 prices and exchange rates.

[61] Consisting of the military budget ($680 million), the NSIP budget (*c.* $750 million) and the civil budget (*c.* $180 million). 'NATO: military budget remains constant', *Atlantic News*, vol. 31, no. 2973 (12 Dec. 1997), p. 1.

[62] These estimates are presented in George, P. *et al.*, 'Military expenditure', *SIPRI Yearbook 1997: Armaments, Disarmament and International Security* (Oxford University Press: Oxford, 1997), p. 179, fn. 79.

[63] 'Ministerial meeting of the North Atlantic Council held at NATO Headquarters, Brussels, on 16 Dec. 1997: Final Communiqué', *Atlantic News*, vol. 31, no. 2976 (18 Dec. 1997), annex, pp. 2–3. The NATO study on the costs of enlargement is based on estimates made by NATO's 2 main military commands, SHAPE and ACLANT, and is classified. 'NATO/enlargement: study on costs approved— $1.3 to 1.5 billion over ten years', *Atlantic News*, vol. 31, no. 2969 (29 Nov. 1997), p. 1 *bis*.

[64] 'NATO/enlargement: Mr Solana confirms that costs will be relatively low', *Atlantic News*, vol. 31, no. 2967 (21 Nov. 1997), pp. 2–2 bis.

[65] US General Accounting Office, NATO enlargement: NATO's requirements and costs for commonly funded projects, GAO/NSIAD-98-113, Mar. 1998, p. 6.

[66] US General Accounting Office (note 65), p. 6.

enlargement will be around $400 million over 10 years.[67] In similar fashion, the three invitees and NATO have agreed to their future contributions to the common budgets—0.90 per cent, 0.65 per cent and 2.48 per cent for the Czech Republic, Hungary and Poland, respectively.[68]

Military expenditure and procurement in the prospective member states

Leaders of the Czech Republic, Hungary and Poland assert that their countries will be willing and able to shoulder the additional costs of joining the alliance[69] but neither they, NATO officials nor allied military leaders can say how much will be required in terms of their national defence for harmonization of equipment to NATO standards and other forms of military modernization. Nor is it clear to what extent military modernization would have been necessary in any case, without NATO membership.

Since the beginning of the 1990s the three candidate countries have been in the process of reorganizing their armed forces. Economic difficulties have forced them to prioritize manpower and O&M at the expense of procurement and R&D. As economic recovery and the restructuring of national defence industries gather momentum, defence planners are confronted with difficult procurement policy issues. The restructuring and procurement options under discussion would require substantially higher levels of military expenditure than current levels, as presented in table 6.6. The trend in all three countries indicates that the expense of new weapon systems predicates generous sales agreements in terms of financing, offsets or international collaboration for any major arms import deal.

The Czech Republic

The military expenditure of the Czech Republic fell by 15 per cent in real terms over the five years 1993–97 (see table 6.6). As a share of GDP this represents a decline from 2.5 per cent in 1993 to 1.9 per cent in 1997. The Czech contribution to NATO has been estimated by the Czech Ministry of Finance at between 1.62 billion and 2.02 billion korunas by 1999, accounting for 0.08–0.10 per cent of GDP. In order to pay for this the government has decided to increase the share of military expenditure in GDP from 1.8 per cent in the budget adopted for 1998 to 2 per cent by the year 2000.[70]

Procurement is taking up an increasing share of the defence budget, having risen from 2 per cent in 1993 to 13 per cent in 1997, and in 1997 was 3.5 times higher in real terms than in 1993. A major part of the procurement

---

[67] US Department of Defense, Report to the Congress on the military requirements and costs of NATO enlargement, URL <http://www.defenselink,mil/pubs/NATO/, Feb. 1998>, pp. 1, 3, 7.
[68] 'NATO/enlargement: negotiations are almost over, save for a few formalities', *Atlantic News*, vol. 31, no. 2964 (13 Nov. 1997), p. 1.
[69] Barker, A., 'East Europe to seek US backing on NATO', *New Europe*, 15–21 Feb. 1998, p. 5.
[70] 'We will, evidently, contribute to the Alliance in 1999', *Prague Hospodarske Noviny*, in Foreign Broadcast Information Service, *Daily Report–East Europe (FBIS-EEU)*, FBIS-EEU-97-259, 16 Sep. 1997, p. 4.

Table 6.6. Procurement and total military expenditure for the Czech Republic, Hungary and Poland, 1993–98

	1993	1994	1995	1996	1997	1998
Czech Republic						
Total military expenditure						
(m. current korunas)	22 802	23 479	23 879	26 055	27 771	. .
(US $m. in 1995 prices and exchange rates)	1 031	965	900	902	880	. .
Procurement (m. current korunas)	549	1 865	2 978	3 779	3 516	. .
(US $m. in 1995 prices and exchange rates)	25	77	112	131	112	. .
Procurement as % of total military expenditure	2	8	12	15	13	. .
GDP (m. current korunas)	910 600	1 037 500	1 252 100	1 414 000	1 442 300	. .
Military expenditure as % of GDP	2.5	2.3	1.9	1.8	1.9	. .
Hungary						
Total military expenditure						
(m. current forints)	67 492	67 966	76 937	85 954	96 814	122 502
(US $m. in 1995 prices and exchange rates)	819	694	612	554	530	. .
Procurement (m. current forints)	3 089	1 282	1 319	1 907	1 994	1 852
(US $m. in 1995 prices and exchange rates)	37	13	10	12	11	. .
Procurement as % of total military expenditure	5	2	2	2	2	2
GDP (m. current forints)	3 537 800	4 351 000	4 831 400	5 409 300	5 687 300	. .
Military expenditure as % of GDP	1.9	1.6	1.6	1.6	1.7	. .
Poland						
Total military expenditure						
(m. current new zlotys)	3 980	5 117	6 595	8 313	9 883	10 635
(US $m. in 1995 prices and exchange rates)	2 773	2 675	2 720	2 853	2 935	. .
Procurement (m. current new zlotys)	493	565	712	700	960	1 258
(US $m. in 1995 prices and exchange rates)	343	295	294	240	287	. .
Procurement as % of total military expenditure	12	11	11	8	10	12
GDP (m. current new zlotys)	155 780	210 407	286 026	301 757	318 354	. .
Military expenditure as % of GDP	2.6	2.4	2.3	2.8	3.1	. .

Source: SIPRI questionnaires submitted to the Czech Republic, Hungary and Poland.

budget is for the modernization of T-72 tanks to NATO standards. The total cost of the programme is estimated at 14 billion korunas, of which 958 million is funded by the 1997 procurement budget. After prototypes have been tested the army plans to modernize roughly 100–300 tanks.[71] Another major deal, worth an estimated 23 billion korunas ($720 million), was signed in September 1997, for 72 L-159 light combat/advanced trainer aircraft for the air force.[72]

Hungary

Hungary's military budget declined by 35 per cent in the period 1993–97 and its share of GDP fell from 1.9 to 1.7 per cent during the same period. The share of procurement is only 2 per cent (see table 6.6). In order to pay its 0.65 per cent contribution to the NATO common budgets (around 2.3 billion forints a year[73]), the government has proposed that the share of military expenditure in GDP should increase by 0.1 per cent per year from 1998 for four years, from 1.4 per cent in the 1998 budget to 1.8 per cent by the year 2001.[74]

Extra funds have been requested for 1998 to finance an increase in the salaries of professional soldiers (5 billion forints) and for a deal made with France in 1997 and worth 10 billion forints for an air defence system based on French Mistral surface-to-air missiles and Italian SHORAR-2D surveillance radars and other equipment.[75] Defence Minister Gyorgy Keleti has pointed out that this programme is not a formal condition of NATO membership but a necessity since the Soviet-made air defence system currently in operation is obsolete.[76]

Poland

The recent growth of military expenditure in real terms—by almost 6 per cent in the period 1993–97—resulted from the inclusion of military retirement pensions and disabled personnel benefits in the military budget. Up to 1993 these were financed directly from the national budget, but they have gradually been taken over by the Ministry of Defence. The 1997 military budget was 9883 million zlotys ($2.9 billion in 1995 prices).[77] Procurement expenditure at 960 million zlotys ($287 million) or 10 per cent of the military budget was to be spent mostly on spare parts and repair of equipment.

[71] 'The army of the Czech Republic will further converge to NATO standards', *Prague Hospodarske Noviny*, in FBIS-EEU-97-009, 13 Jan. 1997, p. 4.
[72] 'Czech combat aircraft comes into view', *Jane's Defence Weekly*, vol. 27, no. 24 (18 June 1997), p. 3.
[73] Interview with Hungarian Prime Minister Gyula Horn, 10 Nov. 1997. 'Hungary's Horn views NATO referendum, cost of membership', Budapest MTI, 11 Nov. 1997, in FBIS-EEU-97-315, 11 Nov. 1997.
[74] Interview with Hungarian Foreign Minister Lazlo Kovacs, 'Hungarian foreign minister discusses NATO, Slovakia', Budapest Kossuth Radio, 4 Oct. 1997, in FBIS-EEU-97-278, 5 Oct. 1997.
[75] See also chapter 8 in this volume.
[76] Interview with Hungarian Defence Minister Gyorgy Keleti, 'NATO membership is cheaper than neutrality', *Nepszabadsag*, 23 Aug. 1997, pp. 1, 7, in FBIS-EEU-97-237, 25 Aug. 1997.
[77] Of the 1997 defence budget, 39% is allocated to personnel, 30% to O&M, about 10% to procurement, and 19.2% to military and disability pensions.

Poland's Military Foreign Affairs Department estimated in January 1997 that the costs over four to five years for adjustments in particular parts of the military infrastructure, including command systems, communications, air defence and logistics, would be about 4.8 billion zlotys ($1.55 billion).[78] In September 1997 the government approved a military modernization and restructuring programme for the 15-year period 1998–2012. It included an allocation of 40 billion zlotys for technical modernization to achieve compatibility with NATO in command, control and communications,[79] a personnel cut from 220 000 to 180 000 and a reduction in compulsory military service from 18 to 12 months as of the year 2000. However, in 1998, the first year of programme implementation, a budget shortfall will make it impossible to fulfil the plan.[80] Poland is working on a detailed military development plan under which the needs of the military units designated for cooperating with NATO should be a priority and which will specify the cost estimates for integration with NATO.[81] It is to be financed by an increase in military expenditure at an average rate of 3.2 per cent per year during the period 1998–2012, somewhat slower than forecast growth in GDP.[82]

Fighter procurement

The three NATO candidate countries wish to launch programmes to replace their ageing Soviet-type fighter aircraft as soon as possible, despite the sluggish performance of their respective economies and the lack of resources for procurement. The Czech Republic is interested in purchasing 24 advanced fighter aircraft, Hungary 30, and Poland has been considering offers from several manufacturers to provide 50–100 fighter aircraft. Apart from politics, the major hurdle on the way to procurement of a new fighter is financing.

Combat aircraft are expensive. The unit cost of a new JAS-39 Gripen is about $35 million and of the F-16 C/D fighter aircraft around $25 million.[83] It is difficult to estimate the aggregate value of the deals being discussed but for a combined requirement of 100–150 aircraft it would be in the range of $2.5–5.3 billion, excluding system costs. Representatives of industry have estimated the size of this market at $10 billion.[84] The financing problems of

[78] Wieczorek, P. and Zukrowska, K., *Costs of the Polish Integration with the Euroatlantic Structures*, COPRI Working Paper no. 11 (Copenhagen Peace Research Institute: Copenhagen, Nov. 1997), p. 7.
[79] Zygulski, W., 'Squeezing into NATO, the government proposes an overhaul anticipating negotiations with Poland's new allies', *Warsaw Voice*, vol. 46, no. 38 (21 Sep. 1998), p. 5 (in English).
[80] According to the Chief of General Staff, General Henryk Szumski. Wronski, P., 'Deputies and generals on funds and pensions for servicemen: armed forces full of anxiety', *Gazeta Wyborcza*, 6–7 Dec. 1997, in FBIS-EEU-97-343, 9 Dec. 1997, p. 4.
[81] Polak, R., Deputy Director of the Budget Department of the Polish Defence Ministry and chief of a team that edited the 15-year military modernization programme 'Financing of the Army 2012', *Polska Zbrojna*, 19 Sep. 1997, pp. 12, 22, in FBIS-EEU-97-266, 23 Sep. 1997.
[82] Polak (note 81), p. 6.
[83] Latawski, P., 'Another aircraft sale of the century? Central Europe and the multi-role aircraft market', *RUSI Journal*, June 1997, pp. 51–57; and *Jane's all the World Aircraft 1997–98* (Jane's Information Group: Coulsdon, 1998), p. 488.
[84] The higher estimate is provided by US Aerospace Industries Association's Vice-President of International Affairs, Joel Johnson. 'NATO candidates not eager to buy new arms', *Interavia Airletter*, 7 July 1997, p. 5.

purchasing new fighter aircraft are clear if these estimates are compared with the combined 1997 procurement budgets of the three countries—$410 million at 1995 prices.

In more than one way, the situation illustrates the tightening international competition in the arms industry and the changing company strategies. For the time being, the leading contenders for the three nations' fighter programmes are the US F-16 (Lockheed Martin) and F/A-18 (McDonnell Douglas) aircraft, the Swedish JAS-39 Gripen (Saab/BAe), the Russian MiG-29 (MiG-MAPO) and the French Mirage-2000-5 (Dassault). At the time of writing there does not appear to be any likelihood of the three national programmes achieving even some loose form of coordination: they are being run completely independently. The need for compatibility of equipment as between NATO members is one of the sales argument used by Western suppliers. For this reason it is unlikely that Russia, which was once the main supplier in this market, will make any major deals.

For the suppliers it is important to introduce at least some military products into service in Central and Eastern Europe, if necessary almost free of charge in the interests of building up a long-term dependence. 'Whoever gets in first will have a lock for the next quarter century', said a US Aerospace Industries Association official.[85] There is stiff competition between the USA and Europe and between US companies. Sales offices have been set up in the capitals of the prospective member countries, aircraft demonstrations arranged and offset arrangements prepared to ease the financial burden. Lockheed Martin has air force generals on its team, while Saab and Dassault count on support from their diplomats and military. US manufacturers have come up with what is described as a 'creative option' of leasing used aircraft[86] and the US Navy has offered to lease seven used F/A-18s under a no-cost, five-year agreement.

The three candidate countries are armed with old Soviet equipment and redundant Warsaw Pact facilities the maintenance and repair of which consume much of the resources available for modernization. Any new procurement, on the other hand, will require a major increase in spending not currently planned in any of the three countries' military procurement budgets.

---

[85] Fairhall, D., 'West lures newcomers with hard sell on arms', *The Guardian*, 9 July 1997, p. 7.
[86] Bonner, R., 'Arms: jet-fighter dealers set up a bazaar for Central Europe', *International Herald Tribune*, 16 July 1996, pp. 1, 7.

Appendix 6A. Tables of military expenditure

ELISABETH SKÖNS, AGNÈS COURADES ALLEBECK, EVAMARIA LOOSE-WEINTRAUB and PETTER STÅLENHEIM

Sources and methods are explained in appendix 6C. Notes and explanations of the conventions used appear below table 6A.4.

Table 6A.1. Military expenditure by region, in constant US dollars, 1988–97

Figures are in US $b, at constant 1995 prices and exchange rates.

	1988	1989	1990	1991	1992	1993	1994	1995	1996	1997
World total	**1 066**	**1 047**	**1 003**	..	**810**	**779**	**756**	**716**	**708**	**[704]**
Geographical regions[1]										
Africa	12.6	13.3	12.3	11.2	10.6	10.7	9.7	9.2	9.4	[8.8]
North Africa (excl. Libya)	2.2	2.8	2.4	2.5	2.7	3.0	3.3	3.0	3.2	3.2
Sub-Saharan Africa	10.4	10.4	9.9	8.7	7.9	7.7	6.4	6.1	6.2	[5.6]
Americas	410	405	386	338	358	342	325	309	295	[290]
North America	390	385	369	325	342	325	307	289	273	268
Central America	0.8	0.8	0.9	0.6	0.6	0.6	0.6	0.6	0.5	0.5
South America	19.2	18.9	16.0	12.1	15.3	16.5	16.6	[19.6]	[21.2]	[21.9]
Asia (excl. Central Asia)	95.0	99.5	102	105	108	110	112	115	119	120
Central Asia	..	..	..	..	..	..	..	..	..	..
East Asia	83.8	88.3	90.6	93.4	96.6	98.1	99.7	102	106	106
South Asia	11.2	11.2	11.4	11.2	11.2	12.2	12.1	12.6	13.0	13.6
Europe	500	483	447	..	279	265	259	235	235	[234]
Middle East (excl. Iraq)	39.6	36.9	[47.0]	[64.2]	[45.0]	42.1	41.2	38.5	42.1	43.3
Oceania	8.9	8.8	8.8	8.8	9.1	8.9	9.2	8.9	8.7	8.8

MILITARY EXPENDITURE AND ARMS PRODUCTION

Organizations[1]										
ASEAN	12.2	13.2	14.0	14.1	15.1	15.9	16.5	18.1	18.9	18.6
CIS (excl. CIS Asia)	..	..	..	..	50.2	44.1	43.5	27.6	26.0	[26.4]
EU	218	219	219	216	205	198	192	185	185	184
NATO	604	601	586	538	546	522	498	472	458	451
OECD	676	677	661	613	622	597	575	548	535	528
OPEC	28.0	25.5	33.8	50.9	33.1	31.7	30.1	27.5	31.1	32.0
OSCE	889	868	815	..	621	589	565	523	506	[500]
Income group[1]										
Low-income economies	25.7	26.3	29.2	28.1	29.5	30.0	28.8	28.9	29.9	30.5
Middle-income economies	292	272	237	..	85.0	79.5	80.9	64.4	63.5	[64.2]
Upper-middle-income economies	56.8	57.8	55.3	64.2	53.8	57.1	55.5	56.8	62.0	[62.0]
High-income economies	691	690	682	639	642	613	591	566	553	548

Table 6A.2. Military expenditure by region and country, in local currency, 1988–97

Figures are in local currency, current prices.

State	Currency	1988	1989	1990	1991	1992	1993	1994	1995	1996	1997
Europe											
Albania[2]	m. leks	955	1 075	1 030	895	2 368	3 837	4 412	4 922	4 400	4 927
Armenia[3]	m. roubles	. .	. .	. .	. .	. .	. .	. .	. .	. .	. .
Austria	m. shillings	16 597	17 849	17 537	18 208	19 600	20 500	21 200	21 500	21 700	21 900
Azerbaijan[3]	m. manats	. .	. .	. .	. .	1 642	13 290	120 000	. .	. .	. .
Belarus[2,3]	b. B. roubles	. .	. .	. .	. .	. .	17.7	365	1 723	2 231	4 278
Belgium	m. francs	150 647	152 917	155 205	157 919	132 819	129 602	131 955	131 156	131 334	134 835
Bulgaria[2]	m. leva	1 752	1 605	1 615	4 434	5 748	8 239	12 917	21 840	37 853	357 192
Croatia[4]	m. kuna	. .	. .	. .	21.0	200	3 422	7 149	9 282	7 760	7 000
Cyprus	m. C. pounds	77.0	82.0	127	131	191	90.0	99.0	91.0	141	(200)
Czech Rep.[5]	m. korunas	. .	. .	. .	. .	. .	22 802	23 479	2 879	26 055	27 771
Czechoslovakia[6]	m. korunas	29 236	43 784	4 900	43 037	4 503	. .	. .	. .	. .	. .
Denmark	m. kroner	15 620	15 963	16 399	17 091	17 129	17 390	17 293	17 468	17 896	18 594
Estonia[7]	m. kroons	. .	. .	. .	. .	68.0	174	327	417	483	798
Finland[8]	m. markkaa	6 445	6 853	7 405	8 903	9 298	9 225	9 175	8 336	9 157	9 653
France	m. francs	215 073	225 331	231 911	240 936	238 874	241 199	246 469	238 432	237 375	242 485
Georgia[9]	th./m. lari	. .	. .	. .	. .	3.5	200	[40.0]	[55.0]	76.7	95.0
German DR[10]	m. marks	21 647	. .	. .	. .	. .	. .	. .	. .	. .	. .
Germany[11]	m. D. marks	61 638	63 178	68 376	65 579	65 536	61 529	58 957	58 986	58 671	57 947
Greece	m. drachmas	471 820	503 032	612 344	693 846	835 458	932 995	1 052 760	1 171 377	1 343 276	1 510 684
Hungary[2]	m. forints	49 157	47 763	52 367	53 999	61 216	67 492	67 996	76 937	85 954	96 814
Ireland[12]	m. I. pounds	254	264	290	314	324	332	415	429	460	488
Italy	b. lire	25 539	27 342	28 007	30 191	30 813	32 364	32 835	31 561	36 170	37 190
Latvia[13]	m. lai	. .	. .	. .	. .	. .	12.0	19.0	23.0	21.0	26.0
Lithuania[7]	m. litai	. .	. .	. .	. .	. .	85.0	79.0	110	169	325
Luxembourg	m. francs	3 163	2 995	3 233	3 681	3 963	3 740	4 214	4 194	4 380	4 612
Malta[14]	th. liri	7 998	7 426	6 722	7 029	8 513	9 419	10 533	10 996	11 807	12 105

MILITARY EXPENDITURE AND ARMS PRODUCTION 217

Country	Unit	1988	1989	1990	1991	1992	1993	1994	1995	1996	1997
Moldova³	th. lei	..	..	..	..	..	..	..	..	..	65 000
Netherlands	m. guilders	13 300	13 571	13 513	13 548	13 900	13 103	12 990	12 864	13 240	13 441
Norway	m. kroner	18 865	20 248	21 251	21 313	23 638	22 528	24 019	21 433	23 704	23 598
Poland	m. new zlotys	74.0	215	1 495	1 830	2 624	3 980	5 117	6 595	8 313	9 833
Portugal	m. escudos	194 036	229 344	267 299	305 643	341 904	352 504	360 811	403 478	401 165	448 544
Romania	b. lei	28.0	29.0	30.0	80.0	196	420	1 185	1 785	1 959	..
Russia/USSR¹⁵	b. roubles	[138.3]	[133.7]	[123.4]	..	(1 049)	(9 037)	(35 409)	(60 542)	(82 310)	(101 500)
Slovak Rep.⁵	m. korunas	..	..	..	..	18 229	8 211	9 614	12 932	13 412	14 340
Slovenia⁴	m. tolars	..	..	..	..	18 229	20 864	24 520	31 730	29 823	..
Spain	m. pesetas	835 353	923 375	922 808	947 173	927 852	1 054 902	994 689	1 078 805	1 091 432	1 099 202
Sweden	m. kronor	28 035	31 037	34 974	35 744	35 302	36 309	37 608	39 908	40 973	42 373
Switzerland	m. francs	4 956	5 431	5 947	6 104	6 014	5 524	5 723	5 668	5 417	5 299
Turkey	b. lira	3 789	7 158	13 866	23 657	42 320	77 717	156 724	302 864	611 521	1 101 665
UK¹⁶	m. pounds	19 290	20 868	22 287	24 380	22 850	22 686	22 490	21 439	22 095	21 824
Ukraine¹⁷	m. hryvnya	..	..	..	..	..	[11.4]	477	2 222	3 660	3 517
Yugoslavia (former)	m. new dinars	568	6 113	5 180	..	..	678	1 200	1 611	4 210	..
Yugoslavia¹⁸	m. dinars	..	..	..	..	..	..	..	..	..	7 593
Middle East											
Bahrain	m. dinars	70.4	73.6	81.2	89.2	94.6	94.4	96.3	103	[106]	[135]
Egypt	m. E. pounds	3 118	3 048	3 504	4 223	4 703	5 117	5 767	4 539	..	..
Iran¹⁹	b. rials	719	832	1 040	1 268	1 521	2 340	4 188	..	5 643	7 111
Iraq	m. dinars	..	..	..	..	..	..	..	..	..	..
Israel	m. new shekels	9 121	10 566	12 940	14 776	16 919	17 539	19 836	22 216	26 489	30 000
Jordan²⁰	m. dinars	257	252	255	270	273	300	348	387	417	444
Kuwait	m. dinars	476	610	2 585	3 674	1 852	900	979	1 102	1 108	(1 037)
Lebanon	m. L. pounds	10 573	..	97 874	139 979	498 541	518 482	703 981	795 168	759 944	702 181
Oman²¹	m. riyals	589	601	742	643	778	738	779	776	737	698
Saudi Arabia	m. riyals	50 080	47 812	[50 000]	[100 000]	54 000	61 636	53 549	49 501	(64 000)	(67 000)
Syria	m. S. pounds	14 612	16 654	18 429	32 483	33 412	29 948	37 270	40 500	41 741	..
UAE²²	m. dirhams	(5 827)	(5 827)	(5 827)	(5 827)	7 163	7 750	7 342	7 160	[7 400]	..
Yemen, North	m. rials	5 533	6 030	..	..	..	..	..	..	..	..
Yemen, South	m. dinars	..	..	..	..	..	..	..	..	..	..

State	Currency	1988	1989	1990	1991	1992	1993	1994	1995	1996	1997
Yemen[23]	m. rials	..	..	10 382	13 227	16 812	19 752	30 273	3 897	..	..
Asia											
Central Asia											
Kazakhstan[24]	m. tenge	..	..	..	..	69.0	744	15 581	26 000	..	..
Kyrgystan[3]	m. soms	..	..	..	..	..	38.0	105	232	..	..
Tajikistan[3]	m. T. roubles	..	..	..	..	3.0	243	347	..	21 210	..
Turkmenistan[3]	m. T. manats	..	..	..	..	..	..	..	4 600	2 651	..
Uzbekistan[3]	m. sum	..	..	..	..	11.7	1 164	991	3 355	..	..
South Asia											
Bangladesh	m. taka	10 750	11 450	11 965	13 980	16 095	17 290	18 080	19 110	..	..
India	b. rupees	129	140	151	160	171	206	228	260	288	341
Nepal	m. rupees	738	828	981	1 111	1 306	1 597	1 794	1 895	2 027	2 269
Pakistan	m. rupees	46 808	50 261	57 898	69 682	81 604	90 610	97 816	(108 425)	(123 000)	(132 500)
Sri Lanka	m. rupees	4 732	4 073	6 736	10 317	12 876	15 413	19 415	(34 000)	(46 000)	(44 000)
East Asia											
Brunei[25]	m. B. dollars	359	363	419	..	..	..	[371]	[390]	[475]	[490]
Cambodia	b. riels	..	..	..	..	..	..	..	..	298	267
China, P. R.[26]	m. yuan	21 800	25 100	28 780	32 750	37 470	42 250	54 710	63 270	75 000	80 600
Indonesia	b. rupiahs	2 427	2 647	3 156	3 512	4 067	4 282	5 135	5 914	6 941	[7 600]
Japan	b. yen	3 789	4 041	4 130	4 329	4 510	4 618	4 673	4 714	4 815	4 917
Korea, North	m. won	3 863	4 060	4 314	4 466	4 582	4 692	4 817	..	..	..
Korea, South	b. won	5 268	5 921	6 665	7 892	8 709	9 040	10 057	11 114	12 538	14 014
Laos	b. kip	..	..	..	..	..	..	..	87.6	..	..
Malaysia	m. ringgits	2 241	2 761	3 043	4 323	4 500	4 951	5 565	6 121	6 091	6 183
Mongolia	m. tugriks	900	850	592	[888]	1 184	4 795	7 017	9 339	11 663	..
Myanmar	m. kyats	1 632	3 689	5 160	5 924	8 366	12 695	16 742	22 283	..	..
Philippines	m. pesos	14 906	15 907	14 707	15 898	17 461	20 130	23 271	27 793	35 530	4 917
Singapore	m. S. dollars	2 414	2 735	3 159	3 340	3 684	3 846	4 112	5 226	5 686	(6 100)
Taiwan	b. T. dollars	160	188	211	227	239	255	257	(265)	(273)	(262)

MILITARY EXPENDITURE AND ARMS PRODUCTION 219

Country	Currency										
Thailand	m. baht	42 812	44 831	48 846	55 502	64 961	73 708	78 300	88 983	93 960	97 200
Viet Nam	b. dong	792	2 047	3 319	4 292	3 730	3 168	4 730	. .	. .	. .
Oceania											
Australia	m. A. dollars	7 963	8 538	[9 206]	9 665	[10 385]	10 382	10 721	10 778	10 946	11 196
Fiji[27]	m. F. dollars	35.3	43.1	45.2	47.9	45.9	49.5	49.3	48.8	. .	. .
New Zealand[28]	m. N.Z. dollars	1 336	1 341	1 300	1 210	972	914	1 167	1 251	1 063	1 158
Papua New Guinea	m. kina	45.6	65.6	. .	50.1	56.5	67.1	54.3	. .	. .	. .
Tonga	th. pa'anga	1 115	1 565	1 980	. .	2 269	. .	. .	. .	. .	. .
Africa											
North Africa											
Algeria[29]	m. dinars	6 084	6 500	[8 470]	10 439	[20 125]	29 810	46 800	58 847	79 519	101 126
Libya	m. dinars	582	. .	. .	. .	. .	. .	. .	. .	. .	. .
Morocco	m. dirhams	7 530	11 264	8 816	10 002	10 488	11 640	12 565	12 246	[12 350]	. .
Tunisia	m. dinars	234	269	287	315	319	347	364	326	343	369
Sub-Saharan Africa											
Angola[19]	m./b. kzr	44.0	58.3	52.4	102	388	7 204	31 100	[1 142]	. .	78 200
Benin	m. francs	11 000	9 100	8 935	. .	. .	. .	. .	. .	. .	. .
Botswana[30]	m. pulas	171	207	291	348	376	450	458	460	471	504
Burkina Faso	m. francs	17 033	21 315	22 997	19 608	18 824	17 139	17 372	10 517	15 408	20 199
Burundi	m. francs	4 809	6 014	6 782	7 760	8 121	8 805	10 589	[64 300]	. .	. .
Cameroon	m. francs	52 315	52 525	57 135	54 795	50 055	46 745	55 420	. .	. .	. .
Cape Verde	m. escudos	366	. .	. .	. .	. .	220	. .	. .	368	424
Central Afr. Rep.[29]	m. francs	. .	. .	. .	6 093	6 137	5 421	5 935	6 496	6 239	. .
Chad	m. francs	. .	. .	. .	. .	. .	11 085	12 333	10 000	. .	. .
Congo	m. francs	. .	. .	. .	. .	. .	. .	. .	. .	. .	. .
Congo, Dem. Rep.	th/m./b. new zaïres	13.0	9.0	14.0	235	33.0	1 258	10 816	122 000	. .	28 916
Côte d'Ivoire	m. francs	38 155	41 368	39 199	40 671	41 503	42 088	46 677	. .	. .	. .
Djibouti	m. D.francs	4 701	4 705	4 709	4 809	. .	. .	. .	7 204	6 092	. .
Eritrea[31]	m. birr	. .	. .	. .	. .	. .	539	439	771	. .	. .
Ethiopia	m. birr	1 508	1 751	1 740	1 121	667	703	710	726	762	. .
Gabon	m. francs	. .	. .	. .	. .	. .	. .	. .	. .	. .	. .

State	Currency	1988	1989	1990	1991	1992	1993	1994	1995	1996	1997
Gambia[29]	m. dalasis	14.5	20.7	27.3	34.9	31.2	23.3	22.2	30.1	40.9	. .
Ghana	m. cedis	4 603	6 106	9 006	15 230	23 242	39 481	36 147	58 823	72 644	93 148
Guinea-Bissau	m. pesos	. .	8 027	. .	. .	. .	. .	. .	7 580	. .	. .
Kenya[29]	m. shillings	4 090	4 350	5 240	4 890	4 290	5 170	6 570	7 580	. .	. .
Lesotho	th. maloti	36 836	38 523	59 321	62 505	62 393	69 100	72 400	91 900	126 000	. .
Liberia	m. dollars	26.5	[27.4]	28.3	21.7	23.6	37.3	41.3			
Madagascar	b. francs	46.3	48.5	56.7	63.7	68.9	72.4	84.6	116	135	95.1
Malawi	m. kwachas	51.7	62.9	66.3	66.5	67.8	69.6	151	232	259	. .
Mali	b. francs	14.3	14.7	14.2	. .	. .	. .	. .	. .	. .	. .
Mauritania	m. ouguiyas	3 235	3 229	3 239	3 232	3 427	3 640	3 640	3 750	. .	. .
Mauritius	m. rupees	62.9	96.1	136	164	178	190	221	248	246	830
Mozambique[32]	b. meticais	58.2	102	136	178	259	417	1 016	626	704	830
Namibia[33]	m. rand	. .	. .	. .	309	355	229	202	247	286	385
Niger	m. francs	5 493	5 749	12 315	. .	. .	. .	. .	. .	. .	. .
Nigeria	m. nairas	1 720	2 220	2 286	[3 554]	4 822	6 382	6 608	9 361	15 500	17 450
Rwanda	m. francs	2 800	3 336	7 964	13 184	11 863	12 900	5 700	14 700	. .	. .
Senegal	m. francs	30 300	31 300	31 300	29 928	29 056	. .	. .	. .	. .	. .
Seychelles	m. rupees	65.4	73.6	79.2	87.6	105	67.1	60.1	55.2	52.4	51.0
Sierra Leone	m. leones	230	577	1 369	4 792	10 081	13 244	15 546	18 898	17 119	9 315
Somalia	m. shillings	7 918	4 200	. .	. .	. .	. .	. .	. .	. .	. .
South Africa	m. rand	8 615	9 749	10 038	9 408	9 576	9 428	10 721	10 697	11 121	10 475
Sudan[29]	m. S. pounds	1 297	3 050	4 420	7 420	13 750	29 500	49 900	80 600	208 200	. .
Swaziland	m. emalangeni	18.7	22.2	35.8	41.7	56.4	73.1	86.3	98.3	117	112
Tanzania	m. shillings	8 855	10 823	12 196	16 130	13 000	14 200	33 467	15 400	. .	. .
Togo	m. francs	12 834	13 354	13 817	12 950	59 335	14 200	14 100	15 400	. .	. .
Uganda	m. shillings	11 583	31 194	45 891	53 995	59 335	74 852	137 204	193 889	248 835	35 100
Zambia[19]	m. kwachas	. .	2 315	4 220	5 575	16 835	23 149	42 083	47 756	(45 000)	35 100
Zimbabwe	m. Z. dollars	707	803	954	1 117	1 269	1 439	1 826	2 214	2 330	3 874

MILITARY EXPENDITURE AND ARMS PRODUCTION   221

Americas

North America

Canada[16]	m. C. dollars	12 336	12 854	13 473	12 830	13 111	13 293	13 008	12 457	11 511	10 741
Mexico	m. new pesos	2 077	1 964	2 665	3 661	4 530	5 445	7 554	7 860	11 034	12 111
USA[16]	m. dollars	293 093	304 085	306 170	280 292	305 141	297 637	288 059	278 856	271 417	272 955

Central America

Belize[19]	th. B. dollars	7 926	8 711	9 538	9 466	10 584	13 011	16 049	17 529	. .	. .
Costa Rica[34]	m. colones	1 640	1 870	9 160	10 700	13 180	16 020	23 210	29 460	. .	. .
El Salvador	m. colones	777	926	975	1 011	975	888	829	849	843	850
Guatemala	m. quetzals	337	368	593	600	785	869	1 008	(1 124)	714	630
Honduras	m. lempiras	150	247	276	(252)	(280)	(263)	(385)	(445)	(530)	360
Nicaragua[35]	th./m. gold córdoba	[5.8]	[206]	[32 160]	211	211	224	232	242	269	260
Panama	m. balboas	102	101	74.1	80.1	86.7	94.6	98.7	96.8	98.0	. .

South America

Argentina[36]	th./m. pesos	1 806	51.7	1 248	2 276	2 925	3 411	3 582	3 750	3 458	3 291
Bolivia	m bolivianos	180	225	357	440	473	537	569	632	371	. .
Brazil[37]	reais/th./m. reais	(429)	(6 790)	(142)	(448)	(7 028)	188	4 108	10 008	(14 000)	[15 919]
Chile[38]	b. pesos	136	167	203	254	304	351	396	439	489	509
Colombia	b. pesos	150	211	281	347	470	588	815	646	. .	. .
Ecuador	b. sucres	61.3	102	156	273	532	841	982	. .	. .	. .
Guyana[39]	m. dollars	137	. .	142	227	454	562	759	801	780	1 000
Paraguay	b. guaranies	32.6	59.7	81.4	142	159	181	202	240	(266)	. .
Peru	th./m. new soles	[84.0]	[2 046]	130	480	1 001	[1 390]	(1 778)	1 878	2 000	. .
Uruguay	m. new pesos	58.0	114	233	363	813	974	2 083	1 816	2 228	. .
Venezuela[41]	m. bolivares	12 934	14 110	24 350	46 896	(110 769)	(110 885)	(137 960)	(212 427)	(286 750)	(473 390)

Table 6A.3. Military expenditure by region and country, in constant US dollars, 1988–97

Figures are in US $m., at constant 1995 prices and exchange rates.

State	1988	1989	1990	1991	1992	1993	1994	1995	1996	1997
Europe										
Albania[2]	82.4	92.8	88.9	76.7	62.4	54.6	51.3	53.1	42.1	33.2
Armenia[3]	. .	. .	. .	. .	. .	. .	. .	. .	. .	. .
Austria	2 046	2 146	2 041	2 051	2 121	2 141	2 151	2 133	2 115	2 100
Azerbaijan[3]	. .	. .	. .	. .	1 260	826	423	. .	259	279
Belarus[2,3]	. .	. .	. .	. .	. .	589	523	305	. .	. .
Belgium	6 145	6 051	5 939	5 855	4 808	4 566	4 540	4 449	4 362	4 410
Bulgaria[2]	1 319	1 136	1 218	772	548	476	500	322	250	205
Croatia[4]	. .	. .	. .	1 005	1 305	1 410	1 421	1 775	1 422	1 105
Cyprus	192	197	289	296	415	209	222	201	321	. .
Czech Rep.[5]	. .	. .	. .	. .	. .	1 031	965	900	902	880
Czechoslovakia[42]	1 816	2 683	2 334	1 520	1 547	. .	. .	. .	. .	. .
Denmark	3 304	3 224	3 226	3 283	3 224	3 230	3 150	3 118	3 126	3 170
Estonia[7]	. .	. .	. .	. .	21.4	28.9	36.7	36.4	34.2	51.9
Finland[8]	1 858	1 854	1 887	2 180	2 219	2 155	2 120	1 909	2 084	2 160
France	51 429	52 099	51 851	52 198	50 527	49 979	50 233	47 768	46 596	47 061
Georgia[9]	. .	. .	. .	. .	121	214	[273]	[142]	144	140
German DR[10]	. .	. .	. .	. .	. .	. .	. .	. .	. .	. .
Germany[11]	54 022	53 840	56 760	52 533	49 951	44 930	41 906	41 160	40 343	39 106
Greece	5 340	5 001	5 059	4 797	4 987	4 866	4 950	5 056	5 359	5 702
Hungary[2]	1 818	1 511	1 284	987	910	819	694	612	554	530
Ireland[12]	496	495	527	552	553	559	682	688	726	755
Italy	22 667	22 846	21 974	22 283	21 643	21 758	21 220	19 376	21 369	21 582
Latvia[13]	. .	. .	. .	. .	. .	38.6	45.0	43.6	33.8	38.1
Lithuania[7]	. .	. .	. .	. .	. .	51.1	27.6	27.5	33.9	59.3
Luxembourg	132	121	126	139	145	132	146	142	147	151
Malta[14]	27.7	25.5	22.4	22.8	27.2	28.9	31.0	31.2	32.6	. .

MILITARY EXPENDITURE AND ARMS PRODUCTION 223

Moldova	..	..	..	..	..	..	..	30	29	24
Netherlands	9 809	9 907	9 628	9 362	9 308	8 549	8 249	8 011	8 076	8 014
Norway	3 645	3 745	3 774	3 660	3 968	3 697	3 885	3 383	3 696	3 591
Poland	4 119	3 442	3 661	2 536	2 502	2 773	2 675	2 720	2 853	2 935
Portugal	2 321	2 435	2 503	2 569	2 639	2 547	2 484	2 670	2 573	2 815
Romania	1 373	1 411	1 401	1 362	1 072	647	771	878	694	..
Russia/USSR[15]	[258 800]	[240 000]	[203 000]	..	1 (47 500)	(41 900)	(40 000)	(24 600)	(23 300)	(24 100)
Slovak Rep.[5]						344	356	435	426	430
Slovenia[4]					274	238	233	268	230	
Spain	9 824	10 164	9 517	9 225	8 529	9 275	8 347	8 652	8 451	8 342
Sweden	5 687	5 881	6 031	5 654	5 435	5 351	5 404	5 595	5 744	5 885
Switzerland	5 321	5 653	5 874	5 699	5 395	4 795	4 928	4 793	4 542	4 415
Turkey	3 936	4 552	5 502	5 655	5 948	6 578	6 431	6 606	7 396	7 461
UK[16]	42 560	42 714	41 649	43 022	38 890	38 022	36 771	33 896	34 096	32 837
Ukraine[3]						[538]		2 222	2 033	1 628
Yugoslavia (former)[43]	4 562	3 699	458							
Yugoslavia[18]								597		
Middle East										
Bahrain	205	211	231	251	267	260	263	273	[282]	[360]
Egypt	2 487	2 005	1 973	1 987	1 946	1 890	1 968			
Iran[19]	1 903	1 799	2 089	2 175	2 076	2 635	3 586	2 597	2 504	2 715
Iraq										
Israel	7 795	7 516	7 851	7 534	7 707	7 200	7 250	7 378	7 716	8 054
Jordan[20]	669	520	454	444	432	453	508	552	570	585
Kuwait	2 075	2 574	9 928	12 933	6 555	3 174	3 369	3 693	3 597	(3 325)
Lebanon	94.1		300	283	458	382	480	490	428	
Oman[21]	1 794	1 802	2 022	1 676	2 008	1 882	1 999	2 018	1 879	1 745
Saudi Arabia	15 413	14 580	[14 927]	[28 459]	15 382	17 375	15 010	13 218	(16 789)	(17 455)
Syria	2 953	3 020	2 801	4 529	4 197	3 322	3 585	3 608	3 435	..
UAE[22]	(3 718)	(2 279)	(2 149)	(1 905)	..	2 300	2 096	1 950	[1 951]	..
Yemen, North	491	536								
Yemen, South	..	..								

224 MILITARY SPENDING AND ARMAMENTS, 1997

State	1988	1989	1990	1991	1992	1993	1994	1995	1996	1997
Yemen[23]	. .	. .	2 289	2 013	1 699	1 230	1 097	879	. .	. .
Asia										
South Asia										
Bangladesh	389	376	364	397	438	470	475	474	. .	. .
India	7 574	7 737	7 660	7 126	6 814	7 718	7 752	8 018	8 153	9 015
Nepal	28.4	29.3	32.1	31.4	31.5	35.9	37.2	36.5	35.8	36.7
Pakistan	2 959	2 945	3 111	3 349	3 582	3 617	3 473	(3 427)	(3 522)	(3 410)
Sri Lanka	204	157	214	293	328	351	408	(663)	(775)	(665)
East Asia										
Brunei[25]	426	425	480	. .	. .	. .	[262]	[269]	[319]	. .
Cambodia	. .	. .	. .	. .	. .	. .	. .	. .	113	. .
China, P. R.[26]	5 833	5 675	6 314	6 940	7 466	7 348	7 658	7 576	7 823	7 920
Indonesia	1 896	1 943	2 150	2 187	2 354	2 262	2 499	2 630	2 859	[2 900]
Japan	45 419	47 391	46 982	47 672	48 815	49 373	49 635	50 117	51 095	51 355
Korea, North[44]	(1 756)	(1 845)	(1 961)	(2 030)	(2 083)	(2 133)	(2 190)	. .	. .	. .
Korea, South	10 594	11 261	11 675	12 648	13 140	13 011	13 624	14 410	15 488	16 615
Laos	. .	. .	. .	. .	. .	. .	. .	109	. .	. .
Malaysia	1 167	1 399	1 502	2 044	2 032	2 159	2 339	2 444	2 349	2 295
Mongolia	79.2	69.8	79.2	[37.6]	14.3	5.8	4.1	10.7	11.4	. .
Myanmar	1 424	2 530	3 008	2 610	3 023	3 480	3 699	3 932	. .	. .
Philippines	1 217	1 158	938	854	861	923	978	1 081	1 274	[920]
Singapore	2 048	2 265	2 530	2 587	2 788	2 846	2 953	3 687	3 959	4 157
Taiwan	7 899	8 886	9 584	9 952	10 023	10 397	10 067	(10 007)	(9 998)	(9 460)
Thailand	2 424	2 409	2 478	2 664	2 996	3 289	3 321	3 571	3 563	3 445
Viet Nam	1 631	1 036	964	681	504	372	485	. .	. .	. .
Oceania										
Australia	7 709	7 690	[7 727]	7 861	[8 366]	8 214	8 325	7 992	7 914	8 000
Fiji[27]	34.9	40.1	38.8	38.6	35.3	36.2	35.8	34.7	. .	. .
New Zealand[28]	1 089	1 034	945	858	682	633	795	821	682	730

MILITARY EXPENDITURE AND ARMS PRODUCTION

Country											
Papua New Guinea	56.4	..	..	..	..	51.8	77.7	..	49.9	..	..
Tonga	1.2	1.7	1.9	..	1.9	..	..	..	..	..	..
Africa											
North Africa											
Algeria[29]	555	..	542	[606]	593	[868]	1067	1298	1235	1401	1550
Libya	..	..	..	..	..	..	..	..	..	..	..
Morocco	1303	1890	1383	1453	1441	1521	1561	1434	[1404]	..	..
Tunisia	377	402	402	407	390	409	409	345	349	360	
Sub-Saharan Africa											
Angola[19]	..	..	598	613	584	733	301	[417]	..	385	
Benin	..	..	29.7	..	..	..	..	..	..	..	
Botswana[30]	139	151	190	204	189	198	182	166	154	150	
Burkina Faso	45.8	57.5	62.6	52.0	51.0	46.2	37.4	..	..	..	
Burundi	38.4	42.9	45.3	47.5	48.8	48.3	50.6	42.1	48.8	50.0	
Cameroon	155	159	171	163	149	144	126	[129]	..	..	
Cape Verde	7.6	..	..	..	..	3.2	..	..	4.6	5.0	
Central Afr. Rep.[29]	..	..	..	17.4	17.7	16.1	14.2	13.0	12.0	..	
Chad	..	..	..	..	..	34.0	26.9	20.0	..	..	
Congo	..	..	..	..	..	..	..	..	..	..	
Congo, Dem. Rep.	209	71.0	60.8	45.3	143	274	9.9	17.4	..	..	
Côte d'Ivoire	119	128	123	125	122	121	107	..	33.0	..	
Djibouti	..	..	44.7	36.5	..	..	..	40.5	..	..	
Eritrea[31]	..	..	..	..	..	104	78.5	125	130	..	
Ethiopia	511	550	520	247	133	135	127	118	..	..	
Gabon	..	..	..	..	..	..	..	..	..	..	
Gambia[29]	2.5	3.4	3.9	4.6	3.8	2.7	2.5	3.2	4.2	..	
Ghana	23.3	24.7	26.5	38.0	52.7	71.6	52.5	49.0	45.2	45.5	
Guinea-Bissau	..	3.9	..	..	..	..	..	..	..	..	
Kenya[29]	306	288	300	234	158	131	129	147	..	..	
Lesotho	25.1	33.7	31.8	27.0	25.5	23.6	27.7	34.8	..	..	
Liberia	35.6	[33.8]	45.6	31.8	31.4	45.2	45.5	..	..	..	
Madagascar	37.5	36.0	37.7	39.0	36.8	35.2	29.6	27.2	26.4	18.0	

State	1988	1989	1990	1991	1992	1993	1994	1995	1996	1997
Malawi	17.4	18.8	17.7	15.8	13.1	11.3	18.1	15.2	15.9	. .
Mali	38.3	39.4	37.8	. .	. .	. .	. .	. .	. .	. .
Mauritania	42.4	37.5	35.2	33.3	32.1	31.1	29.9	28.9	. .	. .
Mauritius	6.5	8.8	11.0	12.4	12.9	12.5	13.5	14.3	13.3	. .
Mozambique[32]	92.2	116	104	103	103	116	174	69.4	53.8	56.0
Namibia[33]	. .	. .	. .	133	129	76.9	61.3	68.1	73.0	. .
Niger	13.9	15.0	32.3	. .	. .	. .	. .	. .	. .	. .
Nigeria	884	759	728	[1 001]	939	791	522	428	548	520
Rwanda	32.9	38.8	89.0	123	101	97.9	26.4	56.1	. .	. .
Senegal	85.2	87.6	87.3	85.0	82.6	. .	. .	. .	. .	. .
Seychelles	15.7	17.4	18.0	19.6	22.7	14.3	12.6	11.6	11.1	. .
Sierra Leone	6.6	10.3	11.6	20.1	25.5	27.4	25.9	25.0	18.4	9.0
Somalia[45]	46.4	8.6	. .	. .	. .	. .	. .	. .	. .	. .
South Africa	5 315	5 243	4 719	3 836	3 428	3 076	3 208	2 949	2 854	2 440
Sudan[29]	588	830	727	546	465	495	176	153	204	. .
Swaziland	11.4	12.5	18.2	19.1	23.9	26.4	27.3	27.1	28.6	. .
Tanzania	89.4	86.8	72.0	74.0	. .	. .	75.6	. .	. .	. .
Togo	41.0	43.1	44.1	41.2	40.8	44.5	32.7	30.9	. .	. .
Uganda	63.5	106	117	107	77.5	92.1	154	200	240	. .
Zambia[19]	. .	173	152	104	117	55.7	65.9	55.7	(36.5)	. .
Zimbabwe	384	387	391	372	297	264	274	256	235	. .
Americas										
North America										
Canada[16]	11 055	10 965	10 976	9 897	9 963	9 917	9 686	9 077	8 262	7 595
Mexico	1 104	869	932	1 043	1 118	1 225	1 589	1 224	1 279	1 165
USA[16]	377 620	373 618	356 994	313 647	331 280	313 784	296 188	278 856	263 727	258 963
Central America										
Belize[19]	4.6	5.0	5.4	5.2	5.7	6.9	8.3	8.8	. .	. .
Costa Rica[34]	30.5	29.8	123	111	113	125	159	164	. .	. .

MILITARY EXPENDITURE AND ARMS PRODUCTION 227

El Salvador	237	241	204	185	161	123	104	97.0	87.8	84.6
Guatemala	179	176	201	152	181	179	188	(193)	111	88.8
Honduras	54.6	81.8	74.1	(50.5)	(51.6)	(43.7)	(52.6)	(47.0)	(45.2)	25.6
Nicaragua[35]	[153]	[112]	[231]	49.8	40.2	35.5	34.1	32.1	31.9	..
Panama	109	108	78.5	83.7	89.1	96.7	99.6	96.8	96.7	..
South America										
Argentina[46]	5 614	5 043	5 043	3 381	3 487	3 676	3 702	3 751	3 450	3 266
Bolivia	88.9	96.4	131	133	127	133	131	132	68.8	..
Brazil[47]	(7 940)	(9 060)	(6 240)	(3 933)	(5 513)	7 270	7 429	10 902	(13 175)	[13 900]
Chile[38]	963	1 018	977	1 002	1 038	1 069	1 077	1 106	1 148	1 130
Colombia	813	908	936	887	946	965	1 080	708	..	..
Ecuador	325	308	317	373	471	514	470	..	..	..
Guyana[48]	3.7	..	3.6	5.6	11.0	13.0	15.4	14.5	13.2	..
Paraguay	66.9	96.8	95.6	134	130	126	116	122	(123)	..
Peru	[1 772]	[1 243]	1 042	754	908	[848]	(877)	834	796	..
Uruguay	378	412	396	306	406	316	467	286	273	..
Venezuela[41]	1 190	703	863	1 238	(2 227)	[1 613]	(1 247)	(1 201)	(811)	(870)

Table 6A.4. Military expenditure by region and country, as percentage of gross domestic product, 1988–96

State	1988	1989	1990	1991	1992	1993	1994	1995	1996
Europe									
Albania[2]	5.6	5.8	6.1	3.1	2.7	2.5	2.1	2.0	1.5
Armenia[3]	. .	. .	. .	. .	. .	. .	. .	. .	. .
Austria	1.1	1.1	. .	. .	. .	0.1	0.9	0.9	0.9
Azerbaijan[3]	. .	. .	0.1	0.1	0.1	7.0	4.5	. .	. .
Belarus[2, 3]	. .	. .	. .	. .	6.5	1.8	2.0	1.4	1.2
Belgium	2.7	2.5	2.4	2.3	1.9	1.8	1.7	1.7	1.6
Bulgaria[2]	4.6	4.1	3.6	3.4	2.8	2.9	2.3	2.3	1.8
Croatia[4]	. .	. .	. .	. .	. .	. .	14.0	17.9	14.5
Cyprus	3.9	3.7	5.1	5.0	6.2	2.8	2.8	2.3	3.4
Czech Rep.[5]	. .	. .	. .	. .	. .	2.5	2.3	1.9	1.8
Czechoslovakia[6]	4.4	6.2	5.4	4.2	4.6	. .	. .	. .	. .
Denmark	2.1	2.1	2.1	2.1	2.0	2.0	1.9	1.8	1.8
Estonia[7]	. .	. .	. .	. .	3.7	1.3	1.5	1.4	1.2
Finland[8]	1.5	1.4	1.4	1.9	2.0	1.9	1.8	1.5	1.6
France	3.8	3.7	3.6	3.6	3.4	3.4	3.3	3.1	3.0
Georgia[9]	. .	. .	. .	. .	1.8	1.3	[2.9]	[1.5]	1.3
German DR[10]	. .	. .	. .	1	. .	. .	. .	. .	. .
Germany[11]	2.9	2.8	2.8	2.3	2.1	2.0	1.8	1.7	1.7
Greece	5.2	4.6	4.7	4.3	4.5	4.4	4.4	4.4	4.5
Hungary[2]	3.4	2.8	2.5	2.2	2.1	1.9	1.6	1.6	1.6
Ireland[12]	1.1	1.0	1.1	1.1	1.1	1.0	1.2	1.1	1.1
Italy	2.3	2.3	2.1	2.1	2.1	2.1	2.0	1.8	1.9
Latvia[13]	. .	. .	. .	. .	. .	0.8	0.9	0.1	0.8
Lithuania[7]	. .	. .	. .	. .	. .	0.8	0.5	0.5	0.5
Luxembourg	1.3	1.1	1.1	0.9	0.9	0.8	0.8	0.7	0.7
Malta[14]	1.3	1.1	0.9	0.9	0.1	1.0	1.0	0.1	0.1
Moldova[3]	. .	. .	. .	. .	. .	0.4	0.6	0.8	0.8

MILITARY EXPENDITURE AND ARMS PRODUCTION

Country								
Netherlands	2.9	2.8	2.6	2.5	2.3	2.1	2.0	2.0
Norway	3.0	3.0	2.9	2.8	2.7	2.8	2.3	2.3
Poland	2.5	1.8	2.7	2.3	2.6	2.4	2.3	2.8
Portugal	2.8	2.8	2.8	2.8	2.6	2.5	2.6	2.4
Romania	3.3	3.6	3.5	3.6	2.1	2.4	3.4	3.5
Russia/USSR[15]	[15.8]	[14.2]	[12.3]	(5.5)	(5.3)	(5.8)	(3.7)	(3.7)
Slovak Rep.[5]	:	:	:	—	2.2	2.2	2.5	2.3
Slovenia[4]	:	:	:	:	1.5	1.4	1.8	1.6
Spain	2.1	2.1	1.8	1.7	1.7	1.5	1.6	1.5
Sweden	2.5	2.5	2.6	2.5	2.5	2.5	2.4	2.4
Switzerland	1.8	1.9	1.9	1.8	1.6	1.6	1.6	1.5
Turkey	3.0	3.3	3.5	3.7	3.8	3.9	3.8	4.3
UK[16]	4.2	4.1	4.0	4.2	3.6	3.4	3.0	3.0
Ukraine[3]	:	:	:	:	[0.8]	4.0	4.1	4.5
Yugoslavia (former)	3.7	3.7	:	:	:	:	:	:
Yugoslavia[18]	:	:	:	:	:	5.7	4.2	:
Middle East								
Bahrain	5.5	5.4	5.4	5.6	5.4	5.3	5.4	[5.4]
Egypt	4.5	3.5	3.4	3.4	3.1	3.0	3.0	:
Iran[19]	3.2	3.1	2.9	2.6	2.6	3.4	2.6	2.5
Iraq	:	:	:	:	:	:	:	:
Israel	13.0	12.3	12.3	10.9	10.5	8.9	8.5	8.7
Jordan[20]	11.4	10.6	9.5	9.4	7.8	8.3	8.4	8.8
Kuwait	8.2	8.5	48.5	117	31.8	13.3	13.9	11.9
Lebanon	:	:	:	3.5	11.7	8.0	7.7	6.3
Oman[21]	20.1	18.6	18.3	14.8	16.2	15.7	14.7	13.2
Saudi Arabia	17.6	15.4	[12.8]	[22.6]	11.7	11.9	10.6	(13.2)
Syria	7.9	8.0	6.9	10.4	9.0	7.4	7.3	6.7
UAE[22]	(6.7)	(5.8)	(4.7)	(4.7)	5.9	5.5	4.9	[4.5]
Yemen, North	:	:	:	:	:	:	:	:
Yemen, South	:	:	:	:	:	:	:	:
Yemen[23]	:	:	:	19.8	18.1	16.9	:	:

State	1988	1989	1990	1991	1992	1993	1994	1995	1996
Asia									
Central Asia									
Kazakhstan[24]	. .	. .	. .	. .	. .	. .	. .	. .	. .
Kyrgystan[3]	. .	. .	. .	. .	. .	. .	. .	. .	. .
Tajikistan[3]	. .	. .	. .	. .	. .	. .	. .	. .	. .
Turkmenistan[3]	. .	. .	. .	. .	. .	. .	. .	. .	. .
Uzbekistan[3]	. .	. .	. .	. .	. .	. .	. .	. .	. .
South Asia									
Bangladesh	1.7	1.6	1.5	1.6	1.7	1.8	1.6	1.6	. .
India	3.4	3.2	2.9	2.7	2.5	2.6	2.5	2.5	2.5
Nepal	0.9	0.9	0.9	0.8	0.8	0.9	0.9	0.8	0.8
Pakistan	6.5	6.2	6.2	6.2	6.4	6.2	5.7	(5.4)	(5.6)
Sri Lanka	2.1	1.6	2.1	2.8	3.0	3.1	3.4	(5.1)	(6.0)
East Asia									
Brunei[25]	6.2	6.2	6.2	. .	. .	. .	[.]	[.]	[.]
Cambodia	. .	. .	. .	. .	. .	. .	. .	. .	4.7
China, P. R.[26]	1.6	1.6	1.6	1.5	1.4	1.2	1.2	1.1	1.1
Indonesia	1.7	1.6	1.6	1.5	1.6	1.3	1.3	1.3	1.3
Japan	1.0	1.0	0.1	0.9	0.1	0.1	0.1	0.1	0.1
Korea, North	. .	. .	. .	(84.4)	(83.3)	(83.6)	. .	. .	. .
Korea, South	4.0	4.0	3.7	3.7	3.6	3.4	3.3	3.2	3.2
Laos	. .	. .	. .	. .	. .	. .	. .	6.3	. .
Malaysia	2.5	2.7	2.6	3.3	3.0	3.0	2.9	2.8	2.4
Mongolia	8.7	7.9	5.7	[4.7]	2.5	2.9	2.5	2.2	2.2
Myanmar	2.2	3.3	3.6	3.3	3.6	3.8	3.8	3.9	. .
Philippines	1.9	1.7	1.4	1.3	1.3	1.4	1.4	1.5	1.6
Singapore	4.7	4.6	4.7	4.4	4.6	4.1	3.8	4.3	4.3
Taiwan	4.6	4.9	4.9	4.7	4.5	4.3	4.0	(3.9)	(3.7)
Thailand	2.7	2.4	2.2	2.2	2.3	2.3	2.2	2.1	1.9

MILITARY EXPENDITURE AND ARMS PRODUCTION

Viet Nam	..	..	8.7	6.1	3.7	2.9	4.0	..	..
Oceania									
Australia	2.7	2.5	[2.5]	2.6	[2.7]	2.6	2.5	2.4	2.3
Fiji[27]	2.2	2.3	2.2	2.2	1.9	1.9	1.8	1.7	..
New Zealand[28]	2.2	2.1	1.9	1.7	1.4	1.2	1.5	1.5	1.2
Papua New Guinea	1.4	2.2	..	1.4	1.3	1.2	1.1	..	..
Tonga	0.8	1.1	1.3	..	1.2	..	..	..	..
Africa									
North Africa									
Algeria[29]	1.9	1.7	[1.5]	1.2	[1.9]	2.6	3.2	3.0	3.4
Libya	..	..	..	..	..	..	..	..	..
Morocco	4.1	5.8	4.1	4.1	4.3	4.7	4.5	4.4	[3.9]
Tunisia	2.7	2.8	2.7	2.6	2.3	2.4	2.3	1.9	1.8
Sub-Saharan Africa									
Angola[19]	13.0	11.5	11.5	12.5	10.5	25.6	36.8	[7.9]	..
Benin	2.3	1.9	1.8	..	..	..	..	..	..
Botswana[30]	4.4	3.6	4.5	4.7	4.5	4.9	4.1	3.7	3.2
Burkina Faso	2.6	2.9	3.0	2.3	2.3	2.1	..	..	..
Burundi	3.2	3.4	3.5	3.8	3.6	3.2	4.2	3.5	4.9
Cameroon	1.4	1.5	1.7	1.7	1.6	1.5	1.6	[1.6]	..
Cape Verde	1.8	..	..	..	..	..	..	..	..
Central Afr. Rep.[29]	..	..	..	1.6	1.7	1.6	1.3	1.1	1.1
Chad	..	..	..	..	..	3.8	2.7	2.0	..
Congo	..	..	..	..	..	..	..	..	..
Congo, Dem. Rep.	2.2	0.8	0.6	0.5	1.9	4.7	0.2	0.3	..
Côte d'Ivoire	1.2	1.4	1.5	1.4	1.4	1.4	1.1	..	..
Djibouti	..	..	..	..	..	..	..	..	..
Eritrea[31]	..	..	..	..	1.6	..	..	..	..
Ethiopia	9.8	10.7	9.6	5.6	2.8	2.6	2.3	2.0	1.8
Gabon	..	..	..	..	..	..	..	..	..
Gambia[29]	0.8	0.1	1.1	1.3	1.1	0.9	0.8	1.1	1.4
Ghana	0.4	0.4	0.4	0.6	0.8	1.1	0.7	0.8	0.6

232 MILITARY SPENDING AND ARMAMENTS, 1997

State	1988	1989	1990	1991	1992	1993	1994	1995	1996
Guinea-Bissau	. .	2.2	. .	. .	. .	. .	. .	. .	. .
Kenya[29]	2.7	2.5	2.7	2.2	1.6	1.6	1.6	1.7	. .
Lesotho	3.1	3.8	3.8	3.3	3.1	2.7	2.9	3.3	. .
Liberia	2.3	[2.3]	. .	. .	. .	. .	. .	. .	. .
Madagascar	1.4	1.2	1.2	1.3	1.2	1.1	0.9	0.9	0.8
Malawi	1.5	1.5	1.3	1.1	1.0	0.8	1.4	1.0	0.8
Mali	2.4	2.3	2.1	. .	. .	. .	. .	. .	. .
Mauritania	4.5	4.0	3.8	3.5	3.4	3.1	2.9	2.7	. .
Mauritius	0.2	0.3	0.4	0.4	0.4	0.3	0.4	0.4	0.3
Mozambique[32]	9.2	10.3	10.1	8.7	8.3	7.6	11.7	4.6	3.4
Namibia[33]				4.7	4.5	2.7	1.9	2.2	2.3
Niger	0.8	0.9	1.9	. .	. .	. .	. .	. .	. .
Nigeria	1.2	0.1	0.9	[1.1]	0.9	0.9	0.7	0.6	0.7
Rwanda	1.5	1.7	4.1	6.2	5.4	6.2	3.5	4.5	. .
Senegal	2.0	2.1	2.0	1.9	1.8	. .	. .	. .	. .
Seychelles	4.3	4.3	4.0	4.4	4.7	2.8	2.5	2.3	2.2
Sierra Leone	0.5	0.8	. .	. .	2.5	2.6	2.5	2.6	1.8
Somalia	. .	7.5	. .	. .	. .	. .	. .	. .	. .
South Africa	4.3	4.1	3.6	3.0	2.8	2.5	2.5	2.2	2.1
Sudan[29]	2.0	3.2	2.9	2.3	1.9	1.9	1.5	1.2	1.6
Swaziland	1.1	1.1	1.5	1.6	1.9	2.1	2.2	2.2	2.3
Tanzania	1.8	1.7	1.5	1.5	. .	. .	1.5	. .	. .
Togo	3.1	3.1	3.1	2.8	2.9	4.0	2.7	2.5	. .
Uganda	1.8	2.7	2.9	2.4	1.6	1.9	2.7	3.3	3.8
Zambia[19]	. .	4.2	3.7	2.6	3.0	1.6	2.0	1.7	(1.1)
Zimbabwe	6.2	5.9	4.4	3.8	3.7	3.4	3.2	3.3	2.7
Americas									
North America									
Canada[16]	2.0	2.0	2.0	1.9	1.9	1.9	1.7	1.6	1.4

MILITARY EXPENDITURE AND ARMS PRODUCTION 233

Mexico	0.5	0.4	0.4	0.4	0.4	0.5	0.4
USA[16]	5.8	5.6	5.3	4.7	4.9	4.5	4.2	3.8	3.6
Central America								
Belize[19]	1.3	1.2	1.2	1.1	1.1	1.3	1.5	1.5
Costa Rica[34]	0.5	0.4	1.8	1.6	1.5	1.5	1.8	1.8
El Salvador	2.8	2.9	2.7	2.4	2.0	1.5	1.2	1.0
Guatemala	1.6	1.6	1.7	1.3	1.5	1.4	1.3	(1.3)
Honduras	1.6	2.4	2.2	(1.5)	(1.5)	(1.2)	(1.3)	(1.2)
Nicaragua[35]	[8.7]	[6.5]	[2.1]	2.8	2.3	2.0	1.9	2.0
Panama	2.1	2.1	1.4	1.4	1.3	1.3	1.3	1.2
South America								
Argentina[36]	1.6	1.6	1.8	1.3	1.3	1.3	1.3	1.2
Bolivia	1.7	1.8	2.3	2.3	2.1	2.2	2.1	1.9
Brazil[37]	(1.4)	(1.7)	(1.3)	(0.8)	(1.1)	1.3	1.1	1.5	[1.9]
Chile[38]	2.3	2.2	2.2	2.1	2.0	1.9	1.8	1.6
Colombia	1.3	1.4	1.4	1.3	1.4	1.3	1.4	0.9
Ecuador	2.0	2.0	1.9	2.2	2.7	3.1	2.7	..
Guyana[39]	3.3	..	0.9	0.6	1.0	1.0	1.0	0.9	0.8
Paraguay	1.0	1.3	1.3	1.7	1.6	1.5	1.4	1.4	(1.3)
Peru[40]	[2.0]	[1.9]	2.0	1.5	1.9	[1.7]	(1.6)	1.4	1.3
Uruguay	2.1	2.4	2.4	1.8	2.3	1.8	2.5	1.6	1.5
Venezuela[41]	1.5	0.9	1.1	1.5	(2.7)	(2.0)	(1.6)	(1.6)	(1.0)

Notes: Data should not be compared with those in previous SIPRI Yearbooks. Some series have been significantly revised. Figures for NATO member countries are NATO standardized data, which do not correspond to national data because of differences in definition.

[1] Throughout the series, organizations include all those countries that were members in 1997. Geographical regions and organizations have been harmonized with those used for the SIPRI arms transfers statistics (appendix 8A). Income groups are based on figures of 1995 GNP per capita as calculated by the World Bank and presented in its *World Development Report 1997* (International Bank for Reconstruction and Development and Oxford University Press: Washington, DC and New York, June 1997). Africa excludes Egypt and Libya; Asia excludes Central Asia, Afghanistan, Cambodia and Laos; Europe excludes Yugoslavia before 1991 and Yugoslavia (Serbia and Montenegro) after 1992; the Middle East includes Egypt and excludes Iraq. ASEAN excludes Laos; OPEC excludes Iraq and Libya; OSCE excludes Yugoslavia before 1991 and Yugoslavia (Serbia and Montenegro) after 1992; 'low-income' excludes Afghanistan, Cambodia and Laos; 'middle-income' excludes Yugoslavia before 1991 and Yugoslavia (Serbia and Montenegro) after 1992.

2 Figures exclude pensions and expenditure for internal security.
3 Became independent after the disintegration of the Soviet Union in Dec. 1991.
4 Declared its independence from the former Yugoslavia in June 1991 and was recognized by the European Community in Jan. 1992 and by the United Nations in May 1992.
5 Formed on 1 Jan. 1993 after the breakup of Czechoslovakia.
6 Divided into the Czech Republic and the Republic of Slovakia on 1 Jan. 1993.
7 Became independent in Sep. 1991.
8 Figures exclude expenditure on internal security and from 1991 onward include pensions.
9 Became independent after the disintegration of the Soviet Union in Dec. 1991. Figures include expenditure for military border troops.
10 Integrated into the Federal Republic of Germany on 1 Jan. 1991.
11 Figures up to and including 1990 refer to the former Federal Republic of Germany (West Germany).
12 Figures exclude military pensions.
13 Became independent in Sep. 1991. Figures include expenditure on frontier and home guards.
14 Figures exclude pensions and include expenditure on internal security.
15 Figures up to and including 1991 are for the USSR. For sources and methods of the military expenditure figures for the USSR and Russia, see appendix 6D in this volume.
16 Figures are for fiscal year rather than for calendar year.
17 Became independent after the disintegration of the Soviet Union in Dec. 1991. Apart from national defence, figures include expenditure for military pensions, housing construction, conversion, destruction of strategic arms, interior troops, frontier troops and the national guard.
18 Serbia and Montenegro announced the creation of the Federal Republic of Yugoslavia in Apr. 1992. Figures include pensions.
19 Figures include expenditure for public order and safety.
20 Figures are expenditure for defence and security.
21 Recurrent expenditure only. Figures are expenditure for defence and national security.
22 Figures exclude individual military spending by each of the 7 emirates that form the United Arab Emirates.
23 The People's Democratic Republic of Yemen (South Yemen) and the Yemen Arab Republic (North Yemen) merged in May 1990 to form the Republic of Yemen.
24 Became independent after the disintegration of the Soviet Union in Dec. 1991. Figures include expenditure for law enforcement.
25 Expenditure for the Royal Brunei Armed Forces only.
26 Figures are official data, although these are known to be an underestimate.
27 Figures exclude military pensions.
28 Figures exclude pensions.
29 Recurrent expenditure only.

30 Figures are for recurrent and development expenditure.
31 Became independent from Ethiopia in May 1993. Figures for 1995 include demobilization costs.
32 Figures include expenditure for the demobilization of government and RENAMO soldiers and the formation of a new unified army from 1994 onward.
33 Became independent on 21 Mar. 1990.
34 Figures include expenditure for the Guardia de Assistencia Rural (Rural Guard) and pensions for its personnel, within the Ministry of Public Security. Costa Rica abolished its armed forces in 1948 but the security forces have a military function, i.e., the maintenance of the country's territorial integrity.
35 Figures are uncertain because of extremely rapid inflation and a change in the currency. All figures have been converted to the most recent currency.
36 This state has changed currency during the period. All figures have been converted to the most recent currency. Figures include expenditure for gendarmerie and coastguard and exclude expenditure on the intelligence services. The full amount of pension payments is not included and payments on the military debt has not been identified.
37 This state has changed currency during the period. All figures have been converted to the most recent currency. Figures include only expenditure for the air force, army and navy.
38 Figures exclude expenditure for public order and security (Carabineros and Investigaciones), supporting services, military industries and pensions.
39 Figures include pensions and expenditure on internal security.
40 This state has changed currency during the period. All figures have been converted to the most recent currency.
41 Figures exclude special credits for military equipment. These figures are therefore essentially recurrent expenditure.
42 Divided into the Czech Republic and the Republic of Slovakia on 1 Jan. 1993. Figures are at 1990 prices and exchange rate.
43 At 1990 prices and exchange rate.
44 At current prices and 1995 exchange rate.
45 At current prices and exchange rates.
46 Figures are uncertain because of very rapid inflation and a change in the currency. Figures include expenditure for gendarmerie and coastguard and exclude expenditure on the intelligence services. The full amount of pension payments is not included and payments on the military debt have not been identified.
47 Figures are uncertain because of very rapid inflation and a change in the currency. Figures include only expenditure for the air force, the army and navy activities.
48 At 1990 prices and exchange rate. Figures include pensions and expenditure on internal security.

Source: SIPRI military expenditure database.

Appendix 6B. Tables of NATO military expenditure

Table 6B.1. NATO distribution of military expenditure by category, 1988–97

Figures are in US $m. at 1995 prices and exchange rates. Figures in italics are percentage changes from previous year.

State	Item	1988	1989	1990	1991	1992	1993	1994	1995	1996	1997
North America											
Canada	Personnel	5 019	5 252	5 488	4 889	4 972	4 730	4 979	4 339	3 792	3 821
	Person. change	*–0.3*	*4.6*	*4.5*	*–10.9*	*1.7*	*–4.9*	*5.3*	*–12.9*	*–12.6*	*0.7*
	Equipment	2 222	2 018	1 866	1 791	1 853	1 904	1 685	1 679	1 289	1 246
	Equip. change	*–4.9*	*–9.2*	*–7.5*	*–4.0*	*3.4*	*2.7*	*–11.5*	*–0.4*	*–23.2*	*–3.4*
USA	Personnel	141 985	142 722	130 660	135 496	130 193	121 748	115 513	110 985	102 326	102 808
	Person. change	*2.4*	*0.5*	*–8.5*	*3.7*	*–3.9*	*–6.5*	*–5.1*	*–3.9*	*–7.8*	*0.5*
	Equipment	93 650	94 525	88 535	85 626	75 863	69 032	86 487	77 243	70 943	65 259
	Equip. change	*–8.5*	*0.9*	*–6.3*	*–3.3*	*–11.4*	*–9.0*	*25.3*	*–10.7*	*–8.2*	*–8.0*
Europe											
Belgium	Personnel	3 915	4 060	4 062	4 034	3 140	3 178	3 147	3 163	3 010	3 021
	Person. change	*–1.7*	*3.7*	*0.0*	*–0.7*	*–22.2*	*1.2*	*–1.0*	*0.5*	*–4.8*	*0.4*
	Equipment	737	599	469	480	394	320	354	240	231	229
	Equip. change	*–12.2*	*–18.8*	*–21.7*	*2.3*	*–17.9*	*–18.9*	*10.8*	*–32.2*	*–3.8*	*–0.8*
Denmark	Personnel	1 916	1 928	1 884	1 878	1 828	1 835	1 849	1 886	1 867	1 892
	Person. change	*7.1*	*0.6*	*–2.3*	*–0.3*	*–2.7*	*0.4*	*0.8*	*2.0*	*–1.1*	*1.4*
	Equipment	476	422	481	519	574	472	501	390	391	475
	Equip. change	*–1.5*	*–11.2*	*13.8*	*7.9*	*10.6*	*–17.8*	*6.2*	*–22.2*	*0.3*	*21.7*
Germany	Personnel	26 849	27 512	29 572	29 734	29 271	26 689	25 479	25 354	25 053	24 402
	Person. change	*0.3*	*2.5*	*7.5*	*0.5*	*–1.6*	*–8.8*	*–4.5*	*–0.5*	*–1.2*	*–2.6*
	Equipment	10 426	10 230	10 047	8 195	6 643	4 987	4 568	4 692	4 478	4 575
	Equip. change	*–4.7*	*–1.9*	*–1.8*	*–18.4*	*–18.9*	*–24.9*	*–8.4*	*2.7*	*–4.6*	*2.2*

MILITARY EXPENDITURE AND ARMS PRODUCTION

Greece	Personnel	3 108	3 076	3 243	3 089	3 062	3 027	3 119	3 201	3 280	3 547
	Person. change	−0.3	−1.0	5.4	−4.7	−0.9	−1.2	3.0	2.6	2.5	8.1
	Equipment	1 244	1 095	1 083	974	1 167	1 202	1 208	1 001	1 131	1 106
	Equip. change	43.2	−12.0	−1.2	−10.1	19.8	3.0	0.5	−17.1	12.9	−2.2
Italy	Personnel	13 101	13 410	13 536	14 284	13 787	13 686	13 921	13 059	14 787	14 935
	Person. change	4.1	2.4	0.9	5.5	−3.5	−0.7	1.7	−6.2	13.2	1.0
	Equipment	4 647	4 683	3 845	3 632	3 246	3 742	3 289	2 906	3 056	3 108
	Equip. change	5.7	0.8	−17.9	−5.5	−10.6	15.3	−12.1	−11.6	5.1	1.7
Luxembourg	Personnel	99	93	100	98	110	102	114	115	121	118
	Person. change	10.7	−5.4	7.4	−2.1	12.0	−7.1	11.6	1.0	5.0	−2.4
	Equipment	4	5	4	8	7	4	3	3	6	7
	Equip. change	−18.3	24.4	−12.4	86.4	−11.1	−44.5	−17.3	11.6	76.0	13.3
Netherlands	Personnel	5 326	5 320	5 189	5 168	5 352	5 078	4 809	4 807	4 507	4 335
	Person. change	0.8	−0.1	−2.5	−0.4	3.6	−5.1	−5.3	−0.0	−6.2	−3.8
	Equipment	2 001	1 744	1 723	1 461	1 322	1 197	1 386	1 250	1 510	1 466
	Equip. change	14.1	−12.9	−1.2	−15.3	−9.5	−9.4	15.8	−9.8	20.8	−2.9
Norway	Personnel	1 662	1 596	1 634	1 695	1 738	1 331	1 356	1 262	1 297	1 347
	Person. change	0.3	−4.0	2.4	3.7	2.5	−23.4	1.9	−6.9	2.8	3.8
	Equipment	685	929	853	805	968	1 020	1 107	859	998	869
	Equip. change	−12.2	35.5	−8.2	−5.6	20.2	5.4	8.5	−22.4	16.1	−12.9
Portugal	Personnel	1 538	1 739	1 830	1 924	2 125	2 032	1 955	2 077	2 076	2 094
	Person. change	12.3	13.0	5.2	5.2	10.4	−4.3	−3.8	6.2	0.0	0.9
	Equipment	244	290	258	218	58	183	104	158	162	411
	Equip. change	15.6	18.9	−11.0	−15.3	−73.4	215.8	−43.1	51.0	2.9	153.6
Spain	Personnel	5 354	5 824	5 901	5 968	5 928	5 778	5 526	5 684	5 687	5 606
	Person. change	2.5	8.8	1.3	1.1	−0.7	−2.5	−4.4	2.9	0.1	−1.4
	Equipment	2 034	1 860	1 209	1 190	930	1 252	1 018	1 177	1 132	1 151
	Equip. change	−21.7	−8.5	−35.0	−1.6	−21.9	34.7	−18.7	15.5	−3.8	1.7

Turkey	Personnel	1 401	2 098	2 657	2 743	2 897	3 585	3 280	3 363	3 417	3 260
	Person. change	-9.6	49.8	26.6	3.2	5.6	23.8	-8.5	2.5	1.6	-4.6
	Equipment	886	783	1 100	1 284	1 475	1 506	1 884	1 962	2 278	2 432
	Equip. change	-6.1	-11.6	40.6	16.7	14.9	2.1	25.1	4.1	16.1	6.8
UK	Personnel	17 322	16 872	16 826	18 069	17 034	16 540	15 223	14 168	13 741	12 610
	Person. change	-0.3	-2.6	-0.3	7.4	-5.7	-2.9	-8.0	-6.9	-3.0	-8.2
	Equipment	10 810	9 397	7 455	8 346	7 039	9 886	9 156	7 457	8 149	8 603
	Equip. change	-1.8	-13.1	-20.7	12.0	-15.7	40.4	-7.4	-18.6	9.3	5.6
NATO Europe	Personnel	81 592	83 527	86 434	88 684	86 271	82 861	79 776	78 141	78 842	77 166
	Person. change	1.0	2.4	3.5	2.6	-2.7	-4.0	-3.7	-2.1	0.9	-2.1
	Equipment	34 193	32 036	28 527	27 112	23 824	25 772	24 579	22 096	23 522	24 434
	Equip. change	-1.8	-6.3	-11.0	-5.0	-12.1	8.2	-4.6	-10.1	6.5	3.9
NATO total	Personnel	228 596	231 501	222 582	229 069	221 435	209 340	200 268	193 464	184 961	183 795
	Person. change	1.8	1.3	-3.9	2.9	-3.3	-5.5	-4.3	-3.4	-4.4	-0.6
	Equipment	130 065	128 579	118 927	114 529	101 540	96 708	112 751	101 018	95 754	90 938
	Equip. change	-6.8	-1.1	-7.5	-3.7	-11.3	-4.8	16.6	-10.4	-5.2	-5.0

Note: France does not return figures giving this breakdown to NATO. NATO data on the distribution between spending categories include two other categories—infrastructure and other operating expenditure—which are not included here. The NATO data show percentage shares; the dollar figures have been calculated using these percentages and the total expenditures shown in table 6A.2. Calculations are based on rounded input data.

Sources: NATO, Financial and economic data relating to NATO defence, Press release (97)147, 2 Dec 1997, URL <http://www.nato.int/docu/pr/1997/p97-147e.htm>, version current on 16 Dec. 1997; and NATO Press releases M-DPC-2(91)105 (12 Dec. 1991), M-DPC-2(92)100 (10 Dec. 1992) and M-DPC-2(93)76 (8 Dec. 1993).

Table 6B.2. Military equipment expenditure of France, 1988–97

Figures are in US $m. at 1995 prices and exchange rates. Figures in italics are percentage changes from previous year.

Item	1988	1989	1990	1991	1992	1993	1994	1995	1996	1997
Equipment	21 784	22 242	22 273	22 110	20 673	19 859	19 397	16 657	16 469	16 255
Equipment change	*3.3*	*2.1*	*0.1*	*–0.7*	*–6.5*	*–3.9*	*–2.3*	*–14.1*	*–1.1*	*–1.3*

Note: This table was compiled on the basis of domestic data on equipment expenditure as presented in the French defence budget. These figures refer to expenditure which actually took place. Budgetary freezes and cancellations are taken into account. Equipment expenditure includes all items covered by Titles V and VI of the French defence budget (i.e., research and development, prototype construction, procurement of finished equipment, infrastructure and technical and industrial investments, and investment subsidies). This equipment expenditure is not comparable to the equipment expenditure as defined by NATO and presented in table 6B.1. Equipment maintenance and munitions, which fall under operating costs according to the NATO definition, are included in Titles V and VI of the French budget. French equipment expenditure in 1996, according to the NATO definition, has been estimated as 20 per cent lower than the figure given above. The data in this table should therefore be used with caution.

Sources: Assemblée Nationale, *Rapport fait par M. Didier Migaud, au nom de la Commission des Finances, de l'Economie Générale et du Plan sur le projet de loi de finances pour 1998* (no. 230), Document no. 305 (Assemblée Nationale: Paris, 4 Oct. 1997); *Rapport fait par M. Phillippe Auberger, au nom de la Commission des Finances, de l'Economie Générale et du Plan sur le projet de loi de finances pour 1997* (no. 2993), Document no. 3030 (Assemblée Nationale: Paris, 10 Oct. 1996), p. 18; Assemblée Nationale, *Avis présenté, par M. Arthur Paecht, au nom de la Commission des Finances, de l'Economie Générale et du Plan sur le projet de loi (no. 2766) relatif à la programmation militaire pour les années 1997 à 2002*, Document no. 2826 (Assemblée Nationale: Paris, 29 May 1996), p. 25; and Assemblée Nationale, *Avis présenté, par M. Arthur Paecht, au nom de la Commission des Finances, de l'Economie Générale et du Plan sur le projet de loi (no. 1153) relatif à la programmation militaire pour les années 1995 à 2000*, Document no. 1217 (Assemblée Nationale: Paris, 10 May 1994), p. 30.

Table 6B.2 was prepared by Agnès Courades Allebeck.

Appendix 6C. Sources and methods for military expenditure data

This appendix provides only the most basic information.[1] The military expenditure tables in appendix 6A cover 158 countries for the 10-year period 1988–97. These data cannot be combined with the series for earlier years as published in previous SIPRI Yearbooks, since these are updated each year and the revisions can be extensive—not only are significant changes made in figures which were previously estimates, but entire series are revised when new and better sources come to light. As a result there is sometimes considerable variation between data sets for individual countries in different Yearbooks.

I. Purpose of the data

The main purpose of the data on military expenditures is to provide an easily identifiable measure of the scale of resources absorbed by the military. Military expenditure is an input measure which is not directly related to the output of military activities, such as military capability or military security. Long-term trends in military expenditure and sudden changes in trend may be signs of a change in military output, but such interpretations should be made with caution.

Military expenditure data as measured in constant dollars (table 6A.3) are an indicator of the trend in the volume of resources used for military activities with the purpose of allowing comparisons over time for individual countries and comparisons between countries. The share of gross domestic product (GDP—table 6A.4) is a rough indicator of the proportion of national resources used for military activities, and therefore of the economic burden imposed on the national economy.

II. Sources

The sources for military expenditure data are, in order of priority: (*a*) primary sources, that is, official data provided by national governments, either in their official publications or in response to questionnaires; (*b*) secondary sources which quote primary data; and (*c*) other secondary sources.

The first group consists of national budget documents, defence white papers and public finance statistics published by ministries of finance and of defence, central banks and national statistical offices. It also includes government responses to questionnaires about military expenditure sent out by SIPRI, the United Nations or the Organization for Security and Co-operation in Europe (OSCE).

The second group includes international statistics, such as those of NATO and the International Monetary Fund (IMF). Data for NATO countries are taken from NATO defence expenditure statistics as published in a number of NATO sources. Data for many developing countries are taken from the IMF's *Government Financial Statistics*

---

[1] There are many conceptual problems and sources of uncertainty involved in the compilation of military expenditure data, which cannot be dealt with here. The reader is referred to Brzoska, M., 'World military expenditures', eds. K. Hartley and T. Sandler, *Handbook of Defense Economics*, vol. 1 (Elsevier: Amsterdam, 1995).

Yearbook, which provides a defence line for most of its member countries. This group also includes publications of other organizations which provide proper references to the primary sources used. The three main sources in this category are the *Europa Yearbook* (Europa Publications Ltd, London), the *Country Reports* of the Economist Intelligence Unit (London), and *Länderberichte* (German Federal Statistical Office, Wiesbaden).[2]

The third group of sources consists of specialist journals and newspapers.

The main source for economic data (on exchange rates, consumer price indexes and GDP) is for most countries *International Financial Statistics* of the IMF. The source for purchasing power parity rates is the European Bank for Reconstruction and Development (EBRD) statistics.

III. Methods

Definition of military expenditure

Although the lack of sufficiently detailed data makes it difficult to apply a common definition of military expenditure on a worldwide basis, SIPRI has adopted a definition of military expenditure, based on the NATO definition, as a guideline. Where possible, SIPRI military expenditure data include: (*a*) all current and capital expenditure on the armed forces and in the running of defence departments and other government agencies engaged in defence projects and space activities; (*b*) the cost of paramilitary forces when they are judged to be trained and equipped for military operations; (*c*) military research and development, testing and evaluation expenditure; and (*d*) costs of retirement pensions. Military aid is included in the military expenditure of the donor country and excluded from that of the recipient country. Excluded are civil defence, interest on war debts and veterans' payments.

In practice it is not possible to apply this definition for all countries, since this would require much more detailed information than is available about what is included in military budgets and off-budget military expenditure items. In many cases SIPRI cannot make independent estimates but is confined to using the national data provided. Priority is given to the choice of a uniform definition over time for each country to achieve consistency over time, rather than to adjusting the figures for single years according to a common definition. In cases where it is impossible to use the same source and definition for all years, the percentage change between years in the deviant source is applied to the existing series in order to make the trend as correct as possible. In the light of these difficulties, military expenditure data are not suitable for close comparison between individual countries, and are more appropriately used for comparisons over time.

Calculations

The SIPRI military expenditure figures are presented on a calendar-year basis with a few exceptions. The exceptions are Canada, the UK and the USA, for which NATO statistics report data on a fiscal-year basis. Calendar-year data are calculated on the assumption of an even rate of expenditure throughout the fiscal year.

---

[2] *Länderberichte* ceased publication in 1995.

A difficult methodological problem is the reliability of national official data. As a general rule, SIPRI takes national data to be accurate until there is convincing information to the contrary. Where that is the case, estimates have to be made.

The deflator used for conversion from current to constant prices is the consumer price index (CPI) of the country concerned. This choice of deflator is connected to the purpose of the SIPRI data—that they should be an indicator of resource use on an opportunity cost basis.[3]

For most countries the conversion to dollars is made by use of the average market exchange rates. The exceptions are countries in transition whose economies are still so closed that market exchange rates, which are based on price ratios in foreign transactions only, do not accurately reflect the price ratios of the entire economy. For these countries conversion to dollars is made by use of purchasing power parity (PPP) rates.

The ratio of military expenditure to GDP is calculated in domestic currency at current prices and for calendar years.

Table 6A.1 presents aggregate military expenditure data for geographical regions, organizations and economic groupings. The geographical regions and organizations have been harmonized with those used for the SIPRI arms transfers statistics (appendix 8A). The economic groupings are based on figures for 1995 gross national product (GNP) per capita as calculated by the World Bank and presented in its *World Development Report 1997*. For the purpose of calculating aggregate totals estimates have to be made for the countries for which data are lacking for some years. These estimates are made on the assumption that the trend for these countries is the same as for the geographical region in which they are located.

Estimates and the use of brackets

Where accurate military expenditure data are not available, estimates are made as far as possible. SIPRI estimates are presented in square brackets in the tables and are often highly approximate. Estimates are made in two types of case: (*a*) when data are not available; and (*b*) when there is sufficient evidence that the data provided are unreliable. Estimates are always based on empirical evidence and never on assumptions, in order not to build in assumptions in the military expenditure statistics.

Round brackets are used when data are uncertain for other reasons, such as the reliability of the source or the economic context. Figures are more unreliable when inflation is rapid and unpredictable. Supplementary allocations made during the course of the year to cover losses in purchasing power often go unreported and recent military expenditure can appear to be falling in real terms when it is in fact increasing.

Data for the most recent years include two types of estimate which apply to all countries: (*a*) figures for the most recent years are for adopted budget, budget estimates or revised estimates, and are thus more often than not revised in subsequent years; and (*b*) the deflator used for the last year in the series is an estimate. Unless exceptional uncertainty is involved in these estimates, they are not bracketed.

Countries which require special studies for the preparation of a complete and reliable set of military expenditure tables include China, Russia and the member countries of the Commonwealth of Independent States (CIS). For this edition of the Yearbook a special study was commissioned for Russia (appendix 6D).

---

[3] A military-specific deflator would be the more appropriate choice if the objective were to measure the purchasing power in terms of military personnel, goods and services.

Appendix 6D. The military expenditure of the USSR and the Russian Federation, 1987–97

JULIAN COOPER

I. Introduction

Unravelling the mysteries of the military expenditure of the Soviet Union generated a sizeable industry of government and academic analysts, above all in the United States. The issue became politically charged: the US Central Intelligence Agency (CIA) and other organizations responsible for rival estimates were frequently targeted for criticism on the grounds that they under- or over-estimated the true magnitude of the Soviet 'threat'. With the collapse of the Soviet Union, this industry has contracted sharply and the passions and methodological controversies are now fading into history. The problem of assessing the scale of the military expenditure of the Russian Federation and other Soviet successor states has not acquired a similar salience and, with a greater degree of openness, the difficulties of generating estimates of an acceptable accuracy are not nearly as acute. However, problems remain. This appendix reviews the principal issues and provides a summary of the trend of military expenditure first in the USSR and then in Russia over the 11-year period 1987–97.

Any analysis of Soviet and Russian military expenditure encounters a number of methodological problems. For the former command economy of the USSR the problems are well known. The Soviet budgetary process was non-transparent and published information on the military budget and actual outlays was inadequate, especially before 1989. Prices were systematically distorted and the authorities resorted to complex and opaque systems of subsidization of military-related activities, especially with regard to the development and procurement of weapons. In addition, many items of military spending were concealed under budget headings other than 'defence'. For post-communist Russia the problems have changed. With price liberalization, initiated at the beginning of 1992, price distortions have been progressively eliminated, although in 1997 the process was still incomplete, especially with regard to energy prices. Most of the old Soviet-era subsidies have disappeared. However, a new problem arose for Goskomstat (Gosudarstvenny komitet statistiki, the State Committee on Statistics)—accounting for very high inflation, especially during the period 1992–95. In circumstances of rapid inflation, the federal budget underwent revisions after its formal adoption by the Russian Parliament, complicating the assessment of budget fulfilment. As the output of the economy declined and budgetary stringency intensified, actual disbursements to the military increasingly fell below the planned allocations set out in the approved budget. Published information on the Russian defence budget, in particular on actual disbursements, has remained inadequate and assessments of the military burden have been complicated by revisions to the official series for gross domestic product (GDP).

Comparison of Soviet and post-Soviet military spending is especially problematic as it is impossible to derive a series for spending by the Russian Federation before 1992, Soviet data for 1991 are unreliable, and the radical price changes accompanying the transition make it impossible to link the two series directly in a meaningful

Table 6D.1. Expenditure of the Ministry of Defence and Ministry of Atomic Energy of the USSR, 1987–90[a]

	Military expenditure (b. current roubles)	GNP[b] (b. current roubles)	Military expenditure as a percentage of:	
			GNP	Total budget
1987	69.4	825	8.4	16.1
1988	72.8	875	8.3	15.8
1989	76.9	943	8.2	15.9
1990	70.7	1 000	7.1	13.8

[a] Includes expenditure on nuclear weapons.
[b] GNP = gross national product.

Sources: (*a*) for military expenditure: Alexashenko, S., 'The budgetary system in the USSR: impossibility of transformation', *European Economy*, no. 49 (1993), p. 7. These estimates were first published in the Russian newspaper *Megapolis-Express*, no. 8 (1991) (in Russian); and (*b*) for GNP and total budget expenditure: USSR, State Committee on Statistics, *Narodnoye Khozyaystvo SSSR v 1990 g.* [National economy of the USSR, 1990] (Finansy i Statistika: Moscow, 1991), pp. 9, 16.

manner. Finally, for Russia, as a transitional economy, the official exchange rate provides an inadequate basis for international comparisons of military spending, necessitating resort to a purchasing power parity (PPP) rate.

II. Soviet military expenditure, 1987–91

Russian analysts have shown little interest in reassessing military expenditure in the former Soviet system. Much of the relevant evidence remains inaccessible and a substantial research effort would be required to assemble a consistent series taking full account of all the concealed forms of spending and subsidization. The memoir material now available on the late Soviet period tends to confirm the view that no one, not even President Mikhail Gorbachev himself or the Minister of Defence, had anything more than an approximate understanding of the real scale of military expenditure and of the military burden on the economy. As Gorbachev confirms in his memoirs, 'All statistics concerning the military–industrial complex were top secret, inaccessible even to members of the Politburo . . . only two or three people had access to data on the military–industrial complex'.[1] He adds that when, in the face of opposition, new data were published, 'it turned out that military expenditure was not 16 per cent of the state budget, as we had been told, but rather 40 per cent; and its production was not 6 per cent but 20 per cent of the gross national product'.[2] It should be noted that neither at the time nor since have the 40 and 20 per cent figures been explained and it is impossible to say whether they provide a more accurate indication of the true scale of Soviet military expenditure than others provided by other Western and Russian sources. When in 1989 a more complete version of the military budget was published, it still did not present the real level of expenditure of the

---

[1] Gorbachev, M., *Memoirs* (Bantam Books: London, 1997), p. 174.
[2] Gorbachev (note 1), p. 277.

Ministry of Defence (MOD); still less did it provide an accurate picture of the true resource cost of the USSR's military effort, not least because no attempt was made to correct for the chronic price distortions which led to a substantial understatement of expenditure, especially on the procurement of weapons.[3] In addition, the Soviet authorities did not reveal the scale of other military-related expenditure falling outside the 'national defence' chapter of the state budget.

Accepting the limits of the defence budget as revealed in 1989, there is still some interest in additional data that were made public in 1991—an apparently consistent series of estimates for budget allocations to the MOD, together with expenditure on the development and production of nuclear weapons by the Ministry of Atomic Energy (Minatom), for the period 1976–90.[4] Up to and including 1989 it indicates a stable share in gross national product (GNP) of roughly 8 per cent and a share of total budget expenditure of 16–17 per cent. Table 6D.1 shows the expenditure indicated in this source for the four years 1987–90. It should be noted that the estimated expenditure for 1988 differs from another figure (82.5 billion roubles) provided in 1990 by then First Deputy Finance Minister, V. Vladimir Panskov, but no explanation of this higher total was provided.[5]

In the West also, little new data have appeared but there has been some useful reconsideration of the methodologies employed for estimating Soviet military expenditure. In a judicious review of the issues and achievements, James Noren concluded that the 'building-block' method adopted by the CIA probably gave better results than alternative approaches.[6] This is perhaps not surprising, as Noren is a former CIA analyst, and the building-block method had merit at a time when other evidence was sparse. However, the CIA's dollar estimate was based on the use of US prices and wages, that is, it estimated the cost of buying the Soviet defence effort in the United States—a procedure that is open to criticism. It should be noted that the estimates of the CIA and other Western agencies were often mistaken for measures of Soviet military capability and, as such, became highly politicized. In fact, they measured only the resources devoted to sustaining that capability and, in relation to total government spending, provided an indication of government priorities.

Of attempts to use the available Soviet statistical data to estimate defence expenditure, the most comprehensive appeared shortly after the collapse of the USSR. The late Dmitri Steinberg undertook an impressive reconstruction of the Soviet national accounts and derived a series for military expenditure which, with one modification, is presented in table 6D.2.[7] In an attempt to capture the full resource cost of the Soviet military effort, Steinberg introduced what he termed a 'revenue adjustment' factor. The validity of this procedure is also open to question: here, it has been eliminated from the estimates. In the author's opinion, these estimates must be regarded as a first approximation only, but they have been used here because any future recalculation of Soviet military expenditure will almost certainly be based on a reconsideration of Soviet statistics and not on the use of the building-block method or other techniques employed in the absence of adequate statistical evidence.

[3] *Pravda*, 8 June 1989.
[4] Alexashenko, S., 'The budgetary system in the USSR: impossibility of transformation', *European Economy*, no. 49 (1993), p. 7.
[5] *Ekonomika i Zhizn*, no. 15 (1990), p. 7.
[6] Noren, J. H., 'The controversy over Western measures of Soviet defense expenditures', *Post-Soviet Affairs*, vol. 11, no. 3 (1995), pp. 238–76.
[7] Steinberg, D., 'The Soviet defence burden: estimating hidden defence costs', *Soviet Studies*, vol. 44, no. 2 (1992), pp. 237–63.

Table 6D.2. Estimated total military expenditure of the USSR, 1987–90
Figures are in billion current roubles.

	Military expenditure	GNP	Military expenditure as % of GNP
1987	137.3	825	*16.6*
1988	138.3	875	*15.8*
1989	133.7	943	*14.2*
1990	123.4	1 000	*12.3*

Note: The CIA's rouble current price estimate for 1988 was 163.3 billion roubles, giving a GNP share of 18.7%. Includes Minatom expenditure on nuclear weapons.

Sources: Adapted from Steinberg, D., 'The Soviet defence burden: estimating hidden defence costs', *Soviet Studies*, vol. 44, no. 2 (1992), p. 263. On GNP: USSR, State Committee on Statistics, *Narodnoye Khozyaystvo SSSR v 1990 G.* [National economy of the USSR, 1990] (Finansy i Statistika: Moscow, 1991), p. 9.

The GNP data presented are the official Soviet series, also employed by Steinberg in the article cited. Western assessments of the Soviet military burden depended on independent estimations of GNP and these were also controversial: it has been acknowledged that the CIA tended to overstate Soviet GNP in relation to that of the USA.[8] However, as Noren points out, the CIA did not recalculate Soviet GNP to take account of the growing 'second economy' in the final years of the USSR: if this had been done, the estimate of the military burden would have been lower.

Any improvement of the data on Soviet military expenditure is now unlikely until Russian analysts undertake the daunting task of reviewing all the available evidence and find methods of reliably correcting for price distortions affecting the measurement of both outlays on the military and GNP.

III. Military expenditure in the Russian Federation, 1992–97

Since 1991 the Russian Federation has been undergoing a difficult and protracted process of economic transformation, of which the first modest signs of success appeared only in 1997. For the first four years, 1992–95, the country experienced high rates of inflation, and for the entire period the government has been attempting to cope with severe budgetary problems. In early 1992, in an attempt to reduce the budget deficit, expenditure on military procurement was cut by approximately two-thirds and it has remained at a very low level ever since. As a consequence, the production by the defence industry of weapons and other military equipment, including items for export, has fallen sharply—by the end of 1997 to less than 10 per cent of the 1991 level.[9] At the same time the armed forces have steadily contracted in terms of personnel and face further reduction as the long-delayed military reform gathers pace. In addition to these significant changes, Russia has experienced political uncertainties and has been undergoing institutional change of a far-reaching character, including efforts to establish a stable and effective parliamentary system. In these

---

[8] Schroeder, G., 'Reflections on economic Sovietology', *Post-Soviet Affairs*, vol. 11, no. 3 (1995), pp. 197–234.
[9] Calculated from data of the Russian Ministry of the Economy, available on URL <http://server.vpk/www-vpk/vpk>, version current Jan. 1998.

Table 6D.3. The original budget request of the Russian Ministry of Defence and the final budget allocation to national defence, 1992–97
Figures are in trillion current roubles. Figures in italics are percentages.

	1992	1993	1994	1995	1996	1997
Ministry of Defence request	1.06	10.70	87.00	111.00	134.00	260/160[a]
Budget approved[b]	0.85	7.21	39.75	58.09	78.34	102.20
% of proposal approved	*78*	*74*	*47*	*52*	*58*	*39/64*

[a] The MOD originally requested 260 trillion roubles, but later reduced its claim to 160 trillion roubles.

[b] For 1992 and 1993, the total for national defence as the revised final budget for the Ministry of Defence is not known. For 1994–97 figures are for MOD only.

Sources: (a) MOD budget requests: Rogov, S., *Military Reform and the Defense Budget of the Russian Federation,* Report no. CIM 527 (Center for Naval Analyses: Alexandria, Va., Aug. 1997), pp. 15–16; and (b) budget as approved: as table 6D.4.

circumstances it is not surprising that there have been problems of managing and measuring expenditure on the armed forces.

The budgetary process[10]

The budgetary process in the Russian Federation has now settled down to a standard pattern, although it is still subject to long delays. Only on one occasion since 1991 has the state budget been approved in advance of the new budget year, and then only just. (President Boris Yeltsin signed the federal budget for 1996 on 31 December 1995. The budget for 1997 was finally approved at the end of February 1997.) The first stage of the process is the preparation by the Ministry of the Economy of a forecast of the development of the economy, establishing targets for the new budget year for gross domestic product (GDP), the inflation rate, the exchange rate and other basic parameters. This provides a general framework enabling the Ministry of Finance to draft a federal budget, key variables of which are total revenue and expenditure and their shares of GDP, the size of the deficit and the manner in which it is to be financed. At an early stage of this process, the MOD and other government departments submit their own proposals for expenditure in the year ahead. These are taken into account by the Ministry of Finance, but since 1991 the budget requests of the MOD have been consistently ignored—most strikingly in 1994—sometimes because they have been based on a much more pessimistic assumption as to the future rate of inflation than those forecast by the Ministry of the Economy (see table 6D.3).

The Ministry of Finance's draft budget is reviewed by the government and amendments may be made before it is submitted to the Federal Assembly for approval. In parliament the budget undergoes four readings in each house (the State Duma and the Federation Council). Detailed examination takes place in the principal committees of parliament, in particular the Duma's Budget and Defence Committees.

[10] See also section III by the present author in George, P., 'World military expenditure', *SIPRI Yearbook 1995: Armaments, Disarmament and International Security* (Oxford University Press: Oxford, 1995), pp. 399–408.

The first reading ends with the approval of total revenue and expenditure and the size of the deficit. The second reading ends with the approval of expenditure according to the principal budget categories. During the third stage, the budget chapters are reviewed in detail and amendments made. This can be a protracted process. If serious problems arise at any stage, a conciliation commission may be created with the participation of government officials in order to amend the budget or the underlying economic forecast in an attempt to improve the prospects for its approval. Finally, at the fourth reading, deputies vote on the entire budget. When both houses have approved the federal budget, it goes to the president for signing into law. Since 1992, despite some vigorous lobbying by the MOD, its newspaper, *Krasnaya Zvezda*, and supporters in parliament, the final allocation has not deviated much from that set out in the Ministry of Finance's original draft.

The budget chapter 'national defence'

The chapter headings of the budget and their component items are established by occasional laws on the budget classification, the most recent being that of August 1996. For the four years 1994–97 the budget chapter 'national defence' consisted of: (*a*) expenditure of the MOD (personnel and maintenance, pensions, procurement, construction, and research and developmen, (R&D); (*b*) expenditure of Minatom on the development and production of nuclear weapons; (*c*) an allocation to the Russian Defence Sport and Technical Organization (ROSTO), a public body associated with the armed forces; and (*d*) outlays on the maintenance of mobilization capacities in the economy. According to the law of August 1996, national defence includes allocations to the MOD (minus pensions), the military programmes of Minatom, the maintenance of mobilization capacities, expenditure on military cooperation in the Commonwealth of Independent States (CIS), and military aid to foreign states. This new definition appears to have been adopted for the 1998 draft budget. Pensions of servicemen and civilian employees of the MOD, which have represented a growing share of the national defence allocation as the armed forces have been reduced (13 per cent in the 1997 budget, or 0.5 per cent of forecast GDP), have been transferred to the 'social expenditure' chapter. A new military-related expenditure chapter has been introduced covering the destruction of armaments and their reuse for civilian purposes, including the fulfilment of international agreements. Formerly, the fulfilment of international agreements for the elimination of weapons was funded under the 'international activity' chapter.[11]

The budget chapter 'national defence', while it covers most of the allocations to the MOD, does not account for all military-related budgetary expenditure.

1. The Russian Federation possesses paramilitary forces on a quite substantial scale. These include the internal troops of the Ministry of the Interior, the border troops of the Federal Border Service, the guard for the protection of the government and president, and forces attached to the Federal Security Service and the Federal Agency for Government Communications and Information. Since 1992 about 40 per cent of total expenditure under the 'law enforcement and state security' chapter has been devoted to these paramilitary forces.

---

[11] *Sobraniye Zakonodatelstva Rossiyskoy Federatsii* [Collection of legislative acts of the Russian Federation], no. 34 (1996), art. 4030.

2. One significant omission is subsidies to the 'closed' towns and settlements of the MOD. These so-called 'closed administrative–territorial formations' (known in Russian by the acronym ZATO (Zakrytoye administrativno-territorialnoye obrazovaniye), are very-high-security zones around missile launch sites and other sensitive installations. In addition there are separate budget subsidies to the closed towns of Minatom, where nuclear weapons are developed, produced and stored. These come under the 'other outlays' chapter.

3. In some years the budget has included additional military-related items, such as a separate allocation for housing for servicemen or for social support for their children.

4. In addition to expenditure on the maintenance of mobilization capacities, there is a separate allocation for mobilization preparation and civil defence.

5. As noted above, there is also an allocation to fund the destruction of weapon systems withdrawn from use and other measures to fulfil international arms control agreements. This has been included as military expenditure in so far as the principal recipients of this funding are organizations of the MOD and, at a time of severe budgetary stringency, this additional money must help in sustaining their activities.

6. Insofar as some of its activity is of a military character and involves the employment of Russian military personnel, it may be necessary to include in a broad category of military expenditure subsidies for the Baikonur space launch centre and its associated town of Leninsk in Kazakhstan.

7. The budget chapter 'fundamental research and support for scientific and technical progress' includes allocations to the defence industry and to the Russian Space Agency but, while some of it probably helps to sustain R&D organizations involved in military work, much of the funding is devoted to civilian programmes undertaken by defence industry organizations. In the author's view it is an exaggeration to assume, as is sometimes done,[12] that half the total science budget should be considered of a military-related character; one-third is probably more appropriate and is the proportion used here.

8. Under the 'industry, energy and construction' chapter there is an allocation to cover some of the costs of the conversion of the defence industry. It is debatable whether this should be considered as military-related expenditure, and the matter is of little importance if actual expenditure is the concern: only a small proportion of the modest volume of planned expenditure has actually been disbursed.[13]

Allocations to military expenditure in the federal budget for the six years 1992–97, according to the most important chapters and items, are shown in table 6D.4.

A complication since 1992 has been the fact that in most years the federal budget has been revised after its initial adoption. Unfortunately, details of the revised budget are not always made available. This occurred most recently in 1997, when the government decided that the budget was unrealistic and reduced expenditure by a tough policy of sequestration.

---

[12] International Institute for Strategic Studies, *The Military Balance 1997–1998* (Oxford University Press: Oxford, 1997), p. 111.
[13] In 1995, e.g., only 24% of planned spending on conversion programmes was disbursed, falling to 18% in 1996. Salo, V., 'Rossiya sokhranit oboronny potentsial' [Russia is preserving its defence potential], *Ekonomika i Zhizn*, no. 41 (1997).

Table 6D.4. Military expenditure in the Russian federal budget, 1992–97
Figures are in billion current roubles.

	1992[a]	1993[b]	1994[c]	1995[d]	1996[e]	1997[f]
National defence						
Ministry of Defence						
Personnel/O&M	392	1 556	22 105	31 881	41 120	48 661
Pensions	22	171	1 994	4 867	9 899	13 859
Procurement	115	570	8 442	10 275	13 213	20 963
R&D	76	225	2 433	4 936	6 474	11 575
Construction	91	514	4 778	6 138	7 637	7 141
Total MOD	696	3 036	39 752	58 097	78 343	102 199
Minatom (nuclear weapons)	20	49	874	1 017	1 512	2 095
Total MOD/Minatom	**716**	**3 085**	**40 626**	**59 114**	**79 855**	**104 294**
ROSTO[g]	..	..	[9]	15	23	24
Mobilization capacity	..	30	[61]	250	307	– [h]
Total national defence	**716**	**3 115**	**40 626**	**59 379**	**80 185**	**104 318**
Other military expenditure						
Paramilitary forces:						
Interior troops	..	..	1 129	1 798	3 252	4 147
Border troops	..	..	1 800	2 901	3 988	5 765
Security services	..	..	2 130	3 153	5 142	6 930
Total paramilitary[i]	(87)	(371)	5 050	7 852	12 382	16 842
Subsidies to closed towns						
MOD	..	..	249	(483)[j]	898	1 552
Minatom (nuclear weapons)	..	..	334	(595)[j]	1 035	1 183
Housing for troops	..	13	..	..	..	..
Mobilization preparation/ civil defence	..	16	70	68	81	888
For intl. arms agreements	9	28	837	..	3 324	3 111
Baikonur space centre	..	..	..	161	720	582
Military-related R&D[k]	(35)	(228)	(1 683)	(2 485)	(3 855)	(5 086)
Total other mil. exp.	(131)	(656)	(8 293)	(11 644)	(22 295)	(29 244)
Total military exp.	**(847)**	**(3 771)**	**(48 919)**	**(71 023)**	**(102 480)**	**(133 562)**
Total federal budget	3 319	18 725	194 495	284 778	435 750	529 765
Ministry of Defence as % of total federal budget	21.6	16.6	20.9	20.4	18.0	19.3
National defence as % of total federal budget	21.6	16.6	20.9	20.8	18.4	19.7
Total military exp. as % of total fed. budget	(25.5)	(20.1)	(25.2)	(24.9)	(23.5)	(25.2)
Budget GDP estimate	18 000	..	725 000	1 650 000	2 300 000	2 725 000
National defence as % of GDP estimate	4.0	..	5.6	3.6	3.5	3.8
Total military exp. as % of GDP estimate	4.7	..	6.7	4.3	4.5	4.9

Notes: O&M = operations and maintenance.

[a] Budget adopted on 17 July 1992. The budget was revised on 18 Dec. 1992 to national defence—848 billion roubles; total expenditure—3871 billion roubles, but no breakdown of the defence allocation was provided. *Vedomosti Syezda Narodnykh Deputatov Rossiyskoy*

Federatsii i Verkhovnogo Soveta Rossiyskoy Federatsii [Proceedings of the Congress of People's Deputies and Supreme Soviet of the Russian Federation], no. 3 (1993), art. 94.

b Budget adopted 14 May 1993. The budget was revised on 21 Dec. 1993 to national defence—7210 billion roubles; total expenditure—22 247 billion roubles. *Vedomosti Syezda Narodnykh Deputatov Rossiyskoy Federatsii i Verkhovnogo Soveta Rossiyskoy Federatsii*, no. 52 (1993), art. 5063.

c Budget adopted on 1 July 1994.

d Final version of budget adopted on 27 Dec. 1995. The initial version of 31 Mar. 1995 included national defence—48 577 billion roubles; total budget expenditure—248 344 billion roubles. *Rossiyskaya Gazeta*, 7 Apr. 1995, in Russian. It was then revised on 12 Aug. 1995 to national defence—50 854 billion roubles; total expenditure—248 344 billion roubles. *Sobraniye Zakonodatelstva Rossiyskoy Federatsii* [Collection of legislative acts of the Russian Federation], no. 35 (1995), art. 3502.

e Budget adopted on 31 Dec. 1995. This budget was not revised.

f Budget adopted on 26 Feb. 1997. On 30 Apr. 1997 it was revised when a law on sequestration was approved; national defence was reduced to 83 177 billion roubles and total budget expenditure to 421 649 billion roubles. *Sobraniye Zakonodatelstva Rossiyskoy Federatsii*, no. 35 (1997), art. 3502.

g ROSTO = Russian Defence Sport and Technical Organization.

h Transferred to a separate budget chapter, 'mobilization preparation of the economy' (total allocation 888 billion roubles, as indicated).

i When no details available, estimated as 40% of total for 'law and order'.

j Estimated, using proportions of total in initial 1995 federal budget in *Rossiyskaya Gazeta*, 7 Apr. 1995.

k Estimated as one-third of total science budget.

Sources: (*a*) 1992: *Vedomosti Syezda Narodnykh Deputatov Rossiyskoy Federatsii i Verkhovnogo Soveta Rossiyskoy Federatsii* [Proceedings of the Congress of People's Deputies and the Supreme Soviet of the Russian Federation], no. 34 (1992), art. 1979; (*b*) 1993: *Vedomosti Syezda Narodnykh Deputatov Rossiyskoy Federatsii i Verkhovnogo Soveta Rossiyskoy Federatsii*, no. 22 (1993), art. 794; (*c*) 1994: *Sobraniye Zakonodatelstva Rossiyskoy Federatsii* [Collection of legislative acts of the Russian Federation], no. 10 (1994), art. 1108; and Ministry of Finance, Proyekt, Federalny byudzhet Rossiyskoy Federatsii na 1995 god [Draft federal budget, 1995], Moscow, Oct. 1994; (*d*) 1995: *Rossiyskaya Gazeta*, 4 Jan. 1996; (*e*) 1996: *Rossiyskaya Gazeta*, 10 Jan. 1996; (*f*) 1997: *Rossiyskaya Gazeta*, 4 Mar. 1997; and (*g*) GDP estimates on which federal budgets are based: for 1992 and 1994, Sinelnikov, S., *Byudzhetny Krizis v Rossii 1985–1995 Gody* [The budget crisis in Russia 1985–95] (Evraziya: Moscow, 1995), pp. 110, 152; and for 1995–97, calculated from the sources for budget above.

Other sources of funding for the military

A more difficult issue is the extent to which budget allocations for national defence, and under other budget chapters, represent the totality of military expenditure. Several possible forms of such expenditure can be distinguished. First, concealed budgetary allocations certainly existed in Soviet times and it cannot be ruled out that additional allocations have been made to the MOD, above all from the substantial 'other expenditures' chapter, details of which are sparse. This may explain a discrepancy in reported expenditure in 1995: according to Goskomstat, actual expenditure on 'national defence' was 47.6 trillion roubles, but in the Russian Government's return of military expenditure to the United Nations[14] the expenditure of the MOD (excluding expenditure on nuclear weapons of some 1 trillion roubles and other

[14] See chapter 6, section I in this volume.

Table 6D.5. Actual outlays on Russian national defence and Ministry of Defence, 1992–97

Figures are in billion current roubles. Figures in italics are percentages.

	Nat. defence	MOD	GDP	As % of GDP, exp. on National defence	MOD
1992	855	829	19 006	*4.50*	*4.36*
1993	7 213	6 979	171 510	*4.21*	*4.07*
1994	22 018	..	610 956	*4.59*	..
1995	47 553	52 107	1 630 956	*2.92*	*3.20*
1996	63 891	..	2 256 000	*2.84*	..
1997	(75 500)	..	2 675 000	*(2.82)*	..

Sources: (*a*) national defence: 1992–95, Russia, State Committee on Statistics, *Rossiyskiy Statisticheskiy Ezhegodnik 1996* [Russian statistical yearbook, 1996], (Finansy i Statistika: Moscow, 1997), pp. 418–49; 1996, *Russian Economic Trends*, no. 1 (1997), p. 18; and 1997, estimated on the basis of GDP share in first 11 months, Institut Ekonomicheskikh Problem Perekhodnogo Perioda, *Belaya Kniga: Ekonomika i Politika Rossii v 1997 Godu* [The white book: the economy and politics of Russia in 1997], (Institut ekonomicheskikh problem perekhodnogo perioda: Moscow, Feb. 1998), p. 172; (*b*) MOD: reports of the Russian Federation to the United Nations; and (*c*) GDP: 1992–95, Russia, State Committee on Statistics, *Rossiyskiy Statisticheskiy Ezhegodnik 1996* [Russian statistical yearbook, 1996], (Finansy i Statistika: Moscow, 1997), p. 285; 1996, *Russian Economic Trends*, no. 1 (1997), p. 18; and 1997, BBC, *Summary of World Broadcasts*, SUW/0522 WA/3, 30 Jan. 1998.

expenditure of approximately 200 billion roubles) was reported to be 52.1 trillion roubles (see table 6D.5). A possible explanation is that additional money was made available for the war in Chechnya: it may not be a coincidence that the difference, 5.7 trillion roubles, is identical to the reported MOD expenditure in 1995 on military operations in Chechnya.[15] It may also explain another puzzle: reported actual military expenditure in 1996 was 63.9 trillion roubles, but General Lev Rokhlin, then Chairman of the Duma's Defence Committee, has claimed on more than one occasion that expenditure was actually not less than 130 trillion roubles.[16] Until the Russian authorities release more information, such discrepancies are likely to remain mysteries.

Budget outlays may understate the true level of costs if the armed forces acquire goods and services at subsidized or artificially low prices or without payment. The limited evidence available suggests that the prices of weapons have risen more slowly that those of most other industrial goods. If this is so, the real trend of arms procurement may not be reflected reliably in the data on expenditure. According to one source, comparing the 1991 average with the 1996 average, industrial prices for Russian industry as a whole increased by 5498 per cent, prices for the production of weapons and other military hardware by 2142 per cent, and prices for the civilian output of the defence industry by 1683 per cent.[17] These data provide only a hint, as the source provides no indication of the scope of the prices and it is difficult to relate

---

[15] *Moskovskiy Komsomolets*, 10 Apr. 1996.
[16] See, e.g., *Krasnaya Zvezda*, 20 May 1997, p. 1.
[17] Data of the Russian Ministry of Defence Industry, available on URL <http://server.vpk.ru/www-vpk/vpk>, version current Oct. 1997.

these figures to other evidence on the Russian industrial price index. In addition, while almost all prices have been liberalized, energy prices for most of the period have been well below world levels. This makes it difficult to assess the full resource cost of the Russian military effort.

Problems of non-payment have been acute in the Russian economy since 1992. It is known that the MOD has frequently failed to pay for electricity, transport services, and other goods and services or has settled debts with long delay, by which time they have been reduced in real terms by high rates of inflation. By these means more military services have been obtained than are indicated by the monetary outlays.

In addition to budget sources of finance, the armed forces have some opportunities to earn money by the sale of goods and services. The principal activities are the production and sale of civilian goods, including consumer items, by the repair works and other industrial facilities of the armed forces; the provision of transport services, in particular air freight transport by the air force; civilian building work undertaken by military construction organizations; the leasing of property and facilities to civil organizations; and the sale of surplus military property and equipment, including export sales. Sales of surplus property and equipment have been the responsibility of a specially created 'state economic enterprise', established in late 1992. In 1994 it earned 46 billion roubles; in 1995 it earned 133 billion roubles, equivalent to a mere 0.3 per cent of total expenditure on national defence in the same year.[18]

The scattered evidence suggests that the total income earned by these activities has been very modest in relation to expenditure, and it is unlikely that it has supplemented the budget by anything more than 2–3 per cent of budgetary allocations to the MOD. According to the rules for the sale of surplus property and equipment, most of the proceeds are used to fund housing construction or other social measures for servicemen. Some funding for housing has also been received from abroad: by March 1995 more than 22 000 flats had been built for servicemen with funding provided by the German Government under an agreement of 1990 intended to ease the return to Russia of troops previously located in the German Democratic Republic (GDR).[19]

Actual expenditure

For most countries, including the USSR in 1989–90, the approved state budget provides an acceptable approximation to actual outlays. This has not been the case for the Russian Federation. The divergence between planned expenditure and actual outlays has been substantial and the share of military expenditure in GDP has consistently fallen below the share envisaged at the time of the budget's approval.

Unfortunately, the Russian authorities have been very restrictive in publishing information on actual military expenditure. Almost all that has been available has been a single total figure for expenditure under the budget chapter 'national defence', with no breakdown by main categories of expenditure. In addition, there is information supplied to the UN, which for some years provides a figure for the total expenditure of the MOD. These data are discussed further below and shown in table 6D.5.

It can be seen from table 6D.3 that the greatest divergence between planned and actual allocations occurred in 1994, but in other years the gap was still substantial. These shortfalls in expenditure have been associated with the accumulation of substantial debts. At the end of each year the Ministry of Finance has been in debt to the

[18] *Krasnaya Zvezda*, 19 Sep. 1996, p. 4.
[19] *Armeyskiy Sbornik*, no. 6 (1995), p. 5.

Table 6D.6. Structure of actual and planned expenditure of the Russian Ministry of Defence, 1992–97

Figures are percentages of total expenditure.

	1992 B	1992 A	1993 B	1993 A	1994 B	1994 A	1995 B	1995 A	1996 B	1996 A	1997 B
Personnel and O&M	58.1	56.0	54.3	62.2	53.9	..	59.9	67.0	60.1	70.4	55.3
Procurement	17.1	22.3	19.9	9.1	24.9	..	19.3	17.9	19.3	16.4	23.9
R&D	11.2	8.7	7.8	5.7	7.2	..	9.3	7.2	9.4	5.4	13.2
Construction	13.6	13.0	18.0	13.0	14.0	..	11.5	7.9	11.2	7.8	7.6
Total	**100.0**	**100.0**	**100.0**	**100.0**	**100.0**	**100.0**	**100.0**	**100.0**	**100.0**	**100.0**	**100.0**

Notes: B = federal budget as approved. A = actual expenditure as reported to the UN. Expenditure excludes pensions. Data on the structure of actual expenditure are not available for 1994 and 1997. O&M = operations and maintenance.

Sources: (*a*) official budget: as table 6D.4; and (*b*) actual expenditure: reports of the Russian Federation to the United Nations.

MOD; in turn the MOD has owed money to the defence industry and other suppliers. Over time, an increasing proportion of the allocations for the current year has been to settle debts accumulated in earlier years, further eroding the current value of budget funding. When the rate of inflation was very high, especially during the four years 1992–95, there is evidence that some of the delays in payment were caused by the MOD itself: budget money was kept in commercial banks for a period in order to earn income before being disbursed to the intended recipients.

For the first time in 1990, the Soviet Union provided the United Nations with a detailed report on actual military expenditure in the previous year, broadly in accordance with the UN instrument for the standardized reporting of military expenditure. The Russian Federation has continued this practice, although there have been some inconsistencies in the data supplied. It has not always been made clear whether the data are actual expenditure or intended budget allocations (in particular, this is true of the year 1994) and some information provided in earlier reports has been later omitted, for example, expenditure on nuclear weapon development and production disappeared in 1995 and information on pensions in 1996. Some information has been provided on expenditure on paramilitary forces (4987 billion roubles in 1995 and 5443 billion roubles in 1996), but its scope is not clear. It may cover the troops of the Ministry of the Interior and the border troops.

For 1992 and 1993 some information was provided on expenditure associated with UN peacekeeping operations, but since then the columns for 'military assistance' have remained blank. There have also been some unexplained reallocations of expenditure between categories and the attached explanatory notes have in general been inadequate. Nevertheless, the information illuminates some important aspects of Russian defence expenditure.

As table 6D.6 indicates, expenditure on personnel has absorbed an ever-increasing share of the budget and more than intended when each budget was adopted. As a result the shares of procurement, R&D and construction expenditure have fallen.

Table 6D.7. USSR and Russia, expenditure by service, 1990–97

Figures are percentages of total Ministry of Defence expenditure.

	Ground forces	Navy	Air Force	Other forces[a]	Central[b]	Total
Total expenditure						
USSR						
1990[c]	29.6	17.1	17.4	23.7	12.2	**100.0**
Russia						
1992[c]	27.6	20.2	11.6	19.9	20.7	**100.0**
1993[c]	29.4	19.4	9.9	19.0	22.3	**100.0**
1994[d]	27.5	15.9	12.4	19.7	24.5	**100.0**
1995[c]	28.7	15.9	11.5	18.6	25.3	**100.0**
1996[c]	38.0	16.5	10.5	23.2	11.8	**100.0**
1997[d]	36.6	15.7	11.3	24.8	11.6	**100.0**
Procurement						
USSR						
1990[c]	28.5	20.0	21.3	16.8	13.4	**100.0**
Russia						
1992[c]	18.5	30.1	19.6	16.8	15.0	**100.0**
1993[c]	22.0	28.0	13.5	18.9	17.6	**100.0**
1994[d]	20.0	23.2	20.2	20.7	15.9	**100.0**
1995[c]	31.9	22.5	16.9	17.4	11.3	**100.0**
1996[c]	34.8	16.1	13.7	26.6	8.8	**100.0**
1997[d]	41.6	17.8	14.6	17.7	8.3	**100.0**
Research and development						
USSR						
1990[c]	7.0	15.6	19.7	53.9	3.8	**100.0**
Russia						
1992[c]	6.7	16.6	19.5	50.8	6.4	**100.0**
1993[c]	6.9	16.1	18.4	52.2	6.4	**100.0**
1994[d]	8.8	13.7	17.2	56.5	3.8	**100.0**
1995[c]	8.8	15.1	15.6	45.8	16.7	**100.0**
1996[c]	12.4	12.7	11.1	55.3[e]	8.5	**100.0**
1997[d]	11.3	12.5	12.3	56.7[e]	7.2	**100.0**

Note: Figures exclude pensions and nuclear weapons. No data are provided for 1991 as those available are not sufficiently reliable.

[a] Strategic missile forces, air defence forces and other forces of the MOD.
[b] Central support administration and command.
[c] Reported actual expenditure.
[d] Federal budget as approved (no data on actual expenditure available).
[e] Figures for R&D specify that in 1996 38.9% and in 1997 35.5% was spent on the strategic missile forces.

Source: Reports of the Russian Federation to the United Nations.

The reports to the UN omit separate data on the strategic missile forces and the air defence forces, but the trends in expenditure on the other services are much as expected: the army's share has increased and the navy and to a lesser extent the air

Table 6D.8. Estimated actual total Russian military-related expenditure, 1992–96
Figures are in billion current roubles. Figures in italics are percentages.

	National defence	Other military expenditure	Total military expenditure	GDP	Total military exp. as % of GDP
1992	855	194	1 049	19 006	*5.5*
1993	7 213	1 842	9 037	171 510	*5.3*
1994	28 018	7 391	35 409	610 745	*5.8*
1995	47 553	12 989	60 542	1 630 079	*3.7*
1996	63 891	18 419	82 310	2 256 120	*3.7*
1997	(75 500)	26 000[a]	(101 500)	2 675 000	*(3.8)*

[a] Estimated on the basis of the law on sequestration of 30 Apr. 1997.

Sources: (*a*) national defence and GDP: as table 6D.5; (*b*) other military: estimated as text above; and (*c*) expenditure on law and order and science: 1992–95, Russia, State Committee on Statistics, *Rossiyskiy Statisticheskiy Ezhegodnik 1996* [Russian statistical yearbook, 1996] (Finansy i Statistika: Moscow, 1997), pp. 418–49; and 1996, *Russian Economic Trends 1997*, no. 1 (1997), p. 18.

force have experienced diminishing shares, as shown in table 6D.7. The land forces have also gained in terms of their share of total procurement expenditure, with the navy and air force shares being squeezed markedly. In R&D expenditure, the strategic missile and ground forces have in relative terms improved their position.[20]

The Russian authorities do not provide detailed information on actual expenditure below the level of the main chapters of the budget. It is therefore possible to arrive at only a very approximate estimate of actual total military-related expenditure from the reported aggregate expenditure on national defence, law and order and science. Assuming 40 per cent of expenditure on law and order and one-third of expenditure on science to be military-related, it is still necessary to estimate actual outlays on the closed cities, mobilization preparedness, the fulfilment of international arms agreements and other minor categories of expenditure. Taking the 1996 federal budget, as shown in table 6D.4, planned expenditure on these items amounted to 7.5 per cent of planned expenditure on national defence, and this proportion has been used for the period 1992–96 in table 6D.8.

The military burden

Tables 6D.5 and 6D.8 provide an indication of the military burden, the share of expenditure on defence in GDP. Measurement of Russia's military burden has been complicated by the difficulty of accurately measuring GDP during a time of rapid economic transformation and high rates of inflation. The GDP series for Russia has undergone more than one revision, with the result that the share of military expenditure has fallen as the estimate of GDP has risen, partly to take account of revised assessments of the scale of the new business sector and of unregistered economic activity which, according to official estimates, accounts for about 25 per

---

[20] Arnett, E., 'Military research and development', *SIPRI Yearbook 1997: Armaments, Disarmament and International Security* (Oxford University Press: Oxford, 1997), pp. 221–22.

Table 6D.9. Soviet and Russian military expenditure, 1987–96

	GDP*a* (constant 1995 US $b., PPP terms)	MOD and Minatom (constant 1995 US $b., PPP terms)	Index (1995=100)	Total military expenditure (constant 1995 US $b., PPP terms)	Index (1995=100)
USSR					
1987	1 548	130.0	..	257.0	..
1988	1 638	136.0	..	258.8	..
1989	1 689	136.8	..	240.0	..
1990	1 650	122.1	..	203.0	..
Russian Federation					
1992	863	38.8	201	47.5	193
1993	790	33.3	173	41.9	170
1994	690	31.5*b*	163	40.0	163
1995	664	19.3*b*	100	24.6	100
1996	631	17.8*b*	92	23.3	95
1997	(634)	(17.8)	(92)	(24.1)	(98)

Note: No data are provided for 1991 as those available are not sufficiently reliable.
a GNP for USSR.
b For 1994–96, expenditure of the MOD plus nuclear weapons was estimated by taking 99.5% of actual expenditure on national defence.
Sources: Calculated from GDP/GNP shares, tables 6D.1, 6D.2, 6D.5 and 6D.8. PPP rate for 1995: *World Bank Atlas 1997* (World Bank: Washington, DC, 1997), p. 37.

cent of GDP.[21] The military share of GDP at the time when the budget was adopted thus appeared to be higher than it actually was and the use of notional GDP shares as a guide to setting budget allocations has worked to the disadvantage of the MOD.

IV. The trend of Soviet and Russian military expenditure in 1995 dollar terms

Comparison of Russian military expenditure with that of other countries is complicated by the fact that the official exchange rate cannot be used, as it substantially understates the level of expenditure. In 1995 dollar terms, for instance, using the exchange rate, total 1996 military-related expenditure amounts to a mere $13 billion, which is not credible. This is a problem typical of all transforming economies, especially during the early years of transition. In order to generate more reliable estimates, it is necessary to use purchasing-power parity rates, although problems remain. The World Bank's international PPP rate, derived from GDP data, has been used here. The World Bank figures are useful for comparing the overall output of economies, and for resource use measures of military expenditure, while comparisons of military output would require a PPP rate specifically for military expenditure. The resulting estimates of Soviet and Russian military expenditure in constant 1995 dollar terms are shown in table 6D.9. It must be emphasized that they are provisional and

---

[21] Goskomstat's estimate for the first quarter of 1997 was 25%. BBC, *Summary of World Broadcasts*, SUW/0488 WA/4, 30 May 1997.

Table 6D.10. Military expenditure in the Russian Federation and the USSR, 1987–97

	National defence (b. current roubles)	National defence as % of		Total military expenditure (b. current roubles)	Total military exp. as % of	
		Total budget[a]	GDP[b]		Total budget[a]	GDP[b]
USSR						
1987	69.4	*16.1*	*8.4*	137.3	*31.9*	*16.6*
1988	72.8	*15.8*	*8.3*	138.3	*30.1*	*15.8*
1989	76.9	*15.9*	*8.2*	133.7	*27.7*	*14.2*
1990	70.7	*13.8*	*7.1*	123.4	*24.0*	*12.3*
Russia						
1992	855	*14.3*	*4.5*	1 049	*17.6*	*5.5*
1993	7 213	*12.5*	*4.2*	9 037	*15.7*	*5.3*
1994	28 018	*11.9*	*4.6*	35 409	*15.1*	*5.8*
1995	47 553	*8.8*	*2.9*	60 542	*11.3*	*3.7*
1996	63 891	*8.3*	*2.8*	82 310	*10.7*	*3.7*
1997	(75 500)	..	*2.8*	(101 500)	..	*3.8*

Notes: No data are provided for 1991 as those available are not sufficiently reliable.

[a] USSR state budget for the USSR; consolidated budget for the Russian Federation (i.e., federal budget plus local budgets).

[b] GDP for the Russian Federation; GNP for the USSR.

Sources: (*a*) national defence: as table 6D.1 and 6D.5; (*b*) total military expenditure: author's estimates; as tables 6D.2 and 6D.8; and (*c*) Russian consolidated budget: 1992, Russian Federation State Committee on Statistics, *Statisticheskiy Ezhegodnik Rossiyskoy Federatsii 1996* (Finansy i Statistika: Moscow, 1997), p. 415; and 1993–96, *Russian Economic Trends*, no. 4 (1997), p. 11.

approximate, especially for the USSR (for which the official Soviet index for real GNP has been employed) and are intended to provide only a very general indication of the overall trend. It is likely that the use of a PPP rate specific to military expenditure would increase the estimate of Russian military expenditure in dollar terms since 1992.

Current issues of Russian military expenditure

Analysis of Russian military expenditure faces new uncertainties. For 1998 the budget classification has been changed, including the removal of pensions for armed forces personnel from the 'national defence' chapter. As reform of the armed forces gathers momentum, activities previously under the MOD, such as the network of military stores and the military construction system, are being transferred to other agencies or allowed to privatize as independent economic agents. Other armed forces are also undergoing reform and administrative change. President Yeltsin has decreed an upper limit of 3.5 per cent to the military share of GDP, but the meaning of this remains uncertain. It is inevitable that there will be problems of comparability and consistency in the Russian military expenditure series during the next few years. On the other hand, there is active discussion in Russia of moving towards a much greater degree of openness in relation to the defence budget. The MOD appears to support publication of more details of the main headings of expenditure, and while the Ministry of Finance has been more cautious, probably fearing that it will be held to public account for shortfalls in budget allocations in a more detailed manner than hitherto, there is now a real possibility that Russia will come into line in this respect with the practice of other leading industrial nations.

Comparing the openness and accuracy of information on military expenditure in the Russian Federation today with the situation in the USSR in 1987 it is clear that very substantial progress has been made. The budget is published in greater detail, price distortions have been reduced substantially and it is now possible to obtain an acceptable estimate of total military expenditure. International comparisons remain difficult and will do so until the Russian exchange rate becomes usable for such comparative purposes: in time, this can be predicted with confidence. As the economy stabilizes further and recovery strengthens, the budgetary process should become more predictable and planned budget allocations should increasingly approximate to actual outlays. It is to be hoped that the Russian Government will retain its commitment to greater openness in reporting military expenditure and that its reporting of such expenditure will be brought fully into line with internationally accepted standards.

Appendix 6E. The 100 largest arms-producing companies, 1996

ELISABETH SKÖNS, REINHILDE WEIDACHER and the SIPRI ARMS INDUSTRY NETWORK*

Table 6E contains information on the 100 largest arms-producing companies in the OECD and the developing countries ranked by their arms sales in 1996.[1] Companies with the designation 'S' in the column for rank in 1995 are subsidiaries; their arms sales are included in the figure in column 6 for the holding company. Subsidiaries are listed in the position in which they would appear if they were independent companies. In order to facilitate comparison with data for the previous year, the rank order and arms sales figures for 1995 are also given. Where new data for 1995 have become available, this information is included in the table; thus the 1995 rank order and the arms sales figures for some companies which appeared in table 8A in the *SIPRI Yearbook 1997* have been revised.

Sources and methods

Sources of data. The data in the table are based on the following sources: company reports, a questionnaire sent to over 400 companies, and corporation news published in the business sections of newspapers, military journals and on the Internet. Company archives, marketing reports, government publication of prime contracts and country surveys were also consulted. In many cases exact figures on arms sales were not available, mainly because companies often do not report their arms sales or lump them together with other activities. Estimates are therefore made.

Definitions. Data on total sales, profits and employment are for the entire company, not for the arms-producing sector alone. Profit data are after taxes in all cases when the company provides such data. Employment data are either a year-end or a yearly average figure as reported by the company. Data are reported on the fiscal-year basis reported by the company in its annual report.

Key to abbreviations in column 5. A = artillery, Ac = aircraft, El = electronics, Eng = engines, Mi = missiles, MV = military vehicles, SA/O = small arms/ordnance, Sh = ships, and Oth = other. Comp ( ) = components of the product within the parentheses. It is used only for companies which do not produce any final systems.

---

[1] For the membership of the Organisation for Economic Co-operation and Development, see the glossary in this volume. For countries in the developing world, see notes to appendix 8A.

---

* Participants in the SIPRI Arms Industry Network: Peter Batchelor, Centre for Conflict Resolution (Cape Town), Paul Dunne, Middlesex University (London), Ken Epps (Ontario), Jean-Paul Hébert, CIRPES (Paris), Gruppo di Studio su Armi e Disarmo, Universitá Cattolica (Milano), Peter Hug (Bern), Christos Kollias, Center of Planning and Economic Research (Athens), Luc Mampaey, Groupe de Recherche et d'Information sur la Paix et la Sécurité (Brussels), Rita Manchanda (New Delhi), Arcadi Oliveres, Centre d'Estudis sobre la Pau i el Desarmament (Barcelona), Ton van Oosterhout, University of Twente (Enschede), Sharon Sadeh (London), and Gülay Günlük-Senesen (Istanbul).

Table 6E. The 100 largest arms-producing companies in the OECD and developing countries, 1996

Figures in columns 6, 7, 8 and 10 are in current US $m.[a]

1	2	3	4	5	6	7	8	9	10	11
Rank[b]					Arms sales					
1996	1995	Company[c]	Country	Sector[d]	1996	1995	Total sales 1996	Col. 6 as % of col. 8	Profit 1996	Employment 1996
1	1	Lockheed Martin	USA	Ac El Mi	18 010	13 800	26 875	67	1 347	190 000
2	2	McDonnell Douglas	USA	Ac El Mi	9 510	9 620	13 834	69	788	63 870
3	3	British Aerospace	UK	A Ac El Mi SA/O	8 340	7 150	11 621	72	486	47 000
4	6	Northrop Grumman	USA	Ac El Mi SA/O	6 700	5 700	8 100	83	234	52 000
5	4	General Motors, GM	USA	El Eng Mi	6 660	6 550	164 069	4	4 963	647 000
S	S	Hughes Electronics (GM)	USA	El Mi	6 340	5 950	15 918	40	1 029	86 000
6	7	Thomson	France	El	4 570	4 630	14 473	32	-466	93 920
S	S	Thomson-CSF (Thomson)	France	El	4 540	4 620	7 090	64	146	46 510
7	9	GEC	UK	El Sh	4 460	4 100	17 409	26	637	79 850
8	10	Raytheon	USA	El Mi	4 030	3 960	12 331	33	761	75 300
9	8	Boeing	USA	Ac El Mi	4 000	4 200	22 681	18	1 182	143 000
10	12	DCN	France	Sh	3 470	3 520	3 536	98	-37	20 400
11	11	United Technologies	USA	El Eng	3 380	3 650	23 512	14	906	173 800
12	13	Daimler Benz, DB	FRG	Ac El Eng MV Mi	3 360	3 350	70 667	5	1 861	290 030
13	18	TRW	USA	Comp (El MV)	3 360	2 800	9 857	34	480	65 220
S	S	Daimler–Benz Aerospace, DASA (DB)	FRG	Ac El Eng Mi	3 330	3 250	8 674	38	799	44 240
14	15	General Dynamics	USA	MV Sh	3 310	2 930	3 581	92	353	23 100
15	14	Litton	USA	El Sh	3 220	3 030	3 612	89	151	33 500
16	20	Mitsubishi Heavy Industries[e]	Japan	Ac MV Mi Sh	3 030	2 430	28 888	10	1 136	67 120
17	16	IRI	Italy	Ac El Eng Mi Sh	2 740	2 810	49 056	6	279	132 490
18	17	Aérospatiale Groupe	France	Ac Mi	2 310	2 800	9 947	23	159	38 450
S	S	Finmeccanica (IRI)	Italy	Ac El Eng Mi	2 290	2 330	8 998	25	-350	60 010

Rank 1996	Rank 1995	Company	Country	Industry	Arms sales 1996	Arms sales 1995	Total sales 1996	Col. 6 as % of col. 8	Profit 1996	Employment 1996
19	21	Rockwell International[f]	USA	El Mi	2 200	2 430	14 343	15	726	58 640
20	23	Alcatel Alsthom	France	El	2 070	2 000	31 688	7	533	190 600
21	22	Rolls Royce	UK	Eng	2 010	2 050	6 702	30	−73	42 900
S	–	Matra BAe Dynamics[g] (Matra HT/BAe, UK)	France	Mi	1 950	0	1 955	100	. .	6 000
S	S	Pratt & Whitney (UTC)	USA	Eng	1 860	1 840	6 201	30	637	3 000
22	26	General Electric	USA	Eng	1 800	1 700	79 179	2	7 280	23 900
23	25	Texas Instruments	USA	El	1 770	1 740	11 713	15	63	59 930
24	S	Newport News	USA	Sh	1 730	1 670	1 822	95	90	18 000
25	24	CEA	France	Oth	1 510	1 740	3 661	41	−32	16 680
26	34	GKN	UK	Ac MV	1 500	1 180	5 212	29	−66	30 000
27	5	Loral[h]	USA	El Mi	1 500	6 500	. .	. .	. .	14 270
28	30	GIAT Industries	France	A MV SA/O	1 340	1 280	1 642	82	−407	76 600
29	33	Allied Signal	USA	Ac El	1 260	1 220	13 971	9	1 020	12 040
30	31	Dassault Aviation Groupe	France	Ac	1 230	1 270	2 541	48	224	113 350
31	36	Mitsubishi Electric[e]	Japan	El Mi	1 210	1 150	33 073	4	76	11 530
32	32	Celsius	Sweden	A El SA/O Sh	1 200	1 270	1 657	72	42	47 170
33	41	Lagardère SCA	France	Mi	1 190	980	11 026	11	203	20 590
S	S	Matra Hautes Technologies (Lagardère SCA)	France	El Mi	1 190	. .	3 820	31	113	
34	35	Samsung[i]	S. Korea	A El MV Mi Sh	1 160	1 160	78 100	1	3 802	206 410
35	43	Siemens	FRG	El	1 060	910	62 586	2	1 655	379 000
36	37	Alliant Tech Systems	USA	SA/O	1 050	1 150	1 089	96	59	6 800
37	42	FMC	USA	A MV	1 020	970	4 969	21	218	22 050
S	S	United Defense (FMC/Harsco)	USA	MV	1 020	970	1 020	100	99	5 800
38	40	ITT Industries	USA	El	1 010	1 010	8 718	12	223	59 000
39	29	Textron	USA	Ac El Eng MV	1 000	1 300	9 274	11	253	57 000

MILITARY EXPENDITURE AND ARMS PRODUCTION   263

		Company	Country	Industry	Arms sales 1998	Arms sales 1997	Total sales	%	Profit	Employment
40	46	FIAT	Italy	Eng MV SA/O	990	840	50 554	2	1 470	237 400
S	S	Thomson–CSF Communications (Thomson–CSF)	France	El	980	. .	1 222	80	. .	6 500
S	S	Eurocopter Group (Aérospatiale/DASA, FRG)	France	Ac	960	960	1 870	51	–88	9 530
41	39	Israel Aircraft Industries	Israel	Ac El Mi	950	1 050	1 466	65	–40	13 300
42	47	Thyssen	FRG	MV Sh	910	780	25 700	4	233	123 750
43	38	SNECMA Groupe	France	Eng	910	1 080	3 657	25	–76	21 300
44	27	Kawasaki Heavy Industries[e]	Japan	Ac Eng Mi Sh	910	1 670	11 254	8	208	24 210
S	S	Samsung Aerospace (Samsung)[j]	S. Korea	Ac El Eng	900	900	1 490	60	14	8 000
45	52	Tracor	USA	Comp (Ac El Mi)	850	720	1 083	78	37	10 450
S	–	Thyssen Werften[j] (Thyssen)	FRG	MV Sh	840	0	1 579	53	. .	5 110
46	S	EDS	USA	El	750	. .	14 441	5	432	95 000
47	–	Lucent Technologies[k]	USA	El	750	. .	23 286	3	1 054	. .
48	56	SAGEM Groupe	France	El	690	650	3 012	23	77	14 350
49	51	Harris	USA	El	690	720	3 621	19	178	27 600
50	60	Ishikawajima-Harima[e]	Japan	Eng Sh	660	600	9 853	7	126	25 430
51	92	Preussag	FRG	Sh	650	320	16 643	4	182	65 470
S	S	HDW (Preussag)	FRG	Sh	650	320	1 107	59	42	3 530
52	55	Hunting	UK	Comp (El Mi)	640	670	2 002	32	–17	12 740
53	19	Westinghouse Electric[l]	USA	El	640	2 550	8 449	8	30	59 280
54	49	Oerlikon–Bührle	Switzerl.	A Ac El Mi SA/O	630	730	2 923	22	49	15 540
55	64	BDM International	USA	El Oth	630	550	1 002	63	27	9 000
56	45	Diehl	FRG	SA/O	620	870	1 790	34	. .	12 590
57	61	Ordnance Factories	India	A SA/O	620	590	734	85	. .	. .
58	50	GTE	USA	El	600	730	21 339	3	2 798	102 000
S	S	SAGEM (SAGEM Groupe)	France	El	600	430	1 828	33	134	8 460
S	S	LFK (Daimler Aerospace)	FRG	Mi	590	730	590	100	–34	1 870
59	71	Saab	Sweden	Ac El Mi	580	470	1 230	47	–105	8 460
60	58	Dassault Electronique	France	El	570	610	891	64	23	4 090
61	S	STN Atlas Elektronik[m]	FRG	El	560	620	930	61	. .	4 700

264   MILITARY SPENDING AND ARMAMENTS, 1997

1	2	3	4	5	6	7	8	9	10	11
Rank					Arms sales					
1996	1995	Company	Country	Industry	1996	1995	Total sales 1996	Col. 6 as % of col. 8	Profit 1996	Employment 1996
S	S	FIAT Aviazione[n] (FIAT)	Italy	Eng	560	330	1 392	40	. .	6 960
62	66	Racal Electronics	UK	El	550	540	1 851	30	49	14 320
63	68	Ceridian	USA	El	550	510	1 496	37	182	10 800
S	S	Bofors (Celsius)	Sweden	A MV SA/O	550	500	629	87	−24	4 540
64	63	Rheinmetall	FRG	A El MV SA/O	540	550	2 429	22	30	14 320
65	54	SEPI[o]	Spain	Ac El Oth	540	670	15 775	3	1 109	76 110
66	62	Vickers	UK	Eng MV SA/O	540	560	1 870	29	88	10 190
S	S	MTU (Daimler Aerospace)	FRG	Eng	540	440	1 534	35	25	6 280
S	S	Rheinmetall Ind. (Rheinmetall)	FRG	A El MV SA/O	540	550	737	74	2 711	. .
67	67	Dyncorp	USA	Comp (Ac)	530	540	1 020	52	15	. .
68	48	NEC[e]	Japan	El	520	780	45 490	1	842	151 970
69	65	Toshiba[e]	Japan	El Mi	480	540	48 416	1	596	186 000
70	79	Avondale Industries	USA	Sh	480	430	625	77	31	52 000
71	82	Logicon	USA	Oth	480	410	566	85	33	5 000
72	70	Gencorp	USA	El Eng	470	490	1 515	31	42	8 950
S	S	SNECMA (SNECMA Groupe)	France	Eng	470	630	1 788	26	−93	11 380
S	S	Aerojet (Gencorp)	USA	El Eng	470	490	494	94	42	3 010
73	69	Rafael	Israel	SA/O Oth	460	490	500	93	−77	4 200
74	59	Eidgenössische Rüstungsbetr.	Switzerl.	A Ac Eng SA/O	460	610	537	86	1	3 220
75	—	Allegheny Teledyne	USA	El Eng Mi	460	250	. .	. .	. .	. .
76	57	Denel	S. Africa	A Ac El MV Mi SA/O	450	650	701	64	20	14 200
77	—	AIE[o]	Spain	SA/O Sh Oth	450	. .	. .	. .	. .	. .
78	76	Koor Industries	Israel	A El	440	440	3 591	12	184	21 530
79	73	Honeywell	USA	El Mi	440	460	7 312	6	403	530 000
80	78	Daewoo[i]	S. Korea	El SA/O Sh	430	430	51 215	1	. .	196 000
S	S	Agusta (Finmeccanica)	Italy	Ac	430	390	600	72	38	5 340

MILITARY EXPENDITURE AND ARMS PRODUCTION 265

	S	Company	Country	Sector						
	S	Hollandse Signaalapparaten (Thomson–CSF, France)	Netherl.	El	420	400	420	100	33	2 670
81	80	Mitre	USA	Oth	410	420	454	90		4 500
	S	Fincantieri Gruppo (IRI)	Italy	Sh	410	440	2 278	18	33	11 650
82	83	Hyundai[i]	S. Korea	MV Sh	400	400	23 221	2		..
83	74	Hindustan Aeronautics	India	Ac Mi	390	450	423	92		..
	S	Bazan (AIE)[o]	Spain	El Eng Sh	390	..	487	81	−28	36 000
	S	Tadiran (Koor Industries)	Israel	El	380	370	1 138	33	94	7 420
	S	CASA (SEPI)	Spain	Ac	380	490	869	44	35	..
	S	Saab Military Aircraft (Saab)	Sweden	Ac	380	280	467	82		7 930
84	98	Babcock International Group	UK	Sh	370	290	1 009	37	−37	3 530
85	–	Primex Technologies[q]	USA	SA/O	370	0	472	78	−8	9 030
	S	Babcock Rosyth Defence (Babcock International)	UK	Sh Oth	370	..	370	100	13	2 600
86	–	Israel Military Industries	Israel	A MV SA/O	360	270	511	70	−14	..
87	84	MKEK	Turkey	SA/O	360	380	699	51	163	4 150
88	81	Smiths Industries	UK	El	360	410	1 575	23	184	10 980
89	85	EG&G	USA	Comp (El Oth)	360	370	1 427	25	60	12 800
90	90	Bombardier	Canada	El Mi	340	330	5 849	6	298	..
	S	Sextant Avionique (Thomson–CSF)	France	El	340	360	878	39	..	41 150
	S	Hyundai Precision (Hyundai)[j]	S. Korea	MV	340	340	2 575	13	..	5 950
91	86	Wegmann Group	FRG	MV	330	350	665	50	..	..
92	–	Hitachi[e]	Japan	El MV	330	230	78 352	0.4	812	..
93	–	Mannesmann	FRG	MV	320	210	23 048	1	401	330 150
	S	GM Canada (GM, USA)	Canada	Eng	320	..	20 022	2	498	119 710
	S	IVECO (FIAT)	Italy	MV	320	220	4 446	7	..	..
94	94	Australian Submarine[q]	Australia	Sh	310	300	313	100	..	17 570
95	96	Elbit Systems	Israel	El	310	300	310	100	18	..
96	91	Vosper Thornycroft	UK	Sh	300	330	376	80	32	2 950
97	88	Esco Electronics	USA	El	300	350	439	69	26	..

1	2	3	4	5	6	7	8	9	10	11
Rank					Arms sales					
1996	1995	Company	Country	Industry	1996	1995	Total sales 1996	Col. 6 as % of col. 8	Profit 1996	Employment 1996
98	99	ADI	Australia	El SA/O Sh	290	280	420	68	4	3 190
99	72	Lucas Industries	UK	Comp (Ac)	290	460	4 668	6	..	..
100	–	Sema Group	UK	Oth	290	260	1 448	20	50	13 110

a The period average of market exchange rates of the International Monetary Fund's *International Financial Statistics* is used for conversion to US dollars.
b Rank designations in the column for 1995 may not correspond to that given in table 8A in the *SIPRI Yearbook 1997* because of subsequent revision. A dash (–) in this column indicates either that the company did not produce arms in 1995, or that it did not exist as it was structured in 1996, in which case there is a zero (0) in column 7, or that it did not rank among the 100 top companies in 1995. Companies with the designation S in the column for rank are subsidiaries.
c Names in brackets are names of parent companies.
d A key to abbreviations in column 5 is provided on p. 260.
e For Japanese companies, data in the arms sales column represent new military contracts rather than arms sales.
f Arms sales data for Rockwell International are estimates for 11 months. The company's arms-producing unit was acquired by Boeing in Dec. 1996.
g Matra BAe Dynamics, a missile joint venture between Lagardere and BAe, has been operative since Nov. 1996. The data here are full-year estimates.
h Arms sales data for Loral are estimates for 3 months. The company's arms-producing branch was acquired by Lockheed Martin in Apr. 1996.
i Data for South Korea are for 1995.
j Thyssen Werften was established in 1996 and includes the former Thyssen Nordseewerke and Blohm&Voss.
k Lucent Technologies was spun off from AT&T in Apr. 1996.
l Arms sales data for Westinghouse Electric are estimates for 2 months. Its arms-producing unit was acquired by Northrop Grumman in Mar. 1996.
m STN Atlas is presented as an independent company in 1996 because it was in the process of transfer from Bremer Vulkan to its new owners (Rheinmetall 26%, Badenwerke 25%, British Aerospace 49%) until July 1997 when the acquisition was approved by the relevant monopoly authorities. The arms sales figure is an estimate based on the figure for its arms sales share in 1995.
n The figure for Fiat Aviazione's arms sales includes Alfa Romeo Avio, although it was acquired only in Jan. 1997.
o SEPI, Sociedad Estatal de Participaciones Industrial, was established in Aug. 1995 to take over the profit-making subsidiary companies of INI (Instituto Nacional de Industria). Teneo, a sub-holding of SEPI, was dissolved in 1996 in order to accelerate the privatization process. Loss-making companies of the former INI were taken over by AIE (Agencia Industrial del Estado). In Sep. 1997 AIE was dissolved and Bazan and Santa Barbara were integrated into SEPI.
p The Ordnance & Aerospace business of Olin was spun off as Primex Technologies in late 1996.
q Australian Submarine Corporation is owned 49.5% by Kockums (Celsius) of Sweden and 48.5% by the Australian Government.

7. Military research and development

ERIC ARNETT

I. Introduction

Global military research and development (R&D) expenditure continues to decline, mainly because of reductions in the US budget. Of the major investors, only South Korea has continued to increase its effort and apparently will continue to do so despite economic difficulties and a new government. The most notable developments in 1997 were the Japan Defense Agency's decision to reduce R&D investment for the first time since 1976, the Russian Government's new approaches to diversify funding of the military technology base, and the US Quadrennial Defense Review (QDR), which continued the controversial post-cold war policy of reducing R&D less than other accounts, especially procurement. US R&D is the main focus of this chapter.

After a discussion of global trends with special attention to new policies in Russia, section II examines trends in military R&D in the Organisation for Economic Co-operation and Development (OECD) states and India between 1983 and 1996. It shows that by the mid-1990s most OECD states had returned to spending less than 110 per cent of their 1983 funding levels, but few have reduced their military R&D much below that. The UK is a major exception, having reduced its R&D budget substantially, even during the 1980s. Spain, which joined NATO during that period, India, Japan and South Korea are still spending at much higher levels than in 1983. The fear commonly expressed that Western science would be irreversibly militarized by the build-up in the 1980s has not been borne out, the military share of government and national R&D having returned to its previous level or lower in most cases. The exceptions are Japan, Spain and to a lesser extent India, which is finally seeing an expansion of independent R&D on civilian technologies in the era of economic reform.

Section III addresses US military R&D policy. The QDR was most significant for its emphasis on continuity in R&D programmes at the expense of the technologies often grouped under the rubric of the Revolution in Military Affairs (RMA). Critics claimed that the QDR and related policies of the Clinton Administration would leave US forces vulnerable to new threats, particularly from ballistic and cruise missiles, but the brief analyses presented in this chapter suggest that these fears are exaggerated. The debate over the QDR is essentially over whether the policies promulgated by presidents Bill Clinton and George Bush, under which new technologies are developed but not necessarily built and deployed, were sustainable. For the time being, the answer appears to be 'yes', a result of importance for researchers interested in the relationship between military R&D and arms-race behaviour.

SIPRI Yearbook 1998: Armaments, Disarmament and International Security

Table 7.1. Official figures for government military R&D expenditure[a]

Country	Military R&D expenditure Current local currency	1995 US$ m.	Year	Share of total military exp. (%)	Source
Nuclear weapon states					
USA (m. dollars)	38 000	37 000	1996	*14.0*	OECD
France (b. francs)	25	4 900	1996	*11.0*	OECD
UK (b. pounds)	2.1	3 200	1996	*9.5*	OECD
Russia (tr. roubles)	3.06	990	1996	*5.1*	OSCE
China[b]	..	1 000	1994	*< 4.0*	Chinese Govt
Non-nuclear weapon and threshold states					
Germany (m. D. marks)	3 200	2 200	1996	*5.5*	OECD
Japan (b. yen)	170	1 800	1996	*3.5*	OECD
Sweden (b. kronor)	4.1	570	1995	*10.0*	OECD
India (b. rupees)	14.9	510	1994	*6.5*	Indian Govt
South Korea (b. won)	370	460	1996	*3.0*	Korean Govt
Taiwan (b. T. dollars)	8.9	350	1994	*3.3*	Taiwan Govt
Spain (b. pesetas)	40	310	1996	*3.7*	OECD
Italy (b. lire)	480	300	1995	*1.5*	OECD
Australia (m. A. dollars)	220	170	1994	*2.0*	OECD
South Africa (m. rand)	572	150	1996	*5.1*	RSA Govt
Canada (m. C. dollars)	170	120	1996	*1.5*	OECD
Ukraine (b. karbonavets)	416	120	1994	*2.3*	UN
Switzerland (m. francs)	117	100	1995	*2.0*	UN
Netherlands (m. guilders)	170	100	1996	*1.3*	OECD
Brazil (m. reais)	84.7	78	1996	*0.8*	UN
Norway (m. kroner)	460	71	1996	*1.9*	OECD
Finland (m. markkaa)	110	25	1996	*1.2*	OECD
Poland (m. new zlotys)	69.9	24	1996	*0.7*	UN
Czech Republic (m. korunas)	630	15	1996	*2.6*	UN
Argentina (m. pesos)	11.6	11	1996	*0.3*	UN
Philippines (m. pesos)	249	10	1994	*1.2*	UN
Romania (b. lei)	18.6	9.1	1995	*1.0*	UN
Portugal (b. escudos)	1.0	6.9	1995	*0.3*	OECD
Belgium (m. francs)	210	6.9	1996	*1.6*	OECD
Ecuador (b. sucres)	16.0	6.2	1995	*1.4*	UN
Turkey (b. lira)	140	5.7	1994	*0.1*	UN
Denmark (m. kroner)	30	5.3	1996	*1.7*	OECD
Greece (b. drachmas)	1.0	4.3	1995	*0.1*	OECD
New Zealand (m. N.Z. dollars)	5.4	3.6	1995	*0.4*	OECD
Slovakia (m. korunas)	99	3.1	1996	*0.7*	UN
Hungary (m. forints)	164	1.7	1994	*0.2*	UN
Luxembourg (m. francs)	45.3	1.6	1994	0.9	UN

[a] Includes only states spending more than $1 million on military R&D. Figures are for the year indicated only. [b] Figures for China are accurate to only 1 significant digit.

Sources: OECD Main Science and Technology Indicators no. 2 (1997); UN documents A/49/190, 29 June 1994; A/49/190/Add. 1, 30 Aug. 1994; A/51/209, 24 July 1996; and A/52/310, 25 Aug. 1997; other data provided by governments as cited below; and chapter 6 in this volume.

Table 7.2. Government expenditure on military R&D in select countries, 1983–96[a]
Figures are in US $m. in 1995 prices and exchange rates.

Country	1983	1986	1989	1992	1993	1994	1995	1996	1992–95
USA	38 000	51 000	51 000	44 000	43 000	39 000	37 000	37 000	163 000
France	5 400	6 200	7 100	6 800	6 200	6 000	5 200	4 900	24 200
UK	5 500	5 400	4 100	3 500	3 800	3 300	3 500	3 200	14 100
Germany[b]	1 700	2 300	3 100	2 400	1 900	1 900	2 000	2 200	8 200
Japan	520	[820]	1 100	1 400	1 500	1 500	1 600	1 800	6 000
Sweden	540	660	680	690	650	500	570	..	2 410
Italy	270	540	750	600	620	590	300	..	2 110
India	170	340	410	380	470	510	[500]	[490]	1 860
S Korea	[140]	120	170	330	400	400	440	460	1 570
Spain	66	75	460	410	340	280	300	310	1 330
S Africa	160	390	480	210	170	160	160	150	700
Canada	180	220	230	190	180	180	150	120	700

[a] Figures in square brackets are author's estimates.
[b] Figures for 1983, 1986 and 1989 are for the Federal Republic of Germany (West Germany) only.

Sources: *OECD Main Science and Technology Indicators*, no. 2 (1997), no. 2 (1995), no. 1 (1990) and 1981–87; India, Department of Science and Technology, *Research and Development Statistics* (various publishers, various years); Republic of Korea, Ministry of National Defense, *Defense White Paper* (Ministry of National Defense: Seoul, various years); and Batchelor, P., 'Balancing arms procurement with national socio-economic imperatives', paper submitted to the SIPRI Arms Procurement Project, 21 June 1997.

II. Global trends

Total annual expenditure on military R&D has fallen to about $58 billion,[1] of which $37 billion is accounted for by the USA, $48 billion by NATO and $51 billion by the OECD countries. With the Japanese Defense Agency reducing its R&D request for fiscal year (FY) 1998, only South Korea continued to increase military R&D expenditure significantly.[2] As seen in table 7.2, few of the leading states of the OECD have reduced their military R&D budgets to

---

[1] This figure is derived from the sum of best publicly known estimates and 1% of military expenditure in states where no figure for military R&D is publicly known. The estimate of China's expenditure is elaborated in Arnett, E., 'Military technology: the case of China', *SIPRI Yearbook 1995: Armaments, Disarmament and International Security* (Oxford University Press: Oxford, 1995), pp. 375–77. The estimate that China spends of the order of $1 billion to 1 significant digit means that it spends $0.5–$1.5 billion, but no more precise estimate is possible.

[2] The Japanese 143.4-billion yen budget request represents a 17.6% cut in real terms from FY 1997, but still a real increase from 1996. Usui, N., 'JDA seeks small hike in weapon procurement budget', *Defense News*, 8–14 Sep. 1997, p. 32. Korean military R&D funding for FY 1997 was increased 10% in real terms. After the economic crisis, the KTX-2 trainer project received an emergency 20% budget increase, which almost completely compensates for the devaluation of the won and the programme's 50% foreign-exchange content, and a final funding commitment. Proctor, P., 'KTX-2 eyes T-38, F-5 replacement market', *Aviation Week & Space Technology*, 16 Mar. 1998, p. 13; and Proctor, P., 'Basic defense work still on track in Asia', *Aviation Week & Space Technology*, 23 Feb. 1998, p. 66. The long-term trend in Japanese and South Korean military R&D is described in Arnett, E., 'Military research and development', *SIPRI Yearbook 1997: Armaments, Disarmament and International Security* (Oxford University Press: Oxford, 1997), pp. 226–35.

their 1983 levels but, with the exceptions of Germany and Spain, the leading NATO allies are within 110 per cent of their 1983 budgets.³ As has long been the case, the main area of emphasis for most of the states spending most heavily on R&D is combat aircraft.⁴ The long-anticipated first flights of two Asian aircraft prototypes—the Chinese J-10 and the Indian Light Combat Aircraft (LCA)—did not take place in 1997, despite some observers' expectations that they would.⁵

A note on sources of information

As discussed more comprehensively in the *SIPRI Yearbook 1996*,⁶ publicly available information on military R&D has improved since the mid-1980s but is still quite limited. The most complete information is available from certain national governments, in particular that of the USA. Data from any one state, however, are not easily compared with those from another. Often only R&D undertaken by the defence ministry is counted and other projects of military importance are neglected. The largest set of comparable data on military R&D comes from the OECD, which compiles a survey of national budgets to produce aggregate figures for total civil and military R&D investment in member states.⁷ South Korean figures appeared in the OECD survey for the first time in 1997, but covered only a single year and—as with other new members of the OECD, the Czech Republic, Hungary and Poland—gave no estimate for R&D funded by the government for military purposes.

Although considerable effort was put into collecting comparable data for the UN register of military budgets, it is difficult to know how governments derive the figures they submit, and some do not disaggregate military R&D at all. (The same instrument is used to submit budget information to the Organization for Security and Co-operation in Europe (OSCE), but these submissions are only available from the governments of origin. They are not published by the OSCE.) Moreover, although the register still enjoys unanimous support in the First Committee of the UN General Assembly, only 63 states have submitted R&D data in any year since the register was started in

---

³ Germany reduced its military R&D budget to within 15% of its 1983 level in 1993 and 1994 by underfunding some major programmes, but has since increased it by 5%. On the dramatic increase in Spain, which joined NATO in 1982 and confirmed its membership by referendum in 1986, see Arnett, E., 'Military research and development', *SIPRI Yearbook 1996: Armaments, Disarmament and International Security* (Oxford University Press: Oxford, 1996), pp. 392–403.

⁴ In China and Russia, nuclear delivery systems appear to have a greater emphasis, as discussed in Arnett (note 2), pp. 219, 221.

⁵ A Chinese engineer familiar with the J-10 project has said that the 'prototype' discussed in the Western press is actually a full-scale model and will not fly. He contradicted Western predictions that the J-10 would fly in 1997, putting the date past the turn of the century. Personal communication with a Chinese engineer, Chengdu, Nov. 1996.

⁶ Arnett (note 3), pp. 387–88.

⁷ Definitions and methods are described in OECD, *Frascati Manual 1993* (OECD: Paris, 1993). Data generally refer to expenditures by organizations carrying out R&D but may include budgeted disbursements from funding organizations. Some OECD members report R&D figures to the UN which are counted as education and training or other funds by OECD methods. In cases where the OECD method gives a nil return for a member, table 7.1 gives the figure submitted to the UN.

1980; 17 of these (mainly African and Latin American states) have only ever filed a nil report and only 32 have given figures for any year since 1993. The USA reported in 1997 for the first time since 1990. Among the 20 largest investors in military R&D among UN members, China, India, South Africa and South Korea have never filed a return, although India has given figures to the *Unesco Statistical Yearbook*.

This chapter uses OECD figures where possible, falling back when necessary on UN or OSCE submissions and other national data, in that order of preference. Independent R&D undertaken by firms with the expectation that it will be reimbursed during procurement is not included, although it may constitute more than half of all military R&D investment in some cases, such as that of Japan.

In general, this chapter seeks to evaluate and compare the results of R&D programmes rather than the opportunity cost to governments of the relevant expenditure and human resources. Current figures are deflated using the local consumer price index and converted to US dollars at the 1995 exchange rate in order to facilitate comparisons between figures in this chapter of the *SIPRI Yearbook* and the military expenditure chapter. Purchasing power parity (PPP) conversions are usually preferable for comparing R&D figures, but are difficult to derive for military goods. Using the OECD's PPP factors for R&D gives lower results for some currencies (by about 20 per cent for the yen and the deutschmark, and over 35 per cent in the case of the Swedish krona). Similar PPP factors could increase results by as much as a factor of four for currencies like the rouble, yuan and rupee.

New sources of support for the Russian military technology base

The Russian Government's funding for military R&D has fallen dramatically from the levels sustained by the Soviet Union during the cold war—having reached a level perhaps 90 per cent lower in real terms, and with as much as half of the amount budgeted actually being spent on other things.[8] Russia is struggling to maintain a military technology base without adequate funds in the budget. The situation became even more dire for R&D institutes in 1997 when, shortly after the appointment of Igor Sergeyev as Defence Minister, it was announced that funding for at least 220 of 1670 R&D institutes would be cut off.[9]

Two new approaches are being tried in the hope of preserving the technology base without additional funding from the central government. Russian design bureaux will receive a 5 per cent royalty on exported arms, despite

---

[8] Other R&D funding, especially Ministry of Atomic Energy funds, may be used for military purposes. This may amount to as much as 75% more than the figures reported in table 7.1. See also appendix 6D in this volume.

[9] Babadzhanyan, N., ITAR-TASS, 4 Sep. 1997, in Foreign Broadcast Information Service, *Daily Report–Central Eurasia* (hereafter FBIS-SOV), FBIS-SOV-97-248, 9 Sep. 1997.

being independent of production firms in many cases;[10] and they are encouraged to sell their services directly to foreign firms, offering either technology transfer or simply modification of arms produced in Russia for export.[11]

The most prominent of these arrangements has been India's agreement to fund the further development of the Sukhoi Su-30M as part of a $1.8 billion deal for 40 of the multi-role aircraft. Aside from the unit costs of the aircraft delivered, India has already paid $200 million directly to Sukhoi for the development of more advanced variants, the Su-30MK and Su-30MKI.[12] The Su-30s will be delivered in batches as the modifications are completed. Sukhoi has relied on exports for its survival, while the Russian Government has supported MiG-MAPO as its supplier of combat aircraft.[13] India is also thought to be funding an upgrade of the MiG-27 and development of an airborne warning and control aircraft at Ilyushin with cooperation from Israel Aircraft Industries (IAI).[14] Other reports claim that Russian R&D institutes are transferring technology to China's submarine and ballistic missile projects and Iran's ballistic missile projects, but these are difficult to verify.[15]

While the new Russian approach goes beyond the familiar strategy of supporting arms industries through export of arms developed for the domestic market, it is not without precedent. During its period of conversion and diversification in the mid-1980s, the Chinese industry developed new arms with its own money and loans from Chinese banks specifically for export markets. Western firms, too, have occasionally developed systems solely for export, and in some cases have received R&D funds directly from recipient governments for 'indigenous' projects, as US firms have done most recently from Taiwan and are doing in the development of the LCA. The USA has also funded Israeli military R&D on 'indigenous' projects, including the Merkava tank, the Lavi fighter and the Chetz anti-missile interceptor. Nevertheless, Russia's expectation that the export of arms and military technology will save

---

[10] Felgengauer, P., 'Selling Russian arms and transferring arms-building technology to China: a short-term policy with long-term consequences', paper presented to the RAND–CAPS workshop on Foreign Military Assistance to the People's Republic of China and Taiwan, Oxford, 26 June 1997, p. 2.

[11] Felgengauer (note 10), p. 6.

[12] Then Indian Prime Minister P. V. Narasimha Rao reportedly agreed to provide Rs 5.5 billion (c. $200 million) for the development of the Su-30. Mehta, A. K., 'Under a cloud', *Sunday* (Calcutta), 4 May 1997. A Russian source gives the figure of $150 million. Felgengauer (note 10), p. 8.

[13] An upgrade of the MiG-31 strategic air defence interceptor was the only combat aircraft project being funded by the government in 1996. Lambeth, B. S., *Russia's Air Power at the Crossroads* (RAND: Santa Monica, Calif., 1996). In 1997, Defence Minister Sergeyev promised to fund MiG-MAPO's more advanced 1-42 MFI fighter to the tune of 15–16 million roubles. Butowski, P., 'Russia plans first flight for long-awaited fighter', *Jane's Defence Weekly*, 18 Feb. 1998, p. 3.

[14] Novichkov, N. and Taverna, M. A., 'Russia, Israel plan A-50', *Aviation Week & Space Technology*, 23 June 1997, p. 27; and Aneja, A., 'India seeks arms transfers from Russia', *The Hindu*, 11 Nov. 1997. It is not clear whether India is funding Russian R&D on the MiG-27 upgrade or is contributing as a co-developer. 'India, Russia to devise new arms systems', *The Hindu*, 23 Dec. 1997.

[15] Sharpe, R., *Jane's Fighting Ships 1997–98* (Jane's Information Group: Coulsdon, 1997), p. 114; Knowlton, B., 'US warns Russians on SS-18 sales to Chinese', *International Herald Tribune*, 22 May 1996, p. 1; George, A., 'China uses Russian know-how on ICBM', *Flight International*, 22 Dec. 1993–4 Jan. 1994; and Fitchett, J., 'Ousting Iranian, Russia signals US on arms', *International Herald Tribune*, 9 Dec. 1997, pp. 1, 4. The Russian Government has specifically denied transferring missile technology to Iran. Interfax, 15 Sep. 1997, in FBIS-SOV-97-258, 16 Sep. 1997; and Romanenkova, V., ITAR-TASS, 16 Sep. 1997, in FBIS-SOV-97-259, 17 Sep. 1997.

Table 7.3. Government expenditure on military R&D as a fraction of total government R&D expenditure in select countries, 1983–96[a]
Figures are percentages.

Country	1983	1986	1989	1992	1993	1994	1995	1996
USA	64.3	69.4	65.5	58.6	59.0	55.3	54.1	54.7
UK	49.6	49.3	43.6	40.7	42.0	38.9	40.8	37.0
France	32.7	34.0	37.0	35.7	33.3	33.1	30.3	29.0
India	18.7	24.1	25.1	25.2	26.2	28.1	..	..
Sweden	21.4	25.9	24.7	24.3	23.5	18.9	20.9	..
South Korea	[30]	16	14	20	21	19	16	13
Spain	6.4	5.8	19.1	14.6	12.5	10.6	10.4	10.8
Germany[b]	9.6	12.1	12.8	10.0	8.5	8.6	9.1	9.8
Japan	2.4	[3.5]	5.1	5.9	6.1	6.0	6.2	5.9
Canada	6.0	7.1	7.5	6.0	5.5	5.5	4.9	4.3
Italy	5.7	8.5	10.3	7.1	8.5	8.9	4.7	..

[a] Figures in square brackets are author's estimates.
[b] Figures for 1983, 1986 and 1989 are for the Federal Republic of Germany only.

Sources: *OECD Main Science and Technology Indicators*, no. 2 (1997), no. 2 (1995), no. 1 (1990) and 1981–87; India, Department of Science and Technology, *Research and Development Statistics*, various years; Republic of Korea, Ministry of Science and Technology, *Annual Survey Report on R&D Activities*, various years; and *UNESCO Statistical Yearbook*, various years.

its military industrial and technology bases from oblivion is the grandest to date. It remains to be seen whether the strategy underlying these new policies can succeed and do so without recourse to more reckless practices.

Military R&D and national technology bases

When Western investment in military technology increased dramatically in the early 1980s, one concern (apart from the potential for a renewed arms race) was the possibility that science policy would be difficult to return to a civilian emphasis if the international situation changed for the better. Now that military R&D expenditure has nearly returned to its earlier levels in most Western states, it is instructive to see how much the balance between military and civilian science has been altered. As seen in table 7.3, by 1996 NATO governments (with the exceptions of Germany and Spain) were spending a similar or smaller fraction of their government R&D funds on military projects than in 1983, the year in which the USA launched its Strategic Defense Initiative (SDI).[16] Furthermore, since more R&D is now funded privately in most West-

---

[16] US military R&D spending in 1983 was already about 35% higher than it had been in 1979 and 12% higher than its average between 1960 and 1979. US civilian R&D was cut significantly during the 8 years of Ronald Reagan's presidency, in part because of conservative Republicans' ideological opposition to intervening in civilian markets. If civilian R&D had not been cut to such an extent, the post-cold war reduction of the military fraction of government-funded R&D would have been even greater. There is now bipartisan support in the USA for an increase in civilian R&D funding of as much as 100% over 10 years, which would result in the military portion of government-funded R&D falling

Table 7.4. Government expenditure on military R&D as a fraction of national R&D expenditure in select countries, 1983–96
Figures are percentages.

Country	1983	1986	1989	1992	1993	1994	1995	1996
USA	28.3	30.3	28.0	24.3	24.9	22.4	20.8	20.5
India	14.6	19.9	19.8	16.0	17.4	18.4	..	..
UK	29.0	25.4	18.0	16.3	16.8	14.4	15.6	..
France	21.4	22.3	21.0	19.0	17.1	16.9	14.5	13.8
Sweden	11.6	[10.6]	9.8	..	9.6	..	9.8	..
Spain	3.8	3.1	13.0	8.4	6.9	6.2	6.6	6.4
Germany[a]	4.3	[6.0]	4.6	4.1	3.5	3.4	3.6	4.0
South Korea	[10]	3.5	[3.2]	4.1	4.0	3.7	3.6	..
Italy	5.3	5.4	6.0	4.4	4.7	4.8	2.4	..
Canada	3.0	3.1	3.1	2.4	2.0	1.9	1.6	1.3
Japan	0.6	[0.8]	0.8	0.9	1.0	1.0	1.1	..

[a] Figures for 1983, 1986 and 1989 are for the Federal Republic of Germany (West Germany) only.

Sources: OECD Main Science and Technology Indicators, various years; India, Department of Science and Technology, *Research and Development Statistics*, various years; Republic of Korea, Ministry of Science and Technology, *Annual Survey Report on R&D Activities*, various years; and *UNESCO Statistical Yearbook*, various years.

ern countries, the share of national R&D investment (government plus private firms, institutes and universities) accounted for by government-sponsored military R&D has declined even further, as seen in table 7.4. While the proportion remains high, especially in the nuclear weapon states—and missile defence continues to claim a large share of US military R&D funding, as seen in the next section—the fear that science would be permanently militarized by the build-up in the 1980s has not been borne out. Whether the proportion will continue to drop remains to be seen.

In contrast, two of the three Asian states for which accurate figures are available—India and Japan—show continued increases in the share of the government R&D budgets devoted to military projects. This suggests that the dynamic underlying their build-ups had little to do with the cold war. Japanese investment in military R&D has nearly quadrupled since 1983 to a level that rivals Germany's as the highest among the world's non-nuclear weapon states.[17] Japanese investment in civilian technology has also increased steadily, so that the balance of national investment still strongly favours the civilian side. Furthermore, one reason cited by the Japan Defense Agency for 'the stagnation of [military] R&D investment' in 1997 is 'personnel reduction

below 40%. American Association for the Advancement of Science, *Federal Spending on Defense and Nondefense R&D* (AAAS: Washington, DC, 1998).

[17] Japanese firms invest heavily in independent military R&D, so that it is likely that total national funding of military R&D is greater in Japan than in Germany.

in the defense industry, including transfer of engineers and technicians', who presumably are moving to civilian projects.[18]

In the case of India, military R&D expenditure increased dramatically in the early 1980s but appears to have stabilized in the mid-1990s. In the era of economic reform, civilian R&D in the private sector is gradually growing, leading to a notable decrease in the fraction of national R&D investment accounted for by military projects since the 1980s, despite increases in military R&D expenditure in some years. This trend is likely to continue to favour independent investment in civilian R&D as that continues to increase, since funding for military R&D has not increased in real terms since 1994/95.[19]

South Korea shows a similar pattern of diversification in the technology base despite dramatic increases in government military R&D expenditure. Although it increased by more than 280 per cent between 1986 and 1996, the ratios of government military R&D expenditure to government civilian R&D expenditure and to national R&D expenditure have been falling since 1993 because of even larger increases in other accounts. The explosion of civilian R&D spending—government-funded civilian R&D increased by 250 per cent between 1986 and 1996, while R&D funded by other sources increased by over 380 per cent—ensures that the national technology base is more balanced, despite increases on the military side, and is a dramatic departure from the practices of the late 1970s and early 1980s when military R&D dominated a much smaller R&D effort. It is not clear that such rapid increases in the technology base are sustainable or cost-effective.

III. The USA

With a military R&D budget more than seven times that of France, its closest competitor, the USA clearly maintains the wherewithal to continue its dominance in the realm of military technology. Events in 1997 raised new questions about that dominance and policies to preserve it. The QDR and the new National Security Strategy[20] from which it was derived signalled yet another continuation of the policy of preparing for two near-simultaneous wars against Iran or Iraq and North Korea using established conventional technologies. Criticism of the QDR focused on the lack of imagination in applying new technologies, especially information technology, as well as the necessity and feasibility of preparing to fight two near-simultaneous wars. Further, critics claimed that US policies were inadequate to compensate for areas of potential

---

[18] Japan Defense Agency, *Defense of Japan 1997* (Japan Defense Agency: Tokyo, 1997), p. 176.

[19] For the long-term trend in funding of the Defence Research and Development Organisation, which funds roughly 85% of military R&D, see Arnett (note 2), p. 223. For the long-term trends in military, nuclear, space and other civilian R&D see Arnett, E., 'Nuclear weapons and arms control in South Asia after the test ban', ed. E. Arnett, *Nuclear Weapons and Arms Control in South Asia after the Test Ban*, SIPRI Research Report No. 14 (Oxford University Press: Oxford, 1998), p. 5. Official statistics may underestimate independent civilian R&D by as much as 30%. Alagh, Y. K., 'Technological change in Indian industry', *Economic and Political Weekly*, 24 Jan. 1998, p. 181.

[20] *National Military Strategy: Shape, Respond, Prepare Now—A Military Strategy for a New Era* (White House: Washington, DC, 1997).

vulnerability that might still exist despite the enormous and growing US qualitative lead.

This section summarizes developments in 1997, then looks more closely at remedies to two areas of possible vulnerability: ballistic missile defence and cruise missile defence. While there is little doubt that the USA can maintain its fighting edge, weaknesses in these areas are thought to give potential adversaries the possibility of inflicting unacceptable losses. The risk of suffering casualties might therefore deter the USA from intervening under certain circumstances.[21] The section concludes with a brief discussion of developments in 1997 related to anti-satellite weapons.

The Quadrennial Defense Review

As President Bill Clinton began his second term in office, the US military was set for its first assessment of the success and durability of policy adjustments made in the early 1990s. Clinton's new Secretary of Defense, William Cohen, noted in May 1997 that the post-cold war era had ended, by which he meant that the time was ripe for a stable defence policy appropriate to the potentially long-lasting condition of uncertainty without acute threats.[22] Cohen was preparing to make a case for steady or increasing defence budgets after 10 years of reductions, totalling 38 per cent of the defence budget, 33 per cent of force structure and 67 per cent of procurement funding.[23]

There was considerable speculation as to whether the USA could continue its policy of maintaining the military technology base through relatively high R&D expenditure—R&D has been cut only 27 per cent from its 1986 high, as table 7.2 shows—despite the 67 per cent reduction in procurement.[24] Sceptics questioned whether the USA could maintain this comparatively high level of R&D expenditure if little hardware was ever bought. Enthusiasts hoped that Cohen would increase investment in R&D on the new technologies that characterize the RMA, especially information technology, a shift that might allow for large reductions in procurement and troop strength in the long run.[25]

---

[21] There are related fears regarding nuclear, biological and chemical weapons. According to US counter-proliferation doctrine, these are being addressed primarily through arms control, technology denial, nuclear deterrence, the capability to pre-empt and protective measures. Nuclear arms control is discussed in chapter 10 in this volume, chemical and biological arms control and protection in chapter 11 and export controls in chapter 9.

[22] Cohen, W. S., 'Time has come to leap into the future', *Defense Issues*, vol. 12, no. 9 (12 May 1997).

[23] US Department of Defense, *Report of the Quadrennial Defense Review* (US Department of Defense: Washington, DC, 1997). Procurement funding fell from about $120 billion to about $40 billion between 1985 and 1997. US Congress, Senate Committee on Armed Services, *Quadrennial Defense Review*, S. Hrg. 105-197, 20–21 May 1997, p. 12.

[24] The outlook as Clinton took office is reviewed in Arnett, E. H. and Kokoski, R., 'Military technology and international security: the case of the USA', *SIPRI Yearbook 1993: World Armaments and Disarmament* (Oxford University Press: Oxford, 1993), p. 328.

[25] For a good brief summary of RMA technologies see Binnendijk, H., *1997 Strategic Assessment: Flashpoints and Force Structure* (National Defense University Institute for National Strategic Studies: Washington, DC, 1997), pp. 273–81.

MILITARY RESEARCH AND DEVELOPMENT 277

The QDR was expected to have profound implications for the US military technology base, but did not. In presenting the QDR, Cohen explicitly did not move decisively towards the RMA and did not cancel any programmes for the major weapon systems that the RMA is meant to render obsolete.[26] The only programme in development to get a decisive boost from Cohen in parallel with the QDR was National Missile Defense (NMD), which will receive an additional $2.3 billion over FYs 1998–2002. NMD and other new technologies are to be developed as 'options' that will not necessarily ever be deployed.

Even with the QDR's emphasis on continuity and a stable budget, funding for military R&D is likely to fall an additional 13.8 per cent in real terms from its FY 1998 level of $40.4 billion by 2001, after which it is expected to increase again after 2001 as some prominent projects reach full-scale development.[27] If the Department of Defense gets its hoped-for increase to $60 billion in annual procurement funding by 2001, the fraction of R&D in equipment expenditure will drop from its current 54 per cent to 38 per cent—still an unusually high level even among the Group of Seven industrialized countries (G7).[28] Furthermore, it is possible that mergers and acquisitions among arms-producing firms are diverting funds from independent R&D performed by firms in anticipation of future profits, thereby reducing the total amount being devoted to programmes embodying new technologies.

While some critics of the QDR were dismayed that it did not raise R&D expenditure as much as they would have liked,[29] the outcome of the review, favouring as it does the status quo plus 'options', suggests that the US post-cold war approach to military technology is more resilient than might have been expected by some conceptions of arms-race dynamics.[30] A greater test will come in the early years of the next decade, by which time Cohen has

[26] US Department of Defense, News Briefing—Subject: Quadrennial Defense Review, 19 May 1997. According to a military source, 'RMA thinking is still just the parsley on the plate'. Graham, B., 'Cohen weighing three possible courses for shape of future US military', *Washington Post*, 4 Apr. 1997. See also Vickers, M. G. and Kosiak, S. M., *The Quadrennial Defense Review: An Assessment* (Center for Strategic and Budgetary Assessments: Washington, DC, 1997). In defence Cohen countered: 'Information technologies will clearly be in the forefront of our activities . . . [But] we must pursue this transformation prudently'. Cohen, W. S., *Response to the National Defense Panel's Final Report* (US Department of Defense: Washington, DC, 1997).

[27] The FY 1998 level is in turn 2.7% lower than the FY 1994 level after a slight increase in FY 1997. American Association for the Advancement of Science, *Congressional Action on Research and Development in the FY 1998 Budget* (AAAS: Washington, DC, 1997); American Association for the Advancement of Science, *Projected Effects of President's FY 1999 Budget on Defense R&D* (AAAS: Washington, DC, 1998); and US Department of Defense, Background Briefing, 30 Jan. 1998.

[28] On the membership of the G7 see the glossary. Compare statistics for the G7 and leading NATO members given in Arnett (note 2), p. 213; and Arnett (note 3), p. 386. Between 1988 and 1996 the share of R&D in US military equipment expenditure varied between 44% (in 1994) and 62% (in 1993). During the same period in other G7 countries this share varied between 9.9% (Canada in 1988) and 51% (France in 1990).

[29] US National Defense Panel, *Transforming Defense: National Security in the 21st Century* (US National Defense Panel: Arlington, Va., 1997); Friedman, N., 'World naval developments: the Quadrennial Defense Charade', *US Naval Institute Proceedings*, July 1997, pp. 91–92; and Hunter, D., 'QDR misses the point', *US Naval Institute Proceedings*, Oct. 1997, pp. 30–32. In response to the congressionally mandated NDP report, Cohen created an RMA oversight council within the Pentagon. Cohen (note 26).

[30] See discussion in Arnett (note 3), pp. 385–86.

Table 7.5. Appropriations for major US R&D programmes, 1998
Figures are in current US $m.

Programme	R&D budget	Service or agency
Aircraft and associated weapons		
F-22 fighter	2 077	Air Force
Joint Strike Fighter	464	Navy
F/A-18E/F fighter-bomber	294	Navy
B-1B bomber upgrades	221	Air Force
Airborne reconnaissance	197	DARPA
Endurance unpiloted aerial vehicles	193	DARPA
E-8A JSTARS surveillance aircraft	152	Air Force
Joint Air-to-Surface Stand-off Missile (JASSM)	128	Air Force
C-17 transport aircraft	111	Air Force
Sub-total	**3 940**	
Missile defence		
National Missile Defense	979	BMDO
Theater High-Altitude Area Defense (THAAD)	667	BMDO
Joint theatre missile defence	605	BMDO
Navy Theater-Wide (Upper Tier)	410	BMDO
Navy Area Defense (Lower Tier)	290	BMDO
Space Based Infrared (SBIR) satellite	217	Air Force
Sub-total	**2 694**	
Other		
Defence assets	1 049	Department of Energy
Naval reactors	648	Department of Energy
New SSN attack submarine	323	Navy
Information systems security	254	DARPA
Brilliant Anti-armour Technology (BAT) submunition	237	Army
Chemical and biological warfare defence	191	DARPA
Total	**9 336**	

Notes: Includes only those programmes allocated more than $100 million. DARPA = Defense Advanced Research Projects Agency, JSTARS = Joint Surveillance and Target Attack Radar, BMDO = Ballistic Missile Defense Organization.

Sources: US Congress, House of Representatives, *Conference Report on Department of Defense Appropriations Act, 1998* (US Government Printing Office: Washington, DC, 1997).

promised to increase procurement funding by 50 per cent. A number of combat aircraft and missile-defence programmes are due to enter production at the same time as the federal budget will be under unprecedented pressure from deficit-reduction laws and social security payments to retiring baby-boomers. Moreover, the QDR can only be financed if the Congress accepts two more rounds of base closures, which were initially greeted with hostility.

Ballistic missile defence

Among the weapon systems identified as potentially vulnerable, ballistic missiles are by far the most familiar. There are two distinct US concerns regarding ballistic missiles: intercontinental missiles might be launched against the US homeland, and short- to intermediate-range missiles might be launched against US security partners or intervention forces. Both concerns are as controversial as their suggested remedies. At present, the intercontinental threat to the US homeland resides in only two countries, both of which are generally treated more as promising partners for cooperation than potential enemies—China and Russia. While there are fears that Iran or North Korea could develop or buy intercontinental missiles, the existence and viability of even intermediate-range ballistic missile (IRBM) programmes are uncertain in both cases.

Upon assuming office, Cohen—once a Republican senator and therefore sensitive to the ideological fixation of some in that party on the issue—suggested that NMD, the primary strategic missile-defence programme, had been underfunded and the budget should be doubled to $979 million for 1998. Cohen noted that the Joint Chiefs of Staff did not see the need for theatre missile defences (TMD): 'They are saying, wait a minute, let's see what the threat is'.[31]

The Republican-dominated Congress eagerly accepted the increase for NMD, ignored the service chiefs' hesitation and increased two TMD programmes by $100 million or more each: Navy Theater-Wide ($215 million) and Theater High-Altitude Area Defense (THAAD, $111 million). They also increased the budget for the strategic Space-Based Laser (SBL) to $98 million. When congressional Republicans tried to add $325 million to the missile defence budget over and above these increases, the Director of the Ballistic Missile Defense Organization (BMDO), Lester Lyles, said that he could not use any more money.[32]

NMD is being developed under conditions that will offer a strong test of the current approach to military technology. Under a compromise programme known as 3 + 3, the administration seeks to develop technology for NMD within three years that will constitute a capability to deploy defences within three more years if a threat to the homeland can be identified with greater certainty than exists today (or if the political impetus behind NMD increases after the presidential election in the year 2000). It remains to be seen whether the technological push behind strategic defences will overcome economic and political obstacles, especially if relations with China and Russia improve and Iranian and North Korean programmes do not come to fruition. In any case, there are doubts that the technology can be developed as scheduled, or at all.[33]

---

[31] Cohen is quoted in Rosenfeld, S. S., 'Still on a cold-war footing', *Washington Post*, 31 Oct. 1997, p. A25.

[32] Asker, J. R., 'Going ballistic', *Aviation Week & Space Technology*, 10 Nov. 1997, p. 31.

[33] Mann, P., 'Republicans lose steam on missile defense', *Aviation Week & Space Technology*, 8 Sep. 1997, p. 63.

Table 7.6. Ballistic missile programmes in select countries and corresponding tactical ballistic missile defence programmes

Local desig.	Export desig.	NATO desig.	Status[a]	Country	BMD programme	Country
Short-range missiles (< 500 km)					*Defences comparable to Patriot*	
R-17	..	SS-1c Scud-B	O	DPRK, Iran, Libya, Syria	Aster 30	France, Italy
					S-300 (SA-10/-12)	Russia
DF-11	M-11	CSS-7	O	China	Patriot/PAC-3	USA
Samed	..		D	Iraq	MEADS	USA, Germany, Italy
Medium-range missiles (500–1000 km)					*Improved endo-atmospheric defences*	
..	..	Scud-C	O	DPRK, Iran, Syria	Arrow	Israel
					S-400	Russia
DF-15	M-9	CSS-6	O	China	THAAD	USA
					Navy Area Defense	USA
Intermediate-range missiles (> 1000 km)					*Exo-atmospheric defences*	
DF-3A		CSS-2	O?	China	Navy Theater-Wide	USA
JL-1		CSS-N-3	O	China		
DF-21A		CSS-5	O	China		
Ro-dong	..		D?	DPRK		
Shihab	..		D?	Iran		

[a] O = operational; O? = may have been retired; D = development; D? = development may have been interrupted or has not been confirmed.

Notes: DPRK = Democratic People's Republic of Korea (North Korea); DF = Dongfeng; PAC = Patriot Advanced Capability; MEADS = Medium Extended Area Defense System; THAAD = Theater High-Altitude Area Defense; JL = Julang.

As can be seen from table 7.6, the situation is somewhat more complex in the case of TMD. Potential adversaries already possess ballistic missile capabilities and tactical defences have already been deployed. With the resolution of US–Russian negotiations on differentiating between tactical and strategic defence capabilities in the context of the 1972 Anti-Ballistic Missile (ABM) Treaty,[34] the question for US policy makers becomes one of cost and technological risk. Russia and the USA have already deployed defences with some capability against existing short-range ballistic missiles, like those deployed by Iran, Libya, North Korea and Syria. The additional capability hoped for in improved endo-atmospheric (working within the earth's atmosphere) programmes like the Israeli Arrow-2, the Russian S-400 and the US THAAD and Navy Area Defense entails technological risk and considerable expense, but may offer greater hope of intercepting IRBMs which cannot be intercepted reliably by systems like the Patriot.[35] The US projects in particular involve a

---

[34] See chapter 10 in this volume.

[35] The Arrow failed in its last flight test of 1997. Work on the S-400 and similar systems has not been accorded a high priority in Russia. 'The S-400s now under development will be unable to compete with THAAD.' Goryainov, S. A., 'Intercept point: ABM defence as a political argument', *Nezavisimoye Voyennoye Obozreniye*, no. 25 (12–18 July 1997), p. 3, in FBIS-SOV-97-161-S, 21 Aug. 1997.

new 'hit-to-kill' approach that has not been successful in most of its flight tests thus far and may still turn out to be unworkable.[36] Still more ambitious is the Navy Theater-Wide programme, which is exo-atmospheric: it aims to intercept missiles outside the atmosphere and is therefore literally useless against missiles of a range less than about 1000 km. As with strategic defences, questions remain as to whether a threat exists or will emerge to justify this system.[37] Navy Theater-Wide was not considered a high priority until congressional Republicans insisted that it join PAC-3, THAAD and Navy Area Defense as a 'core' programme.

Despite the claims of its opponents that undue regard for the ABM Treaty has prevented a proper appreciation of the most advanced missile-defence programmes in the USA, other states which remain unconstrained by the treaty have evinced little if any interest in these technologies. Doubts about the threat, cost and technological feasibility have made it difficult for the USA to convince them to further strain their smaller R&D budgets by cooperating on missile defence.[38] The TMD capability of the Franco-Italian Aster 30 is limited, having been added late in the missile's development in hopes of boosting its export potential and preventing a US monopoly on the technology.[39] The USA bears 60 per cent of the cost of the Medium Extended Air Defense System (MEADS), in which Germany and Italy are junior partners, and Pentagon officials have proposed phasing out the project, which has already lost its patrons in the US armed services.[40] After years of encouragement from Washington, Japanese interest in funding missile-defence research has still not been sparked.[41] China, France and the UK appear to be concerned

---

[36] Of 17 hit-to-kill flight tests since 1993, 11 have failed, including all 7 of those related to THAAD or similar systems. Dornheim, M. A., 'Missile defence design juggles complex factors', *Aviation Week & Space Technology*, 24 Feb. 1997, p. 54. According to Paul Kaminski, head of acquisition in the Department of Defense, 'I would describe [THAAD] as high risk'. Asker, J. R., 'Do or die?', *Aviation Week & Space Technology*, 24 Feb. 1997, p. 19.

[37] China and Russia have agreed to observe the guidelines specified by the Missile Technology Control Regime. See chapter 9 in this volume. North Korea's missile programmes are being dealt with under the aegis of the Agreed Framework with the USA. Iranian officials say that they are not developing IRBMs and reports to the contrary cannot be confirmed. North Korean cooperation with Iran has apparently been terminated. Arnett, E., 'Beyond threat perception: assessing military capacity and reducing the risk of war in southern Asia', ed. E. Arnett, SIPRI, *Military Capacity and the Risk of War: China, India, Pakistan and Iran* (Oxford University Press: Oxford, 1997), p. 5.

[38] Allied reservations are discussed further in Arnett (note 2), pp. 218, 231. NMD in particular has been unpopular. According to the former head of the US BMDO, Malcolm O'Neill, 'Not one of our allies has offered to bring their significant talents and technical capabilities to the development of our national missile defense system'. 'Lack of allied interest in NMD "frustrating", ex-BMDO chief says', *Armed Forces Newswire Service*, 15 Apr. 1997.

[39] Because of lateral jets at the centre of gravity, the Aster 30 has an inherent capability against ballistic missiles. The manufacturer claims that this includes the ability to intercept 1000-km range ballistic missiles. 'Impact direct pour l'Aster' [Direct hit for Aster], *Air & Cosmos* (Paris), 20 June 1997, p. 42.

[40] MEADS, under the name Corps SAM (surface-to-air missile), was originally intended to be a replacement for the Army's Hawk.

[41] Japan has spent only 460 million yen on missile defence since 1995 and funding for 1998 amounts to only 80 million yen. Japanese officials cite 'feasibility, likely effectiveness, and cost' in explaining their reluctance. Kyodo (Tokyo), 18 July 1997, in Foreign Broadcast Information Service, *Daily Report–East Asia* (hereafter FBIS-EAS), FBIS-EAS-97-199; and *Mainichi Shimbun* (Tokyo), 23 Aug. 1997, p. 3, in FBIS-EAS-97-237, 26 Aug. 1997.

that missile defences will undermine the effectiveness of their nuclear forces or lead to greater investment in countermeasures.[42]

Cruise missile defence

A rapidly emerging concern for US planners is the proliferation of cruise missiles. Although cruise missile technology is most familiar from its use as a land-attack weapon like the US Tomahawk, the main concern expressed in 1997 was the threat that new types of anti-ship cruise missiles pose to US intervention forces.[43] Specifically, it has been claimed that supersonic P-80/3M80 Moskit (SS-N-22 Sunburn) anti-ship missiles sought by China from Russia might deter or defeat US intervention on behalf of Taiwan and that Chinese anti-ship missiles transferred to Iran create new risks for forces in the Persian Gulf. Chinese and Iranian interest in anti-ship missiles is also said to demonstrate malign intentions.[44]

The issue of Chinese anti-ship capabilities was already sensitive because of a 1994 simulation conducted at the US Naval War College, in which Chinese anti-ship missiles deterred effective US naval intervention in the South China Sea.[45] Although such simulations are not meant to be models of actual combat so much as points of departure for pondering strategy and politics, the perceived threat posed by Chinese anti-ship missiles has since taken on a political life of its own. Arthur Waldron, a civilian professor at the Naval War College, claims that the Moskit is 'capable of defeating the Aegis anti-missile defences of the US Navy and thus sinking American aircraft carriers'.[46] In the same vein, Representative James Lightfoot of the House Committee on Appropriations has said: 'For those of you unfamiliar with the Sunburn-class missile . . . our Navy has no defense against such a missile'.[47] Representative Dana Rohrabacher asserts that the Moskit 'could alter the balance of power in

---

[42] For an overview of European attitudes see Lara, B., *ATBM Systems and European Security*, UNISCI Papers no. 6 (Faculty of Political Science, Complutense University: Madrid, 1997).

[43] The proliferation of land-attack cruise missiles is discussed in Arnett, E., American Association for the Advancement of Science, 'The most serious challenge of the 1990s? Cruise missiles in the developing world', *The Proliferation of Advanced Weaponry: Technology, Motivations, and Responses* (AAAS: Washington, DC, 1992); and Arnett, E., *Sea-Launched Cruise Missiles and US Security* (Praeger: New York, 1991). Not all anti-ship missiles are cruise missiles, but the problems of defence are similar. This section does not exclude anti-ship missiles from consideration if they are not cruise missiles.

[44] 'China's military buildup in fact is clearly directed at US vulnerabilities—in the form of anti-ship cruise missiles, air-to-air missiles, and wake-homing torpedos that could do serious damage to US forces in the near term.' Rodman, P. W., 'Chinese puzzles', *National Review*, 13 Oct. 1997, pp. 28–29. See also the comments of Congressmen Rohrabacher and Solomon on the Moskit in, respectively, 'National Defense Authorization Act for Fiscal Year 1998', *Congressional Record*, 23 June 1997, p. H4198, and 'Reauthorization of the Export–Import Bank', *Congressional Record*, 6 Oct. 1997, p. H8380.

[45] Chanda, N., 'China: aiming high', *Far East Economic Review*, 20 Oct. 1994, p. 15; and Opall, B., 'China sinks US in simulated war', *Defense News*, 30 Jan.–5 Feb. 1995, pp. 1, 26.

[46] Waldron, A., 'How not to deal with China', *Commentary*, Mar. 1997, p. 45. See also Fisher, R. D., *Dangerous Moves: Russia's Sales of Missile Destroyers to China* (Heritage Foundation: Washington, DC, 1997).

[47] 'Foreign Operations, Export Financing, and Related Programs Appropriations Act, 1994', *Congressional Record*, 17 June 1993, p. H3720.

key strategic areas such as the Straits of Taiwan'.[48] In a 1997 best-seller, two journalists express their fear that the US President will be reluctant to support Taiwan against China in a future war because 'there is always the danger of losing a ship to submarine-launched missiles'.[49] Representative Benjamin A. Gilman, chair of the House Committee on International Relations, has said that 'China is said to have sold Iran about 40 [C802] missiles, against which the US Navy does not have a reliable defense'.[50] In 1997, Senator Jesse Helms agreed that the C802 missiles 'pose a serious risk to US naval presence in the region'.[51]

Despite the emphasis placed on the risks posed by Chinese anti-ship missiles by conservative legislators and commentators, US military spokesmen have consistently dismissed both the Chinese and the Iranian threats to the fleet, in part because they are more confident with respect to existing US defences. As a senior Pentagon official explained to reporters in Bahrain, 'The Aegis [system is] designed specifically to handle the cruise missile threat . . . It can certainly track and engage any cruise missile in the Gulf today'.[52] Further, China's force of maritime bombers has not been modernized for decades and the state of readiness of its missile boats is deteriorating.[53] Nevertheless, the popularity of conflict scenarios involving anti-ship missiles suggests that the issue merits closer attention. The salience of the issue is made clear by measures passed by the House of Representatives in July that would have cut off all foreign aid to Russia, including Nunn–Lugar aid and Export–Import Bank loans, if any Moskits were sold to China or Iran.[54]

New aspects of the problem posed by anti-ship missiles are rooted as much in the different political milieu created by the end of the cold war as in technology. In the changed international system, the US Navy expects to play

[48] Rohrabacher goes on to claim that the Moskit will allow China 'to develop lethal parity with the United States Navy'. 'Division C—Miscellaneous Provisions [of the Foreign Relations Authorization Act for Fiscal Years 1998 and 1999]', *Congressional Record*, 10 June 1997, p. H3626.

[49] Bernstein, R. and Munro, R. H., *The Coming Conflict with China* (Alfred A. Knopf: New York, 1997), p. 196. Bernstein and Munro assume that China will have cruise missiles comparable to the US Tomahawk by 2004. Submarine-launched anti-ship cruise missiles are identified as the primary threat to US forces from China and Iran in Blair, D., 'How to defeat the United States: the operational military effects of the proliferation of weapons of precise destruction', ed. H. Sokolski, *Fighting Proliferation: New Concerns for the Nineties* (Air University Press: Maxwell Air Force Base, Ala., 1996).

[50] US Congress, House of Representatives, *Consequences of China's Military Sales to Iran* (US Government Printing Office: Washington, DC, 1996), pp. 2, 28.

[51] 'Foreign Affairs Reform and Restructuring Act of 1997', *Congressional Record*, 17 June 1997, p. S5739.

[52] US Department of Defense, Background Briefing—Subject: Iranian cruise missile launch, 17 June 1997. Similarly, Secretary of Defense William Cohen: 'We have the capability to defeat any weapon that the Iranians might possess . . . The United States has the full capability to defeat any operation that the Iranians might seek to launch against us or our allies'. US Department of Defense, Press Briefing—William Cohen, 17 June 1997. US Secretary of State Madeleine Albright informed the Senate that 'the known transfers [of anti-ship missiles to Iran] are not of a destabilizing number and type'. 'Senate Resolution 82: Expressing the sense of the Senate to urge the Clinton Administration relative to C-802 cruise missiles', *Congressional Record*, 5 May 1997, p. S3969. See also testimony of Robert Einhorn in US Congress, Senate Committee on Governmental Affairs, *Proliferation: Chinese Case Studies,* S. Hrg. 105-242 (US Government Printing Office: Washington, DC, 1997), pp. 14–15.

[53] Only some of these boats carry the YJ-8, an earlier variant of the C802 that was of concern to Gilman. The rest carry older missiles based on the obsolete Soviet P-15 Termit (SS-N-2 Styx). Preston, A., 'World navies in review', *US Naval Institute Proceedings*, Mar. 1996, p. 110.

[54] On Nunn–Lugar funding see chapter 10 in this volume.

a role in regional conflicts on land by operating close to shore and supporting the land war from the sea. The problem of ship defence in the cold war primarily involved fighting in the open sea where identifying and destroying aircraft, ships and submarines that might launch anti-ship missiles was relatively straightforward. For ships operating closer to shore, hostile cruise-missile launchers may be more difficult to detect and objects that are detected may not be unambiguously legitimate targets for pre-emptive attack. A reluctance to fire in crowded airspace led to the frigate USS Stark's being struck by an Exocet launched from an Iraqi fighter in 1987, while the cruiser USS Vincennes shot down an Iranian airliner it mistook for a diving bomber.

The political problems of ship defence are aggravated by new and proliferating technologies. Among these are subsonic missiles like the Exocet that are becoming more sophisticated in order to defeat ships' self-defence systems, supersonic missiles that can fly at low altitudes, and submarine-launched anti-ship missiles, which are becoming available to a larger number of states.

Subsonic anti-ship missiles

The capabilities of advanced subsonic anti-ship missiles are the most difficult to counter, as well as the most difficult to characterize. While the sophistication of the guidance programmes in missiles like the French Exocet and the US Harpoon is constantly improving, the basic airframes have hardly changed since the missiles were introduced in 1973 and 1977, respectively. The difficulty is compounded by the increasing number of producers, even if most of them are dependent on a small number of suppliers for state-of-the-art electronics. Subsonic anti-ship missiles roughly comparable to the Exocet have been produced by China, France, Germany, Israel, Italy, Japan, Russia, South Africa (under licence from Israel), Sweden, Taiwan, the UK and the USA, and have been exported to at least 50 more countries. Norway produces a smaller anti-ship missile.

Ship-defence specialists have been energetically addressing the question how to defeat missile attacks since the first successful use of missiles to sink a warship in 1967.[55] Point-defence guns and defensive missiles as well as passive defences (jamming, false targets and so on) have been introduced into a spiralling competition of measure against countermeasure involving the most advanced Russian and Western electronics firms. Uncertainty over the outcome of a contest between a naval task force and an anti-ship missile attack has increased with the availability of missiles designed to destroy air-defence radars, including those that coordinate fleet air defence, such as the US Aegis system. Anti-radar missiles are produced by France, Russia, the UK and the USA and have been exported to at least 14 countries over the past 15 years, but of those only Iraq (which received the French Armat) is among the potential adversaries identified in the QDR. Aérospatiale has promoted the

[55] Ship defence is budgeted $163 million for fiscal year 1998. US Congress, House of Representatives, *Conference Report on Department of Defense Appropriations Act, 1998* (US Government Printing Office: Washington, DC, 1997).

Armat and the earlier Martel as being highly effective against the US Aegis air defence system, but has not been targeted for punishment by US legislators in the way Chinese and Russian missile firms have.

There may be some uncertainty about the ability of one advanced arms supplier to defeat another, but this is not the challenge faced by US defence planners. Among the potential adversaries identified by US officials—Iran, Iraq and North Korea—none produces state-of-the-art anti-ship systems, nor can they continuously upgrade the electronics and software of the missiles already in their arsenals. Furthermore, they run the risk that their arms suppliers will share secrets about how to defeat their missiles in the event of war, as Iraq's suppliers did in 1990.

Nevertheless, there remains the risk that Chinese anti-ship missiles supplied to Iran could inflict damage on US warships with loss of life comparable to that suffered when an Iraqi ballistic missile struck a US barracks in Saudi Arabia in 1991, the single greatest US loss during the 1991 Persian Gulf War. Iran is known to operate the Chinese C201, C801 and C802 anti-ship missiles.[56] These are Chinese copies of the obsolete Soviet P-15 Termit (SS-N-2 Styx) or are similar to the Exocet, but are likely to feature electronics far behind the state of the art. China itself is phasing out missiles like the C201 which are based on the Termit. Ship-defence measures adopted by Western navies after the successful use of the Exocet against the British Royal Navy in 1982 and the US Navy in 1987 should minimize the risk posed by the similar C802. Indeed, none of the C201s launched by Iran at US warships in 1987 struck its target and, of the two anti-ship missiles launched by Iraq during the 1991 Persian Gulf War, one crashed and the other was intercepted by a British Sea Dart defensive missile. Iranian aircraft, warships and shore-based cruise missile batteries are vulnerable to attack.

Supersonic anti-ship missiles

Soviet planners sought to overcome Western ship defences with the speed of their anti-ship missiles, thereby reducing the effectiveness of some defensive measures and the time available to intercept an attack. One of the supersonic missiles developed for this purpose, the Moskit, may have been included in a 1996 agreement by which Russia would transfer two Sovremenny Class warships to the Chinese Navy. The possible transfer of the Moskit has been noted with alarm by observers concerned about China's increasing military capabilities.

---

[56] A C802 was launched from a Chinese-supplied missile boat for the first time in 1996. The air-launched K variant of the C801 was tested from a US-supplied F-4 aircraft for the first time in 1997. US Department of Defense, *Iranian Cruise Missile Launch* (US Department of Defense: Washington, DC, 20 June 1997). China promised in 1997 not to transfer any more anti-ship missiles to Iran. Associated Press, 'China vows to halt cruise missile shipments to Iran', 18 Oct. 1997.

Table 7.7. Chinese anti-ship missiles

Local desig.	Export desig.	NATO desig.	NATO nickname	Comments
Copies of Soviet P-15 Termit (SS-N-2 Styx) and derivatives				
SY-1	..	CSS-N-1	Silkworm	In service 1960s; copy of Soviet P-15 Termit
SY-1A	..	CSS-N-2	Silkworm	In service 1983; also called FL-1, CSSC-1 Sold to Iraq; modified for low altitude flight
SY-2	..	CSS-N-5	..	Sea skimmer; certification test 1989; unsuccessful Also called FL-2; fits SY-1 launcher
HY-1	..	CSSC-2	Silkworm	In service 1974; sold to North Korea
HY-2	C201	CSSC-3	Seersucker	HY-1 with extended range; in service 1970 Sold to Bangladesh, Egypt, Iran, North Korea, Pakistan; also called FL-3A
HY-4	C201W	..	Sadsack	HY-2 with improved engine; in service 1985 Licensed to Egypt; sold to Iran, Pakistan
YJ-6	C601	CAS-1	Kraken	Air-launched HY-2; in service 1986; sold to Iraq
YJ-6A	C611	..	..	YJ-6 with improved propellant
Other subsonic missiles				
YJ-8	C801	CSS-N-4	Sardine	Sea skimmer; sold to Iran, Pakistan, Thailand In service 1987, also called YL-1, HY-5
YJ-8A	C802	CSS-N-8	Saccade	YJ-8 with improved engine; in service 1991 Sold to Iran; also called YL-2 C801K air-launched variant tested by Iran in 1997
Supersonic missiles				
FL-7	..	..	..	In service 1992; 30-km range; fits SY-1 launcher
HY-3	C301	..	..	Sea skimmer? In production 1994; 100-km range
YJ-1	C101	..	..	Sea skimmer? In development 1997; 45-km range
..	..	SS-N-22	Sunburn	P-80/3M80 Moskit may be imported from Russia

Sources: China, Committee on Science, Technology and Industry for National Defence, *China Today: Defence Science and Technology* (National Defence Industry Press: Beijing, 1993); Forecast International, 'Chinese antiship cruise missiles', *DMS Market Intelligence Report*, June 1996; Hooten, E. R., *Jane's Naval Weapon Systems* (Jane's Information Group: Coulsdon, 1992); International Institute for Strategic Studies, *Strategic Survey 1996/97* (Oxford University Press: Oxford, 1997); and SIPRI arms transfers database.

As seen in table 7.7, Chinese military production centres have been developing anti-ship cruise missiles energetically and have fielded supersonic missiles for about five years.[57] It is the Moskit's supersonic sea-skimming attack profile that has concerned US planners since it was introduced to the Soviet Navy in 1984.[58] The US Navy's main countermeasure for large, long-range

---

[57] China's military production centres developed several systems in the 1980s without support from the Chinese Government in hopes of recouping development costs from sales to the Chinese military or export customers. Some of these projects may have failed because of lack of customer interest. Arnett (note 1).

[58] *Soviet Military Power: An Assessment of the Threat 1988* (Department of Defense: Washington, DC, 1988), p. 83. Only China, Russia and Ukraine produce supersonic anti-ship missiles. A European joint project, ANS (anti-navire supersonique) is in limbo, but may be replaced by an anti-ship variant of the French strategic ASMP (air-sol moyenne portée) called the ANNG (anti-navire nouvelle génération).

missiles like the Moskit is destroying the launch platform before the missiles take flight. For the foreseeable future, Chinese warships (the Moskit exists only in a surface-launched variant) will remain highly vulnerable to US aircraft because of poor Chinese air defences and electronic warfare capabilities. Furthermore, the Moskit and China's indigenous supersonic missiles (FL-7, HY-3 and YJ-1) fly at higher altitudes for most of their flight profiles. Since supersonic missiles are large (to carry more fuel) and hot (due to drag), they are generally easy to detect and destroy by radar- or infrared-guided air-defence missiles. Supersonic missiles are also susceptible to the passive ship-defence measures taken to defend against subsonic missiles, and Chinese missiles are likely to lag far behind in relevant electronic warfare capabilities.

Nevertheless, each increment in Chinese anti-ship capabilities increases the risk for US naval operations and creates an incentive for the US Navy to keep its distance from the mainland. Recent developments in the region suggest that the United States can support its interests in East Asia without bringing carrier task forces close to the Chinese coast or into the South China Sea. Most significantly, China's potential adversaries—especially Taiwan—are bolstering their own defences to such an extent that China will find it difficult to defeat them, even if US support is limited.[59]

Submarine-launched anti-ship missiles

Submarine-launched anti-ship missiles are of concern because they offer the possibility of avoiding pre-emptive attack on missile-launching platforms. Submarines are the original stealth platforms, but are easily detectable once they surface. Missile designers have therefore sought to develop missiles that can be launched while the submarine is submerged. At present, only French, Russian and US anti-ship missiles are known to have this submerged-launch capability, but it has been sold to a number of other states and US planners must fear that Russian anti-ship missiles will be offered as submerged-launch weapons to China and Iran, which operate the Russian 877 EKM (Kilo Class) submarine.

While submerged-launch weapons would represent a new danger to US intervention forces in regional scenarios, US anti-submarine warfare capabilities have been funded lavishly for the express purpose of defeating the missile threat to aircraft-carriers. Most Russian submerged-launch weapons require direction from a ship on the surface or an aircraft in order to select the most appropriate target without being diverted by ship-defence measures. These target-direction platforms are likely to be destroyed quickly in combat, although they are more difficult to identify and destroy in heavily trafficked waters like the Persian Gulf or the South China Sea. Finally, the Moskit is too large to be launched from the Kilo Class submarine's torpedo tubes, but the

---

Reports that the Moskit has been sold to Iran appear to have been in error. Zaloga, S. J., 'Russia's Moskit anti-ship missile', *Jane's Intelligence Review*, Apr. 1996, p. 158.

[59] Arnett (note 37).

newer AFM-L Alpha (SS-N-27) may be supersonic and compatible with Kilo torpedo tubes.[60]

Anti-satellite weapons

In October 1997, the US Air Force illuminated a satellite in space with a 30-watt laser on the ground. It justified the experiment on the basis of the latent threat to US satellites.[61] The US effort is unique since the demise of the Soviet Union, and critics expressed doubts about the need for protective research,[62] suggesting instead that a mission was being created for the laser facility, which has strong supporters in Congress, especially in Secretary Cohen's Republican Party. The facility had originally been intended to develop methods for using lasers against ballistic and cruise missiles in flight, but was found to be less than promising in those roles. In any case, the test was largely unsuccessful and there are no plans to repeat it or to develop the laser into an operational weapon.[63] Indeed, the US programme for an anti-satellite weapon—based on a projectile and not directed energy—was the only military R&D programme excised from the Defense Appropriations Bill in 1997 by President Clinton in the first use of his 'line-item veto' authority.

IV. Conclusions

Since military R&D is the ultimate source of proliferation, horizontal or vertical, it is worth considering what the major developments of 1997 portend. For the most part, the indications are encouraging, but not without reservation.

With its continuing technological dominance, the USA is the most likely source of vertical proliferation, meaning entirely new technologies entailing some risk of instability. With R&D funding still as high as $37 billion in 1997 and unlikely to fall below $30 billion, significant innovation is inevitable. Nevertheless, the QDR's preference for familiar technologies rather than the most exotic of those associated with the RMA suggests that technological determinism will not necessarily win the day. Other decisions made in 1997 reinforce this conclusion, particularly the veto on funding for anti-satellite weapons.

---

[60] The Alpha may have been demonstrated for the Iranian Navy. Friedman, N., 'Soviet-built Kilos gettings SS-N-27s?', *US Naval Institute Proceedings*, Nov. 1997, p. 92. The supersonic 3K55 Oniks (SS-N-26), offered for export under the name Yakhont, may be fielded in surface-, submarine- and air-launched variants, but is associated with special launchers not featured on the Kilo Class. It reportedly was offered to Iran in the early 1990s but not accepted. Zaloga, S. J., 'Russia's enigmatic gem: the Yakhont/Oniks supersonic ASM', *Jane's Intelligence Review*, Feb. 1998, p. 19.

[61] US Department of Defense, 'Secretary of Defense approves laser experiment to improve satellite protection', News Release no. 526-97, 2 Oct. 1997; and US Department of Defense, News Briefing, 2 Oct. 1997.

[62] The Soviet Union conducted research on anti-satellite lasers at Dushanbe, Tajikistan, and had an operational anti-satellite rocket facility. Anti-satellite capabilities are unlikely to proliferate. Arnett, E., American Association for the Advancement of Science, *Antisatellite Weapons* (AAAS: Washington, DC, 1990), p. 6.

[63] US Department of Defense, *News Briefing*, 23 Oct. 1997.

If there is an exception to the trend, it is ballistic missile defence. Although the development of NMD and TMD will be kept within the confines of the ABM Treaty for the immediate future, the desire to deploy both strategic defences and very capable TMD is growing in some influential quarters with little reference to the actual threats they are meant to counter. While Clinton Administration officials have been frankly sceptical of claims made about the necessity for and capability of the most provocative systems, they have shown a willingness to entertain options that pose the risk of stimulating countermeasures and further slowing the process of nuclear disarmament. The situation could deteriorate rapidly if pro-missile defence ideologues succeed in pushing through deployments in coming years.

Most of the other major investors in military R&D are much less likely to contribute to vertical proliferation. They still aspire mainly to emulate parts of the US technology and industrial bases, for reasons based on their understandings of their political and economic situations. As a result, the main concern is their contribution to horizontal proliferation as new suppliers of technologies that could reach users to whom US technology is not available. Even this problem, however, is much smaller than was expected even a few years ago. Indeed, it is surprising that the 1991 Persian Gulf War did not lead second-tier arms producers to increase their R&D budgets in hopes of developing or countering technologies demonstrated by the USA, which itself cancelled several programmes at that time.[64] While Russia's new willingness to allow its design bureaux to sell their expertise on the international market was a notable development in 1997, the more important trends are towards tighter technology controls, even as the Russian technology base quickly falls further behind the state of the art.

Finally, Japan's decision in 1997 to halt its 20-year crescendo of military R&D effort—if it holds in the years to come—will serve as an important additional example that major states need not necessarily express their stature and sovereignty through the development of an extensive military technology base. Indeed, all the G7 countries have reduced their military R&D budgets and only France and the USA are developing a broad range of systems. If this trend continues, the international system is likely to be characterized by a greater dependence on US technology for friendly militaries and on US military intervention in the event of conflict. The prospects for the emergence of a global challenger to US power—or even a very capable regional foe—remain remote. The impetus to arm should therefore be that much more possible to resist.

---

[64] This was the expectation, for instance, of Marek Thee. Thee, M., *Whatever Happened to the Peace Dividend? The Post-Cold War Armaments Momentum*, European Labour Forum (Russell Press: Nottingham, 1991). Of the major arms producers, only Italy, Japan, South Korea, Sweden and perhaps China increased their military R&D budgets between 1991 and 1993. Arnett (note 2), p. 213. As seen in table 7.2, Italy and Sweden then cut their R&D budgets to even lower levels.

8. Transfers of major conventional weapons

SIEMON T. WEZEMAN and PIETER D. WEZEMAN

I. Introduction

The global SIPRI trend-indicator value of international transfers of major conventional weapons for 1997 was 12 per cent higher than that for 1996.[1] The trend-indicator value for 1997 was $25 156 million at constant (1990) prices, up from the value of $22 542 million for 1996.[2] As figure 8.1 shows, there has been a clear trend of increasing arms transfers since 1994, when the trend-indicator value stood at $20 231 million, the lowest since 1970. The figure for 1997 is 24 per cent higher than that for 1994, but only 62 per cent of the value of $40 582 million for 1987, when arms transfers reached their highest level since 1950.

Section II of this chapter highlights some of the most important developments in 1997 and surveys the dominant trends among the exporters and importers of major conventional weapons. Section III focuses on Sub-Saharan Africa as a recipient of arms in the light of continuing warfare in the region, which has suffered some of the most violent conflicts since 1945. A brief report on international arms embargoes is given in section IV.

Section V examines the transparency of arms transfer data in government publications. Since the early 1990s, increased transparency has featured prominently on the agenda of several governments, international organizations and non-governmental organizations (NGOs). In 1997 a number of governments began or promised to begin publishing details, and others agreed to publish more comprehensive details, of arms transfers from their respective countries. A group of government experts evaluated the first five years of operation of the United Nations Register of Conventional Arms (UNROCA) with a view to recommending further steps in its development. The results of this 1997 review and an evaluation of the 1996 reports to the UNROCA are also presented in section V.

---

[1] The index produced using the SIPRI valuation system enables the aggregation of data on physical arms transfers. The SIPRI system for evaluating arms transfers was designed as a *trend-measuring device*, to permit the measurement of changes in the total flow of major weapons and its geographical pattern. A description of the method used in calculating the trend-indicator value is given in appendix 8C. A more extensive description of the SIPRI Arms Transfers Project methodology, including a list of sources used and examples of calculations, is available on the SIPRI Internet website, URL <http://www.sipri.se/projects/armstrade/atmethods.html>.

[2] The figures for years before 1997 differ from those given in previous SIPRI Yearbooks. The SIPRI database on arms transfers is constantly updated as new data become available, and the trend-indicator values are revised each year. For this reason it is advisable for readers who require time series data for periods before the years covered in this Yearbook to contact SIPRI.

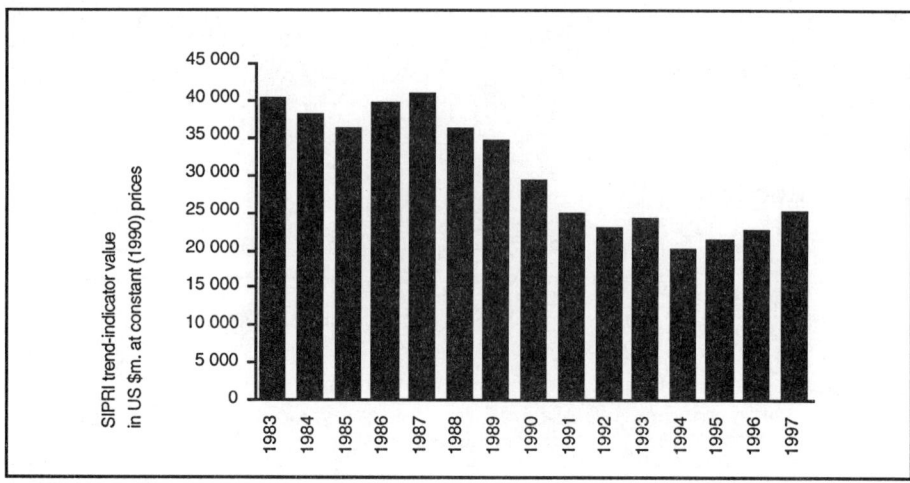

Figure 8.1. The trend in transfers of major conventional weapons, 1983–97

II. Main developments in 1997

According to the arms export guidelines of many supplier countries, human rights violations in a recipient country are one of the reasons for following a restrictive arms transfer policy. Internationally agreed guidelines such as those of the European Union (EU), the Organization for Security and Co-operation in Europe (OSCE) and the Permanent Five (P5) members of the United Nations Security Council also follow this principle.[3] While the principle of restraints on arms transfers to countries with poor human rights records is unquestioned, all these guidelines are open to interpretation by national governments and there is little agreement among the main supplier countries as to when restraints are called for or how far they should go. Because the economic advantages of arms exports seem to take priority for some countries, decision makers in the more restrained countries might have serious misgivings in cases where emphasizing the human rights records of potential buyers might lead to the loss of orders.

There were two clear cases in 1997 when refusals to deliver weapons to countries that had abused human rights led would-be buyers to seek and find willing suppliers elsewhere. Turkey cancelled a $150 million order for US AH-1W combat helicopters and part of an order for medium transport helicopters after the US Congress repeatedly denied export permission on the grounds of human rights abuses in Turkey. A $430 million order for transport helicopters was instead awarded to French Eurocopter, and Turkish officials warned that any future US stalling on export permissions would probably lead

---

[3] Anthony, I. et al., 'The trade in major conventional weapons', *SIPRI Yearbook 1992: World Armaments and Disarmament* (Oxford University Press: Oxford, 1992), pp. 295–96; and Anthony, I. et al., 'Arms production and arms trade', *SIPRI Yearbook 1993: World Armaments and Disarmament* (Oxford University Press: Oxford, 1993), p. 461. The 1991 P5 Guidelines for Conventional Arms Transfers and the 1993 OSCE Criteria on Conventional Arms Transfers are reproduced in Anthony, I. (ed.), SIPRI, *Russia and the Arms Trade* (Oxford University Press: Oxford, 1998), pp. 233–53.

Turkey to look elsewhere.[4] In a similar case, US criticism of Indonesia's human rights and democracy records led Indonesia to cancel a planned order for 9 F-16 fighter/ground attack (FGA) aircraft and other weapons and to opt for a $1 billion Russian package, which included 12 Su-30M FGA aircraft.[5]

European cooperation in the development and production of major systems experienced a new set-back in 1997. The European Future Large Aircraft (FLA) military transport aircraft programme was partly undermined when Italy placed a $1.2 billion order for 18 C-130J transport aircraft from the USA, following the lead of the UK, which had ordered 55 of these aircraft in 1996.

In a move that seems consistent with the increasing interest among developing and newly industrialized countries in the only 'stealth' item available on the market, both Indonesia and Singapore placed orders for submarines.[6] Indonesia bought two second-hand Type-206 submarines from Germany (originally five were ordered, but after the financial crash in Indonesia three were cancelled or postponed), and Singapore bought four second-hand Sjöormen Class submarines from Sweden. Their delivery will raise the total number of submarines owned by South-East Asian countries from two to eight.

The suppliers of major conventional weapons

The list of the leading suppliers of major conventional weapons was largely unchanged for 1997. As in 1996, the USA was by far the largest supplier, with Russia ranking second. For 1997 alone France was the third largest supplier, followed by the UK, but for 1993–97 overall Britain's share of weapon exports was higher than that of France (see table 8.1). Of the six major suppliers, France, the UK and the USA all exported more weapons, while China, Germany and Russia exported fewer weapons than in 1996. Together these countries accounted for nearly 84 per cent of all deliveries in 1997.

The remaining 16 per cent of international transfers of major conventional weapons was accounted for by 29 smaller suppliers.[7] Exports from these suppliers are mainly based on a limited number of designs, mostly in areas not well covered by any of the major suppliers. Some were nonetheless involved in major deals or recorded significant changes in percentage terms, mostly because of occasional large deals that are very time-limited. An example of a country that suddenly moved up the SIPRI list of suppliers is Spain, which experienced a 546 per cent increase in exports for 1997 as compared with 1996. This was mainly the result of one high-value delivery which is unlikely to be repeated—that of an aircraft-carrier to Thailand.

[4] 'Turkey will pick Eurocopter if Seahawk buy stalls', *Defense News*, 10–16 Feb. 1997, p. 20; *Rotor & Wings*, Jan. 1997, p. 10; and 'US–Turk spat buoys Russian exporters', *Defense News*, 3–9 Mar. 1997, pp. 3 and 26.

[5] 'No meddling', *Far Eastern Economic Review*, 19 June 1997, pp. 16–17. At least part of the Russian deal was postponed after the fall of the Rupiah, however (see also below).

[6] Foxwell, D., 'Sub proliferation sends navies diving for cover', *Jane's International Defense Review*, Aug. 1997, pp. 30–39.

[7] In addition to the 6 major and 21 smaller suppliers shown in table 8.1 to have exported weapons in 1997, 8 other countries—Austria, Egypt, Ethiopia, Greece, Singapore, Taiwan, the United Arab Emirates and Yugoslavia (Serbia and Montenegro)—exported major conventional weapons in 1997.

Table 8.1. The 30 leading suppliers of major conventional weapons, 1993–97

The list includes only countries with aggregate exports of $100 million or more for 1993–97. The countries are ranked according to 1993–97 aggregate exports. Figures are trend-indicator values expressed in US $m. at constant (1990) prices.

Rank 1993–97	Rank 1992–96[a]	Supplier	1993	1994	1995	1996	1997	1993–97
1	1	USA	12 504	10 434	9 823	9 528	10 840	53 129
2	2	Russia	3 541	1 117	3 218	3 904	3 466	15 246
3	4	UK	1 585	1 506	1 726	1 975	2 631	9 423
4	5	France	898	704	811	2 004	3 343	7 760
5	3	Germany	1 562	2 392	1 255	1 399	569	7 177
6	6	China	1 108	687	887	679	170	3 531
7	7	Netherlands	351	502	381	440	504	2 178
8	8	Italy	353	289	338	393	408	1 781
9	9	Canada	220	365	434	239	81	1 339
10	14	Spain	94	260	120	117	639	1 230
11	11	Israel	186	140	237	260	335	1 158
12	12	Ukraine	127	189	188	192	399	1 095
13	10	Czech Republic	267	377	193	137	19	993
14	13	Sweden	58	59	179	315	273	884
15	24	Moldova	–	175	–	–	392	567
16	16	Korea, North	422	48	48	21	–	539
17	17	Uzbekistan	–	238	272	–	–	510
18	19	Belgium	–	20	296	69	93	478
19	25	Belarus	–	8	24	129	263	424
20	32	Australia	30	24	22	10	318	404
21	21	Norway	93	186	54	9	56	398
22	18	Poland	–	130	185	61	18	394
23	15	Switzerland	79	37	90	107	72	385
24	20	Slovakia	151	28	85	91	–	355
25	23	Brazil	26	38	40	28	28	160
26	29	Qatar	49	51	15	–	29	144
27	27	Japan	15	16	16	86	3	136
28	31	Korea, South	28	8	41	22	12	111
29	26	South Africa	54	10	10	33	1	108
30	33	Indonesia	25	25	38	–	13	101
		Others[b]	173	168	245	294	181	1 061
		Total	**23 999**	**20 231**	**21 271**	**22 542**	**25 156**	**113 199**

[a] The rank order for suppliers in 1992–96 differs from that published in the *SIPRI Yearbook 1997* (p. 268) because of the subsequent revision of figures for these years.

[b] Includes 32 countries with aggregate 1993–97 exports of less than $100 million.

Note: The index produced using the SIPRI valuation system is not comparable to official economic statistics such as gross domestic product, public expenditure or export/import figures. To enable the aggregation of data on transfers of different types of weapon, SIPRI has created an index which gives similar values to similar weapon systems. The SIPRI system was designed as a *trend-measuring device* to permit the measurement of changes in the total flow of major weapons and its geographical pattern. For a description of the method used in calculating the trend-indicator value see appendix 8C.

Source: SIPRI arms transfers database.

The leading suppliers

In 1997 the *United States* was again by far the major supplier, accounting for 43 per cent of all major weapon deliveries. This was not a significant increase over its 42 per cent share for 1996. While its average share for 1993–97 was 47 per cent, its share of deliveries has fallen each year since 1993.

There were no remarkable changes in US arms export policies in 1997. The impact of a sale on regional stability is still an important element of the Clinton Administration's conventional arms transfer policy. However, the US Government's reactions to the plans of several South American countries to acquire advanced weapons from non-US producers showed its sensitivity to economic factors and possible infringements on what it considers to be a US market.[8] Industry, the Department of Defense and certain members of Congress pressured the government to relax its restrictive 1977 policy on sales of advanced weapons to Latin America.[9] By the end of 1997, US companies were allowed to market their advanced F-16 and F/A-18 FGA aircraft and, in accordance with a presidential decision of 1 August 1997, export requests for these aircraft would be considered on a case-by-case basis.[10]

The introduction of a 'Code of Conduct' severely limiting arms exports to countries with poor human rights records and countries with very limited transparency concerning arms imports (including those not reporting to the UNROCA) was discussed in the Congress. The House of Representatives passed a code in its version of the State Department Authorization Act, but no agreement could be reached between the House and the Senate versions of the code and the issue was omitted from the final Authorization Act.[11]

Russia retained its second position, although its share of world exports of major conventional arms decreased from 17 per cent for 1996 to 14 per cent for 1997. Close ties to India were reaffirmed by the sale of two Kilo Class submarines and three Krivak-4 Class frigates, as well as three Ka-31 airborne early-warning (AEW) helicopters. Russia also introduced the first air-refuelling technology in South Asia by selling a number of Il-78 tanker aircraft to India. Eight Su-30M FGA aircraft were delivered to India in 1997—the first Russian export of combat aircraft more sophisticated than those used by Russia's own armed forces. China became more firmly established as one of Russia's major clients with the start of licensed production of the Su-27 FGA aircraft and final confirmation of an order for two Sovremenny Class

---

[8] In a similar but less dramatic way, the US Department of State argued very strongly against Kuwaiti plans to buy self-propelled guns from China. US State Department, Daily Press Briefing, 15 July 1997, URL <http://www.state.gov/www/briefings/9707/970715db.html>, version current 15 July 1997.

[9] This policy is discussed in Anthony, I., Wezeman, P. D. and Wezeman, S. T., 'The trade in major conventional weapons', *SIPRI Yearbook 1995: Armaments, Disarmament and International Security* (Oxford University Press: Oxford, 1995), pp. 497–99; and Anthony, I., Wezeman, P. D. and Wezeman, S. T., 'The trade in major conventional weapons', *SIPRI Yearbook 1997: Armaments, Disarmament and International Security* (Oxford University Press: Oxford, 1997), pp. 269–71.

[10] Press release from the White House, 1 Aug. 1997, URL <http://www.clw.org/pub/clw/cat/policy.html>, version current on 9 Mar. 1998; and 'Sharp debate likely over Latin exports', *Aviation Week & Space Technology*, 15 Sep. 1997, pp. 38–42.

[11] *AIA update*, vol. 2, no. 6 (Dec. 1997), URL <http://www.access.digex.net/~aia/nu2_6.html#code>, version current on 9 Mar. 1998.

destroyers. These acquisitions will mean a technological quantum leap for the Chinese forces and have already given rise to concern in the region.[12]

Russia's hopes for massive increases in arms exports were expressed in early 1997, for example, by Mikhail Timkin—first deputy director of Russia's only official arms marketing agency, Rosvooruzheniye—who even believed that Russia would bypass the USA as the main arms exporter by 1998.[13] While this seems extremely unlikely, known orders indicate that Russia is likely to maintain its position as the second largest exporter for at least the next few years. Stagnating investment in military research and development (R&D), however, may lead to diminishing competitiveness in the field of military technology.[14] Both Russian industry and the Russian military have pressured President Boris Yeltsin to relax arms export regulations, and to permit export of the newest technology, in the hope that exports of weapons will generate enough income to finance procurement for the armed forces and R&D. To some extent this is already government policy—part of the income from arms transfers has been used for R&D and for the procurement of limited numbers of advanced systems such as the Su-30, Su-37 and S-37 FGA aircraft.[15]

Following the changes made in 1996 in the procedures for marketing Russian arms, further changes were made in 1997. In September/October, under a cloud of corruption and charges of misuse of funds, Rosvooruzheniye was reorganized and two other organizations, PromExport and Rossiyskiye Tekhnologii, were mandated to act as agents for the industry to increase flexibility in marketing.[16]

France increased its share of conventional arms deliveries dramatically from 9 per cent in 1996 to 13 per cent in 1997. Deliveries of the first 24 Mirage-2000-5 FGA aircraft, associated air-to-air missiles and three La Fayette Class frigates to Taiwan, and of an estimated 76 Leclerc main battle tanks (MBTs) to the United Arab Emirates (UAE), made up 62 per cent and 15 per cent, respectively, of French exports in 1997. Continuing deliveries to these two countries alone for the next two to three years would be enough to maintain French exports at approximately the same level as in 1997.

The UK recorded a smaller increase in its share of deliveries than that of France, from 9 per cent in 1996 to 10 per cent in 1997. As in previous years, exports of ships and combat aircraft to the Persian Gulf countries and South-East Asia made up the bulk of British arms exports in 1997. On 28 July, British Foreign Secretary Robin Cook announced a new set of criteria for

---

[12] See, e.g., Berry, W. E., Jr, *Threat Perceptions in the Philippines, Malaysia and Singapore* (US Air Force Academy, Colo, 1997).

[13] 'Russia exports hit $3.5b with aircraft sales', *Jane's Defence Weekly*, 12 Feb. 1997, p. 4.

[14] See also chapter 7 in this volume.

[15] *Jane's Defence Weekly* (note 13); 'Russian Air Force is down but not out', *Jane's Defence Weekly*, 19 Mar. 1997, p. 22; and Butowski, P., 'Russia plans first flight for long-awaited fighter', *Jane's Defence Weekly*, 18 Feb. 1998, p. 3.

[16] *Jane's Intelligence Review*, Oct. 1997, p. 434. Rosvooruzheniye provides marketing support for the arms industry. Radio Free Europe/Radio Liberty, *RFE/RL Newsline*, vol. 1, no. 113, part I (9 Sep. 1997). While some companies have the right to market weapons on their own, most preferred to use Rosvooruzheniye as their agent. In 1996 only $100 million worth of arms exports from the Russian total of exports worth $3.5 billion were arranged without Rosvooruzheniye. *Jane's Defence Weekly* (note 13).

arms exports, according to which the government 'would not permit the sale of arms to regimes that might use them for internal oppression or international aggression'. The new criteria would stop the export of equipment 'which has obvious application for internal repression, in cases where the recipient country has a significant confirmed record of repression'.[17] At the same time, however, the government committed itself to 'a strong and successful defence industry' and maintaining 'its leading position'.[18] With the exception of some export licence refusals to Indonesia, regarding equipment for internal security, by early 1998 this new policy did not seem to have changed much in the usual practice of British arms exports.[19]

Germany's share of arms exports decreased significantly, from 6 per cent of the world total for 1996 to just over 2 per cent for 1997. During 1990–96 Germany exported large quantities of surplus weapons from its own stocks or from those inherited from the former German Democratic Republic, but by 1997 these stocks were largely exhausted. About half of all German arms exports in 1990–96 consisted of surplus equipment. Deliveries of Leopard-2 MBTs to Sweden and MEKO-200 Type frigates to Australia, Greece and Turkey tipped the balance in favour of new systems in 1997, when surplus equipment made up only 30 per cent of total deliveries, but German arms exports were much reduced overall.

The decrease in arms transfers by *China* was even more remarkable. While China was still ranked as the sixth largest supplier for the period 1993–97, it exported 75 per cent fewer weapons in 1997 than in 1996. China's efforts to compete with other suppliers by offering cheap weapons have met with little success. It seems that even the poorer countries no longer want the old technology embodied in Chinese designs, and they are also put off by the often shoddy workmanship encountered in Chinese weapons.[20] While unable to compete with other countries in terms of technology, China remained one of the few suppliers that did not yield to US pressure to refrain from deliveries to Iran, and it was also Pakistan's main ally and supplier. Exports to Iran and Pakistan accounted for 51 per cent of total Chinese deliveries for the period 1993–97. However, according to US Government sources, in October 1997 and in early 1998 China seemed to be bowing to US pressure and promising restraint in its arms transfers to Iran, in particular those of advanced anti-ship missiles.[21] China denied having made such a promise, however.[22]

---

[17] 'Foreign Secretary announces criteria to ensure responsible arms trade', *FCO Daily Bulletin*, 28 July 1997, URL <http://www.fco.gov.uk/texts/1997/jul/28/bulletin.txt>, version current on 9 Mar. 1998.
[18] *FCO Daily Bulletin* (note 17).
[19] 'Approval for Jakarta defence deals likely', *Financial Times*, 3 Oct. 1997, p. 9.
[20] Even major client Pakistan would consider buying the latest Chinese combat aircraft, the Super-7, only for a 'second line of defence'. Reuters, 'Pakistan airchief says India's planes have the edge', URL <http://customnews.cnn.com/cnews>, version current on 19 Jan. 1998.
[21] AP, 'China vows to halt cruise missile shipments to Iran', 18 Oct. 1997; 'Cohen Finds Progress in China Ties', *International Herald Tribune*, 21 Jan. 1998, p. 6; and Voice of America, URL <gopher://gopher.voa.gov;70/00/newswire/mon/CHINA_CRUISE_MISSILES-L>, version current on 19 Jan. 1998.
[22] 'China vows to continue arms sales', United Press Institute, 20 Jan. 1998, URL <http://biz.yahoo.com/upi/98/01/20/international_news/chinacohe_1.html>, version current on 20 Jan. 1998.

The recipients of major conventional weapons

The data on arms importers in 1997 tend to reinforce the main trends identified in the past few years. As can be seen in table 8A.1, three regions—Asia, Europe and the Middle East—remain the predominant markets for exported major conventional weapons.[23] However, the relative importance of these regions is changing. As a share of the total the demand from European countries has decreased, while that from Asian, particularly North-East Asian, countries has grown.

Among the importers, the 10 leading recipients for 1993–97—Saudi Arabia, Taiwan, Turkey, Egypt, South Korea, China, Japan, India, Greece and Kuwait—remained the same as for 1992–96, with only an internal change in ranking. Together these countries accounted for 52 per cent of world arms imports for the period and for 57 per cent in 1997.

Asia and Oceania

For the period 1988–97 the share of deliveries of major conventional weapons to Asian countries rose from 31 per cent to 49 per cent. In Asia, in particular North-East Asia, several countries initiated programmes in the early 1990s which are now being reflected in the data on equipment deliveries.

In 1997 *North-East Asia* accounted for nearly 30 per cent of global imports, with three of the five countries of the region—China, South Korea and Taiwan—being among the top 10 recipients.[24] The most important deliveries included a third Kilo Class submarine and the first licence-built Su-27 FGA aircraft for China; 24 Mirage-2000-5 and 24 F-16A-MLU FGA aircraft, 3 La Fayette and 2 Perry Class frigates for Taiwan; and the first licence-produced F-16C/D FGA aircraft for South Korea.

In *South-East Asia*, Malaysia took delivery of two Lekiu Class frigates and eight F/A-18 FGA aircraft, while Thailand received the aircraft-carrier *Chakri Naruebet* (the first for an East Asian country since 1945) and related Harrier (AV-8A) FGA aircraft from Spain.

In *South Asia*, adversaries India and Pakistan maintained high levels of arms imports. While India has been trying to produce indigenous tanks and combat aircraft, its programmes have encountered technical problems, forcing the country for the time being to continue licensed production of Russian T-72 tanks and import of Russian Su-30M FGA aircraft. Pakistan's much smaller production facilities also seem to be facing problems in the development of the Al Khalid tank, leaving Pakistan no option but to import the Chinese Type-85-IIM and the more modern Ukrainian T-80UD tanks.

---

[23] Demand for major conventional weapons is heavily concentrated in North America and Western Europe, where it is largely covered by domestic procurement rather than international transfers. The countries included in each region are listed in appendix 8A in this volume.

[24] For a discussion of the implications of defence modernization by China and Taiwan, see Gill, B. and Bitzinger, R., *Gearing up for High-Tech Warfare? Chinese and Taiwanese Defense Modernization and Implications for Military Confrontation across the Taiwan Strait, 1995–2005*, CAPS paper no. 11 (Chinese Council of Advanced Policy Studies: Taipei, 1996). See also Arnett, E. (ed.), SIPRI, *Military Capacity and the Risk of War: China, India, Pakistan and Iran* (Oxford University Press: Oxford, 1997).

Most North-East and South-East Asian countries, notably Indonesia, South Korea, Malaysia, the Philippines and Thailand, saw their currencies lose significantly against the US dollar during the closing months of 1997, in many cases by between 35 and 70 per cent, with further major losses in early 1998. While this did not affect arms transfers in 1997, several countries postponed acquisitions or even cancelled important orders. Thailand is trying to pull out of a $390 million deal for eight F/A-18 FGA aircraft; Malaysia postponed and slimmed down its acquisition of up to 27 light frigates, combat helicopters and armoured vehicles; Indonesia cut parts of its planned $1 billion purchases from Russia; and South Korea postponed the purchase of four airborne early-warning and control (AEW&C) aircraft and may acquire a cheaper aircraft than the planned new heavy FGA aircraft.[25]

Other regions: Europe and the Middle East

The *European* share of world imports of major conventional weapons declined from 33 per cent in 1993 to 19 per cent in 1997. Reduced procurement expenditure by many European countries after 1990 has led to the slowing down, postponement or deferment of equipment modernization programmes, which has had a major impact on arms imports.

Deliveries of weapons to Central and East European countries were limited to less than 1 per cent of the world total. In 1996 three of the Visegrad countries—the Czech Republic, Hungary and Poland—published in broad outline their equipment priorities, and in 1997 these countries were invited to become members of NATO. By early 1998 neither of these events had led to the signature of major contracts, but US and European companies had strengthened their positions by forming partnerships with Czech, Hungarian and Polish companies, especially (but not only) in preparation for the competition for the most important planned acquisition, that of new fighter aircraft to replace those of Soviet design.[26]

The share of deliveries to the *Middle East* remained constant at around 20–25 per cent of the world total. The positions of Egypt, Kuwait, Saudi Arabia and the United Arab Emirates on the list of importers of major conventional weapons for the period 1993–97 are little changed. There were some noteworthy deliveries in 1997 to the smaller arms-importing countries in the region. The UAE took delivery of the first of two refitted ex-Dutch Navy Kortenaer Class frigates ordered in 1996 as a direct reaction to Iran's acquisition of Russian Kilo Class submarines.[27]

The developing arms trade relations between Israel and Turkey are also noteworthy. After awarding a $650 million contract for upgrading 54 F-4E

---

[25] *Air Letter*, 2 Feb. 1998, p. 1; 'Cash crisis threatens Southeast Asian arms market', Inter Press Service/CNN, 9 Jan. 1998; and 'Arms makers scramble to keep Asia contracts', *International Herald Tribune*, 14 Jan. 1998, p. 7. See also chapter 6 in this volume.
[26] 'Boeing has big plans for Aero Vodochody', *Aviation Week & Space Technology*, 16 June 1997, p. 61; 'Selling arms to Central Europe', *The Economist*, 8 Nov. 1997 (via CDI listserver); and 'Aircraft groups swoop on new markets', *Financial Times*, 19 Aug. 1997, p. 2.
[27] 'UAE defence posture', *Military Technology*, Apr. 1993, p. 32.

Table 8.2. The 72 leading recipients of major conventional weapons, 1993–97

The list includes only countries with aggregate imports of $100 million or more for 1993–97. The countries are ranked according to 1993–97 aggregate imports. Figures are trend-indicator values expressed in US $m. at constant (1990) prices.

Rank 1993–97	Rank 1992–96[a]	Recipient	1993	1994	1995	1996	1997	1993–97
1	1	Saudi Arabia	2 799	1 460	1 259	1 946	2 370	9 834
2	9	Taiwan	907	614	1 138	1 530	4 049	8 238
3	2	Turkey	1 983	1 373	1 253	1 127	1 276	7 012
4	3	Egypt	1 267	1 941	1 680	937	867	6 692
5	6	Korea, South	482	642	1 553	1 591	1 077	5 345
6	8	China	1 097	341	697	1 102	1 816	5 053
7	5	Japan	1 580	703	1 021	666	584	4 554
8	7	India	582	468	1 062	1 231	1 085	4 428
9	4	Greece	991	1048	947	248	715	3 949
10	10	Kuwait	650	45	962	1 323	411	3 391
11	14	UAE	751	636	475	684	808	3 354
12	13	Thailand	135	835	688	522	1 031	3 211
13	21	Malaysia	17	448	1 143	199	1 346	3 153
14	15	Pakistan	825	719	225	644	572	2 985
15	16	USA	639	504	499	478	656	2 776
16	17	Iran	1149	295	223	514	11	2 192
17	11	Germany	1246	649	161	108	–	2 164
18	18	Spain	361	625	384	409	316	2 095
19	19	Finland	564	189	155	574	492	1 974
20	22	Indonesia	267	600	359	547	171	1 944
21	12	Israel	613	829	233	54	41	1 770
22	27	Brazil	38	235	238	562	384	1 457
23	24	Hungary	1 190	4	67	135	–	1 396
24	25	Australia	420	303	71	304	215	1 313
25	26	Chile	127	166	536	220	180	1 229
26	32	Italy	137	131	168	222	552	1 210
27	20	Canada	213	519	182	171	97	1 182
28	29	Oman	66	201	175	326	173	941
29	31	Switzerland	77	117	106	199	391	890
30	28	Portugal	364	431	15	3	14	827
31	38	Peru	77	142	92	166	258	735
32	33	Singapore	88	170	214	118	108	698
33	37	Myanmar	308	–	283	–	100	691
34	30	Netherlands	114	218	77	185	93	687
35	43	Qatar	15	14	15	349	286	679
36	35	Norway	125	78	118	168	155	644
37	45	Kazakhstan	–	–	–	408	172	580
38	40	Viet Nam	–	–	265	224	84	573
39	39	Algeria	15	161	332	5	–	513
40	44	Sweden	20	220	84	45	123	492
41	47	Argentina	65	148	85	44	148	490
42	23	UK	64	38	92	216	71	481
43	41	Slovakia	211	3	228	36	–	478
44	42	Armenia	8	310	51	106	–	475
45	46	Morocco	98	129	40	89	104	460

Rank 1993–97	1992–96[a]	Recipient	1993	1994	1995	1996	1997	1993–97
46	64	New Zealand	48	16	4	18	343	429
47	50	Mexico	125	92	43	63	96	419
48	34	France	138	26	65	30	160	419
49	60	Colombia	22	39	95	39	190	385
50	53	Cyprus	–	61	29	177	110	377
51	51	Sri Lanka	36	56	77	144	41	354
52	48	Yemen	–	205	142	–	–	347
53	49	Denmark	38	80	129	53	46	346
54	36	Syria	194	63	43	21	–	321
55	54	Bahrain	–	14	38	219	13	284
56	52	Poland	–	6	159	117	–	282
57	67	Austria	12	56	54	14	139	275
58	57	Philippines	52	109	49	15	47	272
59	58	Bangladesh	29	89	118	4	13	253
60	55	Belgium	115	64	27	–	34	240
61	61	Angola	81	96	1	7	–	185
62	63	Tunisia	–	32	45	60	37	174
63	62	Bulgaria	–	1	–	123	40	164
64	74	Jordan	1	–	24	74	62	161
65	68	Croatia	24	–	86	2	37	149
66	66	Lebanon	38	13	40	24	10	125
67	59	South Africa	7	19	38	51	8	123
68	83	Bosnia and Herz.		–	–	51	68	119
69	80	Eritrea		18	1	38	53	110
70	73	Cambodia	–	61	–	47	–	108
71	65	Nigeria	35	72	–	–	–	107
72	56	Romania	8	45	1	35	12	101
		Others[b]	249	199	310	385	200	1 343
		Total	**23 999**	**20 231**	**21 271**	**22 542**	**25 156**	**113 199**

[a] The rank order for recipients in 1992–96 differs from that published in *SIPRI Yearbook 1997* (pp. 272–73) because of the subsequent revision of figures for these years.

[b] Includes 58 countries with aggregate 1993–97 imports of less than $100 million.

Note: The index produced using the SIPRI valuation system is not comparable to official economic statistics such as gross domestic product, public expenditure or export/import figures. To enable the aggregation of data on transfers of different types of weapon, SIPRI has created an index which gives similar values to similar weapon systems. The SIPRI system was designed as a *trend-measuring device* to permit the measurement of changes in the total flow of major weapons and its geographical pattern. For a description of the method used in calculating the trend-indicator value see appendix 8C.

Source: SIPRI arms transfers database.

FGA aircraft to Israel in 1996, Turkey ordered Popeye air-to-surface missiles (ASMs) in 1997. At the same time Turkey was also discussing other projects, including more aircraft upgrades and the acquisition of tanks.[28]

[28] Reuters, 'Arms deals, military ties on Israel–Turkey agenda', 7 Dec. 1997; and 'Turkey's Mid East arms ties', *The Middle East*, Feb. 1998, pp. 5–7.

III. Arms transfers to Sub-Saharan Africa

Only two of the 47 Sub-Saharan African countries (Angola and South Africa) imported weapons for more than $100 million (SIPRI trend-indicator value) for the period 1993–97. Total arms imports by the region were only 0.5 per cent of the world total in 1997, and the yearly average of $243 million for the period 1993–97 was the lowest for any five-year period since 1960. The strong decline in the trend after 1990 (see table 8A.1) is explained by a decrease in imports by Angola. Angola's share of the region's imports was 62 per for 1988–90 and had dropped to 12 per cent for the period 1991–97. As the level of imports of major conventional weapons by the rest of Sub-Saharan Africa for 1988–97 was consistently low, a few deliveries of small batches of major conventional weapons cause strong fluctuations in the time series.

After years of being a minor importer because of a UN arms embargo, the only country in Sub-Saharan Africa that is likely to become an importer of sizeable quantities of major conventional weapons is South Africa, which has serious plans to import up to 40 fighter aircraft, 4 submarines, 4 corvettes, 60 light helicopters and 150 main battle tanks for about $2.5 billion.[29] If no financing problems occur and the plans materialize this would lead to a sharp rise in deliveries to South Africa in the first decade of the next century.

Arms transfers to countries in conflict

The many new and continuing conflicts in Sub-Saharan Africa in the period 1993–97 have not led to significant imports of major conventional weapons.[30] No clear pattern or relation can be discerned between imports of major conventional weapons and the outbreak or outcome of recent conflicts in this region. The most recent conflict in which major weapons were used on an intensive scale was that in Angola, where they were used both by Angola and by South Africa in 1975–88. In other major conflicts in Sub-Saharan Africa, mainly low-technology weapons and small arms are used. Most of the wars are fought on a technological level little different from that which characterized similar wars in the region in the 1960s and 1970s. Almost all the major weapons delivered in the past five years to the countries in conflict have been second-hand, the most advanced being small numbers of Mi-24 combat helicopters and six Chinese F-7M fighter aircraft. While the latter were new they represent the lowest level of fighter aircraft technology available on the market.

It is difficult to assess the importance of the few major conventional weapons being used. Most casualties are caused by small arms or by side-effects of the conflicts, and while the possession of major weapons can influence the outcome of the conflicts much depends on how they are used. The origins of smaller weapons delivered to the region are not easily traced. A few

---

[29] Campbell, K., 'South Africa seeks arms package', *Military Technology*, Nov. 1997, pp. 32–38.
[30] Chapter 1 in this volume lists 7 'major conflicts' in Sub-Saharan Africa during 1997. There have also been some smaller conflicts, e.g., in Chad, Comoros and Nigeria.

case studies have uncovered information indicating that small arms are being delivered from outside the region, but they also stress the importance of intra-regional transfers in which governments in the region support and supply rebel groups fighting in neighbouring countries.[31]

The arms transfer dynamics in some conflicts going on in 1993–97 in Sub-Saharan Africa for which substantial information is available are illustrated below.

Congo (Brazzaville) received three G-222 transport aircraft from Italy and three Mi-8 helicopters from Russia in 1995–96. The most recent deliveries of combat equipment were some 12 ex-Soviet MiG-21 fighter aircraft in the late 1980s. However, the only major weapons that seem to have influenced the conflict belonged not to the Congolese armed forces but to Angolan units supporting the rebels which ousted the government in 1997.[32]

Probably the most significant use of major weapons in the conflict in *Rwanda* was the shooting down, with two portable SA-16 missiles, of the aircraft in which President Juvénal Habyarimana of Rwanda was travelling home in April 1994 after having reached preliminary agreements on peace at a regional summit meeting in Dar es Salaam. This incident signalled the start of the 1994 massacres. Rwanda received a small number of light armoured vehicles from France in the late 1980s and about six howitzers from Egypt in the early 1990s; Rwanda's only aircraft that could perhaps be used for combat purposes were six SA-342L helicopters delivered by France in the mid-1980s, but none of these major weapons is reported to have had a discernible impact on the conflict. Information on supplies of small arms to Rwanda has been uncovered, showing the government to have been armed mainly by France, Egypt and South Africa, and the rebels by the Ugandan Government.[33]

Burundi received nine M-3 armoured personnel carriers (APCs), 18 AML-60/90 armoured cars and four SA-342L helicopters from France, and four SF-260TP trainer aircraft suitable for light combat duties from Italy in the early 1980s. No further major weapons were received. As in the case of Rwanda, information on supplies of small arms has emerged, showing that there have been deliveries from several countries including some in Africa.[34]

The conflict between the Alliance of Democratic Forces for the Liberation of Congo-Kinshasa (ADFL) and the Government of President Sese Seko Mobutu in *Zaire* in 1996 and 1997 led to very few transfers of major conventional weapons. There was only evidence for the transfers of some (two to four) ex-Yugoslavian Galeb light combat aircraft and a small number of Mi-24 combat helicopters from an unidentified East European source, flown by mercenaries. Some 20 Fahd APCs were delivered from Egypt in 1988–90. More substantial deliveries of armoured vehicles date from the early 1980s while the latest deliveries of jet combat aircraft (17 Mirage-5s) took place as

[31] E.g., *Arming Rwanda: The Arms Trade and Human Rights Abuses in the Rwandan War*, Human Rights Watch Arms Project, vol. 6, issue 1 (Jan. 1994); and *Stoking the Fires: Military Assistance, Arms Trafficking, and the Civil War in Burundi* (Human Rights Watch Arms Project: Washington, DC, 1997).
[32] 'Angola assists overthrow', *Air Forces Monthly*, Mar. 1998, p. 8.
[33] *Arming Rwanda, The Arms Trade and Human Rights Abuses in the Rwandan War* (note 31).
[34] *Stoking the Fires: Military Assistance, Arms Trafficking, and the Civil War in Burundi* (note 31).

Table 8.3. Suppliers of major conventional weapons to Sub-Saharan countries engaged in conflicts, 1993–97[a]

Supplier	Tanks	Armoured vehicles	Combat aircraft	Combat helicopters	Artillery	Transport aircraft and helicopters
Belarus	9	–	–	8	–	–
Bulgaria	24	50	–	–	–	–
China	–	–	6	–	–	–
Czech Republic	–	7	–	–	–	–
Italy	–	–	–	–	–	3
Kyrgyzstan	–	–	–	1	–	–
Poland	–	52	–	–	–	–
Portugal	–	–	–	–	–	4
Russia	30	218	–	–	14	(3)
Slovakia	(19)	–	–	–	40	–
South Africa	–	(19)	–	–	–	2
Spain	–	–	–	–	–	(2)
Ukraine	(64)	(6)	–	(2)	–	–
Yugoslavia	–	–	(2)	–	–	–
Unknown	–	–	–	(7)	–	–
Total	**(144)**	**(352)**	**(8)**	**(11)**	**54**	**(14)**

( ) = number uncertain.

[a] Angola, Burundi, Congo, Rwanda, Sierra Leone, Sudan, Uganda and Zaire. Liberia did not import any major conventional weapons during the period.

Source: SIPRI arms transfers database.

early as 1975. The limited numbers of major weapons still in service with the Zairean armed forces saw little use and did not influence the fighting in any spectacular way. Even the vulnerable railway system, used by the ADFL as a logistic system in their final offensive towards Kinshasa, did not suffer from Zairean air force attacks.[35] The rebels gained victory mainly with small arms. The mercenaries from Serbia were probably less well organized than those of the South African Executive Outcomes (EO) in Sierra Leone and were unable to help the Mobutu Government.

During the conflict between the government and the Revolutionary United Front (RUF) in *Sierra Leone*, Sierra Leone received two Mi-24V Hind-E combat helicopters in 1994–95 (its first combat aircraft) and two T-72 tanks from Belarus (although the usefulness of the tanks in this war is unclear) and 10 OT-64A SKOT APCs from Slovakia. It also leased two Mi-17 transport helicopters, which were brought in and used by Executive Outcomes. Their use, mainly by these government-hired mercenaries, is well documented[36] and shows how the effective use of small numbers of major weapons can have a decisive influence. Earlier small deliveries of major weapons date from the

[35] Boyne, S., 'The white legion in Zaire', *Jane's Intelligence Review*, June 1997, pp. 278–81.

[36] Hooper, J., 'Peace in Sierra Leone: a temporary outcome?', *Jane's Intelligence Review*, Feb. 1997, pp. 91–94.

late 1970s. Major weapons have also been used in this conflict by Nigeria, which supported the former government with air strikes against RUF rebels using Alpha Jet fighter aircraft delivered by Germany between 1981 and 1986 and which is involved in the new military conflict in Sierra Leone.[37]

Liberia received two transport aircraft and one small patrol craft in 1989–90, neither of which was well suited for use in the conflict. The only major weapons in the country were 20 artillery pieces bought in 1987 from Romania, but there is no evidence that they influenced the conflict in any way. Here, too, the main use of major conventional weapons was by foreign (mainly Nigerian) forces from the Economic Community of West African States Monitoring Group (ECOMOG) peacekeeping force.[38]

Uganda's largest arms import since the mid-1980s took place in 1995 when it received 62 second-hand T-55 tanks from Ukraine. Further weapons and equipment were bought from South Africa in 1995, including 10 Mamba APCs, and Uganda is reported to have ordered some AB-412 helicopters with advanced night-vision equipment in 1996.[39] It has received several batches of major weapons in the past 20 years, including MiG-21 fighter aircraft in the late 1970s, but most of the older equipment is reported to be unserviceable.[40]

The rebel forces in Uganda are reported to receive weapons from the Government of *Sudan*, while the latter accuses the Government of Uganda of supplying the Sudanese People's Liberation Army. Both governments also support rebels in other countries that would fight on their side.[41]

Table 8.3 gives an overview of the suppliers of major conventional weapons to the Sub-Saharan countries in which there were major conflicts during the period 1993–97. Several Central and East European countries—mainly Belarus, Russia, Slovakia and Ukraine—have delivered most of the small amounts of major weapons delivered to the warring countries. While in the cold war period arms transfers were important as an instrument of foreign policy,[42] the primary motive for the suppliers now seems to be financial.

Some of the major weapons, mainly aircraft, used in the conflicts were brought into the region by mercenaries who owned the weapons and leased them to those for whom they fought. The combination of small numbers of major weapons and the high military professionalism of the South African EO mercenaries led to important victories for the Government of Sierra Leone.

IV. International embargoes on arms transfers

In 1997 a number of countries were under international arms embargoes. Table 8.4 lists all the countries subject to partial or complete embargo on arms transfers, military services or other military related transfers during 1993–97.

[37] Hooper (note 36).
[38] United Nations Institute for Disarmament Research, Disarmament and Conflict Resolution Project, *Managing Arms in Peace Processes: Liberia* (United Nations: New York and Geneva, 1996).
[39] *Air Force Monthly*, Jan. 1997, p. 7.
[40] *Jane's Defence Weekly*, 18 Sep. 1996, p. 17.
[41] 'Uganda's three-sided war of attrition', *Jane's Defence Weekly*, 25 Sep. 1996, p. 41.
[42] See, e.g., Arlinghaus, B. E., *Arms for Africa* (Lexington Books: Lexington, Mass., 1983).

Table 8.4. Arms embargoes by international organizations in effect, 1993–97

Target	Entry into force[a]	Lifted	Legal basis	Organization
Afghanistan[b]	27 Oct. 1996	–	UNSCR 1076	UN
Afghanistan	1 Dec. 1996	–	–	EU
Bosnia and Herzegovina	..	–	–	EU
China	27 June 1989	–	–	EU
Croatia	..	–	–	EU
Haiti	30 Sep. 1991	15 Oct. 1994	–	OAS
Haiti[c]	13 Oct. 1993	15 Oct. 1994	UNSCR 841	UN
Iraq	6 Aug. 1990	–	UNSCR 661 + 687	UN
Liberia	19 Nov. 1992	–	UNSCR 788	UN
Libya	27 Jan. 1986	–	–	EU
Libya	31 Mar. 1992	–	UNSCR 748+883	UN
Myanmar	28 Oct. 1996	–	–	EU
Nigeria[d]	20 Nov. 1995	–	–	EU
Nigeria	24 Apr. 1996	–	–	Commonwealth
Rwanda	17 May 1994	17 Aug. 1995[e]	UNSCR 918	UN
Sierra Leone	8 Oct. 1997	–	UNSCR 1132	UN
Slovenia	..	–	–	EU
Somalia	23 Jan. 1992	–	UNSCR 733	UN
South Africa[f]	4 Nov. 1977	24 May 1994	UNSCR 418	UN
Sudan	15 Mar. 1994	–	–	EU
UNITA (Angola)	25 Sep. 1993	–	UNSCR 864 + 834	UN
Yugoslavia	25 Sep. 1991	1 Oct. 1996	UNSCR 713	UN
Yugoslavia	26 Feb. 1996	–	–	EU
Zaire	7 Apr. 1993	–	–	EU

[a] All non-UN embargoes are voluntary.
[b] Voluntary (non-mandatory) embargo.
[c] Originally imposed in June 1993, but temporarily suspended until Sep. 1993.
[d] The embargo does not apply to deliveries under existing contracts.
[e] The arms embargo was suspended on this date and formally ended on 1 Sep. 1996.
[f] A voluntary arms embargo commenced on 7 Aug. 1963 (US Security Council Resolution [UNSCR] 181); a voluntary embargo on equipment and material for arms production on 4 Nov. 1963 (UNSCR 182); and a voluntary embargo on arms imports from South Africa on 13 Dec. 1985 (UNSCR 558).

Source: SIPRI arms transfers database.

One new UN embargo on arms exports was implemented in 1997, to force the coalition of soldiers and former rebels in Sierra Leone to reinstate the democratically elected government that they had displaced in a coup.

V. National and international transparency in transfers of conventional weapons

Official data on arms exports

Government statistics on the value of arms exports are presented in table 8.5. A time series of data illustrates trends in arms exports as recorded in official data. SIPRI reports official data on the value of arms exports for three reasons: to make such information more accessible; to underline the lack of useful current government data and the fact that the data available are compiled in a manner that prevents comparative analysis; and, as the statistics present real values (in contrast to the SIPRI trend-indicator values), to provide an indication of the financial scale of arms exports.

The data are from official national documents, official statements or official replies to SIPRI's requests for information. Off-the-record statements by government officials are excluded since it is impossible to determine the basis of such statements. Using the SIPRI estimates of deliveries of major conventional weapons as a baseline, the countries publishing statistics together probably account for around 92 per cent of total arms exports.

Readers are cautioned in using these data in analysis. The table is not comprehensive and there are certainly other countries whose exports would be larger than some of those shown in the table. Governments' arms export definitions are not consistent from country to country, and not all countries which produce export statistics explain them fully.

In cases where explanations are given they underline the difficulty of using the data in analysis. Some countries aggregate figures for exports of arms and dual-use equipment; others release only an arms export figure; and different countries have different definitions of what is included in the category 'arms'. Some countries release data on the value of items delivered, others on the value of items approved for export. Moreover, the statistics are not necessarily consistent within countries across time. No attempt has been made to compensate for these inconsistencies.

A number of countries report exports of 'Weapons and Ammunition' as one of the categories in the trade statistics supplied to the UN Statistics Division and published by the International Trade Centre of the United Nations Conference on Trade and Development (UNCTAD)/World Trade Organization (WTO). These reports are made in accordance with the Standard International Trade Classification (SITC) 891.[43] Although these figures are more comparable than those presented in table 8.5, they are only of limited use for analysing the international arms trade. First, reporting is voluntary and some of the major arms exporters, for example, China and Russia, do not report statistics in the 'Weapons and Ammunition' category. Second, the SITC 891 definition of 'Weapons and Ammunition' only includes armoured vehicles, missiles, ordnance, ammunition, firearms and a range of non-military small arms. It does not cover, for example, warships, combat aircraft and military electronics, which make up a considerable part of the international arms trade.

---

[43] These data can be found in the COMTRADE databank, part of which is available on the International Trade Centre Internet website, URL <http://www.intracen.org/itc/infobase/data/chap33/e891.htm>. For the exact description of SITC 891 see the UN International Computing Centre Internet website, URL <gopher://gopher.unicc.org:70/00/itc/dir3/dir31/file313.txt>.

Table 8.5. Official data on arms exports, 1992–96

Country	Currency unit (current prices)	1992	1993	1994	1995	1996	1996 (US $m.)	Explanation of data
Australia[a]	m. A. dollars	57	67.3	28.4	39.2	435.2	555.9	Value of shipments of military goods (fiscal years)
Belgium[b]	b. B. francs	15.116	11.684	11.403	8.230	8.180	264	Value of arms exports
Brazil[c]	m. US dollars	. .	. .	2.6	12.4	8.7	8.7	Value of arms exports
Canada[d]	m. C. dollars	361.8	335.9	497.4	447.3	459.4	338	Shipments of military goods, excluding exports to the USA
Czech Rep.[e]	m. US dollars	n.a.	167	194	154	117	117	Value of arms exports
Finland[f]	m. FIM	30	62	61	132	69	15	Value of export of defence *matériel* based on customs statistics
France[g]	b. francs	20.8	14.6	11.6	10.9	18.6	3 636	Value of exports of defence equipment
	b. francs	29	20.6	16.8	19	29.4	5 747	Value of deliveries of defence equipment and associated services
Germany[h]	m. D. marks	2 638	2 577	2 131	1 982	1 006	669	Value of exports of weapons of war
Italy[i]	b. lire	1 270	1 080	920	1 230	1 196	775	Value of deliveries of military equipment
Netherlands[j]	m. guilders	1 007	1 475	1 006	1 029	922	547	Value of export licences for military goods
Norway[k]	m. kronor	. .	. .	. .	. .	985	153	Value of actual deliveries of defence *matériel*
Portugal[l]	m. escudos	. .	. .	. .	6 803	4 157	96	Value of exports of defence materials, equipment and technology
Russia[m]	b. US dollars	2.3	2.5	1.7	3.1	3.5	3 500	Value of exports of military equipment
Slovakia[n]	m. koruna	n.a.	2 257	3 320	2 452	2 214	72	Value of exports of military production
South Afr.[o]	m. rand	. .	. .	. .	855	524	122	Value of export permits issued
Spain[p]	m. pesetas	17 659	17 867	9 478	16 400	19 473	153	Value of exports of defence *matériel*
Sweden[q]	m. kronor	2 753	2 863	3 181	3 313	3 087	460	Value of actual deliveries of military equipment; changes in the coverage of data occurred in 1992–93
Switzerland[r]	m. S. francs	258.8	260.2	221	141.2	232.9	188	Value of exports of war *matériel*
UK[s]	m. pounds	1 530	1 914	1 798	2 076	3 402	5 313	Value of deliveries of defence equipment
USA[t]	b. dollars	10.1	10.9	9.3	11.6	12.6	12 590	Value of transfers made through the US Government in fiscal years
	b. dollars	2.7	3.8	2.1	3.6	0.7	705	Value of military and certain dual-use equipment transfers from US commercial suppliers in fiscal years

. . = no data available or received; n.a. = not applicable

TRANSFERS OF MAJOR CONVENTIONAL WEAPONS 309

Sources: The table is based on official government publications, official statements or information received on request from governments. Comments are worded as closely as possible to details in the documents cited. Sources refer to the last year reported here, for earlier years see earlier SIPRI Yearbooks.

[a] Annual Report: Exports of Defence and Related and Dual-Use Goods from Australia, Industry and Procurement Infrastructure Division, Department of Defence, Canberra, February 1998.

[b] Rapport van de regering aan het parlement over de toepassing van de wet van 5 augustus 1991 betreffende de in-, de uit-, en de doorvoer van wapens, munitie, en speciaal voor militair gebruik dienstig materieel en de daaraan verbonden technologie, 1 januari 1996 tot 31 december 1996, Ministry of Foreign Affairs, Brussels, 1996.

[c] Information received from the Brazilian Embassy, Stockholm, 24 Nov. 1997.

[d] Annual Report: Export of Military Goods from Canada, 1996, Exports Controls Division, Export and Import Controls Bureau, Department of Foreign Affairs and International Trade, Ottawa.

[e] 'Czech armaments industry wants to draw on tradition', *Narodna Obroda*, 27 Mar. 1997, in Foreign Broadcast Information Service, *Daily Report–East Europe (FBIS-EEU)*, FBIS-EEU-97-090, 31 Mar. 1997.

[f] Information received from the Finnish Ministry of Defence.

[g] Rapport fait au nom de la commission des finances, annexe nr 40, Assemblée Nationale, nr 305, Paris, 9 Oct. 1997, p. 174.

[h] Information received from the Ministry of Economics, Bonn.

[i] Consiglio dei ministri, Relazione sulle operazioni autorizzate e svolte per il controllo dell'esportazione, importazione e del transito dei prodotti di alta technologia, Roma, Camera dei Deputati, 1990–96.

[j] Letter from the Minister of Foreign Affairs to the Chairman of the Second Chamber, 22054 nr. 26, The Hague, 22 May 1997.

[k] Eksport av forsvarsmateriell frå Noreg 1996, Eksportkontroll og ikkje-spreiing, St meld nr 57 (1996–97), Oslo, May 1997.

[l] Anuário Estatístico da Defesa Nacional 1996, Ministry of Defence, July 1997, p. 63.

[m] 'Russia exports hit $3.5 b with aircraft sales', *Jane's Defence Weekly*, 12 Feb. 1997, p. 4. The values are reported by the official Russian arms marketing agency, Rosvooruzheniye. For a discussion of reports on the value of Russian arms exports see Anthony. I., 'Economic dimensions of Soviet and Russian arms exports', ed. I. Anthony, SIPRI, *Russia and the Arms Trade* (Oxford University Press: Oxford, 1998), p. 72.

[n] Information received from the Ministry of Economy of the Slovak Republic

[o] Information received from the Directorate of Conventional Arms Control, Republic of South Africa.

[p] Exportaciones realizadas de material de defensa para el período 1991–1996, Ministry of Economy and Agriculture, Madrid, Feb. 1998.

[q] Regeringens skrivelse 1996/97:134, Redogörelse för den svenska krigsmaterielexporten år 1996, Stockholm, 1997.

[r] Pressemitteilung, Ausfuhr von Kriegsmaterial 1996, Eidgenössisches Militärdepartement Information, 5 Feb. 1997.

[s] UK Defence Statistics, 1996 and 1997 edn, Government Statistical Service, London.

[t] Foreign Military Sales, Foreign Military Construction Sales and Military Assistance Facts, as of September 30, 1996 Financial Policy Division Comptroller, Department of Defense Security Assistance Agency, Washington, DC.

Countries which regularly make available information on their overall arms exports remain the exception and not the rule. In the majority of democracies the parliament does not exercise effective oversight of arms exports.

Six countries—Australia, Canada, Italy, Sweden, Switzerland and the USA—produce publicly available annual information on arms exports, showing the exact value of arms and military equipment exported to individual countries.[44] Sweden and the USA have chosen a very open approach, in which detailed information is provided and actively disseminated to the general public. The information is very readily available.[45] A less open approach, for example, is that of the Belgian and Dutch governments, which only publish aggregate arms export figures and provide confidential country-by-country information to the relevant parliamentary commissions.

The most common form of reports on arms exports, reporting their monetary value, is only useful for assessments of the economic aspects of arms exports. To examine the military consequences of arms exports, such as destabilizing accumulations of weapons, more information on the number and type of equipment items being exported is needed. Ideally, a complete list of export licences and actual deliveries should be provided, stating the recipient, the weaponry in question and the value. Only if this information is easily available is it possible for a parliament to hold the government accountable for its export policy and to have a well-informed and meaningful national debate on arms transfers. As British Foreign Secretary Cook stated: 'An informed public debate is the best guarantee of responsible regulation of the arms trade'.[46]

A major step towards greater openness is the report published in September 1997 by the US Departments of State and Defense on US arms exports. It provides information on arms exports in 1996, including details of the types of equipment (in some cases the actual designation), the number of items transferred and their value.[47]

The argument often given by governments for not disclosing more details or for not disclosing anything at all on arms exports is the need for commercial confidentiality. Transparency could hurt the interests of arms-producing companies by giving competitors useful information, and certain customers only want to buy if deals are kept secret. Protection of the arms industry seems to override the principle of transparency, which is the basis of the UN Register of Conventional Arms, for example.

In several European countries parliamentarians and NGOs have actively pressured governments to change this position and to release more informa-

---

[44] Canada's report omits sales to its largest customer, the USA, however, for which export licences are not required.

[45] The Swedish Government publishes an annual report on arms exports on the Internet. Swedish Government Report to Parliament 1996/97:138, Swedish arms exports in 1996, URL <http://www.sb.gov.se/info_rosenbad/departement/utrikes/vapenexport>, version current on 9 Mar. 1998.

[46] *FCO Daily Bulletin* (note 17).

[47] US Department of State, US Department of Defense, Foreign Military Assistance Act Report to Congress, Authorized U.S. Commercial Exports, Military Assistance and Foreign Military Sales and Military Imports, Fiscal Year 1996, Washington, DC, Sep. 1997.

tion on arms exports. In presenting new criteria for arms exports in July 1997, the British Labour Government announced that it would publish annual reports on their application.[48] In 1997 the Norwegian Government published for the first time a comprehensive report on arms transfers in 1996 along the same lines as the Swedish report. The Spanish Parliament passed a motion in March 1997 in which the government was urged to make public essential data on arms exports, and the first such report was published in February 1998.[49] The Netherlands Government started a study into the possible effects of declassifying the disaggregated arms export data provided to parliament after the latter had urged greater transparency.[50]

The UN Register of Conventional Arms[51]

On 28 August 1997 the UN Secretary-General released the fifth annual report of information received from governments on their arms imports and/or exports.[52] By that time, 84 countries had responded in some way to the request for information.[53] As of 1 April 1998, the number had increased to 93 countries.[54] The geographical pattern of participation in 1997 was very similar to that recorded in previous years, participation being high among the OSCE participating states and countries in the Americas and in Asia, and extremely low in the Middle East and Africa. By the time the Secretary-General's report was released, Israel was the only Middle Eastern country that had responded. Iran, which had submitted data for each of the four previous years after the release of the report, did so on 10 October. However, on behalf of the League of Arab States, Mauritania sent in a *note verbale* which, while 'fully supporting the cause of transparency in armaments', accused the UNROCA of being discriminatory as long as it does not include data on 'advanced conventional weapons, on weapons of mass destruction, particularly nuclear weapons, and on high technology with military applications'. It claimed that in its present form the UNROCA favours Israel in the Middle East.[55]

---

[48] *FCO Daily Bulletin* (note 17).
[49] Estévez, A., 'Killing secrets: the story of a success', *Network,* summer 1997; see also table 8.4.
[50] 'Nederlandse wapenexporten worden mogelijk openbaar' [Dutch arms exports may become public], *De Volkskrant,* 11 Dec. 1997; and Letter from the Minister of Foreign Affairs and the state secretaries of Economy and of Defence to the Chairman of the Second Chamber, 22054 nr. 30, The Hague, 27 Feb. 1998.
[51] SIPRI research on the UN register in 1997 was generously supported by a grant from the United States Institute for Peace, Washington, DC.
[52] United Nations, United Nations Register of Conventional Arms, Report of the Secretary-General, United Nations document A/52/312, 28 Aug. 1997.
[53] Only 23 countries, some of them reporting nil exports or imports, or providing only background information or *notes verbales*, had reported before the 'deadline' of 30 Apr. 1997.
[54] This does not include all Arab League countries, for whom Mauritania as Chairman of the Arab Group sent in a *note verbale*. Reply by Mauritania dated 2 Sep. 1997, as included in United Nations document A/52/312, 28 Aug. 1997, pp. 71–72. By comparison, by the same time in 1993 the UN had received 82 replies from members; in 1994, 84 replies; in 1995, 87; and in 1996, 92 replies. However, some countries have routinely submitted information retrospectively for calendar years other than that requested by the Secretary-General.
[55] Reply by Mauritania dated 2 Sep. 1997, as included in United Nations document A/52/312, 28 Aug. 1997, pp. 71–72.

Table 8.6. Government returns to the UN Register for calendar years 1992–96, as of 1 April 1998

e = export data, en = nil report on exports, i = import data, in = nil report on imports, b = background information, nv = explanation in *note verbale*, – = no reports received

Country	1992	1993	1994	1995	1996
Afghanistan	–	nv	–	–	–
Albania	en, in	–	–	en	–
Antigua & Barbuda	en, in	en, in	–	–	–
Andorra	–	–	in	en, in, nv	en, in
Argentina	e, in	en, i, b	en, i, b	e, i, b	en, i, b
Armenia	–	en, in	en, in, b	en, in, b	en, in, b
Australia	en, i, b	en, i, b	en, i, b	en, i	e, i, b
Austria	b	en, in, b	en, i, nv, b	en, i, b	e, in, b
Azerbaijan	–	–	–	en, in, b	en, in, b
Bahamas	–	–	en, in	en, in	–
Barbados	–	–	en, in	en, in	–
Belarus	e, in	e, in, b	e	i, b	e, in
Belgium	en, i, b	i, b	e, in, b	e, in, b	e, in, b
Belize	–	–	en, in	–	en, in
Benin	–	–	en, in	–	–
Bhutan	en, in	en, in	en, in	en, in	en, in
Bolivia	i, b	–	–	–	–
Brazil	e, i, b	en, i, b	en, i, b	en, i, b	en, i, b
Brunei	–	–	–	–	i
Bulgaria	e, i, b	e, in, b	e, b	en, in, b	en, i, b
Burkina Faso	–	en, in	en, in	en, in	–
Cameroon	–	–	en, in	–	en, in
Canada	e, i, b	e, i, b	e, i, b	e, in, b	e, i, b
Central African Rep.	–	–	–	in	–
Chad	–	e	en, in	–	–
Chile	en, i, b	en, in, b	en, i	en, i	en, i
China	e, i	e, in	e, i	e, i	e, i, b, nv
Colombia	en, i	–	–	–	–
Comoros	–	en, in, b	–	–	–
Cook Islands					in
Côte d'Ivoire	–	en, in, b	–	–	–
Croatia	en, in, nv	en, in, nv	en, in, nv	–	en, in
Cuba	en, in, nv	en, in	en, in	en, in	en, in
Cyprus	–	en, in	en, i	en, i	en, i
Czech Republic	e, in, b	e, i, b	e, in, b	e, in, b	e, in, b
Denmark	en, i, b	e, in, b	en, i, b	en, in, b	en, i, b
Dominica	en, in	en, in	en, in	en, in	–
Dominican Republic	–	en, in	–	–	b
Ecuador	–	–	en, in	–	en, in
Egypt	en, in, nv	–	–	–	–
El Salvador	–	–	–	b	–
Estonia	–	–	en, i	en, in	en, in
Ethiopia	–	–	–	en, in, nv	en
Fiji	en, in, nv	en, in	en, in	en, in	en, in
Finland	e, i, b	e, i, b	e, i	e, i, b	e, i
France	e, in, b	e, in, b	e, i, b	e, in, b	e, i, b

TRANSFERS OF MAJOR CONVENTIONAL WEAPONS

Country	1992	1993	1994	1995	1996
Gabon	–	–	–	en, in	–
Georgia	en, in, nv	en, in	en, in	–	en, in
Germany	e, i, b	e, in, b	e, i, b	e, in, b	e, in, b
Greece	e, i, nv, b	i, b	i, b	i, b	e, i, b
Grenada	in	en, in	en, in	–	en, in
Guatemala	–	–	–	–	en, in
Guyana	–	–	en, in	–	en, in
Honduras	–	–	–	–	en, in
Hungary	en, in, b	en, i, b	i	en, i	en, i
Iceland	en, in, nv	en, in	en, in	en, in	en, in
India	e, i	e, in	en, i	i	en, i
Indonesia	in	i	i	i	i
Iran	en, i	en, i, nv	en, i	en, i	en, i
Ireland	en, in	en, in	en, i	en, in, b	en, in, b
Israel	e, i, b	e, i, b	e, i	e, i	e, i, b
Italy	e, i, b	e, i, b	e, i, b	e, i, b	e, i, b
Jamaica	nv	nv	en, in, b, nv	en, in	–
Japan	en, i, b	en, i, b	en, i, b	en, i, b	en, i, b
Jordan	–	en, in	–	en, in	–
Kazakhstan	en, in, nv	–	en, in	e, i	e, in
Korea, South	en, i, b	e, i, b	e, i, b	en, i, b	en, i
Kyrgyzstan	–	–	–	en, in, nv	–
Latvia	–	–	–	en, i	en, in
Lebanon	en, in, nv	–	–	–	–
Lesotho	en, in, nv	–	–	–	–
Libya	en, in, nv	–	en, in, nv	–	–
Liechtenstein	en, in, nv	en, in	en, in	en, in	en, in
Lithuania	i	–	–	en, i	en, in
Luxembourg	en, in	en, in	en	en, in	en, in, b
Macedonia	–	–	–	–	en, in, b
Madagascar	–	en, in	–	en, in	en, in
Malawi	–	en, in	–	–	–
Malaysia	en, in	en, i	en, i	i	en, i
Maldives	en, in	en, in	en, in	en, in	en, in
Malta	en, i	en, in	en, in, b	en, in	en, in
Marshall Islands	–	en, in	en, in, b	–	en, in
Mauritania	nv	en, in	en, in	–	–
Mauritius	en, nv	en, in	–	en, in	en, in
Mexico	nv	en, in, b	en, i, b	en, i, b	en, i, b
Moldova	–	–	e, i	en, i	–
Monaco	–	–	–	en, in	en, in
Mongolia	en, in, nv	en, in	en, in	en, in	en, in
Namibia	en, in	–	–	en, in	en, in
Nepal	i	en, in	en, in	en, in, nv	–
Netherlands	e, i, b, nv	e, i, b, nv	e, i, b	e, i, b	e, in, b
New Zealand	en, i, b	en, i, b	en, i, b	en, in, b	en, in, b
Nicaragua[a]	e, nv, b	e, b, nv	–	–	–
Niger	nv	en, in, b	en, in, nv	–	–
Norway	en, i, b	en, i	en, in	en, i	en, i
Oman	nv	–	–	–	–

Country	1992	1993	1994	1995	1996
Pakistan	en, i	en, i	en, i	i	i
Panama	nv, b	–	en, in	–	–
Papua New Guinea	en, in	–	en, in, nv	en, in, nv	–
Paraguay	nv	b	b	–	en, in
Peru	i	en, i	en, i	en, i	en, i
Philippines	en, i, nv	i	i	en, i	en, i
Poland	e, i, b	e, in, b	e, in, b	e, i, b	en, i, b
Portugal	en, i, b	en, i, b	en, i, b	en, i, b	en, i, b
Qatar	b	–	–	–	–
Romania	e, i	e, in	e, i	e, in	e, i
Russia	e, in	e, in	e, in	e, i	e, in
Saint Kitts & Nevis	–	–	–	en, in	–
Saint Lucia	en, in	en, in	en, in	–	en, in
Saint Vincent & the Grenadines	–	en, in	–	en, in	–
Samoa	–	en, in	en, in	en, in	en, in
Senegal	en, in, b	–	–	–	–
Seychelles	en, in,	–	–	–	en, in
Sierra Leone	–	b	–	–	–
Singapore	en, i	en, i	en, i	en, i	e, i
Slovakia	e, in, nv	e, i, nv	e, i	e, i	e, i, b
Slovenia	en, in, nv	en, in	en, in	en, in	en, i
Solomon Islands	en, in, nv	–	en, in	–	–
South Africa	nv	–	e, in, b	e, in, b	e, in
Spain	en, i, b	en, i, b	en, i, b	en, i, b	en, i, b
Sri Lanka	i, nv	i	i	i	–
Sweden	e, i, b	e, i, b	en, i, b	en, i, b	e, i, b
Switzerland	en, in, b	e, in, b	en, in, b	e, in, b	e, i, b
Tajikistan	–	–	en, in	en, in	–
Tanzania	en, in	en, in	en, in	en, in	en, in
Thailand	–	i	en, i	i	i
Trinidad and Tobago	–	en, in	–	en, in	en, in
Tunisia	nv	–	–	–	–
Turkey	en, i, b	en, i	en, i	en, i, b	en, in, b
Turkmenistan	–	–	–	en, in	e
Ukraine	en, in	e, in	e, in	e, in	e
UK	e, i, b	e, in, b	e, i, b	e, i, b	e, i, b
USA	e, i, b, nv	e, i, b, nv	e, i, b, nv	e, i, b, nv	e, i, b
Vanuatu	en, in	en, in	–	en, in	–
Viet Nam	–	–	in	en, i	en, in
Yugoslavia (S & M.)	en, in, b, nv	en, in, b	en, in, b	–	–
Total reports	92	90	94	95	93
On exports (en)	22 (51)	24 (55)	22 (64)	21 (65)	26 (61)
On imports (in)	38 (41)	31 (53)	42 (48)	42 (51)	37 (50)
Background data	34	37	31	31	33
Notes verbales	32	8	7	6	1

[a] While submitting a comprehensive aggregate report for 1992/93, Nicaragua did not submit data for exports in the standard format.

Note: Non-UN members Switzerland and the Holy See (Vatican) were asked to provide data. The Republic of China (Taiwan), also a non-member, was not asked for information.

Four countries, Brunei, Guatemala, Honduras and Macedonia, submitted returns to the register for the first time in 1997, for calendar year 1996. On the other hand 21 countries which had submitted returns to the register in 1996 did not do so in 1997. As noted above for Iran, some of these countries are likely to supply information at a later date.

While the number of states reporting to the register has not changed, there is a greater willingness to go beyond the minimum reporting requirements. Several states, including China and the UK, have provided more details in their 1996 report than in earlier reports. Information on the exact designation of the weapons would be especially useful to enable the possible impact of arms transfers on stability to be assessed. The main exporters of weapons in the seven UNROCA categories, Russia and the USA, have not yet provided such qualitative details. The USA did, however, publish a very comprehensive public report on its 1996 arms exports, which included many of the details that would make the US report to the UNROCA really useful.[56]

There are still widespread discrepancies between the information submitted by exporting and importing states for their bilateral transfers in the same year. In some cases exporters report as much as 500 per cent higher or lower deliveries than the importers. These discrepancies make the data in the register difficult to interpret.[57] There are also cases in which exports and/or imports have been clearly overlooked by the reporting countries, or in which major transfers have taken place without the knowledge of those government departments responsible for policy on this matter. Examples of cases in which reports were not made to the UNROCA, but for which ample and official sources document the transfers, are the delivery of three F-16 FGA aircraft by the USA to Denmark in 1994, which neither country reported, and, more serious from the viewpoint of 'destabilizing arms build-ups', the transfer of 84 T-72 tanks, 50 BMP-2 infantry fighting vehicles (IFVs), 90 pieces of artillery and 24 SS-1 Scud-B surface-to-surface missiles (SSMs) from Russia to Armenia in 1993–96.[58] On the Russian side it is clear that the central authorities responsible for arms exports were not informed by the local military authorities that effected the transfers, but the Armenian 'nil' reports for 1993 to 1996 are more difficult to explain, unless the Armenian authorities responsible for importing the equipment have also kept those responsible for the compilation of the report to the UN uninformed.[59]

---

[56] See under 'Official data on arms exports' above.

[57] The problem of discrepancies led some government experts to suggest the creation of a consultative mechanism by which the UN Secretariat could question member states about the contents of their annual returns with a view to harmonizing the information presented by exporters and importers. However, there was no consensus supporting this idea. See also Laurence, E. J., Wezeman, S. T. and Wulf, H., *Arms Watch: SIPRI Report on the First Year of the UN Register of Conventional Arms*, SIPRI Research Report no. 6 (Oxford University Press: Oxford, 1993).

[58] Anthony, I., 'Illicit arms transfers', ed. Anthony (note 3), pp. 224–25.

[59] 'Rokhlin details arms supplies to Armenia', *Sovetskaya Rossiya* (Moscow), 3 Apr. 1997, in Foreign Broadcast Information Service, *Daily Report–Central Eurasia (FBIS-SOV)*, FBIS-SOV-97-067, 3 Apr. 1997. See also chapter 12 in this volume.

The 1997 Review

In early and mid-1997 the Group of Governmental Experts met to review the operation of the UNROCA and to consider improvements and additions to the reporting procedures. The group completed its work on 15 August 1997, presenting a consensus report on 29 August 1997.[60] Despite the fact that panel members stressed their intention to be productive, the results, as in 1994, were disappointing. The group discussed expanding the UNROCA to include procurement from national production, and additional types of conventional weapon. Once again, however, the issue of the inclusion of weapons of mass destruction blocked all substantial progress. The group was unable to reach agreement on any measure to expand or strengthen the UNROCA, referring the issue once more to the next review, which was recommended for 2000. The only positive decision was to make public the background information provided by several states instead of only providing an index of such information as had been done previously. However, most if not all background information is already publicly available and the decision is, therefore, only of minor importance.

The aim of the UNROCA was to contribute to the prevention of destabilizing accumulations of conventional weapons by giving early warning through transparency. Despite the fact that some of the information reported gave unique insights into patterns of arms transfers not revealed in other public sources, five years of experience with the UNROCA has shown no evidence of preventing destabilizing weapon accumulations and in many cases has led to confusion where importer and exporter reports differ widely. The fact that procurement from national production is still not part of the UNROCA is a further hindrance in analysing arms transfers and their military–political impact.

The disappointing performance of both reviews, the continuous low quality of some of the reported data and the lack of reports from certain key countries and regions does not inspire strong confidence in any future review.

The idea of setting up regional registers tailored specifically to the wishes and needs of regions, included as an option for future development in the original UN resolution for the UNROCA, has been discussed in several regions and forums—in Africa, the Association of South-East Asian Nations (ASEAN), the EU and Latin America—but it has so far met with only lukewarm receptions. Generally there has been scepticism about the usefulness of reproducing the UNROCA on a regional level unless agreement can be reached on which additional weapon systems of specific importance for regional stability should be covered. There is no mandate from an existing institution such as ASEAN or any other regional institution with which reports could be deposited. An additional problem is that in some cases it would be difficult to define the region. Clearly the Americas are at least militarily independent of the rest of the world and could, therefore, have their own

[60] United Nations, Report on the continuing operation of the United Nations Register of Conventional Arms and its further development, UN document A/52/316, 29 Aug. 1997.

regional register with their own organization—the Organization of American States. However, regions such as the Middle East or South-East Asia are more difficult to define. While ASEAN may set up a regional register this would not contribute much to arms transparency or stability in the region, since the main concern for the ASEAN countries is China.

Appendix 8A. The volume of transfers of major conventional weapons, 1988–97

IAN ANTHONY, PIETER D. WEZEMAN and
SIEMON T. WEZEMAN

Table 8A.1. Volume of imports of major conventional weapons
Figures are SIPRI trend-indicator values expressed in US $m. at constant (1990) prices. Regional and group figures include transfers between countries in the same region or group.

	1988	1989	1990	1991	1992	1993	1994	1995	1996	1997
World total	36 331	34 412	29 137	24 936	22 858	23 999	20 231	21 271	22 542	25 156
Developing world	21 658	19 822	18 117	14 074	10 930	13 205	12 370	14 944	16 204	18 327
LDCs	1 822	2 967	2 701	1 690	122	357	149	482	163	233
Industrialized world	14 673	14 590	11 019	10 862	11 927	10 794	7 862	6 326	6 337	6 830
Africa	2 104	1 496	1 322	835	395	274	575	583	485	260
Sub-Saharan	1 670	413	725	172	303	160	254	166	330	119
Americas	1 773	1 916	1 515	2 447	1 908	1 396	1 847	1 785	1 785	2 058
North	966	543	453	1 468	1 287	977	1 114	724	712	850
Central	210	249	321	160	6	6	–	4	3	12
South	597	1 123	740	819	615	414	733	1 057	1 070	1 197
Asia	11 421	12 361	10 169	8 421	6 030	6 422	5 903	8 923	9 005	12 344
North-East	3 837	3 682	3 399	3 448	3 485	4 083	2 311	4 440	4 891	7 527
South-East	1 376	1 107	1 265	1 235	1 003	867	2 223	3 001	1 683	2 934
South	5 191	5 354	3 295	2 352	1 536	1 472	1 345	1 482	2 025	1 711
Europe	11 827	11 530	8 899	7 561	8 733	7 895	5 855	4 577	4 469	4 872
Middle East	8 313	6 142	6 806	5 425	5 401	7 544	5 717	5 310	6 471	5 049
Oceania	893	967	426	246	391	468	335	92	327	574
ASEAN	1 354	940	959	1 061	964	559	2 161	2 718	1 636	2 934
CSCE/OSCE	12 621	12 035	9 323	9 009	9 999	8 746	6 901	5 258	5 476	5 729
CIS	..	..	..	..	101	60	360	76	514	172
EU	4 011	4 354	3 392	5 205	5 845	3 568	3 341	2 357	2 111	2 755
GCC	2 021	2 654	3 677	2 093	2 439	4 281	2 370	2 924	4 847	4 061
NATO	6 460	6 265	4 959	7 604	8 687	6 528	5 783	4 116	3 421	4 186
P5	2 457	2 273	1 413	2 755	3 278	1 930	909	1 372	1 826	2 703
OECD	9 095	9 235	7 176	10 017	11 439	9 249	7 418	5 655	5 325	6 576
OPEC	5 535	5 863	5 552	3 499	2 813	5 731	3 284	3 624	5 378	4 069
WEU	3 843	3 967	3 328	4 992	5 799	3 530	3 230	1 936	1 425	1 955

Note: Tables 8A.1 and 8A.2 show the volume of arms transfers for different geographical regions and subregions, selected groups of countries and international organizations. Since countries can belong to only one region, the regional values add up to the world total. As many countries are included in more than one group or organization, totals cannot be derived from these figures. Countries are included in the values for the different international organizations from the year of joining. The following countries are included in each group.

Developing world: Afghanistan, Algeria, Angola, Argentina, Bahamas, Bahrain, Bangladesh, Barbados, Belize, Benin, Bhutan, Bolivia, Botswana, Brazil, Brunei, Burkina Faso, Burundi, Cambodia, Cameroon, Cape Verde, Central African Republic, Chad, Chile, China, Colombia, Comoros, Congo (Brazzaville), Congo (Dem. Rep.), Costa Rica, Côte d'Ivoire, Cuba, Cyprus, Djibouti, Dominica, Dominican Republic, Ecuador, Egypt, El Salvador, Equatorial Guinea, Eritrea, Ethiopia, Fiji, Gabon, Gambia, Ghana, Guatemala, Guinea, Guinea-Bissau, Guyana, Haiti, Honduras, India, Indonesia, Iran, Iraq, Israel, Jamaica, Jordan, Kenya, Kiribati, North Korea, South Korea, Kuwait, Laos, Lebanon, Lesotho, Liberia, Libya, Madagascar, Malawi, Malaysia, Maldives, Mali, Marshall Islands, Mauritania,

Table 8A.2. Volume of exports of major conventional weapons
Figures are SIPRI trend-indicator values expressed in US $m. at constant (1990) prices. Regional and group figures include transfers between countries in the same region or group.

	1988	1989	1990	1991	1992	1993	1994	1995	1996	1997
World total	36 331	34 412	29 137	24 936	22 858	24 000	20 232	21 271	22 542	25 156
Developing world	3 224	2 009	1 591	1 570	1 364	1 987	1 065	1 358	1 169	713
LDCs	3	–	–	–	–	–	–	–	–	13
Industrialized world	33 107	32 403	27 546	23 366	21 494	22 013	19 166	19 913	21 373	24 444
Africa	106	4	51	38	94	54	10	10	33	14
Sub-Saharan	53	4	16	38	94	54	10	10	33	14
Americas	10 282	9 718	9 049	11 297	13 143	12 790	10 843	10 300	9 866	10 949
North	10 077	9 642	8 955	11 243	13 003	12 725	10 800	10 257	9 767	10 921
Central	–	1	5	3	79	25	–	–	21	–
South	205	75	89	52	60	41	43	43	78	28
Asia	2 536	1 635	1 343	1 336	958	1 602	1 034	1 392	821	266
North-East	2 516	1 527	1 243	1 327	934	1 573	759	992	810	197
South-East	18	108	6	6	24	25	32	40	–	69
South	1	1	94	3	–	3	4	3	1	–
Europe	23 011	22 739	18 446	12 033	8 470	9 243	8 086	9 260	11 544	13 202
Middle East	377	294	103	144	185	280	233	286	268	408
Oceania	18	22	144	88	8	30	26	22	10	318
ASEAN	18	60	6	6	24	25	32	40	–	69
CSCE/OSCE	33 088	32 381	27 401	23 247	21 473	21 967	19 124	19 875	21 320	24 123
CIS	..	..	..	..	2 977	3 668	1 727	3 813	4 234	4 520
EU	5 818	6 825	5 821	5 699	4 658	4 854	5 692	5 129	6 774	8 516
GCC	–	–	2	–	–	49	52	42	4	67
NATO	15 907	16 554	14 805	17 105	17 667	17 676	16 678	15 238	16 205	19 354
P5	29 494	29 119	24 667	19 447	18 766	19 636	14 448	16 465	18 090	20 450
OECD	16 517	17 052	15 529	17 736	18 199	17 871	16 844	15 569	16 890	19 906
OPEC	224	42	46	26	–	75	77	80	4	81
WEU	5 769	6 826	5 709	5 689	4 660	4 845	5 653	4 631	6 358	8 146

Mauritius, Mexico, Micronesia, Mongolia, Morocco, Mozambique, Myanmar, Namibia, Nepal, Nicaragua, Niger, Nigeria, Oman, Pakistan, Palau, Panama, Papua New Guinea, Paraguay, Peru, Philippines, Qatar, Rwanda, St Vincent & the Grenadines, Samoa, Saudi Arabia, Senegal, Seychelles, Sierra Leone, Singapore, Solomon Islands, Somalia, South Africa, Sri Lanka, Sudan, Suriname, Swaziland, Syria, Taiwan, Tanzania, Thailand, Togo, Tonga, Trinidad & Tobago, Tunisia, Tuvalu, Uganda, United Arab Emirates, Uruguay, Vanuatu, Venezuela, Viet Nam, North Yemen (–1990), South Yemen (–1990), Yemen (1991–), Zambia, Zimbabwe

Least developed countries (LDCs): Afghanistan, Bangladesh, Benin, Bhutan, Botswana, Burkina Faso, Burundi, Cape Verde, Central African Republic, Chad, Comoros, Djibouti, Equatorial Guinea, Eritrea, Ethiopia, Gambia, Guinea, Guinea-Bissau, Haiti, Laos, Lesotho, Liberia, Malawi, Maldives, Mali, Mauritania, Mozambique, Myanmar, Nepal, Niger, Rwanda, Samoa, Sierra Leone, Somalia, Sudan, Tanzania, Togo, Uganda, Vanuatu, North Yemen (–1990), South Yemen (–1990), Yemen (1991–)

Industrialized world: Albania, Armenia (1992–), Australia, Austria, Azerbaijan (1992–), Belarus (1992–), Belgium, Bosnia and Herzegovina (1992–), Bulgaria, Canada, Croatia (1992–), Czechoslovakia (–1992), Czech Republic (1993–), Denmark, Estonia (1991–), Finland, France, Georgia (1992–), German DR (–1990), Germany, Greece, Hungary, Iceland, Ireland, Italy, Japan, Kazakhstan (1992–), Kyrgyzstan (1992–), Latvia (1991–), Liechtenstein, Lithuania (1991–), Luxembourg, Macedonia (1992–), Malta, Moldova (1992–), Monaco, Netherlands, New Zealand, Norway, Poland, Portugal, Romania, Russia (1992–), Slovakia (1993–), Slovenia (1992–), Spain, Sweden, Switzerland, Tajikistan (1992–), Turkey, Turkmenistan (1992–), UK, Ukraine (1992–), USA, USSR (–1991), Uzbekistan (1992–), Yugoslavia (–1991), Yugoslavia (Serbia and Montenegro) (1992–)

Africa: Algeria, Angola, Benin, Botswana, Burkina Faso, Burundi, Cameroon, Cape Verde, Central African Republic, Chad, Comoros, Congo (Brazzaville), Congo (Dem. Rep.), Côte d'Ivoire, Djibouti, Equatorial Guinea, Eritrea, Ethiopia, Gabon, Gambia, Ghana, Guinea, Guinea-Bissau, Kenya, Lesotho, Liberia, Libya, Madagascar, Malawi, Mali, Mauritania, Mauritius, Morocco, Mozambique, Namibia, Niger, Nigeria, Rwanda, Senegal, Seychelles, Sierra Leone, Somalia, South Africa, Sudan, Swaziland, Tanzania, Togo, Tunisia, Uganda, Zambia, Zimbabwe

Sub-Saharan Africa: Angola, Benin, Botswana, Burkina Faso, Burundi, Cameroon, Cape Verde, Central African Republic, Chad, Comoros, Congo (Brazzaville), Congo (Dem. Rep.), Côte d'Ivoire, Djibouti, Equatorial Guinea, Eritrea, Ethiopia, Gabon, Gambia, Ghana, Guinea, Guinea-Bissau, Kenya, Lesotho, Liberia, Madagascar, Malawi, Mali, Mauritania, Mauritius, Mozambique, Namibia, Niger, Nigeria, Rwanda, Senegal, Seychelles, Sierra Leone, Somalia, South Africa, Sudan, Swaziland, Tanzania, Togo, Uganda, Zambia, Zimbabwe

Americas: Argentina, Bahamas, Barbados, Belize, Bolivia, Brazil, Canada, Chile, Colombia, Costa Rica, Cuba, Dominica, Dominican Republic, Ecuador, El Salvador, Guatemala, Guyana, Haiti, Honduras, Jamaica, Mexico, Nicaragua, Panama, Paraguay, Peru, St Vincent & the Grenadines, Suriname, Trinidad & Tobago, Uruguay, USA, Venezuela

North America: Canada, Mexico, USA

Central America: Bahamas, Barbados, Belize, Costa Rica, Cuba, Dominica, Dominican Republic, El Salvador, Guatemala, Haiti, Honduras, Jamaica, Nicaragua, Panama, St Vincent & the Grenadines, Trinidad & Tobago

South America: Argentina, Bolivia, Brazil, Chile, Colombia, Ecuador, Guyana, Paraguay, Peru, Suriname, Uruguay, Venezuela

Asia: Afghanistan, Bangladesh, Bhutan, Brunei, Cambodia, China, India, Indonesia, Japan, Kazakhstan (1992–), North Korea, South Korea, Kyrgyzstan (1992–), Laos, Malaysia, Maldives, Mongolia, Myanmar (Burma), Nepal, Pakistan, Philippines, Singapore, Sri Lanka, Taiwan, Tajikistan (1992–), Thailand, Turkmenistan (1992–), Uzbekistan (1992–), Viet Nam

North-East Asia: China, Japan, North Korea, South Korea, Taiwan

South-East Asia: Brunei, Cambodia, Indonesia, Laos, Malaysia, Myanmar, Philippines, Singapore, Thailand, Viet Nam

South Asia: Bangladesh, Bhutan, India, Maldives, Nepal, Pakistan, Sri Lanka

Europe: Albania, Armenia (1992–), Austria, Azerbaijan (1992–), Belarus (1992–), Belgium, Bosnia and Herzegovina (1992–), Bulgaria, Croatia (1992–), Cyprus, Czechoslovakia (–1992), Czech Republic (1993–), Denmark, Estonia (1991–), Finland, France, Georgia (1992–), German DR (–1990), Germany, Greece, Hungary, Iceland, Ireland, Italy, Latvia (1991–), Liechtenstein, Lithuania (1991–), Luxembourg, Macedonia (1992–), Malta, Moldova (1992–), Monaco, Netherlands, Norway, Poland, Portugal, Romania, Russia (1992–), Slovakia (1993–), Slovenia (1992–), Spain, Sweden, Switzerland, Turkey, UK, Ukraine (1992–), USSR (–1991), Yugoslavia (–1991), Yugoslavia (Serbia and Montenegro) (1992–)

Middle East: Bahrain, Egypt, Iran, Iraq, Israel, Jordan, Kuwait, Lebanon, Oman, Qatar, Saudi Arabia, Syria, United Arab Emirates, North Yemen (–1990), South Yemen (–1990),Yemen (1991–)

Oceania: Australia, Fiji, Kiribati, Marshall Islands, Micronesia, New Zealand, Palau, Papua New Guinea, Samoa, Solomon Islands, Tonga, Tuvalu, Vanuatu

Association of South-East Asian Nations (ASEAN): Brunei, Indonesia, Laos (1997–), Malaysia, Myanmar (Burma) (1997–), Philippines, Singapore, Thailand, Viet Nam (1995–)

Organization for Security and Co-operation in Europe (OSCE): Albania (1991–), Andorra, Armenia (1992–), Austria, Azerbaijan (1992–), Belarus (1992–), Belgium, Bosnia and Herzegovina (1992–),

TRANSFERS OF MAJOR CONVENTIONAL WEAPONS

Bulgaria, Canada, Croatia (1992–), Cyprus, Czechoslovakia (–1992), Czech Republic (1993–), Denmark, Estonia (1991–), Finland, France, Georgia (1992–), German DR (–1990), Germany, Greece, Holy See, Hungary, Iceland, Ireland, Italy, Kazakhstan (1992–), Kyrgyzstan (1992–), Latvia (1991–), Liechtenstein, Lithuania (1991–), Luxembourg, Macedonia (1995–), Malta, Moldova (1992–), Monaco, Netherlands, Norway, Poland, Portugal, Romania, Russia (1992–), San Marino, Slovakia (1992–), Slovenia (1992–), Spain, Sweden, Switzerland, Tajikistan (1992–), Turkey, Turkmenistan (1992–), UK, Ukraine (1992–), USA, USSR (–1992), Uzbekistan (1992–), Yugoslavia (–1991), Yugoslavia (Serbia and Montenegro, suspended since 1992)

Commonwealth of Independent States (CIS): Armenia, Azerbaijan, Belarus, Georgia (1993–), Kazakhstan, Kyrgyzstan, Moldova, Russia, Tajikistan, Turkmenistan, Ukraine, Uzbekistan

European Union (EU): Austria (1995–), Belgium, Denmark, Finland (1995–), France, Germany, Greece, Ireland, Italy, Luxembourg, Netherlands, Portugal, Spain, Sweden (1995–), UK

GCC (Gulf Co-operation Council) Bahrain, Kuwait, Oman, Qatar, Saudi Arabia, United Arab Emirates

NATO: Belgium, Canada, Denmark, France, Germany, Greece, Iceland, Italy, Luxembourg, Netherlands, Norway, Portugal, Spain, Turkey, UK, USA

P5 (5 Permanent members of the UN Security Council) China, France, Russia (1992–)/USSR (–1992), UK, USA

Organisation for Economic Co-operation and Development (OECD): Australia, Austria, Belgium, Canada, Czech Rep. (1995–), Denmark, Finland, France, Germany, Greece, Hungary (1996–), Iceland, Ireland, Italy, Japan, South Korea (1996–), Luxembourg, Mexico (1994–), Netherlands, New Zealand, Norway, Poland (1996–), Portugal, Spain, Sweden, Switzerland, Turkey, UK, USA

Organisation of Petroleum Exporting Countries (OPEC): Algeria, Ecuador (–1992), Gabon (–1995), Indonesia, Iran, Iraq, Kuwait, Libya, Nigeria, Qatar, Saudi Arabia, United Arab Emirates, Venezuela

Western European Union (WEU): Belgium, France, Germany, Greece, Italy, Luxembourg, Netherlands, Portugal, Spain, UK

Appendix 8B. Register of the transfers and licensed production of major conventional weapons, 1997

IAN ANTHONY, PIETER D. WEZEMAN and SIEMON T. WEZEMAN

This register lists major weapons on order or under delivery, or for which the licence was bought and production was under way or completed during 1997. 'Year(s) of deliveries' includes aggregates of all deliveries and licensed production since the beginning of the contract. Sources and methods for the data collection are explained in appendix 8C. Conventions, abbreviations and acronyms used are explained at the end of this appendix. Entries are alphabetical, by recipient, supplier and licenser.

Recipient/ supplier (S) or licenser (L)	No. ordered	Weapon designation	Weapon description	Year of order/ licence	Year(s) of deliveries	No. delivered/ produced	Comments
Algeria							
L: UK	3	Kebir Class	Patrol craft	(1990)		. .	Algerian designation El Yadekh Class
Angola							
S: USA	6	C-130K Hercules	Transport aircraft	(1997)		. .	Ex-UK Air Force; sold back to US producer and resold to Angola
Argentina							
S: Italy	20	Palmaria 155mm turret	Turret	(1983)	1996	(2)	Turret for TAMSE VCA-155 self-propelled gun
Russia	8	Su-29	Trainer aircraft	1997	1997	8	
USA	36	A-4M Skyhawk-2	FGA aircraft	1994	1997	5	Ex-US Marines; deal worth $282 m; incl 18 refurbished before delivery and 18 refurbished from kits; Argentine designation A-4AR Fightinghawk; incl 4 refurbished to TA-4AR trainer version
	16	Bell-205/UH-1H	Helicopter	1996	1997	8	Ex-US Army; EDA aid; incl 8 for Navy
	1	Boeing-707-320C	Transport aircraft	(1997)	1997	1	Second-hand

	6	P-3B Orion	ASW/MP aircraft	1996	(6)	Ex-US Navy; for Navy; EDA aid
	2	Schweizer-330	Helicopter	(1997)	2	For Coast Guard; for training
	(15)	Super King Air-200	Light transport ac	(1993)	(1)	Ex-US Air Force and US Army
L: Germany	..	TAM	Main battle tank	1994	(106)	

Australia

S: Israel	..	Popeye-1	ASM	1996	(10)	For F-111C fighter/bomber aircraft
Sweden	8	9LV	Fire control radar	(1991)	(1)	For 8 MEKO-200ANZ Type (Anzac Class) frigates
	8	Sea Giraffe-150	Surveillance radar	1991	(1)	For 8 MEKO-200ANZ Type (Anzac Class) frigates
UK	12	Hawk-100	FGA/trainer aircraft	1997	..	Deal worth $640 m incl 21 licensed production
USA	12	C-130J-30 Hercules	Transport aircraft	1995	..	Deal worth $670 m; option on 24 more
	3	P-3B Orion	ASW/MP aircraft	1994	2	Ex-US Navy; modified in Australia to TAP-3 for training; 1 more for spares only
	11	SH-2G Super Seasprite	ASW helicopter	1997	..	Ex-US Navy SH-2Fs rebuilt to SH-2G; for Navy; US export designation SH-2G(A); deal worth $600 m
	8	127mm/54 Mk-45	Naval gun	(1989)	2	For 8 MEKO-200ANZ Type (Anzac Class) frigates
	8	AN/SPS-49	Surveillance radar	1993	(1)	For 8 MEKO-200ANZ Type (Anzac Class) frigates
	8	Seasparrow Mk-48	ShAM system	(1991)	(1)	For 8 MEKO-200ANZ Type (Anzac Class) frigates
	(32)	RIM-7P Seasparrow	ShAM	(1991)	(16)	For 2 MEKO-200ANZ Type (Anzac Class) frigates
	12	RGM-84A Harpoon	ShShM	1995	..	Deal worth $38 m incl 21 training missiles
L: Germany	8	MEKO-200ANZ Type	Frigate	1989	1	Australian designation Anzac Class; more produced for export
Italy	6	Gaeta Class	MCM ship	1994	..	Australian designation Huon Class
Sweden	6	Type-471	Submarine	1987	2	Deal worth $2.8 b; Australian designation Collins Class; option on 2 more
UK	21	Hawk-100	FGA/trainer aircraft	1997	..	Deal worth $640 m incl 12 delivered direct

Austria

S: France	22	RAC	Surveillance radar	1995	(7)	Deal worth $129 m (offsets $344 m) incl Mistral missiles

MILITARY SPENDING AND ARMAMENTS, 1997

Recipient/ supplier (S) or licenser (L)	No. ordered	Weapon designation	Weapon description	Year of order/ licence	Year(s) of deliveries	No. delivered/ produced	Comments
Germany	87	RJPz-1 Jaguar-1	Tank destroyer (M)	1996	1997	(44)	Ex-FRG Army; deal worth $1.4 m; incl 18 for spares only
	(828)	HOT-2	Anti-tank missile	1996	1997	(828)	For 69 RJPZ-1 tank destroyers; Austrian designation PAL-4000
	(552)	HOT-3	Anti-tank missile	1996	1997	..	For 69 RJPZ-1 tank destroyers
Netherlands	114	Leopard-2	Main battle tank	1996	1997	(10)	Ex-Dutch Army; deal worth $236 m
Sweden	..	RBS-56 Bill-2	Anti-tank missile	1996	1997	..	
USA	54	M-109A5 155mm	Self-propelled gun	1995	1997	(54)	Austrian designation M-109A5Ö; deal worth $48.6 m
Bahamas							
S: USA	2	Bahamas Class	Patrol craft	1997		..	
Bahrain							
S: USA	14	Bell-209/AH-1E	Combat helicopter	1994	1995–97	(14)	Ex-US Army
	10	Bell-209/AH-1E	Combat helicopter	1995		..	Ex-US Army; status uncertain
	6	Bell-209/AH-1E	Combat helicopter	1995		..	Ex-US Army; refurbished before delivery; status uncertain
	1	I-HAWK SAMS	SAM system	1995		..	Ex-US Army; EDA aid
	..	MIM-23B HAWK	SAM	1995		..	Ex-US Army; for 1 I-HAWK SAM system
Bangladesh							
S: China	4	T-43 Class	Minesweeper	(1993)	1994–97	(2)	Bangladeshi designation Sagar Class
Belgium							
S: Austria	54	Pandur	APC	1997		..	Incl 5 APC/CP, 4 ARV and 4 ambulance version; deal worth $42 m
France	14	LG-1 105mm	Towed gun	1996	1997	14	Deal worth $11 m

Netherlands	3	Scout	Surveillance radar	1995	1997	(3)	For refit of 3 Wielingen Class frigates
Singapore	2	A-310-200	Transport aircraft	1997	1997	1	Deal worth $36 m; second-hand
USA	2	MD Explorer	Helicopter	1996	1997	2	For Gendarmerie
	(72)	AIM-120B AMRAAM	Air-to-air missile	1995		..	For F-16A/B-MLU FGA aircraft
Bosnia and Herzegovina							
S: Egypt	10	T-55	Main battle tank	(1997)	1997	10	Ex-Egyptian Army
UAE	(41)	AML-90	Armoured car	1996	1997	41	Ex-UAE Army; gift
	42	AMX-30B	Main battle tank	1996	1997	(42)	Ex-UAE Army; gift
USA	15	Bell-205/UH-1H	Helicopter	1996		..	Ex-US Army; part of Train and Equip Program; incl 2 UH-1V version
	(126)	M-114A1 155mm	Towed gun	1997	1997	126	Ex-US Army; part of Train and Equip Program; incl 10 for spares only
Botswana							
S: Canada	13	CF-5A Freedom Fighter	FGA aircraft	1996	1996-97	13	Ex-Canadian Air Force; refurbished before delivery; deal worth $50 m; incl 3 CF-5D trainer version
UK	36	Scorpion	Light tank	(1994)	1995-97	(36)	Ex-Belgian Army sold back to UK producer; refurbished before delivery; probably incl some Spartan APCs
USA	2	C-130B Hercules	Transport aircraft	(1996)		..	Ex-US Air Force; EDA aid
Brazil							
S: Belgium	87	Leopard-1A1	Main battle tank	1995	1997	33	Ex-Belgian Army
France	2	Mirage-3E	Fighter aircraft	1996	1997	2	Ex-French Air Force
	(100)	Mistral	Portable SAM	1994	1996-97	(100)	
Germany	2	Grajau Class	Patrol craft	1996	1997	(2)	
Italy	6	Albatros Mk-2	ShAM system	1995		..	For refit of 6 Niteroi Class frigates; deal worth $111.5 m incl 13 RTN-30X and 7 RAN-20S radars
	13	Orion RTN-30X	Fire control radar	1995		..	For refit of 6 Niteroi Class frigates
	7	RAN-20S	Surveillance radar	1995		..	For refit of 6 Niteroi Class frigates
	(144)	Aspide	ShAM	1996		..	For 6 refitted Niteroi Class frigates; deal worth $48.5 m

Recipient/ supplier (S) or licenser (L)	No. ordered	Weapon designation	Weapon description	Year of order/ licence	Year(s) of deliveries	No. delivered/ produced	Comments
Sweden	5	Erieye	AEW radar	1994		..	Deal worth $143 m; for 5 EMB-120SA AEW aircraft
	..	RBS-56 Bill	Anti-tank missile	1995	1996–97	(100)	Deal worth $9.3 m; for Marines
UK	9	Super Lynx	ASW helicopter	1993	1996–97	(9)	Deal worth $221 m incl refurbishment of 5 Brazilian Lynx to Super Lynx; for Navy; UK export designation Lynx Mk-21A; Brazilian designation SAH-11
	4	Broadsword Class	Frigate	1994	1995–97	4	Ex-UK Navy; Brazilian designation Greenhalgh Class
	4	MM-38/40 ShShMS	ShShM system	1994	1995–97	4	On 4 ex-UK Broadsword Class frigates
	8	Seawolf GWS-25	ShAM system	1994	1995–97	8	On 4 ex-UK Broadsword Class frigates
	(128)	Seawolf	ShAM	1994	1995–97	(128)	For 4 Broadsword Class frigates
	8	Type-911	Fire control radar	1994	1995–97	8	On 4 ex-UK Broadsword Class frigates; part of Seawolf ShAM system
	4	Type-967/968	Surveillance radar	1994	1995–97	4	On 4 ex-UK Broadsword Class frigates
	4	River Class	Minesweeper	1997		..	Ex-UK Navy; Brazilian designation Do Valle Class; minesweeping gear removed before transfer, mainly for use as buoy tenders, and survey and training ships
USA	22	Bell-205/UH-1H	Helicopter	1996	1996–97	22	Ex-US Army
	4	S-70A/UH-60L	Helicopter	1997	1997	4	
	14	LVTP-7A1	APC	1995	1997	14	Deal worth $23 m incl 1 ARV and 1 APC/CP version
	6	AN/TPS-34	Surveillance radar	1997		..	For SIVAM air-surveillance system; US export designation TPS-B-34
L: Germany	2	SNAC-1	Submarine	1995		..	Brazilian designation Tikuna Class
	3	Type-209/1400	Submarine	1984	1994–96	2	Brazilian designation Tupi Class
Singapore	2	Grajau Class	Patrol craft	1995		..	
Brunei							
S: France	3	MM-38/40 ShShMS	ShShM system	(1997)		..	For 3 Yarrow-95m Type frigates

TRANSFERS OF MAJOR CONVENTIONAL WEAPONS 327

Recipient/Supplier	No.	Weapon designation	Weapon description	Year of order	Year of delivery	No. delivered	Comments
Indonesia	(48)	MM-40 Exocet	ShShM	(1997)			For 3 Yarrow-95m Type frigates
	1	CN-235-110	Transport aircraft	1995	1997	1	
	3	CN-235MPA	MP aircraft	1995			
Netherlands	3	Goalkeeper	CIWS	(1997)			For 3 Yarrow-95m Type frigates
Switzerland	4	PC-7-2	Trainer aircraft	(1996)	1997	4	
UK	3	Yarrow-95m Type	Frigate	(1997)			
	3	AWS-9	Surveillance radar	(1997)			On 3 Yarrow-95m Type frigates
	3	Seawolf GWS-26	ShAM system	(1997)			On 3 Yarrow-95m Type frigates
	(96)	Seawolf VL	ShAM	(1997)			On 3 Yarrow-95m Type frigates
	3	ST-1802SW	Fire control radar	(1997)			On 3 Yarrow-95m Type frigates; part of Seawolf ShAM system
USA	4	S-70A/UH-60L	Helicopter	1995	1996–97	(3)	US export designation S-70A-14
Bulgaria							
S: Russia	12	Mi-24D Hind-D	Combat helicopter	1995	1997	(12)	Ex-Russian Air Force; gift; status uncertain
Cambodia							
S: Czech Republic	6	L-39Z Albatros	Jet trainer aircraft	(1994)	1996	2	Ex-Czech Air Force; deal worth $3.6 m incl refurbishment and training in Israel
Canada							
S: France	28	LG-1 105mm	Towed gun	1994	1996–97	(15)	Deal worth $13 m
Germany	(123)	Leopard-1A5 turret	Turret	(1996)	1997	(75)	Ex-FRG Army; deal worth $105 m; for refurbishment of 114 Canadian Leopard-1 tanks
UK	15	EH-101-500	Helicopter	1997			Deal worth $415 m; for SAR; Canadian designation AW-520 Cormorant
	18	Hawk-100	FGA/trainer aircraft	1997			For civilian company for training of pilots from Canadian and other NATO air forces; option on 7 more
USA	(152)	MSTAR	Battlefield radar	1994	1995–97	(152)	For use on 152 LAV-25 (Coyote) AIFVs
	2	C-130H-30 Hercules	Transport aircraft	1996	1997	2	Deal worth $79 m; Canadian designation CC-130
	24	PC-9	Trainer aircraft	1997			For civilian company for training of pilots from Canadian and other NATO air forces

Recipient/ supplier (S) or licenser (L)	No. ordered	Weapon designation	Weapon description	Year of order/ licence	Year(s) of deliveries	No. delivered/ produced	Comments
L: Switzerland	240	Piranha-3 8x8	APC	1997			Deal worth $1.49 b incl option on 411 more
	203	Piranha/LAV-25	IFV	1993	1996–97	(200)	Deal worth $367 m; Canadian designation Coyote
USA	100	Bell-412	Helicopter	1992	1994–97	(96)	Deal worth $558 m; Canadian designation CH-146 Griffon
Chile							
S: France	11	AMX-30D	ARV	1996		..	Ex-French Army
	..	AM-39 Exocet	Air-to-ship missile	1992		..	For 6 Navy AS-532SC helicopters
	1	Scorpene Class	Submarine	1997		..	Deal worth $400 m incl 1 from Spain
Germany	6	Combattante-2 Type	FAC(M)	1996	1997	2	Ex-FRG Navy; FRG designation Tiger Class or Type-148
	6	Castor-2B	Fire control radar	1996	1997	2	On 6 ex-FRG Navy Combattante-2 Type FAC; for use with 76mm and 40mm guns
	6	MM-38/40 ShShMS	ShShM system	1996	1997	2	On 6 ex-FRG Navy Combattante-2 Type FAC
	6	TRS-3050 Triton-G	Surveillance radar	1996	1997	2	On 6 ex-FRG Navy Combattante-2 Type FAC
Israel	2	Reshef Class	FAC(M)	1996	1997	(2)	Ex-Israeli Navy; Chilean designation Casma Class
	2	Orion RTN-10X	Fire control radar	1996	1997	(2)	On 2 ex-Israeli Reshef Class FAC; for use with 76mm guns
	2	THD-1040 Neptune	Surveillance radar	1996	1997	(2)	On 2 ex-Israeli Reshef Class FAC
	2	Gabriel ShShMS	ShShM system	1996	1997	(2)	On 2 ex-Israeli Reshef Class FAC
	(24)	Gabriel-2	ShShM	(1996)	1997	(24)	For 2 Reshef Class FAC
	(192)	Python-3	Air-to-air missile	(1988)	1992–97	(192)	For modified Mirage-50 (Pantera) and F-5E (Tigre-3) FGA aircraft
Italy	128	M-113A2	APC	(1996)	1997	3	Probably ex-Italian Army
Spain	3	C-212-300 Aviocar	Transport aircraft	(1996)	1997	..	For Army
	1	Scorpene Class	Submarine	1997			Deal worth $400 m incl 1 from France
UK	..	Rayo	MRL	1995	1997	1	Assembled in Chile from kits
USA	1	Boeing-737-500	Transport aircraft	1996	1997	1	For VIP transport
	10	Cessna-337/O-2	Light aircraft	(1996)	1997	(10)	Ex-US Air Force; for Navy

L/S: Supplier	No.	Weapon designation	Weapon description	Year of order	Year(s) of deliveries	No. delivered	Comments
L: Switzerland	(120)	Piranha 8x8D	APC	(1991)		(69)	
China							
S: France	(5)	Castor-2B	Fire control radar	(1986)	1994–96	(4)	For refit of 2 Luda-1 Class (Type-051) and 3 Luhu Class (Type-052) destroyers; deal worth $91.5 m incl 5 Crotale ShAM systems and missiles
	(5)	Crotale Naval EDIR	ShAM system	1986	1994–96	(4)	For refit of 2 Luda-1 Class (Type-051) and 3 Luhu Class (Type-052) destroyers
	(5)	DRBV-15 Sea Tiger	Surveillance radar	1986	1987–96	4	For 3 Luhu Class (Type-052) and some Luda-2 Class (Type-051) destroyers
Israel	(4)	EL/M-2075 Phalcon	AEW radar	(1996)		. .	For modification of 4 Il-76 transport aircraft to AEW&C aircraft
Russia	24	Su-27S Flanker-B	FGA aircraft	1995	1996–97	24	Deal worth $2.2 b; incl 6 Su-27UB trainer version
	2	Kilo Class/Type-636	Submarine	1993	1997	2	
	2	Sovremenny Class	Destroyer	1996		. .	Originally ordered for Soviet/Russian Navy, but cancelled before completion
	4	AK-130 130mm	Naval gun	1996		. .	On 2 Sovremenny Class destroyers
	4	Bass Tilt	Fire control radar	1996		. .	On 2 Sovremenny Class destroyers; for use with AK-630 30mm guns
	12	Front Dome	Fire control radar	1996		. .	On 2 Sovremenny Class destroyers; for use with SA-N-7 ShAMs
	2	Kite screech	Fire control radar	1996		. .	On 2 Sovremenny Class destroyers; for use with AK-130 130mm guns
	6	Palm Fond	Surveillance radar	1996		. .	On 2 Sovremenny Class destroyers
	2	Top Plate	Surveillance radar	1996		. .	On 2 Sovremenny Class destroyers
	4	SA-N-7 ShAMS/Shtil	ShAM system	1996		. .	On 2 Sovremenny Class destroyers
	(88)	SA-N-7 Gadfly/Smerch	ShAM	1996		. .	For 2 Sovremenny Class destroyers
	2	SS-N-22 ShShMS	ShShM system	1996		. .	On 2 Sovremenny Class destroyers
	(32)	SS-N-22 Sunburn/P-80	ShShM	1996		. .	For 2 Sovremenny Class destroyers
	(4)	SA-10c/S-300PMU	SAM system	1992	1993–97	(4)	
	(144)	SA-10 Grumble/5V55R	SAM	1992	1993–97	(144)	For 4 SA-10c/S-300PMU SAM systems
	15	SA-15 SAMS	AAV(M)	(1996)	1997	15	
	(255)	SA-15 Gauntlet/9M330	SAM	(1996)	1997	(255)	For 15 SA-15 SAM systems

Recipient/ supplier (S) or licenser (L)	No. ordered	Weapon designation	Weapon description	Year of order/ licence	Year(s) of deliveries	No. delivered/ produced	Comments
UK	(6)	Searchwater	AEW radar	1996		. .	Deal worth $62 m; for use on Y-8 MP aircraft
L: France	. .	AS-350B Écureuil	Helicopter	(1992)	1994–97	4	Chinese designation Z-11
	. .	AS-365N Dauphin-2	Helicopter	1988	1992–97	(11)	Chinese designation Z-9A-100 Haitun; more produced for civilian customers
	. .	SA-321H Super Frelon	Helicopter	(1981)	1989–97	(13)	Chinese designation Z-8; for Navy
Israel		Python-3	Air-to-air missile	1990	1990–97	(6 474)	Chinese designation PL-8
Russia	(200)	Su-27SK Flanker-B	FGA aircraft	1996	1997	(21)	Incl assembly from kits; Chinese designation J-11
Colombia							
S: Germany	3	Do-328-100	Transport aircraft	1996	1996–97	3	For military airline SATENA
	1	Lüneburg Class	Depot ship	1997	1997	1	Ex-FRG Navy; Colombian designation Cartogena de Indias Class
Russia	10	Mi-17 Hip-H	Helicopter	1997	1997	10	For Army; deal worth $49 m
Spain	3	CN-235-100	Transport aircraft	1997	1997	(1)	Deal worth $55 m
	2	Lazaga Class	Patrol craft	1997		. .	Ex-Spanish Navy; deal worth $137 m; refitted before delivery
USA	6	S-70A/UH-60L	Helicopter	1993	1994–97	6	
	(10)	S-70A/UH-60L	Helicopter	1996	1997	(10)	
Congo, Democratic Republic of the							
S: Yugoslavia	(2)	G-2A Galeb	Jet trainer aircraft	(1996)	1997	(2)	Ex-Yugoslav Air Force
Unknown	(7)	Mi-24D Hind-D	Combat helicopter	(1996)	1997	(7)	Second-hand; possibly from Ukraine or Belarus
Croatia							
S: Canada	10	Bell-206B JetRanger-3	Helicopter	1996	1997	(10)	
Switzerland	17	PC-9	Trainer aircraft	1996	1997	17	Deal worth $15 m
Turkey	3	CN-235-100	Transport aircraft	1997		. .	

TRANSFERS OF MAJOR CONVENTIONAL WEAPONS 331

Cyprus						
S: Canada	1	Bell-412EP	Helicopter	(1997)	1997	For Police
Greece	(50)	AMX-30B2	Main battle tank	(1993)	1996–97	Ex-Greek Army; refurbished before delivery
Russia	41	T-80U	Main battle tank	1996	1996–97	Deal worth $174 m
	..	SA-10a/S-300P	SAM system	1996		
	..	SA-10 Grumble/5V55K	SAM	1996		
Czech Republic						
S: Poland	11	W-3 Sokol	Helicopter	1995	1996–97	Exchanged for 10 ex-Czech Air Force MiG-29 fighter aircraft
Denmark						
S: Canada	1	Challenger-604	Transport aircraft	1997		For MP, SAR and VIP transport; lease
France	8	RAC	Surveillance radar	1996	1997	Deal worth $35 m
Germany	14	TRS-3D	Surveillance radar	1990	1993–96	For 14 Flyvefisken Class (Stanflex-300 Type) patrol craft/MCM ships
Italy	1	RAT-31SL	Surveillance radar	1995		
Switzerland	26	Eagle	Scout car	1996	1996–97	
USA	3	F-16A Fighting Falcon	FGA aircraft	1994	1997	Ex-US Air Force
	1	F-16B Fighting Falcon	FGA/trainer aircraft	1996	1997	Ex-US Air Force
	8	MLRS 227mm	MRL	1996		
	4	Seasparrow Mk-48	ShAM system	1993		Deal worth $20 m; option on more; for 4 Flyvefisken Class (Stanflex-300 Type) patrol craft/MCM ships
	..	RIM-7M Seasparrow	ShAM	(1994)		For 4 Flyvefisken Class (Stanflex-300 Type) patrol craft/MCM ships
	..	AIM-120A AMRAAM	Air-to-air missile	1994		For F-16A/B-MLU FGA aircraft
Ecuador						
S: Argentina	36	M-114A1 155mm	Towed gun	1995		Ex-Argentine Army; illegal deal worth $34 m incl 18 M-101A1 guns and small arms; status uncertain
Egypt						
S: Netherlands	12	M-577A1	APC/CP	1994	1997	Ex-Dutch Army; deal worth $135 m incl 599 AIFVs

Recipient/ supplier (S) or licenser (L)	No. ordered	Weapon designation	Weapon description	Year of order/ licence	Year(s) of deliveries	No. delivered/ produced	Comments
	599	AIFV	IFV	1994	1996–97	599	Ex-Dutch Army; incl 210 AIFV-TOW tank destroyers, 6 AIFV-CP APC/CPs and 79 AIFV-APC APCs
Russia							
	20	Mi-17 Hip-H	Helicopter	(1997)	1997	(10)	
USA							
	12	AH-64A Apache	Combat helicopter	1995	1996–97	(12)	Deal worth $518 m incl armament
	927	AGM-114K Hellfire	Anti-tank missile	1996			Deal worth $45 m; for AH-64A helicopters Aid
	21	F-16C Fighting Falcon	FGA aircraft	1996			For F-16C/D FGA aircraft; deal worth $80 m
	271	AIM-7M Sparrow	Air-to-air missile	1996			
	2	Gulfstream-4	Transport aircraft	1996			Deal worth $80 m; for VIP transport
	2	S-70A/UH-60L	Helicopter	1995	1997	(2)	Deal worth $42 m incl 2 spare engines; for VIP transport
	10	SH-2G Super Seasprite	ASW helicopter	1994	1997	3	Ex-US Navy SH-2F rebuilt to SH-2G; US export designation SH-2G(E)
	24	M-109/SP-122 122mm	Self-propelled gun	1996	1997	(12)	Deal worth $28 m; FMF aid
	130	M-901 ITV	Tank destroyer (M)	1995			Ex-US Army; gift
	1	Perry Class	Frigate	1996	1997	1	Ex-US Navy; aid; deal worth $47 m; Egyptian designation Sharm el-Sheik Class
	1	AN/SPS-55	Surveillance radar	1996	1997	1	On 1 ex-US Perry Class frigate
	1	Phalanx Mk-15	CIWS	1996	1997	1	On 1 ex-US Perry Class frigate
	1	Standard Mk-13 ShAMS	ShAM system	1996	1997	1	On 1 ex-US Perry Class frigate
	34	RIM-66B Standard-1MR	ShAM	1996	1997	(34)	For 1 Perry Class frigate
	40	RIM-66B Standard-1MR	ShAM	1996	1997	(40)	For 1 Perry Class frigate
	1	AN/SPG-60 STIR	Fire control radar	1996	1997	1	On 1 ex-US Perry Class frigate; part of Standard ShAM system
	1	WM-28	Fire control radar	1996	1997	1	On 1 ex-US Perry Class frigate; for use with 76mm gun
	8	I-HAWK SAMS	SAM system	(1996)			Ex-US Army; EDA aid; refurbished before delivery
	180	MIM-23B HAWK	SAM	1996			
	..	BGM-71D TOW-2	Anti-tank missile	1996			Deal worth $59 m

TRANSFERS OF MAJOR CONVENTIONAL WEAPONS

	No.	Weapon designation	Weapon description	Year of order	Years of deliveries	No. delivered	Comments
L: Germany	. .	Fahd	APC	1978	1986–97	(587)	Developed for Egyptian production; more produced for export
USA	499	M-1A1 Abrams	Main battle tank	1988	1992–97	(499)	Deal worth $2.7 b incl 25 delivered direct
	31	M-1A1 Abrams	Main battle tank	1996	1997	31	
	. .	AIM-9P Sidewinder	Air-to-air missile	(1988)	1990–97	(3 665)	
Eritrea							
S: Ethiopia	1	Osa-2 Class	FAC(M)	(1997)	1997	1	Ex-Ethiopian Navy
	1	Drum Tilt	Fire control radar	(1997)	1997	1	On 1 ex-Ethiopian Osa-2 Class FAC; for use with 30mm guns
	1	SS-N-2 ShShMS	ShShM system	(1997)	1997	1	On 1 ex-Ethiopian Osa-2 Class FAC
	1	Square Tie	Surveillance radar	(1997)	1997	1	On 1 ex-Ethiopian Osa-2 Class FAC
Italy	6	MB-339C	Jet trainer aircraft	1996	1996–97	(6)	Deal worth $45 m; Italian export designation MB-339CE
Estonia							
S: Finland	19	M-61/37 105mm	Towed gun	1997		. .	Ex-Finnish Army; gift
France	. .	Rasit-E	Battlefield radar	1996		. .	
Germany	2	Frauenlob Class	Minesweeper	1996	1997	2	Ex-FRG Navy; aid worth $26 m; Estonian designation Kalev Class
Sweden	8	RBS-56 Bill	Anti-tank missile	1997		. .	Ex-Swedish Army; loan; deal also incl 2 launchers
USA	1	Balsam Class	Depot ship	1997	1997	1	Ex-US Coast Guard; Estonian designation Valvas Class
Finland							
S: USA	57	F/A-18C Hornet	FGA aircraft	1992	1996–97	(18)	Assembled in Finland
	(250)	AIM-120A AMRAAM	Air-to-air missile	1992	1996–97	(75)	For 64 F/A-18C/D FGA aircraft
	480	AIM-9S Sidewinder	Air-to-air missile	1992	1996–97	(150)	For 64 F/A-18C/D FGA aircraft
France							
S: Belgium	3	Aster Class	MCM ship	1997	1997	3	Ex-Belgian Navy; French designation Eridan Class
Brazil	50	EMB-312 Tucano	Trainer aircraft	1991	1993–97	(50)	Deal worth $170 m; option on 30 more; Brazilian export designation EMB-312F

Recipient/ supplier (S) or licenser (L)	No. ordered	Weapon designation	Weapon description	Year of order/ licence	Year(s) of deliveries	No. delivered/ produced	Comments
South Africa	5	Husky	AMV	1996	1996–97	(5)	Part of 'Chubby' mine-clearing system; for use in Bosnia
	5	Meerkat	AMV	1996	1996–97	(5)	Part of 'Chubby' mine-clearing system
Spain	7	CN-235-100	Transport aircraft	1996		..	Deal worth $90 m (offsets 100%, incl Spanish order for 15 AS-552UL helicopters)
USA	2	E-2C Hawkeye	AEW&C aircraft	1995		..	For Navy (offsets incl French production of components)
	5	KC-135A Stratotanker	Tanker aircraft	1994	1997	(2)	Ex-US Air Force; deal worth $220 m; refurbished to KC-135R before delivery
Germany							
S: France	13	AS-365N Dauphin-2	Helicopter	1997		..	For Border Guard; option on 2 more
Netherlands	3	APAR	Surveillance radar	(1997)		..	For 3 Sachsen Class (Type-124) frigates; option on 1 more
	3	SMART-L	Surveillance radar	(1997)		..	For 3 Sachsen Class (Type-124) frigates
Sweden	(9)	HARD	Surveillance radar	1995		..	For 3 ASRAD SAM systems
UK	7	Super Lynx	ASW helicopter	1996		..	Deal worth $154 m; UK export designation Lynx Mk-88A; for Navy
USA	96	AIM-120A AMRAAM	Air-to-air missile	1991	1995	48	For F-4F FGA aircraft, deal worth $53.6 m
	96	AIM-120B AMRAAM	Air-to-air missile	1995		..	
Ghana							
S: Italy	(4)	Bell-412/AB-412	Helicopter	1995	1996–97	(2)	
Greece							
S: Germany	5	TRS-3050 Triton-G	Surveillance radar	(1986)	1994–96	(2)	For 5 Jason Class landing ships; probably ex-FRG Navy; refurbished before delivery
	5	TRS-3220 Pollux	Fire control radar	(1986)	1994–96	(2)	For 5 Jason Class landing ships; probably ex-FRG Navy; refurbished before delivery

TRANSFERS OF MAJOR CONVENTIONAL WEAPONS

Supplier	No.	Weapon designation	Description	Year of order	Year of delivery	No. delivered	Comments
Netherlands	1	Kortenaer Class	Frigate		1997	1	Ex-Dutch Navy; Greek designation Elli Class; deal worth $50 m
	1	LW-08	Surveillance radar	1997	1997	1	On 1 ex-Dutch Navy Kortenaer Class frigate
	1	ZW-06	Surveillance radar	1997	1997	1	On 1 ex-Dutch Navy Kortenaer Class frigate
	1	STIR	Fire control radar	1997	1997	1	On 1 ex-Dutch Navy Kortenaer Class frigate
	1	WM-25	Fire control radar	1997	1997	1	On 1 ex-Dutch Navy Kortenaer Class frigate; for use with 76mm gun
	1	RGM-84 ShShMS	ShShM system	1997	1997	1	On 1 ex-Dutch Navy Kortenaer Class frigate
	1	Seasparrow Mk-29	ShAM system	1997	1997	1	On 1 ex-Dutch Navy Kortenaer Class frigate
	4	DA-08	Surveillance radar	(1989)	1992–96	(2)	For 4 MEKO-200HN Type (Hydra Class) frigates
	4	MW-08	Surveillance radar	(1989)	1992–96	(2)	For 4 MEKO-200HN Type (Hydra Class) frigates
	8	STIR	Fire control radar	1989	1992–96	(4)	For 4 MEKO-200HN Type (Hydra Class) frigates; for use with 127mm guns and Seasparrow ShAM system
Norway	(24)	Penguin Mk-2-7	Air-to-ship missile	1996	1997	(24)	For 6 Navy S-70B/SH-60B helicopters
UK	1	Martello-743D	Surveillance radar	1995		..	Deal worth $376 m
	7	CH-47D Chinook	Helicopter	1997		..	
USA	40	F-16C Fighting Falcon	FGA aircraft	1993	1997	(16)	'Peace Xenia' programme worth $1.8 b; incl 8 F-16D trainer version
	50	AIM-120B AMRAAM	Air-to-air missile	1996		..	For F-16C/D FGA aircraft; deal worth $90 m incl 84 AGM-88B missiles
	84	AGM-88B HARM	Anti-radar missile	1996		..	Deal worth $70 m
	100	AIM-120A AMRAAM	Air-to-air missile	(1995)		..	Deal worth $27 m; for F-16C/D FGA aircraft
	52	AGM-88B HARM	Anti-radar missile	1994		..	
	4	P-3B Orion	ASW/MP aircraft	1994	1996	(1)	Ex-US Navy; lease worth $69 m; refurbished before delivery
	2	S-70B/SH-60B Seahawk	ASW helicopter	1997		..	For Navy; US export designation S-70B-6 Aegean Hawk
	1	S-70B/SH-60B Seahawk	ASW helicopter	(1996)	1997	1	For Navy
	12	M-109A5 155mm	Self-propelled gun	1997		..	Option on 12 more
	4	Phalanx Mk-15	CIWS	1996		..	Deal worth $46 m; for refit of 4 Adams (Kimon) Class destroyers
	4	127mm/54 Mk-45	Naval gun	(1989)	1992–96	(2)	For 4 MEKO-200HN Type (Hydra Class) frigates
	8	Phalanx Mk-15	CIWS	1988	1992–96	4	For 4 MEKO-200HN Type (Hydra Class) frigates

Recipient/ supplier (S) or licenser (L)	No. ordered	Weapon designation	Weapon description	Year of order/ licence	Year(s) of deliveries	No. delivered/ produced	Comments
	4	RGM-84 ShShMS	ShShM system	1989	1992–96	(2)	For 4 MEKO-200HN Type (Hydra Class) frigates
	4	Seasparrow Mk-48	ShAM system	1988	1992–96	(2)	For 4 MEKO-200HN Type (Hydra Class) frigates
	(64)	RIM-7M Seasparrow	ShAM	(1988)	1992–96	(32)	For 4 MEKO-200HN Type (Hydra Class) frigates
	(32)	UGM-84A Sub Harpoon	SuShM	(1989)	1993–97	(24)	For 4 refitted Type-209 (Glavkos Class) submarines
	40	MGM-140A ATACMS	SSM	1996		..	Deal worth $28.6 m
L: Germany	3	MEKO-200HN Type	Frigate	1988	1996	1	Deal worth $1.2 b incl 1 delivered direct (offsets $250 m); partly financed by FRG 'Rüstungssonderhilfe' aid programme and USA; Greek designation Hydra Class
Hungary							
S: France	..	Mistral	Portable SAM	1997		..	Deal worth $100 m incl SHORAR-2D radars, ATLAS launchers and UNIMOG trucks
Italy	..	SHORAR-2D	Surveillance radar	1997		..	Sold through France
Russia	97	BTR-80	APC	1995		..	
India							
S: Italy	(6)	Seaguard TMX	Fire control radar	1993	1997	(2)	For 3 Brahmaputra Class (Project-16A Type) frigates; for use with AK-630 30mm CIWS
Netherlands	3	DA-05	Surveillance radar	(1996)	1997	(1)	For 3 Delhi Class (Project-15 Type) destroyers; incl assembly in India; Indian designation RAWS
	3	LW-08	Surveillance radar	(1996)	1997	(1)	For 3 Delhi Class (Project-15 Type) destroyers; incl assembly in India; Indian designation RALW
	3	LW-08	Surveillance radar	(1989)	1997	(1)	For 3 Brahmaputra Class (Project-16A Type) frigates
	6	ZW-06	Surveillance radar	(1989)	1997	(2)	For 3 Brahmaputra Class (Project-16A Type) frigates
Russia/USSR	3	Ka-31 Helix	AEW helicopter	(1997)		..	For Navy; deal worth $29 m
	40	Su-30M Flanker	FGA aircraft	1996	1997	8	Deal worth $1.8 b; incl 12 Su-30MKI version and 20 other improved version
	(720)	AA-10a Alamo/R-27R	Air-to-air missile	1996	1997	(144)	For 40 Su-30MK/MKI FGA aircraft

No. ordered	Weapon designation	Weapon description	Year of order	Year of delivery	No. delivered	Comments
(720)	AA-11 Archer/R-73M1	Air-to-air missile	(1996)	1997	(144)	For 40 Su-30MK/MKI FGA aircraft
2	Kilo Class/Type-877E	Submarine	1997	1997	1	Incl 1 originally built for Russian Navy, but sold to India before completion
3	Krivak-4 Class	Frigate	1997			Deal worth $360 m
3	100mm L/59	Naval gun	(1997)			On 3 Krivak-4 Class frigates
3	SS-N-25 ShShMS	ShShM system	(1997)			On 3 Krivak-4 Type frigates
(96)	SS-N-25/X-35	ShShM	(1997)			For 3 Krivak-4 Type frigates
3	Head Net-C	Surveillance radar	1989	1997	(1)	For 3 Brahmaputra Class (Project-16A Type) frigates
3	Muff Cob	Fire control radar	(1989)	1997	(1)	For 3 Brahmaputra Class (Project-16A Type) frigates; for use with 57mm guns
3	SS-N-2 ShShMS	ShShM system	1993	1997	(1)	For 3 Brahmaputra Class (Project-16A Type) frigates
(24)	SS-N-2e Styx/P-27	ShShM	1993	1997	(8)	For 3 Brahmaputra Class (Project-16A Type) frigates
3	SA-N-4 ShAMS	ShAM system	(1989)	1997	(1)	For 3 Brahmaputra Class (Project-16A Type) frigates
(60)	SA-N-4 Gecko/Osa-M	ShAM	(1989)	1997	(20)	For 3 Brahmaputra Class (Project-16A Type) frigates
3	100mm L/59	Naval gun	(1986)	1997	(1)	For 3 Delhi Class (Project-15 Type) destroyers
6	Bass Tilt	Fire control radar	(1986)	1997	(2)	For 3 Delhi Class (Project-15 Type) destroyers; for use with AK-650 30mm guns
3	SS-N-25 ShShMS	ShShM system	1992	1997	(1)	For 3 Delhi Class (Project-15 Type) destroyers
(96)	SS-N-25/X-35	ShShM	1992	1997	(32)	For 3 Delhi Class (Project-15 Type) destroyers
3	SA-N-7 ShAMS/Shtil	ShAM system	(1986)	1997	(1)	For 3 Delhi Class (Project-15 Type) destroyers
(66)	SA-N-7 Gadfly/Smerch	ShAM	(1986)	1997	(22)	For 3 Delhi Class (Project-15 Type) destroyers
8	Cross Dome	Surveillance radar	(1983)	1989–97	(5)	For 8 Khukri Class (Project-25/25A Type) corvettes
8	Plank Shave	Surveillance radar	(1983)	1989–97	(5)	For 8 Khukri Class (Project-25/25A Type) corvettes
8	Bass Tilt	Fire control radar	1983	1989–97	(5)	For 8 Khukri Class (Project-25/25A Type) corvettes; for use with 76mm gun and AK-630 30mm CIWS
8	SS-N-2 ShShMS	ShShM system	1983	1989–97	(5)	For 8 Khukri Class (Project-25/25A Type) corvettes
(64)	SS-N-2d Styx/P-21	ShShM	1983	1989–97	(40)	For 8 Khukri Class (Project-25/25A Type) corvettes
(320)	SA-N-5 Grail/Strela-2M	ShAM	(1983)	1989–97	(200)	For 8 Khukri Class (Project-25/25A Type) corvettes
7	Plank Shave	Surveillance radar	(1987)	1991–97	(7)	For 7 Tarantul-1 (Vibhuti) Class FAC
7	Bass Tilt	Fire control radar	(1987)	1991–97	(7)	For 7 Tarantul-1 (Vibhuti) Class FAC; for use with 76mm gun and AK-630 30mm CIWS
7	SS-N-2 ShShMS	ShShM system	1987	1991–97	(7)	For 7 Tarantul-1 (Vibhuti) Class FAC
(56)	SS-N-2d Styx/P-21	ShShM	1987	1991–97	(56)	For 7 Tarantul-1 (Vibhuti) Class FAC
(280)	SA-N-5 Grail/Strela-2M	ShAM	1987	1991–97	(280)	For 7 Tarantul-1 (Vibhuti) Class FAC

Recipient/ supplier (S) or licenser (L)	No. ordered	Weapon designation	Weapon description	Year of order/ licence	Year(s) of deliveries	No. delivered/ produced	Comments
Singapore	3	Tara Bai Class	Patrol craft	1995	1997	2	For Coast Guard
Slovakia	89	VT-72B	ARV	1997		. .	Deal worth $71 m
UK	2	Harrier T-Mk-4	FGA/trainer aircraft	1996		. .	Ex-UK Navy; refurbished to Harrier T-Mk-60 before delivery; for Navy
Uzbekistan	(4)	Il-78 Midas	Tanker aircraft	1997		. .	Sold via Russia
L: France	. .	PSM-33	Surveillance radar	1988	1990–96	(7)	
Germany	33	Do-228-200MP	MP aircraft	1983	1989–97	(18)	For Coast Guard
	(27)	Do-228-200MP	MP aircraft	(1989)	1991–97	(7)	For Navy
	2	Type-209/1500	Submarine	(1997)		. .	Indian designation: Shishumar Class
Korea, South	(7)	Sukanya Class	OPV	1987	1990–97	6	Incl 3 Samar Class for Coast Guard
Netherlands	212	Flycatcher	Fire control radar	(1987)	1988–97	(182)	Indian designation PIW-519
UK	15	Jaguar International	FGA aircraft	1993	1995–97	(12)	Indian designation Shamsher
	2	Magar Class	Landing ship	1985	1997	1	Indian designation Bahadur
Russia/USSR	165	MiG-27L Flogger-J	FGA aircraft	1983	1984–97	(165)	Indian designation Vibhuti Class
	7	Tarantul-1 Class	FAC(M)	1987	1991–97	7	
Indonesia							
S: Australia	(16)	N-22B Missionmaster	Transport aircraft	1996	1997	(16)	Ex-Australian Army; for Navy
	(7)	N-24A Nomad	Transport aircraft	1996	1997	(7)	Ex-Australian Army; for Navy
France	18	VBL	Scout car	1996	1997	18	Option on 46 more
	(240)	Mistral	Portable SAM	1996		. .	For SIMBAD launchers on 6 refitted Van Speyk Class (Ahmad Yani Class) frigates
	. .	Mistral	Portable SAM	1996		. .	
Germany	5	Wiesel-1	Scout car	1996		. .	
	2	Wiesel-2	APC	1996		. .	
	2	Type-206	Submarine	1997	1997	2	Ex-FRG Navy; 3 more cancelled
Russia	8	Mi-17 Hip-H	Helicopter	1997		. .	Status uncertain after financial crisis
	12	Su-30M Flanker	FGA aircraft	1997		. .	Status uncertain after financial crisis
UK	8	Hawk-100	FGA/trainer aircraft	1993	1996–97	(8)	UK export designation Hawk Mk-109

TRANSFERS OF MAJOR CONVENTIONAL WEAPONS 339

	16	Hawk-200	FGA aircraft	1993	1996–97	(16)	UK export designation Hawk Mk-209
	16	Hawk-200	FGA aircraft	1996		. .	Deal worth $266m; Indonesian designation Hawk Mk-209
	50	Scorpion-90	Light tank	1997		. .	
	(91)	Stormer	APC	1995	1996–97	(17)	Incl 2 APC/CPs and some ambulance version
L: Germany	. .	Bo-105CB	Helicopter	1976	1978–91	(45)	For Army, Navy and Police
	4	PB-57 Type	Patrol craft	1993		. .	Indonesian designation Singa Class
Spain	6	C-212-200MPA Aviocar	MP aircraft	1996		. .	For Navy
USA	1	Bell-412	Helicopter	1996		. .	Deal worth $4.2 m; for Navy
Iran							
S: China	(7)	C-801/802 ShShMS	ShShM system	(1995)	1996–97	(2)	For refit of 7 Combattante-2 Type (Kaman Class) FAC
	(80)	C-802/CSS-N-8 Saccade	ShShM	(1995)	1996–97	(16)	For 10 refitted Combattante-2 Type (Kaman Class) FAC
USSR	(200)	T-72	Main battle tank	1989	1993–96	122	
Ireland							
S: UK	1	BN-2T-4S Defender	Light transport ac	1996	1997	1	For Police
Israel							
S: France	(7)	AS-565SA Panther	ASW helicopter	1994	1996–97	5	Ordered through USA; partly financed by USA; Israeli designation Atalef
Germany	2	Dolphin Class	Submarine	1991		. .	Deal worth $570 m; financed by FRG
	1	Dolphin Class	Submarine	1994		. .	
	(16)	Bell-209/AH-1E	Combat helicopter	1995	1996–97	(16)	Ex-US Army
USA	21	F-15I Strike Eagle	Fighter/bomber ac	1994		. .	Deal worth $1.76 b (offsets $1 b); financed by USA; Israeli designation Ra'am
	4	F-15I Strike Eagle	Fighter/bomber ac	1995		. .	
	15	S-70A/UH-60L	Helicopter	1997		. .	Deal worth $200 m
	42	MLRS 227mm	MRL	1995	1995–97	(30)	Deal worth $108 m incl 1500 rockets
	36	M-48 Chaparral	AAV(M)	1996		. .	Ex-US Army; EDA aid
	500	MIM-72C Chaparral	SAM	1996		. .	Ex-US Army; EDA aid

340 MILITARY SPENDING AND ARMAMENTS, 1997

Recipient/ supplier (S) or licenser (L)	No. ordered	Weapon designation	Weapon description	Year of order/ licence	Year(s) of deliveries	No. delivered/ produced	Comments
Italy							
S: UK	24	Tornado ADV F-Mk-3	Fighter aircraft	1994	1995–97	(24)	Ex-UK Air Force; 10-year lease worth $360 m incl $200 m for logistical support
	(96)	Sky Flash	Air-to-air missile	1994	1995–97	(96)	For 24 Tornado ADV fighter aircraft
USA	13	AV-8B Harrier-2 Plus	FGA aircraft	1992	1996–97	13	Deal worth $522 m; assembled in Italy; for Navy
	18	C-130J Hercules-2	Transport aircraft	1997		..	
	42	AGM-65G Maverick	ASM	1994	1996–97	(42)	Deal worth $25 m; for Navy AV-8B+ FGA aircraft
	33	AIM-120A AMRAAM	Air-to-air missile	1994	1996–97	(33)	Deal worth $23 m; for Navy AV-8B+ FGA aircraft
	233	AIM-120B AMRAAM	Air-to-air missile	1997		..	Deal worth $116 m; for Navy; for AV-8B+ FGA aircraft
L: France	23 000	Milan-2	Anti-tank missile	1984	1985–97	(21 000)	Option on 2 more
Germany	2	Type-212	Submarine	1996		..	
USA	77	Bell-412SP/AB-412SP	Helicopter	1980	1983–97	(75)	Incl 18 for Army, 34 for Police and 25 for Coast Guard; more produced for export and civilian customers; incl Bell-412HP/EP versions
Japan							
S: Italy	4	127mm/54	Naval gun	(1988)	1993–96	(3)	For 4 Kongo Class destroyers
Sweden	2	Saab 340B SAR-200	MP aircraft	1996		..	For Coast Guard; for SAR; deal worth $21 m
UK	6	BAe-125-800	Transport aircraft	1992	1994–97	(6)	
USA	8	BAe-125/RH-800	Transport aircraft	1995	1997	(2)	For SAR; Japanese designation U-125A; 'HS-X' programme
	4	BAe-125/RH-800	Transport aircraft	1997		..	Deal worth $80 m; for SAR; option on 12 more; 'HS-X' programme
	2	Boeing-767/AWACS	AEW&C aircraft	1993		..	Deal worth $840 m
	2	Boeing-767/AWACS	AEW&C aircraft	1994		..	Deal worth $773 m
	(9)	Gulfstream-4	Transport aircraft	1994	1996–97	2	

TRANSFERS OF MAJOR CONVENTIONAL WEAPONS

(15)	Super King Air-350	Light transport ac	1996				For Army
(72)	MLRS 227mm	MRL	1993	1994–97	36		
12	AN/SPG-62	Fire control radar	(1988)	1993–96	(9)		For 4 Kongo Class destroyers; part of Standard ShAM system
4	AN/SPY-1D	Surveillance radar	1988	1993–96	(3)		Part of AEGIS air defence system for 4 Kongo Class destroyers
4	ASROC VLS	ShSuM system	(1988)	1993–96	(3)		For 4 Kongo Class destroyers
8	Phalanx Mk-15	CIWS	1988	1993–96	(6)		For 4 Kongo Class destroyers
4	RGM-84 ShShMS	ShShM system	1993	1993–96	(3)		For 4 Kongo Class destroyers
4	Standard Mk-41	ShAM system	(1988)	1993–96	(3)		For 4 Kongo Class destroyers
9	ASROC VLS	ShSuM system	(1993)	1996–97	(2)		For 9 Murasame Class frigates
18	Phalanx Mk-15	CIWS	(1993)	1996–97	(4)		For 9 Murasame Class frigates
9	Seasparrow Mk-48	ShAM system	(1993)	1996–97	(2)		For 9 Murasame Class frigates
..	RIM-7M Seasparrow	ShAM	1993	1996–97	(32)		Deal worth $13.4 m
2	LCAC	Landing craft	1994	1997	(2)		

L: France
Germany
USA

..	MO-120-RT-61 120mm	Mortar	1992	1993–97	(240)		
..	FH-70 155mm	Towed gun	(1982)	1984–97	(440)		
(88)	Bell-209/AH-1S	Combat helicopter	1982	1984–97	(86)		For Army
(52)	CH-47D Chinook	Helicopter	(1984)	1986–97	(40)		For Army
(22)	CH-47D Chinook	Helicopter	(1984)	1986–96	(16)		
3	EP-3C Orion	ELINT aircraft	1992	1995–96	2		For Navy
(44)	F-15DJ Eagle	FGA/trainer aircraft	1978	1988–97	28		
(169)	F-15J Eagle	FGA aircraft	1978	1982–97	154		
..	Hughes-500/OH-6D	Helicopter	1977	1978–97	(208)		For Army and Navy
..	P-3C Orion Update-3	ASW/MP aircraft	1988	1991–97	32		For Navy
(67)	S-70/UH-60J Blackhawk	Helicopter	1988	1991–97	(29)		Incl 18 for Navy and 6 for Army
(100)	S-70B/SH-60J Seahawk	ASW helicopter	1988	1991–97	(56)		For Navy; incl 21 for SAR
(3)	UP-3D Orion	EW aircraft	1994	1997	1		For Navy
1 330	AIM-7M Sparrow	Air-to-air missile	1990	1990–97	(1 326)		Deal worth $477 m
..	BGM-71C I-TOW	Anti-tank missile	(1983)	1985–97	(9 254)		
(1 000)	MIM-104 Patriot	SAM	1986	1989–97	(900)		

Recipient/ supplier (S) or licenser (L)	No. ordered	Weapon designation	Weapon description	Year of order/ licence	Year(s) of deliveries	No. delivered/ produced	Comments
Jordan							
S: USA	4	Bell 209/AH-1P	Combat helicopter	1995		. .	Ex-US Army; incl 2 TAH-1P trainer version; EDA aid
	1	C-130H Hercules	Transport aircraft	(1996)	1997	1	Ex-US Air Force; aid
	12	F-16A Fighting Falcon	FGA aircraft	1996	1997	(4)	Ex-US Air Force; lease; 'Peace Falcon' deal worth $220 m incl 4 F-16B trainer version; refurbished before delivery
	4	F-16B Fighting Falcon	FGA/trainer aircraft	1996		. .	Ex-US Air Force; lease; refurbished before delivery
	4	S-70A/UH-60L	Helicopter	1995	1995	2	Ex-US Army; deal worth $67 m incl 2 spare engines
Kazakhstan							
S: Russia	(17)	MiG-29 Fulcrum-A	Fighter aircraft	(1995)	1996–97	(17)	Ex-Russian Air Force; aid
	(14)	Su-25 Frogfoot-A	Ground attack ac	(1995)	1996–97	(14)	Ex-Russian Air Force
	(38)	Su-27S Flanker-B	FGA aircraft	(1995)	1996–97	(10)	Ex-Russian Air Force; payment for Russian debt to Kazakhstan
	. .	BMP-2	IFV	1995	1996	55	Ex-Russian Army
	. .	BTR-80	APC	(1995)	1996	10	Ex-Russian Army
	. .	T-72	Main battle tank	1995	1996	63	Ex-Russian Army
Korea, North							
L: China	(550)	HN-5A	Portable SAM	(1985)	1987–97	(550)	
USSR	. .	SA-16 Gimlet/Igla-1	Portable SAM	(1989)	1992–96	(100)	
Korea, South							
S: France	5	F-406 Caravan-2	Light aircraft	1997		. .	Deal worth $24 m; for Navy; for use as target tugs
	(67)	Crotale NG SAMS	SAM system	(1989)		. .	Korean designation Pegasus
	984	Mistral	Portable SAM	1992	1993–96	(800)	Deal worth $180 m (offsets 25%); deal also incl 130 launchers
	(1 294)	Mistral	Portable SAM	(1997)		. .	Deal worth $300 m

TRANSFERS OF MAJOR CONVENTIONAL WEAPONS

Supplier	No.	Weapon designation	Weapon description	Year of order	Year of delivery	No. delivered	Comments
Indonesia	8	CN-235-220	Transport aircraft	1997			
Israel	(101)	Harpy	Anti-radar missile	1997			
Italy	3	127mm/54	Naval gun	(1993)	1996–97	(2)	For 3 Okpo Class (KDX-2000 Type) frigates
	2	Goalkeeper	CIWS	(1991)			For 1 Okpo Class (KDX-2000 Type) frigate
	4	Goalkeeper	CIWS	1995			For 2 Okpo Class (KDX-2000 Type) frigates
Netherlands	3	MW-08	Surveillance radar	1994			For 3 Okpo Class (KDX-2000 Type) frigates
	6	STIR	Fire control radar	(1992)			For 3 Okpo Class (KDX-2000 Type) frigates; for use with Seasparrow and 127mm gun
Russia	(70)	BMP-3	IFV	1995	1996–97	(60)	Payment for Russian debt to South Korea; for Marines
	(480)	AT-10 Bastion/9M117	Anti-tank missile	1995	1996–97	(480)	For BMP-3 AIFVs
	..	T-80U	Main battle tank	1995	1996–97	(57)	Payment for Russian debt to South Korea
	(342)	AT-11 Sniper/9M119	Anti-tank missile	1995	1996–97	(342)	For 57 T-80U tanks
UK	13	Super Lynx	ASW helicopter	1997			For Navy
USA	10	RH-800XP	Reconnaissance ac	1996			Deal worth $460 m; also for use in SIGINT role
	30	T-38 Talon	Jet trainer aircraft	1996			Ex-US Air Force; lease
	29	MLRS 227mm	MRL	1996	1996–97	(30)	Deal worth $624 m incl 1626 rockets, 111 ATACMS SSMs, 14 M-577A2 APC/CPs, 4 M-88A1 ARVs, 9 simulators and 54 trucks
	110	ATACMS	SSM	1997			
	14	M-577A2	APC/CP	1996			
	4	M-88A1	ARV	1996			
	3	AN/SPS-55	Surveillance radar	1994			For 3 Okpo Class (KDX-2000 Type) frigates
	3	RGM-84 ShShMS	ShShM system	(1992)			For 3 Okpo Class (KDX-2000 Type) frigates
	2	Seasparrow Mk-48	ShAM system	(1994)			For 2 Okpo Class (KDX-2000 Type) frigates; deal worth $57 m
	1	Seasparrow Mk-48	ShAM system	(1995)			For 1 Okpo Class (KDX-2000 Type) frigate
	45	RIM-7M Seasparrow	ShAM	1992			For Okpo Class (KDX-2000 Type) frigates; deal worth $19 m
	116	AGM-130	ASM	1996			Deal worth $250 m incl modification of 30 F-4E FGA aircraft and 116 Popeye-1/AGM-142 missiles
	116	Popeye-1	ASM	1996			
	132	AGM-88A HARM	Anti-radar missile	1995			For F-16C/D FGA aircraft
	(46)	RGM-84A Harpoon	ShShM	1996			Incl some UGM-84A SuShM version

344 MILITARY SPENDING AND ARMAMENTS, 1997

Recipient/ supplier (S) or licenser (L)	No. ordered	Weapon designation	Weapon description	Year of order/ licence	Year(s) of deliveries	No. delivered/ produced	Comments
	2	Edenton Class	Salvage ship	1996	1997	2	Ex-US Navy; Korean designation Pyong Taek Class
L: Germany	3	Type-209/1200	Submarine	1989		3	Korean designation Chang Bogo Class
	3	Type-209/1200	Submarine	1994		. .	Deal worth $510 m; Korean designation Chang Bogo Class
USA	72	F-16C Fighting Falcon	FGA aircraft	1991	1997	(20)	Deal worth $2.52 b incl 48 delivered direct
	57	S-70A/UH-60P	Helicopter	(1994)	1995–97	(37)	
	(528)	M-109A2 155mm	Self-propelled gun	1992	1993–97	(528)	Developed for Korean production; incl 5 prototypes
	(1 085)	K-1 ROKIT/Type-88	Main battle tank	1981	1984–97	(1 085)	Incl 3 prototypes
	. .	K-1A1/Type-88	Main battle tank	(1994)	1996–97	(3)	Incl ARV and APC/CP versions; deal worth $91 m; for Marines
	57	LVTP-7A1	APC	1995	1996–97	(48)	
	. .	M-167 Vulcan	AAA system	(1986)	1986–97	(205)	Incl some fitted on KIFV APC chassis
Kuwait							
S: Australia	22	S-600 APC	APC	1997	1997	(2)	For National Guard; deal worth $12 m
Egypt	2	AN/TPS-63	Surveillance radar	(1993)	1994	1	
France	8	P-37BRL Type	FAC(M)	1995		. .	Deal worth $475 m
	8	MRR-3D	Surveillance radar	1995		. .	On 8 P-37BRL Type FAC
	1	TRS-22XX	Surveillance radar	1995		. .	Deal worth $54 m
Italy	11	Skyguard SAMS	SAM system	(1988)	1989–97	(11)	Delivered via Egypt, incl partly assembled in Egypt; Kuwaiti designation Amoun
UK	254	MCV-80 Desert Warrior	IFV	1993	1995–97	(254)	Deal worth $740 m (offsets 30%); incl 21 APC/CP, repair and ARV version
	(80)	Sea Skua SL	ShShM	1997		. .	For 8 PB-37BRL Type FAC; deal worth $89 m
USA	16	AH-64D Longbow	Combat helicopter	1997		. .	Deal worth $800 m incl 384 AGM-114K missiles
	384	AGM-114K Hellfire	Anti-tank missile	1997		. .	For 16 AH-64D Longbow helicopters
	218	M-1A2 Abrams	Main battle tank	1992	1995–97	(218)	Deal worth $4 b incl. 16 M-113A3 APCs, 30 M-577A3 APC/CPs, 46 M-88A1 ARVs and ammunition

TRANSFERS OF MAJOR CONVENTIONAL WEAPONS 345

	Pandur	APC	1996	70		Incl IFV, APC/CP, APC/mortar carrier, ARV, ambulance and armoured car versions; option on 200 more
	I-HAWK SAMS	SAM system	1992	6		
	MIM-23B HAWK	SAM	1992	342		
	AGM-84A Harpoon	Air-to-ship missile	1988	40	1997	For F/A-18C/D FGA aircraft
	BGM-71C I-TOW	Anti-tank missile	1993	(466)	1995–97	For 233 MCV-80 IFVs
Laos						
S: Russia	Mi-17 Hip-H	Helicopter	1997	12	1997	2
Latvia						
S: Poland	Mi-2 Hoplite	Helicopter	(1994)	(4)	1995–97	Second-hand
Sweden	RBS-56 Bill	Anti-tank missile	1997	8	1997	Ex-Swedish Army; loan; deal also incl 2 launchers
Lebanon						
S: Iran	SA-7b Grail	Portable SAM	(1993)	(50)	1993–97	For Hezbollah
Syria	AT-4 Spigot/9M111	Anti-tank missile	(1995)	(50)	1996–97	For Hezbollah
USA	Bell-205/UH-1H	Helicopter	1996	16		Ex-US Army; aid
	M-113A2	APC	1994	(460)	1995–97	Ex-US Army; aid; may incl M-577A2 APC/CP version
Lithuania						
S: Sweden	RBS-56 Bill	Anti-tank missile	1997	8		Ex-Swedish Army; loan; deal also incl 2 launchers
Malaysia						
S: France	MM-38/40 ShShMS	ShShM system	1993	2	1997	For 2 Lekiu Class frigates
	MM-40 Exocet	ShShM	1993	(20)	1996–97	For 2 Lekiu Class frigates
Indonesia	CN-235-220	Transport aircraft	1995	6		Option on 12 more; deal worth $102 m (offsets incl Indonesian order for 20 MD-3-160 trainer aircraft and 500 cars)

Recipient/ supplier (S) or licenser (L)	No. ordered	Weapon designation	Weapon description	Year of order/ licence	Year(s) of deliveries	No. delivered/ produced	Comments
Italy	2	Assad Class	Corvette	1995	1997	2	Originally built for Iraq but embargoed; Malaysian designation Laksamana Class
	2	RAN-12L/X	Surveillance radar	1995	1997	2	On 2 Assad Class corvettes
	4	RTN-10X	Fire control radar	1995	1997	4	On 2 Assad Class corvettes; for use with Albatros ShAM system and 76mm and 40mm guns
	2	Albatros Mk-2	ShAM system	1995	1997	2	On 2 Assad Class corvettes
	(12)	Aspide	ShAM	1995	1997	(12)	For 2 Assad Class corvettes
	2	Otomat/Teseo	ShShM system	1995	1997	2	On 2 Assad Class corvettes
	(24)	Otomat Mk-2	ShShM	1995	1997	(24)	For 2 Assad Class corvettes
	2	Assad Class	Corvette	1997		..	Originally built for Iraq but embargoed; Malaysian designation Laksamana Class
	2	RAN-12L/X	Surveillance radar	1997		..	On 2 Assad Class corvettes
	4	RTN-10X	Fire control radar	1997		..	On 2 Assad Class corvettes; for use with Albatros ShAM system and 76mm and 40mm guns
	2	Albatros Mk-2	ShAM system	1997		..	On 2 Assad Class corvettes
	(12)	Aspide	ShAM	(1997)		..	For 2 Assad Class corvettes
	2	Otomat/Teseo	ShShM system	1997		..	On 2 Assad Class corvettes
	(24)	Otomat Mk-2	ShShM	(1997)		..	For 2 Assad Class corvettes
Netherlands	2	DA-08	Surveillance radar	1992	1997	2	For 2 Lekiu Class frigates
Russia	(96)	AA-12 Adder/R-77	Air-to-air missile	(1997)		..	For 16 MiG-29S FGA aircraft
Sweden	2	Sea Giraffe-150	Surveillance radar	1992	1997	2	For 2 Lekiu Class frigates
	2	Lekiu Class	Frigate	1992	1997	2	Deal worth $600 m incl training
UK	4	ST-1802SW	Fire control radar	1992	1997	4	On 2 Lekiu Class frigates; for use with Seawolf SAM system
	2	Seawolf GWS-26	ShAM system	1992	1997	2	On 2 Lekiu Class frigates
	32	Seawolf VL	ShAM	1993	1997	32	For 2 Lekiu Class frigates
	504	Starburst	Portable SAM	1993	1995–97	(504)	
USA	2	S-70A/UH-60L	Helicopter	1996	1997	1	For VIP transport
	8	F/A-18D Hornet	FGA/trainer aircraft	1993	1997	8	(Offsets $250 m)
	30	AGM-65D Maverick	ASM	1993	1997	30	For F/A-18D FGA/trainer aircraft

TRANSFERS OF MAJOR CONVENTIONAL WEAPONS

25	AGM-84A Harpoon	Air-to-ship missile	1993	1997	25	For F/A-18D FGA/trainer aircraft
20	AIM-7M Sparrow	Air-to-air missile	1993	1997	20	For F/A-18D FGA/trainer aircraft
40	AIM-9S Sidewinder	Air-to-air missile	1993	1997	40	For F/A-18D FGA/trainer aircraft
L: Germany						
(6)	MEKO-A-100	OPV	1997		. .	
Mexico						
S: Russia						
12	Mi-8T Hip-C	Helicopter	1997	1997	. .	Deal worth $15 m; for Navy
53	Bell-205/UH-1H	Helicopter	1996	1997	53	Ex-US Army; refurbished before delivery; for anti-drugs operations
USA						
4	Metro-3	Transport aircraft	1996	1997	4	Ex-US Air Force; aid
4	S-70A/UH-60L	Helicopter	1994		. .	Deal worth $14 m
Micronesia						
S: Australia						
1	ASI-315	Patrol craft	1997	1997	1	'Pacific Patrol Boat'/'Defence Cooperation' aid programme
Morocco						
S: France						
1	LSS-69m Type	Support ship	1995	1997	1	Moroccan designation Dakhla Class
2	OPV-64 Type	OPV	1994	1996–97	2	Moroccan designation Rais Bargach Class
1	OPV-64 Type	OPV	1996	1997	1	Moroccan designation Rais Bargach Class
Myanmar						
S: China						
24	A-5C Fantan	FGA aircraft	(1992)		. .	Status uncertain
(144)	PL-2B	Air-to-air missile	1992		. .	For 24 A-5C FGA aircraft; status uncertain
6	Hainan Class	Patrol craft	1994	1995–97	6	Myanmar designation Yan Sit Aung Class
Russia						
5	Mi-17 Hip-H	Helicopter	1996	1997	(5)	
Netherlands						
S: Finland						
90	XA-188	APC	1997		. .	Deal worth $82 m (offsets 100%); incl 20 for Marines
France						
1	AS-355 Twin Écureuil	Helicopter	1997	1997	1	Operated by civilian company for Navy and Coast Guard in Dutch Antilles

Recipient/ supplier (S) or licenser (L)	No. ordered	Weapon designation	Weapon description	Year of order/ licence	Year(s) of deliveries	No. delivered/ produced	Comments
Germany	17	AS-532U2 Cougar-2	Helicopter	1993	1996–97	17	Deal worth $242 m (offsets 120%)
	874	FIM-92C Stinger	Portable SAM	(1992)	1993–97	(749)	
Italy	2	127mm/54	Naval gun	1996		. .	For 2 LCF Type frigates; option on 2 more; ex-Canadian Navy; sold back to producer and refurbished before delivery
Switzerland	3	PC-7 Turbo Trainer	Trainer aircraft	1997	1997	3	Deal worth $6.2 m
USA	30	AH-64D Longbow	Combat helicopter	1995		. .	Deal worth $686 m (offsets $873 m)
	605	AGM-114K Hellfire	Anti-tank missile	1995	1996	(50)	For AH-64D helicopters; deal worth $127 m
	6	CH-47D Chinook	Helicopter	1993		. .	
	1	Schweizer-330	Helicopter	1997	1997	1	Operated by civilian company for Navy and Coast Guard in Dutch Antilles
	2	Standard Mk-41	ShAM system	(1996)		. .	Deal worth $54 m; for 2 LCF Type frigates
	36	AGM-65G Maverick	ASM	1997		. .	Deal worth $6 m
	200	AIM-120A AMRAAM	Air-to-air missile	1995		. .	For F-16A/B-MLU FGA aircraft

New Zealand

Recipient/ supplier (S) or licenser (L)	No. ordered	Weapon designation	Weapon description	Year of order/ licence	Year(s) of deliveries	No. delivered/ produced	Comments
S: Australia	2	MEKO-200ANZ Type	Frigate	1989	1997	1	Deal worth $554.7 m; New Zealand designation Te Kaha Class; option on 2 more not used
France	23	Mistral	Portable SAM	1996	1997	(11)	Deal worth NZ$22.8 m incl 12 launchers and 2 radars and 7 thermal sights
Sweden	2	9LV	Fire control radar	1991	1997	1	For 2 MEKO-200ANZ Type frigates; for use with Seasparrow ShAM system and 127mm gun
USA	2	Sea Giraffe-150	Surveillance radar	1991	1997	1	For 2 MEKO-200ANZ Type frigates
	2	Bell-205/UH-1H	Helicopter	1996	1997	2	Ex-US Air Force
	4	SH-2F Seasprite	ASW helicopter	1997	1997	1	Ex-US Navy
	4	SH-2G Super Seasprite	ASW helicopter	1997		. .	For Navy; deal worth $185 m (offsets 36%); option on 2 more; US export designation SH-2G(A)
	2	127mm/54 Mk-45	Naval gun	(1989)	1997	(1)	For 2 MEKO-200ANZ Type frigates
	2	AN/SPS-49	Surveillance radar	(1993)	1997	1	For 2 MEKO-200ANZ Type frigates

TRANSFERS OF MAJOR CONVENTIONAL WEAPONS   349

Supplier/recipient	No. ordered	Weapon designation	Weapon description	Year of order	Year of deliveries	No. delivered	Comments
Nigeria							
L: USA	2	Seasparrow Mk-48	ShAM system	1992	1997	1	For 2 MEKO-200ANZ Type frigates
	(16)	RIM-7P Seasparrow	ShAM	(1991)	1997	(8)	For 2 MEKO-200ANZ Type frigates
Norway							
S: France	60	Air Beetle	Trainer aircraft	1992	1993–97	(60)	
	7 200	Eryx	Anti-tank missile	1993	1995–97	(4 700)	Deal worth $115 m incl 424 launchers; option on more (offsets incl production of components)
	400	Mistral	Portable SAM	1990	1992–97	(400)	Deal worth $60 m (offsets 75%); for 9 Oksøy MCM ships and 14 refitted Hauk FAC
Italy	3	RAT-31S	Surveillance radar	1994		..	
Sweden	104	CV-9030	IFV	1994	1996	4	Deal worth $241 m (offsets $184 m); option on more
	..	Arthur	Tracking radar	1997	1997	(5)	Deal worth $85 m
UK	2	S-61/Sea King HAR-3	Helicopter	1993	1996–97	(2)	Deal worth $22.2 m; UK export designation Sea King Mk-43B
USA	12	MLRS 227mm	MRL	1995	1997	6	Deal worth $199 m incl 360 rockets and practice rockets
	24	AN/TPQ-36A	Tracking radar	1994	1995–96	(12)	For Norwegian Advanced Surface-to-Air Missile System (NASAMS)
	..	AGM-114A Hellfire	Anti-tank missile	1996	1996	(4)	For coast defence; deal worth $36 m (offsets 100%); assembled in Sweden; Norwegian designation N-HSDS
	..	AIM-120A AMRAAM	SAM	1994	1995–96	152	Deal worth $106 m; for NASAMS
	500	AIM-120A AMRAAM	Air-to-air missile	1996	1997	(100)	For F-16A/B-MLU FGA aircraft; deal worth $150 m
	..	BGM-71F TOW-2A	Anti-tank missile	1996		..	Deal worth $46 m (offsets 100%)
Oman							
S: France	51	VBL	Scout car	1996	1997	(25)	
	2	MM-38/40 ShShMS	ShShM system	1992	1996–97	2	For 2 Qahir Class corvettes
	(32)	MM-40 Exocet	ShShM	1992	1996–97	(32)	For 2 Qahir Class corvettes
Switzerland	5	Skyguard	Fire control radar	1995	1997	(2)	For use with 10 GDF-005 35mm AA guns

Recipient/ supplier (S) or licenser (L)	No. ordered	Weapon designation	Weapon description	Year of order/ licence	Year(s) of deliveries	No. delivered/ produced	Comments
UK	20	Challenger-2	Main battle tank	1997		. .	Deal worth $172 m
	80	Piranha 8x8	APC	1994	1995–97	(80)	Deal worth $138 m; incl ARV, APC/CP, 81mm APC/mortar carrier, ambulance and artillery observation versions; option on 46 more
USA	2	Qahir Class	Corvette	1992	1996–97	2	Deal worth $265 m; 'Muheet' programme
	. .	BGM-71D TOW-2	Anti-tank missile	(1996)	1997	(50)	For use on VBL scout cars
Pakistan							
S: Belarus	(1 920)	AT-11 Sniper/9M119	Anti-tank missile	1996	1997	(600)	For 320 T-80UD tanks
China	. .	K-8 Karakorum-8	Jet trainer aircraft	1987	1994	6	Incl some assembled in Pakistan; some components produced in Pakistan; status of planned licensed production uncertain
	(6)	LY-60N ShAMS	ShAM system	(1994)	1996–97	(6)	For refit of 6 Tariq (Amazon) Class frigates
	(96)	LY-60N	ShAM	(1994)	1996–97	(96)	For 6 refitted Tariq (Amazon) Class frigates
France	20	Mirage-3E	Fighter aircraft	1996		. .	Ex-French Air Force; refurbished before delivery; deal worth $120 m incl 20 second-hand
	20	Mirage-3E	Fighter aircraft	1996	1997	(20)	Ex-French Air Force
	2	Agosta-90B Type	Submarine	1994		. .	Incl 1 assembled in Pakistan; deal worth $750 m incl 1 licensed production
	. .	SM-39 Exocet	SuShM	1994		. .	Deal worth $100 m; for 3 Agosta-90B Type submarines
Netherlands	6	DA-08	Surveillance radar	1994		. .	For refit of 6 Tariq (Amazon) Class frigates
USA	10	Bell-209/AH-1S	Combat helicopter	1990	1997	(10)	Deal worth $89 m; delivery embargoed between 1992 and 1995
Ukraine	(320)	T-80UD	Main battle tank	1996	1997	(105)	Deal worth $550 m
L: China	. .	HN-5A	Portable SAM	(1988)	1989–97	(850)	Pakistani designation Anza-1
	. .	Hongjian-8	Anti-tank missile	1989	1990–97	(700)	
	. .	QW-1 Vanguard	Portable SAM	(1993)	1994–97	(275)	Pakistani designation Anza-2
France	1	Agosta-90B Type	Submarine	1994		. .	Deal worth $750 m incl 2 delivered direct

TRANSFERS OF MAJOR CONVENTIONAL WEAPONS

Sweden	1	Eridan Class	MCM ship	1992	1997	1	Pakistani designation Munsif Class
	..	Supporter	Trainer aircraft	1974	1981–97	(133)	Pakistani designation Mushshak; more produced for export
Panama							
S: Taiwan	5	Bell-205/UH-1H	Helicopter	1997	1997	5	Ex-Taiwanese Army; gift; for Police
USA	6	Bell-205/UH-1H	Helicopter	1997	1997	6	Ex-US Army; for Police; aid; for anti-drugs operations
Papua New Guinea							
S: Singapore	3	Vosper Type-A/B	Patrol craft	1996	1997	(3)	Ex-Singaporean Navy; Papua New Guinean designation Aitape Class
	3	WM-26	Fire control radar	1996	1997	(3)	On 3 ex-Singaporean Navy Vosper-A/B Type patrol craft
Paraguay							
S: Taiwan	12	F-5E Tiger-2	FGA aircraft	1997	1997	(2)	Ex-Taiwanese Air Force; incl 2 F-5F trainer version; gift
Peru							
S: Belarus	(12)	MiG-29 Fulcrum-A	Fighter aircraft	1996	1997	(12)	Ex-Belarus Air Force; incl 2 MiG-29UB trainer version
	(180)	AA-10a Alamo/R-27R	Air-to-air missile	1996	1997	(180)	For 10 MiG-29 fighter aircraft
	(144)	AA-8 Aphid/R-60	Air-to-air missile	1996	1997	(144)	For 12 MiG-29/MiG-29UB fighter aircraft; designation uncertain
Netherlands	2	Dokkum Class	Minesweeper	1996	1997	2	Ex-Dutch Navy; Peruvian designation Carrasco Class
USA	11	A-37B Dragonfly	Ground attack ac	1996	1997	..	Ex-US Air Force; gift
Philippines							
S: Australia	2	Transfield 56m Type	Patrol craft	1997	1997	..	For Coast Guard; partly financed by Australia
UK	3	Peacock Class	OPV	1997	1997	3	Ex-UK Navy; deal worth $9.7 m; Philippine designation Jacinto Class

352 MILITARY SPENDING AND ARMAMENTS, 1997

Recipient/ supplier (S) or licenser (L)	No. ordered	Weapon designation	Weapon description	Year of order/ licence	Year(s) of deliveries	No. delivered/ produced	Comments
L:	142	FS-100 Simba	APC	1992	1994–97	142	Deal worth $46 m incl 8 delivered direct; incl 4 assembled from kits
Portugal							
S: UK	21	L-119 105mm	Towed gun	1997		..	
USA	1	Stalwart Class	Survey ship	1996	1997	1	Ex-US Navy; Portugese designation Dom Carlos I Class
Qatar							
S: France	12	Mirage-2000-5	FGA aircraft	1994	1997	3	Deal worth $1.25 b; French export designation Mirage-2000-5EDA; incl 3 Mirage-2000DDA trainer version
	..	Apache/MAW	ASM	1994			For Mirage-2000-5 FGA aircraft
	(144)	MICA-EM	Air-to-air missile	1994	1997	(36)	Deal worth $280 m incl R-550 missiles; for 12 Mirage 2000-5 FGA aircraft
	(144)	R-550 Magic-2	Air-to-air missile	1994	1997	(36)	For 12 Mirage 2000-5 FGA aircraft
	10	AMX-30B	Main battle tank	(1996)	1997	10	Ex-French Army; gift
	4	MM-38/40 ShShMS	ShShM system	1992	1996–97	4	For 4 Vita (Barzan) Class FAC
	4	MRR-3D	Surveillance radar	(1992)	1996–97	4	For 4 Vita (Barzan) Class FAC
	4	TRS-3051 Triton	Surveillance radar	(1992)	1996–97	4	For 4 Vita (Barzan) Class FAC
	(64)	MM-40 Exocet	ShShM	1992	1996–97	(64)	For 4 Vita (Barzan) Class FAC
Netherlands	4	Goalkeeper	CIWS	1992	1996–97	4	For 4 Vita (Barzan) Class FAC
	4	STING	Fire control radar	(1992)	1996–97	4	For 4 Vita (Barzan) Class FAC; for use with 76mm gun
UK	(8)	Hawk-100	FGA/trainer aircraft	1996		..	
	4	Piranha 8x8	APC	1996	1997	(4)	
	36	Piranha 8x8 AGV-90	Armoured car	1996	1997	(10)	
	..	Starburst	Portable SAM	1996		..	
	2	VT-46M Type	Patrol craft	1996		..	Deal worth $155 m

TRANSFERS OF MAJOR CONVENTIONAL WEAPONS 353

	4	Vita Class	FAC(M)	1992	4	Deal worth $200 m; Qatari designation Barzan Class
Romania						
S: France	(200)	R-550 Magic-2	Air-to-air missile	1996	..	For MiG-21, MiG-23 and MiG-29 fighter aircraft
USA	4	C-130B Hercules	Transport aircraft	1995	1996-97	Ex-US Air Force
	5	AN/FPS-117	Surveillance radar	1995	4	Deal worth $82 m
L: France	..	SA-330 Puma	Helicopter	1977	(125)	More produced for export
USSR	..	SA-7 Grail/Strela-2	Portable SAM	(1978)	(475)	
Saudi Arabia						
S: Canada	1 117	Piranha/LAV-25	IFV	1990	655	Deal worth $700 m; incl 111 LAV-TOW tank destroyers, 130 LAV-90 armoured cars, 73 LAV-120 APC/mortar carriers and 449 other version; for National Guard
France	12	AS-532U2 Cougar-2	Helicopter	1996	..	For SAR
	2	La Fayette Class	Frigate	1994	..	Deal worth $3.42 b incl other weapons, construction of a naval base and training (offsets 35%); French export designation F-3000S Type
	2	100mm Compact	Naval gun	1994	..	On 2 La Fayette Class frigates
	2	Arabel	Fire control radar	(1994)	..	On 2 La Fayette Class frigates
	2	Castor-2J	Fire control radar	1994	..	On 2 La Fayette Class frigates
	2	DRBV-26C Jupiter-2	Surveillance radar	1994	..	On 2 La Fayette Class frigates
	2	MM-38/40 ShShMS	ShShM system	1994	..	On 2 La Fayette Class frigates
	(32)	MM-40 Exocet	ShShM	1994	..	For 2 La Fayette Class frigates
	2	Crotale Naval EDIR	ShAM system	1994	..	On 2 La Fayette Class frigates
	(48)	VT-1	ShAM	(1994)	..	For 2 La Fayette Class frigates; for use with Crotale ShAM system
	2	EuroSAAM VLS	ShAM system	(1994)	..	On 2 La Fayette Class frigates
	48	ASTER-15	ShAM	(1997)	..	For 3 La Fayette Class frigates
	1	La Fayette Class	Frigate	1997	..	French export designation F-3000S Type
	1	100mm Compact	Naval gun	(1997)	..	On 1 La Fayette Class frigate
	1	Arabel	Fire control radar	1997	..	On 1 La Fayette Class frigate
	1	Castor-2J	Fire control radar	(1997)	..	On 1 La Fayette Class frigate

354 MILITARY SPENDING AND ARMAMENTS, 1997

Recipient/ supplier (S) or licenser (L)	No. ordered	Weapon designation	Weapon description	Year of order/ licence	Year(s) of deliveries	No. delivered/ produced	Comments
	1	DRBV-26C Jupiter-2	Surveillance radar	(1997)		..	On 1 La Fayette Class frigate
	1	MM-38/40 ShShMS	ShShM system	(1997)		..	On 1 La Fayette Class frigate
	(16)	MM-40 Exocet	ShShM	(1997)		..	For 1 La Fayette Class frigate
	1	Crotale Naval EDIR	ShAM system	(1997)		..	On 1 La Fayette Class frigate
	(24)	VT-1	ShAM	(1997)		..	For 1 La Fayette Class frigate; for use with Crotale ShAM system
	1	EuroSAAM VLS	ShAM system	1997		..	On 1 La Fayette Class frigate
Switzerland	(20)	PC-9	Trainer aircraft	1994	1995–97	(20)	Sold through UK company; part of 'Al Yamamah-2' deal
UK	20	Hawk-50	Jet trainer aircraft	1993	1997	(20)	Part of 'Al Yamamah-2' deal; UK export designation Hawk Mk-65A
	48	Tornado IDS	FGA aircraft	1993	1996–97	(18)	Part of 'Al Yamamah-2' deal
	73	AMS 120mm	Mortar	1996	1996–97	(30)	Deal worth $57 m incl ammunition; for 73 LAV-25 APC/mortar carriers
	3	Sandown Class	MCM ship	1988	1991–97	3	Option on 3 more; Saudi designation Al Jawf Class
USA	8	C-130H Hercules	Transport aircraft	1990	1992	(1)	Deal worth $320 m incl 2 C-130H-30 version
	72	F-15S Strike Eagle	Fighter/bomber ac	1992	1995–97	30	Deal worth $9 b incl AGM-65D/G, AIM-7M and AIM-9S missiles
	900	AGM-65D Maverick	ASM	1992	1995–97	(450)	For 72 F-15S fighter/bomber aircraft; incl AGM-65G version
	300	AIM-7M Sparrow	Air-to-air missile	1992	1995–97	(140)	For 72 F-15S fighter/bomber aircraft
	300	AIM-9S Sidewinder	Air-to-air missile	1992	1995–97	(140)	For 72 F-15S fighter/bomber aircraft
	(8)	S-70A/UH-60L	Helicopter	(1992)		..	Deal worth $225 m; for Medevac
	13	Patriot SAMS	SAM system	1992	1995–97	(13)	Deal worth $1.03 b incl 1 SAM system for training and 761 MIM-104 PAC-2 missiles
	761	MIM-104 PAC-2	SAM	1992	1995–97	(761)	
Singapore							
S: Israel	6	Barak ShAMS	ShAM system	(1992)	1996–97	(3)	For 6 Type-62-001 (Victory Class) corvettes
	(96)	Barak	ShAM	(1992)	1996–97	(48)	For 6 Type-62-001 (Victory Class) corvettes

TRANSFERS OF MAJOR CONVENTIONAL WEAPONS

	No. ordered	Weapon designation	Weapon description	Year of order	Year(s) of delivery	No. delivered	Comments
	6	EL/M-2221	Fire control radar	1992		(3)	For 6 Type-62-001 (Victory Class) corvettes; part of Barak ShAM system
	12	EL/M-2228	Fire control radar	(1993)		(7)	For 12 Fearless Class patrol craft/FAC; for use with 76mm gun
Russia	(50)	Python-4	Air-to-air missile	(1997)		..	For F-5E and F-16 FGA aircraft
	350	SA-16 Gimlet/Igla-1	Portable SAM	1997		..	Incl 30 launchers; option on 500 more
Sweden	3	Sjöormen Class	Submarine	1997		..	Ex-Swedish Navy; refitted before delivery; Singaporean designation Challenger Class
UK	18	FV-180 CET	AEV	1995	1996-97	(16)	
	6	CH-47D Chinook	Helicopter	1994	1996-97	(6)	Incl 3 for SAR
USA	8	F-16C Fighting Falcon	FGA aircraft	1994		..	'Peace Carven-2' deal worth $890 m incl 10 F-16D trainer version, 50 AIM-7M and 36 AIM-9S missiles
	10	F-16D Fighting Falcon	FGA/trainer aircraft	1994			
	50	AIM-7M Sparrow	Air-to-air missile	1994			
	36	AIM-9S Sidewinder	Air-to-air missile	1994			
	12	F-16C Fighting Falcon	FGA aircraft	1996		..	Lease with option to buy in 1999; for training in USA only
	4	KC-135A Stratotanker	Tanker aircraft	1997		..	Ex-US Air Force; deal worth $280 m incl refurbishment to KC-135R before delivery
	24	AGM-84A Harpoon	Air-to-ship missile	1996		..	Deal worth $39 m; for Fokker-50 ASW/MP aircraft
L:	(2)	LPD Type	Landing ship	1994		..	Designed for production in Singapore; option on 2 more
Slovakia							
S: France	2	AS-350B Ecureuil	Helicopter	1997		..	
	(5)	AS-532U2 Cougar-2	Helicopter	1997		..	
Russia	1	SA-10c/S-300PMU	SAM system	1997		..	
	..	SA-10 Grumble/5V55R	SAM	1997		..	
Slovenia							
S: Israel	..	Model-839 155mm	Towed gun	1996	1996-97	(18)	Incl assembly in Slovenia

Recipient/ supplier (S) or licenser (L)	No. ordered	Weapon designation	Weapon description	Year of order/ licence	Year(s) of deliveries	No. delivered/ produced	Comments
South Africa							
S: Switzerland	1	PC-12	Light transport ac	1997	1997	1	Deal worth $2.4 m
USA	2	C-130B Hercules	Transport aircraft	1995		..	Ex-US Air Force; gift
	3	C-130B Hercules	Transport aircraft	1996	1996–97	(3)	Ex-US Marines; gift
Spain							
S: France	15	AS-532U2 Cougar-2	Helicopter	1997		..	Deal worth $205 m (offsets 100%)
	840	Mistral	Portable SAM	1991	1992–96	(750)	Deal worth $154 m incl 200 launchers (offsets 50%)
Germany	200	Leopard-2A5	Main battle tank	1997		..	Spanish designation Leopard-2A5E; assembled in Spain; deal worth $2.7 b
Italy	1	RAN-30X	Surveillance radar	(1993)		..	For use with Meroka CIWS on 1 LPD Type AALS
	2	RAT-31S	Surveillance radar	1992		..	Deal worth $23.4 m (offsets 150%); option on 2 more
Qatar	10	Mirage F-1C	FGA aircraft	1994	1994–97	10	Ex-Qatari Air Force; deal worth $132 m incl 3 Mirage F-1B trainer version; Spanish designation C-14
	3	Mirage F-1B	FGA/trainer aircraft	1994	1994–97	3	Ex-Qatari Air Force
UK	56	L-118 105mm	Towed gun	1995	1996–97	(48)	Deal worth $63 m incl ammunition
USA	8	AV-8B Harrier-2 Plus	FGA aircraft	1992	1996–97	8	Deal worth $257 m; for Navy; assembled in Spain; Spanish designation VA-2 Matador-2
	2	Cessna-560 Citation-5	Light transport ac	(1996)	1997	2	
	24	F/A-18A Hornet	FGA aircraft	1995	1995–97	18	Ex-US Navy; option on 6 more; deal worth $288 m; refurbished before delivery; Spanish designation C-15
	83	M-110A2 203mm	Self-propelled gun	1991	1991–97	(83)	Ex-US Army; CFE cascade
	(31)	M-577A2	APC/CP	1993	1996–97	(31)	Ex-US Army
	4	AN/SPY-1F	Surveillance radar	1996		..	Deal worth $750 m; part of AEGIS air defence system for 4 F-100 Class frigates
	4	Standard Mk-41	ShAM system	(1997)		..	For 4 F-100 Class frigates
	(128)	RIM-66M Standard-2	ShAM	1997		..	For 4 F-100 Class frigates

TRANSFERS OF MAJOR CONVENTIONAL WEAPONS 357

		Weapon designation	Weapon description	Year of order	Year(s) of deliveries	Number delivered	Comments
	(256)	RIM-7PTC ESSM	ShAM	(1997)			For 4 F-100 Class frigates
	2	AN/VPS-2 Modified	Fire control radar	(1993)			For 2 Meroka CIWS on 1 LPD Type AALS
	(200)	AIM-120A AMRAAM	Air-to-air missile	(1996)			
	100	AIM-7P Sparrow	Air-to-air missile	1997			For F-18A/B FGA aircraft
L: UK	4	Sandown/CME Type	MCM ship	1993	1995-96		Deal worth $381 m
USA	(2 000)	BGM-71F TOW-2A	Anti-tank missile	1987		(245)	Deal incl also 200 launchers
Sri Lanka							
S: China	2	Haiqing Class	Patrol craft	(1995)	1997	2	
	1	Yuhai Class	Landing ship	(1996)	1997	1	
Sweden							
S: France	..	TRS-2620 Gerfaut	Surveillance radar	1993	1997	(10)	Deal worth $17.7 m; for CV-90 AAV(G)s
Germany	15	BMP-1	IFV	1993	1995-97	15	Former GDR equipment; refurbished before delivery; for trials
	350	BMP-1	IFV	1994		..	Former GDR equipment; refurbished in Czech Republic before delivery; 66 more delivered for spares only
	610	MT-LB	APC	1993	1994-97	(610)	Former GDR equipment; refurbished before delivery incl to ARV and tank destroyer; incl 60 MT-LBu (ACRV) APC/CPs; deal worth $10.3 m (not incl refurbishment) incl 215 MT-LB and 228 2S1 SP gun chassis for spares only; Swedish designation Pbv-401 (APC), Bgbv-4102 (ARV) and Pbv-4020 (APC/CP)
Switzerland	3	Piranha-3 10x10	APC/CP	1996	1997	3	Option on 50 more
USA	100	AIM-120A AMRAAM	Air-to-air missile	1994		..	Deal worth $190 m (offsets 100%); for JAS-39 FGA aircraft
L: Germany	120	Leopard-2A5+	Main battle tank	1994	1996-97	(41)	Deal worth $770 m incl 160 ex-FRG Army Leopard-2 tanks (offsets 120%); option on 90 more; Swedish designation Strv-122

Recipient/ supplier (S) or licenser (L)	No. ordered	Weapon designation	Weapon description	Year of order/ licence	Year(s) of deliveries	No. delivered/ produced	Comments
Switzerland							
S: USA	34	F/A-18C/D Hornet	FGA aircraft	1993	1996–97	(11)	Deal worth $2.3 b; incl 8 F/A-18D trainer version; incl assembly of 32 in Switzerland
	150	AIM-120A AMRAAM	Air-to-air missile	(1993)	1997	(50)	For 34 F/A-18C/D FGA aircraft
	12 000	BGM-71D TOW-2	Anti-tank missile	(1985)	1988–97	(9 750)	Deal worth $209 m incl 400 launchers and night vision sights; assembled in Switzerland
Taiwan							
S: Canada	30	Bell-206B JetRanger-3	Helicopter	1997		..	For training
France	60	Mirage-2000-5	FGA aircraft	1992	1997	24	Deal worth $2.6 b (offsets 10%); French export designation Mirage-2000-5Ei; incl 12 Mirage-2000-5Di trainer version; option on 40 more
	(960)	MICA-EM	Air-to-air missile	(1992)	1996–97	(400)	Deal worth $1.2 b incl 400 R-550 missiles; for 60 Mirage-2000-5 FGA aircraft
	(400)	R-550 Magic-2	Air-to-air missile	1992	1997	(130)	
	6	La Fayette Class	Frigate	1991	1996–97	5	Deal worth $2.8 b; Taiwanese designation Kang Ding Class; 'Kwang Hua-2' project
	12	Castor-2C	Fire control radar	1995	1996–97	10	On 6 La Fayette Class frigates; for use with 76mm and 40mm guns
	6	DRBV-26C Jupiter-2	Surveillance radar	1995	1996–97	5	On 6 La Fayette Class frigates
	6	TRS-3050 Triton-G	Surveillance radar	1995	1996–97	5	On 6 La Fayette Class frigates
USA	42	Bell-209/AH-1W	Combat helicopter	1992	1993–97	(36)	
	4	C-130H Hercules	Transport aircraft	1996	1997	(3)	Deal worth $200 m
	150	F-16A-MLU	FGA aircraft	1992	1997	(24)	Deal worth $5.8 b incl spare engines, 600 AIM-7M and 900 AIM-9S missiles; incl 30 F-16B-MLU trainer version
	600	AIM-7M Sparrow	Air-to-air missile	1992	1996	(240)	
	900	AIM-9S Sidewinder	Air-to-air missile	1992	1997	(100)	
	11	S-70B/SH-60B Seahawk	ASW helicopter	1997		..	For Navy; US export designation S-70C(M)-2 Thunderhawk

TRANSFERS OF MAJOR CONVENTIONAL WEAPONS   359

160	M-60A3 Patton-2	Main battle tank	(1994)	1995–97	(160)	Ex-US Army; deal worth $91 m; refurbished before delivery
. .	AN/FPS-117	Surveillance radar	1992			
6	Phalanx Mk-15	CIWS	1995	1996–97	(4)	Deal worth $75 m incl 6 Mk-75 76mm guns and ammunition; for 6 La Fayette Class frigates
7	AN/SPG-60 STIR	Fire control radar	(1989)	1993–97	(5)	For 7 Perry Class frigates; part of Standard ShAM system
7	AN/SPS-49	Surveillance radar	(1989)	1993–97	(5)	For 7 Perry Class frigates
7	Phalanx Mk-15	CIWS	1991	1993–97	(5)	For 7 Perry Class frigates
7	WM-28	Fire control radar	(1989)	1993–97	(5)	For 7 Perry Class frigates
7	Standard Mk-13 ShAMS	ShAM system	1989	1993–97	(5)	For 7 Perry Class frigates
. .	RIM-66B Standard-1MR	ShAM	(1995)	1995–96	(63)	For Perry Class frigates
1 786	BGM-71D TOW-2	Anti-tank missile	1997		. .	Deal worth $80 m
1 299	FIM-92A Stinger	Portable SAM	1997		. .	Deal worth $200 m incl 79 Avenger AAV(M)s, 50 man-portable launchers and training
3	Patriot MADS	SAM system	1994	1996–97	3	Deal worth $1.3 b incl 200 MIM-104 Patriot missiles
200	MIM-104 PAC-2	SAM	1994	1996–97	(200)	
2	Newport Class	Landing ship	1995	1997	2	Ex-US Navy; lease; refitted before delivery; Taiwanese designation Chung Ho Class
2	AN/SPS-67	Surveillance radar	1994	1997	2	On 2 ex-US Newport Class landing ships
2	Phalanx Mk-15	CIWS	1995	1997	2	On 2 ex-US Newport Class landing ships
1	Newport Class	Landing ship	1997		. .	Ex-US Navy; lease; refitted before delivery
1	AN/SPS-67	Surveillance radar	1997		. .	On 1 ex-US Newport Class landing ship
1	Phalanx Mk-15	CIWS	1997		. .	On 1 ex-US Newport Class landing ship
L: 7	Perry Class	Frigate	1989	1993–97	6	Taiwanese designation Cheng Kung Class; 'Kwang Hua' project

Thailand

S: Canada						
20	Bell-212	Helicopter	1993		. .	Deal worth $130 m
Czech Republic						
4	L-39Z Albatros	Jet trainer aircraft	1996	1996–97	(4)	
France						
3	AS-332L2 Super Puma-2	Helicopter	1995	1996–97	3	For VIP transport
. .	Mistral	Portable SAM	1996		. .	For Navy
Italy						
2	Gaeta Class	MCM ship	1996		. .	Deal worth $120 m

Recipient/ supplier (S) or licenser (L)	No. ordered	Weapon designation	Weapon description	Year of order/ licence	Year(s) of deliveries	No. delivered/ produced	Comments
Spain	2	C-212-300 Aviocar	Transport aircraft	(1995)	1996–97	2	For Army
	9	Harrier Mk-50/AV-8A	FGA aircraft	1995	1997	9	Ex-Spanish Navy; incl 2 Harrier Mk-54/TAV-8A trainer version; deal worth $90 m; for Navy; refurbished before delivery
Sweden	1	Chakri Naruebet Class	Aircraft-carrier	1992	1997	1	Deal worth $230 m without armament and radars
	(1)	Giraffe-40	Surveillance radar	1996	1997	(1)	For Air Force; for use with RBS-70 SAMs
	15	RBS-70 Mk-2	Portable SAM	1996	1997	15	Deal worth $4 m incl 3 launchers
USA	12	F-16A Fighting Falcon	FGA aircraft	1991	1995–97	(12)	'Peace Naresuan-2' programme worth $547 m incl 6 F-16B trainer version
	8	F/A-18C/D Hornet	FGA aircraft	1996		..	Incl 4 F/A-18D trainer version; deal worth $578 m; status uncertain after financial crisis
	6	S-70B/SH-60B Seahawk	ASW helicopter	1993	1997	6	Deal worth $186 m; for Navy; US export designation S-70B-7
	2	127mm/54 Mk-42/9	Naval gun	1992	1994–97	2	On 2 ex-US Knox Class frigates
	(101)	M-60A3 Patton-2	Main battle tank	1995	1995–97	(101)	Ex-US Army; deal worth $127 m
	12	M-106A3	APC/mortar carrier	1995	1997	(10)	Deal worth $85 m incl 18 M-901A3 tank destroyers, 21 M-125A3 APC/mortar carriers, 12 M-577A3 APC/CPs and 19 M-113A3 APCs
	19	M-113A3	APC	1995	1996–97	(19)	
	21	M-125A3 81mm	APC/mortar carrier	1995	1997	(21)	
	12	M-577A3	APC/CP	1995	1997	(12)	
	18	M-901 ITV	Tank destroyer (M)	1995	1997	(18)	
	2	Knox Class	Frigate	1992	1994–97	(2)	Ex-US Navy; 5-year lease worth $4.3 m; Thai designation Phutthayotfa Chulalok Class
	2	AN/SPG-53	Fire control radar	1992	1994–97	2	On 2 ex-US Knox Class frigates
	2	AN/SPS-10	Surveillance radar	1992	1994–97	2	On 2 ex-US Knox Class frigates
	2	AN/SPS-40B	Surveillance radar	1992	1994–97	2	On 2 ex-US Knox Class frigates
	2	Phalanx Mk-15	CIWS	1992	1994–97	2	On 2 ex-US Knox Class frigates
	2	RGM-84 ShShMS	ShShM system	1992	1994–97	2	On 2 ex-US Knox Class frigates

TRANSFERS OF MAJOR CONVENTIONAL WEAPONS

	8	RGM-84A Harpoon	ShShM	(1996)	1997	(8)	For 1 Phutthayotfa Chulalok Class (Knox) Class frigate
	1	AN/SPS-52C	Surveillance radar	1994	1997	1	For 1 Chakri Naruebet Class aircraft carrier; ex-US Navy
	4	Phalanx Mk-15	CIWS	1994	1997	(4)	For 1 Chakri Nareubet Class aircraft carrier
	3	W-2100	Surveillance radar	1995		..	Deal worth $180 m incl communication network and training
L: UK	3	Khamronsin Class	OPV	1997			
Tunisia							
S: Austria	26	M-30 107mm	Mortar	1996	1997	26	Ex-Austrian Army
Czech Republic	12	L-59	Jet trainer aircraft	1994	1995–97	12	Ex-US Air Force
USA	(5)	C-130B Hercules	Transport aircraft	1996	1996–97	(5)	Ex-US Army; deal worth $1.3 m; EDA aid
	4	S-61R Pelican	Helicopter	1994		..	
Turkey							
S: France	2	AS-532UL Cougar-1	Helicopter	1997		..	Deal worth $430 m incl 28 licensed production; incl 1 for Army and 1 AS-532AL version for SAR
	5	Circe Class	MCM ship	1997		..	Ex-French Navy; refitted before delivery; deal worth $50 m
Germany	197	RATAC-S	Battlefield radar	1992	1995–97	(110)	Incl assembly in Turkey; Turkish designation Askarad
	1	Kilic Class	FAC(M)	1993		..	Deal worth $250 m incl 2 licensed production
	1	MEKO-200T-2 Type	Frigate	1994		..	Deal worth $525 m incl licensed production of 1; partly financed by FRG aid; Turkish designation Barbaros Class
Israel	40	Popeye-2	ASM	1997	1997	40	Prior to licensed production
Italy	3	RAT-31SL	Surveillance radar	1995		..	
	4	Seaguard	CIWS	(1994)		..	For 2 MEKO-200T-2 Type (Barbaros Class) frigates; for use with Sea Zenith 25mm CIWS
	2	Seaguard TMX	Fire control radar	(1991)	1996–97	(2)	For 2 FPB-57 Type (Yıldız Class) FAC; for use with 76mm and 35mm guns

Recipient/ supplier (S) or licenser (L)	No. ordered	Weapon designation	Weapon description	Year of order/ licence	Year(s) of deliveries	No. delivered/ produced	Comments
Netherlands	3	MW-08	Surveillance radar	1995		..	For 3 Kilic Class FAC
	3	STING	Fire control radar	1995		..	For 3 Kilic Class FAC; for use with 76mm and 35mm guns
	4	STIR	Fire control radar	(1994)		..	For 2 MEKO-200T-2 Type (Barbaros Class) frigates; for use with Seasparrow VLS ShAM system and 127mm gun
UK	2	AWS-6 Dolphin	Surveillance radar	(1991)	1996–97	(2)	For 2 FPB-57 Type (Yildiz Class) FAC
	2	AWS-6 Dolphin	Surveillance radar	(1994)		..	For 2 MEKO-200T-2 Type (Barbaros Class) frigates
	2	AWS-9	Surveillance radar	(1994)		..	For 2 MEKO-200T-2 Type (Barbaros Class) frigates
USA	7	KC-135A Stratotanker	Tanker aircraft	1994	1997	3	Ex-US Air Force; refurbished to KC-135R before delivery
	4	S-70B/SH-60B Seahawk	ASW helicopter	1997		..	For Navy; deal worth $120 m incl AGM-114 missiles; US export designation S-70B-28
	..	AGM-114A Hellfire	Anti-tank missile	1997		..	For 4 S-70B/SH-60B helicopters; for Navy
	3	Perry Class	Frigate	1995	1997	3	Ex-US Navy; incl 2 SAP aid and 1 lease; Turkish designation Gaziantep Class
	3	WM-28	Fire control radar	1995	1997	3	On 3 ex-US Perry Class frigates; for use with 76mm gun
	3	AN/SPS-49	Surveillance radar	1995	1997	3	On 3 ex-US Perry Class frigates
	3	AN/SPS-55	Surveillance radar	1995	1997	3	On 3 ex-US Perry Class frigates
	3	Phalanx Mk-15	CIWS	1995	1997	3	On 3 ex-US Perry Class frigates
	3	RGM-84 ShShMS	ShShM system	1995	1997	3	On 3 ex-US Perry Class frigates
	3	Standard Mk-13 ShAMS	ShAM system	1995	1997	3	On 3 ex-US Perry Class frigates
	3	AN/SPG-60 STIR	Fire control radar	1995	1997	3	On 3 ex-US Perry Class frigates; part of Standard ShAM system
	(108)	RIM-66B Standard-1MR	ShAM	(1995)	1997	(108)	For 3 Perry Class frigates
	2	127mm/54 Mk-45	Naval gun	(1994)		..	For 2 MEKO-200T-2 Type (Barbaros Class) frigates
	2	RGM-84 ShShMS	ShShM system	(1992)		..	For 2 MEKO-200T-2 Type frigates

TRANSFERS OF MAJOR CONVENTIONAL WEAPONS 363

	No.	Weapon designation	Description	Year of order	Year(s) of delivery	No. delivered	Comments
	16	RGM-84A Harpoon	ShShM	1995		..	Deal worth $15.3 m; for 1 MEKO-200T-2 Type (Barbaros Class) frigate
	2	Seasparrow Mk-48	ShAM system	1994		..	For 2 MEKO-200T-2 Type frigates
	..	RIM-7M Seasparrow	ShAM	(1994)		..	For 2 MEKO-200T-2 Type frigates
	5	AN/TPQ-36	Tracking radar	1992	1995–96		Deal worth $28 m
	2	RGM-84 ShShMS	ShShM system	(1991)	1996–97	(4)	For 2 FPB-57 Type (Yildiz Class) FAC
	(32)	RGM-84A Harpoon	ShShM	(1991)	1996–97	(2)	For 2 FPB-57 Type FAC
	2	RGM-84 ShShMS	ShShM system	1993		(32)	For 3 FPB-57 Type FAC
	..	RGM-84A Harpoon	ShShM	1993		..	For 3 FPB-57 Type FAC
	(48)	AIM-120A AMRAAM	Air-to-air missile	1993		..	Deal worth $52 m; for F-16C/D FGA aircraft
	80	AIM-9M Sidewinder	Air-to-air missile	(1992)	1996	..	Deal worth $23 m
	200	AIM-9S Sidewinder	Air-to-air missile	1994		(100)	Deal worth $55 m incl 30 training missiles
	500	MLRS 227mm	MRL	1993		..	Deal worth $289 m incl 1772 rocket pods
	24	MGM-140A ATACMS	SSM	(1996)		..	Deal worth $47.9 m
	72	RGM-84A Harpoon	ShShM	1994		..	
	16	UGM-84A Sub Harpoon	SuShM	(1993)	1994	(6)	For 4 Type-209/1400 (Preveze Class) submarines
L: France	28	AS532UL Cougar-1	Helicopter	1997		..	Deal worth $430 m incl 20 delivered direct; incl 9 for Army and 19 AS-532AL version for SAR
Germany	2	FPB-57 Type	FAC(M)	1991	1996–97	2	Deal worth $143 m; Turkish designation Yildiz Class
	2	Kilic Class	FAC(M)	1993		..	Deal worth $250 m incl 1 delivered direct
	1	MEKO-200T-2 Type	Frigate	1994		..	Deal worth $525 m incl 1 delivered direct; partly financed by FRG aid; Turkish designation Barbaros Class
Israel	4	Type-209/1400	Submarine	1987	1994–97	(3)	Turkish designation Preveze Class
	60	Popeye-2	ASM	1997		..	
Spain	50	CN-235-100	Transport aircraft	1991	1992–97	(45)	Deal worth $550 m incl 2 delivered direct
UK	..	Shorland S-55	APC	(1990)	1994–96	(30)	For Gendarmerie
USA	40	F-16C Fighting Falcon	FGA aircraft	1992	1996–97	(30)	'Peace Onyx-2' programme worth $2.8 b
	40	F-16C Fighting Falcon	FGA aircraft	1994		..	'Peace Onyx-2' programme worth $1.8 b
	650	AIFV	IFV	1988	1990–97	(128)	Deal worth $1.08 b incl 830 APC, 48 tank destroyer and 170 APC/mortar carrier version (offsets $705 m)

364 MILITARY SPENDING AND ARMAMENTS, 1997

Recipient/ supplier (S) or licenser (L)	No. ordered	Weapon designation	Weapon description	Year of order/ licence	Year(s) of deliveries	No. delivered/ produced	Comments
	830	AIFV-APC	APC	1988	1991-97	(796)	
United Arab Emirates							
S: France	30	Mirage-2000-9	FGA aircraft	1997		..	Deal worth $3 b incl upgrade of 33 UAE Air Force Mirage-2000
	(7)	AS-565SA Panther	ASW helicopter	1995		..	For Abu Dhabi; deal worth $230 m incl AS-15TT missiles
	(56)	AS-15TT	Air-to-ship missile	(1997)		..	For Dubai; deal worth $30 m incl 5 SA-342K helicopters
	2	AS-565SA Panther	ASW helicopter	1997		..	
	5	SA-342K Gazelle	Helicopter	1997		..	
	390	Leclerc	Main battle tank	1993	1994-97	(164)	Deal worth $4.6 b incl 46 Leclerc ARVs (offsets 60%)
	46	Leclerc DNG	ARV	1993	1996	(2)	
Germany	12	G-115T Acro	Trainer aircraft	1995	1997	(12)	Deal worth $5.5 m; option on 12 more
Netherlands	85	M-109A3 155mm	Self-propelled gun	1995		..	Ex-Dutch Army; refurbished before delivery for $33 m; for Abu Dhabi
	2	Kortenaer Class	Frigate	1996	1997	1	Ex-Dutch Navy; refitted before delivery; deal worth $320 m incl training; UAE designation Abu Dhabi Class
	2	LW-08	Surveillance radar	1996	1997	1	On 2 ex-Dutch Kortenaer Class frigates
	2	WM-25	Fire control radar	1996	1997	1	On 2 ex-Dutch Kortenaer Class frigates; for use with 76mm gun
	2	STIR	Fire control radar	1996	1997	1	On 2 ex-Dutch Kortenaer Class frigates; for use with Seasparrow ShAM system
	2	RGM-84 ShShMS	ShShM system	1996	1997	1	On 2 ex-Dutch Kortenaer Class frigates
	2	Seasparrow Mk-29	ShAM system	1996	1997	1	On 2 ex-Dutch Kortenaer Class frigates
	2	Goalkeeper	CIWS	1996	1997	1	For refit of 2 Kortenaer Class frigates
	10	Scout	Surveillance radar	1996	1997	(1)	For refit of 2 Kortenaer Class Frigates and 8 other ships

TRANSFERS OF MAJOR CONVENTIONAL WEAPONS

Supplier	No.	Weapon designation	Weapon description	Year of order	Year(s) of deliveries	No. delivered	Comments
Romania	10	SA-330 Puma	Helicopter	1994			Deal worth $37 m; for Abu Dhabi
Russia	6	BM-9A52/BM-23	MRL	1996	1997	(3)	For Dubai
	(200)	BMP-3	IFV	(1994)	1994–97	(200)	For refit of 6 TNC-45 Type (Ban Yas Class) FAC
Sweden	6	Sea Giraffe-50	Surveillance radar	(1994)	1996–97	(4)	For Dubai; incl 75 artillery support version; deal worth $75 m incl 8 ARV version
Turkey	128	AIFV-APC	APC	1997			
	8	AIFV-ARV	ARV	1997			
UK	..	Al Hakim	ASM	1985	1989–97	(1 191)	For Mirage-2000 FGA aircraft; UK export designation PGM-1A/B and possibly PGM-2
USA	636	AGM-114A Hellfire	Anti-tank missile	1996			For AH-64A helicopters
	24	RGM-84A Harpoon	ShShM	1997			For 2 Kortenaer (Abu Dhabi) Class frigates
	72	RIM-7M Seasparrow	ShAM	1997			Deal worth $27 m; for 2 Kortenaer Class frigates
UK							
S: Canada	9	Bell-412EP	Helicopter	1996	1996–97	9	Operated by civilian company for UK armed forces pilot training
France	38	AS-350B Ecureuil	Helicopter	1996	1997	(12)	Operated by civilian company for UK armed forces pilot training
Netherlands	2	Goalkeeper	CIWS	(1996)			For 2 Albion Class AALS
USA	25	C-130J-30 Hercules	Transport aircraft	1994			Deal worth $1.56 b (offsets 100%); UK designation Hercules C-Mk-4; option on 5 more
	6	CH-47D Chinook	Helicopter	1995	1997	(2)	Deal worth $365 m incl 8 MH-47E version; UK designation Chinook HC-Mk-2
	8	MH-47E Chinook	Helicopter	1995			UK designation Chinook HC-Mk-3
	..	AGM-114 Longbow	Anti-tank missile	1996			For AH-64D Longbow helicopters; assembled in UK
	210	AIM-120A AMRAAM	Air-to-air missile	1992	1995–97	(210)	Deal worth $235 m; for Navy Sea Harrier FRS-Mk-2 fighter aircraft
	65	BGM-109 T-LAM	SLCM	1995			Deal worth $142 m; for 1 or 2 Swiftsure and 7 Trafalgar Class submarines
L:	67	AH-64D Longbow	Combat helicopter	1995			Deal worth $3.95 b (offsets 100%)
USA							
S: Canada	17	Piranha 8x8	APC	1995	1997	(6)	Chassis for LAV-AD AAV(G/M); for Marines

366 MILITARY SPENDING AND ARMAMENTS, 1997

Recipient/ supplier (S) or licenser (L)	No. ordered	Weapon designation	Weapon description	Year of order/ licence	Year(s) of deliveries	No. delivered/ produced	Comments
France	. .	Box Mortar 120mm	Mortar	1997		. .	For Marines
Israel	2	Astra SPX	Transport aircraft	1996	1997	2	Deal worth $20.8 m; US designation C-38A; option on 2 more
	1 254	K-6 120mm	Mortar	1990	1991–97	(1 254)	Incl for use in M-106A3 APC/mortar carrier, US designations M-120 and M-121
	50	Popeye-1	ASM	1996		. .	Deal worth $39 m; US designation AGM-142A Have Nap
Moldova	6	MiG-29 Fulcrum-A	Fighter aircraft	1997	1997	6	Ex-Moldovan Air Force; deal worth $80 m incl 15 MiG-29UB/C version and AA-10, AA-11, AA-2c and AA-8 missiles
	14	MiG-29S Fulcrum-C	FGA aircraft	1997	1997	14	Ex-Moldovan Air Force
	1	MiG-29UB Fulcrum-B	Fighter/trainer ac	1997	1997	1	Ex-Moldovan Air Force
	(150)	AA-10a Alamo/R-27R	Air-to-air missile	1997	1997	(150)	Ex-Moldovan Air Force
	(125)	AA-11 Archer/R-73M1	Air-to-air missile	1997	1997	(125)	Ex-Moldovan Air Force
	(100)	AA-2c Atoll-C/R-13R	Air-to-air missile	1997	1997	(100)	Ex-Moldovan Air Force
	(125)	AA-8 Aphid/R-60	Air-to-air missile	1997	1997	(125)	Ex-Moldavan Air Force
UK	8	UFH 155mm	Towed gun	1997		. .	Option on 190 more; for Marines
L: Italy	12	Osprey Class	MCM ship	1986	1993–97	10	
Japan	180	Beechjet-400T	Light transport ac	1990	1991–97	(180)	Deal worth $925 m; for training; US designation T-1A Jayhawk; 'TTTS' programme
Switzerland	(711)	PC-9	Trainer aircraft	1995		. .	Incl 339 for Navy; 'JPATS' programme; US designation Beech Mk-2 or T-6A Texan-2
UK	172	Hawk/T-45A Goshawk	Jet trainer aircraft	1981	1988–97	(85)	For Navy; US designation T-45A Goshawk; 'VTXTS' or 'T-45TS' programme; incl 2 prototypes
	1	Cyclone Class	Patrol craft	1997		. .	Deal worth $23.2 m
Uruguay							
S: Israel	15	T-55 Model-S	Main battle tank	(1997)	1997	15	Ex-Israeli Army

TRANSFERS OF MAJOR CONVENTIONAL WEAPONS

	No.	Weapon designation	Weapon description	Year of order	Year of delivery	No. delivered	Comments
UK	6	Wessex	Helicopter	1997	1997	6	Ex-UK Air Force
	5	Wessex	Helicopter	1997	1997	..	Ex-UK Air Force
Venezuela							
S: Canada	3	Bell-412EP	Helicopter	1997		..	
Netherlands	2	Reporter	Surveillance radar	1997		..	
Poland	6	M-28 Skytruck	Light transport ac	(1995)	1996–97	6	For National Guard
	(6)	M-28 Skytruck	Light transport ac	1997	1997	(2)	For National Guard; deal worth $20 m
Viet Nam							
S: Russia	6	Su-27UB Flanker-C	FGA/trainer aircraft	(1996)	1997	2	
	2	Bass Tilt	Fire control radar	1996		..	For 2 BPS-500 Type FAC; for use with 76mm and AK-630 30mm guns
	2	Cross Dome	Surveillance radar	1996		..	For 2 BPS-500 Type FAC
	2	SS-N-25 ShShMS	ShShM system	1996		..	For 2 BPS-500 Type FAC
	(32)	SS-N-25/X-35	ShShM	1996		..	For 2 BPS-500 Type FAC
	(48)	SA-N-5 Grail/Strela-2M	ShAM	(1996)		..	For 2 BPS-500 Type FAC; designation uncertain
L:	2	BPS-500 Type	FAC(M)	1996		..	
Zimbabwe							
S: Italy	6	SF-260E/F	Trainer aircraft	1997		..	

Abbreviations and acronyms

ac	Aircraft	(M)	Missile-armed
AAA	Anti-aircraft artillery	MCM	Mine countermeasures
AAV	Anti-aircraft vehicle	Medevac	Medical evaluation
AALS	Amphibious assault landing ship	MP	Maritime patrol
ACRV	Armoured command and reconnaissance vehicle	MRL	Multiple rocket launcher
AEV	Armoured engineer vehicle	OPV	Offshore patrol vessel
AEW	Airborne early-warning	SAM	Surface-to-air missile
AEW&C	Airborne early-warning and control	SAP	Southern Amendment Program
AIFV	Armoured infantry fighting vehicle	SAR	Search and rescue
AMV	Anti-mine vehicle	ShAM	Ship-to-air missile
APC	Armoured personnel carrier	ShShM	Ship-to-ship missile
APC/CP	Armoured personnel carrier/command post	ShSuM	Ship-to-submarine missile
ARM	Anti-radar missile	SIGINT	Signals intelligence
ARV	Armoured recovery vehicle	SLCM	Submarine-launched cruise missile
ASM	Air-to-surface missile	SSM	Surface-to-surface missile
ASW	Anti-submarine warfare	SuShM	Submarine-to-ship missile
CIWS	Close-in weapon system	VIP	Very important person
EDA	Excess Defense Articles	VLS	Vertical launch system
ELINT	Electronic intelligence		
EW	Electronic warfare	**Conventions**	
FAC	Fast attack craft		
FGA	Fighter/ground attack	. .	Data not available or not applicable
FMF	Foreign Military Funding		
FRG	Federal Republic of Germany	( )	Uncertain data or SIPRI estimate
(G)	Gun-armed		
GDR	German Democratic Republic	m	million (10^6)
IFV	Infantry fighting vehicle		
incl	Including/includes	b	billion (10^9)

Appendix 8C. Sources and methods[1]

I. The SIPRI sources

The sources for the data presented in the arms transfer registers are of a wide variety: newspapers; periodicals and journals; books, monographs and annual reference works; and official national and international documents. The common criterion for all these sources is that they are open—published and available to the general public.

Published information cannot provide a comprehensive picture because not all arms transfers are fully reported in the open literature. Published reports provide partial information, and substantial disagreement among reports is common. Therefore, the exercise of judgement and the making of estimates are important elements in compiling the SIPRI arms transfers database. Order dates, delivery dates and exact numbers of weapons ordered and delivered may not always be known and are sometimes estimated—particularly with respect to missiles. It is common for reports of arms deals involving large platforms—ships, aircraft and armoured vehicles—to ignore missile armaments. Unless there is explicit evidence that platforms were disarmed or altered before delivery, it is assumed that a weapon fit specified in one of the major reference works is carried. As new data become available, the SIPRI arms transfers database is constantly updated.

II. Selection criteria

SIPRI arms transfer data cover six categories of major conventional weapons or systems: aircraft, armoured vehicles, artillery, guidance and radar systems, missiles and ships. Only transfers of systems in these six categories are presented in the statistics. The categories are defined below.

    1. Aircraft: all fixed-wing aircraft and helicopters, with the exception of microlight aircraft and powered and unpowered gliders.

    2. Armoured vehicles: all vehicles with integral armour protection, including all types of tank, tank destroyer, armoured car, armoured personnel carrier, armoured support vehicle and infantry combat vehicle.

    3. Artillery: multiple rocket launchers, naval, fixed and towed guns, howitzers and mortars, with a calibre equal to or above 100-mm, as well as all armoured self-propelled guns, regardless of calibre.

    4. Guidance and radar systems: all land- and ship-based surveillance and fire-control radars, and all non-portable land- and ship-based launch and guidance systems for missiles covered in the SIPRI 'missile' category.

    5. Missiles: all powered, guided missiles with explosive conventional warheads. Unguided rockets, guided but unpowered shells and bombs, free-fall aerial munitions, anti-submarine rockets, drones and unmanned air vehicles (UAV) and all torpedoes are excluded.

    6. Ships: all ships with a standard tonnage of 100 tonnes or more, and all ships armed with artillery of 100-mm calibre or more, torpedoes or guided missiles.

---

[1] A more extensive description of the SIPRI Arms Transfers Project methodology, including a list of sources used and examples of calculations, is available on the SIPRI Internet website, URL <http://www.sipri.se/projects/armstrade/atmethods.html>.

The registers and statistics do not include transfers of small arms, trucks, towed or naval artillery under 100-mm calibre, ammunition, support items, services and components or component technology. Publicly available information is inadequate to track these items satisfactorily on a global scale.

To be included in the SIPRI registers of arms transfers, items must be destined for the armed forces, paramilitary forces or intelligence agencies of another country. Arms supplied to guerrilla forces pose a problem. For example, if weapons are delivered to the Contra rebels they are listed as imports to Nicaragua with a comment in the arms trade register indicating the local recipient.

III. The SIPRI trend-indicator value

The SIPRI valuation system is not comparable to official economic statistics such as gross domestic product, public expenditure and export/import figures. The monetary values chosen do not correspond to the actual prices paid, which vary considerably depending on different pricing methods, the length of production runs and the terms involved in individual transactions. For instance, a deal may or may not cover spare parts, training, support equipment, compensation, offset arrangements for the local industries in the buying country, and so on. Furthermore, using only actual sales prices—even assuming that the information were available for all deals, which it is not—would exclude military aid and grants, and the total flow of arms would therefore not be measured.

The SIPRI system for valuation of arms transfers is designed as a *trend-measuring device*, to permit the measurement of changes in the total flow of major weapons and its geographical pattern. Expressing the valuation in trend-indicator values, in which similar weapons have similar prices, reflects both the quantity and the quality of the weapons transferred. Values are based only on *actual deliveries* during the year/years covered in the relevant tables and figures.

Production under licence is included in the arms transfers statistics in such a way as to reflect the import share embodied in the weapon. In reality, this share is normally high in the beginning, gradually decreasing over time. SIPRI has attempted to estimate an average import share for each weapon produced under licence.

Part III. Non-proliferation, arms control and disarmament, 1997

Chapter 9. Multilateral security-related export controls

Chapter 10. Nuclear arms control

Chapter 11. Chemical and biological weapon developments and arms control

Chapter 12. Conventional arms control

Chapter 13. The ban on anti-personnel mines

9. Multilateral security-related export controls

IAN ANTHONY and JEAN PASCAL ZANDERS

I. Introduction

Developments in 1997 underlined that multilateral export control regimes can play an important role in creating the conditions for effective approaches to non-proliferation. However, events also demonstrated that in some cases where the possibility of weapon proliferation is creating security concerns—in particular in the Middle East—the triangular relationship between China, Russia and the United States is the main focus of political activity.[1]

In bilateral discussions with Russia, the USA raised the issue of alleged transfers from Russia to Iran that are inconsistent with the rules accepted by Russia in the Missile Technology Control Regime (MTCR). This has provoked the question of what impact participation in the MTCR has had on Russia's national export control policies and procedures.

In bilateral discussions with China, the USA criticized China's transfers of nuclear and chemical materials and technologies to Iran as well as its transfers of nuclear and missile-related materials and technologies to Pakistan. Although until October 1997 China was not a member of any of the multilateral security-related export control regimes, the USA considered these actions to be inconsistent with China's unilateral declaration of support for non-proliferation and the bilateral undertakings between China and the USA.

In 1997 changes occurred in the membership of two of the multilateral security-related export control regimes discussed in this chapter: the MTCR and the Zangger Committee. Turkey participated in the 1997 MTCR plenary meeting, bringing the membership to 29 states. China, South Korea and Ukraine joined the Zangger Committee, bringing its membership to 33 states.

In 1997 there were changes to the common control lists developed in the framework of the MTCR, Nuclear Suppliers Group (NSG) and the Wassenaar Arrangement.

Sections II, III, V and VI address recent developments in five multilateral security-related export control regimes. The Wassenaar Arrangement on Export Controls for Conventional Arms and Dual-Use Goods and Technolo-

---

[1] For background information on the export control regimes, see Anthony, I. *et al.*, 'Multilateral weapon-related export control measures', *SIPRI Yearbook 1995: Armaments, Disarmament and International Security* (Oxford University Press: Oxford, 1995), pp. 597–633; Anthony, I. and Stock, T., 'Multilateral military-related export control measures', *SIPRI Yearbook 1996: Armaments, Disarmament and International Security* (Oxford University Press: Oxford, 1996), pp. 537–51; and Anthony, I., Eckstein, S. and Zanders, J. P., 'Multilateral military-related export control measures', *SIPRI Yearbook 1997: Armaments, Disarmament and International Security* (Oxford University Press: Oxford, 1997), pp. 345–63.

SIPRI Yearbook 1998: Armaments, Disarmament and International Security

Table 9.1. Membership of multilateral military-related export control regimes, as of 1 January 1998

State	Zangger Committee[a] 1974	NSG[b] 1978	Australia Group[a] 1985	MTCR[c] 1987	EU dual-use regulation 1995	Wassenaar Arrangement 1996
Argentina	x	x	x	x	n.a.	x
Australia	x	x	x	x	n.a.	x
Austria	x	x	x	x	x	x
Belgium	x	x	x	x	x	x
Brazil		x		x	n.a.	
Bulgaria	x	x			n.a.	x
Canada	x	x	x	x	n.a.	x
China	x[d]				n.a.	
Czech Republic	x	x	x		n.a.	x
Denmark	x	x	x	x	x	x
Finland	x	x	x	x	x	x
France	x	x	x	x	x	x
Germany	x	x	x	x	x	x
Greece	x	x	x	x	x	x
Hungary	x	x	x	x	n.a.	x
Iceland			x	x	n.a.	
Ireland	x	x	x	x	x	x
Italy	x	x	x	x	x	x
Japan	x	x	x	x	n.a.	x
Korea, South	x[d]	x	x		n.a.	x
Luxembourg	x	x	x	x	x	x
Netherlands	x	x	x	x	x	x
New Zealand		x	x	x	n.a.	x
Norway	x	x	x	x	n.a.	x
Poland	x	x	x		n.a.	x
Portugal	x	x	x	x	x	x
Romania	x	x	x		n.a.	x
Russia	x	x		x	n.a.	x
Slovakia	x	x	x		n.a.	x
South Africa	x	x		x	n.a.	
Spain	x	x	x	x	x	x
Sweden	x	x	x	x	x	x
Switzerland	x	x	x	x	n.a.	x
Turkey				x[d]	n.a.	x
UK	x	x	x	x	x	x
Ukraine	x[d]	x			n.a.	x
USA	x	x	x	x	n.a.	x
Total	**33**	**34**	**30**	**29**	**15**	**33**

Note: The years in the column headings indicate when the export control regime was formally established, although the groups may have met on an informal basis before then.

n.a. = not applicable

[a] The European Commission is represented in this regime as an observer.

[b] The Nuclear Suppliers Group. The European Commission is represented in this regime as an observer.

[c] The Missile Technology Control Regime.

[d] This state became a member of the regime in 1997.

gies is discussed in section II as is a new agreement reached in 1997 in the framework of the Organisation for Economic Co-operation and Development (OECD) which is related to international transfers of computer software used to encrypt electronic messages. Section III deals with two nuclear export control regimes, the Zangger Committee and the NSG.

The Australia Group (AG) is an informal arrangement in which like-minded states discuss issues related to chemical and biological weapon (CBW) proliferation. In 1997 the entry into force of the 1993 Chemical Weapons Convention (CWC) added importance to the question of whether or not the activities of the group (all of whose members have signed and ratified the CWC) are consistent with the commitments of states parties under the convention.[2] This issue and the recent activities of the AG are discussed in section IV.

The MTCR and the European Union (EU) system for dual-use export control are dealt with in sections V and VI, respectively. Table 9.1 lists the members of these regimes.

II. The Wassenaar Arrangement

In 1996 the Wassenaar Arrangement on Export Controls for Conventional Arms and Dual-Use Goods and Technologies was established by 33 states. No new states participated in 1997.[3] The Wassenaar Arrangement seeks to contribute to regional and international security and stability by promoting transparency and greater responsibility in transfers of conventional arms and dual-use goods and technologies. The Wassenaar Arrangement is itself not a decision authority, and agreements are implemented through national export and import control mechanisms. Participating states seek to ensure that: (*a*) transfers of items described in equipment and technology annexes (that are agreed by consensus) do not contribute to the development or enhancement of military capabilities which undermine security and stability; and (*b*) these transfers are not diverted to support such capabilities.

The development of the Wassenaar Arrangement has been a slow process of evolution, reflecting the fact that there is less agreement among governments about norms and principles that should apply to transfers of conventional arms than in the cases of nuclear, biological and chemical (NBC) weapons. In part, this also reflects the fact that at the end of 1997 the Wassenaar Arrangement had not yet agreed internal rules and procedures. For example, no decision had been reached on appointing a head of the secretariat.

In 1997 the participating states agreed to conduct a study on criteria for assessing destabilizing weapon accumulations. This study may contribute to a modification of the elements guiding the activities of the Wassenaar Arrange-

---

[2] The Convention on the Prohibition of the Development, Production, Stockpiling and Use of Chemical Weapons and on their Destruction is reproduced in *SIPRI Yearbook 1993: World Armaments and Disarmament* (Oxford University Press: Oxford, 1993), pp. 735–56; and at the SIPRI CBW Project Internet URL <http://www.sipri.se/cbw/docs/cw-cwc-mainpage.html>.

[3] The tasks and organization of the Wassenaar Arrangement are described in Anthony, Eckstein and Zanders (note 1), pp. 345–48.

ment—a process envisaged when it began its work.⁴ A review of the scope of conventional arms to be covered by the regime is part of this study and may lead to voluntary notification of information beyond the categories currently used (i.e., the seven categories of arms identified in the United Nations Register of Conventional Arms).⁵ The participating states will also make a wider assessment of the Wassenaar Arrangement in 1999.

These states also made clear that the Wassenaar Arrangement is not the only arrangement or organization dealing with issues of stability and security arising out of international arms transfers. The Wassenaar Arrangement has encouraged other efforts and established contact with several initiatives, including the EU Programme for Preventing and Combating Illicit Trafficking in Conventional Arms and regional initiatives taken by states in West Africa and by the Organization of American States.

Controls on encryption technology

In March 1997 the OECD Council issued a set of recommendations to its members related to national cryptography policies.⁶ The background to the recommendations was the recognition that the rapid development of electronic communications is likely to have an important impact on economic development and world trade provided that users are confident that the information they exchange is secure (i.e., it cannot be modified by an unauthorized person) and confidential (i.e., the contents cannot be read or used by an unauthorized person). Without these assurances the full potential of new technologies might not be realized. Cryptography was recognized to have an important role in creating the necessary assurance for users. At the same time, it was feared that unrestricted access to cryptography might have negative consequences for national and international security. In the 1980s a group of concerned states began to discuss the issue of a common approach to encryption policy. In 1995 these discussions were transferred to the OECD, which hosted a meeting at which member countries could explain and compare their national policies and discuss possible changes.⁷

Until the 1980s the issue of cryptography was of relevance almost exclusively to the military, police and security services—which had a virtual

---

⁴ The Initial Elements of the Wassenaar Arrangement included an agreement that 'work on further guidelines and procedures will continue expeditiously and taking into account experience acquired'. This document is available at the SIPRI Internet site at URL <http://www.sipri.se/projects/armstrade/wass_initialelements.html>.

⁵ Public Statement by the participating states in the Wassenaar Arrangement on Export Controls for Conventional Arms and Dual-Use Goods and Technologies, 10 Dec. 1997. This document is available at the SIPRI Internet site at URL <http://www.sipri.se/projects/armstrade/wass_press97.html>. See also chapter 8 in this volume.

⁶ OECD, 'Recommendation of the Council concerning guidelines for cryptography policy', 27 Mar. 1997, available at URL <http://www.oecd.org/dsti/iccp/crypto_e.html>, version current on 24 Feb. 1998. The OECD defines cryptography as the transformation of data in order to 'hide its information content, establish its authenticity, prevent its undetected modification, prevent its repudiation and/or prevent its unauthorized use'.

⁷ Kamata, H. and Peters, T., 'A consensus on cryptography', *OECD Observer*, Aug./Sep. 1997, pp. 13–15.

monopoly on encrypted electronic information distribution. Export and import controls were one way this monopoly was maintained. States which had the capacity to produce cryptographic technology made it subject to national export controls, and this technology was subject to the Coordinating Committee on Multilateral Export Controls (COCOM) embargo. In some cases states operated import controls or their equivalent—for example, by prohibiting the use of foreign encryption technology. With the political changes and developments in technology that occurred in the 1980s and 1990s the question was raised whether maintaining existing controls was feasible or desirable.

In the 1980s wide-area networks crossing national borders became more common in industry. The development of the Internet accelerated this process with the growing use of public telecommunications networks for data communication. There was increased commercial demand for message encryption, and it became possible to download software that included encryption technology from servers located in other countries via the Internet.

Under these conditions it became an open question whether export controls could play any role in managing international communications. There was pressure in several countries—notably in the USA—for a relaxation or lifting of export controls on encryption technology.[8] It was argued that if the USA maintained national export controls on a wider range of technologies than its commercial competitors, or if US national implementation was more restrictive, US companies might lose commercial advantages in what was likely to become an increasingly important market for communications software.

There were counter-arguments put forward in the United States against removing export controls, largely based on security concerns of different kinds. First, companies would no longer be obliged to keep customer records and report information in a systematic way to the government licensing authorities. This would reduce the level of knowledge about end-use and end-users of encryption technology. Second, unrestricted access to encryption technology might make it easier for hostile forces to penetrate the information systems of the exporting country. It is possible that for cost reasons a growing number of military and security forces will use commercial encryption software as an important element of their internal and external communications. Third, secure communications would give military advantages to potentially hostile foreign powers. Fourth, access to advanced encryption technology

---

[8] Until Dec. 1996 encryption technology was controlled by both the State Department (which has responsibility for licensing exports under the Arms Export Control Act) and the Commerce Department. On 30 Dec. 1996 the USA published new regulations that transferred responsibility for licensing exports of commercial encryption products to the Commerce Department (eliminating the need for companies to submit 2 sets of applications). 'Reinsch of Commerce on export controls, sanctions', *Washington File* (United States Information Service, US Embassy: Stockholm, 8 July 1997). The issue was raised in the context of revising the 1979 Export Administration Act (EAA), which provides the legal basis for licensing US exports of dual-use technologies. The EAA expired in 1994 and has not been renewed by Congress. Its controls remain in force because successive presidents have invoked the International Emergency Economic Powers Act (which gives the president broad authority to regulate financial and commercial transactions with foreign countries in national emergencies). Separate legislation related specifically to encryption was considered by 5 different congressional committees in 1997, but no text was agreed.

would be an advantage to criminal and terrorist groups in that surveillance by police and security forces would become more difficult.

These factors led to the conclusion that unrestricted access to advanced encryption technology was not desirable while traditional forms of export control were unfeasible. As a result, an alternative form of control was sought through harmonization of national objectives at the intergovernmental level.

The OECD created a working group of experts and officials from member states, and in 1996 the OECD Committee for Information, Computer and Communications Policy completed a set of guidelines for consideration by the OECD Council. The guidelines were intended to promote, among other things, the use of cryptography without unduly jeopardizing public safety, law enforcement and national security; to raise the awareness of the need for compatible cryptography policies and laws among states operating in the global information network; and to foster cooperation between the public and private sectors in developing and implementing national and international policies.

The guidelines incorporated a set of eight principles which the OECD member states were to implement through national measures and cooperation in other international forums.[9] The OECD also recognized that exports of encryption technology were already controlled by the members of the European Union (in its dual-use export control system) and the Wassenaar Arrangement (in its list of dual-use goods and technologies). Further discussions about the impact on export controls of national implementation of the OECD principles are more likely to take place in the framework of these bodies.[10] The eight agreed OECD principles were:

1. Cryptographic methods should be trustworthy in order to generate confidence in the use of information and communications systems.

2. Users should have a right to choose any cryptographic method, subject to applicable law.

3. Cryptographic methods should be developed in response to the needs, demands and responsibilities of individuals, businesses and governments.

4. Technical standards, criteria and protocols for cryptographic methods should be developed and promulgated at the national and international level.

5. The fundamental rights of individuals to privacy, including secrecy of communications and protection of personal data, should be respected in national cryptography policies and in the implementation and use of cryptographic methods.

6. National cryptography policies may allow lawful access to plaintext, or cryptographic keys, of encrypted data. These policies must respect the other principles contained in the guidelines to the greatest extent possible.

---

[9] Although the OECD guidelines argue the need for national measures, in Oct. 1997 the European Commission published a draft policy framework for security on open communications networks. The Commission argued that divergent legal and technical approaches in EU member states could, if national regulations were preferred, have a significant impact on the EU single market. Moreover, national approaches would have to be consistent with existing Community law. Therefore, the Commission announced its intention to propose EU-wide legislation in 1998. European Commission, 'European Commission adopts policy framework for more security on the Internet', Press Release no. IP/97/862, Brussels, 8 Oct. 1997.

[10] In addition, the European Commission has been working on a draft regulation on a common legal basis for EU information security.

7. Whether established by contract or legislation, the liability of individuals and entities that offer cryptographic services or hold or access cryptographic keys should be clearly stated.

8. Governments should co-operate to co-ordinate cryptography policies. As part of this effort, governments should remove, or avoid creating in the name of cryptography policy, unjustified obstacles to trade.[11]

The discussion that led to these principles underlined some of the difficulties of developing regulations to address problems that could not easily be allocated exclusively to either the military or the civilian domain, or to either the government or the non-government domain. For example, the idea of a single technical standard defined by governments (which might have been a basis for controls) either through regulation or by using their collective 'buying power' in a coordinated way was not accepted, and there was a preference for promoting market-based technology development. The guidelines recognized that governments have 'separable and distinct responsibilities for the protection of information which requires security in the national interest' and stated that the guidelines were not intended to be applied in such cases. However, it became clear that governments had different perceptions of their interests and responsibilities with regard to issues such as the right of individuals and companies to privacy. Consensus could not be reached on the main specific proposal being discussed—a control based on a 'key escrow' or 'Trusted Third Party' approach.

Trusted Third Parties

The most widely used form of encryption is to place an algorithm in a transmitted message which makes the contents unintelligible without access to a valid decryption 'key'. One proposed approach to regulation was to license a non-governmental agent—a Trusted Third Party (TTP)—to maintain a register of these keys to which authorized government agencies would have access under certain conditions.[12] In this way a balance might be struck between allowing individuals and companies secure and confidential communications without disallowing interception and monitoring by government where necessary for security reasons.

This approach (which was emerging as the preferred basis for national control systems in several countries, including all the 'P8' members) was not acceptable to all the OECD countries.[13] Given the international nature of modern communications traffic, the TTPs would have to hold both national and

---

[11] 'Recommendation of the Council concerning guidelines for cryptography policy' (note 6).

[12] UK, Department of Trade and Industry, Commercial IT Security Unit, 'Government sets out proposals for encryption on public telecommunications networks', Press Release no. P/96/430, London, 10 June 1996.

[13] The P8 (Political 8) countries are the Group of 7 (G7)—Canada, France, Germany, Italy, Japan, the UK and the USA—plus Russia. In the statement at the end of the 1997 Summit of the Eight in Denver, Colo., the 8 heads of government and heads of state invited all states 'to promote the use of encryption which may allow, consistent with OECD guidelines, lawful government access to combat terrorism'. US Department of State, 'Communiqué: the Denver Summit of the Eight', 22 June 1997, URL <http://www.state.gov/www/issues/economic/summit/communique97.html>, version current on 9 Mar. 1998.

international keys. Multiplying the number of bodies holding these keys could make it easier for unauthorized users to gain access to encrypted information and thereby compromise information security systems. Moreover, national legislation would define the conditions under which individual government users could gain access to keys from a domestic TTP. These keys could then be used to penetrate foreign information systems.

In the absence of a harmonized approach to national encryption policies it is unlikely that international transfers of encryption technologies will be completely unregulated in spite of the commercial and technological changes which have occurred.

III. Nuclear export controls

Nuclear export controls are discussed in two separate multilateral arrangements: the Zangger Committee and the Nuclear Suppliers Group.

The Zangger Committee

The Zangger Committee is an informal group of 33 states which meets twice a year with two main objectives: (*a*) to reach a common understanding of what constitutes nuclear material and equipment or material especially designed or prepared for the processing, use or production of special fissionable material;[14] and (*b*) to discuss procedures for exporting nuclear materials and some types of equipment 'in the light of the commitment of states pursuant to Article III.2 of the NPT [1968 Non-Proliferation Treaty]' so that parties to the treaty can feel confident that they are implementing their commitments effectively.[15]

The main task of the Zangger Committee has been to identify the items that fall into the category nuclear material and equipment or material specially designed or prepared for the processing, use or production of special fissionable material (the Trigger List, so called because any export of a listed item to a non-nuclear weapon state triggers the need for IAEA safeguards).[16]

The new model protocol on nuclear safeguards

Approximately 70 countries have nuclear reactors or major facilities of different kinds containing nuclear materials on their territories. Many other coun-

---

[14] The term means plutonium-239, uranium-233, uranium enriched in the isotopes 235 or 233, any material containing one or more of the foregoing, and such other fissionable material as the IAEA Board of Governors shall from time to time determine, but the term does not include source material. Oak Ridge National Laboratory, 'Special fissionable material', URL <http://www.ornl.gov/risk/t_section 1.html>, version current on 20 Feb. 1998.

[15] Histories of the Zangger Committee include URL <http://www.iaea.or.at/worldatom/infcircs/inf 209r1.html>, version current on 23 Feb. 1998; and Schmidt, F., 'The Zangger Committee: its history and future role', *Nonproliferation Review*, fall 1994, pp. 39–44. See also Anthony et al. (note 1), p. 601; and Anthony and Stock (note 1), p. 546.

[16] The Trigger List is available as an IAEA Information Circular; the most recent is INFCIRC/209/ Rev.1, Nov. 1974, URL <http://www.iaea.or.at/worldatom/infcircs/inf209r1.html>, version current on 21 Apr. 1998.

tries possess smaller nuclear facilities. While the safety of nuclear installations and the physical security of nuclear material are the primary responsibility of states, the International Atomic Energy Agency (IAEA) has developed a set of activities—known as safeguards—by which it seeks to verify that a state is not using nuclear material or equipment to develop or produce nuclear weapons. While these IAEA safeguards are not directly a part of the activities of the Zangger Committee or the Nuclear Suppliers Group, as noted above, they do have an impact on how the regimes function.

The specific safeguards that should be required prior to the transfer of Trigger List items have never been harmonized. This issue re-emerged in 1997 with the development of enhanced safeguards (the so-called Programme 93+2 safeguards) by the IAEA.[17]

According to Zangger Committee Chairman Fritz Schmidt the effect of Article III of the NPT should be to bring all non-nuclear weapon states under the IAEA full-scope safeguards regime whether or not they are parties to the NPT. Under Article III.2 of the NPT all parties would then insist that non-parties should be brought under full-scope safeguards as a condition of supply of Trigger List items.[18] There has not been a decision by the Zangger Committee members to make full-scope safeguards a condition of supplying Trigger List items, although this is a condition which has been adopted by all members of the Nuclear Suppliers Group. As discussed below, China has become a member of the Zangger Committee but not of the NSG. China has not given a specific undertaking that full-scope safeguards will be a condition of supplying Trigger List items.

In May 1997 the Board of Governors of the IAEA adopted an additional Model Protocol supplementing existing safeguards agreements. The new protocol (the Programme 93+2 safeguards) is intended to address a perceived weakness in the previous system. Whereas the previous safeguards were designed to check that statements by IAEA members were accurate, they did not check whether the statements offered a complete picture of nuclear activities. Evidence that North Korea had produced a greater quantity of plutonium than it had declared to the IAEA and the discovery that Iraq had a secret nuclear weapon programme led to a review of the safeguards system.

The new protocol has three types of provision: (a) measures to strengthen IAEA access to information; (b) increased physical access to sites, including agreed access beyond nuclear sites on a case-by-case basis; and (c) a rationalization of the safeguards system through closer cooperation between the

---

[17] The IAEA's Committee on Strengthening the Effectiveness and Improving the Efficiency of the Safeguards System agreed on 21 Apr. 1997 on the text of the Model Protocol to implement Part 2 of the measures of the IAEA's Programme 93+2. The Board of Governors approved the protocol on 15 May, and it was presented publicly on 16 May 1997. *PPNN* [Programme for Promoting Nuclear Non-Proliferation] *Newsbrief*, no. 38 (2nd quarter 1997), p. 7.

[18] 'Full-scope safeguards' are those described in the IAEA Information Circular Model Protocol Additional to the Agreement(s) Between State(s) and the International Atomic Energy Agency for the Application of Safeguards, INFCIRC/540, Sep. 1997.

IAEA, its member states and international organizations, such as the European Atomic Energy Community (known as the EAEC or Euratom).[19]

One element of the new safeguards system will be an enhanced information system managed by the IAEA based on expanded declarations related to nuclear transfers. These declarations will include (among many things) information from exporters and importers related to specific transfers. The IAEA can combine these declarations with other information in a 'country profile' which should give detailed insight into the activities which may be related to the possible existence of a nuclear weapon programme in that country. If these safeguards are implemented successfully it is hoped that they will reduce the probability that any country could pursue a clandestine nuclear weapon programme. At the September 1997 meeting of the IAEA Board of Governors, six states—Armenia, Australia, Georgia, the Philippines, Poland and Uruguay—signed an Additional Protocol. Armenia and Georgia announced their intention to apply the Additional Protocol provisionally pending parliamentary ratification. Before the end of 1997 Lithuania also accepted the Additional Protocol.[20]

China and the Zangger Committee

In 1997 China stated its intention to apply for membership of the Zangger Committee at the same time as it announced changes to its national nuclear export controls.[21] China participated in the October 1997 meeting of the Zangger Committee[22] and therefore is included as a member in table 9.1.

For many years after the NPT entered into force China (itself a nuclear weapon state) remained outside the international nuclear non-proliferation regime. China often drew attention to the potential negative consequences of efforts to restrict international technology transfers in pursuit of non-proliferation objectives. In the 1990s China became persuaded that it had a national interest in cooperative approaches to non-proliferation, and in 1992 it acceded to the NPT. Subsequently, the question has been raised how China interprets its obligations under Article III.2 of the NPT in the light of continued Sino-Pakistani cooperation in the nuclear field.

In 1997 the desire to make a public statement on non-proliferation issues at the Chinese–US summit meeting in Washington in October 1997 spurred changes in China's national policy. Non-proliferation issues were repeatedly

---

[19] Keynote Address of Hans Blix, Director-General of the IAEA, at the NSG Seminar on the Role of Export Controls in Nuclear Non-Proliferation, Vienna, 7 Oct. 1997.

[20] Hooper, R., 'The system of strengthened safeguards', *IAEA Bulletin* (Internet edn), vol. 39, no. 4 (Dec. 1997), URL <http://www.iaea.or.at/worldatom/inforesource/bulletin/bull394/hooper.html>, version current on 3 Mar. 1998.

[21] *Australia–United States Ministerial Consultations 1997 Joint Communiqué*, 9 Oct. 1997, at the US State Department gopher, URL <gopher://198.80.36.82:70/0R53350581-53381379-range/archives/1997/pdq.97>, version current on 23 Feb. 1998.

[22] Fitchett, J., 'A new China embracing nuclear nonproliferation', *International Herald Tribune*, 11 Dec. 1997, pp. 1, 4.

raised by the US representative in bilateral discussions with the USA's Chinese counterparts throughout the year.[23]

In September 1997 the Chinese Foreign Ministry issued a statement and a Decree of the State Council on Regulations on the Control of Nuclear Exports. The statement outlined three principles that guide Chinese nuclear export policy: (*a*) nuclear technology which is transferred may only be used for peaceful purposes; (*b*) the use of the technology should be subject to IAEA safeguards; and (*c*) the technology may not be transferred to a third country without the prior written permission of the China Atomic Energy Authority. The statement by the Foreign Ministry repeated and underlined previous statements by China that 'no assistance whatsoever' may be provided to countries or regions not subject to IAEA supervision.[24]

Ideally, the USA would like China to join all the multilateral regimes addressing weapon proliferation.[25] However, the issue of nuclear export controls played a particularly important part in Chinese–US relations in 1997. From a political perspective, the USA has been particularly concerned about China's nuclear cooperation with Pakistan, which is not a party to the NPT, and Iran, which is a party to the treaty.

Generation of nuclear power will form part of China's future energy strategy and international cooperation is likely to play an important role in developing China's nuclear industry. The USA has made it clear that China's commitment to nuclear weapon non-proliferation would need to be accompanied by effective national nuclear export controls before cooperation with US industry could be developed.[26]

The US Department of Commerce noted in May 1997 that the most difficult problem in deciding on specific applications for the export of dual-use items to China was 'determining the legitimacy of the end-user and assuring that the ultimate consignee uses the item in the approved end-use. This approach is not easily monitored and data is difficult to gather'.[27] This point was emphasized by a State Department spokesman who explained that 'China is a big country.

[23] Interview with Deputy Assistant Secretary of State Robert Einhorn, United States Information Service, *Washington File*, 7 Jan. 1998, URL <http://www.usia.gov/current/news/topic/intrel/98010703. ppo.html?/products/washfile>, version current on 12 Jan. 1998.

[24] Central People's Radio Network (Beijing), 15 Sep. 1997, in 'China: Spokesman on 3 principles of nuclear export regulations', Foreign Broadcast Information Service, *Daily Report–China (FBIS-CHI)*, FBIS-CHI-97-258, 16 Sep. 1997. The Regulations of the People's Republic of China on Control of Nuclear Exports can be viewed at URL <http://www.sipri.se/projects/armstrade/natexpcon/country_matrix.html>.

[25] Statement by James B. Steinberg, Deputy Assistant to the President for National Security Affairs, at the Carnegie Endowment for International Peace, 9 June 1997. Steinberg said, 'Ultimately, the effectiveness of these multilateral efforts depends on the full participation of all potential suppliers. In particular, Russia and China are key to meeting the supply challenge'.

[26] China and the USA concluded a Peaceful Nuclear Cooperation Agreement in 1985 which was never activated. As a consequence of developments in 1997 President Bill Clinton was considering certifying to Congress that China was cooperating in nuclear non-proliferation. This certification is required under the 1978 US Nuclear Nonproliferation Act before industrial cooperation can be developed. *International Herald Tribune*, 19 Sep. 1997, p. 1.

[27] Letter from William M. Daley, Secretary of Commerce, to the United States General Accounting Office, 12 May 1997, reproduced in General Accounting Office, *Hong Kong's Reversion to China: Effective Monitoring Critical to Assess US Nonproliferation Risks*, GAO/NSIAD-97-149, May 1997, pp. 35–36.

There are many companies that trade. In order to maintain the credibility of China's international commitments, there has to be a nationwide export control system that will assure China's partners that commitments are being met.... [T]he construction of that system and the tightening of that system [are] going to be very important to the credibility of China'.[28]

A second export control issue related to China that received attention in 1997 was the implications of the change in the status of Hong Kong. On 1 July 1997 Hong Kong became a Special Administrative Region under the jurisdiction of China. Under the principle of 'one country–two systems' Hong Kong retained a great deal of autonomy in regulating its affairs, including its trade policy. Although prior to July 1997 some specific transaction types were referred to the United Kingdom for licensing (mostly those to proscribed destinations), Hong Kong processed the majority of licences locally.[29] After July 1997 the intention of Hong Kong authorities was to continue operating an autonomous export licensing system under which Hong Kong authorities would continue to require licences for exports of controlled items. Transfers to other parts of China would also require licences.[30]

Under these conditions other countries had to decide whether to change their approach to exports to Hong Kong. Different countries reached different decisions.

Comparing the licensing arrangements in place for Hong Kong and China (across the full range of controlled goods, not only nuclear items), the US General Accounting Office (GAO) concluded that: 'export control rules applied to China are more stringent: more categories of exports require licenses, and the US government has refused to export certain items owing to concerns over proposed end users and end uses'.[31] The UK and the USA both intend to continue treating China and Hong Kong differently for licensing purposes by maintaining the existing simplified procedures for Hong Kong. Other countries conducting large volumes of trade with Hong Kong, for example Australia and Japan, intend to treat China and Hong Kong identically by requiring licences for all exports of controlled items to both destinations.

The Nuclear Suppliers Group

The Nuclear Suppliers Group is an informal group of 34 nuclear supplier countries which 'seeks to contribute to the non-proliferation of nuclear weapons through the implementation of two sets of guidelines for nuclear exports and nuclear related exports'.[32] The guidelines are adopted by consen-

---

[28] Press Briefing following bilateral meeting between US Secretary of State Madeleine Albright and Vice Premier Qian Qichen of China, Washington, DC, 28 Apr. 1997.

[29] The Hong Kong licensing system is described in Cupitt, R. T., 'Nonproliferation export controls in East Asia', *Journal of East Asian Affairs*, vol. 11, no. 2 (1997).

[30] Xinhua (Beijing), 6 Oct. 1997, in 'China: Hong Kong, US to cooperate on strategic trade controls', FBIS-CHI-97-279, 7 Oct. 1997.

[31] General Accounting Office (note 27).

[32] In Aug. 1997 the NSG sent a letter to the IAEA Director-General which was intended to clarify the origin, roles and activities of the group. The letter and associated information were reproduced by the IAEA as Communication Received from the Permanent Mission of Australia on Behalf of the Member

sus and are implemented through national export control systems. The guidelines for nuclear transfers and nuclear-related dual-use transfers are both published as information circulars by the IAEA.[33]

The Nuclear Suppliers Group applies its guidelines to two common lists which are published by the IAEA as annexes to its information circulars. At its meeting in Canada in May 1997 the NSG indicated that it had clarified some elements of the Trigger List with respect to nuclear reactors, fuel-fabrication facilities and non-nuclear material as well as adopting additional measures to facilitate the sharing of information among member states.[34]

The activities of the NSG are of three kinds. First, the regular work of the NSG consists of plenary and working group meetings. Working groups are established to address a specific issue of interest or concern. Second, the NSG has two standing bodies which report to the plenary. Third, the plenary meeting can decide to initiate ad hoc activities.[35]

The plenary meeting typically focuses on reports by the working groups and the NSG Chair (which rotates among the members). The standing bodies are the Dual-Use Consultations (in which NSG members review the guidelines on nuclear-related dual-use transfers) and a Joint Information Exchange. Consultation and information exchange procedures were outlined in a Memorandum of Understanding (MOU) adopted in 1992, when the original set of guidelines related to nuclear-related dual-use transfers was finalized. Until 1997 this MOU was a restricted document. However, in the 1997 Ottawa plenary meeting NSG members decided to publish it.[36]

The membership of the NSG continues to expand. In 1997 the decision was taken to admit Latvia, which applied for membership of the NSG in January 1996. Latvia meets all the NSG membership criteria having signed the NPT in 1992, signed (in 1993) and ratified (in 1996) the CWC, and ratified the 1972 Biological and Toxin Weapons Convention (BTWC) in 1997. In April 1997 Latvia deposited an instrument of acceptance of the Statute of the IAEA and became a member of the organization (although a safeguards agreement had been concluded in 1993). Latvia was obliged to create an effective national export control system. This system was completed and operating in 1997.[37]

States of the Nuclear Suppliers Group, INFCIRC/539, 16 Sep. 1997. It can be viewed at the IAEA homepage URL <http://www.iaea.org> or at URL <http://www.sipri.se/projects/armstrade/NSG_documents.html>.

[33] The most recent are Communication Received from Certain Member States Regarding the Guidelines for the Export of Nuclear Material, Equipment and Technology: Nuclear Transfers, INFCIRC/254/Rev.3/Part 1, 16 Sep. 1997; and Communication Received from Certain Member States Regarding the Guidelines for the Export of Nuclear Material, Equipment and Technology: Nuclear-related Dual-use Transfers, INFCIRC/254/Rev.2/Part 2/Mod.1, 19 Mar. 1996. NSG members have all adopted full-scope safeguards as a condition of supply for nuclear transfers but not for transfers of nuclear-related, dual-use items.

[34] Press Statement from the Nuclear Suppliers Group Plenary Meeting, Ottawa, Canada, 8–9 May 1997.

[35] The history and past activities of the NSG are described in Anthony, Eckstein and Zanders (note 1), pp. 348–51.

[36] See appendix 9A in this volume.

[37] The system is described in the document Export Control System in the Republic of Latvia available at URL <http:www.sipri.se/projects/armstrade/natexpcon/country_matrix.html>.

At present the NSG member states are implementing a programme of outreach and transparency activities aimed at increasing the level of knowledge about the group among non-member states.[38]

IV. Export control regimes for chemical and biological weapons and technologies

Since 1985 a steadily increasing number of countries have coordinated their national export controls on chemical and biological weapons in the Australia Group. The AG lists of controlled items have meanwhile been incorporated in other export control regimes. CBW are also prohibited by multilateral disarmament treaties which require their parties not to assist any other state, group or individual in acquiring such weaponry. The Chemical Weapons Convention includes export control mechanisms and requires states to report the transfer of certain chemicals listed in the convention. The Biological and Toxin Weapons Convention, however, lacks these instruments.[39] Since both conventions permit the transfer of CBW-related dual-use technologies and commodities for non-prohibited purposes, some developing countries have expressed grave concerns about the continued functioning of supplementary export control mechanisms outside the BTWC and CWC. The controversy hampers and may even threaten the further development of the disarmament treaty regimes.

The Australia Group

The Australia Group is an informal arrangement whose objective is to limit the transfer of precursors to chemical weapons, equipment used in the production of CBW and biological warfare agents. The participating states have agreed to apply decisions taken collectively through their national export control systems. Created in 1985 when it was clear that Iraq was using CW in its war against Iran, the original objective of the AG was to prevent CW proliferation while the negotiations to complete the CWC were being undertaken. Subsequently, it has acted to prevent BW proliferation during the process of developing improved measures to ensure compliance with the BTWC. Its most recent annual meeting was held in Paris on 6–9 October 1997. As in 1996, 30 states attended and the European Commission participated as an observer. No changes were made to the agreed common control lists.[40] By 1997 all participants had become parties to both the BTWC and the CWC.

---

[38] Described in section IV of INFCIRC/539 (note 32).

[39] The Convention on the Prohibition of the Development, Production and Stockpiling of Bacteriological (Biological) and Toxin Weapons and on their Destruction is reproduced in Geissler, E. and Woodall, J. P. (eds), *Control of Dual-Threat Agents: The Vaccines for Peace Programme*, SIPRI Chemical & Biological Warfare Studies, no. 15 (Oxford University Press: Oxford, 1994), pp. 243–45; and at the SIPRI CBW Project Internet URL <http://www.sipri.se/cbw/docs/bw-btwc-mainpage.html>.

[40] The Australia Group agreed common control lists include CW precursors; dual-use chemical manufacturing facilities and equipment, and related technology; biological agents; animal pathogens; dual-use biological equipment; and plant pathogens.

The Australia Group has no charter and, apart from the support provided by the Australian Department of Foreign Affairs and Trade as point of contact and the Australian embassy in Paris as meeting place, it has no institutional foundations. Because of its informal nature, the AG cannot enforce implementation of its decisions. Each member must incorporate the agreed measures into its national export control legislation. As decisions are reached by consensus, the other participants can exert moral and political pressure to ensure the maximum harmonization of policies. The Australia Group also provides a forum to share information from a variety of sources, including intelligence agencies, on the activities, programmes and methods of acquisition of CBW proliferators; to express concerns; and to discuss items on the export control lists and policy measures to control CBW proliferation.[41] Some of the shared information comes from the exporting companies themselves. It does not appear that the Australia Group maintains an official list of target countries or differentiates between levels of restriction on the export of listed commodities on the basis of CBW proliferation threat evaluations of the targeted countries.[42] There are approximately two and one-half days of expert group meetings and a plenary meeting, which is a policy consultation meeting attended by diplomats and experts. Chemical and biological weapon experts and law enforcement and customs officials of the various countries participate in the expert groups, depending on the matters under consideration. In keeping with the informal character of the AG, procedures and practices at these meetings are adjusted as considered necessary.

The Australia Group also has no formally agreed policy on membership. An informal practice has developed instead under which decisions to admit applicant countries are taken by consensus, based on the collective judgement of the states participating in the AG meeting that the prospective member can contribute to furthering the AG's non-proliferation objectives. In this process the adequacy of a prospective member's CBW-related export controls and its overall approach to non-proliferation issues are taken into account.[43]

Coordination of export control procedures is the principal policy instrument in the effort to stem CBW proliferation within the framework of the AG. In June 1993 the Australia Group adopted a so-called 'no undercut' policy.[44] The policy seeks to avoid a situation in which an AG member competing for a lucrative business deal tendered by a potential proliferator would grant an export licence under the presumption that otherwise another AG state would do so. The AG countries honour the decisions of other AG states to deny a

[41] Morel, B., 'How effective is the Australia Group?', eds K. Bailey and R. Rudney, *Proliferation and Export Controls* (University Press of America: Lanham, Md., 1993), p. 57; Perry Robinson, J. P., 'Chemical and biological weapons proliferation and control', *Proliferation and Export Controls: An Analysis of Sensitive Technologies and Countries of Concern* (Deltac Limited and Saferworld: Chertsey, Surrey, 1995), pp. 41, 43; and Vachon, G. K., 'The Australia Group and proliferation concerns', *UNIDIR Newsletter*, no. 33 (1996), p. 59.

[42] Perry Robinson (note 41).

[43] Private communication with the author by officials attending AG meetings, Nov. 1997 and Apr. 1998.

[44] US Arms Control and Disarmament Agency, 'Australia Group' (28 Oct. 1997), URL <http://www.acda.gov/factshee/wmd/cw/aus496.htm>, version current on 16 Feb. 1998.

particular export. If an AG country does not grant an export licence it notifies the other AG states of its decision and provides them with information regarding the goods, their destination and the end-user. If, however, a second AG member has doubts about or disagrees with the proliferation risk assessment on which the original denial was based, it is obliged to consult with the country that denied the export licence before proceeding with a sale, which otherwise would undercut the original denial. The outcome of this consultation mechanism can be either that the state which has issued the denial notification revokes it, and thus allows the export to proceed, or that both countries agree on the soundness of the denial and, consequently, refuse the licence. All denials are subject to periodic review with the issuing country stating whether a particular denial should continue to stand or not.[45]

This practice strengthens the export control regime in two ways. First, it signals to a potential proliferator that it will not be able to play off one Australia Group member against another. Second, the commitment of the AG participants to the regime is strengthened by their refusal to grant an export licence on the grounds that otherwise a competitor in another AG country might win the business.[46]

There have been some efforts to streamline Australia Group policies and coordinate them with other export control regimes. In its 29 June–2 July 1992 meeting the MTCR made its membership identical to that of the AG by admitting Greece, Ireland, Portugal and Switzerland, and extended the scope of the MTCR to include missiles capable of delivering chemical and biological warheads.[47] In May 1994 the AG held a joint meeting with MTCR licensing and enforcement experts.[48] No further joint meetings have apparently been held since then and membership is no longer identical. The AG lists of controlled goods have also been included in the Wassenaar Arrangement and the EU regulation on exports of dual-use goods.

The legal status of CBW-related export control mechanisms

Chemical and biological weapons and related dual-use commodities are the object of six export control regimes: (*a*) treaty-based regimes—the CWC and the EU regulation on dual-use goods;[49] (*b*) non-treaty-based regimes—the Australia Group and the Wassenaar Arrangement on export controls for conventional arms and dual-use technologies; and (*c*) sanction regimes, such as

---

[45] UK, Department of Trade and Industry, Export Control Organisation, 'Export controls: a guide for business', URL <http://www.dti.gov.uk/export.control>, version current on 9 Apr. 1998; and private communication with the author by an official attending AG meetings, Apr. 1998.

[46] The practice, however, also creates legal problems for the exporting companies. According to business experts the AG members produce case law for each other, and companies are consequently expected to be aware of decisions that are not disclosed to the public. For transfers to potentially sensitive destinations companies are essentially forced to consult with the authorities. Jokinen, A. and Stephenson, J., 'Trade controls, growing uncontrollably', *Kemia–Kemi*, vol. 20, no. 9–10 (1993), p. 833.

[47] '29 June–2 July', *Chemical Weapons Convention Bulletin*, no. 17 (Sep. 1992), p. 17.

[48] '16–19 May', *Chemical Weapons Convention Bulletin*, no. 25 (Sep. 1994), p. 16.

[49] The BTWC does not have a specific export control regime, but such measures are currently the subject of negotiations as part of a future protocol to the convention (see below).

multilateral sanctions imposed by the UN Security Council and the unilateral sanctions imposed by one state or group of states against another state.[50] These regimes differ in legal status, the identity of the participants, the goods controlled and, notably for the sanction regimes, the objectives and duration. The BTWC and the CWC aim to be universal and therefore constitute inclusive regimes: the strength and relevance of both conventions are correlated to the number of participating states. All the other regimes are exclusive: the number of participating states in the export control arrangements is limited, and membership does not follow automatically from a national decision to join the forum,[51] although any state may opt to implement similar measures unilaterally.

On 29 April 1997 the CWC entered into force.[52] The convention deals with the threat of CW proliferation by requiring all parties to destroy existing CW stockpiles and to undertake not to acquire chemical weapons under any circumstances. Article I of the CWC also commits parties never to 'assist, encourage or induce, in any way, anyone to engage in any activity prohibited' under the convention. The CWC will benefit greatly from universal adherence and will progressively introduce a discriminatory regime for trade with non-parties in the chemicals listed in schedules 1–3 of the convention.[53] It is hoped that the negative impact on their economic development will induce non-parties to join the convention. In support of this aim Article XI of the CWC requests parties not to maintain barriers which restrict or impede trade for legitimate purposes with other parties and to review their national regulations on the trade of chemicals in order to render them consistent with the object and purpose of the CWC. The verification and inspection regime of the CWC enhances the effectiveness and credibility of the trade controls.

The BTWC, in contrast, lacks both verification mechanisms and treaty-specified trade controls. Under Article III parties undertake not to transfer to any recipient whatsoever biological agents, toxins, weapons, equipment or means of delivery and never to assist, encourage or induce, in any way, any state, group of states or international organizations to acquire BW. Article X commits parties to facilitate the fullest possible exchange of equipment, materials, and scientific and technological information for peaceful purposes and declares that the convention shall be implemented in such a manner as to avoid hampering the legitimate economic or technological development of parties. Verification measures and trade controls are currently the subject of

[50] Sanction regimes are not discussed in the present chapter. Multilateral sanctions by the UN Security Council, for example, were imposed on Iraq following its defeat in the 1991 Persian Gulf War. Cuba, on the other hand, faces unilateral sanctions by the USA. Cuba has called for their abolition under Article XI of the CWC. Statement by the Delegation of Cuba to the Sixteenth Plenary Session, 9 Apr. 1997, Preparatory Commission document PC-XVI/16, 9 Apr. 1997, p. 2.

[51] These issues are discussed in more detail in Zanders, J. P., 'Chemical weapons between disarmament and nonproliferation', *The Monitor*, vol. 3, no. 3 (summer 1997), pp. 18–23.

[52] See appendix 11A and annexe A in this volume.

[53] Toxic chemicals and their precursors are categorized in 3 schedules in the convention by the degree of risk which they pose to the purposes of the CWC and their relevance to legitimate industrial and commercial activities. Schedule 1 chemicals pose the greatest risk and are least relevant to legitimate purposes, and schedule 3 chemicals are deemed to pose the least risk to the convention and have widespread legitimate application.

negotiations in the Ad Hoc Group of the parties to the BTWC in Geneva to make them part of a future protocol to the BTWC. The proposed language in Article VII of the 'rolling text' seems to indicate that the transfer of relevant materials under Article X of the BTWC might be made explicitly contingent on full compliance with Article III of the convention: 'Transfers of materials, equipment and technology of concern [shall] [should] [only] take place in full compliance with [all] the provisions of [Article III and] [Article X] of the BTWC [and subject to the protection of commercial and propriety information and national security information] [taking into consideration the international law relating to the protection of commercial and propriety information]'.[54] The many brackets indicate the level of disagreement. The document does not prejudice the position of delegations, so the bracketed sections merely indicate preliminary concerns.[55]

The EU dual-use regulation also creates a treaty-based regime, which may pose a problem with respect to the CWC. On signing the CWC in January 1993, most EU member states added a written clarification similar to the following: 'As a member state of the European Community, the Government of Belgium will implement the provisions of the Convention on the prohibition of chemical weapons, in accordance with its obligations arising from the rules of the treaties establishing the European Communities to the extent that such rules are applicable'.[56] For the EU member states community law is self-executing and therefore takes precedence over national law. Following ratification of the CWC, a party must enact national legislation, subject to approval by the respective parliaments, to implement the convention. That national legislation cannot contravene EU law.

Two main areas of conflict may arise. First, the EU dual-use regulation is not applicable to transfers of commodities among EU member states unless it is known that they are intended for use in connection with non-conventional weapons.[57] Restrictions imposed by the CWC on transfers of scheduled chemicals thus do not apply to transactions among EU member states as long as these chemicals are also listed in the EU dual-use regulation. Second, the EU dual-use regulation contains a 'catch-all' clause. A transfer involving dual-use goods which are not on the control lists to a party outside the EU requires authorization if it is known that these goods are intended for programmes involving non-conventional weapons.[58] Moreover, national legislation may include a clause requiring an exporter to inform the government of his suspi-

---

[54] Article VII, (B), 3, (i), (b). Procedural Report of the Ad Hoc Group of the States Parties to the Convention on the Prohibition of the Development, Production and Stockpiling of Bacteriological (Biological) and Toxin Weapons and on Their Destruction, BWC/AD HOC GROUP/38, 6 Oct. 1997, p. 65.

[55] Procedural Report of the Ad Hoc Group of the States Parties (note 54), p. 3.

[56] *Multilateral Treaties Deposited with the Secretary-General: Status as at 31 December 1995* (United Nations: New York, 1996), pp. 872–74.

[57] Council Regulation (EC) no. 3381/94 of 19 Dec. 1994 setting up a Community regime for the control of exports of dual-use goods, *Official Journal of the European Communities*, L367, 31 Dec. 1994, especially Article 2 (b) and Articles 3 and 4.

[58] The national interpretations of the catch-all clause still require harmonization among EU members. In some countries the clause becomes operational if the exporter has been informed by the government.

cion that the goods are intended for such armament programmes.[59] To summarize, the EU dual-use regulation creates a legal framework under which EU member states could be exempted from licensing and reporting requirements under the CWC and establishes an export control regime for all countries irrespective of whether or not they are a party to the CWC. However, all EU members are also parties to the CWC, and its national implementation has thus far not caused any problems with the EU obligations. Practice will demonstrate how these potential conflicts—if they arise—can be resolved.

The international debate concerning the Australia Group

The debate between the Australia Group participants and several developing countries focuses on the relationship between Articles III and X of the BTWC and between Articles I and XI of the CWC. The CWC contains its own set of trade controls in Article VI,[60] and many developing countries view the maintenance of an export control regime outside the CWC as undermining the commitment made in Article XI (Economic and technological development).

A chemical industry is recognized to be one of the key elements necessary for sustainable development. For some developing countries Article XI of the CWC and the adverse effects of trade restrictions on scheduled chemicals as regards non-parties were important reasons for joining the convention.[61] For example, Algeria, Morocco and Tunisia—together with South Africa the main importers and only exporters of schedule 2 and 3 chemicals in Africa[62]—defected from the position adopted by the League of Arab States not to ratify the CWC unless Israel joins the Non-Proliferation Treaty because of the

[59] Council Regulation (EC) no. 3381/94 (note 57), Article 4.

[60] Schedule 1 chemicals can only be transferred between 2 parties for research, medical, pharmaceutical or protective use and in quantities defined in the General Provisions of Part VI of the Verification Annex. They cannot be retransferred to a 3rd state. Both parties must notify the Technical Secretariat (TS) not less than 30 days before any transfer. All parties must submit detailed annual reports to the TS regarding the transfer of Schedule 1 chemicals. Three years after entry into force of the CWC its parties will be allowed to transfer Schedule 2 chemicals, but only among themselves. Such transactions will not be subject to the stringent quantitative conditions or reporting requirements that apply to Schedule 1 chemicals. In the interim 3-year period, parties may transfer Schedule 2 chemicals to non-parties if they obtain an end-use certificate specifying *inter alia* the conditions laid down in the CWC. The transfer of Schedule 3 chemicals is only addressed in relation to non-parties. There are no quantitative limits, but the exporting party must ensure that Schedule 3 chemicals will not be used for purposes prohibited by the CWC. An end-use certificate which meets the stipulations imposed by the CWC is required. Five years after entry into force of the CWC, the Conference of the States Parties will consider the need to establish other measures regarding the transfer of Schedule 3 chemicals to non-parties. The regimes that govern the transfer of chemicals are detailed in the Verification Annex (Part VI, B for Schedule 1 chemicals; Part VII, C for transfer of Schedule 2 chemicals to non-parties; and Part VIII for transfer of Schedule 3 chemicals to non-parties). Initial and annual declarations must be made of the import and export of Schedule 2 and Schedule 3 chemicals to other parties according to Part VII, A and Part VIII, A of the Verification Annex, respectively.

[61] Zanders, J. P., 'Putting the horse before the cart: some thoughts on controlling unconventional arms in the Middle East', Paper presented at the conference the EU's Common Foreign and Security Policy and World Responsibilities, organized by the Institut d'études européennes, Université Libre de Bruxelles and the Olof Palme International Center (Stockholm), Brussels, 3–5 Oct. 1997, publication forthcoming.

[62] Kifleyesus, M., 'Article XI: the driving force for African CWC ratification', Paper presented to the 7th Workshop of the Pugwash Study Group on the Implementation of the Chemical and Biological Weapons Conventions, Noordwijk, The Netherlands, 6–8 June 1997.

adverse effect non-ratification would have on their economic development. For other developing countries, which have limited or no trade in scheduled chemicals, the technology transfer aspects of Article XI and the assistance provisions of Article X provided a greater incentive to join the convention.

At the 16th and final session of the Preparatory Commission (PrepCom) of the Organisation for the Prohibition of Chemical Weapons (OPCW) in April 1997 Kenya elaborated on the balance between global security and national development. On the one hand, the country recognized that the CWC was the first 'multilateral treaty with a universal application geared to offer us an opportunity towards total elimination of weapons of mass destruction', which therefore required full and effective implementation. On the other hand, Kenya 'attaches equal importance to Article XI which provides an expanded international cooperation in the field of chemical activities for purposes not prohibited under the Convention' and its 'fast growing chemical industrial base looks upon this as an opportunity for speedy industrialization and economic growth'. It called for a balanced approach between the security and development components during implementation of the CWC.[63]

Fearing further obstacles to economic development, certain developing countries called for the abolition of the AG. They were supported by Yuri Klyukin, head of the Russian delegation to the 16th session of the PrepCom, who stated that all restrictions on trade in chemicals should be lifted for any country that ratified the CWC after it entered into force.[64]

In contrast, many industrialized states perceive a rapidly changing security environment in which the use of CBW, despite the disarmament conventions, is a distinct possibility. The emergence of a multipolar global system with its increased regional insecurity after 1989, the 1991 Persian Gulf War against Iraq, which was then known to possess CBW, and the use of a nerve agent by religious extremists in Japan in 1994 and 1995 have added to calls to strengthen the Australia Group's export control regime. In particular the difficulties encountered by the United Nations Special Commission on Iraq (UNSCOM), and the fact that after six years of intrusive inspections no guarantee can yet be given that the full extent of the Iraqi CBW programmes is known, raised doubts about the effectiveness of the elaborate verification mechanisms of the CWC.[65] Further justification for the continued functioning of the AG follows from the lack of verification mechanisms in the BTWC. Progress towards a protocol to the BTWC was modest in 1997. The success of these negotiations will depend largely on that of the CWC regime.[66]

---

[63] Statement by the Delegation of Kenya at the Sixteenth Plenary Session of the Preparatory Commission for the Prohibition of Chemical Weapons, 9–15 Apr. 1997, The Hague, Preparatory Commission document PC-XVI/28, 14 Apr. 1997, pp. 1–2.

[64] Statement made by the Delegation of the Russian Federation at the Sixteenth Plenary Session of the OPCW Preparatory Commission on 9 April 1997, Preparatory Commission document PC-XVI/18, 9 Apr. 1997, p. 2.

[65] See also the sections 'Chemical and biological warfare proliferation concerns' and 'UNSCOM developments' in chapter 11 in this volume.

[66] See also the section 'Biological weapon disarmament' in chapter 11 in this volume.

In view of the continued debate the Australia Group took care to define its relationship with the BTWC and the CWC, although some passages in the October 1997 press release reiterate earlier statements: the national export licensing arrangements are 'aimed at preventing inadvertent assistance to the production of chemical and biological weapons' and provide 'practical support for the global bans on these weapons'.[67] While acknowledging that 'full adherence to the BTWC and CWC will be the best way to rid the world of these heinous weapons of mass destruction for all time', the AG noted that 'continued informal cooperation in the maintenance of effective licensing measures remains relevant and reinforces the effective implementation of the Conventions'.[68]

The persisting debate has also made the Australia Group participants aware of the necessity to ensure the continued transparency of their national export controls. To this end they conduct briefings for non-participants. Australia, as the chair of the AG, has for some years maintained a practice of briefing a significant number of non-participants on the outcome of the AG meetings. These briefings have sometimes resulted in countries exploring the possibility of membership or adopting similar export control measures unilaterally. In order to further awareness and understanding the AG initiatives also include regional seminars. After the October 1996 meeting of the Australia Group a regional CBW export control seminar was also held in October for the countries of Central and Eastern Europe and the Commonwealth of Independent States, and in January 1997 Japan organized an Asian regional seminar on export controls.[69] At the 16th session of the PrepCom the European Union declared that it was willing to address all matters of substance regarding the CWC, including those related to Article XI.[70]

At the heart of the discussion is the fact that neither the BTWC nor the CWC gives guidance about the relationship between the conventions and other non-proliferation regimes. Both conventions prohibit parties from assisting in any way in the BW or CW armament programmes of other countries or individuals but give no indication how that goal should be achieved. In other words, the BTWC and the CWC do not prohibit export control arrangements such as the Australia Group, nor do they indicate that such supply-side groups are the sole option. Developing countries, however, perceive a continuous strengthening and institutionalization of the AG regime: its members meet annually; the lists of controlled goods have been incorporated in other export control arrangements; and, although it merely reflects US policy, one of the

---

[67] Australia Group meeting, 6–9 Oct. 1997, Press release, Australia Group document DOC AG/Oct97/Press/Chair/20, Paris, 9 Oct. 1997.
[68] Australia Group meeting (note 67).
[69] Australia Group meeting (note 67).
[70] Statement on behalf of the European Union delivered by Jan Zaadhof, Head of the Netherlands Delegation to the Sixteenth Plenary Session of the Preparatory Commission of the OPCW, The Hague, Preparatory Commission document PC-XVI/33, 15 Apr. 1997, p. 2.

conditions under which the US Senate ratified the CWC in April 1997 was the 'continuing vitality of the Australia Group and national export controls'.[71]

At the time of the entry into force of the CWC the export licensing issue appeared near resolution. Several parties provided information that their trade in dual-use chemicals with potential application as CW precursors was less than 1 per cent of their total trade in chemicals and that few license applications for these chemicals were refused.[72] In November 1996 Iran submitted a working paper to the PrepCom suggesting a compromise: the CWC parties could agree on a supplementary system of import controls based on end-user certificates, to be issued by the recipient, for chemical compounds listed in the AG warning list (but not in the CWC schedules) and for certain chemical manufacturing facilities and equipment. Under the proposal, the OPCW would be the sole body responsible for verifying compliance with the CWC, and its parties would undertake no unilateral action to prevent CW proliferation.[73]

The issue, however, has not been fully resolved. Some developing countries view the existence of the AG as a major impediment to full, equitable implementation of the BTWC and the CWC. Neither convention was devised for some of the security challenges which exist in the post-cold war world, so some measures may be required to reinforce the global disarmament regimes. The negotiators currently working on a protocol to the BTWC, in fact, may be pointing to a solution to the unresolved issue: a conventional system of trade controls among states whereby the recipient state also exercises import controls and offers verifiable guarantees that the imported goods are not diverted for purposes prohibited by either the BTWC or the CWC.

V. The Missile Technology Control Regime

The MTCR is a voluntary arrangement among countries which share a common interest in stopping certain kinds of missile proliferation. The regime applies a common set of guidelines to an agreed list of controlled items. The aim of the MTCR is to restrict the acquisition of missiles, unmanned air vehicles (UAVs) and related technology for systems capable of carrying a 500-kilogram (kg) payload at least 300 kilometres (km), as well as systems intended for the delivery of NBC weapons.[74] Controlled items include ballistic

---

[71] USA, *Congressional Record*, 24 Apr. 1997, p. S3653. In particular, the president must certify prior to the deposit of the instrument of ratification that, among other things, each AG member understands and agrees that 'export control and non-proliferation measures which the Australia Group has undertaken are fully compatible with the provisions of the Convention, including Article XI (2), and its commitment to maintain in the future such export controls and non-proliferation measures against non-Australia Group members'.

[72] Mathews, R. J., 'Preparing for implementation of the Chemical Weapons Convention: progress during 1996', *Verification 1997* (Verification Technology Centre: London, 1997), p. 104, fn 43.

[73] Islamic Republic of Iran, Implementation of Article XI in the field of chemical trade, Preparatory Commission document PC-XV/B/WP.6, 5 Nov. 1996.

[74] The MTCR was originally concerned only with nuclear-capable delivery systems. In Jan. 1993 the MTCR Guidelines were expanded to cover delivery systems capable of delivering all NBC weapons. The document is available at URL <http://www.sipri.se/projects/armstrade/mtcrguidelines.html>.

missiles, cruise missiles, space launch vehicles (SLVs), sounding rockets, drones and remotely piloted vehicles (RPVs).

Despite the gradual increase in the membership of the MTCR, its members have acknowledged the need for increased cooperation with countries outside the regime. Events in 1997 underlined that some of the most pressing issues related to missile proliferation are beyond the scope of the MTCR. The regime can only make a limited contribution to managing potential security problems stemming from bilateral transfers between non-members. Issues such as reported Chinese missile-related transfers to Pakistan and North Korean missile transfers to countries in the Middle East have usually been addressed directly by the United States.

In October 1994 China gave the USA assurances that it adheres to the original 1987 MTCR Guidelines and Annexe.[75] In spite of press reports that China has transferred to Pakistan missile components, unassembled missiles, and equipment and know-how for use in missile production, the US Government has stated that it has 'no evidence that China has conducted activities inconsistent with this commitment'.[76] According to Israel and South Korea, North Korea has exported approximately 300 Scud-C missiles to Iran and Syria.[77] Despite a series of bilateral discussions with the USA on the issue of missile proliferation, North Korea has not agreed to any controls on its exports.[78]

Given that the Soviet Union was one of the most important suppliers of surface-to-surface and cruise missiles, it appeared to be a significant step forward for the MTCR when Russia became a member in 1995. However, in 1997 it was alleged that Russia was engaged in practices that would be very difficult to reconcile with the MTCR Guidelines.

In particular, Israel alleged that Russia was making missile-related transfers to Iran—said to be developing several surface-to-surface missiles.[79] According to the Israeli Minister of Defence, Iran has received assistance from Russian technicians to develop a guidance system for its missiles.[80] The Russian Space

---

[75] 'China and nonproliferation', US Department of State Fact Sheet, Washington, DC, 17 June 1997, URL <http://www.state.gov/www/regions/eap/fs-china_nonprolif_970617.html>, version current on 23 Feb. 1998; see also Statement of Assistant Secretary of State Stanley Roth before the Senate Foreign Relations Committee, 17 Sep. 1997, URL <gopher://198.80.36.82:70/0R47838619-47854927-range/archives/1997/pdq.97>, version current on 23 Feb. 1998.

[76] US State Department Daily Press Briefing, DPB no. 131, 10 Sep. 1997, URL <gopher://gopher.state.gov:70/00ftp%3ADOSFan%3AGopher%3A02%20Public%20Affairs%3APress%20Briefings%20-%20Conferences%3A1997%20Press%20Briefings%3A9709%20Press%20Briefings%3A970910%20Daily%20Briefing>, version current on 5 Mar. 1998.

[77] Israel held a series of bilateral talks with North Korea on missile sales to the Middle East in 1992 and 1993 but apparently with no result. In Aug. 1997, during a visit to South Korea by Israeli Prime Minister Benjamin Netanyahu, Israel and South Korea agreed to exchange information and to cooperate in opposing the proliferation of missiles and nuclear weapons. *Korea Newsreview*, 30 Aug. 1997, p. 6.

[78] In Apr. 1996 representatives of the USA and North Korea held talks on missile proliferation in Berlin. Additional talks were scheduled to take place in New York in Aug. 1997. However, after the North Korean Ambassador to Egypt sought political asylum in the USA the North Korean representatives withdrew from the New York talks. *International Herald Tribune*, 28 Aug. 1997, p. 1; and *Korea Newsreview*, 30 Aug. 1997, p. 11.

[79] See chapter 7 in this volume.

[80] *Jerusalem Post* (international edn), 4 Oct. 1997, p. 2.

Agency was also said to be providing solid-fuel technology to the Iranian missile programme.[81]

Under these circumstances several commentators raised the question of whether Russia—which, because it joined the MTCR in 1995, accepted the MTCR Guidelines as revised in January 1993—was implementing its commitments in good faith. One leading expert on the MTCR suggested that if the allegations were proved 'continued Russian membership [of the MTCR] is no longer in the interests of the regime'.[82]

The January 1993 version of the MTCR Guidelines included language intended to move the regime away from the approach of relying strictly on technical parameters (such as range and payload) and towards an approach of slowing/preventing all programmes of concern. Missile programmes of concern were defined to include those that might be linked to the delivery of weapons of mass destruction—not only nuclear weapons, but also chemical and biological weapons.

This change was reflected in the new guidelines in the statement: 'Particular restraint will also be exercised in consideration of transfers of any items in the [Equipment and Technology] Annex, or of any missiles (whether or not in the Annex), if the Government judges, on the basis of all available, persuasive information, evaluated according to factors including those in paragraph 3, that they are intended to be used for the delivery of weapons of mass destruction, and there will be a strong presumption to deny such transfers'.[83] This language incorporated the basic principle of the US Enhanced Proliferation Control Initiative[84] into the multilateral guidelines. The principle (sometimes called the 'catch-all' or 'know' rule) is that, if an exporter is aware that an item will contribute to the proliferation of weapons of mass destruction, the export should be prevented whether or not it conforms to technical parameters in a commodity control list.

At the same time it is the responsibility of the individual governments to decide whether or not a given transfer should be approved, taking into account five factors listed in the MTCR Guidelines (although other factors may also be taken into account). The five factors are:

---

[81] *Moskovskiy Komsomolets*, 15 Sep. 1997, in Foreign Broadcast Information Service, *Daily Report–Central Eurasia (FBIS-SOV)*, FBIS-SOV-97-258, 15 Sep. 1997; and *Defense News*, 15–21 Sep. 1997, p. 8.

[82] Speier, R., 'Russia and missile proliferation', Statement before the Subcommittee on International Security, Proliferation and Federal Services of the Committee on Governmental Affairs, US Senate, 5 June 1997, reproduced in *The Monitor*, vol. 3 no. 3 (summer 1997), pp. 31–34.

[83] The Equipment and Technology Annex of the MTCR is a restricted document. However, it is known to be divided into 2 categories of items. Category I, considered most sensitive and to which the greatest restrictions apply, consists of complete systems and specially designed production facilities for these systems along with complete subsystems usable in these systems and production facilities and production equipment for the subsystems. Category II consists of a range of materials, components and equipment which can be of use in missile programmes.

[84] *Fact Sheet on Enhanced Proliferation Control Initiative* (White House, Office of the Press Secretary: Washington, DC, 13 Dec. 1990).

A. Concerns about the proliferation of weapons of mass destruction;

B. The capabilities and objectives of the missile and space programs of the recipient state;

C. The significance of the transfer in terms of the potential development of delivery systems (other than manned aircraft) for weapons of mass destruction;

D. The assessment of the end-use of the transfers, including the relevant assurances of the recipient states referred to in sub-paragraphs 5.A and 5.B below; [and]

E. The applicability of relevant multilateral agreements.[85]

The assurances from recipient states refer to an end-use assurance from the buyer that 'the items will be used only for the purpose stated and that such use will not be modified nor the items modified or replicated without the prior consent of the [supplier] Government' and an assurance that 'Neither the items nor replicas nor derivatives thereof will be retransferred without the consent of the [supplier] Government'.[86]

In 1997 the question of how Russia applies the MTCR Guidelines through its national export control system in cases of transfers of category II items to Iran was raised by the United States in bilateral meetings in the framework of the US–Russian Joint Commission on Technological Cooperation (the Gore–Chernomyrdin Commission).[87] The Gore–Chernomyrdin Commission report found no evidence of Russian deliveries of missile technology to Iran. The allegations were also investigated by a group of US officials led by Ambassador Frank Wisner, who visited Israel and Russia in mid-1997.[88]

Officials from the Russian Government stressed that, while Russia has bilateral cooperation of various kinds with Iran (including military–technical matters), no assistance was being given to Iran's missile programme. The Russian Space Agency explained that its bilateral contact with Iran related to the possible use of Russian SLVs to carry Iranian civilian satellites.[89] The director of the Federal Security Service of Russia noted that a case had been revealed in which Iranian representatives who were interested in developing a natural gas pumping station tried to purchase parts which could be used in the manufacture of a liquid-propellant rocket engine from a Russian enterprise. However, permission to export these parts was denied and no transfer took place.[90] It has also been reported that the Federal Security Service detected efforts by Iran to

[85] The MTCR Guidelines are available at URL <http://www.sipri.se/projects/armstrade/mtcrguidelines.html>.

[86] Note 85.

[87] The Gore–Chernomyrdin Commission, which was established in 1993 as a joint initiative of US Vice-President Al Gore and Russian Prime Minister Viktor Chernomyrdin, meets regularly to promote cooperation on a wide range of issues related to energy, environmental protection, science and technology, health, space exploration and defence conversion. US Department of State, *Fact Sheet: Gore–Chernomyrdin Commission* (Bureau of Public Affairs: Washington, DC, 21 Sep. 1994). See also chapter 10 in this volume.

[88] US State Department Press Briefing, DPB no. 142, 2 Oct. 1997, URL <gopher://gopher.state.gov:70/00ftp%3ADOSFan%3AGopher%3A02%20Public%20Affairs%3APress%20Briefings%20-%20Conferences%3A1997%20Press%20Briefings%3A9710%20Press%20Briefings%3A971002%20Daily%20Briefing>, version current on 5 Mar. 1998.

[89] ITAR-TASS, 16 Sep. 1997, in FBIS-SOV-97-259, 16 Sep. 1997; and ITAR-TASS World Service, 26 Sep. 1997, in FBIS-SOV-97-269, 26 Sep. 1997.

[90] ITAR-TASS World Service, 29 Oct. 1997, in FBIS-SOV-97-302, 29 Oct. 1997.

acquire ballistic missile-related technologies in Russia and provided some information on these efforts to US counterparts during the discussions led by Ambassador Wisner.[91]

To summarize, the public information is insufficient to establish which, if any, missile-related technology transfers have occurred between Russia and Iran. The Russian Government has undoubtedly taken significant steps to establish an effective national export control system, but there is evidence of weakness in that system. Cooperation between government agencies, between government and industry, and within industry all appear to fall short of international 'best practices'.

In January 1998 the Russian Government issued a new regulation that apparently introduced a 'catch-all' provision into Russia's national export control system for dual-use goods and technologies.[92]

During the cold war Turkey participated in the COCOM embargo on exports of strategic goods to state socialist countries.[93] In the 1990s significant changes were made in Turkey's national export control system, including the introduction of measures designed to enable Turkey to implement the provisions of the MTCR. The measures designed to implement the provisions of the MTCR in Turkey took effect on 19 March 1997.

The primary legal foundation of the Turkish national export control system is the Law on the Control of Private Industrial Enterprises Producing War Weapons, Vehicles, Equipment and Ammunition, Law no. 3763 of 1940. Under this law the Ministry of National Defence issues an annual notification in the *Official Gazette* setting out which goods and technologies require special permission prior to export from or transit through Turkey. In 1996 a direct reference to the MTCR control list was introduced in this notification.[94] Goods referred to in the annual notification cannot be exported without the prior permission of the Ministry of National Defence (MND).

In 1995 Turkey introduced a system of registration for exporters of controlled goods. In order to be eligible to export controlled goods it is necessary to belong to the Union of Exporters of Metals and Metallurgical Items (IMMIB), an association that is under the supervision of the Undersecretariat for Foreign Trade.[95] An exporter must have an export manifest validated by the IMMIB before controlled items can be transferred to a customer. If the IMMIB experts consider that the items fall under the MTCR Guidelines, the export is submitted to the relevant agency within the MND for approval

---

[91] *International Herald Tribune*, 9 Dec. 1997, pp. 1, 4; and Schweid, B., 'Russia promises to curb missile deals', URL <http://www.foxnews.com/news/newswires2/0116/n_ap_0116_15.sml>, version current on 16 Jan. 1998.

[92] 'Dual technologies under double control', Interview with Foreign Ministry spokesman Gennadiy Tarasov in *RIA Novosti Daily Review*, 10 Feb. 1998, URL <http://www.ria-novosti.com/products/dr/1998/02/10-002-1.htm>, version current on 9 Mar. 1998.

[93] COCOM was disbanded on 31 Mar. 1994.

[94] Notification no. 96/2, Regarding the goods the export of which are prohibited or subject to prior license, *Official Gazette*, no. 22515 (6 Jan. 1996). Information provided by the Embassy of Turkey in Stockholm, 16 Dec. 1997.

[95] Export Regime Decree no. 95/7623, 21 Dec. 1995. Information provided by the Embassy of Turkey in Stockholm, 16 Dec. 1997.

before the validation is given. The exporter is required to provide the Turkish customs authority with documents that confirm both the prior permission of the MND and the validation of the IMMIB in order for the goods to leave Turkey.

VI. European Union dual-use export controls

In 1995 the EU established an export control system based on Community legislation in the form of a Council Decision and a Council Regulation.[96] Responsibility for implementing the system and developing it further is divided between the Council of the European Union and the European Commission.

The Council of the European Union (usually known as the Council of Ministers) is where the member states legislate for the EU, set its political objectives, coordinate national policies and resolve differences between themselves and with other institutions. The European Commission is tasked with ensuring that EU legislation is applied by the member states and taking action if there is evidence of breaches of treaty obligations. The Commission also proposes new legislation for consideration by the member states.

There is legal ambiguity about how authority is allocated between the member states and the Commission. In two cases the European Court of Justice has ruled that dual-use goods fall within the scope of the common commercial policy of the EU as defined in Article 113 of the 1957 Treaty Establishing the European Economic Community (Treaty of Rome).[97] However, most aspects that have an impact on the system fall under a Joint Action taken in the framework of the Common Foreign and Security Policy—and are therefore outside the competence of EU institutions. As the necessary information and licensing procedures remain at the national level, in practice the export control system is controlled by the member states.

The security implications of the proliferation of dual-use goods and technology are discussed in an ad hoc group of the Council of Ministers, the Committee on Nonproliferation (CONOP), as part of its Common Foreign and Security Policy 'pillar'. The meetings focus on general policy preparation and information exchange. Non-proliferation is usually on the agenda at the regular high-level and expert meetings between the European Union and the USA.

---

[96] The legal basis for the system is formed by 2 documents: Council Regulation (EC) 3381/94 (note 57); and Council Decision of 19 Dec. 1994 on the joint action adopted by the Council on the basis of Article J.3 of the Treaty on European Union concerning the control of exports of dual-use goods, Decision 94/942/CFSP, *Official Journal of the European Communities*, L367/37, 31 Dec. 1994, as amended. The system is described in more detail in Anthony, Eckstein and Zanders (note 1), pp. 359–63.

[97] European Commission, 'Action plan for the defence-related industries', COM(97)583 final/ Annex II, 12 Nov. 1997, URL <http://europa.eu.int/en/comm/dgiii/publicat/aerospac/com583e.htm>, version current on 24 Feb. 1998. Article 113 could give the European Commission a far greater role in developing the dual-use export control system in that it calls for a policy based on 'uniform principles' (and makes specific reference to export policy in this context). This article also authorizes the Commission to open and conduct negotiations with states and international organizations on matters related to commercial policy.

Based on the first 18 months of operation of the export control system it seems unlikely that a common EU position on non-proliferation will emerge in the short term. Member states prefer to discuss these issues in the informal multilateral regimes described in this chapter (to which they all belong). Similarly, because member states can introduce recommendations and views on the modification of equipment lists in the other multilateral regimes, there is little incentive to develop an EU list different from those adopted elsewhere.

The EU system seems to have led to practical improvements in export control implementation. There will be some advantages to industry in having simplified procedures for obtaining a licence and managing their shipments of goods. The common acceptance of countries listed in Annex II of the Council Decision (destinations to which simplified export licensing procedures may be adopted) could lead to harmonized practices with regard to general licences (i.e., licences to make multiple shipments of a given product without the need for repeated applications to a national authority).

Eleven countries now appear to be using standard documentation for export licensing, which will ease the problem for customs authorities in recognizing valid licences at points of exit. The four remaining countries (Greece, Portugal, Spain and the United Kingdom) are also expected to adopt the standard documentation in time as they have no objection to the idea in principle.

Information exchange has been stimulated between member states both on a bilateral basis and by the use of a common communication system. Greater awareness of how other countries implement export controls could lead to a convergence around best practices as well as allow countries to build a more complete picture of potential proliferation risks.

Further steps

The European Commission may recommend new legislation because of the apparent failure of the current mechanism to evolve towards a genuine EU export control system. Among the proposals which could be included in such legislation might be: (*a*) harmonization of procedures and practices in issuing general licences; (*b*) extension of 'catch-all' provisions to transfers of dual-use goods to countries under a United Nations mandatory embargo; and (*c*) development of procedures that would require detailed discussion and explanation of a decision by an EU member state to export a controlled item to a state which had previously been denied a licence for the same item by another EU member state.

Appendix 9A. Nuclear Suppliers Group consultation and information exchange procedure guidelines

MEMORANDUM OF UNDERSTANDING ON IMPLEMENTATION OF 'DUAL-USE' GUIDELINES

Warsaw, 31 March–3 April 1992

The Governments subscribing to this Memorandum of Understanding (MOU) (hereinafter referred to as 'Subscribing Governments') intend to implement the Guidelines for Transfers of Nuclear-Related Dual-Use Equipment, Material and Related Technology and its accompanying Annex in accordance with their national legislation and relevant international commitments in the following manner:

Scope of application

1. The aforementioned Guidelines will be applied to each transfer of any item in the Annex. However, in the case of transfers to destinations within the jurisdiction or control of Subscribing Governments, it is a matter for the discretion of a Subscribing Government to determine the expedited export licensing measures to apply and whether to apply paragraph 5 of the Guidelines.

Further, in the case of transfers to destinations within the jurisdiction or control of other Governments agreed upon by Subscribing Governments through consultations:

(i) it is a matter for the discretion of a Subscribing Government to determine the particular export licensing measures to apply consistent with obtaining the information and, as appropriate, the assurance required by paragraph 5 of the Guidelines; and

(ii) paragraph 6 of the Guidelines may be implemented by a requirement that the recipient notify the supplier sufficiently in advance of a retransfer to a third country of any equipment, material, or related technology, identified in the Annex, or any replica thereof, to permit the supplier to communicate its views, as appropriate.

Consultations

2. The Government should consult with other Subscribing Governments through regular channels and through the convening of at least one annual meeting. These consultations should address such matters as:

(*a*) Information exchanges, as appropriate:
 (i) in pursuit of the Basic Principle and paragraphs 4 and 5 of the Guidelines;
 (ii) concerning decisions by Subscribing Governments not to authorize transfers of equipment, material or related technology;
 (iii) on measures taken to implement the Guidelines; and
 (iv) on proposed and authorized transfers, on a voluntary basis;

(*b*) Additional measures, as referred to in paragraph 7 of the Guidelines, as appropriate.

(*c*) Updating the Annex, as necessary.

Violations

3. In the event that one or more Subscribing Governments believes that there has been a serious violation of supplier–recipient understandings resulting from the application of the Guidelines, Subscribing Governments, as appropriate, should consult promptly through regular channels to discuss appropriate responses.

Decisions on transfers

4. (*a*) The Government should provide prompt notification to other Subscribing Governments of a decision it has made pursuant to the Guidelines not to authorize a transfer of equipment, material, or related technology identified in the Annex.

(*b*) The Government should not authorize a transfer of equipment, material, or related technology identified in the Annex which is essentially identical to a transfer which was not authorized by another Subscribing Government where this decision was notified pursuant to subparagraph (*a*), without consulting the Subscribing Government which provided the notice. After such consultations, the Government, in the event of its authorization of the transfer, should notify other Subscribing Governments of its authorization. Thereafter the restriction on transfers set forth in the first sentence of this subparagraph will no longer apply.

(*c*) Three years after the issuance of a notification of non-authorization, the Government which provided the notice should review the basis for that decision and advise the other Subscribing Governments of its conclusions through regular channels. If the conclusion is to confirm that the basis for the decision still obtains, the procedure outlined above in subparagraph 4(*b*) should apply once more. The conclusions called for in this subparagraph should also be reviewed at the meetings to be held pursuant to paragraph 2 above.

Commercial confidentiality

5. The Government should not take commercial advantage of information exchanged under this MOU and should strictly protect the commercial confidentiality of such information.

Subscribing Governments

6. (*a*) Those governments that exchange notes of acceptance of this MOU and both the Guidelines and the Annex on [DATE TO BE DETERMINED IN WARSAW MEETING] are thereafter Subscribing Governments.

(*b*) Subsequently, upon the unanimous consent of all existing Subscribing Governments, any other government becomes a Subscribing Government based on an exchange of notes of acceptance of this MOU and both the Guidelines and the Annex with all existing Subscribing Governments.

Concluding provision

7. Any changes to the Guidelines, Annex, or the MOU require the unanimous consent of the Subscribing Governments.

Source: Document supplied by the Nuclear Suppliers Group. It is available at Stockholm International Peace Research Institute, 'Memorandum of understanding', URL <http://www.sipri.se/projects/armstrade/NSG_MOU.html>, version current on 15 Dec. 1997.

10. Nuclear arms control

SHANNON KILE*

I. Introduction

In 1997 efforts to advance the nuclear arms control and non-proliferation agenda yielded mixed results. The year ended with key pieces of 'unfinished business' remaining unfinished. The landmark Comprehensive Nuclear Test-Ban Treaty (CTBT), which had been adopted overwhelmingly in the United Nations General Assembly in 1996, remained in limbo as proponents struggled to win the ratifications of the 44 states needed to bring it into force. The Conference on Disarmament (CD) had yet to form a committee to negotiate a global convention banning the production of fissile material for nuclear explosives. One of the keystones of US–Russian nuclear arms control endeavours, the 1993 Treaty on Further Reduction and Limitation of Strategic Offensive Arms (START II Treaty), remained unratified by the Russian Federal Assembly (Parliament), despite a political agreement reached in March between US President Bill Clinton and Russian President Boris Yeltsin on a set of measures to improve the treaty's prospects of ratification.

There were also positive developments in nuclear arms control during the year. In the USA and across the former Soviet Union, the large-scale dismantlement of strategic nuclear weapons and associated infrastructure proceeded ahead of the interim deadlines set out in the 1991 Treaty on the Reduction and Limitation of Strategic Offensive Arms (START I Treaty). The impasse in the negotiations between Russia and the USA over a US proposal to clarify the scope of the 1972 Anti-Ballistic Missile Treaty (ABM Treaty) was formally resolved when the two sides reached agreement on the demarcation between strategic and theatre (non-strategic) missile defence systems, although some arms control advocates warned that the permissive terms of the agreement will undermine the ABM Treaty and actually impede progress in nuclear arms control. In addition, Clinton and Yeltsin agreed on the outline of a START III accord that could bring about further reductions in the Russian and US nuclear arsenals and make those cuts permanent and irreversible.

This chapter reviews the principal developments in nuclear arms control and non-proliferation in 1997. Section II highlights the progress made by the five parties to START I in eliminating strategic nuclear weapons and associated infrastructure. It focuses on the stalled START II ratification proceedings in the State Duma (the lower house of the Federal Assembly) and describes the Clinton–Yeltsin agreement on a package of treaty amendments and follow-on measures aimed at addressing Russian deputies' objections to that treaty.

---

* Data for figure 10.1 were provided by Robert S. Norris and William M. Arkin.

SIPRI Yearbook 1998: Armaments, Disarmament and International Security

Section III summarizes the long-running controversy over US theatre missile defence (TMD) programmes and examines the demarcation agreement. Section IV reviews the principal denuclearization activities under way in the former Soviet republics supported by the US-funded Cooperative Threat Reduction (CTR) programme and describes Russia's agreement to convert three nuclear reactors so that they can no longer produce plutonium for use in weapons. Section V examines the status of multilateral nuclear arms control and disarmament initiatives, highlighting developments related to the CTBT, and section VI presents the conclusions.

Appendix 10A presents data on the nuclear forces of the five declared nuclear weapon states. Appendix 10B analyses the nuclear weapon-free zones established in Africa and South-East Asia and assesses their contribution to the global nuclear non-proliferation regime.

II. The START treaties

Implementation of the START I Treaty

The START I Treaty was signed by the USA and the USSR in 1991 after nearly 10 years of negotiations.[1] Ratification and implementation of the treaty were complicated by the dissolution of the Soviet Union, which resulted in the creation of 15 new states, four of which—Belarus, Kazakhstan, Russia and Ukraine—had former Soviet strategic nuclear weapons based on their territories. On 23 May 1992 the foreign ministers of Belarus, Kazakhstan, Russia, Ukraine and the USA signed the Lisbon Protocol, which made these five states parties to START I.[2] The treaty's future was cast into doubt by the Ukrainian Parliament's attachment of a set of conditions to its resolution of ratification. Following a period of intense high-level diplomatic bargaining, START I entered into force on 5 December 1994.[3]

Under START I, Russia and the USA have undertaken to make phased reductions in their strategic offensive nuclear forces over a seven-year period, with interim limits on strategic nuclear delivery vehicles (SNDVs) and accountable warheads to be reached within three and five years, respectively, after the treaty's entry into force (table 10.1). In accordance with their denuclearization commitments made in the Lisbon Protocol and associated

---

[1] For a description of the provisions of the START I Treaty, see Cowen Karp, R., 'The START Treaty and nuclear arms control', *SIPRI Yearbook 1992: World Armaments and Disarmament* (Oxford University Press: Oxford, 1992), pp. 13–26; excerpts from the treaty and related documents are reproduced in appendix 1A, pp. 38–63. For a summary of the provisions and the list of parties, see annexe A in this volume.

[2] Excerpts from the text of the Lisbon Protocol are reproduced in *SIPRI Yearbook 1993: World Armaments and Disarmament* (Oxford University Press: Oxford, 1993), appendix 11A, pp. 574–75. The leaders of the 3 non-Russian former Soviet republics committed their respective countries to accede to the 1968 Non-Proliferation Treaty (NPT) as non-nuclear weapon states 'in the shortest possible time'. In accompanying letters to US President George Bush they also pledged to eliminate all the nuclear weapons based on their territories within 7 years of the START I Treaty's entry into force.

[3] For more detail on the developments clearing the way for the START I Treaty's entry into force, see Goodby, J., Kile, S. and Müller, H., 'Nuclear arms control', *SIPRI Yearbook 1995: Armaments, Disarmament and International Security* (Oxford University Press: Oxford, 1995), pp. 636–39.

Table 10.1. START I limits in 1997, 1999 and 2001[a]

Category	Phase I limits 5 Dec. 1997	Phase II limits 5 Dec. 1999	Final limits 5 Dec. 2001
Strategic nuclear delivery vehicles (SNDVs)[b]	2 100	1 900	1 600
Total treaty-accountable warheads	9 150	7 950	6 000
ICBM and SLBM warheads	8 050	6 750	4 900

[a] These ceilings applied equally to the USA and the Soviet Union as the signatories of the START I Treaty. The USSR's obligations were assumed by Russia as its legal successor state and later by Belarus, Kazakhstan and Ukraine. Only Russia will retain SNDVs and nuclear warheads at the end of the 7-year implementation period on 5 Dec. 2001.

[b] Deployed ICBMs and their associated launchers, deployed SLBMs and their associated launchers and deployed heavy bombers.

Source: START I Treaty.

documents, Belarus, Kazakhstan and Ukraine agreed not to retain any of the strategic nuclear arms based on their territories. At the end of the START I implementation period on 5 December 2001, Russia and the USA may deploy no more than 1600 SNDVs and 6000 treaty-accountable nuclear warheads each, of which no more than 4900 may be deployed on intercontinental ballistic missiles (ICBMs) and submarine-launched ballistic missiles (SLBMs). The treaty also places limits on inventories of mobile and heavy ICBMs and on aggregate ballistic missile throw-weight.

In 1997 Russia and the USA continued to proceed ahead of schedule in implementing the reductions in launchers and accountable warheads mandated by the treaty (table 10.2).[4] The USA had already deactivated all the land-based missile launchers it plans to eliminate under the treaty, and all the B-52 heavy bombers scheduled for dismantlement had been retired to a central elimination facility at Davis–Monthan Air Force Base, Arizona.[5] By the end of 1997 the USA had met the final limit on deployed missile launchers and heavy bombers and was very close to meeting the Phase II limit on total accountable warheads that comes into effect in December 1999.

Russia also continued to proceed ahead of schedule with the elimination or conversion of its strategic nuclear weapons. The sharp decline in the number of Russian delivery systems in part reflected the fact that older weapon systems were not being replaced with new systems, as envisioned in the modernization plans for the Soviet strategic forces at the time of the signing of the START I Treaty.[6] By January 1998 the Russian strategic forces (together with the former Soviet heavy bombers and ICBMs remaining in Ukraine) were

---

[4] With the START I Treaty's entry into force in Dec. 1994, the parties are required to update every 6 months the Sep. 1990 START Memorandum of Understanding data on the number, type and location of the strategic nuclear weapons on their territories.

[5] The missiles were deactivated by removing the nuclear warheads from the launch vehicles. The deactivated missiles remain START-accountable, however, until they have been destroyed in accordance with the procedures specified in the START Protocol on Conversion or Elimination.

[6] Sokov, N., *Russia's Approach to Deep Reductions of Nuclear Weapons: Opportunities and Problems*, Occasional Paper no. 27 (Henry L. Stimson Center: Washington, DC, June 1996), pp. 18–19.

Table 10.2. START I aggregate numbers of strategic nuclear delivery vehicles and accountable warheads, 1 January 1998[a]

Category	Belarus	Kazakhstan	Russia	Ukraine[b]	Ex-Soviet total	USA
Deployed SNDVs	0	0	1 484	110	1 594	1 486
Total treaty-accountable warheads	0	0	6 680	932	7 612	7 986
ICBM and SLBM warheads	0	0	6 110	580	6 690	6 205

[a] The numbers given in this table are in accordance with the START I Treaty counting rules and include delivery vehicles which have been deactivated; the estimates of the number of operational systems in figure 10.1 and appendix 10A are smaller.

[b] The transfer of strategic nuclear warheads from Ukraine to Russia was completed in May 1996. The warheads remain START-accountable until their associated delivery vehicles have been eliminated.

Source: START I Treaty Memorandum of Understanding, 1 Jan. 1998.

under the Phase II limit on total warheads and were also under the final limit on SNDVs.

The START I Treaty proved instrumental in settling the fate of the former Soviet strategic nuclear arsenal in Belarus, Kazakhstan and Ukraine. With the dissolution of the USSR these new states had inherited over 3400 strategic nuclear warheads carried on ICBMs and long-range heavy bombers based on their territories, although operational control over the weapons remained in Moscow's hands. A key concern in the international community, particularly in the United States, was to preserve a centralized command and control system for the post-Soviet strategic nuclear forces and to ensure their security and custodial safety. Within the START I framework, the Lisbon Protocol provided the basis for consolidating Soviet nuclear warheads in Russia and for eliminating the delivery vehicles and associated infrastructure in Belarus, Kazakhstan and Ukraine.[7] The removal to Russia of all strategic nuclear warheads from Kazakhstan was completed in April 1995, from Ukraine in May 1996 and from Belarus in November 1996.[8] The completion of the transfers, which left Russia as the sole nuclear weapon state on the territory of the former Soviet Union, was a milestone in the handling of the Soviet nuclear weapon legacy and provided a boost for global nuclear non-proliferation efforts.

In 1997 Ukraine made some progress in eliminating the former Soviet ICBM launchers based on its territory.[9] By 1 July, in accordance with the

---

[7] In addition, the presidents of Russia, Ukraine and the USA signed a Trilateral Statement in Jan. 1994, which helped to pave the way for Ukraine to fulfil its pledge to eliminate former Soviet nuclear weapons from its territory. The Trilateral Statement is reproduced in *SIPRI Yearbook 1994* (Oxford University Press: Oxford, 1994), pp. 677–78.

[8] The transfer from Ukraine to Russia of c. 2500 former Soviet tactical nuclear warheads was completed in May 1992.

[9] Although all nuclear warheads have been transferred to Russia, under START counting rules the ICBMs and heavy bombers based in Ukraine are assumed to carry attributed force loadings until they have been destroyed.

START rules, Ukraine had destroyed 66 of 130 SS-19 ICBMs but none of the 46 SS-24 ICBMs. Russian officials have complained about the slow pace of nuclear weapon destruction in Ukraine and expressed concern about calls from certain Ukrainian parliamentarians to retain some delivery vehicles and silos.[10] In May 1997 US Secretary of Defense William Cohen and Ukrainian Minister of Defence Olexander Kuzmuk signed an agreement under which the USA will provide additional assistance, worth $47 million, to help Ukraine to complete destruction of the remaining SS-19 ICBMs and silos and to begin eliminating the SS-24 ICBMs based in silos at Pervomaysk.[11] The funding, provided under the CTR programme, was additional to the $404 million in assistance that the USA had already committed to Ukraine (see section IV).

The fate of the 44 START-accountable former Soviet heavy bombers (19 Tu-160 'Blackjack' and 24 Tu-95MS 'Bear' aircraft) based at Priluki and Uzin in Ukraine remained unclear. Russian and Ukrainian negotiators had reached an agreement in November 1995 under which the bombers would be returned to Russia in exchange for a reduction in Ukraine's energy debt to Russia. However, this deal was still in limbo at the end of 1997, and some observers speculate that the prospects for its implementation are doubtful.[12] The aircraft, particularly the Blackjack bombers, reportedly have seriously deteriorated and are not expected to return to service.

Compliance with START I provisions

The START I Treaty establishes a complex and intrusive verification regime for monitoring the parties' compliance with the provisions of the agreement; the regime will also apply to START II, except where it has been specifically modified (e.g., to take into account differences in bomber counting rules). In addition to relying on national technical means of verification, the START regime follows the trend set in recent arms control agreements in emphasizing cooperative verification measures. These measures include the exchange of data on relevant weapon inventories and the distribution of telemetry tapes following missile flight-tests. The verification regime also provides for 12 types of on-site inspection (OSI). The START I Treaty set up a Joint Compliance and Inspection Commission (JCIC) as the forum in which the parties can resolve compliance questions, clarify ambiguities and discuss ways to facilitate implementation of the treaty.

The encouraging progress made towards reaching the START I force limits has been accompanied by a relative lack of controversy over the parties' treaty compliance behaviour. A dispute in 1995 between Russia and the USA over Russia's conversion of SS-25 ICBMs for space-launch purposes was resolved

---

[10] Obolensky, G., 'Russia forced to take responsibility', *Krasnaya Zvezda*, 5 Sep. 1996, p. 3, in Foreign Broadcast Information Service, *Daily Report–Central Eurasia (FBIS–SOV)*, FBIS-SOV-96-176, 10 Sep. 1996, p. 5.

[11] Reuters, 'US provides more nuclear funds', 1 May 1997, URL <http://www.yahoo.com/headlines/970501/International/storics/ukraine_1.html>, version current on 2 May 1997.

[12] Butowski, P., 'Russia's air forces face up to their dilemmas: part one', *Jane's Intelligence Review*, vol. 9, no. 10 (Oct. 1997), p. 451.

in the JCIC with an agreement that space-launch vehicles derived from missiles limited by START I would remain subject to the restrictions of the treaty.[13] Following the conclusion of the 15th session of the JCIC in June 1997, US officials reported that the five parties had agreed to reduce the area of installations and sensitive facilities to be inspected; in addition, a number of sites in the USA and in the former Soviet Union were removed from the inspection list following close-out (concluding) inspections.[14] The former Soviet republics have suggested that START's extensive OSI requirements be eased in order to reduce the costs of implementing the treaty.

The START II Treaty

The START II Treaty was signed by the USA and the USSR in 1993. Under the original terms of the treaty, the signatories committed themselves to reduce their strategic nuclear forces in two phases: the first phase runs simultaneously with the START I Treaty's seven-year implementation period, which ends on 5 December 2001; and the second phase will end on 1 January 2003, by which date the two parties may not deploy more than 3500 strategic nuclear warheads each.[15] However, on 26 September 1997, in New York, the Russian and US foreign ministers signed a Protocol to the START II Treaty which will extend this implementation timetable, contingent upon the approval of the legislatures of both countries (see below). In addition to lowering force levels, the treaty also bans all land-based strategic ballistic missiles carrying multiple independently targetable re-entry vehicles (MIRVs). This ban, which represents a key arms control breakthrough and forms the core of the treaty, will rid the Russian and US nuclear arsenals of what many experts consider to be their most destabilizing weapons.

The fate of the START II Treaty continued to be uncertain in 1997. In the US Senate, the treaty had encountered little organized opposition and won overwhelming endorsement in January 1996.[16] In Russia, however, START II faced significant opposition on budgetary and technical grounds even before

---

[13] The agreement reportedly allows Russia to sell space-launch services to other countries, but Russia must maintain ownership and control over the converted missiles. Woolf, A., *Strategic Arms Reduction Treaties (START I & II): Verification and Compliance Issues,* Congressional Research Service (CRS) Issue Brief, 22 Nov. 1996, URL <http://www.fas.org/spp/starwars/crs/91-139.htm>, version current on 9 Oct. 1997.

[14] 'Joint statement on compliance as to strategic weapons', *European Wireless File* (United States Information Service, US Embassy: Stockholm, 17 June 1997), URL <http://www.usis.usemb.se/wireless/200/eur210.htm>, version current on 18 June 1997. Although all nuclear warheads have been withdrawn from Belarus, Kazakhstan and Ukraine, inspections will continue to be carried out in these countries.

[15] This ceiling represents c. one-third of the size of the US and Soviet strategic nuclear arsenals before the signing of START I in 1991. For a description of the provisions of the START II Treaty, see Lockwood, D., 'Nuclear arms control', *SIPRI Yearbook 1993* (note 2), pp. 554–59.

[16] Kile, S., 'Nuclear arms control', *SIPRI Yearbook 1997: Armaments, Disarmament and International Security* (Oxford University Press: Oxford, 1997), p. 371. The US Senate's resolution of ratification contained 8 binding conditions, including 1 stipulating that if START II is not ratified by Russia the US President must consult the Senate prior to undertaking to reduce US strategic nuclear forces below START I levels.

its submission to the Duma for ratification by President Yeltsin in June 1995.[17] Hostility to the treaty intensified as the ratification issue became linked to the wider security policy controversies over US ballistic missile defence (BMD) programmes and NATO enlargement, which were generating strains in Russia's relations with the USA. NATO's proposal to invite former Warsaw Treaty Organization member states in Central and Eastern Europe to open membership accession talks has provoked a particularly fierce backlash against START II; in the view of many parliamentarians, it has transformed the ratification vote from an arms control debate into a high-stakes political conflict involving Russia's fundamental national security interests.[18] In addition, the treaty has to some extent become hostage to the vicissitudes of domestic politics—a situation which prompted Vladimir Lukin, chairman of the Duma Foreign Affairs Committee, to warn that such an important document should not become 'a ball in the game played by various forces'.[19] As 1997 ended, START II ratification remained a relatively low priority for a parliamentary leadership preoccupied with pressing domestic issues, and the treaty continued to languish in multiple committees in the Duma.[20]

The Helsinki initiatives

Against the background of hardening opposition in the Duma to START II ratification, presidents Clinton and Yeltsin held a summit meeting in Helsinki on 20–21 March 1997. Two issues dominated the agenda: (*a*) the acrimonious dispute over NATO enlargement, which the two leaders sought to defuse by finding a formula for a cooperative Russia–NATO relationship that would reassure Russia that its security concerns were being taken into account;[21] and (*b*) the uncertain future of the START II Treaty and prospects for further bilateral nuclear arms control cooperation. In reaffirming their governments' commitment to take 'concrete steps to reduce nuclear danger and to strengthen strategic stability and nuclear security', Clinton and Yeltsin agreed on a package of amendments to the terms of START II and to follow-on arms control

---

[17] Under the provisions of the 1993 Russian Constitution, treaty ratification requires a simple majority vote in both the lower (State Duma) and upper (Federation Council) houses of the Federal Assembly (Parliament). Some observers believe that the Federation Council is likely to defer to the deliberations of the Duma with regard to START II. Woolf, A., *START II in the Russian Duma: Issues and Prospects*, CRS Report 97-359F (Library of Congress, Congressional Research Service: Washington, DC, 14 Mar. 1997), p. 1; and Lepingwell, J., 'START II and the politics of arms control in Russia', *International Security*, vol. 20, no. 2 (fall 1995), p. 78.

[18] The Communist Party (which emerged after the 1995 parliamentary elections as the largest single party in the Duma with 157 seats out of 450) and other parties allied with the Communists have taken an increasingly negative position on START II ratification in the light of NATO's enlargement plans. Interfax (Moscow), 15 Feb. 1997, in 'Opposition to block START ratification if NATO expands', FBIS-SOV-97-032, 15 Feb. 1997; and Interfax (Moscow), 7 Jan. 1997, in 'Duma committee chairmen opposed to ratification of START-2 Treaty', FBIS-SOV-97-005, 7 Jan. 1997.

[19] ITAR-TASS (Moscow), 17 Dec. 1997, in 'State Duma to debate START 2 Treaty soon', FBIS-SOV-97-351, 17 Dec. 1997.

[20] Hoffman, D., 'START II approval imperiled, Russian says', *Washington Post*, 7 Dec. 1997, p. A34. Within the Duma, the International Affairs Committee and the Defence Committee are the principal parliamentary committees responsible for considering the treaty. The Security Committee and Geopolitics Committee are also actively involved in the ratification proceedings.

[21] See chapter 5 in this volume.

measures aimed at encouraging the Duma to ratify the long-stalled treaty.[22] They issued a draft START II Protocol, spelling out a number of proposed amendments to those treaty provisions which had raised the greatest concern among Russian parliamentarians and defence officials. In a separate joint statement, the two presidents sought to resolve the impasse in US–Russian negotiations to clarify the ABM Treaty by issuing guidelines for a demarcation between strategic missile defence systems (which are sharply limited by the provisions of the ABM Treaty) and TMD systems (which are not constrained by the treaty). They also reached agreement in principle on the outline of a START III treaty which would mandate still deeper cuts in nuclear arms and establish a new set of nuclear transparency and confidence-building measures (CBMs).

The presidential commitments made in Helsinki were codified in two sets of legal agreements which were signed in New York on 26 September 1997. The first set, signed by US Secretary of State Madeleine Albright and Russian Foreign Minister Yevgeniy Primakov, consisted of a Protocol to the START II Treaty and several associated documents detailing proposed amendments to the terms of the treaty. The second set, signed by the foreign ministers of Belarus, Kazakhstan and Ukraine as well as by Primakov and Albright, consisted of four agreements relating to the ABM Treaty (see section III). Significantly, both sets of agreements must be submitted for ratification or approval by the signatories 'in accordance with the constitutional procedures of each state'.[23] This has led some arms control advocates to express concern that the agreements will become embroiled in domestic political controversy and may ultimately founder.[24]

The START II Protocol

The Protocol to the START II Treaty codified the Helsinki summit meeting agreement to extend the treaty's deadline for final reductions. This amendment is aimed at meeting objections in Russia that the START II implementation timetable is financially not feasible given the poor condition of the Russian economy. The Protocol, when ratified by Russia and the USA, will extend the date by which the final START II reductions must be completed from 1 January 2003 to 31 December 2007; it will also extend the interim reduction deadline from 5 December 2001 (i.e., seven years after the entry into force of the START I Treaty) to 31 December 2004.[25]

Proponents of the treaty argue that extending its interim and final reduction deadlines will give Russia several important benefits. First, it will enable plan-

---

[22] Joint Statement on Parameters of Future Reductions in Nuclear Forces, The White House, Office of the Press Secretary, 21 Mar. 1997.

[23] 'State Department on signing of two arms control accords', *Washington File* (United States Information Service, US Embassy: Stockholm, 26 Sep. 1997), URL <http://www.usisusemb.se/wireless/500/eur503.htm>, version current on 30 Sep. 1997.

[24] See, e.g., Keeny, S., 'Helsinki: a pyrrhic victory?', *Arms Control Today*, vol. 27, no. 1 (Mar. 1997), p. 2.

[25] The deadline for completing reductions originally specified in START II—1 Jan. 2003—was predicated on the assumption that the accord would enter into force in 1993, the year in which it was signed.

ners in Moscow to spread over additional years the financial burden connected with safely eliminating large numbers of missiles and destroying or converting their silos. Second, the decommissioning of the MIRVed land-based missiles, particularly the SS-18 heavy ICBMs which constitute the backbone of the Russian Strategic Rocket Forces (SRF), will then coincide with the end of their useful service lives. This will give Russia more time to manufacture and deploy new single-warhead ICBMs in order to maintain a rough numerical parity with the USA's strategic nuclear forces—a goal that has acquired great symbolic significance in the Russian domestic debate. In the view of many politicians and editorial writers, nuclear equality with the USA is Russia's sole remaining claim to superpower status and guarantees that the USA will continue to treat Russia with respect.[26] Finally, proponents argue that the proposed delay will give Russia a 'political breathing space' lasting up to a full decade in which to assess the consequences of NATO enlargement and to monitor ABM Treaty developments.[27]

Accompanying the START II Protocol was an exchange of letters between Albright and Primakov on the early deactivation of SNDVs. The letters codified the presidential commitment made at Helsinki to deactivate by 31 December 2003 all missiles slated for elimination, either by removing their re-entry vehicles or by 'taking other jointly agreed steps'.[28] The agreement on early deactivation was seen by many observers as being essential for securing the US Senate's approval of the proposed extension of the START II implementation deadline; that body was considered unlikely to approve an extension that would allow Russia to continue to deploy operational MIRVed ICBMs for an additional five years. However, Russian military officials have previously objected to deactivation measures requiring the removal of warheads from missiles on the grounds that Russia already lacks adequate secure storage space for its burgeoning stockpile of nuclear warheads resulting from START I and unilateral force reductions.[29] A number of proposals for deactivating missiles are under consideration, including disabling silo lid-opening mechanisms, dismounting missile nose-cones, inserting metal pins into rocket engine firing-switches and removing guidance system power supplies.[30]

---

[26] Arbatov, A., 'Eurasian letter: a Russian–US security agenda', *Foreign Policy*, no. 104 (fall 1996), p. 109. Among Russian military planners, the predominant view is that aggregate force numbers provide only a very approximate estimate of the strategic balance and that strict numerical parity is not necessary to ensure a robust retaliatory capability. Sokov, N., 'Russia's approach to nuclear weapons', *Washington Quarterly*, vol. 20, no. 3 (summer 1997), pp. 111–12.

[27] Giacomo, C., 'US, Russia signs arms accords', Associated Press, 27 Sep. 1997.

[28] 'Fact Sheet on START II Protocol, Letters on Early Deactivation', *Washington File* (United States Information Service, US Embassy: Stockholm, 26 Sep. 1997), URL <http://www.usis.usemb.se/wireless/500/eur509.htm>, version current on 30 Sep. 1997.

[29] Jones, R. and Sokov, N., 'After Helsinki, the hard work', *Bulletin of the Atomic Scientists*, vol. 53, no. 4 (July/Aug. 1997), p. 28. Complaints have also been raised that Russia will be disproportionately affected by an ICBM deactivation agreement since a larger fraction of its strategic forces are made up of land-based missiles compared with those of the USA.

[30] Blair, B. *et al.*, 'Taking nuclear weapons off hair-trigger alert', *Scientific American*, vol. 277, no. 5 (Nov. 1997), pp. 74–80.

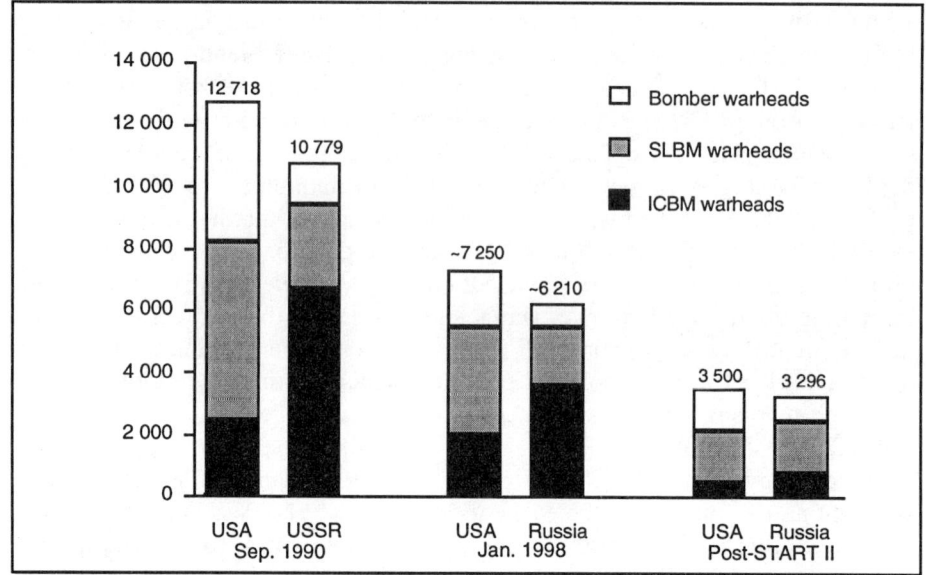

Figure 10.1. US and Soviet/Russian strategic nuclear forces: deployed warheads, 1990, 1998 and after implementation of the START II Treaty

Note: Figures for Jan. 1998 do not include warheads on strategic nuclear delivery systems which have been deactivated or retired, although they remain treaty-accountable according to the START counting rules.

Source: Data provided by Robert S. Norris, of the Natural Resources Defense Council (NRDC), and William M. Arkin.

Strategic nuclear forces, September 1990

US delivery vehicles

   ICBMs: 450 Minuteman II; 500 Minuteman III; 50 Peacekeeper (MX).
   SLBMs: 192 Poseidon (C-3); 384 Trident I (C-4); 96 Trident II (D-5).
   Bombers: 66 B-52G; 95 B-52H; 97 B-1B.

Russian delivery vehicles

   ICBMs: 326 SS-11; 40 SS-13; 188 SS-17; 308 SS-18; 300 SS-19; 56 SS-24 (silo-based); 33 SS-24 (rail-mobile); 288 SS-25 (road-mobile).
   SLBMs: 192 SS-N-6; 280 SS-N-8; 12 SS-N-17; 224 SS-N-18; 120 SS-N-20; 112 SS-N-23.
   Bombers: 17 Tu-95 Bear A/B; 46 Tu-95 Bear G; 57 Tu-95 Bear-H (equipped to carry 16 nuclear-armed cruise missiles each); 27 Tu-95 Bear-H (equipped to carry 6 nuclear-armed cruise missiles each); 15 Tu-160 Blackjack.

Current strategic nuclear forces, January 1998

US delivery vehicles

   ICBMs: 500 Minuteman III; 50 Peacekeeper (MX).
   SLBMs: 192 Trident I (C-4); 240 Trident II (D-5).
   Bombers: 71 B-52H; 21 B-2.

Russian delivery vehicles

ICBMs: 180 SS-18; 160 SS-19; 10 SS-24 (silo-based); 36 SS-24 (rail-mobile); 360 SS-25 (road-mobile).

SLBMs: 192 SS-N-18; 80 SS-N-20; 112 SS-N-23.

Bombers: 35 Tu-95 Bear-H16 (equipped to carry 16 nuclear-armed cruise missiles each); 29 Tu-95 Bear-H6 (equipped to carry 6 nuclear-armed cruise missiles each); 6 Tu-160 Blackjack.

Post-START II strategic nuclear forces, projected

US delivery vehicles

ICBMs: 450/500 Minuteman III downloaded to 1 warhead each.

SLBMs: 336 Trident II (D-5) downloaded to 5 warheads each.

Bombers: 32 B-52H (equipped to carry 20 air-launched cruise missiles, ALCMs/advanced cruise missiles, ACMs each); 30 B-52H (equipped to carry 12 ALCMs/ACMs each); 21 B-2.

Russian delivery vehicles

ICBMs: 605 SS-25 (road-mobile); 90 SS-25 (based in converted SS-18 silos); 105 SS-19 downloaded to 1 warhead each.

SLBMs: 176 SS-N-18; 120 SS-N-20 downloaded to 6 warheads each; 112 SS-N-23.

Bombers: 35 Tu-95 Bear-H (equipped to carry 16 nuclear cruise missiles each); 20 Tu-95 Bear-H (equipped to carry 6 nuclear cruise missiles each); 10 Tu-160 Blackjack.

Note: Assumptions for the Russian strategic forces after the implementation of the START II Treaty are increasingly untenable, given the serious shortfalls in defence spending and lack of investment to replace strategic nuclear delivery systems now reaching the end of their service lives. Some analysts suggest that the Russian strategic forces could easily decline to 1500–2000 deployed warheads, even without a START III accord.

Sources: For US forces: START I Treaty Memorandum of Understanding, 1 Sep. 1990; START I Treaty Memorandum of Understanding, 5 Dec. 1994; START I Treaty Memorandum of Understanding, 1 July 1995; START I Treaty Memorandum of Understanding, 1 Jan. 1996; START I Treaty Memorandum of Understanding, 1 July 1996; START I Treaty Memorandum of Understanding, 1 July 1997; Senate Committee on Foreign Relations, START II Treaty, Executive Report 104–10, 15 Dec. 1995; Cohen, W. S., Secretary of Defense, *Annual Report to the President and the Congress*, 1998, pp. 57–62; US Air Force Public Affairs, personal communications; and Natural Resources Defense Council (NRDC), 'Nuclear notebook', *Bulletin of the Atomic Scientists*; various issues; and authors' estimates.

For Russian forces: Arbatov, A. (ed.), *Implications of the START II Treaty for US–Russian Relations* (Henry L. Stimson Center: Washington, DC, 1993), p. 6; Sorokin, K. E., 'The nuclear strategy debate', *Orbis*, vol. 38, no. 1 (winter 1994), pp. 19–40; Statement of Ted Warner, Senior Defense Analyst, RAND Corporation, before the Senate Foreign Relations Committee, 3 Mar. 1992, as cited in *The START Treaty*, Senate Hearing 102–607, Part 1 (US Government Printing Office: Washington, DC, 1992), pp. 228–29; START I Treaty Memorandum of Understanding, Sep. 1990; Gromov, F., 'Reforming the Russian Navy', *Naval Forces*, vol. 14, no. 4 (1993), p. 10; US Office of Naval Intelligence, Director of Naval Intelligence Posture Statement (June 1994), p. 13; and authors' estimates.

Towards a START III treaty

In an effort to further boost the START II Treaty's prospects for ratification by the Duma, presidents Clinton and Yeltsin reached an agreement in principle at Helsinki on the framework of a START III treaty designed to address some of what Russian critics perceive to be the main shortcomings in START II.[31] The Helsinki understanding marked a retreat from the Clinton Administration's insistence that the USA would not discuss a follow-on accord until the Duma had ratified START II. US officials had previously discouraged discussion of proposals to move beyond the unratified treaty, fearing that key deals contained in START II (above all, the hard-won ban on MIRVed ICBMs) would come undone; they chose instead to emphasize that the benefits of the treaty outweighed its perceived shortcomings. The hostile reception accorded to then US Secretary of Defense William J. Perry when he appeared before the Duma in October 1996 to appeal for its approval of START II reportedly convinced Clinton that a new approach was needed to jump-start the stalled ratification process in Russia.[32]

As outlined at the Helsinki meeting, a START III accord would reduce aggregate levels of strategic nuclear warheads to between 2000 and 2500 for each of the parties. The implementation timetable would run simultaneously with the extended period for completing START II reductions, with final reductions to be made by 31 December 2007. The two presidents committed their governments to opening formal negotiations on the new accord immediately upon the entry into force of the START II Treaty.

The idea of linking START II ratification to a successor agreement further reducing Russian and US strategic nuclear forces has gained increasing favour in Russia. It is particularly appealing insofar as it offers a framework for addressing the treaty's allegedly inequitable impact on the structure of Russia's strategic forces. Critics have long complained that even under the reduced START II force ceilings the ban on MIRVed ICBMs, which comprise the largest and most powerful component of the Russian nuclear triad, will force Moscow to allocate scarce defence resources to build approximately 500 single-warhead SS-27 ICBMs (a follow-on to the SS-25 ICBM, designated the Topol M in Russia) if it intends to maintain rough numerical parity with the USA's strategic forces.[33] Treaty ratification proponents point out that the agreement between Clinton and Yeltsin to implement simultaneously the START II and the deeper START III reductions will greatly reduce the need for Russia to undertake an expensive interim build-up of single-warhead

---

[31] This approach has a precedent in the June 1992 US–Russian Joint Understanding on Further Substantial Reductions in Strategic Offensive Arms (the De-MIRVing Agreement), which formed the basis for START II; senior political officials reached an agreement in principle to ban land-based MIRVed missiles and then let technical specialists hammer out the details. Lockwood (note 15), p. 555.

[32] Jones and Sokov (note 29), p. 26.

[33] Some Russian opponents of START II argue that deploying a new generation of MIRVed ICBMs would be much more cost-effective than deploying single-warhead ICBMs, particularly in the light of the US Congress' strong interest in building a nationwide missile defence system. Surikov, A., 'START II ratification is inadvisable: Russia needs new missile instead of treaty', *Segodnya*, 5 Apr. 1996, p. 5, in FBIS-SOV-96-068, 8 Apr. 1996, pp. 15–17.

missiles in order to maintain parity under the START II ceilings. They also point out that large-scale reductions in Russia's strategic nuclear forces are unavoidable since the country cannot afford to replace the inventory of former Soviet missiles now reaching the end of their service lives.[34] A ceiling of 2000–2500 warheads will help Russia maintain numerical parity with the USA by requiring US reductions to force levels that Russia can afford to sustain as it eliminates ageing MIRVed ICBMs and older ballistic missile submarines.[35]

Dismantling nuclear warheads

In a potential, ground-breaking advance for nuclear arms control cooperation, Clinton and Yeltsin also agreed in Helsinki that START III would contain 'measures relating to the transparency of strategic nuclear warhead inventories and the destruction of strategic nuclear warheads'.[36] These measures are specifically aimed at allaying Russian concerns that the START II Treaty places the USA in a better position than Russia to stage a rapid 'break-out' from the treaty regime and achieve a strategically significant advantage in the number of deployed nuclear warheads.[37] In particular, a requirement to dismantle warheads removed from ballistic missiles in a transparent and verifiable manner will help to compensate for the absence in the START II Treaty of a rule requiring that a 'downloaded' missile (i.e., a missile from which one or more warheads have been removed to meet the START numerical limits) must be fitted with an entirely new 'bus', or front-end platform, able to hold only the smaller number of warheads.

More broadly, the establishment of a nuclear warhead dismantlement regime will 'lock in' US–Russian achievements in shrinking their strategic nuclear arsenals.[38] By making those cuts permanent and irreversible, such a regime will contribute to enhancing stability in times of high political tension by reducing the potential for a 'break-out' by one side. It would be particularly useful in this regard if numerical limits eventually were to be applied not only

---

[34] Gen. Igor Sergeyev, then Commander-in-Chief of the Russian SRF, warned in early 1997 that c. half of the missiles in the SRF had reached the end of their certified service lives. Interfax, 9 Mar. 1997, in 'Rocket troops commander supports ratifying START II', FBIS-SOV-97-068, 9 Mar. 1997.

[35] Litovkin, V., 'Who will stand to lose if the Duma does not ratify START II?', *Izvestiya*, 17 June 1997, in *RIA Novosti–Daily Review*, URL <http://www.ria-novosti.com/products/dr/199>, version current on 26 June 1997. Some leading US analysts believe that Russian strategic nuclear force levels, particularly for the submarine- and bomber-based legs of the nuclear 'triad', will probably decline precipitously over the next decade and may fall below 2000 deployed warheads, even without a START III treaty. Norris, S. and Arkin, W., 'Nuclear notebook: Russian strategic nuclear forces, end 1997', *Bulletin of the Atomic Scientists*, vol. 54, no. 2 (Mar./Apr. 1998), pp. 70–71.

[36] Joint Statement on Parameters of Future Reductions in Nuclear Forces (note 22).

[37] Russian critics complain that START II requires Russia to destroy the bulk of its MIRVed missiles—in particular, the 10-warhead SS-18 heavy ICBM—while the USA can 'download' and retain all its Minuteman III ICBMs and highly accurate Trident II SLBMs. See, e.g., Belous, V., 'What to do with nuclear warheads? No one has yet to ponder their destruction', *Nezavisimoye Voyennoye Obozreniye* (Moscow), 26 July–1 Aug. 1997, p. 5, in FBIS-SOV-97-161-S, 1 Aug. 1997.

[38] Some analysts have argued that a nuclear warhead dismantlement and transparency regime could reinforce the informal limitations on the tactical nuclear weapons currently in place and eventually form a verifiable and legally binding basis for controlling these weapons. Sokov, N., 'The advantages and pitfalls of non-negotiated arms reductions: the case of tactical nuclear weapons', *Disarmament Diplomacy*, no. 21 (Dec. 1997), pp. 6–10.

to operational nuclear warheads deployed on launchers but also to those held in storage, since the number of stored warheads figures more prominently in calculations of the strategic balance as the number of deployed nuclear warheads declines.[39]

However, if the experience of the recent past is any indication, proposals for building what might be called 'nuclear *glasnost*' face an uncertain future. Earlier bilateral negotiations on an ambitious US proposal to establish a nuclear warhead transparency regime were broken off by Russia in the autumn of 1995.[40] Russian officials, particularly those in the Ministry of Atomic Energy (Minatom), have shown little enthusiasm for confidence-building and transparency measures that involve sharing highly sensitive nuclear weapon design and stockpile data. In the light of Russian resistance to creating a transparency regime, US officials have been careful not to link progress in this area to the proposed START III force reductions.

The prospects for START II ratification

Although the agreements reached at Helsinki address the principal technical and economic criticisms of the START II Treaty raised in the Duma, it remains unclear whether they will tip the balance in favour of the treaty's ratification. The missile defence demarcation agreement promises to be a contentious political issue in Moscow; as 1997 ended, the government had not announced whether the demarcation agreement would be submitted to the Federal Assembly as a package with the START II Protocol. Furthermore, a number of issues were left unresolved at Helsinki, such as the method for deactivating delivery vehicles slated for elimination and the clarification of proposed CBMs related to tactical nuclear weapons and nuclear-armed sea-launched cruise missiles (SLCMs).[41] This has led to demands from some deputies for a legally binding elaboration of the START III framework to be presented to the Duma before START II is brought up for a vote. Parliamentary leaders have also expressed disquiet that the Helsinki deal requires the

---

[39] The START I and START II treaties do not require the dismantlement of nuclear warheads, nor do they limit the number of non-deployed warheads held in storage. According to the US DOD's 'lead but hedge' strategy set out in the 1994 Nuclear Posture Review, the USA will retain a reserve stockpile of nuclear warheads (reportedly *c.* 2500) in order to be able to rapidly reconstitute its strategic forces in the event of a 'reversal of reform' in Russia. Transcript of press conference remarks by Secretary of Defense William J. Perry, Office of Assistant Secretary of Defense for Public Affairs, News release no. 546-94, 22 Sep. 1994; and Hitchens, T., 'Study underestimates nuclear arsenal numbers, cost', *Defense News*, vol. 10, no. 29 (17–23 July 1995), p. 14.

[40] Bunn, M. and Holdren, J., 'Managing military uranium and plutonium in the United States and the former Soviet Union', *Annual Review of Energy and the Environment*, vol. 22 (1997), pp. 433–35. These talks were held in the Joint Working Group on Safeguards, Transparency and Irreversibility (ST&I), a forum created for negotiations to establish a new arms control regime covering US and Russian stockpiles of nuclear weapons and fissile materials. The measures being discussed were based on a comprehensive notion of transparency, in which a regular bilateral exchange of classified data on aggregate warhead and fissile material stockpiles would be linked with intrusive reciprocal monitoring and inspection arrangements. See also Kile, S. and Arnett, E., 'Nuclear arms control', *SIPRI Yearbook 1996: Armaments, Disarmament and International Security* (Oxford University Press: Oxford, 1996), p. 649.

[41] Clinton and Yeltsin called for the creation of a forum within the START III framework to discuss 'possible measures' related to tactical nuclear weapons and SLCMs, including confidence-building measures. Joint Statement on Parameters of Future Reductions in Nuclear Forces (note 22).

Duma to go first in taking action on START II and the amending protocol and TMD accords, before they are brought before the US Senate for action; Lukin has urged Congress to respond positively to calls for a dialogue on the issue, warning that Russian ratification will be possible only if the process is 'coordinated' between the two legislatures.[42]

Despite these concerns, the prospects for the START II Treaty in the Duma appeared somewhat brighter at the end of 1997 than when the year began. In addition to the Helsinki initiatives, several other developments seemed to boost the treaty's chances of ratification. First, the government of Prime Minister Viktor Chernomyrdin provided the Duma with a document drafted by the Ministry of Defence which analysed the impact of START II on the structure of Russia's strategic forces and its nuclear deterrent capabilities; this document had long been requested by deputies as a prerequisite for bringing the treaty up for a vote. Second, on 23 May General Igor Sergeyev, then the commander of the Russian Strategic Rocket Forces, was named to replace ousted General Igor Rodionov as the new Russian Defence Minister. Rodionov, who had been dismissed the previous day by Yeltsin ostensibly for his failure to carry out an overhaul of the Russian armed forces, had been a tepid public supporter of START II.[43] By contrast, Sergeyev has long been one of the treaty's most consistent champions and has taken the lead in urging its ratification;[44] his views are expected to carry considerable weight in the ratification debate, even among conservative circles in the Duma. Finally, the Chernomyrdin Government began to push with greater vigour for approval of the treaty as the initial domestic furore over the signing of the NATO–Russia Founding Act subsided.[45] On 15 September Sergeyev and Foreign Minister Primakov met the leaders of parliamentary factions to convince them that the ratification of START II was in Russia's national interest.[46] However, President Yeltsin, who had come under mounting criticism for having done little to rescue the floundering accord other than to offer rhetorical support for it at summit meetings, showed few signs of taking a more active role in pushing for the treaty.[47] Some START II proponents have argued that the treaty will be able to win the Duma's approval only if Yeltsin fully commits himself—and

---

[42] ITAR-TASS (note 19).
[43] Gertz, B., 'Russian defense chief stalls START', *Washington Times*, 13 May 1997, p. 6.
[44] Interfax (Moscow), 22 Sep. 1997, in 'Defence Minister Sergeev: START II Treaty must be ratified', in FBIS-SOV-97-265, 22 Sep. 1997.
[45] The NATO–Russia Founding Act was signed on 27 May 1997. The text of the Founding Act is reproduced in appendix 5A in this volume.
[46] Interfax (Moscow), 15 Sep. 1997, in 'Yeltsin supports ratifying START II Treaty', FBIS-SOV-97-258, 15 Sep. 1997. Following this meeting, however, Communist Party leader Gennadiy Zyuganov linked the treaty's approval to another controversial military issue, declaring that 'until the issue of reducing the general force is resolved, cutting nuclear arms cannot be debated'. Interfax, 16 Sep. 1997, in 'Russian minister, officer on discussions on START II', FBIS-SOV-97-259, 16 Sep. 1997.
[47] On 2 Dec. 1997, during an official visit to Sweden, Yeltsin made a surprise announcement that Russia would unilaterally reduce its nuclear arsenal by one-third. Presidential aides subsequently explained that Yeltsin was referring to previously proposed US–Russian joint reductions within the framework of a START III accord. Reuters, 'Kremlin moves to tone down Yeltsin nuke remark', 2 Dec. 1997; and Arbatov, A., 'The President's word and nuclear warheads', *Moskovskiye Novosti*, no. 49 (7–14 Dec. 1997), p. 5, in 'Aides urged to curb Yeltsin's arms "inflation"', FBIS-SOV-97-346, 12 Dec. 1997.

the considerable powers of the Russian presidency—to leading a vigorous ratification campaign.[48]

The START reductions and changes in US nuclear doctrine

In anticipation of the deeper cuts in strategic nuclear arsenals envisioned in the START III framework agreement, President Clinton approved in November 1997 new targeting guidelines for US nuclear weapons intended to pave the way for an arsenal limited to 2000–2500 warheads.[49] The top-secret Presidential Decision Directive (PDD) 60, which marked the first formal adjustment of the US Government's nuclear targeting policy since 1981, reportedly describes in a general manner the purposes that US nuclear weapons serve and provides broad guidance for military planners who prepare operational plans and target lists for the strategic nuclear forces. According to senior administration officials, the emphasis in the updated guidelines is on deterring the use of nuclear weapons; the previous, Reagan-era guidance for the US military to prepare to fight and win a protracted nuclear war has been dropped. The new directive confirms the judgement set out in the 1994 Nuclear Posture Review that the principal targets of US strategic nuclear weapons are other nuclear weapons and associated infrastructure (i.e., for so-called counterforce attacks), not cities and industrial centres. At the same time, it retains a long-standing policy allowing the USA to use nuclear weapons first in a conflict. It also leaves in place the 1978 declaratory policy of offering negative security assurances while retaining the current ambiguity over whether the USA would use nuclear weapons to retaliate against a chemical or biological weapon attack launched by a non-nuclear weapon state. This ambiguity has been strongly criticized by some arms control advocates as running contrary to the USA's commitments under the 1968 Non-Proliferation Treaty (NPT) as well as to broader efforts to devalue the role of nuclear weapons in conflict and to convince states that they do not need nuclear weapons; concern has also been raised that it may lead to the development of new types of nuclear weapon.[50] Administration officials have stressed, however, that the new directive does not mark a change in US nuclear policy on negative security assurances and the non-use of nuclear weapons or sanction an expansion of the role of nuclear weapons in military planning.[51]

---

[48] Hoffman, D., 'Why is Yeltsin not getting off to a new START?', *International Herald Tribune*, 29 May 1997, p. 5.

[49] Smith, R. J., 'Clinton orders changes in nuclear-war strategy', *International Herald Tribune*, 8 Dec. 1997, pp. 1, 10.

[50] Erlich, J., 'New US nuclear policy maintains ambiguity', *Defense News*, vol. 13, no. 1 (5–11 Jan. 1998), pp. 4, 19.

[51] Robert Bell, Senior Director for Defense and Arms Control Policy, National Security Council, and an architect of the new guidance, has explained that the USA reserves the right to use nuclear weapons first in a conflict if, among other circumstances, 'a state is not a state in good standing under the Non-Proliferation Treaty or equivalent international convention'. Cited in Cerniello, C., 'Clinton issues new guidelines on US nuclear weapons doctrine', *Arms Control Today*, vol. 27, no. 10 (Nov./Dec. 1997), p. 23.

Reducing alert rates

Although not on the formal START II or START III agendas, proposals for parallel unilateral measures aimed at reducing alert rates for strategic nuclear forces have attracted considerable interest as the political momentum towards deeper arms cuts builds up. These proposals, many of which involve steps similar to those for deactivating launchers, have gathered growing support as important CBMs for reducing nuclear weapon-related tensions between Russia and the USA. The overarching goal is to reduce the threat of the accidental or unauthorized use of nuclear weapons.[52] A number of prominent defence analysts and expert panels have called for urgent action to move Russian and US nuclear forces away from the hair-trigger postures of the cold war.[53] They point to reports of deficiencies in Russia's early-warning and nuclear command-and-control networks as clear evidence of the dangers of military planning still dominated by the fear of surprise attack and of the need to adjust the operational status of the thousands of nuclear weapons in Russia and the USA still primed for rapid launch.[54]

III. The ABM Treaty and ballistic missile defence

The debate over ballistic missile defences and the future of the ABM Treaty showed few signs of abating in 1997, despite the formal resolution of a protracted dispute between Russia and the USA over the permissibility under the ABM Treaty of advanced-capability TMD systems.[55] The demarcation guidelines agreed upon by Clinton and Yeltsin at the Helsinki summit meeting provided the basis for resolving the deadlock in negotiations on the issue in the Standing Consultative Commission (SCC).[56] However, the resulting demarcation agreement reached in the SCC in August did little to settle the political controversy about the future of missile defences and faces an uphill struggle to win the formal endorsement of the Russian and US legislatures. The Republican leadership in Congress continued to press the Clinton Administration to

[52] Russia and the USA have taken some modest parallel unilateral steps in this regard, including removing strategic bombers from alert and 'detargeting' ICBMs. Miller, S., 'Dismantling the edifice: strategic nuclear forces in the post-Soviet era', ed. C. Hermann, *American Defense Annual, 1994* (Lexington Books: New York, 1995), pp. 69–71.

[53] See, e.g., National Academy of Sciences, Committee on International Security and Arms Control, *The Future of US Nuclear Weapons Policy* (National Academy Press: Washington, DC, 1997); and Blair, B., *Global Zero Alert for Nuclear Forces*, Brookings Occasional Papers (Brookings Institution: Washington, DC, 1995).

[54] Blair *et al.* (note 30).

[55] The ABM Treaty was signed by the USA and the USSR on 26 May 1972 and entered into force in Oct. of that year. Amended in a protocol in 1974, the treaty obligates the parties not to undertake to build nationwide defence against strategic ballistic missile attack and sharply limits the development and deployment of permitted missile defences. Among other provisions, it prohibits the parties from giving air defence missiles, radars or launchers the technical ability to counter strategic ballistic missiles and from testing them in a strategic ABM mode. For the text of the ABM Treaty; the Agreed Statements, Common Understandings and Unilateral Statements; and the 1974 Protocol, see Stützle, W., Jasani, B. and Cowen, R., SIPRI, *The ABM Treaty: To Defend or Not to Defend?* (Oxford University Press: Oxford, 1987), pp. 207–13.

[56] Article XIII of the ABM Treaty provides for the establishment of the SCC as the forum for the parties to discuss treaty-related questions and to ensure its 'continuing viability and effectiveness'.

renegotiate—or to abandon outright—the ABM Treaty in order to proceed with developing and deploying a multi-site nationwide BMD system; these moves have been vigorously contested by Russia, which insists on the immutability of the treaty as a prerequisite for further nuclear arms control progress. The year ended with a growing chorus of complaints from arms control advocates that the way had been cleared for the USA's ambitious pursuit of new missile defences that threatened to eviscerate the ABM Treaty and undo progress in reducing nuclear armaments.

The ABM Treaty demarcation agreement

The controversy over theatre missile defences has been one of the thorniest disputes in US–Russian relations and has contributed to fostering an atmosphere of mistrust that has hindered arms control cooperation. The TMD issue appeared on the arms control agenda in November 1993 when the USA put forward a proposal in the SCC to clarify the ABM Treaty to permit the testing and deployment of a new generation of advanced-capability TMD systems.[57] The Clinton Administration argued that the new TMD systems are needed to protect US allies and troops operating overseas in future conflicts from adversaries who might be armed with long-range ballistic missiles.[58] However, its attempts to move ahead with developing the new systems while at the same time remaining in compliance with the ABM Treaty have elicited strong criticism from the Republican-controlled Congress for being unduly constrained by the treaty and strong criticism from Russia for exceeding what is permitted by the treaty.

Although concern about the emergence along the southern rim of the Russian Federation of potentially hostile states armed with ballistic missiles has sparked renewed interest in TMD in Moscow, Russian officials and defence experts approached the demarcation talks in the SCC primarily from the perspective of the US–Russian strategic nuclear balance. They expressed concern that some of the planned TMD systems which the USA wanted to exclude from the strict limitations imposed by the ABM Treaty would have considerable capabilities against Russian strategic ballistic missiles and would thereby undermine the stabilizing logic of mutual assured destruction codified in that treaty. Russian officials were also anxious to forestall an expensive arms race that the country could ill afford.

---

[57] TMD systems occupy a 'grey zone' and are not formally subject to the restrictions of the ABM Treaty, which limits only strategic ABM systems. However, the demarcation between strategic and theatre ballistic missiles is not clearly defined and the technical characteristics of defences against them overlap considerably. For a description of planned US TMD systems, see Arbatov, A., 'The ABM Treaty and theatre missile defence', *SIPRI Yearbook 1995* (note 3), pp. 681–717.

[58] Critics within the US policy-making and arms control communities have challenged the plausibility of the threat assessments upon which this argument is based, claiming that there is little to justify the most technologically advanced TMD systems currently under development. Cerniello, C., 'Panel uphold NIE assessment of ballistic missile threat to US', *Arms Control Today*, vol. 26, no. 10 (Jan./Feb. 1997), p. 22. For further discussion of the relationship between possible threats and US missile defence programmes, see chapter 7 in this volume.

In 1997 agreement on TMD demarcation was finally reached in the SCC. The demarcation talks had revolved around a series of proposals and counter-proposals for distinguishing between strategic and theatre missile defence systems; these were based largely on the technical and performance parameters of interceptor and target missiles. The goal was to establish a verifiable set of demarcation criteria that would permit the deployment of new theatre missile defences while preserving the ABM Treaty. A key point of contention was the insistence by Russian negotiators that a strict maximum speed limit be imposed on permitted TMD interceptor missiles in order to prevent them from having a significant 'inherent capability' against strategic ballistic missiles. A breakthrough was achieved in the SCC on the issue of lower-velocity TMD systems (i.e., systems with interceptor speeds below 3.0 kilometres per second) in the autumn of 1996.[59] However, a full demarcation agreement remained beyond reach until Clinton and Yeltsin issued guidelines to their respective countries' SCC commissioners for concluding an understanding on higher-velocity (above 3.0 kilometre/second) TMD systems. These guidelines were set out at the Helsinki summit meeting in the Joint Statement Concerning the Anti-Ballistic Missile Treaty. They built upon the principles contained in previous presidential agreed statements, including the commitment of both Russia and the USA to preserve the ABM Treaty as the 'cornerstone of strategic stability'.[60]

On the basis of the elements outlined in the Joint Statement, the SCC announced on 21 August that it had reached a formal agreement clarifying the demarcation line between strategic and theatre missile defence systems within the framework of the ABM Treaty.[61] The documents legally codifying the TMD demarcation agreement were signed by the foreign ministers of Belarus, Kazakhstan, Russia, Ukraine and the USA on 26 September at the ceremony in New York at which the START II Protocol was signed.[62] These consisted of: (*a*) a First Agreed Statement (Agreed Statement Relating to Lower-Velocity Theater Ballistic Missile Defense (TMD) Systems), in which lower-velocity TMD systems are defined as having interceptor missiles with maximum velocities below 3.0 km/s; (*b*) a Second Agreed Statement (Agreed Statement Relating to Higher-Velocity Theater Ballistic Missile Defense (TMD) Systems), in which higher-velocity TMD systems are defined those with interceptor missiles faster than 3.0 km/s; (*c*) an associated Confidence-

---

[59] This limit would permit all the new US TMD systems—including the Army's Theater High-Altitude Area Defense (THAAD) interceptor—currently under development, except for the Navy's Theater-Wide System. It would also permit Russia's new S-400 air defence system.

[60] Joint Statement Concerning the Anti-Ballistic Missile Treaty, The White House, Office of the Press Secretary, 21 Mar. 1997.

[61] 'Geneva negotiations conclude on ABM demarcation', *Washington File* (United States Information Service, US Embassy: Stockholm, 26 Sep. 1997), URL <http://www.usis.usemb.se/wireless/400/ eur403. htm>, version current on 26 Aug. 1997.

[62] At the 26 Sep. ceremony, the 5 foreign ministers signed a Memorandum of Understanding on Succession (MOUS) that formally designated Belarus, Kazakhstan, Russia and Ukraine as the USSR successor states. Pursuant to the MOUS, these states collectively assume the rights and obligations of the USSR under the ABM Treaty. This means *inter alia* that only a single ABM site is permitted among the 4 states.

Building Measures Agreement (CBMA); and (*d*) new regulations that will govern the multilateral operation of the SCC.

The Agreed Statements codify a permissive definition of TMD systems. The demarcation criteria are based on the performance parameters of the target missiles and not on those of the interceptor missiles. Specifically, the Agreed Statements declare that the land-, sea- and air-based components of both lower-velocity and higher-velocity TMD systems will be deemed compliant with the ABM Treaty if, during the testing of the TMD components or systems, the target missile does not exceed a velocity of 5.0 km/s or a range of 3500 km; only systems using space-based kill vehicles (which no country is now developing) are prohibited outright. Significantly, they do not impose a maximum limit on the speed of interceptor missiles. However, each party did issue non-legally binding unilateral statements associated with the Second Agreed Statement in which they reaffirmed that they had 'no plans' to develop TMD systems with interceptor missiles exceeding a velocity of 5.5 km/s for land- and air-based systems or with interceptor missiles exceeding a velocity of 4.5 km/s for sea-based systems. Higher-velocity TMD systems (i.e., those with interceptor speeds above 3.0 km/s) will not be tested against target missiles before 1999.[63] As two prominent missile defence analysts have pointed out, this means that TMD systems with considerable capabilities against strategic missiles (indeed, even systems designed for defence against strategic missiles) can be legally developed and deployed within the framework of the ABM Treaty as long as they are not tested against target missiles moving faster than 5 km/s.[64]

Assessment

The demarcation agreement essentially satisfies the US concern expressed in the SCC that specific performance limits on TMD should relate only to the target missiles being tested and not to the interceptor systems themselves.[65] Russian officials had insisted throughout the demarcation talks on imposing maximum speed limits on TMD interceptors as a way to limit the capabilities of non-strategic missile defence systems for intercepting strategic missiles. However, US officials, under intense congressional pressure not to agree to wording that would constrain current US missile defence programmes, managed to parry this demand. Indeed, the Second Agreed Statement imposes no meaningful limitations on planned US TMD systems; it clears the way for the US Navy to develop and deploy its controversial Theater-Wide (formerly referred to as Upper Tier) TMD system, which will have an interceptor missile

---

[63] 'Fact Sheet on Second Agreed Statement on ABM Treaty', *Washington File* (United States Information Service, US Embassy: Stockholm, 26 Sep. 1997), URL <http://www.usis.usemb.se/wireless/400/eur506.htm>, version current on 30 Aug. 1997. The parties also stated that they had no plans to test TMD systems against strategic ballistic target missiles or against MIRVed re-entry vehicles deployed on such missiles.

[64] Lewis, G. and Postol, T., 'Portrait of a bad idea', *Bulletin of the Atomic Scientists*, vol. 53, no. 4 (July/Aug. 1997), pp. 21–22.

[65] Mendelsohn, J. and Cerniello, C., 'The arms control agenda at the Helsinki summit', *Arms Control Today*, vol. 27, no. 1 (Mar. 1997), pp. 17–18.

with a velocity exceeding 3.0 km/s.⁶⁶ This system had already been certified by the USA as being in compliance with the ABM Treaty, as had all other US TMD programmes currently under development, despite the absence of a TMD demarcation agreement in the SCC.⁶⁷

The demarcation agreement is also notable for its lack of constraints on the characteristics of TMD target-acquisition and tracking systems. In particular, the Agreed Statements and associated documents do not prohibit or limit TMD systems from operating with tracking and guidance information (known as 'cueing' data) supplied by satellites and external sensors.⁶⁸ A ban on space-based sensors had been a Russian demand in the SCC negotiations and had been highlighted in a 1996 letter from Foreign Minister Primakov to then Secretary of State Warren Christopher listing Russia's guidelines for a demarcation deal on higher-velocity TMD systems.⁶⁹ Russian officials have been especially concerned that even a limited use of space-based cueing data will greatly expand the areas that can be defended by systems such as the US Army's Theater High-Altitude Area Defense (THAAD) interceptor and the US Navy's Theater-Wide interceptor.⁷⁰ This concern has been compounded by the fact that THAAD and the other advanced-capability TMD systems under development by the USA are mobile.⁷¹ Defence experts in Russia and the USA point out that in conjunction with a network of early-warning radars and satellites, such as the USA's Space and Missile Tracking System satellite (formerly known as Brilliant Eyes) which is scheduled to go into operation in the year 2004, these systems provide the foundation for a rapid US break-out from a theatre-defence technical base leading to the deployment of a nation-wide ABM system.⁷²

Reactions to the demarcation agreement

While formally ending the deadlock in the SCC, the signing of the demarcation agreement did little to still the debate over the future of missile defences and the ABM Treaty. The politically charged agreement also faced a difficult

---

⁶⁶ Also accompanying the Second Agreed Statement is a Joint Statement in which each party undertakes to update annually the status of its TMD plans. The USA has emphasized that nothing in the Joint Statement or in the Agreed Statements limits the rights of a party to change its plans.

⁶⁷ Prepared statement of Paul G. Kaminski, Under-Secretary of Defense for Acquisition and Technology, to the Military Research and Development Subcommittee, House National Security Committee, 6 Mar. 1997. The USA maintains that determining the compliance of particular TMD systems with the ABM Treaty is a national responsibility. Russian officials dispute that parties to the ABM Treaty can unilaterally decide the compliance of particular TMD systems with that treaty.

⁶⁸ 'Fact Sheet on Second Agreed Statement' (note 63).

⁶⁹ Excerpts from the letter are reproduced in Institute for Defense and Disarmament Studies (IDDS), *Arms Control Reporter* (IDDS: Brookline, Mass.), sheet 603.B.278, July 1996.

⁷⁰ Based on conservative assumptions about the quality of cueing data, one independent analysis has shown that if THAAD works as claimed against theatre-range ballistic missiles it will also be effective against strategic missiles. Gronlund, L. *et al.*, 'Highly capable theatre missile defences and the ABM Treaty', *Arms Control Today*, vol. 24, no. 3 (Apr. 1994), pp. 3–8.

⁷¹ Russian negotiators abandoned efforts to impose restrictions on the basing areas and deployment patterns of these systems.

⁷² Dyakov, A. *et al.*, 'ABM Treaty is still assessed as the basis of strategic stability, but agreements signed recently in New York practically destroy it', *Nezavisimoye Voyennoye Obozreniye* (Moscow), 3–9 Oct. 1997, pp. 1, 6, in FBIS-SOV-97-307, 3 Nov. 1997.

struggle to win the approval of the US and Russian legislatures, making it a potential 'show stopper' that could block progress towards deeper nuclear arms reductions.[73]

In the USA, the TMD controversy has been part of a broader domestic debate over the desirability of national missile defences and of continued adherence to the ABM Treaty. At the root of this debate is a doctrinal dispute over whether the ABM Treaty should still function as one of the cornerstones of the strategic balance in the post-cold war world. The demarcation agreement has come under fire from critics who are opposed to any approach that would shore up the ABM Treaty and constrain US BMD programmes; at the same time, it has been criticized by arms control advocates for undermining that treaty. Republican leaders in the US Congress were quick to denounce the demarcation criteria set out at Helsinki for hindering the development of effective missile defences to protect the population of the United States as well as US troops overseas.[74] They also complained about its prohibition on space-based interceptor systems and about the statement declaring that the USA has 'no plans' for TMD interceptors with speeds exceeding 5.5 km/s for land- or air-based systems or 4.5 km/s for sea-based systems.[75]

The demarcation agreement faces opposition in the Duma as well, where deputies have complained that Yeltsin gave away too much. They argue that his failure to secure explicit limitations on higher-velocity TMD interceptor speeds, on the number and areas of deployment of TMD systems and on external sensor support jeopardizes Russia's nuclear deterrent and effectively eviscerates the ABM Treaty. However, the demarcation accord has received the cautious support of Defence Minister Sergeyev, who emphasized at the same time the importance of strictly observing the ABM Treaty.[76] It has also received only muted criticism from senior Russian military officers, whose support for the accord will be crucial. It has been suggested that Yeltsin may believe that the USA's commitment to preserving the ABM Treaty, coupled with the extended START II implementation period, may be sufficient to persuade the Duma to accept the permissive definition of TMD systems contained in the accord. In turn, this could help persuade the Republican majority in the US Senate to abandon efforts to repudiate the ABM Treaty and deploy a multi-site national missile defence shield.[77]

The governments of the other three declared nuclear weapon states have reacted cautiously to the demarcation deal. France and the United Kingdom have been largely silent on the issue apart from stressing the importance of preserving the integrity of the ABM Treaty. Chinese officials have been more

---

[73] The Clinton Administration had agreed to submit a TMD demarcation deal to the Senate for its approval as part of a compromise aimed at winning ratification of the Chemical Weapons Convention.

[74] Joint Statement on Anti-Ballistic Missile Defence Agreement by the Hon. Newt Gingrich, Bob Livingston and Chris Cox, US House of Representatives, Speaker's Press Office, 23 Mar. 1997.

[75] Graham, B., 'Missile deal with Russia sharpens defense dispute', *International Herald Tribune*, 26 Mar. 1997, p. 5.

[76] Interfax, 5 Sep. 1997, in 'Russia favours strategic, tactical delimitation accords', FBIS-SOV-97-248, 5 Sep. 1997.

[77] Keeny (note 24).

vocal in expressing concern about the deployment of new advanced-capability US TMD systems as well about US moves towards developing a nationwide BMD network.[78] Although such defences are unlikely to be very effective against a large-scale attack with nuclear-armed long-range ballistic missiles, some analysts warn that the dictates of prudent military planning in these states may compel them to take compensatory measures, presumably by expanding and modernizing their nuclear arsenals.[79] These measures, which might require a resumption of nuclear testing, would undermine the emergent norm against nuclear modernization and set back efforts within the global non-proliferation regime to cap 'vertical proliferation' among the nuclear weapon states.

IV. Cooperative threat reduction

The Nunn–Lugar programme

The Cooperative Threat Reduction programme (often called the Nunn–Lugar programme after the two senators who co-sponsored the original authorizing legislation) has played the central, albeit sometimes controversial, role in the US Government's efforts to reduce the nuclear weapon-related dangers that accompanied the dissolution of the Soviet Union.[80] The CTR programme began in 1991 under the auspices of the Department of Defense (DOD). Its immediate aim was to provide bilateral US financial and other assistance to Belarus, Kazakhstan, Russia and Ukraine for consolidating the former Soviet nuclear arsenal and ensuring its custodial safety. The programme has since evolved to encompass a wide range of nuclear non-proliferation and demilitarization activities across the former Soviet Union. The CTR programme also provides financial and technical assistance for the destruction of chemical weapons.[81] Several important Nunn–Lugar initiatives in the former Soviet republics are now funded and administered by the US Departments of Energy and State.[82]

---

[78] Lamson, J. and Bowen, W., '"One arrow, three stars": China's MIRV programme, Part One', *Jane's Intelligence Review*, vol. 9, no. 5 (May 1997), p. 18; and Shen, D., 'China', ed. E. Arnett, SIPRI, *Nuclear Weapons After the Comprehensive Test Ban: Implications for Modernization and Proliferation*, (Oxford University Press: Oxford, 1996), p. 26.

[79] Lewis and Postol (note 64), pp. 24–25.

[80] For more detail about the CTR programme, see Kile and Arnett (note 40), pp. 640–42; and Kile (note 16), pp. 379–84.

[81] The Clinton Administration's FY 1998 budget request included $55.4 million for chemical weapon destruction activities, of which $35.4 million was for the design and construction of a chemical weapons destruction facility to be built in Russia. Report of the Committee on National Security, House of Representatives, National Defense Authorization Act for Fiscal Year 1998, 105th Congress, 1st Session, Report 105-132, 16 June 1997. See also chapter 11 in this volume.

[82] On 10 Nov. 1997 Defense Secretary Cohen announced as part of his Defense Reform Initiative that responsibility within the Pentagon for administering the CTR programme would be transferred to the Defense Treaty Compliance and Threat Reduction Agency, a new agency which is also being given responsibility for overseeing the verification of a growing list of arms control treaties. Erlich, J., 'Defense officials disagree about nonproliferation consolidation', *Defense News*, vol. 12, no. 46 (17–23 Nov. 1997), p. 10.

CTR projects fall into three general categories of activity: weapon destruction and dismantlement; chain of custody (i.e., ensuring proper control and safeguards over nuclear weapons and fissile material); and demilitarization and defence conversion. By the end of fiscal year (FY) 1997, the USA had committed over $1.28 billion to the support of CTR activities.[83]

The largest share of CTR programme funds has been earmarked for the dismantlement and destruction of SNDVs and their associated launchers in the former Soviet Union. The money has been used to provide technical assistance and US-made equipment for use in the dismantlement and elimination of ICBM silos, SLBM tubes and heavy bombers. It has also been used to upgrade transport infrastructure (including railway carriage security upgrades and 'supercontainers' for warhead transport) in order to safely move nuclear weapons from Belarus, Kazakhstan and Ukraine to storage facilities in Russia. Supporters of the programme argue that it was instrumental in creating incentives for Ukraine to fulfil its pledges to eliminate the former Soviet nuclear weapons based on its territory; they also credit it with helping Russia to overcome obstacles in meeting its arms reduction obligations under the START I Treaty.[84]

After bureaucratic delays, the pace of CTR-funded projects to dismantle and destroy strategic offensive arms is accelerating. The Clinton Administration's FY 1998 budget request contained $77.9 million for strategic nuclear arms elimination projects in Russia, an increase from the $52.0 million appropriated in FY 1997, and $76.7 million for strategic nuclear arms elimination in Ukraine. This money, which represents an increase of 63 per cent over the level appropriated for FY 1997, is to be used to fund a new project to eliminate additional ICBMs and associated silos and launch control centres.[85]

Since 1995, the creation of an effective fissile material physical control and accounting (MPC&A) regime has become one of the programme's highest priorities. In 1997 MPC&A projects accounted for 26 per cent of the CTR budget. The serious security shortcomings identified at many nuclear facilities (such as research reactors and laboratories, fuel fabrication facilities, uranium enrichment plants, nuclear material storage sites and nuclear weapon production plants) have spurred the launching of a variety of measures aimed at preventing the theft or unauthorized diversion of highly enriched uranium (HEU), plutonium and other weapon-usable nuclear material. One of the most successful of these has been the Department of Energy (DOE)-sponsored laboratory-to-laboratory programme, which brings US laboratory personnel together with their counterparts across the former Soviet Union to collaborate on improving fissile material control and accounting at nuclear research centres. By the end

---

[83] In Mar. 1997 the USA suspended CTR assistance obligated for Belarus (c. $40 million) because of its poor human rights record. 'Factfile: Chronology of US–Soviet–CIS nuclear relations', *Arms Control Today*, vol. 27, no. 4 (June/July 1997), p. 30.

[84] Bunn and Holdren (note 40), pp. 424–25. According to a Pentagon official, until early 1997 CTR programme assistance had supported the deactivation or destruction of 3800 nuclear warheads, 276 SLBM launchers, 597 ICBM silos and 53 bombers. Franklin C. Miller, Assistant Secretary of Defense for International Security Policy, Statement before the Senate Armed Services Committee, 7 Mar. 1997.

[85] Report of the Committee on National Security (note 81).

of 1997, MPC&A upgrades had been completed at 17 sites throughout the former USSR, with more than 50 facilities handling weapon-usable nuclear material (including facilities in Belarus, Georgia, Kazakhstan, Latvia, Ukraine and Uzbekistan) scheduled to receive help in improving nuclear material security and accounting by the end of the year 2002.[86]

In addition, CTR funds have been used to support other activities, such as the expansion of US defence and military contacts with the newly independent states of the former Soviet Union, aimed at promoting the development of democratic and civilian control of military establishments in these states. CTR funds have also been used to support wider US non-proliferation efforts. In October 1997, for example, the Pentagon purchased 21 Russian-made MiG-29C jet fighters from Moldova to prevent their sale elsewhere.[87]

The reactor conversion agreement

Following the ninth meeting of the US–Russian Joint Commission on Economic and Technical Cooperation (also known as the Gore–Chernomyrdin Commission), US Vice-President Al Gore and Russian Prime Minister Chernomyrdin announced on 23 September 1997 that they had reached an agreement resolving outstanding issues connected with an earlier pledge by Russia to halt the production of plutonium for use in weapons.[88] The September announcement followed up on an agreement signed at the June 1994 meeting of the commission in which both Russia and the USA had committed themselves to ending the production of plutonium for military purposes; a side-agreement reached at that meeting, which prohibited the restarting of plutonium production reactors already closed, was reaffirmed by the two sides in September.[89]

Under the new deal, Russia promised to convert the cores of three nuclear reactors located in the Siberian cities of Seversk (reactors ADE-4 and ADE-5, in a complex formerly known as Tomsk) and Zheleznogorsk (reactor ADE-2, in a complex formerly known as Krasnoyarsk) so that they will no longer produce plutonium for use in weapons.[90] Minatom officials had previously

---

[86] 'United States and Russia complete nuclear control systems at four sites: Department of Energy participates in commissioning ceremony in Moscow', DOE press release R-98-020, 25 Feb. 1998.

[87] According to Defense Secretary Cohen, the purpose of the purchase of the aircraft was to prevent their possible sale to 'rogue states, including Iran'. Aldinger, C., 'US buys 21 Russian-made MiGs from Moldova', Reuters, 5 Nov. 1997, URL <www.yahoo.com/headlines/971105/news/ stories/migs_1.html>, version current on 6 Nov. 1997.

[88] US–Russian Joint Commission on Economic and Technological Cooperation, 'US–Russian agreement on plutonium production reactors', *Washington File* (United States Information Service, US Embassy: Stockholm, 23 Sep. 1997), URL <http://www.usis.usemb.se/wireless/ 200/eur221.htm>, version current on 24 Sep. 1997; and Williams, C., 'Russia vows not to make plutonium for bombs', *Los Angeles Times,* 24 Sep. 1997, URL <http://www.latimes.com/HOME/NEWS/FRONT/leadstory.html>, version current on 25 Sep. 1997.

[89] US Department of State, Bureau of Public Affairs, 'Fact Sheet: Gore–Chernomyrdin Commission', 21 Sep. 1994. The USA had shut down the 14 reactors producing plutonium for military purposes by 1989. Russia declared that it had halted the production of plutonium for military purposes on 1 Oct. 1994; however, the 3 dual-purpose reactors continued in operation.

[90] Specifically, Russia agreed to halt by 31 Dec. 2000 the production of spent fuel in the 3 reactors 'containing plutonium (Pu) whose combined Pu-240 plus Pu-238 isotopic concentration is less than

rejected calls to shut down these dual-purpose reactors since they also produce heat and electricity for the surrounding communities. Furthermore, Minatom had insisted that the USA pay, or at least help secure financing, for a new advanced reactor programme to replace the existing plants.[91] Under the terms of the September deal, the USA agreed to provide approximately half of the projected $150 million cost of the conversion project.[92]

The agreement provides for intrusive monitoring arrangements at the three reactors to verify that the production of plutonium for weapons has ceased. These arrangements, the scope of which had been a major sticking-point in earlier bilateral discussions, will include the monitoring of agreed fuel types and fuel discharge schedules. They also include measures for checking seals and tags on plutonium storage containers to permit US inspectors to verify that recently produced plutonium is not used to manufacture nuclear weapons. In addition, Russian and US inspectors will install seals and other monitoring equipment at closed reactors to provide assurance that they cannot be restarted without detection.[93] Together, these arrangements constitute a step towards creating greater transparency in fissile material production and stockpiles and offer a useful precedent that can be applied at other facilities. The reactor conversion agreement also reinforces support for a convention prohibiting the production of fissile material for military purposes.

V. Other nuclear non-proliferation and disarmament developments

The Comprehensive Nuclear Test-Ban Treaty

In 1997 the future of the CTBT remained unclear. The treaty had been adopted by an overwhelming vote of the UN General Assembly on 10 September 1996, an historic achievement which marked the culmination of four decades of fitful negotiations to ban testing of nuclear weapons.[94] As of 1 January 1998, the CTBT had been ratified by 8 states and signed but not ratified by 141 states.[95]

---

20 percent of total Pu, averaged over the total fuel discharged in any one batch'. US–Russian Joint Commission on Economic and Technological Cooperation, 'Joint Statement on plutonium production reactors', *Washington File* (United States Information Service, US Embassy: Stockholm, 23 Sep. 1997), URL <http://www.usis.usemb.se/wireless/ 200/eur220.htm>, version current on 24 Sep. 1997. In addition, Russia is prohibited from using any of the plutonium produced in the 3 reactors for the manufacture of nuclear weapons prior to their conversion.

[91] Medeiros, E., 'Gore–Chernomyrdin talks resolve several outstanding issues', *Arms Control Today*, vol. 25, no. 7 (Sep. 1995), pp. 26, 32.

[92] In FY 1997 Congress authorized and appropriated $10 million for implementation of the reactor conversion agreement; an additional $70 million has been earmarked for the project. US–Russian Joint Commission on Economic and Technological Cooperation (note 88).

[93] 'Fact sheet on plutonium production reactor agreement', *Washington File* (United States Information Service, US Embassy: Stockholm, 25 Sep. 1997), URL <http://www.usis.usemb.se/wireless/400/eur430.ht>, version current on 26 Sep. 1997.

[94] For a summary of developments leading up to the CTBT's adoption by the General Assembly, see Arnett, E., 'The Comprehensive Nuclear Test-Ban Treaty', *SIPRI Yearbook 1997* (note 16), pp. 403–407. The text of the CTBT is reproduced in *SIPRI Yearbook 1997*, pp. 414–31.

[95] For the list of states which have signed or ratified the CTBT, see annexe A in this volume.

Although the international norm against nuclear testing embodied in the CTBT is now universally accepted, India's steadfast refusal to sign the treaty continued to cast doubt on whether it would enter into full legal force. India is one of 44 states with nuclear programmes listed in Annexe 2 of the CTBT which must ratify the accord before it can enter into force.[96] Of these 44 states, North Korea and Pakistan had also not signed the treaty at the end of 1997, with the latter stating that it would not do so until India had signed it. Officials in New Delhi have denounced India's inclusion in the list of states whose ratification is necessary for the CTBT's entry into force.[97] They have also vowed to resist international pressure to accede to the accord, complaining that the treaty contains language which implicitly threatens India with sanctions if it fails to ratify the test ban.[98]

The USA faced a difficult struggle to gain the Senate's approval of ratification. Opponents of ratification argued that a permanent halt to nuclear testing was unverifiable and would undermine the safety and reliability of the USA's nuclear arsenal. President Clinton sought to address some of these concerns in his letter transmitting the treaty to the Senate on 22 September 1997. He emphasized that the Administration remained committed to ensuring a 'high level of confidence in the safety and reliability of nuclear weapons in the active stockpile' as well to maintaining 'the basic capability to resume nuclear test activities' if the safety or reliability of a nuclear weapon type deemed vital to the US nuclear deterrent could no longer be certified.[99] The centre-piece of these efforts is the Stockpile Stewardship and Management Programme (SSMP). This technologically ambitious 10-year $40 billion programme, which is managed under the auspices of the DOE and the national nuclear weapon laboratories, involves using a set of computational and experimental simulations as a way of maintaining confidence in the long-term safety and reliability of the US stockpile of nuclear weapons.

Despite the uncertainty over when the CTBT would enter into force, preparations for implementing the treaty and its verification provisions proceeded apace in 1997. The Preparatory Commission of the Comprehensive Test-Ban Treaty Organization (CTBTO) reached agreement in March on a budget for establishing a Provisional Technical Secretariat at the Vienna International Centre. It also made further progress on working out organizational and administrative arrangements for the International Monitoring System (IMS) and the International Data Centre (IDC). The CTBT verification system is

[96] These 44 states are listed in annexe A in this volume.
[97] India's opposition had prevented the CTBT from being adopted by consensus in the CD in 1996. For a discussion of Indian attitudes to the CTBT, see Deshingkar, G., 'India', Arnett (note 78), pp. 41–55.
[98] If the CTBT has not entered into force 3 years after the date of the anniversary of its opening for signature (i.e., Sep. 1999), the treaty provides for the parties to convene an annual review conference to consider measures 'consistent with international law' to facilitate bringing it into force (Art. XIV).
[99] 'Clinton letter to Senate on nuclear test ban', *Washington File* (United States Information Service, US Embassy: Stockholm, 23 Sep. 1997), URL <http://www.usis.usemb.se/wireless/200/eur209.htm>, version current on 24 Sep. 1997. Clinton also pledged that the USA would continue to carry out a comprehensive research and development programme to improve treaty monitoring capabilities and operations.

expected to become operational by September 1998, pending the allocation of funds requested from signatory states. Proponents argue that the $100 million verification system, which will consist of 321 seismic and hydro-acoustic stations around the world, will be of considerable value in reinforcing the no-testing norm whether or not the CTBT enters into force.[100]

Significantly, the partially operational verification system was able to help determine that a suspicious seismic event which occurred in August 1997 in the ocean about 100 km east of the now-closed Russian nuclear test site at Novaya Zemlya was in fact an underwater earthquake.[101] The seismic event had precipitated a flurry of accusations in the USA that Russia had clandestinely carried out a nuclear test prohibited by the CTBT. These accusations were fuelled by earlier reports of activities at Novaya Zemlya which suggested that a nuclear test was being prepared.[102] By November, however, the US Government acknowledged that it had concluded that the seismic event was an earthquake.[103]

The issue of subcritical testing gained prominence in 1997 when on 2 July and 15 September the US DOE conducted the first two in a planned series of subcritical experiments as part of its SSMP.[104] The DOE stressed that the tests were in conformity with Article I of the CTBT, which prohibits nuclear explosions but does not prohibit laboratory tests.[105] However, many observers complained that they contravened the spirit of the CTBT. The experiments drew widespread criticism from both within and outside the USA, including a condemnatory resolution from the European Parliament. The Indian Government used the experiments as evidence supporting its contention that the CTBT's provisions fail to prevent the nuclear weapon states from developing and refining nuclear weapon technology.[106]

---

[100] Ambassador Wolfgang Hoffman, Executive Secretary of the Preparatory Commission for the CTBTO, quoted in Gunther, S., 'Progress and challenges in bringing the comprehensive test ban into force', *The Nuclear Roundtable* (Henry L. Stimson Center: Washington, DC, 21 Oct. 1997).

[101] Some treaty proponents pointed out that the seismic event was of a smaller magnitude than the completed system's estimated detection capability. Kenny, S., 'Aftershocks from the Novaya Zemlya earthquake', *Arms Control Today*, vol. 27, no. 5 (Aug. 1997), p. 2.

[102] Programme for Promoting Nuclear Non-Proliferation (PPNN), *PPNN Newsbrief*, no. 39 (fourth quarter 1997), p. 3. In addition, it was disclosed that the USA had remotely monitored 2 subcritical tests conducted at Novaya Zemlya.

[103] Macilwain, C., 'Seismologists claim quake data being "mis-read" as bomb test', *Nature*, vol. 389, no. 650 (2 Oct. 1997), p. 425; and Holland, S., 'US says Russia did not detonate nuclear test', Reuters, 4 Nov. 1997, URL <www.yahoo.com/headlines/971104/news/ stories/nuclear_1.html>, version current on 5 Nov. 1997.

[104] The experiments are called 'subcritical' because the configuration and quantities of explosives and nuclear materials used do not produce a critical mass (i.e., a self-sustaining nuclear fission chain reaction).

[105] 'Fact sheet: energy experiments comply with test ban', *Washington File* (United States Information Service, US Embassy: Stockholm, 23 Sep. 1997), URL <http://www.usis.usemb.se/wireless/ 200/eur209.htm>, version current on 24 Sep. 1997. The purpose of the first experiment, code-named Rebound, was to monitor the response of plutonium to shock-wave compression under different high pressure conditions; the purpose of the second experiment, code-named Holog, was to obtain data on the characteristics of plutonium when subjected to a shock wave of high explosive.

[106] Cited in *Arms Control Reporter*, sheet 608.B.467, Sep. 1997.

A ban on the production of fissile material for nuclear explosives

The CD concluded its 1997 session without having opened formal talks on a Fissile Material Cut-off Treaty (FMCT), despite having agreed a mandate for negotiations two years earlier.[107] Little headway was made towards resolving underlying political differences over how the proposed convention should contribute to nuclear disarmament. The differences between the 61 members of the CD, which had produced such a weak negotiating mandate, remained unbridged—a stalemate which contributed to the already widespread sense that the CD is in crisis. At the same time, however, the discussions throughout the year on the issue did highlight the importance of the CD as the only regular forum for negotiating global nuclear disarmament measures in which the non-nuclear weapon states can make their voices heard.

There continued to be two main obstacles to opening negotiations on the proposed convention. The first was the insistence of Egypt, Pakistan and other states that the convention should go beyond mandating a cut-off of fissile material production and include existing stockpiles of fissile material as well, with these stockpiles to be placed under international safeguards. This proposal has generated strong opposition from the five permanent members of the UN Security Council (i.e., the five declared nuclear weapon states), which have large inventories of fissile material for military purposes, and, among others, India. These states argue that the mandate should apply only to the future production of fissile material.[108] The second obstacle continued to be the Indian-led demand that the negotiations on an FMCT be placed in the context of a time-bound framework for general nuclear disarmament. This demand gained some support in 1997. The Group of 21 (G-21) submitted a Programme of Work calling for the establishment of an ad hoc committee on nuclear disarmament to commence negotiations on a phased programme to eliminate nuclear weapons.[109] However, several G-21 states, including Chile, Morocco and South Africa, argued that discussions should first be held to consider feasible steps towards nuclear disarmament, with an appropriate negotiating mandate to follow.[110] France, Russia, the UK and the USA have refused to consider the establishment of an ad hoc committee on nuclear disarmament. As the year ended, the prospects for moving ahead on an FMCT seemed remote in the absence of a broader political consensus on the role of the convention in promoting nuclear disarmament.

---

[107] A mandate had been agreed in Mar. 1995 for a committee to 'negotiate a non-discriminatory, multilateral and effectively verifiable treaty banning the production of fissile material for nuclear weapons or other nuclear explosive devices'. Conference on Disarmament document CD/1299, 24 Mar. 1995.

[108] None of the 5 permanent members of the UN Security Council is believed to be currently producing plutonium or HEU for weapon purposes.

[109] 'Conference on Disarmament concludes 1997 session', United Nations Press Release, DCF 315, 9 Sep. 1997. The G-21 is a group of 30 (originally 21) non-aligned CD member states; they are listed in the glossary in this volume.

[110] Johnson, R., 'Geneva update no. 35', *Disarmament Diplomacy*, no. 15 (May 1997), pp. 13–14.

The NPT Preparatory Committee

The first meeting of the Preparatory Committee for the 2000 Non-Proliferation Treaty Review Conference was held in New York on 7–18 April 1997.[111] The meeting was attended by 148 states parties to the NPT.[112] The substantive issues for review were grouped into three clusters: (*a*) nuclear disarmament; (*b*) safeguards and nuclear weapon-free zones; and (*c*) the peaceful use of nuclear energy. Discussions at the meeting underscored the division between the nuclear 'haves' and 'have nots' within the NPT regime. They also revealed considerable disagreement between the delegations about the role of the Preparatory Committee in the review process, its principles and objectives and the procedures governing its activities. The meeting adjourned following the issuing of a Final Report containing, among other elements, recommendations to the next Preparatory Committee (which is scheduled to convene in May 1998) about the categories of issues to be addressed.[113]

VI. Conclusions

In 1997 Russia and the USA undertook to reinvigorate their bilateral nuclear arms control cooperation amid clear signs that the political momentum behind the arms control accomplishments of the past decade was declining. The Russian and US presidents reaffirmed the overarching importance of maintaining a constructive arms control relationship in which the two former cold war adversaries cooperate—however fitfully—to achieve common goals. They reached several political agreements aimed at overcoming key obstacles that were blocking progress towards further nuclear arms cuts and CBMs. These included a set of amendments to the START II Treaty designed to make that treaty more palatable to the Duma and a resolution of the US–Russian dispute over clarification of the ABM Treaty to permit new advanced-capability TMD systems. However, the year ended with these agreements embroiled in domestic political controversies. Their uncertain fate provides yet another illustration of why the promise of arms control often remains unfulfilled: agreements must not only balance the national interests of the signatory states but also the agendas of influential domestic interests, legislators and political parties.

The question 'how low can we go?' once again moved to the fore of the bilateral nuclear arms control agenda in 1997. In the aftermath of the collapse of the Soviet Union, this question had been eclipsed to some extent by more basic concerns about preserving the physical security of and centralized con-

---

[111] The May 1995 NPT Review and Extension Conference had sought to strengthen the review process by requiring that Preparatory Committee meetings be held in each of the 3 years leading up to the 5-yearly Review Conferences. The purpose of the Preparatory Committee meetings is to 'consider principles, objectives and ways in order to promote the full implementation of the Treaty, as well as its universality, and to make recommendations thereon to the Review Conference'. 'Strengthening the review process for the treaty', New York, 11 May 1995, NPT/CONF.1995/32 (Part I), reproduced in *SIPRI Yearbook 1996* (note 40), appendix 13A, pp. 590–91.

[112] For the list of the 187 parties to the treaty, see annexe A in this volume.

[113] Johnson (note 110), pp. 9–24.

trol over nuclear weapons and not least about forestalling the emergence of new nuclear weapon states. With domestic political pressure mounting to channel defence expenditures into other areas, Clinton and Yeltsin agreed in principle to reduce the US and Russian strategic nuclear forces, albeit to levels that many arms control advocates consider to be disappointingly high nearly 10 years after the end of the cold war. The START III framework outlined by the two presidents reflects a continuation of the trend towards gradually declining strategic nuclear force levels as target lists and modernization plans are brought into line with changing political and fiscal circumstances. However, the question of what to do about their countries' large inventories of non-strategic nuclear weapons remained largely unaddressed.[114]

One of the potential breakthroughs on the nuclear arms control agenda in 1997 was the agreement in principle to establish a warhead dismantlement regime within the START III framework. This step, which has long been urged by arms control advocates, highlights the direction in which strategic nuclear arms control is heading. The previous focus on limiting launchers and their warheads is turning to physically dismantling those warheads in a transparent and verifiable way. The immediate aim in requiring warheads to be dismantled is to allay Russian concern about the USA's potential to stage a 'break-out' from the START II Treaty limits. However, the broader objective is to lock in the force reductions being made by Russia and the USA and make them permanent and irreversible.

Clearly, the nuclear arms control agenda remains a full one. The ratification of the START II Treaty is in jeopardy as opposition to the accord mounts in the Duma. The landmark CTBT is facing an uncertain future. The efforts in the CD to negotiate a legally binding global ban on the production of fissile material for weapons have also stalled. Furthermore, the encouraging progress already made in eliminating nuclear weapons has added a new set of issues to the arms control agenda: namely, how to enhance the security and the safe disposal of the vast quantity of fissile material left over from the former Soviet nuclear weapon complex.[115] Disposing of the fissile material extracted from dismantled nuclear warheads is becoming an increasingly urgent challenge, one which poses serious technical and financial challenges for both Russia and the USA. Thus, despite the encouraging progress of recent years, much remains in the way of unfinished business on the arms control agenda. Its completion will require the decisive and sustained commitment of all states, particularly that of the nuclear weapon and threshold states.

---

[114] According to an authoritative estimate, at the beginning of 1998 the Russian stockpile contained c. 22 500 nuclear warheads: of these, 10 240 are thought to be operational (6240 in strategic forces and c. 4000 in non-strategic forces). The other c. 12 000 warheads are non-strategic and are thought to be in reserve and/or awaiting dismantlement. Of the 12 070 nuclear warheads in the US stockpile at the beginning of 1998, 8420 are operational (7450 in strategic forces and 970 in non-strategic forces). Approximately 2300 warheads are held in reserve, and 1350 are awaiting dismantlement. Arkin, W., Norris, R. and Handler, J., *Taking Stock: Worldwide Nuclear Deployments 1998* (Natural Resources Defense Council: Washington, DC, 1998), pp. 1–2, 14, 26–27.

[115] Bunn and Holdren (note 40).

Appendix 10A. Tables of nuclear forces

ROBERT S. NORRIS and WILLIAM M. ARKIN

The reductions in Russian and US strategic nuclear delivery vehicles mandated by the 1991 Treaty on the Reduction and Limitation of Strategic Offensive Arms (START I Treaty) proceeded ahead of schedule in 1997. Russia's plans to modernize its strategic nuclear forces continued to be severely constrained by shortfalls in the Russian defence budget. Tables 10A.1 and 10A.2 show the composition of the operational strategic nuclear forces of the United States and Russia, respectively, with notes about the developments in 1997.

The nuclear arsenals of the three other declared nuclear weapon states—the United Kingdom, France and China—are considerably smaller than those of the USA and Russia; data are presented in tables 10A.3–10A.5, respectively. In recent years France and the UK have scaled back their nuclear force modernization plans; the UK is considering changes in its nuclear policy as part of a Strategic Defence Review, which is due to be completed in 1998. China's plans for the size and composition of its arsenal are unknown.

The figures contained in the tables are estimates based on public information but contain some uncertainties, as reflected in the notes. The acronyms which appear in the tables are defined in the list at the front of this volume.

Table 10A.1. US strategic nuclear forces, January 1998

Type	Designation	No. deployed	Year first deployed	Range (km)[a]	Warheads x yield	Warheads
Bombers						
B-52H[b]	Stratofortress	71/44	1961	16 000	ALCM 5–150 kt	400
					ACM 5–150 kt	400
B-2[c]	Spirit	21/9	1994	11 000	Bombs, various	1 000
Total		**92/53**				**1 800**
ICBMs						
LGM-30G[d]	Minuteman III					
	Mk-12	200	1970	13 000	3 x 170 kt	600
	Mk-12A	300	1979	13 000	3 x 335 kt	900
LGM-118A	MX/Peacekeeper	50	1986	11 000	10 x 300 kt	500
Total		**550**				**2 000**
SLBMs						
UGM-96A[e]	Trident I (C-4)	192	1979	7 400	8 x 100 kt	1 536
UGM-133A[f]	Trident II (D-5)					
	Mk-4	192	1992	7 400	8 x 100 kt	1 536
	Mk-5	48	1990	7 400	8 x 475 kt	384
Total		**432**				**3 456**

[a] Range for aircraft indicates combat radius, without in-flight refuelling.

[b] B-52Hs can carry up to 20 air-launched cruise missiles (ALCMs)/advanced cruise missiles (ACMs) each. Because of a shrinking bomber force, only about 400 ALCMs and 400 ACMs

are deployed, with over 900 other ALCMs in reserve. The Nuclear Posture Review (NPR) released on 22 Sep. 1994 recommended retaining 66 B-52Hs. The Air Force has since recommended retaining 71. The B-52Hs have been consolidated at 2 bases, the 2nd Bomb Wing at Barksdale Air Force Base (AFB), Louisiana, and the 5th Bomb Wing at Minot AFB, North Dakota. The 1st figure in the *No. deployed* column is the total number of B-52Hs in the inventory, including those for training, test and backup; the 2nd figure is the operational number available for nuclear and conventional missions.

Under the START II Treaty the B-1Bs will not be counted as nuclear weapon carriers. The USA has completed a reorientation of its B-1Bs to conventional missions. By the end of 1997 all B-1Bs were out of the strategic war plan altogether and are not included in the table. Of the original 100 B-1Bs, 6 have crashed: 1 in 1987, 2 in 1988, 1 in 1992, 1 on 19 Sep. 1997 and the most recent on 18 Feb. 1998.

[c] The 1st B-2 bomber was delivered to the 509th Bombardment Wing at Whiteman AFB, Missouri on 17 Dec. 1993. By the end of 1995, 8 B-2s had arrived at Whiteman; 5 more were delivered in 1996 and 4 more in 1997, bringing the total to 17. All 6 aircraft from the test programme are being modified to achieve an operational capability, which will bring the total number to 21.

The B-2 is configured to carry various combinations of nuclear and conventional munitions. The 1st 16 bombers were produced as Block 10 versions, able to carry the B83 nuclear bomb (and the Mk 84 conventional bomb). These were followed by 3 production Block 20 versions, able to carry the B61 nuclear bomb. Finally, the last 2 bombers were production Block 30 versions (able to carry both types of nuclear bomb and an assortment of conventional bombs, munitions and missiles). Earlier Block 10 and 20 aircraft are being upgraded to Block 30 standards at the Northrop Grumman factory in Palmdale, California. In the year 2000 the upgrades will be completed and there will be 21 Block 30 B-2s.

The B-2 bomber came under criticism from the General Accounting Office in a 14 Aug. 1997 report which stated that 'Testing indicated that B-2s are also sensitive to extreme climates, water, and humidity—exposure to water or moisture can damage some of the low-observable enhancing surfaces on the aircraft'. There is also criticism about the high operations and maintenance costs. For each flight hour the B-2 requires 119 hours of maintenance, compared with 53 hours for the B-52 and 60 hours for the B-1B. The 1st figure in the *No. deployed* column is the totla number of B-2s delivered to Whiteman; the 2nd figure is an approximate number of those available for nucler and conventional missions.

[d] The 500 Minuteman IIIs are being consolidated from 4 bases to 3. Minuteman III missiles are being transferred from Grand Forks AFB, North Dakota, to Malmstrom AFB, Montana, at a rate of about 1 per week, with completion of the transfer now due by the spring of 1998. When completed there will be 200 Minuteman IIIs at Malmstrom, and 150 each at Minot AFB, North Dakota, and F. E. Warren AFB, Wyoming.

To comply with the ban on MIRVs when the START II Treaty enters into force, each of the 500 Minuteman III missiles will have the number of warheads reduced from 3 to 1. Currently, 300 missiles have the higher-yield W78 warhead and 200 have the W62 warhead. Several de-MIRVing options are possible. One would be to place a single W87 warhead on each Minuteman III. Five hundred W87s will be removed from the 50 MX missiles when they are retired. The W87 warhead has the preferred safety features, including insensitive high explosive (IHE), fire-resistant pit (FRP) and the enhanced nuclear detonation system (ENDS), whereas the W78 only has ENDS. A drawback is the difficulty of putting multiple warheads back on the missiles if the force is reconstituted. A 2nd option is to use a single W78 on each missile. The 3rd and perhaps preferred option would be to put W78s on a portion of the force, e.g., 150 of the 500 missiles, and W87s on the rest. This choice uses the newer warhead and permits easier re-MIRVing. Previously, the downloading was to have been accomplished within 7 years of the entry into force of START I, i.e., by 5 Dec. 2001. Under the new protocol it does not have to be completed until the end of 2007.

Table 10A.1 *Notes, contd*

In 1997 work proceeded on blowing up Minuteman II silos in accordance with the START I Treaty Protocol on Conversion or Elimination. The silo destruction programme was completed in Sep. 1996 at Ellsworth AFB, South Dakota. On 18 Dec. the last of the 150 silos was blown up at Whiteman AFB. Thus far none of the empty silos that once housed the Minuteman IIIs at Grand Forks has been blown up.

A 3-part programme to upgrade the Minuteman missiles continued: (*a*) the launch control centres have been updated with Rapid Execution and Combat Targeting (REACT) consoles; (*b*) improvements to the missile's guidance system are being conducted by Boeing Autonetics and will continue until 2002—these measures will eventually increase the accuracy of the Minuteman III to near that of the current MX, a circular error probable (CEP) of 100 metres; and (*c*) the 1st and 2nd stages are being 'repoured', incorporating the latest solid-propellant and bonding technologies, and the 3rd stage will be either refurbished or rebuilt. Some estimates put the total cost as high as $7 billion.

In an effort to save money the Air Force has transferred responsibility for maintaining the readiness of the 550 ICBMs to TRW, Inc., a private contractor. The $3.4 billion contract was awarded on 22 Dec. 1997 and runs until 2012.

^{e} The W76 warheads from the Trident I missiles have been fitted on Trident II submarines home-ported at Kings Bay, Georgia, and are supplemented by 400 W88 warheads, the number built before the nuclear weapon complex ceased production in 1990.

^{f} One new Ohio Class submarine, the *USS Louisiana* (SSBN-743), the 18th and last of the class, joined the fleet on 6 Sep. 1997. The 1st 8 Ohio Class submarines carry the Trident I (C-4) missile; the final 10 are equipped with the Trident II (D-5) missile.

The 1994 NPR recommended completing construction of 18 Ohio Class SSBNs (nuclear-powered ballistic-missile submarines) and then retiring 4 older SSBNs. The Navy has chosen the submarines that will be upgraded and those that will be retired. The 4 newest Trident I-equipped SSBNs based in the Pacific at Bangor, Washington, will be backfitted to fire Trident II missiles. In order of their upgrade they are: *Alaska* (732), *Nevada* (733), *Jackson* (730) and *Alabama* (731). The 4 older submarines (*Ohio, Michigan, Florida* and *Georgia*) will probably be retired. A remote possibility would be to retire 2 and convert or modify 2 others to be special-purpose submarines. Conversion is permitted but is a more costly and extensive process as the submarine's missile launch tubes must be removed. Modification leaves the tubes empty but must be agreed by both sides. START I contained an Agreed Statement allowing for 2 US special-purpose Poseidon submarines. If the Navy wanted to replace those 2 with 2 Trident submarines it would have to be agreed upon in a future treaty. Given those complexities and the cost involved it is unlikely that this option will be pursued.

The Navy continues to purchase Trident II SLBMs. In the FY 1998 Pentagon budget 7 missiles were purchased, bringing the total bought so far to 357. The NPR called for 4 Trident I-equipped SSBNs to be backfitted with Trident IIs, increasing the number of missiles to be procured from 390 to 434, at an extra cost of $2.2 billion. Twenty-eight additional missiles were bought for the research and development programme. The total cost of the programme is now $27.5 billion, or $60 million per missile. Through FY 1998 over $23 billion has already been authorized. Some critics have questioned the need to continue to buy missiles if the future force under START III is going to be fewer than 14 SSBNs. E.g., a force of 10 submarines requires 347 missiles and would result in significant savings.

The Bangor base will have to undergo some adaptation to support the Trident II, although activities such as training can be carried out at Kings Bay, Georgia. The backfitting of the 4 SSBNs will take place from FY 2000 to FY 2005. Eventually 2 or 3 submarines will be shifted from Kings Bay to Bangor to balance the 14-submarine fleet. To comply with START II warhead limits the Navy will have to download its SLBMs, retire additional SSBNs or do both. Under the new timetable set out in the START II Protocol, SLBMs can have no more than 2160 warheads by the end of 2004 and no more than 1750 warheads by the end of 2007. If there is a START III treaty with limits of 2000–2500 deployed strategic warheads, the SSBN portion would probably account for c. one-half. This would mean a fleet of 10–12 submarines, depending on the number of warheads per SLBM. Some speculate that with an SSBN fleet of a dozen or fewer the Bangor base could be closed, although war planners object because China would not be adequately targeted.

While much has changed, some things have not. In 1998, at any given time, between 8 and 11 US SSBNs are on patrol, a rate equal to that at the height of the cold war. The practice of each SSBN having 2 crews also continues.

Sources: Cohen, W. S., Secretary of Defense, *Annual Report to the President and the Congress*, Feb. 1998, pp. 57–61; Cohen, W. S., Secretary of Defense, *Annual Report to the President and the Congress*, Apr. 1997, pp. 207–11; Perry, W. J., Secretary of Defense, *Annual Report to the President and the Congress*, Mar. 1996, pp. 213–18; START I Treaty Memoranda of Understanding, 1 Sep. 1990, 5 Dec. 1994, 1 July 1995, 1 Jan. 1996, 1 July 1996, 1 Jan. 1997 and 1 July 1997; Senate Committee on Foreign Relations, START II Treaty, Executive Report 104-10, 15 Dec. 1995; US Air Force Public Affairs, personal communications; and Natural Resources Defense Council (NRDC), 'Nuclear notebook', *Bulletin of the Atomic Scientists* various issues.

Table 10A.2. Russian strategic nuclear forces, January 1998

Type	NATO designation	No. deployed	Year first deployed	Range (km)[a]	Warheads x yield	Warheads
Bombers						
Tu-95M[b]	Bear-H6	29	1984	12 800	6 x AS-15A ALCMs, bombs	174
Tu-95M[b]	Bear-H16	35	1984	12 800	16 x AS-15A ALCMs, bombs	560
Tu-160[c]	Blackjack	6	1987	11 000	12 x AS-15B ALCMs or AS-16 SRAMs, bombs	72
Total		70				806
ICBMs[d]						
SS-18[e]	Satan	180	1979	11 000	10 x 550/750 kt	1 800
SS-19[f]	Stiletto	160	1980	10 000	6 x 550 kt	960
SS-24 M1/M2[g]	Scalpel	36/10	1987	10 000	10 x 550 kt	460
SS-25[h]	Sickle	360	1985	10 500	1 x 550 kt	360
Total		746				3 580
SLBMs[i]						
SS-N-18 M1	Stingray	192	1978	6 500	3 x 500 kt	576
SS-N-20[j]	Sturgeon	80	1983	8 300	10 x 200 kt	800
SS-N-23	Skiff	112	1986	9 000	4 x 100 kt	448
Total		384				1 824

[a] Range for aircraft indicates combat radius, without in-flight refuelling.

[b] According to the 1 July 1997 START I Memorandum of Understanding, the Bear bombers are deployed as follows: Bear H16s—19 at Mozdok (Russia), 16 at Ukrainka (Russia), and 14 at Uzin (Ukraine); Bear H6s—2 at Mozdok, 27 at Ukrainka and 3 at Uzin. The 40 Bear-H bombers (27 Bear H6s and 13 Bear-H16s) that were based in Kazakhstan were withdrawn to Russia, including some 370 AS-15 ALCM warheads. The 17 Bear bombers in Ukraine, at Uzin, are poorly maintained and are not considered operational. Seven additional Bear bombers at Uzin are in storage.

Table 10A.2 *Notes, contd*

c Nineteen Blackjack bombers are based in Ukraine at Priluki; the remaining 6 are in Russia at Engels AFB near Saratov. The Blackjacks at Priluki are poorly maintained and are not considered operational. An agreement announced on 24 Nov. 1995 that called for Ukraine to eventually return the Blackjack and Bear bombers and more than 300 cruise missiles to Russia collapsed in the spring and summer of 1997.

d Deactivation and retirement of ICBMs and their launchers proceed through at least 4 stages. In step 1, an ICBM is removed from alert status by electrical and mechanical procedures. Next, warheads are removed from the missile. In step 3 the missile is withdrawn from the silo. Finally, to comply with START-specified elimination procedures, the silo is blown up and eventually filled in. The number of missiles and warheads will vary depending upon which step the analyst chooses to feature.

e In the Sep. 1990 START I Treaty Memorandum of Understanding, the Soviet Union declared 104 SS-18s in Kazakhstan (at Derzhavinsk and Zhangiz-Tobe) and 204 in Russia (30 at Aleysk, 64 at Dombarosvki, 46 at Kartaly and 64 at Uzhur). All the SS-18s in Kazakhstan and 24 in Russia are considered to be non-operational, leaving 180 in Russia. Beginning in Apr. 1995 the 1st SS-18 silos in Kazakhstan were blown up. By Sep. 1996 all 104 had been destroyed. Under the START I Treaty Russia is permitted to retain 154 SS-18s. If the START II Treaty is fully implemented, all SS-18 missiles will be destroyed, but Russia may convert up to 90 SS-18 silos for deployment of single-warhead ICBMs.

f In the Sep. 1990 START I Treaty Memorandum of Understanding, the Soviet Union declared 130 SS-19s in Ukraine and 170 in Russia. A Nov. 1995 agreement included the sale of 32 SS-19s, once deployed in Ukraine, back to Russia. Some SS-19s in Russia are being withdrawn from service. Under START II Russia may keep up to 105 SS-19s downloaded to a single warhead.

g Of the original 56 silo-based SS-24 M2s, 46 were in Ukraine at Pervomaysk and 10 are in Russia at Tatishchevo. At the beginning of 1998 only the 10 in Russia are considered operational. All 36 rail-based SS-24 M1s are in Russia—at Bershet, Kostroma and Krasnoyarsk.

h By 27 Nov. 1996 the last remaining SS-25 missiles in Belarus and their warheads had been shipped back to Russia. The new variant of the SS-25 is called the Topol-M by the Russians and designated the SS-27 by NATO. It is assembled at Votkinsk in Russia and is the only Russian strategic weapon system still in production. Flight-testing began on 20 Dec. 1994 and continued during the period 1995–97. In Jan. 1998 Defence Minister Igor Sergeyev announced that 2 silo-based SS-27s were in 'trial service' with a regiment of the Taman division in south-western Russia's Saratov region at Tatishchevo. The silos formerly housed SS-19 missiles. The 1st regiment of 9–10 launchers is expected to be fully operational in 1998, although at a production rate of 10–20 missiles per year it will take some time for significant numbers of them to be fielded.

i About one-half of the SSBN fleet has been withdrawn from operational service. The table assumes that all the Yankee Is, Delta Is and Delta IIs and 2 Delta IIIs have been withdrawn from operational service, leaving 23 operational SSBNs of 3 classes (12 Delta IIIs, 7 Delta IVs and 4 Typhoons). According to a Russian Navy vice-admiral, 2 Typhoons are 'unfit for combat'; hence they are not included in the table of operational forces. All these SSBNs are based on the Kola Peninsula (at Nerpichya, Olenya and Yagelnaya) except for 9 Delta IIIs based at Rybachi (15 km south-west of Petropavlovsk) on the Kamchatka Peninsula. The keel of the new Borey Class SSBN was laid in Nov. 1996.

j A new SLBM, for the Borey Class SSBN, designated the SS-NX-28, is under development but has yet to have a successful test-flight.

Sources: START I Treaty Memoranda of Understanding, 1 Sep. 1990, 5 Dec. 1994, 1 July 1995, 1 Jan. 1996, 1 July 1996, 1 Jan. 1997 and 1 July 1997; International Institute for Strategic Studies (IISS), *The Military Balance 1997–1998* (Oxford University Press: Oxford, 1997), p. 108; and Natural Resources Defense Council (NRDC), 'Nuclear notebook', *Bulletin of the Atomic Scientists,* various issues.

Table 10A.3. British nuclear forces, January 1998

Type	Designation	No. deployed	Year first deployed	Range (km)^a	Warheads x yield	Warheads in stockpile
Aircraft						
GR-1/1A	Tornado	96^b	1982	1 300	1–2 x 200–400 kt	100^c
SSBNs/SLBMs^d						
D-5	Trident II	32	1994	7 400	4–6 x 100 kt	160^e

^{a} Range for aircraft indicates combat radius, without in-flight refuelling.

^{b} The Royal Air Force operates 8 squadrons of dual-capable Tornado GR.1/1A aircraft. These include 4 squadrons at RAF Bruggen, Germany (Nos. 9, 14, 17, 31); 2 squadrons previously at RAF Marham were redeployed to RAF Lossiemouth in 1994. They replaced the Buccaneer S2B in the maritime strike role and were redesignated Nos. 12 and 617; and 2 reconnaissance squadrons at RAF Marham (Nos. 2, 13). Each squadron has 12 aircraft. By the end of Mar. 1998 Tornadoes will no longer have a nuclear role.

^{c} The total stockpile of WE-177 tactical nuclear gravity bombs was estimated to have been about 200, of which 175 were versions A and B. The C version of the WE-177 was assigned to selected Royal Navy (RN) Sea Harrier FRS.1 aircraft and ASW helicopters. The 1992 White Paper stated: 'As part of the cut in NATO's stockpile we will also reduce the number of British free-fall nuclear bombs by more than half'. A number of British nuclear bombs were returned to the UK from bases in Germany. The 1993 White Paper stated that the WE-177 'is currently expected to remain in service until well into the next century'. The government announced in Mar. 1994 that this would be until the year 2007. On 4 Apr. 1995 the government announced that the remaining WE-177s would be withdrawn by the end of 1998. This was later advanced to the end of Mar. 1998. On 1 May 1996 Defence Secretary Michael Portillo announced that RAF Bruggen would close in 2002. The Tornadoes (4 years after becoming non-nuclear) will be reassigned to bases in the UK.

^{d} The UK built and deployed 4 Resolution Class SSBNs, commonly called Polaris submarines after the missiles they carried. The 1st boat (*HMS Resolution*) went on patrol in mid-June 1968, the 4th (*Revenge*) in Sep. 1970. The total number of patrols for the 4 boats over the 28-year period was 229. *Revenge* was retired on 25 May 1992, after 56 patrols; *Resolution* was decommissioned on 22 Oct. 1994, after 61 patrols; *Renown* was decommissioned on 24 Feb. 1996, after 52 patrols; and *Repulse* was withdrawn from service on 28 Aug. 1996, after 60 patrols. The Chevaline warheads are being dismantled.

The 1st Trident submarine of the new class, *HMS Vanguard*, went on its 1st patrol in Dec. 1994. The 2nd submarine, *Victorious*, entered service in Dec. 1995. The 3rd submarine, *Vigilant*, was launched in Oct. 1995 and will enter service in the summer or autumn of 1998. The 4th and final boat of the class, *Vengeance*, is under construction. Its estimated launch date is 1998, with service entry in late 2000 or early 2001. The current estimated cost of the Trident programme is $18.8 billion.

Each Vanguard Class SSBN carries 16 US-produced Trident II D-5 SLBM. It has never been publicly stated exactly how many missiles the UK is purchasing from the USA. The number is estimated here to be 70, but it should be noted that there are no specifically US or British Trident II missiles. There is a pool of SLBMs at Strategic Weapons Facility Atlantic at the Kings Bay Submarine Base, Georgia. The UK has title to a certain number of SLBMs but does not actually own them. A missile that is deployed on a US SSBN may at a later date be deployed on a British one, or vice versa.

^{e} It is assumed here that the UK will only produce enough warheads for 3 boatloads of missiles, a practice followed by the UK with Polaris. Thus, it is estimated that 240 warheads for 48 missiles (assuming 5 warheads per missile) will be produced, plus another 10% for spares and maintenance. This would mean a future British stockpile in the 275-warhead range of only

Table 10A.3 *Notes, contd*

1 type. The Ministry of Defence has announced that 'each submarine will deploy with no more than 96 warheads [i.e., MIRV x 6], and may carry significantly fewer'. The number will certainly be lower as the 'sub-strategic' mission for Trident is fully implemented. A MOD official described it as follows: 'A sub-strategic strike would be the limited and highly selective use of nuclear weapons in a manner that fell demonstrably short of a strategic strike, but with a sufficient level of violence to convince an aggressor who had already miscalculated our resolve and attacked us that he should halt his aggression and withdraw or face the prospect of a devastating strategic strike'.

Under plans formulated by the Conservative Government of Prime Minister John Major, the future British stockpile was to have increased slightly from the present 260 to about 275 warheads of 1 type (Trident) around the turn of the century. With the victory of the Labour Party in May 1997 there could be further developments. Changes in nuclear policy are being considered as part of a Strategic Defence Review scheduled to be completed in early 1998. Among the proposals being considered are fewer warheads per Trident missile (placing the total stockpile in the 175–200 warhead range), a no-first-use policy and the ending of continuous SSBN patrols. The implementation of a 'sub-strategic' Trident plan in the UK—deployment of dual strategic and non-strategic Trident II missiles on submarines, some allocated to national tasks and some to NATO—will probably lead to a future operational stockpile of about 200 warheads. When a 4-submarine force is fully operational in 2001, the number on patrol at any given time would be 2 SSBNs with about 120–130 warheads of mixed types. A 3rd SSBN could put to sea fairly rapidly while the 4th is undergoing overhaul and maintenance.

The sub-strategic mission has begun with *Victorious* and 'will become fully robust when *Vigilant* enters service', according to the 1996 White Paper. The plan is to put a single warhead on some Trident II SLBMs and have them assigned to targets once covered by WE-177 gravity bombs. E.g., a submarine could be armed with 10, 12 or 14 of its SLBMs carrying an average of 5 warheads per missile, and the other 2, 4 or 6 missiles armed with just one. There is some flexibility in the choice of yield of the Trident warhead. (Choosing to only detonate the unboosted primary could produce a yield of 1 kt or less. Choosing to detonate the boosted primary could produce a yield of a few kilotons.) With the sub-strategic mission the submarine would have *c*. 56–72 warheads on board during its patrol. Following this logic it is concluded that a more accurate future operational stockpile for the SSBN fleet is about 200 warheads.

Sources: Norris, R. S., Burrows, A. S. and Fieldhouse, R. W., *Nuclear Weapons Databook Vol. V: British, French, and Chinese Nuclear Weapons* (Westview: Boulder, Colo., 1994), p. 9; British Secretary of State for Defence, *Statement on the Defence Estimates 1996*, Cmnd 3223 (HMSO: London, May 1996); and Natural Resources Defense Council (NRDC), 'Nuclear notebook', *Bulletin of the Atomic Scientists*, Nov./Dec. 1996, pp. 64–67.

Table 10A.4. French nuclear forces, January 1998[a]

Type	No. deployed	Year first deployed	Range (km)[b]	Warheads x yield	Warheads in stockpile
Land-based aircraft[c]					
Mirage 2000N/ASMP	45	1988	2 750	1 x 300 kt ASMP	45
Carrier-based aircraft					
Super Étendard[d]	24	1978	650	1 x 300 kt ASMP	20
SLBMs[e]					
M4A/B	48	1985	6 000	6 x 150 kt	288
M45	16	1996	6 000	6 x 100 kt	96

a On 22 and 23 Feb. 1996 President Jacques Chirac announced several reforms for the French armed forces for the period 1997–2002. The decisions in the nuclear area were to withdraw several obsolete systems and to modernize those that remain.

After officials considered numerous plans to replace the silo-based S3D IRBM during President François Mitterrand's tenure, President Chirac announced that the missile would be retired and that there would be no replacement. On 16 Sep. 1996 all 18 missiles on the Plateau d'Albion were deactivated. It will take 2 years and cost $77.5 million to fully dismantle the silos and complex.

In July 1996, after 32 years of service, the Mirage IVP was converted from its nuclear role and retired. Five Mirage IVPs will be retained for reconnaissance missions at Istres. The other aircraft will be put into storage at Châteaudun.

b Range for aircraft assumes combat mission, without refuelling, and does not include the 90- to 350-km range of the Air-Sol Moyenne Portée (ASMP) air-to-surface missile.

c The 3 squadrons of Mirage 2000Ns have now assumed a 'strategic' role, in addition to their 'pre-strategic' one. A 4th Mirage 2000N squadron at Nancy—now conventional—is scheduled to be replaced with Mirage 2000Ds. Those aircraft may be modified to carry the ASMP and be distributed to the 3 2000N squadrons at Luxeuil and Istres, along with the Mirage IVP's ASMP missiles. In Feb. 1997 President Chirac said that a longer-range ASMP (500 km as opposed to 300 km, sometimes called the 'ASMP Plus') will be developed for service entry in about a decade.

The Rafale is planned to be the multi-purpose Navy and Air Force fighter/bomber for the 21st century. Its roles include conventional ground attack, air defence, air superiority and nuclear delivery of the ASMP and/or ASMP Plus. The carrier-based Navy version will be introduced 1st with the Air Force Rafale D attaining a nuclear strike role in *c.* 2005. The Air Force still plans to buy a total of 234 Rafales.

d France built 2 aircraft-carriers, 1 of which entered service in 1961 (*Clemenceau*) and the other in 1963 (*Foch*). Both were modified to handle the AN 52 nuclear gravity bomb with Super Étendard aircraft. The *Clemenceau* was modified in 1979 and the *Foch* in 1981. The AN 52 was retired in July 1991. Only the *Foch* was modified to 'handle and store' the replacement ASMP, and *c.* 20 were allocated for 2 squadrons—*c.* 24 Super Étendard aircraft. The *Clemenceau* was never modified to 'handle and store' the ASMP. The 32 780-ton aircraft-carrier was decommissioned in Sep. 1997. The new aircraft-carrier *Charles de Gaulle* is scheduled to enter service in Dec. 1999, 3 years behind schedule. At that time the *Foch* will be laid up. The *Charles de Gaulle* will have a single squadron of Super Étendards (with presumably about 10 ASMPs) until the Rafale M is introduced in 2002. At about that time a 2nd carrier may be ordered. The Navy plans to purchase a total of 60 Rafale Ms, of which the 1st 16 will perform an air-to-air role. Missions for subsequent aircraft may include the ASMP and/or the ASMP Plus.

e The lead SSBN, *Le Triomphant*, was rolled out from its construction shed in Cherbourg on 13 July 1993. It entered service in Sep. 1996 armed with the M45 SLBM and new TN 75 warheads. The 2nd SSBN, *Le Téméraire*, is under construction and will not be ready until 1999. The schedule for the 3rd, *Le Vigilant*, has slipped and it will not be ready until 2001. The service date for the 4th SSBN is *c.* 2005. It is estimated here that there will eventually be 288 warheads for the fleet of 4 new Triomphant Class SSBNs, because only enough missiles and warheads will be purchased for 3 boats. This loading is the case today, with 5 submarines in the fleet—only 4 sets of M4 SLBMs were procured. President Chirac announced on 23 Feb. 1996 that the 4th submarine would be built and that a new SLBM, known as the M51, will replace the M45 and be ready for service in the period 2010–15.

Sources: Norris, R. S., Burrows, A. S. and Fieldhouse, R. W., *Nuclear Weapons Databook Vol. V: British, French, and Chinese Nuclear Weapons* (Westview: Boulder, Colo., 1994), p. 10; and *Air Actualités*; *Le Magazine de l'Armée de l'Air,* Address by M. Jacques Chirac, President of the Republic, at the École Militaire, Paris, 23 Feb. 1996.

Table 10A.5. Chinese nuclear forces, January 1998

Type	NATO designation	No. deployed	Year first deployed	Range (km)[a]	Warheads x yield	Warheads in stockpile
Aircraft[a]						
H-6	B-6	120	1965	3 100	1–3 bombs	120
Q-5	A-5	30	1970	400	1 x bomb	30
Land-based missiles[b]						
DF-3A	CSS-2	50	1971	2 800	1 x 3.3 Mt	50
DF-4	CSS-3	20	1980	4 750	1 x 3.3 Mt	20
DF-5A	CSS-4	7	1981	13 000+	1 x 4–5 Mt	7
DF-21A	CSS-6	36	1985–86	1 800	1 x 200–300 kt	36
SLBMs[c]						
Julang-1	CSS-N-3	12	1986	1 700	1 x 200–300 kt	12
Tactical weapons						
Artillery/ADMs, Short-range missiles					Low kt	120

[a] All figures for bomber aircraft are for nuclear-configured versions only. Hundreds of aircraft are also deployed in non-nuclear versions. The Hong-5 has been retired and the Hong-7 will not have a nuclear role. Aircraft range is equivalent to combat radius. Assumes 150 bombs for the force, with yields estimated between 10 kt and 3 Mt.

[b] China defines missile ranges as follows: short-range, < 1000 km; medium-range, 1000–3000 km; long-range, 3000–8000 km; and intercontinental range, > 8000 km. The nuclear capability of the medium-range M-9 is unconfirmed and not included. China is also developing 2 other ICBMs: the DF-31, with a range of 8000 km and carrying one 200- to 300-kt warhead, may be deployed in the late 1990s; and the DF-41, with a range of 12 000 km, is scheduled for deployment around 2010 and may be MIRVed if China develops that capability.

[c] The 8000-km range Julang-2 (NATO designation CSS-N-4), to carry one 200- to 300-kt warhead, will be available in the late 1990s.

Sources: Norris, R. S., Burrows, A. S. and Fieldhouse, R. W., *Nuclear Weapons Databook Vol. V: British, French, and Chinese Nuclear Weapons* (Westview: Boulder, Colo., 1994), p. 11; Lewis, J. W. and Hua, D., 'China's ballistic missile programs: technologies, strategies, goals', *International Security*, vol. 17, no. 2 (fall 1992), pp. 5–40; Allen, K. W., Krumel, G. and Pollack, J. D., *China's Air Force Enters the 21st Century* (Rand: Santa Monica, Calif., 1995); International Institute for Strategic Studies (IISS), *The Military Balance 1996–1997* (Oxford University Press: Oxford, 1996), p. 179; and Natural Resources Defense Council (NRDC), 'Nuclear notebook', *Bulletin of the Atomic Scientists*, Nov./Dec. 1996, pp. 64–67.

Appendix 10B. The nuclear weapon-free zones in South-East Asia and Africa

AMITAV ACHARYA and SOLA OGUNBANWO*

I. Introduction

The increasing number of nuclear weapon-free zones (NWFZs) either in existence or under consideration reflects the disapproval of the international community of the acquisition, use or threat of use of nuclear weapons. Regional arrangements establishing such zones are important legal components of the global nuclear non-proliferation regime and supplement international efforts to prevent the emergence of new nuclear weapon states. The establishment of NWFZs has also been an instrument for regulating nuclear weapon deployments by the five declared nuclear weapon states—China, France, Russia, the UK and the USA—and, during the cold war years, for constraining the superpower military competition.

The establishment of NWFZs, which first received widespread attention in the 1950s with respect to Central Europe, has gained considerable momentum. Zones have been created in five regions: Latin America and the Caribbean, the South Pacific, the Korean Peninsula, South-East Asia and Africa.[1] Proposals are being discussed or negotiated for NWFZs in Central Asia, North-East Asia, South Asia, Central and Eastern Europe, the Middle East and the southern hemisphere.[2]

This appendix examines two initiatives which recently culminated in treaties establishing NWFZs in South-East Asia and Africa; these accords illustrate some of the problems and possibilities attending the creation of such zones. Sections II and III describe the background to and provisions of the 1995 Southeast Asia Nuclear Weapon-Free Zone Treaty and the 1996 African Nuclear-Weapon-Free-Zone Treaty, respectively, and point out the implications of these treaties for the nuclear weapon policies of the nuclear weapon states and for the different security dynamics in these two regions.

II. South-East Asia

On 15 December 1995, at a summit meeting of the Association of South-East Asian Nations (ASEAN) held in Bangkok, the Southeast Asia Nuclear Weapon-Free Zone Treaty, known as the Treaty of Bangkok, was signed by all the states of South-East

---

[1] Four of the agreements establishing NWFZs have entered into force: the 1967 Tlatelolco Treaty, for Latin America and the Caribbean; the 1985 Treaty of Rarotonga, for the South Pacific; the 1992 Joint Declaration on the Denuclearization of the Korean Peninsula; and the 1995 Treaty of Bangkok, for South-East Asia. The 1996 Pelindaba Treaty, for Africa, has been opened for signature but has not yet entered into force. The provisions of these and other arms control and disarmament agreements are summarized in annexe A in this volume.

[2] Certain uninhabited areas have also been formally denuclearized: Antarctica, in the 1959 Antarctic Treaty; outer space, the moon and other celestial bodies, in the 1967 Outer Space Treaty and the 1979 Moon Agreement; and the seabed, the ocean floor and the subsoil thereof, in the 1971 Seabed Treaty. All these agreements have entered into force.

* A. Acharya contributed section II of this appendix and S. Ogunbanwo section III.

Asia—Brunei, Cambodia, Indonesia, Laos, Malaysia, Myanmar (Burma), the Philippines, Singapore, Thailand and Viet Nam.[3] At that time, seven of these states were members of ASEAN.[4] On 28 March 1997 Cambodia became the seventh signatory to deposit its instrument of ratification with the Government of Thailand, the treaty depositary. This marked the treaty's entry into force.[5]

The Bangkok Treaty is a major initiative of ASEAN in its search for a new order in the region. Two features of the treaty set it apart from other efforts to create nuclear weapon-free zones. It is the first such treaty to include the land territory, territorial sea, 200-mile exclusive economic zone (EEZ) and continental shelf of each state party. It is also the first such treaty in which, in the protocol, the five nuclear weapon states are to undertake to refrain from using or threatening to use nuclear arms not only against parties to the treaty but also anywhere within the zone.

Background

The idea of a NWFZ in South-East Asia was first mooted in the early 1970s when ASEAN (then comprising the original five members) considered a proposal to establish a South-East Asian Zone of Peace, Freedom and Neutrality (ZOPFAN).[6] ZOPFAN was aimed at limiting the scope for great-power intervention in the region by calling on these states to refrain from forging alliances with South-East Asian countries, establishing military bases on their territories or interfering in their domestic affairs. At that time, ASEAN took note of zone initiatives elsewhere, particularly the 1967 Treaty for the Prohibition of Nuclear Weapons in Latin America and the Caribbean (Treaty of Tlatelolco)[7] and the proposals for an African NWFZ (see section III), indicating a desire to establish a similar zone in the ZOPFAN framework.

The ZOPFAN initiative was suspended by ASEAN following Viet Nam's invasion of Cambodia in December 1978. The perceived threat from Viet Nam caused ASEAN to seek strategic support from China and the USA. Its focus shifted to isolating Viet Nam and searching for a negotiated settlement of the Cambodia conflict. At the same time, a NWFZ was seen by ASEAN as an interim measure which could be advanced as a prelude to the realization of ZOPFAN. In 1984 the ASEAN foreign ministers, meeting in Jakarta, considered the prospects for a NWFZ treaty for South-East Asia. Two years later, the ministers asked a committee of officials working on ZOPFAN to study the principles, objectives and elements of a zone and begin preliminary work on drafting a treaty.

The proposed treaty met serious objections from the United States. The USA pointed out that, because the tensions between ASEAN and Viet Nam made acceptance of the proposed zone by Viet Nam unlikely, the treaty would not be able to pre-

---

[3] The text of the Bangkok Treaty is reproduced in *SIPRI Yearbook 1996: Armaments, Disarmament and International Security* (Oxford University Press: Oxford, 1996), pp. 601–608.

[4] ASEAN was established by the 1967 Bangkok Declaration. The founding members were Indonesia, Malaysia, the Philippines, Singapore and Thailand. Brunei joined in 1984, Viet Nam in 1995, and Laos and Myanmar in 1997. Cambodia's membership was postponed in July 1997 because of its internal problems.

[5] The Bangkok Treaty requires that 7 of the 10 South-East Asian countries ratify it for it to enter into force (Art. 16.1). For the list of signatories and parties to the treaty as of 1 Jan. 1998, see annexe A in this volume.

[6] Alagappa, M., *Towards a Nuclear-Weapons-Free Zone in Southeast Asia*, ISIS Research Note (Institute of Strategic and International Studies: Kuala Lumpur, 1987).

[7] In 1967 the Tlatelolco Treaty was called the Treaty for the Prohibition of Nuclear Weapons in Latin America; it was amended in 1990–92 and the name was changed to include 'and the Caribbean'.

vent Viet Nam's principal ally, the Soviet Union, from being able to station nuclear forces in Viet Nam. Consequently, a South-East Asian NWFZ would restrict deployments of US nuclear forces without imposing similar constraints on the USSR. Because of the strong US position, three ASEAN countries—the Philippines, Singapore and Thailand—were reluctant to go forward with the initiative. The Philippines and Thailand maintained bilateral defence treaties with the USA, while Singapore believed that its security was best served by a strong and unrestricted US military presence in the region.[8] The proposed NWFZ thus divided the ASEAN members, with Indonesia and Malaysia remaining more enthusiastic about the proposal than the other four members at that time.

The end of the cold war and the thaw in relations between ASEAN and Viet Nam following the signing of the 1991 Paris Peace Agreement on Cambodia removed a major obstacle to the NWFZ proposal. ASEAN's decision in 1992 to begin dealing with regional security issues more directly and regularly gave a new impetus to the proposed zone.[9] Although no South-East Asian country possessed nuclear weapons or was suspected of developing them, ASEAN was concerned that North Korea's nuclear programme might encourage Japan to 'go nuclear'. Another concern was China's expanding nuclear arsenal and its territorial claims in the South China Sea, which involved it in disputes with four South-East Asian countries (Brunei, Malaysia, the Philippines and Viet Nam). Against this backdrop, a NWFZ covering the land mass and extended maritime zones of South-East Asia could be helpful in addressing ASEAN's long-term concerns regarding the nuclear weapon policies of the major powers of the Asia–Pacific region and the implications of their rivalry for the region.[10]

At the 26th ASEAN ministerial meeting, held in Singapore in 1993, the ASEAN foreign ministers reaffirmed their commitment to ZOPFAN. As an essential component of ZOPFAN, they decided to create a NWFZ in the region. These efforts culminated in the 1995 Bangkok Treaty.

The treaty provisions

The provisions of the Bangkok Treaty may be analysed in terms of six key areas.

1. *Basic undertakings* (Article 3). The parties undertake not to develop, manufacture or otherwise acquire, possess or have control over nuclear weapons, or to station, transport, test or use such weapons anywhere inside *or outside* the NWFZ. They also undertake to conclude safeguards agreements with the International Atomic Energy Agency (IAEA) and not to allow any other state to develop, manufacture or otherwise acquire, possess or have control over nuclear weapons, or station, test or use them in their territory. The treaty prohibits the dumping of radioactive substances on land, at sea or in the atmosphere.

2. *Peaceful uses of nuclear energy* (Articles 4 and 5). While the treaty allows the use of nuclear energy for economic development, any such programme must be

---

[8] Acharya, A., *A New Regional Order in Southeast Asia: ASEAN in the Post-Cold War Era*, Adelphi Paper no. 279 (International Institute for Strategic Studies: London, 1993).
[9] Until 1992 the ASEAN members stressed the group's socio-economic objectives, while playing down its role in regional security affairs.
[10] The Asia–Pacific region includes the states of South-East Asia plus Australia, Canada, China, Japan, North Korea, South Korea, Mongolia, New Zealand, Papua New Guinea, Russia, Taiwan and the USA.

submitted for rigorous safety assessment before it is embarked upon. This assessment must be made available to other member states when requested. Signatories undertake to ensure the safe disposal of radioactive waste. Prompt notification is required in the event of nuclear accidents.

3. *Rights of passage* (Articles 2 and 7). The treaty does not prejudice the rights of states in this regard under the 1982 United Nations Convention on the Law of the Sea (UNCLOS), such as those concerning freedom of the high seas, rights of innocent passage, and transit of ships and aircraft. Each state may decide for itself whether to allow visits by foreign ships and aircraft to its ports and airfields, transit of its airspace by foreign aircraft, navigation by foreign ships through its territorial sea or archipelagic waters, and overflight of foreign aircraft above those waters in a manner not governed by the rights of innocent passage, archipelagic sea-lane passage or transit passage.

4. *Implementation, compliance and verification mechanisms* (Articles 5 and 10–13). The treaty's verification regime relies on: (*a*) the IAEA safeguards system; (*b*) mutual reporting and exchange of information among the parties to the treaty; and (*c*) requests for fact-finding missions by treaty signatories. The Commission for the Southeast Asia Nuclear Weapon-Free Zone was established by the treaty (Article 8) to oversee implementation and ensure compliance. All parties are members, represented by their foreign ministers or their representatives. It should be noted that the treaty contains no provision for challenge inspections. Instead, it provides for loosely defined fact-finding missions (in the annex). Every member state has the right to ask for a fact-finding mission to be sent to another state to clarify and resolve doubts about compliance with the treaty.

5. *Settlement of disputes* (Article 21). Disputes regarding interpretation of the treaty should be settled by peaceful means, including negotiation, mediation, enquiry and conciliation. If no settlement can be reached within one month, then the dispute may be referred to the International Court of Justice. Despite the availability of this legal mechanism, ASEAN officials have stressed the importance of political dialogue as a means of dispute settlement. Legal procedures are to be used only as a last resort.

6. *Undertakings by the nuclear weapon states* (protocol). Like treaties creating NWFZs elsewhere, the Bangkok Treaty contains a protocol under which the nuclear weapon states are to undertake not to use or threaten to use nuclear weapons against any state party to the treaty. They are also to declare their intention to help achieve 'the general and complete disarmament of nuclear weapons'.

The attitude of the nuclear weapon states

Since no South-East Asian country currently possesses or is suspected of developing nuclear weapons, the main purpose of a NWFZ in this region is to regulate the policies of the nuclear weapon states. However, none of these five states had signed the protocol as of 1 January 1998, despite ASEAN's offer to make amendments or revisions to the treaty just before it was opened for signature.[11]

At that time, the nuclear weapon powers complained about ASEAN's failure to consult them adequately prior to the signing of the treaty, a charge which ASEAN rejected. The more serious reasons behind their refusal to sign the protocol, however, pertained to its language and specific provisions. In this regard, the two most distinc-

[11] Dacanay, A., 'Nuclear-free zone, liberalization moves herald a deeper, broader ASEAN', *Nikkei Weekly*, 18 Dec. 1995, p. 20.

tive features of the Bangkok Treaty have also proved to be the most controversial. These concern the zone's coverage of maritime areas and the restraints it seeks to place on the nuclear weapon states; these states, particularly the USA, consider the restraints to be too sweeping and restrictive.[12]

In registering the strongest objection to the treaty in its original form, the USA argues that the treaty implies territorial rights on the part of the signatories which it does not and cannot accept and which may threaten its ability to move warships around the globe. The USA particularly objects to the application of the treaty's provisions to the continental shelves and the EEZs. In the US view, these provisions violate UNCLOS, which—while allowing coastal nations to exercise sovereign rights over resource development in exclusive economic waters and on continental shelves—does not permit them to exercise political control, such as that entailed in the restrictions on nuclear activity imposed by the Bangkok Treaty anywhere within the zone. The USA is also concerned that extending security rights 200 nautical miles seaward (an idea explicitly rejected in the UNCLOS negotiations) would invite increased, excessive maritime claims and promote conflicts.[13]

The Bangkok Treaty leaves it unclear who interprets the right of innocent passage. Despite ASEAN's assurances that innocent passage of nuclear-armed or -powered vessels through South-East Asian waters is allowed under the treaty, the USA fears that the treaty restricts the free passage of nuclear weapon-capable warships, including submarines. The USA is also concerned that the provisions concerning the rights of innocent passage of warships and aircraft are 'too restrictive'.[14] Against this backdrop, US officials insist that the text of the Bangkok Treaty and its protocol be modified to meet the US criteria for supporting such nuclear weapon-free zones. Furthermore, the USA objects that the ambiguous treaty language potentially interferes with standing US visitation policies for its ships and aircraft.

While China has indicated its support for the general objectives of the treaty it, too, objects to its territorial scope. As Chinese Foreign Ministry spokesman Chen Jian stated, 'The issue at present is the geographical area of the zone. We have expressed our concern to Asean'. At the same time, China issued a reminder that it already had a long-standing policy of no-first-use of nuclear weapons, under which it is obliged not to 'use . . . nuclear arms . . . against non-nuclear states or in nuclear-free zones'.[15] The reasons behind the Chinese objection may be understood in the context of the treaty's coverage of areas in the South China Sea which are under dispute between China and several of the South-East Asian countries. China's concerns are aggravated by the enthusiasm for the treaty shown by Viet Nam, which alone among the ASEAN members has a history of direct military confrontation with China.[16]

On a visit to Singapore in early 1996, French President Jacques Chirac stated that his country was 'predisposed to sign the Treaty'.[17] He conceded, however, that some

---

[12] Editorial, 'Leap toward united, N-free S. E. Asia', *Daily Yomiuri*, 16 Dec. 1995, p. 11.

[13] Rosen, M., 'Nuclear weapon-free zones', *Naval War College Review*, vol. 49, no. 4 (autumn 1996), p. 59.

[14] Johnson, C., 'Southeast Asia asks world to back nuclear pact', Reuters World Service Dispatch, 15 Dec. 1995.

[15] Lee, S. H., 'Study investment prospects, Asem told', *Straits Times*, 2 Mar. 1996, p. 18.

[16] 'Nuclear-free zones', *Mainichi Daily News*, 19 Dec. 1995, p. 2. China carried out a 'punitive' attack on Viet Nam in retaliation against Viet Nam's invasion of Cambodia in 1978 and has since then fought 2 naval battles with Viet Nam in the South China Sea.

[17] 'France likely to sign S-E Asia N-pact soon', *Straits Times*, 3 Mar. 1996, p. 18.

'technical details' (which he did not specify) remained to be sorted out.[18] By appearing to be less hard-line on the treaty than the USA, Chirac was clearly trying to restore the country's image in the region, which had suffered when France resumed nuclear testing in the South Pacific in 1995. It is noteworthy that, while expressing France's 'constructive attitude' towards the creation of a NWFZ in South-East Asia,[19] Chirac also announced his decision to sign the three protocols to the 1985 South Pacific Nuclear Free Zone Treaty (Rarotonga Treaty) after France had conducted its last series of nuclear tests in the South Pacific, completed in January 1996.[20]

The Russian attitude towards the Bangkok Treaty has been somewhat more positive.[21] The Russian Ambassador to Indonesia expressed Russia's support for the treaty 'in principle'. While Russia did not 'want its contents changed', it 'need[ed] clarification on how the treaty will be implemented'. This includes details of the boundaries covered by the treaty and the regulations covering ships operating in the zone.[22] Despite its generally supportive position, however, Russia has not signed the protocol.

Prospects

The ASEAN countries have expressed great disappointment at the refusal of the nuclear weapon states to accept the Bangkok Treaty in its present form.[23] As Malaysian Foreign Ministry Secretary General Ahmed Kamil Jaafar put it, 'If we succumb to their fancies, it will make nonsense of that treaty'.[24] Viet Nam's Prime Minister, Vo Van Kiet, urged the nuclear weapon states to 'respect Southeast Asia's aspiration and commitment' by accepting the treaty.[25] However, realizing that without the support of the nuclear weapon states its hopes for a NWFZ will remain a pipedream, ASEAN agreed to a dialogue with the USA to accommodate its reservations. President Fidel Ramos of the Philippines stated that the treaty and protocol had enough 'flexibility' to accommodate the big powers, adding, 'ASEAN is going to be very patient about this'.[26]

The United States has proposed two ways to resolve the protocol issue.[27] The first option is to delete all references to continental shelves and EEZs in the text of the treaty. This is its preferred option. A less desirable option from the US point of view is for all the parties to the treaty to issue an 'interpretive statement' which specifies that the treaty's provisions concerning continental shelves and EEZs will apply only to the parties to the treaty and not to the protocol signatories. This statement should

---

[18] Jacques Chirac, as cited in Ganz, S., 'France ready to sign on SE Asian nuclear-free zone', Kyodo News Service Dispatch, Japan Economic Newswire, 2 Mar. 1996.
[19] Teo, P. K., 'France seeks warmer ties, larger role in Asia', *Nikkei Weekly*, 4 Mar. 1996, p. 23; and 'Chirac gives his word', *New Straits Times*, 3 Mar. 1996, p. 2.
[20] France signed the protocols to the Rarotonga Treaty in Mar. and ratified them in Sep. 1996.
[21] Dacanay (note 11), p. 20; and ITAR-TASS (in English), 27 July 1997, in 'Primakov calls for nuclear free zone in South East Asia', Foreign Broadcast Information Service, *Daily Report–Central Eurasia (FBIS-SOV)*, FBIS-SOV-97-208, 27 July 1997.
[22] Dacanay (note 11), p. 20.
[23] Chaiyapinunt, N., 'Nuclear weapon free zones and ASEAN', Paper presented to the Eighth Regional Disarmament Meeting in the Asia Pacific Region, 21–24 Feb. 1996, Kathmandu, Nepal, p. 2.
[24] Cited in Dacanay (note 11), p. 20.
[25] Cited in Dacanay (note 11), p. 20.
[26] Cited in Coloma, R., 'Big powers' doubts pose problems for Southeast Asia nuclear ban', Agence France Presse Dispatch, 16 Dec. 1996.
[27] Conversation by the author with Ambassador Thomas Graham, US Special Representative for Arms Control, Nonproliferation and Disarmament, in Kuala Lumpur, 8 June 1996.

be accompanied by the deletion of the second sentence of Article 2 of the protocol, which now reads: 'It [each party] further undertakes not to use or threaten to use nuclear weapons within the Southeast Asia Nuclear Weapon-Free Zone'. In subsequent talks with ASEAN, the USA has pointed out that this sentence prohibits it from launching nuclear missiles from platforms, such as ships or submarines, sailing within the zone against targets outside the zone.[28] The modified Article 2, in the US view, should only contain its current first sentence: 'Each State Party undertakes not to use or threaten to use nuclear weapons against any State Party to the Treaty'.

Although both the USA and ASEAN seem hopeful that mutually acceptable amendments to the treaty will be found, several exchanges between them to resolve the difference over the language of the protocol have failed to produce the desired breakthrough.[29] Moreover, an agreement reached between the USA and ASEAN may not allay China's concerns regarding the implications of the treaty for its territorial claims in the South China Sea.

Conclusions

Despite the problems encountered in securing agreement from the nuclear weapon states, the Bangkok Treaty remains an important milestone for ASEAN. It also strengthens the global non-proliferation regime by signalling the growing acceptance of NWFZs around the world. The opening for signature of the Bangkok Treaty added momentum to regional approaches to nuclear non-proliferation: less than six months later a treaty was opened for signature that established a NWFZ in Africa, and progress was made towards securing ratification of the relevant protocols to the Treaty of Rarotonga by the nuclear weapon states.[30] Although non-proliferation problems in Asia are more salient in the Korean Peninsula and South Asia, a NWFZ in South-East Asia sets an important precedent in dealing with proliferation issues in the wider Asia–Pacific region.

It is interesting to note that in the wake of the signing of the Bangkok Treaty ASEAN sought to put pressure on India to forgo nuclear testing.[31] A successful agreement between ASEAN and the nuclear weapon states on the treaty's protocol will be an important demonstration of the relevance of NWFZs and a helpful signal of the desire and commitment of the nuclear weapon states to halt proliferation trends in other areas of the Asia–Pacific region and in the rest of the world.

[28] According to Tariq Rauf, Director of the International Organizations and Nonproliferation Project, Monterey Institute of International Studies and consultant to the Canadian Government, a source familiar with the negotiations, Malaysia has proposed language that allows the nuclear weapon powers to launch nuclear weapons from within the zone targeted against non-zonal states, but the USA insists on deleting this sentence altogether.

[29] E.g., no progress was made in the talks held in Kuala Lumpur on 2–4 June 1997 to consider a series of compromises to resolve the differences between the ASEAN members and the nuclear weapon states over the language of the protocol. Institute for Defense and Disarmament Studies, *Arms Control Reporter* (IDDS: Brookline, Mass.), sheet 459.B.4, Sep. 1997.

[30] Of the nuclear weapon states, the USA is the only signatory which has not ratified all the protocols. See annexe A in this volume.

[31] 'Southeast Asia opposes any Indian nuclear test', Reuters World Service Dispatch, 16 Dec. 1995. The Bangkok Treaty was opened for signature at a time when speculation was rife concerning an imminent Indian nuclear test. Ajit Singh, then Secretary General of ASEAN, stated ASEAN's opposition to nuclear testing by any power, including India. However, in 1996, when India joined the ASEAN Regional Forum (ARF)—a multilateral forum established in 1993 for the countries of Asia–Pacific to discuss regional security issues—the ASEAN countries did not seem to challenge India's refusal to accept the 1996 Comprehensive Nuclear Test-Ban Treaty or to use ARF to discuss South Asian nuclear proliferation issues.

III. Africa

On 11 April 1996 representatives of the African nations, the nuclear weapon states and other concerned extra-regional states met in Cairo to participate in the historic signing ceremony of the African Nuclear-Weapon-Free Zone Treaty, known as the Treaty of Pelindaba.[32] As of 1 January 1998, 47 African states had signed the treaty and 2 had ratified it.[33] The treaty will enter into force on the date of the deposit of the 28th instrument of ratification with the Secretary-General of the Organization of African Unity (OAU), the treaty depositary.

In their 1996 and 1997 resolutions both the OAU and the UN drew the attention of the African states to their responsibilities and called upon them to ratify the treaty as soon as possible so that it may enter into force without delay. Moreover, at a meeting of the African Group at UN Headquarters in New York on 13 November 1997, several signatories indicated that their processes of ratification had reached an advanced stage. It is expected that like-minded African states and other strong supporters of the treaty will speed up the ratification process by organizing similar meetings in 1998 at either the regional or the subregional level. This has led to the conclusion that the required 28 ratifications may be attainable by the end of 1998.

The opening of the treaty for signature was a source of justifiable satisfaction for those African nations which have shared the NWFZ goal for decades and represents a significant achievement for Africa.[34]

Background

The origin of the efforts of African states to pursue the denuclearization of Africa can be traced to their opposition to France's nuclear testing in the Sahara Desert, announced in 1958 and first carried out in 1960.[35] Alongside opposition to the colonial powers' use of their former African colonies for nuclear testing, the African states also advanced other reasons, such as the need to prevent Africa from being drawn into the cold war rivalry of the nuclear weapon powers, to do away with the South African nuclear weapon capability (in the period 1970–90), to maintain security and stability, and to avoid a regional nuclear arms race. They also wished to contribute to general and complete disarmament as part of an international effort to strengthen global peace and security and to halt the proliferation of nuclear weapons. It is significant that the early initiatives of the African states to denuclearize Africa led to the adoption by the UN General Assembly of the first resolution on a nuclear

---

[32] The text of the Pelindaba Treaty is reproduced in *SIPRI Yearbook 1996* (note 3), pp. 593–601. The treaty is called the Pelindaba Treaty after the name of the area near Pretoria where South Africa's nuclear weapon development took place and where the UN–OAU Group of Experts completed the treaty draft on 2 June 1995.

[33] The treaty is open for signature by all the states of Africa. By Apr. 1998, 6 states had ratified the treaty. For the list of signatories and parties to the treaty, see annexe A in this volume.

[34] For a discussion of regional proliferation and efforts to curb it, see Goodby, J. E., Kile, S. and Müller, H., 'Nuclear arms control', *SIPRI Yearbook 1995: Armaments, Disarmament and International Security* (Oxford University Press: Oxford, 1995), pp. 653–63. For a general assessment and history of nuclear weapon-free zones, see Goldblat, J., *Nonproliferation Review*, spring–summer 1997, pp. 18–32.

[35] France conducted 17 nuclear tests in this programme; 13 tests were conducted underground (in In Ecker) and 4 in the atmosphere (in Reganne). For the full list of nuclear explosions, see Ferm, R., 'Nuclear explosions, 1945–96', *SIPRI Yearbook 1997: Armaments, Disarmament and International Security* (Oxford University Press: Oxford, 1997), pp. 432–36.

weapon-free zone.[36] In 1963 five Latin American presidents issued a Joint Declaration on the Denuclearization of Latin America, the first example of cross-fertilization between the African and Latin American denuclearization concepts.

The OAU, established in 1963, held its first Assembly of Heads of State and Government in Cairo in 1964, where it adopted the Declaration on the Denuclearization of Africa (Cairo Declaration).[37] Signed by 34 OAU member states, the declaration stated their willingness to undertake, through an international agreement to be concluded under UN auspices, not to manufacture or have control of nuclear weapons and requested the General Assembly to take the necessary measures to convene an international conference for the purpose of concluding an agreement to that effect. Thus Africa was the first region to undertake a unilateral renunciation of the right to develop nuclear weapons.

The General Assembly did not convene such a conference but in General Assembly Resolution 2033 (XX) of 3 December 1965 endorsed the Cairo Declaration and expressed the hope that the African states themselves would initiate studies and take the necessary measures through the OAU to implement the declaration. This resolution also requested the UN Secretary-General to extend to the OAU the facilities and assistance that it might require to achieve its aims.

The delay in implementing the Cairo Declaration may be attributed to several factors. First, France terminated its nuclear testing in the Sahara Desert in 1966, thereby removing the African states' original motivation for creating the zone. Another factor was the suspicion of the African nations that the South African apartheid government was developing a nuclear weapon capability, which was perceived by them as a threat to security in the region. In this situation it became difficult to achieve consensus on implementation of the declaration. A third factor was the fact that the African states themselves did not take adequate political initiatives or plan a strategy for capitalizing on the Cairo Declaration and Resolution 2033. Thus, from 1970 until 1990 the UN General Assembly and the OAU adopted annual resolutions in which the focus shifted from concluding a treaty on an African NWFZ to matters considered to be obstacles to its achievement. This was in sharp contrast to the intense negotiations of 1963–67 by the Latin American states that resulted in the Treaty of Tlatelolco.

From 1990 a series of dramatic changes at the regional and international levels led the African states to believe that the time was ripe to pursue their plan for denuclearization of Africa. The first significant change was the political confidence created in the nuclear field by South Africa's accession to the 1968 Non-Proliferation Treaty (NPT) in 1991 and its quick acceptance of IAEA safeguards. Of critical importance was the historic disclosure by President F. W. de Klerk, on 24 March 1993, that South Africa had developed and produced nuclear weapons but had dismantled and destroyed them before joining the NPT.[38] This announcement meant that the Pelindaba Treaty would vary significantly from the existing NWFZ treaties since, in contrast to the other zones, there existed a nuclear weapon-capable state in the region. It also meant that the treaty should ensure not only that no new nuclear explosive devices would be introduced into the region but also that those already developed

---

[36] UN General Assembly Resolution 1652 (XVI) of 24 Nov. 1961, 'Consideration of Africa as a "denuclearized zone"'.

[37] OAU document AHG/Res.11(1), 21 July 1964.

[38] Albright, D., 'South Africa's secret nuclear weapons', *ISIS Report* (Institute of Strategic and International Studies, Kuala Lumpur), vol. 1, no. 4 (May 1994). See also Ferm, R., 'Chronology 1993', *SIPRI Yearbook 1994* (Oxford University Press: Oxford, 1994), p. 796; and Goodby, Kile and Müller (note 34), pp. 661–62.

would be destroyed together with the facilities for their production. South Africa went from playing an obstructionist role in the global non-proliferation regime to a positive one and was instrumental in pushing forward the negotiations to establish an African NWFZ. These measures by South Africa meant that a vital precondition for the military denuclearization of Africa had been fulfilled.

Other significant changes related to South Africa's successful peace process with the front-line and neighbouring states and the improved political situation within South Africa itself through the abolition of the universally condemned apartheid system and the holding of democratic elections, which led to the installation of the Government of National Unity in April 1994. These developments greatly changed the threat perceptions of the African states and their general attitude towards regional security and the establishment of an African NWFZ.

In 1990, at the initiative of the African nations, the General Assembly had adopted a measure in General Assembly Resolution 45/56A of 4 December which was later to prove decisive for the success of the African NWFZ concept—the creation of the OAU/UN Group of Experts, specifically instructed to examine the modalities and elements for the preparation and implementation of a treaty on the denuclearization of Africa. The Group of Experts held six sessions between 1991 and 1995. At the last session, in June 1995, the group completed the draft text of the African Nuclear-Weapon-Free Zone Treaty and it was amended by the OAU Council of Ministers on 23 June 1995. The OAU Assembly of Heads of State and Government approved the treaty at its 31st Ordinary Session, held on 26–28 June 1995. The treaty was forwarded to the UN Secretary-General on 2 August, and during the celebration of the 50th anniversary of the founding of the UN, the General Assembly welcomed the Pelindaba Treaty with special satisfaction in General Assembly Resolution 50/78 of 12 December 1995.

The treaty provisions

The nuclear non-proliferation provisions of the Pelindaba Treaty include the renunciation of nuclear explosive devices, the prevention of the stationing of nuclear explosive devices and the prohibition of testing of nuclear explosive devices. As to the definition of a nuclear weapon state, the treaty follows Article IX of the NPT, which defines a nuclear weapon state as 'one which has manufactured and exploded a nuclear weapon or other nuclear explosive device prior to 1 January, 1967', that is, the five declared nuclear weapon states. Nuclear threshold states are thus not included in that category of states.

The treaty has several unique features not found in other NWFZ treaties, including the ban on research aimed at acquiring nuclear explosive devices (Article 3) and the provisions of Article 6: parties undertake to declare their capabilities for manufacturing nuclear explosive devices, to dismantle and destroy any such device that it has manufactured before the treaty enters into force; to destroy or convert facilities for production; and to permit international inspection of the processes of dismantling and destruction of nuclear explosive devices and destruction or conversion of production facilities. The text of Article 6 was prompted by de Klerk's admission in 1993 that South Africa had developed a nuclear 'deterrent' capability. Subsequently, the IAEA verified and assessed the correctness and completeness of South Africa's declared inventory and later confirmed that South Africa had in fact destroyed all its nuclear explosive devices.[39] The provisions in Article 11, by which parties will not take, assist or encourage any action aimed at an armed attack by conventional or other means against nuclear installations in the zone, are also unique to this NWFZ treaty.

Among the other provisions of the treaty, Article 10 sets the highest standards of security and physical protection of nuclear materials and facilities, which must be maintained by the parties. Article 5 prohibits nuclear testing by the parties, thereby constituting a regional test ban. Annex IV (paragraph 4) permits complaints against the parties to Protocol III. Article 1 defines the terms 'nuclear installation' and 'nuclear material', and Article 4 contains the requirement that the parties' sovereign rights to allow visits by foreign ships and aircraft to their ports and airfields, transits of their airspace by foreign aircraft and navigation by foreign ships in their territorial waters, and so on, are subject to the qualification contained in the phrase 'without prejudice to the purposes and objectives of the treaty'.

Article 7 contains an important provision, the prevention of the dumping of radioactive waste in the zone, which reflects the long-standing environmental concern of the African states that their continent should not be used as a dumping site. For this purpose, the parties are obliged 'to use as guidelines the measures contained in the [1991] Bamako Convention on the Ban of the Import into Africa and Control of Transboundary Movement and Management of Hazardous Wastes within Africa in so far as it is relevant to radioactive waste'.

Article 8 contains elaborate provisions on the peaceful uses of nuclear technology. Accordingly, it encourages parties to make use of the programme of assistance for Africa available through the IAEA and the African Regional Cooperative Agreement for Research, Training and Development Related to Nuclear Science and Technology (AFRA).[40] Parties also undertake to promote individually and collectively the use of nuclear technology for economic and social development and to establish and strengthen mechanisms for cooperation at the bilateral, subregional and regional levels. In Article 9, parties are obliged to conclude safeguards agreements with the IAEA and to apply full-scope safeguards when supplying source material to non-nuclear weapon states. Africa is an important source of nuclear fuel. A few African states produce large amounts of uranium minerals and engage in significant commercial activities which provide valuable and needed sources of income. The African suppliers of uranium minerals include Gabon, Namibia, Niger and South Africa.

In Article 12 the parties agree to establish the African Commission on Nuclear Energy (AFCONE) for the purposes of implementation and ensuring compliance with their undertakings. The commission will be composed of 12 members elected by the parties for a three-year period, 'bearing in mind the need for equitable geographical distribution as well as to include Members with advanced nuclear programmes. Each Member shall have one representative nominated with particular regard for his/her expertise in the subject of the Treaty' (Annex III). The commission shall be responsible for the operation of the treaty and is comparable to the Agency for the Prohibition of Nuclear Weapons in Latin America and the Caribbean (OPANAL) under the Tlatelolco Treaty, with its own headquarters, secretariat and executive branch. Any disputes that cannot be resolved in negotiations between the parties concerned will be

---

[39] For a discussion, see Goodby, Kile and Müller (note 34).

[40] AFRA is an African intergovernmental organization established in 1990; 21 African states are members. It promotes regional collaboration in the development and application of science and technology, in cooperation with the IAEA.

brought to the commission, which, if appropriate, will request the IAEA to conduct an inspection or establish its own mechanism.

The highest body created by the treaty is the Conference of Parties (Article 14). However, its main functions are to elect members of the commission, to adopt the commission's budget, and, occasionally, to convene in extraordinary session to receive and deliberate on the commission's findings regarding complaints against a party.

The attitude of the nuclear weapon states

The extent of the zone of application of the treaty is defined in Article 2 and illustrated in the map in Annex I. Preparation of the map of the zone and the wording of Article 2 proved problematic because of existing disputes between extra-regional states and certain African nations over contested territories and islands that might lie within the African NWFZ. To compound the problem, two of the concerned extra-regional states are nuclear weapon states whose support for the protocols to the treaty is crucial for its effectiveness. The problem was solved through extensive consultations with the extra-regional states concerned. In the case of the Chagos Archipelago, including the island of Diego Garcia, the compromise solution was to encircle the archipelago, claimed by both the UK and Mauritius, with a footnote which reads: 'Appears without prejudice to the question of sovereignty'. The UK considers Diego Garcia to be part of the British Indian Ocean Territory (BIOT), while Mauritius considers the Chagos Archipelago to be part of its territory. The UN–OAU Group of Experts acknowledged that resolution of the sovereignty issue could only occur outside the framework of the treaty.[41]

Protocols I and II are addressed to the nuclear weapon states. Protocol I relates to negative security assurances: these states undertake not to use or threaten to use a nuclear explosive device against any party to the treaty or territory within the zone. Protocol II deals with nuclear tests: the nuclear weapon states undertake not to test a nuclear explosive device within the zone. All the nuclear weapon states have signed these two protocols, but only France and China have ratified them.

Protocol III is not addressed to the nuclear weapon states but to the extra-regional states which are, *de jure* or de facto, responsible for territories within the zone, that is, France and Spain. They undertake to apply the relevant provisions of the treaty to those territories. France has ratified Protocol III, but Spain has not yet signed it.

It is both significant and commendable that all the nuclear weapon states signed the relevant Pelindaba protocols immediately after they were opened for signature in 1995 and that France and China quickly ratified the protocols addressed to them.

Conclusions

The establishment of an African NWFZ advances international nuclear non-proliferation norms and contributes to efforts to strengthen the global non-

---

[41] In 1996 the UK stated that neither the treaty nor Protocol III applies to the activities of the UK, the USA or any other state not party to the treaty on the island or elsewhere in the BIOT. Russia stated that as long as a nuclear weapon state had a military base on the islands of the archipelago and as long as certain nuclear weapon states consider themselves free from the obligations under the protocols with regard to these islands, Russia could not regard them as meeting the requirements of nuclear weapon-free territories. For summaries of the interpretive statements and understandings issued by France, Russia and the UK in connection with the protocols, see annexe A in this volume.

proliferation regime. It is also an important achievement for the continent in regional security cooperation.

The Pelindaba Treaty is the first NWFZ accord to be negotiated under the auspices of the United Nations in cooperation with a regional organization—in this case the OAU. The ability of the UN to extend assistance if requested by other regions or subregions in similar circumstances has been amply demonstrated. It is also the only NWFZ treaty that establishes a zone with a former nuclear weapon state, South Africa, which played a constructive role in the efforts to conclude the treaty. The 1993 Harare meeting of the UN–OAU Group of Experts was significant in that for the first time in the history of the efforts to denuclearize Africa the conjuncture of circumstances made it possible to invite representatives of the South African Government to participate in that and future meetings of the group. Indeed, this was the first major cooperative undertaking between post-apartheid South Africa and the rest of the African continent.

Just as the African negotiators drew on the experience and operation of earlier NWFZ treaties, the Pelindaba Treaty will add to this experience and may provide lessons in confidence building and non-proliferation for other regions. The combined areas of the zones created by the Antarctic, Bangkok, Pelindaba, Rarotonga and Tlatelolco treaties constitute about 45 per cent of the earth's surface. With the entry into force of the Pelindaba Treaty, virtually all of the southern hemisphere and parts of the northern hemisphere will be covered by NWFZs.

With regard to the issues of drawing up the map of the areas of application of NWFZ treaties, as well as securing the support of nuclear weapon states and other concerned extra-regional states, certain lessons can be learned from the African experience. The most important lesson is that states wishing in the future to create a NWFZ in their region should seriously seek to establish adequate contacts at an early stage—certainly before the treaty is finalized and signed—with the nuclear weapon states and the other concerned extra-regional states. In the African context, this proved to be mutually beneficial. In addition to extensive informal consultations, representatives of the nuclear weapon states and the other concerned extra-regional states participated in special meetings of the UN–OAU Group of Experts. This provided opportunities to ascertain in a timely fashion their viewpoints regarding the treaty protocols which are addressed to them.

In addition to its non-proliferation, disarmament, verification and compliance, and environmental protection provisions, the Treaty of Pelindaba will enhance regional and international cooperative efforts in the application of nuclear technology for sustainable development in Africa. Thus, the treaty will represent an important contribution to a holistic approach to African security.

11. Chemical and biological weapon developments and arms control

JEAN PASCAL ZANDERS and JOHN HART

I. Introduction

The year 1997 was marked by the entry into force of the 1993 Chemical Weapons Convention (CWC) and the start of work to establish an effective disarmament regime. Progress in the negotiations on a protocol to the 1972 Biological and Toxin Weapons Convention (BTWC) was modest, although the introduction of a 'rolling text' allows for a more structured approach.[1]

Despite efforts to establish or strengthen disarmament regimes for chemical and biological weapons (CBW) concern about their proliferation and use increased in 1997. In Iraq officials continued to obstruct inspections by the United Nations Special Commission on Iraq (UNSCOM) teams, and at the end of the year the crisis between the UN and Iraq escalated to the point that military intervention became a serious possibility. Tear-gas was used for the first time after the entry into force of the CWC—by military forces in Bosnia and Herzegovina. This event highlighted a grey area in the convention. Cuba formally accused the United States of waging biological warfare and initiated the BTWC procedure to discuss such types of allegation, the first time this has occurred since the convention entered into force in 1975. Measures to counter proliferation increased in Western countries.

Section II of this chapter deals with the declarations regarding past chemical weapon programmes, the destruction of chemical weapons in Russia and the USA, and abandoned CW in China. The relation to the CWC of the use of riot-control agents by peacekeeping forces is also investigated. The efforts to strengthen the BTWC disarmament regime are discussed in section III. Sections IV and V deal with CBW proliferation concerns and allegations of use and the UNSCOM activities in Iraq, respectively. The Gulf War illnesses are addressed in section VI.

II. Chemical weapon disarmament

The creation of a disarmament regime

The CWC entered into force on 29 April 1997, and after four years of preparation the Organisation for the Prohibition of Chemical Weapons (OPCW) became operational and began its mandated tasks. As of 1 January 1998, 106 states had deposited their instruments of ratification or acceded to the

---

[1] A brief summary of both conventions and lists of parties are given in annexe A in this volume.

CWC (including the five permanent members of the UN Security Council), and 59 states had signed but not ratified the convention.[2] France and the United Kingdom deposited their instruments of ratification in 1995 and 1996, respectively. Although the US Senate earlier refused to give its consent, the United States ratified the CWC on 24 April 1997. In Congress a vigorous campaign mounted by the Clinton Administration and supported by a broad coalition of non-governmental organizations (NGOs), the chemical industry and former governmental officials overcame the resistance of conservative Republicans. The Senate nonetheless attached 28 conditions to the ratification, which focus on the Senate's views on aspects of the CWC; reporting, consultation and notification of Congress; financial and resource commitments; implementation tasks; and US safeguards, especially as regards the ability of the USA to defend itself effectively.[3] By the end of 1997 Congress had not passed national implementation legislation, and the USA thus failed to meet some CWC requirements. China approved the CWC on 30 December 1996 but waited for the US ratification before depositing its instrument of ratification on 25 April 1997. The ratification process in Russia was more arduous as a consequence of internal political developments, concern about the high cost of implementation in view of the frailty of the economy and the local environmental impact of the destruction of Russia's huge CW stockpile. The Duma initially considered ratification on 23 April[4] but delayed action until the autumn. Russia deposited its instrument of ratification on 5 November, before the Second Conference of the States Parties on 1–5 December 1997. Several countries waited for the US cue before taking action on the CWC and, consequently, some of them failed to ratify the convention before it entered into force; they could thus neither become original parties nor attend the First Conference of the States Parties, held on 6–24 May 1997, as full members.[5]

Despite controversy over the interpretation of some articles, the CWC has attracted the ratification of states in regions of high tension. In some cases, joining the convention amounted to an act of unilateral disarmament in the face of a hostile neighbour believed to possess CW or superior conventional or nuclear weapons, thus expressing confidence in the security regime offered by the CWC. Some of these countries are presumed CW possessors or have admitted to having a CW programme. South Korea became an original party to the CWC despite continuing reports that North Korea might launch a surprise missile strike with chemical agents against South Korea. In October 1997 Pakistan joined India as a party to the CWC. Pakistan's delay in ratifica-

[2] States that accede to the CWC or deposit their instruments of ratification after 29 Apr. 1997 become parties only 30 days after deposit of the instrument of ratification or accession. See appendix 11A in this volume for a discussion of the entry into force of the convention.

[3] US Senate, *Congressional Record*, 24 Apr. 1997, pp. S3651–57. The effects of the conditions are discussed in Gordon, A., 'Implications of the US resolution of ratification', *CBW Conventions Bulletin*, no. 38 (Dec. 1997), pp. 1–6.

[4] 'Duma to consider Chemical Weapons Convention ratification soon', Interfax via Maximov Online, 16 Apr. 1997, URL <http://www.maximov.com/scripts/recent.pl?ref=2058>, version current on 25 Apr. 1997.

[5] A chronological overview of ratifications and accessions is available at the SIPRI CBW Project web site, URL <http://www.sipri.se/cbw/docs/cw-cwc-ratchrono.html>.

tion may partially have been the consequence of political instability in early 1997. Some senior active and retired military officers also voiced concern about abandoning an important military option in the face of Indian hegemony both before and after Pakistan's ratification. Although the government was not required to seek parliamentary consent, it was criticized for depositing the instrument of ratification without doing so—thus denying public debate on the security value of retaining the military option of chemical warfare.[6] India, which became a party on 3 September 1996, threatened in March 1997 to withdraw from the CWC on the grounds that its two main regional rivals, China and Pakistan, and the two possessors of the world's largest stocks, Russia and the United States, were not parties.[7] India's threat was not carried out since China and the USA deposited their instruments of ratification in April 1997. The statement, which was repeated on 6 August,[8] was probably made to allay domestic fear that India was compromising its national security by joining the CWC and to emphasize some Indian positions on the CWC to other parties.

The number of Arab parties to the CWC rose to nine in 1997, despite the position adopted by the League of Arab States not to ratify the CWC unless Israel joins the 1968 Non-Proliferation Treaty (NPT). The countries in the geographical periphery of the Arab–Israeli conflict—the Maghreb and the Persian Gulf region—became parties in part because of the negative economic impact the convention would otherwise have had on their oil and chemical industries.[9] Jordan, which borders Israel and with which it has a peace treaty, acceded to the CWC on 29 October. The Middle East, however, also has the highest concentration of non-signatory states, most of which are widely considered to be actively involved in CW armament programmes: Egypt, Eritrea, Iraq, Lebanon, Libya, Sudan and Syria. In early September 1997 speculation increased as to whether Israel would become a party,[10] but on 4 September Eytan Bentsur, Director-General of the Ministry of Foreign Affairs, told the Conference on Disarmament in Geneva that Israel would not do so because of the increasing CW threat from its neighbours.[11] Following a 10 April verdict by the Berlin Criminal Court (Berliner Kammergericht) that Iranian author-

[6] Jilani, F. (Brig.), 'Indian chemical warfare capability', *NDC Journal*, vol. 9, no. 1 (National Defence College: Islamabad, 1996), pp. 71–73; and *Rawalpindi Nawa-i-Waqt*, 12 Jan. 1998, pp. 5, 8, in 'Pakistan: retired generals criticize signing of CWC', Foreign Broadcast Information Service, *Daily Report–Near East and South Asia (FBIS-NES)*, FBIS-NES-98-089, 15 Jan. 1998. In the latter article, one general wrongly claimed that India had not yet signed the CWC. H. A., 'Pakistan to ratify CWC if others do: FO', *Dawn* (Karachi), 25 Apr. 1997.

[7] 'India threatens to quit chemical weapons treaty', *The Muslim* (Islamabad), 18 Mar. 1997; 'Chemical reactions', *Times of India*, 19 Apr. 1997, p. 10; and *Navbharat Times* (New Delhi), 28 Apr. 1997, in 'India: signing of chemical weapons treaty', FBIS-NES-97-083, 1 May 1997.

[8] P. H., 'India can walk out of chemical pact: PM', *The Hindu* (Madras), 7 Aug. 1997.

[9] See the section on 'The international debate concerning the Australia Group' in chapter 9 in this volume.

[10] Eshel, D. (Lt-Col, ret.), 'Israel grapples with CWC ratification', *Armed Forces Journal*, Sep. 1997, p. 24; and Associated Press, 'Israel might OK chemical weapon ban', via *The Wire*, 3 Sep. 1997, URL <http://wire.ap.org/APnews/center?STORYOID=206b.8924&FRONTID=MIDEAS>, version current on 5 Sep. 1997.

[11] Permanent Mission of Israel (Geneva), Statement by H. E. Mr Eytan Bentsur, Director-General of the Ministry of Foreign Affairs of Israel, before the Conference on Disarmament, 4 Sep. 1997, pp. 7–8.

ities were involved in the bombing of a restaurant, Iran delayed the deposit of its instrument of ratification until 3 November 1997.

Declarations of CW possession and programmes

Under Article III of the CWC each party must declare its chemical weapon stockpile, old and abandoned chemical weapons, and production facilities not later than 30 days after the convention enters into force for it. Unless the party chooses to make such information public, it remains confidential to the OPCW and available to other parties. Few such announcements were made in 1997. The OPCW began its preliminary inspections on 1 June in the USA.

Data on the Russian and US stockpiles and programmes have been available for some time.[12] In an effort to set a precedent of transparency the UK published part of its detailed declaration to the OPCW relating to its former offensive CW programme at the end of May 1997.[13] On 26 June India submitted details of what an Indian foreign affairs spokesman called 'its chemical weapons hoards and production facilities' to the OPCW.[14] The details were not made public, although a New Delhi-based military analyst suggested that the Indian Army had no access to the CW stockpiles, which remain at a laboratory of the Defence Research and Development Organisation (DRDO) which produced the weapons.[15] The OPCW inspected a DRDO chemical weapon facility at Gwalior in July and a laboratory at Ozra in August.[16]

On 31 October 1997, the OPCW completed its draft report on the implementation of the convention for the Second Conference of the States Parties.[17] One hundred states were then parties to the CWC: 68 of these states had submitted the required initial declarations and 32 had not. Sixty-five states made declarations under Article III, five states under Article V on CW production facilities,[18] and 56 states under Article VI on non-prohibited activities. Inferences, which cannot be confirmed, can be drawn about CW programmes after

---

[12] Zanders, J. P., Eckstein, S. and Hart, J., 'Chemical and biological weapon developments and arms control', *SIPRI Yearbook 1997: Armaments, Disarmament and International Security* (Oxford University Press: Oxford, 1997), pp. 445–51.

[13] United Kingdom of Great Britain and Northern Ireland, Declaration of past activities relating to its former offensive chemical weapons programme, via British Embassy, Stockholm, May 1997. Some 40 pages (of 238 pp.) were blanked out for national security reasons.

[14] 'India calls on Pakistan to reveal chemical weapon arsenals', Agence France-Presse via Nando.net, 26 June 1997, URL <http://pele.nando.net/newsroom/ntn/world/062697/world16_25025.html>, version current on 26 June 1997; and 'India opens its chemical weapons for scrutiny', *Times of India* (New Delhi), 27 June 1997. For years India had formally denied the existence of a CW armament programme. The declaration therefore caused a controversy about the trustworthiness of India in disarmament and non-proliferation questions. Dixit, A., 'India must reclaim position as leader in nonproliferation', *Defense News*, vol. 18, no. 32 (11–17 Aug. 1997), p. 15; and Kremmer, C., 'Ten years later, Indians come clean', *Sydney Morning Herald*, 28 June 1997, URL <http://www.smh.com.au>, version current on 22 July 1997.

[15] Kremmer (note 14).

[16] Bedi, R., 'Indian chemical bases come under scrutiny', *Jane's Defence Weekly*, vol. 28, no. 6 (13 Aug. 1997), p. 5.

[17] Organisation for the Prohibition of Chemical Weapons, Draft report of the Organisation on the implementation of the Convention, OPCW document C-II/2, 31 Oct. 1997.

[18] The 5 countries were China, France, Japan, the UK and the USA. India and South Korea requested that the information pertaining to their declarations not be included in OPCW document C-II/2 (note 17).

World War II from the initial inspections conducted under Article V (i.e., the first visit to a declared production facility). Inspectors visited two such installations in China, six in France, one in Japan, eight in the UK and nine in the USA. India and South Korea both requested that information regarding inspections on their territories be excluded from the OPCW inspections report to the First Conference of the States Parties. However, four initial Article V inspections were conducted three different times in unnamed states, so it may be presumed that both countries had CW production facilities.[19]

This tentative picture is of necessity incomplete because many parties did not submit declarations within 30 days of the entry into force of the CWC for them or were not yet required to do so at the time the OPCW draft report was completed because of the date of their accession. In addition, the publicly available information does not reveal when the CW programmes were active or terminated. As the OPCW is bound to its confidentiality obligation and in view of persistent allegations of CW proliferation, confidence in the emerging CWC regime would be greatly strengthened if individual parties were more forthcoming with public information on relevant past activities. For at least two parties, France and India, the limited publicly available data appear to be or are at odds with past formal statements on the non-possession of chemical weapons or CW-related programmes.[20]

Destruction of chemical weapons

The United States

In the USA, CW destruction continued in 1997. The US stockpile is stored at nine locations,[21] but only two disposal facilities were operational: the Johnston Atoll Chemical Agent Disposal System (JACADS) and the Tooele Chemical Agent Disposal Facility (TOCDF).[22] By the end of October, 2191 tons or 6.96 per cent of the total stockpile had been destroyed at these sites. At JACADS 69 per cent of the CW stored there had been destroyed. This comprised 49 327 sarin-filled, 105-mm projectiles; 100 811 sarin-filled, 155-mm projectiles; 2570 MK–94 (500-pound or approximately 227-kilogram) bombs filled with sarin; 3047 MC–1 (750-pound or c. 340-kg) bombs filled with sarin; 72 242 M-55 sarin and VX-filled rockets and warheads; 45 108 blister agent-filled, 105-mm projectiles; 68 blister agent-filled ton containers; and

---

[19] On the basis of the press reports regarding India mentioned above, it would appear that South Korea declared 1 facility.

[20] In Oct. 1997 it was revealed, e.g., that France had conducted CW tests in Algeria until 1978, 16 years after Algeria's independence. Jauvert, V., 'Quand la France testait des armes chimiques en Algérie' [When France tested chemical weapons in Algeria], *Le Nouvel Observateur*, 23–29 Oct. 1997, pp. 10–22.

[21] The locations are Edgewood Chemical Activity, Aberdeen Proving Ground, Maryland; Anniston Chemical Activity, Anniston, Alabama; Blue Grass Chemical Activity, Richmond, Kentucky; Newport Chemical Depot, Newport, Indiana; Pine Bluff Chemical Activity, Pine Bluff, Arkansas; Pueblo Chemical Depot, Pueblo, Colorado; Deseret Chemical Depot, Tooele, Utah; Umatilla Chemical Depot, Hermiston, Oregon; and Johnston Atoll Chemical Agent Disposal System, Johnston Atoll (south-west of Hawaii). For further details, see Zanders, Eckstein and Hart (note 12), pp. 449–51.

[22] There is also a Chemical Demilitarization Training Facility located in Maryland.

66 sarin-filled ton containers. The TOCDF destroyed 11 592 M55 sarin-filled rockets, 970 sarin-filled ton containers and 1 619 587 pounds (c. 736.2 tonnes) of sarin.[23]

At most locations CW destruction activities are estimated to be completed by 2004 or 2005. On 19 June 1997, Alabama issued a hazardous waste permit for the Anniston Chemical Disposal Facility, which enabled construction work to proceed. It is expected that 32 months will be needed for construction, with an additional 18–22 months for setting up and testing the disposal system before destruction can begin.[24] There are no estimated dates of completion for the Blue Grass Chemical Activity and the Pueblo Chemical Depot because the US Army was still assessing technologies which could be used instead of incineration, and meanwhile construction work is prohibited.[25] The JACADS stockpile is scheduled to be eliminated by 2000.[26] However, serious concern has been expressed about whether the projected completion dates will be met.[27] The army has consistently underestimated the time needed to reach agreements with states and local communities on the disposal method to be used at the stockpile sites. In the 1997 Authorization and Appropriation Acts Congress directed that research and development (R&D) be carried out on alternative CW destruction technologies, in response to public concern.[28] The General Accounting Office (GAO) forecast that the stockpile programme will exceed its $12.4 billion estimated cost and take longer than the projected completion date of 31 December 2004.[29] According to other estimates, it will be difficult to achieve total stockpile destruction by 2007, the CWC deadline.[30]

The army's Non-Stockpile Chemical Materiel Project deals with five categories of chemical warfare *matériel*: (*a*) binary CW; (*b*) miscellaneous chemical warfare items, including unfilled munitions, support equipment and devices to be employed in conjunction with the use of CW; (*c*) recovered chemical weapons; (*d*) former production facilities; and (*e*) buried chemical

---

[23] US Army Program Manager for Chemical Demilitarization, 'World's first chemical weapons disposal facility reaches new milestone', Press Release, 30 Oct. 1997, URL <http://www-pmcd.apgea.army.mil/CSDP/csdp_ip_pr_103097.html>, version current on 11 Mar. 1998.

[24] US Army Program Manager for Chemical Demilitarization, 'RCRA permit granted for construction of Anniston Chemical Agent Disposal Facility', *CSDP Newsletter*, Sep. 1997, URL <http://www-pmcd.apgea.army.mil/CSDP/csdp_ip_nl997_001.html>, version current on 11 Mar. 1998.

[25] Zanders, Eckstein and Hart (note 12), p. 451; and Miller, C. and Larson, C., 'US dilemmas in meeting the CWC's destruction deadline', *Nonproliferation Review*, vol. 5, no. 2 (winter 1998), p. 105.

[26] US Army Program Manager for Chemical Demilitarization, 'CSDP site locations', URL <http://www-pmcd.apgea.army.mil/CSDP/csdp_sl.html>, version current on 1 Feb. 1998.

[27] According to Public Law 102-484, National Defense Authorization Act for Fiscal Year 1993, the CW destruction deadline is 31 Dec. 2004. However, the US Army already accepts a closure date of 2005 for the Anniston Chemical Disposal Facility.

[28] US General Accounting Office, *Chemical Weapons and Materiel: Key Factors Affecting Disposal Costs and Schedule*, GAO/NSIA-97-18 (General Accounting Office: Washington, DC, Feb. 1997), p. 6.

[29] US General Accounting Office (note 28), pp. 28–29. Another estimate placed the total cost of destroying the stockpile at $15.7 billion. Smith, H., 'DOD chemical demilitarization program', Presentation at Fall Meeting of the Board on Army Science and Technology of the National Research Council, 18 Nov. 1997, quoted in Miller and Larson (note 25), p. 102.

[30] Miller and Larson (note 25), pp. 102, 103, 106.

warfare *matériel*.[31] The US Army has identified 64 potential locations in 31 states where CW *matériel* is believed to be buried. It is estimated that it will take 40 years to implement the programme with respect to buried CW *matériel* and cost approximately $15.2 billion.[32] The other categories of non-stockpile chemical *matériel* must be destroyed according to the convention-mandated time-lines.

The Russian Federation

While the Duma delayed Russian ratification of the CWC until the autumn of 1997, it passed a comprehensive destruction act, Federal Law 76-FZ, on 25 April 1997, which President Boris Yeltsin signed into law on 2 May.[33] The cost of destruction of the Russian CW stockpile of approximately 40 000 agent tonnes is generally estimated at $3.5–5 billion.[34] On 17 March, the day on which Yeltsin submitted the CWC to the Duma, commander of the Russian NBC [nuclear, biological and chemical] Protection Troops[35] Colonel General Stanislav Petrov stated that the programme will cost 24 000 billion roubles,[36] a much higher figure than the cost estimate of 16 642 billion roubles in Presidential Decree 305, which was introduced on 21 March 1996. That decree also stated that destruction would begin in 1998, but the starting date remained unclear throughout 1997. Approximately 120 billion roubles ($24 million) were allocated for CW destruction-related activities in the 1997 budget, although funding needs had been assessed at over 10 times that figure, and 500 billion roubles will reportedly be allocated in 1998.[37] Insufficient funding to date has led to an estimated delay of two to three years in the implementation of Decree 305. Such delays also increase the overall cost. According to one estimate, a 15-year delay in the destruction programme would raise the cost by 25 per cent, and a 20-year delay would lead to a 50 per cent increase.[38]

---

[31] US Army Program Manager for Chemical Demilitarization, 'Five categories of non-stockpile chemical materiel', URL <http://www-pmcd.apgea.army.mil/NSCMP/nscmp_h_5cat.html>, version current on 1 Feb. 1998.

[32] US General Accounting Office (note 28), p. 4, fn 1 and p. 42.

[33] 'Ob unichtozhenii khimicheskogo oruzhiya' [On the destruction of chemical weapons], Federal Law no. 76-FZ, 25 Apr. 1997, in *Krasnaya Zvezda*, 17 May 1997; and Georgiyev, V., 'Minoborony gotovo k unichtozheniyu khimicheskogo oruzhiya' [Ministry of Defence prepared for chemical weapon destruction], *Nezavisimaya Gazeta*, 21 June 1997, p. 2.

[34] Sergey Baranovsky, Executive Secretary of Green Cross, Russia, has stated that the cost could be $6–9 billion. 'News headlines for 10/17/97', Interfax, *Today's News*, 17 Oct. 1997, URL <http://www.interfax-news.com/TodayFSUNews/today.html>, version current on 17 Oct. 1997.

[35] The name in Russian is Rossiyskye Khimicheskye Voiska (RKhV).

[36] Kortunov, S., 'Russia must become a full-fledged member of the OPCW', *Chemical Weapons and Problems of Their Destruction*, no. 4 (PIR Center: Moscow, summer/autumn 1997), p. 6. The figure includes 1150 billion roubles for environmental monitoring, 1800 billion roubles for regional infrastructure and 400 billion roubles for medical and sanitary services to the local population.

[37] Averre, D. and Khripunov, I., 'Russian chemdemil coaxing communities', *Jane's Intelligence Review*, vol. 9, no. 6 (June 1997), pp. 257–59; and 'Russia: law on Chemical Weapons Convention ratification detailed', Foreign Broadcast Information Service, *Daily Report–Soviet Union (FBIS-SOV)*, FBIS-SOV-97-310, 6 Nov. 1997.

[38] Kortunov (note 36), pp. 8, 11.

In addition Russia must pay the costs of OPCW inspections on its territory, which have been estimated at $13 million per year.[39]

At the end of 1997, three documents formed the legal basis for the destruction of CW in Russia: the 'Special federal programme, destruction of chemical weapons stockpiles in the Russian Federation',[40] Federal Law 76-FZ[41] and the CWC ratification act.[42]

Federal Law 76-FZ defines terms and concepts and the responsibilities of the bodies involved in CW destruction. It also envisages the creation of special zones around CW storage and destruction facilities and the establishment of a network of laboratories and health institutions to monitor for signs of adverse health effects from the activities of such facilities and to deal with the possible consequences.

The CWC ratification act outlines the responsibilities and obligations of the Russian President, the Russian Federation Government and the Federation Council. The president is given the responsibility for overseeing the implementation of CW destruction and ensuring compliance with the provisions of the CWC. The act also requires him to take into account Russia's economic situation when implementing CWC destruction deadlines and mandates that the safest available destruction technologies be used. The government is responsible for implementation of activities such as coordinating international destruction assistance and carrying out related health and safety measures. The Federation Council is to provide 'oversight'. In particular, it will review the annual report prepared by the government and submitted by the president. The information on destruction activities which is to be included in the report consists of the status of the implementation of the CWC, the amount of chemical weapons destroyed, the status of the construction of CW destruction facilities and of the destruction or conversion of former CW production facilities, the condition of the CW stockpiles, the environmental situation at the CW storage and destruction areas, and the health of CW facility personnel and civilians living in the vicinity of such facilities. The act also explicitly leaves open the possibility of the conversion of CW production facilities. If there is disagreement between the Russian Government and the OPCW regarding the OPCW's refusal of Russian conversion requests, for example, Russia 'shall implement

---

[39] Kalyadin, A., 'Russia's dilemmas in the area of chemical disarmament', *Chemical Weapons and Problems of Their Destruction* (note 36), p. 31. The amount to be repaid has yet to be agreed by the OPCW.

[40] 'Federalnaya tselevaya programma' [Special federal programme], *Rossiyskaya Gazeta*, Presidential decree no. 305, 2 Apr. 1996, pp. 5–6; and Russian Federation, Special federal programme, destruction of chemical weapons stockpiles in the Russian Federation, Preparatory Commission document PC-XIV/B/WP.7, 25 June 1996, pp. 19–20.

[41] 'Ob unichtozhenii khimicheskogo oruzhiya' (note 33), pp. 3, 7.

[42] 'O ratifikatsii Konventsii o zapreshenii razrabotki, proizvodstva, nakopleniya i primeneniya khimicheskogo oruzhiya i ob ego unichtozhenii' [On the ratification of the Convention on the Prohibition of the Development, Production, Stockpiling and Use of Chemical Weapons and on their Destruction], Federal Law no. 138-FZ, 5 Nov. 1997. An unofficial translation is published in *CBW Conventions Bulletin*, no. 38 (Dec. 1997), pp. 6–8.

procedures in accordance with generally recognized principles and standards of international law and international treaties of the Russian Federation'.[43]

Because in the former Soviet Union chemical weapons were generally produced in a relatively small area of the large industrial chemical complexes, Russia continues to attach great importance to the issue of conversion of former CW manufacturing installations. According to the CWC, a state party must obtain permission from the OPCW to convert such facilities for non-prohibited purposes. For Russia, obtaining such permission may be critical to the success of joint ventures with foreign companies. For instance, on 12 September 1997 DuPont and Khimprom announced a joint venture to produce pesticides at Khimprom's Novocheboksarsk site, located some 640 kilometres east of Moscow. Prior to the agreement, DuPont had asked the Science Applications International Cooperation (SAIC) to conduct an assessment to ensure that no part of the facility involved in the joint venture had previously produced CW.[44] The Russian Government does not wish to risk a negative response from the OPCW. It has also expressed concern that it could be forced to pay for the inspection of an entire chemical complex although only a small part may have been used for CW production in the past.[45]

Finland, Germany, the Netherlands, Sweden and the USA continued to provide CW destruction assistance in 1997. Finland has reportedly offered assistance totalling 2 million Finnish marks.[46] Germany and Russia reached agreement on 2 April 1997 on the distribution of 7.7 million Deutschmarks for the Russian CW destruction programme.[47] On 18 June 1997 the Netherlands and Russia signed a memorandum of understanding on Dutch CW destruction assistance.[48] In addition, the European Council of the European Union (EU) decided on 21 May 1997 to offer assistance for activities related to the implementation of the CWC worth up to 10–15 million European Currency Units (ECU), equivalent to $11.5–17.2 million, for the period 1997–99 through the programme for Technical Assistance for the Commonwealth of Independent States (Tacis). There is an expectation that the Tacis programme will be accompanied by a dialogue between the EU and Russia on the implementation of the CWC. At its 17 November meeting the Working Group on Global Disarmament and Arms Control agreed to initiate the dialogue in 1998 in the

---

[43] Federal Law no. 138-FZ (note 42), Article 4, para. 1, as translated in *CBW Conventions Bulletin*, no. 38 (Dec. 1997), p. 8.

[44] DuPont, 'DuPont and A. O. Khimprom to form JV for crop protection products in Russia', Press Release, 12 Sep. 1997, URL <http://biz.yahoo.com/prnews/97/09/12/dd_y0006_1.html>, version current on 12 Sep. 1997; and Ember, L., 'Converting chemical arms plants to peaceful uses', *Chemical & Engineering News*, vol. 75, no. 38 (22 Sep. 1997), p. 10.

[45] The details of the verification regime for converted plants are outlined in Part V, D of the Verification Annex of the CWC.

[46] '17 March', *CBW Conventions Bulletin*, no. 36 (June 1997), p. 21; and Kapashin, V. (Maj.-Gen.), 'Expert opinion: who and what will help Russia to eliminate chemical weapons?', RIA Novosti, *Russian Executive and Legislative Newsletter*, no. 37 (19 Sep. 1997), URL <http://www.ria-novosti.com/products/reln/1997/09/19-1-12.htm>, version current on 19 Sep. 1997. Finnish assistance reportedly consists of the provision of monitors, including X-ray fluorescence detectors. Private communication by the author with a Dutch government official, 12 Dec. 1997.

[47] '2 April', *CBW Conventions Bulletin*, no. 36 (June 1997), p. 23.

[48] Private communication by the author with a Dutch government official, 19 June 1997.

first semester of the British presidency of the EU.[49] In 1997 the USA allocated a total of $135.5 million under the Cooperative Threat Reduction (CTR) programme to support Russian CW destruction at Shchuchye.[50]

Old and abandoned chemical weapons

More information about old and abandoned chemical weapons became public in 1997.[51] By the end of October 1997, Belgium, China, France, Germany, Italy, Japan and the UK had made declarations related to old and abandoned chemical weapons to the OPCW under Part IV(B) of the CWC Verification Annex.[52] In one interesting case, Poland did not make such a declaration as regards the 9.326 tonnes of adamsite which are located on its territory. The adamsite is presumed to be of German origin, but because Poland needed to repackage it for storage it is no longer possible to determine the country of origin, the reason for its import and the identity of the importer.[53]

The entry into force of the CWC and the 25th anniversary of the 1972 Sino-Japanese peace and friendship agreement[54] prompted China and Japan to intensify efforts to resolve their long-standing dispute over the chemical weapons which Japanese troops abandoned in China in World War II. Between April and August 1997 working-level talks stalled over disagreement about the number of shells—China estimates them at nearly 2 million, while Japan places the figure at approximately 700 000—and how to destroy them.[55] However, on 1 October Japan created the Abandoned Chemical Weapons Coordination Division, a special team within the Cabinet Councillor's Office on External Affairs, to develop a plan for the disposal of the chemical weapons. Japan hoped to start the CW disposal in April 1998 in order to meet the CWC requirements. It sent two additional investigative teams to China in May and November 1997, bringing the total number of such missions to nine.

---

[49] 'Tacis chemical weapons assistance programme to Russia', Information Note of the Commission Services, CODUN (Cooperation on Disarmament in the UN System) document, session no. 4/98, 26 Feb. 1998. The 1997 Tacis Action Programme included 3 million ECU ($3.4 million) for Russia's former CW facilities and 4 million ECU ($4.6 million) for a 2nd project to start in 1998.

[50] On CTR funding see Zanders, Eckstein and Hart (note 12), p. 448; and chapter 10 in this volume. The areas designated to receive CTR funding at Shchuchye are: (a) chemical processing equipment, (b) munitions processing equipment, (c) safety monitoring equipment, (d) process chemicals storage, (e) maintenance, (f) waste water treatment, (g) industrial waste storage and landfill, (h) emergency support, and (i) a camp for construction workers. The Shchuchye CW destruction facility is designated 'Object 1597'. Lajoie, R. (Maj.-Gen.), 'U.S. support to the Russian CW destruction program', Paper presented at intergovernmental meeting, Moscow, 22 Oct. 1997, pp. 3, 4, 8.

[51] Stock, T. and Lohs, Kh. (eds), *The Challenge of Old Chemical Munitions and Toxic Armament Wastes*, SIPRI Chemical & Biological Warfare Studies, no. 16 (Oxford University Press: Oxford, 1997).

[52] OPCW document C-II/2 (note 17). The declarations may pertain both to the presence of old and abandoned CW on the territory of a state party and to the recognition by a state party that it has abandoned CW on the territory of another country.

[53] Witkiewicz, Z. and Szarski, K., 'The history of chemical weapons in Poland', eds Stock and Lohs (note 51), p. 117.

[54] Joint Communiqué of the Government of Japan and the Government of the People's Republic of China, Peking, 29 Sep. 1972, *White Papers of Japan 1973–74* (Japan Institute of International Affairs: Tokyo, 1975), pp. 61–62.

[55] Tokyo Kyodo News Service, 26 Aug. 1997, in 'Japan: Kajiyama on creation of chemical weapons disposal office', Foreign Broadcast Information Service, *Daily Report-East Asia (FBIS-EAS)*, FBIS-EAS-97-238, 27 Aug. 1997.

After cutting open some shells, one team found that the munitions were still highly explosive and that great care will need to be taken during disposal.[56]

The CWC and the use of riot-control agents in peacekeeping operations

On 28 August 1997 heavily armed troops of the North Atlantic Treaty Organization (NATO)-led Stabilization Force (SFOR) had to evacuate more than 40 officers of the International Police Task Force from the Bosnian Serb town of Brcko after clashes erupted between peacekeeping forces and civilians. In what was described as one of NATO's worst confrontations in Bosnia and Herzegovina since the 1995 Dayton Agreement,[57] US helicopters dropped tear-gas and soldiers fired warning shots to disperse the crowd.[58] Another US unit used tear-gas in a second incident on 1 September after being attacked by about 250 people armed with sticks and stones near Bijeljina, a village close to Brcko.[59]

Under the CWC riot-control agents are classified as toxic chemicals;[60] they therefore fall under the general purpose criterion.[61] Their use is consequently prohibited as a method of warfare but permitted for law enforcement purposes, including domestic riot control.[62] The line between law enforcement and use as a method of warfare can become thin if troops are deployed between hostile factions as could occur, for example, in UN peacekeeping missions.[63] The resort to tear-gas by UN peacekeeping forces has been extremely rare. The only known documented instance occurred on 10 March 1957, when Danish

---

[56] Ministry of Foreign Affairs of Japan, 'Press conference by the Press Secretary', 13 June 1997, URL <http://www.mofa.go.jp/press/1997/6/613.html>, version current on 11 Mar. 1998; Tokyo Kyodo News Service, 20 Oct. 1997, in 'Japan: WWII chemical weapons found still "live" in China', FBIS-EAS-97-293, 22 Oct. 1997; and Tokyo Kyodo News Service, 13 Nov. 1997, in 'Japan: Japan to send chemical weapons disposal mission to China', FBIS-EAS-97-317, 17 Nov. 1997.

[57] The text of the General Framework Agreement for Peace in Bosnia and Herzegovina is reproduced in *SIPRI Yearbook 1996: World Armaments, Disarmament and International Security* (Oxford University Press: Oxford, 1996), pp. 232–33.

[58] 'UN police evacuated in troubled Bosnian town', CNN Interactive, 28 Aug. 1997, URL <http://www.cnn.com/WORLD/9708/28/bosnia.update/index.html>, version current on 28 Aug. 1997; and Associated Press, 'NATO troops attacked in Serb-held towns, one American injured', *Boston Globe Online*, 28 Aug. 1997, URL <http://www.boston.com/dailynews/wirehtml/240/NATO_troops_attacked _in_Serb_held_t.htm>, version current on 28 Aug. 1997.

[59] Dinmore, G., 'US unit repels Serb mob with tear gas', *Financial Times*, 2 Sep. 1997, p. 1.

[60] Article II, paras. 2 and 7.

[61] Under the general purpose criterion of the CWC certain purposes for which objects may be employed are prohibited, but not the objects themselves. Article II of the CWC thus defines CW as any toxic chemical or its precursors *intended for purposes other than those not prohibited by the CWC* as well as munitions, devices or equipment specifically designed to be used with them.

[62] Article 1, para. 5 and Article II, paras. 1, 2, 7, and 9 (d) of the CWC. The term 'riot-control agent' should be used with caution. As part of a NATO Partnership for Peace exercise near Riga, Latvia, in Sep. 1997, chloropicrin—a World War I lachrymator and asphyxiating agent—was used to simulate chemical contamination. NATO officials immediately halted the practice when, according to a statement from the Public Affairs Office of the US Army V Corps, it was learned that 'this riot-control compound was being used on the initiative of one station monitor'. Chloropicrin is listed in Schedule 3 of the CWC and can, according to Article II, para. 7, therefore not be considered as a riot-control agent. '8–11 September', *CBW Conventions Bulletin*, no. 38 (Dec. 1997), p. 26.

[63] For an in-depth discussion of the possible use of riot-control agents by armed forces, see Chayes, A. and Meselson, M., 'Proposed guidelines on the status of riot control agents and other toxic chemicals under the Chemical Weapons Convention', *Chemical Weapons Convention Bulletin*, no. 35 (Mar. 1997), pp. 13–18.

military policemen of the United Nations Emergency Force (UNEF) deployed in the Gaza Strip following Israel's invasion of Egypt in 1956 were authorized to use 'tear-gas bombs' against rioting civilians attempting to take over the UN post.[64] Recent calls to equip forces with so-called non-lethal weapons, to which riot-control and other incapacitating agents belong, increase the possibility of the use of riot-control agents during interventions in local or regional wars or peacekeeping missions.[65]

The key question concerns the authority to release such agents for use by troops (i.e., determining that a particular situation calls for law enforcement measures to be taken by peacekeeping troops). Two days before the 10 March 1957 incident the UNEF commander had issued a proclamation, approved by UN headquarters, which included a statement that UNEF had assumed responsibility for civil affairs in the Gaza Strip.[66] The increasingly common UN practice of contracting regional security organizations for peacekeeping missions further complicates the issue. Three sources of authority can be discerned in the SFOR incident mentioned above.

The first source of authority was the United Nations Security Council, which decided on the deployment and mandate of the peacekeeping forces. In Resolution 1088 (1996), the Security Council recognized 'the right of [SFOR] to take all necessary measures to defend itself from attack or threat of attack'.[67] However, SFOR did not receive responsibility for civil affairs: its tasks were to implement and ensure compliance with Annex 1-A of the Dayton Agreement, the Agreement on the Military Aspects of the Peace Settlement.[68] NATO was the second source of authority. NATO leads SFOR and was ultimately responsible for the choice of troops and equipment to be deployed in accordance with the UN mandate and the subordinate commands in charge of the daily management of operations. The third source of authority in the incident comprised the US president, armed forces and Congress, which were responsible for the type of weaponry with which the US forces were equipped and the operational guidance for its use.

US policy regarding the use of riot-control agents is defined in Executive Order 11850, 'Renunciation of certain uses in war of chemical herbicides and riot control agents', which was signed in the wake of the Viet Nam War by President Gerald Ford on 8 April 1975.[69] During the 1991 Persian Gulf War President George Bush invoked the executive order to authorize the use of

[64] Burns, E. L. M. (Lt-Gen.), *Between Arab and Israeli* (George G. Harrap & Co. Ltd: London, 1962), pp. 260–63.
[65] Lewer, N. and Schofield, S., 'Non-lethal weapons for UN military operations', *International Peacekeeping*, vol. 4, no. 3 (autumn 1997), pp. 71–93.
[66] Burns (note 64), p. 193.
[67] UN Security Council Resolution 1088 (1996), UN document S/RES/1088, 12 Dec. 1996, para. 20.
[68] The General Framework Agreement, Annex 1A, Agreement on the Military Aspects of the Peace Settlement, Article I, para. 1a, URL <http://www.nato.int/ifor/gfa/gfa-an1a.htm>, version current on 23 Jan. 1998. In addition, the UN Security Council created a UN civilian police force for Bosnia and Herzegovina, the International Police Task Force. UN Security Council Resolution 1035 (1995), UN document S/RES/1035, 21 Dec. 1995. See also chapter 2 in this volume.
[69] Document reprinted in McCullough, J. M. and Randall, B. (IV), *Chemical and Biological Warfare: Issues and Developments during 1975*, CRS document 7-30 SP (Library of Congress, Congressional Research Service: Washington, DC, 5 Jan. 1976), p. 76.

riot-control agents in search-and-rescue operations.⁷⁰ The US Senate agreed to ratify the CWC in April 1997, on the understanding that the convention does not restrict the use of riot-control agents, including use against combatants, in the following cases: (*a*) the conduct of peacetime military operations within an area of continuing armed conflict when the United States is not a party to the conflict (e.g., Bosnia, Rwanda and Somalia); (*b*) consensual peacekeeping operations when the use of force is authorized by the receiving state, including operations pursuant to Chapter VI of the UN Charter;⁷¹ and (*c*) peacekeeping operations in which force is authorized by the Security Council under Chapter VII of the UN Charter.⁷² The US Senate accepted the definition of a riot-control agent in Article II of the CWC but stated explicitly that the 'President shall take no measure, and prescribe no rule or regulation, which would alter or eliminate Executive Order 11850'.⁷³

The use of tear-gas in Brcko and Bijeljina was in conformity with the US Senate's ratification of the CWC. The lack of comment on the incident by either NATO or SFOR indicates that they, too, regarded the actions which were taken to be unexceptional.⁷⁴ However, the incident appears to fall in a grey zone between warfare and riot control that is inadequately covered by the CWC. It raises questions about the extent to which the actions taken can be considered as law enforcement or *domestic* riot control, the stipulation in the CWC, in view of the mandate and nationality of the SFOR troops. Questions can also be asked about the extent to which the lachrymator agents and their disseminating devices are of types (and quantities) consistent with purposes not prohibited by the convention.⁷⁵ If the CWC does prohibit these agents and disseminating devices, it would appear that the possessor state must declare and destroy them in order to meet its obligations under the convention. The OPCW must unambiguously clarify these issues before the practice of nations leads to acceptance of the *use* of lachrymators and other chemical incapacitants in armed conflict and adoption of the view that their *use* does not constitute chemical warfare.

---

[70] Perry Robinson, J. P., 'The chemical weapons of Desert Storm forces and the wider implication of tear gas and other incapacitants', ed. J. P. Zanders, *The 2nd Gulf War and the CBW Threat*, Proceedings of the 3rd Annual Conference on Chemical Warfare, Vredesonderzoek, Special issue (Interfacultair Overlegorgaan voor Vredesonderzoek van de Vrije Universiteit Brussel: Brussels, Nov. 1995), pp. 83–95.
[71] Chapter VI of the UN Charter deals with the peaceful settlement of disputes.
[72] Chapter VII of the UN Charter deals with action with respect to threats to peace, breaches of the peace and acts of aggression.
[73] US Senate, *Congressional Record*, 24 Apr. 1997, p. S3657.
[74] Aldinger, C., 'Two US troops injured in Bosnia operation', Reuters via Yahoo! News, URL <http://www.yahoo.com/headlines/970828/news/stories/bosnia_27.html>, version current on 28 Aug. 1997; 'Joint Press Conference', SFOR LANDCENT Transcript, 29 Aug. 1997, URL <http://www.nato.int/ifor/landcent/t970829a.htm>, version current on 4 Sep. 1997; and Dinmore, G., 'US unit repels Serb mob with tear gas', *Financial Times*, 2 Sep. 1997, p. 1.
[75] In one instance, tear-gas was dropped from helicopters.

III. Biological weapon disarmament

In December 1996 the Fourth Review Conference of the BTWC parties endorsed further intensification of the discussions on a legally binding protocol to the BTWC in its Ad Hoc Group.[76] The Ad Hoc Group was established by the 1994 Special Conference to consider verification measures and other proposals to strengthen the BTWC treaty regime. It held its 6th, 7th and 8th sessions on 3–21 March, 14 July–1 August and 15 September–3 October 1997, respectively. Friends of the Chair (FoC) were appointed to preside over particular topics in order to facilitate the negotiation process.

As requested at the 6th session, Ad Hoc Group chairman Tibor Tóth produced and circulated an initial version of a rolling text in June in preparation for the 7th session. The document provides a basic structure for the negotiations. However, it was presented 'without prejudice to the positions of delegations on the issues under consideration in the Ad Hoc Group and does not imply agreement on the scope or content'.[77] The rolling text, which is now an annexe to the Procedural Report of the Ad Hoc Group and has more than doubled in size, reflects the discussions. The negotiators are still far from agreement on a final document. Much of the text contains bracketed language indicating the variant positions. Annexes A–E to the rolling text provide an indication of the types of programme and facility to be declared.

Some positions are diametrically opposed to others. Article II of the draft protocol seeks to define some of the terminology used in Article I of the BTWC including the basic terms 'bacteriological (biological) and toxin weapons' and 'biological agents'. According to the majority view, any proposal to define these Article I terms would have the effect of amending the BTWC, which is contrary to the provisions of Article XI of the convention and also falls outside the mandate of the Ad Hoc Group. (The group's mandate authorizes it to define only those terms necessary to devise an effective, legally binding protocol.) The USA, for example, has suggested that the fuzzy definitions of the BTWC will be defined by decisions on disputed issues.[78] The minority view, supported by Russia, holds that such definitions are indispensable for the purposes of a verification mechanism and do not have the effect of amending the convention.[79] The issue is delicate because the outcome

---

[76] Zanders, Eckstein and Hart (note 12), pp. 452–57.

[77] Rolling Text of a Protocol to the Convention on the Prohibition of the Development, Production and Stockpiling of Bacteriological (Biological) and Toxin Weapons and on Their Destruction, Ad Hoc Group of the States Parties to the Convention on the Prohibition of the Development, Production and Stockpiling of Bacteriological (Biological) and Toxin Weapons and on Their Destruction, Ad Hoc Group document BWC/AD HOC GROUP/35/Rev.1, 29 July 1997.

[78] Pearson, G. S., 'Strengthening the Biological and Toxin Weapons Convention', *CBW Conventions Bulletin*, no. 38 (Dec. 1997), p. 19; and Wright, S., 'Cuba case tests treaty', *Bulletin of the Atomic Scientists*, vol. 53, no. 6 (Nov./Dec. 1997), p. 19.

[79] Procedural Report of the Ad Hoc Group of the States Parties to the Convention on the Prohibition of the Development, Production and Stockpiling of Bacteriological (Biological) and Toxin Weapons and on Their Destruction, Ad Hoc Group of the States Parties to the Convention on the Prohibition of the Development, Production and Stockpiling of Bacteriological (Biological) and Toxin Weapons and on Their Destruction, Ad Hoc Group document BWC/AD HOC GROUP/38, 6 Oct. 1997, Annex 1, p. 16, fn. 3.

of the debate could affect the scope of the prohibition in Article I of the BTWC, which is based on the general purpose criterion.[80]

The CWC contains a similar general purpose criterion, a definition of the term 'toxic chemical' (Article II) and a list of toxic chemicals grouped in three schedules depending on the level of threat which they pose to the purpose of the convention. Reporting requirements for parties and some types of inspection and export control mechanism in the CWC are based on the schedules. Concern exists that unlisted chemicals (including potential novel CW agents) may go undetected or unchallenged in practice unless there is firm evidence of a violation, despite the fact that these unlisted chemicals are covered by the general purpose criterion.

The mandate of the BTWC's Ad Hoc Group, however, calls for the definition of terms and objective criteria, including lists of biological and toxin agents and their threshold quantities, and of facilities, equipment and types of activity that should be covered by the protocol.[81] The annexe to the draft protocol contains elaborate definitions, lists of and criteria for human, animal and plant pathogens and toxins, equipment and thresholds.[82] The lists of and criteria for agents and toxins were originally presented in a 1996 FoC paper, and brackets have been introduced to address the concerns of some delegations.[83] The section on programmes and facilities remains blank.

The opposing positions on definitions highlight a fundamental difference between the BTWC and the CWC. The CWC deals mainly with mature technologies, substances and processes which have been available for decades and in some cases since the 19th century. The global expansion of the chemical industry has made them widely available throughout the world. Breakthroughs in the mid-1970s, when the BTWC entered into force, revolutionized the biological sciences.[84] Diverse biotechnological research establishments and industries have since emerged which operate at the leading edge of science and which, in the near future, may produce discoveries that are unimaginable today. At the First BTWC Review Conference, in 1980, the parties to the BTWC confirmed that the scope of the prohibition in Article I of the BTWC was sufficiently comprehensive to cover the relevant new scientific and technological developments of the 1970s. The Second Review Conference stated that the article also covered all relevant future developments.

This difference between the BTWC and the CWC also explains why the verification and inspection regimes of the CWC cannot simply be adapted and applied to the protocol to the BTWC. For non-military research establishments

---

[80] In Article I the parties to the BTWC undertake never under any circumstances to develop, produce, stockpile or otherwise acquire or retain biological agents or toxins that cannot be justified for prophylactic, protective or other peaceful purposes.

[81] Final Declaration of the Fourth Review Conference, BTWC Fourth Review Conference document BWC/CONF.IV/9, part II, p. 29.

[82] Procedural Report . . . (note 79), Annex A, pp. 106–31.

[83] Procedural Report . . . (note 79), Annex A, p. 112, fn. 85. See also Zanders, Eckstein and Hart (note 12), p. 454.

[84] Bartfai, T., Lundin, S. J. and Rybeck, B., 'Benefits and threats of developments in biotechnology and genetic engineering', *SIPRI Yearbook 1993: World Armaments and Disarmament* (Oxford University Press: Oxford, 1993), pp. 293–305.

and companies, investments in R&D are costly, and the returns—generated by relatively few commercially viable products in a highly competitive environment—cannot be expected for years or decades. Novel processes, techniques and products are key elements of innovative research, and the loss of proprietary information as a consequence of inspection routines could spell the ruin of an enterprise. Some representative organizations of the various branches of the biotechnology industry oppose an intrusive verification regime based on routine inspections, like that of the CWC. The Dutch association of biotechnology companies, Niaba, does not oppose inspections, taking the position that its members have nothing to hide and are already being inspected regularly by national authorities and the US Food and Drug Agency, following procedures with guarantees against the disclosure of proprietary information. The Dutch Foreign Ministry and the EU are also in favour of including inspections in the verification regime but do not want it to include such elaborate inspection routines as those in the CWC. The Dutch Ministry of Economic Affairs has conducted negotiations with the biotechnology industry with respect to challenge inspections on 24 hours' notice.[85] Some companies, however, prefer to wait for a decision on the matter by EuropaBio, a trade organization representing more than 600 European companies. EuropaBio recognizes the need for a verification regime but fears that on-site inspections and the removal of samples could threaten commercial confidentiality. The Association of Pharmaceutical Research and Manufacturers of America (PhRMA) wants to reduce the BW threat but opposes any protocol that does not fully protect confidential business information.[86]

Article III, paragraph F of the draft protocol distinguishes between 'investigations' and 'visits'.[87] Investigations are intended to address concerns regarding non-compliance with Article I of the BTWC. Two types are currently under consideration: field and facility investigations. A field investigation would be carried out if there is a 'release of, or exposure of humans, animals or plants to microbial or other biological agents and toxins' which could be attributable to biological warfare-related activities. An alternative formulation, reflecting a minority view supported by Russia, proposes 'investigation of the alleged use of biological weapons', which is more restrictive because suspicious accidental outbreaks might be excluded from the procedure. A facility investigation would take place when concern exists that a particular facility is conducting prohibited activities.

The draft protocol contains elaborate language on the initiation, organization, conduct and reporting of non-compliance investigations and proposes procedures to guard against abusive requests for such investigations. In addi-

[85] Evenblij, M., 'Zoeken naar biologische wapens' [Searching for biological weapons], *De Volkskrant*, 5 Apr. 1997.

[86] 'PhRMA position on a compliance protocol to the Biological Weapons Convention', reproduced in Chevrier, M. I. et al., *Biological Weapons Proliferation: Reasons for Concern, Courses of Action*, report no. 24 (Henry L. Stimson Center: Washington, DC, Jan. 1998), appendix 3, pp. 135–36; Butler, D., 'Talks start on policing bio-weapons ban', *Nature*, vol. 388 (24 July 1997), p. 317; and Ehrlich, J., 'US experts cite weakness of biological war treaty', *Defense News*, vol. 12, no. 34 (25–31 Aug. 1997), p. 6.

[87] Procedural Report . . . (note 79), pp. 32–36, 40–57.

tion to field and facility investigations, Article III, paragraph F, III also mentions investigation of any other breach of the BTWC obligation as an alternative to facility investigations. In addition, transfers which are alleged to be in violation of Article III of the BTWC could be investigated.

Annex D of the draft protocol expands in detail on the procedures for investigations.[88] The language is heavily bracketed and some parts duplicate sections from Article III, paragraph F of the protocol. Annex D also contains sections which elaborate on the types of investigation, although the section on the investigation of illegal transfers remains blank, apart from its headings.[89] In order to guard against abuse, a request for an investigation must be submitted to a screening process. Currently, it is unclear whether the delegates will opt for a procedure whereby a significant majority of the representative body must formally approve the investigation (the 'green-light' procedure) or one in which the investigation will proceed unless a three-quarter majority of all members of the representative body votes against it (the 'red-light' procedure), in a process similar to that of the CWC.[90]

The 'non-challenge visits' are verification routines other than those for non-compliance concerns. Article III, paragraph F, I defines five types of non-challenge visit: (*a*) random visits, which are a limited number of visits to declared facilities selected at random that would be carried out annually in cooperation with the visited party to confirm that the declarations are consistent with the facts; (*b*) ambiguity-related visits to declared facilities to resolve ambiguities in the declarations of parties; (*c*) clarification visits, which would be conducted to resolve ambiguity, uncertainty, anomaly or omission in the declaration obligations of a party and to promote accuracy and comprehensiveness in future declarations;[91] (*d*) request visits, to help compile individual facility and national declarations and to further the cooperation and assistance envisaged by the protocol; and (*e*) voluntary visits to clarify ambiguities, which are to be based on arrangement and agreement between the party and the organization to be set up to implement the protocol with respect to the number, intensity, duration, timing and mode of visits to a particular facility.[92]

The non-challenge visits remain controversial, and Annex B to the draft protocol, which should detail the procedures, is blank.[93] Some delegations fear that the efficiency of visits will be low and that the goals could be met by other measures. Visits would require additional national structures to provide organizational support and, consequently, would increase the cost of the

---

[88] Procedural Report . . . (note 79), Annex D, pp. 134–97.
[89] The issue of transfers is dealt with in chapter 9 in this volume.
[90] Procedural Report . . . (note 79), Article III, F, III (E), para. 20, p. 46. The alternatives are presented as bracketed language. In the green-light procedure proposal, the suggested majorities are 'at least a two-thirds majority' and 'a three-quarters majority' of either all members of the future organization or only the members 'present and voting'.
[91] This category could include visits to undeclared facilities.
[92] Procedural Report . . . (note 79), pp. 32–35.
[93] Procedural Report . . . (note 79), p. 132.

envisaged verification mechanism.⁹⁴ According to another view, a regime of non-challenge visits would include visits to facilities to review the observance of declaration obligations and thus would contribute to the overall effectiveness of the BTWC treaty regime.⁹⁵ As noted above, some biotechnology industries strongly oppose such visits, which is also one of the reasons why references to 'routine inspections', as in the CWC, are studiously avoided.

Implementation of the future BTWC protocol will inevitably require an organizational structure, and the rolling text contains some language to this effect. The shape and size of such an organization will depend on the ultimate verification regime, which, apart from different kinds of inspection, also consists of the declarations which the parties will be required to submit. The ideas which have been discussed include a new structure, a total or partial integration with the OPCW in The Hague or no new structure at all. The practice of the CWC verification regime and the experience of UNSCOM will undoubtedly have a major impact on the outcome of these discussions. At the 8th session of the Ad Hoc Group, the delegates agreed to intensify the negotiations.

IV. Chemical and biological warfare proliferation concerns

Threat and response

The CBW proliferation threat appraisal appears to be shifting from a quantitative to a qualitative threat. Until recently the threat level was essentially determined by the number of CBW-capable states, which was assumed to be rising rapidly. In 1997 proliferation analyses tended to converge on a figure of 'at least 20 countries' that 'already have or may be developing nuclear, biological, or chemical weapons, or their missile delivery systems'.⁹⁶ As the figure now comprises four categories of weapon, it is no longer possible to isolate the CBW threat assessment. The US Department of Defense (DOD) listed nine countries as having a CW programme in various stages of development and seven as having a BW programme in its annual *Proliferation: Threat and Response* report. However, some countries are conspicuously absent.⁹⁷

---

⁹⁴ Procedural Report . . . (note 79), p. 32, fn. 27. Random inspections are strongly opposed by Russia and resisted by, among others, Japan and the USA. Wright (note 78). According to one estimate, verifying compliance with the BTWC could cost up to $100 million annually. Butler (note 86).

⁹⁵ Procedural Report . . . (note 79), p. 32, fn. 28. Proponents of this view include most European and South American countries, Australia, Canada, New Zealand and South Africa. Wright (note 78).

⁹⁶ Counterproliferation Program Review Committee, *Counterproliferation: Chemical Biological Defense*, CPRC Annual Report to Congress (1997), chapter 3, URL <http://www.acq.osd.mil/cp/cprc97.htm>, version current on 12 Mar. 1998.

⁹⁷ The countries are, notably, Egypt, Israel, South Korea and Taiwan. Compare with, e.g., Office of Technology Assessment, *Proliferation of Weapons of Mass Destruction: Assessing the Risks*, OTA-ISC-559 (US Government Printing Office: Washington, DC, Aug. 1993), pp. 65–66. As noted above, South Korea made a declaration under Article V of the CWC. US Department of Defense, *Proliferation: Threat and Response* (Department of Defense: Washington, DC, Nov. 1997), via DefenseLINK, URL <http://www.defenselink.mil/pubs/prolif97/>, version current on 12 Mar. 1998 lists the following countries as having a CW programme: China, India, Iran, Iraq, North Korea, Libya, Pakistan, Russia and Syria. The countries which it lists as having a BW programme are China, India, Iran, Iraq, North Korea, Pakistan and Russia. Libya is said to lack the scientific and technical base for a BW programme; Syria is said to possess the biotechnical infrastructure to support a BW programme.

The qualitative debate follows from the rapidly growing importance in the USA of counter-proliferation policies instead of sole reliance on export controls on strategic dual-use commodities targeted against certain countries to stem the spread of non-conventional weapons.[98] The principal goal of the counter-proliferation strategy is to ensure that military forces can operate effectively and decisively even if the enemy resorts to non-conventional weapons. The strategy supports the traditional non-proliferation policies but adds counterforce assets to plan and conduct interdiction operations if proliferation prevention and deterrence fail, active (e.g., anti-ballistic missile defences) and passive (e.g., protective suits, chemical and biological agent detectors and antidotes) defence capabilities, and targeted intelligence gathering.[99] In addition, civil emergency plans are set up in which specialized military personnel and municipal emergency services develop and test their rapid-response capability in case of terrorist attacks with CBW.[100] Arms control and disarmament—together with export control activities—are also subsumed under the proliferation prevention strategies, which may have a major impact on the debate on the non-security clauses of complex disarmament treaties such as the BTWC and CWC.

The US view of the reason why CBW proliferation poses a threat to the security of Western states, and the USA in particular, has been stated clearly: the possession of non-conventional weapons may enable a hostile, less powerful country to equalize the military balance with an advanced, well-equipped military power. The 1997 US Quadrennial Defense Review expressed the fear that 'U.S. dominance in the conventional military arena may encourage adversaries to use such asymmetric means to attack our forces and interests overseas and Americans at home' in order to exploit US vulnerabilities.[101]

Sensitivity to these vulnerabilities has resulted in major US R&D and arms acquisition efforts specifically to counter proliferation. For fiscal year (FY) 1998 the US DOD and Department of Energy (DOE) will invest $5.4 billion, an increase of 15 per cent over FY 1997. The DOD's share is almost $4.9 billion for FY 1998, an increase of $0.6 billion over the previous fiscal year. The bulk of the money is allocated to air and missile defence ($3.2 billion). Other major areas include: the detection and characterization of BW agents

---

[98] Following the analysis of Operation Desert Storm to liberate Kuwait in 1991, the 1992 Defense Science Board summer study produced the US Counterproliferation Initiative (CPI), which was formally announced in Dec. 1993. The CPI was actively promoted and now is broadly accepted by the appropriate government agencies, including the DOD and the Department of State. Larsen, J. A., *NATO Counterproliferation Policy: A Case Study in Alliance Politics*, INSS Occasional Paper no. 17 (USAF Institute for National Security Studies, US Air Force Academy: Colorado Springs, Colo., Nov. 1997), p. 15.

[99] Counterproliferation Program Review Committee (note 96), chapter 1, pp. 1.5–1.6; and United States Information Service, 'Asst. Defense Sec. Miller 3/5 testimony on proliferation', *Washington File* (United States Information Service, US Embassy: Stockholm, 6 Mar. 1997), URL <http://www.usis.usemb.se/wireless/400/eur408.htm>, version current on 6 Mar. 1997.

[100] US Department of Defense, *Domestic Preparedness Program in the Defense of Weapons of Mass Destruction*, Report to Congress, 1 May 1997, URL <http://www.defenselink.mil/pubs/domestic/>, version current on 17 Sep. 1997.

[101] US Department of Defense, *Report of the Quadrennial Defense Review* (Department of Defense: Washington, DC, May 1997), section II, 'The global security environment', URL <http://www.defenselink.mil/pubs/qdr/sec2.html>, version current on 12 Mar. 1998.

($191.1 million); BW vaccine research, development, testing and evaluation (RDT&E) and production ($64.5 million); maintenance of an NBC passive defence capability ($364.9 million); support of Special Operations Forces and defence against paramilitary, covert delivery and terrorist NBC threats ($151.1 million); and support of the inspection, monitoring and verification of arms control agreements ($569.9 million).

The significance of these rising budgetary commitments must also be viewed in the light of the budgetary constraints faced by the DOD. The DOE requested $489.4 million for FY 1998 to invest in non-proliferation activities, an increase of 19 per cent over FY 1997. At the request of the US Congress, the DOE has begun technology development efforts in detection, identification and characterization of CBW agents ($41 million).[102] For FY 1998, $48.7 million was requested for DOD support of the Domestic Preparedness Program, which aims to enhance the capability of the federal, state and local response agencies to prevent and respond to domestic terrorist incidents involving NBC weapons.[103] After a computerized war-game was held which simulated a campaign on the Korean Peninsula and showed that there were serious deficiencies in the protection of US forces against CW, the US Secretary of Defense announced that an additional $1 billion would be spent in FYs 1999–2003 to procure more CW personal protective equipment.[104] The level of concern in the United States is also reflected in the announcement by the DOD on 15 December 1997 of plans to vaccinate all US military personnel against anthrax, beginning in 1998.[105]

After the Persian Gulf War, NATO also began to consider military options to counter proliferation. The two greatest threats were considered to be posed by non-conventional weapons against NATO forces engaged in regional conflicts and against NATO territory. In June 1996 the Senior Defence Group on Proliferation (DGP) presented its third report on *Capabilities and Shortfalls* to the North Atlantic Council (NAC).[106] It examined current NATO and national capabilities, identified deficiencies, and suggested areas for improvement and cooperation regarding proliferation. The report prioritized defence system requirements and recommended that NATO institutionalize the threat assessment process in future defence planning. In June 1997 NATO endorsed the 'Guidance for effective military operations in an NBC environment', which

[102] Counterproliferation Program Review Committee (note 96), executive summary, p. ES-3, chapter 5, pp. 5–10, table 5.2.

[103] US Department of Defense (note 100).

[104] Starr, B., 'USA will add $1b to chemical protection', *Jane's Defence Weekly*, vol. 27, no. 22 (4 June 1997), p. 19.

[105] 'Defense Department to start immunizing troops against anthrax', News Release no. 679-97, Office of Assistant Secretary of Defense (Public Affairs), Washington, DC, 15 Dec. 1997, URL <http://www.defenselink.mil/news/Dec1997/b12151997_bt679-97.html>, version current on 15 Dec. 1997.

[106] In 1994 NATO created 3 bodies to examine the proliferation threat and response: the DGP, the Senior Political-military Group on Proliferation (SGP) and the Joint Committee on Proliferation (JCP). The membership of the DGP is identical to that of the Nuclear Planning Group Staff Group, but the DGP designation is used when non-proliferation matters are discussed. The SGP and DGP were created to conduct parallel studies in a collegial atmosphere, but under US influence the latter body became the focus of NATO military efforts involving policy, force structure and acquisition. The JCP meets irregularly to report SGP and DGP findings to the NAC. Larsen (note 98), pp. 24–25.

comprises the plans for counter-proliferation doctrine and training exercises and planning guidance.[107] The NAC had also authorized the exceptional procedure of an accelerated phase of force proposals to be added to the 1996 Force Goals, which the NATO defence ministers approved in June 1996. A further analysis by the DGP of the progress NATO has made towards intensifying and expanding its defence efforts against proliferation risks is expected to be submitted to the spring 1998 meeting of the NAC in the Defence Ministers Session.[108]

Many European partners which do not have overseas military commitments (Germany, in particular) emphasize diplomatic, economic and political measures to prevent proliferation. Consequently, the US term 'counterproliferation initiative' is politically unacceptable in NATO documents, but the alliance has adopted some of the core elements of the initiative, while maintaining a wide range of non-military measures to prevent, rather than counter, the proliferation of non-conventional weapons.[109] In the short term, NATO will rely on traditional forms of deterrence and focus on passive defence to protect troops in situations where it is feared that CBW may be used. In a short period the force planning, training and acquisition processes have been adapted to meet the proliferation threats.[110]

Allegations of CBW programmes

The reported continuation of CBW programmes in Russia continued to be a concern. For several years the existence of two nerve agents, A–232 and A–234, has been known in the West, and according to a leaked *Military Intelligence Digest* report 'the Russians can produce sizeable quantities of their new chemical agents within weeks to meet military requirements'.[111] The chemical structure of these compounds is not publicly known, but it is believed that neither the compounds nor their key precursors are included in the schedules of the CWC. Russia is also reported to have developed a genetically engineered variant of anthrax that is totally resistant to all known antibiotics.[112]

An officer of a Russian secret service reportedly defected to a Nordic country, believed to be Sweden, bringing with him a sample of an unnamed new

[107] Final communiqué of the ministerial meeting of the North Atlantic Council in Sintra, Portugal, 29 May 1997, Press release M-NAC-1(97)65, 29 May 1997.

[108] Final communiqué of the meeting of the North Atlantic Council in Defence Ministers Session, Press release M-NAC-D-2(97)149, 2 Dec. 1997.

[109] Larsen (note 98), pp. 56–57.

[110] Final communiqué of the meeting of the North Atlantic Council in Defence Ministers Session, Press release M-NAC-D-1(97)71, 12 June 1997; and Final communiqué of the ministerial meetings of the Defence Planning Committee and the Nuclear Planning Group, Press release M-DPC/NPG-1(97)70, 12 June 1997.

[111] 'Secret report cites Russian capability to make chemical arms', Associated Press via Fox News, 5 Feb. 1997, URL <http://foxnews.com/news/wires/n_0205_49.sml>, version current on 5 Feb. 1997; and Ember, L., 'Russian chemical agent flouts treaty', *Chemical & Engineering News*, vol. 75, no. 11 (17 Mar. 1997), p. 22.

[112] Cullen, T. and Foss, C. F. (eds), *Jane's Land Based Air Defence 1997–98* (Jane's Information Group: Coulsdon, Surrey, 1997), p. 9.

type of CW agent.¹¹³ The agent, which is said to be extremely potent and to leave no trace because of its high volatility, was reportedly tested in Chechnya,¹¹⁴ which would account for some unexplained deaths there.

In early 1997 a South African newspaper published details from a summary of a secret 1992 report by General Pierre Steyn, who investigated the role of the so-called Third Force, an obscure apartheid-era group within the South African Government which was involved in assassinations, beatings and other similar actions in the violence that racked South Africa. The report, prepared for former President F. W. de Klerk, was reputed to be so sensitive that President Nelson Mandela chose not to make it public in order not to jeopardize the post-election transition. The document was given to the Truth and Reconciliation Commission¹¹⁵ in December 1996 for further investigation.¹¹⁶ A summary document, *The Steyn Portfolio*, reveals that the 7th Medical Battalion of the South African Defence Forces under Brigadier Wouter Basson was involved in a CBW programme called Project Jota, which planned to employ poison for murder and drugs for operational use. A chemical attack was conducted against Frelimo (Frente de Libertação de Moçambique, Front for the Liberation of Mozambique), which—according to the document—was confirmed by a British team from the Chemical and Biological Defence Establishment at Porton Down in the UK. This operation appears to have been part of the attempts to discredit the African National Congress (ANC).¹¹⁷ Basson founded and was head of South Africa's CBW programme, known as Project B or Project Coast in 1980–93 and revealed by de Klerk in 1994, and was also one of the South African CW experts linked by the US State Department in 1995 to the Libyan CW programme.¹¹⁸

Allegations of the presence of chemical weapons in the former Yugoslavia were detailed in a report published by the Human Rights Watch.¹¹⁹ The Middle East continued to be of major concern with respect to CBW proliferation.¹²⁰ Libya, however, apparently stopped construction of its CW plant at Tarhuna, according to a statement based on information from intelligence

---

¹¹³ Deutsche Presse Agentur, 'Russische Überläufer brachte neuartiges Giftgas in den Westen' [Russian defector brought new type of poison gas to the West], dispatch no. 3904, 12 Mar. 1997; and Private communication by the author with a Deutsche Presse Agentur journalist.

¹¹⁴ Claims of Russian chemical warfare in Chechnya were made in 1994 and 1995. Stock, T., Haug, M. and Radler, P., 'Chemical and biological weapon developments and arms control', *SIPRI Yearbook 1996* (note 57), p. 663.

¹¹⁵ The Truth and Reconciliation Commission is investigating abuses which occurred during the apartheid era. Its chairman is Archbishop Desmond Tutu.

¹¹⁶ 'Shocks from the Steyn Report', *Weekly Mail & Guardian*, 31 Jan. 1997, URL <http://wn.apc.org/wmail/issues/970131/NEWS1.html>, version current on 31 Jan. 1997.

¹¹⁷ *The Steyn Portfolio*, mimeographed, no date, pp. 7, 11.

¹¹⁸ Duke, L., 'Drug bust exposes S. African arms probes', *Washington Post*, 1 Feb. 1997, p. A15; and 'Poison gas secrets were sold to Libya', *Weekly Mail & Guardian*, 7 Feb. 1997, URL <http://wn.apc.org/wmail/issues/970207/NEWS1.html>, version current on 7 Feb. 1997. See also Leklem, E. and Boulden, L., 'Exorcising Project B: Pretoria probes its shady chemical past', *Jane's Intelligence Review*, vol. 9, no. 8 (Aug. 1997), pp. 372–75.

¹¹⁹ Human Rights Watch, 'Clouds of war: chemical weapons in the former Yugoslavia', *Human Rights Watch Arms Project*, vol. 9, no. 5 (Mar. 1997).

¹²⁰ Note 97.

agencies by John Holum, Director of the US Arms Control and Disarmament Agency.[121]

The Cuban allegation of biological warfare

On 30 June 1997 Cuba submitted a request to Russia, one of the three co-depositaries of the BTWC, to convene a formal consultative meeting to investigate an alleged US attack with BW agents in October 1996.[122] This was the first time since the entry into force of the BTWC in 1975 that a party had formally requested the international community to investigate a breach of the convention. Cuba did not lodge a complaint with the UN Security Council under Article VI of the BTWC but invoked a procedure to strengthen the implementation of Article V which was adopted by the 1991 Third Review Conference of the BTWC. According to this procedure, the formal consultative meeting must be preceded by bilateral or other consultations among the states involved in the dispute. Following the submission of the request, the depositaries of the BTWC must convene a formal consultative meeting within 60 days of receipt of the request.[123]

According to the allegation, a US anti-narcotics fumigation plane flying from Florida to Grand Cayman crossed Cuba with Cuban authorization on 21 October 1996 and was observed by a Cuban civilian aircraft to spray unknown substances intermittently. On 18 December the first signs appeared of a plague of *Thrips palmi*, a polyphagous insect pest. While Thysanoptera, to which thrips belong, live on plants, Cuba stated that this particular insect was indigenous to Asia and exotic to Cuban territory, although since 1985 its presence has been noted on several Caribbean islands. By January 1997 other parts of Cuba had also been affected.[124] In October the Cuban Government reported that 20 000 tonnes of produce had been lost to *thrips palmi*.[125]

Cuba dismissed the US explanation that the pilot had used the smoke generator of his aircraft to signal his presence to the Cuban pilot and that the tanks of the sprinkling system had carried extra fuel for the long flight.[126] On 28 April, in a note to the UN Secretary-General, Cuba accused the USA of biological warfare.[127] In a letter, dated 27 June, Cuba formally rejected the US

[121] United Press International, 'Libya halts chemical arms plant', 19 Mar. 1997, URL <http://www.brook.edu/fp/projects/nucwcost/tarhunah.htm>, version current on 8 Apr. 1997.

[122] Prensa Latina (Havana), 0904 GMT, 1 July 1997, in 'Cuba: UN asked to investigate US use of bacteriological weapons', Foreign Broadcast Information Service, *Daily Report–Latin America (FBIS-LAT)*, FBIS-LAT-97-182, 1 July 1997.

[123] Final Document of the Third Review Conference of the Parties to the Convention on the Prohibition of the Development, Production and Stockpiling of Bacteriological (Biological) and Toxin Weapons and on Their Destruction, Part II, Final Declaration, BTWC Third Review Conference document BWC/CONF.III/22, 27 Sep. 1991, Article V.

[124] Note verbale dated 28 April 1997 from the Permanent Mission of Cuba to the United Nations addressed to the Secretary-General, UN document A/52/128, 29 Apr. 1997.

[125] Radio Rebelde Network (Havana), 1800 GMT, 25 Oct. 1997, in 'Cuba: Lage stresses increased watch against biological warfare', FBIS-LAT-97-301, 28 Oct. 1997.

[126] The US version of events was presented on 6 May: 'Transcript: State Dept. noon briefing, May 6, 1997', *Washington File* (United States Information Service, US Embassy: Stockholm, 7 May 1997), URL <http://www.sis.usemb.se/wireless/300/eur303.htm>, version current on 7 May 1997.

[127] Note verbale . . . (note 124).

version of the incident.[128] The formal consultative meeting began in Geneva on 25 August in closed session but after three days of talks failed to resolve Cuba's claim because, according to its chairman, British ambassador Ian Soutar, 'it was not possible to draw a direct causal link' between the overflight and the outbreak.[129] As *thrips palmi* occur in the Dominican Republic, Florida, Haiti and Jamaica, the main unresolved question is whether the insect could have been introduced into Cuba in another way.[130] The meeting mandated Soutar to further investigate the allegation and prepare a report by 31 December 1997.[131]

The allegation and the subsequent procedure are further evidence of one of the BTWC's most significant weaknesses, the lack of a verification regime. The incident added urgency to the work of the Ad Hoc Group to complete negotiations on a verification protocol, as discussed above in section III.

Other events related to CBW proliferation

Iran was at the centre of several international incidents involving the shipment of controlled goods which, taken together, may indicate an active Iranian interest in the manufacture of chemical weapons. On 24 January 1997 two men were arrested in Portland, Oregon, for trying to ship impregnated alumina to Iran despite the US embargo against that country. Impregnated alumina is a catalyst used in the plastics and rubber industry but can also be used to produce phosphorus oxychloride, a precursor to nerve agents.[132] In Tel Aviv a French-based Israeli businessman was charged in May 1997 with supplying components for CW, including mustard and nerve agents, to Iran.[133] Later in May, pursuant to the 1991 Chemical and Biological Weapons and Warfare Elimination Act,[134] the USA levied sanctions against three Chinese companies and five individuals for knowingly selling equipment and ingredients which can be used for the manufacture of CW agents to Iran. The offending companies, two of which are based in China and the third in Hong Kong, cannot import goods into the USA or buy US products for one year. Chinese authorities maintained that the companies had conducted normal business and that

---

[128] Letter dated 27 June 1997 from the Permanent Representative of Cuba to the United Nations addressed to the Secretary-General, UN document A/52/213, 27 June 1997.

[129] 'Cuba accuses US of biological attack', CNN Interactive, 25 Aug. 1997, URL <http://www.cnn.com/WORLD/9708/25/biological.cuba.ap/index.html>, version current on 25 Aug. 1997; and Higgins, A. G., 'Panel cannot resolve Cuban claim against US, sets plan for study', Fox News, 27 Aug. 1997, URL <http://foxnews.com/news/wires2/n_0827_170.sml>, version current on 27 Aug. 1997.

[130] Wright (note 78), p. 18. The insects can travel long distances on the wind.

[131] Deen, T., 'Cuban pest strike claim tests UN Convention', *Jane's Defence Weekly*, vol. 28, no. 10 (10 Sep. 1997), p. 17.

[132] Associated Press, 'O. C. man held in nerve gas shipment probe', *Los Angeles Times*, 25 Jan. 1997, p. A17.

[133] Marcus, R., 'Israeli indicted for helping Iran get chemical arms', *Jerusalem Post* (international edn), 17 May 1997, p. 24.

[134] Cornell Law School, Legal Information Institute, 'Sanctions against the use of chemical or biological weapons', URL <http://www.law.cornell.edu/uscode/22/ch65.html>, version current on 8 Apr. 1998.

China strictly enforces controls on the trade in such materials.[135] In July the Hong Kong Government closed a local subsidiary of a Chinese state arms manufacturer after alleging that the firm had supplied CW materials to Iran.[136]

In October it became known that the Israeli secret service, Mossad, had attempted to assassinate a Hamas political leader, Khaled Meshal, in Amman by use of poison. When the operation went wrong and Meshal survived, the Israeli agents were imprisoned in Jordan, leading to a major crisis between Israel and Jordan. The poison reportedly leaves no traces and can therefore not be detected in an autopsy. The antidote is known only to Israeli experts, but King Hussein of Jordan forced Israel to provide it to treat the victim.[137]

In an incident in April, which raised fear of BW terrorism in the USA, a package with a broken Petri dish and a note indicating that the Petri dish contained anthrax and plague was left outside the Washington headquarters of the Jewish organization B'nai B'rith. Tests proved negative for a variety of BW agents. During the incident, over 100 people were trapped inside the building for over eight hours, an event which highlighted the inadequacies of the then-existing emergency measures against CBW terrorism.[138]

Israel operates a biological research laboratory, the Institute for Biological Research, in Nes Tsiona, which is known to conduct defence work. Marcus Klingberg, who was sentenced to an 18-year prison term in 1983 for passing BW secrets to the Soviet Union, was refused a request to be released on health grounds because, according to the court, he could possess information that 'if exposed could cause unimaginable damage to national security'.[139]

V. UNSCOM developments

After the defeat of Iraq in the Persian Gulf War, the UN Security Council created UNSCOM to uncover Iraq's CBW and missile programmes;[140] to ensure destruction of its stockpiles, production facilities and other related installations; and to establish a long-term monitoring programme so that Iraq would be unable to acquire a new non-conventional weapon capability.

---

[135] 'US levies sanctions against Chinese companies', CNN Interactive, 22 May 1997, URL <http://cnn.com/WORLD/9705/22/us.china/index.html>, version current on 22 May 1997; US Information Service, 'US imposes CW sanctions against Chinese entities', 22 May 1997, URL <gopher://198.80.36.82:70/0R28127762-28131581-range/archives/1997/pdq.97>, version current on 22 May 1997; and Reuters, 'China slams US sanctions on Iran Trade', via Fox News, 23 May 1997, URL <http://foxnews.com/news/052397/china2.sml>, version current on 23 May 1997.

[136] Guyot, E., 'Hong Kong closes unit of Norinco in arms case', *Wall Street Journal Europe*, 16 July 1997, p. 2.

[137] Cowell, A., 'The daring attack that blew up in Israel's face', *New York Times*, 15 Oct. 1997, pp. A1, A8; and Tsur, B. and Bushinsky, J., 'Panel probes botched assassination', *Jerusalem Post* (international edn), 18 Oct. 1997, pp. 1–2. See also chapter 3 in this volume.

[138] 'FBI: leaking package at B'nai B'rith not life-threatening', CNN Interactive, 24 Apr. 1997, URL <http://www.cnn.com/US/9704/24/bnai.brith.wrap/index.html>, version current on 24 Apr. 1997; and 'FBI considers B'nai B'rith package as terrorism', Fox News, 25 Apr. 1997, URL <http://foxnews.com/news/wires/n_0425_122.sml>, version current on 25 Apr. 1997.

[139] 'Israeli germ war lab "no danger"', *Electronic Telegraph*, 20 Feb. 1997, URL <http://www.telegraph.co.uk:80/>, version current on 7 Jan. 1998.

[140] The International Atomic Energy Agency (IAEA) is responsible for uncovering and dismantling Iraq's nuclear weapon programme with the assistance and cooperation of UNSCOM.

Table 11.1. UNSCOM inspections, 1997

Type of inspection/date	Team
Biological	
2 Apr.–4 July	BG 9
9–14 May	BW 49/UNSCOM 184
16–20 May	BW 50/UNSCOM 187
13–19 June	CBW 4/UNSCOM 190
5 July–present [into 1998]	BG 10
7–21 July	BW 51/UNSCOM 189
26 July–4 Aug.	BW 52/UNSCOM 192
8–15 Aug.	BW 53/UNSCOM 193
21–25 Aug.	BW 54/UNSCOM 197
8–20 Sep.	BW 55/UNSCOM 199
9–13 Sep.	BW 56/UNSCOM 200
15 Oct.–21 Nov.	BG 11
22 Nov.–5 Jan. 1998	BG 12
Chemical	
16 Jan.–23 Apr.	CG 9
9–17 Apr.	CW 37/UNSCOM 186
24 Apr.–17 July	CG 10
5–14 May	CW 31/UNSCOM 153
13–19 June	CBW 4/UNSCOM 190
1–4 July	CW 38/UNSCOM 195
18 July–13 Oct.	CG 11
26–30 Aug.	CW 40/UNSCOM 198
10–20 Sep.	CW 42/UNSCOM 203
22–26 Sep.	CW 41/UNSCOM 202
29 Sep.–8 Oct.	CW 39/UNSCOM 196
14 Oct.	CG 12
Ballistic missile	
26 Feb.–4 May	MG 12
24 Mar.–3 Oct.	BM 50/UNSCOM 175
5 May–3 Aug.	MG 13
2–13 June	BM 56/UNSCOM 188
12–17 July	BM 57/UNSCOM 191
4 Aug.–14 Oct.	MG 14
11–16 Aug.	BM 58/UNSCOM 204
18–26 Aug.	BM 59/UNSCOM 205
5–19 Sep.	BM 60/UNSCOM 206
26 Sep.–4 Oct.	BM 61/UNSCOM 208
7–11 Oct.	MG 14A
15 Oct.–14 Jan. 1998	MG 15
10–19 Dec.	BM 64/UNSCOM 220
10–21 Dec.	MG 15A
27 Dec.–1 Jan. 1998	MG 15B
Export/import	
27 Mar.–6 June	EG–5
7 June–23 July	EG–6
24 July–5 Oct.	EG–7
6 Oct.–15 Jan. 1998	EG–8

Type of inspection/date	Team
Concealment investigation missions	
2–13 June	CIM 6/UNSCOM 194
19–24 Sep.	CIM 7/UNSCOM 201
26 Sep.–2 Oct.	CIM 8/UNSCOM 207
18–24 Dec.	CIM 9/UNSCOM 218
Special missions to Baghdad	
21–24 June	Deputy Executive Chairman's visit
21–25 July	Executive Chairman's visit
5–9 Sep.	Executive Chairman's visit
12–16 Dec.	Executive Chairman's visit

BG = Biological Monitoring Group, BM = ballistic missiles, BW = biological weapons, CBW = chemical and biological weapons, CIM = Concealment Investigation Mission, CG = Chemical Monitoring Group, CW = chemical weapons, EG = Export/Import Monitoring Group, MG = Missile Monitoring Group.

Source: Information provided by UNSCOM spokesman.

In July 1997 Swedish ambassador Rolf Ekéus stepped down as UNSCOM's Executive Chairman and was replaced by Australian ambassador Richard Butler. The long-term monitoring system, which includes an export/import control mechanism for dual-use goods, continued to function. More than 100 people, including approximately 20 scientists and specialists in nuclear physics, chemistry, biology and missile technology, now work at the Baghdad Monitoring and Verification Centre (BMVC) and carry out 'no-notice' inspections of relevant facilities. (Table 11.1 lists the inspections conducted by UNSCOM in Iraq in 1997.) Their work is supported by advanced sensors, detectors and field laboratories, and by approximately 150 cameras that monitor machines, production lines and missile test stands, among other things, and which beam real-time imagery to the BMVC.[141]

After more than six years UNSCOM is still unable to certify that the full extent of the Iraqi CBW programmes has been discovered. Inspectors have collected hard and circumstantial evidence which suggests that the programmes were either more advanced or wider in scope than previously thought. The 'full, final and complete' declarations submitted by Iraq in 1997 again proved to be of limited value.

Under UNSCOM supervision more than 53 000 chemical weapons were destroyed in 1991–94, including 38 537 filled and unfilled munitions, 690 tonnes of agents, more than 3000 tonnes of precursor chemicals for the manufacture of chemical warfare agents, and thousands of pieces of production equipment and analytical instruments. In 1996 UNSCOM found new evidence of CW production. Many analytical tools and precursor chemicals had been exempted from destruction in 1995 on the basis of Iraqi declarations of their past use or intended purpose, which proved to be false. Between August

[141] Interview with Ambassador Rolf Ekéus in 'Ambassador Rolf Ekéus: leaving behind the UNSCOM legacy in Iraq', *Arms Control Today*, vol. 27, no. 4 (June/July 1997), p. 3.

and October 1997 UNSCOM supervised the destruction of 325 newly identified pieces of production equipment, 125 analytical instruments and 275 tonnes of precursor chemicals. In addition, 120 pieces of production equipment were declared by Iraq in August 1997.[142]

However, no full account of the CW programme has been possible for a variety of reasons. First, Iraq removed CW, equipment and materials from the main site of the al-Muthanna State Establishment before the first UNSCOM inspection team arrived, and a full account of their destruction has not been forthcoming. Second, Iraq claims that it unilaterally destroyed 15 620 chemical munitions and 130 tonnes of CW agents, a fact and total that remain unverified. Third, in 1997 UNSCOM found fresh evidence that Iraq had developed a production capability for VX, the most toxic nerve agent in military arsenals. Iraq had obtained at least 750 tonnes of VX precursor chemicals and had produced a further 55 tonnes domestically. Iraq claimed that 460 tonnes were destroyed through aerial bombardment in the Gulf War and that it destroyed an additional 212 tonnes. The remainder was said to have been consumed in VX production attempts. However, UNSCOM was able to verify the destruction of only 155 of the 212 tonnes of VX precursor chemicals. (It also supervised the destruction of an additional 36 tonnes.)

Until 1995 Iraq denied that it had produced VX, and attempts were made to eliminate all traces of such activity.[143] The amount of VX precursor chemicals which Iraq appears to have possessed would have enabled it to produce up to 200 tonnes of VX. UNSCOM has determined that 3.9 tonnes of VX were actually produced in industrial plants.[144] Inspectors were reportedly about to uncover more evidence of the VX-production programme when a dispute began between Iraq and the UN Security Council in the autumn of 1997. According to Ekéus, UNSCOM possesses documentary evidence that Iraqi scientists have been ordered by the government to retain the capability to manufacture CW at short notice.[145]

Iraq's BW programme was so secret that, according to Ekéus, even Iraq's Deputy Prime Minister Tariq Aziz was initially not aware of it.[146] Iraq has been least cooperative as regards its BW programme. According to an October 1997 UNSCOM report, Iraqi declarations are inaccurate and BW-related

[142] Report of the Secretary-General on the activities of the Special Commission established by the Secretary-General pursuant to paragraph 9 (b) (i) of resolution 687 (1991), UN document S/1997/774, 6 Oct. 1997.

[143] Report of the Secretary-General . . . (note 142).

[144] United States Information Service, 'Fact sheet: Iraq's program of mass destruction' (United Sttes Information Service, US Embassy: London, 19 Nov. 1997), URL <http://www.usembassy.org.uk/midest26.html>, version current on 19 Nov. 1997; Mann, P., 'Iraq's stratagem: conceal and comply', *Aviation Week & Space Technology*, vol. 147, no. 21 (24 Nov. 1997), p. 24; Deen, T., 'UNSCOM report exposes extent of Iraq's projects', *Jane's Defence Weekly*, vol. 28, no. 22 (3 Dec. 1997), p. 16; and United States Information Service, 'UNSCOM Chairman Butler report on visit to Baghdad', *Washington File* (United States Information Service, US Embassy: Stockholm, 26 Jan. 1998), URL <http://www.usis.usemb.se/wireless/100/eur110.htm>, version current on 26 Jan. 1998.

[145] '10 June', *CBW Conventions Bulletin*, no. 37 (Sep. 1997), p. 22.

[146] Address by Rolf Ekéus to a conference in Washington hosted by the Carnegie Endowment, as reported in '10 June', *CBW Conventions Bulletin*, no. 37 (Sep. 1997), p. 22; and Marshall, R., *Ekéus: Weapons of Mass Destruction of Higher Value to Iraq than Oil*, United States Information Agency, 10 June 1997.

activities are greatly under-reported. In some cases, Iraq reported that it had destroyed more munitions than the number which it had declared that it had produced.[147] According to some accounts, Iraq may have produced up to 10 billion doses of anthrax, botulinus toxin and aflatoxin.[148] The discovery that Iraq was researching aflatoxin, which is not a traditional BW agent, was surprising. Aflatoxin is a carcinogen whose effects would manifest themselves only after many years, and some Western experts have speculated that the Iraqi programme had genocidal goals.[149] If aflatoxin were used against the Kurds, for example, it would probably be impossible to prove biological warfare at the time the symptoms appeared. The Iraqi BW research programme focused on other agents, such as camel pox and gas gangrene, and included animal testing. A variety of delivery systems were developed and produced, including 155-mm artillery shells, 122-mm rockets, R400 aircraft bombs, warheads for the al-Hussein ballistic missile and an experimental spray tank converted from drop tanks, which would have held 2000 litres of anthrax.[150] The delivery systems faced serious developmental problems and may therefore have been ineffective. The BW programme remains a major cause of concern as Iraq can easily hide small quantities of freeze-dried organisms in a variety of locations and resurrect its research and production programme within a brief span of time.

As of October 1997, Iraq had also declared the production of 80 special warheads for the al Hussein ballistic missile: 50 for CW agents, 25 for BW agents and 5 for trials. These figures also differed from previous declarations. UNSCOM has evidence of the probable existence of additional special warheads. It can only confirm the destruction of 30 CW warheads under its supervision and some of the 45 other warheads which Iraq claims to have destroyed. No response was made to a request in September 1997 to document the destruction of the remainder.[151]

In 1997 the number of incidents between UNSCOM inspectors and Iraqi officials increased, leading to the unanimous adoption of UN Security Council Resolution 1115 on 21 June 1997. In the autumn a major crisis erupted when Iraq refused inspectors access to several facilities, including presidential sites (which comprise both buildings and the surrounding area), and objected to the nationality of some inspectors. Although escalation was initially prevented by Russian diplomatic efforts, the crisis flared up again in early 1998 following the submission of a negative report by Richard Butler to the UN Security Council after his January 1998 visit to Baghdad to resolve the crisis.[152]

---

[147] Report of the Secretary-General . . . (note 142).
[148] United States Information Service, 'Fact sheet . . .' (note 144); and Mann (note 144).
[149] Discussion at the NATO Advanced Study Institute meeting, 'New Scientific and Technological Aspects of Verification of the Biological and Toxin Weapons Convention (BTWC)', Budapest, Hungary, 6–16 July 1997.
[150] United States Information Service, 'Fact sheet . . .' (note 144); and Mann (note 144).
[151] Report of the Secretary-General . . . (note 142).
[152] United States Information Service, 'UNSCOM Chairman Butler . . .' (note 144).

VI. The Gulf War illnesses

The so-called Gulf War Syndrome is a variable cluster of symptoms and physical conditions with different causes and to which individual susceptibility varies. The health complaints are mainly reported by British and US veterans of the war, but an increased incidence of symptoms and conditions has also been noted among veterans from Australia, Canada, the Czech Republic, Hungary, Kuwait, New Zealand and Norway, and among the civilian populations of Iraq, Kuwait and Saudi Arabia.[153] The Danish Army has also commissioned an epidemiological study to investigate the health problems which exist among nearly one-half of the 840 Danish soldiers and civilians who served in the Gulf War.[154] The ailments include influenza-like symptoms, chronic fatigue, rashes, joint and muscle pain, headaches, memory loss, reproductive problems, depression, loss of concentration and gastrointestinal problems.[155] While official sources in the UK and the USA maintained that post-traumatic stress disorder (PTSD) was the main source of the various symptoms, there is growing recognition that exposure to CBW agents, depleted uranium, oil-well fire smoke, pesticides, petroleum products, the experimental nerve agent pre-treatment pyridostigmine bromide (PB) or vaccines, alone or in combination, may be the real cause of the wide range of health disorders.[156] French troops serving in the Gulf War, however, do not complain of such symptoms. It is noteworthy that, according to Colonel Françoise Rota, a French medical officer in the Gulf War, French troops did not use any of the chemical and biological agent pre-treatments administered to British and US personnel or the organophosphate spray which was used to control insect pest populations.[157]

In 1997 attention increasingly focused on the exposure of the veterans to toxic chemical substances following the disclosure in 1996 that the demolition of a munition bunker containing 8.5 tonnes of nerve agent at Khamisiyah in southern Iraq may have contaminated tens of thousands of US troops. Before this admission, the US DOD categorically denied that any US or other coalition soldiers had been exposed directly or indirectly to CBW agents. This was despite the fact that during the military operations in January and February 1991 the chemical alarms went off repeatedly. Although many of these alarms were false, NBC specialists with sophisticated detection equipment also confirmed the presence of CW agents in southern Iraq and Kuwait both during

---

[153] Tucker, J. B., *Chemical/Biological Weapons Exposures and Gulf War Illness*, Report to the Subcommittee on Human Resources and Intergovernmental Relations, Committee on Government Reform and Oversight, US House of Representatives, 29 Jan. 1996.

[154] '8 January', *Chemical Weapons Convention Bulletin*, no. 35 (Mar. 1997), p. 33.

[155] *Gulf War Veterans' Illnesses: VA, DoD Continue to Resist Strong Evidence Linking Toxic Causes to Chronic Health Effects*, Second Report by the Committee on Government Reform and Oversight together with additional views, US House of Representatives, 7 Nov. 1997 (US Government Printing Office: Washington, DC, 1997), pp. 6–7.

[156] US General Accounting Office, *Gulf War Illnesses: Improved Monitoring of Clinical Progress and Reexamination of Research Emphasis are Needed*, GAO/NSIA-9-163 (General Accounting Office: Washington, DC, June 1997), appendix IV, pp. 54–64.

[157] 'Darkness at noon', *The Economist*, 11 Jan. 1997, p. 84.

and after the fighting.[158] Coalition troops may have been exposed to low levels of CW agents as a consequence of the chemical fallout from the aerial bombardment of Iraqi CW depots, the demolition of munition depots containing CW after the cease-fire, and the sporadic and uncoordinated Iraqi use of CW in the ground campaign.[159] The DOD's position is based on a lack of evidence of mass incidents of morbidity and mortality. Consequently, funding for research on the health effects of such exposure, especially at low levels, has been refused.[160] In the 1980s the US Air Force conducted animal studies of low-level exposure because of concern that some personnel, such as bomb loaders, might have to work in a contaminated environment.[161] The delayed toxic effects of various CW agents have been described in the medical literature since World War I.[162]

British and US troops, in particular, were required to take experimental drugs and vaccines to counter the effect of potential exposure to CBW agents in the Gulf War and these may have caused some of the reported symptoms. The anti-nerve agent pyridostigmine bromide, which was administered in tablet form, has been studied for its possible connection with the complaints of ill health. Like nerve agents and organophosphate pesticides, PB inhibits the functioning of the enzyme acetylcholinesterase (AChE), which leads to nerve and muscle degeneration moments after a single dose and worsens with multiple doses.[163] The PB tablets therefore, according to some claims, can have masked the acute effects of chemical exposure and contributed to the conclusion by the DOD that no such exposure occurred.[164] Laboratory research has suggested that exposure to PB, the insecticide permethrin and the insect repellent diethyltoluamide (DEET)—all of which were used routinely in the Gulf War theatre—may have caused increased neurotoxicity. Since the war it has also been established that with the onset of stress PB can leak through the blood/brain barrier, increasing its ability to cause damage to the central nervous system.[165] According to testimony before a US congressional committee, the US Army's chemical warfare research centre in Aberdeen, Maryland,

---

[158] See various testimonies in *Persian Gulf Veterans' Illnesses*, Hearings before the Subcommittee on Human Resources and Intergovernmental Relations of the Committee on Government Reform and Oversight, House of Representatives, 104th Congress, 2nd session, 10–11 Dec. 1996 (US Government Printing Office: Washington, DC, 1997).

[159] Tucker, J. B., 'Low-level chemical weapons exposures during the 1991 Persian Gulf War', Prepared statement before the Subcommittee on Human Resources, Committee on Government Reform and Oversight, US House of Representatives, 24 Apr. 1997, p. 2; and US General Accounting Office (note 156), p. 62.

[160] US General Accounting Office (note 156), pp. 62, 64.

[161] The results are summarized in Hartgraves, S. L. and Murphy, M. R., 'Behavioral effects of low-dose nerve agents', ed. S. M. Somani, *Chemical Warfare Agents* (Academic Press: San Diego, Calif., 1992), pp. 125–54.

[162] Lohs, Kh., SIPRI, *Delayed Toxic Effects of Chemical Warfare Agents* (Almqvist & Wiksell: Stockholm, 1975). Also available at the SIPRI CBW Project Internet site, URL <http://www.sipri.se/cbw/cbw-info.html>.

[163] *Gulf War Veterans' Illnesses* (note 155), p. 33. Unlike the nerve agents, PB slowly restores the functioning of the AChE. Pre-treatment is intended to block a percentage of the action of the AChE before exposure to the nerve agent. The blocked AChE cannot then be destroyed by the nerve agent and is available for recovery from nerve agent poisoning.

[164] *Gulf War Veterans' Illnesses* (note 155), pp. 38, 86.

[165] *Gulf War Veterans' Illnesses* (note 155), pp. 33–34, 87.

established in the early 1980s that: '1) PB would be harmful in healthy individuals; 2) PB was worthless, even counterproductive, as a protectant against chemical warfare; and 3) PB was more toxic than sub-lethal doses of chemical warfare agents'.[166] It is therefore surprising that in December 1990 the Food and Drug Administration agreed to grant a waiver to the DOD allowing the military to issue the experimental drug PB without the prior informed consent of the soldiers.

In the UK an estimated 1800 soldiers suffer from Gulf War-related illnesses. On the basis of the revised Pentagon data on the destruction of the munition dump at Khamisiyah, the British Ministry of Defence stated at the end of July 1997 that British units may also have been exposed to minute amounts of chemical agents.[167] This news followed the admission in December 1996 by Conservative Nicholas Soames, then Armed Forces Minister, that troops with no training and no protective clothing had been told during the Gulf War to spray camps with the organophosphate pesticides Fenitrothion and Diazanon, which are not used for public hygiene.[168] The British Government had also approved large-scale vaccination of troops against CBW agents but was unaware of concerns raised by the Department of Health in late 1990 as it did not receive the relevant document until 7 April 1997. A programme has been set up to investigate the interaction of vaccines and anti-nerve agent tablets as a possible cause of the Gulf War Syndrome. Soldiers serving on land, for example, were given simultaneous inoculations against anthrax and whooping cough, the latter having been administered as an adjuvant to enhance the anthrax vaccine. According to Armed Forces Minister John Reid, one of the reasons for the new focus was that during the Gulf War the commander of the French forces had refused 'to allow any of his men to have the vaccines or any of the anti-nerve agent tablets'.[169]

VII. Conclusions

Two contradictory forces regarding the future of chemical and biological weapons seem to have been at work in 1997. On the one hand, the international norms against their possession and use were strengthened with the entry into force of the Chemical Weapons Convention and the intensification of the negotiations to create an effective, equitable and verifiable verification regime for the Biological and Toxin Weapons Convention. On the other hand, there is a growing fear that states or sub-state actors might gain disproportionate military advantage from violating or failing to adhere to these norms by

---

[166] *Gulf War Veterans' Illnesses* (note 155), pp. 33, 87–88, 110–11.

[167] Associated Press via CNN Interactive, 'British as well as US troops were exposed to poison gas in Iraq', 30 July 1997, URL <http://www.cnn.com/WORLD/meast/9707/29/AP000531.ap.html>, version current on 30 July 1997.

[168] Zanders, Eckstein, and Hart (note 12), p. 466; and Burrell, I., 'Veterans ignored in Whitehall inquiry', *The Independent*, 10 Mar. 1997, p. 5.

[169] 'Gulf veterans: new care plans', *Survey of Current Affairs*, vol. 27, no. 5 (1997), p. 167; Bellamy, C., 'Gulf War syndrome research stepped up', *The Independent*, 15 July 1997, p. 9; and Fairhall, D., 'New Gulf syndrome inquiry', *The Guardian*, 15 July 1997, p. 4.

having such weapons ready for use without fear of retaliation in kind. In particular, the difficulties UNSCOM experiences in accounting for and eliminating Iraq's CBW capabilities, despite operating under the most intrusive inspection mandate ever, appear to challenge the belief in the effectiveness of the verification measures of arms control and disarmament regimes. In addition, the fact that more British and US soldiers have died after than during the Persian Gulf War as a consequence of various ailments, which are increasingly being attributed to exposure to a variety of toxic chemicals, seems to underscore the fear that even the limited CBW capabilities of a small power can inflict long-term damage on the best-equipped forces. The Gulf War experience has led the Western powers to launch major R&D and acquisition programmes to counter these threats. While the chances of a war or a major terrorist attack in which CBW are used remain relatively low, the consequences of a lack of preparation are extremely serious and at present few Western governments feel that they can safely neglect the issue. However, the institutionalization of policy, military and emergency planning and acquisition across many governmental bodies also perpetuates and enhances the threat perception as many organizations inside and outside government, including research institutes and commercial companies, develop a vested interest in the continuation of the situation in which the use of CBW is viewed as a major threat.

The changing environment in which a treaty must operate can quickly erode the degree of international consensus at a given moment regarding a particular prohibition. For the future of the CWC disarmament regime, for instance, it is imperative that the convention achieves universal adherence as soon as possible, that parties provide complete and accurate declarations, and that certain grey areas are clarified. Similarly, greater public transparency on the part of governments regarding past CW programmes should alleviate international proliferation concerns. Speedy international agreement on verification and confidence-building measures for the BTWC is imperative before biotechnological developments turn biological weapons into controllable battlefield weapons. The manner in which the international community meets these challenges in the near future will determine the strength and future of the CBW disarmament regimes.

Appendix 11A. Entry into force of the Chemical Weapons Convention

ROBERT J. MATHEWS

I. Introduction

The Chemical Weapons Convention (CWC) specifies that the convention will enter into force 180 days after the date of deposit of the 65th instrument of ratification, but not earlier than two years after it was opened for signature, and that upon entry into force the CWC will be administered by the Organisation for the Prohibition of Chemical Weapons (OPCW) in The Hague. At the time of the signing ceremony in 1993 there was an expectation in some quarters that there would be 65 ratifications by mid-1994, enabling entry into force at the earliest possible date, 13 January 1995. However, the 'trigger point' was not reached until Hungary deposited the 65th ratification on 31 October 1996, making the date of entry into force 29 April 1997.

The fact that it took longer to achieve 65 ratifications gave the Preparatory Commission (PrepCom) of the OPCW 'extra time' over the originally assumed two years for its preparations for entry into force of the convention. The time was well spent on the establishment of the OPCW (including substantial progress on tasks which experienced unanticipated delays, such as the OPCW building and laboratory, and staff recruitment) and 'outreach' to signatory states (e.g., seminars in The Hague, regional seminars and workshops). However, the development of verification provisions by the Expert Groups[1] allowed some signatory states—particularly a minority which appeared more interested in minimizing the cost and intrusiveness of the OPCW and protecting confidential information than in effective verification—to attempt to renegotiate provisions of the CWC (rather than developing practical implementation procedures which accurately reflected the agreed CWC text). This resulted in a virtual stalemate in attempts to resolve many issues.[2]

At the 14th plenary session of the PrepCom, in July 1996, the Committee on the Preparations for the First Conference of the States Parties (FCSP) was established, and its first meetings were held in August 1996. Various administrative preparations and decisions were required for the FCSP on issues such as: the dates, duration and agenda of the FCSP; the content and format of the Final Report of the PrepCom to the FCSP; the rules of procedure for the FCSP and the Executive Council; and allocation of the responsibilities of the host state (the Netherlands) and the OPCW for the facilities to be provided at the FCSP. These administrative measures became a major focus of the work of the PrepCom, particularly after the trigger point was reached.

The PrepCom made a last, and largely unsuccessful, attempt to resolve the outstanding issues in February 1997 through extensive efforts by the Expert Groups of

---

[1] The Expert Groups are discussed in Zanders, J. P., Eckstein, S. and Hart, J., 'Chemical and biological weapon developments and arms control', *SIPRI Yearbook 1997: Armaments, Disarmament and International Security* (Oxford University Press: Oxford, 1997), pp. 442–44.

[2] However, in 1996 most signatory states accepted that the issues related to verification which were critical in the first year or more after entry into force had been sufficiently resolved by the PrepCom to enable the OPCW successfully to tackle its most critical tasks immediately after entry into force of the CWC. Mathews, R. J., 'Preparing for implementation of the Chemical Weapons Convention: progress during 1996', *Verification 1997* (Verification Technology Centre: London, 1997), pp. 81–105.

Working Group B, which was responsible for the development of detailed procedures for verification and technical cooperation and assistance. In March 1997 there was extensive informal discussion of how the unresolved issues should be presented to the FCSP. The 16th plenary session of the PrepCom, on 9–15 April, agreed on the format of the Final Report, which contained a separate section listing the unresolved issues.[3] In addition, a separate report listed background papers which had been prepared by the signatory states.[4] A draft agenda for the FCSP and for the first meeting of the Executive Council were also adopted, but the rules of procedure for the FCSP and the Executive Council were not agreed.

The FCSP began on 6 May 1997, more than four years after the PrepCom commenced its work. The PrepCom had developed a large number of draft decisions relating to the work of the OPCW, but, as mentioned above, numerous issues and procedures had not been agreed by the signatory states. Agreement had not been reached on the rules of procedure for the various bodies and the top management structure of the OPCW, and these issues were turned over to the FCSP. Similarly, the PrepCom was unable to finalize negotiations on the first OPCW budget, and the FCSP was also given this task to complete.

II. The First Conference of the States Parties

The Conference of States Parties, which is the principal organ of the OPCW, is composed of all the parties to the CWC. Each member has one representative. The Conference meets in regular sessions, which will be held annually unless it decides otherwise. The United Nations as depositary of the CWC was required to convene the FCSP not later than 30 days after entry into force of the CWC.[5]

The FCSP took place on 6–24 May in The Hague, and 80 parties, 3 contracting states[6] and 34 signatory states participated. Representatives from a number of governmental and non-governmental organizations also attended. The opening statement was made by UN Secretary-General Kofi Annan, and high-level representatives of the participating states and international organizations addressed the FCSP in its first four days. The remainder of the FCSP consisted of sessions of the Conference and the Executive Council to take the decisions necessary to establish the OPCW and enable the commencement of its operations. The delegates confronted a wide range of issues that the Expert Groups had been unable to resolve. The issues on which there was not full agreement in the PrepCom included:

(*a*) the scope of the CWC—in particular, concerns that the CWC could not be effectively verified if the OPCW Analytical Database were limited to the chemicals listed in the three CWC schedules of chemicals;

---

[3] Final Report of the Preparatory Commission for the Organisation for the Prohibition of Chemical Weapons to the First Session of the Conference of the States Parties of the Organisation for the Prohibition of Chemical Weapons and to the First Meeting of the Executive Council of the Organisation for the Prohibition of Chemical Weapons, Preparatory Commission document PC-XVI/37, 15 Apr. 1997.

[4] List of associated papers to unresolved issues, Preparatory Commission document PC-XVI/39, 5 May 1997.

[5] Article VIII, B of the CWC. For an overview of the structure of the OPCW under the CWC, see Perry Robinson, J. P., Stock, T. and Sutherland, R. G., 'The Chemical Weapons Convention: the success of chemical disarmament negotiations', *SIPRI Yearbook 1993: World Armaments and Disarmament* (Oxford University Press: Oxford, 1993), pp. 721–23.

[6] Cuba, Turkey and Singapore deposited their instruments of ratification after the entry into force of the CWC and, consequently, became parties only 30 days after their respective deposits.

(b) cost of verification of destruction—the requirement that declared possessors should bear the primary cost of destruction and verification of destruction of CW stocks and related facilities;

(c) old chemical weapons—in particular the 'usability' and level of verification required;

(d) conversion of former chemical weapons production facilities (CWPFs)—the development of criteria to permit the conversion of former CWPFs for production of chemicals for civilian purposes;

(e) low concentrations—the extent to which the chemical industry monitoring provisions are to be applied to mixtures containing a low concentration of a Schedule 2 or 3 chemical;

(f) aggregate national data—the method of calculation of aggregate national data in relation to production, processing, consumption, and the import and export of scheduled chemicals;

(g) discrete organic chemicals—including whether the term 'production by synthesis' includes chemicals produced by biochemical and biologically mediated processes;

(h) challenge inspections—including the political question of establishment of political filters on the verification process; and

(i) economic and technological development—including the development of mechanisms to facilitate the exchange of information relating to economic and technological development in the field of chemicals, such as an Article XI (economic and technological development) database.

The Executive Council

The 41-member Executive Council, which is responsible for overseeing the day-to-day operations of the OPCW, was elected without major controversy at the beginning of the second week of the FCSP, based on the regional group representation.[7] However, final agreement on the rules of procedure of the Executive Council was more problematic, in particular with respect to the rules of access for non-members. Concern was expressed that the rules as drafted may not allow non-members to make their views known in an appropriate manner.[8]

The first decision adopted by the Executive Council was the recommendation that the FCSP appoint José Maurício Bustani of Brazil as Director-General of the OPCW for a four-year period. Following his appointment, one of Bustani's early tasks was to undertake intensive consultations with the regional groups to enable finalization of

[7] Article VIII, para. 23 of the CWC. The elected members of the Executive Council are the *Africa Group*: Algeria, Kenya, Morocco and South Africa (for 1 year) and Cameroon, Côte d'Ivoire, Ethiopia, Tunisia and Zimbabwe (2 years); the *Asia Group*: Bangladesh, Oman, Philippines and Sri Lanka (1 year) and China, India, Japan, South Korea and Saudi Arabia (2 years); the *Eastern European Group*: Belarus, Bulgaria and Romania (1 year) and Hungary and Poland (2 years); the *Latin American and the Caribbean Group*: Ecuador, Peru, Suriname and Uruguay (1 year) and Argentina, Brazil, Chile and Mexico (2 years); and the *Western European and Other States Group*: Australia, Malta, Netherlands, Norway and Spain (1 year) and France, Germany, Italy, UK and USA (2 years).

[8] As regards the rules of procedure of the Executive Council, the Irish delegation, speaking also on behalf of the Austrian, Canadian, Greek, Swiss and New Zealand delegations, stated that, as drafted, rules 22 and 57 could potentially restrict non-members of the Executive Council from making their views known in an appropriate manner and proposed a new agenda item for consideration of this issue at the Second Session of the Conference of the States Parties.

the top management structure of the OPCW.[9] However, because of delays caused by a misunderstanding on the level of appointment of the Director-General formal announcement of the top management structure was not made until 24 May 1997.

Action on PrepCom recommendations

The FCSP adopted a number of recommendations by the PrepCom on the less controversial issues,[10] in most cases without serious debate. These included recommendations on declarations and on detailed procedures for verification and for the conduct of inspections. The FCSP also approved the draft OPCW policies on confidentiality, media and public affairs, and visa procedures for OPCW inspectors and inspection assistants. The FCSP endorsed other PrepCom recommendations, including those on the Information Management System, the voluntary fund for assistance and the data bank on protection against chemical weapons.

Prior to the FCSP concern existed that a few states might reopen issues agreed by the PrepCom, but this did not occur. While certain states clearly had been prepared to disrupt the PrepCom Expert Groups, for example, by overstating differences in perspectives and interests between the developed and the developing countries,[11] a more constructive atmosphere prevailed at the FCSP (particularly between the different regional groups) which was conducive to the endorsement of the PrepCom recommendations. The reasons for the relatively straightforward adoption of the recommendations by the FCSP included the fact that the Hague-based delegates, many of whom were relatively junior diplomats, were fatigued and weary after months of difficult negotiation. In addition, the representatives who were based in the national capitals, in many cases at the ambassadorial level and with a broader arms control perspective, greater negotiating experience and a better appreciation of the benefits of having an effective organization, chose not to attempt to reopen agreed positions. Despite their differences of view, the more active states also recognized that there are core interests shared by all parties to the convention.

The OPCW programme and budget

Issues related to the OPCW programme and budget provoked the most intensive and controversial discussions. These issues included the staff levels in the Technical Secretariat, the costs of verification of Articles IV (chemical weapons) and V (CWPFs), and the budget for technical cooperation and assistance.[12] On 24 May 1997, it was agreed that the OPCW budget for the remainder of 1997 would total 88.87 million

---

[9] The FCSP confirmed the appointment of John Gee (Australia) as Deputy Director-General and appointed the following as directors of the various divisions: Jean-Louis Roland (France), Verification; Ichiro Akiyama (Japan), Inspectorate; Huang Yu (China), External Relations; David Clements (USA), Administration; John Makhubalo (Zimbabwe), International Cooperation and Assistance; Rodrigo Yepes Enriquez (Ecuador), Legal; Mohamed Louati (Tunisia), Internal Oversight; and Sylwin Gizowski (Poland), Secretary of the Policy-Making Organs.

[10] As recorded in PrepCom document PC-XVI/37, 15 Apr. 1997, sections 2 and 3. See also the discussion of unresolved PrepCom issues above.

[11] E.g., a small number of developing countries suggested that the developing countries have less at stake in security terms from the elimination of chemical weapons, despite their historic and intrinsic greater vulnerability to CW attack, and that developed countries are less committed to the economic and development provisions of the CWC.

[12] During the negotiation of the OPCW budget many parties expressed the view that the OPCW should be 'lean and cost-effective'.

Dutch guilders (NLG), or approximately $44.50 million.[13] Many issues, such as the formula for payment of verification of Articles IV and V, were agreed on an interim basis on the understanding that decisions taken at the FCSP for the 1997 OPCW budget would not prejudice decisions on subsequent budgets.[14] In terms of personnel resources, the PrepCom had already approved 233 posts at entry into force as well as an additional 140 posts for inspectors and 32 posts for the Technical Secretariat.[15]

In the latter stages of the PrepCom there were concerns that Article XI may have become a major issue during the FCSP. However, apart from the references to technical cooperation assistance which were made in plenary meeting statements,[16] the major issue related to Article XI was the availability of OPCW inspection equipment to all parties.[17] The issue was resolved in the final hours of the FCSP with an agreement that the Director-General would undertake a range of measures to ensure that the parties would be familiar with all items of equipment that the inspectors are permitted to use in an inspection. However, this issue and related Article XI export licensing issues will require further consideration.[18]

The FCSP also adopted a number of other administrative arrangements, including the OPCW Staff Rules and Regulations, the transfer of property (from the PrepCom to the OPCW), and the Headquarters Agreement with the Host Country. On behalf of the OPCW, Director-General Bustani signed the Headquarters Agreement with the Dutch Ministry of Foreign Affairs. In addition, on 22 May 1997 the UN General Assembly approved a resolution on cooperation between the United Nations and the OPCW whereby the General Assembly invited the UN Secretary-General to conclude an agreement with the Director-General of the Technical Secretariat of the OPCW for the two bodies to regulate their relationship.[19]

The FSCP considered how to deal with the issues that had not been resolved by the PrepCom and took a decision that between the FCSP and the Second Conference of the States Parties (SCSP) these unresolved issues would be addressed by a flexible, informal and transparent consultation process. Particular attention would be given to issues requiring resolution in accordance with the time-lines stipulated by the CWC, as well as other issues identified by the parties or the Director-General as requiring

---

[13] The verification component of the budget was agreed at NLG 59.15 million (c. $29.61 million) and administrative and other costs at NLG 29.71 million (c. $14.88 million).

[14] A major issue was the payment of inspectors' salaries while inspections are being conducted. The principle that payment should be made was agreed, but the method of calculation of the salaries remained to be determined.

[15] It was agreed that the remaining 71 inspectors would not join the OPCW until 1998. Including inspectors, the proposed number of posts for 1997 was 405, to be increased to 476 posts in 1998.

[16] In their opening statements a number of delegations, including Cuba's, stressed the importance of Article XI related to economic and technological development for developing countries, which they regarded as requiring further resolution in the intersessional period.

[17] In 1996 a number of signatory states had argued that for items to be approved as OPCW equipment, they should be freely available to all parties. There were 2 concerns: that unavailability of these items would not be consistent with Article XI of the CWC; and that every party should be able to be familiar with all items of equipment that may be used during OPCW inspections on its territory.

[18] E.g., the delegations of Cuba and Iran both made statements at the FCSP regarding the availability of the approved inspection equipment, stating that inspection equipment should be commercially available to all parties, and if this were not so, then parties should have the right to exclude such equipment from their territories.

[19] The General Assembly authorized the Secretary-General, pending conclusion of an appropriate relationship agreement, to enter into a temporary arrangement with the Director-General of the OPCW Technical Secretariat to allow UN *laissez-passer* travel documents to be issued to members of the OPCW inspection teams. United Nations General Assembly, Press Release GA/9243, May 1997. This is an example of the time-consuming arrangements which were necessary to achieve an operational convention.

urgent resolution. Facilitators from among interested delegates of the parties would be designated and made responsible for conducting consultations on particular unresolved issues. The facilitators would subsequently present a report to the SCSP based on the outcome of their consultations, including a description of the consultation process and the rationale for the proposed solution. It was also decided that signatory states would have a reasonable opportunity to express their views during the consultation process by the facilitators.

III. The Second Conference of the States Parties

Between the FCSP and the SCSP the Executive Council held regular sessions for approximately one week each month.[20] The most time-consuming and difficult task was the consideration and development of the draft 1998 OPCW budget. The Executive Council reviewed the status of implementation of the CWC. A particular concern was the number of parties that either had not submitted a national declaration or had submitted an incomplete one. At each meeting, the Executive Council assessed the status of the contributions of the parties and urged those parties in arrears to fully meet their financial obligations forthwith. Part of the problem of non-payment of contributions was related to the scale of assessment. The financial situation improved after the decision at the fourth session that the ceiling for any one party's contribution for 1997 would be 25 per cent of the annual OPCW budget.[21] The Executive Council also considered several requests for conversion of CWPFs for purposes not prohibited under the CWC. It was recommended that the SCSP approve some of these requests, but others were deemed to require further consideration before they could be recommended for approval. The Executive Council also dealt with various issues associated with the handling and protection of confidential information, including access to declarations by the least possible number of Technical Secretariat personnel, the confidentiality audit on the electronic document management system and the decision not to use the electronic document management system for declaration data until the security environment for the system was brought up to an appropriate level. Many other administrative and technical issues were considered between the FCSP and the SCSP, both in the meetings of the Executive Council and also in the less formal meetings convened by the facilitators of unresolved issues.[22]

The SCSP was held on 1–6 December 1997. Delegates from 81 parties, 27 signatory states and 2 non-signatory states (Botswana and Libya) participated. As required by its rules of procedure, the SCSP elected a new chairman (Ambassador Simbarashe Simbanenduku Mumbengegwi of Zimbabwe) and two vice-chairmen from each regional group.[23]

---

[20] Regular meetings were held on 13–23 May, 23–27 June, 28 July–1 Aug., 1–4 Sep., 29 Sep.–1 Oct. and 28–31 Oct. An additional specially scheduled 7th session was held on 18–20 Nov.

[21] It was reported just prior to this decision that the OPCW may have had to suspend all inspections and staff recruitment. Delaere, M., 'CW agency owed "tens of millions of dollars"', *Jane's Defence Weekly*, vol. 28, no. 9 (3 Sep. 1997), p. 3. After the decision, the USA and several other states paid their 1997 contributions.

[22] The issues included the unresolved issues outlined in section II above and also a number of new issues including the transfer of saxitoxin (a chemical listed in Schedule 1 of the convention) for medical/diagnostic use.

[23] The vice-chairmen were from the following countries and groups: Algeria and Kenya (African), Pakistan and South Korea (Asian), Belarus and Bulgaria (Eastern European), Chile and Mexico (Latin American and the Caribbean), and France and the USA (West European and Other).

The Director-General reported on the activities of the OPCW since the FCSP. He also highlighted a number of important issues facing the OPCW, including the need for all parties to provide complete declarations, to develop and maintain a culture of transparency, to promote the universality of the convention, to protect confidential information and to fully implement the provisions of Article XI on economic and technological development.[24]

Approximately 30 parties presented national statements. The statements were generally of a positive nature, many noting the progress which had been made in the universality and implementation of the CWC since its entry into force. A number of issues were also raised which reflected various concerns of the parties from the days of the PrepCom and the first six months of operation of the CWC. These included the need to: (*a*) promote universality; (*b*) ensure that all parties fully comply with all provisions of the CWC in a timely manner, in particular in their initial declarations;[25] (*c*) approve a lean and cost-effective budget for operations in 1998, including the need to ensure that the costs of verification related to CW facilities should be reimbursed by the party inspected in accordance with the provisions of the CWC; (*d*) ensure that the OPCW be as transparent as possible in its activities, including making public the maximum amount of information related to former CW programmes; (*e*) implement the convention in a fair, balanced and non-discriminatory manner;[26] and (*f*) address concerns regarding how some unresolved issues before the OPCW might be resolved.

Under its new Chairman, Ambassador Bjørn Barth (Norway), the Committee of the Whole discussed the OPCW Programme of Work and Budget for 1998 and the outstanding issues before the SCSP. These included the terms of reference for the Scientific Advisory Board; the costs of verification, assistance and protection against chemical weapons; economic and technological development; industry declarations; confidentiality concerning samples taken off site; and old chemical weapons. Progress was made on only a limited number of issues.

The 1998 OPCW budget was the most difficult issue facing the SCSP. As in the negotiation of the 1997 budget at the FCSP, the cost of verification related to Articles IV and V was problematic. There was general agreement on the application of the 'possessor pays' principle, but agreement could not be reached on how the reimbursements of verification costs should be calculated. Eventually, it was decided that the interim reimbursement criteria in the 1997 budget also should apply to the 1998 budget. A final decision on attribution of costs, including the calculation of inspectors' salaries, will be made at the meeting of the Executive Council in June 1998 in the light of the experience gained in the first half of 1998. The SCSP tasked the Technical Secretariat with obtaining more definitive details of the various costs of verification so that reimbursement criteria can be fully developed and applied in the 1999 budget.

---

[24] Statement by the Director-General to the Conference of the States Parties at its Second Session, Conference of the States Parties document C-II/DG.10, 1 Dec. 1997.

[25] Concerns were expressed that incomplete declarations of Article VI could result in an unfair competitive advantage and all parties were urged to provide full declarations so as to avoid discriminatory verification. In this context, the USA stated that it hoped that its implementing legislation, which would allow industry declarations, would be passed in early 1998.

[26] E.g., China stressed the need to ensure that the challenge inspection provisions of the CWC were not abused. Russia noted that the policy of the OPCW on the conversion of former CWPFs should be 'rational'. See the discussion of the Russian Federation in the section 'Destruction of chemical weapons' in chapter 11 in this volume.

Staffing levels within the Technical Secretariat were also a major concern. The new ratifications—in particular that of the Russian Federation, which holds the largest stocks of chemical weapons—clearly will create an extra workload in 1998. There was also a need to have a reasonable representation of the states which had become parties after entry into force. Eventually, 15 new posts were created, bringing the total number of posts approved in the 1998 budget to 491. The scale of assessments, on the basis of which the financial contributions of parties are determined, also became a major issue and a ceiling of 25 per cent for the 1998 contributions was eventually accepted. The SCSP approved a total OPCW budget for 1998 of NLG 140.79 million (approximately $70.50 million), with NLG 57.47 million (c. $28.78 million) for administrative and NLG 83.33 million (c. $41.73 million) for verification costs.

The budget agreements were of primary importance. Some other decisions that will affect the future activities of the OPCW were taken. Among other things, the SCSP approved the use of two converted CWPFs for purposes not prohibited under the CWC, adopted revised procedures for addressing unresolved issues in the next intersessional period,[27] decided on the terms of reference of the Scientific Advisory Board and approved the recommendations related to the functioning of the Confidentiality Commission mandated by the CWC.

Two important decisions related to the implementation of the CWC by the chemical industry were also taken. First, parties are required to clearly indicate the concentration limits approved for their 1998 and subsequent annual declarations in relation to industrial plant sites. They are also required to indicate the concentration levels applied to their 1997 declarations. Previously, parties had been required to take a national decision on an interim basis. Several chose a 30 per cent level[28] for declarations of 'low concentrations' of Schedule 2 and 3 chemicals based on the value which had received considerable support in the PrepCom Expert Group on Industry Issues. A final decision will ultimately be taken on the basis of experiences in the preparation of initial declarations. Second, the term 'production' as used in the CWC will be understood to include a scheduled chemical produced by a biochemical or biologically mediated reaction.

IV. Future issues and concerns

Some of the problems that remained unresolved in the PrepCom as well as some important new issues which have emerged since entry into force of the convention challenge the new disarmament regime.

After entry into force of the CWC its parties were required to meet several important deadlines so that an effective verification regime could be established as soon as possible. For example, the CWC specifies that parties are required to submit complete initial declarations within 30 days of entry into force and that initial inspections and facility agreements for Schedule 1 facilities are to be completed within 180 days of entry into force. There are also several verification-related administrative obligations and declaration requirements with specific deadlines. A significant number of parties failed to meet these obligations.[29] As of 9 January 1998, only 53 of the 106 parties

---

[27] The Third Session of the Conference of the States Parties will be convened in Nov. 1998.

[28] In the situation where a Schedule 2 or 3 chemical is a component of a chemical mixture, a declaration on the production (and, in the case of Schedule 2 chemicals, processing and consumption) of the chemical is only provided when the Schedule 2 or 3 chemical constitutes 30% or more of the mixture.

[29] See also the section 'Declarations of CW possession and programmes' in chapter 11 in this volume.

had notified points of entry for inspection teams (required 30 days after entry into force) and only 68 parties had given notification of their National Authority, despite the requirement to do so at the time of entry into force. In addition, only 27 parties had provided information on the assistance to be provided pursuant to Article X (assistance and protection against chemical weapons), although notification is required within 180 days of entry into force.[30] The complexity of the requirements makes it difficult for all parties to meet all the CWC time-lines. This implies that the CWC will not have a particularly smooth transition to its operational phase. While it is important not to overdramatize the problem, all parties should make every reasonable effort—with the encouragement and support of the OPCW where appropriate—to fulfil their obligations within the specified time-lines.

Universal adherence to the CWC contributes to its strength and is therefore a key objective. There are 106 parties to the convention and an additional 59 states had signed but not ratified it as of 1 January 1998.[31] Critical to the overall credibility and long-term effectiveness of the CWC is the situation whereby certain Arab and North African nations (including Egypt, Iraq, Libya and Syria), in a region where concerns about CW proliferation have been acute, have yet to sign the CWC and argue that they will not do so until Israel accedes to the 1968 Non-Proliferation Treaty (NPT). In his report to the SCSP the Director-General expressed the hope that other countries would join the convention in the near future. In particular, he mentioned Kazakhstan and Ukraine in the Commonwealth of Independent States, as well as Indonesia, North Korea, Malaysia, Myanmar, Thailand and Viet Nam. He pointed out that accession by North Korea would be a major boost to regional security in Asia.

The OPCW also faces several technical challenges. The FCSP adopted many verification-related decisions on an interim basis for 1997 on the understanding that the issues would be further considered and decided upon as the OPCW gains experience. Certain technical questions cannot be resolved because of political factors so that during the early implementation of the CWC a number of decisions will have to be taken on a case-by-case basis. The CWC will be evolutionary, and procedures will be further developed and refined as experience is gained. As a dynamic organization, the OPCW will continue to face new and sometimes unexpected challenges, including those caused by changing technology and industry practices. Issues which may require consideration in the near future to facilitate the development of a more effective verification regime are discussed below.

OPCW analytical database

The lack of analytical data for the majority of members of the various families of scheduled chemicals is a serious gap, which should be addressed as a priority.[32] In the interest of effective verification, it is also hoped that spectra of other relevant chemicals will be promptly added to the OPCW analytical database.

---

[30] Report of the Director-General: status of implementation of the Convention as of 9 January 1998, OPCW document EC-VIII/DG.1, 21 Jan. 1998, para. 3.6.

[31] A list of the parties is given in annexe A in this volume.

[32] However, it will not be necessary to obtain the spectra of all the family members of the scheduled chemicals. Adequate recognition has been shown to be feasible if a representative number of spectra are obtained and pattern recognition techniques are then applied. Borrett, V. T., Mathews, R. J. and Mattsson, E. R., 'Verification of the Chemical Weapons Convention: mass spectrometry of alkyl methylphosphonofluoridates', *Australian Journal of Chemistry*, vol. 47, no. 2065 (1994).

Schedules of chemicals

Additions to the three schedules of chemicals may have to be considered in the light of the early experiences of the OPCW, especially if there are declarations of novel chemical warfare agents.[33]

Refinement of the inspection procedures

There will need to be a refinement of the inspection procedures in the light of the early experiences of the OPCW Inspectorate, including issues related to the safety of inspectors during the conduct of OPCW inspections when following the OPCW health and safety regulations[34] and the ability of 'blinded analytical instruments' to provide unambiguous analysis results.[35]

Relative proportion of inspection effort for Article I verification activities

During the PrepCom, there was a focus on the development of guidelines for inspections of Schedule 1 and 2 facilities, in particular, as against the need to take into account all relevant facilities (e.g., Schedule 3 and other chemical production facilities). Several delegations argued against indefinite postponement of Schedule 3 inspections, which many experts regard as most applicable with respect to recent CW proliferation programmes.[36]

Off-site analysis

This issue will clearly need to be addressed to ensure that accurate and reliable analysis of samples is possible in situations where analysis using OPCW on-site equipment does not provide unambiguous results. Unfortunately, the issue of off-site analysis was brought into question with one of the conditions attached to the US ratification of the CWC, which specified that samples taken during an inspection at US facilities will not be taken to a laboratory outside the USA for analysis.[37] An alternative approach suggested in the 'margins' of the FCSP was the possibility of analysis of samples in national laboratories (for industry or military samples) in the event that on-site analysis yields ambiguous results.[38]

---

[33] E.g., there have been reports of the development of a class of binary nerve agents called Novichok, which apparently are not covered by the CWC schedules. '4 February', *Chemical Weapons Convention Bulletin*, no. 35 (Mar. 1997), p. 38; and the section 'Allegations of CBW programmes' in chapter 11 in this volume.

[34] OPCW inspectors will have to rely on the assurances of the inspected state party regarding the absence of hazards in the inspection site during the conduct of inspections.

[35] Blinded analytical equipment uses special 'blinded software' and a restricted database to provide only 'presence/absence' information of CWC-related chemicals.

[36] E.g., Iraq used a number of Schedule 3-type facilities in its CW production programme. Gee, J., 'The destruction, removal or rendering harmless of Iraq's chemical warfare capability', *Disarmament*, vol. 15, no. 2 (1992), pp. 77–93.

[37] US Senate, *Congressional Record*, 24 Apr. 1997, p. S3656.

[38] However, a small number of designated laboratories which are fully accredited by the OPCW will be needed to analyse samples taken during investigations of alleged use. It is unlikely that a party which has alleged that CW have been used on its territory would oppose the analysis of samples in the best-quality, off-site laboratories.

V. Conclusions

By the end of 1997 significant progress had been made on the creation of the CWC regime. The OPCW, with its Technical Secretariat, was established and became operational. The OPCW still faces problems, including the difficulties for a significant number of parties to adhere to the CWC time-lines and a number of other unresolved issues. However, most parties now appear confident that these difficulties can and will be overcome. The situation was much better at the end of 1997 than most participants would have thought possible at the beginning of 1997. As stated by the Director-General in his report to the SCSP, 'The first 200 days of the OPCW show that multilateral disarmament can be made to work'.[39]

Despite this progress, it is unrealistic to expect the CWC to have a smooth transition from its preparatory phase to an operational convention. However, at the end of the painful PrepCom process the basic balances and compromises of the CWC text appear to have been sufficiently retained to allow the verification regime to function as intended, in particular to provide the necessary confidence that parties are complying with their obligations under the CWC and to provide an effective deterrent to states which may be considering violating the provisions of the CWC. At this stage, there are good prospects that the CWC verification regime will achieve these objectives, be affordable, have an acceptably small impact on the affected operations (such as the chemical industry) and will not jeopardize national security information.

Just as the conclusion of the negotiation of the CWC and the signing ceremony were not the end of all problems, but merely a change to a new set of them, neither will the transition from the PrepCom to an operational CWC be the end of difficulties, but the beginning of a new set of issues. It will still take at least a few years until the CWC can be regarded as an effective operational treaty. This will put it in good company with the NPT, which, after its own teething troubles, is now regarded as a major success in arms control.[40]

---

[39] Note 24.

[40] Although the NPT is much less complex than the CWC and the path from signature to entry into force of the NPT was easier, there were a number of minor problems in the early years of the NPT. However, despite these problems the NPT has evolved into a successful arms control treaty. Mathews (note 2), pp. 125–50.

12. Conventional arms control

ZDZISLAW LACHOWSKI

I. Introduction

Europe remained the world's main arena of conventional arms control achievements in 1997. In other regions efforts at creating security arrangements, including military confidence and stability building, saw mixed results. While progress was noted in Sino-Russian relations and some headway was discernible in the Asia–Pacific region, there was little change elsewhere.

Negotiations began in January 1997 on the adaptation of the 1990 Treaty on Conventional Armed Forces in Europe (the CFE Treaty) to the new security environment and resulted in a mid-year 'framework agreement' mapping out the course of further talks. The Flank Document, setting out a special regime for the former flank zone, entered into force on 15 May 1997 after it was approved by all states parties.[1] Reductions of heavy weapons under the 1996 Agreement on Sub-Regional Arms Control (the Florence Agreement)[2] were successfully completed, in contrast to the various difficulties in implementing other parts of the 1995 General Framework Agreement for Bosnia and Herzegovina (the Dayton Agreement).[3] There were signals in the latter half of the year of Russia's willingness to discuss regional security in the Baltic Sea area in the context of a long-needed military reform of the Russian armed forces.

The entry into force of the 1992 Open Skies Treaty was still deadlocked in 1997, mainly because of Russia's failure to ratify it.

In the volatile Caucasus region, the Armenian–Azerbaijani conflict has led to an excessive build-up of armaments and resulting CFE compliance problems, and other CFE states parties urged both sides to the conflict to fulfil their commitments and obligations under the treaty.

This chapter describes the major issues and developments relating to conventional arms control in 1997. Section II deals with critical aspects of CFE Treaty implementation and the adaptation negotiations, and section III covers regional arms control efforts in Europe. Steps to keep the Open Skies Treaty

---

[1] CFE, Final Document of the First Conference to Review the Operation of the Treaty on Conventional Armed Forces in Europe and the Concluding Act of the Negotiation on Personnel Strength, Vienna, 15–31 May 1996, CFE-TRC/DG.2 Rev. 5, 31 May 1996, Annex A: Document Agreed Among the States Parties to the Treaty on Conventional Armed Forces in Europe of 19 November 1990 (the Flank Document). Excerpts from the Flank Document are reproduced in *SIPRI Yearbook 1997: Armaments, Disarmament and International Security* (Oxford University Press: Oxford, 1997), pp. 512–17. For the complete text of the Final Document see URL <http://www.osia.mil/osialink/history/cfe book/appendd.html>, version current on 10 Feb. 1998.
[2] The text of the Florence Agreement is reproduced in *SIPRI Yearbook 1997* (note 1), pp. 517–24.
[3] Excerpts from the Dayton Agreement are reproduced in *SIPRI Yearbook 1996: Armaments, Disarmament and International Security* (Oxford University Press: Oxford, 1996), pp. 235–50.

SIPRI Yearbook 1998: Armaments, Disarmament and International Security

regime alive are addressed in section IV. Section V reviews conventional arms control-related developments outside Europe, and the conclusions are presented in section VI. Appendix 12A reviews developments in the field of European confidence- and security-building measures (CSBMs) and the implementation of and debate on those agreed in the Vienna Document 1994,[4] and the framework agreement as elaborated in the decision concerning certain 'basic elements' for treaty adaptation is reproduced in appendix 12B. The ban on anti-personnel mines is the subject of chapter 13.

II. Conventional arms control in Europe: the CFE Treaty

The CFE Treaty set equal ceilings within its Atlantic-to-the-Urals (ATTU) application zone on the major categories of heavy conventional armaments and equipment of the groups of states parties, originally the NATO and the Warsaw Treaty Organization (WTO) states. There are now 30 individual parties.[5] The reduction of excess treaty-limited equipment (TLE) was carried out in three phases from 1993. By the 16 November 1995 deadline, several parties had not met all their treaty commitments. Some but not all of the outstanding compliance issues were resolved in 1996 and 1997.

Compliance issues

Belarus completed its reduction obligation, Ukraine complied with all the treaty limits and several major concerns about Russia's non-compliance were addressed in 1996 and 1997. Surpluses of decommissioned equipment awaiting export were removed in 1996, but the issue of decommissioned TLE (in excess of treaty limits) awaiting disposal in 1997 was not fully cleared up. The Flank Document was agreed and progress was made concerning Russian equipment east of the Urals—some three-quarters of which had been destroyed or converted by early 1998.

Other compliance issues were still unresolved in early 1997: the division of Black Sea Fleet naval infantry/coastal defence-related weapons between Russia and Ukraine remained unsettled;[6] Armenia and Azerbaijan still exceeded TLE ceilings in one or more categories and had not declared their reduction obligations; and the former Soviet republics had still not resolved the discrepancy between the former USSR's reduction liabilities and the total collective obligation of the successor states. There was still some unaccounted-for TLE in Chechnya. In the flank zone, Russia excluded a number of armoured personnel carriers (APCs) from treaty accountability, seeking to categorize them as ambulances. Belarus and Bulgaria declared the temporary storage in the ATTU zone of excess TLE awaiting export. There were

---

[4] The Vienna Document 1994 is reproduced in *SIPRI Yearbook 1995: Armaments, Disarmament and International Security* (Oxford University Press: Oxford, 1995), pp. 799–820.

[5] A list of states parties to the CFE Treaty is given in annexe A in this volume. For discussion of conventional arms control in Europe before 1997, see the relevant chapters in previous SIPRI Yearbooks.

[6] By 31 Dec. the situation was unchanged, with *c*. two-thirds of the liabilities destroyed or converted.

also minor, more technical concerns, such as late notifications, unreported TLE, undeclared sites and denials or delays of on-site inspections.[7]

At its first session in January 1997, the CFE Joint Consultative Group (JCG) decided to form: (*a*) a negotiation group (set up on 18 February) to address treaty adaptation; and (*b*) a treaty operation and implementation group to tackle other issues listed in the Final Document of the First CFE Review Conference.[8] The latter group was also to deal with non-compliance.

Non-compliance in the Caucasus

Continuing non-compliance by Armenia and Azerbaijan was primarily related to the Nagorno-Karabakh conflict.[9] Since their formation both states have failed to declare accurate reduction liabilities, provide accurate information, participate fully in the inspection regime, complete their TLE reductions or cooperate in resolving the problem of unaccounted-for and uncontrolled TLE.

In mid-February 1997 there were reports of illegal arms shipments from Russia to Armenia, and the Russian State Duma assigned three standing committees to investigate these allegations.[10] In April the Duma Defence Committee reported illegal deliveries to Armenia of some $1 billion worth of Russian weapons in 1993–96—apparently for use against Azerbaijan and said to have included equipment limited under the CFE Treaty: 84 T-72 tanks, 50 BMP-2 armoured infantry fighting vehicles (AIFVs), 36 152-mm and 36 122-mm artillery pieces, and 18 122-mm Grad multiple rocket launchers.[11]

A comparison with the JCG's official figures on Armenian holdings showed that these deliveries raised Armenia's artillery holdings above the CFE Treaty ceiling (315 as against 285 allowed). Azerbaijan also noted the additional Russian TLE stationed in Armenia: 74 tanks, 108 armoured combat vehicles (ACVs) and 84 artillery pieces. Armenia is also accused of having deployed large quantities of unaccounted-for weapons on the occupied territories in Azerbaijan which, while insignificant in overall TLE terms, create a serious

---

[7] E.g., Russia had denied or delayed inspections in the North Caucasus Military District on the grounds of safety, even after fighting had ended in Chechnya. In late 1996, however, Russia stated that this practice would cease in 1997. 'Adherence to and compliance with arms control agreements', *ACDA 1996 Annual Report,* chapter VII (Arms Control and Disarmament Agency: Washington, DC, 1997), URL <http://www.acda.gov/reports/annual/ch7.htm>, version current on 15 Aug. 1997.

[8] CFE Final Document (note 1). The Final Document lists the issues as follows: (*a*) unaccounted-for and uncontrolled TLE (para. 9); (*b*) TLE in internal security organizations (para. 12); (*c*) temporary deployments (para. 14); (*d*) updating the Protocol on Existing Types of Conventional Armaments and Equipment (POET) (para. 15); (*e*) most effective use of the CFE provisions concerning the work of the JCG (para. 18); and (*f*) 15 issues requiring 'further consideration and resolution' in the JCG (Annex C).

[9] See also chapter 4 in this volume.

[10] Open Media Research Institute (OMRI), *OMRI Daily Digest,* vol. 3, no. 33 (17 Feb. 1997) and vol. 3, no. 37 (21 Feb. 1997), URL <http://www.omri.cz>. Hereafter, references to the *OMRI Daily Digest* refer to the Internet edition at this URL address. On 18 Apr. 1997 the Duma ratified the 25-year Russian–Armenian agreement on bases, which strengthened Russia's position regarding the Nagorno-Karabakh conflict, oil exploration and exploitation in the Caspian Sea, and so on.

[11] 'Summary of presentation by Lev Rokhlin, chairman of State Duma Defense Committee, at State Duma session on violations in arms deliveries to Republic of Armenia: "Shady-deal city" (Aferograd)', *Sovetskaya Rossiya* (Moscow), 3 Apr. 1997, in 'Armenia, Russia: Rokhlin details arms supplied to Armenia', Foreign Broadcast Information Service, *Daily Report–Central Eurasia (FBIS-SOV),* FBIS-SOV-97-067, 3 Apr. 1997. See also chapter 8 in this volume.

regional imbalance. Consequently, Azerbaijan refuses to comply with the treaty unless the Nagorno-Karabakh issue is resolved.[12]

In response to Azerbaijani allegations, the US Senate mandated the president to report by 1 August on whether or not Armenia was in compliance with the CFE Treaty in allowing the transfer of weapons through Armenian territory to Nagorno-Karabakh.[13] The US review of treaty compliance by states parties in the Caucasus attributed a number of cases of non-compliance to Armenia and Azerbaijan. Apart from the accusations that over 200 TLE items had been transferred from Russia to Armenia, Armenia's declaration of reduction liability was questioned; the 1 January 1997 data exchange also showed that Armenia had more AIFVs/heavy armoured combat vehicles (HACVs) than permitted under its declared limits. Azerbaijan has never declared a reduction liability, but its January 1997 data showed it to have too many tanks, ACVs, AIFV/HACVs and artillery. Azerbaijan also exceeded the 1992 Tashkent Agreement[14] ceilings on armoured vehicle launched bridges (AVLBs) and is said to have failed to comply with other treaty obligations (notifications of deliveries of TLE, inspection quotas and reporting on units).[15]

On 23 July, the JCG agreed on general procedures for the conduct of on-site visits to assess and account for TLE unaccounted for and uncontrolled within the treaty (UTLE).[16]

Entry into force of the Flank Document

The Flank Document was to enter into force upon confirmation of its approval by all states parties, or by 15 December 1996. Since it was already clear at the Organization for Security and Co-operation in Europe (OSCE) Lisbon summit meeting (2–3 December 1996) that the document would not be approved by all parties by 15 December (only 12 states had approved it by that date), the deadline was extended until 15 May 1997.[17]

Four Commonwealth of Independent States (CIS) flank states in particular—Georgia, Ukraine, Azerbaijan and Moldova (referred to as 'GUAM')—expressed concern that Russia might use the Flank Document to pursue its security interests at their expense.[18] As well as giving Russia too much mili-

---

[12] Armenia reportedly has 253 tanks, 278 ACVs and 298 artillery pieces in Nagorno-Karabakh. Statement by the Azerbaijani Deputy Defence Minister, Col M. A. Beydullaev, at the JCG session, 29 Apr. 1997, Joint Consultative Group document JCG.REF(AZ)/92/97, Vienna, 29 Apr. 1997.

[13] Resolution of Advice and Consent to Ratification of the Document Agreed Among the States Parties to the Treaty on Conventional Armed Forces in Europe of November 19, 1990 ('the CFE Flank Document'), Adopted by the Senate of the United States, 14 May 1997.

[14] The text of the Agreement on the Principles and Procedures for Implementing the Treaty on Conventional Armed Forces in Europe, of the Tashkent Document, is reproduced in *SIPRI Yearbook 1993: World Armaments and Disarmament* (Oxford University Press: Oxford, 1993), pp. 672–77.

[15] Statement by the US delegation to the JCG, Joint Consultative Group document JCG.DL/12/97, Vienna, 28 Oct. 1997.

[16] Decision of the JCG on modalities for UTLE on-site visits, Joint Consultative Group document JCG.DEC/9/97, Vienna, 23 July 1997.

[17] For more on the Flank Document, see Lachowski, Z., 'Conventional arms control', *SIPRI Yearbook 1997* (note 1), pp. 476–79.

[18] None of these countries wants Russia to station troops permanently either on its territory or in its vicinity. Georgia is keen to secure the withdrawal of the Russian troops if they fail to quell separatist

tary power in various regions of the flank area, they felt that the Flank Document might effectively override the Tashkent Agreement and enable Russia to seek bilateral solutions and perhaps coerce individual countries into allowing Russia to use part of their TLE entitlements and thereby put pressure on third countries (as in the case of Nagorno-Karabakh). A clear definition of 'temporary deployments' of troops in the flank zone was called for as well as a ceiling on permitted equipment in conflict areas, such as Nagorno-Karabakh or Abkhazia, to avoid potential concentrations of weapons not formally in violation of the treaty.[19] JCG officials faced a difficult task of addressing the concerns of these countries without provoking Russia.

An active stance was taken by the USA. On 14 May, the US Senate approved a resolution on the ratification of the Flank Document with 14 conditions addressing the concerns of the United States and the affected CIS states, especially with regard to the Russian troops and equipment deployed on the territory of states parties.[20] Proceeding from the finding that Russian forces are deployed in the GUAM states 'without full and complete agreement of these states', the conditions set out by the Senate included:

1. The president should certify that: (*a*) NATO governments have issued a statement to the effect that the Flank Document does not allow any party to station, reallocate or temporarily deploy TLE without the 'freely expressed consent' of the receiving state party, and that each state party retains the right to fully utilize its declared maximum levels for holdings;[21] and (*b*) the Secretary of State has initiated discussions to secure the immediate withdrawal of Russian troops and equipment deployed on the territories of flank states without their approval (Condition 2).

2. The USA, acting as an intermediary, should ensure that the GUAM states retain the right to 'reject or accept conditionally' any (in fact, Russian) request to temporarily deploy forces or reallocate GUAM allotments, as established under the Tashkent Agreement (Condition 3).

3. From 1 January 1998, monitoring and the verification regime should be strengthened by quarterly US Government briefings to Congress on compliance and annual reports by the president (classified and unclassified) on compliance, withdrawal of Russian armed forces and military equipment, the status of 'uncontrolled' TLE and equipment subject to the treaty and their transfer to secessionist, terrorist or paramilitary groups. There should also be a report on compliance by Armenia and other states in the Caucasus region by 1 August 1997 (Condition 5).

movements in Abkhazia and South Ossetia; Ukraine seeks the ending of the naval infantry dispute in the Black Sea; Azerbaijan is protesting against Russian support for Armenia in the Nagorno-Karabakh conflict; and Moldova wants to address the question of the Russian troops stationed in the Trans-Dniester separatist region. See also chapter 4 in this volume.

[19] Goble, P. A., 'Outflanked: how non-Russian countries view the proposed CFE flank modifications', Testimony prepared for a hearing of the Committee on Foreign Relations, US Senate, 29 Apr. 1997.

[20] Resolution of Advice and Consent (note 13).

[21] As stated by NATO on 8 May 1997 at the JCG. Joint Consultative Group document JCG.REF (US+)/95/97, Vienna, 8 May 1997.

4. The president should certify that 'temporary deployments' are measured 'in days or weeks or, at most, several months, but not years' (Condition 11) and warn against any acts of intimidation with the use of TLE (Condition 12).

Russia announced its approval of the Flank Document on 14 May 1997 with a reservation establishing a linkage between its observance of the document's provisions and future limitations on overall ceilings for 'military alliances' and additional permanent stationing of foreign armed forces. Like other notifications, this was not acknowledged by the JCG Chairman as constituting a reservation to the Flank Document.

President Bill Clinton notified Congress on 15 May 1997 that the conditions attached to the Senate resolution had been met.[22] On the same day, the Netherlands announced that all approvals of the Flank Document had been filed and that it had entered into force.[23] On 21 May Azerbaijan and the USA issued a joint statement reiterating Condition 2 of the US Senate resolution, acknowledging the absence of foreign military bases and supporting the Azerbaijani position that foreign troops might only be stationed temporarily on its territory under an agreement duly concluded in accordance with its constitution and in conformity with international law. Both sides urged all states parties to resolve the issue of unaccounted-for and uncontrolled TLE in a cooperative manner within the JCG. The USA also supported Azerbaijan's position on non-use of temporary deployments and reallocation of quotas on its territory, as expressed in the statement of the Chairman of the First CFE Review Conference on 31 May 1996.[24]

Nevertheless, the flank issue was not conclusively resolved. The adaptation negotiation launched in early 1997 led to the re-emergence of the problem in connection with new arrangements proposed for adjusting the CFE regime to the new security environment.

Towards adaptation of the CFE Treaty

The CFE states parties agreed at the CFE Review Conference and at the OSCE Lisbon summit meeting in 1996 that negotiations to adapt the CFE Treaty to the security challenges that have emerged since it was signed would start in early 1997.[25] The negotiations opened on 21 January in Vienna.

Russia made the first explicit link between CFE Treaty adaptation and NATO enlargement, to which it was relentlessly opposed, on 8 January 1997.

---

[22] 'Clinton implements conditions of Senate CFE ratification', Text of the president's statement of certification connected with the conditions of the CFE Flank Document, Office of the Press Secretary, White House, Washington, DC, 15 May 1997, URL <gopher://198.80.36.82:70/0R26211650-26217401-range/archives/1997/pdq.97>, version current on 15 May 1997.

[23] For the list of approvals by states parties, see Institute for Defense and Disarmament Studies, *Arms Control Reporter* (IDDS: Brookline, Mass.), sheet 407.B.563, 1997.

[24] Statements of the Chairman of the First Conference to Review the Operation of the Treaty on Conventional Armed Forces in Europe and the Concluding Act of the Negotiation on Personnel Strength, attached to the CFE Final Document (note 1); and Lachowski (note 17), p. 477, footnote 18.

[25] On the developments in 1996 clearing the way towards the adaptation talks, see Lachowski (note 17), pp. 479–84.

Russian Foreign Minister Yevgeniy Primakov announced that Russia would use NATO's approach to planned talks on the CFE Treaty 'to evaluate whether the Alliance was serious about negotiating a substantive Russia–NATO charter'. Hinting that Russia wanted the adapted treaty strictly to limit NATO deployments, Primakov signalled that Moscow intended to use the CFE Treaty as a means of containing NATO enlargement.[26] In the spring of 1997, the CFE issue was used by Russia for two purposes: (*a*) to achieve the maximum curtailment of NATO armaments and their deployments within the future, enlarged alliance and thus to reduce the alleged NATO military 'threat' (a goal to some degree shared by NATO, seeking to assure Russia and other states that NATO enlargement will not have a destabilizing effect on military capabilities in Europe); and (*b*) indirectly, either to hinder or to delay the NATO enlargement process. To this end, Moscow made successive demands regarding CFE Treaty adaptation and other CFE questions.

Since the 10 December 1996 North Atlantic Council (NAC) statement (approved by the prospective NATO members) that the alliance has 'no intention, no plan and no reason'[27] to deploy nuclear forces on the territory of its new members, Russia has focused on the conventional weapon dimension of European military security. In early 1997, insisting that NATO enlargement should not create a military advantage for the alliance, Russia contended that the existing collective ceilings should remain and that NATO should not allow the additional weaponry of new member states to raise its total beyond treaty limits. Russia also demanded that the adapted treaty should impose national ceilings. While NATO indicated its readiness to reduce arms ceilings for its member states, Russia proposed that the starting-point for reductions be the 17 November 1995 holdings (which were much lower than the ceilings). Russia also sought limitations on new force deployments in new NATO states, the inclusion of new weapons in the treaty and the prevention of the build-up of any allied military infrastructure on the newcomers' territories.[28]

The NATO proposal

In drawing up its proposal, NATO sought to address two conflicting issues: Russia's objections to the eastward enlargement of NATO and the right of future members to host NATO forces on their soil.[29] The Central and East European (CEE) candidates were consulted in advance and supported the NATO proposal (although with some hesitation).

On 20 February 1997, NATO submitted its treaty adaptation proposal to the JCG.[30] Its main suggestions were the abolition of the group (bloc) structure, unchanged TLE ceilings within the ATTU zone, avoidance of potentially des-

[26] *OMRI Daily Digest*, vol. 3, no. 6 (9 Jan. 1997).
[27] NATO Press Communiqué M-NAC-2 (96) 165, 10 Dec. 1996.
[28] 'Tarasov: Russia wants to hasten CFE negotiations', ITAR-TASS (Moscow), 21 Jan. 1997, in FBIS-SOV-97-014, 21 Jan. 1997; and 'MFA official stresses seriousness of new CFE proposals', Interfax (Moscow), 24 Jan. 1997, in FBIS-SOV-97-017, 24 Jan. 1997.
[29] See also chapter 5 in this volume.
[30] NATO Proposal on Basic Elements for Adaptation of the CFE Treaty, Joint Consultative Group document JCG.PRO(4)/2/97, Vienna, 20 Feb. 1997.

tabilizing force accumulations in different regions and elimination of the structure of nested zones; however, the Flank Document would be retained as adopted in May 1996. Two types of ceiling were proposed instead:

1. *National* ceilings would cover all TLE categories which each state may hold in the area of application (they would not exceed notified maximum national levels for holdings, MNLHs, as of signature of the CFE adaptation agreement).

2. *Territorial* ceilings would be derived from current notified MNLHs, covering the three categories of ground equipment: tanks, ACVs and artillery. Territorial ceilings would be set up for each territorial unit with the aim of enhancing conventional stability by preventing any dangerous concentration of forces and helping to resolve the problem of stationed forces in all states parties. All states would have the right to decide whether they wish to use up their entire territorial quotas themselves or to what extent they wish to permit foreign forces to be stationed on their territory within their limit.

In short, national ceilings would define *what* states parties could have, and territorial ceilings would define *where* the ground TLE (national plus possible foreign stationed forces) could be located. The national/territorial concept marked a departure from the agreement in the adaptation agenda adopted at the Lisbon summit meeting to preserve zonal limitations.[31] NATO pledged that under the new agreement the total aggregate national ceilings of ground TLE of its 16 members would be much lower than the current group ceiling, although without specifying the reductions. According to NATO officials, reductions would lead to the disbandment of eight army divisions and the USA would cut back its heavy ground weapon inventory in Europe by half.

The proposal suggested storage modification: states would either retain their designated permanent storage site (DPSS) entitlements or eliminate 80 per cent of them and include the remainder in active units. In June NATO opted for the latter solution.[32] Under this scheme, on 19 June NATO's High Level Task Force agreed substantial reductions in future aggregate ceilings for its ground forces: 2800 tanks, 2160 ACVs and 2400 artillery pieces.[33] Moreover, it would renounce 756 items of its unallocated active entitlements[34] and declared that future cuts would be about 5–6 per cent of the total.[35] NATO's pro-

---

[31] The Lisbon Summit Declaration, Document adopted by the States Parties to the Treaty on Conventional Armed Forces in Europe on the Scope and Parameters of the Process Commissioned in Paragraph 19 of the Final Document of the First CFE Treaty Review Conference, para. 9. The text is reproduced in *SIPRI Yearbook 1997* (note 1), pp. 157–59.

[32] Of its 9200 pieces of stored equipment in Europe NATO would destroy 7360 items and convert 1840 (20%) to active entitlements. Russia has 3690 pieces in storage, of which it could transfer 738 items to active units while scrapping the remaining 2952. Russia insists on locating *all* TLE stored in DPSS in active units.

[33] Statement by the delegation of Italy on behalf of the sixteen members of the Atlantic Alliance at the Joint Consultative Group, Vienna 26 June 1997, Joint Consultative Group document JCG.DEC/8/97, Annex 5, Vienna, 23 July 1997.

[34] This equipment comprised 406 tanks, 122 ACVs and 228 artillery pieces.

[35] Originally France ruled out any cuts in its conventional weapon limits but altered this decision during the year. 'France: no cuts in upper conventional arms limits', Agence France-Presse (Paris), 21 Feb.

Table 12.1. Accommodation of new members' holdings and allocations within NATO TLE headroom

	NATO ceilings	NATO holdings	NATO headroom	New member[a] allocations	New member[a] holdings
Battle tanks	19 142	14 101	5 041	3 522	3 478
ACVs	29 825	21 464	8 361	5 217	4 109
Artillery	18 286	14 010	4 276	3 217	3 188
Combat aircraft	6 662	4 218	2 444	870	668
Attack helicopters	2 026	1 221	805	288	189
Total	**75 941**	**55 014**	**20 927**	**13 114**	**11 632**

[a] The Czech Republic, Hungary and Poland.

Source: Consolidated matrix on the basis of data available as of 1 January 1997, Joint Consultative Group, Vienna, 18 Mar. 1997. The matrix is reproduced in Lachowski, Z., 'Conventional arms control', *SIPRI Yearbook 1997: Armaments, Disarmament and International Security* (Oxford University Press: Oxford, 1997), pp. 470–71.

posal would result in an overall reduction of the current ceiling by some 10 000 TLE items. Since NATO's aggregate holdings of tanks, ACVs and artillery are 25 per cent (*c.* 17 700 pieces) below its current group ceiling, such a reduction could be readily accommodated.

Freedom to move equipment between states with their agreement and a consultative mechanism for national and territorial ceiling revisions were envisaged in the NATO proposal. Any state party might exceed its territorial limits during a notified military exercise, an OSCE- or UN-mandated peacekeeping operation or a temporary deployment.

Of particular importance in the NATO proposal was the idea of creating a 'stability zone' consisting of the Visegrad states (the Czech Republic, Hungary, Poland and Slovakia), the Russian Kaliningrad exclave (thus treating the Kaliningrad *oblast* as a territorial unit), Belarus and Ukrainian territory not covered by the Flank Document. By putting forward this concept NATO sought to quell Russia's fears of a Western military build-up near its borders. At the same time, it insisted on including countries other than new NATO members in that zone. The zone would have a regime of special stabilizing measures in which:

1. Territorial and national ceilings would be the same for each state/territorial unit and would not be revised upward until 2001. (Because their current holdings would limit the capacity of the applicant countries to receive NATO equipment (see table 12.1) this gave rise to some apprehensions among their governments, but army modernizations and concomitant reductions in equipment will leave some headroom for deployment of allied TLE on their territories.) Territorial limits in the zone could, however, be exceeded temporarily in specific cases.

1997, in Foreign Broadcast Information Service, *Daily Report–West Europe (FBIS-WEU)*, FBIS-WEU-97-036, 21 Feb. 1997.

2. Additional information would be provided on stationed forces and temporary CFE deployments.

3. Special additional inspection quotas would be set for declared sites.

The concept of a special zone provoked particular anxiety among the CEE applicants to NATO, anxious not to be 'singled out' from other states parties or given a second-class status either within or outside NATO.[36]

The Russian position

While welcoming and promising to study the NATO proposal, Russia found it insufficient in the face of NATO enlargement. Both the Russian interventions in the JCG and the Russian position paper[37] circulated on 22 April aimed at constraining the alliance and alleviating the disparity between Russian and NATO forces (allegedly between 1:3 and 1:4) through asymmetrical reductions. Consequently, Moscow drew attention to two major issues:

1. The collective ceiling (sufficiency rule) for a group or alliance (i.e., NATO), irrespective of its number of members, would be 'substantially' lower than at the end of the period of CFE Treaty reductions, while other individual states would not be required to make similar reductions.[38]

2. Regarding the future stationing of NATO forces, Russia reiterated the proposal to ban the stationing of foreign TLE not stationed on 16 November 1995. This would prevent NATO from deploying forces in new member states, while Russian assets in the Caucasian states or Ukraine would remain intact.

Russia favoured aggregate rather than territorial limits to forestall 'destabilizing accumulations of forces by a particular military–political alliance', and considered that national and alliance limits would make zonal limitations (including the flank regime) superfluous. Russia proposed to solve the matter of DPSS entitlements by locating *all* land-based forces in active units. It also criticized the omission of aviation from the territorial ceilings.

The Russian 'basic elements' proposal would not prevent NATO enlargement but would limit it to just a few states, and the ban on stationing would discriminate against new members. NATO therefore found the Russian proposal unacceptable on principle. The attempt to deny a state's right to host allied forces was rejected by both NATO and the CEE applicants as impairing their vital security interests and the sovereign right of states to decide whether to become party to treaties of alliance, as laid down in the mandate for the CFE

---

[36] Consequently, the Czech Republic has suggested that the concept of such a zone could best be reflected in a political declaration rather than in the adapted treaty. Poland has made the inclusion of the Kaliningrad region in the stability zone a condition *sine qua non*. It also insisted that the territorial and national limits be applied for a limited period (until 2001).

[37] Basic Elements of an Adapted CFE Treaty (Position of the Russian Federation), Joint Consultative Group document JCG.REF(RU)/88/97, Vienna, 22 Apr. 1997.

[38] This concept of correcting the imbalance was reportedly dropped later by Russian Foreign Minister Yevgeniy Primakov during US Secretary of State Madeleine Albright's visit to Moscow on 2 May.

adaptation negotiation. It also ran counter to the NATO proposal for a new treaty structure based on national and territorial ceilings. At the same time, while rejecting the demand for November 1995 collective ceilings, the CEE states confirmed that they were not interested in permanent massive stationing of NATO forces on their territories.

Accommodating Russia's demands and concerns

On 14 March the NAC made a declaration remarkable for its impact on the course of the CFE adaptation negotiations: 'In the current and foreseeable security environment, the Alliance will carry out its collective defence and other missions by ensuring the necessary interoperability, integration and capability for reinforcement rather than additional permanent stationing of substantial combat forces'[39] (i.e., in future member states). It thereby rejected Russia's demand for a complete ban on stationing new forces to be introduced in the adapted treaty.

The US–Russian summit meeting held on 20–21 March 1997 in Helsinki brought an agreement to accelerate the CFE negotiations to conclude a framework agreement setting forth the basic elements of an adapted CFE Treaty by late spring or early summer.[40] President Clinton reassured Russian President Boris Yeltsin that, in line with the NAC declaration, NATO does not envisage a build-up of its stationed forces close to Russia. However, he firmly rejected Moscow's insistence that NATO make absolute commitments to the non-deployment of nuclear and conventional weapons on the territory of new members. Such commitments were seen as bound to compromise NATO security guarantees and lead to the creation of a 'second-class' membership.

In the spring of 1997, the focus of attention shifted to the NATO–Russia talks on the envisaged charter guiding their relations. In order to dispel Russian concerns, the talks between Foreign Minister Primakov and US Secretary of State Madeleine Albright in Moscow in early May brought an agreement to establish national TLE ceilings as binding limits (to be agreed by the consensus of all 30 states parties, and reviewed in 2001 and at five-year intervals thereafter); to maintain only such military capabilities as are commensurate with individual or collective legitimate security needs; to establish measures to prevent destabilizing concentrations of forces in agreed areas, including the CEE countries; and to retain the Flank Document with the understanding that in the course of adaptation it will need to be expressed in the same conceptual terms as the adapted treaty.

A set of confidence-building measures (CBMs) addressed to Russia, although not directly related to the CFE Treaty, was also prepared. NATO offered to provide information on transfers of troops and equipment, and permit attendance at military exercises, inspections of bases and monitoring of

---

[39] NATO Press Release 97 (27), 14 Mar. 1997.
[40] Joint Statement on European Security released at the US–Russian Summit Meeting in Helsinki, 21 Mar. 1997, URL <gopher://198.80.36.82:70/00s/current/news/latest/9703211.tlt>, version current on 21 Mar. 1997.

NATO airspace.[41] Although Russia had wanted to discuss CBMs on military infrastructure within the CFE negotiations, a package of transparency measures (concerning airfields, storage facilities, fixed air defence sites, training areas and ranges, headquarters and pipelines serving military facilities) was tabled at the OSCE Forum for Security Co-operation.[42]

Facing NATO's firm opposition to a ban on the stationing of new forces, Russia modified its position and put forward a proposal for a binding sub-ceiling on foreign forces on the territory of new NATO member states. Russia would have liked to have it set at the level of 5 per cent of the national limit (then, e.g., Poland could only receive forces equivalent to less than a US brigade; and for Hungary the numbers would be ridiculously small), while NATO opted for 20 per cent of territorial ceilings and demanded that the sub-ceilings encompass *all* the countries in the proposed CEE stability zone.[43] Russia insisted on the inclusion of the limits in the NATO–Russian document. NATO had not yet agreed on its future stationing requirements; this was considered premature as the candidate states had not yet been chosen. In effect, both NATO and the candidates deemed it appropriate that the sub-ceilings be settled at the CFE negotiation in Vienna.

The NATO–Russia Founding Act and the 'basic elements' decision

On 14 May, NATO Secretary General Javier Solana and Russian Foreign Minister Primakov announced in Moscow that the NATO–Russia Founding Act on Mutual Relations, Cooperation and Security was to be signed on 27 May 1997 in Paris by all the NATO heads of state or government, the NATO Secretary General and the Russian President.[44] Both NATO and Russia reiterated their commitment to work for prompt adaptation of the CFE Treaty.

Section IV of the Founding Act[45] is devoted to conventional forces in Europe and sums up the series of Primakov–Solana negotiations; nevertheless it failed to address a number of key proposals made by both sides in Vienna. Its main points are:

1. Both sides confirmed an intention to speedily adapt the CFE Treaty and, in the meantime, to conclude a framework agreement setting forth the basic elements of an adapted treaty.

2. Significant reductions in overall ceilings, enhanced stability and transparency were to be pursued by both sides.

---

[41] 'NATO–Russia talks hit "red lines" and stall', *International Herald Tribune*, 16 Apr. 1997.

[42] OSCE Forum for Security Co-operation (FSC), NATO proposal on transparency measure on infrastructure, FSC document REF.FSC/158/97, 16 Apr. 1997. The CEE countries opposed these measures, considering them to be excessively intrusive, particularly since considerable investments will be required to rebuild their military infrastructure. *Rzeczpospolita*, 9 Apr. 1997, p. 7.

[43] The percentage idea was eventually dropped by Russia, perhaps realizing that it might later harm its interest to have more than 5% of its stationed equipment in the Caucasus region. *Arms Control Reporter*, sheet 407.B.567, 1997.

[44] See also chapter 5 in this volume.

[45] The text of the NATO–Russia Founding Act is reproduced in appendix 5A in this volume.

3. The future agreement was to be based on legally binding national ceilings, which should be well below current levels.

4. Both sides supported further measures to strengthen stability in order to prevent any potentially threatening build-up of conventional forces 'in agreed regions of Europe, to include Central and Eastern Europe'.

5. The 14 March NAC declaration was reaffirmed and complemented with an additional point to the effect that NATO 'accordingly ... will have to rely on adequate infrastructure commensurate with the above tasks [i.e., ensuring the necessary interoperability, integration and capability for reinforcement]'. In turn, Russia managed to have the following passage inserted into the Founding Act: 'In this context, reinforcement may take place, when necessary, in the event of defence against a threat of aggression and missions in support of peace consistent with the United Nations Charter and the OSCE governing principles, as well as for exercises consistent with the adapted CFE Treaty, the provisions of the Vienna Document 1994 and mutually agreed transparency measures'. In conclusion, Russia undertook to 'exercise similar restraint in its conventional force deployments in Europe'.

In late June and early July 1997 the states parties intensely pursued the goal of a framework agreement setting forth the main guidelines governing the adaptation of the treaty. NATO tabled further proposals for DPSSs (suggesting a renunciation of 80 per cent of the quotas and of the unused storage quotas, with the United States assuming the bulk of these cuts) and held internal discussions on the interrelationships between territorial limits, temporary deployments, stationed foreign forces and their impact on NATO military activities. Russia submitted a new proposal in early July, accepting the concept of national ceilings (in line with the NATO–Russia Founding Act) and indicating, among other things, that it would like to have restrictions on permanently stationed land-based TLE. Regarding foreign military presence Russia proposed that no state may host more than an amount of TLE equivalent to the size of one German brigade (106 tanks, 120 ACVs and 34 artillery pieces) but that no more than three brigades should be permanently stationed in all the new NATO member states. Russia also wished to see aircraft included in the territorial limits. On 12 July, Albright and Primakov achieved another breakthrough: Russia abandoned its demand for collective group ceilings (as national ceilings would effectively provide for a limit on NATO forces) and accepted that the flank issue should be modified within the adapted treaty. Three other issues remained unsolved, however: the definition of territorial limits, limitations on the stationing of forces and permanent stationing of aircraft. On 18–20 July the US–Russian consultations in Vienna brought further progress: Russia withdrew its demand that any revisions of national limits dealt with at the review conferences held every five years should be arrived at by consensus (this would constrain NATO's room for manoeuvre and was found unacceptable). Moreover, a formula was found for territorial limits which did not rule out defining part of the territory of a state party as a territorial unit.[46] These developments paved the way for a partial framework agreement.[47]

The basic elements for CFE Treaty adaptation

On 23 July the JCG approved a partial framework agreement on 'certain basic elements for treaty adaptation'.[48] The CFE states parties agreed on a system of national and territorial ceilings to replace the bloc-to-bloc structure, pledged restraint in maintaining military capabilities and agreed that initial national ceilings should not exceed MNLHs. National ceilings would be codified as binding limits and reviewed in 2001 and at five-year intervals thereafter. Destabilizing accumulations of forces would be avoided; to this end, territorial ceilings would be established covering whole territories or parts of territories of each state.[49] The states declared that they would consider establishing stabilizing measures in particular regions and areas of the treaty's area of application and limitations on additional stationing of TLE (sub-ceilings) to enhance stability and predictability. It would be permissible to exceed territorial limits for notified military exercises and peace-supporting missions. The states parties agreed that the substance of the Flank Document would be 'maintained but reconciled' with the structure of the adapted treaty. New accessions were envisaged, and cooperative and consultative rules and mechanisms for revising ceilings, enhancing verification and information exchange would be established.

The status of the negotiations

Following NATO's June 1997 statement of its intention to cut back collectively its weapon levels by some 10 000 items, and the adoption of the basic elements decision, NATO states made individual pledges to make further reductions in their arsenals, ranging from some 5 to 55 per cent (only Greece and Spain envisaged no reductions—see table 12.2). Some former WTO states have also expressed their readiness either to make (e.g., the Czech Republic and Hungary[50]) or to consider reductions in their holdings. Similarly, Russia has confirmed that it has no plans to seek an increase in the levels of its

---

[46] Zellner, W., 'Die Anpassung des KSE-Vertrags Regimewandel unter sich ändernden Bedingungen' [The adaptation of the CFE Treaty's change of regime under changing conditions], *S&F: Vierteljahresschrift für Sicherheit und Frieden*, vol. 15, no. 2 (1997), p. 97; and *Arms Control Reporter*, sheets 407.B. 569–71, 1997.

[47] A few days before approving the decision, Azerbaijan, Poland and Turkey sought to assuage the concerns of the other parties. Poland managed to remove the idea of limiting stabilizing measures to Central and Eastern Europe and to keep open the option of developing additional limitations and sub-ceilings on additional stationing of TLE. Turkey unsuccessfully opposed any departure from the Flank Document. It was supported by Azerbaijan, which also resisted any possibility of increasing the weapon limits of its neighbours (Armenia and Russia).

[48] The framework agreement is laid down in the Decision of the Joint Consultative Group Concerning Certain Basic Elements for Treaty Adaptation, Vienna, 23 July 1997. The text is reproduced in appendix 12B in this volume.

[49] Russia continued to insist that the whole of its territory be acknowledged as a single territorial unit.

[50] The Czech Republic declared that it would reduce its tank holdings from 957 to 700. Hungary will cut its holdings as follows: tanks—from 835 to 710; ACVs—from 1700 to 1500; and artillery—from 840 to 750. The territorial limits of Hungary and Poland are intended to equal their current MNLHs.

Table 12.2. Current entitlements and adjusted national ceilings proposed by NATO states, July–September 1997

Figures in parentheses are the proposed ceilings.

State[a]	Battle tanks		ACVs[b]		Artillery		Combat aircraft		Attack helicopters	
Belgium[c]	334		1 099		320		232		46	
Canada	77	(77)	277	(263)	38	(32)	90	(90)	13	(13)
Denmark[d]	353		336		503		106		12	
France[e]	1 306		3 820		1 292		800		352	
Germany	4 166	(3 644)	3 446	(3 281)	2 705	(2 255)	900	(765)	306	(280)
Greece[f]	1 735		2 534		1 878		650		18	
Italy	1 348	(1 267)	3 339	(3 172)	1 955	(1 818)	650	(618)	142	(142)
Netherlands	743	(669)	1 080	(972)	607	(546)	230	(230)	69	(69)
Norway[g]	170		225		527		100		0	
Portugal[h]	300		430		450		160		26	
Spain[i]	794		1 588		1 310		310		71	
Turkey[j]	2 795		3 120		3 523		750		43	
UK	1 015	(843)	3 176	(3 017)	636	(583)	900	(855)	384	(365)
USA	4 006	(1 812)	5 372	(3 037)	2 492	(1 553)	784	(784)	518	(404)

[a] Iceland and Luxembourg have no weapon limits in the application zone.
[b] Armoured combat vehicles.
[c] Reductions will be made but are still under study.
[d] Reductions are not excluded but are still under consideration.
[e] MNLHs for the 3 ground force categories are to be reduced by c. 5%.
[f] Reductions cannot be made because of security requirements.
[g] Adjustments are under review and will depend on flank limits.
[h] Ceilings will not be higher than current MNLHs and adjustments are possible.
[i] The intention is to keep the ceiling and give up the share of unassigned equipment.
[j] Reductions are under review and the preservation of the flank regime is seen as essential.

Sources: Joint Consultative Group document JCG.DEC/8/97, Vienna, 23 July 1997, Annexes 1–19, 21; and Joint Consultative Group document JCG.JOUR/275, Vienna, 30 Sep. 1997, Annexes 1–2.

armed forces during the negotiation and, in the event of a satisfactory outcome, is prepared 'to consider the possibility of not exceeding' its current holdings in the CFE Treaty area.[51]

In mid-September the JCG resumed its work in Vienna, and on 30 September it set up two subgroups within the negotiation group to negotiate the adaptation agreement text and new ceilings: (*a*) the limitation group (chaired by the French representative) to elaborate new national and territorial ceilings and their definitions; and (*b*) the verification group (chaired by the Bulgarian representative) to work on modifications of the verification system and additional measures relating to stationed forces, information exchange and the protocols.

[51] Joint Consultative Group document JCG.DEC/8/97, Vienna, 23 July 1997, Annexes 1–19, 21; and Joint Consultative Group document JCG.JOUR/275, Vienna, 30 Sep. 1997, Annexes 1–2.

Table 12.3. 'Initial illustrative ceilings' proposed by Germany

	Tanks	ACVs	Artillery
1. MNLHs	4 166	3 646	2 505
2. Intended reallocation to Spain	97	365	60
3. Residual German MNLHs	4 069	3 281	2 445
4. 20% of DPSS	– 117	– 0	– 0
5. Final MNLHs	3 952	3 281	2 445
6. Entitlements of other states parties	1 260	3 491	1 152
7. Derived territorial ceilings (5 + 6)	5 212	6 772	3 597
8. Unilateral reduction	– 308	– 0	– 190
9. Illustrative territorial ceilings	**4 904**	**6 772**	**3 407**
Entitlements of other states parties			
USA	761	1 346	839
UK	295	1 506	181
France	60	180	20
Netherlands	65	100	50
Belgium	2	96	30
Canada	77	263	32
Total	**1 260**	**3 491**	**1 152**

Source: Joint Consultative Group document JCG.DEL/24/97, Vienna, 2 Dec. 1997.

Reports at the end of the year indicated 'slow but methodical' progress in Vienna. Among the most difficult issues were the national and territorial ceilings: states parties wanted to ensure that the adapted treaty would allow them to reconcile their new national and territorial limits. It is generally assumed within NATO that territorial limits would be higher than national limits.[52] There is consensus that any increase in the national/territorial ceiling of one state party should be compensated for by a corresponding decrease in the national ceilings of one or more other states parties to avoid excessive concentrations of equipment. The relationship between national and territorial limits is not yet resolved. Germany proposed new 'illustrative' territorial ceilings to accommodate non-German forces stationed in Germany (table 12.3).[53] The discussion within NATO resulted in the drawing up in early December of 'initial illustrative ceilings'.[54] Another concern is how to create mechanisms for revising or reallocating the ceilings once they are in force.

The problem of restrictions in the stability zone and of stationing foreign troops on the territories of the new NATO states remains.[55] Russia is also

[52] This is a problem for states with a large part of their equipment stationed outside their territories (e.g., France and the UK). To avoid double counting, they would have to have higher national than territorial ceilings. Bringing home their troops would require upward revisions of their territorial ceilings.

[53] *Arms Control Reporter*, sheets 407.B.570 and 407.B.575–7, 1997.

[54] *Arms Control Reporter*, sheet 407.B.577, 1997. As Spain plans to deploy a new armoured division, Germany reallocated part of its entitlement to Spain. Canada and the USA, with no territorial ceilings in the area of application, will distribute their entitlements among various territorial units with the consent of the host states (all the Canadian entitlements will be counted within the German territorial ceiling).

[55] The NATO candidates have reportedly found the ceilings which NATO would like them to adopt to be too restrictive. According to a Polish official, Poland would rather negotiate the adapted treaty as a full NATO member. *Defense News*, 15–21 Dec. 1997, p. 4.

CONVENTIONAL ARMS CONTROL 517

pressing for the adaptation of the flank regime. Another issue is how to define exemptions for exercises and temporary deployments. Verification in the new, more complicated agreement stands out as an important technical problem. At the end of the year delegates at the negotiations expressed the hope that the adapted treaty could be agreed by the end of 1998.[56]

Verification of aircraft

The NATO proposal excluded aircraft from territorial limits, including the CEE zone. Russia, however, insists on limiting these units, too. Aircraft may be verified in different ways; a central database could account for their locations and activities at all times. Since aircraft can fly long distances very quickly, they do not need to be concentrated within the ATTU zone. In effect, verification costs may become prohibitively high, with the confidence-building value of verification rather marginal. Moreover, poorer states parties, already coping with other treaty-related costs, appear to be lukewarm towards incurring the costs of supporting aircraft verification.[57]

III. Regional arms control in Europe[58]

Phase II of the implementation of the Florence Agreement

The Agreement on Sub-Regional Arms Control (the Florence Agreement) of 14 June 1996 set numerical ceilings on five categories of heavy armaments of the former combatants in the former Yugoslavia: Bosnia and Herzegovina and its two entities (the Muslim–Croat Federation of Bosnia and Herzegovina and the Bosnian Serb Republika Srpska), Croatia and Yugoslavia (Serbia and Montenegro). Phase I of the reductions under the agreement was concluded on 31 December 1996 with the disposal of some 1700 items, predominantly artillery (75-mm and above), of an estimated total of more than 6000 liabilities.

At the beginning of 1997 uncertainty still surrounded the reduction process. Despite successive exchanges of data it was not clear how many weapons had been held or how many should have been destroyed. The data provided by the NATO Stabilization Force (SFOR) differed substantially from those provided by the parties in the Sub-Regional Consultative Commission (SRCC).[59] Parties

[56] According to Gregory Govan, chief US negotiator on CFE, the attitude of states was critical: 'One group of countries at the talks has strong ideas on how a future treaty . . . should look. There are other countries that don't have this outlook. Some have difficulties adjusting to a new kind of treaty that is not based on a bloc-to-bloc approach'. He also acknowledged that even some NATO countries are 'nostalgic for the ease of decision-making under the old system'. Egglestone, R., 'Slow progress on new conventional arms treaty', *RFE/RL Newsline*, 12 Dec. 1997, URL <http://www.rferl.org/newsline/1997/12/121297.html>.

[57] Chung, R., 'The road to a new CFE treaty', Verification Matters Briefing Paper, 97/3, *VERTIC Briefing* (Verification and Technology Information Centre: London, Sep. 1997), p. 4.

[58] There is some confusion about the use of the terms 'subregional' and 'regional' in the European debate. Sometimes Europe is referred to as a region; accordingly, its parts should then be referred to as subregions. The former Yugoslavia was considered a 'subregion' of the Balkan region, and, accordingly, the Florence Agreement is 'subregional'. For the purpose of this chapter, and in keeping with OSCE usage, 'regional' refers to areas beneath the continental/OSCE area level.

[59] Later in the year it transpired that the differences stemmed from the different counting methods and criteria. The OSCE had carried out systematic inspections, while SFOR, concerned with monitoring

Table 12.4. Five per cent exemptions under Article III of the Florence Agreement, as agreed on 30 January 1997

Party	Ceilings (total)	Ratio of limits	Holdings 16 Dec. 1996[a]	5% of holdings[a]
Yugoslavia (Serbia and Montenegro)	5 833	5	7 372	369
Croatia	2 333	2	2 514	126
Bosnia and Herzegovina	2 333	2	5 086	254
Federation of Bosnia and Herzegovina	1 555	(2)	2 841	142
Republika Srpska	778	(1)	2 245	112

[a] The numbers were to be corrected as the detailed information was provided.

Source: Sub-Regional Consultative Commission document SRCC/23/97, Vienna, 30 Jan. 1997.

accused each other of: (*a*) under-reporting and concealing their holdings; (*b*) abusing exemptions under Article III (on items in the process of manufacture, used for the purposes of research and development, belonging to historical collections, or awaiting export or re-export); (*c*) failing to report equipment supplied under the Train and Equip (T&E) Program (largely remaining under SFOR control because of continued disagreement on its distribution between the Croat and Muslim armed forces within the Federation of Bosnia and Herzegovina); and (*d*) denying or blocking declared-site inspection rights—mainly because of the dispute as to the right of Bosnia and Herzegovina to carry out inspections in Yugoslavia (Serbia and Montenegro) and Croatia.[60] The failure to agree on the division of the Federation of Bosnia and Herzegovina's overall reduction liabilities continued. It was decided that all the weapons that should have been destroyed in Phase I should be destroyed in Phase II (1 January–31 October 1997).[61] In mid-January SFOR ordered the Croat, Muslim and Serb communities to declare any previously undeclared weapons by 15 February and move all their weapons to approved cantonment sites by mid-March or face 'strong action' if they failed to comply.[62]

The first breakthrough took place in late January. The very controversial Article III exceptions were agreed in principle, allowing exceptions to be made of 5 per cent of the holdings of each party, although other interpretations

military movements and exercises, had conducted spot checks of cantonments, its estimates being less systematic. In Aug. SFOR and the OSCE agreed that OSCE verification staff would accompany SFOR staff on armaments inspections. The Bosnian Serbs, however, rejected the arrangement for reasons other than the counting rules. *Arms Control Reporter*, sheets 402.B-Bosnia.7–8, 1997.

[60] Bosnia and Herzegovina is a party to the Florence Agreement but has no forces of its own, and thus it is unable to host inspections.

[61] Status of Implementation of the Vienna and Florence Agreements (Dayton Annex 1-B, Art II, IV), OSCE document REF.SEC/230/97, Vienna, 16 Apr. 1997. The Implementation Force (IFOR) estimated that the Republika Srpska had failed to declare some 1250 weapon systems, mostly artillery. The Federation of Bosnia and Herzegovina had failed to report 100–120 artillery pieces; however, these came under the 5% rule explained below.

[62] 'SFOR demands declaration of all weapons by 15 Feb', Agence France-Presse (Paris), 17 Jan. 1997, in Foreign Broadcast Information Service, *Daily Report–East Europe (FBIS-EEU)*, FBIS-EEU-97-012, 17 Jan. 1997.

were to emerge later (e.g., decommissioning of equipment). Parties were then able to agree on numbers for exceptions (based on the 16 December 1996 exchange, with no acknowledgement of under-reporting).[63] The agreed numbers are shown in table 12.4.

At the third data exchange, in February 1997, the Republika Srpska reported a total of 2149 holdings, including 292 items to be classed as exceptions. In March, at the SRCC meeting, it raised its reduction liabilities from a total of 77 to 1082. These were welcomed as more realistic data, although according to Western estimates the Republika Srpska would have to dispose of a total of 2200–2300 heavy weapons to comply fully with the agreement.[64] The Republika Srpska's delaying tactics during the reduction process were interpreted by observers as partly motivated by alarm at the ongoing US-sponsored T&E Program, which was providing the Federation of Bosnia and Herzegovina with modern equipment and the possibility of using tactics similar to those that had been used against Serb forces in Croatia in May and August 1995.[65]

A new inspection plan was also adopted at the SRCC meeting, giving inspection rights to the central government of Bosnia and Herzegovina.[66]

On 11 April Croatia announced that it had fulfilled its Phase II reduction obligations, having destroyed 400 artillery pieces.[67] The Federation of Bosnia and Herzegovina had still not distributed its reduction obligations between the Croat and Muslim forces, evidently waiting for the Republika Srpska to begin its Phase II reduction process. It was only in June that the two forces in the Federation of Bosnia and Herzegovina agreed on the distribution of their liabilities and military personnel. Battle tanks, artillery, combat aircraft and attack helicopters were divided in a ratio of 2:1; ACVs in a ratio of 1.9:1; and military personnel in a ratio of 2.3:1 for the Muslim and Croat Federation army sections, respectively. The combined personnel ceiling for the Federation of Bosnia and Herzegovina was set at 45 000 troops.[68]

In June–July the Republika Srpska, the Federation and, later, Yugoslavia (Serbia and Montenegro) started their Phase II reductions, under which they were to destroy some 2000, 1460 and 960 pieces of weaponry, respectively. Within two months they had reduced some 550, 500 and 30, respectively.[69] In early August, an OSCE spokesman announced that about 30 per cent of the

---

[63] *Arms Control Reporter*, sheet 402.B-Bosnia.2, 1997.

[64] US General Accounting Office (GAO), *Bosnia Peace Operation: Progress Toward Achieving the Dayton Agreement's Goals*, GAO/NSIAD-97-132 (General Accounting Office: Washington, DC, May 1997), p. 40.

[65] *A Peace or Just a Cease-Fire? The Military Equation in Post-Dayton Bosnia and Herzegovina*, ICG [International Crisis Group] Bosnia Project, Report no. 28, 15 Dec. 1997, p. 14.

[66] *Arms Control Reporter*, sheet 402.B-Bosnia.3, 1997.

[67] Its Phase II liability was 374 pieces of artillery.

[68] The former ceiling was 55 000. *Arms Control Reporter*, sheet 402.B-Bosnia.6, 1997.

[69] In July the Republika Srpska reported an additional 840 weapons for reduction, mostly artillery, thus raising its reduction liability to almost 2000. The Federation of Bosnia and Herzegovina had increased its liability by acquiring additional artillery through the Train and Equip Program and the addition of newly discovered items. *Arms Control Reporter*, sheet 402.B-Bosnia.7, 1997. Yugoslavia (Serbia and Montenegro) announced that it would destroy only 151 tanks, 9 ACVs and 457 pieces of artillery, and the rest would be exported. This would account for one-third of its Phase II reductions, contravening the 25% ceiling allowed by Article VI of the agreement.

Table 12.5. Reductions completed under the Florence Agreement, as of 31 October 1997

Equipment	Yugoslavia (Serbia and Montenegro)	Croatia	Federation of Bosnia and Herzegovina	Republika Srpska	**Total**
Battle tanks	422	–	–	280	702
ACVs	29	–	–	52	81
Artillery	1 090	697	2 219	1 731	5 737
Combat aircraft	59	–	–	1	60
Attack helicopters	–	–	–	–	–
Total	**1 600**	**697**	**2 219**	**2 064**	**6 580**

Source: Sub-Regional Consultative Commission document SRCC/48/97, Vienna, 20 Nov. 1997.

liabilities had been reduced in Bosnia and Herzegovina. The parties were assisted in their destruction procedures by teams from France, Germany, Italy and the UK; 10 states provided assistance for reductions (training, advice, equipment and financial support) and 18 states assisted in inspections.

The OSCE announced on 21 November that as of the end of the reduction period (31 October) the former warring parties had destroyed a total of 6580 weapons, including over 700 tanks, 80 ACVs, more than 5700 pieces of artillery and 60 combat aircraft, with the Federation of Bosnia and Herzegovina and the Republika Srpska each having destroyed roughly one-third of the total (see table 12.5). The reductions were even somewhat in excess of the liabilities notified by the parties to meet the limits required by the Florence Agreement.[70] The Personal Representative of the OSCE Chairman-in-Office (CIO) for the agreement, Ambassador Vigleik Eide, called this a milestone in the peace process and drew attention to other achievements: the establishment of an effective inspection regime (185 inspections were conducted in the period August 1996–October 1997), the routine exchange of information on military forces and a constructive working relationship within the SRCC.[71]

The residual-level validation inspections were scheduled for 1 November 1997 to 31 February 1998. The SRCC was to hold a review conference on the agreement in June 1998.

The successful implementation of the Florence Agreement has created a stable military environment in Bosnia and Herzegovina.[72] Now that all the par-

---

[70] OSCE and SFOR arms control monitors agree that there might still be some discrepancies in the count of heavy weapons in Bosnia and Herzegovina since local commanders could have hidden some of them, but not in sufficient numbers to make a difference. *A Peace or Just a Cease-Fire?* (note 65), p. 15.

[71] Reduction period ends for parties to the Agreement on Sub-Regional Arms Control, Press Release no. 80/97, OSCE document SEC.INF/130/97, Vienna, 21 Nov. 1997.

[72] According to US estimates, of the 410 000 troops deployed during the war until Nov. 1995, 350 000 had returned to civilian life and 80 000 active-duty troops and their equipment are under SFOR supervision; of the 7700 heavy weapons deployed, 6600 items had been destroyed and 2600 remain in supervised cantonments. Fact Sheet: Background on Bosnia and Herzegovina, *USIS Washington File* (United States Information Agency: Washington, DC), URL <gopher://198.80.36.82:70/0R68311220-

ties have complied with Article IV of the Agreement on Regional Stabilization annexed to the Dayton Agreement, attention can turn to the Article V provisions on broader regional stabilization 'in and around the former Yugoslavia' and the pursuit of a stable military balance in the region.[73]

Article V negotiations on a regional balance

Prior to the OSCE Ministerial Council meeting on 18–19 December 1997 in Copenhagen, the CIO appointed Ambassador Henry Jacolin of France as his Special Representative to help organize and conduct negotiations under Article V. The Copenhagen meeting invited the Special Representative to start consultations on a precise mandate and initiate a process as early as possible with a view to achieving initial results by summer 1998. The following premises for the negotiations were put forward by the Ministerial Council:

1. States not parties to the Dayton Agreement should participate on a voluntary basis depending on their specific security environment.

2. Bosnia and Herzegovina must be represented by a single delegation appointed by the common institutions at all Article V-related negotiations.

3. The development of CSBMs and other appropriate measures adapted to specific regional security challenges can be considered, and information exchange and verification activities can be agreed in line with regimes already in place.

4. Such activities can be agreed between states which do not at present have the opportunity to exchange information with each other or inspect each other under legally binding arms control agreements.

5. The guiding principles should include military significance, practicality and cost-effectiveness.

6. Steps in this context should not prejudice the integrity of existing arms control and CSBM agreements. In particular, Article V talks should not alter obligations under the CFE Treaty or under the Article II or Article IV agreements.[74]

The Train and Equip Program

Within the specific ceilings, the parties are free to structure, equip and train their forces as they choose. In 1996, with the aim of creating a balance of

---

68319063-range/archives/1997/pdq.97>, version current on 18 Dec. 1997. Since the figures do not add up, it can be surmised that in the meantime there had been increases in the numbers of troops and equipment. The number of weapons said to have been destroyed in Bosnia and Herzegovina is surprising as it equals the overall reductions for the subregion.

[73] Germany has made several proposals with regard to Article V negotiations, aiming at 3 goals: (*a*) expanded CSBMs for the region similar to the sets of bilateral CSBMs between Bulgaria and its neighbours; (*b*) the creation of a framework for mutual data exchange and verification between the CFE Treaty and the Florence Agreement; and (*c*) arms ceilings in the countries currently not parties to any (conventional) arms limitation agreements (i.e., Albania, Austria, Macedonia and Slovenia). *Arms Control Reporter*, sheet 402.B-Bosnia.8, 1997.

[74] OSCE Ministerial Council document MC(6).DEC/2, 19 Dec. 1997, Decision No. 2, URL <http://www.osceprag.cz/news/mc06ej02.htm>, version current on 19 Dec. 1997.

forces in Bosnia and Herzegovina, the USA began its T&E Program envisaging the shipment of weapons and services to the underarmed Federation of Bosnia and Herzegovina.[75] As of April 1997, 14 countries had pledged at least $376 million in cash, equipment, training and technical support. The European Union (EU) reaffirmed its dissatisfaction over this endeavour and renewed its ban on arms transfers to the former Yugoslavia in January 1997.[76] Russia also expressed concern about the weapon deliveries. By early December 1996, the bulk of heavy weapons was being supplied by the USA. The United Arab Emirates delivered 36 105-mm howitzers; Egypt shipped 12 M59 130-mm guns and 12 D-30 122-mm howitzers; and ammunition, spare parts, light arms and other equipment and training were provided by other donors (Bangladesh, Germany, Indonesia, Morocco, Pakistan, Qatar and Turkey).[77]

In May 1997 the USA confirmed that it would send 116 M114 155-mm towed howitzers with a range of 9 miles (*c.* 14 km) to the Federation of Bosnia and Herzegovina.[78] The USA was also to pay for 51 D-30 122-mm guns to be manufactured in the Federation of Bosnia and Herzegovina for its own forces. The new artillery was to arrive in September–October 1997, but it was not supposed to be handed over to the Federation Army until US officers were satisfied with the cohesiveness of the Muslim–Croat forces. Agence France Presse reported in late May that arms for the Federation were unloaded in the port of Ploce from two ships from the United Arab Emirates. The shipment was said to contain about 4000 tonnes of arms, including 50 French-made AMX-30 tanks and 41 Panhard AML-90 APCs.[79] In the meantime, there were reports that the Republika Srpska would receive deliveries of modern artillery and tanks from Russia.[80] On 29 October a US State Department spokesman announced that the Federation Army must destroy some 100 older artillery pieces before the USA would deliver new howitzers. Ten Soviet-designed T-55 tanks from Egypt also reached Ploce at the end of October.[81]

Although the arms package falls within the limits of the Florence Agreement, the rate and scope of the rearming of the Federation Army during the year led NATO observers (as well as the Republika Srpska) to claim that the

---

[75] The US training is provided by the private-sector company Military Professional Resources Inc. (MPRI), which is licensed to provide assistance to foreign governments. Its operations are coordinated by the US Department of State Task Force for Military Stabilization in the Balkans. In 1996 the USA reportedly offered to extend the programme to the Republika Srpska if its leaders agreed to implement the Dayton Agreement. *Bosnia Peace Operation* (note 64), p. 82. In May 1996 the USA offered a $2 million payment to the Republika Srpska for its weapons, a step criticized by the OSCE. The Serbs declined, partly because of NATO's expected departure from Bosnia and Herzegovina in 1998, and also claiming that they needed to maintain their forces to balance the US Train and Equip Program. *Arms Control Reporter*, sheet 402.B-Bosnia.5, 1997.

[76] Germany offered to provide training on US-furnished equipment. *Bosnia Peace Operation* (note 64), p. 85.

[77] *Bosnia Peace Operation* (note 64), p. 87; and Arbuckle, T., 'Building a Bosnian army', *Jane's International Defense Review*, no. 8 (1997), pp. 58–59.

[78] The number of howitzers was later increased to 126.

[79] 'Bosnian Serbs discuss disarmament, Muslims–Croats get arms', Tanjug (Belgrade), 3 June 1997, in FBIS-EEU-97-154, 3 June 1997. Another source states that there were 42 AMX 30 tanks and 44 AML-90 APCs. *A Peace or Just a Cease-Fire?* (note 65), p. 18.

[80] *International Herald Tribune*, 14 May, p. 6.

[81] *Atlantic News*, no. 2962 (3 Nov. 1997), p. 3.

CONVENTIONAL ARMS CONTROL 523

qualitative military balance had been clearly tipped in its favour. Since in reality there is no integrated Federation of Bosnia and Herzegovina force, this was to the benefit of the Muslims. The equipment they had received was far more modern than the Soviet-pattern equipment that the Republika Srpska forces had largely inherited from the former Yugoslav Army.[82] In the autumn, the USA encouraged the Bosnian Serbs to participate in the T&E Program—thus altering the original goal of the programme. In November, the Government of Bosnia and Herzegovina pledged conditional support for the Republika Srpska to join the programme.[83]

The US-led rearmament programme could not but invite a reaction and countermeasures. At the end of the year a Russian–Yugoslav military agreement was concluded during the visit by Yugoslav Prime Minister Radoje Kontic to Moscow. Under the terms of the deal, Yugoslavia (Serbia and Montenegro) was promised sizeable but undisclosed quantities of Russian tanks, combat aircraft, assault helicopters and other weapons.[84] Since Yugoslavia is at the limit in all heavy weapon categories except for artillery, concerns have been voiced that some of the excess weapons could be transferred to the Bosnian Serbs.[85]

Russian arms control and security initiatives in the Baltic Sea region

Russian diplomatic activity in the Baltic Sea region in the latter half of 1997 related to the broader European security dialogue in general and the progress of NATO enlargement, including membership prospects for the Baltic states, in particular.

In early September, then Russian Prime Minister Viktor Chernomyrdin offered the three Baltic states a set of additional CSBMs if they would agree to remain outside military alliances.[86] In late October, the Moscow-based Council on Foreign and Defence Policy issued a report on 'Russia and the Baltic States', setting out a new agenda for Russia's relations with its north-western neighbours.[87]

---

[82] 'The question no longer is if the Muslims will attack the Bosnian Serbs, but when', a senior NATO commander asserted, declaring himself in favour of extending the mandate of SFOR. *International Herald Tribune*, 4–5 Oct. 1997, pp. 1, 4.

[83] *Jane's Defence Weekly*, 19 Nov. 1997, p. 3. The Republika Srpska is interested in receiving new equipment but is lukewarm about the training component of the Train and Equip Program, seeing the training offer as a NATO stalking-horse to get it involved in closer cooperation with the Federation of Bosnia and Herzegovina. See also *A Peace or Just a Cease-Fire?* (note 65), pp. 22–23.

[84] According to a Yugoslav source, the deliveries would include at least 1 squadron of MiG-29 fighters with enhanced radar and greater payload, the Russian version of an AWACS, 4 MiG-31 strategic pursuit aircraft and attack helicopters (Mi-24s, Mi-28s and Ka-50s—reportedly it has already received 2 of them). It is also to receive S-300 anti-aircraft missile systems and a range of sea-based weapons—torpedoes, ship-to-ship missiles, anti-aircraft missiles, etc. 'Missiles in the contract', *Vecernje Novosti* (Belgrade), 8 Dec. 1997, in 'Serbia: FRY–Russian arms deal seen result of US policy on FRY', FBIS-EEU-97-346, 12 Dec. 1997.

[85] *International Herald Tribune*, 26 Mar. 1997, p. 4. Another aspect of the rearmament risks is that attack helicopters have been used in quelling the demonstrations in Kosovo in Mar. 1998.

[86] See also appendix 12A in this volume.

[87] 'Rossiya i Pribaltika' [Russia and the Baltic region], *Nezavisimaya Gazeta*, 28 Oct. 1997; and *Russia and the Baltic States,* Executive Summary of the Report by the Council on Foreign and Defence Policy of Russia (Council on Foreign and Defence Policy of Russia: Moscow, 1997).

During his visit to Sweden, President Boris Yeltsin pledged on 3 December to unilaterally cut Russian land and naval forces, particularly in north-western Russia, by 40 per cent by January 1999. The units stationed in the Kaliningrad and Leningrad military districts will not exceed division and brigade levels. Yeltsin also reiterated the earlier proposal regarding CSBMs in the Baltic region and border areas. Then Defence Minister General Igor Sergeyev confirmed the Russian offer when speaking in Brussels on a 'spectacular reduction' of the Russian military and troop reductions in the regions of Kaliningrad and Leningrad, as well as the Russian fleet in the Baltic Sea.[88] Later, Deputy Foreign Minister Aleksandr Avdeyev elaborated on the proposal. Russia envisaged three stages of wide-ranging talks on Baltic security: (*a*) measures aimed at improving military, political and other relations with the three Baltic states to ensure 'a more predictable military policy and closer cooperation in customs and border protection areas'; (*b*) negotiation between Russia and the Baltic states of a 'well-defined security and stability-enhancing agreement' for the region; and (*c*) bringing together all the elements conducive to military, political, economic and environmental cooperation in one document, which would be 'part of the overall process of European security and the European security architecture for the next century'.[89]

It is unclear whether the Yeltsin proposal on unilateral reduction pertains solely to troops or also covers equipment; nor is it certain to what extent it would concern the strategic component of the Northern Fleet. It is also unclear whether it really is a new initiative or a part of the overall Russian Army reform announced in July 1997, which envisages a reduction in personnel to 1.2 million by 1999.[90] The new proposals for the Baltic region seem to be motivated as much by political will and military reform as by the very difficult financial situation of the Russian Federation.

IV. Open Skies

The 1992 Open Skies Treaty did not enter into force in 1997 because of the continuing failure of Belarus, Russia and Ukraine to ratify it.[91] The main

---

[88] 'Text of Yeltsin address on Baltic security', ITAR-TASS World Service (Moscow), 3 Dec. 1997, in FBIS-SOV-97-337, 3 Dec. 1997; and *Atlantic News*, no. 2971 (5 Dec. 1997), p. 2. 'It [the Baltic Sea] is the most stable region of Europe and therefore we can afford it [i.e. 40% arms reductions]'. *Rzeczpospolita*, 4 Dec. 1997, pp. 1, 6. It is not clear whether the 40% reduction concerns the north-west territory exclusively or other parts of Russia, too. Yeltsin said '*particularly* in north-western Russia', which suggests that other regions might also be affected by the reductions. *Nezavisimaya Gazeta*, 4 Dec. 1997, p. 1.

[89] 'Russia's Avdeyev outlines Yeltsin's Baltic security plans', Voice of Russia World Service (Moscow), 17 Jan. 1997, in FBIS-SOV-97-017, 17 Jan. 1997.

[90] *Kontseptsiya Voyennoy Reformy Rossiyskoy Federatsii* [The concept of military reform of the Russian Federation], Institute of World Economy and International Relations (IMEMO) of the Russian Academy of Sciences (IMEMO: Moscow, 1997). The text was also published as an annex in *Yezhegodnik SIPRI 1997: Vooruzheniya, Razoruzheniye y Mezhdunarodnaya Bezopasnost* [Russian edition of the *SIPRI Yearbook 1997*] (IMEMO: Moscow, 1997), pp. 445–76. See also 'Yeltsin decree cuts authorized army strength by 500 000', Interfax (Moscow), 25 July 1997, in FBIS-SOV-97-206, 25 July 1997.

[91] For the status of the Open Skies Treaty see annexe A, and for details of Open Skies trial overflights in Bosnia and Herzegovina see appendix 12A in this volume.

obstacle is Russia's reluctance to go ahead with ratification. The opposition in the Russian Duma claims that the treaty discriminates against Russia because the NATO states have agreed not to conduct overflights of each other's territory, and therefore Russia (and Belarus) would have to accept an excessive number of overflights compared with, for example, Germany and the USA. Although the Western European Union states voluntarily offered Russia additional overflights, the Duma opponents did not change their minds. Belarus is apparently just waiting for Russia's ratification and will probably follow suit but Ukraine, having failed to ratify the treaty in January 1996, cites financial reasons for not renewing its efforts. On the other hand, the Western governments were and are more anxious to see other prominent arms control agreements enter into force—the 1993 Chemical Weapons Convention, the 1993 Treaty on Further Reduction and Limitation of Strategic Offensive Arms (the START II Treaty) and an adapted CFE Treaty. Pending the entry into force of the Open Skies Treaty, signatories continue to conduct informal operations.

Signatories carried out a fairly intensive programme of reciprocal overflights in 1997, and its failure to ratify the treaty did not prevent Russia from participating in the informal trial flights. After a stalemate of more than a year, the Russian Defence Ministry consented to a new round of bilateral trial flights. In July–August Russia conducted its first surveillance flight over the United States (following Ukraine, which was the first former WTO country to fly over the USA in April), covering US sites on the East Coast including Cape Canaveral, and Canada, and flew over Turkey in October. The USA conducted six overflights of other countries and received the same number of observation flights over its territory. NATO missions flew over Russia in August–October. Some of the flights were 'taxi' flights, that is, crews flew in the host country's aircraft and used the host's sensors.[92]

The concept of Open Skies is gaining ground in South America, too. Four to five South American countries have reportedly expressed their interest in bilateral or trilateral arrangements of this kind with their neighbours. The idea is promoted by the United States, which proposed to display its Open Skies aircraft at a major air show in Santiago de Chile in March 1998 and offered to bring its aircraft to all the capitals of the interested countries.[93]

V. Conventional arms control endeavours outside Europe

Some relative progress in conventional arms control was made in the Asia–Pacific area in 1997. Because of the different conditions and experience that prevail, conventional arms control endeavours outside Europe tended to focus more on CBMs combined with various peacekeeping, preventive diplomacy and stabilizing activities rather than on disarmament and arms reduction steps. A combination of financial turmoil, economic uncertainty, and political and

[92] *Arms Control Reporter*, sheet 840.B.31, 1997; *Atlantic News*, no. 2939 (31 July 1997), p. 4 and no. 2974 (18 Dec. 1997), p. 3; and 'Russia to overfly Turkey according to Open Skies Treaty', Interfax (Moscow), 13 Oct. 1997, in FBIS-SOV-97-286, 13 Oct. 1997.
[93] *Trust and Verify*, issue 75 (May/June 1997), p. 5.

security considerations led countries in South-East Asia to develop an interest in arms control measures in the second half of the year.

In the Middle East, the arms control dialogue initiated in 1992 remained deadlocked[94] and the Arms Control and Regional Security Working Group (ACRS) was still inactive in 1997.[95] In addition, the Euro-Mediterranean Partnership, based on the 1995 Barcelona Declaration aiming at the creation of a 'zone of peace and stability' in the Mediterranean, has shown that the region is not ready for CBMs and arms control. However, it is encouraging that all parties maintain a regular dialogue on security alongside economic and cultural cooperation.[96]

In Latin America, the Clinton Administration decision of August 1997 to remove US restrictions on exports of advanced weapons to the region was criticized as liable to prompt rearmament despite the assertions that the decision 'will take into account the goals of strengthening democracy, supporting transparency and confidence-building, preventing an arms race, and other policy considerations'.[97] The 1995 Central American Democratic Security Treaty provisions envisaging arms limitations and CBMs have so far not been implemented.[98]

Russia–China

On 24 April 1997, China, Kazakhstan, Kyrgyzstan, Russia and Tajikistan signed a Treaty on Mutual Reduction of Military Forces in Border Areas. The text of the agreement was not disclosed and is to remain secret until it has been ratified by all five parliaments. It provides measures to reduce and limit the size of their armies, air forces and units of air defence to the minimum level required for solely defensive needs. Reportedly, the forces of China and the forces of the other four countries combined should be limited to 130 400 each within a depth of 100 km from the border lines between them. The treaty is valid until 31 December 2020. The parties pledged not to seek unilateral military advantage or to wage any offensive against one another. They will also regularly exchange relevant military information about the border areas, which will be kept secret from any third party. The implementation of the agreement will be subject to mutual supervision. There are said to be four protocols, detailing stipulations on such issues as geographical scope, reduction procedures, exchanges of relevant military data, supervision and verifica-

---

[94] See also chapter 3 in this volume.

[95] Jones, P., 'Arms control in the Middle East: some reflections on ACRS', *Security Dialogue*, vol. 2, no. 1 (1997), pp. 55–70.

[96] Tanner, F., 'The Euro-Med Partnership: prospects for arms limitations and confidence-building after Malta', *International Spectator*, vol. 32, no. 2 (Apr.–June 1997), pp. 3–25.

[97] 'White House statement on Latin American arms transfers', *USIS Washington File* (United States Information Agency, Washington, DC), 1 Aug. 1997, URL <gopher://198.80.36.82:70/0R42192651-42196250-range/
archives /1997/pdq.97>, version current on 1 Aug. 1997.

[98] *Arms Control Reporter*, sheets 840.B.32–33, 1997. The treaty was signed in San Pedro Sula, Honduras, on 15 Dec. 1995 by the presidents of Costa Rica, El Salvador, Guatemala, Honduras, Nicaragua and Panama.

tion.⁹⁹ Along with the Shanghai CBM border agreement signed a year earlier,¹⁰⁰ it is hoped that the treaty will exert a positive impact on security and stability in the region and in the Asia–Pacific area as a whole.

In the Soviet era, the approximately 8000-km border between China and the USSR witnessed occasional armed incidents and clashes. Now the security concerns of China and Russia are of a different character: China is worried about the Uighur minority in its western parts, and Russia is faced with the problem of Tajik Islamic rebels and their allies in Afghanistan. The intention of both states was to send a clear signal of Sino-Russian *rapprochement* as a sort of counterbalance *vis-à-vis* 'enlarging and strengthening military blocs' (in fact, NATO). However, despite assurances about building a 'security model', contributing to a 'multi-polar world' and creating a 'strategic coordination partnership oriented toward the 21st century', as stated in the Sino-Russian declaration of 23 April 1997,¹⁰¹ a major change in relations between the two countries, which are still divided by diverse interests and world outlooks, seems unlikely.¹⁰²

Asia–Pacific

There is a growing network of bilateral and multilateral security relationships in the Asia–Pacific region. Immediately after the cold war, countries in the region started to increase their military expenditures and acquisitions of advanced military technology. In parallel, however, there was a more pragmatic approach that saw the evolution of bilateral and multilateral cooperative diplomacy. In 1993 the Association of South-East Asian Nations (ASEAN) Regional Forum (ARF) and the Council for Security Cooperation in the Asia Pacific (CSCAP), an unofficial forum for security issues, were established to provide platforms for regional security dialogue.¹⁰³ The agendas of both forums include security-related CBMs and maritime cooperation. There has also been a flurry of bi-, tri- and multilateral security-related conferences (over 100 annually) and security policy activities of an official, semi-official or non-governmental/expert character in the region.¹⁰⁴

The developments of 1997 and especially the interplay of the major powers—China, Russia and the USA—show that the policies of countries in the region are increasingly aimed at cooperation. The USA is actively engaged

---

⁹⁹ 'China: spokesman on 5-nation border disarmament agreement', *Wen Wei Po* (Hong Kong), 24 Apr. 1997, in Foreign Broadcast Information Service, *Daily Report–China (FBIS-CHI)*, FBIS-CHI-97-114, 24 Apr. 1997; 'China: more on border reduction accord', Xinhua (Beijing), 24 Apr. 1997, in FBIS-CHI-97-114, 24 Apr. 1997; and *International Herald Tribune*, 25 Apr. 1997, p. 2.

¹⁰⁰ Lachowski (note 17), p. 494.

¹⁰¹ 'China: statement expresses concern over growing military blocs', Xinhua (Beijing), 23 Apr. 1997, in FBIS-CHI-97-113, 23 Apr. 1997.

¹⁰² 'China: Yeltsin, Jian discuss strategic coordination partnership', Xinhua (Beijing), 23 Apr. 1997, in FBIS-CHI-97-113, 23 Apr. 1997; and 'Russia and China: can a bear love a dragon?', *The Economist*, 26 Apr. 1997, pp. 19–23.

¹⁰³ Members of ASEAN, ARF and CSCAP are listed in the glossary in this volume.

¹⁰⁴ Klintworth, G., 'Regional security dialogues grow', *Asia–Pacific Reporter*, Oct./Nov. 1997, pp. 12, 14.

in the regional dialogue, carefully transforming the network of bilateral defence arrangements with countries of the region into a more flexible and multilateral system, including subregional confidence-building efforts (such as the trilateral China–Japan–USA and Japan–South Korea–USA dialogues). Its position, however, is that multilateral mechanisms are important as long as they are built on the basis of 'solid bilateral relationships and continued US presence in the region'; confidence-building initiatives are supported unless they undermine US operational flexibility or military posture in the region.[105]

China and the USA have taken several steps to increase mutual confidence and decrease the risk of miscalculation (exchanges of military personnel, reciprocal ship visits and calls by the US Navy to Hong Kong ports). During the visit of Chinese President Jiang Zemin to the USA in October 1997, the first US–Chinese formal Military Maritime Consultative Agreement designed to help avoid incidents at sea and provide a venue for dialogue between operational naval officers was worked out. The agreement was signed on 18 January 1998 during the visit of US Defense Secretary William Cohen to Beijing.[106]

The ARF Intersessional Support Group (ISG), which met in Beijing on 6–8 March 1997, was the first formal, multilateral security dialogue held in China.[107] Although the agenda of the CBM talks did not go beyond earlier discussions (exchanges of views on the regional security environment and security perceptions, information on regional CBM cooperation, dialogues on defence policies and conversion, exchange of information on observation and prior notification of military exercises, non-military CBMs, the implementation of the agreed CBMs and discussion of other proposed maritime security issues), it showed that participation in the security dialogue is expanding. The work continued in Brunei in November 1997 and in March 1998 another meeting of the ISG on CBMs was to be held in Sydney.[108] In March 1997 the ARF held a Second Intersessional Meeting (ISM) on maritime search and rescue in Singapore. China established its CSCAP committee in April and vowed to participate actively in Council activities. It is increasingly apparent that a Pacific community with shared values and objectives is gradually emerging.

The South-East Asian financial plunge in the autumn of 1997 affected the rate of arms purchases in the region. Analysts predict that the prospect of several years of shrinking budgets will, among other things, make the military establishments intensify cooperation with neighbouring countries. Appeals to

---

[105] Excerpts: Cohen speech 1/15 Asia Pacific security strategy, 15 Jan. 1998, *USIA Public Diplomacy Query*, URL<http://pdq2.usia.gov/scripts/cqcgi.exe/@pdqtest1.env>, version current on 15 Jan. 1998.
[106] *Washington Times*, 19 Jan. 1997, p. 1.
[107] ARF (ASEAN Regional Forum) Chairman's Statement: Annex C: Intersessional Support Group on Confidence Building Measures, 6–8 Mar. 1997, Beijing, China, URL <http://www.dfat.gov.au/arf/arf_1_confid.html>, version current on 15 Jan. 1998. See also Ying, A., 'New security mechanism needed for Asian–Pacific region', *Beijing Review*, vol. 40, no. 33 (18–24 Aug. 1997), pp. 6–7.
[108] In addition work on preventive diplomacy and enhancing the 'good offices' role of the ARF Chairman is envisaged for 1998; the ASEAN ministers agreed to move meetings on disaster relief and search and rescue to the technical/expert level. 'The fourth meeting of the ASEAN Regional Forum', URL <http://www.dfat.gov.au/arf/regional_97. html>, version current on 15 Jan. 1998.

South Asia

South Asia has a mixed record of declaratory CBMs. Except for the pledge not to attack each other's nuclear facilities (1992), joint declarations by India and Pakistan not to interfere in each other's internal affairs (1966), use force (1971) or develop, produce, acquire or use chemical weapons (1992) have not been respected. As CBMs have little influence on national policies, such declarations have been widely viewed with scepticism.[110] On the other hand, the concept of operational CBMs adapted to regional conditions for South Asia is broadly accepted. The main sticking-point surrounds the conflicting perspectives on the insurgency in Kashmir: India contends that it is supported by Pakistan, while the Pakistani view is that the insurgency has domestic roots and finds only moral support in Pakistan. The issue of whether to place CBMs in a bilateral (as proposed by India) or an international (as advanced by Pakistan) framework remains unresolved.

On 23 June 1997, the foreign ministers of India and Pakistan agreed in Islamabad to establish a negotiating framework for the discussion of all outstanding mutual concerns, including the disputed area of Jammu and Kashmir and issues of peace and security, including CBMs. Accordingly, a mechanism was to be established including working groups 'at appropriate levels' to address all these issues 'in an integrated manner'.[111] This did not prevent another round of clashes between the two sides' armed forces across the Line of Control in Kashmir in August–September 1997. The meeting of Indian and Pakistani foreign ministers in New Delhi on 18 September 1997 ended in deadlock and no mutually acceptable framework was reached. In October, Pakistani Prime Minister Nawaz Sharif, both in his talks with Indian Prime Minister Inder Kumar Gujral and at the UN forum, proposed that the issues of Kashmir and peace and security, including CBMs, be addressed at the foreign minister level and declared readiness to 'conclude and strengthen CBMs starting with agreement "on a set of principles to guide future bilateral arms control agreements"'.[112] At the end of the year, it remained an open question whether these steps are simply symbolic tactical gestures or concrete moves in the political game between the two South Asian powers—all the more so as domestic politics in India were in a state of flux, which rendered difficult any meaningful dialogue on such sensitive issues as Kashmir or CBMs.

---

[109] *International Herald Tribune*, 19 Nov. 1997, p. 6.
[110] Krepon, M., 'Opportunities for Indo-Pak. ties', *The Hindu* (Delhi), 14 Oct. 1997.
[111] 'Joint statement, Islamabad, 23 June 1997', *The News* (Islamabad), 22 Sep. 1997.
[112] Krepon (note 110); and 'Pak. not insisting on Working Groups', *The Hindu*, 1 Oct. 1997.

VI. Conclusions

There were new elements in conventional arms control in 1997, particularly in Europe. Despite earlier fears that Russia's opposition to NATO enlargement would adversely affect the CFE Treaty adaptation negotiations, developments were marked by good will and *rapprochement* between NATO and Russia. Both the NATO–Russia Founding Act and the July decision concerning certain basic elements for treaty adaptation opened the way for businesslike negotiations on a CFE adaptation agreement, which is expected to be finalized in the latter half of 1998. The states parties are challenged by the fact of an expanding NATO, on the one hand, and the need for innovative thinking on military security in the post-cold war environment, on the other. The enlarging alliance is beginning to redefine its strategic doctrine in the new Europe, which, among other things, calls for adaptation of the mission, tasks and deployments of its forces to the new requirements. This runs in parallel with the CFE adaptation talks, which will also contribute to shaping the future strategic concept of the alliance. Russia, in turn, is striving to curtail NATO's freedom in redeployment and reinforcement capabilities as the alliance gets closer to its borders. The difficult negotiations require a departure from or a change in some axioms of the traditional arms control approach, but, if the cooperative atmosphere prevails, states parties should be able to resolve the outstanding issues and arrive at a satisfactory agreement.

The Florence Agreement has contributed to improved military stability in the former Yugoslavia, especially in Bosnia and Herzegovina. Its implementation established a balance of armed forces and increased transparency and predictability. This was the result of considerable work and good will, not only on the part of the parties to the agreement, but also on that of the international community: the OSCE, SFOR and individual states that lent different forms of assistance and expertise. It is hoped that the success of arms control in the former Yugoslavia will continue to have a favourable impact on the overall situation in this unstable region and translate into better relations between the parties in civilian spheres, as well as enable further steps towards a stable military balance in the Balkans as a whole. However, the disquieting trend towards rearming parties to the recent conflict is potentially destabilizing.

Regional arms control is addressed in different forums in Europe, notably the OSCE. The Baltic Sea region seems to offer good prospects for a genuine dialogue, especially in the wake of the substantial cuts that Russia has pledged to make in its land and naval forces deployed in the north-west. However, as long as progress is linked to conditions that are unacceptable to Russia's neighbours, the chances for a genuine dialogue will remain bleak.

Outside Europe, only the Asia–Pacific region witnessed a promising security dialogue that touched upon conventional arms control. Other parts of the world are either bogged down in political and security crises, as in South Asia, the Middle East, the Mediterranean and Africa, or facing the risk of rearmament, as in South America.

Appendix 12A. Confidence- and security-building measures in Europe

ZDZISLAW LACHOWSKI and PATRICK HENRICHON

I. Introduction

Confidence- and security-building measures (CSBMs) remained on the agenda of the Organization for Security and Co-operation in Europe (OSCE), both on the pan-European and on the regional level, in 1997. Suggestions submitted at the Annual Implementation Assessment Meeting (AIAM) aimed to improve and adapt the Vienna Document 1994 of the Negotiations on Confidence- and Security-Building Measures to the new security environment. The OSCE Forum for Security Co-operation (FSC) agreed on a number of amendments and undertook to launch a process of general 'modernization' of the Vienna Document with a view to completing it in 1998. The 1996 Agreement on Confidence- and Security-Building Measures in Bosnia and Herzegovina was in its second year of successful operation. Elsewhere in Europe, confidence- and security-building efforts continued to have a mixed record: in one area they raised hopes for progress (the Baltic Sea region), while in the south-eastern part of the continent they failed after a short-lived accord (on Greek–Turkish relations).

II. The Annual Implementation Assessment Meeting

On 3–5 March 1997, the FSC held the seventh Annual Implementation Assessment Meeting to review the implementation of the Vienna Document 1994 and to discuss ways to improve the document. The proposals tabled can be seen broadly as a continuation of the framework established by the suggestions made in 1996.[1] In order to formulate these proposals, six working groups addressed the following topics:

1. *Annual Exchange of Military Information.* Mechanisms were proposed for the Conflict Prevention Centre (CPC) to inform, remind and assist participating states regarding their obligations to submit information on time; to broaden the CPC survey to highlight tendencies and developments more clearly; to present the Annual and Global Exchanges of Military Information simultaneously, preferably on a given date (15 January; there was no consensus on combining them into a single document); and to include paramilitary forces in the Annual Exchange of Military Information.

2. *Defence planning.* Suggestions were made to broaden the information provided to the CPC from 'publicly available information' to 'all information'; to establish a more transparent format for the exchange of defence planning information; and to submit all defence planning documentation on a given date.

3. *Risk reduction.* It was proposed that verification by multinational inspections be introduced in crisis areas to enable information to be gathered in an impartial manner.

---

[1] Lachowski, Z., 'Confidence- and security-building measures in Europe', *SIPRI Yearbook 1997: Armaments, Disarmament and International Security* (Oxford University Press: Oxford 1997), appendix 14A, pp. 502–503.

4. *Contacts*. The following topics were addressed: a possible role for the CPC in monitoring new weapon systems and in reminding participating states of their obligation to demonstrate such systems before introducing them into their armed forces; the creation by the CPC of a bulletin board to inform participating states of planned events; the extension of time-frames for inspections/invitations; publication of lists of invited countries and countries accepting the invitation(s); and distribution to participating states of regular information on contacts throughout the year.

5. *Military activities, annual calendars and constraining provisions*. Applying the document's constraining provisions to joint military activities and including multinational military forces and activities in the document were considered. Reducing thresholds for observation and participating troops was discussed, along with the possible reporting by participating states on their largest military activity if their exercises did not reach threshold numbers. Putting artillery under the constraining provisions was also debated, a measure which would constitute a significant change in the scope of the document.

6. *Compliance and verification*. The proposals included the use by participating states of their unexhausted inspection quotas for evaluation visits; the development of a mechanism to ensure the conduct of inspections and evaluations during crisis situations; the distribution of quotas over the year and among participating states; and a suggestion that states should not be obliged to host more than one visit/inspection per month. Limiting the size of inspection areas and a less encompassing definition of the term 'restricted area' were also discussed.

7. *Communications*. Monthly rather than weekly and quarterly overviews of messages sent were proposed, and ways to ensure that all states participated in the OSCE Communications Network were also debated.

8. *Other agreed CSBMs*. Three other CSBM documents were discussed. First, proposals were made to include paramilitary forces with combat capabilities in the Global Exchange of Military Information (GEMI) and to include GEMI information in the document. Second, it was proposed to establish a pool of experts to supervise the implementation of the Code of Conduct on Politico-Military Aspects of Security; to give a role to the CPC in controlling the implementation; and to develop verification mechanisms for the code.[2] Finally, the adaptation of the document on Stabilizing Measures for Localized Crisis Situations to cases of internal conflicts was discussed.[3]

III. Improving and reviewing the Vienna Document 1994

Amending the Vienna Document

During 1997, the FSC continued to adapt the Vienna Document 1994 to the new European security context by annexing the following amendments:

---

[2] The first Follow-up Conference to examine the 1994 OSCE Code of Conduct on politico-military aspects of security and its implementation was held in Vienna on 22–24 Sep. 1997. Many proposals and suggestions were discussed, and a number of concrete measures to improve implementation and control of the code were raised. These included CSBM- and arms control-related measures, such as making the CPC a point of contact for the follow-up of the code, developing and following up implementation in regular assessment meetings in connection with the AIAM or in separate meetings, verification of implementation in conjunction with CSBMs, and the potential value of the confidence- and security-building function of the code at the regional level of arms control. Follow-up Conference on the OSCE Code of Conduct on politico-military aspects of security, Summary, FSC.GAL/15/97, Vienna, 30 Sep. 1997.

[3] For the suggestions and proposals of the AIAM, see OSCE, CPC Survey of Suggestions tabled at the AIAM, OSCE document REF.SEC/199/97, Conflict Prevention Centre, Vienna, 27 Mar. 1997.

1. A decision on multinational evaluation teams to enable more countries to make use of existing evaluation quotas (Decision 2/97, 19 Feb. 1997).

2. A decision on *force majeure* to clarify the procedures to be followed if inspections or evaluation visits cannot be conducted as previously requested or scheduled (Decision 6/97, 9 Apr. 1997).

3. The strengthening of Chapter VII on constraining provisions by including the armoured combat vehicle parameter in all relevant paragraphs (Decision 7/97, 9 Apr. 1997).

4. A standardized declaration format for countries with no armed forces (Decision 8/97, 21 May 1997).

5. A feedback modality included in Annex II for replies to invitations for visits to events or military sites (Decision 9/97, 25 June 1997).[4]

It was decided that from 1998 an obligatory information exchange would be annexed to the Document on Principles Governing Conventional Arms Transfers with regard to the transfers of weapon and equipment systems in the categories and formats as set out in the UN Register of Conventional Arms (Decision 13/97, 16 July 1997).

A statement regarding the extension of the application zone for CSBMs as defined by Annex I to the territories of the former Yugoslav Republic of Macedonia and of Andorra was made in order to reflect their earlier accession to the status of OSCE participating states.[5]

Towards a new Vienna Document

On 22 October 1997, the FSC Chairman commissioned an exploratory study on a complete revision of the Vienna Document 1994[6] to enable the FSC to make a proper contribution to the OSCE's Copenhagen Ministerial Council. After presenting the initial report in early December,[7] the FSC made the formal decision to review the document. It was hoped that the review would be completed during 1998. It would be based on existing documents and aim to: (*a*) update the document to reflect agreements already reached; (*b*) consider the addition of new measures and amendments to improve the transparency, predictability and cooperative nature of the Vienna CSBM process (including the regional level); and (*c*) consider the relationship of the document to other FSC documents.[8]

This attempt to consolidate the Vienna framework and to adapt it to the new political challenges in Europe will focus on both general and technical aspects of the document. According to a proposal submitted by France, Germany and Poland, the review should seek to accomplish four main reforms: (*a*) an enhancement of transparency and predictability and a strengthening of verification procedures; (*b*) a lowering of

---

[4] For texts of the FSC decisions see OSCE CSBM/FSC Documents, on the the OSCE Internet homepage, URL <http://www.osceprag.cz/docs/csbmfsc.htm>.

[5] OSCE Forum for Security Co-operation, 179th Plenary meeting, FSC.JOUR/185, *Journal*, no. 185 (23 Apr. 1997)

[6] OSCE Forum for Security Co-operation, 198th Plenary Meeting, FSC.JOUR/204, *Journal*, no. 204 (22 Oct. 1997).

[7] FSC, Report by the co-ordinator on the initial review of the Vienna Document 1994, FSC.DEL/127/97, Vienna, 3 Dec. 1997.

[8] OSCE Forum for Security Co-operation, 205th Plenary Meeting, FSC.DEC/15/97, *Journal*, no. 211 (10 Dec. 1997).

Table 12A. Calendar of planned notifiable military activities in 1998, exchanged by 18 December 1997

States/Location	Dates/Start window	Type/Name of activity	Area	Level of command	No. of troops	Type of forces or equipment	Comments
1. Canada, Denmark, France, Germany, Greece, Netherlands, Portugal, Spain, Turkey, UK, USA	15 Feb–31 Mar.	Strong Resolve 1998	Norwegian Sea, Norway, Portugal, Spain	SACLANT, SACEUR	..	Amphibious, ground and air forces	Amphibious forces; deployment of NATO task forces and land/air elements of SCE reaction forces
1a. Belgium, Bulgaria, Czech Rep., France, Germany, Greece, Hungary, Italy, Lithuania, Netherlands, Poland, Portugal, Romania, Slovakia, Slovenia, Spain, Sweden, FYROM, Turkey, UK, USA	9–21 Mar.	Livex Strong Resolve 98	Iberian Peninsula	SACLANT, SACEUR	..	Ground, naval and air forces	Combined NATO/PFP exercise to cope with simultaneous crises in separate geographical regions
1b. Canada, Denmark, Germany, Italy, Netherlands, Norway, UK, USA	16–21 Mar.	FTX Strong Resolve 98	Norway	Div. level, responsibility of Norway COMITFNON	18 500[a]	Amphibious, ground and air forces; 1 light mech. div.	Exercise forces in deployment operations, practice cooperation and interoperability between Norway and allied formations
2. Netherlands, Norway, UK	23 Feb.–1 Mar.	Unitex South 1998	Norway	Brig. level	4 600[b]	Amphibious and ground forces	Exercise forces in amphibious operations, planning and drill
3. France, Greece, Italy, Netherlands, Spain, UK, USA	1–30 Apr.	Destined Glory 98	Southern Spain	COMSTRIK–FORSOUTH NAVSOUTH	..	Amphibious and naval forces	Training of HQ staffs, amphibious units and maritime forces in development of combined amphibious forces concept
4. France, Germany, Greece, Italy, Netherlands, Spain, Turkey, UK, USA	1 Sep.–30 Oct.	Dynamic Mix 98	Central/Eastern Mediterranean	CINC–SOUTH	..	Marine forces	Fleet Livex operations to improve readiness, implement strategy in NATO southern region

Notes: brig. = brigade; CINCSOUTH = Commander-in-Chief Allied Forces Southern Europe; COMJTFNON = Commander Joint Task Force Northern Norway; COMSTRIK-FORSOUTH = Commander Striking and Support Forces Southern Europe; div. = division; FTX = field training exercise; FYROM = Former Yugoslav Rep. of Macedonia; Livex = Live exercise; mech. = mechanized; NAVSOUTH = Allied Naval Forces Southern Europe; PFP = Partnership for Peace; SACEUR = Supreme Allied Commander Europe; SACLANT = Supreme Allied Commander Atlantic.

[a] Canada 1500; Denmark 500; Germany 1500; Italy 1000; Netherlands 1500; Norway 7500; UK 1500; USA 3500.
[b] Netherlands 500; Norway 800; UK 3300.

notification thresholds to reflect the replacement of the large-scale military exercises of the cold war period by limited multilateral training exercises, peacekeeping operations and paramilitary activities; (c) the inclusion of *à la carte* provisions under which regional CSBM agreements could be reached; and (d) an increase and consolidation of cooperation between participating states at the political and military levels, especially by the establishment of a regular dialogue on defence planning and military doctrine. The proposal suggested including paramilitary forces in the information exchange; reducing the notification threshold for planned increases in personnel strength and for temporary reactivation of non-active formations; introducing a particular verification regime for multinational inspections in crisis situations; reducing the threshold values needed for notification and introducing special notification thresholds for peacekeeping operations.[9]

Technical recommendations made at the 1996 and 1997 AIAMs were compiled for further study in a document addressing each of the 10 chapters of the Vienna Document 1994.[10] In April 1997 the NATO countries, led by the USA, tabled their 'transparency measure on infrastructure' proposal at the FSC. This measure was designed to alleviate Russian concerns about NATO infrastructures in new member states and would provide increased transparency on, for example, military airfields, camp sites, headquarters, exercise and practice ranges, fixed air defence sites, and pipelines used for military purposes. It would be verified in accordance with the Vienna Document.[11] NATO also proposed to include new aircraft types (transport, tanker and airborne early-warning and control) in the annual exchange of military information.[12] In the spring and autumn Russia made proposals for naval CSBMs .[13]

IV. The implementation record for 1997

Nearly half of the participating states failed to submit annual calendars and information regarding constraining provisions by the end of 1997.

By 18 December 1997, a total of 34 inspections had been requested and conducted in 22 countries. Participating states also asked for 76 evaluation visits (although only 73 actually took place) to 42 countries. However, the CPC had only received reports on 29 inspections and 64 evaluation visits.[14] Despite these shortcomings, the number of inspections and evaluation visits confirms the trend of a constant annual increase in transparency-oriented and confidence-building activities.

SIPRI has received information about six manoeuvres (including three notifications within the framework of 'Strong Resolve 1998') subject to notification and planned for 1998. They are listed in table 12A. Moreover, there were 5 voluntary prior notifications (i.e., for exercises to be conducted below the notification thres-

---

[9] OSCE Forum for Security Co-operation, 187th Plenary Meeting, Proposal on a further development of the Vienna Document 1994 (Submitted by the delegations of France, Germany and Poland), *Journal*, no. 193 (18 June 1997).

[10] OSCE, Conflict Prevention Centre, Synopsis on suggestions relating to the Vienna Document 1994, FSC.GAL/33/97, Vienna, 4 Nov. 1997.

[11] OSCE Forum for Security Co-operation, NATO proposal on transparency measure on infrastructure, FSC document REF.FSC/158/97, 16 Apr. 1997.

[12] OSCE Forum for Security Co-operation, Proposal on information on additional types of aicraft, FSC document FSC.DEL/135/97, 10 Dec. 1997.

[13] OSCE Forum for Security Co-operation, CSBMs in the field of naval activities, FSC documents REF.FSC/137/97, 19 Mar. 1997 and FSC.DEL/96/97, 29 Oct. 1997.

[14] OSCE, Conflict Prevention Centre, Quarterly CPC Survey on CSBM Information Exchanged 4/97, FSC document FSC.GAL/55/97, Vienna, 19 Dec. 1997.

holds). Two of the planned activities ('Baltic Challenge 1998', which is not subject to notification, and the live exercise portion of 'Strong Resolve 1998') would involve NATO troops working alongside soldiers from Partnership for Peace (PFP) countries.

V. Regional CSBMs

Agreement on CSBMs in Bosnia and Herzegovina

The Agreement on Confidence- and Security-Building Measures in Bosnia and Herzegovina of 26 January 1996 (negotiated under Article II of Annex 1-B of the 1995 General Framework Agreement for Peace in Bosnia and Herzegovina, the Dayton Agreement) was basically modelled on the Vienna Document 1994, with some of its provisions, particularly those concerning the exchange of data and inspections, derived from the 1990 Treaty on Conventional Armed Forces in Europe (the CFE Treaty). The CSBM Agreement outlined a set of measures to enhance mutual confidence and reduce the risk of conflict. The parties are Bosnia and Herzegovina and its two entities: the Federation of Bosnia and Herzegovina and the Republika Srpska.

As in 1996, the overall record of CSBM implementation in Bosnia and Herzegovina was found satisfactory. No major problems were noted during inspections in the first two years of implementation. Some general concerns were voiced: incomplete implementation of certain measures, vulnerability of implementation to political problems, attempts to misuse arms control for political purposes, and so on.[15] During 1997, the atmosphere between the parties to the agreement was improving: transparency and confidence between the armed forces of the two entities were growing; a synergy developed between CSBMs and the regional arms control process; and voluntary measures were carried out including voluntary open skies measures. The minor problems and difficulties of CSBM implementation in 1997 were as follows:[16]

1. *Military information exchange.* The problems stemmed chiefly from the process of moving from wartime mobilization to peacetime deployments, the reduction of cantonments and barracks (under the instructions of the Stabilization Force, SFOR) and the reorganization of the armed forces under the 1996 Agreement on Sub-Regional Arms Control (the Florence Agreement). Information was sometimes imprecise and felt to be inadequate as regards the role of the police and internal security forces in the internal crisis in the Republika Srpska.

2. *Demonstration of new types of major weapons and equipment systems.* Some concerns arose in connection with the Train and Equip (T&E) Program. The equipment was to be demonstrated by October 1997.

3. *Notifications of changes in command structures or equipment holdings.* Because the permanent military structures of the armed forces are still being worked out, there are frequent information exchanges instead of notifications.

4. *Risk reduction.* The mechanism had been initiated three times by September 1997 and oral complaints had been answered.

---

[15] Talking points for Ambassador Marton Krasznai, Personal Representative of the OSCE Chairman-in-Office, FSC document CIO.GAL/6/97, 10 Sep. 1997.

[16] The following review is based on Status of Implementation of the Vienna and Florence Agreements (Dayton Annex 1-B, Art II, IV), OSCE Secretariat document REF.SEC/230/97, 16 Apr. 1997; Talking points (note 15); and 'Review Meeting measures progress in implementation of confidence- and security-building measures in Bosnia and Herzegovina', OSCE Press Release, 23 Feb. 1998.

5. *Notification, observation and constraints.* These measures were observed. The Republika Srpska notified two activities which would have violated the agreement, but later said it was scaling down the exercises.

6. *Withdrawal of forces and heavy weapons to cantonments and barracks.* The agreement was modified twice to bring it into line with Florence Agreement reductions and SFOR requirements. Regular notifications were provided under the CSBM Agreement.

7. *Identification and monitoring of weapons-manufacturing capabilities.* The parties provided their lists. The Federation offered a detailed and quite comprehensive list. The Republika Srpska first notified that it had no capabilities to report but later provided a list. The scope of confidence-building visits to entity armaments factories is still under discussion, and two voluntary visits were planned to solve the problem.

8. *Military contacts and cooperation.* Two seminars and four visits were conducted in 1997. One contact was downgraded because of political tension in the Republika Srpska and one was cancelled. A voluntary visit in June 1997 to Hadzici, where the T&E *matériel* was stored, was important in dispelling Bosnian Serbs' concerns.

9. *Visits to military bases.* The OSCE recorded full compliance. There were four visits in 1996 and two more by September 1997. An HVO (Croatian) guard brigade undergoing T&E training was also visited.

10. *Verification and inspection.* By 31 December 1997, 131 inspections had been completed 'in a professional and friendly manner'. These are said to have been the most successfully implemented measures. With OSCE assistance, verification agencies were created to help the parties gain experience and professional skills.

11. *Communication.* A military 'hot line' was established in June 1996. After the relocation of the Republika Srpska General Staff to the north-east (Bijelijna) direct communication became impossible. In 1997, this measure was implemented in part.

12. *Implementation assessment.* Bi-monthly (instead of twice-yearly) meetings of the Joint Consultative Commission (JCC) played a key role in implementation.

CSBM-related meetings

The international community sought to improve cooperation between the parties on issues relating to military security. An OSCE Seminar on Regional and Bilateral Confidence and Security Building and Open Skies took place in Sarajevo on 12–13 February 1997. Participants learned of the experience of a number of states which have implemented and monitored CSBMs. They also discussed the importance of confidence-building measures (CBMs) for Bosnia and Herzegovina.[17]

The first voluntary informal meetings between officers of the Federation and the Republika Srpska were held under OSCE auspices at the initiative of Regional Stabilization officers in Tuzla and Sokolac on 16 April. This first meeting, at Corps Commander level, was widely acknowledged as a breakthrough in the implementation of CBMs.[18]

On 11 and 12 June in Jahorina, Republika Srpska, a seminar on military doctrines was organized by the Office for Regional Stabilization. It was designed to encourage dialogue between local authorities on military doctrines, their impact on training and their consequences for military structures in a changing security environment.[19]

---

[17] *OSCE Newsletter*, vol. 4, no. 2 (Feb. 1997).
[18] *OSCE Newsletter*, vol. 4, no. 4 (Apr. 1997).
[19] *OSCE Newsletter*, vol. 4, no. 6 (June 1997).

The OSCE Ministerial Council in Copenhagen in December 1997 noted 'considerable progress' in implementation of the CSBM Agreement.[20] The first review conference to assess the implementation, overcome problems and amend the agreement where necessary took place under the chairmanship of the Personal Representative of the OSCE Chairman-in-Office (CIO), Carlo Jean, in Vienna from 16 to 20 February 1998. In his words, the conduct of the parties had been 'very constructive and open', demonstrating the OSCE's success in creating an atmosphere of trust and confidence. In the light of the two-year experience, several decisions were taken at the conference to update existing articles and measures, and other decisions were referred to working groups. The next review conference is planned for February 1999.[21]

Open skies flights in Bosnia and Herzegovina

Open skies voluntary demonstration overflights of Bosnia and Herzegovina in 1997 awoke interest and were praised as a useful CBM. On 17 and 18 June, Hungary and Romania undertook the first two joint trial flights, involving representatives of the three parties to the CSBM Agreement and international observers. Photographs were taken of military sites of the entities and made available to all the parties to the agreement.[22]

On 27 August another trial overflight of Bosnia and Herzegovina was carried out under OSCE auspices, using the German Tu-154M aircraft. The flight covered 2300 km, photographing 120 civilian and military sites, 60 each in the Federation and the Republika Srpska.[23] The next open skies flight, a joint US–Russian project, took place between 3 and 7 November 1997.[24]

Russia's CSBM initiative in the Baltic Sea region

On 5 September 1997, Russian Prime Minister Viktor Chernomyrdin, speaking at a conference organized by Lithuania and Poland in Vilnius, proposed a set of CSBMs for the Baltic Sea states with the aim of turning the region into a zone of low military activity.[25] Some of these suggestions were reiterated and supplemented with others in President Boris Yeltsin's speech in Stockholm on 3 December.[26] The proposed measures included: (*a*) a hot line between the military commands of the Kaliningrad region and the Baltic states for fast decision making on safe sea and air passage;[27] (*b*) Russia's commitment to hold only training manoeuvres in the Kaliningrad *oblast*;

---

[20] OSCE Ministerial Council document MC(6).DEC/2, 19 Dec. 1997, Decision No. 2, URL <http://www.osceprag.cz/news/mc06ej02.htm>, version current on 19 Dec. 1997.
[21] OSCE Press Release (note 16).
[22] *Trust and Verify*, issue 75 (May/June 1997), p. 4–5.
[23] *Trust and Verify*, issue 77 (Sep. 1997), p. 2.
[24] *OSCE Newsletter*, vol. 4, no. 11 (Nov. 1997).
[25] 'Russia: Chernomyrdin offers incentive for Baltic nonalignment', Interfax (Moscow), 5 Sep. 1997, in Foreign Broadcast Information Service, *Daily Report–Central Eurasia (FBIS-SOV)*, FBIS-SOV-97-248, 5 Sep. 1997.
[26] 'Text of Yeltsin address on Baltic security', ITAR-TASS World Service (Moscow), 3 Dec. 1997, FBIS-SOV-97-337, 3 Dec. 1997.
[27] After the Stockholm address, Commander of the Russian Baltic Fleet Admiral Vladimir Yegorov stressed that the strengthening of CBMs in the region is a priority, particularly lines of direct communication between the commanders and between their duty services and rescue teams. He said that such a communication line had already been installed between the Russian Baltic Fleet air-defence command and Poland's air-defence command. 'Russia: Baltic Fleet chief calls for military cooperation in region', ITAR-TASS (Moscow), 8 Dec. 1997, in FBIS-SOV-97-342, 8 Dec. 1997.

CONVENTIONAL ARMS CONTROL 539

(c) mutual notification of large-scale military exercises in the Baltic states and the neighbouring parts of Russia, including exercises involving forces from non-Baltic states, and the invitation of observers; (d) agreement on procedures for visiting military sites, going beyond the provisions of the Vienna Document; (e) the definition of Baltic Sea areas in which countries would refrain from naval exercises; (f) more reciprocal visits by warships; (g) a zone for joint military control over the airspace of the Baltic states including these states, the neighbouring parts of Russia, Poland, Finland and other Scandinavian countries; (h) joint exercises of military transport aviation; and (i) measures to prevent natural and man-made disasters.

Chernomyrdin also stressed that Russia would like to see additional restrictions on military exercises in the Baltic Sea region, over and above the framework of the CFE Treaty. However, all these arrangements were on condition that the Baltic states remain outside any military alliance (e.g., NATO or a bloc with Finland and Sweden).

The Russian proposals were received with caution. The rhetoric notwithstanding, the other Baltic Sea rim countries are concerned about the effect that the Russian suggestions would have on their security and political status. Criticism has therefore been voiced. Participation in major exercises, as proposed by Moscow, can and does take place through PFP activities; Russia has so far been a reluctant participant in this kind of endeavour. The idea of joint control of airspace, a critical question for military integration, would effectively hamstring the states' aspirations to join NATO. Moreover, leaving Norway, a NATO member, out of the confidence-building area in the Baltic region suggests that the goal is not so much military security collaboration in the eastern Baltic Sea as to control the security policies of the states concerned.[28]

South-eastern Europe

This part of the continent attracted considerable attention in 1997 owing to the arms control and confidence-building efforts under the Dayton Agreement in the former Yugoslavia, a move to start a military security debate among eight south-east European countries (Albania, Bulgaria, the Former Yugoslav Republic of Macedonia, Greece, Italy, Romania, Slovenia and Turkey), and continuing tension between Greece and Turkey, mainly over Cyprus.

The successful conclusion of weapon reductions under the Florence Agreement and the smooth implementation of CSBMs in Bosnia and Herzegovina enabled the start of the process of regional stabilization 'in and around the former Yugoslavia', as foreseen under Article V of Annex 1-B of the Dayton Agreement.[29] The OSCE Copenhagen Ministerial Council encouraged the Special Representative of the CIO, Ambassador Henry Jacolin, to start consultations on a precise mandate for the Article V negotiation, including the development of CSBMs and other appropriate measures adapted to specific regional security challenges.[30]

In early October defence ministers from the eight south-east European countries plus US Secretary of State for Defense William Cohen attended the South East Defence Ministerial meeting in Sofia, Bulgaria. The goal was to foster communication and cooperation among the defence ministers, to facilitate interoperability with

[28] Wagrowska, M., 'Jelcynowska strefa zaufania' [Yeltsin's confidence zone], *Rzeczpospolita*, 8 Dec. 1997, p. 7.
[29] See chapter 12 in this volume.
[30] OSCE (note 20).

NATO forces and to encourage NATO partners to play a more active role in the region. The CBMs discussed included high-level meetings, exchanges between military units, joint exercises and a possible regional conflict prevention and crisis management centre.[31]

Following numerous disputes and tensions between Greece and Turkey in the Aegean Sea over the US and NATO headquarters and over Cyprus in 1997, hopes for reducing the risk of accidental conflict were pinned on CSBMs between these two NATO states brokered by the USA in May 1997.[32] Cyprus promised not to invite Greek aircraft to overfly the island during the Greek military exercise; Turkey, in turn, committed itself not to overfly Cyprus as long as Greek aircraft did not do so. This step followed other CBMs such as hot lines between Athens and NATO and between Turkey and NATO and, from February 1997, a test programme sending pictures of Aegean activity to NATO headquarters in Naples.[33] However, renewed incidents and the military exercises carried out in the autumn of 1997 soon revived tensions in the region. In October, Greece and Cyprus held the Nikiforos exercise; in November, Turkey and Turkish Cypriots responded with the Toros manoeuvre. By holding these exercises, the parties involved violated and broke the moratorium on military overflights of Cyprus signed only six months previously.

VI. Conclusions

In spite of all the amendments added in recent years, the Vienna Document 1994 no longer provides an adequate framework for the security requirements of Europe. By initiating a review of the entire document, the FSC has taken an important step towards its adaptation in the light of new measures to enhance transparency, predictability and cooperation, which will complement the process of CFE Treaty adaptation. It is hoped that by the end of 1998 this process will lead to broader and more effective CSBMs for Europe. Within the framework of the security dialogue, the FSC decided to organize a seminar on defence policies and military doctrines in January 1998 to promote discussions on the evolution of military doctrines and their relationship to changes in the armed forces of the OSCE states.

Headway was made on the regional plane. Apart from the above-mentioned developments, a plethora of meetings and seminars in 1997 were devoted to regional endeavours, including confidence building and stability enhancement. In early June, the OSCE seminar on regional security and cooperation was held in Vienna in line with the 1996 Lisbon Summit Declaration, providing its participants with the opportunity to discuss a broad spectrum of relevant issues. In the FSC, the Netherlands has submitted a 'menu' of measures for use on a regional or subregional basis. In February 1998, Hungary and Slovakia signed an agreement on mutual CSBMs outside the framework of the Vienna Document. In late February 1998, the Black Sea countries (Bulgaria, Georgia, Romania, Russia, Turkey and Ukraine) agreed on guidelines for the conduct of negotiations on CSBMs relating to naval activities in the Black Sea.

---

[31] 'SE Europe ministers pledge defence steps', *New Europe*, issue 229 (12–18 Oct. 1997), p. 5.
[32] 'Text: Burns statement May 9 on Cyprus overflights', 9 May 1997, URL<gopher://198.80.36.82:70/0R23998315-23999557-range/archives/1997/pdq.97>, version current on 3 Apr. 1998.
[33] Migdalovitz, C., *Greece and Turkey: Aegean Issues—Background and Recent Developments*, CRS Report for Congress (Congressional Research Service, Library of Congress: Washington, DC, 21 Aug. 1997), p. 4.

Appendix 12B. Basic elements for CFE Treaty adaptation

DECISION OF THE JOINT CONSULTATIVE GROUP CONCERNING CERTAIN BASIC ELEMENTS FOR TREATY ADAPTATION

23 July 1997

1. In accordance with the document agreed at Lisbon on 1 December 1996, defining the scope and parameters for the process commissioned in paragraph 19 of the Final Document of the First CFE Treaty Review Conference, the States Parties have agreed upon certain of the Basic Elements which will govern the adaptation of the CFE Treaty; and have identified certain other Basic Elements upon which further work will be done. Both are recorded below.

GENERAL

2. The States Parties have decided that the bloc-to-bloc structure upon which the existing Treaty is based should be replaced. The Treaty will be adjusted to incorporate a specific system of national and territorial ceilings for Treaty Limited Equipment (TLE). The States Parties are agreed that there will be no increase in total numbers of TLE permitted in each category within the Treaty's area of application. Each State Party will base its agreement to the provisions of the adapted Treaty on its projections of the current and future situation in Europe.

A. National ceilings

3. National ceilings will be set, for each of the Treaty's five categories of TLE, at levels which recognize the legitimate security concerns of all States Parties and the need to ensure that the security of no State Party is diminished. While eliminating the group-to-group system of limitations, the setting of ceilings will be guided by the extant security circumstances within the area of application, including the relative security situation of each State Party whether individually or in association with others, with the purposes of ensuring equal security for all States Parties irrespective of their membership of a politico-military alliance and of strengthening their security relations and building trust and mutual reassurance.

4. In setting these ceilings, the States Parties reaffirm that they will take a restrained approach, maintaining only such military capabilities, individually or in conjunction with others, as are commensurate with individual or collective legitimate security needs, taking into account their international obligations, including the CFE Treaty.

5. For the existing 30 States Parties initial national ceilings may equate to, but not exceed, the up-to-date Maximum National Levels for Holdings (MNLHs) which have been notified under the existing Treaty. From this basis, in the spirit of restraint which States Parties are showing during the period of negotiation, and through a transparent and co-operative process, they will reach conclusions regarding reductions they might be prepared to take, with the aim of achieving a significant lowering in the total amount of TLE permitted in the area of application compatible with the legitimate defence requirements of each State Party. All relevant information on TLE within the area of application will be taken into account. National ceilings will be:

– Codified as binding limits in the adapted Treaty for all TLE in the area of application once agreed by consensus of all States Parties;

– Reviewed at the Treaty review conference in 2001 and at five-year intervals thereafter, taking into account relevant developments in the security situation and security structures. In conducting these reviews, States Parties, using agreed procedures, will balance the requirement for certainty and continuity of ceilings once established with flexibility to reflect new security realities as they may emerge and the need to ensure that the security of no State Party is diminished;

– Subject to rules and procedures which will be devised to govern the process of revisions to ceilings between Treaty review conferences, to ensure that no destabilizing accumulations of forces may occur. These should, *inter alia*, permit States Parties freely to declare and notify lower national ceilings at any time between such Treaty review conferences.

6. In setting national ceilings, States Parties will take into account all the levels of TLE established for the Atlantic-to-the-Urals area by the original CFE Treaty, the substantial reductions that have been carried out since then and those which States Parties will decide to carry out in the future, the changes to the situation in Europe, and the need to ensure that the security of no State Party is diminished.

7. They take note of the statements by certain States Parties which are annexed to this Decision.

8. Each State Party will base its agreement to the provisions of the adapted Treaty on all national ceilings of the States Parties, on its projections of the current and future security situation in Europe.

9. The States Parties will undertake further work to determine how to handle the Treaty's existing provisions relating to Designated Permanent Storage Sites (DPSS) in the context of Treaty adaptation.

B. Preventing destabilizing accumulations of forces

10. The States Parties are determined to sustain and strengthen the Treaty's effectiveness in preventing destabilizing accumulations of indigenous and stationed forces. They will seek to strengthen stability by further developing measures to prevent any potentially threatening build-up of conventional forces in particular regions. Treaty adaptation will include the following measures to this end:

Territorial ceilings

11. The existing structure of zones will be replaced by a system of territorial ceilings covering both national and stationed TLE, thus establishing total levels permitted on a permanent basis on the territory in the area of application of each State Party, or, if so decided, a portion thereof. These might be termed territorial units.

12. Individual territorial ceilings will be derived from current notified MNLHs, taking account of decisions reached in relation to DPSS provisions (paragraph 9) and of stationed forces. This does not preclude States Parties from notifying lower territorial ceilings.

Specific stabilizing measures

13. The adaptation process will include consideration of the possibility of establishing specific stabilizing measures, which might include measures of restraint or constraints in particular regions and areas of the Treaty's area of application, including Central and Eastern Europe, in order to prevent any potentially threatening build-up of conventional forces.

Stationed forces

14. In relation to stationed forces, the States Parties:

– Consider that the decisions taken at the First CFE Treaty Review Conference in relation to the provisions of Article IV, paragraph 5, must be fulfilled;

– Decide to develop additional information requirements and measures of transparency in respect of stationed forces, including pre-notification of changes in the equipment holdings of a stationed forces unit;

– Confirm that stationed forces must count against the national ceilings of the stationing State Party;

– Agree that territorial ceilings may constitute a means to constrain the TLE held by stationed forces;

– Take note that the statement made by the North Atlantic Council on 14 March 1997 covers all five categories of TLE;

– Will welcome further statements clarifying the intentions of States Parties on this issue.

15. In addition, and in conjunction with their efforts to promote the goals of enhancing stability and predictability in Europe, the States Parties will consider the possibility of developing, where appropriate, limitations or sub-ceilings on additional stationing of TLE. If such sub-ceilings are agreed to be feasible, the format, scope of application and details will be determined accordingly. Such limitations would have to be consistent with the inherent right of States to choose the means to ensure their own security. They would also be contingent upon detailed provisions for setting territorial ceilings and temporarily exceeding them being worked out to the satisfaction of all States Parties.

C. Relationship between treaty adaptation and Article V as modified by the Document agreed among the States Parties to the Treaty on Conventional Armed Forces in Europe of November 19, 1990, which forms Annex A to the Final Document of the First CFE Treaty Review Conference, May 1996

16. States Parties agree that the substance of Article V as modified by the Document

agreed among the States Parties to the Treaty on Conventional Armed Forces in Europe of November 19, 1990, which forms Annex A to the Final Document of the First CFE Treaty Review Conference, May 1996, which has recently entered into force, will be maintained but reconciled with the structure of the adapted Treaty as it emerges in detail throughout the negotiation, ensuring that the security of each State Party is not affected adversely at any stage.

D. Provisions for temporarily exceeding territorial ceilings

17. The States Parties have decided to include provisions to allow a State Party temporarily to receive, with its express consent, forces on its territory that would exceed its territorial ceiling for notified military exercises or as temporary deployments provided both are consistent with the objectives of an adapted Treaty.

Definitions, modalities, transparency, verification and consultation arrangements, and appropriate limitations will be negotiated.

18. The provisions developed for an adapted Treaty will allow for territorial ceilings to be temporarily exceeded by missions in support of peace under a mandate from the United Nations or the OSCE.

E. Accession by new Parties

19. The States Parties have decided that the adapted Treaty will be open to accession by States who may request it. This would be upon a case-by-case basis and would require the agreement of all States Parties. They will work together to draft the necessary accession clause, the details of which will reflect the revised Treaty structure as set out above.

F. Co-operative and consultative mechanisms

20. The States Parties will work co-operatively to establish:

– The necessary rules and mechanisms to govern arrangements for revising territorial ceilings, in accordance with the considerations set out in paragraphs 3 and 4;

– The necessary rules and mechanisms to govern arrangements for revising territorial ceilings, ensuring that such revisions do not lead to destabilizing accumulations of forces.

21. The States Parties recognize that the basis upon which they intend to adapt the Treaty, as outlined above, also requires certain modifications to the verification arrangements established in the Treaty, while retaining all their scope and detail, including possible additional inspection quotas and adjustments to quotas. The adaptation process also provides an opportunity for enhancement to the Treaty's verification and information exchange provisions. They will adopt a co-operative approach to devising the necessary modifications and in order to establish:

– The additional information requirements in respect of stationed forces referred to in paragraph 14;

– The definitions, modalities, transparency, verification and consultation arrangements and limitations referred to in paragraph 17;

– The provisions referred to in paragraph 18.

CONCLUSION

22. This Decision does not preclude other suggestions that are consistent with the Scope and Parameters agreed at Lisbon from being raised as the negotiation proceeds on this basis to its conclusion in accordance with the timetable established in the Scope and Parameters Document.

Source: Joint Consultative Group document no. JCG.DEC/8/97, Vienna, 23 July 1997.

13. The ban on anti-personnel mines

ZDZISLAW LACHOWSKI

I. Introduction

On 18 September 1997 agreement was reached in Oslo on the text of a convention to ban anti-personnel mines (APMs). The Convention on the Prohibition of the Use, Stockpiling, Production and Transfer of Anti-Personnel Mines and on their Destruction (the APM Convention)[1] was opened for signature in Ottawa on 3–4 December, where it was signed by 121 states, and from 5 December it could be signed at the United Nations Headquarters in New York. This achievement was the culmination of the 'Ottawa Process', the initiative launched by the Canadian Government in October 1996[2] and strongly supported by non-governmental organizations (NGOs) led by the International Campaign to Ban Landmines (ICBL) which, together with its coordinator Jody Williams, was awarded the Nobel Peace Prize for 1997.

'Landmine' is the broad term most commonly used for this type of weapon. The convention prohibits only APMs. It defines an APM as 'a mine designed to be exploded by the presence, proximity or contact of a person and that will incapacitate, injure or kill one or more persons', and a 'mine' as 'a munition designed to be . . . exploded by the presence, proximity or contact of a person or vehicle' (Article 2). Thus anti-tank and other anti-vehicle mines, and anti-ship mines at sea or in inland waterways, are not covered by the convention.

The pursuit of a ban on landmines has long been an international, public and governmental concern. Their military utility has been increasingly questioned and it has been estimated that they kill or maim over 2000 people each month, some 80 per cent of whom are civilians. It is estimated by the United Nations that more than 110 million landmines are deployed in some 70 countries.[3]

---

[1] The text of the convention is reproduced in appendix 13A in this volume.

[2] For more on the Ottawa Process, see Lachowski, Z., 'Conventional arms control', *SIPRI Yearbook 1997: Armaments, Disarmament and International Security* (Oxford University Press: Oxford, 1997), pp. 498–99.

[3] The UN Department of Humanitarian Affairs has published internationally accepted figures on the number of landmines deployed worldwide. Alongside these figures there has been an abundance of unfounded estimates. A tendency to exaggerate the numbers, e.g., by pro-ban activists, has sometimes created a sense of hopelessness that could adversely affect the process of mine clearance. Many such estimates are being reassessed. Even a UN estimate that 35 million mines had been laid in Afghanistan was later revised—to 10 million, and this is still considered to be an overestimate. Some sources claim that the total number deployed worldwide is closer to half the estimated over 110 million. World stockpiles (unreliably estimated at over 100 million) are being steadily reduced and fewer than 25 countries now produce landmines. UN estimates locate 85% of the landmine casualties in Afghanistan, Angola and Cambodia. Land Mine Facts, United Nations Demining Database, URL <http://www.un.org/Depts/Landmine/index.html>, version current on 18 Mar. 1998; Canadian Department of Foreign Affairs and International Trade, 'What is the extent of the anti-personnel (AP) mine problem?', URL <http://www.mines.gc.ca/faq-e.htm#problem>, version current on 19 Mar. 1998; and King, C., 'Legislation and the landmine', *Jane's Intelligence Review,* Special Report no. 16 (Nov. 1997).

SIPRI Yearbook 1998: Armaments, Disarmament and International Security

Since the early 1990s the efforts of NGOs and a group of like-minded governments have built a huge wave of international public opinion against landmines that has carried the cause of a prohibition forward at an impressive speed.

A significant shift in attitudes towards the elimination of APMs occurred in the mid-1990s. Progress was made in the wake of the 1995/96 Review Conference of the 1981 Convention on Prohibitions or Restrictions on the Use of Certain Conventional Weapons which May be Deemed to be Excessively Injurious or to Have Indiscriminate Effects (the CCW Convention). Often referred to as the 'Inhumane Weapons' Convention, this is the only convention in force that prohibits the use of 'mines, booby-traps and other devices' (Protocol II). The Review Conference underscored the extent of the problem, gained widespread support for a ban and, at its concluding session in May 1996, adopted an amended version of Protocol II of the convention, replacing and strengthening the provisions of the original protocol and adding further restrictions on the use, production and transfer of APMs. Despite the progress made it was largely the deficiencies of this amended protocol that led to a series of further steps and initiatives.[4] The subsequent momentum, especially after the initiative of the International Strategy Conference held in Ottawa on 3–5 October 1996 to pursue a complete ban on these weapons, was unprecedented, and the number of states supporting a ban grew during 1997 from some 50 to more than 120.

The vigorous and innovative anti-landmine campaign and constant pressure by NGOs generated wide-ranging public interest. It forced governments to take a more active position on the goal of a ban and stood in contrast to the lame efforts in a parallel forum, the Conference on Disarmament (CD). Unlike the successful Ottawa Process, grouping like-minded participants around a moral and humanitarian goal, the attempt to approach a ban on landmines in the CD failed in 1997. These two different approaches are examined in section II. The successful conclusion of the convention within the Ottawa Process is reported in section III, and the conclusions of the chapter are presented in section IV.

II. A two-track approach

During 1997 the ban on landmines was raised in two separate forums. The approaches of the CD and the Ottawa Process can be roughly classified as the 'arms control' and 'humanitarian' tracks, respectively.

Within the framework of this two-track approach, four different positions on a ban could be broadly distinguished at the beginning of the year:

[4] For a discussion of the CCW Review Conference and the amended Protocol II to the CCW Convention, see Goldblat, J., 'Land-mines and blinding laser weapons: the Inhumane Weapons Convention Review Conference', *SIPRI Yearbook 1996: Armaments, Disarmament and International Security* (Oxford University Press: Oxford, 1996), pp. 754–61; and Lachowski (note 2), pp. 496–97. As of 1 Jan. 1998 there were 71 parties to the CCW Convention and the amended Protocol II had been ratified by 12 states, with 8 more ratifications needed for its entry into force (see annexe A in this volume). The text of Protocol II, as amended on 3 May 1996, is reproduced in appendix 13A in this volume.

1. Many countries backed the Canadian-sponsored Ottawa Group, believing it to be the best forum in which to achieve their goal of a speedy prohibition (e.g., Austria, Belgium, Colombia, Denmark, Germany, Ireland, Malaysia, Mexico, Mozambique, the Netherlands, Nicaragua, Norway, Panama, Peru, the Philippines, Slovenia, South Africa, Sweden, Switzerland and Uruguay).

2. Some countries believed the CD to be the best forum because of its international disarmament functions but did not dismiss talks within the Ottawa Process as a complementary track towards the goal of a ban (e.g., Australia, France, Italy, Japan, the UK and the USA).

3. Another group rejected any talks on APMs outside the CD and were only prepared to work towards a ban through a lengthy, step-by-step negotiation process. Together with the second group, these countries saw a complete ban only as a long-term goal, but they were willing to negotiate a ban on transfers as the first step, while allowing the possession, use and manufacture of APMs to remain legitimate for an indefinite period of time (e.g., China, India, Iran, Iraq, Libya, Pakistan, Russia, Syria and Turkey).

4. Because of their location in areas of continuing or potential conflict and/or their inability to afford more costly weapons, other nations were opposed to a ban (e.g., Azerbaijan, Cuba, Ecuador, North Korea, South Korea and Sri Lanka).

During the course of the year a growing number of African, Latin American, Pacific and Western countries came to support the goal of an APM ban as pursued in the Ottawa framework.

The Conference on Disarmament

On 17 January 1997, the United States announced that it would observe a permanent ban on the export and transfer of APMs and that it would cap the US stockpile at the level of the current inventory.[5] In addition it unexpectedly decided to seek to initiate negotiations on a worldwide treaty banning the use, production, stockpiling and transfer of APMs in the Conference on Disarmament, which includes all the major landmine producers and exporters, rather than to pursue the Ottawa track. The CD, the only multilateral negotiating body dealing with the full range of disarmament issues, operates by the mechanism of consensus. The US decision was criticized by the proponents of the 'fast track' on various grounds because it would apply an arms control approach to what the Ottawa Group viewed as a humanitarian question and, as the CD is grappling with a serious institutional crisis, act as a potential brake on progress towards a ban. It was also feared that China and Russia, CD members outside the Ottawa Group and both opposed to a swiftly negotiated ban, and others might bog down or hamstring the entire negotiation process.

[5] Letter dated 21 January 1997 addressed to the Secretary-General of the Conference on Disarmament from the Permanent Representative of the United States of America to the Conference on Disarmament transmitting a Statement by the Press Secretary of the White House and a Fact Sheet on United States Initiatives on Anti-Personnel Landmines, CD document CD/1442, 22 Jan. 1997.

The US resistance to a complete ban that would mean giving up the US stockpile stemmed chiefly from the military's reluctance to abandon high-technology mines. According to Pentagon estimates (especially in the context of the Korean Peninsula) the proper use of 'smart' mines (i.e., those with self-destruction and self-deactivation mechanisms) can considerably reduce US casualties (reportedly by one-third) by limiting the mobility of an adversary's forces and offering early warning of attack.[6] The USA saw the Ottawa Process as leading to a double standard for the use of mines, with some states continuing to possess and use these weapons while parties to the treaty would be unable to use them in self-defence.[7] The military view was that the USA should focus on a comprehensive ban on the use of 'dumb' mines (those without self-destruction or self-deactivation mechanisms) and do all it could to slow down the whole process pending the development of alternative weapons.[8] In January 1997 the US Department of Defense announced that it was starting a programme to seek replacement technologies and would spend more than $9 million in the coming years on research and development (R&D) of alternative technologies.[9]

Nevertheless the USA retained the option of participating in the Ottawa Group either as a complementary effort which might give momentum to the work of the CD[10] or, if the CD failed to achieve anything substantial towards the goal of a landmine ban, as an alternative course.[11] Although doubtful of the US motives, the Ottawa Group states decided not to put obstacles in the way of introducing a landmine ban on the CD agenda and took the view that the two tracks—the Ottawa Process and the CD—could be complementary and mutually reinforcing.

Australia, France, the UK and, later, Italy followed the example of the Clinton Administration and supported its initiative to start phased talks in the CD beginning with negotiations to ban exports. In January the CD began the first part of its 1997 session. With two major proposals to be considered—a fissile material cut-off treaty and a landmine ban—it did not manage to agree on either the agenda or a programme of work until mid-February. The UK called for 'a universal, effectively verifiable and legally-binding international agreement to ban the use, stockpiling, production and transfer of anti-personnel landmines' and 'as a vital first step' towards a global ban on APM

---

[6] 'Pentagon may resist effort to ban anti-personnel mines', *Defense News*, 30 June–6 July 1997, p. 11.

[7] However, similar arguments were made regarding the CWC, which was eventually ratified by the USA on 27 Apr. 1997.

[8] US Department of Defense, Background Briefing on US Landmine Policy, 17 Jan. 1997.

[9] The Department of Defense was to spend $1.3 million in 1997 and requested $3 million for fiscal year 1998 and $5 million for fiscal year 1999. Report to the Secretary of Defense on the Status of DoD's Implementation of the US Policy on Anti-Personnel Landmines, Office of the Under Secretary for Policy, May 1997, URL <http:/www.defenselink.mil/pubs/landmines/#PURSUE>, version current on 12 Aug. 1997. In early 1998 the US Army Armament Research, Development and Engineering Center (ARDEC) awarded 3 contracts for the development and production of alternatives to landmines; 12 other companies have been invited to submit their offers.

[10] Interview with chief US negotiator Stephen Ledogar, *International Herald Tribune*, 27 Jan. 1997, p. 9.

[11] 'Tale of two treaties', *Washington Post*, 14 Apr. 1997, p. A16.

exports, imports and transfers.[12] The main motive for this step-by-step approach was the attempt by Western diplomats to encourage China, India and Russia to enter into landmine negotiations in the CD.[13] Nevertheless, the agenda for 1997 adopted by the CD on 14 February did not include a comprehensive landmine ban, confirming the fears of the proponents of the Ottawa approach that the ban would not be raised there during the year.

Russia, reluctant to seek an immediate ban for the same reason as China (the need to defend long borders), argued that mine-clearance efforts should be intensified and that moratoria on exporting APMs should be imposed and maintained. Russia questioned the feasibility and costs of verifying the ban effectively and warned of the use of APMs by non-state actors. At the Ottawa Process meeting in Vienna in February 1997 (see below) Russia was reported to have signalled its willingness to discuss a step-by-step approach to a total ban on mines, starting with an export ban, to be followed by outlawing production and, eventually, the destruction of all stockpiles.[14]

China also showed signs of changing its position during the year. In late June its representative at the CD announced that, while it could not agree to an immediate prohibition, China was in favour of imposing restrictions on APMs and their use as a step towards achieving a ban.[15]

A dozen or so CD participants did not want to ban APMs or discuss restrictions in either the CD or any other context. On 12 June the Mexican representative reiterated that his delegation was not convinced that the CD was the appropriate forum in which to deal with a ban on APMs.[16] A number of states shared the view that the priority of the CD was nuclear disarmament,[17] and the May/June part of the 1997 session of the CD therefore saw a stalemate on APMs. The CD was unable to reach agreement on establishing an ad hoc committee and almost failed to adopt the Australian proposal to appoint a special coordinator to conduct consultations on the 'most appropriate arrangement' to deal with landmines.[18] It was only on 26 June, on the eve of the closure of the second part of the session, that the deadlock was overcome and the CD adopted a decision to appoint a special coordinator to conduct consultations on a possible mandate on landmines, thus de-linking the question from nuclear issues and paving the way for more substantial action.[19]

[12] United Kingdom of Great Britain and Northern Ireland proposal. Draft mandate for an Ad Hoc Committee on a 'Ban on Anti-Personnel Landmines', CD document, CD/1443, 30 Jan. 1997.
[13] Robert Bell, Senior Director for Defense Policy and Arms Control for the US National Security Council, stressed the military utility of APMs and claimed that a ban not including the participation of China and Russia would amount to 'giving up the military benefit but not achieving your humanitarian goal'. *Guardian Weekly*, 26 Jan. 1997, p. 8.
[14] Agence France-Presse (Paris), 'Russia considers "step-by-step approach" on mines', 14 Feb. 1997, in Foreign Broadcast Information Service, *Daily Report–West Europe (FBIS–WEU)*, FBIS-WEU-97-032, 14 Feb. 1997.
[15] Conference on Disarmament document CD/PV.770, 26 June 1997.
[16] Conference on Disarmament document CD/PV.767, 12 June 1997.
[17] Conference on Disarmament (note 15); and Johnson, R., 'Geneva update no. 37', *Disarmament Diplomacy*, no. 17 (July/Aug. 1997), p. 20.
[18] See the Australian proposal, CD/1458, 22 May 1997, in *Disarmament Diplomacy*, May 1997, p. 13.
[19] Conference on Disarmament document CD/1466, 26 June 1997.

After the Ottawa Process International Conference on a Global Ban on Anti-Personnel Mines, held in Brussels on 24–27 June, it was evident that this movement at the CD would not affect the Canadian-sponsored track of negotiations. Moreover, in another volte-face on 18 August the USA announced its intention to participate fully in the Oslo meeting of the Ottawa Group in September.[20]

Having consulted with CD delegations, appointed special coordinator John Campbell, Australian Ambassador to the CD, identified four possible options for dealing with APMs in 1998: (*a*) a comprehensive mandate; (*b*) a phased or step-by-step approach towards a global ban, starting with a ban on exports, imports and transfers of APMs; (*c*) a partial approach focusing on discrete issues (without the overall declared goal of the total elimination of landmines); and (*d*) an ad hoc committee, without a negotiating mandate, to review and discuss the situation.[21] According to Campbell the greatest support was for option *b*; however, it was evident that most delegations preferred to decide on a specific mandate only after the APM Convention was signed, that is, in early 1998.[22]

The CD concluded the final part of its 1997 session in September. It had been unable to agree on a work programme earlier in the year and remained torn between the non-aligned states, advocating the priority of nuclear issues, and the Western states, wanting to focus on a fissile material cut-off and landmine negotiations.

The failure of the CD in 1997, not only on APMs but also on all other disarmament issues (prevention of nuclear war, prevention of an arms race in outer space, control of new types of weapons of mass destruction, comprehensive disarmament, negative assurances and transparency in armaments), many of which have been on the CD agenda for some 20 years, showed the institution to be in deep crisis. This led to strong criticism and proposals for quickly breaking the deadlock.[23]

The Ottawa Process

The Ottawa Process, however, picked up steam during 1997 and the Ottawa Group augmented its ranks at an unexpected rate. In October 1996 Canada's Foreign Minister Lloyd Axworthy had entrusted Austria, host of the next Ottawa Process meeting, with drafting an agreement. Experts from 111 states met behind closed doors on 12–14 February 1997 in Vienna to discuss the

[20] 'US to join Ottawa treaty process on landmines', *USIS Washington File*, URL <gopher://198.80.36.82:70/0R44066250-44069169-range/archives/1997/pdq.97>, version current on 18 Aug. 1997. The USA formally reported its decision to the CD on 21 Aug. 1997. Conference on Disarmament document CD/PV.755, 21 Aug. 1997.

[21] Conference on Disarmament document CD/PV.774, 14 Aug. 1997.

[22] Johnson (note 17), p. 20. In fact the issue of landmines was not included on the agenda adopted in Feb. 1998 (which was identical to the 1997 agenda).

[23] For more on the crisis of the CD and proposed remedies see, e.g., Johnson, R., 'Making the Conference on Disarmament accountable to the United Nations', *Disarmament Diplomacy*, no. 17 (July/Aug. 1997), pp. 2–6; and Goldblat, J., 'The CD on the brink', *Disarmament Diplomacy*, no. 18 (Sep. 1997), pp. 2–3.

Austrian draft as a basis for the Ottawa Group discussions on banning the development, production, acquisition, storage, sale or use of APMs. China did not participate but Cuba, Egypt, Finland, India, Pakistan, Russia, Turkey and Ukraine sent observers.

The points in the Austrian draft which led to most discussion were the definition of APMs and the mechanisms for the verification and implementation of the intended ban. Clarification was requested regarding a clause on the acquisition or retention of APMs in 'small amounts'. The comprehensiveness of the agreement was the subject of debate, and only Cuba, Ecuador, South Korea and Sri Lanka defended their right to use mines for self-defence.[24]

The verification issue

One of the major sticking-points in addressing the ban was how and to what extent compliance could be verified. At the 120-nation International Expert Meeting on Possible Verification Measures for a Convention to Ban Anti-Personnel Landmines, held in Königswinter, Germany, on 24–25 April 1997, two approaches to verification clashed. Those who considered the convention to be essentially an arms control agreement (led by Germany, which wanted compliance to be made verifiable through an elaborate verification regime) favoured an intrusive verification system based on arrangements similar to those of other conventions (e.g., the Chemical Weapons Convention and the CCW Convention)—that is, regular and comprehensive information exchange, consultations to resolve disputes and substantive issues, prosecution of convention violations, fact-finding to monitor national measures, UN involvement in verification, and so on. In turn, the advocates of a humanitarian approach (with Mexico playing a prominent role) were against such instruments, propounding purist legal arguments and stressing the impracticality of such verification endeavours. They saw APMs as a special category of weapon not appropriate for traditional arms control and would only accept voluntary steps by states, a loose network of cooperative confidence-building and transparency measures, a regular review of the agreement, and systematic reporting and information exchanges. The question of the cost of a strict verification regime was also raised. The emergence of a middle course was reported by the International Expert Meeting, combining comprehensive cooperation and transparency with possible fact-finding measures.[25]

The Ottawa Process strove for a compromise between these divergent approaches to compliance, which led to weaker verification and enforcement components and an increased emphasis on cooperative aspects.

---

[24] Walkling, S., '111 states consider draft treaty banning anti-personnel landmines', *Arms Control Today*, vol. 27, no. 2 (Mar. 1997), p. 23.

[25] Letter dated 21 May 1997 to the Secretary-General of the Conference by the Representative of the Federal Republic of Germany, transmitting a summary of the International Expert Meeting on Possible Verification Measures for a Convention to Ban Anti-Personnel Landmines, held in Königswinter, Germany, on 24 and 25 April 1997, Conference on Disarmament document CD/1459, 22 May 1997.

Keeping up the momentum

In the run-up to the December 1997 Ottawa meeting the 115-state group (plus observers from 37 other states) met on 24–27 June in Brussels at the International Conference for a Global Ban on Anti-Personnel Mines to advance the process towards a comprehensive ban. In a declaration signed by 97 countries the conference affirmed that the essential elements of such an agreement should include: (*a*) a comprehensive ban on the use, stockpiling, production and transfer of anti-personnel mines; (*b*) the destruction of stockpiled and removed anti-personnel mines; and (*c*) international cooperation and assistance in the field of mine clearance in affected countries.[26] The aim of the next conference, held in Oslo on 1–19 September 1997, was to agree on the text of the convention.

In the meantime, numerous conferences were held to broaden the political support for a ban. The ICBL, the International Committee of the Red Cross (ICRC) and other NGOs actively promoted a ban by organizing workshops and coordinating action on several continents, and a growing number of states and international organizations announced their intention to join the pro-ban movement.[27] Africa is the most mine-infested region of the world. The 4th annual International NGO Conference on Landmines organized to support the ICBL in late February in Maputo, Mozambique, appealed to all governments to enhance their efforts in the conference Toward a Mine-Free Southern Africa[28] and was followed by other regional meetings. Between the October 1996 Ottawa Conference and the May 1997 Organization of African Unity (OAU) Conference Towards a Landmine-Free Africa,[29] Botswana, Burundi, Cape Verde, Guinea-Bissau, Lesotho, Malawi, Mauritius, Sierra Leone and Swaziland committed themselves to the ban. Mozambique, South Africa, Tanzania, Zambia and Zimbabwe also supported the Ottawa Process.[30] In early March the Japanese Government hosted the Tokyo Conference on Anti-Personnel Landmines, attended by 27 states, the European Union (EU) and 10 other international organizations. Five Central Asian states, with other Asian countries attending as observers, held a conference in June to discuss a landmine ban and mine clearance. National and international conferences and seminars took place in East, Central and South Asia, Australia, New Zealand

[26] Letter dated 9 July 1997 addressed to the Secretariat of the Conference on Disarmament by the Office of the Permanent Representative of Belgium to the Conference on Disarmament, transmitting the Closing Document of the Brussels International Conference for a Global Ban on Anti-Personnel Mines, CD/1467, 16 July 1997, p. 2.

[27] One of the goals of the ICBL was to stigmatize mine producers and pressure them to cease producing both mines and components. In the USA 17 of 47 landmine-manufacturing companies pledged to cease production. *Washington Times*, 18 Apr. 1997, p. A26.

[28] Final Declaration of the 4th International NGO Conference on Landmines, Toward a Mine-Free Southern Africa, Maputo, Mozambique, 25–28 Feb. 1997.

[29] This was the first comprehensive government-sponsored conference on landmines in Africa. *Towards a Landmine-Free Africa: The OAU and the Legacy of Anti-personnel Mines,* Proceedings of the First Continental Conference of African Experts on Landmines, 19–21 May 1997, World Trade Centre, Kempton Park (Institute for Security Studies: Johannesburg, 1997).

[30] *Landmine Update* (International Campaign to Ban Landmines), Part I, Ban treaty meetings, no. 5 (June 1997). Egypt is believed to be the only country in Africa still producing APMs.

and Europe, furthering national, regional and international, governmental and non-governmental endeavours to build public awareness of landmines and to effectively promote the ban.[31]

Apart from the impact of the Ottawa Process much depended on the major powers. In the USA the campaign led by Senator Patrick Leahy (Democrat) to revise US landmine policy to follow the Ottawa approach gathered new momentum. For all the opposition of the US Joint Chiefs of Staff, a growing number of military, both retired generals and current commanders, started to call into question the battlefield utility of APMs. In June 56 members of the Senate, led by Leahy and Senator Chuck Hagel (Republican), introduced legislation to ban the use of APMs by US forces from the year 2000, thus supporting the Canadian initiative. In addition, a bipartisan group of 160 congressmen urged the president to support the Ottawa effort.[32]

The newly elected governments in France and the UK also revised their countries' landmine policies. The British, French and German[33] initiative of 4 May, supported by Italy, to work together for a total ban 'in international fora' was expected to strengthen the search to eliminate the mines. Additionally, on 21 May the new British Labour Government pledged the total destruction of British landmines by 2005[34] and backed the Ottawa Process while supporting efforts to enable the CD to make headway on the ban. During the June conference in Brussels, France expressed support for the Ottawa Process and affirmed that it would reverse its earlier insistence on permitting exceptional use[35] by the time the treaty was signed or by 1999, whichever came first, and Italy both supported outlawing the use and production of APMs and pledged to renounce their operational use.

III. From Oslo to Ottawa

The Oslo Conference for a Global Ban on Anti-Personnel Landmines took place on 1–19 September 1997 with the aim of adopting a text for the convention. China, Cuba, Egypt, India, Iran, Iraq, Israel, North Korea, South Korea, Pakistan, Russia and Syria did not participate. Several states had NGO representatives in their delegations. Decisions were made by a two-thirds majority vote, and as a result the language of most of the convention, except for a few articles, was finalized within the first three days. Apart from US demands in Oslo, the main sticking-points were paragraphs in the Austrian draft regarding the definition of APMs, references to the CD and compliance.[36]

---

[31] For more information on anti-landmine activities, see *Landmine Update* (note 30).
[32] *International Herald Tribune*, 13 June 1997, p. 3.
[33] *International Herald Tribune*, 8 May 1997, p. 5. Germany had already renounced the use of APMs and announced that it would destroy its existing stockpiles by the end of the year.
[34] *Financial Times*, 22 May 1997, p. 3.
[35] Lachowski (note 2), p. 499.
[36] Velin, J.-A., 'Stage three of the Ottawa process: the Oslo diplomatic conference', *Disarmament Diplomacy*, no. 18 (Sep. 1997), pp. 6–8.

The Oslo Conference: the US end-game thwarted

On 18 August 1997, two weeks before the Oslo Conference began, the USA announced its intention to take part as a full participant. During the negotiation in Oslo the US Administration sought five 'improvements' to the draft text: (*a*) the strengthening of the verification provisions (enhanced transparency); (*b*) an exemption for the Korean Peninsula;[37] (*c*) the unrestricted right of withdrawal from the treaty; (*d*) a nine-year term for entry into force; and (*e*) an exemption for anti-handling devices placed near anti-tank mines to protect them.[38] Facing strong opposition from other delegations, the USA eventually reduced its preconditions to three: (*a*) the elimination of landmines in Korea within nine years of entry into force; (*b*) the possibility to withdraw from the treaty during a conflict; and (*c*) an exemption for explosive devices combined with anti-tank mines in canisters.[39] As regards *c*, the USA sought to exempt its 'smart' mines—GATOR, Volcano and MOMPS—from the APM category, presenting them as submunitions or anti-handling devices, but was quickly reminded that at the CCW Review Conference it had classified them as APMs. Despite vigorous US efforts, including last-minute compromises, and despite the willingness of a number of states, such as Australia, Germany and Spain, to support some of these demands, the US amendments were effectively opposed by the majority of other states and NGOs determined 'not to pay any price' for the USA climbing on the bandwagon ('no exceptions, no reservations and no loopholes'). On 17 September the Clinton Administration, under heavy pressure from the US Joint Chiefs of Staff, decided to withdraw and not to sign the final text in December. On 18 September, 89 countries accepted the final text of the convention.

Together with the Oslo Conference, the 10 October announcement that the ICBL and Jody Williams, who played the decisive role in finalizing the text of the APM Convention, were to be awarded the Nobel Peace Prize for 1997 gave another impetus to the Ottawa Process and attracted support from other states in the run-up to the Ottawa meeting. In October Australia and Greece,[40]

---

[37] The USA has removed all its landmines except those in Guantanamo, Cuba, which will be removed by 1999, and the Korean Peninsula, where its objective is to have them removed by 2006—by which time alternatives to APMs might have been developed.

[38] 'Transcript: briefing by NSC staffer on US land-mine policy', *USIS Washington File*, 17 Sep. 1997, URL<gopher://198.80.36.82:70/0R48198828-48224531-range/archives/1997/pdq.97>, version current on 17 Sep. 1997; and Institute for Defense and Disarmament Studies, *Arms Control Reporter* (IDDS: Brookline, Mass.), sheet 708.B.26, 1997.

[39] Cohen, W. S., 'Clinton's position is necessary and right', *Washington Post*, 19 Sep. 1997.

[40] This left Turkey and the USA as the only NATO countries outside the Ottawa Process. At the ministerial meeting in Dec. 1997, the NATO ministers stated obliquely that '[w]e will take the necessary action to ensure that national obligations under the Convention are compatible with our obligations under the North Atlantic Treaty'. NATO Final Communiqué, 16 Dec. 1997, *NATO Review*, no. 1 (spring 1998), pp. D1–D5. This showed a measure of disagreement among the Allies, especially regarding US landmines stockpiled in many NATO countries, including Germany, Norway and Turkey. Another signatory with US stockpiles on its territory is Japan. Kyodo (Tokyo), 28 Nov. 1997, in 'Japan: Obuchi hopes for landmine treaty ratification in January', Foreign Broadcast Information Service, *Daily Report–East Asia (FBIS-EAS)*, FBIS-EAS-97-334, 30 Nov. 1997. Among the EU states, only Finland is not prepared to sign the convention in the near future. 'Replacing landmines will cost billions', *Helsinginsanomat* (Helsinki), 23 Nov. 1997, in 'Finland: military studying landmine substitution', FBIS-WEU-97-349, 15 Dec. 1997.

and soon thereafter Romania, announced their support for the convention. On 27 November Japan officially announced that it would sign the convention and it was soon followed by Bulgaria, Croatia and other states. Even Russia seemed to be warming to the goal of a ban.[41]

On 3–4 December 1997 in Ottawa, 121 states signed the convention,[42] and by 1 January 1998 there were 123 signatures and 3 ratifications.[43]

The APM Convention

The APM Convention is a disarmament agreement which aims to eliminate, not just to limit, a category of weapons. The text is short, simple and direct. It comprises 22 articles and envisages no reservations or exceptions for specific types of weapon or their conditional use. Moral and humanitarian considerations are to the fore and APMs are clearly defined as mines designed to be exploded by the direct 'presence, proximity or contact of a person' (Article 2), not just as those 'primarily' designed to do so. (This controversial word from the amended CCW Protocol II was dropped). The definition explicitly excludes anti-tank and anti-vehicle mines equipped with 'anti-handling devices' to ward off tampering. An anti-handling device is defined as a device 'intended to protect a mine and which is part of, linked to, attached to or placed under the mine'. The US proposal at the Oslo Conference to exempt anti-handling devices placed 'near' the mine, which would have meant that three US systems with anti-personnel components would not have been classed as APMs, was not adopted.

Under the terms of the convention, small amounts of APMs—'the minimum number absolutely necessary'—can be retained or transferred for the development of and training in mine detection, clearance or destruction techniques, and the transfer of APMs for the purpose of destruction is permitted (Article 3). All other stockpiled APMs are to be destroyed within four years of entry into force of the convention (Article 4); all those in mined areas under a state party's 'jurisdiction or control' are to be destroyed as soon as possible but not later than 10 years after entry into force; and a party may request an extension of up to 10 years to complete destruction (Article 5). The convention envisages that each party may seek and receive aid from other parties and that states 'in a position to do so' will provide assistance for the care and rehabilitation of mine victims, mine-awareness programmes, mine clearance

---

[41] During his visit to the Council of Europe in Strasbourg on 10 Oct. 1997, President Boris Yeltsin stated that Russia would work to reach a solution and sign the convention. The next day, however, his press service issued a clarifying statement to the effect that Russia will sign the convention 'when necessary conditions are laid for this'. 'Statement clarifies Russia's stance on land mine ban', ITAR-TASS (Moscow), 11 Oct. 1997, in Foreign Broadcast Information Service, *Daily Report–Central Eurasia (FBIS–SOV)*, FBIS-SOV-97-284, 11 Oct. 1997. During a later visit to Canada, Yeltsin announced Russia's extension of its moratorium on landmine exports 'until the convention is signed'. 'Russia to extend moratorium on land mines export', ITAR-TASS World Service (Moscow), 20 Oct. 1997, in FBIS-SOV-97-293, 20 Oct. 1997.

[42] According to the Canadian hosts, 125 states had asked to sign the convention; several did not come with the proper signing authority from their governments and were expected to sign later in New York.

[43] These are listed in annexe A in this volume. Canada, Ireland and Mauritius ratified the convention in 1997. The Holy See and Turkmenistan did so in Jan. 1998.

and the destruction of stockpiled APMs (Article 6). Within one year of the convention's entry into force, states parties are to submit to the UN Secretary-General (the depositary of the convention) detailed information on their stockpiled mines and the locations of all their minefields and mined areas known to them; this information is to be updated annually. Regarding compliance the absence of such terms as 'verification' or 'inspection' shows that the states parties have practically abandoned enforcement and verification (Article 8).[44] Instead fact-finding missions authorized by a regular or special meeting of states parties are envisaged. In short, the focus is on the good will and cooperation of the participating states and on the prevention of widespread use rather than on minor individual violations. Review conferences are to be convened every five years after entry into force. Amendments to the convention may be proposed at any time after entry into force and may be adopted by a two-thirds majority vote of states parties present and voting at a specially convened Amendment Conference.

The convention will enter into force six months after the 40th instrument of ratification, acceptance, approval or accession has been deposited with the UN Secretary-General (Article 17). When the convention has entered into force, ratification or accession by a state will take effect after six months. The convention will be of unlimited duration. No article is subject to reservation (Article 19), but states parties may withdraw from the convention with six months' notice, except in time of conflict (Article 20).

Demining

In 1997, in parallel with the pursuit of a ban, increasing attention was paid to mine-clearance programmes. Simply banning APMs neither reduces casualties nor facilitates the restoration of land to agriculture or development; these objectives must be achieved by demining.[45]

International demining activities are sponsored, carried out and coordinated by different international organizations. The United Nations has continued its mine-clearance actions (initiated through its mine action centres established in cooperation with national governments in poor countries) since the first operation in Afghanistan in 1989. By October 1997 more than 40 countries and organizations had contributed a total of $32.5 million and pledged an additional $9 million to the UN Voluntary Trust Fund for Assistance in Mine Clearing (established in 1994). Among the largest contributors are the EU, Denmark, Germany, Italy, Japan, Norway, Sweden, Switzerland, the UK and the USA.[46] The UN currently coordinates mine-clearance programmes in 13

[44] The convention also does not mention 'non-state actors', or terrorists, guerrillas and other criminal groups.

[45] According to UN estimates, removing all mines currently in the ground will cost $50–100 billion, and at the present rate of clearance it will take a decade to complete the job (in contrast to the figure of more than 1100 years, which has been widely quoted). 'Banning, clearing mines a top priority for UN, US', *USIS Washington File,* 17 Dec. 1997, URL <gopher://198.80.36.82:70/R67968305-67977625-range/archives/1997/pdq.97>, version current on 17 Dec. 1997.

[46] UN Department of Public Information, Fighting landmines: the Ottawa process and the United Nations role, Report no. DPI/1942, 10 Nov. 1997.

countries—Afghanistan, Angola, Bosnia and Herzegovina, Cambodia, Croatia, Georgia, Guatemala, Iraq, Laos, Mozambique, Somalia, Sudan and Tajikistan.

In August 1997 the World Bank agreed, for the first time in its history, to finance landmine clearance. A $16.2 million effort is now under way in Bosnia and Herzegovina.[47] In November the European Commission earmarked 15 million European currency units (c. $17 million) for a research programme to promote new technologies to identify and deactivate APMs.[48]

The USA has provided remarkable support to landmine removal. It spent $153 million in 1993–97 and planned to spend $68 million in 1998. Its demining assistance programmes have included 17 mine-infested countries since 1993. On 31 October 1997 Secretary of State Madeleine Albright and Defense Secretary William Cohen announced the US-led Demining 2010 Initiative to remove all APMs from over 64 countries by the year 2010, under which the USA will expand its demining programme by increasing funding to $77 million in 1998.[49] It aims to harness financial and material support from private and public sectors and increase to $1 billion resources to identify and clear landmines. Ambassador Karl Indefurth was appointed special representative of the US President and Secretary of State for global humanitarian demining. In 1998 the USA will host a conference on the initiative, bringing together donors, afflicted countries, international demining organizations and NGOs to coordinate the mine-removing efforts.[50]

IV. Conclusions

The conclusion of the APM Convention in 1997 illustrates a significant change in the basis of security in the post-cold war world. Security is no longer a matter of limiting the levels of military forces and equipment. It reaches beyond traditional arms control into the realm of the laws of war and, more broadly, the humanitarian and development dimensions. The APM Convention differs significantly from other disarmament and arms control agreements in its concern not so much with the military utility of weapons as with their longer-term impact—it calls for the elimination of a whole category of weapons that pose a residual threat long after a conflict has ended. It seeks broad humanitarian benefits rather than the reduction of unnecessary suffering on the battlefield. In the face of the vigorous landmine ban campaign many countries felt compelled to set aside military considerations, seeing political expedience in signing the convention.[51] For the first time, a grassroots cam-

---

[47] *Atlantic News*, no. 2942 (21 Aug. 1997), p. 2.

[48] Reuters, 'EU to launch into landmine removal', 18 Nov. 1997.

[49] 'Albright, Cohen announce U.S. demining initiative', *USIS Washington File*, URL <gopher://198.80.36.82:70/0R58684819-58702252-range/archives/1997/pdq.97>, version current on 31 Oct. 1997.

[50] For more detail, see 'Colonel G. K. Cunningham details global demining effort', *USIS Washington File*, URL <gopher://198.80.36.82:70/0R68460202-68477393-range/archives/1997/pdq.97>, version current on 19 Dec. 1997.

[51] Vinson, N., 'The demise of the anti-personnel mine: a military perspective', *RUSI Journal*, vol. 143, no. 1 (Feb. 1998), pp. 18–23.

paign cum interstate negotiation led to a disarmament agreement outside the framework of the United Nations and without the decisive involvement of the major powers.

Meanwhile, the CD is in the grip of a crisis. Although proceeding from different perspectives, the Ottawa Process and the CD tracks have not been mutually exclusive. They share some participants and the same ultimate goal—a total ban on a category of indiscriminate weapons whose value has been increasingly questioned, on the one hand, and that has continued to cause civilian casualties, on the other. Each track has followed its own methods and procedures. Taking advantage of the continuing momentum the world over, the Ottawa Group strove to achieve the goal swiftly, thoroughly and with the greatest possible number of like-minded participants—and succeeded. Enjoying the support of networks of NGOs, it was organized around a measure of idealism, a clear, unambiguous purpose and the strong motivation to rid the world of these weapons effectively and once and for all. The Canadian initiative reinforced a norm of moral behaviour; it aimed to make landmines universally unacceptable and compel the 'hold-outs' ultimately to accept the terms of the convention. The main challenges for the Ottawa Process are to keep up the momentum and gather the 40 ratifications required for the convention's entry into force as soon as possible and, in the longer term, to assure universal adherence.

It remains to be seen whether the convention will result in a truly workable ban and the eventual elimination of APMs throughout the world. Its critics are keen to point out that nearly three-quarters of the Ottawa Group participants are virtually unaffected by landmines. The timetable and costs of implementation of the destruction provisions of the convention are challenging and will require a great deal of effort by individual states parties and considerable international cooperation and assistance. Apart from the lack of strong compliance guarantees and enforcement provision, another shortcoming is the lack of measures to ensure that landmines are not used by non-state actors (terrorists, guerrillas and insurgents). In addition, the issue of storage of US APMs on the territories of US allies which have signed the convention is bound to emerge as they embark upon ratification.

The achievement of the Ottawa Process could well be strengthened by complementary efforts by the CD. The CD is an exclusive body of participants working laboriously by consensus and on a step-by-step basis, overcoming disparate political and security interests, aims and world outlooks. It is handicapped by a group of developing countries that link the issue of nuclear disarmament to the other issues before it, including the landmine ban. Nevertheless the CD is believed to have a role to play in negotiating and elaborating verification arrangements and in engaging reluctant participants, notably China and Russia, in the ban. The main advantage of the CD is that it is a body representing different groups of countries and includes all the major producers and exporters of landmines. It remains to be seen how quickly it will manage to overcome its stalemate, embark upon businesslike talks and contribute to the effective elimination of landmines.

Appendix 13A. Documents on the prohibition of anti-personnel mines

PROTOCOL ON PROHIBITIONS OR RESTRICTIONS ON THE USE OF MINES, BOOBY-TRAPS AND OTHER DEVICES AS AMENDED ON 3 MAY 1996 (PROTOCOL II AS AMENDED ON 3 MAY 1996)

Annexed to the Convention on Prohibitions or Restrictions on the Use of Certain Conventional Weapons which may be Deemed to be Excessively Injurious or to have Indiscriminate Effects

ARTICLE 1: AMENDED PROTOCOL

The Protocol on Prohibitions or Restrictions on the Use of Mines, Booby-Traps and Other Devices (Protocol II), annexed to the Convention on Prohibitions or Restrictions on the Use of Certain Conventional Weapons Which May Be Deemed to Be Excessively Injurious or to Have Indiscriminate Effects ('the Convention') is hereby amended. The text of the amended Protocol shall read as follows:

Article 1

SCOPE OF APPLICATION

1. This Protocol relates to the use on land of the mines, booby-traps and other devices, defined herein, including mines laid to interdict beaches, waterway crossings or river crossings, but does not apply to the use of anti-ship mines at sea or in inland waterways.
2. This Protocol shall apply, in addition to situations referred to in Article 1 of this Convention, to situations referred to in Article 3 common to the Geneva Conventions of 12 August 1949. This Protocol shall not apply to situations of internal disturbances and tensions, such as riots, isolated and sporadic acts of violence and other acts of a similar nature, as not being armed conflicts.
3. In case of armed conflicts not of an international character occurring in the territory of one of the High Contracting Parties, each party to the conflict shall be bound to apply the prohibitions and restrictions of this Protocol.
4. Nothing in this Protocol shall be invoked for the purpose of affecting the sovereignty of a State or the responsibility of the Government, by all legitimate means, to maintain or re-establish law and order in the State or to defend the national unity and territorial integrity of the State.
5. Nothing in this Protocol shall be invoked as a justification for intervening, directly or indirectly, for any reason whatever, in the armed conflict or in the internal or external affairs of the High Contracting Party in the territory of which that conflict occurs.
6. The application of the provisions of this Protocol to parties to a conflict, which are not High Contracting Parties that have accepted this Protocol, shall not change their legal status or the legal status of a disputed territory, either explicitly or implicitly.

Article 2

DEFINITIONS

For the purpose of this Protocol:
1. 'Mine' means a munition placed under, on or near the ground or other surface area and designed to be exploded by the presence, proximity or contact of a person or vehicle.
2. 'Remotely-delivered mine' means a mine not directly emplaced but delivered by artillery, missile, rocket, mortar, or similar means, or dropped from an aircraft. Mines delivered from a land-based system from less than 500 metres are not considered to be 'remotely delivered', provided that they are used in accordance with Article 5 and other relevant Articles of this Protocol.
3. 'Anti-personnel mine' means a mine primarily designed to be exploded by the presence, proximity or contact of a person and that will incapacitate, injure or kill one or more persons.
4. 'Booby-trap' means any device or material which is designed, constructed, or adapted to kill or injure, and which functions unexpectedly when a person disturbs or approaches an apparently harmless object or performs an apparently safe act.
5. 'Other devices' means manually-emplaced munitions and devices including improvised explosive devices designed to kill, injure or damage and which are actuated manually, by remote control or automatically after a lapse of time.
6. 'Military objective' means, so far as objects are concerned, any object which by its

nature, location, purpose or use makes an effective contribution to military action and whose total or partial destruction, capture or neutralization, in the circumstances ruling at the time, offers a definite military advantage.

7. 'Civilian objects' are all objects which are not military objectives as defined in paragraph 6 of this Article.

8. 'Minefield' is a defined area in which mines have been emplaced and 'mined area' is an area which is dangerous due to the presence of mines. 'Phoney minefield' means an area free of mines that simulates a minefield. The term 'minefield' includes phoney minefields.

9. 'Recording' means a physical, administrative and technical operation designed to obtain, for the purpose of registration in official records, all available information facilitating the location of minefields, mined areas, mines, booby-traps and other devices.

10. 'Self-destruction mechanism' means an incorporated or externally attached automatically-functioning mechanism which secures the destruction of the munition into which it is incorporated or to which it is attached.

11. 'Self-neutralization mechanism' means an incorporated automatically-functioning mechanism which renders inoperable the munition into which it is incorporated.

12. 'Self-deactivating' means automatically rendering a munition inoperable by means of the irreversible exhaustion of a component, for example, a battery, that is essential to the operation of the munition.

13. 'Remote control' means control by commands from a distance.

14. 'Anti-handling device' means a device intended to protect a mine and which is part of, linked to, attached to or placed under the mine and which activates when an attempt is made to tamper with the mine.

15. 'Transfer' involves, in addition to the physical movement of mines into or from national territory, the transfer of title to and control over the mines, but does not involve the transfer of territory containing emplaced mines.

Article 3

GENERAL RESTRICTIONS ON THE USE OF MINES, BOOBY-TRAPS AND OTHER DEVICES

1. This Article applies to:
(*a*) mines;
(*b*) booby-traps; and
(*c*) other devices.

2. Each High Contracting Party or party to a conflict is, in accordance with the provisions of this Protocol, responsible for all mines, booby-traps, and other devices employed by it and undertakes to clear, remove, destroy or maintain them as specified in Article 10 of this Protocol.

3. It is prohibited in all circumstances to use any mine, booby-trap or other device which is designed or of a nature to cause superfluous injury or unnecessary suffering.

4. Weapons to which this Article applies shall strictly comply with the standards and limitations specified in the Technical Annex with respect to each particular category.

5. It is prohibited to use mines, booby-traps or other devices which employ a mechanism or device specifically designed to detonate the munition by the presence of commonly available mine detectors as a result of their magnetic or other non-contact influence during normal use in detection operations.

6. It is prohibited to use a self-deactivating mine equipped with an anti-handling device that is designed in such a manner that the anti-handling device is capable of functioning after the mine has ceased to be capable of functioning.

7. It is prohibited in all circumstances to direct weapons to which this Article applies, either in offence, defence or by way of reprisals, against the civilian population as such or against individual civilians or civilian objects.

8. The indiscriminate use of weapons to which this Article applies is prohibited. Indiscriminate use is any placement of such weapons:

(*a*) which is not on, or directed against, a military objective. In case of doubt as to whether an object which is normally dedicated to civilian purposes, such as a place of worship, a house or other dwelling or a school, is being used to make an effective contribution to military action, it shall be presumed not to be so used;

(*b*) which employs a method or means of delivery which cannot be directed at a specific military objective; or

(*c*) which may be expected to cause incidental loss of civilian life, injury to civilians, damage to civilian objects, or a combination thereof, which would be excessive in relation to the concrete and direct military advantage anticipated.

9. Several clearly separated and distinct military objectives located in a city, town, village or other area containing a similar con-

centration of civilians or civilian objects are not to be treated as a single military objective.

10. All feasible precautions shall be taken to protect civilians from the effects of weapons to which this Article applies. Feasible precautions are those precautions which are practicable or practically possible taking into account all circumstances ruling at the time, including humanitarian and military considerations. These circumstances include, but are not limited to:

(*a*) the short- and long-term effect of mines upon the local civilian population for the duration of the minefield;

(*b*) possible measures to protect civilians (for example, fencing, signs, warning and monitoring);

(*c*) the availability and feasibility of using alternatives; and

(*d*) the short- and long-term military requirements for a minefield.

11. Effective advance warning shall be given of any emplacement of mines, booby-traps and other devices which may affect the civilian population, unless circumstances do not permit.

Article 4

RESTRICTIONS ON THE USE OF ANTI-PERSONNEL MINES

It is prohibited to use anti-personnel mines which are not detectable, as specified in paragraph 2 of the Technical Annex.

Article 5

RESTRICTIONS ON THE USE OF ANTI-PERSONNEL MINES OTHER THAN REMOTELY-DELIVERED MINES

1. This Article applies to anti-personnel mines other than remotely-delivered mines.

2. It is prohibited to use weapons to which this Article applies which are not in compliance with the provisions on self-destruction and self-deactivation in the Technical Annex, unless:

(*a*) such weapons are placed within a perimeter-marked area which is monitored by military personnel and protected by fencing or other means, to ensure the effective exclusion of civilians from the area. The marking must be of a distinct and durable character and must at least be visible to a person who is about to enter the perimeter-marked area; and

(*b*) such weapons are cleared before the area is abandoned, unless the area is turned over to the forces of another State which accept responsibility for the maintenance of the protections required by this Article and the subsequent clearance of those weapons.

3. A party to a conflict is relieved from further compliance with the provisions of sub-paragraphs 2 (*a*) and 2 (*b*) of this Article only if such compliance is not feasible due to forcible loss of control of the area as a result of enemy military action, including situations where direct enemy military action makes it impossible to comply. If that party regains control of the area, it shall resume compliance with the provisions of sub-paragraphs 2 (*a*) and 2 (*b*) of this Article.

4. If the forces of a party to a conflict gain control of an area in which weapons to which this Article applies have been laid, such forces shall, to the maximum extent feasible, maintain and, if necessary, establish the protections required by this Article until such weapons have been cleared.

5. All feasible measures shall be taken to prevent the unauthorized removal, defacement, destruction or concealment of any device, system or material used to establish the perimeter of a perimeter-marked area.

6. Weapons to which this Article applies which propel fragments in a horizontal arc of less than 90 degrees and which are placed on or above the ground may be used without the measures provided for in sub-paragraph 2 (*a*) of this Article for a maximum period of 72 hours, if:

(*a*) they are located in immediate proximity to the military unit that emplaced them; and

(*b*) the area is monitored by military personnel to ensure the effective exclusion of civilians.

Article 6

RESTRICTIONS ON THE USE OF REMOTELY-DELIVERED MINES

1. It is prohibited to use remotely-delivered mines unless they are recorded in accordance with sub-paragraph 1 (*b*) of the Technical Annex.

2. It is prohibited to use remotely-delivered anti-personnel mines which are not in compliance with the provisions on self-destruction and self-deactivation in the Technical Annex.

3. It is prohibited to use remotely-delivered mines other than anti-personnel mines, unless, to the extent feasible, they are equipped with an effective self-destruction or self-neutralization mechanism and have a back-up self-deactivation feature, which is designed

so that the mine will no longer function as a mine when the mine no longer serves the military purpose for which it was placed in position.

4. Effective advance warning shall be given of any delivery or dropping of remotely-delivered mines which may affect the civilian population, unless circumstances do not permit.

Article 7

PROHIBITIONS ON THE USE OF BOOBY-TRAPS AND OTHER DEVICES

1. Without prejudice to the rules of international law applicable in armed conflict relating to treachery and perfidy, it is prohibited in all circumstances to use booby-traps and other devices which are in any way attached to or associated with:

(*a*) internationally recognized protective emblems, signs or signals;

(*b*) sick, wounded or dead persons;

(*c*) burial or cremation sites or graves;

(*d*) medical facilities, medical equipment, medical supplies or medical transportation;

(*e*) children's toys or other portable objects or products specially designed for the feeding, health, hygiene, clothing or education of children;

(*f*) food or drink;

(*g*) kitchen utensils or appliances except in military establishments, military locations or military supply depots;

(*h*) objects clearly of a religious nature;

(*i*) historic monuments, works of art or places of worship which constitute the cultural or spiritual heritage of peoples; or

(*j*) animals or their carcasses.

2. It is prohibited to use booby-traps or other devices in the form of apparently harmless portable objects which are specifically designed and constructed to contain explosive material.

3. Without prejudice to the provisions of Article 3, it is prohibited to use weapons to which this Article applies in any city, town, village or other area containing a similar concentration of civilians in which combat between ground forces is not taking place or does not appear to be imminent, unless either:

(*a*) they are placed on or in the close vicinity of a military objective; or

(*b*) measures are taken to protect civilians from their effects, for example, the posting of warning sentries, the issuing of warnings or the provision of fences.

Article 8

TRANSFERS

1. In order to promote the purposes of this Protocol, each High Contracting Party:

(*a*) undertakes not to transfer any mine the use of which is prohibited by this Protocol;

(*b*) undertakes not to transfer any mine to any recipient other than a State or a State agency authorized to receive such transfers;

(*c*) undertakes to exercise restraint in the transfer of any mine the use of which is restricted by this Protocol. In particular, each High Contracting Party undertakes not to transfer any anti-personnel mines to States which are not bound by this Protocol, unless the recipient State agrees to apply this Protocol; and

(*d*) undertakes to ensure that any transfer in accordance with this Article takes place in full compliance, by both the transferring and the recipient State, with the relevant provisions of this Protocol and the applicable norms of international humanitarian law.

2. In the event that a High Contracting Party declares that it will defer compliance with specific provisions on the use of certain mines, as provided for in the Technical Annex, sub-paragraph 1 (*a*) of this Article shall however apply to such mines.

3. All High Contracting Parties, pending the entry into force of this Protocol, will refrain from any actions which would be inconsistent with sub-paragraph 1 (*a*) of this Article.

Article 9

RECORDING AND USE OF INFORMATION ON MINEFIELDS, MINED AREAS, MINES, BOOBY-TRAPS AND OTHER DEVICES

1. All information concerning minefields, mined areas, mines, booby-traps and other devices shall be recorded in accordance with the provisions of the Technical Annex.

2. All such records shall be retained by the parties to a conflict, who shall, without delay after the cessation of active hostilities, take all necessary and appropriate measures, including the use of such information, to protect civilians from the effects of minefields, mined areas, mines, booby-traps and other devices in areas under their control.

At the same time, they shall also make available to the other party or parties to the conflict and to the Secretary-General of the United Nations all such information in their possession concerning minefields, mined areas, mines, booby-traps and other devices laid by them in areas no longer under their control; provided, however, subject to reciprocity, where the forces of a party to a conflict are in the territory of an adverse party, either party may withhold such information from the Secretary-General and the other party, to the extent that security interests require such withholding, until neither party is in the territory of the other. In the latter case, the information withheld shall be disclosed as soon as those security interests permit. Wherever possible, the parties to the conflict shall seek, by mutual agreement, to provide for the release of such information at the earliest possible time in a manner consistent with the security interests of each party.

3. This Article is without prejudice to the provisions of Articles 10 and 12 of this Protocol.

Article 10

REMOVAL OF MINEFIELDS, MINED AREAS, MINES, BOOBY-TRAPS AND OTHER DEVICES AND INTERNATIONAL COOPERATION

1. Without delay after the cessation of active hostilities, all minefields, mined areas, mines, booby-traps and other devices shall be cleared, removed, destroyed or maintained in accordance with Article 3 and paragraph 2 of Article 5 of this Protocol.

2. High Contracting Parties and parties to a conflict bear such responsibility with respect to minefields, mined areas, mines, booby-traps and other devices in areas under their control.

3. With respect to minefields, mined areas, mines, booby-traps and other devices laid by a party in areas over which it no longer exercises control, such party shall provide to the party in control of the area pursuant to paragraph 2 of this Article, to the extent permitted by such party, technical and material assistance necessary to fulfil such responsibility.

4. At all times necessary, the parties shall endeavour to reach agreement, both among themselves and, where appropriate, with other States and with international organizations, on the provision of technical and material assistance, including, in appropriate circumstances, the undertaking of joint operations necessary to fulfil such responsibilities.

Article 11

TECHNOLOGICAL COOPERATION AND ASSISTANCE

1. Each High Contracting Party undertakes to facilitate and shall have the right to participate in the fullest possible exchange of equipment, material and scientific and technological information concerning the implementation of this Protocol and means of mine clearance. In particular, High Contracting Parties shall not impose undue restrictions on the provision of mine clearance equipment and related technological information for humanitarian purposes.

2. Each High Contracting Party undertakes to provide information to the database on mine clearance established within the United Nations System, especially information concerning various means and technologies of mine clearance, and lists of experts, expert agencies or national points of contact on mine clearance.

3. Each High Contracting Party in a position to do so shall provide assistance for mine clearance through the United Nations System, other international bodies or on a bilateral basis, or contribute to the United Nations Voluntary Trust Fund for Assistance in Mine Clearance.

4. Requests by High Contracting Parties for assistance, substantiated by relevant information, may be submitted to the United Nations, to other appropriate bodies or to other States. These requests may be submitted to the Secretary-General of the United Nations, who shall transmit them to all High Contracting Parties and to relevant international organizations.

5. In the case of requests to the United Nations, the Secretary-General of the United Nations, within the resources available to the Secretary-General of the United Nations, may take appropriate steps to assess the situation and, in cooperation with the requesting High Contracting Party, determine the appropriate provision of assistance in mine clearance or implementation of the Protocol. The Secretary-General may also report to High Contracting Parties on any such assessment as well as on the type and scope of assistance required.

6. Without prejudice to their constitutional and other legal provisions, the High Contracting Parties undertake to cooperate and transfer technology to facilitate the implementation of the relevant prohibitions and restrictions set out in this Protocol.

7. Each High Contracting Party has the right to seek and receive technical assistance, where appropriate, from another High Contracting Party on specific relevant technology, other than weapons technology, as necessary and feasible, with a view to reducing any period of deferral for which provision is made in the Technical Annex.

Article 12

PROTECTION FROM THE EFFECTS OF MINEFIELDS, MINED AREAS, MINES, BOOBY-TRAPS AND OTHER DEVICES

1. Application

(*a*) With the exception of the forces and missions referred to in sub-paragraph 2 (*a*) (i) of this Article, this Article applies only to missions which are performing functions in an area with the consent of the High Contracting Party on whose territory the functions are performed.

(*b*) The application of the provisions of this Article to parties to a conflict which are not High Contracting Parties shall not change their legal status or the legal status of a disputed territory, either explicitly or implicitly.

(*c*) The provisions of this Article are without prejudice to existing international humanitarian law, or other international instruments as applicable, or decisions by the Security Council of the United Nations, which provide for a higher level of protection to personnel functioning in accordance with this Article.

2. Peace-keeping and certain other forces and missions

(*a*) This paragraph applies to:
(i) any United Nations force or mission performing peace-keeping, observation or similar functions in any area in accordance with the Charter of the United Nations; and
(ii) any mission established pursuant to Chapter VIII of the Charter of the United Nations and performing its functions in the area of a conflict.

(*b*) Each High Contracting Party or party to a conflict, if so requested by the head of a force or mission to which this paragraph applies, shall:
(i) so far as it is able, take such measures as are necessary to protect the force or mission from the effects of mines, booby-traps and other devices in any area under its control;

(ii) if necessary in order effectively to protect such personnel, remove or render harmless, so far as it is able, all mines, booby-traps and other devices in that area; and
(iii) inform the head of the force or mission of the location of all known minefields, mined areas, mines, booby-traps and other devices in the area in which the force or mission is performing its functions and, so far as is feasible, make available to the head of the force or mission all information in its possession concerning such minefields, mined areas, mines, booby-traps and other devices.

3. Humanitarian and fact-finding missions of the United Nations System

(*a*) This paragraph applies to any humanitarian or fact-finding mission of the United Nations System.
(*b*) Each High Contracting Party or party to a conflict, if so requested by the head of a mission to which this paragraph applies, shall:
(i) provide the personnel of the mission with the protections set out in sub-paragraph 2(*b*)(i) of this Article; and
(ii) if access to or through any place under its control is necessary for the performance of the mission's functions and in order to provide the personnel of the mission with safe passage to or through that place:
(*aa*) unless on-going hostilities prevent, inform the head of the mission of a safe route to that place if such information is available; or
(*bb*) if information identifying a safe route is not provided in accordance with sub-paragraph (*aa*), so far as is necessary and feasible, clear a lane through minefields.

4. Missions of the International Committee of the Red Cross

(*a*) This paragraph applies to any mission of the International Committee of the Red Cross performing functions with the consent of the host State or States as provided for by the Geneva Conventions of 12 August 1949 and, where applicable, their Additional Protocols.
(*b*) Each High Contracting Party or party to a conflict, if so requested by the head of a mission to which this paragraph applies, shall:
(i) provide the personnel of the mission with the protections set out in sub-paragraph 2 (*b*) (i) of this Article; and
(ii) take the measures set out in sub-

paragraph 3 (*b*) (ii) of this Article.

5. *Other humanitarian missions and missions of inquiry*

(*a*) In so far as paragraphs 2, 3 and 4 of this Article do not apply to them, this paragraph applies to the following missions when they are performing functions in the area of a conflict or to assist the victims of a conflict:

(i) any humanitarian mission of a national Red Cross or Red Crescent society or of their International Federation;

(ii) any mission of an impartial humanitarian organization, including any impartial humanitarian demining mission; and

(iii) any mission of enquiry established pursuant to the provisions of the Geneva Conventions of 12 August 1949 and, where applicable, their Additional Protocols.

(*b*) Each High Contracting Party or party to a conflict, if so requested by the head of a mission to which this paragraph applies, shall, so far as is feasible:

(i) provide the personnel of the mission with the protections set out in sub-paragraph 2 (*b*) (i) of this Article; and

(ii) take the measures set out in sub-paragraph 3 (*b*) (ii) of this Article.

6. *Confidentiality*

All information provided in confidence pursuant to this Article shall be treated by the recipient in strict confidence and shall not be released outside the force or mission concerned without the express authorization of the provider of the information.

7. *Respect for laws and regulations*

Without prejudice to such privileges and immunities as they may enjoy or to the requirements of their duties, personnel participating in the forces and missions referred to in this Article shall:

(*a*) respect the laws and regulations of the host State; and

(*b*) refrain from any action or activity incompatible with the impartial and international nature of their duties.

Article 13

CONSULTATIONS OF HIGH CONTRACTING PARTIES

1. The High Contracting Parties undertake to consult and cooperate with each other on all issues related to the operation of this Protocol. For this purpose, a conference of High Contracting Parties shall be held annually.

2. Participation in the annual conferences shall be determined by their agreed Rules of Procedure.

3. The work of the conference shall include:

(*a*) review of the operation and status of this Protocol;

(*b*) consideration of matters arising from reports by High Contracting Parties according to paragraph 4 of this Article;

(*c*) preparation for review conferences; and

(*d*) consideration of the development of technologies to protect civilians against indiscriminate effects of mines.

4. The High Contracting Parties shall provide annual reports to the Depositary, who shall circulate them to all High Contracting Parties in advance of the conference, on any of the following matters:

(*a*) dissemination of information on this Protocol to their armed forces and to the civilian population;

(*b*) mine clearance and rehabilitation programmes;

(*c*) steps taken to meet technical requirements of this Protocol and any other relevant information pertaining thereto;

(*d*) legislation related to this Protocol;

(*e*) measures taken on international technical information exchange, on international cooperation on mine clearance, and on technical cooperation and assistance; and

(*f*) other relevant matters.

5. The cost of the Conference of High Contracting Parties shall be borne by the High Contracting Parties and States not parties participating in the work of the conference, in accordance with the United Nations scale of assessment adjusted appropriately.

Article 14

COMPLIANCE

1. Each High Contracting Party shall take all appropriate steps, including legislative and other measures, to prevent and suppress violations of this Protocol by persons or on territory under its jurisdiction or control.

2. The measures envisaged in paragraph 1 of this Article include appropriate measures to ensure the imposition of penal sanctions against persons who, in relation to an armed conflict and contrary to the provisions of this Protocol, wilfully kill or cause serious injury to civilians and to bring such persons to justice.

3. Each High Contracting Party shall also require that its armed forces issue relevant military instructions and operating procedures and that armed forces personnel receive training commensurate with their duties and responsibilities to comply with the provisions of this Protocol.

4. The High Contracting Parties undertake to consult each other and to cooperate with each other bilaterally, through the Secretary-General of the United Nations or through other appropriate international procedures, to resolve any problems that may arise with regard to the interpretation and application of the provisions of this Protocol.

Technical Annex

1. Recording

(a) Recording of the location of mines other than remotely-delivered mines, minefields, mined areas, booby-traps and other devices shall be carried out in accordance with the following provisions:

(i) the location of the minefields, mined areas and areas of booby-traps and other devices shall be specified accurately by relation to the coordinates of at least two reference points and the estimated dimensions of the area containing these weapons in relation to those reference points;

(ii) maps, diagrams or other records shall be made in such a way as to indicate the location of minefields, mined areas, booby-traps and other devices in relation to reference points, and these records shall also indicate their perimeters and extent; and

(iii) for purposes of detection and clearance of mines, booby-traps and other devices, maps, diagrams or other records shall contain complete information on the type, number, emplacing method, type of fuse and life time, date and time of laying, anti-handling devices (if any) and other relevant information on all these weapons laid. Whenever feasible the minefield record shall show the exact location of every mine, except in row minefields where the row location is sufficient. The precise location and operating mechanism of each booby-trap laid shall be individually recorded.

(b) The estimated location and area of remotely-delivered mines shall be specified by coordinates of reference points (normally corner points) and shall be ascertained and when feasible marked on the ground at the earliest opportunity. The total number and type of mines laid, the date and time of laying and the self-destruction time periods shall also be recorded.

(c) Copies of records shall be held at a level of command sufficient to guarantee their safety as far as possible.

(d) The use of mines produced after the entry into force of this Protocol is prohibited unless they are marked in English or in the respective national language or languages with the following information:

(i) name of the country of origin;
(ii) month and year of production; and
(iii) serial number or lot number.

The marking should be visible, legible, durable and resistant to environmental effects, as far as possible.

2. Specifications on delectability

(a) With respect to anti-personnel mines produced after 1 January 1997, such mines shall incorporate in their construction a material or device that enables the mine to be detected by commonly-available technical mine detection equipment and provides a response signal equivalent to a signal from 8 grammes or more of iron in a single coherent mass.

(b) With respect to anti-personnel mines produced before 1 January 1997, such mines shall either incorporate in their construction, or have attached prior to their emplacement, in a manner not easily removable, a material or device that enables the mine to be detected by commonly-available technical mine detection equipment and provides a response signal equivalent to a signal from 8 grammes or more of iron in a single coherent mass.

(c) In the event that a High Contracting Party determines that it cannot immediately comply with sub-paragraph (b), it may declare at the time of its notification of consent to be bound by this Protocol that it will defer compliance with sub-paragraph (b) for a period not to exceed 9 years from the entry into force of this Protocol. In the meantime it shall, to the extent feasible, minimize the use of anti-personnel mines that do not so comply.

3. Specifications on self-destruction and self-deactivation

(a) All remotely-delivered anti-personnel mines shall be designed and constructed so that no more than 10% of activated mines will fail to self-destruct within 30 days after emplacement, and each mine shall have a back-up self-deactivation feature designed and constructed so that, in combination with the self-destruction mechanism, no more than one in one thousand activated mines will function as a mine 120 days after emplacement.

(b) All non-remotely delivered anti-personnel mines, used outside marked areas, as defined in Article 5 of this Protocol, shall comply with the requirements for self-destruction and self-deactivation stated in sub-paragraph (a).

(c) In the event that a High Contracting Party determines that it cannot immediately comply with sub-paragraphs (a) and/or (b), it may declare at the time of its notification of consent to be bound by this Protocol, that it will, with respect to mines produced prior to the entry into force of this Protocol, defer compliance with sub-paragraphs (*a*) and/or (*b*) for a period not to exceed 9 years from the entry into force of this Protocol.

During this period of deferral, the High Contracting Party shall:

(i) undertake to minimize, to the extent feasible, the use of anti-personnel mines that do not so comply; and

(ii) with respect to remotely-delivered anti-personnel mines, comply with either the requirements for self-destruction or the requirements for self-deactivation and, with respect to other anti-personnel mines comply with at least the requirements for self-deactivation.

4. International signs for minefields and mined areas

Signs similar to the example attached and as specified below shall be utilized in the marking of minefields and mined areas to ensure their visibility and recognition by the civilian population:

(*a*) size and shape: a triangle or square no smaller than 28 centimetres (11 inches) by 20 centimetres (7.9 inches) for a triangle, and 15 centimetres (6 inches) per side for a square;

(*b*) colour: red or orange with a yellow reflecting border;

(*c*) symbol: the symbol illustrated in the Attachment, or an alternative readily recognizable in the area in which the sign is to be displayed as identifying a dangerous area;

(*d*) language: the sign should contain the word 'mines' in one of the six official languages of the Convention (Arabic, Chinese, English, French, Russian and Spanish) and the language or languages prevalent in that area; and

(*e*) spacing: signs should be placed around the minefield or mined area at a distance sufficient to ensure their visibility at any point by a civilian approaching the area.

ARTICLE 2: ENTRY INTO FORCE

This amended Protocol shall enter into force as provided for in paragraph 1 (*b*) of Article 8 of the Convention.

Source: United Nations Centre for Disarmament Affairs, *Status of Multilateral Arms Regulation and Disarmament Agreements, Fifth Edition: 1996* (United Nations: New York, 1997), pp. 189–207.

CONVENTION ON THE PROHIBITION OF THE USE, STOCKPILING, PRODUCTION AND TRANSFER OF ANTI-PERSONNEL MINES AND ON THEIR DESTRUCTION

3 December 1997

Preamble

The States Parties,

Determined to put an end to the suffering and casualties caused by anti-personnel mines, that kill or maim hundreds of people every week, mostly innocent and defenceless civilians and especially children, obstruct economic development and reconstruction, inhibit the repatriation of refugees and internally displaced persons, and have other severe consequences for years after emplacement,

Believing it necessary to do their utmost to contribute in an efficient and coordinated manner to face the challenge of removing anti-personnel mines placed throughout the world, and to assure their destruction,

Wishing to do their utmost in providing assistance for the care and rehabilitation, including the social and economic reintegration of mine victims,

Recognizing that a total ban of anti-personnel mines would also be an important confidence-building measure,

Welcoming the adoption of the Protocol on Prohibitions or Restrictions on the Use of Mines, Booby-Traps and Other Devices, as amended on 3 May 1996, annexed to the Convention on Prohibitions or Restrictions on the Use of Certain Conventional Weapons Which May Be Deemed to Be Excessively Injurious or to Have Indiscriminate Effects, and calling for the early ratification of this Protocol by all States which have not yet done so,

Welcoming also United Nations General Assembly resolution 51/45 S of 10 December 1996 urging all States to pursue vigorously an effective, legally binding international agreement to ban the use, stockpiling, production and transfer of anti-personnel landmines,

Welcoming furthermore the measures taken over the past years, both unilaterally and multilaterally, aiming at prohibiting, restricting or suspending the use, stockpiling, production and transfer of anti-personnel mines,

Stressing the role of public conscience in furthering the principles of humanity as evidenced by the call for a total ban of anti-personnel mines and recognizing the efforts to that end undertaken by the International

Red Cross and Red Crescent Movement, the International Campaign to Ban Landmines and numerous other non-governmental organizations around the world,

Recalling the Ottawa Declaration of 5 October 1996 and the Brussels Declaration of 27 June 1997 urging the international community to negotiate an international and legally binding agreement prohibiting the use, stockpiling, production and transfer of anti-personnel mines,

Emphasizing the desirability of attracting the adherence of all States to this Convention, and determined to work strenuously towards the promotion of its universalization in all relevant fora including, *inter alia*, the United Nations, the Conference on Disarmament, regional organizations, and groupings, and review conferences of the Convention on Prohibitions or Restrictions on the Use of Certain Conventional Weapons Which May Be Deemed to Be Excessively Injurious or to Have Indiscriminate Effects,

Basing themselves on the principle of international humanitarian law that the right of the parties to an armed conflict to choose methods or means of warfare is not unlimited, on the principle that prohibits the employment in armed conflicts of weapons, projectiles and materials and methods of warfare of a nature to cause superfluous injury or unnecessary suffering and on the principle that a distinction must be made between civilians and combatants,

Have agreed as follows:

Article 1. General obligations

1. Each State Party undertakes never under any circumstances:

(*a*) To use anti-personnel mines;

(*b*) To develop, produce, otherwise acquire, stockpile, retain or transfer to anyone, directly or indirectly, anti-personnel mines;

(*c*) To assist, encourage or induce, in any way, anyone to engage in any activity prohibited to a State Party under this Convention.

2. Each State Party undertakes to destroy or ensure the destruction of all anti-personnel mines in accordance with the provisions of this Convention.

Article 2. Definitions

1. 'Anti-personnel mine' means a mine designed to be exploded by the presence, proximity or contact of a person and that will incapacitate, injure or kill one or more persons. Mines designed to be detonated by the presence, proximity or contact of a vehicle as opposed to a person, that are equipped with anti-handling devices, are not considered anti-personnel mines as a result of being so equipped.

2. 'Mine' means a munition designed to be placed under, on or near the ground or other surface area and to be exploded by the presence, proximity or contact of a person or a vehicle.

3. 'Anti-handling device' means a device intended to protect a mine and which is part of, linked to, attached to or placed under the mine and which activates when an attempt is made to tamper with or otherwise intentionally disturb the mine.

4. 'Transfer' involves, in addition to the physical movement of anti-personnel mines into or from national territory, the transfer of title to and control over the mines, but does not involve the transfer of territory containing emplaced anti-personnel mines.

5. 'Mined area' means an area which is dangerous due to the presence or suspected presence of mines.

Article 3. Exceptions

1. Notwithstanding the general obligations under Article 1, the retention or transfer of a number of anti-personnel mines for the development of and training in mine detection, mine clearance, or mine destruction techniques is permitted. The amount of such mines shall not exceed the minimum number absolutely necessary for the above-mentioned purposes.

2. The transfer of anti-personnel mines for the purpose of destruction is permitted.

Article 4. Destruction of stockpiled anti-personnel mines

Except as provided for in Article 3, each State Party undertakes to destroy or ensure the destruction of all stockpiled anti-personnel mines it owns or possesses, or that are under its jurisdiction or control, as soon as possible but not later than four years after the entry into force of this Convention for that State Party.

Article 5. Destruction of anti-personnel mines in mined areas

1. Each State Party undertakes to destroy or ensure the destruction of all anti-personnel mines in mined areas under its jurisdiction or control, as soon as possible but not later than ten years after the entry into force of this Convention for that State Party.

2. Each State Party shall make every effort to identify all areas under its jurisdiction or control in which anti-personnel mines are known or suspected to be emplaced and shall ensure as soon as possible that all anti-personnel mines in mined areas under its jurisdiction or control are perimeter-marked, monitored and protected by fencing or other means, to ensure the effective exclusion of civilians, until all anti-personnel mines contained therein have been destroyed. The marking shall at least be to the standards set out in the Protocol on Prohibitions or Restrictions on the Use of Mines, Booby-Traps and Other Devices, as amended on 3 May 1996, annexed to the Convention on Prohibitions or Restrictions on the Use of Certain Conventional Weapons Which May Be Deemed to Be Excessively Injurious or to Have Indiscriminate Effects.

3. If a State Party believes that it will be unable to destroy or ensure the destruction of all anti-personnel mines referred to in paragraph 1 within that time period, it may submit a request to a Meeting of the States Parties or a Review Conference for an extension of the deadline for completing the destruction of such anti-personnel mines, for a period of up to ten years.

4. Each request shall contain:

(*a*) The duration of the proposed extension;

(*b*) A detailed explanation of the reasons for the proposed extension, including:

(i) The preparation and status of work conducted under national demining programmes;

(ii) The financial and technical means available to the State Party for the destruction of all the anti-personnel mines; and

(iii) Circumstances which impede the ability of the State Party to destroy all the anti-personnel mines in mined areas;

(*c*) The humanitarian, social, economic, and environmental implications of the extension; and

(*d*) Any other information relevant to the request for the proposed extension.

5. The Meeting of the States Parties or the Review Conference shall, taking into consideration the factors contained in paragraph 4, assess the request and decide by a majority of votes of States Parties present and voting whether to grant the request for an extension period.

6. Such an extension may be renewed upon the submission of a new request in accordance with paragraphs 3, 4 and 5 of this Article. In requesting a further extension period a State Party shall submit relevant additional information on what has been undertaken in the previous extension period pursuant to this Article.

Article 6. International cooperation and assistance

1. In fulfilling its obligations under this Convention each State Party has the right to seek and receive assistance, where feasible, from other States Parties to the extent possible.

2. Each State Party undertakes to facilitate and shall have the right to participate in the fullest possible exchange of equipment, material and scientific and technological information concerning the implementation of this Convention. The States Parties shall not impose undue restrictions on the provision of mine clearance equipment and related technological information for humanitarian purposes.

3. Each State Party in a position to do so shall provide assistance for the care and rehabilitation, and social and economic reintegration, of mine victims and for mine awareness programmes. Such assistance may be provided, *inter alia*, through the United Nations system, international, regional or national organizations or institutions, the International Committee of the Red Cross, national Red Cross and Red Crescent societies and their International Federation, non-governmental organizations, or on a bilateral basis.

4. Each State Party in a position to do so shall provide assistance for mine clearance and related activities. Such assistance may be provided, *inter alia*, through the United Nations system, international or regional organizations or institutions, non-governmental organizations or institutions, or on a bilateral basis, or by contributing to the United Nations Voluntary Trust Fund for Assistance in Mine Clearance, or other regional funds that deal with demining.

5. Each State Party in a position to do so shall provide assistance for the destruction of stockpiled anti-personnel mines.

6. Each State Party undertakes to provide information to the database on mine clearance established within the United Nations system, especially information concerning various means and technologies of mine clearance, and lists of experts, expert agencies or national points of contact on mine clearance.

7. States Parties may request the United Nations, regional organizations, other States Parties or other competent intergovernmental

or non-governmental fora to assist its authorities in the elaboration of a national demining programme to determine, *inter alia*:

(*a*) The extent and scope of the anti-personnel mine problem;

(*b*) The financial, technological and human resources that are required for the implementation of the programme;

(*c*) The estimated number of years necessary to destroy all anti-personnel mines in mined areas under the jurisdiction or control of the concerned State Party;

(*d*) Mine awareness activities to reduce the incidence of mine-related injuries or deaths;

(*e*) Assistance to mine victims;

(*f*) The relationship between the Government of the concerned State Party and the relevant governmental, intergovernmental or non-governmental entities that will work in the implementation of the programme.

8. Each State Party giving and receiving assistance under the provisions of this Article shall cooperate with a view to ensuring the full and prompt implementation of agreed assistance programmes.

Article 7. Transparency measures

1. Each State Party shall report to the Secretary-General of the United Nations as soon as practicable, and in any event not later than 180 days after the entry into force of this Convention for that State Party on:

(*a*) The national implementation measures referred to in Article 9;

(*b*) The total of all stockpiled anti-personnel mines owned or possessed by it, or under its jurisdiction or control, to include a breakdown of the type, quantity and, if possible, lot numbers of each type of anti-personnel mine stockpiled;

(*c*) To the extent possible, the location of all mined areas that contain, or are suspected to contain, anti-personnel mines under its jurisdiction or control, to include as much detail as possible regarding the type and quantity of each type of anti-personnel mine in each mined area and when they were emplaced;

(*d*) The types, quantities and, if possible, lot numbers, of all anti-personnel mines retained or transferred for the development of and training in mine detection, mine clearance or mine destruction techniques, or transferred for the purpose of destruction, as well as the institutions authorized by a State Party to retain or transfer anti-personnel mines, in accordance with Article 3;

(*e*) The status of programmes for the conversion or de-commissioning of anti-personnel mine production facilities;

(*f*) The status of programmes for the destruction of anti-personnel mines in accordance with Articles 4 and 5, including details of the methods which will be used in destruction, the location of all destruction sites and the applicable safety and environmental standards to be observed;

(*g*) The types and quantities of all anti-personnel mines destroyed after the entry into force of this Convention for that State Party, to include a breakdown of the quantity of each type of anti-personnel mine destroyed, in accordance with Articles 4 and 5, respectively, along with, if possible, the lot numbers of each type of anti-personnel mine in the case of destruction in accordance with Article 4;

(*h*) The technical characteristics of each type of anti-personnel mine produced, to the extent known, and those currently owned or possessed by a State Party, giving, where reasonably possible, such categories of information as may facilitate identification and clearance of anti-personnel mines; at a minimum, this information shall include the dimensions, fusing, explosive content, metallic content, colour photographs and other information which may facilitate mine clearance; and

(*i*) The measures taken to provide an immediate and effective warning to the population in relation to all areas identified under paragraph 2 of Article 5.

2. The information provided in accordance with this Article shall be updated by the States Parties annually, covering the last calendar year, and reported to the Secretary-General of the United Nations not later than 30 April of each year.

3. The Secretary-General of the United Nations shall transmit all such reports received to the States Parties.

Article 8. Facilitation and clarification of compliance

1. The States Parties agree to consult and cooperate with each other regarding the implementation of the provisions of this Convention, and to work together in a spirit of co-operation to facilitate compliance by States Parties with their obligations under this Convention.

2. If one or more States Parties wish to clarify and seek to resolve questions relating to compliance with the provisions of this Convention by another State Party, it may submit, through the Secretary-General of the

United Nations, a Request for Clarification of that matter to that State Party. Such a request shall be accompanied by all appropriate information. Each State Party shall refrain from unfounded Requests for Clarification, care being taken to avoid abuse. A State Party that receives a Request for Clarification shall provide, through the Secretary-General of the United Nations, within 28 days to the requesting State Party all information which would assist in clarifying this matter.

3. If the requesting State Party does not receive a response through the Secretary-General of the United Nations within that time period, or deems the response to the Request for Clarification to be unsatisfactory, it may submit the matter through the Secretary-General of the United Nations to the next Meeting of the States Parties. The Secretary-General of the United Nations shall transmit the submission, accompanied by all appropriate information pertaining to the Request for Clarification, to all States Parties. All such information shall be presented to the requested State Party which shall have the right to respond.

4. Pending the convening of any meeting of the States Parties, any of the States Parties concerned may request the Secretary-General of the United Nations to exercise his or her good offices to facilitate the clarification requested.

5. The requesting State Party may propose through the Secretary-General of the United Nations the convening of a Special Meeting of the States Parties to consider the matter. The Secretary-General of the United Nations shall thereupon communicate this proposal and all information submitted by the States Parties concerned, to all States Parties with a request that they indicate whether they favour a Special Meeting of the States Parties, for the purpose of considering the matter. In the event that within 14 days from the date of such communication, at least one third of the States Parties favours such a Special Meeting, the Secretary-General of the United Nations shall convene this Special Meeting of the States Parties within a further 14 days. A quorum for this Meeting shall consist of a majority of States Parties.

6. The Meeting of the States Parties or the Special Meeting of the States Parties, as the case may be, shall first determine whether to consider the matter further, taking into account all information submitted by the States Parties concerned. The Meeting of the States Parties or the Special Meeting of the States Parties shall make every effort to reach a decision by consensus. If despite all efforts to that end no agreement has been reached, it shall take this decision by a majority of States Parties present and voting.

7. All States Parties shall cooperate fully with the Meeting of the States Parties or the Special Meeting of the States Parties in the fulfilment of its review of the matter, including any fact-finding missions that are authorized in accordance with paragraph 8.

8. If further clarification is required, the Meeting of the States Parties or the Special Meeting of the States Parties shall authorize a fact-finding mission and decide on its mandate by a majority of States Parties present and voting. At any time the requested State Party may invite a fact-finding mission to its territory. Such a mission shall take place without a decision by a Meeting of the States Parties or a Special Meeting of the States Parties to authorize such a mission. The mission, consisting of up to nine experts, designated and approved in accordance with paragraphs 9 and 10, may collect additional information on the spot or in other places directly related to the alleged compliance issue under the jurisdiction or control of the requested State Party.

9. The Secretary-General of the United Nations shall prepare and update a list of the names, nationalities and other relevant data of qualified experts provided by States Parties and communicate it to all States Parties. Any expert included on this list shall be regarded as designated for all fact-finding missions unless a State Party declares its non-acceptance in writing. In the event of non-acceptance, the expert shall not participate in fact-finding missions on the territory or any other place under the jurisdiction or control of the objecting State Party, if the non-acceptance was declared prior to the appointment of the expert to such missions.

10. Upon receiving a request from the Meeting of the States Parties or a Special Meeting of the States Parties, the Secretary-General of the United Nations shall, after consultations with the requested State Party, appoint the members of the mission, including its leader. Nationals of States Parties requesting the fact-finding mission or directly affected by it shall not be appointed to the mission. The members of the fact-finding mission shall enjoy privileges and immunities under Article VI of the Convention on the Privileges and Immunities of the United Nations, adopted on 13 February 1946.

11. Upon at least 72 hours notice, the members of the fact-finding mission shall arrive in the territory of the requested State Party at the earliest opportunity. The requested State Party shall take the necessary administrative measures to receive, transport and accommodate the mission, and shall be responsible for ensuring the security of the mission to the maximum extent possible while they are on territory under its control.

12. Without prejudice to the sovereignty of the requested State Party, the fact-finding mission may bring into the territory of the requested State Party the necessary equipment which shall be used exclusively for gathering information on the alleged compliance issue. Prior to its arrival, the mission will advise the requested State Party of the equipment that it intends to utilize in the course of its fact-finding mission.

13. The requested State Party shall make all efforts to ensure that the fact-finding mission is given the opportunity to speak with all relevant persons who may be able to provide information related to the alleged compliance issue.

14. The requested State Party shall grant access for the fact-finding mission to all areas and installations under its control where facts relevant to the compliance issue could be expected to be collected. This shall be subject to any arrangements that the requested State Party considers necessary for:

(*a*) The protection of sensitive equipment, information and areas;

(*b*) The protection of any constitutional obligations the requested State Party may have with regard to proprietary rights, searches and seizures, or other constitutional rights; or

(*c*) The physical protection and safety of the members of the fact-finding mission.

In the event that the requested State Party makes such arrangements, it shall make every reasonable effort to demonstrate through alternative means its compliance with this Convention.

15. The fact-finding mission may remain in the territory of the State Party concerned for no more than 14 days, and at any particular site no more than 7 days, unless otherwise agreed.

16. All information provided in confidence and not related to the subject matter of the fact-finding mission shall be treated on a confidential basis.

17. The fact-finding mission shall report, through the Secretary-General of the United Nations, to the Meeting of the States Parties or the Special Meeting of the States Parties the results of its findings.

18. The Meeting of the States Parties or the Special Meeting of the States Parties shall consider all relevant information, including the report submitted by the fact-finding mission, and may request the requested State Party to take measures to address the compliance issue within a specified period of time. The requested State Party shall report on all measures taken in response to this request.

19. The Meeting of the States Parties or the Special Meeting of the States Parties may suggest to the States Parties concerned ways and means to further clarify or resolve the matter under consideration, including the initiation of appropriate procedures in conformity with international law. In circumstances where the issue at hand is determined to be due to circumstances beyond the control of the requested State Party, the Meeting of the States Parties or the Special Meeting of the States Parties may recommend appropriate measures, including the use of cooperative measures referred to in Article 6.

20. The Meeting of the States Parties or the Special Meeting of the States Parties shall make every effort to reach its decisions referred to in paragraphs 18 and 19 by consensus, otherwise by a two-thirds majority of States Parties present and voting.

Article 9. National implementation measures

Each State Party shall take all appropriate legal, administrative and other measures, including the imposition of penal sanctions, to prevent and suppress any activity prohibited to a State Party under this Convention undertaken by persons or on territory under its jurisdiction or control.

Article 10. Settlement of disputes

1. The States Parties shall consult and cooperate with each other to settle any dispute that may arise with regard to the application or the interpretation of this Convention. Each State Party may bring any such dispute before the Meeting of the States Parties.

2. The Meeting of the States Parties may contribute to the settlement of the dispute by whatever means it deems appropriate, including offering its good offices, calling upon the States parties to a dispute to start the settlement procedure of their choice and recommending a time-limit for any agreed procedure.

3. This Article is without prejudice to the

provisions of this Convention on facilitation and clarification of compliance.

Article 11. Meetings of the States Parties

1. The States Parties shall meet regularly in order to consider any matter with regard to the application or implementation of this Convention, including:

(a) The operation and status of this Convention;

(b) Matters arising from the reports submitted under the provisions of this Convention;

(c) International cooperation and assistance in accordance with Article 6;

(d) The development of technologies to clear anti-personnel mines;

(e) Submissions of States Parties under Article 8; and

(f) Decisions relating to submissions of States Parties as provided for in Article 5.

2. The First Meeting of the States Parties shall be convened by the Secretary-General of the United Nations within one year after the entry into force of this Convention. The subsequent meetings shall be convened by the Secretary-General of the United Nations annually until the first Review Conference.

3. Under the conditions set out in Article 8, the Secretary-General of the United Nations shall convene a Special Meeting of the States Parties.

4. States not parties to this Convention, as well as the United Nations, other relevant international organizations or institutions, regional organizations, the International Committee of the Red Cross and relevant non-governmental organizations may be invited to attend these meetings as observers in accordance with the agreed Rules of Procedure.

Article 12. Review Conferences

1. A Review Conference shall be convened by the Secretary-General of the United Nations five years after the entry into force of this Convention. Further Review Conferences shall be convened by the Secretary-General of the United Nations if so requested by one or more States Parties, provided that the interval between Review Conferences shall in no case be less than five years. All States Parties to this Convention shall be invited to each Review Conference.

2. The purpose of the Review Conference shall be:

(a) To review the operation and status of this Convention;

(b) To consider the need for and the interval between further Meetings of the States Parties referred to in paragraph 2 of Article 11;

(c) To take decisions on submissions of States Parties as provided for in Article 5; and

(d) To adopt, if necessary, in its final report conclusions related to the implementation of this Convention.

3. States not parties to this Convention, as well as the United Nations, other relevant international organizations or institutions, regional organizations, the International Committee of the Red Cross and relevant non-governmental organizations may be invited to attend each Review Conference as observers in accordance with the agreed Rules of Procedure.

Article 13. Amendments

1. At any time after the entry into force of this Convention any State Party may propose amendments to this Convention. Any proposal for an amendment shall be communicated to the Depositary, who shall circulate it to all States Parties and shall seek their views on whether an Amendment Conference should be convened to consider the proposal. If a majority of the States Parties notify the Depositary no later than 30 days after its circulation that they support further consideration of the proposal, the Depositary shall convene an Amendment Conference to which all States Parties shall be invited.

2. States not parties to this Convention, as well as the United Nations, other relevant international organizations or institutions, regional organizations, the International Committee of the Red Cross and relevant non-governmental organizations may be invited to attend each Amendment Conference as observers in accordance with the agreed Rules of Procedure.

3. The Amendment Conference shall be held immediately following a Meeting of the States Parties or a Review Conference unless a majority of the States Parties request that it be held earlier.

4. Any amendment to this Convention shall be adopted by a majority of two thirds of the States Parties present and voting at the Amendment Conference. The Depositary shall communicate any amendment so adopted to the States Parties.

5. An amendment to this Convention shall enter into force for all States Parties to this Convention which have accepted it, upon the deposit with the Depositary of instruments of acceptance by a majority of States Parties.

Thereafter it shall enter into force for any remaining State Party on the date of deposit of its instrument of acceptance.

Article 14. Costs

1. The costs of the Meetings of the States Parties, the Special Meetings of the States Parties, the Review Conferences and the Amendment Conferences shall be borne by the States Parties and States not parties to this Convention participating therein, in accordance with the United Nations scale of assessment adjusted appropriately.

2. The costs incurred by the Secretary-General of the United Nations under Articles 7 and 8 and the costs of any fact-finding mission shall be borne by the States Parties in accordance with the United Nations scale of assessment adjusted appropriately.

Article 15. Signature

This Convention, done at Oslo, Norway, on 18 September 1997, shall be open for signature at Ottawa, Canada, by all States from 3 December 1997 until 4 December 1997, and at the United Nations Headquarters in New York from 5 December 1997 until its entry into force.

Article 16. Ratification, acceptance, approval or accession

1. This Convention is subject to ratification, acceptance or approval of the Signatories.

2. It shall be open for accession by any State which has not signed the Convention.

3. The instruments of ratification, acceptance, approval or accession shall be deposited with the Depositary.

Article 17. Entry into force

1. This Convention shall enter into force on the first day of the sixth month after the month in which the 40th instrument of ratification, acceptance, approval or accession has been deposited.

2. For any State which deposits its instrument of ratification, acceptance, approval or accession after the date of the deposit of the 40th instrument of ratification, acceptance, approval or accession, this Convention shall enter into force on the first day of the sixth month after the date on which that State has deposited its instrument of ratification, acceptance, approval or accession.

Article 18. Provisional application

Any State may at the time of its ratification, acceptance, approval or accession, declare that it will apply provisionally paragraph 1 of Article 1 of this Convention pending its entry into force.

Article 19. Reservations

The Articles of this Convention shall not be subject to reservations.

Article 20. Duration and withdrawal

1. This Convention shall be of unlimited duration.

2. Each State Party shall, in exercising its national sovereignty, have the right to withdraw from this Convention. It shall give notice of such withdrawal to all other States Parties, to the Depositary and to the United Nations Security Council. Such instrument of withdrawal shall include a full explanation of the reasons motivating this withdrawal.

3. Such withdrawal shall only take effect six months after the receipt of the instrument of withdrawal by the Depositary. If, however, on the expiry of that six-month period, the withdrawing State Party is engaged in an armed conflict, the withdrawal shall not take effect before the end of the armed conflict.

4. The withdrawal of a State Party from this Convention shall not in any way affect the duty of States to continue fulfilling the obligations assumed under any relevant rules of international law.

Article 21. Depositary

The Secretary-General of the United Nations is hereby designated as the Depositary of this Convention.

Article 22. Authentic texts

The original of this Convention, of which the Arabic, Chinese, English, French, Russian and Spanish texts are equally authentic, shall be deposited with the Secretary-General of the United Nations.

Source: United Nations, New York, Dec. 1997.

Annexes

Annexe A. Arms control and disarmament agreements

Annexe B. Chronology 1997

Annexe A. Arms control and disarmament agreements

RAGNHILD FERM

Notes

1. The agreements are listed in the order of the date on which they were opened for signature (multilateral agreements) or signed (bilateral agreements); the date on which they entered into force is also given. Information is as of 1 January 1998 unless otherwise indicated. Where confirmed information on entry into force or new parties became available in early 1998, this information is also given in notes.

2. The main source of information is the lists of signatories and parties provided by the depositaries of the treaties.

3. For a few major treaties, the substantive parts of the most important reservations, declarations and/or interpretive statements made in connection with a state's signature, ratification, accession or succession are given in footnotes below the list of parties.

4. The Russian Federation, constituted in 1991 as an independent state, has confirmed the continuity of international obligations assumed by the Soviet Union. The other former Soviet republics which were constituted in 1991 as independent sovereign states have subsequently signed, ratified or acceded to agreements in order to become signatories/parties.

5. Czechoslovakia split into two states, the Czech Republic and Slovakia, in 1993. Both states have succeeded to all the agreements listed in this annexe to which Czechoslovakia was a party.

6. The Federal Republic of Yugoslavia split into several states in 1991–92. The international legal status of what remains of the former Yugoslavia—Yugoslavia (Serbia and Montenegro)—is ambiguous, but since it considers that it is the same entity 'Yugoslavia' is given as a party to those agreements which it has signed or ratified. (The former Yugoslav republics of Bosnia and Herzegovina, Croatia, Macedonia and Slovenia have succeeded, as independent states, to several agreements.)

7. Taiwan, while not recognized as a sovereign state by some nations, is given as a party to those agreements which it has ratified.

8. Unless otherwise stated, the multilateral agreements listed in this annexe are open to all states for signature, ratification, accession or succession.

9. A complete list of UN member states, with the year in which they became members, appears in the glossary at the front of this volume. Not all the states listed in this annexe are UN members.

Protocol for the Prohibition of the Use in War of Asphyxiating, Poisonous or Other Gases, and of Bacteriological Methods of Warfare (Geneva Protocol)

Opened for signature at Geneva on 17 June 1925; entered into force on 8 February 1928.

The protocol declares that the parties agree to be bound by the prohibition on the use in war of these weapons.

Parties (132): Afghanistan, Albania, Algeria,[1] Angola,[1] Antigua and Barbuda, Argentina, Australia, Austria, Bahrain,[1] Bangladesh,[1] Barbados, Belarus, Belgium, Benin, Bhutan, Bolivia, Brazil, Bulgaria, Burkina Faso, Cambodia, Cameroon, Canada,[4] Cape Verde, Central African Republic, Chile, China,[1] Côte d'Ivoire, Cuba, Cyprus, Czech Republic, Denmark, Dominican Republic, Ecuador, Egypt, Equatorial Guinea, Estonia, Ethiopia, Fiji,[1] Finland, France, Gambia, Germany, Ghana, Greece, Grenada, Guatemala, Guinea-Bissau, Holy See, Hungary, Iceland, India, Indonesia, Iran, Iraq,[1] Ireland, Israel,[2] Italy, Jamaica, Japan, Jordan,[3] Kenya, Korea (North),[1] Korea (South),[1] Kuwait,[1] Laos, Latvia, Lebanon, Lesotho, Liberia, Libya,[1] Liechtenstein, Lithuania, Luxembourg, Madagascar, Malawi, Malaysia, Maldives, Malta, Mauritius, Mexico, Monaco, Mongolia, Morocco, Nepal, Netherlands, New Zealand, Nicaragua, Niger, Nigeria,[1] Norway, Pakistan, Panama, Papua New Guinea,[1] Paraguay, Peru, Philippines, Poland, Portugal,[1] Qatar, Romania, Russia,[4] Rwanda, Saint Kitts (Christopher) and Nevis, Saint Lucia, Saudi Arabia, Senegal, Sierra Leone, Slovakia, Solomon Islands, South Africa, Spain, Sri Lanka, Sudan, Swaziland, Sweden, Switzerland, Syria, Tanzania, Thailand, Togo, Tonga, Trinidad and Tobago, Tunisia, Turkey, Uganda, UK,[4] Uruguay, USA,[4] Venezuela, Viet Nam,[1] Yemen, Yugoslavia

[1] The protocol is binding on this state only as regards states which have signed and ratified or acceded to it. The protocol will cease to be binding on this state in regard to any enemy state whose armed forces or whose allies fail to respect the prohibitions laid down in it.

[2] The protocol is binding on Israel only as regards states which have signed and ratified or acceded to it. The protocol shall cease to be binding on Israel in regard to any enemy state whose armed forces, or the armed forces of whose allies, or the regular or irregular forces, or groups or individuals operating from its territory, fail to respect the prohibitions which are the object of the protocol.

[3] Jordan undertakes to respect the obligations contained in the protocol with regard to states which have undertaken similar commitments. It is not bound by the protocol as regards states whose armed forces, regular or irregular, do not respect the provisions of the protocol.

[4] The protocol shall cease to be binding on this state with respect to use in war of asphyxiating, poisonous or other gases, and of all analogous liquids, materials or devices, in regard to any enemy state if such state or any of its allies fails to respect the prohibitions laid down in the protocol.

Signed but not ratified: El Salvador

Treaty for Collaboration in Economic, Social and Cultural Matters and for Collective Self-defence (Brussels Treaty)

Opened for signature at Brussels on 17 March 1948; entered into force on 25 August 1948.

The treaty provides for close cooperation of the parties in the military, economic and political fields.

Parties (7): Belgium, France, Germany, Italy, Luxembourg, Netherlands, UK

See also the Protocols of 1954.

Convention on the Prevention and Punishment of the Crime of Genocide (Genocide Convention)

Adopted at Paris by the UN General Assembly on 9 December 1948; entered into force on 12 January 1951.

Under the convention any commission of acts intended to destroy, in whole or in part, a national, ethnic, racial or religious group as such is declared to be a crime punishable under international law.

Parties (124): Afghanistan, Albania,* Algeria,* Antigua and Barbuda, Argentina,* Armenia, Australia, Austria, Azerbaijan, Bahamas, Bahrain,* Barbados, Belarus,* Belgium, Bosnia and Herzegovina, Brazil, Bulgaria,* Burkina Faso, Burundi, Cambodia, Canada, Chile, China,* Colombia, Congo (Democratic Republic of, formerly Zaire), Costa Rica, Côte d'Ivoire, Croatia, Cuba, Cyprus, Czech Republic, Denmark, Ecuador, Egypt, El Salvador, Estonia, Ethiopia, Fiji, Finland,* France, Gabon, Gambia, Georgia, Germany, Ghana, Greece, Guatemala, Haiti, Honduras, Hungary,* Iceland, India,* Iran, Iraq, Ireland, Israel, Italy, Jamaica, Jordan, Korea (North), Korea (South), Kuwait, Kyrgyzstan, Laos, Latvia, Lebanon, Lesotho, Liberia, Libya, Liechtenstein, Lithuania, Luxembourg, Macedonia (Former Yugoslav Republic of), Malaysia,* Maldives, Mali, Mexico, Moldova, Monaco, Mongolia,* Morocco,* Mozambique, Myanmar (Burma),* Namibia, Nepal, Netherlands, New Zealand, Nicaragua, Norway, Pakistan, Panama, Papua New Guinea, Peru, Philippines,* Poland,* Romania,* Russia,* Rwanda,* Saint Vincent and the Grenadines, Saudi Arabia, Senegal, Seychelles, Singapore,* Slovakia, Slovenia, Spain,* Sri Lanka, Sweden, Syria, Tanzania, Togo, Tonga, Tunisia, Turkey, Uganda, UK, Ukraine,* Uruguay, USA,* Venezuela,* Viet Nam,* Yemen,* Yugoslavia, Zimbabwe

*With reservation and/or declaration upon ratification, accession or succession.

Signed but not ratified: Bolivia, Dominican Republic, Paraguay

Geneva Convention (IV) Relative to the Protection of Civilian Persons in Time of War

Opened for signature at Geneva on 12 August 1949; entered into force on 21 October 1950.

The convention establishes rules for the protection of civilians in areas covered by war and on occupied territories.

Parties (188): Afghanistan, Albania,* Algeria, Andorra, Angola,* Antigua and Barbuda, Argentina, Armenia, Australia,* Austria, Azerbaijan, Bahamas, Bahrain, Bangladesh, Barbados,* Belarus,* Belgium, Belize, Benin, Bhutan, Bolivia, Bosnia and Herzegovina, Botswana, Brazil, Brunei, Bulgaria,* Burkina Faso, Burundi, Cambodia, Cameroon, Canada, Cape Verde, Central African Republic, Chad, Chile, China,* Colombia, Comoros, Congo (Brazzaville), Congo (Democratic Republic of, formerly Zaire), Costa Rica, Côte d'Ivoire, Croatia, Cuba, Cyprus, Czech Republic,* Denmark, Djibouti, Dominica, Dominican Republic, Ecuador, Egypt, El Salvador, Equatorial Guinea, Estonia, Ethiopia, Fiji, Finland, France, Gabon, Gambia, Georgia, Germany,* Ghana, Greece, Grenada, Guatemala, Guinea, Guinea-Bissau,* Guyana, Haiti, Holy See, Honduras, Hungary,* Iceland, India, Indonesia, Iran,* Iraq, Ireland, Israel,* Italy, Jamaica, Japan, Jordan, Kazakhstan, Kenya, Kiribati, Korea (North),* Korea (South),* Kuwait,* Kyrgyzstan, Laos, Latvia, Lebanon, Lesotho, Liberia, Libya, Liechtenstein, Lithuania, Luxembourg, Macedonia (Former Yugoslav Republic of),* Madagascar, Malawi, Malaysia, Maldives, Mali, Malta, Mauritania, Mauritius, Mexico, Micronesia, Moldova, Monaco, Mongolia, Morocco, Mozambique, Myanmar (Burma), Namibia, Nepal, Netherlands, New Zealand, Nicaragua, Niger, Nigeria, Norway, Oman, Pakistan,* Palau,

Panama, Papua New Guinea, Paraguay, Peru, Philippines, Poland,* Portugal,* Qatar, Romania,* Russia,* Rwanda, Saint Kitts (Christopher) and Nevis, Saint Lucia, Saint Vincent and the Grenadines, Samoa (Western), San Marino, Sao Tome and Principe, Saudi Arabia, Senegal, Seychelles, Sierra Leone, Singapore,* Slovakia,* Slovenia, Solomon Islands, Somalia, South Africa, Spain, Sri Lanka, Sudan, Suriname,* Swaziland, Sweden, Switzerland, Syria, Tajikistan, Tanzania, Thailand, Togo, Tonga, Trinidad and Tobago, Tunisia, Turkey, Turkmenistan, Tuvalu, Uganda, UK, Ukraine,* United Arab Emirates, Uruguay,* USA,* Uzbekistan, Vanuatu, Venezuela, Viet Nam,* Yemen,* Yugoslavia,* Zambia, Zimbabwe

* With reservation and/or declaration upon ratification, accession or succession.

Protocols to the 1948 Brussels Treaty (Paris Agreements on the Western European Union)

Opened for signature at Paris on 23 October 1954; entered into force on 6 May 1955.

The protocols modify the 1948 Brussels Treaty, allowing the Federal Republic of Germany and Italy to become parties in return for controls over German armaments and force levels (annulled, except for weapons of mass destruction, in 1984). The Protocols to the Brussels Treaty are regarded as having created the Western European Union (WEU). *Members of the WEU:* Belgium, France, Germany, Greece, Italy, Luxembourg, Netherlands, Portugal, Spain, UK.

Antarctic Treaty

Opened for signature at Washington, DC, on 1 December 1959; entered into force on 23 June 1961.

Declares the Antarctic an area to be used exclusively for peaceful purposes. Prohibits any measure of a military nature in the Antarctic, such as the establishment of military bases and fortifications, and the carrying out of military manoeuvres or the testing of any type of weapon. The treaty bans any nuclear explosion as well as the disposal of radioactive waste material in Antarctica.

In accordance with Article IX, consultative meetings are convened at regular intervals to exchange information and hold consultations on matters pertaining to Antarctica, as well as to recommend to the governments measures in furtherance of the principles and objectives of the treaty.

The treaty is subject to ratification by the signatories and is open for accession by UN members or by other states invited to accede with the consent of all the parties entitled to participate in the consultative meetings provided for in Article IX.

Parties (43): Argentina,† Australia,† Austria, Belgium,† Brazil,† Bulgaria, Canada, Chile,† China,† Colombia, Cuba, Czech Republic, Denmark, Ecuador,† Finland,† France,† Germany,† Greece, Guatemala, Hungary, India,† Italy,† Japan,† Korea (North), Korea (South),† Netherlands,† New Zealand,† Norway,† Papua New Guinea, Peru,† Poland,† Romania,* Russia,† Slovakia, South Africa,† Spain,† Sweden,† Switzerland, Turkey, UK,† Ukraine, Uruguay,*† USA†

* With reservation and/or declaration upon ratification, accession or succession.
† Party entitled to participate in the consultative meetings.

The Protocol on Environmental Protection to the Antarctic Treaty (**Madrid Protocol**) was signed on 4 October 1991 and entered into force on 14 January 1998.

Treaty Banning Nuclear Weapon Tests in the Atmosphere, in Outer Space and Under Water (Partial Test Ban Treaty, PTBT)

Opened for signature at Moscow on 5 August 1963; entered into force on 10 October 1963.

Prohibits the carrying out of any nuclear weapon test explosion or any other nuclear explosion: (*a*) in the atmosphere, beyond its limits, including outer space, or under water, including territorial waters or high seas; and (*b*) in any other environment if such explosion causes radioactive debris to be present outside the territorial limits of the state under whose jurisdiction or control the explosion is conducted.

Parties (125): Afghanistan, Antigua and Barbuda, Argentina, Armenia, Australia, Austria, Bahamas, Bangladesh, Belarus, Belgium, Benin, Bhutan, Bolivia, Botswana, Brazil, Bulgaria, Bosnia and Herzegovina, Canada, Cape Verde, Central African Republic, Chad, Chile, Colombia, Congo (Democratic Republic of, formerly Zaire), Costa Rica, Côte d'Ivoire, Croatia, Cyprus, Czech Republic, Denmark, Dominican Republic, Ecuador, Egypt, El Salvador, Equatorial Guinea, Fiji, Finland, Gabon, Gambia, Germany, Ghana, Greece, Guatemala, Guinea-Bissau, Honduras, Hungary, Iceland, India, Indonesia, Iran, Iraq, Ireland, Israel, Italy, Jamaica, Japan, Jordan, Kenya, Korea (South), Kuwait, Laos, Lebanon, Liberia, Libya, Luxembourg, Madagascar, Malawi, Malaysia, Malta, Mauritania, Mauritius, Mexico, Mongolia, Morocco, Myanmar (Burma), Nepal, Netherlands, New Zealand, Nicaragua, Niger, Nigeria, Norway, Pakistan, Panama, Papua New Guinea, Peru, Philippines, Poland, Romania, Russia, Rwanda, Samoa (Western), San Marino, Senegal, Seychelles, Sierra Leone, Singapore, Slovakia, Slovenia, South Africa, Spain, Sri Lanka, Sudan, Suriname, Swaziland, Sweden, Switzerland, Syria, Taiwan, Tanzania, Thailand, Togo, Tonga, Trinidad and Tobago, Tunisia, Turkey, Uganda, UK, Ukraine, Uruguay, USA, Venezuela, Yemen, Yugoslavia, Zambia

Signed but not ratified: Algeria, Burkina Faso, Burundi, Cameroon, Ethiopia, Haiti, Mali, Paraguay, Portugal, Somalia

Treaty on Principles Governing the Activities of States in the Exploration and Use of Outer Space, Including the Moon and Other Celestial Bodies (Outer Space Treaty)

Opened for signature at London, Moscow and Washington, DC, on 27 January 1967; entered into force on 10 October 1967.

Prohibits the placing into orbit around the earth of any objects carrying nuclear weapons or any other kinds of weapons of mass destruction, the installation of such weapons on celestial bodies, or the stationing of them in outer space in any other manner. The establishment of military bases, installations and fortifications, the testing of any type of weapons and the conduct of military manoeuvres on celestial bodies are also forbidden.

Parties (95): Afghanistan, Algeria, Antigua and Barbuda, Argentina, Australia, Austria, Bahamas, Bangladesh, Barbados, Belarus, Belgium, Benin, Brazil,* Bulgaria, Burkina Faso, Canada, Chile, China, Cuba, Cyprus, Czech Republic, Denmark, Dominican Republic, Ecuador, Egypt, El Salvador, Equatorial Guinea, Fiji, Finland, France, Germany, Greece, Guinea-Bissau, Hungary, Iceland, India, Iraq, Ireland, Israel, Italy, Jamaica, Japan, Kenya, Korea (South), Kuwait, Laos, Lebanon, Libya, Madagascar,* Mali, Mauritius, Mexico, Mongolia, Morocco, Myanmar (Burma), Nepal, Netherlands, New Zealand, Niger, Nigeria, Norway, Pakistan, Papua New Guinea, Peru, Poland, Portugal, Romania, Russia, San Marino, Saudi Arabia, Seychelles, Sierra Leone, Singapore, Slovakia, South Africa, Spain, Sri Lanka,

Sweden, Switzerland, Syria, Taiwan, Thailand, Togo, Tonga, Tunisia, Turkey, Uganda, UK, Ukraine, Uruguay, USA, Venezuela, Viet Nam, Yemen, Zambia

* With reservation and/or declaration upon ratification, accession or succession.

Signed but not ratified: Bolivia, Botswana, Burundi, Cameroon, Central African Republic, Colombia, Congo (Democratic Republic of, formerly Zaire), Ethiopia, Gambia, Ghana, Guyana, Haiti, Holy See, Honduras, Indonesia, Iran, Jordan, Lesotho, Luxembourg, Malaysia, Nicaragua, Panama, Philippines, Rwanda, Somalia, Trinidad and Tobago, Yugoslavia

Treaty for the Prohibition of Nuclear Weapons in Latin America and the Caribbean (Treaty of Tlatelolco)

Opened for signature at Mexico, Distrito Federal, on 14 February 1967; entered into force on 22 April 1968. The treaty was amended in 1990, 1991 and 1992.

Prohibits the testing, use, manufacture, production or acquisition by any means, as well as the receipt, storage, installation, deployment and any form of possession of any nuclear weapons by Latin American and Caribbean countries.

The parties should conclude agreements with the IAEA for the application of safeguards to their nuclear activities. The IAEA has the exclusive power to carry out special inspections.

The treaty is open for signature by all the independent states of the region.

Under *Additional Protocol I* states with territories within the zone (France, the Netherlands, the UK and the USA) undertake to apply the statute of military denuclearization to these territories.

Under *Additional Protocol II* the nuclear weapon states—China, France, Russia (at the time of signing, the USSR), the UK and the USA—undertake to respect the statute of military denuclearization of Latin America and not to contribute to acts involving a violation of the treaty, nor to use or threaten to use nuclear weapons against the parties to the treaty.

The amended treaty is fully in force for Argentina, Barbados, Brazil, Chile, Guyana, Jamaica, Mexico, Paraguay, Peru, Suriname, Uruguay and Venezuela.

Parties to the original treaty (32): Antigua and Barbuda, Argentina, Bahamas, Barbados, Belize, Bolivia, Brazil, Chile, Colombia, Costa Rica, Dominica, Dominican Republic, Ecuador, El Salvador, Grenada, Guatemala, Guyana, Haiti, Honduras, Jamaica, Mexico, Nicaragua, Panama, Paraguay, Peru, Saint Kitts (Christopher) and Nevis, Saint Lucia, Saint Vincent and the Grenadines, Suriname, Trinidad and Tobago, Uruguay, Venezuela

Parties to Additional Protocol I: France,[1] Netherlands, UK,[2] USA[3]

Parties to Additional Protocol II: China,[4] France,[5] Russia,[6] UK,[2] USA[7]

Signed but not ratified: Cuba

[1] France declared that Protocol I shall not apply to transit across French territories situated within the zone of the treaty, and destined for other French territories. The protocol shall not limit the participation of the populations of the French territories in the activities mentioned in Article 1 of the treaty, and in efforts connected with the national defence of France. France does not consider the zone described in the treaty as established in accordance with international law; it cannot, therefore, agree that the treaty should apply to that zone.

[2] When signing and ratifying Protocols I and II, the UK made the following declarations of understanding: The signing and ratification by the UK could not be regarded as affecting in any way the legal status of any territory for the international relations of which the UK is responsible, lying within the limits of the geographical zone established by the treaty. Should any party to the treaty carry out any act of aggression with the support of a nuclear weapon state, the UK would be free to reconsider the extent to which it could be regarded as bound by the provisions of Protocol II.

[3] The USA ratified Protocol I with the following understandings: The provisions of the treaty do not affect the exclusive power and legal competence under international law of a state adhering to this Protocol to grant or deny transit and transport privileges to its own or any other vessels or aircraft irrespective of cargo or armaments; the provisions do not affect rights under international law of a state adhering to this protocol regarding the exercise of the freedom of the seas, or regarding passage through or over waters subject to the sovereignty of a state. The declarations attached by the USA to its ratification of Protocol II apply also to Protocol I.

[4] China declared that it will never send its means of transportation and delivery carrying nuclear weapons to cross the territory, territorial sea or airspace of Latin American countries.

[5] France stated that it interprets the undertaking contained in Article 3 of Protocol II to mean that it presents no obstacle to the full exercise of the right of self-defence enshrined in Article 51 of the UN Charter; it takes note of the interpretation by the Preparatory Commission for the Denuclearization of Latin America according to which the treaty does not apply to transit, the granting or denying of which lies within the exclusive competence of each state party in accordance with international law. In 1974, France made a supplementary statement to the effect that it was prepared to consider its obligations under Protocol II as applying not only to the signatories of the treaty, but also to the territories for which the statute of denuclearization was in force in conformity with Protocol I.

[6] The USSR signed and ratified Protocol II with the following statement:

The USSR proceeds from the assumption that the effect of Article 1 of the treaty extends to any nuclear explosive device and that, accordingly, the carrying out by any party of nuclear explosions for peaceful purposes would be a violation of its obligations under Article 1 and would be incompatible with its non-nuclear weapon status. For states parties to the treaty, a solution to the problem of peaceful nuclear explosions can be found in accordance with the provisions of Article V of the NPT and within the framework of the international procedures of the IAEA. The USSR declares that authorizing the transit of nuclear weapons in any form would be contrary to the objectives of the treaty.

Any actions undertaken by a state or states parties to the treaty which are not compatible with their non-nuclear weapon status, and also the commission by one or more states parties to the treaty of an act of aggression with the support of a state which is in possession of nuclear weapons or together with such a state, will be regarded by the USSR as incompatible with the obligations of those countries under the treaty. In such cases the USSR reserves the right to reconsider its obligations under Protocol II. It further reserves the right to reconsider its attitude to this protocol in the event of any actions on the part of other states possessing nuclear weapons which are incompatible with their obligations under the said protocol.

[7] The USA signed and ratified Protocol II with the following declarations and understandings: Each of the parties retains exclusive power and legal competence, to grant or deny non-parties transit and transport privileges. As regards the undertaking not to use or threaten to use nuclear weapons against the parties, the USA would consider that an armed attack by a party, in which it was assisted by a nuclear weapon state, would be incompatible with the treaty.

Treaty on the Non-proliferation of Nuclear Weapons (Non-Proliferation Treaty, NPT)

Opened for signature at London, Moscow and Washington, DC, on 1 July 1968; entered into force on 5 March 1970.

Prohibits the transfer by nuclear weapon states, to any recipient whatsoever, of nuclear weapons or other nuclear explosive devices or of control over them, as well as the assistance, encouragement or inducement of any non-nuclear weapon state to manufacture or otherwise acquire such weapons or devices. Prohibits the receipt by non-nuclear weapon states from any transferor whatsoever, as well as the manufacture or other acquisition by those states, of nuclear weapons or other nuclear explosive devices.

Non-nuclear weapon states undertake to conclude safeguard agreements with the International Atomic Energy Agency (IAEA) with a view to preventing diversion of nuclear energy from peaceful uses to nuclear weapons or other nuclear explosive devices.

The parties undertake to facilitate the exchange of equipment, materials and scientific and technological information for the peaceful uses of nuclear energy and to ensure that potential benefits from peaceful applications of nuclear explosions will be made available to non-nuclear weapon parties to the treaty. They also undertake to pursue negotiations in good faith on effective measures relating to cessation of the nuclear arms race at an early date and to nuclear disarmament, and on a treaty on general and complete disarmament.

A Review and Extension Conference, convened in 1995 in accordance with the treaty, decided that the treaty should remain in force indefinitely.

Parties (187): Afghanistan,[†] Albania, Algeria,[†] Andorra, Angola, Antigua and Barbuda, Argentina,[†] Armenia,[†] Australia,[†] Austria,[†] Azerbaijan, Bahamas,[†] Bahrain, Bangladesh,[†] Barbados,[†] Belarus,[†] Belgium,[†] Belize,[†] Benin, Bhutan,[†] Bolivia,[†] Bosnia and Herzegovina, Botswana, Brunei,[†] Bulgaria,[†] Burkina Faso, Burundi, Cambodia, Cameroon, Canada,[†] Cape Verde, Central African Republic, Chad, Chile, China, Colombia, Comoros, Congo (Brazzaville), Congo (Democratic Republic of, formerly Zaire),[†] Costa Rica,[†] Côte d'Ivoire,[†] Croatia,[†] Cyprus,[†] Czech Republic,[†] Denmark,[†] Djibouti, Dominica,[†] Dominican Republic,[†] Ecuador,[†] Egypt,[†] El Salvador,[†] Equatorial Guinea, Eritrea, Estonia,[†] Ethiopia,[†] Fiji,[†] Finland,[†] France,[†] Gabon, Gambia,[†] Georgia, Germany,[†] Ghana,[†] Greece,[†] Grenada,[†] Guatemala,[†] Guinea, Guinea-Bissau, Guyana,[†] Haiti, Holy See,[†] Honduras,[†] Hungary,[†] Iceland,[†] Indonesia,[†] Iran,[†] Iraq,[†] Ireland,[†] Italy,[†] Jamaica,[†] Japan,[†] Jordan,[†] Kazakhstan,[†] Kenya,[†] Kiribati,[†] Korea (North),[†] Korea (South),[†] Kuwait, Kyrgyzstan, Laos, Latvia,[†] Lebanon,[†] Lesotho,[†] Liberia, Libya,[†] Liechtenstein,[†] Lithuania,[†] Luxembourg,[†] Macedonia (Former Yugoslav Republic of), Madagascar,[†] Malawi,[†] Malaysia,[†] Maldives,[†] Mali, Malta,[†] Marshall Islands, Mauritania, Mauritius,[†] Mexico,[†] Micronesia, Moldova, Monaco,[†] Mongolia,[†] Morocco,[†] Mozambique, Myanmar (Burma),[†] Namibia, Nauru,[†] Nepal,[†] Netherlands,[†] New Zealand,[†] Nicaragua,[†] Niger, Nigeria,[†] Norway,[†] Oman, Palau, Panama, Papua New Guinea,[†] Paraguay,[†] Peru,[†] Philippines,[†] Poland,[†] Portugal,[†] Qatar, Romania,[†] Russia,[†] Rwanda, Saint Kitts (Christopher) and Nevis,[†] Saint Lucia,[†] Saint Vincent and the Grenadines,[†] Samoa (Western),[†] San Marino, Sao Tome and Principe, Saudi Arabia, Senegal,[†] Seychelles, Sierra Leone, Singapore,[†] Slovakia,[†] Slovenia,[†] Solomon Islands,[†] Somalia, South Africa,[†] Spain,[†] Sri Lanka,[†] Sudan,[†] Suriname,[†] Swaziland,[†] Sweden,[†] Switzerland,[†] Syria,[†] Taiwan, Tajikistan, Tanzania, Thailand,[†] Togo, Tonga,[†] Trinidad and Tobago,[†] Tunisia,[†] Turkey,[†] Turkmenistan, Tuvalu,[†] Uganda, UK,[†] Ukraine,[†] United Arab Emirates, Uruguay,[†] USA,[†] Uzbekistan, Vanuatu, Venezuela,[†] Viet Nam,[†] Yemen, Yugoslavia,[†] Zambia,[†] Zimbabwe[†]

[†] Party with safeguards agreements in force with the International Atomic Energy Agency (IAEA), as required by the treaty, or concluded by a nuclear weapon state on a voluntary basis.

Treaty on the Prohibition of the Emplacement of Nuclear Weapons and other Weapons of Mass Destruction on the Seabed and the Ocean Floor and in the Subsoil thereof (Seabed Treaty)

Opened for signature at London, Moscow and Washington, DC, on 11 February 1971; entered into force on 18 May 1972.

Prohibits implanting or emplacing on the seabed and the ocean floor and in the subsoil thereof beyond the outer limit of a 12-mile seabed zone any nuclear weapons or any other types of weapons of mass destruction as well as structures, launching installations or any other facilities specifically designed for storing, testing or using such weapons.

Parties (94): Afghanistan, Algeria, Antigua and Barbuda, Argentina,[1] Australia, Austria, Bahamas, Belarus, Belgium, Benin, Bosnia and Herzegovina, Botswana, Brazil,[2] Bulgaria, Canada,[3] Cape Verde, Central African Republic, China, Congo (Brazzaville), Côte d'Ivoire, Croatia, Cuba, Cyprus, Czech Republic, Denmark, Dominican Republic, Equatorial Guinea, Ethiopia, Finland, Germany, Ghana, Greece, Guatemala, Guinea-Bissau, Hungary, Iceland,

India,[4] Iran, Iraq, Ireland, Italy,[5] Jamaica, Japan, Jordan, Korea (South), Laos, Latvia, Lesotho, Libya, Liechtenstein, Luxembourg, Malaysia, Malta, Mauritius, Mexico,[6] Mongolia, Morocco, Nepal, Netherlands, New Zealand, Nicaragua, Niger, Norway, Panama, Philippines, Poland, Portugal, Qatar, Romania, Russia, Rwanda, Sao Tome and Principe, Saudi Arabia, Seychelles, Singapore, Slovakia, Slovenia, Solomon Islands, South Africa, Spain, Swaziland, Sweden, Switzerland, Taiwan, Togo, Tunisia, Turkey,[7] UK, Ukraine, USA, Viet Nam,[8] Yemen, Yugoslavia,[9] Zambia

Signed but not ratified: Bolivia, Burundi, Cambodia, Cameroon, Colombia, Costa Rica, Gambia, Guinea, Honduras, Lebanon, Liberia, Madagascar, Mali, Myanmar (Burma), Paraguay, Senegal, Sierra Leone, Sudan, Tanzania, Uruguay

[1] Argentina precludes any possibility of strengthening, through this treaty, certain positions concerning continental shelves to the detriment of others based on different criteria.

[2] Brazil stated that nothing in the treaty shall be interpreted as prejudicing in any way the sovereign rights of Brazil in the area of the sea, the seabed and the subsoil thereof adjacent to its coasts. It is the understanding of Brazil that the word 'observation', as it appears in para. 1 of Article III of the treaty, refers only to observation that is incidental to the normal course of navigation in accordance with international law.

[3] Canada declared that Article I, para. 1, cannot be interpreted as indicating that any state has a right to implant or emplace any weapons not prohibited under Article I, para. 1, on the seabed and ocean floor, and in the subsoil thereof, beyond the limits of national jurisdiction, or as constituting any limitation on the principle that this area of the seabed and ocean floor and the subsoil thereof shall be reserved for exclusively peaceful purposes. Articles I, II and III cannot be interpreted as indicating that any state but the coastal state has any right to implant or emplace any weapon not prohibited under Article I, para. 1 on the continental shelf, or the subsoil thereof, appertaining to that coastal state, beyond the outer limit of the seabed zone referred to in Article I and defined in Article II. Article III cannot be interpreted as indicating any restrictions or limitation upon the rights of the coastal state, consistent with its exclusive sovereign rights with respect to the continental shelf, to verify, inspect or effect the removal of any weapon, structure, installation, facility or device implanted or emplaced on the continental shelf, or the subsoil thereof, appertaining to that coastal state, beyond the outer limit of the seabed zone referred to in Article I and defined in Article II.

[4] The accession by India is based on its position that it has full and exclusive rights over the continental shelf adjoining its territory and beyond its territorial waters and the subsoil thereof. There cannot, therefore, be any restriction on, or limitation of, the sovereign right of India as a coastal state to verify, inspect, remove or destroy any weapon, device, structure, installation or facility, which might be implanted or emplaced on or beneath its continental shelf by any other country, or to take such other steps as may be considered necessary to safeguard its security.

[5] Italy stated, *inter alia*, that in the case of agreements on further measures in the field of disarmament to prevent an arms race on the seabed and ocean floor and in their subsoil, the question of the delimitation of the area within which these measures would find application shall have to be examined and solved in each instance in accordance with the nature of the measures to be adopted.

[6] Mexico declared that the treaty cannot be interpreted to mean that a state has the right to emplace weapons of mass destruction, or arms or military equipment of any type, on the continental shelf of Mexico. It reserves the right to verify, inspect, remove or destroy any weapon, structure, installation, device or equipment placed on its continental shelf, including nuclear weapons or other weapons of mass destruction.

[7] Turkey declared that the provisions of Article II cannot be used by a state party in support of claims other than those related to disarmament. Hence, Article II cannot be interpreted as establishing a link with the UN Convention on the Law of the Sea. Furthermore, no provision of the Seabed Treaty confers on parties the right to militarize zones which have been demilitarized by other international instruments. Nor can it be interpreted as conferring on either the coastal states or other states the right to emplace nuclear weapons or other weapons of mass destruction on the continental shelf of a demilitarized territory.

[8] Viet Nam stated that no provision of the treaty should be interpreted in a way that would contradict the rights of the coastal states with regard to their continental shelf, including the right to take measures to ensure their security.

[9] In 1974, the Ambassador of Yugoslavia transmitted to the US Secretary of State a note stating that in the view of the Yugoslav Government, Article III, para. 1, of the treaty should be interpreted in such a way that a state exercising its right under this article shall be obliged to notify in advance the coastal state, in so far as its observations are to be carried out 'within the stretch of the sea extending above the continental shelf of the said state'. The USA objected to the Yugoslav reservation, which it considers incompatible with the object and purpose of the treaty.

Convention on the Prohibition of the Development, Production and Stockpiling of Bacteriological (Biological) and Toxin Weapons and on their Destruction (Biological and Toxin Weapons Convention, BTWC)

Opened for signature at London, Moscow and Washington, DC, on 10 April 1972; entered into force on 26 March 1975.

Prohibits the development, production, stockpiling or acquisition by other means or retention of microbial or other biological agents, or toxins whatever their origin or method of production, of types and in quantities that have no justification of prophylactic, protective or other peaceful purposes, as well as weapons, equipment or means of delivery designed to use such agents or toxins for hostile purposes or in armed conflict. The destruction of the agents, toxins, weapons, equipment and means of delivery in the possession of the parties, or their diversion to peaceful purposes, should be effected not later than nine months after the entry into force of the convention. According to a mandate from the 1996 BTWC Review Conference, verification and other measures to strengthen the convention are being discussed and considered in an Ad Hoc Group.

Parties (141): Afghanistan, Albania, Argentina, Armenia, Australia, Austria, Bahamas, Bahrain, Bangladesh, Barbados, Belarus, Belgium, Belize, Benin, Bhutan, Bolivia, Bosnia and Herzegovina, Botswana, Brazil, Brunei, Bulgaria, Burkina Faso, Cambodia, Canada, Cape Verde, Chile, China, Colombia, Congo (Brazzaville), Congo (Democratic Republic of, formerly Zaire), Costa Rica, Croatia, Cuba, Cyprus, Czech Republic, Denmark, Dominica, Dominican Republic, Ecuador, El Salvador, Equatorial Guinea, Estonia, Ethiopia, Fiji, Finland, France, Gambia, Georgia, Germany, Ghana, Greece, Grenada, Guatemala, Guinea-Bissau, Honduras, Hungary, Iceland, India,* Indonesia, Iran, Iraq, Ireland,* Italy, Jamaica, Japan, Jordan, Kenya, Korea (North), Korea (South), Kuwait, Laos, Latvia, Lebanon, Lesotho, Libya, Liechtenstein, Luxembourg, Macedonia (Former Yugoslav Republic of), Malaysia, Maldives, Malta, Mauritius, Mexico,* Mongolia, Netherlands, New Zealand, Nicaragua, Niger, Nigeria, Norway, Oman, Pakistan, Panama, Papua New Guinea, Paraguay, Peru, Philippines, Poland, Portugal, Qatar, Romania, Russia, Rwanda, Saint Kitts (Christopher) and Nevis, Saint Lucia, San Marino, Sao Tome and Principe, Saudi Arabia, Senegal, Seychelles, Sierra Leone, Singapore, Slovakia, Slovenia, Solomon Islands, South Africa, Spain, Sri Lanka, Suriname, Swaziland, Sweden, Switzerland,* Taiwan, Thailand, Togo, Tonga, Tunisia, Turkey, Turkmenistan, Uganda, UK, Ukraine, Uruguay, USA, Uzbekistan, Vanuatu, Venezuela, Viet Nam, Yemen, Yugoslavia, Zimbabwe

* With reservation and/or declaration upon ratification, accession or succession.

Signed but not ratified: Burundi, Central African Republic, Côte d'Ivoire, Egypt, Gabon, Guyana, Haiti, Liberia, Madagascar, Malawi, Mali, Morocco, Myanmar (Burma), Nepal, Somalia, Syria, Tanzania, United Arab Emirates

Note: Lithuania acceded to the convention on 10 February 1998.

Treaty on the Limitation of Anti-Ballistic Missile systems (ABM Treaty)

Signed by the USA and the USSR at Moscow on 26 May 1972; entered into force on 3 October 1972.

The treaty obligates the parties not to undertake to build a nationwide defence system against strategic ballistic missile attack and limits the development and deployment of permitted missile defences.

A *Protocol* to the ABM Treaty, introducing further numerical restrictions on permitted ballistic missile defences, was signed in 1974.

On 26 September 1997, Belarus, Kazakhstan, Russia and Ukraine formally assumed the obligations of the USSR regarding the ABM Treaty. On the same day a *Joint Statement* was made by the parties on the delimitation of strategic and non-strategic ABM systems and an *Agreement* was signed on confidence-building measures in respect to non-strategic ABM systems.

Treaty on the Limitation of Underground Nuclear Weapon Tests (Threshold Test Ban Treaty, TTBT)

Signed by the USA and the USSR at Moscow on 3 July 1974; entered into force on 11 December 1990.

The parties undertake not to carry out any individual underground nuclear weapon test having a yield exceeding 150 kilotons.

Treaty on Underground Nuclear Explosions for Peaceful Purposes (Peaceful Nuclear Explosions Treaty, PNET)

Signed by the USA and the USSR at Moscow and Washington, DC, on 28 May 1976; entered into force on 11 December 1990.

The parties undertake not to carry out any underground nuclear explosion for peaceful purposes having a yield exceeding 150 kilotons or any group explosion having an aggregate yield exceeding 150 kilotons.

Convention on the Prohibition of Military or Any Other Hostile Use of Environmental Modification Techniques (Enmod Convention)

Opened for signature at Geneva on 18 May 1977; entered into force on 5 October 1978.

Prohibits military or any other hostile use of environmental modification techniques having widespread, long-lasting or severe effects as the means of destruction, damage or injury to states party to the convention. The term 'environmental modification techniques' refers to any technique for changing—through the deliberate manipulation of natural processes—the dynamics, composition or structure of the earth, including its biota, lithosphere, hydrosphere and atmosphere, or of outer space. The understandings reached during the negotiations, but not written into the convention, define the terms 'widespread', 'long-lasting' and 'severe'.

Parties (64): Afghanistan, Algeria, Antigua and Barbuda, Argentina, Australia, Austria, Bangladesh, Belarus, Belgium, Benin, Brazil, Bulgaria, Canada, Cape Verde, Chile, Costa Rica, Cuba, Cyprus, Czech Republic, Denmark, Dominica, Egypt, Finland, Germany, Ghana, Greece, Guatemala, Hungary, India, Ireland, Italy, Japan, Korea (North), Korea (South),* Kuwait, Laos, Malawi, Mauritius, Mongolia, Netherlands,* New Zealand, Niger, Norway, Pakistan, Papua New Guinea, Poland, Romania, Russia, Saint Lucia, Sao Tome and Principe, Slovakia, Solomon Islands, Spain, Sri Lanka, Sweden, Switzerland, Tunisia, UK, Ukraine, Uruguay, USA, Uzbekistan, Viet Nam, Yemen

* With reservation and/or declaration upon ratification, accession or succession.

Signed but not ratified: Bolivia, Congo (Democratic Republic of, formerly Zaire), Ethiopia, Holy See, Iceland, Iran, Iraq, Lebanon, Liberia, Luxembourg, Morocco, Nicaragua, Portugal, Sierra Leone, Syria, Turkey, Uganda

Protocol (I) Additional to the 1949 Geneva Conventions, and Relating to the Protection of Victims of International Armed Conflict

Opened for signature at Bern on 12 December 1977; entered into force on 7 December 1978.

The protocol confirms that the right of the parties to an international armed conflict to choose methods or means of warfare is not unlimited and that it is prohibited to use weapons or means of warfare which cause superfluous injury or unnecessary suffering.

Parties (148): Albania, Algeria,* Angola,* Antigua and Barbuda, Argentina,* Armenia, Australia,* Austria,* Bahamas, Bahrain, Bangladesh, Barbados, Belarus, Belgium,* Belize, Benin, Bolivia, Bosnia and Herzegovina, Botswana, Brazil, Brunei, Bulgaria, Burkina Faso, Burundi, Cameroon, Canada,* Cape Verde, Central African Republic, Chad, Chile, China,* Colombia, Comoros, Congo (Brazzaville), Congo (Democratic Republic of, formerly Zaire), Costa Rica, Côte d'Ivoire, Croatia, Cuba, Cyprus, Czech Republic, Denmark,* Djibouti, Dominica, Dominican Republic, Ecuador, Egypt,* El Salvador, Equatorial Guinea, Estonia, Ethiopia, Finland,* Gabon, Gambia, Georgia, Germany,* Ghana, Greece, Guatemala, Guinea, Guinea-Bissau, Guyana, Holy See,* Honduras, Hungary, Iceland,* Italy,* Jamaica, Jordan, Kazakhstan, Korea (North), Korea (South),* Kuwait, Kyrgyzstan, Laos, Latvia, Lebanon,[1] Lesotho, Liberia, Libya, Liechtenstein,* Luxembourg, Macedonia (Former Yugoslav Republic of), Madagascar, Malawi, Maldives, Mali, Malta,* Mauritania, Mauritius, Mexico, Micronesia, Moldova, Mongolia, Mozambique, Namibia, Netherlands,* New Zealand,* Niger, Nigeria, Norway, Oman,* Palau, Panama, Paraguay, Peru, Poland, Portugal, Qatar,* Romania, Russia,* Rwanda, Saint Kitts (Christopher) and Nevis, Saint Lucia, Saint Vincent and the Grenadines, Samoa (Western), San Marino, Sao Tome and Principe,[1] Saudi Arabia,* Senegal, Seychelles, Sierra Leone, Slovakia, Slovenia, Solomon Islands, South Africa, Spain,* Suriname, Swaziland, Sweden,* Switzerland,* Syria,* Tajikistan, Tanzania, Togo, Tunisia, Turkmenistan, Uganda, Ukraine, United Arab Emirates,* Uruguay, Uzbekistan, Vanuatu, Viet Nam, Yemen, Yugoslavia,* Zambia, Zimbabwe

* With reservation and/or declaration upon ratification, accession or succession.

[1] In accordance with the provisions of Article 95.2, the protocol enters into force for a party six months after the deposit of its instrument of ratification or accession. This state ratified or acceded to the protocol in the second half of 1996 and the protocol entered into force for that state in 1997.

Note: Cambodia acceded to the Protocol on 14 January 1998, and the UK ratified the Protocol on 28 January 1998.

Convention on the Physical Protection of Nuclear Material

Opened for signature at Vienna and New York on 3 March 1980; entered into force on 8 February 1987.

The convention obliges the parties to protect nuclear material for peaceful purposes during transport across their territory or on ships or aircraft under their jurisdiction.

Parties (58): Antigua and Barbuda, Argentina,* Armenia, Australia, Austria, Belarus, Belgium,† Brazil, Bulgaria, Canada, Chile, China,* Croatia, Cuba, Czech Republic, Denmark,† Ecuador, Estonia, Euratom,*† Finland, France,*† Germany,† Greece,† Guatemala, Hungary, Indonesia,* Ireland,† Italy,*† Japan, Korea (South),* Liechtenstein, Lithuania, Luxembourg,† Macedonia (Former Yugoslav Republic of), Mexico, Monaco, Mongolia,* Netherlands,*† Norway, Paraguay, Peru,* Philippines, Poland,* Portugal, Romania, Russia,* Slovakia,

Slovenia, Spain,*† Sweden, Switzerland, Tajikistan, Tunisia, Turkey,* UK,† Ukraine, USA, Yugoslavia

* With reservation and/or declaration upon ratification, accession or succession.

† Belgium, Denmark, France, Germany, Greece, Ireland, Italy, Luxembourg, the Netherlands, Spain and the UK signed as Euratom member states.

Signed but not ratified: Dominican Republic, Haiti, Israel, Morocco, Niger, Panama, South Africa

Convention on Prohibitions or Restrictions on the Use of Certain Conventional Weapons which may be Deemed to be Excessively Injurious or to have Indiscriminate Effects (CCW Convention, or 'Inhumane Weapons' Convention)

Opened for signature at New York on 10 April 1981; entered into force on 2 December 1983.

The convention is an 'umbrella treaty', under which specific agreements can be concluded in the form of protocols.

Protocol I prohibits the use of weapons intended to injure by fragments which are not detectable in the human body by X-rays.

Protocol II prohibits or restricts the use of mines, booby-traps and other devices; amendments were adopted on 3 May 1996. The amended Protocol II was not in force as of 1 January 1998.

Protocol III restricts the use of incendiary weapons.

Protocol IV, adopted in Vienna in 1995, prohibits the employment of laser weapons specifically designed to cause permanent blindness to unenhanced vision. Protocol IV will enter into force on 30 July 1998.

The amended Protocol II and Protocol IV will enter into force six months after the date of the deposit of the 20th instrument of ratification, acceptance, approval or accession. Hungary ratified Protocol IV on 30 January 1998, as the 20th state. By 20 April 1998, 19 states had approved the amended Protocol II.

Parties (71): Argentina,* Australia, Austria, Belarus, Belgium, Benin,[1] Bosnia and Herzegovina, Brazil, Bulgaria, Cambodia, Canada, Cape Verde,[4] China, Croatia, Cuba, Cyprus,* Czech Republic, Denmark, Djibouti, Ecuador, Finland, France,*[2] Georgia, Germany, Greece, Guatemala, Holy See,[4] Hungary, India, Ireland, Israel,[2] Italy, Japan, Jordan,[1] Laos, Latvia, Liechtenstein, Luxembourg, Macedonia (Former Yugoslav Republic of), Malta, Mauritius, Mexico, Monaco,[3,4] Mongolia, Netherlands,* New Zealand, Niger, Norway, Pakistan, Panama, Peru,[1,4] Philippines,[4] Poland, Portugal, Romania, Russia, Slovakia, Slovenia, South Africa, Spain, Sweden, Switzerland, Togo, Tunisia, Uganda, UK, Ukraine, Uruguay, USA,[2] Uzbekistan,[4] Yugoslavia

* With reservation and/or declaration upon ratification, accession or succession.

[1] Party only to Protocols I and III.
[2] Party only to Protocols I and II.
[3] Party only to Protocol I.
[4] In accordance with Article 5.2, the convention enters into force for a state six months after the deposit of the instrument of ratification or accession. This state deposited its instruments of ratification or accession in the second half of 1997 and the convention entered into force for this state in 1998.

Signed but not ratified: Afghanistan, Egypt, Iceland, Morocco, Nicaragua, Nigeria, Sierra Leone, Sudan, Turkey, Viet Nam

South Pacific Nuclear Free Zone Treaty (Treaty of Rarotonga)

Opened for signature at Rarotonga, Cook Islands, on 6 August 1985; entered into force on 11 December 1986.

Prohibits the manufacture or acquisition by other means of any nuclear explosive device, as well as possession or control over such device by the parties anywhere inside or outside the zone area described in an annex. The parties also undertake not to supply nuclear material or equipment, unless subject to IAEA safeguards, and to prevent in their territories the stationing as well as the testing of any nuclear explosive device and undertake not to dump, and to prevent the dumping of, radioactive wastes and other radioactive matter at sea anywhere within the zone. Each party remains free to allow visits, as well as transit, by foreign ships and aircraft.

The treaty is open for signature by members of the South Pacific Forum.

Under *Protocol 1* France, the UK and the USA undertake to apply the treaty prohibitions relating to the manufacture, stationing and testing of nuclear explosive devices in the territories situated within the zone, for which they are internationally responsible.

Under *Protocol 2* China, France, Russia, the UK and the USA undertake not to use or threaten to use a nuclear explosive device against the parties to the treaty or against any territory within the zone for which a party to Protocol 1 is internationally responsible.

Under *Protocol 3* China, France, the UK, the USA and Russia undertake not to test any nuclear explosive device anywhere within the zone.

Parties (12): Australia, Cook Islands, Fiji, Kiribati, Nauru, New Zealand, Niue, Papua New Guinea, Samoa (Western), Solomon Islands, Tuvalu, Vanuatu

Signed but not ratified: Tonga

Party to Protocol 1: France, UK; **signed but not ratified:** USA

Parties to Protocol 2: China, France,[1] Russia, UK[2]; **signed but not ratified:** USA

Parties to Protocol 3: China, France, Russia, UK; **signed but not ratified:** USA

[1] France declared that the negative security guarantees set out in Protocol 2 are the same as the CD declaration of 6 April 1995 which were referred to in the UN Security Council Resolution 984 of 11 April 1995.

[2] The UK declared that nothing in the treaty affects the rights under international law with regard to transit of the zone or visits to ports and airfields within the zone by ships and aircraft. The UK will not be bound by the undertakings in Protocol 2 in case of an invasion or any other attack on the UK, its territories, its armed forces or its allies, carried out or sustained by a party to the treaty in association or alliance with a nuclear weapon state or if a party violates its non-proliferation obligations under the treaty.

Treaty on the Elimination of Intermediate-Range and Shorter-Range Missiles (INF Treaty)

Signed by the USA and the USSR at Washington, DC, on 8 December 1987; entered into force on 1 June 1988.

The treaty obliged the parties to destroy all land-based missiles with a range of 500–5500 km (intermediate-range, 1000–5500 km; and shorter-range, 500–1000 km) and their launchers by 1 June 1991. The treaty was implemented by the two parties before this date.

Treaty on Conventional Armed Forces in Europe (CFE Treaty)

Opened for signature at Vienna on 19 November 1990; entered into force on 9 November 1992.

The treaty sets ceilings on five categories of treaty-limited equipment (battle tanks, armoured combat vehicles, heavy artillery, combat aircraft and attack helicopters) in an area stretching from the Atlantic Ocean to the Ural Mountains (the Atlantic-to-the-Urals, ATTU, zone).

The treaty was negotiated and signed by the member states of the Warsaw Treaty Organization (WTO) and NATO within the framework of the Conference on Security and Co-operation in Europe (from 1 January 1995 the Organization for Security and Co-operation in Europe, OSCE).

The **1992 Tashkent Agreement**, signed by the former Soviet republics, with the exception of the Baltic states, with territories within the ATTU zone, set out the division of the former Soviet CFE obligations and entitlements.

All the states which have ratified the CFE Treaty signed, at Oslo in 1992, the Final Document of the Extraordinary Conference of the States Parties to the CFE Treaty (**Oslo Document**), introducing necessary modifications because of the emergence of new states as a consequence of the breakup of the USSR.

The first Review Conference of the CFE Treaty, held in 1996, adopted a **Flank Document** which reorganized the flank areas geographically and numerically, allowing Russia and Ukraine to deploy more treaty-limited equipment along their borders.

In January 1997 negotiations were opened to adapt the treaty to the new security environment in Europe. The **Decision of the Joint Consultative Group Concerning Certain Basic Elements for Treaty Adaptation** of 23 July 1997 mapped out the course of negotiations towards a CFE adaptation agreement.

Parties (30): Armenia, Azerbaijan, Belarus, Belgium, Bulgaria, Canada, Czech Republic, Denmark, France, Georgia, Germany, Greece, Hungary, Iceland, Italy, Kazakhstan, Luxembourg, Moldova, Netherlands, Norway, Poland, Portugal, Romania, Russia, Slovakia, Spain, Turkey, UK, Ukraine, USA

The Concluding Act of the Negotiation on Personnel Strength of Conventional Armed Forces in Europe (CFE-1A Agreement)

Opened for signature by the parties to the CFE Treaty at Helsinki on 10 July 1992; entered into force simultaneously with the CFE Treaty.

The agreement limits the personnel of the conventional land-based armed forces within the ATTU zone.

Vienna Documents 1990, 1992 and 1994 on Confidence- and Security-Building Measures

The Vienna Documents were adopted by all the CSCE states. The Vienna Document 1994 was adopted at Vienna on 28 November 1994.

The **Vienna Document 1990** on confidence- and security-building measures (CSBMs) repeats many of the provisions in the 1986 Stockholm Document on CSBMs and Disarmament in Europe and expands several others. It establishes a communications network and a risk reduction mechanism. The **Vienna Document 1992** on CSBMs builds on the Vienna Document 1990 and supplements its provisions with new mechanisms and constraining provisions. The **Vienna Document 1994** on CSBMs amends and expands the previous Vienna Documents. In 1995–96 several amendments to the Vienna Document 1994 were adopted.

The Vienna Documents were signed by all members of the Conference on Security and Co-operation in Europe (from 1 January 1995 the OSCE).

Treaty on the Reduction and Limitation of Strategic Offensive Arms (START I Treaty)

Signed by the USA and the USSR at Moscow on 31 July 1991; entered into force on 5 December 1994.

The treaty requires the USA and Russia to make phased reductions in their offensive strategic nuclear forces over a seven-year period. It sets numerical limits on deployed strategic nuclear delivery vehicles (SNDVs)—ICBMs, SLBMs and heavy bombers—and the nuclear warheads they carry. In the 1992 Protocol to Facilitate the Implementation of the START Treaty (**Lisbon Protocol**), Belarus, Kazakhstan and Ukraine also assumed the obligations of the former USSR under the treaty. They pledged to eliminate all the former Soviet strategic weapons on their territories within the seven-year reduction period and to join the NPT as non-nuclear weapon states in the shortest possible time.

Treaty on Open Skies

Opened for signature at Helsinki on 24 March 1992; not in force as of 1 January 1998

The treaty obliges the parties to submit their territories to short-notice unarmed surveillance flights. The area of application stretches from Vancouver, Canada, eastwards to Vladivostok, Russia.

The treaty was negotiated between the member states of the Warsaw Treaty Organization (WTO) and NATO. It is open for signature by the NATO states and the former WTO members, including the new states of the former Soviet Union. For six months after entry into force of the treaty, any other OSCE member state may apply for accession. The treaty will enter into force 60 days after the deposit of 20 instruments of ratification, including those of the depositaries (Canada and Hungary), and all the signatories with more than eight 'passive quotas' (i.e., flights which the state is obliged to accept); that is, Belarus, Canada, France, Germany, Italy, Russia, Turkey, the UK, Ukraine and the USA.

22 ratifications deposited: Belgium, Bulgaria, Canada, Czech Republic, Denmark, France, Germany, Greece, Hungary, Iceland, Italy, Luxembourg, Netherlands, Norway, Poland, Portugal, Romania, Slovakia, Spain, Turkey, UK, USA

Signed but not ratified: Belarus, Georgia, Kyrgyzstan, Russia, Ukraine

Treaty on Further Reduction and Limitation of Strategic Offensive Arms (START II Treaty)

Signed by the USA and Russia at Moscow on 3 January 1993; not in force as of 1 January 1998.

The treaty requires the USA and Russia to eliminate their MIRVed ICBMs and sharply reduce the number of their deployed strategic nuclear warheads to no more than 3000–3500 each (of which no more than 1750 may be deployed on SLBMs) by 1 January 2003 or no later than 31 December 2000 if the USA and Russia reach a formal agreement committing the USA to help finance the elimination of strategic nuclear weapons in Russia.

On 26 September 1997 the two parties signed a *Protocol* to the treaty providing for the extension until 2007 of the period of implementation of the treaty.

Convention on the Prohibition of the Development, Production, Stockpiling and Use of Chemical Weapons and on their Destruction (Chemical Weapons Convention, CWC)

Opened for signature at Paris on 13 January 1993; entered into force on 29 April 1997.

The convention prohibits both the use of chemical weapons (also prohibited by the 1925 Geneva Protocol) and the development, production, acquisition, transfer and stockpiling of chemical weapons. Each party undertakes to destroy its chemical weapons and production facilities.

Parties (106): Albania, Algeria, Argentina, Armenia, Australia, Austria, Bahrain, Bangladesh, Belarus, Belgium, Bosnia and Herzegovina, Brazil, Brunei, Bulgaria, Burkina Faso, Cameroon, Canada, Chile, China, Cook Islands, Costa Rica, Côte d'Ivoire, Croatia, Cuba, Czech Republic, Denmark, Ecuador, El Salvador, Equatorial Guinea, Ethiopia, Fiji, Finland, France, Georgia, Germany, Ghana, Greece, Guinea, Guyana, Hungary, Iceland, India, Iran, Ireland, Italy, Japan, Jordan, Kenya, Korea (South), Kuwait, Laos, Latvia, Lesotho, Luxembourg, Macedonia (Former Yugoslav Republic of), Maldives, Mali, Malta, Mauritius, Mexico, Moldova, Monaco, Mongolia, Morocco, Namibia, Nepal, Netherlands, New Zealand, Niger, Norway, Oman, Pakistan, Papua New Guinea, Paraguay, Peru, Philippines, Poland, Portugal, Qatar, Romania, Russia, Saint Lucia, Saudi Arabia, Seychelles, Singapore, Slovakia, Slovenia, South Africa, Spain, Sri Lanka, Suriname, Swaziland, Sweden, Switzerland, Tajikistan, Togo, Trinidad and Tobago, Tunisia, Turkey, Turkmenistan, UK, Uruguay, USA, Uzbekistan, Venezuela, Zimbabwe

Signed but not ratified: Afghanistan, Azerbaijan, Bahamas, Benin, Bolivia, Burundi, Cambodia, Cape Verde, Central African Republic, Chad, Colombia, Comoros, Congo (Brazzaville), Congo (Democratic Republic of, formerly Zaire), Cyprus, Djibouti, Dominica, Dominican Republic, Estonia, Gabon, Gambia, Guatemala, Guinea-Bissau, Haiti, Holy See, Honduras, Indonesia, Israel, Kazakhstan, Kyrgyzstan, Liberia, Liechtenstein, Lithuania, Madagascar, Malawi, Malaysia, Marshall Islands, Mauritania, Micronesia, Myanmar (Burma), Nauru, Nicaragua, Nigeria, Panama, Rwanda, Saint Kitts (Christopher) and Nevis, Saint Vincent and the Grenadines, Samoa (Western), San Marino, Senegal, Sierra Leone, Tanzania, Thailand, Uganda, Ukraine, United Arab Emirates, Viet Nam, Yemen, Zambia

Note: Mauritania ratified the convention on 9 February 1998.

Treaty on the Southeast Asia Nuclear Weapon-Free Zone (Treaty of Bangkok)

Opened for signature at Bangkok on 15 December 1995; entered into force on 27 March 1997.

Prohibits the development, manufacture, acquisition or testing of nuclear weapons inside or outside the zone area as well as the stationing and transport of nuclear weapons in or through the zone. Each state party may decide for itself whether to allow visits and transit by foreign ships and aircraft. The parties undertake not to dump at sea or discharge into the atmosphere anywhere within the zone any radioactive material or wastes or dispose of radioactive material on land. The parties should conclude an agreement with the IAEA for the application of full-scope safeguards to their peaceful nuclear activities.

The zone includes not only the territories but also the continental shelves and exclusive economic zones of the states parties.

The treaty is open for signature by all the states in South-East Asia: Brunei, Cambodia, Indonesia, Laos, Malaysia, Myanmar (Burma), the Philippines, Singapore, Thailand and Viet Nam.

Under a *Protocol* to the treaty China, France, Russia, the UK and the USA are to undertake not to use or threaten to use nuclear weapons against any state party to the treaty. They should further undertake not to use nuclear weapons within the Southeast Asia nuclear weapon-free zone. The protocol will enter into force for each state party on the date of its deposit of the instrument of ratification.

Parties (9): Brunei, Cambodia, Indonesia, Laos, Malaysia, Myanmar (Burma), Singapore, Thailand, Viet Nam

Signed but not ratified: Philippines

Protocol: no signatures, no ratifications

African Nuclear-Weapon-Free Zone Treaty (Treaty of Pelindaba)

Opened for signature at Cairo on 11 April 1996; not in force as of 1 January 1998.

Prohibits the research, development, manufacture and acquisition of nuclear explosive devices and the testing or stationing of any nuclear explosive device. Each party remains free to allow visits, as well as transit by foreign ships and aircraft. The treaty also prohibits any attack against nuclear installations. The parties undertake not to dump or permit the dumping of radioactive wastes and other radioactive matter anywhere within the zone. The parties should conclude an agreement with the IAEA for the application of comprehensive safeguards to their peaceful nuclear activities.

'African nuclear-weapon-free zone' means the territory of the continent of Africa, island states members of the OAU and all islands considered by the OAU to be part of Africa.

The treaty is open for signature by all the states of Africa. It will enter into force upon the 28th ratification.

Under *Protocol I* China, France, Russia, the UK and the USA are to undertake not to use or threaten to use a nuclear explosive device against the parties to the Treaty.

Under *Protocol II* China, France, Russia, the UK and the USA are to undertake not to test nuclear explosive devices anywhere within the zone.

Under *Protocol III* states with territories within the zone for which they are internationally responsible are to undertake to observe certain provisions of the treaty with respect to these territories. This protocol is open for signature by France and Spain.

The protocols will enter into force simultaneously with the treaty for those protocol signatories that have deposited their instruments of ratification.

2 ratifications deposited: Gambia, Mauritius

Signed but not ratified: Algeria, Angola, Benin, Burkina Faso, Burundi, Cameroon, Cape Verde, Central African Republic, Chad, Comoros, Congo (Brazzaville), Congo (Democratic Republic of, formerly Zaire), Côte d'Ivoire, Djibouti, Egypt, Eritrea, Ethiopia, Gabon, Ghana, Guinea, Guinea-Bissau, Kenya, Lesotho, Liberia, Libya, Malawi, Mali, Mauritania, Morocco, Mozambique, Namibia, Niger, Nigeria, Rwanda, Sao Tome and Principe, Senegal, Seychelles, Sierra Leone, South Africa, Sudan, Swaziland, Tanzania, Togo, Tunisia, Uganda, Zambia, Zimbabwe

Note: Algeria ratified the treaty on 11 February 1998, Mauritania on 24 February 1998, South Africa on 27 March 1998 and Zimbabwe on 3 April 1998.

Protocol I ratification: China, France[1]; **signed but not ratified:** Russia,[2] UK,[3] USA

Protocol II ratification: China, France; **signed but not ratified:** Russia,[2] UK,[3] USA

Protocol III ratification: France

[1] When signing Protocol I France stated that the commitment expressed in Article I of the Protocol is equivalent to the negative security guarantee that France has given to non-nuclear states parties to the Non-proliferation Treaty, confirmed in a CD statement of 6 April 1995 and in UN Security Council Resolution 984 of 11 April 1995.

[2] The Russian Government declared that as long as a military base is located on the Chagos archipelago islands it cannot meet the requirements put forward by the treaty for the nuclear weapon-free territories and it considers itself not to be bound by the obligations in respect of these territories. As regards Article 1 of Protocol I Russia interprets it as meaning that it will not use nuclear weapons against a state which is a party to the treaty except in cases of invasion of or any other armed attack on Russia.

[3] The British Government declared that it does not accept the inclusion of the British Indian Ocean Territory within the African nuclear weapon-free zone without its consent and it does not accept any legal obligation in respect of that territory by its adherence to Protocols I and II. The UK will not be bound by Protocol I in case of an invasion of or any other attack on the UK, its dependent territories, its armed forces or its allies or carried out or sustained by a party to the treaty in association or in alliance with a nuclear weapon state.

Agreement on Sub-Regional Arms Control (Florence Agreement)

Signed at Florence on 14 June 1996; entered into force upon signature.

The agreement was negotiated under the auspices of the OSCE in accordance with the mandate in the 1995 General Framework Agreement for Peace in Bosnia and Herzegovina (Dayton Agreement). It sets numerical ceilings on armaments of the former warring parties: Bosnia and Herzegovina and its two entities, Croatia and Yugoslavia (Serbia and Montenegro). Five categories of heavy conventional weapons are included: battle tanks, armoured combat vehicles, heavy artillery (75 mm and above), combat aircraft and attack helicopters. The reductions were completed by 31 October 1997. It is confirmed that 6580 weapon items were destroyed by that date.

Parties (5): Bosnia and Herzegovina and its two entities—the Federation of Bosnia and Herzegovina and the Republika Srpska—Croatia, Yugoslavia (Serbia and Montenegro)

Comprehensive Nuclear Test-Ban Treaty (CTBT)

Opened for signature at New York on 24 September 1996; not in force as of 1 January 1998.

Prohibits the carrying out of any nuclear weapon test explosion or any other nuclear explosion, and urges each party to prevent any such nuclear explosion at any place under its jurisdiction or control and refrain from causing, encouraging, or in any way participating in the carrying out of any nuclear weapon test explosion or any other nuclear explosion.

The treaty will enter into force 180 days after the date of the deposit of the instrument of ratification of the 44 states listed in an annexe to the treaty but in no case earlier than two years after its opening for signature. All the 44 states possess nuclear power reactors and/or nuclear research reactors.

Note: The 44 states whose ratification is required for entry into force are Algeria, Argentina, Australia, Austria, Bangladesh, Belgium, Brazil, Bulgaria, Canada, Chile, China, Colombia, Congo (Democratic Republic of, formerly Zaire), Egypt, Finland, France, Germany, Hungary, India, Indonesia, Iran, Israel, Italy, Japan, Korea (North), Korea (South), Mexico, Netherlands, Norway, Pakistan, Peru, Poland, Romania, Russia, Slovakia, South Africa, Spain, Sweden, Switzerland, Turkey, UK, Ukraine, USA and Viet Nam.

8 ratifications deposited: Czech Republic, Fiji, Japan, Micronesia, Mongolia, Peru, Qatar, Uzbekistan

Signed but not ratified: Albania, Algeria, Andorra, Angola, Antigua and Barbuda, Argentina, Armenia, Australia, Austria, Azerbaijan, Bahrain, Bangladesh, Belarus, Belgium, Benin, Bolivia, Bosnia and Herzegovina, Brazil, Brunei, Bulgaria, Burkina Faso, Burundi, Cambodia, Canada, Cape Verde, Chad, Chile, China, Colombia, Comoros, Congo (Brazzaville), Congo (Democratic Republic of, formerly Congo), Cook Islands, Costa Rica, Côte d'Ivoire, Croatia, Cyprus, Denmark, Djibouti, Dominican Republic, Ecuador, Egypt, El Salvador, Equatorial Guinea, Estonia, Ethiopia, Finland, France, Gabon, Georgia, Germany, Ghana, Greece, Grenada, Guinea, Guinea-Bissau, Haiti, Holy See, Honduras, Hungary, Iceland, Indonesia, Iran, Ireland, Israel, Italy, Jamaica, Jordan, Kazakhstan, Kenya, Korea (South), Kuwait, Kyrgyzstan, Laos, Latvia, Lesotho, Liberia, Liechtenstein, Lithuania, Luxembourg, Madagascar, Malawi, Maldives, Mali, Malta, Marshall Islands, Mauritania, Mexico, Moldova, Monaco, Morocco, Mozambique, Myanmar (Burma), Namibia, Nepal, Netherlands, New Zealand, Nicaragua, Niger, Norway, Panama, Papua New Guinea, Paraguay, Philippines, Poland, Portugal, Romania, Russia, Saint Lucia, Samoa (Western), San Marino, San Tome and Principe, Senegal, Seychelles, Slovakia, Slovenia, Solomon Islands, South Africa, Spain, Sri Lanka, Suriname, Swaziland, Sweden, Switzerland, Tajikistan, Thailand, Togo, Tunisia, Turkey, Turkmenistan, Uganda, UK, Ukraine, United Arab Emirates, Uruguay, USA, Vanuatu, Venezuela, Viet Nam, Yemen, Zambia

Note: Turkmenistan ratified the treaty on 20 February 1998, Slovakia on 3 March 1998, Austria on 13 March 1998, and France and the UK on 6 April 1998.

Joint Statement on Parameters on Future Reductions in Nuclear Forces

Signed by the USA and Russia at Helsinki on 21 March 1997.

In the Joint Statement the two sides agree that once the 1993 START II Treaty enters into force negotiations on a START III treaty will begin. START III will include lower aggregate levels of 2000–2500 nuclear warheads for each side.

Convention on the Prohibition of the Use, Stockpiling, Production and Transfer of Anti-Personnel Mines and on their Destruction (APM Convention)

Opened for signature at Ottawa on 3–4 December 1997 and at the UN Headquarters, New York, on 5 December 1997; not in force as of 1 January 1998.

The convention prohibits anti-personnel mines, which are defined as mines designed to be exploded by the presence, proximity or contact of a person and which will incapacitate, injure or kill one or more persons.

Each party undertakes to destroy all its stockpiled anti-personnel mines as soon as possible but not later that four years after the entry into force of the convention for that state party. Each party also undertakes to destroy all anti-personnel mines in mined areas under its jurisdiction or control not later than 10 years after the entry into force of the convention for that state party.

The convention will enter into force six months after the deposit of the 40th instrument of ratification.

3 ratifications deposited: Canada, Ireland, Mauritius

Signed but not ratified: Algeria, Andorra, Angola, Antigua and Barbuda, Argentina, Australia, Austria, Bahamas, Barbados, Belgium, Benin, Bolivia, Bosnia and Herzegovina, Botswana, Brazil, Brunei, Bulgaria, Burkina Faso, Burundi, Cambodia, Cameroon, Cape Verde, Chile, Colombia, Cook Island, Costa Rica, Côte d'Ivoire, Croatia, Cyprus, Czech Republic, Denmark, Djibouti, Dominica, Dominican Republic, Ecuador, El Salvador, Ethiopia, Fiji, France, Gabon, Gambia, Germany, Ghana, Greece, Grenada, Guatemala, Guinea, Guinea-Bissau, Guyana, Haiti, Holy See, Honduras, Hungary, Iceland, Indonesia, Italy, Jamaica, Japan, Kenya, Lesotho, Liechtenstein, Luxembourg, Madagascar, Malawi, Malaysia, Mali, Malta, Marshall Islands, Mauritania, Mexico, Monaco, Moldova, Mozambique, Namibia, Netherlands, New Zealand, Nicaragua, Niger, Niue, Norway, Panama, Paraguay, Peru, Philippines, Poland, Portugal, Qatar, Romania, Rwanda, Saint Kitts (Christopher) and Nevis, Saint Lucia, Saint Vincent and the Grenadines, Samoa (Western), San Marino, Senegal, Seychelles, Slovakia, Slovenia, Solomon Islands, South Africa, Spain, Sudan, Suriname, Swaziland, Sweden, Switzerland, Tanzania, Thailand, Togo, Trinidad and Tobago, Tunisia, Turkmenistan, Uganda, UK, Uruguay, Vanuatu, Venezuela, Yemen, Zambia, Zimbabwe

Note: Turkmenistan ratified the convention on 19 January 1998, the Holy See on 17 February 1998, San Marino on 18 March 1998, Switzerland on 24 March 1998, Hungary on 6 April 1998, Niue on 15 April 1998, Belize on 23 April 1998, and Trinidad and Tobago on 27 April 1998.

Annexe B. Chronology 1997

RAGNHILD FERM

For the convenience of the reader, key words are indicated in the right-hand column, opposite each entry. They refer to the subject-areas covered in the entry. Definitions of the acronyms can be found on page xiv.

15 Jan.	After a meeting between Israeli Prime Minister Netanyahu, PLO Chairman/President of the Palestinian Authority Arafat and the US representative at the Bayt Hanun checkpoint, the Protocol Concerning the Redeployment in Hebron (Hebron Accord) is signed. According to the document, Israel will withdraw from four-fifths of the territory of Hebron within 10 days. In a Note for the Record attached to the accord, Israel agrees to continue its withdrawal from the West Bank and the Palestinians agree to fight terrorism.	Israel/Palestine
21 Jan.	Negotiations on adaptation of the 1990 Treaty on Conventional Armed Forces in Europe (CFE Treaty) to the new security environment open in Vienna.	CFE
23 Jan.	The People's Assembly of Albania passes a law banning investment 'pyramid schemes'. Most of the schemes have already collapsed, which has caused chaos, crises and violent demonstrations in the country.	Albania
26 Feb.	Israeli Prime Minister Netanyahu announces a decision to build 6500 Israeli housing units in Jabal Abu Ghneim/Har Homa, in the Arab sector of Jerusalem. (This decision was subsequently condemned by international organizations and world opinion.)	Israel/Palestine
28 Feb.	At the annual meeting of the Central Asian heads of state held in Almaty, the presidents of Kazakhstan, Kyrgyzstan, Tajikistan, Turkmenistan and Uzbekistan adopt the Almaty Declaration, calling on all interested countries to support the proclamation of Central Asia as a nuclear weapon-free zone open to all states of the region.	Central Asia; NWFZ
1 Mar.	The People's Assembly of Albania declares a national state of emergency. (See *23 Jan.*)	Albania

SIPRI Yearbook 1998: Armaments, Disarmament and International Security

14 Mar.	In response to the Russian demand that large NATO 'infrastructures' should not be advanced towards the Russian border after NATO enlargement, the North Atlantic Council issues a statement that, in the current and foreseeable security environment, the alliance will carry out its collective defence and other missions by ensuring the necessary interoperability, integration and capability for reinforcement rather than by additional permanent stationing of substantial combat forces.	NATO/Russia
20–21 Mar.	A US–Russian summit meeting is held in Helsinki. The two presidents sign: a Joint Statement on parameters on future reductions in nuclear forces, agreeing that START III negotiations on aggregate levels of 2000–2500 strategic nuclear warheads for each side will begin as soon as START II has entered into force; a Joint Statement concerning the ABM Treaty, clarifying the demarcation between strategic and non-strategic defence systems; and a Joint Statement on European security, agreeing to establish a cooperative relationship between NATO and Russia.	USA/Russia; Nuclear weapons; ABM Treaty; European security; NATO/Russia
27 Mar.	The OSCE Permanent Council establishes the OSCE Presence in Albania to provide the country with advice and assistance in democratization, protection of human rights, and preparation and monitoring of elections.	OSCE; Albania
27 Mar.	The 1995 Treaty on the Southeast Asia Nuclear Weapon-Free Zone (Treaty of Bangkok) enters into force.	South-East Asia; NWFZ
28 Mar.	The UN Security Council adopts Resolution 1101 by a vote of 14 to 0 (China abstains from voting), welcoming the offer by certain member states to establish the temporary and limited Multinational Protection Force (MPF), led by Italy, to help create a secure environment for the missions of international organizations in Albania, including those providing humanitarian assistance. The force begins operations on 15 Apr. and withdraws from Albania on 11 Aug.	UN; Albania
2 Apr.	President Yeltsin of Russia and President Lukashenko of Belarus sign a charter committing the two countries to future integration.	Russia/Belarus
3 Apr.	The Japanese Cabinet approves an amendment to the 1952 Law on Special Measures for Land for the US Military, allowing the Japanese Government to authorize the continued use of the land by the USA on a temporary basis after the expiration of the leases (May 1997). On 22 Apr. the Japanese House of Representatives adopts a resolution urging the government to consolidate, realign, reduce and relocate US military bases in Okinawa.	Japan/USA
7–18 Apr.	The first session of the Preparatory Committee for the 2000 Review Conference of the Parties to the Treaty on the Non-Proliferation of Nuclear Weapons (NPT), to take place on 24 Apr.–19 May 2000, is held in New York.	NPT

8–9 Apr.	On the proposal of Belarus, the Conference on the Prospects for the Establishment of a Nuclear Weapon-Free Space in Central and Eastern Europe is held in Minsk. (The Russian Foreign Minister declares that Russia supports the Belarussian initiative to create such a zone.)	Belarus; Russia; NWFZ
24 Apr.	At a summit meeting in Moscow, the presidents of China, Kazakhstan, Kyrgyzstan, Russia and Tajikistan sign the Treaty on Mutual Reduction of Military Forces in Border Areas. The treaty builds on the agreement signed by Russia and China on 26 Apr. 1996 on military confidence building in border areas.	China; Kazakhstan; Kyrgyzstan; Russia; Tajikistan; CBM
29 Apr.	The 1993 Convention on the Prohibition of the Development, Production, Stockpiling and Use of Chemical Weapons and on their Destruction (Chemical Weapons Convention) enters into force.	CWC
6–24 May	The first session of the Conference of States Parties to the Chemical Weapons Convention is held in The Hague.	CWC
8 May	Moldovan President Lucinschi and leader of the Trans-Dniester region Smirnov sign a memorandum on the normalization of relations between Moldova and the Trans-Dniester region.	Moldova/Trans-Dniester
12 May	Russian President Yeltsin and Chechnyan President Maskhadov, meeting in Moscow, sign a treaty on peace and the principles of Russian–Chechnyan relations. It states the aims of 'firm and equal relations' but contains no mention of Chechnya's status.	Russia/ Chechnya
13 May	The Council of Ministers of the Western European Union (WEU), meeting in Paris, adopts the Paris Declaration on the role of the WEU in the European security system.	WEU
15 May	The IAEA Board of Governors approves a Model Protocol, additional to the agreements between states and the IAEA for the application of safeguards. The new protocol (the 'Programme 93+2' safeguards) strengthens the measures for use by Agency inspectors who verify states' compliance with their commitments not to produce nuclear weapons.	IAEA; Safeguards
15 May	The 1996 Flank Document, stipulating numerical and geographical reorganization of the CFE Treaty flank areas, enters into force.	CFE
16 May	President Mobuto of Zaire flees the capital, thereby surrendering power to insurgents led by Kabila, Chairman of the Alliance of Democratic Forces for the Liberation of Congo-Kinshasa (ADFL). On 17 May ADFL troops enter the capital and the establishment of the Democratic Republic of the Congo is announced.	Dem. Rep. of the Congo

17 May	Ukrainian President Kuchma and US Vice-President Gore issue a declaration that Ukraine will start eliminating the last intercontinental ballistic missiles on its territory with the financial support of the US Government.	Ukraine; USA; Nuclear weapons
23 May	President Yeltsin of Russia and President Lukashenko of Belarus, meeting in Moscow, sign a Charter of the Union of Russia and Belarus. According to the charter, the union will also be open to other CIS countries.	Russia/Belarus
23 May	Mohammed Khatami is elected President of Iran by 70% of the vote. His election is regarded as implying a change towards a more moderate policy in Iran.	Iran
25 May	The democratically elected government in Sierra Leone is toppled in a military coup. On 26 May troops from Nigeria and Guinea, deployed under the auspices of the Economic Community of West African States (ECOWAS) Monitoring Group (ECOMOG), arrive to restore the government in Sierra Leone.	Sierra Leone; ECOWAS; ECOMOG
27 May	The NATO–Russia Founding Act on Mutual Relations, Cooperation and Security is signed in Paris by President Yeltsin and the heads of state of the NATO countries. It establishes the NATO–Russia Permanent Joint Council (PJC) for dialogue and cooperation on security issues. It also reaffirms NATO's pledge (made on 10 Dec. 1996) that its current members have no intention, no plan and no reason to deploy nuclear weapons on the territory of new members.	NATO/Russia
28 May	Prime Ministers Chernomyrdin of Russia and Lazarenko of Ukraine, meeting in Kiev, sign three agreements on the Black Sea Fleet: on the division of the fleet; on the status of the Russian Black Sea Fleet and port installations on the territory of Ukraine; and on the related settlement of debts.	Russia/Ukraine
29 May	At the ministerial meeting of the North Atlantic Council, held in Sintra, Portugal, a set of new initiatives to further strengthen the Partnership for Peace (PFP) is agreed. The enhanced PFP programme will give the PFP a more operational role and provide for stronger political consultations and increased opportunities for partners to participate in decision making and planning of PFP activities.	NATO
30 May	In conjunction with the Sintra meeting (see *29 May*) the members of the North Atlantic Cooperation Council (NACC) and the Partnership for Peace (PFP) decide to establish and inaugurate a new cooperation mechanism, the Euro-Atlantic Partnership Council (EAPC), to enhance practical cooperation between NATO and its PFP partners. NACC thereby ceases to exist. The inaugural meeting of the EAPC defence ministers is held in Brussels on 13 June.	NATO

31 May	Russian President Yeltsin, visiting Ukraine, and Ukrainian President Kuchma sign a 10-year Treaty of Friendship, Cooperation and Partnership. The treaty will enter into force on 14 Jan. 1998.	Russia/Ukraine
5 June	Because of tensions between the rival factions of incumbent President Lissouba and former President Sassou-Nguesso, fighting starts in Congo (Brazzaville). It escalates and spreads to the north of the country.	Congo (Brazzaville)
16–17 June	At the European Council meeting in Amsterdam, the negotiations of the EU Intergovernmental Conference (IGC) on the revision of the Treaty on European Union (Maastricht Treaty) are concluded. The Treaty of Amsterdam confirms that the EU will avail itself of the WEU to elaborate and implement decisions and actions which have defence implications and provides the EU with access to an operational capability in the context of the Petersberg tasks. A protocol on relations between the EU and the WEU is adopted.	EU; WEU
20–22 June	The Group of Seven (G-7) summit meeting is held in Denver, Colorado. For the first time, Russian President Yeltsin participates with the G-7 in the Summit of the Eight.	G-7
24–27 June	In the framework of the Ottawa Process, an International Conference for a Global Ban on Anti-Personnel Mines is held in Brussels. The Brussels Declaration, reaffirming the desire to conclude and sign an agreement banning anti-personnel mines before the end of 1997, is adopted by 97 participants.	APM
27 June	President of Tajikistan Rakhmonov, leader of the United Tajik Opposition (UTO) Nuri and the UN special envoy to Tajikistan, meeting in Moscow, sign a Peace and National Reconciliation Accord, ending the country's five-year civil war.	Tajikistan; UN
30 June/1 July	The UK hands over Hong Kong to Chinese sovereignty. Hong Kong had been ceded to the UK in 1842 under the Treaty of Nanking.	China/UK
3 July	A Treaty of Friendship, Cooperation and Mutual Security is signed in Moscow by Russian President Yeltsin and Azerbaijani President Aliev.	Russia/ Azerbaijan
5–6 July	First Prime Minister of Cambodia Norodom Ranariddh is ousted by Second Prime Minister Hun Sen in a coup. The coup is widely condemned by the international community, and the foreign ministers of the Association of South-East Asian Nations (ASEAN) agree to defer indefinitely Cambodian membership, previously scheduled for July 1997.	Cambodia; ASEAN

8 July	The heads of state and government of the NATO members, meeting in Madrid, issue the Madrid Declaration on Euro-Atlantic Security and Cooperation and invite the Czech Republic, Hungary and Poland to immediately begin negotiations to become members of the alliance.	NATO/Czech Rep.; Hungary; Poland
8 July	A USA-brokered Convergence of Views document is signed, in Madrid, by Greece and Turkey. The two states agree to respect each other's sovereign rights and to renounce the use of force in dealing with each other. Turkish President Demirel and Greek Prime Minister Simitis declare that both states are committed to peace, security and the continuous development of good-neighbourly relations.	Greece/Turkey
9 July	The first meeting of the heads of state and government of NATO and the PFP states, under the aegis of the Euro-Atlantic Partnership Council (EAPC), is held in Madrid. (See *30 May*.)	NATO
9 July	A Charter on a Distinctive Partnership between NATO and Ukraine is signed, in Madrid, by President Kuchma of Ukraine and the NATO heads of state and government. The charter calls for consultations on political and security-related issues.	NATO/Ukraine
11 July	The UN Security Council calls on the parties to the conflict in Cambodia to respect fully their commitments under the 1996 Paris Accords and urges them to resolve their differences by peaceful means.	UN; Cambodia
16 July	UN Secretary-General Annan presents a comprehensive reform programme for the UN Organization, including measures to improve its ability to deploy peacekeeping and other field operations more rapidly and enhance the UN rapid-reaction capacity, to strengthen its capacity for post-conflict peace-building and to advance the disarmament agenda by establishing a Department for Disarmament and Arms Regulation to address the issues of reduction of conventional armaments and weapons of mass destruction and regulation of armaments.	UN
16 July	President of the European Commission Santer presents *Agenda 2000* to the European Parliament. The document addresses among other things the question of admitting new states into the Union.	EU
19 July	The Irish Republican Army (IRA) proclaims the restoration of its 1994 cease-fire (broken in Feb. 1996).	IRA; Northern Ireland

22 July	At an extraordinary meeting in Brussels, the WEU Council of Ministers adopts the Declaration of Western European Union on the role of Western European Union and its relations with the European Union and with the Atlantic Alliance, confirming that the WEU will develop its role as the European politico-military body for crisis management. The declaration is to be annexed to the Amsterdam Treaty (see *16–17 June*).	WEU; EU; NATO
23 July	The states parties to the 1990 Treaty on Conventional Armed Forces in Europe (the CFE Treaty), meeting in Vienna, issue the Decision of the Joint Consultative Group Concerning Certain Basic Elements for Treaty Adaptation, envisaging replacement of the bloc-to-bloc structure of the treaty with a system of national and territorial ceilings for treaty-limited equipment (TLE), taking into account the substantial reductions made since the breakup of the USSR. The 1996 Flank Document will be maintained but reconciled with the adapted treaty. The CFE zone of application (the ATTU zone) will no longer be divided into geographic zones with regional ceilings.	CFE
6 Aug.	In a major foreign policy address on the Middle East held in Washington, DC, US Secretary of State Albright says that Israel and the Palestinians must both forgo unilateral acts which prejudge or predetermine issues reserved for permanent status negotiations. During her visit to the region in Sep., she demands that Israel refrain from expanding or building new settlements on disputed land and that the Palestinians combat terrorism.	USA; Israel/Palestine
14 Aug.	Abkhaz leader Ardzinba and Georgian President Shevardnadze, meeting in Tbilisi, adopt a declaration in which the two sides abjure the use or threat of force against each other.	Georgia/ Abkhazia
28 Aug.	The UN Security Council unanimously adopts Resolution 1127, demanding that UNITA implement its obligations under the 1994 Lusaka Protocol, including demilitarization of all its forces.	UN; Angola
29 Aug.	Russian President Yeltsin and Armenian President Ter-Petrosian sign, in Moscow, a Treaty of Friendship, Cooperation and Mutual Assistance.	Russia/Armenia
15 Sep.	China issues new regulations on the control of nuclear exports. Transferred nuclear technology may only be used for peaceful purposes; the use of the technology should be subject to IAEA safeguards; and the technology may not be transferred to third countries without prior permission of the China Atomic Energy Authority.	China; Nuclear export control; IAEA

15–16 Sep.	More than 60 states and international organizations participate in a conference, held in Tashkent, on a Central Asian nuclear weapon-free zone. The foreign ministers of Kazakhstan, Kyrgyzstan, Tajikistan, Turkmenistan and Uzbekistan sign a statement stressing that declaring Central Asia a nuclear weapon-free zone would strengthen regional security. The UN is requested to set up a group of experts to prepare an agreement on the establishment of such a zone.	Central Asia; NWFZ; UN
18 Sep.	At the Ottawa Group meeting in Oslo, 89 participants agree on the text of a Convention on the Prohibition of the Use, Stockpiling, Production and Transfer of Anti-personnel Mines and on their Destruction (APM Convention).	APM
22 Sep.	US President Clinton transmits the 1996 Comprehensive Nuclear Test-Ban Treaty (CTBT) for the advice and consent of the Senate for ratification.	USA; CTBT
23 Sep.	Russian Prime Minister Chernomyrdin and US Vice-President Gore sign, in Moscow, the US–Russian Plutonium Production Reactor Agreement. According to the agreement Russia will convert by the year 2000, with US assistance, its three remaining plutonium reactors so that they can no longer produce weapon-grade plutonium. The two parties pledge not to restart any of their plutonium production reactors that have already been shut down.	USA/Russia; Weapon-grade material
23 Sep.	The USA and Japan adopt a revision of the 1978 Guidelines for US–Japan Defense Cooperation. The new guidelines will provide for Japan to play a broader, mainly logistical, military role in any US engagement in the region.	USA/Japan
23 Sep.	Representatives of Sinn Féin—the political branch of the Irish Republic Army (IRA)—and the Ulster Unionist Party (UUP) meet for the first time in 15 months in multi-party negotiations on the future of Northern Ireland.	Sinn Féin/UUP; Northern Ireland
26 Sep.	The US Secretary of State and the Russian Foreign Minister, meeting in New York, sign a Protocol to the 1993 START II Treaty providing for the extension until 2007 of the period of implementation of the treaty. The two ministers, together with the foreign ministers of Belarus, Kazakhstan and Ukraine, sign a memorandum according to which Belarus, Kazakhstan, Russia and Ukraine assume the obligations of the former USSR regarding the 1972 ABM Treaty. Statements are made on the delimitation of strategic and non-strategic ABM systems. An agreement is signed on confidence-building measures with respect to non-strategic ABM systems. (See *20–21 Mar.*)	USA/Russia/ Belarus/ Kazakhstan/ Ukraine; START; ABM Treaty

26 Sep.	The first meeting of the NATO–Russia Permanent Joint Council (PJC) at the level of foreign ministers is held in New York. A detailed work programme for the council is approved. (See *27 May*.)	NATO/Russia
29 Sep.–3 Oct.	At the annual session of the IAEA General Conference, held in Vienna, the Joint Convention on the Safety of Spent Fuel Management and on the Safety of Radioactive Waste Management, adopted on 5 Sep., is opened for signature. The convention obligates its parties to take appropriate national measures to ensure the safety of spent fuel and radioactive waste from civilian activities and materials of military origin that have been transferred to the civilian sector.	IAEA; Nuclear waste
2 Oct.	The Treaty of Amsterdam (see *16–17 June*) is signed in Amsterdam by all the EU member states.	EU
8 Oct.	The UN Security Council unanimously adopts Resolution 1132, imposing oil and arms sanctions on Sierra Leone. It authorizes ECOWAS to ensure strict implementation of the sanctions. On 24 Oct. a peace agreement, brokered by ECOWAS negotiators, is signed in Conakry, Guinea, ending the fighting between Nigerian-led ECOMOG intervention forces and supporters of the military coup (see *25 May*). The agreement provides for the reinstatement of the civilian president.	UN; Sierra Leone; ECOWAS; ECOMOG
23 Oct.	Former Congolese President Sassou-Nguesso returns to Brazzaville after having defeated the forces of President Lissouba. He is sworn in as president on 25 Oct.	Congo (Brazzaville)
24 Oct.	Lithuanian President Brazauskas, visiting Moscow, and Russian President Yeltsin sign a border agreement, confirming the demarcation of the border between Lithuania and the Russia Kaliningrad *oblast* and the delimitation of the exclusive economic zone and continental shelf in the Baltic Sea.	Lithuania/Russia
27 Oct.	The presidents of Angola, Congo (Brazzaville), the Democratic Republic of the Congo and Gabon, meeting in Luanda, agree on forms of reciprocal assistance to consolidate peace on the principle of African solidarity. They reiterate their determination and political will not to permit the territories of their countries to be used by armed groups or movements for acts of political and military destabilization against the sovereignty and territorial integrity of their states.	Angola/Congo (Brazzaville)/ Dem. Rep. of the Congo/ Gabon

29 Oct.	At a meeting with US President Clinton, in Washington, DC, Chinese President Jiang Zemin declares that China has introduced new rules to restrict exports of nuclear and dual-use materials and related technology and will take further measures to strengthen dual-use export controls by mid-1998. The USA agrees to sell nuclear technology for peaceful purposes to China. Agreement is reached on a US–Chinese Military Maritime Consultative Agreement, designed to help avoid incidents at sea.	USA/China; Nuclear export control; Incidents at sea
29 Oct.	In a letter to the UN Security Council, Iraqi Deputy Prime Minister Aziz informs the Security Council that Iraq will only cooperate with the UN Special Commission on Iraq (UNSCOM) 'provided that no individuals of American nationality shall participate in any activity of the Special Commission inside Iraq'. In responding to the letter (on 30 Oct.) the Council demands that Iraq cooperate fully with UNSCOM in accordance with the relevant resolutions and without restrictions.	Iraq/UNSCOM; UN
29 Oct.	The UN Security Council unanimously adopts Resolution 1135, strongly deploring the failure of UNITA (National Union for the Total Independence of Angola) to comply fully with its obligations under the 1994 Lusaka Protocol. The Council decides to extend the mandate of the UN Observer Mission in Angola (MONUA) and reaffirms its readiness to consider the imposition of additional measures in accordance with its Resolution 1127.	UN; Angola
31 Oct.	The five parties to the 1996 Agreement on Sub-regional Arms Control (the Florence Agreement)—Bosnia and Herzegovina, its two entities (the Federation of Bosnia and Herzegovina and the Republika Srpska), Croatia and Yugoslavia (Serbia and Montenegro)—complete the reductions of their heavy conventional arms having cut back altogether 6580 weapon items.	Former Yugoslavia
1–2 Nov.	Japanese Prime Minister Hashimoto and Russian President Yeltsin, meeting in Krasnoyarsk, Russia, agree to make maximum efforts to conclude a peace treaty by the year 2000.	Japan/Russia
10 Nov.	Russian President Yeltsin and Chinese President Jiang Zemin, meeting in Beijing, sign a joint declaration on friendship and cooperation for security, stability and economic progress. They declare that the demarcation of the eastern sector of the Russian/Chinese border, based on an agreement of 1991, is implemented and for the first time in history marked on the ground.	Russia/China
10 Nov.	Iraqi Deputy Prime Minister Aziz, addressing the UN Security Council, demands that a timetable be established for ending the sanctions on his country.	Iraq; UN

CHRONOLOGY 1997

12 Nov.	The UN Security Council unanimously adopts Resolution 1137, demanding that Iraq rescind immediately its decision expressed in its letter of 29 Oct. and that it cooperate fully and without conditions or restrictions with UNSCOM. The full inspection team returns to Iraq on 21 Nov.	UN; Iraq
18 Nov.	The WEU Council of Ministers, meeting in Erfurt, Germany, adopts the Erfurt Declaration, establishing better cooperation between the EU and the WEU with regard to crisis management and a new, more effective structure for military cooperation between the WEU member states.	WEU/EU
1 Dec.	The US Secretary of Energy announces that for the first time the IAEA will verify the conversion of US weapon-grade uranium into uranium suitable only for peaceful purposes. The initiative to apply IAEA safeguards verification procedures was launched by the Director General of the IAEA, the US Secretary of Energy and the Russian Minister of Atomic Energy in Sep. 1996.	USA; IAEA; Weapon-grade material
2 Dec.	The NATO Defence Ministers, meeting in Brussels, adopt the five-year forces plan. For the first time, the needs of the WEU for any missions of the Petersberg type are taken into consideration in NATO plans.	NATO; WEU
2–4 Dec.	During his visit to Stockholm, Russian President Yeltsin announces that Russia will reduce its north-western land and naval forces by 40% by Jan. 1999.	Russia; Conventional forces
3–4 Dec.	The Convention on the Prohibition of the Use, Stockpiling, Production and Transfer of Anti-Personnel Mines and on their Destruction (APM Convention) is signed in Ottawa by more than 120 states.	APM
7 Dec.	According to media reports US President Clinton has issued (in Nov.) Presidential Decision Directive (PDD) 60, providing new broad guidelines for military planners. The emphasis is on deterring the use of nuclear weapons. The previous guidance, for the US military to prepare to fight and win a protracted nuclear war, has been dropped.	USA; Nuclear weapons
9–10 Dec.	The first session of the talks involving North and South Korea, China and the USA, proposed in 1996 and aiming at a permanent peace agreement for the Korean peninsula, is held in Geneva.	North Korea/South Korea, China, USA
10 Dec.	The International Campaign to Ban Landmines and its leader, Jody Williams, are awarded the 1997 Nobel Peace Prize.	APM
11 Dec.	The UN General Assembly adopts, without a vote, Resolution 52/38 S, calling upon all states to support the establishment of a nuclear weapon-free zone in Central Asia.	UN; Central Asia; NWFZ

12–13 Dec.	The EU heads of state and government, meeting in Luxembourg, decide to initiate a process leading to the eventual accession of Bulgaria, Cyprus, the Czech Republic, Estonia, Hungary, Latvia, Lithuania, Poland, Romania, Slovakia and Slovenia. Formal invitations are issued to Cyprus, the Czech Republic, Estonia, Hungary, Poland and Slovenia to open negotiations on 30 Mar. 1998 with a view to EU entry early in the next century. Turkey objects to not being included in either group and threatens to integrate the Turkish part of Cyprus into Turkey itself.	EU; Turkey
16 Dec.	At the North Atlantic Council meeting, held in Brussels, the NATO member states sign the Protocols of Accession for the Czech Republic, Hungary and Poland.	NATO/Czech Rep.; Hungary; Poland
19 Dec.	The OSCE Ministerial Council, meeting in Copenhagen, adopts the guidelines for a future Charter on European Security. The charter will enable the OSCE members to better manage their relations and play a more effective role in conflict prevention and peacekeeping.	OSCE
22 Dec.	The Cairo Declaration on Somalia is signed by the leaders of the factions in Somalia, committing them to power-sharing, the establishment of a federal system with regional autonomy and the formation of a transitional government pending democratic elections.	Somalia

About the contributors

Dr Amitav Acharya (Canada) is Associate Professor in the Department of Political Science at York University, Toronto, where he is also a fellow of the Centre for International and Security Studies. He was formerly Associate Director of the University of Toronto–York University Joint Centre for Asia Pacific Studies (1996–98). He is co-editor (with Richard Stubbs) of *New Challenges for ASEAN: Emerging Policy Issues* (1995) and contributed to the SIPRI Research Report *Arms, Transparency and Security in South-East Asia* (1997). His most recent publication is *Avoiding War in Southeast Asia: Prospects for a Security Community* (forthcoming, 1998).

Dr Ramses Amer (Sweden) is Associate Professor and Coordinator of the Southeast Asia Programme (SEAP) at the Department of Peace and Conflict Research, Uppsala University. His recent publications include *Peace-keeping in a Peace Process: The Case of Cambodia* (1995) and *The Cambodian Conflict 1979–1991: From Intervention to Resolution* (1996) which he co-authored with Johan Saravanamuttu and Peter Wallensteen. He has also contributed to international journals and books and has written reports on issues of Asian security. He has contributed to the SIPRI Yearbook since 1993.

Dr Ian Anthony (United Kingdom) is Leader of the SIPRI Project on National Export Controls in the New European Security Environment. In 1992–98 he was Leader of the SIPRI Arms Transfers Project. His most recent publication for SIPRI is *Russia and the Arms Trade* (1998), of which he is editor. He is also the editor of the SIPRI volume *Arms Export Regulations* (1991), the SIPRI Research Report *The Future of Defence Industries in Central and Eastern Europe* (1994), and author of *The Naval Arms Trade* (SIPRI, 1990) and *The Arms Trade and Medium Powers: Case Studies of India and Pakistan 1947–90* (1991). He has written or co-authored chapters for the SIPRI Yearbook since 1988.

William M. Arkin (United States) is an independent expert on Internet and defence matters and a consultant to the Natural Resources Defense Council (NRDC). He was previously Director of Military Research at Greenpeace International (1989–94) in Washington, DC. He is co-editor of the NRDC's *Nuclear Weapons Databook* series and co-author of several of the volumes in the same series. His recent publications include (with Robert S. Norris) *The Internet and the Bomb: A Research Guide to Policy and Information about Nuclear Weapons* (1997) and *The US Military Online: A Directory for Online Access to the Department of Defense* (2nd edn, 1998). He has contributed to the SIPRI Yearbook since 1985 and is a columnist for *Bulletin of the Atomic Scientists*.

Dr Eric Arnett (United States), an engineer, is Leader of the SIPRI Military Technology and International Security Project. In 1988–92 he was Senior Programme Associate in the Program on Science and International Security and Director of the Project on Advanced Weaponry in the Developing World at the American Association for the Advancement of Science. He is the editor of the SIPRI volumes *Nuclear Weapons After the Comprehensive Test Ban: Implications for Modernization and Proliferation*

(1996), *Military Capacity and the Risk of War: China, India, Pakistan and Iran* (1997), and *Nuclear Weapons and Arms Control in South Asia after the Test Ban* (1998) and has contributed to the SIPRI Yearbook since 1993.

Dr Vladimir Baranovsky (Russia) is Deputy Director at the Institute of World Economy and International Relations, Moscow. In 1992–97 he was Leader of the SIPRI Project on Russia's Security Agenda. He has authored or co-edited several monographs including *In from the Cold: Germany, Russia and the Future of Europe* (1992) and *1992: Novye Gorizonty Zapadnoy Evropy* [1992: new horizons of Western Europe] (1993, in Russian). He is editor of the SIPRI volume *Russia and Europe: The Emerging Security Agenda* (1997) and has contributed to a number of journals and books including the SIPRI Yearbook since 1993.

Dr Julian Cooper (United Kingdom) is Director of the Centre for Russian and East European Studies and Professor of Russian Economic Studies at the University of Birmingham. His research is concerned with the Russian economy, defence industry, and science and technology policy. He has undertaken studies for the European Commission, the International Labour Organization, NATO, the Organisation for Economic Co-operation and Development (OECD) and other international organizations. Recent publications include chapters on the Russian defence industry and arms exports in *Cascade of Arms* (1997) and *Security Dilemmas in Russia and Eurasia* (1998). He contributed to the SIPRI Yearbook in 1995 and 1997.

Agnès Courades Allebeck (France) is a Research Assistant on the SIPRI Military Expenditures and Arms Production Project. She is responsible for research on military expenditure in NATO, Africa and the Middle East and is the author of chapters in the SIPRI volumes *Arms Export Regulations* (1991) and *Arms Industry Limited* (1993), and contributed to the SIPRI Yearbooks 1989–94 and 1997.

Susanna Eckstein (Germany) was a Research Assistant on the SIPRI Chemical and Biological Warfare Project and on the Peacekeeping and Regional Security Project in 1996–98. She co-authored a SIPRI fact-sheet on the Chemical Weapons Convention (1997) and contributed to the *SIPRI Yearbook 1997*.

Ragnhild Ferm (Sweden) is Leader of the SIPRI Arms Control and Disarmament Documentary Survey Project. She has published chapters on nuclear explosions, the comprehensive nuclear test-ban and arms control agreements, and the annual chronologies of arms control and political events in the SIPRI Yearbook since 1982. She is the author of fact-sheets on SIPRI research topics in Swedish.

Dr Trevor Findlay (Australia) is Executive Director of the Verification Research, Training and Information Centre (VERTIC), London. In 1993–97 he was Leader of the SIPRI Peacekeeping and Regional Security Project. He is author of *Peace Through Chemistry: The New Chemical Weapons Convention* (1993), the SIPRI Research Report *Cambodia: The Legacy and Lessons of UNTAC* (1995) and editor of *Challenges for the New Peacekeepers* (1996). His most recent publication for SIPRI is *Fighting for Peace: The Use of Force in Peace Operations* (forthcoming, 1998). He has contributed to the SIPRI Yearbook since 1994.

ABOUT THE CONTRIBUTORS

Gunilla Flodén (Sweden) is a Research Assistant on the SIPRI Middle East Security and Arms Control Project. As well as conducting security-related research on the Middle East, she assists in the organization of the project's conferences in the region.

John Hart (United States) was a Research Assistant on the SIPRI Chemical and Biological Warfare Project in 1996–97. He co-authored a SIPRI fact-sheet on the Chemical Weapons Convention (1997) and contributed to the *SIPRI Yearbook 1997*. He is co-editor of the SIPRI volume *Chemical Weapon Destruction in Russia: Political, Legal and Technical Aspects* (forthcoming 1998), of which the Russian edition (Unichtozheniye khimicheskogo oruzhiya v Rossii: politicheskiye, pravonye i tecknicheskiye aspekty) was published by IMEMO in 1997.

Patrick Henrichon (Canada) was an intern on the SIPRI Project on Building a Cooperative Security System in and for Europe in 1998.

Ann-Sofi Jakobsson (Sweden) is a Ph.D. student at the Department of Peace and Conflict Research, Uppsala University. She has contributed to the SIPRI Yearbook since 1995.

Andrés Jato (Sweden) is a Ph.D. student at the Department of Peace and Conflict Research, Uppsala University. He holds an MA from the London School of Economics.

Dr Peter Jones (Canada) is Leader of the SIPRI Middle East Security and Arms Control Project. Before joining SIPRI in 1995, he worked for the Canadian Department of Foreign Affairs and International Trade, focusing on security and arms control issues. He is the author of several articles on the Middle East peace process, Middle East arms control, maritime security, Asian security, peacekeeping, verification and Open Skies. He has contributed to the SIPRI Yearbook since 1996.

Shannon Kile (United States) is a Research Assistant on the SIPRI Project on Russia's Security Agenda. He has contributed to most volumes of the SIPRI Yearbook since 1993 and is the author of a chapter in the SIPRI Research Report *The Future of the Defence Industries in Central and Eastern Europe* (1994).

Dr Zdzislaw Lachowski (Poland) is a Researcher on the SIPRI Project on Building a Cooperative Security System in and for Europe. He was previously a Researcher at the Polish Institute of International Affairs, where he studied problems of European security and the Conference on Security and Co-operation in Europe (CSCE) process and issues concerning West European political integration. He has published extensively on these subjects. He is the author of *Conventional Arms Control in Europe: Adapting the CFE Regime to the New Security Environment* (1998) and has contributed to the SIPRI Yearbook since 1992.

Evamaria Loose-Weintraub (Germany) is a Research Assistant on the SIPRI Military Expenditures and Arms Production Project. She is responsible for research on military expenditure in Europe (except for NATO members), Central and South America, and Oceania. She is the author of chapters in the SIPRI volume *Arms Export Regulations* (1991) and co-author of a chapter in the SIPRI Research Report

The Future of the Defence Industries in Central and Eastern Europe (1994) and contributed to the SIPRI Yearbook in 1984–88 and 1992–97.

Robert J. Mathews (Australia) is Visiting Fellow at the Faculty of Law, University of Melbourne, and Principal Research Scientist in Nuclear, Biological and Chemical Arms Control at the Defence Science and Technology Organisation, Canberra. In addition to his scientific research, he has served as Scientific Adviser to the Australian Delegation to the Conference on Disarmament and in a similar role to the Preparatory Commission of the Organisation for the Prohibition of Chemical Weapons. He has published extensively on chemical weapon and verification issues.

Sola Ogunbanwo (Nigeria) is currently Chief Expert Adviser on the African Nuclear-Weapon-Free Zone and has prepared the various working drafts of the African Nuclear-Weapon-Free Zone Treaty (Treaty of Pelindaba). He is also Secretary General of the Conference of States Parties responsible for preparing the Verification and Compliance Protocol to the Biological Weapons Convention. He has written several papers and articles related to the establishment of an African Nuclear-Weapon-Free Zone and has published extensively on other disarmament and security issues.

Dr Robert S. Norris (United States) is Senior Staff Analyst with the Natural Resources Defense Council (NRDC) and Director of the Nuclear Weapons Databook Project in Washington, DC. He is co-editor of the NRDC's *Nuclear Weapons Databook* series and co-author of several of the volumes in the series. He has contributed to the SIPRI Yearbook since 1985 and is a columnist for *Bulletin of the Atomic Scientists*. One of his recent works (with William M. Arkin) is *The Internet and the Bomb: A Research Guide to Policy and Information about Nuclear Weapons* (1997).

Dr Adam Daniel Rotfeld (Poland) is Director of SIPRI and Leader of the SIPRI Project on Building a Cooperative Security System in and for Europe. He was a member of the Polish Delegation to the Conference on Security and Co-operation in Europe (CSCE) and Personal Representative of the CSCE Chairman-in-Office to examine the settlement of the conflict in the Trans-Dniester region (1992–93). He is the author or editor of over 20 books and more than 200 articles on the legal and political aspects of relations between Germany and the Central and East European states after World War II (recognition of borders, the Munich Agreement and the right of self-determination), human rights, CSBMs, European security and the CSCE process. He has written chapters for the SIPRI Yearbook since 1991.

Elisabeth Sköns (Sweden) is Leader of the SIPRI Military Expenditures and Arms Production Project. She is the author of a chapter on the internationalization of arms production in the SIPRI volume *Arms Industry Limited* (1993) and *Annals of the American Academy of Political and Social Science* (1994) and of a background survey on arms production for the Bonn International Center for Conversion (BICC) *Conversion Survey 1998* (1998). She is co-author (with Reinhilde Weidacher) of a chapter on the economics of arms production for the *Encyclopedia of Violence, Peace and Conflict* (forthcoming, 1998) and of the forthcoming SIPRI Research Report *Arms Production in Western Europe in the 1990s*. She has contributed to most editions of the SIPRI Yearbook since 1983.

ABOUT THE CONTRIBUTORS 615

Margareta Sollenberg (Sweden) is a Research Assistant on the Uppsala Conflict Data Project at the Department of Peace and Conflict Research, Uppsala University. She is the editor of *States in Armed Conflict 1994, 1995* and *1996* and has contributed to the SIPRI Yearbook since 1995.

Petter Stålenheim (Sweden) was an intern on the SIPRI Military Expenditures and Arms Production Project in 1998.

Professor Peter Wallensteen (Sweden) has held the Dag Hammarskjöld Chair in Peace and Conflict Research since 1985 and is Head of the Department of Peace and Conflict Research, Uppsala University. He has most recently edited *International Intervention: New Norms in the Post-Cold War Era?* (1997) and is the author of *From War to Peace: On Conflict Resolution in the Global System* (1994). He has co-authored chapters in the SIPRI Yearbook since 1988.

Reinhilde Weidacher (Italy) is a Research Assistant on the SIPRI Military Expenditures and Arms Production Project. She is the author of a report for the Swedish Defence Research Establishment (FOA) on the Italian arms industry (forthcoming, 1998, in Swedish) and co-author (with Elisabeth Sköns) of the SIPRI Research Report *Arms Production in Western Europe in the 1990s* (forthcoming, 1998).

Pieter D. Wezeman (Netherlands) is a Research Assistant on the SIPRI Arms Transfers Project. He has co-authored (with Siemon T. Wezeman) a paper for the Bonn International Center for Conversion (BICC) on Dutch surplus weapon exports (1996) and has published papers on arms export issues in Dutch. He has contributed to the SIPRI Yearbook since 1995.

Siemon T. Wezeman (Netherlands) is a Research Assistant on the SIPRI Arms Transfers Project. He is the co-author (with Edward J. Laurance and Herbert Wulf) of the SIPRI Research Report *Arms Watch: SIPRI Report on the First Year of the UN Register of Conventional Arms* (1993), (with Bates Gill and J. N. Mak) of *ASEAN Arms Acquisitions: Developing Transparency* (1995) and (with Pieter D. Wezeman) of a paper for BICC on Dutch surplus weapon exports (1996). He has contributed to the SIPRI Research Report *Arms, Transparency and Security in South-East Asia* (1997) and to the SIPRI Yearbook since 1993.

Dr Jean Pascal Zanders (Belgium) is Leader of the SIPRI Chemical and Biological Warfare Project. He was previously Research Associate at the Centre for Peace Research at the Free University of Brussels. He has contributed to the SIPRI volume *The Challenge of Old Chemical Munitions and Toxic Armament Wastes* (1997), co-authored a SIPRI fact-sheet on the Chemical Weapons Convention (1997) and contributed to the *SIPRI Yearbook 1997*. In 1997 he published several papers on regime formation and implementation of the Chemical Weapons Convention as well as on regional security in the Middle East with respect to chemical and biological weapons.

Carl Johan Åsberg (Sweden) is a Ph.D. student at the Department of Peace and Conflict Research, Uppsala University. He has contributed to *States in Armed Conflict* since 1993 and to the SIPRI Yearbook since 1994.

SIPRI Yearbook 1998: Armaments, Disarmament and International Security
Oxford University Press, Oxford, 1998, 638 pp.
(Stockholm International Peace Research Institute)
ISBN 0-19-829454-9

ABSTRACTS

ROTFELD, A. D., 'Introduction: Transformation of the world security system', in *SIPRI Yearbook 1998*, pp. 1–14.

The data and facts in this volume reveal the basic, often contradictory elements of the emerging international security regime: it is characterized by both globalization and fragmentation. The radically diminished threat of world war has been replaced by the reality of intra-state conflicts which undermine stability and security at the domestic and regional levels. If the commitments of the nuclear weapon states to pursue the elimination of nuclear weapons are to be credible, they call not only for a serious debate but also a new arms control agenda. The agenda ahead must seriously consider at least four major security issues: the abolition of nuclear weapons, unilateral nuclear arms control initiatives, prevention of armed conflicts and control of the trade in small arms.

SOLLENBERG, M. and WALLENSTEEN, P., 'Major armed conflicts', in *SIPRI Yearbook 1998*, pp. 17–23.

In 1997, 25 major armed conflicts were waged in 24 locations around the world, compared with 27 major armed conflicts and 24 locations in 1996. The decline in numbers represents a continued downward trend for the period of investigation, 1989–97. By the end of 1997 no major armed conflicts were active in Europe and all major armed conflicts emanating from the breakup of the USSR and Yugoslavia had been ended. All the new conflicts were on the African continent; in fact, Africa was the only region with an increase in the number of conflicts in 1997. Africa also had the largest share of conflicts with a high level of intensity, that is, more than 1000 battle-related deaths in one year. The conflict between India and Pakistan was the only interstate conflict recorded in 1997. However, as in previous years other states contributed regular troops in some of the recorded conflicts.

FINDLAY, T., 'Armed conflict prevention, management and resolution', in *SIPRI Yearbook 1998*, pp. 31–74.

There were several major successes in 1997, with peace accords concluded in some lesser-known conflict situations. Historic all-party negotiations began over the Northern Ireland conflict, while agreement to begin talks on peace treaties was reached by the two Koreas and by Japan and Russia. Peace processes continued to be deeply troubled in Angola, Bosnia and Herzegovina, Chechnya and the Middle East, and diplomatic efforts failed to prevent or halt civil wars in Central Africa. Since the end of the cold war the international community's capacity for conflict prevention, management and resolution has shown steady improvement, although professional conflict resolution and prevention capabilities at the UN and in regional bodies remain underdeveloped and underfunded.

JONES, P. and FLODÉN, G., 'The Middle East peace process', in *SIPRI Yearbook 1998*, pp. 91–107.

After what could have been a breakthrough in early 1997 over Israeli withdrawal from Hebron, renewed Israeli settlement activity stalled the Israeli–Palestinian talks. The process was further marred by new outbreaks of terrorist activity. There were no official talks between Israel and Syria, and the level of violence in Lebanon remained high. Internal fighting in Algeria worsened, conflicts in the Kurdish regions of Turkey and Iraq continued and Islamic terrorists struck in Egypt, calling into question the government's assertion that it had defeated them. One hopeful indication came in Iran, where the pragmatic Khatami was elected president by a wide margin. Although the new president has widespread popular support, he will face an uphill battle in trying to effect change against the wishes of the religious élite.

BARANOVSKY, V., 'Russia: conflicts and peaceful settlement of disputes', in *SIPRI Yearbook 1998*, pp. 111–39.

In 1997 Russia intensified its efforts to promote settlement of the ongoing conflicts over territory and status across the former USSR. At the same time there was growing concern in Moscow about challenges to its position from competing influences, particularly in the oil-rich areas of Central Asia. Russia played a prominent role in launching a political reconciliation process in Tajikistan. It increased pressure for negotiations between the conflicting parties in the Trans-Dniester region, Abkhazia and Nagorno-Karabakh. Russia and Chechnya moved towards a practical *modus vivendi* in their postwar relations, although the future status of Chechnya remained an open question. Although Russia continued to place a high foreign policy priority on developing the Commonwealth of Independent States (CIS) as a reliable Russian-centred power pole, the viability of this policy was called into doubt as CIS member states increasingly sought to distance themselves from Russia.

ROTFELD, A. D., 'Europe: the transition to inclusive security', in *SIPRI Yearbook 1998*, pp. 141–67.

With the absence of an external threat to Europe the main challenges and risks are now of a domestic nature, stemming from economic and social problems. For this reason, the non-military elements of stability are gaining in importance, in particular the attempts to institutionalize the changes taking place in NATO 'from defence of member territory to defence of common interests'. Developments in 1997 in the parallel processes of EU and NATO enlargement brought Europe a step closer to establishing a system of inclusive security. While there was no real breakthrough in the shaping of such a security system, the potential for enhanced Europe-wide cooperation was advanced by the establishment of the Euro-Atlantic Partnership Council. In addition, the NATO–Russia Founding Act offers a basis for a lasting and inclusive peace. While the tasks defined for the OSCE in the cold war period have been largely fulfilled or have outlived their relevance, it has conducted significant activities in the areas of conflict prevention, crisis management and resolution of disputes.

SKÖNS, E., COURADES ALLEBECK, A., LOOSE-WEINTRAUB, E. and WEIDACHER, R., 'Military expenditure and arms production', in *SIPRI Yearbook 1998*, pp. 185–213.

World military expenditure declined to $704 billion in 1997, but the rate of decline was slower than before. SIPRI estimates for the period 1988–97 show that global military expenditure has decreased by around one-third, or at an average annual rate of 4.5%. In the past two years the rate of decline has fallen to 1% per year on average. The deepest cuts were made in Russia and other successor states of the Soviet Union. Regions which have been exceptions to the declining trend are North Africa, the Middle East and Asia. The level of arms sales for the top 100 arms-producing companies in the Organisation for Economic Co-operation and Development (OECD) and developing countries remained virtually unchanged in 1996. This was the combined effect of mergers at the high end of the spectrum, which radically increased companies' size and arms sales, and the diminution of companies at the lower end.

COOPER, J., 'The military expenditure of the USSR and the Russian Federation, 1987–97', in *SIPRI Yearbook 1998*, pp. 243–59.

By detailed critical analysis of the component parts of military expenditure, it is possible to create an acceptable extended time series for the estimated military expenditure of Russia and the former USSR. The problems involved in estimating true military expenditure include lack of transparency (particularly before 1992), inflation, changes to the budget after its adoption, 'military' items under other budget heads—the paramilitary forces, housing for servicemen, military research and development and expenditure on the 'closed cities' among them—and the wide divergence between the budget and actual outlays. Estimates of the total military expenditure of the Soviet Union and Russia are presented in current roubles, as a proportion of gross national product (GNP) and in US dollars using purchasing-power parity rates. The conclusion is that military expenditure has fallen from approximately $257 billion in the USSR in 1987 to $24.1 billion in Russia in 1997, and as a proportion of GNP from 16.6% in 1987 to 3.8% in 1997.

ARNETT, E., 'Military research and development', in *SIPRI Yearbook 1998*, pp. 267–89.

Global military research and development (R&D) expenditure continued to decline in 1997, mainly because of reductions in the US budget, which will be cut by another 14% by the year 2001. Critics claim that US forces are vulnerable to new threats, particularly ballistic and cruise missiles, but these fears are exaggerated. US investment in military R&D is more than seven times that of France, the nearest competitor. It is unlikely that a global challenger to US power will emerge before 2020. Rather, the international system will increase its dependence on US technology and military intervention. Contrary to expectations, the 1991 Persian Gulf War did not lead 'second-tier' arms producers to increase their R&D budgets in the hope of developing or countering technologies demonstrated by the USA, which itself cancelled several programmes at that time. Japan reduced its military R&D investment for the first time since 1976. Russia is allowing its design bureaux to sell their expertise abroad, but has promised to limit technology transfer.

WEZEMAN, S. T. and WEZEMAN, P. D., 'Transfers of major conventional weapons', in *SIPRI Yearbook 1998*, pp. 291–317.

The global SIPRI trend-indicator value of international transfers of major conventional weapons in 1997 was just over $25 billion. There has been a clear trend of increasing arms transfers since 1994, but the volume is still only 62% of the volume in 1987, when the highest level since 1950 was reached. Despite being a region with many conflicts, Sub-Saharan Africa only accounts for a very limited share of global arms transfers. With some important exceptions, most exporters of weapons provide official data on arms exports. However, much of this information is aggregated and there is no common definition of arms transfers upon which countries base their figures. Generally, the official data are difficult to analyse or to compare. In 1997, several countries released, for the first time, data on arms exports or promised to do so in 1998. In 1997 a group of government experts evaluated the UN Register of Conventional Arms but failed to reach a consensus regarding changes or improvements.

ANTHONY, I. and ZANDERS, J. P., 'Multilateral security-related export controls', in *SIPRI Yearbook 1998*, pp. 373–400.

In 1997 China became a member of the Zangger Committee, a continuation of the gradual inclusion of China into the multilateral nuclear non-proliferation effort. This is the first time that China has participated in any multilateral export control regime. Turkey became a member of the Missile Technology Control Regime. The entry into force of the Chemical Weapons Convention and continued uncertainty about the status of chemical and biological weapon (CBW) programmes in some countries drew attention to export controls as they apply to goods and technologies that can be used in the production of CBW. The review of events in 1997 reinforced the view that, although multilateral export controls can create conditions for more effective non-proliferation efforts, in specific cases where actual or alleged proliferation creates a security concern—notably in the Middle East—the triangular relationship of China, Russia and the United States is the main focus of political activity.

KILE, S., 'Nuclear arms control', in *SIPRI Yearbook 1998*, pp. 403–33.

In 1997 there were a number of positive developments in strategic nuclear arms control. The US and Russian presidents agreed on a set of measures to boost the START II Treaty's ratification prospects in the Russian Parliament; they also agreed on the outline of a follow-on treaty that would further reduce nuclear arsenals and help to make those cuts irreversible. The USA and Russia also reached an agreement in their stalemated negotiations to clarify the application of the Anti-Ballistic Missile (ABM) Treaty to theatre missile defence systems. The implementation of the START I Treaty continued to proceed ahead of schedule. Despite these accomplishments, key items on the nuclear arms control and disarmament agenda remained unresolved. START II continued to face an uncertain fate in the Russian Parliament. The Comprehensive Nuclear Test-Ban Treaty had yet to enter into force and at the Conference on Disarmament no progress was made towards negotiating a global convention banning the production of fissile material for military purposes.

ACHARYA, A. and OGUNBANWO, S., 'The nuclear weapon-free zones in South-East Asia and Africa', in *SIPRI Yearbook 1998*, pp. 443–55.

The Southeast Asia Nuclear Weapon-Free Zone Treaty (Treaty of Bangkok) entered into force in 1997. Since no South-East Asian countries currently possess nuclear weapons, the main purpose of the treaty is to regulate the policies of the nuclear weapon states. As of 1 January 1998, owing to disagreement over certain provisions and language, none of the nuclear weapon states had signed the protocol to the treaty, which prohibits these states from using or threatening to use nuclear arms, not only against the parties to the treaty, but also anywhere within the zone. During 1997 progress was made towards securing the entry into force of the African Nuclear Weapon-Free Zone Treaty (Treaty of Pelindaba). It was signed by 47 and ratified by 2 African states as of 1 January 1998. The treaty represents an important achievement for the continent in regional security cooperation and is the only accord of this kind that establishes a zone that includes a former nuclear weapon state—South Africa.

ZANDERS, J. P. and HART, J., 'Chemical and biological weapon developments and arms control', in *SIPRI Yearbook 1998*, pp. 457–89.

The 1993 Chemical Weapons Convention (CWC) entered into force on 29 April 1997. Progress in the negotiations on a verification protocol to the Biological and Toxin Weapons Convention (BTWC) was modest. Despite efforts to establish or strengthen disarmament regimes for chemical and biological weapons, concerns about their proliferation or use increased. Tear-gas was used for the first time after the entry into force of the CWC by military forces in Bosnia and Herzegovina. This highlighted a grey area in the convention. Cuba formally accused the United States of waging biological warfare and initiated a procedure to investigate this type of allegation—the first time this has occurred since the BTWC entered into force in 1975. Measures to counter proliferation increased in Western countries. In Iraq, the crisis between the United Nations Special Commission on Iraq (UNSCOM) and Baghdad escalated to the point that military intervention became a serious possibility.

MATHEWS, R. J., 'Entry into force of the Chemical Weapons Convention', in *SIPRI Yearbook 1998*, pp. 490–500.

The Chemical Weapons Convention (CWC) entered into force on 29 April 1997. It will be administered by the Organisation for the Prohibition of Chemical Weapons (OPCW) in The Hague. By the end of 1997 significant progress had been made on the creation of the CWC regime. The OPCW, with its Technical Secretariat, was established and became operational in 1997. The OPCW still faces problems, including the difficulties for a significant number of parties to adhere to the CWC time-lines and a number of other unresolved issues. However, most parties now appear confident that these difficulties can and will be overcome. It will take at least a few years until the CWC can be regarded as an effective operational treaty, but at the end of 1997 the situation was much better than most participants would have thought possible at the beginning of the year.

LACHOWSKI, Z., 'Conventional arms control', in *SIPRI Yearbook 1998*, pp. 501–30.

Challenged by the fact of NATO enlargement and the need for a new approach to military security, the states parties to the 1990 Treaty on Conventional Armed Forces in Europe (CFE Treaty) pursued businesslike negotiations in 1997 on the adaptation of the treaty, which led to the July Decision by the Joint Consultative Group Concerning Certain Basic Elements for Treaty Adaptation. The implementation of the 1996 Florence Agreement effected reductions in heavy armaments of the former warring parties in the former Yugoslavia and created a militarily stable environment which it is hoped will enable further steps towards a stable military balance in the Balkans as a whole. Russia pledged a 40% reduction in its land and naval forces and proposed confidence- and security-building measures for the Baltic Sea region, offering good prospects for a regional security dialogue. The most promising regional security dialogue outside Europe was in the Asia–Pacific region, with moves towards increased security-related confidence-building and maritime cooperation.

LACHOWSKI, Z. and HENRICHON, P., 'Confidence- and security-building measures in Europe', in *SIPRI Yearbook 1998*, pp. 531–40.

Confidence- and security-building measures (CSBMs) remained on the agenda of the Organization for Security and Co-operation in Europe (OSCE), both on the pan-European and on the regional level, in 1997. The OSCE Forum for Security Co-operation agreed on a number of amendments and undertook to launch a process of general 'modernization' of the Vienna Document 1994. The 1996 Agreement on CSBMs in Bosnia and Herzegovina was in its second year of successful operation. Transparency and confidence between the armed forces of the parties to the Agreement were growing; a synergy developed between CSBMs and the regional arms control process; and voluntary measures were carried out including open skies measures. Elsewhere in Europe, regional confidence- and security-building efforts continued to have a mixed record: in one area they raised hopes for progress (the Baltic Sea region), while in the south-eastern part of the continent they failed after a short-lived accord (on Greek–Turkish relations).

LACHOWSKI, Z., 'The ban on anti-personnel mines', in *SIPRI Yearbook 1998*, pp. 545–58.

In 1997 the issue of a ban on anti-personnel mines was raised in two forums: the Ottawa Process and the Conference on Disarmament (CD), proceeding from different perspectives—humanitarian versus arms control. The Ottawa Process swiftly achieved its goal: the text of the Convention on the Prohibition of the Use, Stockpiling, Production and Transfer of Anti-Personnel Mines and on their Destruction was agreed on 18 September and opened for signature in Ottawa on 3–4 December. By the end of the year, there were 123 signatures and 3 ratifications to the convention. The CD failed to approach the landmine issue, although it may have a role to play in negotiating a phased approach and enhanced verification and at the same time engaging reluctant participants, especially China and Russia, in the ban.

Errata

SIPRI Yearbook 1997: Armaments, Disarmament and International Security

Page 4, footnote 13:	'Alfred von Staden' should read 'Alfred van Staden'.
Page 27, table 1A, Afghanistan conflict:	'Afghanistan' should read 'Afghanistan Govt'.
Page 73, table 2A, first entry, for ONUV:	The ONUV multilateral peace mission should appear in italics because its mandate expired on 31 December 1996 and was not renewed (see the table conventions on page 68).
Page 272, table 9.3:	A new line under the caption should read: 'The countries are ranked according to 1992–96 aggregate imports. Figures are trend-indicator values, as expressed in US $m., at constant (1990) prices.' Position 15 in column 1—rank for the period 1992–96—should be occupied by Pakistan (see table 8.2 in this volume for the correct listing).
Page 346, table 10.1, column for the Zangger Committee membership, entries for Argentina and Brazil:	By Argentina, should read 'x' for membership as of 1 January 1997; by Brazil, there should be a blank, for no membership of that regime.
Page 372, figure 11.1	In the bar for *Russia, Jan. 1997*, the sections of the bar indicating SLBM and ICBM warheads are transposed.
Page 401, table 11A.5, note b, line 5:	'the 1200-km range DF-41' should read 'the 12 000-km range DF-41'.
Page 539, under the CCW Convention, summary of Protocol II:	Second line should read: 'amended in 1996; amendments adopted on on 3 May 1996. Not in force.'
Page 544, footnote 2, line 3:	Should read: 'territories and it considers itself not to be bound by the obligations in respect of these territories. As regards'.
Pages 561–64, Abstracts:	The titles of the chapters and names of the authors should be checked against the table of contents.

INDEX

Abacha, General Sani 63
Abbas, Mahmoud 96
Abidjan Agreement (1996) 62
Abkhazia 35, 58, 117, 127, 129–31, 505, 605
Adede, Andronico 38
ADI 266
Aegis system 283, 284, 285
Aerojet 264
Aérospatiale 202, 206, 284–85
Aérospatiale Groupe 261
Afghanistan 19, 27, 31, 34, 35
aflatoxin 485
AFM-L Alpha missile 288
Africa:
    conflicts in 18, 19, 20, 21, 22, 28–30
    economic vulnerability 194–95
    France and 59, 62, 196
    landmines in 552
    military expenditure 186, 191, 192, 195–96, 214, 219–20, 225–26, 231–32
    peacekeeping and 51–52, 59–63, 71
    UN and 35, 36
    see also following entries and under names of countries
Africa, Central:
    conflicts in 8, 22, 35, 192, 195
Africa, North: military expenditure 192, 195–96, 214, 219, 225, 321
Africa, Sub-Saharan:
    arms imports 302–5
    military expenditure 192, 196, 219–20, 225–26, 231–32
African Crisis Response Initiative 51
African Nuclear Weapon-Free-Zone Treaty (1996) 450–55, 594–95
Agreement on Confidence- and Security-Building Measures in Bosnia and Herzegovina (1996) 536
Agreement on Sub-Regional Arms Control *see* Florence Agreement
Agusta 264
Aideed, Hussain 19, 61
AIE 264
Airbus Industrie 206
aircraft, costs of 212
Alatas, Ali 67
Albania:
    conflict in 45, 57–58
    elections 57
    military expenditure 216, 222, 228
    OSCE in 57, 58, 162, 600
    peacekeeping in 57–58, 600
    pyramid investment schemes 57, 599
    state of emergency declared 599

UN and 36, 45, 53, 600
Albright, Madeleine 96, 97, 102, 410, 411, 511, 513, 557, 605
Alcatel Alsthom 206, 262
Alcatel Satellites 202
Algeria:
    conflicts in 9, 19, 22, 28, 65–66, 106, 107
    elections in 35
    military expenditure 192, 195–96, 197, 219, 225, 231
al Hussein missile 485
Aliev, President Haidar 127, 134
Allegheny Teledyne 264
Alliant Tech Systems 203, 262
Allied Signal 202, 262
Almaty Declaration (1997) 599
America *see* United States of America
America, Central:
    conflicts in 20, 23, 29
    military expenditure 191, 192, 214, 221, 226–27
America, South:
    conflicts in 20, 22, 29
    military expenditure 192, 214, 221, 227, 233, 291
Amsterdam Treaty *see under* EU
ANC (African National Congress) 478
Angola:
    arms imports 302
    conflicts and 17, 18, 21, 31, 41, 61, 605, 607, 608
    military expenditure 196, 219, 225, 231
    peacekeepers and 48
    peace process 41–43
Anjouan 59, 60
Annan, Kofi:
    CWC First Conference of the States Parties and 491
    peacekeeping and 46–47, 60, 62
    report to UN 2
    UN reform and 32–33, 604
Antarctic Treaty (1959) 580
anthrax 477, 485
Anti-Ballistic Missile (ABM) Treaty (1972) 13, 403, 410, 419–25, 586–87, 600, 606
Anti-Personnel Mine (APM) Convention (1997):
    background 545–46
    Brussels Conference 550, 603
    Brussels Declaration (1997) 552, 603
    CD and 547–50
    Oslo Conference 553–55
    Ottawa Process 545, 546, 547, 549, 550–53, 558, 603, 606

parties to 597
provisions of 555–56, 597
text of 567–74
verification 551
anti-satellite weapons 288
Arab League *see* League of Arab States
Arafat, President Yasser 93, 94, 95, 96, 97, 101, 108, 599
Arap Moi, President Daniel 61
Ardzinba, Vladislav 129
Argentina 197, 198, 221, 227, 233
Armat missile 284, 285
Armenia:
  arms imports 128, 315
  Azerbaijan and 128, 501
  CFE Treaty and 502, 503, 504
  military expenditure 216, 222, 228
  Russia and 128, 134, 503, 605
  see also Nagorno-Karabakh
arms industry:
  cross-border cooperation 206
  decline in 198
  demand and 198
  restructuring 186, 198–99, 200–7
  sales 186
  SIPRI top 100 companies 11, 199–200, 260–66
  trends in 11, 186–87, 198–207
arms trade:
  concentration of 11
  control of 292
  data, official, on 306–11
  embargoes on 305–6
  human rights and 292
  pressures for 186
  recipients 298–301
  register of 322–68
  SIPRI's sources and methods 369–70
  suppliers 293–97
  transparency in 12, 306–17
  trends in, 1998 11, 291, 292–301
  volumes of imports and exports 318–21
Arusha 38
ASEAN (Association of South-East Asian Nations):
  arms market, size of 193
  ASEAN Regional Forum (ARF) 527, 528
  Cambodia and 64–65, 603
  military expenditure 193, 215
  South-East Asian nuclear weapon-free zone and 444, 446, 448
Asia:
  arms imports 298–99
  conflicts in 20, 22–23, 27–28
  military expenditure 192, 193–94, 214, 218–19, 224, 230
  peacekeeping organizations 64–65

see also following entries and under names of countries
Asia, Central:
  military expenditure 192, 214, 218, 230
  nuclear weapon-free zone in 606, 609
Asia, East:
  financial crisis in 186, 192, 199, 299, 528
  military expenditure 186, 192, 214, 218–19, 224, 230
Asia, South:
  arms control in 529
  military expenditure 192, 214, 218, 224, 230
Asia, Southeast, Nuclear Weapon-Free Zone Treaty (1995) 443–49, 594, 600
Asia–Europe Meeting, Second 5
Asia–Pacific: arms control in 525–26, 527–29
Assad, President Hafez-al 99
Aster 30 system 281
Australia 198, 204, 219, 224, 231, 310, 548, 554
Australia Group 12, 374, 375, 386–94
Australian Defence Industries 204
Australian Submarine 204, 265
Austria 198, 222, 228, 551, 553
Avdeyev, Aleksandr 524
Avondale Industries 264
Axworthy, Lloyd 550
Azerbaijan:
  Armenia and 128, 501
  cease-fire in 31
  CFE Treaty and 502, 503–4, 505, 506
  military expenditure 222, 228
  Russia and 124, 128, 129, 137, 603
  USA and 127
  see also Nagorno-Karabakh
Aziz, Tariq 484, 608

B-52 bombers 405
Babcock International Group 265
Babcock Rosyth Defence 265
Bahrain 217, 223, 229
Baker, James 21, 43
Balkans summit meeting 68
'Baltic Challenge' exercise 51, 536
Baltic states:
  joint peacekeeping force 49
  NATO and 122, 146–48
  Russia and 9, 14, 118, 121–23, 146–47, 523–24, 538–39, 609
  USA and 148
  see also Estonia; Latvia; Lithuania
Bamako Convention (1991) 453
Bangkok Treaty *see* Asia, Southeast, Nuclear Weapon-Free Zone Treaty
Bangladesh 21, 27, 31, 35, 47, 218, 224, 230
Bangui Agreements (1997) 62

Barcelona Declaration (1995) 526
Barcelona Initiative 102
Bar-On, Roni 94–95
Barth, Bjørn 496
Bashir, President Omar Hassan al- 61
Bashkir Republic 114
Basson, Brigadier Wouter 478
Bazan 265
BDM International 263
Bear aircraft 407
Belarus:
 arms exports 304
 CFE Treaty 502
 military expenditure 222, 228
 nuclear weapons 404, 405, 406
 Russia and 118, 120–21, 600, 602
Belgium: 47, 50, 222, 228, 236, 310
Belize 221, 226, 233
Benin 219, 225, 231
Bentsur, Eytan 459
Bijeljina 467, 469
Biological and Toxin Weapons Convention (BTWC, 1972):
 Ad Hoc Group 390, 471
 definitions and 471
 export controls and 386
 parties to 586
 provisions of 586
 relation to other regimes 393
 Review Conferences 470, 471, 479
 verification and 389–90, 392, 470–74
biological weapons:
 countering, R&D programmes 489
 programmes alleged 477–81
 proliferation concerns 474–81
 terrorist attack with 475, 481, 489
 see also previous entry
Blackjack aircraft 407
Black Sea 119
Black Sea Fleet 9, 118–19, 139, 502, 602
Blair, Prime Minister Tony 21, 66
blister agent 461
Blue Hungwe 52
Boeing 202, 205, 261
Bofors 264
Bolivia 64, 221, 227, 233
Bombardier 265
Bongo, President Omar 60
Border Areas, Treaty on Mutual Reduction of Military Forces in (1997) 526, 601
Bosnia and Herzegovina:
 elections in 54–55, 58
 ethnic cleansing 54, 55
 IFOR 54
 landmine clearance 557
 peace process in 31
 SFOR 9, 38, 40, 54–55, 467
 tear-gas used in 467, 469
 Train and Equip Program 55, 521–23, 536, 537
 UN and 36, 40, 45
 see also following entry and Dayton Agreement; Republika Srpska
Bosnia and Herzegovina, Federation of 517, 519, 520, 522–23, 608
Botswana 196, 219, 225, 231
botulinus toxin 485
Bougainville 31, 67
Brazauskas, President Algirdas 123, 146, 147, 607
Brazil 197, 198, 221, 227, 233
Brcko 39, 45, 58, 467, 469
British Aerospace 202, 206, 207, 261
Brunei 218, 224, 230
Brussels Treaty (1948) 578, 580
Bulgaria 222, 228, 555, 610
Burkina Faso 219, 225, 231
Burnham Declaration (1997) 67
Burundi 18, 22, 29, 31, 34, 35, 40, 219, 225, 231, 303
Bush, George 468
Bustani, José Maurício 492, 494
Butler, Richard 483, 485
Buyoya, Pierre 18

C201 missile 285
C801 missile 285
C802 missile 285
Cairo Declaration on Denuclearization of Africa (1964) 451
Cairo Declaration on Somalia (1997) 610
Cambodia 22–23, 27, 31, 35, 64–65, 69, 218, 224, 230, 603, 604
camel pox 485
Cameroon 39, 219, 225, 231
Campbell, John 550
Canada 47, 50, 221, 226, 232, 236, 310
Cape Verde 219, 225, 231
Carter, Jimmy 61
CASA 206, 265
CEA 262
Celsius 262
Central African Republic 31, 36, 62, 219, 225, 231
Central American Democratic Security Treaty (1995) 526
Centrasbat 51
Ceridian 264
Certain Conventional Weapons (CCW) Convention (1981) 546, 589:
 Protocol II, amended, text of 559–67
 Review Conference 554
Ceylon see Sri Lanka
CFE-1A Agreement (1992) 591

CFE Treaty (Treaty on Conventional Armed Forces in Europe, 1990):
    adaptation of 13, 144, 147, 501, 506–12, 513, 514–17, 541–43, 599, 605
    compliance issues 502–4
    Flank Document 501, 502, 504–6, 508, 511, 591, 601, 605
    NATO's enlargement and 507, 510–11
    parties to 591
    provisions 502
    Review Conference 506
    verification 517
Chad 31, 219, 225, 231
Chagos Archipelago 454
Charter of Paris (1990) 165
Chechnya *see under* Russia
chemical weapons:
    abandoned 13, 466–67
    countering, R&D programmes 489
    declaration of possession and programmes 460–61
    destruction of 461–66
    old 13, 466–67
    programmes alleged 477–81
    proliferation concerns 474–81
    terrorist attack with 475, 489
    use likely 392
    use reports 13
Chemical Weapons Convention (CWC, 1993):
    entry into force 13, 457, 490–500, 601
    export controls and 386
    future issues 497–99
    parties to 593
    provisions of 389
    relation with other regimes 393
    riot-control agents and 467–69
    status 457–60, 460–61, 498
    verification 389, 493, 496, 497, 497–98
    see also Organisation for the Prohibition of Chemical Weapons
Chen Jian 447
Chernomyrdin, Viktor 122, 146, 417, 523, 538, 539
Chibirov, President Ludwig 131
Chile 64, 186, 197, 221, 227, 233
China:
    anti-ship capabilities 282, 283, 284, 285, 286, 287
    APM Convention and 549
    arms exports 272, 283, 285, 293, 297, 298, 302, 395
    arms imports 193, 285, 295–96, 298
    border troop reductions 526, 601
    chemical agents and 480
    conflict in 31
    human rights and 70

international integration of 7
Iran and 383
Japanese CW abandoned in 466–67
military expenditure 197, 218, 224, 230
military expenditure on R&D 271
missile programme 280, 282, 286, 287
missile sales 283, 285, 395
non-proliferation and 382–83
nuclear export policy 383, 605, 608
nuclear forces 442
nuclear industry 383
Pakistan and 382, 383
Russia and 7, 68, 608
South-East Asian nuclear weapon-free zone and 447, 449
Uighur minority 527
UN and 36, 37, 40, 48
USA and 382–83, 528, 608
warships' vulnerability 287
Zangger Committee and 382–84
see also Hong Kong; Taiwan
Chirac, President Jacques 60, 132, 447–48
Chowdhury, Anwarul Karim 47
Christopher, Warren 109, 423
Churkin, Vitaliy 144
CIS (Commonwealth of Independent States):
    activities, 1997 10
    alignments within 138
    military expenditure 191, 215
    peacekeeping and 49, 58–59, 136
    peacekeeping force 45
    Russia and 137–38, 139
Ciubuc, Ion 124
CivPol missions 40, 41, 42, 45, 46
Clerides, Glafkos 43
Clinton, President Bill:
    ABM Treaty and 419, 421
    armaments policy 11
    arms transfer policy 295
    Bosnia and Herzegovina and 55
    CFE Treaty and 506
    CTBT and 429
    Iran and 103–4
    Middle East peace process and 91, 93, 95, 97
    military expenditure on R&D and 267
    START II Treaty and 403
    see also Helsinki summit meeting
COCOM (Coordinating Committee on Multilateral Export Controls) 377, 398
Cohen, William 194, 276, 277, 279, 407, 528, 557
Colombia 23, 29, 31, 35, 221, 227, 233
Comoros 31, 35, 59–60
Comprehensive Nuclear Test-Ban Treaty (CTBT, 1996) 13, 403, 428–30, 596, 606
computer software 375

Conackry Agreement (1997) 63
Conference on Disarmament (CD) 13, 403, 431, 459, 546, 547–50, 558
conflict management 8, 69
conflict prevention 8, 69, 71
conflict resolution 8, 69, 73
conflicts:
　achievements and failures and 1–2, 31
　definitions 17
　interstate 17
　intra-state 1, 2, 3, 17, 31
　locations 17
　new 1, 8–9, 18
　numbers 8, 17
　peace efforts 18, 19, 21, 31
　poverty and 5
　regional patterns 22–23
　trends 18–21
Congo (Brazzaville):
　arms imports 303
　conflict in 17, 18, 19, 21, 22, 29, 31, 34, 35, 36, 60–61, 603, 607
Congo, Democratic Republic of the:
　conflict and 607
　founded 18, 601
　military expenditure 219, 225, 231
　UN and 35
　see also Zaire
conventional arms control 13–14
Cook, Robin 65, 67, 296–97, 310
Copenhagen World Summit for Social Development 5
Cordovez, Diego 43
Costa Rica 221, 226, 233
Côte d'Ivoire 219, 225, 231
Council for Security Cooperation in the Asia Pacific (CSCAP) 527, 528
crime, organized 2, 3, 378
Croatia:
　APM Convention and 555
　Florence Agreement and 519, 608
　military expenditure 197, 222, 228
　OSCE and 162–63
　UN and 46
　war criminals 38
Cuba 457, 479–80, 551
Cyprus 31, 34, 156, 157, 222, 228, 539, 540, 610
Czechoslovakia: military expenditure 222, 228
Czech Republic 155, 197, 208, 209–11, 222, 228, 604, 610

Daewoo 264
Dagestan 116
Daimler Benz 261
DASA 202, 206, 207, 261

Dassault Aviation 202
Dassault Aviation Groupe 262
Dassault Electronique 206, 263
Dayton Agreement (1995):
　Arbitral Tribunal 39
　CSBMs and 536–40
　NATO and 151, 467
　UNMBIH and 45
　violations 55
DCN 202, 261
Declaration of Principles on Interim Self-Government Arrangements *see* Oslo agreements
Demining 2010 Initiative 557
Demirel, President Süleyman 604
Denel 264
Denktash, Rauf 43
Denmark 222, 228, 236, 315
developing countries:
　chemical export controls and 391–92, 394
　military expenditure data 190–92
　peacekeeping and 47
　UN and 34, 47
Diego Garcia 454
Diehl 263
Djibouti 219, 225, 231
drug trafficking 2
DuPont 465
Dyncorp 264

Eastern Slavonia 31
East Timor 34–35, 66–67
ECOMOG (ECOWAS Monitoring Group) 19, 59, 62–63, 602, 607
ECOWAS (Economic Community of West African States) 52, 59, 63, 602, 607
Ecuador 63–64, 221, 227, 233, 551
EDS 263
EG&G 265
Egal, Mohamed Ibrahim 61
Egypt 106, 217, 223, 229, 298, 299, 459, 551
Eide, Vigleik 520
Eidgenössische Rüstungsbetriebe 264
Ekéus, Rolf 483, 484
Elbit Systems 204, 265
Elcibey, President Ebulfez 134
El Salvador 221, 227, 233
encryption technology 376–80
Environmental Modification (Enmod) Convention (1977) 587
Erbakan, Necmettin 105
Erfurt Declaration (1997) 609
Eritrea 39, 53, 219, 225, 231, 459
Esco Electronics 265
Esquipulas II Accord (1987) 64
Estonia 147, 155, 222, 228, 610
　see also Baltic states

INDEX 627

Ethiopia 18, 61, 69, 219, 225, 231
EU (European Union):
   Agenda 2000 154, 155, 604
   Amsterdam Treaty (1997) 154, 155, 159, 177–81, 603, 607
   arms trade guidelines 292
   chemical weapons and 393
   dual-use regulation 374, 378, 390–91, 399–400
   enlargement 10, 154–57, 158–60, 604, 610
   Euro-Mediterranean Partnership 102
   export control system 12
   foreign and security policy 154, 166, 177–81, 399
   IGC (Intergovernmental Conference) 154, 603
   Maastricht Treaty (1992) 154, 603
   military expenditure and 189, 215
   NATO and 151
   peacekeeping and 58
   Russia and 159
   security dimension 154–60
   Tacis (Technical assistance for the CIS) programme 465
   WEU and 158, 159, 603, 605, 609
Euratom 382
Eurocopter Group 263, 292
Eurofighter 2000 aircraft 207
EuropaBio 472
Europe:
   activities, 1997 10
   arms imports 299
   arms industry 186, 199, 201, 206–7
   conflicts in 22, 26
   CSBMs in 531–40
   military expenditure 10–11, 185, 192, 214, 216–17, 222–23, 228–29, 236–39
   peacekeeping organizations 54–59
   regional arms control 517–24
   security documents 168–82
   security organizations, membership 142
Europe, Central and Eastern (CEE): nuclear weapon-free zone in 601
Europe, south-eastern, CSBMs in 539–40
European Commission:
   anti-personnel mines and 557
   arms industry 207
   Australia Group and 386
   dual-use export controls 399, 400
   EU enlargement and 154, 155, 156
European Conference 156, 157
European Council 155, 156, 164, 399
European Security and Defence Identity (ESDI) 151, 154, 158
Evans, Gareth 67
Exocet missile 284, 285
export controls: membership of groups 12
   see also names of groups

FIAT 263
FIAT Aviazione 264
Fiji 219, 224, 231
Fincantieri Gruppo 265
Finland 146, 198, 222, 228, 465, 551
Finmeccanica 261
fissile material control scheme 426–27
fissile material production ban 13, 403, 431
Flank Document *see under* CFE Treaty
Florence Agreement (1996) 13, 501, 517–21, 530, 595, 608
FMC 262
Ford, Gerald 468
France:
   Africa and 59, 62, 196
   APM Convention and 548, 553
   arms exports 211, 293, 296–97, 303
   arms industry 206
   military expenditure 216, 222, 228, 239
   NATO and 158
   nuclear forces 434, 440–41
   nuclear tests 450, 451
   peacekeeping 51
Freetown 63
Future Large Aircraft 293

G7 (Group of Seven) 289, 603
Gabcíkovo-Ngymaros dam project 38
Gabon 219, 225, 231, 607
Gambia 35, 220, 225, 231
Garang, Colonel John 61
gas gangrene 485
Gaza 35, 92, 468
GEC 202, 206, 261
Gencorp 264
General Agreement on Peace Settlement and National Accord in Tajikistan (1997) 45
General Dynamics 202, 203, 205, 261
General Electric 202, 262
General Framework Agreement for Peace in Bosnia and Herzegovina *see* Dayton Agreement
General Motors 261
Geneva Conventions (1949) 579–80, 588
Geneva Protocol (1925) 578
Genocide Convention (1951) 579
Georgia:
   cease-fire in 31
   CFE Treaty and 504, 505
   conflict in 58–59, 67, 130
   military expenditure 216, 222, 228
   OSCE and 59
   Russia and 117, 127–28
   UN and 40
   see also Abkhazia
German Democratic Republic: military expenditure 216, 222, 228

Germany:
  APM Convention 551, 553
  arms exports 293, 297, 305
  arms industry 207
  CW destruction aid to Russia 465
  Iran and 103
  Iranian terrorism and 459
  military expenditure 216, 222, 228, 236
  military expenditure on R&D 270, 274
  UN and 37
Ghana 35, 63, 220, 225, 231
Ghukasian, President Arkadiy 132, 134
GIAT Industries 203, 262
Gilman, Benjamin A. 283
GKN 203, 262
GM Canada 265
Golan Heights 98, 99
Gonzáles, Felipe 163
Gorbachev, Mikhail 244
Gore, Al 427
Gore–Chernomyrdin Commission 397, 427
Great Britain *see* United Kingdom
Greece 57, 68, 197, 198, 204, 216, 222, 228, 237, 298, 539, 540, 554, 604
Group of 21 431
GTE 263
Guatemala 18, 23, 31, 35, 37, 40–41, 221, 227, 233
Guinea-Bissau 220, 225, 232
Gujral, Prime Minister Inder Kumar 529
Gulf War illnesses 486–88, 489
Gusmao, Xanana 67
Guyana 35, 221, 227, 233

Habyarimana, President Juvénal 303
Hagel, Chuck 553
Haiti 35, 40, 46, 48
Hamas 93, 100, 101
Hannay, Sir David 43
Hanish islands 39, 53
Har Homa *see* Jabal Abu Ghneim
Harpoon missile 284
Harris 263
HDW (Preussag) 203, 263
Hebron 67, 68, 91–92, 95, 97, 108–9
Hebron Accord (1997) 91, 91–92, 94, 108, 599
Helsinki Final Act (1975) 165
Helsinki Initiatives 409–10, 411, 414, 415, 416–17, 419, 421, 424, 600
Helsinki summit meeting 12, 143, 409–10, 414, 415, 419, 511, 600
Hezbollah 32, 100
Hindustan Aeronautics 265
Hitachi 265
Holbrooke, Richard 43, 55
Holl, Norbert 35
Hollandse Signaalapparaten 265

Honduras 197, 221, 227, 233
Honeywell 264
Hong Kong 384, 480, 481, 528, 603
Hughes 204, 261
Hungary 155, 197, 198, 208, 209, 210, 211, 216, 222, 228, 604, 610
Hun Sen 64, 65, 603
Hunting 263
Huntington, Samuel 4
Hussein, King 91, 100, 101, 481
Hyundai 265
Hyundai Precision 265

IAEA (International Atomic Energy Agency):
  Additional Protocol 382, 601
  nuclear waste and 607
  safeguards 380, 381, 605
IMF (International Monetary Fund) 73, 191, 193, 194
Indefurth, Karl 557
India:
  APM Convention and 549, 551
  arms imports 295, 298
  CBMs and 529
  chemical weapons 460
  conflict in 27, 32
  CTBT and 429
  CWC and 457–59
  military expenditure 218, 224, 230
  military expenditure on R&D 267, 271, 272, 274, 275
  Pakistan, conflict with 17, 27
Indonesia 28, 32, 66–67, 193, 218, 224, 230, 293, 297
INF Treaty (1987) 590
Ingalls Shipbuilding 203
Ingushetia 112, 116–17
Inhumane Weapons Convention *see* Certain Conventional Weapons Convention
Intergovernmental Authority for Development 61
International Campaign to Ban Landmines 545, 554, 609
International Court of Justice 37, 39
International Criminal Court, permanent 39
International Criminal Tribunal for the Former Yugoslavia 38
International Criminal Tribunal for Rwanda 38
International Peace Academy 59
International Verification and Support Commission 64
Internet 377
IRA (Irish Republican Army) 21, 66, 604, 606
Iran:
  arms imports 297, 299
  chemical weapons and 480

China and 383
conflict in 26
election in 9, 103–4, 602
Germany and 103
Kurds and 18
military expenditure 217, 223, 229
missile attack by 285
missile programme 279, 280, 282, 283, 285, 395–96, 397–98
Russia and 129
satellites 397
Tajikistan and 21
terrorism and 103
USA and 103–4, 107
weapons of mass destruction and 103
Iraq:
 biological weapons 392, 457, 484–85, 489
 chemical weapons 392, 457, 459, 483–84, 485, 489
 chemical weapons use 386, 487
 conflict in 26
 genocidal aims 485
 hidden weapons of 105
 Khamisiyah 486, 488
 Kurds and 18, 22, 31, 106
 military expenditure 217, 223, 229
 missile attack by 285
 missile programme 280
 nuclear weapon programme 381
 sanctions on 52, 53, 104
 UN and 34, 36–37, 608
 USA and 18, 97, 104, 105, 285
 see also UNSCOM
Ireland 198, 216, 222, 228
IRI 261
Ishikawajima-Harima 263
Ismail, Razali 37
Israel:
 arms exports 299–301, 311
 arms industry 204
 biological research laboratory 481
 conflict in 1, 21, 22, 26, 32
 military expenditure 198, 217, 223, 229
 Mossad 481
 peace efforts in 67–68
  see also under Middle East peace process
 poison used by 481
 settlements 91, 92–93, 95, 599, 605
 terrorism in 93, 96, 97
 Turkey and 105
Israel Aircraft Industries 204, 263, 272
Israel Military Industries 204, 265
Italy:
 Albania and 57–58, 162
 APM Convention and 548, 551, 553
 arms exports 211, 310
 arms imports 293
 arms industry 207
 military expenditure 216, 222, 228, 237
 peacekeeping 57–58, 162
 UN and 37
ITT Industries 205, 262
IVECO 265

J-10 aircraft 270
Jabal Abu Ghneim (Har Homa) 92–93, 94, 599
Jacolin, Henry 521
Japan:
 APM Convention and 555
 arms imports 193, 298
 arms industry 200, 201
 chemical weapons abandoned in China 466–67
 Defense Agency 201
 financial crisis in 193
 military expenditure 198, 218, 224, 230
 military expenditure on R&D 267, 269, 274–75, 289
 nerve agent use in 392
 peacekeeping 50
 Russia and 31, 68
 UN and 37
 US bases in 600
 US military cooperation and 606
Jean, Carlo 538
Jennings, Sir Robert 39
Jiang Zemin, President 528, 608
Joint Convention on the Safety of Spent Fuel Management and on the Safety of Radioactive Waste Management (1997) 607
Jordan 100, 217, 223, 229
 see also under Middle East peace process

Kabbah, President Ahmed Tejan 63
Kabila, President Laurent 18, 60, 601
Kalimantan 32
Kappen, Major-General Franklin van 48
Karadzic, President Radovan 54
Karlsson, Mats 4–5
Kashmir 17, 31, 65, 68, 529
Kawasaki Heavy Industries 263
Kazakhstan 218, 230, 249, 404, 405, 406, 526, 601
Keleti, Gyorgy 211
Kenya 38–39, 68, 219, 225, 232
Khamenei, Ayatollah 103
Khasaviurt agreement (1996) 113
Khatami, Mohammed 91, 103, 104, 602
Khimprom 465
Khmer Rouge 64, 69
Kinshasa 60, 304
Klerk, President F. W. de 451, 452, 478
Klingberg, Marcus 481
Klyukin, Yuri 392
Kolelas, Bernard 60

Koor Industries 264
Korea, North:
  arms exports 395
  Korea, South, conflict with 32, 66
  landmines in 554
  military expenditure 218, 224, 230
  missile programme 279
  missile transfers 395
  plutonium production 381
Korea, South:
  APM Convention 551
  arms imports 194, 298, 299
  financial crisis 193
  Korea, North, conflict with 32, 66
  landmines in 554
  military expenditure 193, 194, 198, 218, 224, 230
  military expenditure on R&D 267, 269, 270, 271, 275
Korean peace treaty negotiations 31, 66, 609
Koromo, Major Johnny 59
Kuchma, President Leonid 119, 120
Kurds 18, 22, 31, 32, 106
Kuwait 198, 217, 223, 229, 298, 299
Kuzmuz, Olexander 407
Kyrgyzstan 218, 230, 526, 601

Lagardère 206, 262
landmines:
  definition 545
  demining 556–57
  'dumb' 548
  numbers of 545
  'smart' 548, 554
Laos 218, 224, 230
lasers 279, 288
Latvia 123, 147, 216, 222, 228, 385, 610
  see also Baltic states
law, respect for 6
League of Arab States 391, 459
Leahy, Patrick 553
Lebanon 22, 32, 91, 97, 99–100, 197, 217, 223, 229, 459
  see also under Middle East peace process
Lesotho 219, 225, 232
Levy, David 96, 102
LFK 263
Liberia 31, 35, 52, 62–63, 220, 225, 232, 305
Libya 37, 52, 65, 195, 219, 225, 231, 280, 459, 478–79
Light Combat Aircraft (LCA) 270, 272
Lightfoot, James 282
'Linked Seas' exercise 51
Lisbon Protocol (1992) 404, 406, 592
Lissouba, President Pascal 60, 603, 607
Lithuania 216, 222, 228, 607, 610
  see also Baltic states
Litton 202, 205, 261

Lockerbie air crash 52, 65
Lockheed Martin 202, 204, 205, 261
Logicon 264
Loral 262
Lucas Industries 266
Lucent Technologies 263
Lucinschi, President Petru 123, 601
Lukashenko, President Alexander 120–21, 600, 602
Lukin, Vladimir 409, 417
Lusaka Protocol (1994) 41, 43, 605, 608
Luxembourg 216, 222, 228, 237
Lyles, Lester 279

McDonnell Douglas 204, 261
Macedonia: UN and 45–46
Madagascar 35, 220, 225, 232
Madrid Declaration on Euro-Atlantic Security and Cooperation (1997) see under NATO
Malawi 35, 196, 220, 226, 232
Malaysia 192, 193, 194, 197, 198, 218, 224, 299, 230
Mali 35, 220, 226, 232
Malta 216, 222, 228
Managua Agreement (1997) 64
Mandela, President Nelson 66, 478
Mannesmann 265
Marker, Jamsheed 34
Maskhadov, President Aslan 112, 113, 601
Matra BAe Dynamics 202, 262
Matra Hautes Technologies 262
Mauritania 220, 226, 232
Mauritius 220, 226, 232
Mazen, Abu 96
Mbeki, Thabo 60
Medium Extended Air Defense System 281
Meshal, Khaled 100–1
Mexico 35, 197, 198, 221, 226, 233
Middle East:
  arms control dialogue 526
  arms imports 299–301
  chemical weapons and 459
  conflict in 22, 26, 91
    see also under names of states concerned
  events, 1998 9
  military expenditure 192, 214, 217–18, 223–24, 229
  regional economic meetings 102
  terrorism 91, 93, 96, 97, 106
    see also following entry
Middle East peace process:
  assessment 91
  documents on 108–9
  EU and 95–96
  Israeli–Jordanian track 91, 100–1
  Israeli–Palestinian track 91–97
  Israeli settlements and 91, 92–93, 95, 96, 599

INDEX 631

Israeli–Syrian track 91, 97–99
Lebanon and 91, 97, 99–100
Madrid conference 106
multilateral track 101
USA and 91, 92, 93, 94, 95–97, 605
MiG-27 aircraft 272
MiG-MAPO 272
military activities, notifiable 534, 535, 538–39
military coups 8, 19
military expenditure:
  by country income group 196–98
  civil conflict and 188, 195
  database changes 185–86
  data disaggregation 188, 191
  data on 187–91:
    utility of 187–88
  economic impact of 188
  national statistics 190–91
  SIPRI's questionnaires 191
  SIPRI's sources and methods 187–91, 240–42
  tables 214–39
  trends in 10–11, 185–86, 191–96
military expenditure on R&D:
  SIPRI's sources and methods 270–71
  trends 11, 267–75
  see also under names of countries
military forces, democratic control of 6
Military Maritime Consultative Agreement (1997) 528, 607
military R&D:
  national technology bases and 273–75
  proliferation 288–89
  see also military expenditure on R&D
mine clearance 556–57
MINUGUA (United Nations Verification Mission in Guatemala) 41
MINURSO (UN Mission for the Referendum in Western Sahara) 43
MIPONUH (UN Civilian Police Mission in Haiti) 46
MISAB (Inter-African Mission to Monitor the Implementation of the Bangui Agreements) 53, 62
missiles:
  proliferation of 282, 283, 284
  submarine-launched 287–88
missiles, cruise: proliferation of 282, 283, 284, 285
Mitchell, George 66
Mitre 265
Mitsubishi Electric 262
Mitsubishi Heavy Industries 261
Miyet, Bernard 46
MKEK 265
Mobutu Sese Seko, President 21, 303, 601

Mohamed, Ali Mahdi 61
Moldova 31, 67, 123, 124, 125, 217, 223, 228, 504, 505, 601
  see also Trans-Dniester
MOMEP (Military Observer Mission Ecuador/Peru) 63–64
money laundering 2
Mongolia 35, 197, 218, 224, 230
MONUA (UN Observer Mission in Angola) 41, 43, 608
Moratinos, Miguel 96
Morocco 219, 225, 231
Moskit missile 282, 283, 285, 286
Mostar 55
Mowlam, Mo 66
Mozambique 50, 196, 220, 226, 232, 478
MTCR (Missile Technology Control Regime) 12, 374, 394–99
MTU 264
Mugabe, Prime Minister Robert 59
Mujahideen-e Khalq 104
Multilateral Protection Force 53, 57–58
Multinational Advising Police Element 57
Multinational Interception Force (MIF) 53
Mumbengegwi, Simbarashe Simbanenduku 495
Muna, Bernard 38
mustard agents 480
Myanmar 28, 31, 218, 224, 230

Nagorno-Karabakh 58, 67, 132–35, 161–62, 503, 504, 505
Namibia 39, 196, 220, 226, 232
NATO (North Atlantic Treaty Organization):
  CBW and 476–77
  Combined Joint Task Forces (CJTF) 151, 152, 157, 158
  EU and 151, 157–58
  Europeanization 157
  European Security and Defence Identity (ESDI) 151, 154, 158, 159
  Euro-Atlantic Partnership Council (EAPC) 10, 148–49, 158, 166, 173–75, 602, 604
  Madrid Declaration on Euro-Atlantic Security and Cooperation 149, 150, 159, 175–77, 603
  Mediterranean Cooperation Group 150
  membership costs 207–8
  military expenditure 198, 215, 236–39
  military expenditure on R&D 269
  Partnership for Peace (PFP) 10, 50, 148, 149, 158, 602, 604
  peacekeeping 49, 54–55
  riot-control agents, use of 467–69
  role change 10, 142–43, 149–52, 158–59
  strategic concept, new 152
  WEU and 151, 157, 605, 609

Yugoslavia and 150–51
  see also IFOR/SFOR *under* Bosnia and Herzegovina
NATO enlargement:
  accession documents signed 10, 141, 150, 181–82, 207, 610
  candidates for 149–50, 604
  costs of 152–53, 207, 208–9
  EU enlargement, comparison with 158–60
  military expenditure and 209–12
  military modernization and 152, 209–12
  NATO Security Investment Programme (NSIP) 153, 208
  NATO's requirements 207–9
  new security arrangements and 132–53
  nuclear weapons and 143
  Russia's attitude to 9, 122, 144, 145, 146, 600
NATO–Russia Founding Act (1997) 119, 143–45, 147, 168–73, 417, 512–14, 530, 602
NATO–Russia Permanent Joint Council 144, 606
Navy Area Defense programme 280, 281
Navy Theater-Wide programme 279, 281, 422
NEC 264
Nepal 218, 224, 230
nerve agents 480, 486
Netanyahu, Prime Minister Benjamin 9, 91, 92, 93, 94–95, 96, 97–98, 100, 101, 106–7, 108, 109, 599
Netherlands 217, 223, 229, 237, 310, 311, 465
Newport News 203, 262
New Zealand 67, 198, 219, 224, 231
NGO Conference on Landmines 552
NGOs 70, 73, 546, 557
Niaba 472
Nicaragua 31, 197, 221, 227, 233
Niger 31, 220, 226, 232
Nigeria 19, 63, 195, 220, 226, 232
Nikiforos exercise 540
Non-Proliferation Treaty (NPT, 1968) 432, 583–84, 600
Noren, James 245
North Atlantic Co-operation Council (NACC) 10, 148, 149
North Atlantic Council (NAC) 143, 145, 150, 476, 477, 507, 513
Northern Ireland 21, 22, 26, 31, 65, 604, 606
Northrop Grumman 204, 205, 261
North–South partnership 4–5
Norway 217, 223, 229, 237, 311
Nouri, Akbar Nateq 103
Nuclear Forces, Joint Statement on Parameters of Future Reductions in (1997) 596, 600

nuclear forces, tables of 434–42
Nuclear Material, Convention on the Physical Protection of (1980) 588–89
Nuclear Suppliers Group (NSG) 12, 374, 381, 384–86, 385, 401–2
nuclear weapon-free zones *see under names of regions concerned*
nuclear weapons:
  alert status and 8
  arms control 403–33
  control of 12–13
  dismantlement 403, 415–16, 426
Nuri, Said Abdullo 135, 136
Nyangoma, Leonard 18

OAS (Organization of American States) 64
OAU (Organization of African Unity) 59, 60, 61, 62, 63, 71, 450, 451, 452, 455
Oceania: military expenditure 192, 214, 219, 224–25, 231
OECD (Organisation for Economic Co-operation and Development):
  Committee for Information, Computer and Communications Policy 378–79
  military expenditure 215
  military expenditure on R&D 267, 269–70
  peacekeeping and 73
Oerlikon-Bürle 263
oil 115–16, 117, 127, 129
Oman 197, 198, 217, 223, 229
OPEC (Organisation of Petroleum Exporting Countries) 215
Open Skies Treaty (1992) 524–25, 538, 592
'Operation Nangbeto' 51
'Operation Southern Cross 97' 51
Ordnance Factories 263
Organisation for the Prohibition of Chemical Weapons (OPCW):
  begins work 457
  budget 493–94, 497
  conferences of states parties 491–97, 498, 601
  establishment of 490
  Executive Council 492–93, 495, 496
  future issues 497–99
  PrepCom 392, 393, 394, 490–91, 491, 493
  Technical Secretariat 495, 497
  see also Chemical Weapons Convention
organophosphates 486, 488
OSCE (Organization for Security and Co-operation in Europe):
  achievements of 160
  activities, 1998 10, 161–64
  Budapest Summit Declaration (1994) 165
  Charter on European Security 10, 141, 164–66, 610
  Conflict Prevention Centre 69, 166, 190
  Council of Europe and 16

decisions by consensus 165
evolution of 159–66
Forum for Security Co-operation (FSC) 531, 532
Helsinki Summit Declaration (1992) 165
Lisbon Summit 134
membership 141
military expenditure and 189–90, 215, 270, 271
Minsk Group 132–33, 134, 135, 161
missions 58, 161–64
Office for Democratic Institutions and Human Rights (ODIHR) 162, 164
peacekeeping missions 58
UN and 164
Oslo agreements 92fn, 93, 94, 96, 106
Oslo Conference for a Global Ban on Anti-Personnel Landmines 553, 606
Oslo Document (1992) 591
Ossetia, North 116–17
Ossetia, South 127, 131
Outer Space Treaty (1967) 581–82

Pahad, Aziz 60
Pakistan:
   APM Convention and 551
   arms imports 297, 298, 395
   CBMs and 529
   China and 382, 383
   CWC and 458–59
   India, conflict with 17, 27
   military expenditure 218, 224, 230
   missiles 298, 395
   peacekeeping and 47
Palestine Liberation Organization (PLO) Charter 91, 94
Palestinian Authority 68, 91, 94, 95
Palestinian National Council 94
Palestinians, conflict and 1, 21, 26, 91–97, 96
Panama 221, 227, 233
Panskov, V. Vladimir 245
Papua New Guinea 31, 67, 219, 225, 231
Paraguay 221, 227, 233
Paris Agreements on the Western European Union (1954) 580
Paris Declaration (1997) 601
Partial Test Ban Treaty (PTBT, 1963) 581
Paschke, Karl 38
peace-building 73
Peaceful Nuclear Explosions Treaty (PNET, 1976) 587
peacekeeping 71–73, 75–82
   see also under names of countries, regions and organizations concerned
Pelindaba Treaty *see* African Nuclear Weapon-Free-Zone Treaty
Peres, Simon 98
Perry, William J. 414

Persian Gulf War 11, 192, 285, 289, 392, 468–69
   see also Gulf War illnesses
Peru 23, 30, 31, 63–64, 221, 227, 233
Petersen, Niels Helveg 162
Petrov, Colonel General Stanislav 463
Philippines 21, 23, 28, 31, 69, 192, 218, 224, 230
Plavsic, Biljana 54
plutonium production, end of 427, 428
Poland 155, 208, 209, 210, 211–12, 217, 223, 229, 604, 610
Pol Pot 64
Portugal 198, 217, 223, 229, 237
Pratt & Whitney 202, 262
Preussag 263
Préval, President René 46
Primakov, Yevgeniy 129, 132, 146, 410, 411, 417, 423, 507, 511, 512, 513
Primex Technologies 265

Racal Electronics 264
Rafael 204, 264
Rakhmonov, President Imomali 136
Rakotomanana, Honore 38
Ramos Horta, José 35
Ramos, President Fidel 448
Ranariddh, Prince Norodom 64, 65, 69, 603
Rantisi, Abdel-Aziz 93
Rarotonga, Treaty of (1985) 448, 590
Raytheon 202, 205, 261
regional organizations, peacekeeping and 54
Reid, John 488
Republika Srpska 38, 519, 520, 608
Rheinmetall 203, 264
Rio Conference on Environment and Development 5
Rio Protocol (1942) 63
Robinson, Mary 66
Rockwell International 262
Rodionov, General Igor 417
Rohrabacher, Dana 282–83
Rokhlin, General Lev 252
Rolls Royce 202, 262
Romania 150, 217, 223, 229, 555, 610
Ross, Dennis 92, 107
Rota, Colonel François 486
Ruggiu, Georges 39
Russia:
   APM Convention and 549, 551, 555
   arms exports 285, 293, 295–96, 298, 299, 305, 315
   arms industry 246, 249, 252
   arms procurement expenditure 185, 245, 246, 250, 254, 255
   Baikonur space centre 249, 250
   Baltic states and 9, 14, 118, 121–23, 146–47, 523–24, 538–39, 609

Belarus and 9, 600, 602
biological weapons 477–78
border troop reductions 526, 601
CFE Treaty and 502, 503, 504–5, 506, 506–7, 511–12, 513, 514, 516–17
Chechnya and 18, 19, 111–17, 252, 478, 601
chemical weapons 13, 458, 460, 477–78, 497
chemical weapon destruction 13, 463–66
CWC and 458, 463–65
China and 7, 68, 608
design bureaux 271–72, 289
Euro-Asian strategy 7
foreign policy 7
Japan and 31, 68, 608
military expenditure 6, 10, 185–86, 191, 197, 217, 223, 229, 246–59:
    actual expenditure 253–56
    budgetary process 247–48
    budget chapter 'national defence' 248–49
    current issues 258–59
    data problems 243–44, 248–49, 253–54, 257–58
    figures disaggregated 250
    military burden 256–57
    service breakdown 255
military expenditure on R&D 248, 249, 250, 254, 255, 271–73, 296
missile sales 28, 283, 395–96, 397–98
MTCR and 395–96, 397–98
nuclear alert rates 419
nuclear weapons 251, 403, 404, 405, 411, 434
peacekeeping 9, 45, 49, 58, 67, 123–25, 132–34, 136, 138–39
Plutonium Production Reactor Agreement (1997) 427–28, 606
post-Soviet states and 9–10
Rosvooruzheniye 296
Russian-speakers abroad 122–23, 147
South-East Asia nuclear weapon-free zone and 448
strategic nuclear forces 437–38
Tajik Islamic rebels 527
USA and 7
see also Union of Soviet Socialist Republics *and under* NATO enlargement; *for relations with other countries, see under names of countries concerned*
Rwanda 17, 18, 31, 34, 220, 226, 232, 303

Saab 263
Saab Military Aircraft 265
Saddam Hussein 105
SAGEM 263
SAGEM Groupe 263
Sahnoun, Mohammed 35, 60
Samsung 262
Samsung Aerospace 263
sarin 461, 462
Sassou-Nguesso, President Denis 18, 60, 61, 603, 607
Saudi Arabia 197, 198, 217, 223, 229, 298, 299
Schmidt, Fritz 381
Seabed Treaty (1971) 584–85
'Sea Breeze' exercise 119
Sea Dart missile 285
security:
    global problems of 4–5
    international order and 3–5
    prerequisites for 3
    trans-border problems 4
security system:
    changes in 1–14
    fragmentation 1, 2–3
    globalization 1, 2, 5, 70–71
    regionalization 71
Sema Group 266
Senegal 18, 29, 31, 220, 226, 232
Senegal River 68
Separation of Forces Agreement (1974) 98
SEPI 264
Serbia and Montenegro *see* Yugoslavia
Sergeyev, Igor 271, 417, 424, 524
Serov, Valeriy 124
Sextant Avionique 265
Seychelles 220, 226, 232
SFOR *see under* Bosnia and Herzegovina
Sharif, Nawaz 529
Sheremet, Pavel 121
Shevardnadze, President Eduard 127, 129, 131
Siemens 207, 262
Sierra Leone 19, 29, 31, 36, 40, 52, 62–63, 220, 226, 232, 304–5, 602, 607
Simitis, President Spiros 604
Simon, Paul 163
Singapore 193, 198, 218, 224, 230, 293
Sinn Féin 21, 66, 606
Slovakia 217, 223, 229, 304, 305, 610
Slovenia 150, 155, 197, 217, 223, 229, 610
small arms, proliferation of 7
Smirnov, President Igor 123, 601
Smiths Industries 265
SNECMA 264
SNECMA Groupe 202, 263
Soames, Nicholas 488
Sodere Declarations (1997) 18, 61
Solana, Javier 143, 512
Somalia 18, 19, 22, 31, 36, 47, 52, 61, 220, 226, 232, 610
Soutar, Ian 480

INDEX 635

South Africa:
  African nuclear weapon-free zone and 452
  arms imports 302
  CBW and 478
  military expenditure 196, 197, 198, 220, 226, 232
  military expenditure on R&D 271
  NPT and 451
  nuclear weapons 450, 451, 452–53
  peacekeeping and 50, 65
  Project Jota 478
  Third Force 478
  Truth and Reconciliation Commission 478
South African Development Community 196
South America: peacekeeping organizations 63–64
South China Sea 282, 287, 447
Space-Based Laser programme 279
Space and Missile Tracking System 423
Spain 32, 151, 204, 217, 223, 229, 237, 293, 267, 311
Srebrenica 55
Sri Lanka 19, 28, 69, 218, 224, 230, 551
SS-18 missile 411
SS-19 missile 407
SS-24 missile 407
SS-25 missile 407, 414
SS-27 missile 414
Stark, USS 284
START I Treaty (1991) 12, 403, 404–8, 426, 434, 592
START II Treaty (1993) 12, 407, 408–18, 424, 593:
  Protocol 410–13, 421, 606
  ratification difficulties 403, 408–9, 416–18, 433
START III agreement 12, 13, 403, 410, 414, 416, 433, 600
Steinberg, Dmitri 245, 246
Steyn, General Pierre 478
STN Atlas Elektronik 263
Stoel, Max van der 164
Su-30 aircraft 272
submarines 287–88
Sudan 19, 29, 31, 52, 61, 220, 226, 232, 459
Suharto, President Raden 66, 67
Sukhoi 272
Sukhumi 129, 130
Swaziland 220, 226, 232
Sweden 146, 198, 217, 223, 229, 293, 310, 311, 465
Switzerland 198, 217, 223, 229, 310
Syria 98–99, 197, 217, 223, 229, 280, 395, 459
  see also under Middle East peace process

Tabacaru, Nicolae 125
Tadiran 204, 265

Taiwan 193, 197, 198, 218, 224, 230, 296, 282–83, 287, 298
Tajikistan:
  border troop reductions 526, 601
  CIS and 136
  conflict in 18, 21, 22, 31
  military expenditure 218, 230
  National Reconciliation Commission 45
  OSCE and 135, 137, 164
  peace agreement signed 45, 603
  peace process 135–37
  Russia and 21, 135, 137, 139
  UN and 34, 40, 45, 135, 137, 603
Tanzania 220, 226, 232
Tashkent Agreement (1992) 504, 505, 591
Tatarstan 114
Taylor, President Charles 62
tear-gas 457, 467
Tela Agreement (1989) 64
Termit missile 285
Ter-Petrosian, President Levon 134, 135
terrorism 2, 91, 93, 96, 97, 103, 106, 378, 459, 475, 481, 489
Texas Instruments 262
Textron 262
Thailand 193, 219, 224, 230, 293, 298, 299
Theater High-Altitude Area Defense (THAAD) 279, 280, 281, 423
Thomson 261
Thomson-CSF 202, 206, 207, 261, 263
Thomson DASA Armaments 207
Threshold Test Ban Treaty (TTBT, 1974) 587
Thyssen 203, 263
Thyssen Werften 263
Timkin, Mikhail 296
TIPH (Temporary International Presence in Hebron) 67–68
Tlatelolco Treaty (1967) 444, 451, 452, 582
Togo 220, 226, 232
Tokyo Conference on Anti-Personnel Landmines 552
Tonga 219, 225, 231
Toshiba 264
Tóth, Tibor 470
Tracor 263
Trans-Caucasus 125–35
Trans-Dniester 123–25, 601
Treaty of Rome (1957) 399
TRW 202, 205, 261
Tunisia 219, 225, 231
Turajonzoda, Hoji Akbar 136
Turkey:
  APM Convention 551
  arms imports 105, 292–93, 298, 299–301
  conflict in 19, 22, 26
  EU and 156, 157, 610
  Greece and 68, 539, 540, 604
  human rights abuses and 292

Israel and 105
Kurds in 106
military expenditure 197, 217, 223, 229, 238
MTCR and 398
peacekeeping 57
Turkmenistan 218, 230
Turner, Ted 48–49

Uganda 18, 29, 32, 220, 226, 232, 305
Ukraine:
 APM Convention 551
 arms exports 305
 CFE Treaty and 504, 505
 CIS and 120
 military expenditure 217, 223, 229
 NATO and 119, 145–46, 604
 nuclear weapons 404, 405, 406–7, 602
 Russia and 118–20, 145, 602, 603
UNAVEM II (United Nations Angola Verification Mission) 41
UN Civilian Police Mission in Haiti 46
UN Disengagement Force 99
UN Emergency Force 468
UNIKOM (UN Iraq–Kuwait Observation Mission) 53
Union of Soviet Socialist Republics:
 chemical weapons 465
 dissolution of, dangers posed by 425
 military expenditure 10, 185, 186, 197, 217, 243–46, 257–59:
  data problems 243–44, 245–46, 257–58
UNITA (National Union for the Total Independence of Angola) 21, 41, 43, 52, 605, 608
United Arab Emirates 198, 217, 223, 229, 296, 299
United Defense 203, 205, 262
United Kingdom:
 APM Convention and 548, 553
 arms exports 293, 296–97, 311
 arms imports 293
 arms industry 207
 chemical weapons 460
 Hong Kong and 384
 Lockerbie case 37, 52
 military expenditure 217, 223, 229, 238
 military expenditure on R&D 267
 Northern Ireland 21, 22, 26, 31, 65, 66, 604, 606
 nuclear forces 434, 439–40
 nuclear policy 434
 peacekeeping 51–52
 Strategic Defence Review 434
United Nations:
 African nuclear weapon-free zone and 451, 455
 Agenda for Development 5
 Central Asian nuclear weapon-free zone and 606, 609
 Consultative Committee on Security in Central Africa 63
 Department of Peacekeeping Operations 46–47
 financial crisis 9, 48–49
 future of 73
 General Assembly 37
 Headquarters reforms 49
 human rights abuses and 70
 Logistics Base, Brindisi 48
 military enforcement 53
 military expenditure and 189, 191, 254, 256, 270–71
 mine-clearance and 556
 Multinational Stand-by Forces High Readiness Brigade 50
 NGOs and 37
 peace enforcement 52
 peacekeeping, contracting out 36, 57
 peacekeeping, seminar on 51
 peacekeeping operations 40–52:
  costs 40, 42, 48–49
  debtors for 48
  exercises 50–51
  force, right to use 53
  improvements in capability 49–52
  role of 71–73
  joint units 49–52
  misconduct alleged 47, 50
  personnel numbers 40, 42
  reforms of 46–48
  tear-gas and 467–68
 Rapidly Deployable Mission Headquarters 48
 reform 9, 32–34, 49, 73–74, 604
 Register of Conventional Arms 12, 310, 311–17
 sanctions 52–53
 Secretary-General's and Secretariat's activities 34–36, 40
 Security Council 36–37, 74:
  reform 37, 74
 Security Council Resolution 242 98
 Security Council Resolution 1088 468
 Security Council Resolution 1101 600
 Security Council Resolution 1115 485
 Security Council Resolution 1127 605
 Security Council Resolution 1132 607
 Security Council Resolution 1135 608
 Security Council Resolution 1137 609
 Stand-by Arrangements System 47–48
 state sovereignty and 70
 Trust Fund for Preventive Action Against Conflicts 36

INDEX 637

UN Development Group 33
vetoes 37, 93
for relations with individual countries see under names of countries concerned
United States of America:
  Aberdeen chemical warfare research centre 487–88
  Anniston Chemical Disposal Facility 462
  anti-personnel mine storage 558
  anti-submarine warfare 287
  APM Convention and 548, 553
  arms exports 293, 295, 310, 315
  arms industry 186, 199, 200, 201, 204–5
  Asia–Pacific arms control and 527–28
  Ballistic Missile Defense Organization 279
  barracks struck by missile 285
  bases in Japan 600
  biological weapons scare 481
  biological weapons use alleged 457, 479–80
  Blue Grass Chemical Activity 462
  CBW proliferation and 475–76
  CFE Treaty and 504, 505–6, 513
  chemical weapons 13, 460
  chemical weapons destruction 461–63
  China and 382–83, 528
  Chinese missile transfers and 395
  CIA (Central Intelligence Agency) 243, 245
  Congress:
    ABM Treaty and 424
    arms exports and 292, 295
    base closures and 278
    CFE Treaty and 504, 505, 506
    CTBT and 429, 606
    CWC and 458, 462
    START II Treaty and 408, 411
    UN debts and 33–34, 48
  Cooperative Threat Reduction (CTR) programme 407, 425–28
  cruise missile defence 282–88
  cruise missile threat 282–84
  CTBT and 429–30, 606
  CW destruction aid to Russia 465
  CWC and 393–94, 458, 462
  Davis–Monthan AFB 405
  Enhanced Proliferation Control Initiative 396
  IAEA safeguards applied 609
  Johnston Atoll Chemical Agent Disposal System 461, 462
  landmine clearance and 557
  Libya and 37, 52
  military expenditure 11, 191, 221, 226, 233, 236
  military expenditure on R&D 267, 269, 270, 271, 274, 275–88, 288
  missile defence 274, 277, 278, 279–88, 289
  missile threat to 279, 282–84
  National Security Strategy 275
  NATO and 157, 158
  NATO's budget and 208
  navy, role of 283–84
  nuclear alert rates 419
  nuclear doctrine 418–19, 609
  nuclear weapons 403, 404, 405
  peacekeeping 50, 51, 55–56, 66
  Plutonium Production Reactor Agreement (1997) 427–28, 606
  Pueblo Chemical Depot 462
  Quadrennial Defense Review, 1997 11, 267, 275, 276–78, 288, 475
  Revolution in Military Affairs 267, 277, 288
  Russian reactors and 427, 606
  South China Sea and 282
  South-East Asian nuclear weapon-free zone and 444–45, 447, 448
  strategic nuclear forces 434–37
  Tooele Chemical Agent Disposal Facility 461, 462
  UN and 33, 37, 74
  UN debts and 33, 34, 48, 74
  UN veto 37, 93
  for relations with other countries, see under names of countries concerned
UN Law of the Sea Convention (1982) 39
UN Voluntary Trust Fund for Assistance in Mine Clearing 556
UNFICYP (UN Peacekeeping Force in Cyprus) 43
United Technologies 261
UNMIBIH (UN Mission in Bosnia and Herzegovina) 45
UNMOP (UN Mission of Observers in Prevlaka) 46
UNMOT (UN Military Observers in Tajikistan) 45, 58
UNOMIL (UN Observer Mission in Liberia) 62
UNOMOG (UN Observer Mission in Georgia) 58
UNPREDEP (UN Preventive Deployment Force) 45
UNSCOM (UN Special Commission on Iraq) 1, 7, 9, 13, 53, 104, 105, 392, 481–85, 489, 608
UNSMA (UN Special Mission to Afghanistan) 35
UNSMIH (UN Support Mission in Haiti) 46
UNTAES (UN Transitional Administration for Eastern Slavonia, Baranja and Western Sirmium) 46, 163
UNTMIH (UN Transitional Mission in Haiti) 46
Uruguay 198, 221, 227, 233

Uzbekistan 137, 218, 230

Venezuela 221, 227, 233
Vickers 203, 264
Vienna Document 1990 591
Vienna Document 1992 592
Vienna Document 1994 190, 513, 531–35, 592
Viet Nam 197, 219, 224, 231, 447
Vincennes, USS 284
Vosper Thornycroft 265
Vo Van Kiet 448
Vranitzky, Franz 162
VX 461, 484

Waldron, Arthur 282
war criminals 38, 39, 54
Wassenaar Arrangement:
  aims of 375
  criteria, study of 375–76
  encryption technology 376–80
  encryption technology and 378
  membership 374
  status 375
  Trusted Third Parties 379–80
Wegmann 203
Wegmann Group 265
West Bank *see* Hebron
Western Sahara 21, 31, 34
Westinghouse Electric 263
WEU (Western European Union):
  Combined Joint Task Forces 151, 152, 157, 158
  EU and 158, 159, 603, 605, 609
  NATO and 151, 157, 158, 605, 609
  Paris Declaration 601
  peacekeeping activities 57
Williams, Jody 545, 554, 609
Wisner, Frank 397, 398
World Bank 73, 557
World Economic Forum 102

Yassin, Sheikh Ahmad 101
Yeltsin, President Boris:
  ABM Treaty and 419, 421, 424
  arms exports and 296
  Baltic states, CSBMs and 122, 146, 523–24
  Belarus and 120, 121, 600, 602
  budget and 247, 258
  Chechnya and 113–14, 601
  Moldova and 125
  Nagorno-Karabakh 132
  START II Treaty and 403 417–18
  see also Helsinki summit meeting
Yemen 35, 39, 53, 218, 224, 229
Yemen, North 217, 223, 229

Yemen, South 217, 223, 229
Yere, Pierre 59
Yugoslavia (Serbia and Montenegro):
  elections in 163
  Florence Agreement and 519, 608
  Kosovo 1, 9, 31, 164
  military expenditure 217, 223, 229
  OSCE and 163, 164
  UN and 46
Yugoslavia (former):
  CW, allegations of use 478
  Florence Agreement (1996) 13, 501, 517, 530, 595, 608
  military expenditure 217, 223, 229
  peacekeepers in 48
  see also under names of new states

Zaire 17, 18, 19, 21, 22, 30, 31, 34, 35, 36, 40, 60, 303, 601
  see also Congo, Democratic Republic of the
Zambia 196, 220, 226, 232
Zangger Committee 12, 373, 374, 380–84
Zimbabwe 196, 220, 226, 232